Revenue Law—

Principles and Practice

# Revenue Law—
# Principles and Practice
## Twenty-fourth edition

**Emma Chamberlain** BA (Hons), FTII, TEP, LRAM
*Barrister, Lincoln's Inn*

**Jonathan Cooke** ACIB, TEP
*Partner, Humphrey & Co, Hove*

**Sarah Deeks** LLB, FCA

**Andrew Farley** LLB (Hons)
*Partner, Wilsons, Salisbury*

**Hartley Foster** MA (Hons), Barrister
*Partner, DLA Piper Rudnick Gray Cary LLP*

**David Goepel** BA (Hons)
*Solicitor, Withers LLP*

**Michael Haig**
*Corporate Tax Advisory Manager, KPMG LLP (UK)*

**Richard Hayes** CTA, FCA
*Senior Manager, Tax, KPMG LLP (UK)*

**Mark Ife** LLB MJur
*Associate, Herbert Smith LLP*

**Colin Ives** CTA, ATT
*Professional Practices Tax Director, Smith & Williamson*

**Gordon Keenay** MA (Cantab), PhD
*Deputy Head of KPMG's Stamp Taxes Group*

**Sarah Laing** CTA
*CPE Consulting Ltd, Oxfordshire*

**Natalie Lee** LLB (Hons), Barrister
*Senior Lecturer in Law, Southampton University*

**Aparna Nathan** LLB (Hons), LLM
*Barrister, Gray's Inn Tax Chambers*

**Alison Paines** MA (Cantab)
*Principal, Withers LLP*

**Sinead Reid** LLM Barrister
*DLA Piper Rudnick Gray Cary LLP*

**Rupert Shiers** MA (Cantab), MA BCL (Oxon)
*Solicitor, McGrigors*

**Alec Ure**
*Consultant, Ure Associates, Pensions and Taxation Specialists*

**Peter Vaines** FCA
*Barrister, Squire, Sanders & Dempsey LLP*

**Mahesh Varia** LLB (Hons), ATT
*Partner, Travers Smith*

**Stephen Whitehead**
*Senior Manager, Tax, KPMG LLP (UK)*

**Martin Wilson** MA, FCA
*Partner, The Capital Allowances Partnership*

Tottel
publishing

Tottel Publishing Ltd, Maxwelton House, 41–43 Boltro Road, Haywards Heath, West Sussex, RH16 1BJ

© Tottel Publishing Ltd 2006

Previously published by Butterworths Tolley

A CIP Catalogue record for this book is available from the British Library.

ISBN 13 1 84592 248 4

ISBN 10 978 1 84592 248 1

Typeset by Kerrypress Ltd, Luton, Beds

Printed and bound in Great Britain by William Clowes Ltd, Beccles, Suffolk

# Authors

**Emma Chamberlain** FTII—was for some years a solicitor before being called to the Bar in 1998. She practises at 5 Stone Buildings Lincoln's Inn London WC2A 3XT. She is a member of the Society of Trust and Estate Practitioners (STEP) and sits on their Technical Committee. She is chair of the Chartered Institute of Taxation Capital Taxes Committee. She is co-editor of Dymond's *Capital Taxes* and co-author of *Pre-Owned Assets Income Tax—Capital Tax Planning in the New Era*. She is also a cellist (LRAM).

**Jonathan Cooke** is a founder member of STEP, having served on Council from the foundation of the Society until 2003. At different times during that period he was chairman of the Membership and Branches Committees, Honorary Secretary and Honorary Treasurer. He is currently chairman of the Sussex Branch and he serves on the Probate and Estates Sub-Committee and the Disciplinary Panel of Council. Jonathan has specialised in trust and estate work for the whole of his working life, having started his career in the executor and trustee department of a major bank where he qualified as an Associate of the Chartered Institute of Bankers. Since then he has worked in the offices of both solicitors and chartered accountants and has gained considerable experience of the different approaches of the professions to this work. Currently he is a partner in Humphrey & Co, chartered accountants, with offices in Eastbourne and Brighton.

**Sarah Deeks** has a degree in law from University College London and is a Fellow of the Institute of Chartered Accountants in England and Wales and a member of the Faculty of Taxation. She worked in general practice both as a partner and sole practitioner for sixteen years. Sarah has been writing professionally since 1988. She is the author of *Teach Yourself – Understanding Tax for Small Businesses, Tax Essentials: Family Taxation* and *Tax Practice Management*. She is joint author of *Partnership Taxation*. Sarah is the author/editor of *Personal Tax Service*. She is a regular contributor to *Practical Tax and Taxation*.

**Andrew Farley** studied law at Bristol University from where he graduated with first class honours. He was a partner at Boodle Hatfield, London before joining Wilsons, Salisbury in 2003 where he continues to specialise in all forms of private client work and taxation and also capital allowances. Andrew is a member of STEP and the Association of Pension Lawyers and writes and lectures in his specialised subjects.

**Hartley Foster** qualified as a barrister, after studying philosophy at the Universities of Edinburgh and East Anglia. He is a partner and Head of the Tax Litigation practice at DLA Piper Rudnick Gray Cary. He is responsible for the conduct of high profile complex tax litigation at all levels from the tax tribunals to the House of Lords (and including the European Court of Justice). Hartley practices in all areas of revenue and VAT law, but has particular expertise in the fields of international tax law, tax mitigation and the impact of human rights law on taxation. A large part of his practice comprises advising multinational companies with regard to the impact that EU law has on domestic tax legislation. He writes and lectures widely on tax matters, particularly on the tax appeals system and international tax law, and is the author of a division of *Simon's Direct Tax Services*.

**David Goepel** read History at Christ's College, Cambridge, and qualified as a solicitor in 2000. He is a member of Withers LLP's private client and charity teams, and advises individuals, families and charities on a wide range of tax and trust matters. He specialises in advising on and structuring tax-efficient gifts to charities, particularly in an international context, and has lectured on the uses of US/UK dual qualified charities, and tax issues for charities dealing with development land. David is a member of the Charity Law Association and has contributed to its working party on trustee exoneration clauses.

**Michael Haig** is a Corporate Tax Advisory Manager for KPMG LLP (UK) based in the firm's Gatwick office. Michael is a member of the Chartered Institute of Taxation and has experience of advising individuals, owner managed businesses and large international groups.

**Richard Hayes** is a tax senior manager with KPMG LLP (UK), and specialises in Mergers & Acquisitions.

**Mark Ife** studied law at Durham and is now a solicitor in the Employee Incentives group at Herbert Smith LLP. He has been involved in advising on the establishment and continuing operation of a variety of employee incentive arrangements for both quoted and unquoted companies. In addition, he advises on the employee incentive aspects of corporate actions, including takeovers, IPOs, schemes of arrangement and demergers. Mark is a member of the Share Plan Lawyers Group and the Global Equity Organization and is a regular speaker on share scheme issues.

**Colin Ives** has over 25 years experience of advising professional practices in relation to their tax affairs and also general commercial matters. He was made a partner at Smith & Williamson in 1995 becoming a Director on their incorporation in 2002, and is now their Head of Professional Practice Tax. He is a recognised authority on partnership matters and is a committee member and Hon. Secretary of the Association of Partnership Practitioners (APP) and has served on their working parties dealing with Limited Liability Partnerships, Multi-Disciplinary Partnerships and the Law Commission Review of Partnership Law. He also chairs the APP's Taxation Working Party. Colin advised the Law Commission on the taxation and accounting issues of their proposals to reform UK partnership law.

**Gordon Keenay** joined KPMG's Stamp Taxes practice in June 2001. Previously, business director of Inland Revenue Stamp Taxes, his responsibilities included the provision of policy advice on Stamp Duty and Stamp Duty Reserve Tax to Treasury ministers. Gordon has held other senior positions during 18 years with the head office of Inland Revenue in areas including transfer pricing and international treaties and has worked in a number of government departments, including the Treasury. He has lectured at professional seminars and is a regular contributor to the *Tax Journal* and the author of Tolley's *Tax Digest—A Practical Guide to Stamp Duty Land Tax.* He represented the CBI as a member of the Inland Revenue's consultative committees on Modernising Stamp Duty and is a member of the SDLT working parties of the British Property Federation and the Chartered Institute of Taxation.

**Sarah Laing** is a Chartered Tax Adviser. She is a director of CPE Consulting Ltd, an Oxfordshire-based company which provides technical writing and editorial services for the tax and accountancy profession. Sarah has been writing professionally since joining *CCH Editions* in 1998 as a Senior Technical Editor, contributing to a range of highly regarded publications including the *British Tax Reporter, Taxes - The Weekly Tax News,* the *Red & Green* legislation volumes, *Hardman's, International Tax Agreements* and many others. She became Publishing Manager for the tax and accounting portfolio in 2001 and then went on to help run CCH Seminars (including ABG Courses and Conferences). Sarah originally worked for the Inland Revenue in Newbury and Swindon Tax Offices, before moving out into practice in 1991. She has worked for both small and Big 5 firms.

**Natalie Lee**, who became one of three co-authors of *Revenue Law* in 1993, qualified as a barrister after studying law at Southampton University, where she is now a senior lecturer specialising in revenue law and trusts. She has written and lectured widely on the new system of tax credits. She is a founder member, and currently sits on the steering committee, of the Tax Research Network, and is a panel member of the Revenue group of the Society of Legal Scholars.

**Aparna Nathan** read law to post-graduate level at the London School of Economics. She was called to the Bar in 1994 and came to Gray's Inn Chambers as a pupil; she became a member in 1996. Aparna undertakes all aspects of revenue work, but regards tax planning for domicilaries and non-domicilaries, corporation tax and litigation as her particular specialities. She has collaborated on several books and is a regular contributor to technical journals. She has for several years taught tax and insolvency law to University of London post-graduates and is currently a Visiting Fellow at the LSE.

**Alison Paines** studied classics and law at Cambridge University. She qualified as a solicitor in 1981 and is now a principal at Withers LLP where she is the head of the Charities Group. She advises charities and other not-for-profit entities, their donors and those who have dealings with them on the legal aspects of their operations, including fiscal issues. She is particularly well known for her work with charities related to the NHS and central government and international charity matters. She is on the editorial board of *International Charitable Giving: Laws and Taxation* and is one of the team of writers at Withers LLP who contribute to *Tolley's Charities Manual*. She is currently the Deputy Chairman of the Charity Law Association.

**Sinead Reid** is an Irish qualified barrister with an LLM in European Law and over six years experience in the area of Indirect Tax. She is a senior lawyer within the Tax Litigation team at DLA Piper Rudnick Gary Cary LLP where she assists Hartley Foster, Head of Tax Litigation, in the conduct of a number of high profile and challenging tax cases. Prior to joining DLA Piper, Sinead was a senior manager in one of the Big Four Accountancy Firms where she managed a number of VAT litigation cases through the VAT & Duties Tribunal and advised on a number of indirect tax cases that advanced through the higher courts. From July 2000 until April 2002, Sinead spent time in the Sydney office of one of the Big Four where she advised clients on the goods and services tax (similar to the UK VAT system) that was being implemented; this included detailed advice on the classification of supplies and the procedures that clients needed to introduce in order to comply with the new tax regime.

**Rupert Shiers** is an Associate in the McGrigors tax litigation team, with responsibility for the direct tax litigation practice. He joined McGrigors in 2001 and has specialised ever since then in resolving long-running and deadlocked disputes with HMRC. Rupert's technical background is based on M&A transactions and corporate reorganisations, acquired largely from practice prior to 2001 in the tax department of a top ten City firm. Rupert is a law graduate from the University of Oxford and also the University of Cambridge, both times with first class honours.

**Alec Ure** has more than 30 years of pensions experience. He became a self-employed consultant and author in 2003 and is a leading writer of books and articles on pensions. He had previously worked for Bacon & Woodrow, where he was senior consultant in their legal department and Gissings' Technical Team. Alec advised on many aspects of pensions and taxation issues, and provided UK and offshore pension documentation. Previously, he worked for the Inland Revenue, 15 years being spent in the Pension Schemes Office in a senior role, involving tax and pension enquiries and dedicated work on documentation and pension provision and planning.

**Peter Vaines** is a chartered accountant, a barrister and also a chartered tax advisor. He was senior tax partner of chartered accountants Brebner Allen & Trapp for 24 years and is now with the international law firm Squire, Sanders & Dempsey LLP, where he continues to specialise in UK and international taxation, with a particular focus on domicile issues, providing consultancy advice to professional firms and financial institutions in the UK and abroad. He writes and lectures widely on tax matters and is the tax columnist for the *New Law Journal* as well as being an editorial board member of *Taxation* and the *Personal Tax Planning Review*.

**Mahesh Varia** is a partner at city law firm Travers Smith. He specialises in employee incentives (including employee taxation) and advises companies, directors, trustees and employees on a wide range of issues, both in the context of corporate transactions and on a consultancy basis. Mahesh has been recognised as a leading individual in his field by the Chambers Guide to the UK Legal Profession. He is a member of the Association of Taxation Technicians and the Share Plan Lawyers.

**Stephen Whitehead** was formerly an Inspector of Taxes with the Inland Revenue. He subsequently joined KPMG, dealing with a variety of business and employment tax issues. He currently advises on corporate taxation and tax administration within KPMG's Tax Management Services team.

**Martin Wilson** studied languages at Durham before qualifying as a chartered accountant. After some 15 years with major accounting firms, he founded the Capital Allowances Partnership, a specialist practice dealing with all aspects of capital allowances and tax depreciation. He is the author of many published works on the subject, including *Capital Allowances: Transactions & Planning* (nine editions) and a contributor to *Simon's Tax Planning* and the *Institute of Taxation Finance Act Commentaries 1998–2006*.

# Contents

# Table of statutes

# Table of cases

Decisions of the European Court of Justice are listed numerically after the main table.

PARA

PARA

# References and abbreviations

All statutory references are given in the text.

The standard abbreviations are as follows:

| | | |
|---|---|---|
| ACT | = | Advance corporation tax |
| A&M | = | Accumulation and maintenance trust |
| BES | = | Business Expansion Scheme |
| BPR | = | Business property relief |
| CAA 2001 | = | Capital Allowance Act 2001 |
| CGT | = | Capital gains tax |
| EIS | = | Enterprise Investment Scheme |
| ESC | = | Extra statutory concession |
| FA (year) | = | Finance Act (year) |
| FID | = | Foreign income dividend |
| FII | = | Franked investment income |
| HMRC | = | HM Revenue & Customs |
| IHT | = | Inheritance tax |
| IHTA 1984 | = | Inheritance Tax Act 1984 |
| ITEPA | = | Income Tax (Earnings and Pensions) Act 2003 |
| IRC | = | Inland Revenue Commissioners |
| ITTOIA 2005 | = | Income Tax (Trading and Other Income) Act 2005 |
| LPA 1925 | = | Law of Property Act 1925 |
| MIRAS | = | Mortgage Interest Relief at Source |
| MCT | = | Mainstream corporation tax |
| NIC | = | National Insurance contribution |
| PAYE | = | Pay As You Earn |
| PET | = | Potentially exempt transfer |
| PR | = | Personal representative |

| | | |
|---|---|---|
| RI | = | Revenue Interpretation |
| SA 1891 | = | Stamp Act 1891 |
| SDLT | = | Stamp Duty Land Tax |
| SDRT | = | Stamp Duty Reserve Tax |
| SI | = | Statutory Instrument |
| SP | = | Statement of Practice |
| STI | = | Simon's Tax Intelligence |
| SWTI | = | Simon's Weekly Tax Intelligence |
| TA 1988 | = | Income and Corporation Taxes Act 1988 |
| TCGA 1992 | = | Taxation of Chargeable Gains Act 1992 |
| TMA 1970 | = | Taxes Management Act 1970 |
| TLATA 1996 | = | Trusts of Land and Appointment of Trustees Act 1996 |
| VAT | = | Value added tax |
| VATA 1994 | = | Value Added Tax Act 1994 |

References to the Manuals produced by the Inland Revenue are to the relevant manual (eg IM is Inspector's Manual; CG is Capital Gains Tax Manual) followed by the relevant paragraph number.

Other abbreviations in the text are defined where they appear.

# Section 1     Introduction

**Chapters**

# 1 UK taxation structure and philosophy

*Updated by Peter Vaines, Haarmann Hemmelrath (Solicitors)*

> '*Singleton J*—Your appeal must be dismissed. I will pass you back your documents. If I might add a word to you, it is that I hope you will not trouble your head further with tax matters, because you seem to have spent a lot of time in going through these various Acts, and if you go on spending your time on Finance Acts, and the like, it will drive you silly.
>
> *Mrs Briggenshaw*—I will appeal to the higher court.
>
> *Singleton J*—I cannot stop you, if I would. The advice which I gave you was for your own good, I thought. That is all.'
>
> (*Briggenshaw v Crabb* (1948) 30 TC 331.)
>
> **[1.1]**

## I THE UK TAX PICTURE

### 1 Taxes in general

Taxes imposed in the UK may be classified in various ways. A tripartite division might be adopted into taxes on income, on capital and on expenditure. Alternatively, and arguably more satisfactorily, the classification might be into direct and indirect taxes. This book is concerned with the following direct taxes:

income tax (**Chapters 6–18**)
capital gains tax (CGT) (**Chapters 19–27**)
inheritance tax (IHT) (**Chapters 28–36**)
corporation tax (**Chapters 41–48**)
stamp duty (**Chapter 47**)

and there are also four chapters on VAT (an indirect tax: **Chapters 37–40**).

It omits indirect taxes such as car tax, landfill tax, climate change levy, insurance premium tax and customs and excise duties, as well as such direct taxes as petroleum revenue tax, the tonnage tax and the council tax. In principle, the distinction between direct and indirect taxes is that a direct tax is borne by the taxpayer and is not passed on to any other person, whereas an indirect tax is passed on by the payer so that the burden of the tax is ultimately borne by another, eg VAT which although paid by the business-man, is passed on to the customer. **[1.2]**

## 2   What is a tax?

The basic features of a tax may be simply stated. *First,* it is a compulsory levy. *Secondly,* it is imposed by government or, in the case of council tax, by a local authority. *Finally,* the money raised should be used either for public purposes or, if the purpose of the tax is not to raise money, it should aim to achieve social justice within the community (CGT, for instance, was specifically intended to have that effect). However, to describe the main features of a tax is not to define the concept. Thus, although not treated as taxes for parliamentary purposes, can it be said that social security contributions are, in reality, taxes? Tiley (*Revenue Law,* 2005) has suggested that, on the basis that they are now graduated in a way which does not relate directly to the graduation of the benefit, they *ought* to be treated as taxes. Moreover, taxes shade off into fines and levies imposed for other purposes. So far as the distinction between fines and taxes is concerned, the line is often blurred. HLA Hart in *The Concept of Law* (Oxford, 1975) commented that:

> 'Taxes may be imposed not for revenue purposes but to discourage the activities taxed, though the law gives no express indications that these are to be abandoned as it does when it "makes them criminal". Conversely the fines payable for some criminal offence may, because of the depreciation of money, become so small that they are cheerfully paid. They are then perhaps felt to be "mere taxes", and "offences" are frequent, precisely because in these circumstances the sense is lost that the rule is, like the bulk of the criminal law, meant to be taken seriously as a standard of behaviour.'

It is not really surprising that this 'mere taxes' attitude has spawned the belief that all taxes can be avoided, or even evaded, with complete impunity (see **[1.24]** and chapters 2, 3 and 5). **[1.3]**

## 3   The purpose of taxation

The primary object of taxation is to raise money for government expendi-ture. The twentieth century witnessed increasing expenditure on social welfare whilst the use of taxation both as an economic regulator and for the promotion of the public good (or to discourage certain forms of conduct) may also be discerned in the legislation of this century. Thus, alterations to the rate of VAT can affect the level of economic life in the community as much as adjustments to the money supply and credit regulation. The various tax incentives afforded for gifts to charities may be seen as the promotion of public good and altruism; whilst the duties levied on tobacco and alcohol may be seen as bordering on moral control. The trend of increasing social expenditure has continued into the 21st century, albeit in a different guise, with the new system of tax credits, aimed at both reducing child poverty and encouraging work rather than welfare (**[51.29]**ff). **[1.4]**

## 4 Statistics

Who should pay the bill? Apportioning the burden of taxation fairly amongst the community can turn into the more radical contention that tax should operate as a method for effecting a redistribution of wealth or even the confiscation of wealth above a certain level. One striking feature of the statistics of direct taxation is that the vast proportion of the total yield is from income tax: receipts of income tax in 2004–05 amounted to 71.5% of the total sum raised by direct taxes; corporation tax 19.5% and CGT 1.3%. The comparable figures for 1990–91 were 67% (income tax); 26% (corporation tax); and 2.2% (CGT). The figures for corporation tax are particularly striking: with the substantial cut in the tax rate and the removal of first year capital allowances in 1984, the tax yield from companies increased from £8,341m in 1984–85 to £21,495m in each of 1989–90 and 1990–91. From that peak, the yield fell—to £14,887m in 1993–94—doubtless indicating the depth of the recession, although £34,322m was collected in 1999–2000 and £30,032m in the previous year.

IHT (including its now defunct predecessor, capital transfer tax) accounts for 1.7% of the total tax raised; this should be compared to estate duty that in its final year (1974–75) produced 2.38%. A rise in IHT receipts is likely for two reasons: *first,* as surviving spouses die, estates exempt on the death of the first spouse will fall into the charge to tax; *secondly,* a substantial rise in house prices, combined with a nil rate band threshold that has not risen at the same rate, will boost the value of estates. Receipts from lifetime transfers fell from a peak of £33.9m in 1986–87 to £10.9m in 1991–92 and £5m in 1996–97: this coinciding with the cutback in the tax base which has resulted (generally) in only those lifetime transfers made within seven years of the transferor's death being taxed. However, these too might rise following the, albeit watered-down, changes to the IHT settlement regime. Stamp duty, a tax with strikingly low collection costs, raised 5.2% of the total in 2004–05.

The costs of collection, expressed separately in pence per pound for the major taxes for the last five years, are shown in the table below (taken from the Report of the Board of Inland Revenue for the year ending 5 April 2005).

| | 1999/00[1] | 2000/01[2] | 2001/02 | 2002/03 | 2003/04 | 2004/05 |
|---|---|---|---|---|---|---|
| Income Tax (excluding payable Tax Credits)[3] | 1.59 | 1.36 | 1.38 | 1.41 | 1.42 | 1.34 |
| Corporation Tax | 0.76 | 0.98 | 1.01 | 1.15 | 1.25 | 0.96 |
| Petroleum Revenue Tax | 0.24 | 0.15 | 0.20 | 0.26 | 0.18 | 0.22 |
| Capital Gains Tax | 1.49 | 1.33 | 1.44 | 2.73 | 2.13 | 1.95 |
| Inheritance Tax | 1.46 | 1.23 | 1.21 | 1.38 | 1.25 | 1.14 |
| Stamp duties | 0.11 | 0.09 | 0.11 | 0.17 | 0.43 | 0.44 |

[1] In the 1999–00 report, the published ratio for Income Tax also included NICs costs and receipts, in addition to Tax Credit costs and payments. Since NICs are now shown separately and the reporting of the Tax Credits has also changed, the figures here for 1999–00 have been adjusted and exclude NICs.
[2] The one-off STEPS receipt in 2000–01 has been excluded.
[3] From 2001–02, ratios are now based on Resource rather than Cash.

HMRC's contribution to central government tax revenue has remained fairly constant: for 2004–05, it contributed 67.6% of the total; this compares with 64.1% in 1974–75.                                                              **[1.5]**

## 5   The tax unit

Inherent in the question 'who should pay the bill' posed in [**1.5**] is the issue of the unit of taxation. At various times in the past, the basic taxpaying unit of the individual was expanded to comprise either the nuclear family or the married couple. Thus it was that, prior to the tax year 1972–73, the income of an unmarried infant who was not in regular employment was aggregated with that of its parents; after 1972–73, this ceased to be the case, and the infant became a taxpayer in its own right. However, until 1990–91, the incomes of husband and wife were aggregated, with the husband bearing the responsibility for the tax return and payment of the tax. The inequity of treating a married couple differently from an unmarried couple with equivalent income, together with the lack of privacy afforded to the married woman in her financial affairs, resulted in the current system of independent taxation, with every individual person a taxpayer in their own right.       **[1.6]–[1.20]**

## II   FEATURES OF THE SYSTEM

### 1   Legislation

#### a)   *Interpretation*

Fiscal legislation is both detailed and complex .The aim of the vast amount of detail is to ensure certainty: persons should know whether they are or are not subject to tax or duty on a particular transaction or sum of money; it is complex because the society within which it has to operate is complex. The result, however, has tended to be confusion for all! It has always been held to be a cardinal principle that in a taxation matter the burden lies upon the Crown to show that tax is chargeable in the particular case. In a famous passage, Rowlatt J in *Cape Brandy Syndicate v IRC* (1921) expressed this rule as follows:

> '... It is urged ... that in a taxing Act clear words are necessary in order to tax the subject. Too wide and fanciful a construction is often sought to be given to that maxim, which does not mean that words are to be unduly restricted against the Crown, or that there is to be any discrimination against the Crown in those Acts. It simply means that in a taxing Act one has to look merely at what is clearly said. There is no room for any intendment. There is no equity about a tax. There is no presumption as to a tax. Nothing is to be read in, nothing is to be implied. One can only look fairly at the language used ...'

Where the meaning of the statute is clearly expressed, the court will not consider any contrary intention or belief of Parliament or, indeed, any contrary indication by the Revenue. Apart from this, the question of making allowance for the intendment of Parliament is not clear cut. There are two divergent views on this matter: on the one hand, there are those who view tax statutes to be about revenue collection and nothing else, and accordingly adhere to the literal approach to interpretation. This view can be summed up in the words of Lord Scarman who, in the course of a debate in 1981, said:

> 'If Parliament says one thing but means another, it is not, under the historic principles of the common law, for the courts to correct it. That general principle must surely be accepted in our society. We are to be governed not by Parliament's intentions but by Parliament's enactments.'

On the other hand, there are those who advocate the purposive approach. In *Stenhouse Holdings v IRC* (1972), Lord Reid considered the alternative to the literal approach to interpretation which, he said, was:

> 'to consider the ... general intendment of the provisions ... More recently courts have tended to give at least equal weight to more general considerations, because a strict literal interpretation has been found often to lead to a result which cannot really have been intended, and the object of statutory interpretation must be to find what was the intention of the legislature.'

While there is seen a convergence of these views in cases revealing an actual *ambiguity* within a statutory provision (see, for eg., *Newman Manufacturing Company v Marrable* (1931)), the two opposing approaches continue to be adopted in other cases. In *Frankland v IRC* (1997), while acknowledging that the inheritance tax legislation gave rise to an anomaly, Peter Gibson LJ refused to accept that it revealed any ambiguity. Accordingly, he dismissed the taxpayer's invitation to write words into the provision that would remove the anomaly and, pointing out that the 'court's function is to interpret the legislation and not to legislate under the guise of interpretation'. He concluded that it would be 'impermissible' for the court to write in words that some may conjecture parliament to have intended. In contrast, in *Sutherland v Gustar* (1994), where the statute was silent on the point at issue, the Court of Appeal decided that, in the interests of fairness and justice, it would not 'retreat into adopting a literal approach to the construction of the statutory provisions', but would interpret the legislation 'so as to give effect to Parliament's presumed intention.' Importantly, it is the purposive approach upon which was founded the so-called 'Ramsay' doctrine, which enshrined the judiciary's attempt to defeat artificial tax avoidance schemes (see **[1.24]** and chapters 2, 3 and 5). **[1.21]**

b) *Legislative simplification*

Following criticism from many sources, not least the Tax Law Review Committee of the Institute for Fiscal Studies in its Interim Report on Tax Legislation (1995), that tax law had become lengthy, complex and impenetrable, FA 1995 s 160 required the Inland Revenue to prepare a report on tax simplification. That report—*The Path to Tax Simplification*—was published in December 1995, and gave birth to the Tax Law Rewrite Project, which was charged with the task of rewriting most of the primary tax legislation falling within the remit of the then Inland Revenue. The Capital Allowances Act 2001 was the first piece of rewritten legislation to reach the statute book and this has been followed by the Income Tax (Earnings and Pensions) Act 2003 (ITEPA 2003) and the Income Tax (Trading and Other Income) Act 2005 (ITTOIA 2005) which came into force on 6 April 2005. Remaining income tax provisions are included in a draft Income Tax Bill. **[1.22]**

c)    *Use of Hansard*

The principles of statutory interpretation were revised by the House of Lords decision in *Pepper v Hart* (1993). Speaking for the majority (the then Lord Chancellor, Lord Mackay, dissenting), Lord Browne-Wilkinson accepted that the courts could look at Hansard for guidance on the interpretation of a statute in limited situations:

> 'I therefore reach the conclusion, subject to any question of parliamentary privilege, that the exclusionary rule should be relaxed so as to permit reference to parliamentary materials where:
>
> (a)    legislation is ambiguous or obscure, or leads to an absurdity;
> (b)    the material relied on consists of one or more statements by a minister or other promoter of the bill together, if necessary, with such other parliamentary material as is necessary to understand such statements and their effect;
> (c)    the statements relied on are clear.'

In *Elf Enterprise Caledonia Ltd v IRC* (1994), the court held that Inland Revenue Press Releases could *not* be used as an aid to statutory interpretation, whilst in *IRC v Willoughby* (1995) the Parliamentary Debates of 1936 (on the introduction of what is now TA 1988 s 739) were considered by the Court of Appeal to be of no value:

> 'Whatever might have been the intention of Ministers in 1936, the Court had decided in 1948 and again in 1969 that the words used by Parliament manifest a different intention. Yet in 1952 and again in 1970 the same formula is used and notwithstanding the changes made in 1969. In these circumstances it must be assumed that the original intention, whatever it was, was superseded by an acceptance of the decisions of the Courts' (*Morritt LJ*): note that the House of Lords did not need to consider this matter since they did not find any ambiguity in the statute.

Much of the complexity of recent tax legislation has been prompted by the growth of the tax avoidance industry. Whilst tax evasion is unlawful, the avoidance of tax is both lawful and widely practised. The growth of larger scale schemes, often devoid of all commercial reality, has promoted an increased amount of anti-avoidance legislation and, in 2004, the requirement for detailed advance disclosure of tax avoidance schemes.          **[1.23]**

## 2    Role of the courts—the 'new approach'

The role of the judiciary in the attack on artificial tax avoidance schemes has already been referred to above ([**1.21**]). The so-called 'Ramsay' doctrine (named after *Ramsay Ltd v IRC* (1981), the case in which it began to be developed) and otherwise known as 'the new approach', was a response to the burgeoning tax-avoidance industry in the 1970s, and to the marketing of a myriad of schemes wholly divorced from reality but obtaining a tax advantage because of the precise wording of the relevant legislation. It was felt by some that the methods used for attacking such schemes and neutralising this advantage, namely the canons of statutory construction and the use of limited anti-avoidance legislation, were wholly inadequate for the task.

Hence the development of the new approach to tax-avoidance schemes in the House of Lords and, in particular, in the speeches of the Law Lords in *Furniss v Dawson* (1984) (see **[2.22]**). What the new approach was actually about and how it operated has been the subject of a number of high-profile House of Lords cases, the most recent being *Barclays Mercantile Business Finance Ltd v Mawson* (2004) and *Scottish Provident Institution v IRC* (2004). There were those critics who clearly believed that the early cases demonstrated a willingness on the part of their Lordships to engage in judge-made law and, it has to be said, with some justification as the following words of Lord Scarman demonstrate:

> 'I am aware, and the legal profession (and others) must understand, that the law in this area is in an early stage of development. Speeches in your Lordships' House and judgments in the appellate courts are concerned more to chart a way forward between principles accepted and not to be rejected, than to attempt anything so ambitious as to determine finally the limit beyond which the safe channel of acceptable tax avoidance shelves into the dangerous shallows of unacceptable tax evasion. The law will develop from case to case. Lord Wilberforce in *Ramsay's* case referred to "the emerging principle" of the law. What has been established is that the determination of what does, and what does not constitute unacceptable tax evasion is a subject suited to development by judicial process. Difficult though the task may be for judges, it is one which is beyond the power of the blunt instrument of legislation.'

Other and more recent members of the Judicial Committee of the House of Lords have gone out of their way to demonstrate that the *Ramsay* case did not give rise to a new principle, but was merely an example of purposive statutory interpretation. This will be discussed in far greater detail in **Chapter 2**. Suffice for now to say that the decision in *Ramsay* was critical in so far as the courts have, since that time, at least thought about the issue of artificial tax avoidance, expressed views on it and have brought a greater awareness about it both to advisors and taxpayers. **[1.24]**

## 3 Practice

Given the volume of legislation, it is not surprising that some provisions may impose hardship and cause unforeseen results in individual cases. As a result the Revenue operates a system of extra-statutory concessions (ESCs) and publishes Statements of Practice (SPs) and interpretations ('RI').

An ESC is a relaxation which gives taxpayers a reduction in tax liability to which they would not be entitled under the strict letter of the law: by contrast an SP explains the Revenue's interpretation of legislation and the way in which it is applied in practice (of course the taxpayer may disagree and is free to argue for a different interpretation before the courts!).

The current ESCs are set out in the booklet IR I and comprise over 200 concessions, the effect of which is that tax is not charged despite the case falling within the provisions of a taxing statute. Take for instance the ESC A29 that allows the intensive rearing of livestock or fish to be regarded as 'farming' for the purposes of the averaging provisions in TA 1988 s 96, when it would not be strictly included. A number of concessions have been incorporated in the legislation, particularly in the rewritten legisaltion. An example would be ESC A6 that permitted miners to enjoy free coal or an allowance in lieu which would undoubtedly have been charged as emoluments. This is now the subject of a specific exemption in ITEPA 2003 s 306. It needs to be remembered that the published concessions are prefaced by a warning that 'a concession will not be given in any case where an attempt is made to use it for tax avoidance'. Thus in *R v IRC, ex p Fulford Dobson* (1987) an attempt to take advantage of a CGT concession, which, in certain cases, excluded from charge gains realised by a non resident from the date of his departure from the UK, failed since the relevant asset had been transferred to the non resident by his spouse with the sole object of benefiting from that concession.

The fairness of concessions is open to question as is their constitutional legality. In a pungent judgment Walton J expressed the objection to ESCs as follows:

'I, in company with many other judges before me, am totally unable to understand upon what basis the Inland Revenue Commissioners are entitled to make extra-statutory concessions. To take a very simple example (since example is clearly called for), upon what basis have the commissioners taken it upon themselves to provide that income tax is not to be charged upon a miner's free coal and allowances in lieu thereof? That this should be the law is doubtless quite correct: I am not arguing the merits, or even suggesting that some other result, as a matter of equity, should be reached. But this, surely, ought to be a matter for Parliament, and not the commissioners. If this kind of concession can be made, where does it stop: and why are some groups favoured against others? ...

... This is not a simple matter of tax law. What is happening is that, in effect, despite the words of Maitland, commenting on the Bill of Rights, "This is the last of the dispensing power", the Crown is now claiming just such a power ...' (*Vestey v IRC (No 2)* (1979)).

By contrast, in the *Fulford Dobson* case mentioned above, the judge (McNeill J) accepted the existence and indeed the necessity for extra-statutory concessions, concluding that they fell 'within the concept of good management or of administrative common sense' and that they could fairly be said to be made 'within the proper exercise of managerial discretion'.

SPs set out the view that the Revenue takes of a particular provision and should be treated with caution since they may not accurately state the law (see, for instance, *Campbell Connelly & Co Ltd v Barnett* (1992)). The same can be said of the CGT consequences that ensue when trustees exercise a dispositive power which were set out in a series of Revenue Statements. The first (SP 7/78) was withdrawn as a result of *Roome v Edwards* (1981); its successor (SP 9/81) suffered a similar fate after *Bond v Pickford* (1983); and current Revenue thinking is found in SP 7/84 (issued in October 1984).

There is an argument against inviting the Revenue to express views upon the meaning to be given to particular provisions since in cases where the Revenue indicates that tax is chargeable, it places professional advisers in a difficult position. Do they advise their clients that the Revenue is wrong and that the House of Lords are bound to accept the taxpayer's arguments or do they advise prudence in the face of the risk of protracted and expensive litigation?                                                    **[1.25]–[1.40]**

## III CONCLUSIONS

Tax is often seen as an ephemeral area: as a part of law devoid of principle and subject to the whims of politicians. In part this view is true; the annual (sometimes biannual) Finance Act often effects considerable changes. However, the underlying principles do remain and it is usually only the surface landscape that is altered. The bedrock of income tax, for instance, can be traced back to 1803 and although inheritance tax on gifts is of more recent origin, it is based upon a relatively simple conceptual structure. In understanding tax law the golden rule must be to ignore the form in favour of the substance (see, for instance, Robert Walker LJ giving the judgement of the Court of Appeal in *Billingham v Cooper* (2001)). Given that the whole edifice is man-made and is designed to achieve practical ends, it should also follow that it is fully comprehensible. There is nothing here of the divine and, in the last resort, one should follow the approach of Lord Reid in the House of Lords in *Fleming v Associated Newspapers Ltd* (1972):

> 'On reading it [now TA 1988 s 577(10)] my first impression was that it is obscure to the point of unintelligibility and that impression has been confirmed by the able and prolonged arguments which were submitted to us ... I have suggested what may be a possible meaning, but if I am wrong about that I would not shrink from holding that the subsection is so obscure that no meaning can be given to it. I would rather do that than seek by twisting and contorting the words to give to the subsection an improbable meaning. Draftsmen as well as Homer can nod, and Parliament is so accustomed to obscure drafting in Finance Bills that no one may have noticed the defects in this subsection.' **[1.41]**

It may finally be noted that the long arm of Europe is increasingly to be seen in direct tax matters. Fundamental principles of EC law impact into this area, as seen in the recent decision of the ECJ in *Marks & Spencer plc v Halsey* (2005) (and the subsequent application of it by the High Court (2006)). Following an unsuccessful appeal to the Special Commissioners by the UK-resident company, which had claimed group relief against its UK profits in respect of the losses of its non-resident subsidiaries, the High Court referred the case to the ECJ for a preliminary ruling on whether the UK group relief provisions were compatible with the provisions of the EC Treaty on freedom of establishment (Art 43). The ECJ held that the provisions in principle constituted a restriction on the right of establishment by deterring companies from setting up subsidiaries in other member states, and went beyond what was necessary to attain the legitimate objectives that the relevant provision pursued. Moreover, when UK legislation creates manifest injustice (such as, for example, the settlor charge on offshore trusts: see **Chapter 27**), application to the European Court of Human Rights may be appropriate (compare *National and Provincial Building Society v UK* (1997) and see generally **Chapter 51**). **[1.42]**

# 2     Tax avoidance and the courts

*Written and updated by Natalie Lee, Barrister, Senior Lecturer in Law, University of Southampton*

## I   INTRODUCTION

### 1   The problem of tax avoidance

'There are cases we know of where transactions are completed solely for the benefit of a tax gain, which of course was not intended by Parliament. The question is, is it avoidance or does the activity go beyond avoidance and cross the boundary between avoidance and evasion? This can sometimes be difficult to decide ... It may be that as the legal principles of avoidance become defined in case law, a business which implements an avoidance scheme which has been held by the courts to be avoidance could be embarking on a course of conduct which amounts to evasion.'
> (From the text of the 10th Hardman Memorial Lecture delivered on 14 November 2002 by Richard Broadbent, former Chairman, Customs & Excise, 14 November 2002, BTR Issue No 2, 2003.)

'We will scrutinize artificial schemes very carefully to see whether they involve dishonesty and warrant prosecution.'
> (From the text of a speech to the annual lunch of the Chartered Institute of Taxation, delivered on 9 January 2003 by Sir Nicholas Montagu, former Chairman, Inland Revenue, Inland Revenue Press Release, January 2003.)

'... for a tax system to be effective, everyone must pay their fair share of taxes and receive the reliefs to which they are entitled. We are fully committed to combating all forms of tax avoidance, including VAT avoidance.' (The Paymaster General, Dawn Primarolo, House of Commons, 7 June 2005.)

The desire to escape the payment of tax need scarcely occasion surprise. In some cases, this may be achieved either by non-declaration or by the making of a fraudulent return (eg by deliberately under-declaring), both of which are examples of tax evasion, that is, illegal acts, subject to criminal sanctions. The greater number of situations concern attempts to avoid or minimise the payment of tax. Although there is currently an ongoing debate on questions of tax justice and tax morality, tax avoidance remains something a taxpayer is legally entitled to do. As Lord Templeman said in *Ensign Tankers (Leasing) Ltd v Stokes* (1992), 'there is no morality in a tax and no illegality or immorality in a tax avoidance scheme'.

In the average case it will amount to no more than a sensible use of the available exemptions and reliefs that are provided in all tax legislation. In other cases, where the sums involved are greater, the methods adopted by the 'tax planning industry' to escape the fiscal net may take on a complexity that is beyond the comprehension of most individuals and may involve schemes which are divorced from reality. Two recent Government publications confirm that it is losing considerable amounts of revenue through tax avoidance practices such as these, as well as through tax evasion. In *Protecting Indirect Tax Revenues*, a press notice published alongside the Pre-Budget Report 2002, and in which it was estimated that some £3 billion was being lost to Customs & Excise through VAT avoidance, the Government made clear its determination to maintain the stability of public finances through a strategy aimed at tackling abuse of the tax system and designed to reduce VAT losses, produce additional VAT revenues and put a stop to 'businesses that break or bend the tax law competing unfairly with those that abide by it'. In particular, it was stated that 'tougher action would be taken against those who continue to abuse the VAT system through fraud, avoidance and non-compliance'. Further non-legislative measures directed towards tackling fraud and avoidance of direct tax and national insurance contributions were outlined in *Fairness in Taxation—Protecting Tax Revenues*, a Budget 2003 press release. It was stated that such measures, including what is now HMRC's Anti-Avoidance Group, one of whose functions is the administration of the disclosure rules (see **Chapter 5**), would not only produce additional revenue, but would also ensure that 'the burden of tax does not fall unfairly on taxpayers who play by the rules'. What is clear from these publications, and from the pronouncements made by the former chairmen of the Inland Revenue and Customs & Excise, is that there is currently a deliberate attempt on the part of Government to link tax avoidance and tax evasion, by equating tax avoidance with non-compliance, with a view to prosecuting both. Given that tax evasion involves dishonesty, whereas tax avoidance is based upon the interpretation of tax legislation and the structuring of transactions within the law so as to minimise the tax burden, it is difficult to accept such a policy and, indeed, it has been described by one commentator as an 'abuse of rights' on the part of the authorities. That the Revenue decided to take this stance suggests that it had not previously been successful in combating the effectiveness of artificial tax avoidance schemes. This chapter analyses the way in which the courts have attempted to tackle tax avoidance; **Chapter 3** explores legislative measures designed to neutralise avoidance; and **Chapter 5** provides an overview of the disclosure rules, effective from 1 August 2004 (see **Chapter 5**).    [2.1]

## 2   Tackling tax avoidance

HMRC has three main weapons at its disposal when tackling tax avoidance. The first is legislative and is considered in **Chapter 3**. The second is the disclosure rules, effective from 1 August 2004 and which have recently been extended in their scope; **Chapter 5** provides an overview of these rules. The third weapon in HMRC's armoury, and the subject of this chapter, is to challenge in the courts the legal efficacy of avoidance schemes.          **[2.2]**

## 3   Background

In the past the Revenue won few victories, in part because of the difficulty it had in putting forward the argument that transactions used to avoid tax should be viewed as shams. No matter how artificial a transaction may be, so long as it is genuine and properly implemented, it cannot be ignored as a sham (see *Hitch v Stone* (1999)). The main reason for the Revenue's lack of success, however, was to be found in *IRC v Duke of Westminster* (1936). The object of the scheme in that case was to make servants' wages deductible in arriving at the Duke's total income by paying them by deed of covenant. Hence, although there was no binding agreement to that effect, it was accepted that so long as payments were made under the covenant they would not claim their wages. The House of Lords upheld the scheme saying that, in deciding the consequence of a transaction, the courts will look at the legal effect of the bargain that the parties have entered into and not take account of any supposed artificiality.          **[2.3]**

## 4   The 'new approach'—an overview

Unsurprisingly, the *Westminster* case gave rise to what, in effect, could be called the very first 'taxpayer's charter', instilling a belief in those taxpayers that could afford to do so that the lengths to which they could go to avoid tax were limitless, provided they were not illegal, The growth in tax avoidance schemes became marked in the 1970s, and it seemed that legislative measures, which appeared to be insufficient to keep up with the problem, were met with even more ingenuous schemes. In the early 1980s, however, the Revenue won some outstanding battles in the courts, most importantly before the House of Lords in the leading cases of *WT Ramsay Ltd v IRC, Eilbeck v Rawling* (1981), *IRC v Burmah Oil* (1982) and *Furniss v Dawson* (1984), from which cases there developed what has come to be known as the *Ramsay* principle (named after the first case in the series). At that time, and most notably at the high point of *Furniss v Dawson*, in which case Lord Scarman commented that new law was gradually being developed and that the boundaries remained yet to be fully explored, it was felt that the new principle had sounded the death knell to artificial avoidance schemes. That feeling was given further credence by the high level of hostility shown by the Revenue to such schemes as evidenced by *IRC v Rossminster Ltd* (1980), and it was believed that potential customers would be deterred from purchasing avoidance packages. The status of the *Westminster* case was left unclear by these judgments that showed that judicial attitudes to tax avoidance were very different from those prevailing in the 1930s. Indeed, in *Furniss v Dawson*,

Lord Roskill considered that 'the ghost of the Duke of Westminster has haunted the administration of this branch of the law for too long'.

Concern, however, was expressed that the development of the so-called *Ramsay* principle was nothing short of judicial legislation and, as such, an infringement of the Bill of Rights of 1689 (which established that there should be no taxation without representation). Not surprisingly therefore, subsequent decisions have been concerned with a close analysis of the true effect of *Ramsay* and its subsequent cases. *Craven v White* (1989) and *Fitzwilliam v IRC* (1993), both of which were won by the taxpayer, left the precise ambit of the 'judicial associated operations rule' uncertain, with Lord Oliver in *Craven v White* seeking to explain that the *Ramsay* principle was simply an exercise in statutory construction. In *IRC v McGuckian* (1997), this view was used to the Revenue's advantage in the promotion of purposive statutory interpretation, which certain members of the House of Lords (notably, Lords Steyn and Cooke) believed to be the basis of the *Ramsay* decision. This approach would have given the Revenue almost guaranteed success in challenging tax avoidance schemes, as is evident from Lord Steyn's comment: 'Given the reasoning underlying the new approach it is wrong to regard the decisions of the House of Lords since the *Ramsay* case as necessarily marking the limit of the law on tax avoidance schemes.' Importantly, however, there could be seen an element of retreat in the decision of *MacNiven v Westmoreland* (2001), with Lord Nicholls commenting that 'the *Ramsay* approach is no more than a useful aid ... *Ramsay* did not introduce a new legal principle. It would be wrong, therefore, to set bounds to the circumstances in which the *Ramsay* approach may be appropriate and helpful'. Lord Hoffmann in the same case went further. In rejecting the view that *Ramsay* is a principle of construction, he commented: 'There is ultimately only one principle of construction, namely to ascertain what Parliament meant by using the language of the statute.' He explained further that the formulation of *Ramsay* given in *IRC v Burmah Oil* and *Furniss v Dawson* is simply 'a statement of the consequences of giving a commercial construction to a fiscal concept'. Whilst the approach taken by Lord Hoffmann has already been applied by the Court of Appeal in relation to a PAYE scheme in *DTE Financial Services Ltd v Wilson* (2001), the difficulties inherent in such an approach can be seen in the conflicting decisions of the High Court and the Court of Appeal in *Barclays Mercantile Business Finance Ltd v Mawson* (2002), and in the judgments of both Peter Gibson and Carnwath LLJ in the Court of Appeal in that case. And, whilst in *The Collector of Stamp Revenue v Arrowtown Assets Ltd* (FACV No 4 of 2003) Lord Millett (sitting as a non-permanent judge in the Hong Kong Court of Final Appeal) delivered a challenge to Lord Hoffman's approach, the House of Lords in *Barclays Mercantile Business Finance Ltd v Mawson* (2004) would appear to have finally laid to rest the notion that *Ramsay* had given birth to a special principle affecting tax statutes and tax law, affirming that the case had been decided on the normal basis of statutory construction. If this is the final word on the matter, then it demonstrates that the decisions of the House of Lords in *IRC v Burmah Oil and Furniss v Dawson*, which were believed to have created a principle lying outside the meaning of the statute whereby transactions or elements in transactions that had no commercial purpose were to be disregarded, have been misconstrued.                                   **[2.4]–[2.20]**

## II   ARTIFICIAL SCHEMES AND THE *RAMSAY* PRINCIPLE

### 1   **The decisions in *Ramsay* and *Burmah Oil***

In both *Ramsay* and *Burmah Oil* the taxpayers sought to obtain the benefits of CGT loss relief, in the former case to wipe out large profits, in the latter to turn a large, non-allowable loss into an allowable one. To achieve this end both adopted schemes involving a series of steps to be carried out in rapid succession according to a prearranged timetable. Once started, it was intended that the schemes should be carried through to their conclusion that would be that a capital loss had been incurred. In reality, a comparison of the taxpayer's position at the start and finish showed that either no real loss was suffered, or, in *Ramsay's* case, that the only loss suffered was the professional fees paid for the implementation of the scheme! The House of Lords decided that such schemes should be viewed not as a series of separate transactions, none of which was a sham, but as a whole; the position of the taxpayer in real terms being compared at the start and at the finish. Thus, the scheme involved no real loss and was self-cancelling. In *Ramsay* Lord Wilberforce expounded this new approach to avoidance schemes and sought to explain the decision in *Westminster's* case:

> 'While obliging the court to accept documents or transactions, found to be genuine, as such, it does not compel the court to look at a document or a transaction in blinkers, isolated from any context to which it properly belongs. If it can be seen that a document or transaction was intended to have effect as part of a nexus or series of transactions, or as an ingredient of a wider transaction intended as a whole, there is nothing in the doctrine to prevent it being so regarded; to do so is not to prefer form to substance, or substance to form. It is the task of the court to ascertain the legal nature of any transaction to which it is sought to attach a tax, or a tax consequence, and if that emerges from a series, or combination of transactions, intended to operate as such, it is that series or combination which may be regarded.'
>
> ([1981] STC 174 at 180)

In *Ensign Tankers (Leasing) Ltd v Stokes* (1992) the House of Lords applied the *Ramsay* principle to the single composite transaction made up of 17 documents all dated the same day.                                        **[2.21]**

### 2   **Extending *Ramsay*: *Furniss v Dawson***

#### a)   *The facts*

It was left to Lord Brightman in *Furniss v Dawson*, building upon the words of Lord Diplock in *Burmah Oil*, to set out the conditions necessary for the application of the *Ramsay* principle: *first*, there must be a preordained series of transactions (or one single composite transaction); *secondly*, there must be steps inserted which have no commercial purpose other than the avoidance of tax. Unlike the *Ramsay* and *Burmah Oil* cases, both of which involved circular self-cancelling schemes, the sole object of which was the avoidance of tax, *Furniss v Dawson* was concerned with the deferment of CGT by channelling the sale of chargeable assets through an intermediary company. The facts of the case are simple. The Dawsons decided to sell shares to Wood

Bastow Holdings Ltd ('Wood Bastow') for £152,000. To defer the CGT that would otherwise have been payable, the shares were first sold to a newly incorporated Manx company ('Greenjacket') for the sum of £152,000 that was satisfied by an issue of shares in that company. The purchased shares were then immediately resold by Greenjacket to Wood Bastow for £152,000. The attraction of the scheme was that at no stage did any CGT liability arise: the sale to Greenjacket was specifically exempted from charge under FA 1965 Sch 7 para 6(2) (see now TCGA 1992 s 135(1)), whilst the resale by Greenjacket did not yield any profit to that company (the shares were purchased and sold for £152,000). As the price paid by Wood Bastow was received and retained by Greenjacket the scheme was not circular or self-cancelling: it involved a separate legal entity (Greenjacket) that ended up with the sale proceeds of the shares.                                              **[2.22]**

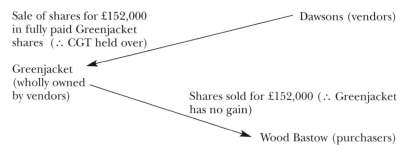

Sale of shares for £152,000
in fully paid Greenjacket
shares ( ∴ CGT held over)

Dawsons (vendors)

Greenjacket
(wholly owned
by vendors)

Shares sold for £152,000 ( ∴ Greenjacket
has no gain)

Wood Bastow (purchasers)

b)   *The decision*

Before the Special Commissioners, Vinelott J, and a unanimous Court of Appeal, CGT was held not to be payable. The sale proceeds had been paid to Greenjacket and, in the phrase of Slade LJ in the Court of Appeal, the existence of Greenjacket had 'enduring legal consequences'. Before the House of Lords it was accepted that for a *scintilla temporis* legal and beneficial title to the shares passed to Greenjacket. Lord Brightman, however, in the only fully argued speech (which was concurred in by the other Lords) viewed the series of transactions as a preplanned scheme:

'The whole process was planned and executed with faultless precision. The meetings began at 12.45pm on 20 December, at which time the shareholdings of the operating companies were still owned by the Dawsons unaffected by any contract of sale. They ended with the shareholdings in the ownership of Wood Bastow. The minutes do not disclose when the meeting ended but perhaps it was all over in time for lunch.'

As its purpose was to obtain a deferral of CGT, he concluded that the scheme should be viewed as a whole, that is as a composite transaction different from the actual transaction entered into by the parties, and that 'the court must then look at the end result. Precisely how the end result will be taxed will depend on the terms of the taxing statute sought to be applied'. Applying that test 'there was a disposal of the shares by the Dawsons in favour of Wood Bastow in consideration of a sum of money paid with the concurrence of the Dawsons to Greenjacket'. The gain on this disposal was subject to CGT. As already mentioned, Lord Brightman considered that there were two basic requirements for the application of the *Ramsay* principle. *First*, there must be a preordained series of transactions ('a scheme'), although he stressed that, so long as a preplanned tax saving scheme existed, no distinction should be drawn between the case where steps were carried out in pursuance of a contract and one where, although the steps were preordained, separate binding contracts only arose at each stage. Although Greenjacket was not contractually bound to resell the shares to Wood Bastow, it was preordained (ie there was an informal arrangement) that this would occur. Hence, 'the day is not saved for the taxpayer because the arrangement is unsigned or contains the magic words "this is not a binding contract"'. In a similar vein, Lord Fraser of Tulleybelton considered that 'the series of two transactions ... were planned as a single scheme and ... it should be viewed as a whole'. Furthermore, the scheme may include the attainment of a legitimate business end: the scheme in that case enabled shares to be sold from the Dawsons to Wood Bastow. *Secondly*, there must be steps in the scheme whose sole purpose is to avoid (or defer) a liability to tax. Such steps may have a 'business effect' but no 'business purpose'. The insertion of Greenjacket was such a step: in the words of Lord Brightman 'that inserted step had no business purpose apart from deferment of tax, although it had a business effect. If the sale had taken place in 1964 before CGT was introduced, there would have been no Greenjacket'.

In *Griffin v Citibank Investments Ltd* (2000), the High Court had to consider the effect of a scheme aimed at producing a capital gain rather than an income profit. It involved the purchase by the taxpayer company of two options, one 'call' and one 'put' with the same exercise date, the combined effect of which would be to produce a guaranteed return when exercised. Each option was entered into on standard terms, and the taxpayer paid the fair market value for each option. Considered separately, each option was a 'qualifying option' within the CGT legislation (TCGA 1992 s 143) and accordingly would be taxed as capital and not as income. The Revenue argued that the two options formed a single composite transaction (resulting in a loan, the interest from which was income) entered into solely for the purpose of tax mitigation. Having decided that the conditions laid down by Lord Brightman in *Furniss v Dawson* were not satisfied (see **[42.39]**), Patten J considered that the Revenue's second argument, that *Ramsay* provided for a 'wider' analysis than *Furniss v Dawson*, and that the court should not be constrained by the preconditions set out therein, must fail. He said that to decide otherwise would be to convert genuine transactions such as the two options under consideration into something quite different, and to do so would be to 'attribute to the options a substance and legal effect which they do not have and which ... the court would not give them upon the application of the ordinary principles of construction ...'                **[2.23]**

c)   *Parliamentary Statement by the Chief Secretary to the Treasury*

Commenting in 1985 on *Furniss v Dawson*, the Rt Hon Peter Rees QC, MP stated that:

> 'Taken with the decision in *Ramsay's* case, it is now clear that the widespread assumption based on the *Duke of Westminster's* case in the 1930s—that the courts will always look at the form rather than the substance of a transaction or various transactions—is no longer valid.

The House of Lords made it clear that this is an evolving area of law, but the emerging principles do not in any way call into question the tax treatment of covenants, leasing transactions and other straightforward commercial transactions. Nor is there any question of the Inland Revenue challenging, for example, the tax treatment of straightforward transfers of assets between members of the same group of companies. I also assure the House that, in accordance with normal practice, the Inland Revenue will not seek to reopen cases when assessments were properly settled in accordance with prevailing practice and became final before that decision.

The Board of Inland Revenue will also see whether clearance for types of case of special importance or general guidance for the benefit of taxpayers and their advisers can be given. The principle in *Furniss v Dawson* should lead, in future, to greater simplicity in our tax system and will, I hope, enable us in time to prune out provisions which owe their existence to the complexities of a high rate—some might say a confiscatory rate—tax system with a multiplicity of special reliefs.'

(HC Deb, vol 58, col 254)

This statement was reiterated and, in some respects, added to in an exchange of correspondence between the Board of Inland Revenue and the Institute of Chartered Accountants (see [1985] STI 568 where the correspondence is set out in full). The following matters are particularly significant.

*First,* that the principle will not be applied retrospectively to cases where assessments have been finalised. It may, of course, be applied to identical cases which arise in the future or are 'in the pipeline', as was evident from the attitude of the Stamp Office to certain pre-FA 1984 conveyancing schemes designed to avoid duty; it took the view that such schemes fell within the scope of *Ramsay* and assessed the transaction accordingly, leaving it up to the taxpayer to challenge their assessment in the courts. Thus, only in a limited sense is *Ramsay* not to be applied retrospectively.

*Secondly,* there is no intention to upset the treatment of 'straightforward commercial transactions'. The phrase 'other straightforward commercial transactions' is not particularly helpful: presumably in *Furniss v Dawson,* although the entire transaction was commercial (the sale of shares to Wood Bastow), it was infected by an artificial step (the insertion of Greenjacket) so that it ceased to be 'straightforward'. Lord Brightman considered that the *Ramsay* approach could apply only if steps were inserted 'which have no commercial (business) purpose apart from the avoidance of a liability to tax' ([1984] STC 153 at 166). Nevertheless, whether the insertion of some relatively insignificant business purpose will be sufficient to save a scheme, is uncertain: it remains possible that the law will develop to frustrate schemes where 'the main purpose, or one of the main purposes, is avoidance of liability to (tax) ...' (as is the case if CGT relief is to be available on a share for share exchange).

*Thirdly,* the Revenue assumes that *Ramsay* applies generally to all taxes and the *Ingram* decision (see [42.43]) offers support for this view. It has also been held that the doctrine is capable of applying to VAT (see [42.44]).

*Fourthly,* the statement itself envisages some simplification of tax legislation in the wake of the decision in *Furniss v Dawson.* At the time, the presumption was that anti-avoidance legislation would be rendered unnecessary so long as the courts preserved the *Ramsay* principle on a broad basis. Particularly in light of the more recent cases, particularly *Westmoreland*, it will be surprising if the existing provisions are removed from the statute book and one of the most puzzling problems is how to marry the new approach with these statutory provisions (see comments on this matter in *McGuckian*).

*Fifthly*, the Chief Secretary expressly exempts from *Ramsay* straightforward transfers of assets between members of the same group of companies. For some taxation purposes, groups are looked at as a whole (see, for instance, the group relief and the group income provisions). There is, however, no provision enabling the pooling of *capital* losses and arrangements designed to remedy this gap in the legislation are to be permitted. The intra-group transfer must, however, be 'straightforward': *Shepherd v Lyntress Ltd; News International plc v Shepherd* (1989) provides a graphic illustration of the kind of arrangement which will be attacked. In that case a company that realised a capital loss was acquired as part of the News International Group with the express object of using its loss relief. Chargeable assets pregnant with gain were transferred to the new group member and immediately sold (some on the day of transfer!). That transfer of the assets intra-group did not attract any tax charge and so the eventual gain on sale was available for offset against the losses. The Revenue, not surprisingly, argued that the whole transaction fell within the scope of *Ramsay*. Vinelott J was unimpressed:

> 'The Commissioners cannot characterise a series of steps as a single composite transaction unless they have first found facts sufficient to support that inference. In the instant case there is no finding by the Special Commissioners that any step had been taken to place the shares of LWT, News Corporation and Broken Hill [these were the assets pregnant with gain transferred intra-group] for sale through the Stock Exchange at the time when these shares were transferred to Lyntress and Salcombe [these were the "loss" companies]. It is not enough to say that they were transferred with a view to a sale and in order that the gain should be realised by Lyntress and Salcombe. That would be to make the fiscal motive alone a sufficient ground for imposing tax.'

The judge, following *Craven v White* ([**2.26**]), concluded that there was no reason to suspect that arrangements had been made for the sale of the shares on the Stock Exchange before their transfer to the loss-making companies: he stressed that it was doubtful whether such sales would have occurred if the price had collapsed immediately after the transfer (see FA 1993 s 88 for provisions aimed at preventing the acquisition of companies in order to utilise their capital losses).                                    [**2.24**]

## III   LIMITS TO THE *RAMSAY* PRINCIPLE

### 1   The difficulty in application

Not only were the requirements just mentioned difficult to apply but, being almost in the nature of a statutory formulation, it was clearly open to later courts to interpret them in 'inventive' ways. Two of their Lordships considered that the *Westminster* case could be distinguished as involving a single and not a composite transaction. Certainly the covenant was a single transaction, but its sole purpose was the avoidance of income tax and it was only entered into on the 'understanding' that the gardeners would not seek to claim their wages. Hence the making of the covenant was a step that had no commercial purpose save for the avoidance of tax. It is arguable, however, that unlike Greenjacket, which was an artificial person under the control of the Dawsons, the gardener's continuing right to sue for his wages serves to distinguish the case. Furthermore, as the covenant was to last for a period of seven years or the joint lives of the parties, it could have continued after the employment had terminated.

Any prearranged scheme which involves either tax avoidance, tax deferral or merely the preservation of an existing tax benefit was potentially within the *Ramsay* principle. A single tax-efficient transaction presumably not since the case does *not* state that persons must so organise their affairs that they pay the maximum amount of tax!

In the case of *Craven v White* (conjoined on appeal with *Baylis v Gregory* and *IRC v Bowater Property Developments Ltd*), the House of Lords was faced with the question of when a series of transactions forms part of a preplanned scheme (or, alternatively, when it constitutes a single composite transaction).

**[2.25]**

## 2    The cases

a)    *Craven v White, Baylis v Gregory and IRC v Bowater Property Developments Ltd*

(*i*)    *The facts*

At first sight, the facts of *Craven v White* closely resemble those of *Furniss v Dawson*. In *Craven v White*, the taxpayers arranged for shares in Q Ltd to be sold to J Ltd after those shares had been transferred to M Ltd, an Isle of Man company which had been specially acquired for the purpose. The proceeds of sale were paid to M Ltd and were loaned to the taxpayers. This loan-back completed the transaction (contrast *Dawson* where it was assumed that the moneys were retained in the Isle of Man company) although the courts did not consider that this final step was of particular significance. Despite the similarities of the two cases, both Peter Gibson J and a unanimous Court of Appeal were not persuaded that the insertion of M Ltd was an artificial step capable of excision and were unable to agree that this case involved a preplanned scheme. The crucial factor was that the taxpayers were, throughout, uncertain whether they would succeed in selling their shares to J Ltd or, indeed, to any other purchaser (although this was what they desired) and they accepted that they might end up merging their company with the business of a third party, C Ltd.    **[2.26]**

In a similar fashion to *Dawson*, the taxpayers in *Baylis v Gregory* were negotiating for the sale of their shares in a family company and envisaged that this would be carried out through an Isle of Man company. However, negotiations were broken off and then the Isle of Man company was incorporated and shares exchanged at a time when no other purchaser was on the horizon. This occurred in March 1974, and the shares were not eventually sold until January 1976. On these facts, assessments to CGT raised on the basis that there had been a direct share sale by the original proprietors to the ultimate purchaser were discharged both at first instance and by the Court of Appeal. In *IRC v Bowater Property Developments Ltd*, the intention of the taxpayer, Bowater (BPD), was to sell land it owned to MP Ltd. Concerned to avoid development land tax (DLT), BPD divided the land in question into five slices among five other companies in the group, none of which had used any part of their annual exemption from DLT. At the time of this fragmentation, there was a firm expectation that the sale to MP Ltd would proceed, although there was no question of any contract being signed at that time and, indeed, some three months later, the projected sale was called off by MP Ltd. It was accepted that the fragmentation was effected without any commercial or business purpose apart from the hope of a tax advantage. In the following year, negotiations were, however, recommenced and the sale duly occurred. Warner J and the Court of Appeal refused to excise the fragmentation step and treat the sale to MP Ltd as having been effected by BPD. They concluded that there was no prearranged scheme: 'in no sense was the second transaction (the sale to MP Ltd) pre-arranged or pre-ordained at the time when the fragmentation was carried out'. **[2.27]**

## (ii) *The House of Lords speeches*

Whilst the Law Lords unanimously rejected the Revenue's appeals in two of the cases (*Baylis v Gregory* and *Bowater Property Developments Ltd*), Lords Templeman and Goff dissented from their colleagues in *Craven v White*, finding for the Revenue. Accordingly, a degree of unanimity could be discerned in the speeches, and there is no doubt that they marked a significant limitation on the *Ramsay* principle.

So far as the actual issue in the case was concerned (namely when a preplanned series of transactions exists (on the question of the ambit of the principle, see **[42.36]** ff)) the majority—Lords Keith, Oliver and Jauncey—adopted a more restrictive view than Lords Templeman and Goff. Lord Jauncey, for instance, suggested the following definition of a 'composite transaction':

'A step in a linear transaction which has no business purpose apart from the avoidance or deferment of tax liability will be treated as forming part of a pre-ordained series of transactions or of a composite transaction if it was taken at a time when negotiations or arrangements for the carrying through as a continuous process of a subsequent transaction which actually takes place had reached a stage when there was no real likelihood that such subsequent transaction would not take place and if thereafter such negotiations or arrangements were carried through to completion without genuine interruption.'

The cases of *Baylis v Gregory* and *Bowater* failed to satisfy such a test whilst in *Craven v White*, at the time of the share exchange, there was a real possibility that the subsequent sale would not occur since negotiations with the prospective purchaser were still continuing and had not been concluded. Accordingly, the majority held that the exchange of shares was a transaction independent from the sale that later occurred.

By contrast with the views of the majority, Lords Templeman and Goff adopted a more flexible approach to the question when a preplanned scheme exists. Lord Templeman, for instance, expressed himself as follows:

'In *Furniss* ... the transactions formed part of a scheme although the Dawsons had no control, direct or indirect over Wood Bastow and could at no stage oblige Wood Bastow to buy shares in the operating company. But both transactions were part of a scheme which was planned by Dawsons, which in the event was successful and which produced a taxable transaction. Two transactions can form part of a scheme even though it is wholly uncertain when the first transaction is carried out whether the taxpayer who is responsible for the scheme will succeed in procuring the second transaction to be carried out at all ... if the shadowy, undefined and indefinable expressions "practically certain", "practical likelihood", and "practical contemplation" possess any meanings, those expressions and those meanings are not to be derived from *Furniss*.'

Lord Goff appeared to adopt an even wider test:

'it is not necessary that the details of the second step should be settled at the time when the first step was taken, nor that they should exactly correspond with those planned in advance.'

Even applying the wider tests advocated above, neither *Bowater* nor *Bayliss v Gregory* involved a preplanned series of transactions: in the former, 'the scheme was frustrated when [the prospective purchasers] abandoned the negotiations' whilst, in the latter, 'the taxpayers placed themselves in a position to escape tax *in the future* but there was no scheme' (Lord Templeman).

As the *ratio decidendi* of the case must be found in the more limited test laid down by the majority, what degree of certainty is necessary for a preplanned scheme? How sure must the taxpayers be that the scheme that was eventually implemented was always going to be so implemented? From the speeches of the majority, it is possible to extract a number of phrases that define this degree of certainty. They are set out below but it must follow, given the vagueness embraced in such phrases, that room has been left for future disagreements:

'The taxpayers were by no means in a position for all practical purposes to ensure that the sale went through.'

(Lord Keith in relation to *Craven v White*)

'a single indivisible composite whole—a concept which may be summed up in homely terms by asking the question whether at the material time that whole is already "cut and dried" ... so certain of fulfilment that it is intellectually and practically possible to conclude that there has indeed taken place one single and indivisible process ... a degree of certainty and control over the end result at the time when the intermediate steps are taken ... it does seem to me to be essential at least that the principal terms should be agreed to the point at which it can be said that there is no practical likelihood that the transaction which actually takes place will not take place.' (Lord Oliver)                                    **[2.28]**

b)    *Fitzwilliam v IRC*

(*i*)    *The facts*

The 10th Earl Fitzwilliam died on 21 September 1979 survived by his 81-year-old wife. Under the terms of his 1977 will, and after leaving a number of pecuniary legacies, his residuary estate was settled on a 23-month discretionary trust for a class of beneficiaries including Lady Fitzwilliam and with a provision that in default of exercise and at the end of that period the estate was to be held for Lady Fitzwilliam for life with remainder to her daughter Lady Hastings. The value of the residuary estate was certified at just over £12.4m and accordingly if the trustees exercised their powers to appoint that property away from Lady Fitzwilliam, CTT at a rate of 75% would apply. By contrast, if the property passed to Lady Fitzwilliam no charge would then be imposed although, given her age and then state of health, there was obviously a considerable danger that she too would die in which case the property would on that occasion be taxed at 75%.

CTT was paid on the pecuniary legacies but not on the property comprised in the residuary estate and therefore subject to the 23-month trust. It is usually thought, despite the fact that a surviving spouse is named as one of the beneficiaries, that tax must be paid in such cases albeit that recovery is then possible if the spouse is appointed the property or alternatively takes in default at the end of the 23-month period. In this case, however, CTT was paid only on the pecuniary legacies and, despite criticism from the Revenue, it appears that the Probate Office were consulted and were agreeable to this. Vinelott J did not comment other than to observe that because of the illiquid nature of the estate 'it would in fact have been very difficult for the executors to have delayed probate until a sum sufficient to pay the whole of the CTT had been raised' and the matter was not considered by the higher courts.

The will trustees and two beneficiaries (Lady Fitzwilliam and Lady Hastings) entered into a series of transactions involving five steps, devised by professional advisers, and intended to mitigate the ultimate CTT bill. The transactions were to a large degree artificial and in some cases circular and the end result was that some £7.8m had been distributed out of the residuary estate—£3.8m to Lady Hastings and £4m to Lady Fitzwilliam—without, it appeared, any CTT liability arising. (For a full analysis of the facts of the case, see earlier editions of this book.) **[2.29]**

*(ii) The House of Lords speeches*

Despite the apparent artificiality of the scheme, the House of Lords concluded (with the dissent of Lord Templeman) that the case did not fall within the *Ramsay* principle as extended by *Furniss v Dawson*. *First*, it should be noted that the Revenue's argument that all five steps formed part of a preplanned series was abandoned after the first instance judge, Vinelott J, decided that at the time the first step was undertaken, no decision had been made as to how matters would proceed. *Secondly*, and critical to the majority decision, although four of the five steps constituted a preplanned series, the House of Lords held that none of those steps could be wholly excised. Rather, the Revenue was forced to rely on all the four steps albeit that some were recharacterised.

As Lord Keith put it:

'The fact of preordainment … is not sufficient in itself, in my opinion, to negative the application of an exemption from liability to tax which the series of transactions is intended to create, unless the series is capable of being construed in a manner inconsistent with the application of the exemption … in my opinion the series in the present case cannot be ... There is no question of running any two or more transactions together as in *Furniss v Dawson* or of disregarding any one or more of them.'

This crucial part of Lord Keith's judgment was strongly rejected by Lord Templeman. In his view, three of the inserted steps that had no purpose other than the avoidance of CTT. In truth, none of the steps had any commercial purpose although they had 'enduring legal consequences' in that they gave rise, albeit for a very short period of time, to an income interest in favour of Lady Hastings or Lady Fitzwilliam. This question of 'enduring legal consequences' was, of course, fully discussed in Lord Bright-man's speech in *Furniss v Dawson*, and yet the distinction therein drawn between *purpose* and *effect* appears to have been ignored by Lord Keith.

For his part, Lord Browne-Wilkinson wished to reserve the question whether *Ramsay* was capable of applying to CTT/IHT given the existence of the wide-ranging associated operations provision in IHTA 1984 s 268:

'This amounts to a statutory statement, in much wider terms, of the *Ramsay* principle which deals with transactions carried through by two or more operations which are inter-related ... it can therefore be argued that there is no room for the Court to adopt the *Ramsay* approach in construing an Act which expressly provides for the circumstances and occasions on which transfers carried through by "associated operations" are to be taxed. It is not necessary in the present case to express any concluded view on this point.' **[2.30]**

## (*iii*)   *Fitzwilliam: an appraisal*

The crusading zeal so evident in *Dawson* appeared to leave the House of Lords: can there really be any doubt that the arrangements in *Fitzwilliam* fell within the spirit and intendment of Lord Brightman's test laid down in *Dawson*? In circular arrangements (typified by *Ramsay* itself and *Burmah Oil*) the taxpayer's position at the beginning and end of a transaction is compared and tax imposed accordingly. Similarly in *Dawson* intervening steps in a preplanned scheme were excised to leave the reconstructed transaction. In *Fitzwilliam*, on the basis of treating four of the five steps as a preplanned operation, at the start of that operation Lady Fitzwilliam owned for CTT purposes £3.8m (ie the property in which she was life tenant) but at the end of those steps she did not. In the light of the post-1984 cases it appears that further refinement is needed to the Brightman test if *Ramsay* is to be established on a coherent basis. The requirement that all steps must be preplanned could, for instance, be widened to include facts like *Fitzwilliam* where, although the precise nature of the later steps was in doubt, it was inevitable that steps aimed at avoiding tax would be undertaken.

There is an interesting contrast between the *Fitzwilliam* decision and that in *Hatton v IRC* (1992), the facts of which are set out in **[22.102]**. Chadwick J concluded in the latter case that the *Ramsay* principle applied. He rejected any suggestion that the taxpayer must have 'control' over the entire operation. In that case the second settlor (Mrs H) could have refused to create her settlement and, indeed, she took separate legal advice (albeit from a recommended adviser who was doubtless familiar with the guidelines of the entire scheme) before doing so. The reality was that a substantial tax liability could only be avoided if the second settlement was created. What actually happened was that legal advice having been taken in England in the morning, the settlement was then established in Jersey in the afternoon and the parties were (in an echo of Lord Brightman's celebrated remark in *Furniss v Dawson*) 'back in England for afternoon tea'! The preordained nature of the arrangement in this case can be contrasted with *Fitzwilliam*. Undoubtedly in *Hatton* the whole operation was planned in advance but, subject to that, it is difficult to distinguish the two cases.

It is possible to see the failure of the House of Lords to adapt *Ramsay* to the facts in *Fitzwilliam* as at root a failure of will. In any event, given the confusing nature of the speeches, it is unlikely that the case will be seen as anything other than a one-off decision on its own facts. **[2.31]**

## IV   REAFFIRMATION OF *RAMSAY*

### 1   *IRC v McGuckian*: the facts

The case involved numerous transactions, the strategy behind which was to reduce the assets held by a company (B), thus minimising the risk of exposure to a possible wealth tax on its shareholders, namely the taxpayer and his wife. At the same time to avoid an income tax liability on moneys paid out by B by ensuring that the proceeds were received in the form of capital rather than income. The main features of the scheme involved:

(1)   the setting up of a trust under which B shares would be held for the benefit of the taxpayer and his wife by a trustee residing outside the jurisdiction; and

(2)   a sale by the trustee of their rights to dividends expected to be declared and paid by B. This was in the form of a written assignment between the trustee and the purchaser, and for a consideration that only just fell short (by 1%) of the eventual dividend declared for that year by B.

The trustees were then—so it was argued—in receipt of a capital sum which could not be attributed to the settlor under eg TA 1988 s 739. As Lord Browne-Wilkinson observed, the crucial question was whether the money received by the trustee as consideration for the assignment of the right to the dividends from B was to be treated as the income of the trustee or as capital. As the proceeds of sale, the sum of money would appear to be capital; however, by applying the *Ramsay* principle, the inserted step (the assignment of the right to the dividends) would be excised, leaving the sum of money to be regarded as income. **[2.32]**

### 2   The House of Lords speeches

Unlike the majority of the Court of Appeal (Northern Ireland), Lord Browne-Wilkinson had no difficulty in applying the *Ramsay* principle; in his judgment, 'nothing in this case turns on the exact scope of the *Ramsay* principle. The case falls squarely within the classic requirements for the application of that principle as stated by Lord Brightman in *Furniss v Dawson* …'. This was a view shared by Lord Steyn who, although feeling the necessity to analyse the basis of the *Ramsay* decision and to question the literal interpretation of taxation statutes, accepted that the present case was 'a classic case for the application of the *Ramsay* principle'. The inserted step had no commercial purpose apart from the avoidance of income tax, with the consequence that it had to be excised. The other members of the court reached the same conclusion, although the reasoning of each of the four Law Lords who delivered judgments was different in emphasis.

Worthy of particular note is the rejection by Lord Browne-Wilkinson of the taxpayer's argument that the *Ramsay* principle can only apply to a series of transactions in the absence of a statutory provision that would reverse the effect of such transactions. He said:

> 'The approach pioneered in *Ramsay* and subsequently developed in later decisions is an approach to construction, viz that in construing tax legislation, the statutory provisions are to be applied to the substance of the transaction, disregarding artificial steps in the composite transaction or series of transactions inserted only for the purpose of seeking to obtain a tax advantage. The question is not what was the effect of the insertion of the artificial steps but what was its purpose. Having identified the artificial steps inserted with that purpose and disregarded them, then what is left is to apply the statutory language of the taxing Act to the transaction carried through stripped of its artificial steps. It is irrelevant to consider whether or not the disregarded artificial steps would have been effective to achieve the tax saving purpose for which they were designed.' (See also Lord Cooke who considered that *Ramsay* was antecedent to or collateral with anti-avoidance provisions.)

The importance of *McGuckian* lies in the language used by the House of Lords in relation to tax avoidance schemes: in terms of clarifying when the principle operates, matters were left as unclear as they ever had been (see, for instance, *Piggott v Staines Investments* (1995) which at first glance would appear to fall within the principle but which was not appealed by the Revenue). Thus, in considering *Craven v White*, Lord Cooke noted that it involved facts 'distant from those of the present case' and categorised it as 'a difficult case, partly because of differences of opinion in Your Lordships' House'. [2.33]

## V   MEANING, SCOPE AND APPLICABILITY OF THE *RAMSAY* PRINCIPLE: THE RECENT CASES

### 1   The earlier cases: a doctrine of fiscal nullity or statutory construction?

That there has been uncertainty as to the basis and extent of the *Ramsay* principle from the start, can be evidenced by the words of Lord Scarman in *Furniss v Dawson*:

> 'I am aware, and the legal profession (and others) must understand, that the law in this area is in an early stage of development. Speeches in your Lordships' House and judgments in the appellate courts are concerned more to chart a way forward between principles accepted and not to be rejected than to attempt anything so ambitious as to determine finally the limit beyond which the safe channel of acceptable tax avoidance shelves into the dangerous shallows of unacceptable tax evasion. The law will develop from case to case. Lord Wilberforce in *Ramsay's* case referred to "the emerging principle" of the law. What has been established with certainty by the House in *Ramsay's* case is that the determination of what does, and

what does not, constitute unacceptable tax evasion is a subject suited to development by judicial process. Difficult though that task may be for judges, it is one which is beyond the power of the blunt instrument of legislation. Whatever a statute may provide, it has to be interpreted and applied by the courts and ultimately it will prove to be in this area of judge-made law that our elusive journey's end will be found.'

Not only does this passage reveal that Lord Scarman appeared to be giving a new meaning to the terms 'tax avoidance' and 'tax evasion', perhaps a forewarning of the current attitude of HMRC, but it also demonstrates a ready acceptance that new law was being created and that this was the proper function of the judiciary. Such sentiments did not, however, commend themselves to the majority of the House of Lords in the later case of *Craven v White* (and conjoined appeals). Indeed, the majority appeared anxious to distance themselves from any notion of judicial legislation, and sought to explain an alternative and more acceptable basis of the *Ramsay* decision. For instance, Lord Oliver commented that the basis was one of statutory construction:

'It has been said that *Furniss v Dawson* is "judge-made law". So it is, but judges are not legislators and if the result of a judicial decision is to contradict the express statutory consequences which have been declared by Parliament to attach to a particular transaction which has been found as a fact to have taken place, that can be justified only because, as a matter of construction of the statute, the court has ascertained that that which has taken place is not, within the meaning of the statute, the transaction to which those consequences attach.'

Having accepted that *Furniss v Dawson* had, in reality, extended the *Ramsay* principle in that it not only applied that principle to a 'linear' transaction, but it also reconstituted the actual constituent transactions into something that they were not in fact, Lord Oliver made this important observation:

'It seems ... that the first and critical point to be borne in mind in considering the true ratio of *Furniss v Dawson* is that it rests not upon some fancied principle that anything done with a mind to minimising tax is to be struck down but upon the premise that the intermediate transfer, whose statutory consequences would otherwise have resulted in payment of tax being postponed, did not, upon the true construction of the [statute], constitute a disposal attracting the consequences set out in [the relevant provision]. That is the first point. The second is that, in reaching the conclusion as a matter of construction, this House did not purport to be doing anything more than applying and explaining the principle that had been laid down ... in [*Ramsay*]. It was that decision that explains why and how the question of construction raised in *Furniss v Dawson* came to be answered in the way that it did and it is ... only if these two considerations are borne in mind that *Furniss v Dawson* itself can be properly understood or rationally justified as a proper exercise of the judicial function.

Such an approach has been used in other tax cases in order to frustrate avoidance schemes: see, for instance, the decision in *Reed v Nova Securities Ltd* (1985) where on a construction of TA 1970 s 274 it was held that shares were not acquired as trading stock (for an analysis of this 'parallel attack' on trading transactions entered into, in whole or in part, for fiscal reasons, see (1990) BTR 52). Without further elaboration (for which, see **[42.39]**), it is difficult to fit decisions in the earlier cases, and certainly the speeches in

*Furniss v Dawson*, into a purely constructional approach. As a simple matter of language, the share exchange carried out in *Furniss, Craven v White* and *Bayliss v Gregory* undoubtedly occurred and involved a disposal of assets. Accordingly, to excise that disposal cannot, without further explanation, be a simple exercise in statutory interpretation but must result from a wholly extraneous rule which is more akin to the striking out of a 'sham' transaction. More recently in *Griffin v Citibank Investments Ltd* (2000), Patten J made it clear that he did not believe that the decision in *Furniss* was in accord with either *IRC v Duke of Westminster* or the ordinary principles of construction and analysis that that decision applied. The considerable level of disagreement on the ambit of the principle and the role of the courts in tax avoidance, was revealed by Lord Templeman in *Craven v White*:

> 'I have read the drafts of the speeches to be delivered in these present appeals. Three of those speeches accept the extreme argument of the taxpayer that *Furniss v Dawson* is limited to its own facts or is limited to a transaction which has reached an advanced stage of negotiation (whatever that expression means) before the preceding tax avoidance transaction is carried out. These limitations would distort the effect of *Furniss*, are not based on principle, are not to be derived from the speeches in *Furniss*, and if followed, would only revive a surprised tax avoidance industry and cost the general body of taxpayers hundreds of millions of pounds by enabling artificial tax avoidance schemes to alter the incidence of taxation. In *Furniss*, Lord Brightman was not alone in delivering a magisterial rebuke to those judges who sought to place limitations on *Ramsay* ... In my opinion, a knife-edged majority has no power to limit this principle which has been responsible for four decisions of this House approved by a large number of our predecessors.'

Lord Templeman always considered that the type of transactions envisaged by *Ramsay* and *Furniss v Dawson* were akin to sham transactions and should be treated accordingly. In *Matrix-Securities Ltd v IRC* (1994) he commented: 'Every tax avoidance scheme involves a trick and a pretence. It is the task of the Revenue to unravel the trick and the duty of the Court to ignore the pretence'. The dictionary definition of a 'sham' is a 'trick' or a 'pretence'.

**[2.34]**

## 2   The later cases: statutory construction confirmed

Later cases, however, sought to lay this matter to rest. In *Fitzwilliam v IRC*, Nourse LJ summarised the position as follows:

> 'In *Craven v White* each of their Lordships said that the *Ramsay* principle is one of statutory construction. That is without doubt true in the sense that once the single composite transaction has been identified the question is whether it is caught by the taxing statute on which the Crown relies. However, it does not always or even usually involve a question of statutory construction in the sense that the meaning of the statute is in doubt. Usually the question is whether a statute whose meaning is clear applies to the single composite transaction. The principle might equally be described as one of statutory application.'

The approach taken by a majority of the House of Lords in *Fitzwilliam*, encapsulated in a statement by Lord Browne-Wilkinson, would appear to support this view:

'Whatever the exact scope of the principles laid down in *W T Ramsay Ltd v IRC ...* as developed and elucidated in *Furniss (HMIT) v Dawson ...* and *Craven (HMIT) v White*, the basic principle cannot be in doubt. The commissioners or the court must identify the real transaction carried out by the taxpayers and, if this real transaction is carried through by a series of artificial steps, apply the words of the taxing provisions to the real transaction, disregarding for fiscal purposes the steps artificially inserted. The provision of the taxing statute is to be construed as applying to the actual transaction the parties were effecting in the real world, not to the artificial forms in which the parties chose to clothe in the surrealist world of tax advisers.'

Of course, this view enabled the majority of the House of Lords to concentrate on matters of detail which, in turn, led to the decision that the transaction undertaken did not form one composite whole (see **[412.33]**) thus allowing £3.8m to pass tax free. As was previously observed (see **[42.34]**), the arrangements in *Fitzwilliam* fell clearly within the spirit and intendment of Lord Brightman's test laid down in *Dawson* and, had Lord Scarman's observations been followed (see **[42.36]**), would have been brought within the tax net.                                                                    **[2.35]**

## 3  Purposive interpretation: *IRC v McGuckian*

That the approach pioneered in *Ramsay* and developed in later decisions is an approach to construction, was again reiterated by Lord Browne-Wilkinson in *IRC v McGuckian*, expressing the view of the majority of the House of Lords. However, in the same case, Lord Steyn (who would have decided the case without the benefit of the *Ramsay* principle) felt the necessity to analyse the basis of the *Ramsay* decision and to question the literal interpretation of taxation statutes. His view (of necessity an *obiter* view and one with which Lord Cooke concurred) was that *Ramsay* was important for two reasons. *First*, was the rejection by the House of pure literalism in the interpretation of tax statutes, and a move to a more purposive method of construction. This he identified in the following statement made by Lord Wilberforce: 'There may, indeed should, be considered the context and scheme of the relevant Act as a whole, and its purpose may, indeed should, be regarded.' *Secondly*, was the acceptance that a series of transactions, intended to be implemented as a whole, could be regarded for fiscal purposes as one composite transaction. Therefore, according to Lord Steyn, the *Ramsay* principle 'was not based on a linguistic analysis of the meaning of particular words in a statute. It was founded on a broad purposive interpretation, giving effect to the intention of Parliament. The principle enunciated in *Ramsay* was therefore based on an orthodox form of statutory interpretation'.

It would appear that the importance of *McGuckian* lies in the acceptance by at least two members of the House of Lords that, in applying *Ramsay*, the court should adopt a *purposive* approach to interpreting the relevant statutory provision. In the immediate aftermath of *McGuckian*, there were few signs of enthusiasm towards the purposive approach to statutory interpretation of fiscal statutes in general. For instance, neither the House of Lords in *Ingram v IRC* (1999) (see **[23.123]**) nor a unanimous Court of Appeal in *Frankland v IRC* (1997) (see **[24.146]**) were willing to apply 'a broad purposive approach' to the interpretation of the relevant statutory provisions before them. But, of course, neither of these cases was concerned with *Ramsay*. However, in the recent case of *MacNiven v Westmoreland Investments Ltd*, both Lord Hoffmann and Lord Nicholls endorsed the views of Lords Steyn and Cooke in *McGuckian*. Indeed, Lord Nicholls referred to 'the established purposive approach to the interpretation of statutes'. He continued:

> 'When searching for the meaning with which Parliament has used the statutory language in question, courts have regard to the underlying purpose that the statutory language is seeking to achieve. Likewise, Lord Cooke of Thorndon regarded *Ramsay* as an application to taxing Acts of the general approach to statutory interpretation whereby, in determining the natural meaning of particular expressions in their context, weight is given to the purpose and spirit of the legislation ...'                                                                [2.36]

### 4   *MacNiven v Westmoreland*: a commercial characterisation of fiscal concepts

The facts in *Westmoreland* revealed a preordained series of transactions designed to secure a tax advantage to Westmoreland (WIL) in the guise of an allowable loss. WIL had incurred debts, including £40m arrears of interest on loans from a pension fund, the trustees of which were its only shareholders. Although WIL's losses were real, under ICTA 1988 s 338 they only became deductible for income tax purposes when actually paid. However, WIL had no assets upon which money could be raised to make the repayment, and thus a simple scheme was devised to make this possible: the pension fund lent money to WIL, which WIL then passed back as payment of interest. The intention was that such payment be a charge on income by virtue of TA 1988 s 338, thus creating a loss that WIL could set against any future profits of the company, even if there was a later change of ownership. (Note that, in making these payments of yearly interest, WIL was obliged to deduct tax at source. However, as the recipient pension fund was an exempt body, it could reclaim the tax. As Lord Hoffmann suggested, it was this to which the Revenue most objected.) Finding in favour of the taxpayer that there had been a payment within the section, the House of Lords rejected the argument advanced by the Revenue that the tax advantage gained by reason of the planned scheme should be vitiated by applying a wide formulation of the '*Ramsay* principle'.

Unlike *McGuckian*, the importance of *Westmoreland* lies in the fact that Lord Hoffmann, who gave the leading speech and with whom all of the members of the House concurred, took the opportunity to review the major cases decided since *Ramsay*, and sought to explain the true basis of that case. For him, as for all the other members of the House, that basis lies in statutory construction (nothing new at this point). However, he readily rejected the notion, advanced by the Revenue, that this principle of construction took the form of an overriding legal principle that sought to nullify any transaction, no matter how genuine, that is (or is part of) some preordained, circular, self-cancelling transaction undertaken for no commercial purpose other than the obtaining of a tax advantage and irrespective of the language or purpose of any particular provision. As he said: 'There is ultimately only one principle of construction, namely to ascertain what Parliament meant by using the language of the statute'. Lord Nicholls was also insistent that '*Ramsay* did not introduce a new legal principle' of the kind advanced by the Revenue. Rather 'the *Ramsay* approach is no more than a useful aid [in ascertaining the legal nature of a transaction]'. Lord Hoffmann believed that some of the confusion that has abounded over the last 20 years stems from the tendency to construe the conditions necessary for the application of *Ramsay* (see [**42.22**]) to particular statutory provisions 'as if it were itself a general principle, applicable to all tax legislation'. According to him, the essence of Lord Wilberforce's judgment in *Ramsay* was the distinction between commercial concepts and juristic analysis. Thus, in that case, it had to be determined whether there had been a 'disposal' giving rise to a 'loss'. By ascribing to those words a commercial meaning, it was permissible to view all the transactions together, rather than considering each step individually, and applying those words to the result of the overall transaction. As Lord Hoffmann explained:

> 'There had never been any commercial possibility that the transactions would not have cancelled each other out. Therefore, notwithstanding the juristic independence of each of the steps of the circular transaction, the commercial view would have been to lump them all together, as the parties themselves intended, and describe them as a composite transaction which had no financial consequences. The innovation in the *Ramsay* case was to give the statutory concepts of "disposal" and "loss" a commercial meaning. The new principle of construction was a recognition that the statutory language was intended to refer to commercial concepts, so that in the case of a concept such as "disposal", the court was required to take a view of the facts which transcended the juristic individuality of the various parts of a preplanned series of transactions.'

This approach taken by Lord Hoffmann was summarised by Lightman J at first instance in *IRC v John Lewis Properties plc* (2001) (whilst Lightman J's decision has recently been upheld by the Court of Appeal in *John Lewis Properties plc v IRC* (2003), the reasoning was very different. It should be noted that leave to appeal to the House of Lords in this very important case was refused). The case concerned the question of whether a lump sum payment received by the company from a bank in return for the assignment of various leases to the bank was a capital or income payment (FA 2000 s 110 contains provisions directed at similar rent factoring schemes, which have the effect of taxing as income the price obtained on such assignments, but the section does not have retrospective effect). In holding the payment to be capital, Lightman J explained that, following *Westmoreland*, the court was required as the first step in the purposive construction of the relevant statute:

> 'to identify the concept to which the statute refers and to determine whether the concept is a legally defined concept or a commercial concept, ie "a concept which Parliament intended to be given a commercial meaning". If the concept is a legally defined concept (eg "payment of interest"), the concept cannot (in the absence of expression of some statutory policy to the contrary) be given a wider or narrower meaning so as to disregard or cancel the effect of transactions answering that description because they have no commercial purpose other than to avoid tax. But if the concept is a commercial concept (eg "disposal" or "loss") and accordingly the statute applies the test of ordinary business, the court is required to look beyond the juristic individuality of component parts of a transaction: steps which have no commercial purpose but have been artificially inserted for tax purposes into a composite transaction will not affect the answer to the statutory question (eg whether there has been a profit or loss).'

In *Barclays Mercantile Business Finance Ltd v Mawson* (2002) (see [**42.40**]), Peter Gibson LJ analysed the situation rather more succinctly. His view was that the *Ramsay* approach is applicable where:

'... it is sought to attach a tax consequence to a transaction which typically consists of a series of pre-ordained transactions or a single composite transaction, in which steps have been inserted which have no business purpose apart from the avoidance of tax. The court gives effect to the statutory language, where the concept to which the statute refers is a commercial one, by disregarding the artificial steps.'

Having established that the attribution of commercial concepts to terms used in tax legislation (most notably the term 'profits or gains') had been occurring for some considerable time, Lord Hoffmann added: 'What was fresh and new about *Ramsay* was the realisation that such an approach need not be confined to well recognised accounting concepts such as profit and loss but could be the appropriate construction of other taxation concepts as well'. Whether such a construction can be applied to other provisions in the tax legislation must depend upon their language and purpose. Lord Hoffmann said that before applying Lord Brightman's conditions:

'... it is first necessary to construe the statutory language and decide that it refers to a concept which Parliament intended to be given a commercial meaning capable of transcending the juristic individuality of its component parts. But there are many terms in tax legislation which cannot be construed in this way. They refer to purely legal concepts which have no broader commercial meaning. In such cases, the *Ramsay* principle can have no application.'

In *Furniss v Dawson*, the relevant concept was whether the disposal that had undoubtedly been made was to one person (G) or to another (D) (see [**42.22**]). According to Lord Hoffmann's analysis, by giving a commercial characterisation to that concept, the House of Lords was able to answer the statutory question to whom was the disposal made by treating the intermediate step involving G as irrelevant. Of significance is the fact that Lord Hoffmann would not disregard or 'excise' the intermediate step; he is merely saying that for the purposes of determining the answer to a particular statutory question, that intermediate step is *irrelevant*. It is because of this rationalisation that Lord Hoffmann sympathised with the view of the Court of Appeal in *McGuckian* that the assignment by Shurltrust of its right to income to Mallard choice in return for a capital payment could not be disregarded (for the facts of *McGuckian*, see [**42.35**]). 'If the assignment had to be disregarded, one could not explain how Shurltrust had received any money at all.' Thus, whilst agreeing with the conclusion of the House of Lords in the same case that the application of the *Ramsay* principle vitiated any tax advantage to the taxpayers, Lord Hoffmann preferred to explain this on the basis that for the purpose of the fiscal concept in question, namely the character of the receipt as income, the assignment to Shurltrust was an irrelevance.

In *Westmoreland* itself, the question that had to be decided was quite simply whether there had been a payment. According to the above analysis, if a commercial attribution can be given to the term 'payment', then that term would be applied only to the end result, ignoring the all-important intermediate steps and, accordingly, no payment would be held to have been made.

However, Lord Hoffmann said that a distinction had to be made between terms that could be construed commercially and those that should be interpreted juristically. In the present context, the term 'payment' was to be construed juristically and, according to its juristic meaning, there was a payment if the legal obligation to pay interest had been discharged.

Although the clear import of *Westmoreland* is that when applying a statutory provision, if a relevant concept is commercial, a transaction can be ignored if it has no commercial purpose apart from the avoidance of tax, Lord Hoffmann himself identified circumstances where that might not be the case. So, a transaction which comes within the statutory language, construed in the correct commercial sense, cannot be disregarded simply on the ground that it was entered into solely for tax reasons. Accordingly, in *Craven v White* (1989), although the initial disposal had no commercial purpose apart from laying the foundation for the avoidance of tax if and when there should be a further disposal to a third party, the transactions were so separate as to make it impossible to treat them in a commercial sense as a single disposal to the third party. Both the lapse of time between the two transactions and the lack of contemplation of any specific later disposal at the time of the first transaction were commercial realities. Similarly, in *Griffin v Citibank Investments Ltd* (2000) (see [**42.22**]), where it had to be decided, *inter alia*, whether two option contracts ('put' and 'call' options) undoubtedly entered into as part of a preplanned scheme to produce a capital gain rather than an income profit, should be treated as a single composite transaction, Patten J held that 'it could not be said that there was no practical likelihood that the preplanned events would not take place'. It is also possible that the use of commercial concepts like 'income' and 'capital' may give the taxpayer a choice of structuring a transaction so as to come within one concept or the other. A transaction that, for the avoidance of tax, has been structured to produce capital, and does in fact produce capital in the ordinary commercial sense of that concept (which, of course, was *not* the position in *McGuckian*), cannot be recharacterised as producing income. Accordingly, in *Citibank Investments*, Patten J held that he was unable to conclude that the transaction (the combined effect of the put and call options) had no other purpose than tax mitigation. He said, 'There seems to me to be a real difference between the taxpayer who sets out to utilise a tax avoidance scheme in order to reduce or eliminate an already existing tax liability and one who makes a legitimate choice between investment options having regard to his own fiscal and financial position.' A similar situation arose on *Scottish Provident Institution v IRC* (2004), where it had to be decided whether or not a loss arising from a scheme involving the use of cross-options in relation to gilts and a collateral loan was deductible in calculating the taxpayer company's tax liability. Although the particular issue did not need to be decided in the wake of the Court's conclusion that the term 'loss' as employed in the relevant statutory provision was a legal concept and accordingly did not attract the application of the *Ramsay* principle, the Court nonetheless gave its opinion in the event that *Ramsay* should apply. As in *Citibank Investments*, the Court was prepared to look at the context in which the scheme was devised and, having done so, did not accept that the two options should be regarded as a composite transaction, precluding a consideration of each option separately. Despite the fact that, in the event, both options *were* exercised, and that the scheme was intended to avoid tax, the Court was of the view that there was a 'genuine commercial possibility and a real practical likelihood that the two options would be dealt with separately, and that option B would not be exercised by [the taxpayers].' The same conclusion was reached by Lightman J at first instance in *IRC v John Lewis Properties plc*, where he held that, for the avoidance of tax, the company was perfectly entitled to structure its commercial transaction with the bank so that in place of an income receipt of rent, it received a capital sum. The sum was not merely the bank's receipt of the rents from the lessees: it was a distinct sum paid out of the resources of the bank under a transaction that had commercial reality. As such, it was not open to the court to recharacterise the sum paid as income. Interestingly, although the majority of the Court of Appeal in *John Lewis Properties v IRC* (2003), agreed with Lightman J that the payment was one of capital, they reached their conclusion with no reference to *Ramsay*, *Westmoreland*, and commercial/legal concepts, basing their argument instead on the traditional and orthodox indicia of capital payments (see **[6.103]–[6.109]**). In contrast, Arden LJ, in her dissenting judgment in which she held the payment to be income, took the view that the conversion of rents into a lump sum had no 'commercial reality' as an exchange of income for capital despite the fact that she found a real commercial motive for the transaction. 'Commercial motive and commercial reality', she said, 'are different concepts'. Such a view, it is suggested, would appear to be completely at odds with Lord Brightman's dictum in *Furniss v Dawson* (see **[42.22]**), where *absence* of commercial purpose (or motive) was one of the factors that caused the scheme in that case to fail.

Despite the feeling that Lord Hoffmann's judgment in *Westmoreland* had provided a definitive view in respect of the application of *Ramsay*, subsequent cases displayed a disparity of approach. In *DTE Financial Services v Wilson* (2001), the Court of Appeal appeared to adopt a pre-*Westmoreland* analysis, although on a broad *Ramsay* basis rather than on the more formalistic *Furniss* approach, by identifying *at the start* the composite transaction and then deciding what would be the result if the *Ramsay* principle applied. Only as a *final step* did the court then consider whether, following *Westmoreland*, the relevant concept ('payment' in the PAYE context) was a commercial concept and thus permitting the *Ramsay* principle to apply (see **[42.40]**). This would appear to be in direct contradistinction to the view expressed by Lord Hoffmann. In contrast, both the High Court in *John Lewis Properties* and the Court of Session in *Scottish Provident v IRC* (2004) did adopt Lord Hoffman's analysis by determining at the start whether the relevant concept was commercial or legal. But it has to be accepted that there are real difficulties with this approach.

*First*, it has to be asked what the position is when the case is concerned with personal rather than commercial tax planning. The difficulty that has always existed is to apply in that context the second of Lord Brightman's conditions, namely that there must be a step inserted that has no business purpose. In *Hatton v IRC* (1992), Chadwick J excised a short-lived interest in possession commenting that neither of the two settlements involved 'had any practical (business) purpose other than the saving of tax'. In a similar fashion,

Millett LJ in his dissenting Court of Appeal judgment in *Ingram v IRC* (1997) sought to explain how the excising of inserted steps operated in a non-commercial context. He said:

> 'What is required to enable the court to disregard a transaction or step in a transaction is not the presence of a tax avoidance motive, but the absence of any other purpose. This is often described as the absence of any business purpose; but in this context "business purpose" does not mean "commercial purpose" but simply "non-fiscal purpose".' (See also *Reynaud v IRC* (1999).)

(The House of Lords in *Ingram v IRC* (1999) took the view that there was no need to discuss the scope of the *Ramsay* principle and the case was decided on the interpretation of the relevant statutory provision: see **Chapter 23**.) However, whilst those judgments are helpful in explaining the notion of business purpose in terms of 'non-fiscal purpose', we now know, of course, that it is wrong to talk of excising intermediate transactions. What has to be done instead is to apply, if permissible, a commercial interpretation to the relevant statutory provision. But, whilst the conditions necessary for the *Ramsay* approach to apply may be satisfied, there must be doubt about being able to characterise commercially a concept that is being applied in the context of a non-commercial transaction. This is not an issue that was addressed by Lord Hoffmann in *Westmoreland*.

*Secondly*, and substantively of the greatest importance, which particular words or concepts will lend themselves to a commercial rather than a juristic interpretation? It has already been seen that Lord Hoffmann spelt out the limitations of *Ramsay* by explaining that not all words or concepts will be capable of being interpreted commercially. However, there is nothing in his speech that lends any guidance to what will undoubtedly become a critical matter in future cases. In *DTE Financial Services Ltd v Wilson* (2001), one of the key issues was whether, in the context of the PAYE system, and for the purposes of TA 1988 s 203(1), the concept of 'payment' was a commercial or legalistic concept. The case concerned a scheme to avoid employer's PAYE on employee bonuses paid in the form of a contingent reversionary interest in an overseas trust. More specifically, the directors of DTE had 'contemplated' (but not, of course, decided) that DTE would pay each of them a bonus of £40,000. In accordance with the devised scheme, a contingent reversionary interest was created in an offshore discretionary settlement. On the following day, DTE took an assignment of the interest for a consideration of £40,600, £600 representing fees. The day after that, the interest was assigned to M, one of the directors. Two days later, the interest fell into possession, and £40,000 was remitted to M. DTE argued that the effect of the scheme was to provide M not with a cash payment of £40,000, but with a contingent reversionary interest and, accordingly, there was no 'payment' within TA 1988 s 203(1). A unanimous Court of Appeal accepted the Revenue's submission that the term 'payment' in the context of the PAYE system was a commercial concept. This conclusion was reached on the basis that the statutory provisions relating to PAYE focus on the actual transfer of money from employer to employee rather than on the discharge of an employer's obligation, and that the term 'payment' means cash or its equivalent.

Given these difficulties, it came as no surprise that Lord Millett, recently retired from the House of Lords and sitting as a non-permanent member of the Hong Kong Court of Final Appeal in *The Collector of Stamp Revenue v Arrowtown Assets Ltd* (2004), sought to destroy Lord Hoffmann's analysis. In this case, concerning the avoidance of Hong Kong stamp duty, the decision in which was that non-voting shares were not share capital and should accordingly be disregarded, Lord Millett said that Lord Hoffmann's approach had led to 'arid debates in an endeavour to fit the statutory language into one or other conceptual category'. In his view, whether a scheme is effective for tax purposes rather than falling foul of the Ramsay principle, had little to do with any distinction between juristic and commercial attribution to certain words in the statute, but depended upon whether 'it fell within the legislative intent of the relevant statutory provision purposively construed'. Thus, in Burmah Oil, on a purposive construction of the statute, the relief for allowable losses was confined to transactions carried out for business purposes, and, therefore, did not apply to a transaction whose only purpose was to generate the tax relief. So also in *Furniss v Dawson*, the word 'disposal' was given its ordinary legal meaning, but was taken to refer to disposals occurring in the course of transactions undertaken for a business purpose other than the avoidance of tax. On this analysis, the share exchange with Greenjacket fell to be disregarded for tax purposes. In granting the tax relief for share exchanges, Parliament could not have intended to include a share exchange undertaken for the sole purpose of obtaining such relief. In distinction, Lord Millett explained why the Ramsay principle did not apply in Westmoreland. He said that there was nothing in the language or the context of the relevant statutory provision (TA 1988 s 338) to indicate that the purpose for which a payment of interest is made is material to the question of whether it should be allowed as a charge against profits. As a consequence, a genuine discharge of a debt (as opposed to a sham transaction) was not disqualified from being a 'payment' in this context merely because its only purpose was to secure a tax deduction under s 388; the granting of relief under this provision in the case of a payment made solely for the purpose of obtaining relief was within the intendment of the statute.          **[2.37]**

## 5   *Barclays Mercantile Business Finance Ltd v Mawson*: **the last piece of the jigsaw?**

Writing extra-judicially, Lord Hoffmann has expressed the view that the decision of the House of Lords in *Barclays Mercantile Business Finance Ltd v Mawson* (*BMBF*) (2004) may well have 'killed off the *Ramsay* doctrine as a special theory of revenue law and subsumed it within the general theory of the interpretation of statutes ...' (2005, BTR 197), although the conclusions of the same members of the Judicial Committee in *Scottish Provident Institution v IRC* (2004) (**[2.45]**) might suggest otherwise. The issue in *BMBF* was whether the lessor (BMBF) was entitled to capital allowances for expenditure on the purchase of a gas pipeline that was leased to the Irish Gas Board (BGE). BMBF was a company in the Barclays group whose principal activity was the provision of asset-based finance. Another member of the same group, BZW (the investment banking arm of the Barclays group), devised a series of transactions involving the various companies in the group under which BMBF agreed to acquire a gas pipeline that had already been constructed between Scotland and the Irish Republic from BGE. The total purchase price was some £91m. On the same date, BMBF borrowed £91m from Barclays. BMBF then leased the pipeline back to BGE on finance lease terms (the rate of which was made more attractive by the availability of capital allowances) and BGE subleased the pipeline to BGE(UK), a UK subsidiary. This sublease was important because, had the end user of the pipeline been a company outside the UK (which BGE was), then BMBF would have been unable to claim capital allowances. It was then agreed that the rent due from BGE(UK) to BGE under the sublease would be paid directly to BMBF. BGE and BGE(UK) then entered into a transportation agreement, under which BGE(UK) would transport, handle and deliver gas to BGE's orders. This agreement provided BGE(UK) with a source of income from the use of the gas pipeline. The security for the lease and transportation agreements was provided by several other transactions, the overall effect of which was that an amount totalling some £91m was passed back to the Barclays group as a security deposit. From an overall perspective, an amount equal to the consideration received by BGE on the sale of the gas pipeline was re-cycled back to the Barclays group. The Revenue refused BMBF's claim for writing-down allowances on the basis that, considering the whole finance lease transaction, there was in fact no finance. Both the Court of Appeal and the House of Lords found in favour of the taxpayer. Giving the leading judgment in the Court of Appeal, Peter Gibson LJ concluded that the purpose of the capital allowances legislation was to encourage the expenditure of capital on plant and machinery. The fact that a trader incurring the expenditure would not himself use the plant or machinery, but would lease it and pass on the benefit of the allowances to the lessee, was not a reason for not conferring capital allowances on that trader. The relevant provision required that expenditure should be incurred by the trader on the provision of plant and machinery wholly and exclusively used for the purposes of his trade. In ascertaining whether that test had been satisfied, the way in which the trader acquired the funds to finance the expenditure and what the vendor of the plant and machinery did with the consideration received, were both immaterial considerations. Also of irrelevance was whether or not the trader's purpose was or included the obtaining of capital allowances. Finally, there was no evidence to establish any artificiality in the arrangements and, accordingly, Peter Gibson LJ could see no scope for the application of the *Ramsay* approach. However, if it was necessary to determine whether the concept of incurring expenditure on the provision of an asset was legal or commercial in accordance with Lord Hoffmann's guidance in *Westmoreland*, the court would have held that it was legal by analogy with the concept of 'payment' which in *Westmoreland* was held to be a legal concept. Peter Gibson LJ said, '… the fundamental question is the true construction of the statutory provisions, and the application of the meaning so ascertained to the facts … the expression "incurring expenditure" archetypally would include a payment.' In the context of the relevant provision, it was irrelevant that the money used in the expenditure was part of a circular transaction and, on that basis, the *Ramsay* approach would not apply. He added further that if that conclusion was wrong, and the concept was a commercial one, even then the *Ramsay* approach would not apply on the basis that there was throughout a genuine business purpose, namely, the acquisition of the pipeline so that it could be leased back to provide the rental stream and enable BMBF to earn the profit it sought. However, in the course of his judgment, Peter Gibson LJ referred to 'the difficult dichotomy between legal and commercial concepts', and it must have been with much relief to all those concerned with tax law to hear that the House of Lords had, most politely, rejected the importance of that dichotomy. Lord Nicholls, expressing the opinion of the judicial committee, said that Lord Hoffmann's approach was not 'intended to provide a substitute for a close analysis of what that statute means. It certainly does not justify the assumption that an answer can be obtained by classifying all concepts a priori as either "commercial" or "legal". That would be the very negation of purposive construction." In dismissing the Revenue's appeal, the view of their Lordships was that a taxing statute was to be applied by reference to the ordinary principles of statutory construction. The essence of the 'new approach' was to give the statutory provision a purposive construction in order to determine the nature of the transaction to which it was intended to apply, and then to decide whether the actual transaction (which might involve considering the overall effect of a number of elements intended to operate together) answered to the statutory description. Accordingly, the question that must always be asked is whether, on its true construction, the relevant statutory provision applies to the facts found. As Lord Nicholls observed,

> 'The simplicity of this question, however difficult it might be to answer on the facts of a particular case, shows that the *Ramsay* case did not introduce a new doctrine operating within the special field of Revenue statutes. On the contrary, as Lord Steyn observed in *McGuckian* ... it rescued tax law from being "some island of literal interpretation" and brought it within generally applicable principles.'

Applying those principles to the case at hand, the House of Lords determined that the object of granting a capital allowance is to provide a tax equivalent to the normal accounting deductions from profits for the depreciation of machinery and plant used for the purposes of the trade. Consistently with that purpose, the relevant statutory provision requires that a trader should have incurred capital expenditure on the provision of machinery or plant for the purposes of the trade. In the case of a trade concerned with finance leasing, where the capital expenditure should have been incurred to acquire the machinery or plant for the purpose of leasing it in the course of the trade, these statutory requirements are concerned entirely with the acts and purposes of the lessor, who suffers the depreciation in the value of the plant and who is, therefore, entitled to the allowance. The Act is silent about what the lessee should do with the purchase price, how he should find the money to pay the rent or how he should use the plant and, accordingly, is not relevant. What arrangements the lessee chooses to make, even if they are pre-ordained, is of no concern to the lessor.                    [2.38]

## 6   Applicability to all taxes

a)   *General*

Given that the House of Lords in *BMBF* (2004) has now so decisively stated that the *Ramsay* line of authorities is based on ordinary principles of statutory construction, it must be the case that they are of common application depending on the facts of each particular case and on the wording of the relevant statutory provision.

Prior to this landmark decision, the Special Commissioners had applied *Ramsay* to a scheme aimed at maximising profit-related pay (see *Colours Ltd (formerly Spectrum Ltd) v IRC* (1998)) and upheld an assessment in a group company scheme designed to avoid the payment of ACT (*Cedar plc v IRC; Larch Ltd v IRC* (1998)), whilst the Court of Appeal has applied *Ramsay* (in the light of *Westmoreland*) to a scheme that sought to avoid having to account for tax on a bonus under the PAYE system (*DTE Financial Services Ltd v Wilson* (2001)). And whilst Lord Browne-Wilkinson queried the application of *Ramsay* to CTT/IHT (see [**42.33**]), he has been the only member of the House of Lords so to do. Moreover, there seems to be no logical reason to assume that *Ramsay* cannot complement IHTA 1984 s 268 and *vice versa*. However, even if *Ramsay* can apply, there is no suggestion that the Revenue would seek to challenge the normal IHT arrangements between spouses designed to ensure that both make full use of the available exemptions and reliefs and nil rate band of tax. Similar arrangements may be entered into in order to take advantage of the independent taxation of spouses.          [**2.39**]

b)   *Stamp duty and stamp duty land tax*

It was thought that there was no room for the application of the *Ramsay* principle to stamp duty because, *inter alia*, it is a duty on documents not transactions. Since stamp duty land tax came into effect on 1 December 2003 (see [**40.3**]), the new tax created thereunder is levied on *transactions* in land rather than on written instruments. Accordingly, there is no longer any rational basis for that original view in relation to land transactions. However, even before that, there were indications that this was simply not the case. In *Ingram v IRC* (1985), Vinelott J held that a stamp duty scheme designed to avoid duty on the purchase of land by splitting the transaction into stages fell within *Furniss v Dawson* and was therefore ineffective. The scheme involved, first, the purchaser agreeing to take a 999-year lease of the property at a premium of £145,000 and small annual rent; secondly, the sale of the property subject to that lease to a company for 500; and finally the resale of the property by the company to the purchaser for 600. As a result of these transactions the taxpayer acquired full title to the land (by merger of the leasehold and freehold interests) but it was intended that the consideration paid for the long lease would escape duty (since agreements for leases exceeding 35 years were excluded from charge under the Stamp Act 1891 s 75) so that only the small sum paid on the transfer of the freehold would be subject to duty.

The judge held that, were it not for the *Ramsay* principle, it was clear that the taxpayer's contentions were correct and that the transfer was what it purported to be—ie of a freehold interest subject to the agreement for the lease which had reduced its value. An application of the *Ramsay* principle, however, required the composite transaction to be 'recharacterised'. Accordingly, the leasehold agreement should be excised as an artificial transaction, leaving the instrument of transfer subject to duty as a transfer of the entire freehold interest at the agreed price (ie £145,600).

Two important matters emerge from this judgment.

*First*, Vinelott J stated that the principle that, if a document was genuine, the court could not go behind it to some supposed underlying substance (derived from *IRC v Duke of Westminster*) had no application to composite transactions entered into for the purpose of avoiding tax and the result of the new approach of the House of Lords was that many decisions (including some of the House of Lords) needed reappraisal. In the light of the House of Lords decision in *Westmoreland*, in particular the speeches of Lords Hoffmann and Nicholls, this view must now be doubted.

*Secondly*, the view that *Ramsay* had no application in the field of stamp duty was rejected '*after considerable hesitation*'. Although the duty was levied on instruments not transactions, in order to determine the nature of a particular instrument, the court had to ascertain the substance of the transaction effected by it—a task which should be carried out by applying the *Ramsay* principle. Since 1 December 2003, stamp duty land tax has been levied on transactions and so, to that extent, there is little difference between this and other direct taxes where land transactions are concerned

The *Westmoreland* decision threw the whole question of the applicability of *Ramsay* to stamp duty back into the melting pot. Lord Hoffmann in illustrating one expression of a taxing statute that referred to a purely legal concept used stamp duty payable upon a conveyance or transfer on sale as an example (FA 1999 Sch 13 para 1(1)). He continued:

'If a transaction falls within the legal description, it makes no difference that it has no business purpose. Having a business purpose is not part of the relevant concept. If the disregarded steps in *Furniss v Dawson* had involved the use of documents of a legal description which attracted stamp duty, stamp duty would have been payable.'

Given that stamp duty in relation to land transactions is no longer the classic tax on form rather than substance, scope for applying *Ramsay* today seems less limited than it had been previously, particularly in the light of *Barclays Mercantile Business Finance Ltd v Mawson* (2004) (it should also be noted as instructive that *Ramsay* was applied in the Hong Kong stamp duty case of *The Collector of Stamp Revenue v Arrowtown Assets Limited* (2004)).

As a postscript, note that the avoidance scheme employed in the *Ingram* case was prohibited by FA 1984 s 111.                                    **[2.40]**

c)    *VAT*

It has already been mentioned that the *Ramsay* doctrine is capable of applying to VAT. This was established in *C & E Comrs v Faith Construction Ltd* (1989), although it was not invoked since the court decided that the relevant scheme amounted to a single genuine transaction. The particular arrangement was designed to avoid the VAT charge on building alterations that came into effect on 1 June 1984. Accordingly, the taxpayers arranged to be paid in full for the alterations before that date and this was achieved as part of an agreement under which the payment in question was lent back to the customer (under a commercial loan) and was then repaid by instalments equal to the amounts periodically certified as payable by the architects. In effect, therefore, payment for the work did occur after the deadline for the introduction of VAT but, because of the legal arrangements entered into, the taxpayers argued that the late instalments represented the repayment of a commercial loan. This abbreviated summary of the facts reveals the high level of artificiality involved in the case and accordingly the decision of the High Court that *Ramsay* did not apply is somewhat surprising. To categorise the scheme as a single transaction is in itself open to doubt and it was even accepted by the taxpayer that the sole reason for the arrangements was to avoid a VAT liability! (*C & E Comrs v Faith Construction Ltd* (1989): the Court of Appeal did not need to consider the possible application of *Ramsay*.)

An explanation for this decision, given by Lord Hoffmann in *Westmoreland*, that 'payment' in the *Faith Construction* case was a legal and not a commercial concept, clearly suggests that Lord Hoffmann considers that *Ramsay* can apply to VAT. Indeed, in the earlier case of *C & E Comrs v Thorn Materials Supply Ltd* (1998), whilst Lord Nolan said that there was no need, and in fact that it was undesirable, to consider the question of whether the *Ramsay* principle had any application to VAT until a case arose when it was necessary to do so, Lord Hoffmann, in contrast, argued in his dissenting judgment that the *Ramsay* principle was potentially relevant, although not applicable on the facts of that particular case. (Note also that in the judicial review case of *R v C & E Comrs, ex p Greenwich Property Ltd* (2001), Collins J suggested that *Ramsay* could apply to VAT cases—although on the facts of the case, no attempt had been made to argue that the scheme in question did in fact fall within *Ramsay*—as could the approach now adopted by the House of Lords in *Westmoreland*.)

A complication with VAT is that it derives directly from the EC Sixth Directive (Directive 77/388), to which principles of European Law apply. Despite the comments made by Lord Hoffmann in *Westmoreland*, it has to be questioned whether these European law principles can incorporate *Ramsay* at all, or whether they would have the effect of restricting the *Ramsay* principle. Moreover, while it is clear that there exists within European law a principle of abuse of rights (see, for example, *Emsland Starke* (2000), the questions arise as to (i) whether this principle applies in the context of VAT, and (ii) if it does, is it in addition, or an alternative, to the *Ramsay* principle. The idea behind the concept (in a fiscal context) is that although taxpayers could arrange their affairs in order to mitigate tax, that right would be deemed to be abused if the purpose was *solely* to avoid tax. The first question appears to have been answered in the affirmative by the ECJ in *Halifax plc v C&E Commrs* (2006) and in a number of other cases heard at the same time, including *University of Huddersfield Higher Education Corp v C&E Commrs* and *BUPA Hospitals Ltd v C&E Commrs*. In all of these cases, the court had to consider various input tax planning arrangements for financial, educational and medical institutions. The court was of the view that the application of Community legislation could not be extended to cover abusive practices, namely transactions carried out solely for the purpose of wrongfully obtaining tax advantages provided for by community law. However, adding two caveats to this conclusion, the court was of the further view that: (i) the measures adopted by member states to ensure the correct levying and collection of tax and for the prevention of fraud, must go no further than is necessary to attain such objectives; and (ii) a finding of abusive practice must not lead to a penalty, but to an obligation to repay. It is yet too early to decide just how influential a decision this is; one commentator is of the view that the message that planning must be associated with a genuine commercial justification is 'undiluted' by the *Halifax* cases, but that 'taxpayer choice, the right to mitigate, proportionality, immunity from penalty, and legal certainty come out of the case intact' (*The Tax Journal*, 27 February 2006). For further comment, see *The Tax Journal*, 6 March 2006; for HMRC's view of the effect of the cases, see 17 April 2006.                                                        **[2.41]**

## 7   'Tax avoidance' versus 'tax mitigation'

Following the Privy Council case of *IRC v Challenge Corpn Ltd* (1986), a distinction emerged between tax mitigation on the one hand and tax avoidance on the other. According to Lord Nolan:

> 'The hallmark of tax avoidance is that the taxpayer reduces his liability to tax without incurring the economic consequences that Parliament intended to be suffered by any taxpayer qualifying for such reduction in his tax liability. The hallmark of tax mitigation, on the other hand, is that the taxpayer takes advantage of a fiscally attractive option afforded to him by the tax legislation, and genuinely suffers the economic consequences that Parliament intended to be suffered by those taking advantage of the option.' (*IRC v Willoughby* (1997)).

Having made the distinction between mitigation and avoidance, the question that then arises is precisely how the distinction affects the *Ramsay* principle. In *Ensign Tankers (Leasing) Ltd v Stokes* (1992), Lord Templeman made it clear that if steps were inserted in order to mitigate tax (and thus resulted in an actual loss or the incurring of actual expenditure) then such mitigation would be outside the *Ramsay* principle. However, where steps were inserted to avoid tax, and thus where the taxpayer sought to reduce his liability to tax without incurring any actual loss or expenditure contrary to the intention of Parliament, such steps would come within the principle. The difficulty with this distinction is that it provides no clear guidance as to the circumstances in which a taxpayer can be said to have suffered genuine economic consequences. Might not the creation of the intermediary company in *Furniss* be considered a genuine economic consequence? The distinction certainly found no favour with Lord Hoffmann who, in *MacNiven v Westmoreland Investments Ltd*, said that, unless the statutory provisions themselves contained words like 'avoidance' or 'mitigation', the terms were not particularly helpful. Thus, in *IRC v Willoughby* (1997), it was necessary for the House of Lords to determine what was meant by the term tax avoidance since the statute expressly provided that certain provisions having the effect of negating any advantage to the taxpayer should not apply if the taxpayer could show that he had not acted with 'the purpose of avoiding liability to tax'. And yet, the distinction may once again become important since it would appear to be the case that, in combating VAT avoidance pursuant to *Protecting Indirect Tax Revenues* (see **[421]**–**[42.20]**), Customs & Excise are most definitely drawing a distinction between tax avoidance and tax mitigation. Their position was put thus:

> 'Some argue that there is no real difference between tax mitigation and tax avoidance, that these are just different ways of describing the same thing. But, while there may be some grey areas, the argument is entirely specious. Horses and donkeys have similarities, but most people can tell one from the other. In the same

way, an objective observer generally has no problem telling an avoidance scheme—a contrived or artificial arrangement that exploits the letter of the law in ways contrary to its spirit and purpose—from tax mitigation.'

(Chris Tailby, former Director of Tax Practice, HM Customs & Excise, *Tax Journal*, 2 December 2002.)

Many would disagree with this view and would argue that, whilst the distinction between tax avoidance and tax evasion is very clear, any distinction between tax avoidance and tax mitigation is not quite so clear cut. That latter distinction is crucial to the success of both the Revenue and Customs & Excise in their efforts to tackle abuse of the tax system through fraud and unacceptable avoidance, but it must necessarily have the effect of blurring the former distinction. It is likely that this will be viewed by most tax practitioners as quite unacceptable. **[2.42]**

## VI   CONCLUSIONS

### 1   Life after *Barclays Mercantile Business Finance Ltd*

It would appear to be the case that the hopes of the Revenue that a broad interpretation of *Ramsay* would permit either the preferment of substance over form (as in the USA) or some form of fiscal nullity doctrine have been dashed in the light of *Barclays Mercantile Business Finance Ltd v Mawson*. The House of Lords has firmly rejected the view that transactions, or elements in a series of transactions, which have no commercial purpose are to be disregarded whatever the taxing statute in question happens to be. Rather, the court must first decide, on a purposive construction, precisely what transaction falls within the statutory description, and then, secondly, establish whether the particular transaction in question actually does so. If, as in *Mawson*, plant is purchased for the purpose of the purchaser's finance leasing trade, that is the only fact that is relevant to the statutory provision and it is of no consequence if the lessee chooses to make arrangements for the sale and leaseback of the plant, which result in the bulk of the purchase price being irrecoverable. There is no scope for the transaction to be disregarded. In contrast, where a taxpayer embarked upon an artificial scheme devised in 1995 to take advantage of a prospective change in the system of taxing gains on options to buy or sell bonds and Government securities ('gilts'), the House of Lords took the view that the relevant statutory provisions required the court to have regard to the whole of the series of transactions that were intended to have a commercial unity (*IRV v Scottish Provident Institution* (2005): see **[42.48]**). Given that the whole purpose of the scheme was to create, not a real profit or loss but, rather, a tax loss, the case closely resembles *Ramsay* itself, and it could be argued that the approach taken in both *Scottish Provident* and in *Barclays Mercantile Business Finance Ltd v Mawson* is simply a return to the uncertainty created by the decision in *Ramsay*. **[2.43]**

### 2   Use by taxpayer?

Although the majority of the Court of Appeal in *Whittles v Uniholdings Ltd (No 3)* (1996) found that the *Ramsay* principle had no application to the facts of this particular case, two of their Lordships were of the view that it could be applied in favour of the taxpayer in appropriate circumstances (see the judgments of Aldous LJ and Sir John Balcombe). In *Bird v IRC* (1985) Vinelott J at first instance, without expressing a concluded view on the matter, had thought it unlikely that when a taxpayer embarked on a series of transactions designed to avoid tax he could later argue (when those transactions were challenged under anti-avoidance legislation such as TA 1988 ss 703 ff) that they should be treated as a fiscal nullity. Further he expressed the view that a party cannot blow 'hot and cold' so that the Revenue could not argue that a scheme fell within TA 1988 s 703 (thereby accepting that all the steps were effective but that the end result was nullified by statute) and, as an alternative, seek to excise certain of those steps under the *Ramsay* approach.

**[2.44]**

## 3   Options

In the wake of the *Furniss* decision the use of options in tax planning needed careful thought. It has in recent years become common to spread the sale of land over a number of years by means of options and part of the attraction has been to mitigate the vendor's CGT and (until its abolition in FA 1985) development land tax (DLT) liability by taking advantage of more than one annual exemption. Assume, for instance, that A wishes to sell Blackacre to B and will realise a gain of £14,000 on that sale. Were he to divide Blackacre into two equal portions and agree to sell the first portion in the tax year 2006–7 and, at the same time, grant a call option to purchase the second portion in the following tax year, it would appear that for CGT purposes the land has been disposed of in two different tax years and A will therefore have two annual exemptions available (notice that A could ensure that B is obliged to purchase the land by taking a 'put' option enabling him to require B to purchase the second parcel if he fails to exercise his 'call' option).

There is no doubt that such schemes amount to a preordained series of transactions and arguably the options represent steps which have been inserted purely for the avoidance of tax, since, in the absence of CGT considerations, A would have sold the whole of Blackacre to B in 2006–07. From a pre-*Westmoreland* view if, under the *Furniss* approach, the steps are excised, it may be argued that there was effectively a sale of the land to B at the time when the contract of sale for the first parcel was made and the put and call options taken. Doubts have always been expressed about the validity of this argument and if the 'option-step' is excised it is by no means clear that the *Ramsay* principle permits the sale of all the land to be treated as occurring in 2006–07. These doubts are endorsed by the decision in *Griffin v Citibank Investments Ltd* (2000) (see **[42.39]**) in which Patten J refused to recharacterise the separate put and call options as a single composite transaction. He said that if he were to 'ignore the terms of each option contract which provide for its independent assignment and exercise, and concentrate instead on the fact that if exercised together the options are guaranteed to produce a fixed return in favour of the taxpayer, then it seems to me that I would be doing the very thing which Lord Wilberforce emphasised in *Ramsay* that the courts cannot do, ie to go behind the transactions and search for some supposed underlying substance which as a matter of ordinary legal analysis they do not possess.' Following *Westmoreland*, further support for this approach was taken by the Court of Session in *Scottish Provident Institution v IRC* (2004) when considering whether a loss arising from the use of cross-options in relation to gilts should be allowed under FA 1994 s 155. Following *Westmoreland*, the Court was of the view that the term 'loss' in s 155(2) should be attributed with a legal meaning, but nonetheless pronounced on whether the *Ramsay* principle would apply had they decided that the provision employed a commercial concept. It was of the view that there was a 'genuine commercial possibility or practical likelihood' that the two options would be dealt with separately and should not be viewed as a composite transaction. However, on appeal, the House of Lords (with the same Law Lords as those sitting in *Barclays Mercantile Business Finance Ltd*) took the opposite view. Proceeding on the basis that the matter was one of construction, they said that there could only be an allowable loss if the option was a 'qualifying contract' within the meaning of FA 1994 s 147(1) and by virtue of FA 1994 ss 147A(1) and 150A(1), for there to be a qualifying contract, the taxpayer had to have an 'entitlement' to gilts. In determining what the statute meant by the term 'entitlement', the Judicial Committee had this to say:

'Since the decision of this House in *W T Ramsay Ltd v Inland Revenue Comrs* [1982] AC 300 it has been accepted that the language of a taxing statute will often have to be given a wide practical meaning of this sort which allows (and indeed requires) the court to have regard to the whole of a series of transactions which were intended to have a commercial unity. Indeed, it is conceded by (*the taxpayer*) that the court is not confined to looking at the ... option in isolation. If the scheme amounted in practice to a single transaction, the court should look at the scheme as a whole. Mr Aaronson, who appeared for (*the taxpayer*), accepted before the special commissioners that if there was 'no genuine commercial possibility' of the two options not being exercised together, then the scheme must fail.'

They went on to conclude that there was no realistic possibility of the options not being exercised simultaneously and that, accordingly, the scheme should be regarded as a single composite transaction. They added that:

'it would destroy the value of the *Ramsay* principle of construing provisions such as section 150A(1) of the 1994 Act as referring to the effect of composite transactions if their composite effect had to be disregarded simply because the parties had deliberately included a commercially irrelevant contingency, creating an acceptable risk that the scheme might not work as planned. We would be back in the world of artificial tax schemes, now equipped with anti-*Ramsay* devices. The composite effect of such a scheme should be considered as it was intended to operate and without regard to the possibility that, contrary to the intention and expectations of the parties, it might not work as planned.'

Returning, then, to the example of Blackacre, it appears that an answer would depend upon the construction of the term 'disposal' in the context of TCGA 1992. Following *Scottish Provident Institution*, it may be possible to say that the disposal of both pieces of land occurred in 2006–07 since, to use the words of Millett J, 'from a commercial point of view, of course, the simultaneous creation of both put and call options puts the parties in much the same position as an unconditional contract of sale would do' (*J Sainsbury Ltd v O'Connor* (1990)). Alternatively, following *Citibank* the commercial context of the transactions may militate against such a conclusion.

In conclusion, commercial reasons may, in particular cases, justify the use of options and the *Ramsay* argument is obviously more difficult to sustain when cross-options are not employed but a call option alone is taken by the purchaser.                                                                      **[2.45]**

# 3    Tax avoidance and legislation

*Updated by Natalie Lee, Barrister, Senior Lecturer in Law, University of Southampton*

## I    INTRODUCTION

This chapter considers the use of legislative measures as a means of tackling tax avoidance. Tax avoidance legislation takes the form of enactments of three types, the first directed at certain transactions, irrespective of whether or not the purpose of the taxpayer is to avoid tax. An example of such legislation is to be found in TA 1988 Part XV relating to settlements. The second type is directed against specific avoidance schemes and includes the provisions designed to prevent artificial transactions in land, those aimed at combating the transfer of assets overseas, those introduced to prevent the use of losses in avoidance schemes, considered at the various provisions aimed at transactions in securities, bond washing and dividend stripping at **[3.9]** ff and the recent provisions introduced by FA (No 2) 2005 to prevent avoidance through arbitrage (that is, the exploitation of the difference between national tax regimes. Interestingly, the legislation will only be engaged if HMRC issues a notice directing that the provisions will apply). The general characteristic of such legislation is that it is designed to deal with a specific problem, normally after it has arisen, but does not purport to prevent new schemes in different areas. A recent example of this type of provision is in FA 1999 and is aimed at reversing the decision of the House of Lords in *Ingram v IRC* (1999). Given a sophisticated legal profession, loopholes in such provisions will be exploited and need constant plugging. IHT is unique in having a legislative provision of the third type: a widely drafted associated operations provision (see IHTA 1984 s 268).                                        **[3.1]**

## II    STATUTORY PROVISIONS TO COUNTER TAX AVOIDANCE

### 1    The legislation

The major provisions that have been enacted in attempts to deal with specific instances of tax avoidance are set out below. In many cases they were designed to prevent the conversion of income profits into capital gains taxed at a lower rate. With the harmonisation in the rates of the two taxes, such provisions are of reduced importance.                                                        **[3.2]**

*Transactions in securities* TA 1988 ss 703–709 (originally enacted in FA 1960) (see **[3.30]**ff).                                                                          **[3.3]**

*Bond washing and dividend stripping* Various provisions deal with these problems, the oldest dating back to FA 1927 with the most recent being in TA 1988 ss 710–728.                                                              **[3.4]**

*Transfer of assets overseas* Originally enacted in FA 1936, these provisions were amended in 1981 as a result of *Vestey v IRC* (1980) and again in 1997, partly as a result of *Willoughby* litigation (see **Chapter 12**).                          **[3.5]**

*Artificial transactions in land* For TA 1988 s 776, see **Chapter 8**. Statutory provisions also regulate sale and leaseback transactions (TA 1988 ss 779–784); see **Chapter 6**.                                                            **[3.6]**

*Sale of income derived from personal activities* TA 1988 s 775 (originally enacted in FA 1969) prevents the conversion of future taxable income into capital gains subject to CGT. The avoidance typically involved entertainers who sold their services to a company formed for that purpose and then sold the shares in that company.                                                                     **[3.7]**

*The use of tax losses and transfer pricing* TA 1988 s 768 (originating in FA 1969) imposes restrictions upon the purchase of tax loss companies (see **Chapter 34**). Sales at under or overvalue may be subject to challenge under TA 1988 s 770, and under the *Sharkey v Wernher* principle (see **Chapter 6**).
                                                                                **[3.8]**

## 2   Typical avoidance schemes involving securities

A company is a legal entity distinct from its shareholders and, therefore, provides fertile ground for such tax avoidance schemes as dividend stripping and bond washing.                                                               **[3.9]**

*Dividend stripping* The simplest illustration of dividend stripping is where A owns A Ltd that has profits available for distribution. A sells the shares to B who is a dealer in securities. A receives a capital sum which reflects the undistributed profits in the company. B will take out the profits from A Ltd (as a dividend) that will be taxed as income but the shares will now be worth less (reflecting the fact that they have been stripped of their dividend). B will, therefore, make a trading loss when he sells the shares that can be set off against the dividend income that B has received (usually under the provisions of TA 1988 s 380). The result is that corporate profits have been extracted free of tax.

The courts were often invited to hold that the purchase and sale of the shares was not a trading transaction. In some cases they decided that it was trading; in others, not (contrast, eg *Griffiths v J P Harrison (Watford) Ltd* (1962) with *FA and AB Ltd v Lupton* (1971) and see *Coates v Arndale Properties Ltd*

(1984) and, for consideration of the effect of fiscal motives, *Ensign Tankers (Leasing) Ltd v Stokes* (1991)). The close company legislation sought to tackle one part of the problem by preventing the accumulation of profits in close companies. In 1960 the problem was attacked with legislation aimed at transactions in securities generally. (See further [3.30].) [3.10]

*Bond washing* Dividends only become a taxpayer's income when they are due and payable; when that happens the shareholder can claim the sum from the company as a debt. Usually there is a time gap between declaration and payment that provides an opportunity to wash the shares (or bonds) of their dividend. The washing process usually involves a taxpayer who is subject to no income tax or to lower rates only. Assume, for instance, that shares are owned by A who is subject to income tax at a high rate. When a dividend is declared on his shares he sells them to his cousin, a student with unused personal allowances. A is, therefore, receiving a capital sum for the shares on which CGT rather than income tax will be charged. The dividends are paid to the cousin who suffers little if any income tax thereon. Finally, the shares may be repurchased by A after payment of the dividend. Legislative provisions (notably TA 1988 s 729 and the accrued income scheme discussed below) prevent the most blatant examples of bond washing. (See further [3.XX].) [3.11]

## 3 The accrued income scheme

TA 1988 ss 710–728 (as amended by ITTOIA 2005 s 294) are designed to prevent the bond washing of fixed interest securities.

The practice of bond washing involved the conversion of income into capital and resulted in that sum being taxed, if at all, to CGT (with the result that as most fixed interest securities were exempt from CGT if held for 12 months or more, tax was often avoided). Accordingly, these provisions treat interest on securities as accruing on a day-to-day basis between the interest payment dates. On a disposal, therefore, the vendor is subject to income tax on the interest accruing from the immediately preceding interest payment date to the date of disposal and the purchaser is treated as owning the income from that date. It follows that when the sale is with accrued interest (*cum div*) the vendor is treated as entitled to extra interest and the purchaser gets relief for a corresponding amount. Conversely, if the sale is without accrued interest (*ex div*), the vendor will obtain relief on an amount equal to the interest to which the purchaser is regarded as entitled. The apportioned sums are treated as received on the day when the interest period ends and are subject to tax for the chargeable period in which they are received. As a result of these provisions appropriate amendments are made in the computation of any capital gains on the disposal of the securities (gilt-edged securities and qualifying corporate bonds are now generally exempt from CGT) and securities covered by the scheme are excluded from the anti-bond washing provisions which preceded this legislation.

### EXAMPLE 3.1

Elena owns £100,000 in nominal value of Government stock paying interest at 5% pa on 30 June and 31 December. She sells that stock *cum div* to Henrietta on 30 September 2006 for £99,780.

(1)   *Elena's tax position*: She is subject to income tax in 2006–07 on three months' accrued interest (£1,250) for the period from 30 June 2006 (the last payment date) to 30 September 2006 (disposal or settlement date).

(2)   *Henrietta's tax position*: Assuming that she retains the stock until 31 December 2006, she will then be subject to income tax on the interest paid as follows:

| | | |
|---|---|---:|
| Interest payment to 31 December 2006 | = | £2,500 |
| Deduct accrued interest purchased (1 July to 30 September) | = | £1,250 |
| Reduced amount taxable | = | £1,250 |

(3)   Had the sale been *ex div* so that the interest payment of £5,000 to 31 December 2006 was retained by Elena, she would be taxed on £1,250 of that figure and the balance of £1,250 (ie interest from the date of disposal to the date of sale) would be taxed in Henrietta's hands.

The securities caught by these provisions are defined in s 710 (as amended) and include bearer bonds, UK and foreign securities, and securities whether secured or unsecured issued by governments, companies, local authorities and other institutions. Excluded from the provisions are ordinary or preference shares, National Savings Certificates, certificates of deposit, bills of exchange, Treasury bills, local authority bills and similar instruments. Individuals (including trustees and PRs) resident or ordinarily resident in the UK are within the provisions, but there are specific exclusions for financial traders (whose profits on sale are taxed as trading income under ITTOIA 2005) and for individuals holding securities with a nominal value not exceeding £5,000. For deaths on or after 6 April 1996 transfers on death to a PR are outside the scheme (FA 1996 s 158); from 1 April 1996 the scheme ceased to apply altogether for corporation tax purposes (being replaced by the new code dealing with corporate loan relationships).          **[3.12]**

### 4   Bed and breakfasting

Bed and breakfasting, which allowed the selling of shares on one day (in order to crystallise a capital gain or loss) and the repurchase of those same shares on the following day, has been stopped for disposals on or after 17 March 1998. Any shares of the same class in the same company sold and repurchased within a 30-day period are now matched, so that the shares sold cannot be identified with those already held. Curiously the rules would appear to be capable of circumvention as follows:

(1)   A sells his shares in X plc: he settles the sale proceeds on a life interest trust for himself and the trustees promptly buy back the shares.

(2)   As in (1) except that A gives the sale proceeds to his wife who buys back the X plc shares. (See further **[20.46]**).          **[3.13]–[3.29]**

### III   TRANSACTIONS IN SECURITIES (TA 1988 ss 703–709)

### 1   Introduction

a)   *Outline history*

In order to understand the present it is necessary to start with the past. It is 1950, rates of income tax (including surtax) are high and destined to rise, accumulated profits (ie after payment of profits tax) retained in certain companies are subject to apportionment (as they have been since the 1920s) and there is no capital gains tax. This is, therefore, an ideal breeding ground for attempts to extract profits from companies in a manner that does not attract income tax.

A number of related techniques have become commonplace:

(1)   '*Dividend stripping*' whereby A purchases shares in X Co for £100 from B, A procures the declaration of a dividend of £20 on which he pays no or little income tax (A is an exempt body or has tax losses), and then sells the shares back to B for £80. A gets 'tax-free' income and (if he can establish himself as a dealer in shares) a trading loss of £20 and B gets a capital profit of £20 which (pre-1965) was free of tax or (post-1965) was chargeable at lower rates (namely CGT rates) than if it were received as income.

(2)   '*Stock stripping*' whereby B, who owns the shares in a company (which in turn owns a plot of land acquired for £20 and now worth £100), sells the shares to A for £100 thereby generating a capital profit free of tax (pre-1965) or chargeable at lower rates (post-1965). A can then extract the land (or profits on a sale) by way of dividend, free of tax (A is an exempt body or has tax losses) and sell the shares at a loss.

(3)   '*Bond washing*' whereby A purchases shares or securities in X Co (upon which a dividend is about to be declared or interest to become payable) for £100 from B, A receives the dividend/interest of £20 on which he pays no or little income tax (A is an exempt body or has tax losses), and then sells the shares back to B for £80. A again gets 'tax-free' income and B gets a capital profit of £20 which (pre-1965) was free of tax or (post-1965) was chargeable at lower rates than if it were received as income.

As is often the case when new 'problems' are identified by the HMRC, attempts were first made to deal with specific concerns. In 1951 the Revenue persuaded Parliament to give it (by FA 1951 s 32) wide discretionary powers where transactions were effected for the avoidance or reduction of liability to profits tax. This—a 'general anti-avoidance rule' or GAAR—was itself modelled on wartime provisions designed to prevent the avoidance of excess profits tax; provision was also made in FA 1951 to deal with the migration of companies (see now TA 1988 ss 765–767) and transfer pricing (see now TA 1988 s 770A and Sch 28AA). In 1955 legislation was introduced to deal with dividend stripping (see F(No 2)A 1955 s 4) and this is currently found in TA 1988 ss 736–738. In 1959 legislation was introduced to deal with bond washing (see FA 1959 ss 23–26, drawing on provisions in FA 1937) and this is currently found in TA 1988 ss 729–735 as amended (and see the 'accrued income scheme' in TA 1988 ss 710–728 as amended). In 1960 legislation was introduced to deal with stock stripping (see FA 1960 ss 21–24) and this is currently found (in a much more limited form) in TA 1988 ss 774, 776 as amended.

These measures were fine as far as they went but did not deal with the more sophisticated transactions. Accordingly, the Revenue persuaded Parliament to tackle the problem on a wider footing. The changes made in FA 1951 for profits tax purposes were the basis for FA 1960 ss 28–29, 43 which—in its amended form—can be found in TA 1988 ss 703–709. The FA

1960 provisions sought to ensure that the Revenue could counteract (by an assessment to income tax under the former Schedule D Case VI) any 'tax advantage' obtained by a person in consequence of a 'transaction in securities' in any of *four* circumstances where the person could not show that the transaction was carried out for (a) 'bona fide commercial reasons or in the ordinary course of making and managing investments' *and* (b) the transaction did not have as its main object, or one of its main objects, 'to enable tax advantages to be obtained'. The four circumstances are what are now found in ss 704A–D. The statute also made provision for advance clearance by the Revenue, for counteraction notices and for the (convoluted and possibly unlawful—see Article 6 of the European Convention on Human Rights) Special Commissioners/Tribunal appeal procedure (see **[52.83]**).

**[3.30]**

b)    *Legislative changes*

The main legislative development in what is now ss 703–709 came in 1966. In that year (see FA 1966 s 39): (1) a fifth circumstance (now s 704E) was added to deal with the case where a shareholder of a close company with assets available for distribution receives shares or securities representing those assets instead of cash; (2) the definition of 'tax advantage' (see **[3.35]**) was extended to meet the argument that an individual shareholder did not gain such an advantage if a company which would otherwise have been liable to a charge under Schedule F avoided such a charge; and (3) the computation of the charge on such a shareholder was clarified to ensure that he was taxed on a sum equal to the former Schedule F charge (taxation of dividend income) before set-off of franked investment income (in other words, any such franked income of the company did not serve to reduce the former Case VI charge on the shareholder).

More recent changes have been made to deal with the abolition of ACT and the introduction of 'shadow' ACT (see FA 1998 Sch 3).    **[3.31]**

c)    *Important cases and key points of interpretation*

There have been numerous cases on the provisions mainly in the 'heyday' of tax avoidance from the 1960s to the early 1980s. The highlights are set out below.    **[3.32]**

'*Cancellation of a tax advantage*'—*the general approach* The Court of Appeal has recently confirmed that, since it was Parliament's intention when introducing the legislation in 1960 to provide for a 'wide and general attack on tax avoidance', s 703 is targeted at all forms of tax avoidance which fall within its scope, and is not limited to contrived transactions carried out otherwise than on the open market (*Sema Group Pension Scheme Trustees v IRC* (2003), following *IRC v Joiner* (1975)).    **[3.33]**

'*In consequence of ... or the combined effect of ...* 'A tax advantage will be regarded as being 'in consequence of' a transaction in securities where it is a product of it, whether or not there is a direct causal link (*Williams v IRC* (1980)). The exact scope of the term 'the combined effect of' is unclear. On the language of the statute, if one step is taken (Step 1) quite independently of a later step

(Step 2) and a tax advantage then arises, the true test is whether there are any s 704 'circumstances' and whether the tax advantage is the product of Steps 1 and 2. If it is, then s 703 applies unless *both* Steps satisfy the 'escape clause' in s 703(1) (see the phrase: 'none of them ...'). The Revenue does not seem to take this line where the Steps are genuinely independent; if Step 2 was inevitable after Step 1 then the two are regarded as a single transaction (*IRC v Brebner* (1967)). **[3.34]**

*'Tax advantage'* A person will obtain a 'tax advantage' where he gets relief or greater relief from tax *or* repayment or greater repayment of tax *or* avoids or gets a reduced charge to tax *or* avoids an assessment or a possible assessment to tax—all by way of a tax-free receipt or a deduction from taxable profits or gains (s 709(1)). It was not clear whether (as the Revenue long contended) an exempt body (eg a charity) would fall within the scope of a person who gets 'relief from' or 'repayment of' tax for these purposes. The High Court (Aldous J) said 'no' in *Sheppard v IRC (No 2)* (1993) on the basis that a person who has no liability to tax cannot gain a tax advantage ('relief') by avoiding what he is not subject to; this was 'reversed' by the High Court (Vinelott J) in *IRC v Universities Superannuation Scheme Ltd* (1997) on the basis that the anti-avoidance context required a broad approach to the term 'relief' and put beyond doubt by FA 1997 s 73 (see s 709(2A)). This is further considered in the recent case of *IRC v Trustees of the Sema Group Pension Scheme* (2003) (see **[3.50]**).

The advantage may arise as a result of one or more transactions or a transaction combined with the liquidation of the company (see s 703(2)). What matters is whether the person has received in non-taxable form cash or property he could have received in a taxable form; it does not matter that what he actually receives is different in nature to what he could have received provided that, in some way, the former represents the latter (*IRC v Parker* (1966), *Emery v IRC* (1981) and *Cleary v IRC* (1987)). In *Cleary* the taxpayers received as capital, in the form of consideration for the sale of shares to the company, sums which would have been received as income, in the form of dividends; notwithstanding that the net assets of the company were not reduced by the transaction, this amounted to a 'tax advantage' (according to the House of Lords).

The amount of the tax advantage is to be computed by looking at all the circumstances—this can be a receipt in cash or kind or even in the form of a loan by a company to a shareholder where the loan is unlikely to be repaid (see *IRC v Williams* (1980) and *Bird v IRC* (1988)). **[3.35]**

*'Tax'* 'Tax' in this context means income tax and corporation tax (see TA 1988 s 832(3)) and so does not include capital gains tax. **[3.36]**

*'Transaction in securities'* A 'transaction in securities' extends to all forms of transaction (sale, exchange, purchase, issue, subscription, alteration of rights) involving 'securities' (s 709(2)). 'Securities' includes shares, stock and any other interest of a member in a company (s 709(2)). Nearly anything can be such a transaction, eg the redemption of debentures (*IRC v Parker* (1966)) and loans to shareholders (*Williams v IRC* (1980))—and two or more steps can be looked at together to see if they amount to a 'transaction' (*IRC v Horrocks* (1968)).

While an 'ordinary' liquidation will not be a transaction for these purposes (see *IRC v Joiner* (1975)) this will not be the case if there is some additional feature which—together with the liquidation—could be so regarded. This can be seen in the following example:

**EXAMPLE 3.2**

(1)    A and B set up a property development company which trades for four years and then sells all of its properties for cash. The shareholders put the company into liquidation and pay CGT (after taper relief) at a lower rate than they would have paid income tax on a dividend of the cash in the company. Absent any other transaction this is not caught by s 703 since it is merely the termination of a trading company and the return to the shareholders of the remaining capital.

(2)    Instead of a simple liquidation, the share rights of the company are altered to give all of the rights to dividends to B and all the rights to capital on a winding up to A. The company declares an abnormal dividend to B and is then wound up with the capital going to A. This falls within s 709(2) since there is a 'transaction' (the alteration of the share rights) and a liquidation; if the capital received by A on the liquidation falls into one of the categories in s 704C then there will be a charge on A. If A suffers a CGT charge on the alteration of the share rights ('a value shift') this will be *additional* to the s 703 charge on the winding up; just as, absent s 703, there could be a CGT charge on an alteration of share rights and another charge on disposal of the shares.

Despite indications to the contrary in the earlier case of *Greenberg v IRC* (1972), the House of Lords has recently held that the payment of a dividend was not a 'transaction in securities' or a 'transaction relating to securities' within the definition in s 709(2) (see *IRC v Laird Group plc* (2003) at **[3.49]**).

**[3.37]**

*Circumstance s 704A* Circumstance s 704A is aimed at dividend stripping where the taxpayer receives an abnormal amount by the way of dividend. There must be a distribution of profits by a company or the sale or purchase of securities in connection with which a person receives an abnormal dividend the amount of which is used in gaining exemption from, relief from or a reduction in tax (eg a charity buys shares, receives the dividend and claims the tax back on the dividend). A dividend is 'abnormal' if it is at an excessive fixed rate or greater than a normal return on the consideration given for the shares, measured by reference to the period of ownership of the shares (s 709(4)(a) (b)(6)) (and see *IRC v Trustees of the Sema Group Pension Scheme* (2003) at **[3.50]**). 'Dividend' encompasses other distributions and interest (s 709(2)), eg a purchase of own shares (*IRC v Universities Superannuation Scheme Ltd* (1997)).    **[3.38]**

*Circumstance s 704B* Circumstance s 704B was aimed at dividend stripping (or stock stripping) where the taxpayer incurs a trading loss as a result of a dividend or from dealing in the assets of a company. There must be a sale or purchase of securities followed by the purchase and sale of the same or similar securities, a trading loss and the payment of a dividend or the sale of assets of the company. This now all falls within TA 1988 ss 729–737 so that s 704B is obsolete (see IM para 4515).    **[3.39]**

*Circumstance s 704C* Circumstance s 704C is aimed at the 'other party' to the dividend stripping arrangement. Thus if the purchaser of shares falls within A or B, the vendor (it is intended) should fall within C. It operates where: (1) a person receives, in a form not chargeable to income tax; (2) consideration which represents assets of a company available for distribution (dividend stripping), future receipts of a company (forward stripping—see *Greenberg v IRC* (1972)) or trading stock of a company (stock stripping); (3) in consequence of a transaction involving shares in a company whereby; (4) another person receives an abnormal dividend (ie Circumstance A) or a deduction in profits attributable to a fall in value of shares (ie Circumstance B). There must be a close enough causal link between the relevant transactions and the abnormal dividend or a deduction in profits (see *IRC v Garvin* (1981)).

The terms of s 704C(1)(i) (and s 704E(3)) ensure that a company cannot reduce its distributable reserves in anticipation of a transaction which would otherwise be caught by s 703. If, however, the reserves are reduced, say, two years before the other transaction at a time when that later transaction is not contemplated, those reserves will not be relevant for s 703 purposes. The legislation could not—does not—apply to all reserves which a company has ever had; what these provisions are aimed at are artificial steps to reduce reserves. Clearance should therefore be given since this is not a transaction that would attract a counteraction notice (see SP 3/80). **[3.40]**

*Circumstance s 704D* Circumstance s 704D is not limited (whatever the original intention of the draftsman) to dividend and stock-stripping activities. It applies to the receipt of consideration, in money or money's worth, 'in connection' with the distribution of profits of a (s 704D) company where the receipt is or represents assets available for distribution or future receipts of the company or trading stock of the company. 'Profts' includes income, reserves and other assets and 'distribution' includes transfers and realisations (s 709(3)(a)(b)). The full extent of the provision is spelt out in the speech of Lord Upjohn in *Cleary v IRC* (1967):

> 'In connection with the distribution, transfer or realisation, including application in discharge of liabilities, of profits, income, reserves or other assets of a company to which this paragraph applies, the person in question so receives ... that he does not pay or bear tax on it as income ... a consideration in money or money's worth which either is, or represents the value of, assets which are (or apart from anything done by the company in question would have been) available for distribution by way of dividend or is received in respect of future receipts of the company or is or represents the value of trading stock of the company.'

In *Cleary v IRC* two sisters owned all the share capital of two companies G (which had substantial accumulated profits) and M. They sold the shares of M to G for cash that would otherwise have been available to pay dividends and counteraction was taken under circumstance s 704D in respect of the consideration for the sale of shares of M. The House of Lords (after commenting on the scope of the imprecise language used in s 704D) rejected the taxpayer's argument that circumstance s 704D only applied if the transfer of assets diminished the company's assets.

Counteraction will be taken in cases of capital distributions (*Addy v IRC* (1975)), a bonus issue of debentures (*Parker v IRC* (1966)) and indirect receipts of proceeds representing trading stock (*IRC v Wiggins* (1979) where the owner of a company procured the transfer of all its business and assets bar one to Newco and then sold the company; the sale proceeds were held to represent the trading stock of the company).

The receipt of consideration will be 'in connection with' the distribution of profits if there is a causal connection which does not need to be as strong as that required by 'whereby' in s 704C (*Emery v IRC* (1981)). There has to be a *link* but it does not have to be *the cause*.

A transaction that falls within ss 704E and D is to be taxed or not under s 704E; s 704D cannot override a conclusion that a sum is not taxable by virtue of s 704E. Thus if a transaction falls within s 704E but with the benefit of a deferral of the charge (s 704E(2)) there will be no immediate charge under s 704D (*Williams v IRC* (1980)).

*Circumstance s 704E* Circumstance s 704E is aimed at transactions that do not fall within s 704D (eg because the person concerned receives shares or securities and not money or money's worth). It applies where a person receives, in connection with the transfer of assets of a s 704D company to another such company, consideration consisting of any share capital or security issued by a s 704D company which is not chargeable to income tax but which represents the assets available for distribution of such a company. The classic case covered by s 704E is the sale of the shares of a s 704D company which has assets available for distribution to another company in return for shares or securities. In effect the assets available for distribution of company A are received in the form of shares in company B.

The provision operates at the time of the receipt of redeemable share capital or securities (they are regarded as 'near cash') or at the time of repayment (on a winding up or otherwise) of non-redeemable share capital (see s 704E(2)). The deferral operates on the latter only. If the receipt of shares or securities gives rise to a charge under s 703 no charge will arise on the redemption of such shares or securities.                                    **[3.41]**

*The 'escape clause'* There are two—cumulative—limbs to this clause so that the commercial purpose must be independent of any tax benefit and (obviously) it is only necessary to meet the second if the first is satisfied. Thus, a taxpayer may have a commercial purpose where a tax advantage is a feature of the transactions but not a main object (the latter is merely a step on the way to the former); in such a case the clause would be satisfied. However, if the taxpayer has both a commercial purpose and a main tax object—they are separate goals in themselves—the clause is not satisfied (see *Hasloch v IRC* (1971)). The heavy—burden of proof lies on the taxpayer.              **[3.42]**

*The 'bona fide commercial' test* The '*bona fide* commercial' test is satisfied where, looking at the subjective intention of the taxpayer, there are genuine commercial reasons for what has been done (*IRC v Brebner* (1966)). If there are two possible courses, one which involves paying more tax than the other, merely choosing to take the latter course does not necessarily mean that the test is not satisfied. Examples of 'commercial' motives include the retention of family control of a company (*IRC v Goodwin* (1975)), the sale of shares to fund the purchase of a farm (*Clark v IRC* (1978)) and a corporate reorganisation to preserve the viability of the group (*Marwood Homes v IRC* (1997)) (but see **[42.120]**).                                              **[3.43]**

*The 'ordinary course of making and managing investments' test* This test is satisfied where the taxpayer takes an ordinary, sensible, investment decision (the 'prudent investor') divorced from tax considerations. In *Clark v IRC* two brothers owned the shares in a company; one, the farming brother, wanted to sell the shares to purchase a farm; the other, the non-farming brother, felt that he had to sell to avoid being left with a less valuable investment. This satisfied the 'making and managing investments' test (see also *Lewis (Trustee of Redrow Staff Pension Scheme v IRC* (1999) at **[42.120]**).                    **[3.44]**

*The 'no main object of obtaining a tax advantage' test* The 'no main object of obtaining a tax advantage' test is satisfied where, looking at the subjective intention of the taxpayer, tax has only played a minor role in the transaction concerned. Indeed, it may be the case that a transaction that relies for its profitability on exemption from tax does not, by virtue of that feature alone, fail the test (*IRC v Kleinwort Benson Ltd* (1969)).

In commercial situations, the test is likely to be satisfied where the transactions are treated as an approved demerger (TA 1988 s 213) or an approved purchase of own shares (TA 1988 s 219) since the requirements in those parts of the tax code are as (or more) stringent than those found in s 703.

Corporate reorganisations will also usually pass the test where what is received is shares; great care should be taken however where any party to a reorganisation receives cash or 'near cash' (see below). It is, however, necessary to examine the particular transaction and not simply the surrounding circumstances: see *IRC v Trustees of the Sema Group Pension Scheme* (2003) at **[42.120]**.                    **[3.45]**

*Counteraction* The Revenue has always taken the view that if a transaction in securities falls within the conditions in TA 1988 s 703, then counteraction can be taken to charge income tax, even if the way in which the transaction is carried out would normally give rise to CGT; similarly in the case of a company, counteraction could be taken (for periods where there was a different rate for chargeable gains) to charge corporation tax at the rate applicable to income. In *IRC v Garvin* (1981) the taxpayer had paid capital gains tax on a sale of shares, but the Revenue subsequently discovered that the sale was part of a series of transactions and sought to take counteraction under s 703. On appeal, the Revenue said that credit would be given 'by concession' against the tax charged under s 703. The House of Lords allowed the taxpayer's appeal on the grounds that the circumstances in s 704 were not present, but was unhappy that double taxation was only avoided by concession. It is rarer now that there is an issue for corporate shareholders unless there are large CGT losses that encourage receipt of consideration in capital form.

Corporate (and indeed individual) shareholders should however be aware of the risk that s 703 will apply as a result of a recharacterisation of the relevant steps under the *Ramsay* principle. While this has not yet happened in the s 703 context, it has in s 739 (*IRC v McGuckian* (1997)) and there is no reason—given that *Ramsay* is a principle of statutory construction—why it does not apply to s 703.                    **[3.46]**

## 2    Current application

### a)    *HMRC's practice*

The avoidance, etc of a charge to CGT is outside the scope of s 703; the avoidance, etc of a charge to ACT is held to be within the definition of 'tax advantage' as ACT is 'an amount of Corporation Tax' which is paid in advance of the normal due date (IM para 4513; TA 1988 s 14).

A dividend is 'abnormal' if it *substantially exceeds* a normal return on the consideration provided by the recipient for the security on which the dividend was paid, taking into account the length of time the shares have been held (IM para 4514). The IM includes an example where the return is an annual yield of 682.5% on the consideration given. Presumably something less than this would also be regarded as 'abnormal'. Note that a reorganisation followed by *any* dividend will be 'abnormal'.

In practice ss 704D and E are unlikely to apply unless there is at least one company involved in the transaction that has (or has recently had) at least some distributable reserves. For TA 1988 s 704E where the shares are non-redeemable it is sufficient for there to be reserves at the time the share capital is repaid (IM paras 4517, 4518).

When a tax advantage is obtained in any of the circumstances, s 703 applies to the whole of the consideration received, irrespective of any CGT liability incurred by the person in question (IM para 4520). In practice, however, the Revenue will only invoke the legislation where the tax on a potential assessment under s 703(3) *significantly* exceeds the CGT liability on the same consideration, eg the gain is wholly covered by retirement relief or substantially reduced by rebasing, indexation or the availability of capital losses.

Where any legislation *other than* the CGT legislation applies to transactions within the general scope of s 703, the latter applies only to any tax advantage which remains after the other legislation has been invoked (IM para 4521).

Where the person who obtained the tax advantage is an individual who has since died TA 1988 s 703(11) enables counteraction to be taken against his personal representatives (IM para 4522).

The types of case that, according to IM para 4524, should be submitted to the specialist s 703 Group in HMRC's Special Investigations Section include:
(1)    the receipt of the dividend (or interest) which represents an excessive return on the cost of the shares or securities on which it is paid and which is taken into account for any of the purposes listed at IM para 4514;
(2)    the payment of a substantial dividend by a company prior to the sale of shares in that company combined with an agreement whereby some or all of the shareholders waive all or part of their dividend rights in return for a greater share of the sale proceeds (see the example at IM para 4516);
(3)    the sale of shares or other securities to a company in which the vendor has a substantial interest (see example 1 at IM para 4517 and the example at IM para 4518);
(4)    the sale of shares or other securities to the trustees of a pension scheme of which the vendor is a member (see example 2 at IM para 4517);

(5)  the transfer or sale by a company of its assets or business to another company having some or all of the same shareholders followed by the liquidation of the company whose assets etc have been acquired (see the example at IM para 4519) or the sale of shares in either company;

(6)  a company reconstruction in which some or all of the shareholders in the original company retain an interest in the second company;

(7)  the sale of shares under any agreement whereby the shares themselves or the underlying assets are capable of being subsequently reacquired by the vendor;

(8)  the acquisition by an individual or a company under his control of shares in a company with accumulated losses at the same time as the assignment to him at a substantial discount of debts due by the loss-making company followed by repayments of the assigned debts (within six years of the end of the year of assessment in which the debts were assigned); and

(9)  the merger of two (or more) companies in which shares or securities form all or part of the consideration and where all the companies concerned are within s 704D(2) (see IM para 4517).          **[3.47]**

b)  *Recent changes in approach*

Take a typical transaction: the sale of the shares in a close company to Newco with a view to bringing in outside investment was often cleared for s 703 purposes whatever the surrounding circumstances. This will no longer be cleared if the vendors receive securities that are 'near cash' and retain some measure of control over Newco. The s 703 Group is now taking a far harder, more commercially aware, line: the test is *not* 'is there a commercial purpose for this deal?' *but* 'is there a commercial purpose for the way in which this deal has been done?' Most cases will satisfy the former but may fail the latter.

The change in approach can be measured in this way: A Co is owned by three shareholders and has ten subsidiaries. Sub7 Ltd has assets available for distribution and a valuable trading site. A third party offers to purchase Sub7 Ltd for cash; because the three shareholders in A Co have personal losses they reorganise the group so that they hold Sub7 Ltd directly and can sell it to the third party. This is done and a claim made to set off the gain against the personal losses.

Bramwell, *Taxation of Companies and Company Reconstructions* (6th edn, 1994) stated, tentatively, that this would meet the escape clause (para 32.23, Example 10); in 1998 the transaction was in fact done by a large plc and counteracted; in the 7th edn (1999), Bramwell says that a clearance is not unknown but each case depends on its facts!          **[3.48]**

c)  *Recent cases*

*Transactions in securities* In *Laird Group plc v IRC* (1999) the Special Commissioners held that where L purchased all of the shares in S Co for *bona fide* commercial reasons, S Co paid an abnormal amount by way of dividend (plus tax credit) to L on 17 December 1990 (outside a group income election) and L gained a tax advantage by setting off the dividend received and tax credit against a dividend and ACT paid to its shareholders on 5 December 1990, there were transactions in securities which failed to satisfy either limb of the escape clause. L plc sought a rehearing in front of the s 703 Tribunal (under s 705(2)). The Tribunal held that the counteraction notice should be struck down since the payment of a dividend is not a transaction in securities, S Ltd's dividend was for *bona fide* commercial reasons since it allowed L plc to avoid surplus ACT and thus prevent the erosion of L plc's earnings per share but that the dividend had as one of its main objects the securing of the tax advantage. On appeal Lightman J upheld the Tribunal's decisions on the basis that a dividend is not a transaction in securities since it merely gives effect to existing rights attached to securities.

The House of Lords (*IRC v Laird Group plc* (2003)) set aside the decision of the Court of Appeal that the declaration or payment of a dividend was plainly a transaction related to securities in the form of the shares in respect of which it was paid, and that it did not just give effect to a shareholder's pre-existing rights, and decided to the contrary that the payment of a dividend was neither a transaction *in* securities, nor a transaction *relating to* securities, Lord Millett (who gave the only full judgment) reached this conclusion by comparing the distribution of profits on an ordinary liquidation (which is not a transaction in securities—see [**42.107**]) with the declaration of a dividend. He said;

> 'Whether the company is in liquidation or continuing to carry on business as a going concern ... the distribution of the undistributed profits of a company to the shareholders entitled thereto merely gives effect to the rights attached to the shares. The funds are released, in the one case from the liquidator's discretion to retain them for the purpose of the winding up, and in the other from the directors' discretion to retain them for the purposes of the undertaking. Given that the former is not 'a transaction relating to securities', neither in my opinion is the latter. The relationship between the payment and the shares in respect of which it is paid is the same in both cases.'

The implications of this important decision are great for those engaged in merger and acquisition planning, although it should be noted that an abnormal dividend could still bring the issue within circumstances A–D where there is already a transaction in securities giving rise to a tax advantage.                                                                           [**3.49**]

*The escape clause* The saga of *Marwood Homes* is a stark reminder of the importance of identifying all relevant evidence *before* commencing s 703 litigation. The basic facts were these: Marwood Homes Ltd (MHL) was making heavy losses; as a way of solving those financial difficulties it acquired four companies from its parent and then procured the payment of dividends by those companies (outside the group income election) and the sale by those companies of their trades and assets. The dividends were, as a result of the reorganisation, necessarily abnormal; the tax credit attaching to them was set against MHL's trading losses. The Revenue (who had refused clearance) issued a notice on the basis of s 704A and the company appealed on the basis that it fell within the escape clause.

In *Marwood Homes Ltd v IRC* (1997) the Special Commissioners held that the transactions were carried out for *bona fide* commercial reasons (getting sufficient funds into MHL to allow it to survive) and did not have a main object of securing a tax advantage; the Revenue, being dissatisfied with this, sought a rehearing (by virtue of s 705(2)) before the Special Commissioners.

The taxpayer challenged this as an abuse of process (on the basis that the reasons given by the Revenue for the rehearing were ones which could have advanced at the first hearing but were not) but this was rejected (see *Marwood Homes (No 2)* (1998)). At the rehearing the Revenue produced evidence—found in an internal note in the files of the taxpayer's accountants—that suggested that the commercial rationale for the transactions had been 'beefed up' so as to outweigh the tax motivation. On the basis of this (and other evidence) the Tribunal overturned the decision of the Special Commissioners and restored the counteraction notice (see *Marwood Homes Ltd v IRC* (1999)). In effect the Tribunal was not satisfied that the tax advantages were not one of the main purposes of the steps taken by MHL.

In *Lewis (Trustee of Redrow Staff Pension Scheme) v IRC* (1999), it was held that the tax advantage obtained by the trustees of a staff pension scheme on their sale of shares in the employer company to the employer company should not be counteracted, because the transaction was carried out for *bona fide* commercial reasons, the trustees were acting in the ordinary course of managing investments and the tax advantage was not the only or main reason for the transaction. The trustees of the scheme held shares in R plc which represented 8.9% of the value of the pension scheme funds. As R plc was about to float, the trustees were told by the Occupational Pensions Board to reduce the employer-related investment to 5% or below as soon as R plc was listed. This was done by a purchase of own shares (which allowed the trustees to reclaim the tax credit) rather than a sale on the flotation. This meant that the trustees did not have to become involved in the flotation and saved them the substantial associated disposal costs. The trustees' appeal against the Revenue's notice under s 703(3) (and assessment under Schedule F) was allowed as the purchase of own shares relieved the trustees of the burden of extra work and the costs involved in the flotation; and the obtaining of a tax advantage was not the main object or one of the main objects in making that choice. The trustees took the simplest and cheapest option available to them, and in doing so were acting in the ordinary course of managing investments. A wish to reduce the excessive holding of employer-related investments was a *bona fide* commercial reason.

In *IRC v Trustees of the Sema Group Pension Scheme* (2003) the trustees of an exempt pension scheme had acquired quoted shares in the market. The company concerned (Powergen) then announced a buy-back of its shares and the trustees sold their shares. The proceeds of sale in excess of the paid up capital of the shares were treated as a distribution in the hands of the trustees that gave them an entitlement to reclaim the tax credit. The Revenue contended that circumstance s 704A was relevant on the basis that the trustees had obtained an abnormal amount by way of dividend. The Special Commissioners decided that the dividend was not abnormal but that the trustees had obtained a 'tax advantage' (in the form of the tax credit repayable to them by virtue of their exempt status) and that had been one of their main objects in selling the shares in the buy-back. The Revenue appealed and the trustees cross-appealed. In the High Court Lightman J concluded that the normalcy (or otherwise) of the dividend had to be determined by looking at the sum received excluding the tax credit but that, on the facts, the dividend was abnormal since it represented a one-off return, by way of distribution, of what was, in reality, capital. Further the judge concluded: (1) although minded to decide otherwise, he was bound to follow the later decision in *IRC v Universities Superannuation Scheme Ltd* (1997) (rather than the earlier one in *Sheppard v IRC (No 2)* (1993)) to the effect that an exemption from tax can be regarded as a 'relief' and thus within the definition of 'tax advantage'; and (2) the Special Commissioners were entitled on the facts to decide that the obtaining of the tax advantage had been a main object of the trustees in deciding to sell in the buy-back. The Court of Appeal, in allowing the trustees' appeal, rejected the view of Lightman J that the amounts in question had to be treated *as if they were dividends.* Section 704(A) requires that the normality of the amount 'received by way of dividends' should be considered. Section 709(2) provides that 'references to dividends include references to other qualifying distributions'. Accordingly, what had to be considered on the facts of the present case was the normality of the amount received by the trustee by way of a qualifying distribution of the kind that in fact occurred. The Court of Appeal did, however, agree with Lightman J on the two further issues. *First*, in holding that the tax credit to which the trustees were entitled was a 'relief from tax', Jonathan Parker LJ opined that:

'what the draftsman was manifestly trying to do when defining "tax advantage" ... was to cover every situation in which the position of the taxpayer vis-à-vis the Revenue is improved in consequence of the particular transaction or transactions.'

*Secondly*, it was held that the Special Commissioners were entitled to hold that the tax credits were crucial to the decision to sell into the buy-backs, and so one of the main objects of the sales was to enable tax advantages to be obtained. These were findings that they were fully entitled to reach on the evidence before them, and there was no basis on which an appellate court could interfere.                                                    **[3.50]**

# 4 Administrative machinery

*Written by Hartley Foster, Partner, DLA Piper Rudnick Gray Cary UK LLP*

## I  GENERAL STRUCTURE

### 1  The merger

In July 2003, a review of HM Customs and Excise, the Inland Revenue and HM Treasury was carried out by Gus O'Donnell. His report, which was published in March 2004, recommended the creation of a new department that would integrate Customs and Excise and the Inland Revenue. Plans to integrate the two departments were introduced in the 2004 Budget. On 7 April 2005 the Commissioners for Revenue and Customs Act 2005 (CRCA) received Royal Assent. It provides the legal basis for the new integrated department—Her Majesty's Revenue and Customs (HMRC), and for the new independent prosecutions office—the Revenue and Customs Prosecutions Office (RCPO). HMRC is responsible now for all the functions (bar prosecutions, for which, as a result of CRCA s 35, RCPO has responsibility) that were previously the responsibility of the Commissioners of Inland Revenue and the Commissioners of Customs and Excise. Customs and Excise had different functions, responsibilities and powers to those of the Inland Revenue; and, although the two bodies are now one department, the actual integration of the two is anticipated to take a number of years. The powers of the Inland Revenue and of HM Customs and Excise were transferred unchanged to HMRC; and the Government has recognised that it is important to consider whether the heterogeneous powers can be rationalised. This would make it easier for taxpayers to understand and comply with their tax obligations and potentially could reduce the administrative burden of the tax system that falls on them. A major review of HMRC's powers, deterrents and safeguards currently is being undertaken.                                              [**4.1**]

### 2  The structure of HMRC

The Commissioners of HMRC answer to the Treasury and, therefore, to the Chancellor of the Exchequer. Below the level of the Commissioners, the structure is complex and has been subject to change, particularly during the last 25 years and partly due to the introduction of self-assessment in the 1990s. Traditionally, the country was divided into tax districts headed by an inspector of taxes, who (after the abolition of the office of assessor by FA 1946 s 62(1)) assessed the taxpayer's tax liability; and the tax was collected by a collector of taxes (appointed by the General Commissioners, but remunerated by the Crown). Now, both those who exercise the roles of inspectors and collectors of taxes are full-time civil servants appointed by the HMRC; they are known, as are all staff who were empowered to exercise the functions of the predecessor departments (eg inspectors, collectors, receivers, authorised persons, etc), as 'Officers of Revenue and Customs' (CRCA s 50(2)). Inspection and collection have been brought together into Taxpayer Service Offices (TSOs). TSOs deal with routine work in respect of assessments and collection and will be most taxpayers' main point of contact. However, for each district, there is also a Taxpayer District Office, which deals with local companies and with technical and compliance issues.

The taxes considered in this book, namely VAT, income tax, corporation tax, capital gains tax, inheritance tax and stamp duty land tax, are under the 'care and management' of the Commissioners of HMRC. However, this chapter considers the administration of income tax and CGT only; the procedures for corporation tax, IHT and stamp duty land tax are dealt with in the appropriate chapters on those taxes. VAT is considered in **Chapter 38**.

**[4.2]–[4.20]**

## II   ASSESSMENT AND COLLECTION OF TAX

### 1   The self-assessment system

The accountability of HMRC to the taxpaying public rests upon the premises that the system of taxation that it administers clearly can be understood and that the way in which it is administered is fair.

As far as the second premise is concerned, the 1990s saw a significant reform of the machinery of administration, particularly in the system for assessing personal tax. The essence of the reform was that those taxpayers who used to be required to make an annual tax return (mainly those self-employed persons who were assessable to tax under Cases I and II of Schedule D) are now allowed to work out their own tax bill. Assessment on a 'preceding year' basis for the self-employed has been abolished, so that all taxpayers pay tax on a current year basis. This enables taxpayers to receive one statement dealing with all their income from whatever source and one tax bill (albeit that there are separate rules for computing the amounts from each source). Self-assessment has reduced the costs of tax administration in the public sector and has increased significantly the government's cash-flow, as tax payments are made more promptly than they were under the old system. Of course, the costs to the private sector, reflected either in taxpayers' own time or in the amounts expended in employing professional advisers, have increased correspondingly.

**[4.21]**

## 2   Returns

As indicated above, the key feature of the self-assessment system is that the primary responsibility for making an assessment of the tax payable each year falls on the individual taxpayer, not HMRC.

The self-assessment cycle is started in April of each year, by HMRC sending notices to complete tax returns, together with blank tax returns, to taxpayers. If a taxpayer does not receive a tax return, but does have taxable income or gains, then he must notify HMRC within six months from the end of the relevant tax year, so that a return can be issued and completed within the normal time limits (under TMA 1970 s 7(1)).

The return must be completed and delivered to HMRC by the 'filing date', which is 31 January following the end of the tax year (ie, 31 January 2007 for the 2005/2006 tax year) or three months from the date of the issue of the return, if it is issued after 31 October. The taxpayer must file the return, calculate and pay the tax due by the filing date. In his review of HMRC's Online Services, published on 22 March 2006, Lord Carter of Coles recommended that the filing dates for personal self-assessment tax returns should be brought forward from 31 January to 30 September for paper filing and 30 November for online filing. That proposal is being considered by the Government.

If a taxpayer wants HMRC to calculate their tax liability for them, on the basis of the information provided by their tax return, and to notify them of the tax payable before the due date for payment, then they must submit the tax return by an earlier date, namely 30 September after the year of assessment (ie 30 September 2006 for the 2005/2006 tax year) or two months from the date of issue of the return, if later (see TMA 1970 s 9(2)).

The tax return operates as a source of information and is the basis of a debt payable by the taxpayer. The due date for payment of the tax (and any balancing payment for the previous year—see [4.26]) is the filing date for the return; the liability to pay tax arises on submission of the return without HMRC having to take any further action. This principle applies also where HMRC has, under TMA 1970 s 9(2), calculated the tax due. Such an assessment is a self-assessment for this purpose (see TMA 1970 s 9(3A)). All relevant figures will be needed for the self-assessment form to be completed; accordingly business accounts made up to (say) 31 March must be ready before the following 31 January. If a provisional figure is used, then, in order for HMRC to accept the return, the taxpayer must provide an acceptable explanation for the delay in providing final figures and a date by which he expects to provide the final figure (see *Tax Bulletin 53*, June 2001). For partnerships, each partner will need to include his share of the adjusted partnership profit. Trustees are subject to the same rules as individuals.

There is a duty to preserve the records that were needed to complete the return properly; generally this duty can be fulfilled by retaining copy documents, but certain original documents must be retained (see TMA 1970 s 12B). If the taxpayer is carrying on a trade, profession or business, then all relevant documents must be kept until the fifth anniversary of the due date for payment (ie records for 2000–2001 must be kept until 31 January 2007). Failure to keep records will render the taxpayer potentially liable to the imposition of a penalty of up to £3,000. HMRC has indicated that the imposition of a penalty, however, is not automatic; and that the maximum penalty will be imposed only 'in the most serious cases' (see Inland Revenue Booklet *Self-assessment—A General Guide to Keeping Records*).

TMA 1970 s 115A allows returns to be returned electronically. However, although HMRC has encouraged personal taxpayers to use this method, filing electronically has yet to become a particularly popular option (and difficulties with the technology have not assisted in this regard). With regard to 2002/2003, about 15% of the self-assessment returns that were filed on time were received electronically by the Revenue.

A taxpayer may amend his self-assessment return within 12 months of the filing date for any reason (TMA 1970 s 9ZA). Also, HMRC may amend a self-assessment return, so as to correct any obvious errors, within nine months of receipt (s 9ZB).

TMA 1970 gives HMRC power to issue notices to certain persons requiring them to make returns containing information relevant to the taxable income of other persons. These include:

(i)    the names of employees, and details of payments to them, from an employer (TMA 1970 s 15);

(ii)    from traders (and certain others), details of payments, such as commissions, made for services to persons other than their employees (TMA 1970 s 16); and

(iii)    interest payments made by banks (TMA 1970 s 17 and 18).

FA 2000 s 145 extends HMRC's powers in relation to savings income (by amending TMA 1970 ss 17 and 18) so that it can collect information on non-residents and provide information to other countries (in the hope of receiving some in return).                                                                    **[4.22]**

## 3    Payment of tax

Under self-assessment, all income is taxed for the year of assessment in which it arises. As the amount of income to be charged to tax for a year of assessment is not known until after the end of that year, and because the date for payment of tax is set at 31 January following the end of the year, in order to ensure that there is a flow of tax to HMRC, payments on account of income tax are made. These payments on account are made in two equal instalments on or before:

(1)    31 January in the year of assessment; and

(2)    31 July next following.

The amount to be paid on account is the sum of:

(a)    the amount of tax in the self-assessment for the immediately preceding year minus the amount of income tax deducted at source; and

(b)    the amount of any discovery assessment made for the immediately preceding year.

### EXAMPLE 4.1

In 2006, tax will be paid as follows:

(1)    payment on account 31 January (50% tax due 2004 to 2005) ;

(2)    payment on account 31 July (50% tax due 2004 to 2005).

Taxpayers who have filed returns are excused from making payments on account if the income tax payable for the previous year was less than £500 or if more than 80% of that tax (and NI contributions) was covered by deduction of tax at source (eg PAYE) or tax credits on dividends.

A taxpayer can reduce the interim payments of tax based on the previous year's income, if they believe that their current year's income is lower than their previous year's, by making a claim specifying the reason for the reduction (TMA 1970 s 59A). HMRC cannot refuse the reduction, but it can impose a penalty if the claim to reduce the instalment was made fraudulently or negligently. **[4.23]**

## 4 Collection of tax

Once the amount of tax due has been finalised, HMRC has a number of powers that it can use to collect the tax (but see *Re Selectmove Ltd* (1995) on the restrictions on HMRC's power to agree to a proposal to pay arrears of tax in instalments). If the taxpayer fails to pay, then HMRC can levy distress (TMA 1970 ss 61–62) or, if the taxpayer is an employee, arrange for the tax to be deducted from his earnings. Alternatively, the tax charged can be recovered in the magistrates' court (for amounts up to £2,000 (see SI 1991/1625)), the county court (without limit (but normally used for amounts between £2,000 to £25,000 (and occasionally up to £50,000) or the High Court (for any amount, but will be used for amounts over £50,000 and may be used for amounts between £25,000 to £50,000) (TMA 1970 ss 65–67).

The insolvency of the taxpayer is no bar to HMRC pursuing the debt. However, the former status given to HMRC as a preferential creditor on insolvency has been abolished (see Insolvency Act 1986 Sch 6), except for those cases where HMRC's claim is for 'quasi-trustee debts' (ie where the taxpayer acts as a collecting agent for HMRC (as, for example, in respect of PAYE or NIC)). In the case of such quasi-trustee debts the preference is limited in the case of PAYE to sums owed in the previous 12 months. HMRC has made public its (apparently long-established) practice of not pursuing its 'legal right to recovery for the full amount where it would be unconscionable to insist on collecting the full amount of tax assessed and legally due'—a practice known as 'equitable liability' (*Tax Bulletin*, 1995, p 245). This practice will be operated if the taxpayer can demonstrate clearly that the liability assessed is greater than it would have been if the documents had been submitted at the right time and acceptable evidence of the correct liability is produced. Operation of the practice will depend on the particular circumstances and it would be very unusual for any taxpayer to benefit from the practice more than once. Taxpayers should not, therefore, *rely* on it applying to them (see further ESC A19). **[4.24]**

## 5 Penalties, Surcharges, and Interest

There are three pecuniary weapons that HMRC has in its arsenal that can be used to control taxpayers under the system of self-assessment. These are penalties, interest on overdue payments and surcharges. Also, to ensure that the correct amount of tax is collected, HMRC has very wide powers to obtain information not only from taxpayers, but also from third parties. These powers are examined in **[4.35]** below. **[4.25]**

a)    *Penalties*

*Introduction*

The penalty regime under self-assessment comprises both tax-geared penalties and fixed penalties. In general, the imposition of penalties by HMRC can be appealed to the General or Special Commissioners. The general time limit for the imposition of penalties is six years from the date when the offence was committed. The exceptions to this rule include, first, that, in the case of tax-geared penalties, there is a further period of three years from the final determination of the amount of tax that the penalty is geared to; and, secondly, that the time limit for the imposition of a penalty on a person for assisting in the preparation of an incorrect return is 20 years (see generally TMA 1970 s 103).                                                                    **[4.26]**

> **EXAMPLE 4.2**
>
> Tax was underpaid because of the taxpayer's fraud in 1992–93. If the assessment only becomes final in May 2003, HMRC has until May 2006 to raise penalties, even though the offence was committed more than six years from the date of the assessment.

The imposition of penalties will not be prevented by the death of the taxpayer (see s 100A); although whether this provision is compatible with the European Convention on Human Rights has yet to be tested in the UK courts.                                                                    **[4.27]**

*Late filing of returns*

TMA 1970 s 93 imposes an automatic fixed penalty of £100 if a return is not filed on time, with a further £100 fine if it still has not been filed six months later. The fixed penalties will be reduced if they amount to more than the tax liability for the relevant year (see s 93(7)); and the penalty is not charged if the taxpayer throughout the 'period of default' had a 'reasonable excuse' for not delivering the return (s 93(8)(a)); see *Steeden v Carver, Tax Bulletin*, December 1999, p 705 and the *Bulletin Working Together* Issue 1, for how these phrases are to be interpreted. If the return is incomplete, then technically s 93 applies, but see *Tax Bulletin*, October 1998, p 593 and December 1999, p 705 with regard to HMRC's approach.

In addition to the fixed penalties, a penalty of up to £60 per day can be imposed by HMRC, but only after permission has been granted by the Special or General Commissioners. HMRC has indicated that it will use this power sparingly; an application might be made if HMRC considers that a substantial amount of tax is probably payable and that the fixed penalty might not provide sufficient encouragement to file the return. If a return has still not been filed one year after the filing date, a penalty related to the amount of tax due can be imposed. The imposition of such a penalty is appealable to the Special or General Commissioners (see, for example, *Caesar v HM Inspector of Taxes*.                                                                    **[4.28]**

*Incorrect information*

The maximum penalty for fraudulently or negligently submitting an incorrect return is 100% of the difference between the amount of tax properly payable and the amount payable on the return or accounts as submitted (TMA 1970 s 95). Although the taxpayer must act negligently or fraudulently for a penalty to be imposed under s 95, they will be deemed to have so acted if they realise that the return is incorrect and do not remedy the error 'without unreasonable delay' (s 97). HMRC may reduce the penalty payable; and, in practice, unless the taxpayer refuses to co-operate, rarely will impose the maximum penalty (*Revenue Booklet 73* sets out HMRC's approach). The imposition of such a penalty is appealable to the Special or General Commissioners.                                                                                     **[4.29]**

*Other penalties*

There are a number of other penalties that HMRC may impose under the self-assessment system. These include:

Failure by a taxpayer, who has taxable income or gains, but does not receive a tax return, to notify HMRC of this in time. The amount of the penalty cannot exceed the tax unpaid on the filing date; and so this penalty can be avoided by paying the correct amount of tax due on or before the filing date.

Assisting in the preparation or delivery of an incorrect return or accounts can lead to a maximum penalty of £3,000 (s 99).                                              **[4.30]**

b)   *Surcharges*

Surcharges are, in effect, penalties for late payment of tax; and exist as a means of preventing taxpayers from obtaining low-interest loans from HMRC. An automatic surcharge of 5% is payable if the tax due on 31 January is not paid by 1 March; and a further 5% is due if the tax is more than six months late. Whilst surcharges are not due on unpaid interim payments, if these payments remain outstanding when the balancing payment becomes due, they are then treated as part of that final payment and will be included for the purpose of calculating the surcharge. Surcharges can be waived if the taxpayer has a 'reasonable excuse' for his failure (see **[4.22]** above and *Bancroft v Crutchfield* (2002)).                                                           **[4.31]**

c)   *Interest*

Similarly to surcharge, the interest regime provides an incentive for taxpayers to pay tax on time. If tax that is due is paid late, then interest will be charged automatically under TMA 1970 s 86. The rate of interest is provided by Statutory Instrument; and the formula is basic rate + 2.5. Interest can be charged on interim payments as well as on the final balancing payment. Also, interest is payable on penalties and surcharges that are not paid by the due date (under TMA ss 59C(6), 69 and 103A).

Where tax has been overpaid or penalties or surcharges paid unnecessarily, the refund will carry interest from the date the tax was paid (see TA 1988 ss 824 and 826 and TCGA 1992 s 283). However, the rate of interest on tax repaid is less than the rate of interest on overdue tax. Usually, repayments will be made automatically. Generally, a claim for repayment must be made within six years from the end of the tax year in question; exceptionally, this period can be extended (ESC B41). **[4.32]**

## 6   Enquiries

There is a statutory procedure that allows HMRC to enquire into the accuracy of a return (ss 9A and 19A). In contrast to the position pre-self-assessment, there is no longer any requirement that a return be incorrect before an enquiry can be commenced. Some enquiries will be made on a random basis, whereas others will arise because of specific queries on a particular return.

Notice of any such enquiry must be 'given' to the taxpayer 'before the end' of the period of 12 months beginning with the filing date or up to 15 months after the return was actually filed, if it was filed late. For returns filed on time an enquiry is valid only if notice is delivered to the taxpayer no later than the following 31 January (see *Tax Bulletin*, Special Edition 3 (2000) Working Together and *Wing Hung Lai v Bale* (1999) and *Holly v Inspector of Taxes* (2000)). If no enquiry notice is served in that period, then (unless it is incorrect because of fraudulent or negligent conduct) the tax return will become final, subject to the power of discovery (see **[4.23]**) and the taxpayer's right to make an 'error or mistake' claim within five years from the normal filing date (under TMA 1970 s 33).

Under s 28A, an enquiry into a personal self-assessment is completed when, by closure notice, the Officer informs the taxpayer that he has completed his enquiries and states his conclusions. The closure notice either must state that no amendment of the return is required or make the amendments of the return that the Officer considers are necessary to give effect to his conclusions. The taxpayer then may appeal any amendments of the return (see **[IV]** below).

Section 28A enables the taxpayer to apply to the Commissioners, during the enquiry, for a direction that the enquiry should be closed. The burden of proof is then on HMRC to show that there are reasonable grounds for not closing the enquiry. This procedural rule is intended to protect taxpayers against protracted and unfocused enquiries. **[4.33]**

## 7   Discovery assessments

Whilst generally HMRC will not issue assessments under the self-assessment regime, it retains the power to make 'discovery assessments' under TMA 1970 s 29 (as amended) if it 'discovers' that income or capital gains that ought to have been assessed have not or that any relief has become excessive. The principle is that HMRC should be able to make assessments to prevent there being any loss of tax. Under the old assessment rules, the concept of 'discovery' covered a variety of different circumstances. For example, it encompassed the discovery of new facts (*Parkin v Cattell* (1971) 48 TC 462), that the wrong conclusion had been drawn from the original facts (*Cenlon Finance Co Ltd v Ellwood* (1962)), as well as that an arithmetical error had been made (*Vickerman v Mason's Personal Representatives* (1984)). In essence, discovery by the Revenue was permissible wherever the Revenue realised that the taxpayer was undercharged to tax (subject to s 54 (see below)). The raising of a discovery assessment did not require any default by the taxpayer. A discovery assessment could be made at any time within a six-year period after the end of the relevant tax year.

The self-assessment rules restrict HMRC's power to make a discovery assessment. If a taxpayer has made a self-assessment, then a discovery assessment can not be made unless either there has been fraudulent or negligent conduct on the part of the taxpayer (or their agent) or the 'officer could not have been reasonably expected, on the basis of the information made available to him' before the final date for opening an enquiry (see above) to be aware that additional tax was due. However, this latter precondition was interpreted in way that does not restrict significantly an Officer's ability to raise a discovery assessment by the Court of Appeal in *Langham v Veltema* [2004] STC 544. In *Veltema*, the Court of Appeal held that an inspector reasonably can be expected to have been aware of tax issues only where there is an actual insufficiency that has been highlighted in the return. There is no obligation on an inspector to make an enquiry, however routine, unless the insufficiency of tax is apparent on the basis of the information before him. This decision suggests that, in order to prevent a discovery assessment being raised, a taxpayer needs to flag, for the Officer's benefit, the fact that a figure in his return may turn out to be incorrect.

If no self-assessment return has been returned by the taxpayer, then the old pre-self-assessment rules still apply.

The relationship between s 54 (see below) and s 29 (pre- its self-assessment amendment) was considered by the House of Lords in *Cenlon Finance Co Ltd v Ellwood* [1962] AC 782. In *Cenlon*, the House of Lords held that an issue in dispute that had been agreed under s 54 could not be re-opened for that year of assessment by the Revenue raising a further assessment. However, the taxpayer is protected only for the particular issue (or issues) agreed and only in respect of the year (or years) that form the subject of the s 54 agreement.

*Scorer v Olin Energy Systems Ltd* (1985) involved the making of a further assessment by a later inspector, after a s 54 agreement had been entered into on what was discovered to have been an erroneous basis (namely allowing a claim for losses to be carried forward from one division of the business to another). The House of Lords held that the Revenue was precluded from making the further assessment. If the Revenue leads the taxpayer reasonably to believe that they are making an offer on particular terms, then they will be estopped from saying subsequently that they did not intend that consequence. Lord Keith (with whom all their Lordships agreed) said that the relevant question was whether the parties had come to an agreement in respect of the claim; and that said that test was an objective one:

'The situation must be viewed objectively, from the point of view of whether the inspector's agreement to the relevant computation, having regard to the surrounding circumstances including all the material known to be in his possession, was such as to lead a reasonable man to the conclusion that he had decided to admit the claim which had been made.'

As the accounts submitted on behalf of the taxpayer set out all the facts relevant to the claim for carry forward of losses, a reasonable man would have concluded that the inspector had agreed to that claim. Thus, the Revenue was bound by the s 54 agreement. (See SP 8/91.)          **[4.34]**

## 8   Powers of HMRC to obtain information

Once an enquiry is in progress, generally HMRC first will seek to obtain information by means of an informal request to the taxpayer. If this does not succeed, then recourse may be had to TMA s 19A. Under s 19A, an Officer can issue a notice to the taxpayer requiring 'such documents as are in the taxpayer's possession or power' and 'such accounts or particulars' as he may reasonably require. A time limit (of not less than 30 days) can be imposed for production of the information (In *Self-assessed v Inspector of Taxes* (1999) a notice was quashed because it required production of documents within 30 days of the date of the notice); and failure to comply will result in the imposition of a penalty of £50 and subsequent daily penalties. The question whether the request is 'reasonable' will depend on the nature of the request in the context of the case. *Mother v Inspector of Taxes* (1999) contains useful guidance as to the nature of documents that can be requested.

Wide and general information powers are given to HMRC under TMA 1970 s 20. Section 20 is distinct from s 19A in two important ways. First, it is a 'free-standing' power that can be used even if there is no open enquiry (see *R v IRC, ex parte Taylor (No 2)* [1990] STC 379); and secondly, it can be used to require third parties to produce information or documents in their power or possession.

There are a number of statutory restrictions on the exercise of powers by the Officer under s 20(1) and (3). This include the following:

(1)   The taxpayer or third party must have been given a reasonable opportunity to produce the requisite information or documents voluntarily; this is usually done by the service of a 'precursor notice' requesting the provision of the documents within a certain time limit (often 30 days).

(2)   Personal records which are excluded from police search powers and journalistic material are protected from disclosure (s 20(8C)).

(3)   Notices under s 20(1) and (3) can be issued by an Officer only after permission has been granted by a General or Special Commissioner, who must be satisfied in all the circumstances that the Officer is justified in proceeding under this section. The exercise of the power thus is limited by the requirement for independent supervision (for discussions of the role of the inspector and his duty to lay all relevant information before the Commissioner and of the role of the latter, see *R v IRC, ex p T C Coombs & Co* (1991), *R v IRC, ex p Continental Shipping Ltd SA* (1996), *R v Macdonald and IRC, ex p Hutchinson & Co Ltd* (1998) and *R v IRC, ex p Archon Shipping Corpn* (1998)). However, the hearing before the Commissioner is *ex parte* (see the decision of the Court of Appeal in *R (on the application of Morgan Grenfell) v Special Commissioner* (2001)).

(4)   Neither the taxpayer nor a third party is obliged to produce documents relating to a pending appeal by the taxpayer. This is a limited form of 'litigation privilege'.

(5)  Tax accountants are protected from disclosing audit papers or working papers that contain tax advice (s 20B(9)).

(6)  An Officer may not give either a s 20 notice to a barrister, advocate or solicitor; the decision to give such a notice must be taken by the Board.

(7)  A barrister, advocate or solicitor is not obliged to produce privileged documents in his possession without the consent of his client in response to a s 20(3) notice (TMA s 20B(8)). (The claim of privilege is not available in relation to notices issued to a legal adviser *in his capacity as taxpayer* (see *R v IRC, ex p Taylor (No 2)* (1990) and *R v IRC, ex p Lorimer* (2000)).

In *R (on the application of Morgan Grenfell) v Special Commissioner* (2002) the House of Lords affirmed that legal professional privilege is a fundamental right. Although s 20(1) contains no express reference to legal professional privilege, it is not possible to draw an 'inescapable inference' from the s 20 provisions that privilege was not intended to be preserved for documents in the possession or power of the taxpayer. Thus, the right can be asserted by taxpayers to prevent HMRC from obtaining production of privileged material.

HMRC possesses further powers to obtain documents where serious fraud is suspected: TMA 1970 s 20BA and s 20C. Section 20C enables an Officer (after obtaining a warrant from a circuit judge) to enter private premises (if necessary by force) to search for and remove documents that he reasonably believes to be evidence of such fraud. No particular offence need be specified in the warrant other than 'serious fraud' (for an illustration of this power see *IRC v Rossminster Ltd* (1980)). Further, the occupier of the premises has no right to be informed of the precise grounds on which the warrant was issued, although he is entitled to a list of the items removed and must be allowed reasonable access to them whilst they are in the possession of HMRC. Section 20C(4) provides that HMRC are not authorised to seize items that are subject to legal privilege. Section 20C(4A) provides a definition of legally privileged documents for the purpose of s 20C. It extends the protection given to such documents to whenever they are held by 'a person who is entitled to possession of them and; provides that 'items held with the intention of furthering a criminal purpose are not subject to legal privilege'.). In *R v IRC, ex p Tamosius and Partners* (1999), the High Court held that s 20C(4) prevented only the removal of documents with respect to which a claim to professional privilege could be 'maintained'—the seizure did not become unlawful merely because the firm of American lawyers that had been raided *claimed* that the documents were privileged. The court also supported the Revenue's approach of taking independent counsel to advise on the issue of privilege in respect of the seized material.

HMRC's ability to obtain possession of documents in the case of suspected serious fraud has been enhanced by the recent introduction of s 20BA (and TMA 1970 Sch 1AA). Section 20BA does not require HMRC to apply for a search and seizure warrant to obtain documents from a third party, who may have evidence relating to suspected fraud; a judge may issue an order requiring the person to deliver the documents to HMRC. A person is entitled to notice of the intention of HMRC to apply for a s 20BA order against them (unless this would seriously prejudice the investigation of the offence), but he may not inform the taxpayer of this, unless he is a 'professional legal adviser' and does so for the purpose of giving legal advice. This 'anti-tipping off' provision stands in contrast to the provisions in respect of s 20(3) notices, where third parties are allowed to (and particularly in the case of tax advisers, frequently do) inform taxpayers of the requests from HMRC. Section 20BA is intended to limit the occasions on which it is necessary for HMRC to enter the premises of persons not themselves suspected of fraud; and a warrant cannot be issued under s 20C if the production order procedure under s 20BA is more appropriate.

Schedule 1AA paragraph 5 provides the same protection to privileged materials with regard to the exercise of a power under s 20BA as s 20C(4) does in the context of s 20C notices. In addition, Regulation 7 of the Orders for the Delivery of Documents (Procedure) Regulations 2000 sets out a procedure for the resolution of disputes as to legal privilege.

A 'tax accountant', who has been convicted of a tax offence or who has been subject to a penalty for making or assisting in making an incorrect tax return, can be required with the consent of a circuit judge or, in certain circumstances, the Board's authority, to produce any documents in their possession or under their authority regarding the tax affairs of any client past or present (see TMA 1970 s 20A; and *Inland Revenue Bulletin* April 2000, pp 743–746 for HMRC's interpretation of the scope of this power).Given the width of the s 20 power it has been recognised that it must be controlled (see [1998] BTR 213 and 278 for a practitioner's view and the Revenue's response), particularly with regard to notices served on third parties. However, the general approach of the courts is not to be overly sympathetic to third parties required to provide information. Although in *R v O'Kane and Clarke, ex p Northern Bank Ltd* (1996), the court quashed notices given by the Revenue to a bank in relation to its customers, on the basis that the notices were too widely drafted (amounting in effect to 'fishing expeditions') and too onerous to comply with, in *R v IRC, ex p Ulster Bank Ltd* (1997), the Court of Appeal allowed far greater leeway to the Revenue. In *R v Commissioners of Inland Revenue (ex parte Banque Internationale a Luxembourg SA* (2000), the High Court noted that, although the notices clearly constituted a prima facie breach of the European Convention on Human Rights Article 8, as they required the disclosure of private and confidential information, there was ample justification for their issue, because 'the notices were issued according to law, in pursuit of a legitimate aim and necessary in a democratic society for the protecting the taxation system and revenue'.

Section 20(8A) was introduced by Finance Act 1988. It enables HMRC to serve a s 20(3) notice without naming the taxpayer to whom the notice relates. The power was introduced primarily for the purpose of enabling the Inland Revenue to obtain information from sponsors of tax avoidance schemes with regard to their clients. Until recently, this power was used only rarely, and almost never for that purpose. Recently, it has started to be used by the department that is now known as the Special Civil Investigations of HMRC to obtain, inter alia, records relating to credit cards issued by card issuers in the UK that are funded from offshore bank accounts held by UK residents whether or not UK domiciled taxpayers. Following the decision in *Re an Application by Revenue and Customs Commissioners to serve a section 20 notice* [2006] STC (SCD) 71, where the Special Commissioner consented to the service of a s 20(8A) notice on a bank that will require the production of a significant amount of documents, it is considered likely that HMRC will make more use of this power in future. **[4.35]**

## 9   Serious investigation cases

A serious investigation case arises when HMRC discovers that a taxpayer may have evaded tax, usually by not disclosing his true income, by supplying inaccurate or incomplete information, or by claiming reliefs and allowances to which he is not entitled. HMRC often discovers this from 'tip-offs' that it receives about the taxpayer, or from a 'confession' from the taxpayer himself. Prior to the enactment of CRCA, it was up to the Inland Revenue, which had power to act as a prosecuting authority, to determine whether or not to commence criminal proceedings, and/or make assessments for the lost tax plus interest and/or claim penalties. What the Inland Revenue chose to do in any case depended largely on the degree of co-operation of the taxpayer.

CRCA set up a separate independent prosecuting authority that is responsible for the prosecution of all HM Revenue and Customs cases in England and Wales—the RCPO. However, HMRC's role in prosecution matters has not disappeared. In April 2005, the Treasury, the Attorney General, the Commissioners for HMRC and the Director of the RCPO entered into a memorandum of understanding concerning the relationship between HMRC and RCPO as to the conduct of criminal investigations and prosecutions by the two entities. It is the Commissioners who are responsible for, and accountable to, Parliament via Treasury Ministers for anything done in the course of an investigation, and policy, including the criteria to be used in deciding whether alternatives to prosecution should be applied.

Criminal proceedings are on the increase but still are taken rarely. It is preferable for HMRC for some settlement to be reached with the taxpayer; criminal prosecutions are expensive and, in prosecutions, the burden of proof lies on the tax authority. In economic terms, HMRC is able to guarantee the recovery of significantly more money (and incur significantly less expenditure) by raising assessments for the lost tax, levying interest and claiming penalties than it would be able to by prosecuting every case of 'tax evasion'.

Small cases are dealt with by local Officers who have the power to agree settlements. In larger cases the approval of the head office is required before any settlement can be reached. When arriving at a settlement, the factors that HMRC considers include the amount of tax lost, interest payable, penalties available, the co-operation of the taxpayer and, most importantly, the need for uniformity in cases of a similar nature. **[4.36]**

a)   *Criminal proceedings*

Prosecutions can be brought against the taxpayer: under the Perjury Act 1911; for forgery; for conspiracy to defraud; under the Theft Acts 1968 and 1978 for obtaining a pecuniary advantage by deception or false accounting; or for the common law offence of cheating the public revenue. Cheating the public revenue exists only as a common law offence. The 'public revenue' includes all taxes and duties levied by central government (but not those imposed by local government). There is no requirement that the revenue actually be defrauded; it is enough that the defendant intended that that occur (see *R v Hunt* [1994] STC 819).

Company officers can be made liable for such offences if committed by the company. Professional tax advisers are likely to be prosecuted for such offences (details of recent prosecutions are now regularly published in the *Tax Bulletin*). One interesting issue is to what extent an ineffective tax avoidance scheme can give rise to a successful criminal prosecution for cheating the public revenue, which was essentially what happened in *R v Charlton* (1996): see [1998] CLR 627 and *Taxation*, 11 February 1999, p 460 for a discussion of this issue and Dawn Primarolo's comments on the new statutory offence described in the following paragraph.

FA 2000 introduced a new statutory offence of fraudulent evasion of income tax, following a report by Lord Grabiner QC (March 2000) on the 'informal economy', designed to facilitate prosecutions in magistrates' courts. The same query as that posed in the previous paragraph was asked in the Committee debates in relation to this offence. The Paymaster General Dawn Primarolo responded: 'A failed scheme whose details have not been hidden from the Revenue amounts not to tax evasion but tax planning ... it does not fall within the remit of this measure.'                                    **[4.37]**

b)    *Hansard and Code of Practice 9*

*The Hansard procedure*

What became known as the Hansard procedure was first introduced on 19 July 1923. It took its name from the official record of parliamentary debates and was set out in a statement made by the Chancellor of the Exchequer (recorded in Hansard). The statement set out the policy of the Board of Inland Revenue as regards serious tax fraud. In short, taxpayers, who are suspected of serious tax fraud, were encouraged to make a full confession and to make good any tax that they have failed to disclose in past years (and, in addition, to pay a substantial penalty (potentially up to 100% of the historic tax lost through their suspected fraud)) in return for an effective immunity from prosecution. The Hansard process was not a 'criminal' process in the sense that that term is widely understood; it was offered in circumstances where the tax authority is not seeking to prosecute the taxpayer. As a result of comments made by Lord Hutton in *R v Allen* (2001), a revised Hansard statement was made on 7 November 2002. It provides an explicit guarantee that if the taxpayer makes a full and complete disclosure of all tax irregularities, then he will not be prosecuted. The Hansard procedure was briefly suspended in 2003 due to the finding by the Court of Appeal in *R v Gill* (2003) that the 'opening meeting' under the Hansard process (where the taxpayer is read the statement from Hansard) should have been subject to the provisions of the Police and Criminal Evidence Act 1984 (PACE). Hansard was subsequently reintroduced in a PACE-compliant way. The modifications include that: (i) the opening meeting will be tape recorded in its entirety (under PACE Code of Practice E); (ii) the taxpayer will be advised in advance of the opening meeting that he has a right to legal advice prior to the meeting and legal representation at the meeting; and (iii) the opening meeting will begin with the reading of the

PACE Code C caution ('You do not have to say anything, but it may harm your defence if you do not mention when questioned something which you later wish to rely on in court.').

Although, potentially, the Crown Prosecution Service (CPS) may still prosecute a taxpayer even if HMRC has decided not to utilise its power to do so, following a settlement negotiated under the Hansard procedure (see *R v W* (1998)), the Attorney-General has made it clear that ordinarily the CPS will bring proceedings that encompass charges relating to tax evasion only where that evasion is incidental to allegations of non-fiscal criminal conduct. (See also *Tax Bulletin* 35.)

The Hansard procedure now applies only with regard to investigations that started before 1 September 2005.

*Code of Practice 9*

With effect from 1 September 2005, following consultation with the relevant professional bodies, HMRC introduced a new combined code, Code of Practice 9 ('COP 9'), governing the civil investigation of fraud. It replaces both the Hansard procedure and HM Customs and Excise's civil evasion procedures. The following statement is given to taxpayers at the outset of the investigation:

1. The Commissioners reserve complete discretion to pursue a criminal investigation with a view to prosecution where they consider it necessary and appropriate.

2. Where a criminal investigation is not considered necessary or appropriate the Commissioners may decide to investigate using the Civil Investigation of Fraud procedure.

3. Where the Commissioners decide to investigate using the Civil Investigation of Fraud procedure they will not seek a prosecution for the tax fraud which is the subject of that investigation. The taxpayer will be given an opportunity to make a full and complete disclosure of all irregularities in their tax affairs.

4. However, where materially false statements are made or materially false documents are provided with intent to deceive, in the course of a civil investigation, the Commissioners may conduct a criminal investigation with a view to a prosecution of that conduct.

5. If the Commissioners decide to investigate using the Civil Investigation of Fraud procedure the taxpayer will be given a copy of this statement by an authorised officer.

Although many of the features of the old Hansard procedure appear in COP 9, one important difference is the absence of the PACE procedures. Thus, meetings will not be tape recorded, nor will the taxpayer be cautioned as to his rights .                                                        **[4.38]**

c)   *Information powers under the Serious Organised Crime And Police Act 2005*

Under the Serious Organised Crime and Police Act 2005 (SOCPA) Part 2 Chapter 1 ss 60–70 new investigatory powers in relation to tax crimes, inter alia, are introduced. Under SCOPA s 60 use of these powers can be delegated by the director of RCPO to any HMRC prosecutor. The offences to which the powers relate include common law cheat of the public revenue and false accounting (Theft Act 1968 s 17), provided that, in the opinion of the investigating officer, the potential loss to the public revenue is of an amount not less than £5,000. The powers came into effect on 1 April 2006.

An HMRC prosecutor can give, or authorise an officer of HMRC to give, a disclosure notice to any person who has information which relates to a matter relevant to the investigation of the offence, provided that there are reasonable grounds for belief that the information in question, whether or not by itself, is likely to be of 'substantial value' to the investigation. A recipient of the notice will not only have to produce documents relevant to the investigation, but also to 'answer questions with respect to any matter relevant to the investigation' and to 'provide information with respect to any such matter as is specified in the notice' (under SOCPA s 62(3)). There is a similar protection for privileged information or documents as is contained in TMA 1970 ss 20B(8) and 20C(4): a person may not be required to answer any privileged question, or provide any privileged information, or produce any privileged document (except that a lawyer may be required to provide the name and address of his client).

Two offences are created with regard to SOCPA disclosure notices. The first is failure to comply with the requirements set out in a disclosure notice (punishable by a maximum sentence of 51 weeks' imprisonment, with a 'reasonable excuse' for failure to comply being a defence); and, second is making a false or misleading statement in response to the requirements imposed by a disclosure notice (punishable by a maximum of two years' imprisonment).

If the recipient of a disclosure notice fails to comply with its terms, then the HMRC prosecutor will be able to obtain a search and seize warrant from a Justice of the Peace. Such a warrant will enable an HMRC prosecutor to enter and search premises, using force where necessary, and to take possession of any documents that appear to be of a description specified in the disclosure notice, or to take any other other steps that appear to be necessary for preserving, or preventing interference with, any such documents. A warrant also will be able to be issued it is not practicable to issue a disclosure notice or where the service of a disclosure notice might seriously prejudice the investigation (under SOCPA s 66(2)).

It is likely that these powers will be used primarily against third parties, including professional advisors. (See the comments of the Parliamentary Under-Secretary of State for the Home Department at the Committee stage of the Serious Organised Crime and Police Bill.)    **[4.39]**

## 10   Assessments for lost tax plus interest

The normal time limit for making an assessment to tax is, in the case of income and capital gains tax, five years after 31 January following the relevant tax year and in the case of corporation tax, six years after the end of the relevant accounting period (TMA 1970 s 34(1)). There is an extended time limit for assessments to recover tax lost through fraudulent or negligent conduct (TMA 1970 s 36): for income tax and capital gains tax the limit is 20 years after 31 January following the relevant tax year. In cases where the defaulting taxpayer had carried on a business in partnership, there may be an extra assessment on the other individuals who were at that time their partners (but based only on their (revised) share of the partnership profit— see *Tax Bulletin*, August 1996, pp 339 and 340). A taxpayer assessed on the basis of fraudulent or negligent conduct is entitled to his full allowances and reliefs for the year in question even though the time limit for claiming them has expired.

A particularly graphic illustration of what was then wilful default and today would be classified as negligent conduct, is afforded by the case of *Pleasants v Atkinson* (1987). The taxpayer's accountants purported to deduct, in arriving at the profits of his trade as a property developer, money that was actually expended on his private residence. The Commissioners were entitled on these facts to conclude that, although the taxpayer was himself innocent of wilful default, his agent (the firm of accountants) was guilty and, furthermore, that it was not necessary to prove any additional requirement, such as personal enrichment, in order to explain that breach of duty. Accordingly, the taxpayer was assessed on profits under-declared (see TMA 1970 s 36(1) which refers to the conduct of a person 'acting on his (ie the taxpayer's) behalf').

For a back duty assessment to be made on a deceased taxpayer's personal representatives (PRs) it must be made within three tax years of the 31 January following the year of death for fraudulent or negligent conduct by the deceased in any of the six years up to and including the year of his death (TMA 1970 s 40). Thus, if the deceased died in the tax year 2001–02, HMRC has until 30 January 2006 in which to assess his PRs for loss of tax because of their fraudulent or negligent conduct in the years from 1995–96 to 2001–02. An assessment is 'made' for these purposes when the certificate of assessment is signed in the assessment book and not when the notice of assessment is received by the taxpayer (TMA 1970 s 40 and *Honig v Sarsfield* (1986)).

In *Baylis v Gregory* (1987) the Court of Appeal had to consider the position when a taxpayer was assessed to CGT, but, because of a typing error, that assessment was stated to be for 1974–75 whereas it should have related to 1975–76. This error went unnoticed until the time limit for making an assessment for 1975–76 had passed. When it was noticed by the inspector he made a note in his records that the assessment for 1974–75 was vacated. On these facts, the court decided, first, that the 1974–75 assessment had not been properly cancelled, since notice had not been given to the taxpayer, but, secondly, that it could not be treated as referring to 1975–76. The correct procedure was for a proper assessment to be made for that year, but as the relevant time limit had passed, the taxpayer could not be taxed on gains realised in 1975–76.                                          **[4.40]–[4.49]**

## III  APPEALS

### 1  Introduction

One of the reasons for introducing self-assessment was to reduce the number of appeals made by taxpayers. Prior to the introduction of the self-assessment regime, there were roughly five million appeals made annually in England and Wales against assessments and, of these, about four million were settled by agreement between taxpayers and HMRC. Under the assessment regime, a taxpayer's failure to provide complete information on time often resulted in HMRC issuing an assessment in estimated figures and such assessments then would be appealed by the taxpayer to the Commissioners. A taxpayer's failure under self-assessment similarly results in HMRC 'determining' the tax due (s 28C). However, the key difference between the regimes is that under self-assessment, the taxpayer simply has to file a self-assessed return in order to replace that determination; there is *no* right of appeal against a determination. Thus, self-assessment has reduced the number of appeals that arose merely because there had been a delay in the taxpayer fulfilling his statutory duties.                                                          **[4.50]**

## 2   Appeals to the Commissioners

### a)   *Notice of Appeal*

An appeal must be brought by a notice of appeal in writing within 30 days after the date that, for example, the amendment to a self-assessment has been made. The notice of appeal must specify the grounds of appeal, but it is normal for the grounds to be stated in a general way only at this stage. The detailed facts and issues of law that form the basis of the appeal can then be set out a later stage, normally in a statement of case and/or in a skeleton argument.

TMA s 49 provides that appeals may be brought out of time provided, first, that there was a reasonable excuse for not bringing the appeal within the time limit, and, secondly, that the application was made thereafter without unreasonable delay. HMRC may consent in writing; and, in practice, normally consents freely to 'reasonable' appeals out of time. In default of consent, the matter must be referred to the Commissioners. The decision of the Commissioners is final (subject to judicial review (see *R, on the application of Browallia Cal, v City of London General Commissioners* (2004)).            **[4.51]**

### b)   *Postponement of tax pending appeal*

Where a taxpayer disagrees with an amendment to his self-assessment (under TMA 1970 s 28A) or other assessment, he must inform the Officer within 30 days of his intention to appeal and the amount of tax he considers excessive. In the event that the taxpayer does not apply for postponement, then the whole of the tax charged is payable as if there had been no appeal, but without prejudice to the appeal (TMA 1970 s 55). In many cases, the taxpayer and the Officer will be able to agree the amount of tax to be postponed (see s 55(7)). However, if agreement cannot be reached, then the taxpayer may apply to the Commissioners for a determination of the amount of tax to be postponed pending the determination of the appeal. Before the Commissioners, the taxpayer does not have to prove all the facts or succeed in the legal arguments that will have to be proved or established at the substantive appeal; instead, the taxpayer just must show 'reasonable grounds' for believing that they have been overcharged to tax. 'Reasonable' means that the grounds must be based on reason and must not be irrational, absurd or ridiculous (See *Sparrow Ltd v Inspector of Taxes* (2001)). There is a right of appeal from the Commissioners to the High Court on a question of law (under TMA 1970 s 56A(4)).

Only the amount of tax that depends on the outcome of the appeal is postponed until the appeal is heard. In the meantime the HMRC is entitled to seek payment of the balance (which is payable within 30 days of the agreement or the Commissioners' decision under s 55(5)—see *Parikh v Back* (1985)).                                                                  **[4.52]**

c)   *Agreements settling appeals*

Litigation which has been commenced before the Commissioners by notice of appeal can be validly settled by agreement only if the agreement complies with the relevant statutory provision, namely TMA 1970 s 54. In short, a s 54 agreement has the same consequences as a determination to the same effect by the Commissioners; and the agreement binds the parties to it in the same way as a determination binds the parties to an appeal (see *Tod v South Essex Motors (Basildon) Ltd* (1988)). It cannot be determinative of tax liabilities for years after that to which the assessment in question relates (See *McNiven v Westmoreland Investments Ltd* (1997), in which, although the inspector's reasoning in the agreement referred to the amount of excess management expenses that were intended to be carried forward, the Court held that this did not bind HMRC to take those into account in future years). Save as otherwise provided in the Taxes Act, the determination of the Commissioners is final and conclusive (under TMA 1970 s 46(2)). Thus, a s 54 agreement is similarly final and conclusive and the issues that are resolved by it can not be re-litigated by the parties.

A s 54 agreement is capable of rectification (*R v Inspector of Taxes, ex p Bass Holdings Ltd* (1993)) and it may be vitiated by mutual mistake (*Fox v Rothwell* (1995)). Moreover, as a consequence of the agreement being final and conclusive, the taxpayer has a statutory 'cooling-off' period of 30 days. During this period, he can resile from the agreement by giving notice in writing to the Officer; and he is not required to show cause in order to resile.

An agreement between HMRC and a taxpayer made outside s 54 will be binding only in limited circumstances. Whilst HMRC, under its care and management powers, may enter into 'back duty' agreements (whereby it agrees to settle for less than the tax that may be due), HMRC does not have power to enter into 'forward tax agreements' (where it is agreed, in advance, that specified amounts will be paid annually in lieu of tax that otherwise would be due (see *Al Fayed v Advocate General for Scotland* (2002)). HMRC does not have power to agree not to perform its duty to collect tax in accordance with the statutory procedure. If a taxpayer enters into such an agreement, it will be enforceable only by way of judicial review proceedings, and HMRC will be bound only if their failure or refusal to abide by the agreement amounts to an abuse of power.                                                        **[4.53]**

d)   *The General and Special Commissioners*

If an appeal cannot be settled by agreement, it is then set down for hearing by the General or the Special Commissioners.

The jurisdiction over direct tax appeals is shared between the General and Special Commissioners. Both bodies are appointed by the Lord Chancellor (TMA 1970 ss 2, 4). Although the status is the same (and there is no appeal from the General to the Special Commissioners), each body has different qualities. The Special Commissioners are legally qualified and have technical expertise; whereas the General Commissioners are able to bring to a dispute local knowledge and commercial experience. The General Commissioners are part-time unpaid laypersons appointed locally for a district, like lay magistrates, and are assisted by a clerk who is usually a solicitor (TMA 1970 s 3). The Special Commissioners, who are 'overseen' by a Presiding Special Commissioner, must be barristers, advocates or solicitors of at least ten years' standing (TMA 1970 s 4).

Although some direct tax issues are exclusive to the Special Commissioners, (such as appeals concerning petroleum revenue tax or international tax issues) direct taxes are generally within the jurisdiction of both the General and Special Commissioners.

For all matters within the jurisdiction of both the General and Special Commissioners, the 'default' rule is that an appeal shall lie to the General Commissioners. A taxpayer who wishes to have their appeal heard before the Special Commissioners must elect for this to occur within the 30-day time limit for making the appeal. If the opportunity to elect is missed, it is still possible, under TMA 1970 s 44(3), to transfer proceedings to the Special Commissioners, but only if HMRC, the General Commissioners and the Special Commissioners consent. Where the taxpayer elects for the Special Commissioners, this election may be disregarded at any time before the determination of the appeal by agreement between the parties or, failing agreement, by a non-appealable direction of the General Commissioners given after hearing the parties (TMA 1970 s 31D(5)).

An appeal is heard either by a panel of General Commissioners or by a single Special Commissioner unless the Presiding Special Commissioner directs otherwise (TMA 1970 s 45). Once started, an appeal cannot be withdrawn except with the agreement in writing of the Officer (TMA 1970 s 54 and see *Beach v Willesden General Comrs* (1982) (see above)). At the hearing, the Crown may be represented by the relevant Officer, but, particularly in cases before the Special Commissioners, frequently is represented by a barrister. The taxpayer may appear in person or be represented by a barrister, solicitor or accountant.

The procedure in respect of the pre-trial stage and at the hearing itself is governed by Regulations that were introduced in 1994 (the Special Commissioners (Jurisdiction and Procedure) Regulations SI 1994/1811 ('the Special Commissioners Regulations') and the General Commissioners (Jurisdiction and Procedure) Regulations SI 1994/1812 ('the General Commissioners Regulations'). On 3 May 2005, the Special Commissioners issued (for a trial period) Preliminary Directions that apply in all cases, and Standard Directions that apply only in so far as the parties do not agree other Directions or request a preliminary hearing in accordance with Regulation 9 of the Special Commissioners Regulations 1994. The directions govern such matters as preparation of witness and documentary evidence. The burden of proof is on the taxpayer to disprove, for example, the amendment to the assessment made by HMRC; and the standard of proof is the ordinary civil standard of 'balance of probabilities'. Whilst it is up to the taxpayer to decide what documents they will produce in order to prove their case, the Commissioners have a power to obtain information and documents from the taxpayer. This power to obtain information is that of the Commissioners'; and it is distinct from HMRC's powers to obtain information under TMA 1970 s 20 (which subsists even after an appeal has been lodged by the taxpayer).

The Commissioners not only may discharge or reduce the amount of tax payable, but also they are empowered to increase the tax payable if they consider that the taxpayer has been undercharged (TMA 1970 s 50 (7)).

[4.54]

e) *Costs*

The General Commissioners have no power to award costs. By virtue of TMA 1970 ss 56B–56D, the Special Commissioners do have such power, but can make an award of costs only where a party has acted 'wholly unreasonably' and has so behaved 'in connection with the hearing'. The power to award costs is used very sparingly (see *Taxation*, 18 June 1998, pp 308–310): in *Gamble v Rowe* (1998) the High Court stated that it would be a rare case in which the Commissioners could say that a party had acted 'wholly unreasonably' and emphasised that the wholly unreasonable behaviour must be 'in connection with the hearing in question' and not at some earlier stage.

In *Carter v Hunt* (2000), the Presiding Special Commissioner commented on the costs rules:

> 'In the present situation the protection given to the Revenue [by the "wholly unreasonably" stipulation] … has imposed a real injustice on the taxpayer. The costs rules are in urgent need of overhaul.'

*Carvill v Frost (Inspector of Taxes)* (2005) is a rare example of an award of costs being made against the Revenue; here the Special Commissioners again indicated that they should have a proper costs jurisdiction. It is to be hoped that with the anticipated introduction of a unified tax tribunal system (see [4.58] below) will be brought also a uniform costs regime (however, in the Leggatt Report, which is the fons et origo of the current recommended changes to the tax appeals system, it was recommended expressly that no change to the existing costs system should be made).

Legal assistance is available in certain limited circumstances: when the proceedings concern a tax penalty that may be 'criminal' under the European Convention on Human Rights (see **Chapter 55**) and it is 'in the interests of justice' (see *Han and Yau* (2001) and the Lord Chancellor's Direction of 2 April 2001). [4.55]

f) *Publicity*

Prior to September 1994, proceedings before both bodies were held in private. Since 1994, proceedings of the Special Commissioners have been held in public; and, in December 2002, legislation was introduced to make General Commissioners' hearings open to the public. A hearing before either tribunal can be in private if the particular tribunal is satisfied that this is necessary under a number of specified grounds, which include the protection of the private life of the individual. (See Regulation 15 of the Special Commissioners Regulations and Regulation 13 of the General Commissioners Regulations.)

The decisions of General Commissioners are not published; the decisions of Special Commissioners have been published since 1994. Anonymity can be given if all or part of the hearing was held in private (see the Special Commissioners Regulations reg 20(2) and *Y Co Ltd v IRC* (1996)).   **[4.56]**

g)   *Review of decisions*

Either body of Commissioners (within strict time limits) can review and set aside or vary its decision on an application by either party or of its own motion (see the Special Commissioners Regulations reg 19 and General Commissioners Regulations reg 17). However, such a review can be one of three grounds only: administrative error; the failure (with good reason) of a party to appear or be represented; or the failure of accounts or other information to reach the tribunal before the hearing.   **[4.57]**

h)   **Reform of the General and Special Commissioners**

The Leggatt Inquiry (which examined the Tribunal system in general) was commenced almost simultaneously with the issue of a consultation document entitled *Tax Appeals* by the Lord Chancellor's Department in 2000. In his Report, a unified tax appeals system was proposed. In July 2004, the Government published a White Paper entitled 'Transforming Public Service: Complaints, Redress and Tribunals', its response to the Leggatt Report. The key proposal that is set out in the White Paper is a unified tribunal service organisation. This was intended to come into being in April 2006; it has yet to be implemented.

Under the White Paper, it is proposed that the current jurisdictions of the VAT and Duties Tribunal, the Special and the General Commissioners will be combined. The High Court's role in tax appeals will be eliminated; and, instead, there will be a two-tier tax tribunal system, with a right of appeal from the second tier tribunal to the Court of Appeal. The first tier will be responsible for hearing most direct and indirect tax appeals at first instance; the second-tier tax tribunal will be an appellate tier to which an appeal will lie with permission from the first tier on a point of law (it will also have a first-instance jurisdiction for cases that are of sufficient size and complexity to justify starting at that level). Decisions of the second tier (almost certainly) would be binding on the lower tier. The Department for Constitutional Affairs has established a Tax Appeals Stakeholders' Group, chaired by His Honour Stephen Oliver QC, to consider the proposals.   **[4.58]**

3   **Further appeals**

Either the taxpayer or the Officer may appeal on a point of law from the decision of the Commissioners to the High Court. As the Commissioners are the final arbiters on questions of fact, a decision of the Commissioners on a pure question of fact can not be overturned (unless it is a finding of fact that no person acting judicially and properly instructed as to the relevant law could have come to (see *Edwards v Bairstow* (1955) 36 TC 207). Thus, it is important that the taxpayer takes the opportunity to establish a factual matrix that supports his appeal at the hearing before the Commissioners.

[**4.59**]

a)  *Appealing from the Special Commissioners*

*High Court*

There is a time limit of 56 days after the issue of the Special Commissioners' decision for appealing to the High Court. Permission to appeal is not required; and the notice of appeal is made by way of an Appellant's Notice to the High Court stating the grounds of the appeal.

[**4.60**]

*Court of Appeal*

Although TMA s 56(5) provides that an appeal from the High Court 'shall lie to the Court of Appeal', the scope for appealing from the High Court to the Court of Appeal in appeals that commenced before the Special Commissioners has been curtailed by the Access to Justice Act 1999. The Act introduced a general requirement to obtain permission to appeal to the Court of Appeal and, under s 55 (1) of that Act: 'second appeals' are to be granted only in exceptional circumstances. No appeal may be made unless the Court of Appeal considers that: (a) the appeal would raise an important point of principle or practice; or (b) there is some other compelling reason for the Court of Appeal to hear it. This test applies even if the taxpayer succeeded before the Special Commissioners, but lost on appeal to the High Court. Although the change was introduced to ensure that: 'second appeals would … become a rarity' (see *Tanfern Ltd v Cameron-McDonald* (2000)) it is often not too difficult to demonstrate an 'important point of principle' in tax matters.

[**4.61**]

*House of Lords*

An appeal from the Court of Appeal to the House of Lords requires either permission of the Court of Appeal or leave of the House of Lords. If permission is refused by the Court of Appeal, a petition for leave to appeal may be made to the House of Lords within one month from the refusal to grant permission by the Court of Appeal. Leave to appeal will be given only to cases: 'which raise an arguable point of law of general public importance which ought to be considered by the House at that time'.

   It is possible to 'leapfrog' either the High Court or the Court of Appeal, but, in practice, these options rarely are exercised (see TMA 1970 s 56A(2) and the Administration of Justice Act 1969 Part II). An unsuccessful attempt to leapfrog the Court of Appeal was made by the Inland Revenue in *Deutsche Morgan Grenfell Group plc v Inland Revenue Commissioners* (2003).

[**4.62**]

b)  *Appealing from the General Commissioners*

In order to appeal from the General Commissioners to the High Court, a 'statement of case' for the opinion of the High Court is required (see TMA s 56 and the General Regulations regs 20–22). The 'case stated' process is complex (for a criticism, see [1970] *British Tax Review* 38). In brief, it is as follows. Any party may, within 30 days of the decision, give notice requiring the General Commissioners to sign and state a case for the opinion of the High Court on a point of law. The General Commissioners may give notice to the party requiring him to identify the point of law; and if the party fails to identify the point of law or the General Commissioners are not satisfied that the question identified is a point of law, then the General Commissioners may refuse to state a case. A case stated must set out the facts and the final determination of the tribunal. Within 56 days of the notice of requirement to state a case or the identification of the question of law involved, a draft of the case must be sent to all parties. The parties are allowed 56 days after the draft case has been sent to them to make written representations on the written case. This gives the taxpayer an opportunity to ensure that the facts are accurately set out. A further 28 days is then allowed to enable any party to make further representations in response to the representations of the other party. When the time limit for making representations has expired and after taking those representations into account, the General Commissioners are to state and sign the substantive case. To appeal the party must then submit the case stated to the High Court within 30 days of receiving it. This time limit is a mandatory one; and HMRC and the taxpayer have no power to extend the time limit by mutual agreement (see *Petch v Gurney* (1994) and *Significant Ltd v Farrel* (2005)).

From the High Court stage onwards, the procedure is the same as appeals that originated before the Special Commissioners.                                   **[4.63]**


### 4   Law or fact?

The question whether an issue is one of fact or of law often can be a difficult one to answer. For example, *Beauchamp v FW Woolworth plc* (1989) concerned whether certain transactions were capital or revenue in nature. The Special Commissioners said that: 'we were invited by both parties to treat the issue as one of fact ... and the authorities seem to us to support that approach'; the Court of Appeal said that it was clear from the judgment of the High Court that the High Court also treated the question as being one of fact and that that was the correct approach. However, the House of Lords not only held that the question was one of law, but also observed that it had correctly been treated as such by the High Court.

Whilst some matters, such as, for example, whether a particular letter was sent to HMRC, are clearly facts, and other matters, such as the technical meaning of a word in a statute, are law, the difficulty in discerning the borderline arises primarily because in reaching their decisions the Commissioners rarely can answer questions such as these in isolation. Tax appeals often concern the application of a statutory meaning to a particular set of circumstances; and in most tax appeals, the Commissioners will have to make findings of primary facts and then draw inferences from those findings. These inferences may be findings of (secondary) facts, answer questions of law or be a mixture of the two.                                   **[4.64]**

## 5  Judicial review

Judicial review is the process by which the courts exercise a supervisory jurisdiction over the conduct of public bodies, on the application of person who has a 'sufficient interest' in the matter. It is well-established that the actions of HMRC, as well as the decisions of the General and Special Commissioners potentially may be judicially reviewed. The remedy of judicial review potentially is available in any situation where HMRC exercises one of its powers, including, for example, obtaining information from individuals; it is not limited to the assessment process. However, a judicial review will not be concerned with the merits of a decision taken by these bodies, but, instead, will evaluate whether the process by which that decision was made was lawful.

There are at least three grounds on which the conduct of HMRC or the Commissioners may be subject to judicial review. The traditional grounds of review are categorised as: (i) illegality, ie, where there has been an error of law; (ii) irrationality: an irrational action is one that is so unreasonable that no reasonable tribunal or official, properly directing itself as to the relevant legal principles, could have reached it, having considered the material before it; and (iii) procedural impropriety, which includes a breach of natural justice, such as not allowing a taxpayer to have a fair hearing, as well a failure by a tribunal to observe the statutory rules of procedure that govern it.

A taxpayer will have a sufficient interest to make an application for judicial review with regard to a decision concerning their own tax affairs. However, they will not have sufficient interest to challenge a decision made in respect of another taxpayer, unless they can show that that decision affects them (adversely) (see *R v Inland Revenue Commissioners, ex p National Federation of Self-Employed and Small Businesses* (1982)).

The courts do not allow judicial review to replace the normal statutory appeal process. If, for example, a taxpayer has a remedy by way of appeal against the decision of HMRC to the General or Special Commissioners, then judicial review will not be appropriate. However, if there is no appeal mechanism, then judicial review will be the only remedy available to the taxpayer.  **[4.65]–[4.90]**

## IV  COMPLAINTS AGAINST HMRC

## 1  Introduction

Although safeguards are built into the system, and there are extensive appeal mechanisms, it has to be recognised that there is still the possibility of a taxpayer's life being badly affected by inappropriate HMRC action without his having a legal remedy (see, for example *Rigby v Jayatilaka* (2000)). The following procedures are aimed at providing protection for taxpayers. **[4.91]**

## 2  Taxpayers' Charter and Revenue Adjudicator

In August 1991, the Taxpayer's Charter was launched, setting out the standard of service to be expected of the Inland Revenue and Customs and Excise. Subsequently the Revenue introduced three new codes of practice in support of the Charter (dealing with the conduct of tax investigations, the conduct of inspections of employers' PAYE records and compensation for serious delays or mistakes) and a Code of Practice for the Provision of Information and Advice (see **[4.91]**). The Taxpayer's Charter has now been replaced by a 'mission statement' ('Our Service Commitment To You') setting out what HMRC's customers can expect to receive by way of service. This is underpinned by two charters, one for taxpayers (IR 167) and one for NI contributors.

In addition there exists an independent adjudicator. The adjudicator's function is to examine complaints from taxpayers. They are not responsible for hearing appeals on matters of law; such appeals continue to rest with the Commissioners. The adjudicator is, instead, concerned with the manner in which HMRC conducts a taxpayer's affairs, eg whether there has been excessive delay, any error or any discourtesy. Unless the circumstances are exceptional, normally HMRC will accept the Adjudicator's decision.

It is still possible to bring complaints about tax matters before the Parliamentary Ombudsman by a taxpayer asking their MP to do so.   **[4.92]**

### 3   Compensation for HMRC mistakes

HMRC's *Redress Handbook* identifies three situations that may result in compensation being paid: unreasonable delay in dealing with correspondence; delay in using information; serious or persistent error. Additional factors in the latter case may give rise to a 'consolatory payment' as well: if, for instance, it results in a significant or unwarranted intrusion into a taxpayer's personal life.   **[4.93]**

# 5  Tax avoidance, the future and the disclosure rules

*Written and updated by Natalie Lee, Barrister, Senior Lecturer in Law, University of Southampton*

## I  INTRODUCTION

### 1  The background

The Chancellor of the Exchequer, Gordon Brown, announced in his Budget speech in July 1997 that it was his intention to curb generally 'the leakage' and avoidance of direct taxes. He said:

> 'I have also instructed the Inland Revenue to carry out a wide-ranging review of areas of tax avoidance, with a view to further legislation in future Finance Bills. I have specifically asked them to consider a general anti-avoidance rule.'

Further to this instruction, the Inland Revenue published in 1998 a Consultation Paper on the proposed general anti-avoidance rule (GAAR). The GAAR, initially planned to apply to direct corporate taxes only, was intended to introduce provisions in the legislation that can be used to strike at tax schemes which the Revenue view as being unacceptable. (Customs and Excise have produced their own Consultation Paper on a series of mini-GAARs.) Although this document was based on a report from the Tax Law Reform Committee (set up in 1994 by the Institute for Fiscal Studies to keep under review the state and operation of tax law), that very same committee subsequently announced that it would be unable to support a GAAR of the type proposed in the consultation. Other professional bodies have also criticised the proposed changes, most notably the Tax Faculty of the Institute of Chartered Accountants, which described the proposals as 'worryingly wide-ranging' with the potential to catch legitimate tax planning. In particular, it was doubted whether the proposed system of pre-transaction rulings would be quick or cheap enough to allow for all taxpayers to make use of it.

Possibly because of the negative response to the Consultation Paper, no provisions have yet been included in any Finance Act.

Other jurisdictions, notably Canada, Australia and New Zealand, have introduced general anti-avoidance provisions to combat the ever-increasing amount of tax avoidance, but with only varying degrees of success. The current Australia provision, which focuses on the concept of a tax avoidance 'scheme', replaced the previous legislation which was so widely worded that the courts tended to restrict its operation so that it became a weak weapon in the hands of the revenue authorities. However, its replacement relies heavily on judicial discretion with the result that there is a great deal of uncertainty surrounding the provision. It is highly unlikely that any such measure will ever find favour in the UK, and it must be asked whether it is really needed. As one commentator has queried, is the rapid growth in complex and often obscure legislation, frequently leading to avoidance possibilities, not a greater evil than uncertain general anti-avoidance legislation? As far as Canada is concerned, the recent case of *The Queen v Canada Trustco Mortgage Co* (2005) highlights just how difficult the application of their GAAR seems to be, and would suggest that, in seeking to apply it, the Supreme Court of Canada is facing exactly the same difficulties with respect to the proper approach to the interpretation of tax statutes as the UK courts did when developing the so-called judicial anti-avoidance doctrine (see **Chapter 2**). [5.1]

Be that as it may, the Government more recently would seem to have chosen a different method of tackling avoidance. With respect to both direct and indirect taxation, the approach appears to be a 'strategic' one, namely, to identify areas of the tax system where the potential loss of revenue is high, and target resources and compliance activity accordingly. In *Fairness in Taxation—Protecting Tax Revenues* (Treasury, 9 April 2003), it was announced that additional resources would be deployed in three particular areas. These are (i) protecting the Exchequer from non-payment of tax and NICs debts and from failure to file tax returns; (ii) tackling fraud involving concealment of undeclared income or profits offshore; and (iii) countering avoidance of corporation tax and of NICs and tax on employment income. FA 2004 (as amended) seeks to start to tackle the third of these by the introduction of new disclosure rules in addition to specific measures to combat particular types of schemes (see, for eg measures to prevent the use of losses in avoidance schemes, finance leasebacks, manufactured dividends and gilt strips). Further measures aimed at reducing tax avoidance include an increase in the rate applicable to trusts (see **[16.21]**), an income tax charge where the former owner continues to enjoy the benefits of ownership of an asset (see **[23.141]**) and restricting the IHT benefits arising from accumulation and maintenance trusts (see **[34.91]**). [5.2]


2   **The disclosure rules**

Rules have been introduced that will enable HMRC to identify avoidance schemes sooner than at present, and to discover schemes and arrangements of which they might not otherwise have been aware, to allow the Government to make a swifter and more targeted response to deliberate abuses of the tax system.

'These new disclosure rules, which are part of an overall package of measures intended to reduce the tax lost from tax avoidance, form a central component in the Revenue's increasingly strategic approach to managing the risk to tax revenues from avoidance. They will help to maintain the integrity of the tax system and ensure that everyone pays their fair share of tax and so contributes to the UK's needs.'

(Regulatory Impact Assessment: Tackling Tax Avoidance – Disclosure Requirements, Inland Revenue, April 2004.)

'The Government's objective is to increase transparency in the tax system. The new rules will provide Customs & Excise with information about tax avoidance schemes, and those using them, much earlier than at present to enable swifter and more effective investigation and, where appropriate, counter action.'

(*Tax Avoidance Impact Assessment*, HM Customs & Excise, July 2004.)

The main objective of the Government is said to be obtaining transparency in the tax system, although some of its detractors would argue that it is 'about the Treasury trying to instill a behavioural change to discourage taxpayers from indulging in 'abusive' tax planning as a follow through to the morality campaign.' (*Tax Journal*, 17 May 2004). Once identified, these schemes and arrangements may then be challenged, as at present, through the courts or with new legislation where appropriate; the new rules do not give HMRC additional powers of challenge. **[5.3]**

## II  THE DIRECT TAX RULES

The essence of the rules is that, as from 1 August 2004, a promoter of a scheme has been required to provide details of certain prescribed arrangements to HMRC within a specified time limit; from 1 August 2006, disclosure of schemes within an extended area is required (SI 2006/1543). These details must include a description of the scheme, including information about each element involved, the expected tax consequences and the statutory provisions sought to be relied upon. HMRC will then register the scheme and allocate it a reference number. The promoter will then be required to provide the reference number to any taxpayer client who uses the scheme or arrangement. For his part, the taxpayer will only be required to include the reference number on his tax return unless he has devised the scheme himself or the scheme was provided by a foreign promoter who has not registered with the Revenue, when the taxpayer will himself be required to disclose the details of the scheme together with his tax return. **[5.4]**

### 1  A promoter

In practice, promoters are likely to be accountants, tax advisers, solicitors and barristers if they provide services relating to taxation, including those who are non-UK resident. Regulations (SI 2004/1865 as amended by SI 2004/2613) seek to ensure that, for example, a member of a firm who provides advice, but not tax advice, in respect of an arrangement, is not treated as a promoter. They also provide that in-house planning need only be disclosed with CTSA filing, thereby relieving each company within a group from the burden of disclosure. FA 2004 s 314 expressly preserves legal professional privilege, although it is said that LPP in itself is not a justification for not disclosing a scheme if it meets the criteria for disclosure. This is because the rules are intended to obtain details of the product and not the technical or legal advice given to the client, and a promoter does not need to reveal the identity of that client. However, following the advice given by the Law Society to its members that advice to clients on tax measures is protected by legal professional privilege and does not have to be revealed to HMRC, thereby casting doubt on the effectiveness of the new rules in relation to advice given by lawyers, amended rules require clients to make a disclosure in place of a promoter where the promoter believes the relevant information is covered by LPP. These amendments are designed to ensure that all promoters of schemes, including the legal profession, can comply with their obligations to HMRC without revealing privileged information.        **[5.5]**

## 2   Schemes and arrangements subject to the disclosure rules

Prior to 1 August 2006, a scheme or arrangement, or a proposal for such a scheme or arrangement, had to be disclosed if:
(1)   it fell within one of the specified structures set out in the legislation and regulations (FA 2004 s 306 and SI 2004/1863 as amended by SI 2994/2429). These original regulations restricted the need to disclose to arrangements that involved employment and financial products (including loans, derivatives, repos, stock loans, shares or 'contracts which in substance represent the making of a loan and are so treated for accounting purposes') but, although the implication was that this list served as a restriction to the categories of notifiable transactions, it was actually a fully comprehensive list, particularly bearing in mind that one or more financial products needed only to be *included* in the relevant scheme to attract the requirement of disclosure;
(2)   it gave rise to a tax advantage, defined in FA 2004 so as to include relief from tax, avoidance of tax, the deferral of any payment to tax and the avoidance of any obligation to account for any tax. It was suggested that this definition left open the question of whether any arrangement which produced a more favourable result in tax terms than some less obvious alternative scheme required disclosure; and
(3)   if the obtaining of that tax advantage was the main benefit, or one of the main benefits, that might be expected to arise under the scheme.
The rules contained a number of 'filters' to ensure that the need for reporting routine tax planning was excluded. Routine planning refers to the situation where taxpayers pay for advice in respect of their affairs and for the implementation of that advice, and must be contrasted with 'off the peg' advice where the taxpayer normally pays a 'premium fee' for making the elements of the scheme itself available and where the promoter wishes to keep the scheme hidden from other promoters. Further, in 2004 the Revenue made clear that 'everyday tax advice' would also be excluded from the obligation to disclose, and the type of products that are deemed acceptable include salary sacrifice arrangements for cars, computers, childcare vouchers or pension funds and standard dual contract arrangements.
Under the new regulations (SI 2006/1543, which replace SI 2004/1863 as amended by SI 2994/2429), the requirement for disclosure is extended to

cover arrangements across the whole spectrum of income tax, corporation tax and capital gains tax, with the restriction to financial and employment products being removed. Moreover, disclosure will no longer be limited by 'filters' but will, instead, be required if one of a specified series of 'hallmarks' applies. The first three hallmarks are virtually the same as the filters existing under the pre-1 August 2006 regime (with the confidentiality hallmark being wider than under the former rules); in addition, there have been added three new 'hallmarks'. The result is that arrangements are required to be disclosed where:

(1) any element of the arrangements giving rise to the tax advantage would be expected to be kept confidential from any competitor promoters or to HMRC;

(2) they are likely to command the payment of a fee, the amount of which is contingent on or attributable to a tax saving by a client with experience of purchasing sophisticated tax services;

(3) the promoter of the scheme is also a party to it (such as a bank or a security house), and the product is not offered on similar terms to those that can be obtained in the open market for a product that is the same or broadly similar;

(4) they are mass-marketed tax products, historically associated with unacceptable tax avoidance. Accordingly, a number of exceptions are specified, encompassing arrangements under approved share incentive plans, approved SAYE option schemes or approved CSOP schemes under ITEPA 2003 Schs 2 (see **[45.65]**), 3 (see **[45.62]**) and 4 (see **[45.64]**) respectively, enterprise management incentives under ITEPA 2003 Sch 5, registered pension schemes, overseas pension schemes in respect of which tax relief is granted in the UK under ICTA 1988 s 615, pension schemes which are relevant non-UK pension schemes, periodical payments of personal injury damages, enterprise investment schemes, venture capital trusts and the corporate venturing scheme (see **Chapter 15**), arrangements consisting solely of one or more plant or machinery leases, arrangements qualifying for community investment tax relief, and accounts which satisfy the Individual Savings Account Regulations;

(5) loss-making schemes of the type commonly used by high-wealth individuals to reduce their income tax or capital gains tax liability; and

(6) leasing arrangements, which concern the lease of high-value plant and machinery and which contain features commonly associated with avoidance. This 'hallmark' will apply where an arrangement includes a plant or machinery lease and:

(a) one of the parties to the arrangement has, or would have, a right or entitlement to claim capital allowances in respect of the expenditure incurred on the plant or machinery, and another party is not, or will not be, within the charge to corporation tax;

(b) either the lower of the cost to the lessor or the market value of any one asset forming part of the plant and machinery leased is at least £10m, or the aggregate of the lower of the costs to the lessor, or the market values, of all the assets forming part of the plant and machinery leased is at least £25m; and

(c)  the lease is not a short-term lease. For the purpose of these rules, a lease for two years or less is a short-term lease unless it is structured in such a way that the term *may* exceed two years. A leasing arrangement will not be notifiable where there is no promoter in relation to it and the tax advantage which may be obtained therefrom is intended to be obtained by an individual or a business which is a small or medium-sized enterprise.    **[5.6]**

## 3  The information that needs to be disclosed

The details (set out in SI 2004/1864 as amended by SI 2004/2613, SI 2005/1869 and SI 2006/1544) that must be given to HMRC in writing are: (i) the name and address of the promoter and, if different, the person giving the notification (in those cases where the *user* is required to make the disclosure); (ii) details of the provision of the disclosure rules under which the scheme is notifiable; (iii) a summary of the scheme and, if it has one, its name or title; (iv) information regarding each step of the arrangement. The regulations do not make it clear whether this is restricted to 'tax-steps' or would include other steps taken for other legal reasons; and (v) the relevant statutory provision relied upon.    **[5.7]**

## 4  Form of disclosure

Disclosures, which will be handled by the Anti- Avoidance Intelligence Group (Intelligence) (AIG) of the Revenue, must be made on the specified form (obtainable from HMRC's website or from the AIG).    **[5.8]**

## 5  Time of disclosure

FA 2004 s 308 together with SI 2004/1864 as amended requires that a promoter must, on or after 1 August 2004, disclose a notifiable scheme or arrangement to HMRC within five days of the earlier of making the proposal available for implementation, or the date on which the promoter first became aware of any transaction forming part of the proposed arrangements. Difficulties may well arise with this provision. What if, say, a barrister is asked to advise on an arrangement structured by an accountant. To the extent that he merely agrees with the arrangement without having to make any changes, he has not initiated the proposal. Does this mean that he can never be said to have made it available for implementation, so that he will only be required to make a disclosure when he becomes aware that a transaction under the arrangement has been implemented, or is he making the proposal available for implementation by simply advising his client that he sees no reason for not going ahead with the arrangement? This lack of clarity raises an important issue, particularly bearing in mind the penalty provisions in FA 2004 s 315.    **[5.9]**

## III  *Stamp duty land tax*

From 1 August 2005, tax schemes seeking a stamp duty land tax advantage are required to be disclosed when they concern property that is not residential property and which has a market value of at least £5m. In distinction to schemes concerning income tax, corporation tax and capital gains tax, HMRC will not issue a reference number, and promoters of SDLT arrangements will not have an obligation to convey a reference number to a client. As a consequence, users will not generally be under an obligation to provide the Revenue with information unless either the promoter is offshore, or the user has devised the scheme in-house, or the promoter is a lawyer bound by legal privilege (although the client may waive the right to privilege and permit the lawyer to make the disclosure). [5.10]

## IV   *The indirect tax rules*

The general thrust of this set of rules is to require all businesses with an annual turnover of more than £600,000 to notify Customs when they use one of eight designated schemes, and all businesses with an annual turnover of more than £10 million to notify HMRC when they carry out a scheme that includes, or is associated with, a provision that has been designated as being tainted with tax avoidance. Both sets of rules refer to schemes entered into to obtain a 'tax advantage', the term 'scheme' being defined so as to include a single supply, whilst 'obtaining a tax advantage' is defined in such a way that any transaction that does not maximise the tax payable is potentially caught (FA 2004 Sch 2). [5.11]

## 1   **Designated transactions (listed schemes)**

Businesses with an annual turnover of more than £600,000 are required to notify Customs when they use one of the eight designated schemes set out in SI 2004/1933. These schemes, all of which are considered by Customs to be 'abusive', include: (i) first grant of a major interest in a building; (ii) credit card or cash handling services; (iii) value shifting (ie, where a retailer supplies a package of goods or services for a single price where part is standard-rated and part zero-rated or exempt); (iv) leaseback agreements (ie, the sale and leaseback of goods by a business making both taxable and exempt supplies); (v) extended approval period (ie, where a retailer supplies goods on approval or sale or return, receives payment, but defers the tax point until the end of the approval period); (vi) groups; third party suppliers (ie, the anti out-sourcing provision); (vii) exempt education or vocational training by a non-profit making body; and (viii) taxable education or vocational training by a non-eligible body. By virtue of the VATA 1994 Sch 11A para 3(1), the Treasury have the power to add to the list of designated schemes further schemes that they believe to be abusive, including those that which they believe as a matter of law could not be tax advantageous! It has recently been proposed that two further schemes will be added to the above list. These are ones that:

(1)   exploit differences between the UK and another Member State's treatment of vouchers; and

(2)   attempt to remove the effect of an election to waive exemption on supplies of land and property.

It is questionable whether some of these schemes can truly be described as being 'abusive'. For example, a value shifting scheme could quite easily cover a normal commercial promotion where a free book (zero-rated) is given away with the sale of a DVD (standard-rated). Because the retailer is charging less overall than had the goods been sold separately, he will account to HMRC for less VAT and will accordingly fall within the 'tax advantage' test, and will be required to notify HMRC. It is interesting to note that for income tax purposes, such a disposal of stock on justifiable commercial grounds will not attract the rigour of the rule in *Sharkey v Wernher* (see **[6.115]**).

Businesses in this category will not have to worry too much about whether or not a tax advantage has been obtained for reporting purposes, since the designated schemes are deemed to produce such an advantage. However, on a failure to report, that advantage will become material, since the 15% penalty is calculated by reference to the VAT saved. For a discussion of the definition of 'tax advantage', see **[42.61]**.                                              **[5.12]**

## 2   Generally notifiable transactions (hallmarked schemes)

In addition to reporting the eight listed schemes, businesses with an annual turnover exceeding £10 million are also required to report *any* transaction in any VAT accounting period that has as it main purpose, or one of its main purposes, the gaining of a tax advantage (see **[42.61]**) **and** that is tainted with avoidance because either:
(1)   it is a confidentiality condition in an agreement; or
(2)   it entails the sharing of the tax advantage with another party to the scheme or with the promoter; or
(3)   it concerns a contingent fee arrangement; or
(4)   there is a prepayment between connected parties; or
(5)   it concerns funding by loan or share subscriptions; or
(6)   it is an off-shore loop; or finally;
(7)   it concerns construction work connected with a property transaction between connected persons (SI 2004/1933).The concern, once again, is that normal commercial transactions are likely to be caught within one of these categories, making notification appear to be a universal requirement. Further, the inclusion of the words 'main purpose, or one of its main purposes' (not defined by HMRC on the basis that they believe that it is a matter for the business using the tax scheme to decide whether gaining a tax advantage is a main purpose) is likely to result in large numbers of transactions undertaken by businesses requiring notification on the basis that, given different ways of structuring a particular business objective, the one involving the least amount of tax will clearly be chosen. Failure to make the required notification for a general transaction will result in a fixed penalty of £5,000.        **[5.13]**

## 3   The tax advantage

A tax advantage is obtained by a person who is, or is liable to be, registered for VAT in any VAT accounting period where:
(1)   the VAT payable (output tax less input tax) is less than it would otherwise have been;
(2)   the VAT repayable (input tax less output tax) is more than it would otherwise have been;

(3)  where the business is the customer, the period of time between which he accounts for the input tax and the supplier accounts for the output tax is greater than would otherwise have been the case (FA 2004 Sch 2). There would appear to be a significant lack of clarity in this 'definition', since there is no indication as to what is meant by 'otherwise' in this context; or

(4)  the amount of non-deductible tax (that is, input tax for which the taxable person is not entitled to credit and the VAT incurred on goods and services which is not input tax and for which the taxable person is not entitled to a refund) is less than it would otherwise have been.

A person who is not liable to be registered for VAT will also obtain a tax advantage if his non-refundable tax is less than it would otherwise be. The term 'non-refundable tax' means the VAT on: (1) goods and services supplied to him; (2) goods acquired by him from other Member States; and (3) goods imported by him from outside the Member States. It excludes any VAT that he is entitled to be refunded under a provision in the VATA 1994.

**[5.14]**

### 4  Notification

Businesses must report the details of the offending scheme or provision to HMRC within 30 days of the due date for filing the VAT return or, where there is a claim for repayment of output tax or an increased input tax claim, within 30 days of making the claim. For a generally notifiable transaction (see **[42.60]**), the details must include:

(1)  the particular provision that taints the scheme with tax avoidance;

(2)  how the scheme gave rise to a tax advantage, which will require a description of each arrangement, transaction or series of transactions, their sequence, their timing or the intervals between them and the goods and services involved;

(3)  the parties involved; and

(4)  the statutory provision relied upon that gives rise to the tax advantage (SI 2004/1029).

Surprisingly, perhaps, although SI 2004/1929 makes provision for HMRC to publish details of the required form and manner in which notification of designated schemes has to be made, no such details are included in those regulations.

**[5.15]**

### V  Assessment of the rules

Much criticism has already been levelled at the disclosure rules. The over-whelming view of practitioners is that they place too great a burden on tax advisers to provide vast amounts of information in respect of transactions which, it must be remembered, are in accordance with the law, and which could in any event be discerned by HMRC from tax returns. Moreover, there is real concern that the rules amount to broadly-based transaction reporting rules that go beyond their US counterparts, and could be counter-productive in so far as the more widely the disclosure legislation is drawn, the less easy it will become to identify the real abuses that most of the profession had been led to believe were the motivating force behind the introduction of the new rules. More specifically, and of vital importance is the fact that both the primary legislation and the regulations leave much room for doubt about certain definitions. On a final note, it has been argued by one commentator that an argument could be maintained that the rules are inconsistent with Art 8 of the European Convention on Human Rights (this article secures the right to respect for private and family life; see **[55.61]**), particularly now that they have been extended (see *The Tax Journal*, 13 March 2006).          **[5.16]**

# Section 2    Income tax

**Chapters**

# 6    General principles

*Updated by Peter Vaines, Squire, Sanders & Dempsey*

'No one has ever been able to define income in terms sufficiently concrete to be of value for taxation purposes ... where it has to be ascertained whether a gain is to be classified as an income gain or a capital gain, the determination of that question must depend in large measure upon the particular facts of the particular case.'

(Abbott J in *Oxford Motors Ltd v Minister of National Revenue* (1959) 18 DLR (2d) 712.)

'In principle, there is little economic difference between income and capital gains, and many people effectively have the option of choosing to a significant extent which to receive. And, insofar as there is a difference, it is by no means clear why one should be taxed more heavily than the other. Taxing them at different rates distorts investment decisions and inevitably creates a major tax avoidance industry.'

(Nigel Lawson, Budget Speech, 15 March 1988.)
[**6.1**]

## I  HISTORY

Income tax is sometimes referred to as the 'tax which beat Napoleon'. Such claims amount to a gross exaggeration although it is true that the tax was first introduced in 1799 by Pitt the Younger as a wartime measure. Pitt's tax was not wholly innovatory; there had always been a tradition of direct taxation even if it had been applied spasmodically. The origins of income tax may be seen in the land tax and in the Triple Assessment of 1798.

Early yields were disappointing; estimates predicted a yield of £10m in the first year, but under £6m was actually raised. Although the tax was repealed when peace with France was concluded in 1802, it was reintroduced by Addington when hostilities recommenced in the following year. Addington included two basic changes which have survived more or less intact: *first*, a requirement that returns should be of income from particular sources and not just a lump sum; and *secondly*, provisions for deduction of tax at source.

The final cessation of hostilities in 1816 led to the repeal of the tax with the resulting financial deficit being made good by increased yields from Customs and Excise. Income tax was brought back, this time for good, by Peel in 1842. It was not revived because of its own inherent merits, but as a way to simplify and reduce the tariff, as a first step towards the repeal of the Corn Laws in 1846.

By the end of the century, the tax, although an accepted part of the fiscal landscape, raised less than either customs or excise. The twentieth century with the extraordinary demands of war and welfare transformed the picture. By the end of the 1914–18 War, the income tax yield was some £585m as compared with the pre-war figure of £34m and the complexity of the modern tax had been established with earned income relief, supertax, a range of personal allowances, and a primitive system of capital allowances. The process was accelerated by the 1939–45 War with the yield rising from £371m in 1938 to £1,426m in 1945. PAYE was introduced in 1944 and the tax avoidance industry maintained a steady growth.

Today, the flood of income tax legislation shows little sign of diminishing; the statutory material was consolidated in 1952, in 1970, and again in 1988 (TA 1988). A further consolidation is needed although this may be overtaken by the complete redraft of the legislation on a piecemeal basis—see, for example, the Capital Allowances Act (CAA) 2001, the Income Tax (Earnings and Pensions) Act (ITEPA) 2003 and the Income Tax (Trading and Other Income) Act (ITTOIA) 2005.                                                    **[6.2]–[6.20]**

## II   STATUTORY BASIS OF THE TAX

### 1   The statutes and case law

The authority for imposing taxation is Act of Parliament and, in the case of income tax, the statutory basis is TA 1988 as amended by later Finance Acts. TMA 1970 deals with the administration of the tax. The legislation on capital allowances (see **Chapter 48**) is now found in the redrafted Capital Allowances Act 2001 and that on employment income and pensions in ITEPA 2003 with trading and other income being contained in ITTOIA 2005 (see **Chapters 8 and 50**).

The meaning of the statute is primarily a question for the judiciary that ranges from Commissioners to the House of Lords. Many concepts are not defined by statute (eg what is a trade? what is an income receipt/expense?), many provisions are obscure, and it is the role of the judiciary to resolve such difficulties. It is questionable whether it should be the job of the courts to create law to deal with sophisticated avoidance schemes but it is a task, which over the last decade or so, they have undertaken with varying degrees of enthusiasm (see, *MacNiven v Westmoreland Investments Ltd* (2001), the Hong Kong case of *Collector of Stamp Revenue v Arrowtown Assets Ltd* (2004) and the more recent cases of *Barclays Mercantile Business Finance Ltd v Mawson* (2005) and *IRC v Scottish Provident Institution* (2005)).                                    **[6.21]**

### 2   Years and rates

The income tax year runs from 6 April to the following 5 April and is termed the 'year of assessment' or simply the 'tax year'. It is referred to by reference to both the calendar years that it straddles—hence, the year of assessment beginning on 6 April 2006 is referred to as the tax year 2006–07. The curious starting date for the year (6 April) is explicable, as is so much of income tax, on historical grounds. The tax year originally ended on Lady Day 25th March but on the change from the Julian to the Gregorian calendar in 1752 11 days were lost and the tax year was extended by 11 days taking it to 5 April.

Income tax needs annual renewal by Parliament. The annual Finance Act receives Royal Assent in late July. By virtue of the Provisional Collection of Taxes Act 1968, however, the Budget resolutions (such as the rates of tax) are given limited statutory force until the Finance Act is enacted.   **[6.22]–[6.40]**

## III   ABOLITION OF SCHEDULAR SYSTEM FOR INCOME TAX

### 1   **The source doctrine**

Before 6 April 2005 the schedular system applied to income tax and charged income and profits as set out below—a system which continues to apply for the purposes of corporation tax.

**The Schedules**

| Schedule | Source | Basis of assessment |
|---|---|---|
| A | Profits from a business of letting land in UK | Income of the current year of assessment |
| D | | |
| Case I | Profits of a trade in UK | |
| Case II | Profits of a profession or vocation in UK | The income of the accounting period ending in the tax year or income of the current year of assessment |
| Case III | Interest, annuities and other annual payments | |
| Case IV | Securities out of the UK | |
| Case V | Possessions out of the UK (but excluding foreign employment) | |
| Case VI | Annual profits or gains not falling under Cases I–V and not charged by virtue of any other Schedule; and certain income directed to be so charged | Income of the current year of assessment |
| F | Dividends and certain other distributions by companies | Income of the current year of assessment |
| ITEPA 2003 | Offices, employments, pensions and chargeable benefits under the social security legislation | Income of the current year of assessment |

The abolition of the schedules means that the various types of income are charged as follows.

| Income category | Income charged | Basis of assessment | Legislation |
|---|---|---|---|
| **Employment** | Employment, pension and social security income | Current year | ITEPA 2003 |
| **Trading** | Profits of a trade, profession or vocation | Current year | ITTOIA 2005 Part 2 |
| **Property** | Rents and income from land | Current year | ITTOIA 2005 Part 3 |
| **Savings and investment income** | Interest, dividends, distributions, securities, deposits, purchased life annuities, life insurance gains, futures and options | Current year | ITTOIA 2005 Part 4 |
| **Miscellaneous** | Intellectual property, non-trade film recordings, telecommunication rights, settlements, income from estates in administration, annual payments and income not otherwise charged | Current year | ITTOIA 2005 Part 5 |
| **Exempt income** | National savings, individual investment plans, FOTRA securities, life annuities, annual payments and other income | N/A | ITTOIA 2005 Part 6 |

Schedules A, D, and F were abolished on 6 April 2005, Schedule B which imposed a charge on commercial woodlands was abolished as from 6 April 1988 and Schedule C, which taxed income from public revenue dividends, from 6 April 1996 (ITEPA 2003 replaced Schedule E.)

The Taxes Act 1988, ITTOIA 2005 and ITEPA 2003 have their own rules for determining the amount of income and the allowable deductions (if any). Property income, for example, is charged to tax by reference to the rents and other receipts which arise as a result of the ownership of land (or of an interest therein) but the landlord may deduct expenses such as repairs to the property.

Income tax is levied according to the source of the income along with the tax levied under ITEPA 2003 which exhaustively lists the various sources. In arriving at the income of a taxpayer it is necessary to identify all his sources of income and, by applying the rules of the relevant provisions, to calculate the income arising under each one. In general *tax is charged only so long as a taxpayer possesses the source of the income.* Tax avoidance opportunities which arise from this general principle are often prevented by legislation. For instance, although the sale of trading stock after the permanent cessation of the relevant trade would not on general principles fall within trading income (because the source—the trade—had ceased when the sale occurred), there is express provision to bring into the tax net the value of stock unsold at the date of the discontinuance. Similar opportunities in connection with earnings (see *Example 6.1* below) and on income arising under TA 1988 Part XV are curtailed by specific rules. Judicious use of the source doctrine can provide an advantage for non-UK domiciliaries taxed on the remittance basis (see **Chapter 18**), but this does not apply to earnings by reason of ITEPA 1003 s17 which applies to charge emoluments received after an employment has ceased, nor to income within the settlements legislation by reason of ITTOIA 2005 s 648(5) which is treated as arising in the year it is remitted.

[6.41]

**EXAMPLE 6.1**

B, having been employed by G Ltd for 20 years, is transferred together with all the other employees to the employment of G Ltd's parent company in the tax year 2006–07. The trustees of a fund for the benefit of employees of G Ltd, including, B accordingly brought that trust to an end and made distributions to B in the following tax year (ie in 2005–06). That distribution will be an emolument (see **Chapter 8**), and although there was no source of income in the year of receipt, ITEPA 2003 s 17 applies the charge to income tax on earnings, even though the employee did not hold the employment in the year of assessment..

## 2 The mutually exclusive rule

The sources of income are mutually exclusive with the result that HMRC cannot assess income to tax under any provision other than the one to which that income is properly attributable (*Fry v Salisbury House Estate Ltd* (1930)). The same principle applies to the taxpayer who may not deduct expenses attributable to a different source nor opt to have his income taxed under a different provision (*Mitchell and Edon v Ross* (1962)). [6.42]

**EXAMPLE 6.2**

(1) Roger lets several properties to university students and works full time in the management of the properties. Tax must be charged as property income (which applies to rent and other receipts from land), not as trading income, because there cannot be a trade of letting properties (see *Griffiths v Jackson* (1983) **[12.23]**).

(2) A firm of solicitors acted as secretary for a number of companies. The profits from the profession of solicitors are assessed as trading income; remuneration from the office of company secretary is, however, charged under ITEPA 2003 (*IRC v Brander and Cruickshank* (1971) see **[8.21]** and ESC A37 for the tax treatment of directors' fees received in such cases).

## 3 What is income?

Income is not defined in the legislation. Furthermore, any definition is a matter for acute debate by both economists and philosophers. How, therefore, can income tax operate if the subject matter of the tax is not defined? The answer is that income for this purpose means all the sums calculated under the Taxes Act 1988, ITTOIA 2005 and ITEPA 2003. Hence, a sum of money falling under these provisions is subject to tax (and is, therefore, 'income'), whilst a sum which escapes them is untaxed (and may, therefore, be termed 'capital'). Critics of income tax (notably the Meade Committee in its report in 1979 on the Structure and Reform of Direct Taxation) argue that it is the distinction between capital and income that has been used to greater effect than many other devices to avoid tax.

Because of the tax avoidance possibilities 'income' is widened in certain cases so that capital sums such as premiums are treated as property income and golden handshakes and restrictive covenant payments under ITEPA 2003 are deemed to be income for the purposes of the tax. This sometimes results in a divergence between the income tax rules and ordinary principles of trust law that identify what sums are income. Take, for instance, ITTOIA 2005 s 568 that imposes an additional charge on income received by discretionary or accumulation trusts. Because the section is limited to 'income arising to the trustees' this is limited to income 'in a trust sense' and hence it does not catch profits which are of a capital nature (eg lease premiums) albeit that those profits are deemed to be income for basic rate purposes in the hands of the trustees (see **Chapter 16**).

Some income is deemed to be exempt such as National Savings ordinary account interest, individual investment plans and FOTRA securities under ITTOIA 2005 Part 6. Although the lack of a definition of income does not generally cause problems, difficulties do arise when the legislation prescribes that only income receipts are subject to tax or only income expenses can be deducted (as for property income and trading and professional income where the tax is levied on the profits that remain after income deductions have been taken from income receipts). The meaning of 'income' has accordingly been debated frequently before the courts and the various tests that have been suggested for resolving the problem are considered in **Chapter 10**.                                              **[6.43]**

# 7 Computation charges, allowances and rates

*Updated by Sarah Deeks LLB FCA*

## I INTRODUCTION: STAGES OF THE INCOME TAX CALCULATION

Income tax is generally levied at three rates; a starting rate of 10%, a basic rate of 22% and a single higher rate of 40%. The issue is complicated by the fact that the 10% credit attaching to dividend income received after 5 April 1999 has resulted in a 'dividend ordinary rate' of 10% and a 'dividend upper rate' of 32.5% (TA 1988 s 1B(2)). The legislation prescribes which source of income is liable at the highest rate. Investment income, and in particular dividend income, is taxable as the top slice. Similarly the tax deducted at 20% (the 'lower rate') on certain investment income (eg interest) is also available to frank any basic rate liability. It may be collected either by direct assessment, or by deduction at source. The following steps are involved in calculating the taxpayer's income and in working out his tax bill for the year:

Step 1    Calculate the individual's 'statutory income', ie the income which is taxable under the rules of the various provisions of the TA 1988 and ITTOIA 2005.

Step 2    Calculate the taxpayer's charges on income, ie tax deductible payments which the taxpayer is bound to make, such as certain interest payments.

Step 3    Deduct charges on income from statutory income to obtain 'total income' (TA 1988 s 835).

Step 4    Deduct personal reliefs from total income to obtain 'taxable income' and extend the basic rate band for reliefs such as personal pension contributions. See Step 6 for other personal allowances.

Step 5    Calculate income tax at starting, basic and higher rate (or the special rate of 32.5% on dividend income) on the taxable income.

Step 6    Deduct any relief attributable to investments in the enterprise investment scheme and venture capital trusts (as to which see **Chapter 15**) and then allowances and reliefs which attract relief at 10%.

Step 7    From the total tax calculated in Step 5 deduct any income tax which has been collected at source. Dividend income from UK resident companies carries a tax credit which is not refundable. The credit is at 10% for higher rate taxpayers and is otherwise available to frank an income tax liability at the basic rate (this is achieved by having a 'dividend ordinary rate').

Step 8    Calculate basic rate tax on any charges on income from which the individual has deducted tax when making the payment.

The result of *Step 7* plus *Step 8* is the final amount of tax payable. All these steps involve terms requiring explanation, and the various stages in the income tax calculation will now be considered in detail. The link between income tax and capital gains tax gets stronger—relief for donations to charities under Gift Aid is, since 6 April 2000, available if the 'basic rate tax deducted' is covered by a capital gains tax liability.          **[7.1]–[7.20]**

## II  STATUTORY INCOME (*STEP 1*)

### 1  General

Statutory income consists of the taxpayer's income from all sources calculated according to the provisions under which it arises and after deducting expenses appropriate to the particular source of income. Since the income tax year runs from 6 April to 5 April following, the basis of the income tax assessment should logically be the statutory income of an individual for that period.          **[7.21]**

### 2  Income received after deduction of tax

a)  *General*

Some income is received and enters the statutory income calculation gross: ie without having suffered any tax. The tax on that income is collected by self-assessment when the tax return is submitted. For certain types of income, however, tax is deducted at source. In such cases, the payer of the income is obliged to act as a tax collector by deducting from the payment an amount of tax and paying it to HMRC. If the recipient is not liable to income tax (or is only liable at a lower rate than the tax deducted), he will be able to obtain a tax repayment from HMRC. If, however, he is liable to higher rate tax, a further tax payment will be necessary. These payments are usually made (and repayments given) through the self-assessment system. For UK dividend income, a tax credit is available (although it is not refundable) which satisfies the taxpayer's starting or basic rate liability.

Any sum received after deduction of tax (or with a tax credit, in the case of UK dividend income) is normally grossed up to discover the amount of income from which the tax was deducted (or deemed deducted). The resulting (gross) figure must be entered in the recipient taxpayer's calculation of statutory income to find his tax liability. The tax that has already been paid on this income is credited against his tax bill.                    **[7.22]**

b)   *Savings income*

Dividends and other company distributions are paid with a tax credit of 10% and are treated as forming the top slice of the individual's income. The credit is treated as satisfying the taxpayer's starting and basic rate liability so that no further tax is charged unless the taxpayer suffers tax at the higher rate (see TA 1988 s 1B and ITTOIA 2005 s 397). This treatment also applies to interest and other savings income which is paid with a tax deduction at the lower rate of 20%. The tax deducted satisfies the taxpayer's starting and basic rate liability so that no further tax is charged unless the taxpayer suffers tax at the higher rate (see TA 1988 s 1A). Basic rate tax must still be deducted in the case of annual payments and annuities, rents paid to foreign landlords and patent royalties.                    **[7.23]**

**EXAMPLE 7.1**

Austin (with other statutory income of £10,000) receives debenture interest of £800 from which lower rate (20%) tax has been deducted and paid to HMRC by the paying company. Austin must include the 'grossed-up' amount of the interest in his statutory income calculation for the year to work out whether the tax deducted is correct.

To gross up multiply the net interest received by

$$\frac{100}{100-R}$$

where R is the rate at which tax was deducted (which in this case is 20%) ie:

$$800 \times \frac{100}{100-20} = 800 \times \frac{100}{80}$$

= £1,000 (gross interest—therefore tax paid is £200)
Austin's statutory income is:

| | |
|---|---:|
| Other sources | £10,000 |
| Interest | £1,000 |
| Statutory income | £11,000 |

When the tax due on this income is calculated, Austin can deduct the £200 tax deducted at source by the company. If his liability to tax is for less than £200, he can reclaim from HMRC the amount for which he is not liable.

c)   *Illustrations*

The main examples of income received after deduction of tax at source are:
(1)   trust income received by a beneficiary after deduction of tax;

(2)   earnings from which tax is deducted under the PAYE system;
(3)   annuities and certain other annual payments from which basic rate tax is deducted;
(4)   income arising from deposit accounts, received after deduction of tax at 20% (see **[7.26]**).                                                                    **[7.24]**

d)   *Irrecoverable tax credits*

Certain forms of income are treated as though they have already suffered income tax when received but that tax is irrecoverable. The main examples are:
(1)   UK dividend income: tax at 10% is treated as having been paid but no further liability arises if the individual is liable at the basic rate. The higher rate of tax on such income is 32.5%.
(2)   Stock dividends: TA 1988 s 249. Tax of 10% treated as paid.
(3)   Loans to participators which are waived: TA 1988 s 421. Tax of 10% treated as paid.

An individual receiving a stock dividend of £90 is therefore treated as if tax of £10 had been paid on income of £100. If he does not pay income tax there is no refund of this sum: if he is a basic rate taxpayer the tax credit satisfies his basic rate tax liability in full: if he is a higher rate taxpayer further tax of £22.50 will be payable (being a liability of £32.50 on the income of £100 less the £10 credit) leaving the individual with £67.50.                                **[7.25]**

## 3   Interest paid by building societies and banks

a)   *Background*

Interest paid to individuals by building societies, banks and other deposit-takers is paid net of lower (20%) rate income tax with non-taxpayers being entitled to recovery of this tax on submitting the appropriate claim (TA 1988 s 480A). To avoid a multiplicity of such claims, there are arrangements whereby non-taxpayers are able to complete a certificate to that effect and to receive interest gross.                                                                              **[7.26]**

b)   *Deposit-takers and 'relevant deposits'*

Deduction of tax at source must be applied in respect of 'relevant deposits' by any deposit-taker who falls within the statutory list (TA 1988 s 481). The list includes any recognised bank, local authorities and specified credit and finance companies but excludes the National Savings Bank. 'Relevant deposits' are widely defined to include deposits which are held by any person for the benefit of UK resident individuals or deposits where the person entitled to the interest receives it in the capacity of personal representative (TA 1988 s 481(4)). Whether the deposit is maintained for private or business purposes is irrelevant; it may, therefore, be held for a partnership of individuals. From 6 April 2005 an alternative finance arrangement is treated as a deposit (FA 2005 ss 46, 55, 56 and Sch 2).                                                          **[7.27]**

c)   *Exclusions*

Excluded from the definition of relevant deposits are those held for companies, associations and charities. There are specific exclusions for 'qualifying time deposits' with a nominal value never falling below £50,000 and, more significantly, when the interest is payable to a person ordinarily resident outside the UK (so long as that person completes a declaration of non-residence: TA 1988 s 480B and s 481). A deposit denominated in a foreign currency can constitute a relevant deposit. **[7.28]**

## 4 Taxation of couples

Irrespective of a person's marital status (single, cohabiting, married or in a civil partnership) all taxpayers are taxed as separate individuals. Prior to 1990 the income of a married woman living with her husband was generally taxed as his income subject to an election for separate assessment and for separate taxation of the wife's earnings. **[7.29]**

## 5 Earned and investment income

With the abolition (in 1984) of the surcharge on investment income, the distinction between earned and investment income is relevant only in relatively few situations (most importantly in calculating 'pensionable earnings').

Under TA 1988 s 833 'earned income' falls into two main categories:
(1) Any income charged to tax under ITEPA 2003 (employment, pension and social security income).
(2) 'Any income which is charged under ITTOIA 2005 Part 2 (trading income) and is *immediately derived* by the individual from the carrying on or exercise by him of his trade, profession or vocation, either as an individual or, in the case of a partnership, as a partner personally acting in the partnership.'

The borderline between earned and unearned income is not always easy to draw. The phrase 'immediately derived' has been strictly construed by the courts (see, for instance, *Northend v White, Leonard and Corbin Greener* (1975) and *Bucks v Bowers* (1970) and, more recently, *Koenigsberger v Mellor* (1993) where the court held that the income must be earned by 'personal exertions'). Generally, income from a trade, profession or vocation is earned income, whereas property income interest and trust income, foreign securities, such as dividends and dividends from UK companies is investment income. Rent from 'furnished holiday lettings' is specifically treated as earned income (see **[12.61]**). **[7.30]–[7.40]**

## III CHARGES ON INCOME (*STEP 2*)

## 1 General

Charges on income are amounts that fall to be deducted in computing total income. Thus, they are deductible from the individual's statutory income and technically may be deducted from investment income first. The 'amounts which fall to be deducted' are not defined, but consist of certain transfers of income which the taxpayer is obliged to make. The theory is that such income ceases to be that of the payer and becomes the income of the payee so that the payer should not be taxed on it. Charges are deducted before personal reliefs.

Charges on income comprise certain annual payments made for *bona fide* commercial reasons, gifts of certain securities, Gift Aid payments to charity and certain interest payments.                                                  **[7.41]**

## 2   Annual payments

The meaning of an annual payment is discussed in **Chapter 14**.

Although annual payments constitute a charge on the payer's income, the payer is used as an agent to collect basic rate tax on the amount paid (see TA 1988 ss 3, 348, 349). He is allowed to deduct and retain from the payment a sum equal to tax at basic rate on that payment which is the mechanism by which he obtains basis rate relief. Relief at the higher rate may be claimed in the self-assessment. A Gift Aid payment is treated as a charge for these purposes: see FA 1990 s 25(6).                                              **[7.42]**

### EXAMPLE 7.2

Viola has statutory income of £40,300. She makes a Gift Aid payment to the NSPCC (a registered charity) of £780 pa (an annual payment). Under TA 1988 s 348 Viola is deemed to have deducted from a gross payment of £1,000 a sum equivalent to basic rate tax on that figure (ie £220). She, therefore, pays £780 and retains £220.

The income on which she is subject to tax (before deducting personal reliefs) is:

|  | £ |
|---|---|
| Statutory income | 40,300 |
| *Less:* charge on income (gross) | 1,000 |
| Total income | £39,300 |

From this Viola may deduct her personal allowance and she will be taxed on the balance. Higher rate tax relief is obtained by extending her basic rate band by the gross amount.

The charity receives the sum of £780 after deduction of basic rate income tax at source with a tax credit for the £220 payable by Viola. As charities are not generally subject to income tax, the NSPCC can reclaim this £220 from HMRC.

## 3   Certain interest payments

An individual obtains income tax relief for certain interest payments by deducting them from his statutory income as a charge except in the case of interest paid on a loan to purchase a life annuity prior to 9 March 1999 when relief is given as an income tax deduction. Some interest payments are deductible in computing income from a particular source only (eg interest payments made for the purposes of a trade are deductible in computing the profits of that trade and interest payments paid in connection with the letting of property are deductible in computing property income). Most interest payments, however, receive no tax relief including interest paid on loans to purchase a main residence. Ordinary bank overdraft, credit card interest, and hire-purchase interest payments, for example, also receive no relief (except, if appropriate, as a trading expense).

The rules governing the deductibility of interest are complex (see TA 1988 ss 353–366 as amended by FA 1994 and FA 1995). To be deductible the interest must be payable on a loan made for one of the qualifying purposes dealt with below. The character of the interest or the status of the lender is irrelevant. As a general rule, interest that is eligible for tax relief is paid gross.

**[7.43]**

a) *Loans to acquire an interest in a close company (TA 1988 ss 360, 361, 363)*

An individual may obtain income tax relief for the interest paid on a loan to acquire ordinary share capital in close trading companies (it has to be shown that the company exists wholly or mainly for the purpose of carrying on a trade: see *Lord v Tustain* (1993)) and on a loan raised to lend money to such a company so long as it is used wholly and exclusively for the business of the company (or of an associated company which is likewise a qualifying close company). To qualify for relief, the borrower has to show *either* that he is a shareholder and works for the greater part of his time in the management or conduct of the company *or* that he controls more than 5% (a 'material interest') of the ordinary share capital (in the latter case the borrower need not work for the company).

To calculate whether the individual has the necessary material interest, shares of associates must generally be aggregated with his own shares. 'Associates' include an individual's relatives, partners, trustees of a settlement which he created, and trustees of a settlement holding shares for the benefit of that individual. However, shares in which the individual has an interest only under an employee benefit trust are not included in deciding whether he has a material interest in the company (see generally TA 1988 s 360A).

To the extent that the borrower recovers any capital from the company during that time (eg by repayment of ordinary share capital), he is treated as having repaid the loan and the amount of interest available for relief is reduced accordingly. Relief is not withdrawn if the company subsequently ceases to be close (see SP 3/78). It is not possible to obtain double tax relief by using the loan to purchase shares qualifying for relief under EIS (Enterprise Investment Scheme).

**[7.44]**

**EXAMPLE 7.3**

Gatty Ltd is the family trading company of the Gatty family. Sam Freebie, a full-time working director owning no shares in the company, borrows £5,000 from his bank to subscribe for ordinary shares. He will own a 4% shareholding and tax relief is available on the interest he pays. If, however, Jack Floor, the caretaker of the company's factory, were to subscribe for a similar number of shares no relief will be available because he is not concerned in the management or conduct of the company.

b) *Loan to acquire an interest in a partnership (TA 1988 s 362)*

Interest relief is available to an individual on a loan used to purchase a share in a partnership or to contribute capital or make a loan to the partnership, if it is used wholly and exclusively for the business purposes of the partnership. Relief is available only if, from the application of the loan to the payment of interest, the individual has been a member of the partnership (otherwise than as a limited partner or a partner in an investment LLP) and has not recovered any capital from the partnership. As a result payments of interest on borrowings to finance the business can be relieved in one of two ways: either under s 353 as described or, alternatively, as a deduction in the partnership accounts. The s 353 deduction has the attraction of enabling the interest to be set against the total income of the individual rather than against the profits of the firm only. For the position of LLPs, see also **[45.12]**.

Where the partnership is subsequently incorporated into a close company and the loan remains outstanding, relief continues to be available so long as relief would be available under the close company provisions considered above if the loan were a new loan taken out on incorporation.          **[7.45]**

c)   *Loan to acquire an interest in a co-operative (TA 1988 s 361)*

Relief is available for interest payments made on a loan to acquire an interest in a co-operative, or to be used wholly and exclusively for the business of that body or a subsidiary. A co-operative is defined as a common ownership enterprise or a co-operative enterprise within the meaning of the Industrial Common Ownership Act 1976 s 2. Relief is available only if the individual shows that from the application of the loan to the payment of the interest he has worked for the greater part of his time as an employee in that co-operative or in a subsidiary thereof.          **[7.46]**

d)   *Loan to invest in an employee-controlled company (TA 1988 s 361)*

Relief is available for interest payments on a loan taken out by an individual to acquire ordinary shares in an employee-controlled company (which must be a UK resident unquoted trading company). An employee-controlled company is one where full-time employees own more than 50% of the ordinary share capital and voting power of the company. When an employee owns more than 10% of the issued share capital, the excess is treated as not being owned by a full-time employee. Other conditions for relief are that the shares must be acquired within 12 months of the company becoming employee-controlled and that the taxpayer or his or her spouse/civil partner must be full-time employees of the company from the time when the loan is applied to the date when interest is paid. Furthermore, in the year of assessment in which the interest is paid the company must either first become employee-controlled or be such a company for at least nine months. Accordingly, interest relief will be withdrawn when the company ceases to be employee-controlled. To the extent that the individual recovers any capital from the company, the same rule operates as for close companies and partnerships.          **[7.47]**

e)   *Loan to purchase plant or machinery (TA 1988 s 359)*

Where a partner borrows money to purchase a car or other items of machinery or plant for which capital allowances are available, he can claim interest relief on that loan for up to three years after the end of the tax year when the debt was incurred. (Note that for a sole trader interest on such loans is a deductible business expense.)

An employee can claim interest relief on a loan to purchase plant and machinery (other than a car, van, motorcycle or bicycle) necessarily provided for use in the performance of the duties of their employment (CAA 2001 s 36). For example, a violinist employed by an orchestra could claim interest relief on a loan to purchase a violin. **[7.48]**

f) *Loan to pay inheritance tax (TA 1988 s 364)*

Personal representatives are eligible for interest relief on a loan used by them to pay IHT attributable to personal property situated in the UK to which the deceased was beneficially entitled and which has vested in them. The relief is limited to a 12-month period. **[7.49]**

g) *Loan to purchase a life annuity (TA 1988 s 365)*

Interest relief is available on loans taken out before 9 March 1999 not exceeding £30,000 by a person aged 65 or over in order to purchase an annuity on his life provided that at least nine-tenths of the loan proceeds are used to buy the annuity and that the annuity is secured on land in the UK (or Republic of Ireland) in which he has an interest and uses as his only or main residence at the time when the interest is paid. Relief is not lost if, after 27 July 1999, the taxpayer ceases to occupy the property as his only or main residence provided it was his only or main residence on 9 March 1999. Relief is given on a replacement loan where at least 90% of the new loan repays the old loan and the above conditions are satisfied. Tax relief is available at 23%, however the interest paid does not reduce the taxpayer's income. Instead relief is given by way of an income tax reduction (see *Step 6,* below). **[7.50]–[7.80]**

## IV  TOTAL INCOME (*STEP 3*)

Charges are deducted from income before any other deductions and the resultant sum is 'total income'. Insofar as charges exceed statutory income, the unabsorbed charge receives no tax relief and cannot be carried forward to a future year. After charges, the individual deducts personal reliefs from total income to arrive at his taxable income. Where losses are available these will be deducted before personal reliefs. Notice that it is the total income figure before any such deduction that is used to calculate (where applicable) the age allowance and (where available) the one-sixth for life assurance premium relief. **[7.81]**

### Loss relief

Sometimes losses arising from one source are deductible only in computing profits from the same source. Such losses, therefore, affect the calculation of the individual's statutory income by reducing income from that source.

**EXAMPLE 7.4**

Anita receives a salary as a lecturer (employment income) of £20,000 pa. She also owns a house in Chelsea which she rents to nurses from the Chelsea Hospital. In the current tax year her allowable expenses on the property exceeded her rental income by £1,000. Her statutory income for the current year is:

|  | £ |
|---|---|
| Employment income | 20,000 |
| Property income (loss £1,000) | Nil |
| Statutory income | £20,000 |

Anita cannot deduct her £1,000 loss on her property income (ITTOIA 2005 Part 3) from income from any other source. All she can do is carry the loss forward to a subsequent year and deduct it from her property income of that year. Thus, if in the following year her rental income exceeds her allowable expenses by £2,000, Anita's statutory income is:

|  | £ | £ |
|---|---|---|
| Employment income |  | 20,000 |
| Property income: profit | 2,000 |  |
| *Less:* loss b/f | 1,000 |  |
|  |  | 1,000 |
| Statutory income |  | £21,000 |

Where the individual makes a loss in his trade, profession or vocation, however, he may choose to deduct that loss from his total income before deducting personal reliefs (see TA 1988 ss 380–381). The danger with claiming this loss relief is that it may so reduce total income that personal allowances are unused.                                          **[7.82]–[7.100]**

**EXAMPLE 7.5**

Andrew is a barrister and a part-time lecturer (employment income) with a salary for the current year of £20,000 pa. He pays £1,000 (gross) to charity under Gift Aid. In the current tax year he makes a loss in his first year at the Bar of £5,000 that he chooses under TA 1988 s 380 to deduct from his total income. His income tax calculation (in part) for the current tax year is as follows:

|  | £ |
|---|---|
| Employment income | 20,000 |
| Trading income (loss £5,000) | Nil |
| Statutory income | 20,000 |
| *Less:* charge on income | 1,000 |
| Total income | 19,000 |
| *Less:* loss (TA 1988 s 380) | 5,000 |
|  | £14,000 |

Andrew has £14,000 income from which he can deduct his personal reliefs.

V   PERSONAL RELIEFS (TA 1988 S 256) *(STEP 4 OR STEP 6)*

1   **General**

Individuals resident in the UK can deduct personal reliefs from their total income. The availability of the reliefs depends not on the type of income involved but on the taxpayer's personal circumstances. Blind person's allowances and the married couple's allowance have to be claimed in the income tax return. If personal allowances exceed the total income of the taxpayer, the surplus is unused and cannot be carried forward for use in future years.

Certain non-residents are also entitled to personal reliefs (see TA 1988 s 278 and also **[18.71]**).

Prior to 6 April 1994 *all* personal reliefs operated by way of deduction from total income. From that date, however, certain allowances and reliefs have been given by subtracting a percentage of the allowance from the individual's total tax liability – 10% from 1999–2000 onwards (see further *Step 6*, below).

A summary of the personal reliefs available for 2006–07 is set out below. Reliefs (marked with a (●)) are linked to increases in the Retail Prices Index between September preceding the year of assessment and the previous September.

| | | |
|---|---|---|
| ● | Personal allowance: | £5,035 |
| ● | Personal allowance (age 65–74)* | £7,280 |
| ● | Personal allowance (age 75 and over)* | £7,420 |
| ● | Married couple's allowance (age 65–74)*† | £6,065 |
| ● | Married couple's allowance (age 75 and over)*† | £6,135 |
| ● | Married couple's allowance (minimum amount)† | £2,350 |
| ● | Blind person's relief | £1,660 |
| | Income limit for age-related allowances | £20,100 |
| * | These allowances are reduced if the taxpayer's income exceeds the income limit. | |
| † | Allowances where relief is restricted to 10%. | |

**[7.101]**

2   **The reliefs**

a)   *Personal allowance (TA 1988 s 257(1))*

The personal allowance (for 2006–07, £5,035) is available to all taxpayers resident in the UK including minor children. The allowance can be set against any form of income but any surplus is wasted since it cannot be used in any other tax year nor transferred to any other taxpayer.   **[7.102]**

b)   *The married couple's allowance (TA 1988 s 257A and 257AB)*

This relief can be claimed by married couples and registered civil partners (from 5 December 2005) provided one party was born before 6 April 1935. Different rules apply to pre-5 December 2005 marriages and to post-5 December 2005 marriages and civil partnerships. The use of the allowance and how it is divided between the couple is considered at [51.26]. For these purposes a couple are treated as living together unless they are separated under a court order, written deed, or are in fact separated in such circumstances that the separation is likely to be permanent. Accordingly this allowance cannot be claimed by a spouse or civil partner who, though separated from his or her spouse or civil partner, continues to maintain them: see further [52.2].

The availability of the married couple's allowance in a case where a man had two wives was confirmed in *Nabi v Heaton* (1983) but in *Rignell v Andrews* (1990) a taxpayer who had lived with the same woman for 11 years and who treated her as his common law wife was not entitled to the allowance as he was not married.                                                                       [7.103]

c)   *Age allowance (TA 1988 s 257(2), (3))*

Higher personal allowances are given by reference to the tax year in which the taxpayer's 65th or 75th birthday falls and curiously they are available even if the taxpayer dies before that birthday.

The personal allowance depends solely on the age of the relevant taxpayer. From £5,035 in 2006–07 it increases to £7,280 (for taxpayers aged 65–74 in the tax year) and then to £7,420 (for those aged 75 and over in the tax year).

By contrast the level of the married couple's allowance depends on the age of the *older spouse/civil partner* in the relevant tax year. The allowance is £6,065 (where the older spouse/civil partner is aged 65–74) and £6,135 (older spouse/civil partner is aged 75 and over).

These higher allowances for taxpayers aged 65 and over are subject to an income limit: this limit (£20,100 for 2006–07) is the same for all taxpayers, male and female, married, in a civil partnership and single. Provided that the taxpayer's total income (see [7.81]) is below this figure *full allowances are due*. However, if total income exceeds £20,100 then the age-related allowances are reduced by half the difference between the taxpayer's total income and the limit (ie the reduction is £1 of allowance for every £2 of income above £20,100). At worst, this reduction will wipe out the higher allowances: no taxpayer, however, will have his personal allowance reduced below the level for those aged under 65 (ie £5,035 for 2006–07). So far as the married couple's allowance is concerned, the reduction is calculated solely by reference to the husband's total income (for pre-5 December 2005 marriages) or the highest earner's total income (for post-5 December marriages and civil partnerships). In calculating any restriction in the married couple's allowance any reduction in the age allowance already suffered will be taken into account. At worst, the reduction will leave the couple with an allowance of £2,350. Note, finally, that married couples and civil partners cannot transfer any unused part of their income limits to each other.                               [7.104]

**EXAMPLE 7.6**

  (1)   Fred is 50; his wife, Wilma, is 73. Fred has income of £8,000 pa; Wilma £21,600.
      (a)   Fred is entitled to a personal allowance of £5,035. Wilma, because of her age, will qualify for an allowance of £7,280 but this will be reduced as follows:

Wilma's income: £21,600
Limit: £20,100
Excess: £1,500
One-half: £750
Age allowance reduced by £750 to £6,530.

(2) Robert is aged 78 with an income of £30,400; his wife, Alison, is aged 68 with an income of £3,000.

  (a) Alison will be entitled to a personal allowance of £7,280 of which £4,280 will be wasted.

  (b) Robert's personal allowance of £7,420 will be reduced to the basic allowance of £5,035 because his income exceeds the £20,100 threshold by more than £4,770. The married couple's allowance of £6,135 will also be reduced by reference to the excess of Robert's income over the income threshold to £2,350.

d) *Blind person's allowance (TA 1988 s 265(1), (2))*

A taxpayer who is a registered blind person for the whole or part of the year of assessment receives an additional relief (for 2006–07) of £1,660. If a husband and wife, or after 5 December 2005 civil partners, are both registered blind they can each claim the blind person's allowance. A married blind person may transfer any surplus allowance to their spouse or civil partner irrespective of whether the spouse or civil partner is themselves blind.                                             **[7.105]–[7.119]**

## VI  METHOD OF CHARGING TAXABLE INCOME (*STEP 5*)

### 1  Rates of tax

Income tax is charged on an individual's taxable income for 2006–07 at the following rates:

|  | *Income band* |
|---|---|
| On the first £2,150 at 10% (starting rate) | £1–£2,150 |
| On the next £31,150 at 22% (basic rate*) | £2,151–£33,300 |
| On the remainder at 40% (higher rate) | Excess over £33,300 |

\* The basic rate on dividends is 10% and on other savings income is 20%.

Increases in the rate bands are linked to the increase in the Retail Prices Index between the September before the year of assessment and the previous September. The indexed rises are, however, subject to a negative resolution of Parliament (ie they occur 'unless Parliament otherwise determines'; TA 1988 s 1(4)). Prior to 1988–89 a relatively complex rate structure existed with the top rate being 60%; from that year until 1991–92 there were only two rates of tax (the basic 25% and the higher 40% rate); 1992–93 witnessed the introduction of the 20% lower rate band and 1999, the starting rate of 10%. F(No 2)A 1997 introduced a complex structure for the taxation of dividends paid on or after 6 April 1999, which was complicated even further by the introduction of the 10% starting rate, but which was retrospectively changed to permit the starting rate to apply to both earned and unearned income.

It should be remembered that where payments are *made by* the taxpayer under deduction of tax at source (eg certain interest payments) those payments are added back to the taxpayer's taxable income for basic rate tax purposes, thereby effectively increasing the figure chargeable to basic rate tax above £33,300. Gifts to charities under Gift Aid are relieved by extending the basic rate band. When payments are *received by* the taxpayer after deduction at source, the tax due from the payee will be reduced by the tax already paid on his behalf by the payer. 10% of the married couple's allowance may be deducted from the tax due and this is considered in the next section. **[7.120]–[7.121]**

**EXAMPLE 7.7**

Brian has a statutory income for 2006–07 of £45,000. He makes gross Gift Aid payments to charity of £3,000 and is entitled to a personal allowance of £5,035. His income tax calculation is as follows:

|  | £ |
|---|---|
| Statutory income | 45,000 |
| *Less:* charge on income | 3,000 |
| Total income | 42,000 |
| *Less:* personal reliefs | 5,035 |
| Taxable income for basic and higher rates | £36,965 |

| Tax payable: | £ |
|---|---|
| First £2,150 at 10% | 215.00 |
| Next £31,150 at 22% | 6,853.00 |
| Balance of £3,665 at 40% | 1,466.00 |
|  | 8,534.00 |
| *Add back* for basic rate tax only payment to charity £3,000 × 22% | 660.00 |
|  | £9,194.00 |

Tax relief on investments in the EIS and in VCTs is considered in **Chapter 15**.

## 2 Dates for payment of tax

The due date for the payment of tax is 31 January following the year of assessment but in some cases with two interim payments falling due on 31 January in the year of assessment and 31 July immediately following that year (TMA 1970 Part VA).

Tax on employment earnings, pension and social security income is collected under the PAYE system at basic and higher rates on a current year basis (ITEPA 2003). If the taxpayer's only source of income is from employment, the correct amount of tax can usually be collected under this system necessitating no further adjustment. Where the taxpayer has other sources of income, either too much or too little tax may be deducted, giving rise to the need for a subsequent adjustment. **[7.122]–[7.125]**

## 3   Specimen income tax calculation

Applying the steps listed at **[7.1]** it is now possible to calculate an individual's income tax liability for a tax year. **[7.126]**

### EXAMPLE 7.8

Benjamin has the following income for 2006–07:

|      |                                                                   | £      |
|------|-------------------------------------------------------------------|-------:|
| (i)  | Pensions (employment, pensions and social security income)        | 25,000 |
| (ii) | Author (trading income)                                           | 3,000  |
| (iii)| Rents from houses (property income)                               | 14,000 |
| (iv) | Dividends from Tenko Ltd (gross—including tax credit of £100)      | 1,000  |

Benjamin who was born on 1 October 1934 is married to Bertha who is ten years younger. He pays £780 pa to the RSPCA (a registered charity) to whom he has made an appropriate declaration that the payments fall within the Gift Aid rules.

|                                                            | £        |
|------------------------------------------------------------|---------:|
| Employment, pensions and social security income            | 25,000   |
| Trading income                                             | 3,000    |
| Property income                                            | 14,000   |
| Savings and investment income                              | 1,000    |
| *Step 1: Statutory income from all sources*                | 43,000   |
| *Step 2: Deduct charges on income:*                        | 1,000    |
| *Step 3: Total income*                                     | 42,000   |
| *Step 4: Deduct personal relief:*                          |          |
|          Personal allowance                                | 5,035    |
| *Step 5: Taxable income for starting basic and higher rates* | £36,965 |

|                                                            | £        |
|------------------------------------------------------------|---------:|
| Tax chargeable at *Step 5:*                                |          |
|          First £2,150 at 10%                               | 215.00   |
|          Next £31,150 at 22%                               | 6,853.00 |
|          Balance of £2,665 at 40%                          | 1,066.00 |
|          £1,000 at 32.5%                                   | 325.00   |
|          Tax on £33,965 at lower, basic and higher rate    | 8,459.00 |
| *Step 6: Deduct 10% of additional allowance (£2,350)*      | (235.00) |
|                                                            | 8,224.00 |

| *Step 7: Give credit for tax deducted at source, ie from the dividends* | 100.00 |
|---|---|
| | 8,124.00 |
| *Step 8: Add back for basic rate tax only sums paid to the RSPCA:* ie £1,000 at 22% | 220.00 |
| Total tax due | £8,344.00 |

*Notes:*
(1)  Tax would have been deducted at source under the PAYE system in respect of the pensions. Credit would be given for this tax in *Step 7*, thereby affecting the actual tax due from Benjamin by self-assessment. Nevertheless, Benjamin is actually liable (however it is collected) for tax of £8,344.00 in 2006–07.
(2)  The dividends are treated as the top slice of Benjamin's taxable income and accordingly suffer tax at the 32.5% higher rate with a credit limited to 10%.
(3)  The married couple's allowance is only given tax relief at the 10% rate: hence it is deducted as shown at *Step 6*. The allowances are reduced due to the total income exceeding £20,100. The reduction leaves Benjamin with the normal personal allowance and £2,350 married couple's allowance.

## 4   Exemptions from income tax

There are a number of exemptions from income tax including the following. It should also be noted that a number of items are exempted from tax by virtue of HMRC ESCs.                                                        **[7.127]**

### a)   *Exempt organisations*

The Crown is not within the tax legislation, whilst charities are generally exempt from income tax in respect of:
(1)  income from land and investment income provided that it is applied for charitable purposes only; and
(2)  trading profits applied purely for charitable purposes where either the trade is part of the main purpose of the charity, or the work is carried out mainly by the beneficiaries (see TA 1988 s 505 and guidance in ESC C4).
    Foreign diplomats and members of overseas armed forces stationed in the UK are exempt (ITTOIA 2005 ss 771–772).
    Other exempt organisations include the British Museum (TA 1988 s 507), agricultural societies (TA 1988 s 510) and scientific research associations (TA 1988 s 508).                                          **[7.128]**

### b)   *Exempt income*

Some of the more important items that are exempt from income tax are set out in ITTOIA Part 6 including:
(a)  National Savings income;
(b)  income and individual investment funds;
(c)  SAYE interest;
(d)  venture capital trust dividends;
(e)  income and FOTRA securities;
(f)  purchased life annuity payments;

g)    scholarship income in the hands of the scholar;
h)    repayment supplement;
i)    interest on damages for personal injury;
j)    benefits paid under sickness and unemployment insurance policies; and
k)    payments to adopters by local authorities and adoption agencies.

Other exempt income includes statutory redundancy, maintenance payments on divorce or separation, and compensation paid by banks for dormant accounts of holocaust victims.                    **[7.129]**

c)    *Life assurance policies, ISAs and PEPs*

These are considered in **Chapter 15**.                              **[7.130]**

# 8 Taxation of employment income

*Updated by Mahesh Varia, LLB (Hons), ATT, Partner, Travers Smith*

## I INTRODUCTION

Earnings from an office or employment are taxed under ITEPA 2003. About 90% of total income tax per annum is raised from such earnings mainly through a deduction-at-source system (Pay As You Earn or PAYE) which ensures timely receipt of the tax by the Treasury.

Whenever an employee receives earnings, national insurance contributions (NICs) have to be considered. NICs are categorised into Classes: Classes 2 and 4 relate to profits from self-employment; Class 3 is a voluntary contribution (for instance, to cover a period when a person has been out of the country). Classes 1, 1A and 1B relate to employment income: both employees and employers pay Class 1 NICs but Class 1A and 1B are employer-only liabilities. Whilst NICs are in theory separate from income tax, from an employee's perspective they seem very similar: primary Class 1 NICs (often known as employees' NICs) are deducted from his salary under the PAYE system and paid to the government. There are, however, differences.

First, not all employee receipts from employment are subject to Class 1 NICs. Second, employees pay primary Class 1 NICs at the following rates: nil on earnings below £5,035 per annum; 11% or 9.4% on earnings between £5,035 and £33,540 per annum (depending on whether the employee is contracted in or out of the State Second Pension—see further **Chapter 50**); and at 1% on earnings over £33,540 per annum. Employers pay secondary Class 1 NICs on their employees' earnings above £5,035 per year, at 12.8% on earnings above £33,540 per annum and at a variety of rates on earnings between £5,035 and £33,540, depending on the type of pension arrangements the employee has. Secondary Class 1 NICs represent a real cost to an employer and many of the tax avoidance schemes in the employment field have had the primary aim of reducing the employers' NIC obligations.

The combination of high marginal tax rates and the PAYE system led to employers providing benefits in kind to minimise the employee's tax or, where tax was payable, escape the PAYE net (and thus give him a cash flow advantage) and avoid NICs. The natural consequence has been frequent legislation making such benefits taxable and widening the PAYE net; further, over the years some benefits in kind were specifically made subject to Class 1 NICs; and since 6 April 2000 the majority of the others have been made subject to Class 1A contributions.

The more the government seeks to increase the tax and NICs raised from employees, the more some workers try to bring themselves within the more beneficial self-employed regime. HMRC's attitude is predictable. The courts' approach has varied over the years: at the moment the case law tests for whether a worker should be classified as employed or self-employed are more helpful to the would-be consultant than they have been for some time.

The tensions created by taxpayers' desire to avoid being taxed as employees and the government's desire to raise as much tax as possible through this source created a regime in which the principles originally at play were swamped by the detailed legislation. Recently, however, a more considered debate has started (see, for instance, the 2001 report by Professor Judith Freedman for the Tax Law Review Committee (established by the Institute for Fiscal Studies) on tax equity between the employed and the self-employed). The need for a fundamental review arises not only from increasingly sophisticated attempts to avoid classification as an employee (for instance, by taking advantage of the beneficial tax regime obtainable through providing a worker's services through his own one-man company) but also from more complex and flexible working patterns in general.

To create a level playing field for all workers, it will be necessary to introduce an approach where people performing the same economic function are treated in the same way. Robert Walker LJ's suggestion in *R (on the application of Professional Contractors Group Ltd) v IRC* (2002), might be the way forward:

> '[I] wonder whether it might not have been possible to bring forward measures which accorded some recognition to the existence of a sort of no man's land between Sch D [the Schedule under which the self-employed used to be taxed] and Sch E [the Schedule under which employees and office-holders used to be taxed] rather than insisting on the gulf which exists in theory (but not, always, in practice) between them.'

The major recent development in this area was the enactment (with effect from 6 April 2003) of the Income Tax (Earnings and Pensions) Act 2003 (ITEPA 2003). Although it made very few changes to the substantive law in this area (it is a consolidation Act, enacted as part of the Tax Law Rewrite Project (see [1.22])), it has restructured the whole regime and in the process abolished its bedrocks—emoluments, Cases and even Schedule E itself.

A subsidiary development is the introduction of tax-avoidance scheme disclosure obligations by FA 2004. Much of the detail of who has the obligation to provide information to HMRC and exactly what arrangements have to be disclosed is set out in statutory instruments. SI 2004/1863 deals with the latter and prescribes two types of arrangement: certain arrangements connected with employment and others related to financial products. Anyone advising in this area on arrangements involving shares, payments to trustees and intermediaries or loans to employees which may give rise to a 'tax advantage' should consider whether a disclosure obligation arises.

HMRC's view on the interpretation and application of ITEPA 2003 can be found in its Employment Income Manual, available on its website (www.hmrc.gov.uk). The old Schedule E Manual is still available on the website for those who are dealing with the application of the old provisions. References in this Chapter to the former manual have the prefix EI and to the latter SE.

Readers of this chapter need also to be aware of the enactment of another consolidation Act, the Income Tax (Trading and Other Income) Act 2005 (ITTOIA 2005) (see further **Chapter 10**). This has restructured the regime for taxing trading income. Persons carrying out a trade, profession or vocation used to be taxed under Case I or II of Schedule D but are now taxed under ITTOIA 2005 Part 2: references to both the old and new regimes will appear in this chapter.                                        **[8.1]–[8.10]**

## II   THE OLD AND NEW STRUCTURES

### 1   The charging provisions

The basic charging provision for income from employment used to be TA 1988 s 19(1) para 1. This provided that emoluments from an office or employment (these terms are considered in Sections III, V and VII) would be taxed under Schedule E if the recipient fell within one of the Cases listed. Although 'Schedule E' had indeed been a schedule to early Income Tax Acts, it had long since been set out in a section of the main taxing Act but the original location remained an official synonym for taxable employment income. Case I of Schedule E caught the emoluments of a person resident and ordinarily resident in the UK; Case II emoluments for UK duties of any person either not resident or resident but not ordinarily resident here; and Case III emoluments for overseas duties remitted to the UK by a person resident, whether or not ordinarily resident, here. Persons who were resident and ordinarily resident but not domiciled in the UK were taxed on their foreign emoluments (broadly, emoluments for non-UK duties provided to a non-UK employer) only if they remitted them here (ie under Case III rather than Case I).

Section 19(1) para 5 contained a residual charging provision: it taxed income which another provision of the Tax Acts directed should be charged under Schedule E. The taxability of such income depended not on the tests in para 1 but on the terms of the relevant provision. *Nichols v Gibson* (1994) provides an example of the application of para 5 (see **[8.149]**).

The taxability of the income of employees was not changed in any significant way by ITEPA 2003 but the whole structure of the charging provisions was altered. Schedule E was abolished. There is only one charging section for employment income—s 9. This imposes a tax charge on 'general earnings', which covers income that was previously charged under s 19(1) para 1 (either because it was an emolument or it was treated as an emolument), and on 'specific employment income', which covers that previously charged by para 5; together these are called 'employment income'. The rest of the employment income Parts of the Act identify what income of employees will be taxed under s 9 as general earnings or specific employment income. ITEPA 2003 Parts 9 and 10 cover pension income and social security income.

Another aspect is that the actual amount charged under ITEPA 2003 is spelt out: in the case of general earnings, it is 'the net taxable earnings from an employment' for the year (ss 9(2), 11(1), 14 and 15(1)); and in the case of specific employment income, it is 'the net taxable specific income from an employment for the year' (ss 9(4) and 12). To ascertain 'taxable earnings', one no longer has to ascertain whether the employee, falls within a Case of Schedule E. Instead, ITEPA 2003 Part 2 Chapters 4 and 5 set out how residence, ordinary residence and domicile affect the taxation of 'general earnings'. To ascertain 'taxable specific income', the position is the same as it was previously under para 5: one has to look at the terms of the relevant provision.

Once taxable earnings and taxable specific income have been ascertained, the net amounts for the purposes of s 9 can be calculated by applying the formulae in ss 11 and 12. These basically provide for the deduction of allowable expenditure (see Section XI).

In so far as employment income involves a foreign element, readers are also referred to **Chapter 18**; this Chapter is limited to the tax position of employees and office-holders who are resident, ordinarily resident and domiciled in the UK.                                                                 **[8.11]**


## 2   Basis of assessment

Prior to 1989–90, tax was charged under Schedule E on a current year basis and was levied on emoluments when earned. Accordingly the date of payment was strictly irrelevant to the tax charge. Inevitably, this led to problems of referring payments back to the tax year when earned: for instance, directors are frequently voted bonuses long after the relevant tax year for which they performed the services. To tidy this area up and to correct certain other defects in the Schedule E legislation, FA 1989 altered the basis of assessment under Schedule E from an earnings to a *receipts* basis. ITEPA 2003 replaces the rather piecemeal approach of the previous legislation with Part 2 Chapters 4 and 5 for employees resident, ordinarily resident and domiciled in the UK, but does not alter the result.

Only general earnings which are 'for a tax year' in which the employee is resident, ordinarily resident and domiciled in the UK fall within Chapter 4 (s 15(1)). Such earnings are subject to charge when they are received (rather than when they are earned) (s 15(2)), even if they are not 'for' that tax year (as to which see **[8.13]–[8.20]**) and even if the employment is not held at the time of receipt (s 15(3)). Not surprisingly, there is a detailed definition of when a payment is received for these purposes (s 18 for money earnings and s 19 for others). In the case of directors, for instance, payment is treated as made when the sum is credited in the company's accounts or records—hence crediting the director's account with that sum will constitute a payment for these purposes (s 18(1)).                                                                 **[8.12]**

## 3  The source doctrine

One of the hallowed principles of income tax (see **[6.41]**) is that a charge can only be made if the source of the income is continuing. This principle has, of course, been much modified by statute. Thus, the possibility of a barrister (who would normally be self–employed) ceasing to practise and, at some time during his peaceful retirement, receiving arrears of fees which, because the source of the fees had ceased, escaped tax, has long since gone under the post-cessation receipts rules. More recently, the case of *Bray v Best* (1988) (see *Example 6.1*) revealed an unsuspected gap in the Schedule E legislation where employees were paid emoluments after the cessation of their employment. That gap was quickly closed by the introduction of paragraph 4A into TA 1988 s 19(1). As a result of FA 1989 s 36(5) this only applied in relation to 1989–90 onwards. Unfortunately, when paragraph 4A was consolidated into ITEPA 2003 s 17, this time limit was not included (though it was included in s 30 (the equivalent provision for employees resident, ordinarily resident or domiciled outside the UK), as a result of ITEPA 2003 Sch 7 para 8), but it is understood that HMRC intends to correct this in due course. Apart from this small omission, ITEPA 2003 clarifies the position further.

   Section 16 sets out the rules for determining whether general earnings are 'for' a particular tax year. This is a great improvement on the old legislation which gave no guidance on how to ascertain what year emoluments were 'for'. Section 16 can be overridden by any provision in ITEPA 2003 Part 3 which specifies when an amount is to be treated as earnings for a particular tax year (s 16(5)). If general earnings are paid to an employee before his employment commences, they will be treated for the purposes of s 9 as earnings for the first year of that employment: if paid after the employment has ceased, they will be related back to the last year of employment (s 17). Accordingly, should the facts of *Bray v Best* recur in the future, the payment will be related back to the last year of the employment. Note, however, that this change merely extends the source doctrine to catch the payment; the tax itself will still remain charged in the year of receipt. The principle that tax is charged in the year of receipt but that the source of the income must be determined in the year when it is earned, applies to the facts of the following example.

#### EXAMPLE 8.1

(1)   In 2004–05, Bert is resident and ordinarily resident in the UK when his UK job ceases. In 2005–06, he becomes non-resident (taking a job as a Eurocrat in Brussels). A bonus paid in 2005–06 in relation to the UK job falls within Part 2 Chapter 4 and is *taxed in year of receipt.*

(2)   Take the opposite case: ie in 2004–05, Henri is non-UK resident when his full–time job in Paris ceases. He comes to the UK in 2005–06 when he receives a bonus in respect of 2004–05. He is not subject to UK tax since he was outside the tax net when the money was earned.

It should be noted that the general rule in s 17 does not apply for the purposes of the benefits code (see Section VIII Part 3) (s 17(4)). Many of the provisions in that code only apply if the benefit is provided in a year when the employment is held: the Chapters of Part 3 identify the year the earnings are 'for' (see, eg s 72). **[8.13]–[8.20]**

## III    OFFICE OR EMPLOYMENT

### 1    Meaning of 'office'

The term '*office*' was described by Rowlatt J in *Great Western Rly Co v Bater* (1920) as 'a subsisting, permanent, substantive position which had an existence independent from the person who filled it, which went on and was filled in succession by successive holders ...'. In *Edwards v Clinch* (1981) the emphasis on permanence and continuity was played down by the House of Lords in favour of the requirement of some degree of continuance and of a position with an existence independent of the individual holding it. In that case a civil engineer who received *ad hoc* appointments as a planning inspector was held not to be an office-holder because the position had no independent existence but lapsed when the particular assignment was completed. Mr Clinch was appointed to *execute a task* not to perform a certain *type* of work (an office).

This distinction was relied on by the Court of Session in *IRC v Brander & Cruickshank* (1971) (affirmed by the House of Lords) in a case dealing with the difficulties which arise when a taxpayer acquires an 'office' by reason of his particular profession: eg solicitor partners (then taxable under Schedule D Case II, now under ITTOIA 2005) who assume trusteeships. Each office will be separately assessed under ITEPA 2003 and not taxed under ITTOIA 2005, unless that office is assumed as an integral part of the trade or profession. In practice, HMRC allows partnerships which receive directors' fees to enter those fees in their self-employed assessment so long as the directorship is a normal incident of the profession and of the particular practice, the fees form only a small part of total profits, and under the partnership agreement the fees are pooled for division amongst the partners (see ESC A37).

Typical examples of office-holders include trustees, personal representatives, company secretaries and auditors. It is generally assumed that a company director who is not an employee (and who probably works part-time in return for fees) is an office-holder and taxable under ITEPA 2003 (*McMillan v Guest* (1942)). Often, the directorship will continue regardless of the person who occupies it; but it may still be an office, it appears, even if it is created for a particular person (see *Taylor v Provan* (1974), cf *Edwards v Clinch* above). Difficulties of interpretation like this explain why ITEPA 2003 s 5 contains only a non-exhaustive definition:

' "office" includes in particular any position which has an existence independent of the person who holds it and may be filled by successive holders'.    **[8.21]**

### 2    Employed or self-employed?

ITEPA 2003 makes no attempt to define 'employment' but s 4 does (in HMRC's view) provide 'a non-exhaustive explanation which [gives] an

indication of the *core* meaning of "employment" by listing certain arrangements that on any view constitute an employment.' (Explanatory Notes to the
Act.)

The arrangements listed in s 4 are any employment under a contract of
service or contract of apprenticeship, or in the service of the Crown. This
leaves open the most significant question: when **is** there a contract of service?

If the taxpayer works for more than one person, the difficulty is to know
whether he holds a number of separate employments or is making a series of
engagements carried out as part of a trade, profession or vocation. The basic
division is between a contract of service (within ITEPA 2003) and a contract
for services (within ITTOIA 2005). Cooke J in *Market Investigations Ltd v
Minister of Social Security* (1969) identified the relevant factors as follows:

> 'a contract of service may exist even though the control does not extend to
> prescribing how the work shall be done ... the most that can be said is that control
> will no doubt always have to be considered although it can no longer be regarded
> as the sole determining factor; and that factors, which may be of importance, are
> such matters as whether the man performing the services provides his own
> equipment, whether he hires his own helpers, what degree of financial risk he
> takes, what degree of responsibility for investment and management he has, and
> whether and how far he has an opportunity of profiting from sound management
> in the performance of his task.'

This test as to whether the person is 'in business on his own account' is
significant but issues of control, integration and mutuality of obligation are
also important (see, for instance, *Future Online Ltd v Faulds* (2004)). The right
of the worker to appoint a substitute has assumed increasing significance. A
genuine right of substitution will make it much more difficult for HMRC to
prove an employment relationship (see paras 1051 to 1060 in HMRC's
Employment Status Manual, *Tilbury Consulting Ltd v Gittins (No2)* (2004) and
the employment law case of *Staffordshire Sentinel Newspapers Ltd v Potter* (2004)
in which the Employment Appeal Tribunal held that an unfettered discretion
to appoint a substitute was inconsistent with a contract of employment).

The main problems arise when a taxpayer works for more than one person,
either consecutively or concurrently. In *Davies v Braithwaite* (1931), for
instance, an actress who entered into a series of separate engagements to
appear on film, stage and radio was held to be taxable under Schedule D.
Rowlatt J looked at her total commitments during the year and, as the
number was considerable, decided that each was a mere engagement in the
course of exercising her profession: compare *Fall v Hitchen* (1973) where the
taxpayer was employed as a professional ballet dancer by Sadler's Wells under
a contract which only allowed him to take other work with their consent
(which was not to be unreasonably withheld). Pennycuick V-C looked at the
characteristics of the contract in isolation and held that the taxpayer was
taxable under Schedule E; undoubtedly, one reason for the decision was that
the taxpayer had only one contract which provided for a first call on his time.

HMRC, adopting this approach of looking at each contract in isolation,
tried to bring persons traditionally taxed under Schedule D (eg actors)
within the old Schedule E. However, the courts reverted to taking an
overview and, in *Hall v Lorimer* (1994), HMRC's attempt to recategorise
technical workers in the film industry as Schedule E taxpayers, whatever the
number and nature of their engagements each year, was successfully resisted.

The Court of Appeal held that the duration of each engagement and the number of people by whom Mr Lorimer was engaged were of critical importance. It said that, in these types of case, the question of whether the taxpayer was 'dependent on or independent of a particular paymaster for the financial exploitation of his talents may well be significant' and that this was a more useful test than the 'business on own account' one since persons who exercise a profession or vocation will often do so 'without any of the normal trappings of a business'. Thus, although the taxpayer only supplied his own expertise, he could still be treated as self-employed.

Successes before the Commissioners suggest that self-employed status may be established even where the number of contracts are few, provided that there is other evidence of self-employment, including that the worker does not have the protections normally given to an employee (eg sick pay or holiday entitlement). Further, Lightman J's decision in *Barnett v Brabyn* (1996) underlines the need for greater subtlety. In that case the taxpayer's situation not only lacked the factors identified in *Market Investigations* above, but Mr Barnett also worked only for one employer and their relationship involved many factors indicating employment, including receipt of holiday pay. However, the court felt that the taxpayer's contractual right to work as much or as little as he liked (which right he exercised) and the parties' agreement that he should be self-employed (as to which, see **[8.23]**) were sufficient to ensure that status. The Special Commissioners' decision in *FS Consulting Ltd v McCaul* (2002) is however a reminder that if a person enters into a full-time contract which requires him to obtain the other party's consent to any absence, he, like Mr Hitchen, will find it hard to prove his self-employed status.

HMRC's summaries of the law (*Tax Bulletin*, April 1997, pp 405–413 and February 2000, pp 715–723 (in relation to personal service companies)) and its Employment Status Manual suggest that it is finally accepting that for each engagement the whole picture needs to be looked at and that its approach must reflect the nuances of the case law. However, clearer guidance, which attempts to reconcile the competing policies at play in this area, is still required (see *Taxation*, 12 July 2001, pp 361 and 363 and *Tax Adviser*, September 2001, pp 26–28 for a warning about the one-sided approach to the case descriptions in the Employment Status Manual; and *Taxation* 26 August 2004, p 553 for criticism of HMRC's leaflet on this subject, IR 56 (reissued July 2004)).

HMRC has also published an 'Employment Status Indicator' which can be accessed through its website and helps taxpayers decide their employment status for tax purposes. While the conclusions of the Employment Status Indicator may be indicative of a person's employment status, they are by no means determinative.                                                        **[8.22]**

## 3   Taxing a partner

A partner in a business is self-employed and, therefore, assessable under ITTOIA 2005. Difficulties may arise, however, as to the status of a salaried partner. Whether he is an employee or is self-employed does not *necessarily* depend upon the labels used or whether his salary is taxed at source under

PAYE. However, in a non-partnership case, *Barnett v Brabyn* (1996), Lightman J stated that whilst the parties' agreement on status:

> 'cannot contradict the effect of a contract as a whole and must be disregarded if inconsistent with the substantive terms or general effect of the contract as a whole, when the terms and general effect of the contract as a whole are consistent with either relationship, the parties' label may be decisive'.

In *Stekel v Ellice* (1973), although the agreement referred to 'salaried partner' and a 'fixed salary', the court found that it was, in substance, a partnership agreement rather than a contract of employment. In *Horner v Hasted* (1995) the rules of the ICAEW prevented a firm of accountants from appointing a non-qualified person as a partner (such an appointment would have led to the firm breaching various statutory rules), so the firm, therefore, went out of its way technically to preserve Mr Horner's employment status (eg by paying employers' NICs). These factors significantly influenced Lightman J's confirmation of his employment status when otherwise he had a 'status in the firm equivalent to that of a partner', including receiving a 'salary' that was a share of the profits, attending and voting at partners' meetings and being held out to clients as a partner! Accordingly, provided that the partnership determines the new partner's status in advance and drafts the agreement accordingly, its terms are likely to be conclusive unless there is strong factual evidence to the contrary (*BSM (1257) Ltd v Secretary of State for Social Services* (1978)). If the partners are in any doubt on the matter, they should seek confirmation of status from HMRC.   **[8.23]**

## 4   Reclassification

If the classification assumed by the parties is later proved to have been wrong, the tax and NIC treatment throughout the relationship will have to be revised (see *Taxation*, 9 October 1997, pp 32–35). Where self-employed status is reclassified as employment, this can cause severe problems for the (newly designated) employer who will be primarily responsible (under the PAYE system) for unpaid income tax and employees' NICs but will have difficulties recovering that from the (possibly former) worker (see further **[8.202]**), as well as having the extra cost of employers' NICs (which it would be unlawful to recover from him) – see *Demibourne v Revenue & Customs Comrs* (2005). *McManus v Griffiths* (1997) illustrates the opposite situation. A golf club stewardess provided catering services at the club under a 'contract of employment' drafted by the club secretary. When she was found to be self-employed, she had to pay interest on 12 years of Schedule D assessments. A simple error of judgment can in this context, because of the uncertainties inherent in any system of classification, have severe financial repercussions.
**[8.24]–[8.30]**

## IV   AGENCY WORKERS AND PERSONAL SERVICE COMPANIES

## 1   Introduction

As discussed in Section I, pressures to avoid taxation as an employee have long existed. Tax avoidance is not, of course, unknown in this area.

Before 1975, workers supplied through agencies and who were self-employed could escape tax on earnings on a particular assignment by disappearing once it was completed. Now, ITEPA 2003 Part 2 Chapter 7 provides that where a worker receives remuneration under a contract with an agency to render personal services to a client under supervision he is taxable under ITEPA (see s 44); the agency has to operate PAYE (*Brady v Hart* (1985) and, on the supervision requirement, see *Bhadra v Ellam* (1988)). Certain workers (such as entertainers) are excluded from the operation of the section (s 47(2)); special rules also apply to self-employed persons working in the construction industry.

At the time of the 1999 Budget, the government announced that it would be introducing provisions to 'counter avoidance in the area of personal service provision', primarily through the use of one-man companies. The effect of using a company to provide a worker's services, rather than those services being provided directly to the client, was that the agency rules would not apply (because there was no contract for the worker to supply his personal services to the client) and the agency could, therefore, pay the company a fee without deducting PAYE or being liable to account for NICs. The worker could take his money out of the personal service company in the form of dividends, which are not subject to NICs, would benefit from the delay before having to pay the higher rate tax to HMRC, and would often pay an overall lower rate of income tax on his income. The announcement was made in Budget Press Release IR 35 and much of the subsequent discussion has used the term 'IR 35' as a catch-all phrase to refer to this whole issue. The legislation itself is now in ITEPA 2003 Part 2 Chapter 8.

Such was the opposition to the introduction of this legislation that judicial review proceedings were brought (*R (on the application of Professional Contractors Group Ltd) v IRC* (2002)), alleging that it infringed EC law on state aid and freedom of establishment. The Court of Appeal dismissed the application.                                                                                                      [8.31]

## 2   The operation of the IR 35 rules

The aim of the legislation is to bring into the ITEPA, PAYE and Class 1 NIC nets workers who provide their services to clients through intermediaries when they would have been classified as employees if they had been providing those services directly to the clients. The essential issue of when a worker would have been classified as an employee is not addressed by the legislation, so that the common law position governs it (see Section III above and note that in some agency and IR35 type situations the courts have implied an employment contract between the worker and the client (*Taxation*, 26 May 2005 p 214), subject to the fact that the decision has to be made within the legislative matrix. HMRC will advise on a person's status before arrangements are implemented.

There is no statutory definition of 'intermediary'. Individuals, companies and partnerships can be intermediaries. It should be noted that it is not only one-man companies that are caught. If the intermediary is a company, it can fall within the statutory provisions if the worker has a 'material interest' in it (basically, 5%); even if he has no interest in the intermediary, the legislation will apply if the intermediary pays him and that pay 'can reasonably be taken to represent remuneration for services' provided by the worker to the intermediary's client.

If the legislation applies and the intermediary receives payments for the worker's services which are not paid to the worker as employment income, the legislation classifies the difference between the receipts of the intermediary and those of the worker as a 'deemed employment payment'. There are detailed rules as to how to calculate the amount of that deemed payment: for instance, one has to take into account not only payments and benefits in kind received by the intermediary in respect of relevant engagements but also those received by the worker and his family from someone other than the intermediary (compare the wide net for 'higher-paid' employees: see **[8.124]**). Expenses incurred and paid for by the intermediary and those borne by the worker and reimbursed by the intermediary are deductible in calculating the deemed payment (provided they would have been deductible in a straightforward employment situation (see Section XI) and see *Tax Bulletin*, December 2004, pp 1165–1168 on claims for travel and subsistence costs).

The deemed employment payment is generally treated as received at the end of the tax year, though in certain cases it can be treated as received earlier (eg if the connection between the worker and intermediary comes to an end before then) (s 50(3)). ITEPA 2003 s 56 sets out how the PAYE provisions apply.

The legislation is particularly complex and this is only a very brief summary of it. HMRC has provided its view of the operation of the legislation in a variety of places: *Tax Bulletin*, June 2000, pp 751–757 and February 2001, pp 819–826; revised guidance issued on 8 June 2005 (to replace leaflet IR175); and a series of Frequently Asked Questions in a section dedicated to this area on its website.                    **[8.32]–[8.40]**


## V ARE THE EARNINGS *FROM* EMPLOYMENT?

### 1 Introduction

The basic charging provision in ITEPA 2003 taxes, inter alia, *earnings from an employment* (see ss 7(3)(a) and 9(2)). This Section considers when it can be said that a receipt by an employee is 'from' his employment (the term 'employee' will be used to cover office-holders as well). The basic charging provision in TA 1988 (s 19) used the term 'emoluments', not earnings, which is why it appears in some of the extracts from cases and discussions in this chapter.

It should be noted that some receipts which are prima facie taxable as earnings from employment are not ultimately taxable as a result of the exemptions in ITEPA 2003 Part 4; and others are removed from the tax net by extra-statutory concessions (the number of which was considerably reduced by the enactment of ITEPA 2003—see *Tax Bulletin*, April 2003, p 1029 for a list of those incorporated into the Act). The final step in calculating taxable earnings is to ascertain if any deductions are available (see Section XI).                    **[8.41]**

## 2   General principles

In *Hochstrasser v Mayes* (1960), Upjohn J said that, in order for a payment received by an employee to be a profit arising from his employment, 'it must be something in the nature of a reward for services past, present or future'. When considering the appeal in the House of Lords, Lord Radcliffe stated:

> 'While it is not sufficient to render a payment assessable that an employee would not have received it unless he had been an employee, it is assessable if it has been paid to him in return for acting as or being an employee.'

The essence of these two statements is that a payment is not taxable merely because it would not have been paid if the recipient had not been an employee—there must be some additional factor to bring the payment within the tax net. The *Hochstrasser* case itself related to a scheme whereby if an employee was transferred within the group, ICI would buy his house at a fair valuation and would also reimburse any capital loss on the sale. Mr Mayes was reimbursed following a move—he would not have received that money unless he was an employee of ICI but that was not sufficient to make it taxable.

The difficulty arises in categorising the additional element that is required to bring a payment within the tax net. The courts have been fairly consistent in their requirement that the payment must be a 'reward for services'. Lord Templeman in *Shilton v Wilmshurst* (1991) (for the facts see [8.43]) said:

> 'Section [19] is not limited to emoluments provided in the course of the employment; the section must therefore apply first to an emolument which is paid as a reward for past services and as an inducement to continue to perform services and, second, to an emolument which is paid as an inducement to enter a contract of employment and to perform services in the future. The result is that an emolument "from employment" means an emolument "from being or becoming an employee". The authorities are consistent with this analysis and are concerned to distinguish in each case between an emolument which is derived "from being or becoming an employee" on the one hand and an emolument which is attributable to something else on the other hand, for example, to a desire on the part of the provider of the emolument to relieve distress or to provide assistance to a home buyer.'

In *Mairs v Haughey* (1993), the House of Lords reaffirmed that payments to compensate for loss or to relieve distress were not taxable under general principles, certainly if they were only payable in certain circumstances after the employment came to an end (the relative significance of these factors was not explained in the judgment). The case involved payments made to employees to compensate them for giving up their contingent rights under a non-statutory redundancy scheme but, in reaching its decision, the House of Lords also considered whether the redundancy payments themselves would have been taxable. Lord Woolf, delivering the judgment of the House, held that they would not have been as 'a characteristic of a redundancy payment is that it is to compensate or relieve an employee for what can be the unfortunate consequences of becoming unemployed'.

The decision in *Mairs* was that a certain type of payment (which was not a 'reward for services' but which was only payable in certain circumstances and then only after the termination of employment) was not an emolument from employment within TA 1988 s 19. No view was expressed on whether any payment which was not a 'reward for services' *could* fall within s 19 and the opportunity to comment on the Court of Appeal decision in *Hamblett v Godfrey* (1987) was forgone by the House of Lords. In *Hamblett*, the court held that a payment of £1,000 made to each employee of GCHQ who relinquished the right to join a trade union was taxable.

This decision was seen as indicating a payment could be taxable even if it was not paid as a reward for services. However, Lord Hutton CJ in the Northern Ireland Court of Appeal in *Mairs v Haughey* (1992) thought that *Hamblett v Godfrey* did not depart from previous authorities because the payment 'was held to be made in return for Miss Hamblett continuing to be an employee at GCHQ': in *Hamblett*, Neill LJ had stated:

'It is plain that the taxpayer received her payments as a recognition of the fact that she had lost certain rights as an employee, *and* by reason of the further fact that she had elected to remain in her employment at GCHQ.' (italics added)

Lord Hutton CJ's explanation of the decision in *Hamblett* would remove one obstacle to a general acceptance of the 'reward for services' test. There have, however, been first instance decisions since *Mairs* which have adopted the approach in *Hamblett v Godfrey* (see *Wilcock v Eve* (1995) and *EMI Group Electronics v Coldicott* (1997) but note that the argument in both these cases that *Hamblett* has been approved by the House of Lords has been criticised ([1998] BTR 364)). Naturally, HMRC has continued to press for the wider *Hamblett* test (see EI 00610). There are, however, signs that the courts are reverting to a more traditional approach.

HMRC's attempt to apply *Hamblett* to payments made by an employer to replace the protective awards that could have been claimed under the Trade Union and Labour Relations (Consolidation) Act 1992 s 189 (for failure to go through the stipulated consultation process when redundancies are planned) was rejected by the Special Commissioner in *Mimtec v IRC* (2001)). Whilst he was, of course, unable to ignore *Hamblett*, the Special Commissioner sought to narrow its application by holding that it does not apply to payments received under statutory provisions in connection with the termination of employment. In *Wilson v Clayton* (2005) the Court of Appeal had to decide whether a payment of compensation under a compromise agreement for unfair dismissal in 1997 was taxable under the general charging provision (then TA 1988 s 19). Peter Gibson LJ (with whom the other two members of the Court of Appeal agreed), reasserted the role of the 'reward for services' test:

'It is not enough that Mr Clayton would not have received [the payment] but for having been an employee. It is not a payment in return or as a reward for past services. It is not a payment in return for acting as or being an employee. It is not an inducement to enter into employment—he was already employed*—or to provide future services. If one looks for what reason it was paid, the answer is obvious ... it was to compensate Mr Clayton for the unfair dismissal.' (*The employer and Mr Clayton had entered into a new contract of employment in 1997.)

In its previous decision on s 19 (*EMI Group Electronics Ltd v Coldicott* (1999)), the Court of Appeal did not refer to *Hamblett* in deciding that a payment in lieu of notice, under a right reserved to the employer in the contract of employment, was taxable. The court concentrated on the fact that at the time of entering into the contract the employee required, as an inducement to enter the employment, the security of knowing he would receive salary for his notice period if forced to seek alternative employment. It is not apparent that the employee actually stipulated for this: in fact, it is much more likely that the right to make a payment in lieu of notice was inserted for the employer's benefit, so that summary dismissal would not bring the restrictive covenants in the contract to an end. The Court of Appeal's approach suggests that the courts should be willing to assume that all contractual benefits act as an inducement and are taxable under ITEPA 2003 s 9 (unless they are not earnings—see Section VII) but, in his judgment in *Mairs v Haughey* (1993) in the House of Lords, Lord Woolf thought otherwise.

The redundancy payments in *Mairs* were payable under the 'conditions of employment': it was not clear whether the written contracts of employment referred to the scheme. In *Comptroller-General of Inland Revenue v Knight* (1973), Lord Wilberforce, delivering the opinion of the Privy Council, said:

> 'Where a sum of money is paid under a contract of employment it is taxable, even though it is received at or after the termination of the employment: see, for example, *Henry v Foster* (1931).'

Lord Woolf stated that this was only 'an agreed general proposition' which is 'subject to exceptions'. Although Lord Woolf's statement is not part of the *ratio decidendi* of *Mairs* (since there was no finding that the redundancy payments would have been 'paid under a contract of employment'), it would have been helpful if the Court of Appeal in *EMI* had addressed this point directly.                                                              [8.42]

## 3   Third party payments

Tips normally form part of an employee's taxable earnings and in some businesses form a substantial part of take-home pay. In such cases, the payment is made by a third party rather than by the employer. In *Shilton v Wilmshurst* (1991) the House of Lords decided that such payments could amount to emoluments even if the third party did not have an interest in the performance of the employment contract. The case concerned Peter Shilton, the former England goalkeeper, who, on his transfer from Nottingham Forest to Southampton, received a payment of £75,000 from Nottingham Forest. Deciding that this sum was an emolument Lord Templeman stressed that:

> 'there is nothing in [the section] or the authorities to justify the inference that an "emolument from employment" only applies to an emolument provided by a person who has an interest in the performance by the employee of the services which he becomes bound to perform when he enters into the contract of employment ... so far as the taxpayer is concerned, both the emoluments of £80,000 from Southampton and £75,000 from Nottingham Forest were paid to him for the same purpose and had the same effect, namely, as an inducement to him to agree to become an employee of Southampton.'                           [8.43]

## 4 Past services

The debate about past services does not, of course, relate to the normal case where salary is paid in arrears. What is in issue is the taxability of a payment which relates to a period of employment for which payment has already been received.

Upjohn J, in the *Hochstrasser* case (**[8.42]**), envisaged that rewards for past services would be taxable. However, Lord Templeman, in the passage from *Shilton* cited above at **[8.43]**, indicated that rewards for past services will only be taxable if they are *also* 'an inducement to continue to perform services'.

In *Brumby v Milner* (1976), the House of Lords held that payments made from an employee trust when it was wound up, to employees who were still in employment, were taxable. In *Bray v Best* (1989), payments in similar circumstances were made to *former* employees. Lord Oliver said:

> 'Although before the Special Commissioners and High Court the taxpayer had contested that the sum paid constituted an emolument from his employment, the decision … in *Brumby v Milner* … effectively precludes further argument on this point and the question has not been pursued either before the Court of Appeal or before your Lordships.'

There is some difficulty in reconciling the idea that the payments in *Bray v Best* were emoluments from employment with Lord Templeman's statement in *Shilton v Wilmshurst*; there *may* also be an argument that the payments were capital in nature and therefore not taxable (see Lord Woolf's comments quoted at **[8.65]**). **[8.44]–[8.60]**

## VI PROBLEM CASES

### 1 Introduction

This Section examines the case law on when particular types of payments can be said to be '*from employment*' and therefore taxable as earnings. When many of these cases were decided, if a payment or benefit did not satisfy that test, it fell outside the income tax net altogether. This is no longer the case: if a payment or benefit is not taxable as earnings, it may well be taxable under another, more specific, provision. If it is not caught by a specific provision in ITEPA 2003 relating to certain types of benefits commonly provided, it may fall within the residual provision bringing benefits within the tax net in Part 3 Chapter 10 or be a payment treated as earnings within Chapter 12. If none of those apply, it could be some form of unapproved retirement payment or benefit taxable under Part 6 Chapter 2. Finally, if the payment or benefit relates to termination of employment (or a change in its nature), it could fall within Part 6 Chapter 3. Since the taxation of termination payments is particularly complicated, the application of the different charging provisions to such payments is considered separately in Section IX. Accordingly, when reading the rest of this Section, it should not be assumed that just because a receipt is not '*from employment*' it is not taxable. **[8.61]**

## 2　**Gifts**

There is a basic distinction between a payment which is a *reward for services* and which is, therefore, taxable under ITEPA 2003 s 9 as earnings and one which is made *in appreciation of an individual's personal qualities,* which is not so taxable (the taxability of a payment made *in appreciation of services rendered* was considered in *Allum v Marsh* (see further **[8.145]**)). Various factors are relevant in drawing this distinction.

*First,* whether the payment is made once only or whether it is recurring (in the former case it is more likely to escape tax).

*Second,* whether it is made to only one employee or to a whole class of employees. In *Laidler v Perry* (1966), for instance, all the employees received a £10 voucher at Christmas instead of the turkey that they had received in previous years. The employees were taxed on the cash value of the voucher.

*Third,* if the payment is by the employer there is a strong presumption that it constitutes earnings, whereas if it is from a third party, it is easier to show that it is a gift for personal qualities. However, tips are generally regarded as being in return for services and so taxable, even though made voluntarily by someone other than the employer. In *Calvert v Wainwright* (1947), a taxi driver was taxable on tips received from customers, although the court suggested that a particularly generous tip from a special customer (eg at Christmas) might escape tax (see also *Blakiston v Cooper* (1909)). In 2003 the Special Commissioners held that payments totalling $7.7m from one of the original investors in Channel 5 to the managers who helped it in its efforts to sell its holding were 'gratuities' and therefore NIC-free (*Channel 5 TV Group Limited v Morehead*): the case contains an extensive survey of the meaning of 'gratuity' but it should be noted that it had been accepted that the payments were taxable (although whether under the general charging provision or the benefits in kind legislation is not clear).

*Fourth,* a payment to which the employee is entitled under the terms of his contract of employment will usually be taxable as a part of his earnings, although this is subject to exceptions (see **[8.42]**).

**EXAMPLE 8.2**

(1) Ham has played cricket for Gloucestershire for many years. At the end of his distinguished career the county grants him a benefit match (ie he is entitled to all the receipts from a particular game). The benefit is a tax-free testimonial paid for Ham's personal qualities (see *Seymour v Reed* (1927)). *Compare:*

(2) Mercenary plays as a professional in the Lancashire League and under the terms of his contract is entitled to have the 'hat passed round' (ie a collection taken) every time he scores 50 runs or takes five wickets in an innings. The sums that he receives will be taxed as earnings because he is entitled to them in his contract of employment (see *Moorhouse v Dooland* (1955)).

*Finally,* the gift rules overlap with the benefit in kind rules. In deciding whether tax is chargeable under ITEPA 2003, the gift rules should be applied first and then the benefit in kind rules (see Sections VII and VIII of this Chapter (particularly *Example 8.13*) and ITEPA 2003 s 64). A gift connected with the termination of an employment is considered at **[8.145]**.　　**[8.62]**

## 3   Inducement payments

*Shilton v Wilmshurst* (1991) (see [**8.42**] and [**8.43**]) illustrates that payments which are made (even by a third party) for 'being or becoming an employee' are taxable. However, payments made to compensate the taxpayer for some sacrifice that he has made by taking up an employment are generally not taxable because they are not in return for services. In *Jarrold v Boustead* (1964) an international rugby union player was not taxable on a £3,000 signing-on fee paid to him when he turned professional. The payment was not an emolument but was to compensate him for permanent loss of his amateur status.

The same principle was applied in *Pritchard v Arundale* (1971) where a chartered accountant was not taxed on a large shareholding transferred to him in return for signing a service contract as managing director of the company. The benefit was held to accrue to him, not for future services as managing director which were to be adequately rewarded, but as compensation for loss of his professional status as a chartered accountant. It may also be noted that the shares were to be transferred in return for the taxpayer's signing the service contract. Hence, even if he had died without performing any services for the company, the shares would have been transferable to his estate. Further, they were given by a third party not by the new employer (see also *Vaughan-Neil v IRC* (1979) at [**8.133**]).

In *Jarrold* Lord Denning MR said (*obiter*) that a church organist appointed for seven months at £10 per month would not be taxable on £500 paid to him in return for giving up golf *for the rest of his life*. On the face of it, *Pritchard* is hard to reconcile with this example, but perhaps the following conclusions can be supported:

(1)   Mr Arundale had been the senior partner in a firm of chartered accountants. Although he could have resumed his status as a chartered accountant on leaving the employment, his age (48) in practice made it 'most unlikely' that he would 'be able to pick up his former profession as soon as his other activities' ended; the organist in Lord Denning's example could never again play golf on a Sunday. In both cases, therefore, the compensation was, in effect, for a permanent loss to the taxpayer. If the loss is merely restricted to the period of the contract, the payment is likely to be viewed as advance remuneration.

(2)   Mr Arundale was fully rewarded for his services under the contract. It seems likely that £10 per month was a reasonable payment, in 1964, for an organist. If the salary is not fair remuneration, again the payment is likely to be viewed as advance remuneration.

In *Glantre Engineering Ltd v Goodhand* (1983) an inducement payment made to a chartered accountant was held to be an emolument as the taxpayer failed to show that he had provided consideration in return for the payment since he was merely moving from one employment to another. It therefore seems that once the taxpayer fails to show that he has been permanently deprived of something akin to amateur status or the status of being a partner, it must follow that the payment is a reward for future services in the new employment.                                                                          [**8.63**]

## 4  Compensation for other losses

Compensation for loss caused to the employee may escape tax even when not paid as part of an inducement payment. The cases discussed at **[8.42]** illustrate that compensation paid for a personal loss suffered by an employee (eg compensation for loss on the sale of a house as in *Hochstrasser v Mayes* (1960)) will usually not be taxable as earnings. Further, compensation for various forms of discrimination prohibited by statute will be taxable, if at all, only under ITEPA 2003 s 401 (see further **[8.148]**).                    **[8.64]**

---

**EXAMPLE 8.3**

Num Ltd paid its employee, Sid, £1,000 to compensate him for the anguish he suffered as a result of his wife running off with the milkman. The payment may be non-taxable in Sid's hands as compensation for his suffering rather than a reward for services.

---

## 5  Payments on variation of terms of employment

Payments are sometimes made to employees when a benefit is withdrawn (and note *Hamblett v Godfrey* (1987), discussed at **[8.42]**, which relates to compensation paid when a right was relinquished). With very few exceptions the courts have held that such payments are taxable whether they were gratuitous—because the employee had no right to the benefit which was removed—or could be seen as compensation for breach of contract on the employer unilaterally withdrawing a contractual right.

Where the employee is to receive a smaller salary in the future, as in *Cameron v Prendergast* (1940) and *Tilley v Wales* (1943), the lump sum is taxable. In *Bird v Martland* (1982) compensation was paid following withdrawal of company cars (which did not cause a breach of contract); in *McGregor v Randall* (1984) a contractual right to receive commission was withdrawn: in both cases the compensation was taxable.

Lump sum compensation payments have, however, been held not to be taxable where the taxpayer gave up a contingent right which would have provided him with a benefit *after* his employment had ceased, even if the benefit would have been taxable: see *Hunter v Dewhurst* (1932) where compensation was payable under the articles of association when a director gave up his office; and *Tilley v Wales* (above) where the taxpayer was (also) entitled to a pension on retirement.

There is some difficulty in reconciling these two groups of cases. In the House of Lords' judgment in *Mairs v Haughey* (1993) (see **[8.42]**), Lord Woolf said that a 'payment made to satisfy a contingent right to a payment derives its character from the nature of the payment which it replaces' (the matching principle). On this basis, sums paid to 'buy out' the employees' contingent rights to redundancy payments under a non-statutory redundancy scheme were not taxable, since the redundancy payments themselves would not have been taxable. This suggests that if the benefit itself would have been taxable, then a lump sum compensation payment following its withdrawal would also be taxable. However, the Northern Ireland Court of Appeal held in *Mairs v Haughey* (1992) that 'even if a payment under the enhanced redundancy scheme was taxable, a payment to secure the termination of [the employee's] rights under the scheme would not be taxable as an emolument from the employment' on the basis of *Hunter v Dewhurst* (above). Although not necessary to the decision, Lord Woolf in *Mairs* indicated that he was not:

'persuaded that this aspect of the Court of Appeal of Northern Ireland's decision was incorrect or that *Hunter v Dewhurst* was wrongly decided. This is because for the Revenue to succeed, the Revenue would have to establish, contrary to my provisional view, that the lump sum payment was in the nature of an income payment before it could begin to qualify as being chargeable to tax under Schedule E.'

This is an unorthodox approach: the income/capital distinction has generally been considered irrelevant to the issue of the taxability of employment income. Given that this was only his provisional view, Lord Woolf's suggestion that the nature of the payment affected whether it was taxable under Schedule E should not be relied on too heavily, particularly as the end–result could be difficult to reconcile with the matching principle he previously had enunciated.

Finally, as these sorts of compensation payments may be taxable under Part 3 Chapter 10, s 225 (restrictive undertakings) or Part 6 Chapter 3 if not taxable under the general charging provision, the reader is referred to Section IX Parts 3–5 of this Chapter.                    **[8.65]**

## 6  Unearned income

A payment may be taxable as earnings even though it would, in other circumstances, be treated as unearned income.

David O'Leary, like Peter Shilton, was a professional footballer. He was domiciled in the Republic of Ireland and entered into an arrangement, designed to avoid income tax, with his employers, Arsenal FC. An offshore trust was established with O'Leary as life tenant and the sum of £266,000 was lent to the trust by Arsenal, interest–free and repayable on demand. The income produced by this sum (£28,985 pa) was payable to O'Leary but, so it was argued, because the sum fell to be taxed under Schedule D Case V and because O'Leary was non-UK domiciled, tax would not arise unless and until that sum was remitted to the UK (see **[18.34]**). Once O'Leary ceased to be employed by Arsenal the loan would be repaid. Vinelott J decided that the annual interest was correctly assessed as an emolument. He commented:

'The fallacy which I think underlies Counsel for the taxpayer's submission can be shortly stated. If an employer lends money to an employee free of interest or at a favourable rate of interest and if the employee is free to exploit the money in any manner he chooses his employment cannot be said to have been the source of the income derived from the exploitation; the employer is the source of the money and the taxpayer is assessable to tax under Schedule E on the benefit to him of obtaining the loan on the terms on which the loan was made; but if the loan is repayable on demand that benefit cannot be quantified and form the basis of an assessment under Schedule E [but see **[8.123]** as employer loans are now subject to tax]. By contrast if an employer were to lend money to a bank on terms that interest was paid to the employee until further order the interest paid to him while he remains an employee would almost inevitably be taxable as an emolument of his employment ...' (*O'Leary v McKinlay* (1991))                                    **[8.66]–[8.90]**


## VII   WHAT ARE EARNINGS?

## 1   **Introduction**

As we have seen in Section II, TA 1988 s 19(1) para 1 taxed 'emoluments' from an office or employment. That term was partially defined in s 131 as including 'all salaries, fees, wages, perquisites and profits whatsoever'. This was wide enough to cover benefits in kind as well as cash payments. Limits were, however, imposed on its meaning by the courts. The major restriction was that a benefit to an employee was only taxable under s 19 if it was convertible into money or was of direct monetary value to the employee (the prime example of the latter being the discharge of a personal debt of the employee).

ITEPA 2003 s 9 taxes 'general earnings' from an employment. General earnings are defined in s 7 and are made up of 'earnings' and amounts treated as earnings. The former replaces 'emoluments' and is defined in s 62 as follows:

'(2)   "earnings" means (a) any salary, wages or fee, (b) any gratuity or other profit or incidental benefit of any kind obtained by the employee if it is money or money's worth, or (c) anything else that constitutes an emolument of the employment.

(3)    "money's worth" means something that is (a) of direct monetary value to the employee, or (b) capable of being converted into money or something of direct monetary value to the employee.'

The change in wording at the beginning of (2)(b) reflects the Rewrite Project's aim of modernising the language of the legislation; the additional words at the end reflect the way the common law had interpreted 'emoluments'; (c) is to ensure that anything which would have been an emolument under the old law but does not fall within (a) or (b) will still be caught, though it is hard to imagine what that could be, given the width of (b). The old authorities on the meaning of emoluments and those on how an emolument is to be valued for tax purposes, which are all reflected in (3), are discussed in **[8.92]** and **[8.93]**.

Clearly, not all the types of benefits that an employee might receive will be 'earnings', so it is not surprising that over the years the legislature has brought other benefits within the tax net; in the main, those statutory provisions now apply to all employees, though 'lower-paid' employees escape some of them. That statutory regime and its relationship with the general charging provision is considered in Section VIII. The remainder of this Section considers further the general principles which apply to all employees.                                                                                    **[8.91]**

## 2 The general principles

### a) *Money or money's worth*

*Tennant v Smith* (1892) is the leading case on the convertibility requirement. In that case, the House of Lords, in interpreting the equivalent of the old s 131, held that the benefit of a house, which the employee was required by his employment to occupy but which he could not assign or sub-let, did not constitute an emolument since it was not convertible into money. The test is whether the benefit *could* be lawfully converted; it is irrelevant whether the employee actually converts it into money. Consider, for instance, a rail season ticket which cannot be sold because it is non-assignable, but which can be converted into cash by surrender.

Although in *Abbott v Philbin* (1961) Lord Reid stated 'if a right can be turned to pecuniary account that in itself is enough to make it a perquisite', the Special Commissioner in *Bootle v Bye* (1996) thought that this was not intended to apply 'regardless of whether any payment obtainable would be heavily depreciated'. He accordingly held that a right to receive a cash sum if the employing company was sold (an event over which the taxpayer had no control) was not a perquisite as, realistically, any payment he could obtain from a third party in relation to that right would in no way reflect the right's intrinsic value. It will be interesting to see whether higher courts adopt this approach.

*Nicoll v Austin* (1935) shows how a payment of direct monetary benefit to an employee will be taxable. In that case a managing director told his employer company that he would have to sell his imposing house, where he entertained potential customers, because he could no longer afford to pay for its upkeep. To prevent the sale, the company paid the outgoings on the house and the employee was taxed on this sum as if he had been given the money to pay the bills himself. Similarly in *Richardson v Worrall* (1985) payment for petrol using an employer's credit card was held taxable since it discharged the taxpayer's liability to the garage.                     **[8.92]**

### EXAMPLE 8.4

Simon is employed as a butler at a wage of £100 pw. He is required to 'live in' and £20 is deducted per week for board and lodging. Simon is assessed to tax on £100 pw (see *Machon v McLoughlin* (1926)). Compare the case of Rosie, who is employed as a housemaid and is paid a weekly wage of £95. She is required to live in but is not charged for board and lodging. She is taxed on £95; the board and lodging is a non-convertible benefit in kind which, therefore, escapes tax under s 9.

### b) *Valuing the benefit*

If the benefit is convertible, tax is levied on the value of the benefit to the employee: this is taken to be its secondhand value. In *Wilkins v Rogerson* (1961) the company arranged with a firm of tailors that each employee would be permitted to obtain clothes of up to £15 in value. The contract provided for payment directly by the company. When HMRC sought to tax an employee on a suit costing £14.50 the court held that the benefit was convertible into money, because the taxpayer could sell the suit, but that he could only be taxed on the secondhand value, estimated at £5 (see also *Jenkins v Horn* (1979), where this test operated to the taxpayer's disadvantage).

The practical application of these two principles can cause problems. For instance, the provision of a non-convertible benefit, such as the free use of a car, is not chargeable as earnings, whereas the provision of money to enable the employee to purchase such a benefit does constitute earnings (see *Bird v Martland* (1982)). A further problem (which mainly arises where an employee agrees to reduce his cash salary in return for a benefit—often known as 'salary sacrifice') is that it may be difficult to decide whether particular facts involve the rules on benefits in kind or not. This is illustrated by the case of *Heaton v Bell* (1970) where a company operated a scheme under which its employees were offered the use of fully insured company cars. If they accepted the offer they thereupon received reduced wages. An employee could withdraw from the scheme on giving 14 days' notice whereupon he would revert to his original wage. The House of Lords by a majority of four to one held that an employee who joined the scheme was entitled to his original unamended wage and that he had merely chosen to spend a portion of that wage on the hire of a car (but see Lord Reid's dissenting judgment). Thus tax was charged on the full wage since what the taxpayer chooses to spend his wages on is not tax-deductible! Three members of the House also considered that, if the full wage was not taxable, then the car was a taxable benefit in kind because, even though the right to use the car could not be assigned, it could be converted into money by withdrawing from the scheme and receiving the original wage again. The value of the benefit was the wage foregone.                                                   **[8.93]**

**EXAMPLE 8.5**

(1)    Employees are given £40 to buy clothes to wear to work. The sum is earnings.
(2)    Employees buy clothes on credit and they send the bills to the employer for payment. As the debt has been incurred by the employee, tax will be charged in accordance with *Nicoll v Austin* (1935).
(3)    The employer enters into an arrangement with Sparks and Menacer Co Ltd that it will pay for work outfits chosen by its employees up to £100 each. The employees are taxable but on the second-hand value of the clothes, not their cost.
NB    It is assumed that the exemption in ITEPA 2003 s 367 for special clothing does not apply.

## 3    Expenses

### a)    *What counts as earnings?*

If a lower-paid employee (ie one not subject to all the provisions of the benefits code—see Section VIII) receives an 'expense allowance', it will be presumed to be a reimbursement of expenditure unless HMRC can show it to be earnings; higher-paid employees and directors have to prove actual deductible expenditure (see **[8.114]**) in order to avoid the reimbursement being taxable.

Where an employee incurs expenses which the employer reimburses, those reimbursements will not be taxed as earnings, provided that the employee could have deducted the money he spent from his employment income as an expense of the employment. In such cases it can be said that the employee has derived no personal profit from the reimbursement (in the sense that he is no better off) and, in addition, no practical purpose would be served by deciding that the reimbursement is earnings but then permitting the employee to reduce those earnings to nil by setting off an equivalent expense (see ITEPA 2003 s 336 and Section XI for a discussion of what expenditure is deductible and **[8.114]** for the position of employees and directors who are not lower-paid). It has been suggested that payments to an employee to reimburse him for the cost of using his home as an office are in fact taxable under ITTOIA 2005, thus avoiding these problems (see *Taxation*, 13 July 2000, p 386 and note that the absence of 'a separate agreement with a specific payment for an office involving use by persons in addition to the taxpayer' was fatal to the claim in *Ainslie v Buckley* (2002)).

In *Pook v Owen* (1970) a doctor holding a part-time hospital appointment and who had to attend the hospital several times a week was reimbursed two-thirds of his travelling expenses. It was held that the reimbursements were not emoluments because he was no 'better off' as a result of them. They were (partial) repayments of actual expenditure which would have been deductible in arriving at the emoluments of the taxpayer.

In other cases, however, reimbursements have been held not to be emoluments even though the relevant expenditure would not have been deductible by the employee. Thus, in *Donnelly v Williamson* (1982), a teacher who was reimbursed for travelling expenses incurred in attending out-of-school functions was not taxable on the reimbursements. The court held that they were not emoluments because they were not derived from her employment (she attended the functions voluntarily) and that they were a genuine attempt to compensate her for actual expenditure. Compare *Perrons v Spackman* (1981) where a mileage allowance paid by the council to one of its rent officers was held to be an emolument because it contained a profit element.

If it is accepted that there is no correlation between the reimbursement rules and the test for deductibility of expenditure under ITEPA 2003, it is not clear exactly what expenses may be reimbursed without giving rise to a tax charge. Presumably, the expense must be directly connected with the employment, since the reimbursement of, eg the employee's private gas bill will be taxed as earnings (*Nicoll v Austin* at **[8.92]**). **[8.94]**

**EXAMPLE 8.6**

Justinian, a part–time and therefore low–paid law lecturer, attends a legal conference and his university employers refund the cost of the conference which he had paid. The reimbursements are not earnings taxable under s 9. If the university had instead paid for the conference so that he had received a benefit in kind, Justinian would be taxed on it if it was convertible. If Justinian had borne the expenses himself, he would have been unable to deduct them from his earnings under ITEPA 2003 s 336 (see **[8.173]**).

b) *Exemptions*

ITEPA 2003 s 240 provides a specific exemption where an employer reimburses (or pays directly for) incidental expenses (eg for newspapers and private telephone calls) incurred by an employee during overnight absences, up to an allowable maximum (currently, £5 for stays in the UK and £10 for those abroad): such expenditure would not normally be deductible under s 336 as it would not be necessarily incurred in the performance of the employee's duties. If the maxima are exceeded, the exemption does not apply to *any* part of the payment (s 241); nor does it apply if the costs of the employee's travel to his overnight rest place are not deductible (unless that is because of an exemption) (s 240(4)). HMRC seem to accept that the exemption applies to round sum allowances to be used to pay such expenses (EI 02760).

ITEPA 2003 ss 250–254 provide an exemption from income tax where the employer (or a third party—for instance, when a manufacturer organises training for a retailer's staff) reimburses (or pays directly for) the cost of 'work-related training' or 'related costs' (see *Tax Bulletin*, April 2003, p 1022 on the application of these provisions where an employer reimburses the cost of training before the employment began, in response to the Special Commissioners' decision in *Silva v Charnock* (2002)). Sections 255–260 exist merely to deal with situations where the employer wishes to contribute to 'non-work-related training' undertaken by employees who are individual learning account holders (eg skills development courses) ('work-related training' is covered by ss 250–254). Individual learning accounts were discontinued throughout the UK in 2001, but were reintroduced in Wales by the Welsh Assembly in 2003 by way of Welsh SI 2003/918.    **[8.95]–[8.110]**

## VIII    AMOUNTS TREATED AS EARNINGS OR COUNTED AS EMPLOYMENT INCOME

### 1    Introduction

Employees are taxed on 'employment income' and this is made up of: (1) earnings (defined in s 62, which constitutes Part 3 Chapter 1 of the Act, and already considered in Section VII 1); (2) amounts treated as earnings; and (3) 'amounts which count as employment income' (ITEPA 2003 s 7 and see **[8.11]**). This Section considers the majority of the taxing provisions covered by the last two categories; others are dealt with elsewhere because of the nature of the benefit to which they relate.

Category (2) incorporates the 'benefits code' (the provisions in Part 3 Chapters 2–11 of the Act) which brings certain benefits in kind within the employment tax net. Chapters 8 and 9 (notional loans in respect of the acquisition of employee shares and disposals of shares by employees for more than market value) had very short legislative histories as they were repealed by FA 2003 in relation to shares acquired after 15 April 2003: their replacements are in ITEPA 2003 Part 7 and are considered in **Chapter 9**. Unfortunately, the neat label 'benefits code' does not encompass all the provisions within (2) (see s 7(5)). As well as those provisions which constitute the code, the following provisions also treat amounts received as earnings: those relating to agency workers and intermediaries (see Section IV); payments (NB not 'amounts') treated as earnings under Part 3 Chapter 12 (ss 221, 225 and 226 are discussed in this Section, ss 222 and 223 in Section XII and s 224 in **Chapter 50**) and balancing charges covered by CAA 2001 s 262.

Category (3) covers share-related income (ITEPA 2003 Part 7, considered in **Chapter 9**) and 'income which is not earnings or share-related' as set out in Part 6 of the Act (Chapters 1 and 2 of which are considered in **Chapter 50** and Chapter 3 of which is considered in Section IX of this Chapter).

Not all payments and benefits which would be 'employment income' are actually taxed as there is a wide range of exemptions. Many can be found in ITEPA 2003 Part 4 (see Section X) but others are scattered throughout the Act. It is therefore important to check carefully whether any exemptions apply when calculating taxable earnings.                                    **[8.111]**

## 2  The purpose of the special rules

It is clear that the consequence of the courts' interpretation of the term 'emoluments' (see Section VII) was that many benefits received by employees were not made subject to income tax under the general charging provision (because they were not convertible); and that those benefits which were brought within the income tax net were often taxed on a low value. The purpose of the special rules introduced over time has been to bring many benefits in kind within the income tax net *even if not convertible into cash* or increase the taxable value of those already within that net.

As a general rule, the old benefits in kind legislation did not apply if the benefit was already taxable under the general charging provision in TA 1988 s 19. There was always a certain ambiguity about the relationship between the two when the amount taxed under s 19 was less than that which would have been taxed under the benefits in kind provisions. This has been resolved by ITEPA 2003: where there might be some overlap, s 64 provides that (except in the case of living accommodation) if the same benefit could give rise to an amount of 'earnings' *and* 'an amount to be treated as earnings under the benefits code', it will first be taxed as earnings and only the excess will be taxed under the benefits code.

### EXAMPLE 8.7

The facts are as in *Wilkinson v Rogerson* (1961) (see **[8.93]**):
(1)   a lower-paid employee would still be taxed on £5;
(2)   any other employee would be taxed on £5 as earnings and £9.50 as an amount to be treated as earnings.

One other purpose of the special rules has been to tax benefits which were not caught by the general charging provision because they were not 'from' employment (see Sections V and VI). TA 1988 s 154 (the old general benefits in kind charging provision) therefore taxed benefits provided 'by reason of employment'.

The Northern Ireland Court of Appeal in *Mairs v Haughey* (1992) thought these words were wider than the word 'therefrom' in s 19 (accepting that s 19 imposed a 'reward for services' test) and that the question to be asked is 'what enabled [the employee] to enjoy the benefit?' In addition, benefits provided by an employer could be *deemed* to have been provided by reason of employment (see TA 1988 s 168(3)). The benefits code in ITEPA adopts the same causation test; when benefits are provided by an employer, the test is deemed to be satisfied (subject to an exception if the employer is an individual and the benefit is provided in the normal course of his personal relationships—see, for instance, ITEPA 2003 s 73). If the benefit is provided by a third party, causation has to be proved.    **[8.112]**

## 3  The benefits code

### a)  *Who is excluded from the benefits code?*

The old approach was to make all employees and directors subject to tax on certain specified non–cash benefits; but only directors and 'higher-paid' employees were subject to the *general* benefit in kind charging provision and also only they were taxed on some other specified benefits. As the amount of employment income which was required to make someone 'higher-paid' (£8,500) did not increase over time, the term was dropped in the recasting of the employment income framework in ITEPA, though the structure of the charging provisions remains the same. ITEPA 2003 now reflects the fact that very few directors and employees do not earn at least £8,500 per annum by applying the 'benefits code' to all employees and then stating in s 216 which parts of it do not apply to lower-paid employees. All the amounts treated as earnings by Part 3 Chapter 12 which are considered in this Section are taxable in the hands of all employees; as are all those which count as employment income as a result of Part 6 Chapter 3 of the Act.

Section 217 defines 'lower-paid employment' as one where the earnings for the year are less than £8,500. To determine whether the employee has earnings of £8,500, it is assumed that the employee is within the special rules; those rules are therefore applied in valuing the benefits and only if the resultant figure for earnings is below £8,500 is he taxed as lower–paid. *Allcock v King* (2004) revealed how the wording of TA 1988 s 167 required the provision of free fuel (paid for using the employer's credit card) to be taken into account twice when calculating whether the threshold was reached: the same is true under ITEPA 2003 s 218 (see s 219(5)) and HMRC has issued ESC A104 to prevent the same benefit being taken into account twice.

#### EXAMPLE 8.8

Aziz receives a salary of £8,100 pa and an expense allowance of £400 (which is taxed as employment income for an employee who is not lower paid). He is treated as receiving employment income of £8,500 pa and is, therefore, within the special rules.

A director whose earnings are less than £8,500 pa is also excluded from certain provisions of the benefits code *provided* he has no material interest in the company (ie he does not control more than 5% of the ordinary share capital) and either works full-time for the company or the company is non-profit making or a charity (ITEPA 2003 s 216(3)). The long-standing debate about whether the benefits in kind legislation extends to 'shadow directors' (see ITEPA 2003 s 67) was resolved in favour of HMRC by *R v Allen* (2001).    **[8.113]**

b)   *Expense payments*

Under ITEPA 2003 ss 70–72, if an employee or director who is not lower–paid receives an expense allowance or a reimbursement of expenses that he has incurred, he is taxed on it in full as an amount treated as earnings unless he can claim any deductible expenses. This forces the employee to justify his expenses. There is an exemption for reimbursements of actual expenditure on 'incidental overnight expenses', up to the permitted maximum (see [8.95]).   [8.114]

### EXAMPLE 8.9

Andy has a salary of £9,000 pa and an expense allowance of £4,000 pa. He is taxed on £13,000 pa as an amount treated as earnings unless he can deduct any expenses under ITEPA 2003 Part 5.

c)   *Vouchers and credit tokens*

An employee or office-holder who (or a member of whose family) receives a benefit in the form of a voucher or credit–token may be charged to tax thereon. The tax charge crystallises when the voucher is received or the token used (unless there is a dispensation under s 96), and therefore the receipt of money, goods or services resulting from its use is not taxable (s 95): this avoids double taxation.

Where the employee receives a cash voucher (ie a voucher which can be exchanged for a sum of money not substantially less than the cost to the person providing it), he is taxed on its exchange value (s 81).

Where he receives a non-cash voucher (ie a voucher or similar document which can be exchanged for goods or services only and not for cash), he is taxed on the cost to the employer of providing the voucher rather than on its exchange value (s 87). Cheque vouchers (ie a cheque provided for an employee to be used by him to obtain goods or services) are treated as non-cash vouchers by s 84 and are therefore similarly charged as earnings.

Where the employee receives a credit–token (including a credit card), he is taxed on the cost to the employer of providing the goods, money and services obtained by the use of that credit token less any part of the cost made good by the employee (s 94).

The employee will not be taxed if the voucher or token is made available to the public generally and he (or a member of his family) does not receive it on more favourable terms (ss 78, 85 and 93). Part 3 Chapter 4 contains other exemptions: for instance, a cash voucher is not taxable if it intended to enable the employee to obtain a payment which would not have been taxable if paid to him directly (s 80). Other exemptions can be found in ITEPA 2003 Part 4, particularly Chapter 6.

Also, HMRC has the power to exempt the provision of certain vouchers and credit tokens as representing a taxable benefit where the voucher or credit token enables an employee to obtain specified benefits which are exempt from taxation under the benefits code (s 96A). HMRC will specify on a case-by-case basis (by way of regulations) the vouchers and credit tokens which benefit from this exemption.   [8.115]

## d)    *Living accommodation*

The leading case on a benefit escaping the general charging provision because it was not convertible into money or money's worth related to employer-provided accommodation (*Tennant v Smith* (1892)—see **[8.92]**). It is not therefore surprising to find that there has long been a statutory provision bringing such a benefit within the tax net.

As a result of ITEPA 2003 s 102, the cash equivalent of the benefit of accommodation is to be treated as earnings for all employees. The charge is divided into two parts: the first calculates the benefit derived from accommodation where the cost of providing it does not exceed £75,000; the second calculates the benefit received when the accommodation costs more than that (see below for how the 'cost' of a property is ascertained). An employee is only taxed on accommodation provided whilst he is actually in employ-ment (s 102(1)).                                                                 **[8.116]**

### i)    *The basic charge*

If an employer *provides* his employee with living accommodation, the employee is taxed on the value to him of that accommodation less any sum that he 'makes good' (normally by paying for the use of the property) (ITEPA 2003 s 105).

In *Stones v Hall* (1989), the court concluded that the provision of services in return for accommodation was, for the purposes of TA 1988 s 145(1) (now ITEPA 2003 ss 105(2) and 106(2)), neither the payment of rent nor the making good of the cost to the company of providing that accommodation. Accordingly, the taxpayer was charged on the value of the accommodation.

If the employee owns a share of the property, so that he and the employer each have an undivided beneficial share in it, there is an argument that, since the employee already has a right to occupy the accommodation rent–free, it is not '*provided*' by the employer. It is clear from HMRC's Employment Income Manual that HMRC sometimes equates 'provided' with 'being avail-able' and claims a tax charge based on the period of availability, not actual use: see *Taxation*, 18 October 2001, pp 51–53 and 15 November 2001, p 170 for two criticisms; and note the interpretation of 'provided' in TA 1988 s 154 in *Templeton v Jacobs* ((1996)—see **[8.124]**).

The value on which the employee is charged is the higher of the rental value of the premises (defined in s 105(3) as based on the annual value, which itself is defined in s 110) and the rent paid by the employer for that accommodation (s 105) (see *Toronto-Dominion Bank v Oberoi* (2004) where the employing bank successfully converted rental payments into a premium and thus reduced the charge under TA 1988 s 145). Using the annual value as the basis for calculating the rental value may result in a lower sum being charged to tax than if the market rent (ie that which would be received if the property were actually let) were used; and if the employer owns the premises, the alternative charge cannot apply.                                                **[8.117]**

### ii)    *The additional charge*

Special rules apply in cases where the cost of providing the accommodation exceeds £75,000 (s 106). First, what would be the cash equivalent under s 105 is calculated. Then, broadly, additional earnings are calculated by applying the official rate of interest (as under beneficial loans—see [8.123]) to the amount by which the cost of providing the accommodation exceeds £75,000. Cost for these purposes will usually be the cost of acquiring the property (though there are special rules in s 107 for calculating the cost under s 106 if the person providing the accommodation has held an interest in it for at least six years when the employee first occupies it). The two amounts added together constitute the taxable benefit.

**EXAMPLE 8.10**

Giles, the managing director of Clam Ltd, sells to the company his house in Manchester for its market value of £160,000. He is granted an option to buy the property back in ten years' time for its present value. The rental value of the house is £750 and Giles continues to live in the property. Giles is assessed to tax under ITEPA 2003 on earnings of £750 pa plus (say) 5% of £85,000 (£160,000 – £75,000), ie £4,250 pa.                                                    [8.118]

*iii)   Increasing and decreasing the charge*

At one time, employers were offering employees a low cash alternative to accommodation, in the hope of reducing the tax charge on accommodation actually occupied (relying on *Heaton v Bell* (1970)—see [8.122]). Now Part 3 Chapter 5 applies even in that situation. Of course, if the cash offered is *higher* than the amount taxable thereunder, that higher amount will be taxed (s 109)!

Where employer-provided accommodation is in multiple occupation, s 108 limits the total amount chargeable to what it would have been if it was occupied by one employee; and this is then apportioned amongst the employees in accordance with what is 'just and reasonable'.            [8.119]

*iv)   Exemptions*

The charge under s 105 does not catch the provision of ancillary services such as cleaning, repairs and furniture. However, if the employee or director is not lower paid, the cost to the employer of providing those services (less any amount paid by the employee for them) will fall within ITEPA 2003 s 203 (but note that there is a cap on the taxable amount if the employee is in 'representative accommodation'—s 315).

No charge arises for 'representative occupation'. This means occupation falling within ss 99(1) and (2) and 100, ie accommodation which is:
(1)   necessary for the proper performance of the employee's duties (eg a caretaker and see *Tennant v Smith* (1892) at [8.92]); or
(2)   customary for the better performance of the employee's duties (eg a police officer who occupies a police house adjacent to the police station); or
(3)   where there is a special threat to his security and special security arrangements are in force as a result of which he resides in that accommodation.
A director can only be a representative occupier under (1) or (2) above if he has no material interest and he is either employed full-time or the company is either non-profit-making or charitable (s 99(3)).

In *Vertigan v Brady* (1988) the owner of a nursery site near Norwich provided his 'right-hand man' with a rent-free bungalow some three miles from the nursery. That employee was in direct charge of the plants and their propagation and was on standby at all hours during the week and on two out of three weekends to make adjustments to the heating and ventilation of the greenhouses. He was able to reach the nursery within five minutes of leaving the bungalow. There was evidence that he had been unable to obtain council accommodation in the area when he took the job and could not afford to buy a house in the vicinity. The court decided that the benefit of the rent-free accommodation was taxable since the exception for accommodation which was customarily provided ((2) above) did not apply. What was customary depended upon three main factors: statistical evidence (how common was the practice?); how long had the practice existed (a custom does not grow up overnight!); and whether the relevant employer accepted the customary practice. In this case, although statistical evidence showed that approximately two-thirds of all key nursery workers were provided with rent-free accommodation, there was insufficient evidence to show that the practice had become so normal as to be an established custom.                    **[8.120]**

*v) Non-domiciliaries*

Whether the charge on living accommodation is capable of applying to shadow directors has long been a matter of debate: the issue is especially important when a non-UK domiciliary purchases a UK house for personal occupation through a foreign company. If it can be shown that he is a shadow director of that company, can he then be assessed on benefits derived from occupying the property? In *R v Allen* (2001) the House of Lords answered this question in the affirmative. However, it should be noted that in that case the money to purchase the UK property derived from the trading profits of the offshore company whereas in most cases it derives from money given or lent to the company by the non-UK domiciliary. For an interesting argument as to whether, in such cases, it can be said that the property is provided at the 'cost' of the non-UK company, as the legislation requires, or whether, if it is, the shadow director 'makes good' that cost, see Brandon, *Offshore and International Taxation Review* (2000) 135 and see *Example 36.2.*                    **[8.121]**

*e) Vehicles and fuel*

ITEPA 2003 Part 3 Chapter 6 brings into the tax net, for employees and directors who are not lower–paid, the benefit that they derive from an employer-provided car or van which is available for their private use (s 114). Tax is not, therefore, charged if the employee can prove that he was forbidden to use the vehicle for private use and did not so use it (*Gilbert v Hemsley* (1981) and see s 118). A lower-paid employee will not be taxed on this benefit because it is not convertible into cash. Generally, any benefit received from the private use of a 'heavier commercial vehicle' is exempt from tax, provided the employee's use of the vehicle is not wholly or mainly private use (s 238).

*i)* *Pooled cars and vans*

The legislation distinguishes between two categories of car and van: the pooled car or van and all others. A pooled vehicle is one which is made available to different employees, is normally garaged overnight at the employer's premises, and any private use is merely incidental to its business use (see ss 167 and 168 for the exact conditions—and see SP 2/96 and s 295 in relation particularly to the position when a pooled car is used for chauffeur-driven home to work journeys for a senior employee; and IR 480 for a discussion of what is 'merely incidental' private use). When these conditions are satisfied, the benefits of using pooled cars or vans are not taxable.

*ii)* *Non-pooled cars*

If a non-pooled car is available for the private use of an employee or his family or household, he is taxed on the cash equivalent of the car as fixed by statute (ITEPA 2003 ss 114 and 120). Section 114 (1) (a) limits the application of Part 3 Chapter 6 to a car which is made available to the employee 'without any transfer of the property in it'. In *Vasili v Christensen* the courts had to decide whether the purchase by the employee of a 5% interest in a car owned by his employer prevented the company car provisions applying (and, if so, whether the (smaller) residual benefit in kind charge applied instead). The Special Commissioner (2003) held that the company car provisions did not apply but the benefits in kind ones did; but the High Court (2004) overturned that decision and held that the former continued to apply on the basis that s 132 must be taken to deal with the situation where the employee acquires an interest in the car following a capital contribution to its purchase.

In *Kerr v Brown* (2002), the Special Commissioners held that the use of vehicles provided to senior officers in the fire brigade which, it was agreed, were not 'cars' for the purposes of these provisions (because they were not commonly used as private vehicles and were unsuitable to be so used—see now s 115(1)) was caught by the general benefits in kind charge (now ITEPA 2003 Part 3 Chapter 10). ITEPA 2003 s 248A now contains an exemption where members of the emergency services take home emergency vehicles when on call.

There are two regimes in ITEPA 2003 for taxing company cars. Readers are referred to earlier editions of this book for that relating to cars registered before 1 January 1998. This edition considers the regime for cars registered after 31 December 1997. The policy behind this regime is to 'help tackle global warming and improve local air quality'. Therefore, the tax charge is linked to the car's $CO_2$ emissions. The starting–point is the car's list price but the percentage of that which is the 'cash equivalent' (the amount to be treated as earnings) depends on the level of $CO_2$ emissions (see s 139); it ranges from 15% to 35%. High business mileage or the fact that the car is older will not decrease the cash equivalent as it did under the old regime; use of a diesel car will in general increase it beyond what it would be based on the $CO_2$ emissions (as diesels emit greater quantities of air pollutants); cars which are capable of running on 'alternative' fuel (such as electric, hybrid and bi-fuel cars) attract a reduced percentage.

In order to avoid the statutory charge (and Class 1A NICs), some employers offered a (low) cash alternative, so that under *Heaton v Bell* (1970) (see [8.93]) earnings would be based only on (and the employers' NICs based on) the salary foregone. Section 119 means that the mere fact that a cash alternative is offered will not make the use of a company car taxable as earnings under the general charging provision. The employee will pay tax on what he actually receives—the car or the cash.

*iii)    Reducing the tax charge*

The amount of tax payable can be reduced if the employee is required to make a payment for the private use of the vehicle or if it is unavailable for at least 30 days (ss 143 and 144 and see s 145 where the car is temporarily replaced); or if the employee makes capital contributions (s 132). Reliance on any of these provisions is not straightforward: for instance, any payments must clearly be for the private use, so a payment for insurance premiums, required by the agreement with the employer, did not reduce the cash equivalent in *IRC v Quigley* (1995) because they were made 'in exchange for the insurance of the vehicle, not for the use of it'.

Problems also arise where contributions are made in order to receive a more expensive car. While HMRC may allow these to be deducted from the cash equivalent if the agreement is properly worded (see *Tax Bulletin*, November 1991, p 3), it is easy to fail to satisfy the (literally interpreted) words of s 144 (previously TA 1988 Sch 6 para 7—see *Brown v Ware* (1995)). It is not even certain that *monthly* contributions will count as capital payments for the purpose of s 132.

HMRC interprets 'unavailability' in s 143 strictly, so the fact that, for instance, the employee is out of the country for three months and cannot in fact then use the car may not be sufficient.

*iv)    Use of own car*

If employees use their own car for business travel, they may get tax relief for their journeys (see [8.174]). If the employer reimburses expenses, the employee will be taxable on any profit element. To support a claim for relief or to calculate if there is any profit, a statutory system of mileage rates now applies (and this extends to payments made to an employee because he carries another employee who is travelling on business) (see ss 229–236 and IR 124).

*v)    Fuel and other benefits*

There is a separate scale charge on the provision of petrol for private use in an employer's car (ss 149–153) which is linked to the $CO_2$ emissions of the company car. See *Tax Bulletin*, August 2005, p 1218 for the advisory fuel rates for company cars. These rates can be used by employers to either reimburse employees for business travel in their company cars and/or require employees to repay the cost of fuel used for private travel. Reimbursement/repayment made within these rates should prevent an employment income and Class 1 NICs charge.

The provision of a personal chauffeur for an employee is a taxable benefit under Part 3 Chapter 10 (but see the comment on pooled cars above). The employee is not taxed on other benefits provided in connection with the car such as insurance, road fund tax and a car parking space provided by the employer (ss 237, 239(4) and (5)). HMRC has confirmed that payment by the employer of the London Congestion Charge, in relation to a non-pooled car (or van) the provision of which gives rise to a benefit charge, is not a taxable benefit ([2003] STI 292 and 303).

*vi)   Non-pooled vans*

Vans available for private use were previously taxed under TA 1988 ss 154–166. Basically, the cash equivalent was £500 if the van was less than four years old at the end of the year; £350 if aged four or more years. There were special provisions to deal with shared vans. In May 2003, the government issued a consultation document on reforming the tax treatment of employer-provided vans to simplify the system and take into account the environmental impact of vans. As a consequence FA 2004 s 80 and Sch 14 substantially changed the tax treatment. From 6 April 2005 there is now no tax charge if any private use of the van other than for 'ordinary commuting' is 'insignificant' (see *Tax Bulletin*, October 2004, pp 1160 and 1161 for how to assess whether other private use is 'insignificant'); and the van is mainly used for the purposes of the employee's business travel (ITEPA s 155 as amended). If unrestricted private use is allowed, the old scale charges continue to apply and to include any private fuel provided by the employer. However, there will be further changes from 6 April 2007, increasing the scale charge to £3,000 and introducing a separate fuel charge of £500 if fuel is provided for unrestricted private use.

FA 2004 Sch 14 further amended ITEPA 2003 to introduce rules to reduce the cash equivalent when the van is unavailable or is shared; and to adjust it if the employee makes payments for its private use. There are similar provisions in relation to the fuel charge. Many of the points made in iii), iv) and v) will also apply in relation to these provisions.                              **[8.122]**

*f)   Beneficial loan arrangements*

Interest-free (or cheap) loans to employees were not caught under TA 1988 s 154 (the old general benefits in kind charge, now the residual liability in ITEPA 2003 Part 3 Chapter 10): if the loan is repayable on demand, the benefit cannot be quantified (see extract from *O'Leary v McKinlay* (1991) at **[8.66]**); in any event, if the money comes from the employer's own funds, then forgoing the opportunity to earn interest may not have been a 'cost' to the employer within s 154. Accordingly, a specific charging provision was introduced (originally TA 1988 s 160, now ITEPA 2003 Part 3 Chapter 7). This provides that where an employee or director who is not lower paid obtains a loan by reason of his employment (as to which, see s 174), either interest–free or at a low rate of interest, he is taxed on the cash equivalent of that loan. This is defined as the difference between interest for the year calculated at the 'official rate' and any interest actually paid by the employee. The 'official rate' is set by the Treasury under FA 1989 s 178 and is linked to commercial mortgage rates, so accordingly varies from time to time.

A beneficial loan is an 'employment-related loan' if it falls within ITEPA 2003 s 174. For the purposes of these provisions 'loan' includes 'any form of credit' (s 173(2)). The width of this definition is illustrated by *Grant v Watton* (1999), in which a service company paid the expenses of a partnership and was reimbursed haphazardly during the year, with the total service fee not being fixed until after the end of the year. It was held that this amounted to the provision of credit to a director of the service company who was also one of the partners because, in the absence of an agreement, the partnership owed the company money as soon as it was expended by the service company.

These provisions apply whenever a benefit is obtained because of an interest-free (or cheap interest) loan and it is not necessary to show that the employee derived any advantage therefrom. In *Williams v Todd* (1988), an inspector of taxes was taxed on an interest-free loan paid as a 'douceur to soften the financial and other disadvantages he had suffered as a result of his compulsory removal from Wigan to the more expensive South': he was taxable on the benefit.

There are two methods of calculating what would be the amount of interest due on the loan at the official rate—the normal and alternative methods (ss 182 and 183 and see s 186 in relation to replacement loans), the latter giving a more accurate figure where the amount outstanding fluctuates during the year. The following example deals with a straightforward situation, using the normal method of calculation.

**EXAMPLE 8.11**

Day, an employee of Digday Ltd, borrows £25,000 from his employer to purchase a suite of Italian furniture. He pays interest at 2% pa and the capital is to be repaid on demand. For 2005–06, Day has received an amount to be treated as earnings equal to:

|  | £ |
|---|---|
| Interest at official rate of 5% on £25,000 | 1,250 |
| Less: interest paid at 2% pa | 500 |
| Taxable amount | £750 |

A loan to a relative of the employee is also taxed unless the employee can show that he derived no benefit from it (s 174(1) and (5)).

If a loan to a relevant employee or director is released or written off, he is treated as receiving earnings equivalent to that amount, even if the release is made after the employment has become an 'excluded employment' (ie lower paid—see s 63(4)) or on (or after) the termination of his employment (unless the termination is due to his death) (ss 188, 189 and s 190). 'Golden handshakes' given in the form of the release of a loan will not have the benefit of the £30,000 exemption under Part 6 Chapter 3 (see **[8.154]**) and should, therefore, be avoided. It may, therefore, be more tax-efficient to make a tax-free payment to the employee which he then uses to repay the loan.

There is no charge to tax where the aggregate amount of all taxable cheap loans (ie loans to which the exceptions in ss 176–179 do not apply—see s 175(2)) outstanding at any time in the tax year does not exceed £5,000; or if the aggregate of 'non-qualifying' loans does not exceed this amount (s 180). This enables small loans (eg to buy a season ticket) to escape the tax net even if the employee has a larger 'qualifying' loan (eg a cheap mortgage). There are special rules on the aggregation of loans by a close company to a director (s 187). Loans provided on 'ordinary commercial terms' are exempted from the charge (s 176). This is to prevent an employee being subject to a tax charge if the rate of interest normally charged by his employer (being in the business of lending money or supplying goods or services on credit) is less than the official rate. There is also an exemption for certain types of fixed interest loan (s 177).

Sums advanced by the employer to cover expenses that will be necessarily incurred in the employment are not treated as earnings provided that the sum advanced is less than £1,000 and that the advance is spent within six months (these conditions may be relaxed on an application by the employer) (s 179).

There has always been a problem reconciling the beneficial loan charge with the provisions which give relief for 'qualifying loans' (basically, loans on which interest is eligible for relief under TA 1988 s 353(1)) when the employee uses the loan for a qualifying purpose. The position now is that loans will not be taxed if interest on the loan would qualify for relief if it were in fact payable and paid (s 178 and see s 184).

The benefit of a cheap or interest-free bridging loan provided when an employee has to move house because of his job may be exempted from tax: see ITEPA 2003 s 288 (**[8.162]**). **[8.123]**

### g)   *Taxable benefits—residual liability*

### i)   *The purpose of these rules*

The object of Part 3 Chapter 10 is to tax all benefits (except those which are taxed under Chapters 3 to 7, or would be but for an exception (s 202)) 'provided by reason of the employment' by any person (not just the employer) to an employee who is not lower-paid or his family *and whether or not convertible into cash*. These are called 'employment-related benefits' (s 201(2)).

In *Templeton v Jacobs* (1996), the court held that a benefit was 'provided' to an employee when the benefit in question became available to be enjoyed by the taxpayer (not when the employer had done everything it had to do to secure the provision of the benefit, as had been held by the Special Commissioner (1995)).

The courts have confirmed that the words 'by reason of the employment' (as used in the old general benefits in kind charging provision, TA 1988 s 154) cast a wider net than the words 'from employment' in the general charging provision—see further **[8.112].**

Generally, the cost incurred in providing the benefit is treated as the cash equivalent which is taxed, subject to a deduction for any payment made by the employee (ITEPA 2003 s 203). In *Rendell v Went* (1964) the managing director of a company had a car accident and was prosecuted at the Old Bailey for dangerous driving. The company paid for the legal services for him and he was acquitted. He was taxed on the cost to the company of providing the legal services (a non-convertible benefit in kind) although he did not request the benefit and could have found cheaper services elsewhere.

Finally, the purpose of s 201 is to bring 'benefits' into the tax net and the Northern Ireland Court of Appeal in *Mairs v Haughey* (1992) indicated that not every payment by an employer to an employee will be caught. In particular, they stated that a 'fair bargain' (in that case, reasonable compensation for employees surrendering rights under a non-statutory redundancy scheme) was not within TA 1988, s 154, the old general benefits in kind provision (see further [8.146]). That HMRC accepts that 'fair bargains' do not fall within ITEPA 2003 s 201 can be seen in the article on reimbursement of employees' bank charges in *Tax Bulletin*, June 2003, p 1039.

It should be noted that, whilst HMRC practice is not to apply s 201 to compensation payments on termination of employment (see [8.146]), it will seek to apply it to compensation for a change to the terms of an ongoing employment (see *Tax Bulletin*, June 2003, pp 1036 and 1037).          [8.124]

*ii)   The cost of providing the benefit*

ITEPA 2003 s 203 provides as follows:

'(1)   The cash equivalent of an employment-related benefit is to be treated as earnings from the employment ...
(2)    The cash equivalent ... is the cost of the benefit less any part of that cost made good by the employee ...'

Section 204 provides:

'The cost of an employment-related benefit is the expense incurred in or in connection with provision of the benefit (including a proper proportion of any expense relating partly to provision of the benefit and partly to other matters).'

In *Pepper v Hart* (1992), the taxpayers were assistant masters at Malvern College and each had one or more sons at the school under a concessionary fees scheme. Payments equal to 20% of the normal school fees were paid and it was accepted that these more than covered any *direct additional expense* resulting from the boys' presence in the school. The issue before the courts was whether what is now s 204 (then s 156(2)) was solely concerned with 'additional direct expenses' or involved a rateable proportion of the expenses incurred in providing the school facilities that were enjoyed generally by *all* the boys. The House of Lords held that, in the case of in-house benefits, the cost of the benefit to the employer was the additional (or marginal) cost and not a *pro rata* share of all the costs of the employer. It reached this decision by taking into account statements made by the Financial Secretary to the Treasury during Standing Committee debates on the Finance Bill 1976. The House's acceptance of the admissibility of extracts from *Hansard* in certain circumstances has wider implications than merely resolving the dispute in that case but taking *Hansard* into account did change the result here: the House would have found 4:1 in favour of HMRC if the argument based on *Hansard* had not been raised.

The effect of s 204 is to enable apportionment if the asset or service provided is used in the employer's business *other than* to provide a benefit for the employee: providing services or assets for the employee to perform his duties does not result in an apportionment because such provision 'is just as much a benefit within [section 204] as provision for the employee's private use' (see *Tax Bulletin*, October 2000). If the asset or service *is* used in performing the duties of his employment, the employee must claim a deduction under s 365 (previously s 156(8)). For a case where apportionment *was* appropriate, see *Kerr v Brown* (2002).

If an employee sells an asset to his employer for its market value, there could still be a charge in respect of the employer's other acquisition costs (eg legal fees). The charge could arise even if the purchase had nothing to do with the employment: if the employer is a company, because the carve–out from the general deeming provision in relation to employers who are individuals could not apply; if the employer is an individual, because the purchase could not be said to be 'in the normal course of his personal relationships' (see **[8.112]**). Section 326 (enacting ESC A85) relieves an employee from charge if the costs would normally have been incurred by any buyer. **[8.125]**

### iii)   Are cash payments caught?

The wording of s 204 would seem to indicate that s 203 does not apply to cash payments. However, the Court of Appeal held in *Wicks v Firth* (1982) that the old s 154 did apply to cash benefits (the House of Lords did not have to decide the point) and this approach was also taken by the Northern Ireland Court of Appeal in *Mairs v Haughey* (1992). **[8.126]**

### iv)   Do the rules apply before commencement and after termination?

A Special Commissioner held, in *Jacobs v Templeton* (1995), that benefits 'provided' to *future* employees in the tax year *before* the employment commenced were not caught by s 154. This point was not considered by the High Court (because it interpreted 'provided' differently) but the Commissioner's view is now made explicit in ITEPA 2003 s 201(4). Benefits provided 'by reason of the employment' to a prospective employee in the tax year in which the employment commences will be caught.

Employers sometimes provide benefits to former employees—for instance, a redundant employee may be allowed to continue his cheap mortgage; a retired employee may still have his private medical insurance premiums paid. For a discussion of whether such benefits could be taxed under the benefits in kind legislation, see **[8.146]**. **[8.127]**

### v)   Special rules for use of an asset

When the benefit consists of the *use* of an asset owned by the employer, the cash equivalent treated as earnings from the employment is the higher of the actual cost to the employer in providing the asset (eg the cost of hiring it) and the 'annual value' of the use of the asset (s 205): see *Tax Bulletin*, October 2000 for HMRC's view that, under the old s 156(5)(b) (now ITEPA 2003 s 205(4)), only the marginal additional cost of running expenses have to be taken into account when calculating the cash equivalent; and *Kerr v Brown* (2002) for the Special Commissioners' interpretation of these difficult provisions.

In the case of land, its annual value is defined in s 207. For any other asset, the annual value is 20% of its market (capital) value when it is first put at the employee's disposal (s 205(3)).

If assets which have previously been used or have depreciated are *transferred* to an employee, the cash equivalent is the market value of the asset *at the date of transfer* less any sum paid by the employee (s 206 and 203(2)). If, however, the employee (or some other person) had previously been subject to an income tax charge for the use of the asset, he is taxed on its market value *at the date when he first used it* less the sum of the annual value(s) on which he has already been taxed (s 206(3)). This alternative method of calculating the taxable benefit does not, however, apply if the asset transferred is an 'excluded asset' (see s 206(3)(a) and (b), as amended by FA 2005 s 17). In such a case, no tax charge will arise provided the employee buys the asset for market value.

**EXAMPLE 8.12**

On 6 April 2003, Mr C Rash was given by his employer the use of a hi-fi system costing £2,000. In October 2005, the employer transferred the system to Mr Rash free of charge when its market value was £800.

| | |
|---|---:|
| Market value at the date when first used by Mr Rash, ie cost | £2,000 |
| *Benefit in kind in 2003–2004: 20% × £2,000 | £400 |
| *Benefit in kind in 2004–2005: 20% × £2,000 | £400 |
| Benefit in kind in 2005–06: £2,000 – £800 (£400 + £400) | £1,200 |

*If the employer had rented the system at £500 pa, this higher figure would be taxed as earnings.

Whenever an employer transfers an asset to an employee, the former's CGT position should be considered in the light of TCGA 1992 s 17, given that HMRC has withdrawn its former concessionary treatment whereby that section was not applied if the employee paid less than market value and was subject to income tax on the difference (*Tax Bulletin*, December 1994, p 181).

[8.128]

*vi)   Scholarships*

Scholarship income is exempt from tax (ITTOIA 2005 s 776—see [8.164] in relation to HMRC practice where employers make payments to employees who are in full-time education). However, scholarships provided under arrangements entered into by the employer which are awarded to the children of employees and directors who are not lower-paid are taxed as earnings of the parents unless not more than 25% of the total payments from the fund are to children of any employees and the award is fortuitous, ie not resulting from the employment (ITEPA 2003 ss 211–215: see further [1984] STI 62).

[8.129]

*vii)   Trivial benefits*

As a final point, it is pleasing to discover that, whilst individual HMRC staff may sometimes be hard-hearted, those ultimately in charge are not, as this extract from *Working Together* (September 2003) shows:

'We have been asked to restate our position about seeking tax/NICs on benefits in kind following an Employer Compliance Review, where the amounts involved may be small. This was brought up with Working Together some time ago and formed the basis of Register of Issues item 9.5, following correspondence about tax/NICs sought on gifts of flowers for staff on sick leave. The item says:

**Issue 9.5 Pay as You Earn:** Flowers for staff who are ill **Current Position** Additional guidance on treatment of benefits that are trivial in nature was issued to network staff in February 2000. Staff are encouraged to exercise discretion and a sense of proportion.'                                            **[8.130]**

### 4   Payments treated as earnings

a)   *Introduction*

Part 3 Chapter 12 sets out those payments which are treated as earnings. These are a sub-set of the category 'amounts treated as earnings' (s 7(5)) and, therefore, form part of 'general earnings' under s 7(3). Not all the provisions of Chapter 12 are considered here: for the whereabouts of the remainder, see **[8.111]**.                                              **[8.131]**

b)   *Sick pay and permanent health insurance*

Sick pay is taxable, whether paid by the employer, a Friendly Society, an insurance company or a third person, if it is paid as a result of arrangements entered into by the employer (ITEPA 2003 s 221). Where an employer runs a sick pay scheme to which both employer and employee contribute, sums paid to him or his family are not treated as earnings to the extent that the sums reflect contributions made by the employee. Similarly, if the employee receives *income* benefits under a permanent health insurance policy which he has taken out then, provided the cost of the insurance premiums was not met by the employer, benefits will be exempt from tax provided that they are only paid while the individual is sick or disabled (including payments during convalescence or rehabilitation and income 'top-ups' following sickness): TA 1988 ss 580A–B and see *Tax Bulletin*, December 1996, p 377, on the types of insurance benefits not covered by the exemption and when and how gross payments can be received.

Statutory sick, maternity, paternity and adoption pay are all taxable under ITEPA 2003 s 656, although as social security (rather than employment) income.                                                              **[8.132]**

c)   *Restrictive undertakings*

The tax treatment of restrictive covenant payments made to employees has undergone substantial revision over the years. Originally, the sum paid escaped tax in the hands of the employee since it was thought not to be a reward for services performed under his contract and usually it was not provided for under the contract itself (*Beak v Robson* (1943)). For the employer, the sum would usually be non-deductible in arriving at his profits since it would be of a capital nature (*Associated Portland Cement Manufacturers Ltd v Kerr* (1946): see **[10.135]**). However, it was accepted that, if the restriction imposed on the employee was for a relatively short period, then the payment by the employer was tax–deductible.

Legislation was introduced (now ITEPA 2003 ss 225 and 226 and FA 1988 s 73) as a result of which all restrictive covenant payments are fully taxed in the hands of the employee and always deductible by the employer in arriving at his profits. In *RCI (Europe) Ltd v Woods* (2004), the High Court held that TA 1988 s 313 extended to payments for covenants entered into after the employment had ceased: this is now reflected in s 225(1).

Limitations on the ambit of s 225 are illustrated by *Vaughan-Neil v IRC* (1979), which involved the payment of £40,000 to a barrister to induce him to leave the planning Bar and work for a company as an employee. This sum was not taxed. It was not a reward for services, being in effect a compensation payment (see *Pritchard v Arundale* at **[8.63]**), nor was it caught by s 225 because the barrister had given no undertaking to the company not to practise at the Bar. His inability to do so was not caused by accepting the particular terms of employment but rather by accepting the employment itself; the payment was merely recognition that the job would prevent his practising at the Bar.

HMRC has in the past argued that the provision charging payments for restrictive covenants applies if the employee gives any sort of undertaking not to sue for breach of contract. This is most likely to occur in a termination agreement, though it could also be a provision in an agreement to change the terms of an ongoing employment: in relation to the former, see **[8.147]**.

**[8.133]**


## 5   Conclusions on the treatment of benefits

The present system is neither logical nor fair and presents a bewildering range of possibilities. Consider, for instance, the following examples (no account is taken of exemptions potentially applicable in the first example).

**[8.134]–[8.140]**


### EXAMPLE 8.13

Rod wants his part-time computer operator, Julie, to work late two evenings per week. Her salary is £4,500 pa. He plans to provide her with meals or a meal allowance on those two evenings. So far as Rod is concerned, the sum that he expends will be a deductible business expense, but Julie's tax position depends upon how the provision is made:

(1)   If Rod, the employer, pays a cash allowance, that sum is earnings.

(2)   If Rod pays the bill incurred by Julie, that sum is earnings (*Nicoll v Austin* (1935)).

(3)   If Rod gives Julie a voucher exchangeable at a restaurant, the cost incurred by Rod in providing the voucher is earnings.

(4)   If Julie buys the food herself and is reimbursed, it may be that there is no charge (see *Donnelly v Williamson* (1982)).

(5)   If the employer has an arrangement with the restaurant, so that food is provided and the expense is directly met by the employer, there is no charge (see *Wilkins v Rogerson* (1961)).

If Julie earned £8,500 or more pa, then method (4) would be caught by s 72 and method (5) by Part 3 Chapter 10.

**EXAMPLE 8.14**

Free Range Ltd gives all its employees a 25lb turkey at Christmas. In deciding whether tax is charged: (1) apply the gift rules (ie is the turkey given in return for services or is it for personal qualities?); then (2) apply the benefit in kind rules (ie is the turkey convertible into money; if not, is it caught by ITEPA 2003 Part 3 Chapters 2–11 in the case of employees and directors who are not lower-paid?). If it is decided that the benefit is a gift, no tax is charged on lower-paid employees, although the benefits code may catch others. If it is decided that it is in return for services, tax may be charged under s 9 on all employees if the turkeys are convertible into cash; if not, employees who are not lower-paid may still be taxable. It is likely in this example that tax would be chargeable.

## IX   TERMINATION PAYMENTS

### 1   Introduction

Over time, the taxability of termination payments under a variety of provisions has been considered by the courts, indicating that the possibility of such payments not being taxable is a recurring issue for HMRC. The application of those provisions is considered in this Section.                **[8.141]**

### 2   The general charging provision

#### a)   *General*

A payment made after the termination of employment is, *prima facie,* not earnings from that employment: however, it may be earnings if it is in the nature of 'deferred remuneration'. Further, as a general proposition, a payment made under the contract of employment will be taxed in full, even though it is paid because of the termination of the employment. In *Dale v de Soissons* (1950), followed in *Williams v Simmonds* (1981), a director's service agreement provided for him to be paid £10,000 if it should be prematurely terminated. The taxpayer argued that the payment was not in return for services. It was held, however, that as the payment was one to which he was contractually entitled, it was taxable. The status of this general proposition is not entirely clear at the moment (see **[8.42]**) but, in view of the generous tax and NIC treatment of non-contractual payments on a termination of employment, it will generally still be advisable from a tax point of view to omit such compensation clauses from contracts of employment (see *4* below).   **[8.142]**

#### b)   *Payments in lieu of notice*

If correct notice is given to the employee and he works out that period or remains employed but on 'garden leave', payments that he receives are earnings under general principles. If the employer terminates the contract and makes a payment in lieu of notice, then it is generally thought that tax is not payable under general principles (as the payment is seen as damages for breach of contract (see *Henley v Murray* (1950)). The position where the contract allows the employer to terminate either by giving notice or by making a payment in lieu was subject to debate after the House of Lords' decision in *Mairs v Haughey* (1993). The Court of Appeal in *EMI Group Electronics Ltd v Coldicott* (1999) held that payments made by the employer in exercise of a contractual right to make a payment in lieu of notice are taxable (see further [**8.42**]).

The tax treatment of damages paid pursuant to a liquidated damages clause following a wrongful dismissal has not been considered by the courts—HMRC's view is probably predictable. It has also been suggested (*Tax Journal*, 18 September 2000, p 19) that HMRC may seek to give *EMI* its widest possible application by arguing:

(1)    that a clause permitting payment in lieu of notice can be implied from the employer's previous practice;

(2)    that a negotiated settlement which results in a payment in lieu falls within *EMI*; and

(3)    even that a payment made following a breach is taxable because it represents a payment of damages for the loss of a sum (the salary) that would have been taxable.

The authors of the above article in the *Tax Journal* had a certain degree of prescience.

In relation to (1), the Employment Income Manual (para 12976) now assumes that an expectation or custom that a payment in lieu of notice will be made on termination will result in its being earnings within s 62. Since a term cannot be implied which conflicts with an express term (the right to notice), it is difficult to see how the employer would not be in breach if he failed to give notice to the employee, so that *Henley v Murray* (above) would apply. HMRC's view appears to be that, because the source of the payment is the employer-employee relationship, this takes precedence over its categorisation as a damages payment.

In relation to (2), Lloyd J in *Richardson v Delaney* (2002) held that a negotiated settlement which resulted in a payment very similar to that which would have been due if the employer had exercised its contractual right to make a payment in lieu was taxable under s 19 (for HMRC's (rather different) analysis see EI 12978, 12979 and 13924).                [**8.143**]

c)    *Redundancy payments*

Statutory redundancy payments can only be taxed as termination payments within s 401 (ITEPA 2003 s 309(3)). Following the House of Lords' decision in *Mairs v Haughey* (1993), HMRC accepts that lump sum payments under non-statutory schemes will also only fall within s 401, provided they are made on a genuine redundancy (as defined (now) in the Employment Rights Act 1996 s 139) and are genuinely made to compensate for the employment lost through redundancy (SP 1/94). Advance clearance for schemes can be obtained. Presumably, genuine one-off redundancy payments will be taxed in the same way but the Statement of Practice does not mention them. In either situation, HMRC will have to be convinced that no part of the payment is what it refers to as a 'terminal bonus' (HMRC will seek to tax those under s 9 as earnings) and that the employee is not really 'retiring' (see [**8.145**]).
[**8.144**]

d)  *Ex gratia payments on termination*

In contrast to payments for redundancy or breach of contract, *ex gratia* payments may be made as a testimonial or present to the employee—to the employee as an individual rather than in return for services rendered (see **[8.62]**). An *ex gratia* payment made to an employee on termination of employment will not be taxable under general principles (see *Cowan v Seymour* (1920)). *McBride v Blackburn* (2003) and *Allum v Marsh* (2005) show how important the payer's description of the reasons for the payment can be in deciding whether it was a gift in recognition of services performed rather than a reward for them.

HMRC treatment of lump sum payments made on termination due to retirement or death was modified by SP 13/91 (see also [1992] STI 869 and 1005 and see *Taxation*, 23 June 2005, p 323 for a criticism of HMRC's approach). Lump sum payments of this nature could be subject to the rules governing payments under retirement benefits schemes. HMRC has the power to approve ex gratia schemes; if approved, the payment will be wholly tax-free (on the conditions for approval): if the payment is made under an unapproved retirement benefits scheme, it will be taxable in full under the retirement benefits provisions (ITEPA 2003 s 386 ff) without the benefit of any £30,000 exemption, since s 401 (see 5(d)(iv) below) only applies if the payment is not otherwise taxable. Whether the SP applied was also considered briefly in *Allum v Marsh* (2005).                                      **[8.145]**

## 3  The residual charging provisions for benefits

Can benefits provided to former employees be taxed under ITEPA 2003 Part 3 Chapter 10? Pensions, lump sums and 'other like' benefits provided to the employee, or his family or dependants, on his death or 'retirement' cannot be so taxed, as a result of s 307.

Certain termination payments *may* escape Chapter 10 as being 'fair bargains' (see **[8.124]**). In *Wilson v Clayton (2005)*, the Court of Appeal supported excluding from the scope of s 154 payments made pursuant to 'fair bargains' and concluded that payments made pursuant to a 'genuine' compromise agreement to settle a dispute could not be a 'benefit'. Peter Gibson LJ did not, however, 'rule out the possibility that it might be shown in some cases that the reason for the payment was to confer a gratuitous benefit within a compromise agreement so that to that extent [Part 3 Chapter 10] might apply.'

In relation to other benefits within Part 3 Chapter 10, s 201(4) makes it clear that the Chapter cannot apply in a year of assessment when the taxpayer has not been employed at all. However, what is the position if benefits which would fall within Chapter 10 are provided in the remainder of the tax year following termination? This will most commonly occur because a pre-termination benefit (for instance, a beneficial loan or use of a car) continues after termination; but could also arise when a new benefit is provided at that time. Whilst s 201(4) suggests that such benefits fall within Chapter 10 for the remainder of the tax year following termination, HMRC has made it clear that it will continue its previous practice of not applying s 201 to 'payments or benefits related to the termination of employment' (*Tax Bulletin*, June 2003, pp 1036–1037). That practice of excluding the benefit in kind charge covered not only benefits newly provided on termination but also the continued provision of a pre-termination benefit (see SE 12815, now EI 12815) (unless, as when beneficial loans are written off, there is a specific provision making that taxable under the benefits code even though the employment has ceased (see, eg ITEPA 2003 s 188)). It is likely that, in most cases, this practice will reflect the strict legal position: the deeming provision in s 201(3) will not apply because an ex-employer is not an 'employer'; and such benefits will not be provided 'by reason of employment'.          **[8.146]**

## 4  Payments treated as earnings

If neither the general charging provision nor the residual benefits charge applies, could the termination payment (or part of it) be regarded as a payment for a restrictive covenant within s 225? Some Revenue officers used to argue that s 225 had a wide ambit and applied, *inter alia*, where an employee agreed, on receiving a compensation payment, to give up his right to claim damages. It appeared from SP 3/96 that HMRC would no longer take this approach. The SP states that 'no chargeable value will be attributed under s [225]' to undertakings to give up legal claims or reaffirmations of restrictive covenants which were in the contract when employment commenced. However, the Special Commissioner in *Appellant v Inspector of Taxes* (2001) held that the SP does not apply if the parties attached a value to the undertakings, an unexpected interpretation of the wording in the SP. Further, whilst there was some evidence that HMRC was seeking to apply s 225 if the ex-employee had to repay the whole (or part of the) termination payment if he commenced legal proceedings, HMRC now 'accepts that such a charge will not arise other than in very exceptional cases' (*Tax Bulletin*, October 2003, p1063).          **[8.147]**

## 5  Amounts counted as employment income

### a)  *Introduction*

Part 6 Chapter 3 applies to payments and benefits received in connection with the termination of a person's employment or a change in his duties or earnings. Thus, if the payment or benefit is not 'in connection with' any of those, it will not fall within Chapter 3. In *Walker v Adams* (2003), HMRC accepted before a Special Commissioner that an award for injury to feelings, made by a Fair Employment Tribunal in Northern Ireland to a man constructively dismissed on grounds of religious discrimination, was not a payment made 'in connection with' the termination of his employment: the Commissioner stated that, in his opinion, HMRC was right. HMRC will, however, seek to tax compensation for discrimination where the discrimination is suffered in respect of the termination itself (EI 12965).

In relation to payments made in connection with a change to the earnings of an employment, no doubt HMRC would consider that s 401 is capable of applying even where, as in *Mairs v Haughey (1992)*, the right given up was not a right to *taxable* emoluments of the employment but the drafting of the section does not make that entirely clear (see [1998] BTR 420 at 422).

Part 6 Chapter 3 sets out a residual liability to tax: it does not apply if the payment or benefit is otherwise chargeable (s 401(3)). Therefore, one has to establish that no other provision applies before considering the applicability of this charge. If no income tax provision applies, TCGA 1992 s 22 (capital sums derived from assets) should be considered carefully when rights are being surrendered.

Part 6 Chapter 3 applies not only when *payments* are received in the circumstances to which it relates but also when 'benefits' are so received. The definition of 'benefit' for these purposes (s 402) is made rather complex because of the distinction drawn in ITEPA 2003 between 'earnings-only exemptions' and 'employment income exemptions' (see Section X).

'Benefit' includes anything which would be taxable as earnings if it were received for the performance of duties; or would be so taxable but for an 'earnings-only exemption'. This means that the provision of all benefits can fall within Part 6 Chapter 3 unless they are subject to an 'employment income exemption'. However, it becomes more complex as s 402(2) goes on to list certain benefits which are subject to an 'earnings-only exemption' (and the provision of which would otherwise, therefore, fall within this Chapter as a result of s 402(1)(b)) but which nevertheless are not within Chapter 3. For completeness, in relation to exemptions, 402(3) exempts removal expenses paid in connection with a change in the duties of a continuing employment; ESC A81 excludes payments of legal costs of a former employee, provided certain criteria are met (eg that the payment is made directly to the employee's solicitor—see also EI 13740 and *Tax Bulletin*, November 1993, pp 94 and 95); and ss 405–414 contain further specific exceptions from this Chapter (see d) below).

It should be noted that s 402 contains a non-exhaustive definition of 'benefit'. Paragraph 13030 of the Employment Income Manual points out that, even though something is not taxed under the rest of the Act, it can still be a benefit, using the ordinary meaning of that word, for the purposes of Part 6 Chapter 3. **[8.148]**

b)  *Lump sum compensation payments—the old regime*

Payments received on termination of employment (often called 'golden handshakes') or to compensate an employee for a change in his conditions (or the emoluments) of employment formerly escaped tax altogether. FA 1960 introduced a special scheme of taxation. The main features of it at 5 April 1998 were:

(1)  TA 1988 s 148 was a residual charging provision, so it only applied if the benefit was not taxable under other provisions, notably ss 19, 313, 595 or 596A (now ITEPA 2003 ss 9, 225, 386 or 394).

(2)  Section 148 was widely drafted. It covered not only cash payments but also payments in kind (eg a dismissed employee being given his company car as compensation). It included payments made by a person other than the employer to someone other than the employee (eg to his spouse or personal representatives); and caught golden handshakes, compensation and damages for wrongful dismissal and redundancy payments not otherwise taxable.

Vinelott J's decision in *Nichols v Gibson* (1994) suggested that s 148 was even wider than generally supposed. An employee received a termination payment on the last day of his employment, being 6 April, the first day of a year of assessment during which he was neither resident nor ordinarily resident in the UK and did not perform any duties here. He argued that the payment was not taxable because at the time of receipt he did not fall within any of the Cases of Schedule E in s 19(1) para 1. The court held, however, that the charge under s 148 was independent of s 19(1) para 1 and fell within para 5. This view was subsequently upheld by the Court of Appeal (1996); and the termination payment was therefore taxable. It is worth noting that *Nichols v Gibson* (1996) was criticised in [1996] BTR 619 on the basis that payments taxable under s 148 were deemed to be emoluments by the old s 148(4) and, therefore, properly fell within s 19(1) para 1. Since 1998, termination payments have no longer been deemed to be emoluments by the charging provision.

(3)    Any payment or benefit was treated as received in the year of the termination (or change in the conditions (or emoluments) of the employment to which it related) and was therefore taxable in that year of assessment. In the case of a termination payment, this overcame the problems that would otherwise have arisen because of the source doctrine but it created two other problems:

(a)    Whenever payments or benefits were received in a later year of assessment, the assessment for the original year had to be reopened; and

(b)    Where continuing benefits were provided, strictly the value of the right to receive those future benefits should have been taxed in the year of termination (s 148(4)). However, such rights were often difficult to value, particularly if it was not known for how long the employee would enjoy the benefit; and if the enjoyment period was shorter than that originally envisaged, there was no mechanism for refunding the excess tax paid.

(4)    Some benefits which would have fallen within s 148 were exempted by s 188, notably the first £30,000 of any payment.

The taxation of continuing benefits became more of an issue as more were provided to ex-employees. FA 1998 therefore repealed s 188 and replaced s 148. The new s 148 applied to any payment or benefit received on or after 6 April 1998 provided it (or the right to receive it) had not already been brought into the charge to tax (eg under the old s 148). These provisions are now in ITEPA 2003 Part 6 Chapter 3.                                    **[8.149]**

c)    *The current regime*

In many respects the current regime mirrors the pre-6 April 1998 one, so that the points noted at (1), (2) and (4) in **[8.149]** still apply (reliefs are discussed below). In relation to (2), in light of *Nichols v Gibson* (1994), the deletion of the deeming provision noted in (2) and the fact that employees are now taxed on a receipts basis, former employees are likely to find HMRC seeking tax on benefits received in years after termination, even if they have become non–resident by the time payment is received.

The main change made in 1998 was to the calculation of the taxable amount for benefits in kind (whenever received) and the timing of the charge when benefits or payments are received in a year of assessment after the termination or change to which they relate. Now, tax is due only if and when a payment or benefit is 'received' and it is charged in the year of receipt. The value of a non-cash benefit is the higher of the value that would be ascribed to it under the common law valuation principles for earnings (see Section VII) or under the benefits code (ie Part 3 Chapters 2 to 11).

One issue which arose under the old provisions remains: the deemed receipt of cash benefits when the recipient 'becomes entitled to require payment of or on account of the benefit' effected by s 403(3) may result in the employee being taxed on a benefit he never receives (eg if the employer becomes insolvent) and there is still no mechanism for refunding the tax paid.                    **[8.150]**

d)   *The exceptions*

i)   *Introduction*

Whilst ITEPA 2003 Part 6 Chapter 3 contains detailed information on the exceptions from s 401 (ss 402 and 405–414), the list is not comprehensive. Payments and benefits subject to 'employment income exemptions' are also excluded (see **[8.148]** and Section X) and there are specific exemptions in Part 4 Chapter 10.

As there is now a wide range of exceptions from s 401, it is not proposed to list them all here but only to consider those that apply most often in practice; readers considering the taxability of any particular payment made in connection with either the termination of an employment or a change in its duties or earnings should check all the applicable exceptions.               **[8.151]**

ii)   *Death, injury and disability*

Section 406 exempts payments and benefits provided in connection with the death of an employee or 'on account of injury to, or disability of, an employee'. Lightman J's view, in *Horner v Hasted* (1995), on the last exemption was that it had to be established as an objective fact that there was a 'relevant disability' (which, reflecting SP 10/81, he considered to be one affecting an employee's ability to perform his duties) and as a subjective fact that the disability was the motive for the payment. HMRC interprets the exemption extremely restrictively.                               **[8.152]**

iii)   *Pension benefits from and contributions to approved schemes*

Pensions received from approved retirement benefits schemes do not fall within s 401 because they are taxed under other provisions. Section 407 exempts from s 401 a lump sum benefit from an approved scheme provided that it can 'properly [be] regarded as earned by past service'; or if it is 'by way of compensation for loss of employment or loss or diminution of earnings and the loss or diminution is due to ill-health' (which may require an objective assessment of why the payment was made (as well as of whether the ill-health caused the loss, in contrast to the position where payments are made 'on account of injury or disability'). There is no blanket exemption for lump sum payments from approved schemes in order to prevent them, in effect, being manipulated to provide non-taxable compensation payments on termination. Section 637 also provides that 'legitimate' lump sum payments from approved schemes are not liable to income tax (for the avoidance of doubt, since s 401 itself establishes a residual liability).

Section 408 gives statutory effect to SP 2/81 by exempting contributions made to approved pension plans as part of arrangements relating to the termination of employment. These special contributions are often made to ensure that the plan is sufficiently funded if the pension is to be drawn earlier than was expected; and they now provide a tax–efficient method of making a termination payment.                        **[8.153]**

*iv)    First £30,000*

The exemption which is still likely to be invoked most often is that for the first £30,000 of payments or benefits received (the threshold is applied to the aggregate of payments made in respect of the same office or employment or made by the same or associated employers—s 404(1)). As termination and compensation payments can now be taxed in more than one year of assessment, the application of this exemption has become more complex but, in essence, the exemption, to the extent that it is not used up by cash and benefits received in the first year of assessment when a charge arises, is applied to successive payments and benefits and, whenever more than one payment or benefit is received in a tax year, it is used first against cash (ss 404(4) and (5)).                        **[8.154]**

**EXAMPLE 8.15**

During the year 2005–06, Joanne has earnings of £25,000 and receives a lump sum payment of £20,000 on termination of her employment. No tax is payable on the £20,000 termination payment.

The next year Joanne receives a further £25,000 of her termination payment. Assuming she has found another job on the same salary and that tax rates, bands and allowances stay the same, then to calculate the *tax payable on the further instalment of the termination payment:*

(1)    Calculate amount of exemption: £30,000 – £20,000 (used in 2005–06) = £10,000 for 2006–07.
(2)    Calculate taxable slice: £25,000 – £10,000 = £15,000.

|  | £ |
|---|---:|
| Earnings from employment | 25,000.00 |
| Other income | Nil |
| Taxable lump sum on termination of employment | 15,000.00 |
| Personal allowance | 5,035.00 |
|  | Tax payable: |
| Taxable income | 40,000.00 |
| *Less:* | 5,035.00 |
|  | 34,965.00 |

| Tax payable: | first £2,150 at 10% | 215.00 |
|---|---|---:|
|  | £31,150 at 22% | 6,853.00 |
|  | remaining £1,665 at 40% | 666.00 |
|  |  | £7,734.00 |

e)   *PAYE and reporting requirements*

PAYE has to be operated on cash termination payments but does not have to be operated on such payments which benefit from the £30,000 exemption. ITEPA 2003 s 404 provides for the £30,000 exemption to be allocated to cash payments in priority to benefits in kind, but employers might still face difficulties in deciding whether the exemption has been used up: for instance, if cash of £28,000 is provided at the time of termination plus continuing benefits and a cash payment is due at the beginning of the next tax year, the employer might find it difficult to calculate how much of that exceeds the tax-free band. The difficulty is exacerbated as the obligation to operate PAYE extends to the provision of 'readily convertible assets' to ex-employees, particularly as, if the employer pays the tax, he can only recover it from cash payments made in the same income tax month and there may well not be any when such assets are provided to ex-employees (see generally Section XII). In the absence of a satisfactory statutory right to recover PAYE from an employee, the need for tax indemnities in termination agreements has become more important (or even a right to retain and realise assets to pay tax, since the employee could remain taxable even if he were non–resident and therefore difficult to pursue—see **[8.149]**).

If the payment is made before the employment has ceased, the deduction should be in accordance with the employee's code for the relevant period; if after, it should be deducted at the basic rate (Income Tax (Pay As You Earn) Regulations 2003, SI 2003/2682 reg 37). Regulation 91 requires a one-off report if the termination settlement includes non-cash benefits and it is estimated that their value will in total exceed £30,000 (this has to be filed if those conditions were not originally fulfilled but are fulfilled later as a result of some change in the arrangements). Further reports are only required if there is a 'material change in the amount of the payments awarded or the nature and amounts of other benefits awarded' (reg 92(4)).

See the October 1998 issue of *Tax Bulletin* which gives HMRC's views on how to apply the £30,000 exemption when operating PAYE and the reporting requirements.                                                              **[8.155]**

f)   *Interaction of £30,000 exemption and a damages claim*

The exemption for the first £30,000 of a termination payment which falls within s 401 can cause problems when assessing the damages payable for breach of the employment contract. *British Transport Commission v Gourley* (1956) and subsequent cases are concerned with the determination of the amount of damages awarded by the courts in tort and for breach of contract. The cases are not concerned with the tax treatment of the sum once it has been awarded. Damages in tort for personal injury are not taxed, but damages for breach of contract and, in tort, for financial loss may be subject to charge if they represent compensation for lost profits or other income (see *London and Thames Haven Oil Wharves Ltd v Attwooll* (1967) at **[10.103]**), especially when they are payable on the termination of an employment contract (although, in certain circumstances, a disposal of contractual rights may attract CGT).

Damages should compensate the innocent party for a breach of contract; they should not normally penalise the contract–breaker. Hence, if an employment contract has been broken, the damages should reflect the fact that, had the employee performed the contract, he would only have been left with the benefit of a net sum after payment of tax. Therefore, the damages awarded should be computed by reference to that net sum. Obviously, this will adequately compensate the claimant so long as the damages are not themselves taxed; if they are, the net sum will be insufficient.

It could be argued that, once a payment is subject to charge (as termination payments are by virtue of s 401), there is no room for the application of the *Gourley* rule and a gross sum should be paid. The courts, however, have generally distinguished between termination payments of less than £30,000 and those in excess of £30,000. A payment below £30,000 is free of tax and, therefore, the amount awarded should be calculated on *Gourley* principles (see *Parsons v BMN Laboratories* (1963)). *Lyndale Fashion Manufacturers v Rich* (1973) shows that the calculation should proceed as if the damages are compensation for income which formed the highest slice of the recipient's income for the year (see *Law Society's Gazette*, 1983, p 346). If the net damages exceed £30,000 (after making the appropriate *Gourley* adjustment for tax), those damages must be increased by a sum equal to the estimated income tax that will be charged on the award under s 403. This final net award will represent, as realistically as possible, the actual loss suffered (*Shove v Downs Surgical plc* (1984) and see (1984) *Modern Law Review* 471 where the conflicting decisions of the courts are discussed).

Raising the unfair dismissal compensatory award ceiling to (currently) £56,800 means that this issue has to be addressed in that context now as well.
**[8.156]**

### g)   *Contemporaneous share sale*

Problems may arise when the employee is also a substantial shareholder in the employer company and a termination payment is made on the change of ownership of that company. In such cases, a payment ostensibly for termination of his service contract may be challenged on the grounds that it represents partial consideration for the shares transferred. To the extent that the challenge is successful, the payment will not be deductible as a business expense of the company (see *James Snook & Co Ltd v Blasdale* (1952)) and will not qualify for the £30,000 exemption. To avoid this, it may be desirable to separate, so far as possible, arrangements for the share sale from the question of compensation for loss of office.                      **[8.157]–[8.160]**

## X   EXEMPTIONS

### 1   Introduction

ITEPA 2003 Part 4 is headed 'Employment income: exemptions'. It is however important to note that not all exemptions are set out in this Part: some can be found in other Parts of the Act—for instance, those in Part 6 Chapter 3 (discussed in Section IX part 5 d) and those in Part 7 listed in s 227(4); others in Extra–Statutory Concessions (though many of these have been incorporated into ITEPA (see Annex 3 to the Explanatory Notes), some remain in force as they would have taken a disproportionate amount of legislation to enact them).

Part 4 contains two types of exemptions: 'earnings–only exemptions' and 'employment income exemptions' (s 227). The former prevent 'liability to tax arising in respect of earnings, either by virtue of one or more particular provisions (such as a Chapter of the benefits code) or at all', but do 'not prevent liability to tax arising in respect of other employment income' (s 227(2)); the latter prevent 'liability to tax arising in respect of employment income of any kind at all'. Although this distinction is not as clear as it might be. Employment income exemptions provide complete exemption from charge under ITEPA. The title 'earnings-only exemption' might lead one to think that they only provide exemption from earnings within Part 3 Chapter 1: however, it is clear from the wording of s 227(2) itself that they also apply to provisions under which amounts are treated as earnings; in other words, they provide an exemption from 'general earnings' (not just 'earnings') but do not provide an exemption from the charges on 'specific employment'. The real distinction in practice (given the nature of the exemptions) is that the earnings-only exemptions do not provide exemption from the charge on termination payments under Part 6 Chapter 3 (though, in fact, even they will apply to that charge if they are listed in s 402) but the employment income exemptions do provide such an exemption.

How is the nature (earnings-only or employment income) of any particular exemption determined? By looking at the wording of the exemption provision. Section 247 provides an example of each: sub-s (2) states that '*no liability to income tax arises by virtue of Chapter 6 or 10 of Part 3 ...* in respect of the benefit [(provision of a car for disabled employees)] if conditions A to C are met' (an earnings-only exemption); sub-s (3) states that '*no liability to income tax* arises in respect of (a) the provision of fuel for the car, or (b) the payment or reimbursement of expenses incurred in connection with it, if conditions A to C are met' (an employment income exception).

Section 228 lists benefits which are exempt from income tax under all statutes, not just ITEPA 2003.

Not all the exemptions in Part 4 will be examined here in detail. To give a flavour of their extent, the headings of the various Chapters are now listed. A few of the exemptions will be considered further in the remainder of this Section. The Chapter headings are:
(1) mileage allowances and passenger payments (see **[8.122]**);
(2) other transport, travel and subsistence (see **[8.95]** and **[8.122]** in relation to some of these);
(3) education and training (see **[8.95]** in relation to some of these);
(4) recreational benefits;
(5) non-cash vouchers and credit-tokens;
(6) removal benefits and expenses;
(7) special kinds of employees;
(8) pension provision;
(9) termination of employment; and
(10) miscellaneous exemptions.                                          **[8.161]**

## 2   Relocation costs

The taxation of benefits provided to a relocating employee is complex.

If the employer offers a guaranteed selling price (GSP) scheme (which normally involves the employer or a relocation company buying the house and subsequently selling it – the employer taking the risk of price fluctuations) then, even if the price paid is no more than the market value of the property, other costs incurred by the employer could be taxable under Part 3 Chapter 10 (eg his legal costs)—see **[8.125]**. However, as a result of s 326, many of these costs will be ignored.

Benefits not covered by s 326, whether or not arising under a GSP scheme, may be relieved under ss 277–289. However, only 'eligible' expenses and benefits are relieved and the maximum relief is limited to £8,000.

Reimbursement of a capital loss is not covered. HMRC's view is that if the employer (or relocation company) pays more than the market value (usually because the house has fallen in value since it was bought), the difference is subject to income tax (*Tax Bulletin*, May 1994, pp 122–124) but this does not seem essentially different from the employee selling to a third party at a loss and being reimbursed by his employer, as in *Hochstrasser v Mayes* (1960) (see **[8.42]**). It is not clear whether HMRC considers that the House of Lords would reverse its previous decision or that the situation would be likely to arise only where Part 3 Chapter 10 applied so that compensation would be taxable thereunder. Even the latter view would not be uncontroversial, particularly if the payment were not made by the employer (see the Northern Ireland Court of Appeal's discussion of the scope of s 154 (the predecessor to Part 3 Chapter 10) in *Mairs v Haughey* (1992)).

If this is not complicated enough, Stamp Duty Land Tax may also be in issue (see *Tolley's Practical Tax Newsletter*, 27 February 2004).    **[8.162]**

### 3    Outplacement counselling

When employees are made redundant, employers sometimes arrange 'outplacement counselling' for them. This is a service provided by a third party to help the employee, for instance, by providing counselling to help him adjust to the redundancy or providing assistance in the preparation of his CV. Section 310 exempts the provision of these services from income tax, provided certain conditions are satisfied. It was extended to cover part-time employees by FA 2005 s 18(2). In addition, the employer can claim a statutory deduction for their cost (see ITTOIA 2005 ss 31 and 73).    **[8.163]**

### 4    Training

If an employer pays up to £15,000 (for the 2005–2006 academic year) of certain costs for employees attending full-time educational courses at universities or technical colleges etc, any benefit which would otherwise be chargeable to tax under ITEPA is not treated as earnings (SP 4/86, revised 16 March 2005). Where an employer meets the cost of a qualifying training course undertaken by his employee or former employee to retrain in skills needed for a new job or self-employment following termination of employment, that payment or reimbursement will not give rise to an income tax charge if the conditions in s 311 are satisfied. This exemption was extended by FA 2005 s 18(3) to cover part-time employees and courses lasting up to two years (rather than one). Relief for other types of external training is given by ss 250–260 (see **[8.95]**).    **[8.164]**

## 5  Homeworker's additional expenses

Section 316A exempts from income tax payments in respect of reasonable additional household expenses incurred in working from home under 'homeworking arrangements'. Budget Note 03 (2003) sets out Revenue practice in relation to this exemption: an employer will be able to pay up to £104 pa tax-free without having to prove the costs the employee has incurred: higher amounts will have to be justified by supporting evidence (see also *Tax Bulletin*, December 2003, pp 1068 and 1069).                    **[8.165]**

## 6  Use of assets

Special treatment applies to the use of certain assets. Section 319 exempts the provision of a mobile phone to an employee. Prior to 6 April 2006, this exemption extended to the provision of mobile phones to members of the employee's family and household. However, FA 2006 narrowed the exemption so as to only apply to employees except where the mobile phone was provided to the employee's family or household member before 6 April 2006. It appears that HMRC accept that a 'BlackBerry' is a mobile phone for these purposes (*Taxation*, 13 January 2005, p 345).

Up to and including the 2005–06 tax year, s 320 exempted the first £500 of the annual value when computer equipment (or any other peripheral device) was made available to employees, provided the arrangement is not confined to directors (or those connected with them) and they cannot obtain use of the equipment on more favourable terms than other employees. The exemption also applied to cases where the benefit would be taxable as earnings (for instance, because the employee had the choice of salary or the lent computer). However, this exemption was repealed by FA 2006 except where the computer equipment was first made available to an employee before 6 April 2006.

To benefit from the exemption for bicycles and cycling safety equipment (s 244), the equipment must be made available generally to all staff and must be mainly used for journeys from home to work or between workplaces (s 249).                    **[8.166]**

## 7  Childcare

Employees who are entitled to Working Tax Credit and who incur childcare costs are entitled to a credit in relation thereto (see **Chapter 51**). For all employees who have children, the deductibility of childcare costs, and the taxability of childcare provided by the employer, is of interest.

Certain employer-provided nursery facilities are excluded from tax by s 318 (which was completely rewritten with effect from 6 April 2005 by FA 2004 s 78 and Sch 13); neither is there any charge when similar provisions are available for older children after school. Whilst the facilities can be provided away from the workplace and jointly with other persons, mere payment of nursery fees to a third party is not enough, nor is a more structured buying-in of places; in HMRC's view s 318(7)(c) requires 'some real and substantial commitment to funding the facility or providing it with capital' (see *Tax Bulletin*, April 1998, p 531). The exemption does not, of course, apply if the employer provides cash to enable his employee to pay for nursery facilities (and HMRC is looking closely at situations where the employee's salary is cut in return for the employer paying for nursery facilities: this may be taxed as if the employee had received the cost as salary). Similar costs incurred by a self-employed taxpayer do not qualify as deductible expenditure, nor can an individual employee deduct the costs of a nanny or child help in the home.

Two new related exemptions have been introduced from 6 April 2005 (by FA 2004, though further amendments have been made by FA 2005 ss 15 and 16). New s 318A exempts from Part 3 Chapter 10 (the residual benefits charge) the first £50 (increased to £55 with effect from 6 April 2006) per week of approved childcare contracted for by the employer, provided that specified conditions are met. New s 270A exempts the first £50 (increased to £55 with effect from 6 April 2006) per week of qualifying childcare vouchers.

For any of these exemptions to apply, the facility will have to be available to the employer's employees generally or to all those working at a particular location (see new s 318(8)).

As this area is now so complex, HMRC have issued a booklet for employees (IR 115) and guidance for employers (E18 (2005)).                    **[8.167]**

## 8   Annual parties and functions, long service awards, subsidised meals and small gifts from third parties

Sections 264 (enacting ESC A70B), 323 (enacting ESC A22) and 324 (enacting ESC A70A) provide limited exemptions for annual parties and functions, long service awards and small gifts from third parties, based on their cost. As a result of ITEPA 2003 s 716, these limits can be increased by Treasury Order. SI 2003/1361 is such an Order and increases the limits to £150, £50 for each year of service, and £150, respectively. It should be noted that, if the limits in ss 264 and 324 are exceeded, the full cost becomes a taxable benefit.

Section 317 exempts free or subsidised meals provided in a workplace canteen. It was amended by FA 2004 Sch 17 para 1 because the old wording did not 'require the same standard of meals or subsidy to be provided to all employees'. This amendment enacts what was apparently originally intended, by ensuring that the same free or subsidised meals have to be available to employees generally (see Explanatory Notes to the Finance Bill 2004).

**[8.168]**

## 9   Minor benefits

Section 316 exempts any benefit obtained from the use of assets and services which is 'not significant' (as to which see *Tax Bulletin*, October 2000), provided that the sole purpose of providing the benefit was to enable the employee to perform his duties and it is not an excluded benefit (for instance, the provision of an aircraft!). Section 210 allows for the exemption by regulation of 'minor benefits' provided they are made available to all employees on similar terms: welfare counselling; cyclists' breakfasts provided on days designated by the employer; lunchtime use of works buses; the private use of equipment or facilities provided to disabled employees to enable them to carry out their duties; the provision of no more than £150 worth of pensions advice per employee per year; and using recreational facilities or being provided with free or subsidised meals on the premises of another employer have all been exempted (see SI 2002/2005, as amended from time to time). **[8.169]–[8.170]**

## XI DEDUCTIBLE EXPENSES

### 1 Introduction

ITEPA 2003 Part 5 sets out the deductions allowed from earnings in computing taxable income. Section 9 charges 'net taxable earnings' and 'net taxable specific income' and so these deductions (as well as the others referred to in s 327) must be taken into account to ascertain the amount ultimately taxable under ITEPA 2003 (see further ss 10–12 and **[8.11]**). In general, the deductions listed in Part 5 can be made from any earnings from the employment in question (s 328), though there are limitations (ss 328–331). Section 329 provides that the amount of allowable deductions may not exceed the earnings from which they are deductible (so that it is not possible to create a loss to offset against other income).

The final provision of Part 5 Chapter 1 lists the 'deductibility provisions'. These are provisions in other Parts of ITEPA which relieve an employee from liability to income tax on a benefit received *provided* that, had the employee paid for the benefit, the cost would have been deductible under Part 5 (eg s 310(6)). **[8.171]**

### 2 Deductions for an employee's expenses

Part 5 Chapter 2 sets out the position when the employee has paid an expense of his employment or when someone else (normally the employer) has paid it on his behalf. Section 333 provides that, to be deductible, an expense must have been paid by the employee; but it is also deductible if it was paid by someone on his behalf *provided* the amount paid forms part of the employee's earnings. Section 333(2) provides that, in Part 5 Chapter 2 (the Part of the Act dealing with the general rules on deductibility), whenever reference is made to an employee 'paying an amount', it includes the latter situation.

Section 334 ensures that, if the employee is reimbursed for an expense he has paid (or any other payment has been made in respect of such an expense—for instance, an expense allowance), he can still claim a deduction for his expense: it states that in such a situation he will still be regarded as having paid the expense (so that he falls within s 333(1)(a)). However, he is only allowed a deduction to the extent that the reimbursement or other payment counts as earnings (s 334(2)—as to which see **[8.94]**).

The general rule for deductibility is set out in s 336; that for the deductibility of travelling expenses in s 337. However, it should be noted that HMRC treats subsistence expenses attributable to business travel in the same way that it treats the travel expenses, rather than in accordance with the general rules relating to other expenses, because it regards them as necessary travelling expenses (IR 490). Sections 336 and 337 are considered separately in a) and b) below; other provisions of Chapter 2 are also dealt with in those paragraphs. **[8.172]**

a)    *Expenses other than travelling expenses*

In general, these expenses are deductible if the employee was 'obliged to incur and pay [them] as holder of the employment' but only if incurred '... wholly, exclusively and necessarily in the performance of the said duties ...' (s 336(1)). These provisions may be contrasted with the more generous expenditure rules in under ITT0IA 2005 (see **[10.137]**). Section 336(2) indicates that Part 5 Chapter 2 contains other rules allowing or preventing deductions. The Explanatory Notes to ITEPA state that s 336(2) 'emphasises the fact that deductions under the later sections in this Chapter do not depend on this section being satisfied first'; but the use of the word 'additional' in s 336(2) does not lead one naturally to the conclusion that the other rules entirely displace this one.

Three requirements must be satisfied if an expense is to be deductible: *first*, it must be incurred 'in performing' the duties. No deduction is allowed for expenses which enable the employee to prepare for his duties or to be better equipped to carry them out. In *Shortt v McIlgorm* (1945), for instance, the taxpayer could not deduct the fee that he paid to an employment agency (contrast ITEPA 2003 s 352 allowing agents' fees paid by actors and other theatrical artists taxed under ITEPA 2003 to be deducted). In *Simpson v Tate* (1952) a medical officer could not deduct the cost of joining learned societies which would enable him to perform his duties better (note the partial reversal of this decision by ITEPA 2003 s 344 and that s 343 permits a deduction for specified professional membership fees (though HMRC did issue a Technical Note in December 2003 to prompt a discussion on how the rules might be changed to provide 'an incentive for membership bodies to provide workforce development')). The House of Lords adopted a similarly strict approach in *Fitzpatrick v IRC (No 2)* and *Smith v Abbott* (1994), which concerned expenses incurred by journalists in purchasing newspapers and journals. It held that when a journalist reads newspapers and periodicals he is *preparing* to perform his duties efficiently but not actually acting 'in the performance of' his duties. Parts of Lord Templeman's speech indicate that the House was to some extent influenced by the amount of tax that would be lost if the journalists' claims were allowed:

'If a journalist or other employee were allowed to deduct expenses incurred by him in his spare time in improving his usefulness to his employer, the imposition of income tax would be distorted and the amount of the expenses claimed by the individual would depend only on his own choice ... if each [journalist] spends £1,000 a year the total deduction for 30,000 journalists will be £30m a year ... the principle of the decision in the present cases does not apply only to journalists; the ramifications of [a] decision in their favour would be enormous.'

This contrasts with the approach of Nolan LJ in the Court of Appeal in *Smith v Abbott* (1993):

'The submission that the reading by the taxpayers of other newspapers and periodicals could only reasonably be regarded as a means of adding to their general qualifications seems to me to ignore the short-lived and almost ephemeral nature of the benefits which they thus acquired.

The purpose which their reading was designed to serve, and did serve, was the production of the next edition of the *Daily Mail* or the *Mail on Sunday*. In these circumstances, the reading seems to me to constitute preparation for a particular assignment.'

Second, the expense must be 'necessarily' incurred in the performance of the duties. This is an objective test: the expenditure must arise from the nature of the employment and not from the personal choice of the taxpayer (see Lord Blanesburgh in *Ricketts v Colquhoun* (1926), as clarified by Lord Wilberforce in *Owen v Pook* (1970)). Nor is it sufficient that the employer requires the expenditure—the nature of the duties must require it. In *Brown v Bullock* (1961), a bank manager was required by his employer to join a London club. He could not deduct his subscription because it was not necessary for the performance of his duties. It seems odd that the employer is not allowed to decide what is necessary to the particular office or employment and these cases may not be as supportive of HMRC's narrow interpretation as they would like to think: see *Taxation Practitioner*, June 1999, pp 14–16.

The *third* requirement is that the expense should be incurred 'wholly and exclusively' in the performance of the duties. This same requirement is found in ITTOIA 2005 (see **[10.137]**).

Few expenses will satisfy all three conditions. In *Kirkwood v Evans* (2002), Patten J refused a claim for home office expenses by a civil servant who opted to join a homeworking scheme. The judge considered that the expenses were not necessarily incurred, even though the scheme required him to provide his own office accommodation at his home, because the scheme itself was voluntary. Further, even ignoring the optional nature of the scheme, it did not oblige Mr Evans to maintain a *separate* room in which to work and therefore he could not claim heating and lighting costs relating to the work space. The case illustrates not only the difficulty of claiming such expenses, but also how strictly the conditions are interpreted in general. See *Tax Bulletin* , October 2005, p 1231 which sets out the conditions which HMRC require to be satisfied in order to claim tax relief under s 336 for unreimbursed homeworking (including additional household) expenses. Even if tax relief is not available under s 336 then relief may be available under ITEPA s 316A — see **[8.165].**

Also, other statutory deductions (eg the flat rate allowance for the costs of tools and special clothing in s 367) mitigate the effect of the way s 336 has been interpreted. The principal statutory deductions are:

*i)  Liability payments*

A person can claim relief if he pays the premiums on liability insurance (including 'D&O' insurance) or pays uninsured work-related liabilities, even for payments made after employment has ceased (at least if made before the end of the sixth year of assessment following that in which the employment ceased) (ss 346–350—and see *Tax Bulletin*, October 1995, p 257 for HMRC's interpretation of the original provisions). It is also possible to claim a deduction for the cost of indemnity insurance premiums in relation to liabilities arising from a previous employment (and for actual payment of liabilities) (ITEPA 2003 Part 8). Since there will rarely be earnings from which to deduct the cost, the deduction is allowed from 'total income' (s 555).

*ii)    Payroll deduction scheme*

The so-called 'payroll deduction scheme' is designed to encourage charitable giving. So long as a recognised scheme is operated by their employer, employees can make donations to the charity of their choice of any amount. These sums are deductible expenses for the employee and are paid gross to an approved charitable agent which then distributes the sums to the charity of the employee's choice (ITEPA 2003 ss 713–715).

The main statutory *restriction* on claiming as a deduction an expense which would be allowable under s 336 is that relating to the expenses of business entertaining in ss 356–358. This also applies to expenses claimed by the self-employed and is discussed at **[10.138]**; for HMRC's view of its application to employees see *Tax Bulletin*, August 1999, pp 679–682.                **[8.173]**

b)    *Travelling expenses*

A deduction for travelling expenses is allowed if 'the employee is obliged to incur them as holder of the employment' and they are expenses *either* 'necessarily incurred on travelling in the performance of the duties of the office or employment' (s 337) *or* 'are attributable to the employee's necessary attendance at any place in the performance of [his] duties' and are not expenses of ordinary commuting or private travel (s 338).

To qualify under s 337 expenses must satisfy the same stringent conditions as applied to all travel expenses under TA 1988 s 198 (now ITEPA 2003 s 336). The requirement that the expenses be incurred 'in the performance' of the duties excludes a deduction for the expense of travelling to work because it is incurred before, rather than in, the performance of the duties. In contrast, travelling between places of work in the course of a single employment is deductible. Section 340 gives some relief for the expenses of an employee of two companies in a group who travels between those companies. The main people, however, who can regularly claim relief under s 337 are those with 'travelling appointments' (eg sales representatives or service engineers).

**EXAMPLE 8.16**

(1)    Sally is employed as a lecturer by the Midtech University and gives seminars at both branches of the University which are two miles apart. Her travelling costs between both branches are deductible under s 337.

(2)    Jim works as a postman and as a barman in a local pub. The cost of travelling between the sorting office and the pub is not deductible under s 337 since Jim has two different jobs and is not therefore travelling between centres of work in the course of a single employment.

The requirement that travelling expenditure be 'necessarily incurred' has been considered in three House of Lords cases. In *Ricketts v Colquhoun* (1926), the travelling expenses of a barrister to and from Portsmouth where he had been appointed Recorder were not deductible. In *Owen v Pook* (1970), a general medical practitioner was allowed to deduct the expenses of travelling to a hospital where he held a part-time appointment, because some of the functions of that post were performed at his home so that he was travelling between two centres of work. Finally, in *Taylor v Provan* (1974) a Canadian director of a UK company was allowed to deduct his travelling expenses to the UK because he performed part of his duties at places outside the UK. What emerges from these cases is that travelling expenses for getting to work will not be deductible under s 337: where a person resides is his personal choice and therefore the expenses of travelling to work will not satisfy the objective test established by the courts (see **[8.173]**). Further, a job will not be treated as having two centres just because the taxpayer *chooses* to perform some of its functions at his home. In *Miners v Atkinson* (1997), the court agreed with the extreme interpretation given to this rule by the Special Commissioner: even if it is an objective requirement of the job that duties are performed at home, if the duties could be performed equally well wherever the taxpayer lived, then doing the work at that precise address should be treated as a matter of personal choice and, therefore, the costs of travelling thereto and therefrom are not deductible (for a criticism of the Special Commissioner's reasoning, see *Taxation*, 27 April 1995, p 79). This decision is, however, in line with HMRC's view that it is extremely difficult to establish home as a place of work except where the employee has a 'travelling appointment' (paras 2.13 and 2.14 of the Consultative Document on travel and subsistence issued in April 1996).

It was widely thought that the old rules were unduly restrictive and so what is now s 338 was introduced. Of course, the costs of getting to the employee's permanent workplace from home (or of private travel) remain non-deductible as does the cost of ordinary commuting. However, the new provisions do allow an employee to claim a deduction when he makes a journey from home to a place he has to attend to carry out the duties of his employment (or *vice versa*)—unless the journey is 'for practical purposes substantially ordinary commuting or private travel': in that case it is treated as such and is non-deductible (see [1998] BTR 425 at 427 for examples of how this operates). So, if an employed solicitor has to attend a meeting at a client's head office and goes there directly from home, his expenses will be deductible, provided the journey was not substantially ordinary commuting (only if he went there from his own office would the costs be deductible under s 337). For the purposes of s 338, the client's office would be designated a 'temporary workplace', and a place can remain 'temporary' even if the employee attends it regularly, provided he only goes there to perform 'a task of limited duration or for some other temporary purpose' (s 339(3)).

There are, however, rules which further circumscribe when a workplace can remain 'temporary' (see *Tax Bulletin*, December 2004, pp 1165–1168 for a detailed discussion of these rules (in relation to composite and managed service companies but nevertheless of general interest)). If an employee spends (or is likely to spend) a significant amount of his time (40% or more, in HMRC's view—see IR 490) performing the duties of his employment at a place for more than 24 months, it will become a 'permanent workplace' and the costs of travelling from home will cease to be deductible (see *Tax Bulletin*,

December 2000 on how HMRC applies these provisions to employees seconded to the UK for up to 24 months). Further, a place cannot be a temporary workplace if the employee's attendance there is 'in the course of a period of continuous work at that place comprising all or almost all of the period for which the employee is likely to hold the employment' (s 339(5)(a)(ii)— discussed in *Philips v Hamilton* (2003)).

The meaning of many of these phrases was considered by Patten J in *Kirkwood v Evans* (2002) (see **[8.173]**) in relation to Mr Evans' weekly trip to his employer's office in Leeds. The decision makes it clear that even under s 338 an employee will face substantial difficulties in claiming a deduction for travel from his home office to his employer's office (although HMRC has pointed out that for many homeworkers the employer's office may not be a permanent workplace, so that the costs of travel thereto could be deductible— *Tax Bulletin*, December 2003, pp 1068 and 1069).

### EXAMPLE 8.17*

(1)    Ernie, who works for Heartless & Co, solicitors, is asked to be at Downsizing Ltd's office at 7 am to deliver the finance director's P45 and ensure he departs without removing any confidential material. He leaves directly from home: his costs of travel are deductible.

(2)    Downsizing Ltd decide to implement a voluntary redundancy programme and changes to the employees' conditions of employment. Over a six-month period, Ernie regularly attends Downsizing's office to meet management, staff and unions. Most meetings are early in the morning, as the company does not want to disrupt the working day, and Ernie travels directly from home. His travel costs are deductible.

(3)    HMRC disputes the taxability of compensation paid for the changes to employment terms, the unions consider that correct procedures were not adopted in relation to the redundancies and the company is sued for failing to meet order deadlines (due to lack of staff). Ernie is sent to work at the company full-time to deal with the legal ramifications and is expected to be there for 30 months. Although he is, in fact, able to leave after eight months when all the cases settle, none of his travel costs for that period are deductible because his attendance was expected to exceed 24 months at the time they were initially incurred (s 339(5)(b)).

*It is assumed none of these journeys are 'substantially ordinary commuting'.

If there is a place regularly attended by employees as their base or to receive their allocation of duties (eg bus drivers attending the bus depot at the beginning and end of each shift), that place is deemed to be a permanent workplace and the costs of travel between home and there is not deductible (s 339(4)). Where a person's job is defined by reference to a particular geographical area (eg a relief manager for a brewery's pubs in Kent), the whole of that area is treated as the permanent workplace so that all travel within it is deductible, but the costs of getting to the edge of it (if, eg the employee lives outside it) are treated as ordinary commuting costs and not deductible.

The other major consequence of the introduction of what is now s 338 is that relief for travel to a temporary workplace when the employee does not in fact have a permanent workplace to go back to is now available. The primary beneficiaries of this change will be site-based employees (eg bank relief staff who are called at home and told to attend a branch where there is a staff shortage).

These are the broad outlines of the new legislation. There are so many permutations that HMRC produced an 80-page booklet (IR 490) and three articles in their *Tax Bulletin* (December 1997 and February and April 1998) to explain its understanding of how the new rules operate (which should now be read in the light of *Kirkwood v Evans* (above)).

Travelling expenses raise two further problems. *First*, allowable expenditure has to be reasonable. In *Marsden v IRC* (1965) an Inland Revenue investigator could not deduct the full cost of travelling by car to perform his duties because he could have used a cheaper form of transport. This is not to say that the cheapest form must always be used, since the matter is one of fact and degree and allowance must be made for the inconvenience of certain forms of transport. For expenditure to be reasonable, the shortest route does not necessarily have to be taken, if the longer route is taken for a good business reason (see IR 490, paras 5.11–5.15). *Secondly*, the relationship between the rules for deductibility of expenditure and the taxation of reimbursements should be carefully noted (see **[8.94]** and **[8.172]**). In the case of employees and directors who are not lower-paid, such reimbursements are automatically treated as earnings (ITEPA 2003 s 70).

It is worth noting that, as a result of s 231, mileage allowance relief can be claimed if an employee uses his own car for business travel and is not reimbursed the full tax-free mileage allowance payments permissible. If that relief is available or if an employee uses his own car and receives mileage allowance payments, no deduction can be claimed under the 'travel deduction provisions' (s 359).  **[8.174]**

## 3  Other deductions

Further provisions relating to deductions are grouped in the remaining Chapters of Part 5 according to the type of deduction. Chapter 3 allows deductions where the employee is taxed under the benefits code but could have claimed a deduction under Part 5 Chapter 2 or 5 if he had paid for the goods or services provided as a benefit in kind. Chapter 4 covers deductions for which an allowance is fixed by Treasury Order (eg if there is a specified allowance for maintaining work equipment for a specified type employment). Chapter 5 allows a deduction in certain limited circumstances where the employer (or a third party) has paid for something and that payment is treated as earnings. In the main it relates to travel and accommodation expenses where duties are performed abroad, though s 377 relates to the provision of personal security assets and services (for an in-depth discussion of the application of its predecessor, FA 1989 s 50, see the Special Commissioners' decision in *Lord Hanson v Mansworth* (2004)). Chapter 6 relates specifically to seafarers.  **[8.175]–[8.190]**

## XII   COLLECTION OF TAX

### 1   The scope of the provisions

Tax relating to employment income is collected by a sophisticated method of deduction at source operated by the employer and known as the PAYE system (ITEPA 2003 Part 11). The employer used to be required by statute to 'deduct' tax when he made a payment (TA 1988 s 203), with the detailed operation of the deduction system being set out in regulations. Most peculiarly, there is no longer primary legislation requiring PAYE to be operated: s 684(1) imposes an obligation on HMRC to make regulations with respect to the collection of all 'PAYE income' and s 684(2) includes in the list of what they may include in those regulations 'provision for requiring persons making payments of PAYE income to make, at the time of the payment, deductions of ... income tax', but this is not quite the same as what the legislation previously required. A payment is treated as made when it is treated as received by the employee (s 686, mirroring s 18—see **[8.12]**). There are difficulties in establishing that there has been a 'deduction' when no actual payment is made at the time of the deemed payment, particularly when money is never actually handed over but a credit is merely given against drawings already made on a director's loan account (see *R v IRC, ex p McVeigh* (1996)).

The system generally applies to all taxable earnings and taxable specific income (defined in s 10). There are far-reaching provisions which extend the PAYE net to cover situations where it would normally be difficult for HMRC to collect the tax due (for instance, if the employer is outside the UK).

Section 689 provides that if the employer (or, if applicable, the person paying the earnings on behalf of the employer) is not subject to the Income Tax (Employments) Regulations 2003, SI 2003/2682 (the PAYE Regulations) (as to which, see *Clark v Oceanic Contractors* (1983), discussed at **[18.51]**), and does not collect PAYE voluntarily, then the person for whom the employee 'works' (in the UK) is treated as making the payment and is, therefore, required to operate PAYE. Typically, this will catch the employee seconded to a UK subsidiary. Section 690 deals with the situation where a non-UK resident employee is liable to UK income tax on his UK earnings because he performs part of his duties in the UK. The employer is required to apply to HMRC for a direction agreeing 'what part of his remuneration is liable to UK income tax'; if no direction is applied for, the employer must operate PAYE in respect of the entire salary. Section 691 enables HMRC to subject a person for whom an employee works (but who is not his employer) to the PAYE Regulations even if the actual employer is taxed in the UK and therefore subject to the PAYE Regulations. HMRC can direct that person to operate PAYE 'if it is likely that income tax will not be deducted or accounted for in accordance with the Regulations'.

ITEPA s 692 allows regulations to make provision for PAYE to be operated where tips are collected and shared amongst employees. The obligation to operate PAYE can be imposed on the person running the arrangement, with a residual liability on the actual employer. This provision used to be in the PAYE Regulations dealing with these arrangements under which the organiser was called the 'troncmaster'. (See HMRC Booklet E24.)          **[8.191]**

2 **Problem cases**

a) *Benefits in kind*

Benefits in kind were generally seen as excluded from the PAYE regime on the basis that there was no payment (but see *Paul Dunstall Organisation Ltd v Hedges* (1999), considered below). However, PAYE has now been imposed where assessable income is provided in the form of 'readily convertible assets' (s 696): PAYE is also imposed where non-cash vouchers and credit-tokens which may be exchanged for such assets (or money, in the case of credit-tokens) are obtained and where cash vouchers to which Part 3 Chapter 4 applies are received (ss 693–695).

Part 11 Chapter 4 and the PAYE Regulations provide how and when the employer is to account for PAYE on these 'notional payments'. They also exclude certain benefits from the scope of these provisions (eg cash vouchers used to defray expenses if the amount for which the voucher can be exchanged would not, if it had been paid directly by the employer to the employee, have been taxable except under Chapter 3 Part 10; some shares received through approved employee share schemes or on exercise of some options granted before 27 November 1996).

Deciding whether or not an asset is readily convertible can be difficult. The definition is set out in s 702 and includes assets for which 'trading arrangements' exist (or are likely to come into existence). On the difficult question of what constitutes 'trading arrangements' see *DTE Financial Services Ltd v Wilson* (2001) (**[8.194]**) and *NMB Holdings Ltd v Secretary of State for Social Security* (2000) (but note that these relate to the legislation before it was amended in 1998). HMRC's interpretation of 'readily convertible' can be seen in *Tax Bulletin*, August 1998, pp 563–567 and April 2000, pp 735 and 736: but it should be noted that in some situations it now views that test as more easily satisfied than there indicated; and that the definition was amended by FA 2003 Sch 22 para 15 so as to include any share the provision of which would not entitle the employing company to a corporation tax deduction under FA 2003 Sch 23 (the main target of this being shares in an unquoted subsidiary of an unquoted parent).

To prevent avoidance, s 697 imposes PAYE where an asset that the employee already owns is enhanced in value, if the asset falls within the definition of 'readily convertible assets'.                    **[8.192]**

b) *Part only of a payment taxed*

Another exclusion derives from the House of Lords decision in *IRC v Herd* (1993). It was held that any payment 'only part of which is assessable to income tax under Schedule E' is excluded from the system because there is no machinery for distinguishing the part that is taxable from the part that is not. In such a situation there is no obligation on the payer to operate PAYE in relation to the taxable part. This type of situation used to arise (as it did in *Herd*) where an employee sells shares acquired by reason of his employment and part only of the purchase price is taxable (eg under ITEPA 2003 Part 7 Chapter 3D—see **[9.28]**) but note that the PAYE treatment changed in that situation as a result of the amendments effected to ITEPA 2003 ss 698 and 700 by FA 2003 (see **[9.34]**)).

The decision in *IRC v Herd* (1993) cast doubt on the practice under which employers operated PAYE on part of an employee's remuneration where the other part was not subject to UK tax (because he performed some of his duties abroad and was not resident or not ordinarily resident). What is now s 690 was therefore introduced to deal with this situation (see **[8.191]**).

As a result of these legislative changes, there is now little scope for the principle established in *IRC v Herd* (1993) to operate.          **[8.193]**

## c)    What is a 'payment'?

Even prior to the introduction of the anti-avoidance provisions, HMRC would try to collect PAYE even though the employee had not actually received cash from the employer (see Press Release IR 24 (30 November 1993) for some examples of the wide interpretation HMRC gave to the word 'payment'). One particularly popular attack was to ascertain whether there had been a declaration of a monetary amount due to the employee (say a bonus of £500,000) which had then been commuted into an asset (say gold bars): HMRC argued that the mere declaration of the amount counted as a 'payment'. In *Paul Dunstall Organisation Ltd v Hedges* (1999), this was in essence what happened (except the payment was in land which the employee immediately sold), but the finding by the Special Commissioners in favour of HMRC was not based on such an approach. Instead, the Special Commissioners seemed to take the view that, since regulation 6 of the (then) PAYE Regulations (SI 1993/744) required the operation of PAYE on the payment of emoluments and that term included non-cash assets, the PAYE obligation extended to such assets (one of the two Special Commissioners in that case applied the same reasoning in *Black v Inspector of Taxes* (2000)). This ignored the fact that it was only emoluments which were 'paid' which triggered the obligation and the reasoning in this part of the decision has been much criticised (see *Taxation*, 4 February 1999, p 429 and 6 May 1999, p 148).

Of course, inserting land in place of cash remuneration could have been regarded as an inserted step under the *Ramsay* principle (as the Commissioners mentioned *obiter* in *Dunstall*). Adopting the approach in *MacNiven v Westmoreland Investments Ltd* (2001) (to ascertain first whether the concept used in the legislation (in this case 'payment') is a practical commercial one and, only if it is, to apply *Ramsay* to the composite transaction), the Court of Appeal in *DTE Financial Services Ltd v Wilson* (2001) found that, when the company satisfied bonuses by assigning its beneficial interest in an offshore trust to the employee, who then received £40,000 from the trustees when his interest fell in, a PAYE liability was triggered. The court's robust approach was to interpret the sequence of events as the company deciding to pay the employee a £40,000 bonus and the employee receiving that bonus—the cash payment received by him was a payment of employment income, so PAYE applied.          **[8.194]**

## 3    Coding and accounting for tax due

### a)    PAYE coding

PAYE is an effective tax collection system which reduces the opportunity and incentive for tax evasion. The employer is given a code for each employee which represents the amount of his (tax-free) allowances less taxable benefits in kind (of which HMRC are aware) for the tax year. This code and the amount of tax paid to date in the tax year determine the amount of tax to be deducted at source. PAYE can be used to collect underpayments of tax by the employee in previous years or tax due on other income by reducing (or eliminating completely) the amount of the employee's (tax-free) allowances for the current year. **[8.195]**

b)  *K codes*

A K code is applied if the employee receives benefits in kind (or has other income not subject to PAYE) the value of which exceeds his personal allowances. The K code is a negative code: normally a non-K code results in a deduction from earnings to arrive at the amount subject to PAYE; the K code results in an addition to earnings, thereby increasing the amount of tax collected. However, an employee's salary cannot entirely be applied in paying tax on his benefits in kind: tax deducted from any payment cannot exceed 50% of the payment (except where tax is being collected on 'notional payments'—see *Tax Bulletin*, May 1994, pp 121–122) (PAYE Regulations reg 23). **[8.196]**

c)  *Returns*

For directors and employees earning at least £8,500 pa, the employer must each year complete Form P11D giving details of benefits in kind and payments by way of expenses (save, in the latter case, those for which a dispensation has been granted: see ITEPA 2003 s 65 and IR 69); for other employees Form P9D must be completed. Other returns may also be required (for instance, in relation to company cars and termination payments). A Form P60 must be given to each employee working for the employer on 5 April, giving details of earnings subject to PAYE and the tax paid; a Form P45 (giving similar details for the tax year to date) is given on cessation of employment. **[8.197]**

d)  *PAYE settlement agreements*

Certain employers regularly agree to pay their employees' tax liabilities on minor items (for instance, the cost of office parties which exceed the exempt amount (see **[8.168]**)—a lump sum is paid for all employees on a grossed–up basis—under what are known as 'PAYE settlement agreements' (or 'PSAs') (ITEPA 2003 ss 703–707). The detailed rules are set out in the PAYE Regulations Part 6, SP5/96, a leaflet (IR 155) and a statement in *Tax Bulletin*, December 1996, p 365. **[8.198]**

e)  *Accounting to HMRC*

Normally, an employer has to account to HMRC within 14 days of the end of the income tax month during which he should have deducted the tax (ie normally by the 19th of the following month); a 17-day delay applies if the employer pays electronically. However, where the amount due is relatively low, the employer can account on a quarterly basis (PAYE Regulations reg 41).

In the event of an overpayment of tax in a previous year, this will be corrected between HMRC and the employee himself either by direct repayment or by set-off against other tax liabilities of that year; alternatively, the employee's code for the current year can be adjusted to take the repayment due into account. If the PAYE due for the tax year is not paid by the following 19 April (22 April if payment is made electronically), interest is payable (PAYE Regulations reg 82).                                                      **[8.199]**

### f)    *Non-deduction of PAYE*

Special provisions operate to ensure that PAYE is operated on remuneration paid to directors. Section 223 provides that, whenever tax on a director's earnings should have been deducted in accordance with the regulations and the whole, or part, of the amount due was not deducted but was accounted for to HMRC by a person other than the director, then, unless the director makes good the tax paid, he will be treated as receiving further earnings equal to the amount of tax that has been accounted for to HMRC. This provision only applies to directors not excluded from the benefits code by Part 3 Chapter 11 (see **[8.113]**).

There is a similar provision if an employer is treated as making a 'notional payment' to an employee or director (generally, a payment treated as made under ss 687, 689, 693–700: see s 710(2)(a)). The employer is required to account for the tax due; and if that tax is neither deducted from actual payments made nor made good by the employee within 90 days, the tax payable is treated as a taxable benefit (s 222) (see *Ferguson v IRC* (2001) for what may be regarded as a liberal interpretation of 'making good'; and EI 11952 for HMRC's harsher view of whether a credit balance in a director's loan account is sufficient to satisfy the statutory requirement that the tax due is 'made good'). Unfortunately for the employer, he only has a statutory right to deduct the tax due from cash payments made in the same income tax month as the notional payment (s 710(7) and see *Tax Bulletin*, April 2000, pp 734 and 735 for a discussion of whether the uncollected tax could be treated as a loan). As the PAYE obligation extends to notional payments made to ex-employees (who may well not be in receipt of cash payments), it has become increasingly important for employers to ensure they have some enforceable means of collecting tax paid from the recipients of these notional payments (see **[8.202]**).                                        **[8.200]**

### g)    *When the employee can be directly assessed*

Under the PAYE system, the liability of the employer to deduct and account for the correct amount of tax is usually exclusive, so that HMRC cannot assess an employee for unpaid tax. Exceptions are provided for in regulations 72(3), (4) and 81 of the PAYE Regulations. Regulation 72(3), which applies when an employee receives the earnings knowing that the employer has wilfully failed to deduct the proper amount of tax, is often relied on by HMRC. In *R v IRC, ex p McVeigh* (1996), May J commented that this provision 'would normally operate where the employer had wilfully paid an employee gross and the employee knew this'. Regulation 81's prime role is to allow an Inspector to determine an amount of PAYE due from an employer if he believes tax is payable; but if the tax so determined is not paid by the employer, it can be collected from the employee if the same conditions as those in regulation 72(4) are satisfied. As a result of amendments effected by SI 2004/851, an employee can now appeal against a direction under regulation 72 or 81.

A heavy burden is placed on HMRC if regulation 72(4) (or 81) is to be satisfied, since not only is actual knowledge on the part of the employee required but also an element of blameworthiness on the part of the employer must be shown. This burden was satisfied in the cases of *R v IRC, ex p Keys and ex p Cook* (1987) where the employees in question were the controlling directors of the employer company which had failed over a number of years to operate PAYE in respect of their salaries (for the public law defence available to an employee in such cases, see *Pawlowski v Dunnington* (1999)).

Regulation 72(3), which can be applied by HMRC if satisfied that the employer took reasonable care to comply with the regulations and the error was made in good faith, is rarely applied. However, as a result of amendments effected by SI 2004/851, an employer can now request HMRC to make a direction if the employer considers an error was made in good faith, so more use may now be made of this mode of recovery.                        **[8.201]**

h)   *Recovery of tax from the employee*

A perennial problem faced by employers is how to recover from employees tax paid over to HMRC but not deducted from their salaries. The statutory rights are extremely limited. Whether recovery is possible at common law was until recently open to debate. In *Bernard & Shaw Ltd v Shaw* (1951) a company failed in a restitutionary claim, but this was not surprising since it had not actually paid over the tax to HMRC; the judge left open the possibility that, if it had done so, it might have been successful in an action for 'money paid to the use of the employee' on the basis that the employee was 'ultimately responsible' for the tax. In the more recent case of *McCarthy v McCarthy & Stone plc* (2006) the employer successfully recovered, from a former director, PAYE income tax and NICs payments it had made to HMRC based on a restitutionary claim. The High Court's decision followed the the possibility left open in *Bernard & Shaw Ltd v Shaw* (1951). The judge accepted that the PAYE payments made by the employer were payments for which the director was 'ultimately responsible' for and therefore the employer was entitled to recover the same from the employee.

A restitutionary action based on mistake of fact will often not be appropriate (as there has not normally been such a mistake), but the removal of the bar to restitutionary claims based on mistakes of law effected by the House of Lords in *Kleinwort Benson v Lincoln City Council* (1998) could also prove helpful to employers (see *Taxation*, 18 March 1999, p 595 and 22 March 2001, p 601 for details of two successful restitutionary claims).                        **[8.202]**

4  **Future reform**

Operating PAYE is a burden for employers, not only because of the uncertainties touched on above and the fact that getting it wrong can be expensive (see *Taxation*, 22 February 2001, p 483 but note the possible right of recovery discussed at **[8.202]**) but also because the basic system is cumulative, aiming to ensure that at any given week in a tax year the tax paid by an employee matches his liabilities. The Treasury's Sixth Report on HMRC advised that, unless the PAYE system could adapt to deal more easily with people commencing and leaving employment during a tax year, 'it may in the longer term, be necessary to consider moving to non-cumulative collection of PAYE or to a form of collection direct from employees'.                    **[8.203]**

# 9 Employee participation: options, incentives and trusts

*Updated by Mark Ife, LLB MJur, Solicitor, Herbert Smith LLP*

## I INTRODUCTION

### 1 Encouraging employee share ownership

Over the last 25 years there has been a substantial growth in employee share option and share incentive schemes. The major attraction of such schemes was stated by the Chancellor in his Foreword to a consultation document on employee share ownership (December 1998) as follows: 'Share ownership offers employees a real stake in their company with shareholders, managers and employees working towards common goals.'

Despite this growth, 'only a fraction of British employees and an even smaller minority of those outside senior management own shares in the companies they work in'. Therefore, the Government's more recent emphasis has been on encouraging companies to introduce schemes which benefit all their employees and on restricting tax relief for schemes which enable large benefits to be provided to senior management, unless the Government perceives substantial macro-economic benefits may result (as with Enterprise Management Incentives (EMIs) introduced by FA 2000).

The Government encourages employees to invest in their employers by enabling such investment to be made out of pre-tax salary through Share Incentive Plans (SIPs), also introduced in 2000. Corporate collapses, such as Marconi and Enron, in which employees have seen their investment become worthless, may, however, act as a disincentive. Nevertheless, the Government still believes that productivity will be increased by encouraging employee participation. The research report 'Employee ownership, motivation and productivity' (November 2002) for Employees Direct by Birkbeck College, University of London and The Work Foundation concludes that there is 'undoubtedly' evidence to support this belief. It is therefore important for the Government to ensure that all the adverse publicity about share benefits provided to 'fat cats' and 'failing executives' does not undermine this key objective.

Various HMRC Manuals deal with share schemes: the Share Schemes Manual (SSM prefix) and the Employee Share Schemes Unit Manual (ESSU prefix), which covers approved schemes, are gradually being replaced by the Employment Related Securities Manual (ERSM prefix) which is available on the HMRC website (www.hmrc.gov.uk/shareschemes). The Employee Shares & Securities Unit at HMRC also publish (now in electronic form only) an irregular newsletter *Share Focus*. HMRC's view of the operation of ITEPA 2003 Part 7, which deals with the taxation of employment-related securities, can also be found in the shares and securities section of its website, in its answers to a series of Frequently Asked Questions (FAQs).                    **[9.1]**


## 2    Taxation of share incentives and options

An individual who is given shares by his employer receives taxable earnings if the shares are 'from employment' and will suffer income tax on the market value of those shares on the date when he receives them: *Weight v Salmon* (1935) and ITEPA 2003 s 9. Similarly, an employee who is sold shares by his employer at an undervalue receives earnings equal to the difference between the price paid and the market value of the shares at the date of purchase. These types of arrangement, where the employee receives shares not share options, are referred to in this **Chapter 9** as *share incentives*.

Various schemes, including the use of *share options*, were introduced by employers in an attempt to circumvent the income tax net. Inevitably, anti-avoidance legislation was then passed in an attempt to widen that net!

Certain employee share schemes are given favourable tax treatment. These are the 'approved schemes'. Profits made by employees under such schemes are, provided the relevant criteria are met, treated as capital gains and are therefore subject to CGT rather than income tax. Although the unification of the rates of income and capital gains tax reduced the tax advantage enjoyed by approved schemes, that advantage has now been restored by the imposition of national insurance contributions (NICs) on benefits received from unapproved schemes and the introduction of CGT taper relief. In addition, where such profits fall to be taxed within the CGT regime, the individual will also benefit from the CGT annual exemption. On the other hand, except for the minority of employees who are eligible to receive approved Enterprise Management Incentive options, the potential to make very large gains is only obtainable under unapproved schemes.

Where employees are offered the opportunity to buy shares they may borrow to finance their acquisition. Readers are referred to **[7.44]** for a discussion of the tax relief available for interest paid on such loans where the company is a close company and to *Revenue Law* (23rd edn) **[5.123]** for a discussion of the tax treatment for employees where the loan is provided interest-free.                    **[9.2]**

### 3   Reporting obligations

At the same time that the taxation of unapproved schemes was fundamentally changed by FA 2003 (see Section II), new reporting requirements were also introduced. There are separate returns for each of the approved share schemes and a single return (Form 42) for all unapproved arrangements. The filing dates for returns for both approved and unapproved arrangements and the penalties for failure to comply with the new rules are set out in *Share Focus*, Issue 3 (March 2004). Essentially, companies will have three months from the end of the tax year in which to file the relevant returns. It is worth noting that the reporting obligations are not limited to shares acquired through specific schemes but will also apply, for instance, to shares acquired through an 'earn-out' (see **[9.20]** (7)). Indeed, the reporting requirements are not limited to cases where an income tax charge arises: they may apply whenever an employee or director acquires shares. HMRC has produced recent guidance on the completion of Form 42, which is available on their website.

The anti-avoidance reporting obligations introduced by FA 2004 Part 7 (see *Revenue Law* (23rd edn) **[42.49]** ff) may also apply to employee share scheme arrangements.                                              **[9.3]–[9.19]**

## II   UNAPPROVED SHARE SCHEMES

### 1   Introduction

The income tax treatment of unapproved schemes was introduced on a piecemeal basis mainly in response to varied attempts over the years to devise arrangements that escaped the income tax net. Although still viewed as complex, this piecemeal approach was replaced with the provisions set out in FA 2003 Sch 22.

> 'By far the lengthiest and most complex part of this year's Finance Bill is Schedule 22 which completely rewrites the rules relating to the tax treatment of non-approved employee share schemes. This is an area of tax law which has always been an active battleground between the Revenue and taxpayers. The Revenue's abiding concern is that share schemes will be used to remunerate employees in a way which avoids income tax. Taxpayer motivation to do just that has been raised by the generous terms on which CGT taper relief has been extended to employee shareholders and by the imposition of national insurance on share schemes.
>
> The main purpose of Schedule 22 is, of course, to close loopholes. But the Revenue accepts that the income tax net should only catch gains which are artificially engineered as opposed to those arising from "real" increases in share values generated by corporate performance.'
>
> (*Tax Journal*, 5 May 2003)

In the remainder of this Section, the operation of the amended Chapters of Part 7 of ITEPA 2003 is examined. It is assumed throughout these Chapters that they, and only they, apply to the shares in question. Therefore, the operative date for each amended provision to come into force is not set out, nor the shares to which each apply (some only apply to shares acquired after 16 April 2003, some to shares whenever acquired). Readers for whom the exact details of the application of a particular provision are important will need to consult FA 2003 Sch 22. Further, whilst in general the provisions of ITEPA 2003 before it was amended by FA 2003 reflected the old legislation, there were one or two changes; and those changes in some cases only applied from 6 April 2003 to 9 or 16 April 2003 and were subject to their own transitional provisions! In relation to the changes effected by ITEPA 2003, readers are referred to *Tax Journal,* 17 April 2003, 11–12.

There are seven further points of general application:

(1)    In the majority of cases employees are given *shares* but as advantage was being taken of the fact that the anti-avoidance legislation only applied to shares, ITEPA 2003 Part 7 now extends to 'securities', as defined in s 420 (and interests therein). However, to reflect the usual position, this Chapter 9 refers to shares.

(2)    In appropriate circumstances it used to be possible to argue that employees/directors had not acquired shares in their company by reason of that status but rather as investors (for instance, on a management buy-out). In most cases such an argument will no longer be possible: now any right or opportunity to acquire shares which is made available by a person's employer (or someone connected with it) will be deemed to be available '**by reason of employment**' (the prerequisite to taxability—s 421B(1)), unless provided by an individual 'in the normal course of the domestic, family or personal relationships' of that individual (s 421B(3)). The proviso might apply, for instance, when a son received shares in his employing company from his father. If the deeming provision does not apply, the Northern Ireland Court of Appeal's consideration of the analogous wording in TA 1988 s 154 (now, ITEPA 2003 s 201) in *Mairs v Haughey* (1992) may provide helpful guidance as to the meaning of the phrase 'by reason of employment'. As a result of this change, ITEPA 2003 Part 7 is wider in scope than the previous provisions which has meant that the Government has had to introduce specific legislation (for example in relation to research institution spinout companies (FA 2005 s 20) —see [**9.31**]) to limit the extent of this legislation.

(3)    Closely connected to (2), section 421B applies Chapters 2 to 4 of Part 7 if shares are acquired 'where the right or opportunity to acquire [them] is **available**' by reason of employment. An almost identical phrase in the old legislation was considered by the Court of Session in *IRC v Herd* (1992). The argument centred around whether an opportunity was 'available' by reason of employment when the employee had stipulated that he must receive the shares as a precondition to taking up the appointment: not surprisingly, the court declined to interpret the provision as requiring it to investigate who instigated the idea of providing share benefits to the employee. However, it should be noted that by virtue of s 421B(2)(b), 'employment' is also taken to cover former and prospective employment.

(4)    There are exceptions from the income tax charges if the event (which would otherwise be a **chargeable** event) affects all shares of the same class as the employee's shares, provided certain conditions are satisfied. Those conditions have been amended with effect from 7 May 2004 by FA 2004 s 86 as it was thought that the previous exceptions were being

exploited to provide an exemption from income tax when employees received value from their shares. Now the exception only applies if: (a) 'the avoidance of tax or national insurance contributions was not the main purpose, or one of the main purposes, of the arrangements under which the right or opportunity to acquire' the employee shares was made available; and (b) either the company is employee-controlled by virtue of shares of that class or the majority of the shares of that class are not held by employees (see, for example, ITEPA 2003 s 429 as amended by FA 2004). Similar anti-avoidance provisions (where HMRC consider avoidance of tax and NIC to be a 'main purpose') have been introduced by F (No 2) A 2005 Sch 2, for example in relation to restricted securities (ITEPA 2003 s 424), convertible securities (ITEPA 2003 s 437) and acquisitions at less than market value (ITEPA 2003 s 446R and new s 446UA).

(5) Prior to FA 2004, ITEPA 2003 s 421F excluded shares acquired on a public offer from the application of Part 7 Chapters 2–4. As a result of FA 2004 s 89, with effect from 18 June (but in relation to shares whenever acquired), only Chapters 2, 3 and 3C are disapplied and then only if tax or NIC avoidance is not the main purpose of the arrangements under which the shares are acquired or held.

(6) In most cases, the charge imposed by Part 7 will arise whether it is the employee or an associate of his who acquires the shares. It is worth noting that, most peculiarly, the legislation does not draw a distinction between the employee and his associates: instead, the employee himself is included in the definition of 'associated person' in s 421C: as a result, on a casual reading of the sections which describe the circumstances when a charge arises and which refer only to an 'associated person' acquiring etc the shares, it looks as if there are no charges when the employee himself holds the shares! Since, in fact, it will usually be the employee himself who acquires the shares, this **Chapter 9** refers only to him.

Sections 421C and 472 (which define 'associated persons' for the purposes of ITEPA 2003 Part 7 Chapter 3) were amended by FA 2004 s 90 to extend the definition of who are 'associated' persons. The current term covers the person who acquires the shares, the employee (if different) and any 'relevant linked person' (ie a current or former connected person or member of the same household). HMRC's reasons for making this change were set out in News Release 30/4:

> 'The changes will ensure that charges cannot be avoided by ensuring that persons, once associated, remain associated and also provide for a charge on a benefit received through the ownership of securities options.'

(7) There are several types of arrangement that could fall within more than one Chapter of Part 7. One example is 'equity ratchets'. These are commonly found in management buyouts and take various forms but all have the same aim—the managers' proportion of the ordinary share capital will increase (and that of the other investors will fall) if certain performance targets are met. Other examples are 'earn-outs' (where the number of shares a purchaser provides to the vendor as consideration for the purchase, or the amount it pays, varies depending on how

the company acquired performs) and 'flowering shares' (where rights provisionally attach to shares when they are acquired but whether they become unconditionally attached depends on future events). How arrangements are structured will affect how, if at all, Part 7 applies. The Memorandum of Understanding between the British Venture Capital Association and the Inland Revenue dated 25 July 2003 and some of the FAQs on the HMRC website discuss how some of those arrangements may be taxed.                                                    **[9.20]**

## 2   Share Incentives

### a)   *Restricted shares*

Some forms of long-term incentive plans (particularly in private companies) involve employees receiving shares subject to a restriction on disposing of them for a certain period and to their being forfeited if the employee leaves service before the end of that period. Sometimes the shares will be held in trust until the end of the period but the employee is entitled to receive dividends and instruct the trustees how to vote in the meantime. These restricted share schemes have become increasingly popular with companies because they not only act as an incentive to the employee to remain in service but also ensure an immediate identity of interest between him and the company. Further, just as companies can make exerciseability of unapproved options subject to satisfying performance criteria, so shares held under these schemes can also be made subject to forfeiture if such criteria are not met. ITEPA 2003 Part 7 Chapter 2 imposes income tax charges in relation to shares that are 'restricted' when acquired. These provisions only apply if the employee was resident and ordinarily resident in the UK at the time of acquisition (s 421E).

Other forms of long-term incentive plans involve employees being given a right to acquire shares in the future, rather than being given the shares themselves. In most such cases, a tax charge on acquiring the shares will arise under the 'option' regime (see **[9.32]**) or as a general employment income charge. If the shares then acquired are restricted, post-acquisition charges can arise under Part 7 Chapter 2.                                       **[9.21]**

### i)   *Meaning of restriction*

The effect of imposing restrictions on shares is to reduce their market value at the time they are acquired. Shares are restricted if their value is less than it would be but for a restriction whereby:

(1)   the shares may be forfeit or the employee can be compelled to sell them for less than their market value at the time of sale (the forfeiture provision);

(2)   their dividend, voting, transfer or any other rights are restricted, or the employee can be compelled to sell the shares (whatever the price); or

(3)   the disposal or retention of the shares or the exercise of rights attached to them may result in some other type of disadvantage (s 423).

Shares will not be restricted merely because the employee can be forced to sell them on termination of employment for misconduct at less than their then market value (s 424(b)). This exemption is narrow and does not apply where employers want to 'punish' employees who resign/are dismissed for other reasons, such as poor performance. Section 424 also provides that forfeiture for non-payment of calls on nil or partly paid shares do not count as restrictions. Previously this also included an exemption for the possibility of redeemable shares being redeemed, but this was removed by F (No 2) A 2005. **[9.22]**

*ii)    The tax charge—acquisition*

Normally, there would be an income tax charge under s 9 on the acquisition of restricted shares if the employee did not pay their (restricted) market value; but if they fall within category (1) listed in **[9.22]**, there will not be such an income tax charge if those restrictions will fall away within five years (even if the shares would remain restricted for another reason) (s 425(2)), unless there is an election under s 425(3). Under this provision it is, therefore, possible for an employee to receive a gift of shares that are subject to forfeiture without paying any tax until the forfeiture provision is lifted or falls away. Even if there is no income tax charge on acquisition under Part 7 Chapter 2, there may still be such a charge if the shares fall within Chapters 3, 3C or 5 (see below). **[9.23]**

*iii)    The tax charge—chargeable events*

Whatever the reason for the shares being restricted, whenever there is a 'chargeable event', the taxable amount calculated under s 428 will 'count as employment income' (see **[8.11]**). There is such an event on the shares ceasing to be restricted, a restriction being varied or on an arm's length sale (s 427). Section 428 sets out a formula for calculating the taxable amount which, basically, results in the taxable amount being the same percentage of the unrestricted market value of the shares immediately after the chargeable event (or percentage of the sale proceeds, if lower) as the percentage difference between the unrestricted market value of the shares when they were acquired and their actual (restricted) value at that time (ie the untaxed proportion).

The policy behind this approach is that the employee should be able to benefit in the same way as an investor would from any increase in value in that part of the share for which he has paid (directly or by paying income tax on its value), so that only the increase in value attributable to that part for which he has not so paid should be within the income tax net.

**EXAMPLE 9.1**

Albert is given shares in his employer, Consort Ltd, which would have an unrestricted market value of £2.50. As the shares have no dividend or voting rights for the first five years, they are actually only worth £1.50. Albert has to pay income tax on £1.50 but has avoided tax on £1 (or two-fifths of the unrestricted value).

Three years later, the restrictions are removed and thereafter the shares are worth £5. Albert will be treated as having employment income of £2 (two-fifths of £5). If the shares were sold at £5, £1.50 (£5 less £1.50 and £2) would be chargeable to CGT (see **[9.39]**).

NB If the shares had been sold before the restrictions were lifted, the same calculation has to be done but if (as would normally be the case with this type of restriction) the restrictions have the same proportionate effect on the share value at the time of the sale as they did at the time of acquisition, the calculation will produce a nil-charge to income tax: this is in line with the policy objective identified above.

Tax charges after acquisition can, however, be avoided by making an election under s 431 for full disapplication of Chapter 2 on acquisition, so that the unrestricted market value of the shares is then taxed (or the difference between that and the price the employee paid as a general charge to income tax under s 9); or the tax charge after acquisition can be reduced by electing for a partial disapplication (ie that the market value on acquisition should be calculated as if some of the restrictions did not apply). The benefit of making such an election is that any future increase in value will generally be subject only to CGT. However, if the share price was to fall, no reclaim of the income tax already paid can be claimed.

**EXAMPLE 9.2**

Assume that Albert made a section 431 election for full disapplication on acquisition.

He would have had to pay income tax on £2.50 on acquisition but there would be no further charges under Chapter 2. If the shares were sold at £5, £2.50 (£5 less £2.50) would be chargeable to CGT.                                    **[9.24]**

b)    *Convertible shares*

The issue of convertible shares to employees, while unusual, is normally associated with the imposition of performance conditions and is most commonly found when the directors have acquired the company with funding from a venture capitalist. It might be the case that the latter holds ordinary shares and the directors have preference shares which will convert to ordinary shares (thus reducing the percentage held by the venture capitalist) on the achievement of performance targets.

HMRC treats convertible shares as two separate assets: the share itself, ignoring the right to convert; and the right to convert. The former is taxed on receipt in the usual way, so the charge will depend upon what, if anything, the employee pays for the shares. Although the latter has a value on receipt, it is not taxed until conversion occurs. When convertible shares are acquired by employees who are resident and ordinarily resident in the UK, there is an income tax charge on their conversion or sale or if the entitlement to convert is released for consideration or if the employee receives a benefit in connection with that entitlement (ss 438–439).

Sections 440–442 set out how to calculate the taxable amount on the occurrence of the chargeable event. Where the shares have been converted, s 441 taxes only the difference in value between the shares converted and the shares acquired.                                                                    **[9.25]**

**EXAMPLE 9.3**

Albert buys 100 preference shares (which are convertible into ordinary shares on achieving performance targets) for £100 (their market value). Ignoring the conversion right, they are worth £150 when he converts them to 100 ordinary shares worth £1,000. He will be charged to income tax on £850.

NB (1) The preference shares are valued as if they were not convertible (s 441(7)) as otherwise the added value that could be acquired by converting would increase their market value to that of the ordinary shares once the right to convert became unrestricted.

(2) It may be possible to avoid any income tax charge by structuring the arrangements differently: see the Memorandum of Understanding referred to at (7) in [9.21].

c) *Artificial depression or enhancement of market value*

Part 7 Chapters 3A and 3B cover the situation when the value of employee shares is enhanced or depressed because of things done other than for genuine commercial reasons. Both Chapters (ss 446A and 446K) include a non-exhaustive definition of 'things that are ... done otherwise than for genuine commercial purposes': this includes where one of the main purposes is the avoidance of tax or NICs; and non-arm's length transactions between group companies.

Section 446B applies to impose a charge on acquisition if, within the seven years preceding the employee's acquisition, the market value of the shares has been artificially depressed by at least 10%. It does not apply if the shares are restricted and fall within s 425(2) where a forfeiture provision applies, provided no election has been made under s 425(3) (see [9.23]). The fact that s 446B applies does not prevent other charges applying (for instance, the ongoing notional loan charge under Chapter 3C (see [9.27])).

Section 446C sets out how to calculate the taxable amount on acquisition (although the formula varies if the shares in question are restricted or convertible (s 446D)). That calculation results in the employee having taxable income equal to the difference between what would have been the market value but for its artificial depression and the actual market value of the shares (or the price paid, if higher). The rest of Chapter 3A sets out how other tax charges (including under ITEPA 2003 s 427 *as originally enacted*) have to be adjusted if the value of the share is artificially depressed *after* acquisition. Further, if the shares are restricted (as will often be the case), a depreciatory transaction will result in a tax charge every 5 April (s 446E).

FA 2004 s 87 introduced an anti-avoidance provision into Chapter 3A. ITEPA 2003 s 446E(1) is amended to introduce other occasions when the market value of the shares which are restricted has to be assessed: when the shares are disposed of in circumstances which are not a chargeable event under Chapter 2 and when they are cancelled. If either of those happens when the shares are restricted and the market value is artificially depressed, there will be a tax charge.

Chapter 3B treats the difference between the actual market value of employee shares on 5 April each year and what would have been their market value if there had not been any non-commercial increases in value during the tax year as employment income for that tax year, even though that increase in value has not been realised (s 446N). No charge arises unless the market value of the shares has been enhanced by at least 10% in the tax year. [9.26]

d)  *Shares acquired for less than market value*

If fully paid shares are issued to a director or employee for less than their market value at that date, the difference between that value and any consideration paid is taxable under s 9. If shares are acquired by a director or 'higher paid' employee and the consideration to be paid is left outstanding as a debt, ITEPA 2003 Part 3 Chapter 7 may apply to that loan. However, if shares are issued at market value but only part of that price is payable on issue (so that the shares are issued partly paid), the resultant benefit to such a director or employee does not fall within either of the foregoing situations but is dealt with by the special provisions in ITEPA 2003 Part 7 Chapter 3C. If these apply, there is deemed to be an interest-free loan, taxable on the same basis as under Part 3 Chapter 7, equal to the undervalue.

Broadly, Chapter 3C applies when a person acquires shares at an undervalue as a result of a right or opportunity made available because of his employment: undervalue is defined as the difference between the market value of fully paid shares of the same class and the amount (if any) actually paid at the time of issue. It therefore applies in more situations than the issue of partly paid shares—for instance, in some cases when shares are acquired on exercise of an unapproved option which was granted to an employee at a time when he was not resident and ordinarily resident in the UK (ERSM70020, *Tax Bulletin*, April 2005, pp 1193 ff and FAQ 3C(c)). It should be noted that Chapter 3C will not apply to the extent that the acquisition of the shares is already taxed as earnings under other provisions; and if the aggregate value of the notional loan and any actual loans is no more than £5,000, or if money borrowed to purchase the shares would have qualified for relief under TA 1988 s 353, no charge arises (s 446S applies ss 178 and 180).

Where a notional loan arises, income tax will be due on the deemed interest (the benefit to the employee) at the official rate of (currently) 5% pa.

Generally, the deemed loan remains outstanding until either:

(1)  the employee dies or the 'loan' is repaid (when liability to income tax will cease); or

(2)  the 'loan' is released or the beneficial interest in the shares is transferred (when the amount of the notional loan outstanding is taxed as employment income of the employee) (s 446U).

ITEPA 2003 s 446UA was introduced as an anti-avoidance provision by F (No 2) A 2005 and provides that where HMRC considers that the avoidance of tax and NIC is a 'main purpose' of the arrangements, the full amount of what would have been the notional loan is treated as employment income and taxed upfront.                                                                                 **[9.27]**

e)  *Shares disposed of for more than market value*

When shares are acquired by reason of employment, there will be a tax charge if they are subsequently disposed of for more than their market value (ITEPA 2003 Part 7 Chapter 3D). The charge is on the difference between the price received and their then market value. This prevents the use of 'stop-loss' protection under which shares acquired under an incentive scheme are bought back by the company if they fall in value. However, the charge applies irrespective of who the purchaser is.                                     **[9.28]**

**EXAMPLE 9.4**

Sandy, the buying manager of Cosifabrics Ltd, is allotted 10,000 £1 shares in the company in 2002. The purchase price of the shares is the market value of £2.25 each but the shares are issued partly paid and Sandy pays only 50p per share. In 2004 he pays a further 50p per share to the company. The tax position is as follows:

(1)    *From 2002 to 2004:* the notional loan per share is £2.25 – 50p = £1.75. This amounts to £17,500 so the deemed interest on that sum at the official rate is treated as employment income each year.

(2)    *After 2004:* the payment of a further 50p per share reduces the notional loan by £5,000 to £12,500. Thereafter, the official rate of interest on that figure is treated as employment income.

In 2005, when the market value of each share is £3, he sells the shares to an employee trust for £4 each. He will pay income tax:

(1)    under Chapter 3C on £12,500; and

(2)    under Chapter 3D on £10,000.

His gain for CGT purposes will be reduced by £22,500 as a result of TCGA 1992 ss 37 and 119A.

f)    *Post-acquisition benefits*

Part 7 Chapter 4 applies whenever a benefit is received 'by virtue of the ownership' of employee shares (the causal connection that this requires has not been considered by the courts but for a discussion of how other provisions imposing a causal connection test have been interpreted, see **[8.42]** and **[8.112]**), if the benefit is not otherwise chargeable to income tax. In such a case, the market value of the benefit counts as employment income (s 448). The predecessor to this provision was rarely invoked by HMRC, but it has indicated that it may now seek to apply this charge in a wide range of circumstances, for instance when an equity ratchet operates to increase the managers' share of the ordinary share capital (see **[9.20]** (7)).          **[9.29]**

g)    *Priority share allocations*

When shares in a company are first offered to the public, employees are sometimes given priority and/or discount offers. Under general principles, the employees would be taxable on the benefit of a priority allocation: if they receive more shares than they would have done as members of the public, then if the share value at the date of allocation is higher than the price paid, they will have received a benefit by reason of their employment. As a result of ITEPA 2003 Part 7 Chapter 10, however, no charge arises merely because of the priority allocation, provided certain conditions are complied with (the statutory provisions are set out in s 542 and are complicated because provisions were added to the previous legislation as privatisations were structured in different ways, so that the employees would continue to be protected). However, if the employees pay less for their shares than members of the public, there will be an income tax charge on that discount.          **[9.30]**

h)    *Research institution spinout companies (FA 2005 s 20)*

As noted above, the provisions of Part 7 are much wider than the previous legislation and this has led the Government into having to introduce specific legislation to deal with certain situations—for example, in relation to university spinout companies.

Universities and similar research institutions often develop their intellectual property (IP) through companies ('spinout' or 'spin-off' companies) created in association with a researcher. There is usually an agreement under which the researcher either shares in the royalties generated by the use of the IP or, where the IP is developed through a spinout into which IP has been transferred, receives shares in that company.

If a researcher is employed by a research institution, acquires shares in a spinout and the research institution transfers IP to that spinout, a charge to income tax could arise under Part 7 Chapter 4 (as a result of the increase in value of existing shares held by the researcher), under s 9 or Chapter 3C (because the shares acquired reflect the value of IP, but are acquired by a researcher at a discount) or under Chapter 5 (if the shares are acquired as a result of the exercise of an option (see below)). The charge would be based on current values when the shares are acquired or the IP transferred.

From 2 December 2004, however, an income tax charge is prevented from arising on an increase in the value of existing shares in a spinout that is due to the transfer of designated IP or where researchers acquire shares following any IP transfer. FA 2005 s 20 (new ITEPA 2003 Part 7 Chapter 4A) sets out the detailed provisions and acts to prevent the value of the IP from being reflected in any consideration as to whether the shares have been acquired at an undervalue, deeming the market value to be the value that the shares would have had if the IP had not been transferred.

The new provisions relate to the researcher's position and does not affect the position of the research institution itself for capital gains tax or corporation tax purposes (although it may make a NI saving—see **[9.35]**). The spinout company and the researcher's shares, remain within the scope of Part 7 in all other respects. **[9.31]**

## 3   Share options and other rights to acquire shares

In *Abbott v Philbin* (1961), the House of Lords held that options are subject to income tax on their value (if any) at the time of grant and that any benefit resulting from the exercise of an option (ie because the shares had grown in value during the option period) was not so taxable.

Naturally, legislation was introduced to reverse this decision. ITEPA 2003 Part 7 Chapter 5 provides that if, by reason of employment, an individual who is resident and ordinarily resident in the UK is granted options to acquire shares, he is not taxed on the value of the options *at that time*. However, the notional gain made on the shares will be subject to income tax *when the option is exercised*. The amount taxed will be reduced by: the price (if any) paid for the option; the price paid for the shares; any relevant expenses (s 480); and any employers' NICs paid by the employee (s 481)—see **[9.35]**.

The previous legislation (TA 1988 s 135) imposed a tax charge on the 'exercise' of a right to acquire shares. Part 7 Chapter 5 applies whenever shares are acquired pursuant to a right to acquire them (s 477(3)(a)) and thus disposing of arguments that either an amount must be paid or something must actually be done by the employee in order to effect an 'exercise'. Thus, if there is a *right* to receive shares after the expiry of a period of time, on meeting performance conditions or under a long-term incentive plan (or otherwise), the receipt of the shares will be a chargeable event under

Chapter 5. In that Chapter the term 'employment-related securities option' is used to describe any type of right to acquire shares to which the Chapter applies.

**EXAMPLE 9.5**

John is granted an option to acquire 10,000 shares in a company at 30p per share. The option can be exercised at any time in the next six years. The price of the shares is fixed at their current market value on grant. John pays £10 for the option, which he exercises five years later when the shares are worth 75p. He sells the shares six months later for 85p per share.

(1)   There is no income tax charge on the grant of the option.
(2)   When the option is exercised, the sum taxed as employment income is calculated as follows:

Market value of shares at exercise:

| | | |
|---|---:|---:|
| 10,000 × 75p | | £7,500 |
| *Deduct:* | | |
| Option price | £10 | |
| Price paid 10,000 × 30p | £3,000 | £3,010 |
| | | |
| Sum assessed to income tax under | | |
| ITEPA 2003 | | £4,490 |

*Note:* Tax is charged on the above sum *despite the fact that the shares have not been sold by the employee;* and it is assumed that the company bears its own NIC liability.

(3)   On the subsequent sale of the shares any further gain is subject to CGT:

| | | |
|---|---:|---:|
| Sale proceeds: 10,000 × 85p | | £8,500 |
| *Deduct:* | | |
| Option price | £10 | |
| Price paid | £3,000 | |
| Sum assessed to income tax | £4,490 | |
| | | £7,500 |
| Gain subject to CGT | | £1,000 |

*Note:* No account is taken of any reliefs or allowable CGT expenses in this example.

If a person holding an employment-related securities option realises a gain by assigning or releasing it (for instance, he might receive a cash payment in return for surrendering his option if his employing company is taken over), that gain also falls within Chapter 5 (s 477(3)(b)).

ITEPA 2003 s 9 and *Abbott v Philbin* will continue to apply to the grant of options where the employee is not both resident and ordinarily resident in the UK; and Part 7 Chapter 3C will sometimes apply on exercise of such options (see **[9.27]**).

*Wilcock v Eve* (1995) illustrated another situation where the general charging provisions used to be relevant. The court held that the old charging provision (TA 1988 s 135) did not apply where an *ex gratia* compensation payment was made following lapse of options under the rules of a scheme (in this case because the employing company had left the group). However, this has been overtaken by s 477(3)(c) which states that there is a chargeable event (for the purposes of s 476) if the employee receives 'a benefit in money or money's worth in connection with' an employment-related securities option. It should be noted that, under the old legislation, when a new employer compensated a new recruit for the share scheme benefits he lost as a result of moving from his former employment, the Special Commissioner was able to find that the payment was an inducement payment and therefore taxable under (now) s 9 (*Teward v IRC* (2001)). It is not entirely clear which of s 9 or Part 7 would now apply if such a payment related to lost securities options, as a result of s 418(1).

There is no charge under Part 7 Chapter 5 where an option is exercised, assigned or released following the death of the employee (s 477(2)).

A subsequent increase in the value of shares acquired by an employee under an employment-related securities option may be subject to income tax, rather than capital gains tax, if other provisions of Part 7 apply (see 2 above). Prior to FA 2004, an exemption from Chapters 2–4 applied in relation to shares acquired under an approved scheme (see **[9.61]**), but this exemption (s 421G) was removed by FA 2004 s 88(13).                    **[9.32]**

## 4  **PAYE and NICs**

Prior to December 1996, the provision of share benefits to employees triggered significant cost and cash flow advantages for both parties since 'own company shares' were outside both the PAYE and NIC nets. A plethora of primary and secondary legislation has since reversed that position to a significant extent.                    **[9.33]**

### a)  *PAYE*

PAYE does not have to be operated on the exercise of an unapproved option over 'own company shares' granted before 27 November 1996, provided that the avoidance of tax or NICs was not 'the main purpose (or one of the main purposes) of any arrangements under which the right was obtained or is exercised' (ITEPA 2003 s 701(2)(c)(iii), as amended by FA 2004 s 88(9)). However, if such an option is exchanged for a new option after that date, PAYE will apply if the employee acquires shares that are 'readily convertible assets' (RCAs) on exercising the new option. Further, the charges in ITEPA 2003 Part 7 Chapters 2–4 can apply to shares acquired on exercise of such options and this could give rise to PAYE obligations.

In relation to options granted on or after 27 November 1996, in general PAYE has to be operated if the employee acquires shares that are RCAs (ss 700(2) and 696). The term 'readily convertible asset' is defined in s 702. It is sometimes difficult to decide whether unquoted shares are readily convertible. HMRC's views on this issue are given in *Tax Bulletin*, August 1998, p 563 and April 2000, pp 735 and 736, but it should be noted that in some situations it now views the PAYE net as rather wider than there indicated (for instance, in relation to the effect of an employee trust). Certain shares that would not have previously been RCAs have, since the addition of s 702(5A) to (5D) by FA 2003 s 140, become RCAs. Essentially this covers shares in respect of which a statutory corporation tax deduction is not available (see **[9.124]** ff). If a tax charge arises under ss 477(3)(b) or (c) because an employee has received consideration in return for assigning or releasing an option, PAYE has to be operated even if the shares subject to the option were not RCAs (s 700(2)).

ITEPA 2003 s 698 sets out the PAYE obligations that apply whenever tax charges arise under Part 7 Chapters 2–4 in relation to shares acquired on or after 16 April 2003 (s 699 applies to the old convertible securities regime— see FA 2003 Sch 22 para 12). When the charges listed in s 698(1) arise, PAYE has to be operated if the shares are RCAs (s 698(2) and s 696). However, if an amount counts as employment income by virtue of the provisions listed in s 698(3)(a), an obligation to operate PAYE can arise even if the shares are not readily convertible.

Where there is a notional loan charge on the acquisition of shares at an undervalue (ITEPA 2003 Part 7 Chapter 3C), the status of the shares is irrelevant and this tax is collected under the self-assessment regime unless the anti-avoidance provisions of ITEPA 2003 s 446UA apply (s 698(1)(ea)).

Employers may face difficulties in recovering from employees (and former employees) the PAYE they have been obliged to pay to HMRC under the above provisions. The statutory right of recovery can only be exercised against cash payments made to the employees in the income tax month in which the notional payment is deemed to have been made (see ITEPA 2003 s 710) and such cash will often be insufficient to cover the PAYE in respect of a substantial share award. It is possible for the terms of the relevant scheme to provide that, by accepting the share award, an employee becomes obliged to reimburse the employer for the amount of tax due. In the absence of such a statutory or contractual right, in certain circumstances a restitutionary claim may be possible.

If the employee does not in fact make good the tax due within 90 days of the date on which the original tax charge is triggered, ITEPA 2003 s 222 results in the employee being taxable on the tax paid (for HMRC's responses to questions raised on the predecessor to this provision, TA 1988 s 144A, see *Tax Bulletin*, April 2000, p 734). **[9.34]**

b) *National Insurance contributions*

Since 1996 there have been periods of time when the PAYE and NIC obligations in relation to share scheme benefits have diverged but over time they have been brought more into line. Where shares are wholly within the new income tax regime introduced by FA 2003, the PAYE and NIC treatment of unapproved benefits will be almost completely aligned, so that whenever there is a PAYE liability under ss 698 or 700, Class 1 NICs are payable. The main exception arises from the exclusion of NICs when shares are acquired on exercise of a pre-6 April 1999 option or on the exercise of an option granted in exchange for a pre-6 April 1999 option (see the Special Edition of the *Tax Bulletin*, December 2003 (and note the erratum notice) on changes to the NIC treatment of such options in particular, as well as on the general position).

Although there is no PAYE liability when there is a notional loan charge under ITEPA 2003 Part 7 Chapter 3C, Class 1A employer NICs are payable.

The effect of extending NICs to employee share benefits is to impose a real cost on employers who cannot, or choose not to, use approved share schemes. It used to be the case that that cost could not be passed on to employees as there was a statutory bar on their reimbursing employers' NICs. Perhaps worse than the fact of this extra cost is its unpredictability. This is a particular strain for small companies if they use share incentives to attract high quality managers and the shares grow significantly in value: the potential NIC charge 'could put at risk investment strategies, damage their future growth by deterring investors and even make them insolvent' (Budget 2000 Press Release 3).

The statutory bar on recovering employers' NICs from employees was removed in 2000 but only in relation to employment-related securities options (see Social Security Contributions and Benefits Act 1992 (SSCBA) Sch 1 paras 3A and 3B). The usual method will be by the employee agreeing to pay the company's liability, so that the company can recover the amount due from him. It is possible for the parties to sign a joint election that will actually transfer the liability to the employee so that the company will no longer have any responsibility for it. The election needs prior HMRC approval. It was introduced to deal with the problem faced by some non-UK companies whose accounting rules require that, unless the liability is transferred completely, it still has to be shown in the company's accounts. It has, however, been suggested that, since the publication by the Accounting Standards Board of UITF 25 (see [9.160]), making an election will also have accounting advantages for UK companies (*Tax Journal*, 16 February 2004, p 10).

Employees can deduct the amount paid to the company (provided that was done no later than 60 days after the year of assessment of the chargeable event) or for which the liability has been undertaken when calculating the amount of gain subject to income tax on option exercise (see [9.32]) (ITEPA 2003 s 481). Employee contributions are not deductible.

The National Insurance Contributions and Statutory Payments Act 2004 (NICSPA) amended, from 1 September 2004, SSCBA 1992 Sch 1 paras 3A and 3B to allow agreements and elections to be made in respect of post-acquisition charges relating to restricted securities and convertible securities. Charges on the acquisition of restricted or convertible securities are excluded. As with options, employees will enjoy income tax relief in respect of any payment of employers' NICs (ss 428A and 442A and *Tax Bulletin*, June 2004, p 1118).

Whilst the NIC charge on an option exercise applies to options granted after 5 April 1999, the legislation allowing the NIC burden to be transferred to employees only came into effect on 20 May 2000. Employers who had granted options between those dates found it difficult to persuade the option holders to agree to accept the NIC liability. The Government, therefore, gave them (and employees who had been persuaded to accept the liability) the option of fixing their NIC liability by reference to the growth in value of the shares subject to the option up to 7 November 2000, provided they notified the Inland Revenue and paid the contribution due (the 'special contribution') by 10 August 2001 (the Social Security Contributions (Share Options) Act 2001 and SI 2001/1817). That notice was deemed to have been given in relation to options which were 'underwater' (that is, the exercise price was more than the market value of the shares) on that day or if the shares were not readily convertible on 7 November 2000; and as, at that time, no NICs would have been payable, no special contribution had to be paid in order to avoid liability in the future.

In relation to employees' NICs, these must be paid to HMRC in the same manner as PAYE. Although an employer is able to immediately recover such amounts from a *cash* payment, it is more difficult when the payment is made in *shares*. In such cases the employer is able to make a recovery from any cash payments made in the same tax year and the next tax year. The addition of this second year for recovery was introduced by SI 2003/1337. If recovery is not made by this time, the amounts become the employer's liability and there is no further right of recovery.

Following the introduction of the additional 1% employees' NICs charge that also applies, uncapped, to earnings over the UEL, the ability to recover NICs from employees has become more important for employers. The National Insurance Contributions and Statutory Payments Act 2004 paved the way to extending the right of recovery when employees and ex-employees receive shares. It amends SSCBA 1992 Sch 1 para 3, which in turn enables the necessary amendments to be made to the Social Security (Contributions) Regulations 2001, in order for NICs to be recovered, with the agreement of the employee, by the withholding of sufficient shares rather than from cash payments (SI 2004/2246). **[9.35]**

## 5  Capital gains tax

a)  *Introduction*

The changes to taper relief introduced in FA 2000 have had a significant effect on the way the provision of employee share benefits is structured; and on the decision by employees as to whether to keep or sell their shares.

When taper relief was introduced, an employee shareholding only counted as a business asset if the employee owned at least 5% of the shares. FA 2000 extended business asset taper relief to all shareholdings in unquoted trading companies and to employees' holdings in trading companies by which they are employed whilst they are in employment, whilst at the same time reducing the time for which assets had to be held to qualify for the full relief (from ten to four years). FA 2001 retrospectively (to 6 April 2000) extended the relief further so that an employee's holding in his non-trading employing company is a business asset provided the employee does not have a material interest (basically a holding of more than 10%) (FA 2001 s 78 and Sch 26). FA 2002 s 46 reduced the four-year period for full business asset taper to only two years in the case of disposals occurring after 5 April 2002 (see generally **Chapter 20**).

These changes have given unapproved share incentive schemes a significant advantage over share option schemes as, in the latter case, the qualifying period for taper relief purposes will only start to run once the option has been exercised (note, however, that, in the case of options granted under approved Enterprise Management Incentive arrangements (see **[9.75]**), taper relief will run from the date of option grant, thus making these schemes extremely attractive).

For employees who held less than 5% of the company's shares on 6 April 2000, calculating any CGT due is complicated: to calculate taper relief there must be an apportionment to reflect the fact that the shares were non-business assets up until that date. Similarly, an apportionment may have to be done if an employee does not sell his shares until after he leaves employment, as they will then become non-business assets if they (or indeed any shares of the company—see TCGA 1992 Sch A1 para 22(1) as amended by FA 2000 s 67(5)) are quoted (see *Revenue Law* (23rd edn) *Examples 15.4 and 15.5* on apportionment generally).

In some cases, the amount of gain subject to CGT can be reduced by the employee transferring some of his shares to his spouse (so that she can make use of her annual exemption if she would not do so otherwise); however, in other cases this may increase the tax payable because of the reduction in taper relief (see *Taxation*, 18 October 2001, pp 60–63, 23 May 2002, pp 206 and 207 and 20 June 2002, p 317) and the application of the identification rules to the spouse transfer (see *Tax Bulletin*, April 2001, pp 839 and 840 and August 2001, pp 876 and 877 and *Taxation*, 12 April 2001 pp 42 and 43, 18 October 2001, pp 64 and 65 and 22 November 2001, pp 188 and 189).

As already discussed, FA 2003 introduced a new regime for the taxation of unapproved share benefits and TCGA was amended in consequence. FA 2003 also amended the CGT treatment when shares are acquired pursuant to a pre-existing right (most often an option). The CGT position set out below is that which applies to shares wholly within the new regime, so that the operative date for the new sections, any transitional provisions and details of shares to which they apply are not set out: for that information, readers will need to consult FA 2003.                                          **[9.36]**

b)   *Employee acquires shares otherwise than pursuant to pre-existing right*

*The employee* The employee is subject to income tax under ITEPA 2003 Part 3 Chapter 1 (ie the general charging provision) on the difference between the market value of the shares and the price, if any, he pays for them (unless the shares are restricted shares by reason of ITEPA 2003 s 423(2), the restrictions are not capable of lasting more than five years and the employee has not elected to be taxed on acquisition (under s 425)—see **[9.23]**). When he has acquired existing shares which are not restricted or convertible (as to which, see below), his base cost will be their market value as a result of the operation of TCGA 1992 s 17(1).

Establishing the CGT position where the employee acquires newly issued shares has always been difficult as TCGA 1992 s 17(2) seems to disapply the deemed market value in s 17(1). However, HMRC's position appears to be that s 17(2) does not apply (see CG 56353 to 56355 but note the position on public offers at CG 56333 ff) on the rather unexpected basis (it would seem, in light of TCGA 1992 s 149A (see **[9.40]**)) that the employee provides market value for the shares in the form of his services; therefore, since one of the two limbs of s 17(2) is not satisfied, s 17(1) applies to uplift the employee's base cost. As a consequence, whether the shares acquired by the employee are newly issued or existing, his base cost is the value by reference to which he pays income tax under the general charging provision (but see below if they are restricted or convertible). HMRC's belief that s 17 applies when newly issued shares are acquired was confirmed in its News Releases on

*Mansworth v Jelley* (2003) (see [**9.44**]); the fact that HMRC felt the need to enact TCGA 1992 s 149AA is further confirmation.

When restricted or convertible shares are acquired, TCGA 1992 s 149AA states that the consideration the employee provided for the shares shall be treated as the aggregate of the price the employee paid and any amount charged to income tax under the general charging provision: this total will be taken into account under TCGA 1992 s 38 and will constitute the employee's base cost (plus any other expenditure allowed under that section). It would seem that s 149AA was introduced to prevent TCGA 1992 s 17 applying when these types of shares are acquired, whether they are *newly issued or existing*. Although, on its face, s 149AA applies if the shares are restricted but employer and employee have elected to ignore all the restrictions (because it applies to 'restricted securities' as defined in Chapter 2 and that definition depends on the nature of the restrictions, not whether or not there is a tax charge under general principles on acquisition), the HMRC view seems to be that s 149AA does not apply (presumably because there will be a tax charge under general principles) and the position set out in the preceding two paragraphs will then apply.

There is one final point in relation to the acquisition of shares. If there is a charge on acquisition because the shares fall within Part 7 Chapter 3A, TCGA 1992 s 119A does not give a CGT uplift for the amount on which tax is charged; nor will there be an uplift under s 149AA even if the shares are restricted or convertible because the taxable amount under Chapter 3A is not 'earnings' under ITEPA 2003 Part 3 Chapter 1 but rather 'counts as employment income' (s 446B) and is, therefore, 'specific employment income'.                                                                                              [**9.37**]

*The transferor or issuer* The transferor of existing shares will be treated as receiving a market value consideration if the requirements of TCGA 1992 s 17 or s 18 are satisfied (as they normally will be). Section 149AA 'is to be disregarded in calculating the consideration received' by the transferor, so s 17 will continue to apply when he transfers restricted or convertible shares. There are no CGT consequences for the issuer when new shares are issued to the employee since there will not be a disposal.                                      [**9.38**]

c)   *Income tax charges following acquisition otherwise than pursuant to pre-existing right*

TCGA 1992 s 119A increases the expenditure to be taken into account under s 38 by reference to any amount taxable under Chapters 2 and 3 and when a notional loan is discharged under ITEPA 2003 Part 7 Chapter 3C.

Section 119A does not cover Chapters 3A, 3B, 3D and the ongoing loan charge under Chapter 3C nor Chapter 4. If shares are sold for more than their market value in circumstances giving rise to a charge under Chapter 3D, the excess over market value will be deducted from the sale price in calculating the employee's gain as a result of TCGA 1992 s 37; but in the other cases not covered by s 119A, the income tax charges will not be taken into account for capital gains tax purposes.                           [**9.39**]

d)    *Grant of right to acquire shares to employee*

As a preliminary matter it must be noted that the income tax treatment whenever shares are acquired pursuant to a pre-existing right was aligned with that of options by FA 2003 (see **[9.32]**). As a consequence, TCGA 1992 was amended, so that every right which falls within ITEPA 2003 Part 7 Chapter 5 will be treated as an option for the purposes of TCGA 1992. In ITEPA 2003 such rights are called 'employment-related securities options' and that terminology is used here.

The CGT position of both the grantor and the employee is established according to normal principles, save that the grant *is* treated as a disposal as a result of TCGA 1992 s 144. The consideration received by the grantor and the employee's base cost are both calculated by reference to what the employee pays for the employment-related securities option, as a result of TCGA 1992 s 149A which disapplies the market value rule in TCGA 1992 s 17 *and* excludes the value of the employee's services in calculating the consideration. It appears that s 149A is sufficient to exclude a deemed market value consideration even if the employment-related securities option is granted to a connected person (within s 18).

If an employment-related securities option is granted in return for the release of an existing option, TCGA 1992 s 237A excludes that release when calculating the consideration received by the grantor. From the point of view of the employee, the section allows him to roll over his employment-related securities option: it states that his allowable expenditure for the new option will be any consideration he gave for the original option and 'any consideration paid for the acquisition' of the new option (this excludes the value of the option released). Finally, the new employment-related securities option is disregarded when calculating the consideration received by the employee for releasing the existing option.                                            **[9.40]**

e)    *Acquisition of shares pursuant to employment-related securities option*

i)    *Introduction*

This subject is complex because the decision in *Mansworth v Jelley* (2003) upset the widely-held view as to the CGT consequences of an employee exercising an option. Amending legislation was introduced but the decision in that case continues to apply to certain options. Paragraphs 56370 to 56392 in HMRC's Capital Gains Manual set out in detail its view of the CGT position in relation to options.                                            **[9.41]**

ii)    *The old position*

*The employee* HMRC's view was that the deemed market value rule in TCGA 1992 s 17 did not apply to an employee's acquisition of existing shares on exercising an option as he acquired those shares as an optionholder, not an employee, and through an arm's length bargain. Accordingly, whether he acquired newly-issued or existing shares, the employee's base cost should be the price paid for the option plus the price paid for the shares plus any amount taxed under TA 1988 s 135 (now ITEPA 2003 Part 7 Chapter 5) (see TCGA 1992 s 120).                                            **[9.42]**

*The grantor* From the point of view of the grantor, grant and exercise of the employment-related securities option are treated as one event as a result of s 144. If the grantor issues new shares to the employee, there is no disposal and, because of the 'one transaction' rule, any CGT assessment raised on the grant of the option will be discharged, so the grantor has no CGT liability, either on payments received on grant of the option or on payments received on its exercise. If existing shares are transferred by the grantor of the option, HMRC's view was that the consideration received by the grantor should be the price he received for the option plus the price he received for the shares.

**[9.43]**

*iii)* *Mansworth v Jelley (2003)*

When Mr Jelley exercised his unapproved option he was not subject to income tax under TA 1988 s 135 (now ITEPA 2003 Part 7 Chapter 5) as he was not a UK resident at grant and so, applying the principles above, his base cost for the shares acquired would have been the price he paid for them (plus anything he paid for the option). He argued (in a bid to reduce the CGT payable on subsequent sale, by which time he was UK resident and subject to CGT) that TCGA 1992 s 17 applied to the exercise, so that his base cost was the market value of the shares at that date. The Court of Appeal's acceptance of his argument, whilst good news for anyone like Mr Jelley who is outside the income tax net but inside the CGT one, gave rise to the following unsatisfactory results in other circumstances (though not on exercise of approved SAYE or Company Share Option Plan options as s 17 was specifically excluded in those cases):

(1) If existing shares were transferred on exercise, the transferor would be deemed to have received not the actual exercise price but market value, thus increasing his taxable gain (unless hold-over relief under TCGA 1992 s 165 was available).

(2) A bizarre outcome of HMRC's interpretation of the effect of the case (see News Releases: 8 January, 17 March and 8 August 2003) was that an employee within s 135 could get a double uplift to his base cost: s 17 would deem him to have paid market value; and s 120 would add to that the amount on which he paid income tax.

The effect of this reversal of HMRC's previous view was that gains previously made on exercise of unapproved (and Enterprise Management Incentive—see **[9.75]**) options should have been lower and in some cases there would have been a capital loss. **[9.44]**

*iv)* *FA 2003*

Given the above, it is not surprising that FA 2003 s 157 inserted s 144ZA into TCGA 1992 to prevent s 17 applying whatever type of option is exercised on or after 10 April 2003. The old position as set out above therefore applies again. **[9.45]**

*v)* *Exercise of employment-related securities options on same day*

When a person acquires assets of the same type on the same day, they are usually pooled and the total acquisition costs averaged to provide the base cost for each (TCGA 1992 s 105). This is disadvantageous to an employee who exercises either an approved option and unapproved employment-related securities option on the same day or two approved options with different exercise prices (which will most often occur in the context of a takeover): the total CGT he has to pay on subsequent sale of the shares acquired could be reduced (and the payment thereof delayed) if the shares could be kept separate and he could sell those with the highest base cost first. This is particularly the case in the first scenario when there will be no chargeable gain if the shares acquired on exercise of the unapproved employment-related securities option are immediately sold (as they often are to pay the exercise price and income tax due) because their base cost will usually be their then market value (see above); and if the employee can hold on to the shares acquired on exercise of the approved option, he may well be able to take advantage of CGT reliefs to reduce the tax payable on later sale (see Explanatory Notes issued by the Inland Revenue on clause 49 of the Finance Bill 2002 for an example).

In relation to shares acquired on or after 6 April 2002, TCGA 1992 ss 105A and 105B have remedied the position in relation to the first scenario by allowing the employee to opt to treat the shares with the higher base cost as disposed of first. The election must be made by the next but one 31 January following the end of the tax year in which the first disposal of (some of) the shares acquired takes place. Unfortunately, it does not seem to extend to the second scenario; and it may be that it will not operate when the acquisition of the option shares is matched with a disposal during the *preceding* 30 days (see **[27.46]**).                                                                          **[9.46]**

*f)   Income tax charges following acquisition of shares pursuant to employment-related securities option*

ITEPA 2003 Part 7 Chapters 2–4 can apply to shares acquired pursuant to an employment-related securities option: the effect on the employee's base cost will be the same as where they apply following a share acquisition (see **[9.39]**). It would be possible to avoid later charges under Chapter 2 by making an election under s 431 (see **[9.24]**). Such an election when shares are acquired pursuant to an employment-related securities option may increase the income tax charge on acquisition under Chapter 5 by deeming the value of the shares acquired to be increased. This would feed through to the employee's base cost via TCGA 1992 s 119A(3)(d).                          **[9.47]**

g)   *Calculating the chargeable gain on eventual sale*

The gain is found by deducting the allowable expenditure from the disposal consideration. The effect of the provisions discussed above is to increase the employee's allowable expenditure and hence his base cost (except for s 37(1) which reduces the amount of the disposal consideration that is taken into account).

To calculate chargeable gains for a year, losses are first deducted from gains (starting with those gains for which there is the least taper relief). Taper relief is then applied to the extent that the gain on the asset with taper relief survives the deduction of losses: in other words, if losses have been used to reduce the chargeable gain on that asset, it is the balance of the gain to which the taper relief percentage is applied, not the original gain on it. A person's annual exemption is set against his gains after the taper relief has been given. For more detailed information on how the CGT liability is calculated, please see **Chapters 19 and 20**. For further detail on CGT arising on a disposal of shares, particularly in relation to the order in which shares are deemed to be sold and the share identification rules, please see **Chapter 26**.

The following example assumes there are no losses to be used in the relevant years. Having the employee acquire his shares after 6 April 2000 avoids the need to do one of the apportionments discussed at **[9.36]** (the other is not relevant because none of the shares in Haythrop Ltd are quoted), or to calculate his indexed pool as at 6 April 1998.                    **[9.48]**

**EXAMPLE 9.6**

In September 2001 Mog exercises unapproved options over 1,000 shares in his employing company, Haythrop Ltd (which is a trading company), paying £1 per share when the market value is £2. The option was granted by deed.

|  | £ |
|---|---|
| Cost | 1,000 |
| Income tax payable on | 1,000 |
| Mog's base cost | £2,000 |

In May 2004 Mog sells 50 of those shares at £5 per share, realising £250. The remaining 950 shares are worth £4,750. The proportion of qualifying expenditure attributable to the shares to be sold is:

$$\frac{£250}{£5000} \times £2,000 = £100$$

Mog therefore realises a gain of £150.

Taper relief then has to be applied. Mog has more than a two-year qualifying period, therefore:

chargeable gain arising in May 2004: £150 × 25% = £37.50

In July 2005 Mog is given 500 shares of the same class by Haythrop Ltd. The market value is still £5 per share. He pays income tax under ITEPA 2003 s 9 on £2,500.

In August 2006 Mog sells 750 shares at £10 each. He is treated as having disposed of: (a) the 500 shares acquired in July 2005; and (b) 250 of the remaining 950 shares acquired in September 2001. His chargeable gain will be calculated as follows:

*The 500 July 2005 shares*

|  | £ |
|---|---|
| Proportion of disposal proceeds | 5,000 |
| Allowable expenditure | 2,500 |
| Gain | 2,500 |
| Taper relief after 1 year: 50% |  |
| Chargeable gain: £2,500 × 50% = | 1,250 |

*250 of the September 2001 shares*

|  | £ |
|---|---|
| Proportion of disposal proceeds | 2,500 |
| Value of remaining 700 shares | 7,000 |

Proportion of qualifying expenditure attributable to shares sold:

$$\frac{£2,500}{£9,500} \times (£2,000 - £100) = £500$$

Taper relief after more than 2 years: 25%
Chargeable gain in August 2006: (£2,500 – £500) × 25% = £500
*Total chargeable gain for sale of 750 shares in August 2006*
£1,250 + £500 = £1,750

## 6 Reassessment of unapproved schemes

The imposition of NICs had shifted the balance of advantage back towards approved schemes. However, the change to the rules on reimbursement of employers' NICs may go some way to redressing that. Between the unapproved schemes themselves, the FA 2000 changes to CGT taper relief, under which all shares acquired by employees count as business assets, has tipped the balance in favour of share incentive, rather than share option, schemes. In particular, there has been an increase in the number of restricted shares schemes which include a forfeiture provision as taper relief will run from the date of the acquisition of the shares notwithstanding that the income tax charge may be at a later date.

The great benefit unapproved schemes offer is flexibility: they can be selective in any way the employer wishes (subject to the requirements of EC and UK non-discrimination legislation); they can relate to any type of share; and they can be more flexible in relation to adjustable performance targets.

**[9.49]–[9.60]**

## III    APPROVED SHARE SCHEMES

### 1 Tax treatment—general

The overriding advantage of approved share schemes is that, provided the rules of the scheme and the requirements of the legislation are complied with, any profit made by the employees on disposal of shares acquired through such schemes will be *subject to CGT and not income tax.*

Whilst there are circumstances where an income tax charge can arise when shares are acquired under an approved scheme (see further below), prior to 18 June 2004 the charges imposed by ITEPA 2003 Part 7 Chapters 2–4 (see Section II 2 above) did not apply to shares acquired under approved schemes, as a result of s 421G. However, the Government removed that exclusion with effect from 18 June 2004 (in relation to shares whenever acquired) because shares acquired through approved schemes were being used 'to give a cash bonus to employees free of tax and National Insurance contributions' (News Release 30/04) (FA 2004 s 88(2)). However, if restricted shares are acquired from an approved scheme after 17 June 2003, in circumstances in which no liability to income tax arises, the election under ITEPA 2003 s 431 (see **[9.24]**) is deemed to be made (ITEPA 2004 s 431A, inserted by FA 2004 s 88(3)). Further, as the revocation of s 421G applies to all shares, whenever acquired, a s 431 election is deemed to have been made in relation to those on 18 June 2004 (FA 2004 s 88(12)). The deemed election in both cases exempts the shares to which it relates from the application of ITEPA 2003 Part 7 Chapter 2 when restrictions are lifted or varied thereafter. However, the other Chapters of Part 7 will apply.

It used to be the case that the charges under Chapters 2–4 could apply to shares acquired on exercise of an approved Enterprise Management Incentive (EMI) option but those under Chapter 2 could be avoided if an election was made under s 431. Section 431A was added to also deem an election to be made on exercise of an EMI option if no income tax is payable on exercise.

The deemed election on acquisition will not affect the tax position of the employee at that time because it only operates where there is a statutory exemption from income tax at that point. If an election to disapply Chapter 2 is made when shares are acquired from an approved share scheme or on the exercise of an EMI option in circumstances where income tax is then payable, a s 431 election may increase the tax then payable.

As a further anti-avoidance measure, FA 2004 s 88 limited the income tax exemptions that apply to the approved schemes. From 18 June 2004, the exemptions are not available if the main purpose (or one of the main purposes) of the arrangements under which the shares were awarded or acquired, or the option was granted or exercised, was 'the avoidance of tax or national insurance contributions'. It was not necessary to introduce this limitation for EMI options because ITEPA 2003 Sch 5 para 4 already excluded options granted for such purposes from the beneficial tax treatment. **[9.61]**

## 2 General requirements for approved share option schemes

Many of the conditions which must be satisfied to gain approved status, and thus have the possibility of avoiding income tax on gains, are common to the SAYE (see **[9.63]**) and CSOP (see **[9.64]**), such as:

(1) *The types of share* The shares must be ordinary, fully paid up, non-redeemable shares in the employing company or its parent (or, if the employer is held by a consortium, in a member of that consortium). Furthermore, the shares must be quoted on a recognised stock exchange (see TA 1988 s 841) or, if not quoted, must be in a company that is either controlled by a quoted company or not controlled by any other company. These rules are aimed at preventing manipulation of the value of the shares to be received under the scheme; or at least at only allowing this if it also affects shareholders who acquired their shares through other means.

(2) *Restrictions attached to the shares* Few restrictions are permitted. The two main kinds allowed are: firstly, restrictions which attach to *all* shares of the *same class*; and, *secondly*, restrictions imposed by the articles of association requiring shares held by directors or employees to be

disposed of *when the holders cease to be directors or employees.* The first is to ensure that, within a class of shares, shares acquired under an approved scheme cannot be disadvantaged; the second recognises that small private companies have a legitimate interest in excluding outsiders from holding shares.

(3)   *The exclusion of persons holding a material interest* An individual who holds (or has within the previous 12 months held) a material interest in a close company which is *either* the company which issues the shares *or* a company which controls the issuing company, is not eligible to participate in one of these approved schemes. An individual holds a material interest for these purposes if he either alone, or together with associates, beneficially owns or controls 25% of the ordinary share capital of the company. 'Associate' means, broadly, a relative or partner or trustee of any settlement in which the employee has an interest. However, an individual who is a beneficiary under an employee trust which owns shares in the company will not have an interest in those shares for these purposes (ITEPA 2003 Sch 3 para 15 and Sch 4 para 13).          **[9.62]**

### 3   Approved Savings-Related Share Option Schemes (ITEPA 2003 Part 7 Chapter 7 and Sch 3)

Savings-related share option schemes (commonly referred to as 'SAYE' or 'Sharesave' schemes) are funded by contributions from the employees themselves. These are accumulated in standard Save-As-You-Earn savings arrangements (ITTOIA 2005 s 703) that are entered into at the time the options are granted. These arrangements require a person to save a regular fixed monthly contribution and they pay out a tax-free bonus: arrangements entered into on or after 1 September 2006 pay a bonus of 1.8 monthly contributions (equal to 3.19% pa) on a three-year contract, and 5.5 monthly contributions on a five-year contract (equal to 3.46% pa); a seven-year contract receives a bonus equal to 10.3 monthly contributions (equal to 3.52%). The proceeds are used to provide funds for the exercise of the options to acquire ordinary shares in the employer company. The maximum permitted monthly contribution into all savings arrangements is currently £250.

The *price* of the shares must be fixed at the time *when the employee is granted* the option and must not be less than 80% of the market value of the shares at that time. Generally, the option must not be exercisable until the SAYE savings arrangements mature at the end of three, five or seven years. The employee is *exempt from any charge to income tax* on the grant (s 518) and, in most cases, on the exercise of the option (s 519). A charge to income tax under s 476 will apply where the option is exercised before the third anniversary of grant, otherwise than in certain specified circumstances. However, by virtue of s 701(2)(c), the shares acquired are not classed as RCAs and so there are no NICs or PAYE, and so gains on exercise are accounted for under self-assessment. Where income tax relief applies the only charge is to CGT *if and when the shares are sold* (see TCGA 1992 Sch 7D for the disapplication of TCGA 1992 s 17 in such a case) and in many cases the employee will be able to take advantage of the annual exemption.

To gain approval, the scheme must be open to *all* full-time employees and directors; part-time employees must also be able to participate in schemes approved after 30 April 1995 but participation of part-time directors remains at the discretion of the company. The scheme may restrict participation to employees who have been in employment for a period of up to five years and it must satisfy the detailed conditions set out in Sch 3.

These schemes are attractive because the employee is not required to find a large sum of money to exercise his option as sufficient funds will have accrued through the SAYE savings arrangements. This encourages the employee to *retain* his shares, since he is not forced to sell to repay a loan or deferred finance arrangements taken out to acquire them. **[9.63]**

### 4 Approved Company Share Option Plans (ITEPA 2003 Part 7 Chapter 8 and Sch 4)

Options granted under these plans can only be approved if: (a) the value of shares subject to options held by any one employee (value to be measured at date of option grant) does not exceed £30,000 (see *Share Focus,* Issue 2 (December 2003) for HMRC's view of the effect of granting options with an aggregate market value which exceeds this limit); and (b) the option exercise price is not manifestly less than the market value of the shares at date of option grant.

Participation in Company Share Option Plans remains subject to the company's discretion: it used to be that a plan could only allow 'qualifying' employees (required to work at least 20 hours per week) and 'full-time' working directors (normally required to devote at least 25 hours per week to their duties) to obtain rights under it; options may, however, be granted to part-time employees (but not directors) under plans approved after 30 April 1995.

As with SAYE schemes, provided the requirements of the legislation are complied with there is *no income tax* charge on the *exercise* of the option. The only charge is to *CGT if and when the shares are sold* (see TCGA 1992 Sch 7D for the disapplication of TCGA 1992 s 17 in such a case). The detailed conditions for approval are set out in Sch 4; and for tax relief in s 524.

To avoid income tax charges on these options, they not only have to be granted under an approved plan but the requirements of s 524 must also be satisfied. To avoid the charges which normally arise on exercise of an unapproved option when a Company Share Option Plan option is exercised:

(1) the option must be exercised between the third and tenth anniversaries of the date of grant; or

(2) if is exercised within three years of grant, the employee must be a 'good leaver' (for instance, leaving as a result of disability, retirement following a specified age or redundancy).

Where an income tax charge arises on exercise, the employee will be taxed in the same way as on exercise of an unapproved option (see Section II) and NICs and PAYE will apply if the shares are RCAs.

Even if there is no income tax charge on option exercise, many option-holders exercise their rights and then immediately sell some or all of their shares. This is because employees often need to borrow in order to finance the exercise of their options. **[9.64]**

## 5    Share Incentive Plans (ITEPA 2003 Part 7 Chapter 6 and Sch 2)

a)    *Introduction*

In December 1998 the Chancellor announced that he wished to double the number of companies in which all the employees had the opportunity to acquire shares. The statutory rules for Share Incentive Plans seek to achieve this by providing a more flexible framework, in an attempt to address some of the concerns that prevented smaller companies adopting approved schemes in the past.                                                                              **[9.65]**

b)    *General requirements*

To operate a Share Incentive Plan (SIP) the company must establish a trust that buys shares and holds them as trustee for the relevant employees to whom they have been awarded or by whom they have been purchased.

Many of the requirements that apply to the approved share option schemes (see **[9.62]**) apply to the all-employee SIP but there are the following differences:
(1)    *The types of share* Shares for a SIP may be non-voting. Most co-operative societies will be able to use redeemable shares. As the Government was concerned that these schemes may be used to replicate profit-related pay schemes (tax-efficient cash bonus schemes that have now been phased out) by using restricted shares in a service company, if the employees of a company perform services for a third party, shares in the employer can only be used for a SIP if it has an 'independent business'.
(2)    *Restrictions attached to the shares* Whilst the restrictions that will be allowed are similar in nature to those under the approved share option schemes, they are more suited to the requirements of small companies. The most important difference is that the shares can be subject to forfeiture in certain circumstances. In addition, provisions requiring compulsory transfer by a departing employee do not have to be in the articles and can extend to permitted transferees. Further, whilst such provisions must extend to all employees, they do not have to apply to all shares held by employees—just those acquired under the plan.    **[9.66]**

c)    *Benefits to be provided*

Employees may receive up to four types of share benefits under a SIP:
(1)    Employers can give up to £3,000 worth of shares each year to each employee (Free Shares—Sch 2 Part 5). The award of some or all of these shares can be linked to performance.
(2)    If the company allows, employees can use up to £1,500 per year (or 10% of salary if that is lower) of pre-tax income to buy shares (Partnership Shares—Sch 2 Part 6).
(3)    If the company chooses, it can give up to two shares for every one Partnership Share purchased (Matching Shares—Sch 2 Part 7).
(4)    If the company allows, up to £1,500 of dividends received on plan shares each year can be reinvested in further shares without the employee paying income tax thereon (Dividend Shares—Sch 2 Part 8).
                                                                              **[9.67]**

d)   *Forfeiture and compulsory transfer*

The tax treatment of these benefits in the hands of employees depends on the length of time they hold the shares in the plan. It is important to note that the plan can (but does not have to) provide for Free and Matching Shares to be forfeited if the employment is terminated within three years (or a shorter period if the company wishes), unless the employee is a 'good leaver' (for instance, if he is leaving as a result of disability, retirement or redundancy—see Schedule 2 para 32(2)). Further, whilst Partnership Shares cannot be forfeited as the employee will have used his own money to buy them, the rules can impose forfeiture of Matching Shares if the Partnership Shares to which they were linked are withdrawn from the plan within three years.

In situations where an employee is leaving and plan shares are not forfeited, it is important for many small companies that the employee is obliged to sell his shares. As described at **[9.66]**, the compulsory transfer provisions are slightly different than under SAYE schemes and CSOPs. The fact that they do not have to extend to all shares held by departing employees is helpful to, for example, founder directors who may want privately negotiated pre-emption provisions to apply to the majority of their shares acquired outside the SIP.                                                      **[9.68]**

e)   *Taxation of the employees*

Obviously, shares that are forfeited are not taxed in the hands of the employee. However, withdrawal of shares from the plan has tax consequences. Employees are able to withdraw their Partnership Shares at any time but have to agree to keep both Free Shares and Matching Shares in for at least three years. Whenever employment ceases, however, all shares are then deemed to have been removed from the plan. The timing of the removal affects the tax liability.

(1)   *Free and Matching Shares (s 505)* No income tax is payable on these shares if they remain in the plan for at least five years. If they are removed between three and five years, tax is payable based on their market value at the time they were originally awarded to the employee (or current market value if that is lower); before then, the tax charge is based on the market value at date of removal.

(2)   *Partnership Shares (s 506)* These are subject to a similar regime: if removal is within three years, tax is charged on market value at time of withdrawal; on removal between three and five years, tax is charged on the amount used to buy the shares (or current market value if lower); no income tax is charged on withdrawal after five years.

(3)   *Dividend Shares (s 515(a)(ii))* If Dividend Shares leave the plan within three years of acquisition, income tax is due on the amount of dividend used to acquire the shares. Removal thereafter is not subject to a charge.

In cases (1) and (2), PAYE and NICs apply if the shares are then 'readily convertible' (see **[9.34]**); in case (3) the tax is charged in accordance with ITTOIA 2005 ss 392 to 396 or ss 405 to 408 (previously known as Schedule F) in the same way as dividends and the trustees must supply the employee with sufficient information in this respect. In addition, in all three cases: no income tax charge arises if the employee is a 'good leaver' (s 498); on removal of shares from the plan, an employee's base cost for CGT purposes is uplifted to their then market value (TCGA 1992 Sch 7D para 5); and the CGT taper relief period then starts to run. **[9.69]**

f)  *Funding the SIP trust*

Tax benefits are given to three types of funding:
(1)  In computing their taxable profits, companies are able to claim a deduction for the costs of setting up and administering the plan, as with SAYE schemes and CSOPs.
(2)  When SIPs were introduced, one novel feature was that the company could claim a statutory corporation tax deduction, at the time either Free Share or Matching Shares were awarded, for the market value of those shares at the time they were acquired by the SIP trustee. This deduction continues to be available (TA 1988 Sch 4AA) and indeed takes precedence over the more generally available relief introduced by FA 2003 (see Section V of this **Chapter 9**). Further, in order to enable SIP trusts to acquire large blocks of shares for distribution over a long period (which private companies might want to do) without substantially delaying the corporation tax deduction, the Employee Share Schemes Act 2002 allows an *immediate* corporation tax deduction for contributions to a SIP trust after 5 April 2003, provided: the SIP trust acquires at least 10% of the ordinary shares in the year following the first acquisition funded by the contribution; and 30% of the shares are distributed in five years and all within ten to avoid a clawback of the deduction.
(3)  A CGT roll-over relief is available for transfers to a SIP trust provided that the rather restrictive conditions are satisfied (see TCGA 1992 s 236A and Sch 7C). **[9.70]**

6   **Enterprise Management Incentives (ITEPA 2003 Part 7 Chapter 9 and Sch 5)**

a)  *Introduction*

The Government not only wants to extend the use of all-employee share schemes but also wishes to encourage 'high-quality managers to share in the risks and rewards of running small- and medium-sized enterprises, particularly early stage high-technology companies, by supporting equity-based remuneration' (Pre-Budget Report 1998). This is the role for Enterprise Management Incentives (EMIs) under which options over up to £100,000 worth of shares can be granted to an individual employee, subject to a beneficial tax regime.

Companies that wish to award EMI options may enter into individual option agreements with selected employees, although many companies continue to prefer to establish a scheme under which options are granted. The main features are discussed below. **[9.71]**

b)   *Qualifying companies*

Given the government's aim, the types of company that can grant EMIs are, of course, limited. Broadly, to qualify a company's gross assets must not exceed £30m; it must be independent; its trading activities must be conducted wholly or mainly in the UK; and it cannot undertake certain activities (eg dealing in land). It used to be the case that shares in a parent company could only be used if it owned at least 75% of all its subsidiaries. FA 2004 s 96 has amended ITEPA 2003 Sch 5 para 11(2), so that, for EMI options granted after 16 March 2004, most subsidiaries need only be 51% owned. The same section introduces new requirements where there is a property managing subsidiary. It is possible to obtain advance assurance from HMRC that a company qualifies.                                                      **[9.72]**

c)   *Eligible employees*

Prior to FA 2001, options could only be granted 'for commercial reasons in order to recruit or retain a *key* employee'. Now they can be granted to any employee who has committed to work at least 25 hours a week for the company (or 75% of his working time, if that is less) and who does not have a material interest (essentially, owning or controlling 30% or more of the ordinary share capital of the company).                                 **[9.73]**

d)   *Maximum value of options*

Prior to FA 2001, the maximum value of options that a company could grant was limited by the fact that only 15 'key' employees could have EMIs. Now any number of 'eligible employees' can benefit (up to an individual limit of £100,000) but the maximum value of shares over which there can be unexercised EMI options is limited to £3m (the value to be measured at the time of option grant).                                              **[9.74]**

e)   *Tax treatment of employees*

The basic position is that if an option granted at market value is exercised within ten years of grant and there are no intervening 'disqualifying events' (see s 533), no income tax charge arises on option grant or exercise (s 530). This applies no matter how short a time the option has been held but, of course, companies will normally impose a contractual retention period. Further, and very beneficially, the taper relief period starts to run from the date of option grant, as opposed to the date of exercise. It is important to note, however, that if HMRC is not notified of the grant of the option within 92 days in accordance with the statutory procedure (Sch 5 Part 7), the beneficial tax treatment is lost.

If the option is granted at a discount, the discount will be taxed under ITEPA 2003 s 476 at the time of option exercise. Additionally, if the option is exercised after ten years, s 476 will apply.

If there has been a 'disqualifying event' before the option is exercised and the option is not exercised within 40 days of that event, there is an income tax charge on exercise but it is based only on the amount (if any) by which the market value of the shares when the option is exercised exceeds their market value immediately before the disqualifying event. Most importantly, failure to exercise before the 40 days expire means that the beneficial taper relief treatment is lost and the taper period runs only from the date of exercise.

It will be clear from the above that, in most cases, any gains will be subject to CGT and not income tax. The CGT taper relief period starts to run at the time of option grant. Since (nearly) all employee shareholdings count as business assets (at least during employment—see **[9.36]**), if the employee exercises his option after two years and then immediately sells his shares, he will only pay CGT on 25% of his gain (equivalent to paying CGT at a 10% rate for a higher rate taxpayer). **[9.75]**

## 7   PAYE and NICs

Originally, benefits from approved schemes fell wholly outside the PAYE and NICs nets but this position has changed significantly over recent years. **[9.76]**

### a)   *PAYE*

PAYE has always applied whenever there is an income tax charge when benefits are acquired from Share Incentive Plans and on the exercise of Enterprise Management Incentive options, provided the shares acquired are readily convertible assets (RCAs—see further **[9.34]**). PAYE now has to be operated in most cases if there is an income tax charge on the exercise of a Company Share Option Plan (CSOP) option, if the shares are RCAs; and PAYE will also apply if there are income tax charges thereafter, in accordance with the usual principles (see **[9.34]**) (ITEPA 2003 s 701, as amended by FA 2004 s 88). However, it is still the case that, even if there is an income tax charge on the exercise of an SAYE option, PAYE is not operated; but it will apply in the usual way if there are charges thereafter (see again **[9.34]**).

Whenever a payment is made for the surrender of any EMI or approved option, there is an income tax charge under ITEPA 2003 s 477(3)(b) and, in such a case, PAYE will apply, whatever the nature of the shares that would have been acquired on exercise of the option (see ITEPA 2003 s 700). **[9.77]**

### b)   *NICs*

The NIC treatment of approved benefits follows the PAYE treatment discussed above. However, as a result of the Social Security Contributions (Share Options) Act 2001 (see **[9.35]**), income-taxable gains made on CSOP options granted before 20 May 2000 are outside the NICs net: the notice that had to be given to the Inland Revenue by 10 August 2001 is deemed to have been given in such a case; and as, at the time, NICs would not have been payable on such options, no payment had to be made in order to avoid liability in the future. Further, in relation to CSOP and EMI options, it is possible for the employee to agree to bear the cost of employer NICs whenever there is an income tax charge (see further **[9.35]**) (but see *Share Focus*, Issue 2 (December 2003) for HMRC's view on how the amount of PAYE and NICs due on existing options can be recovered). **[9.78]–[9.110]**

## IV EMPLOYEE TRUSTS AND TREASURY SHARES

### 1 Unapproved employee trusts

a) *Introduction*

The term 'employee trust' has no statutory definition but, in broad terms, an employee trust is a discretionary trust the actual and potential beneficiaries of which are defined by reference to employment. Such trusts may enjoy favoured treatment for IHT, CGT, income tax and corporation tax. Consequently, they may be used as a tax-efficient means of providing not only incentives to employees but also non-contractual benefits for them (eg to those suffering personal difficulties).

There are several other important functions of employee trusts. *First*, they offer non-quoted companies the opportunity of creating a market for the sale and purchase of their shares: without such a market, non-quoted companies cannot effectively embark upon any share scheme unless current shareholders or the company itself would be prepared to buy shares from employees wishing to sell. *Secondly*, unlike treasury shares (see below) that are treated in the same way as new issue shares, the use of existing shares through a trust does not affect the 'headroom' limits usually contained in the rules of listed companies' schemes (see **[9.164]**). *Thirdly*, they can be used to build up a large shareholding in friendly hands so that the company will be protected against any unwanted takeovers and outside interference. *Fourthly*, they promote good relations between employer and employee since they can be viewed as a demonstration of an employer's concern for the welfare of its staff. *Finally*, they may provide a cost-efficient means for the company to finance a scheme: the tax deductibility of company contributions is considered in Section V of this **Chapter 9**. **[9.111]**

b) *Taxation of the trust*

Trustees pay tax at 40% on any income received other than dividend income that is taxed at 32.5% (TA 1988 s 686, as amended by FA 2004 s 29) (see *Tax Bulletin*, April 2004, p 1113 on what items of expenditure may properly be claimed as trust management expenses by the trustees of discretionary trusts). By ESC A68, to avoid an effective double tax charge trustees may reclaim tax paid by them when payments made to employees are treated as earnings (which will normally be the case).

If the trustees distribute shares to employees, the employee will normally be liable to income tax on the market value of the shares and that value will be treated as his base cost for CGT purposes (TCGA 1992 s 17(1)). The trustees will be liable to CGT on the difference between the market value at the date of distribution and their base cost. ESC D35 relieves the trustees from this CGT liability where the employee is liable to income tax on the full market value of the shares (thus removing the double tax charge). The concession will not normally operate where shares are used to satisfy options held by employees because payment of the option price will mean the employee will not be taxable on the *full* market value of the shares acquired (but see *Tax Bulletin*, April 2000, p 738 for this and other points relating to ESC D35). Where an employee trust is to be used to supply shares for a share scheme, particularly an option scheme, consideration should be given as to whether establishing the trust offshore would avoid this double tax charge. The CGT treatment of offshore employee trusts has been problematical, particularly after the changes introduced by FA 1991, but HMRC's view that, if there is no element of bounty (as with genuine commercial arrangements), ss 86–87 do not apply, is helpful (*Tax Bulletin*, April 1995, p 204).

Transfers of shares or other assets to an employee trust can have CGT consequences for the transferor. TCGA 1992 s 239 will often prevent the market value rule in s 17 being applied, so that the transferor's gain will be based on the actual consideration received and, in the case of close companies, it will limit the effect of s 125. Hold-over relief under TCGA 1992 s 165 may be available when shares are transferred to an employee trust (even if it has a corporate trustee—see *Tax Bulletin*, December 2000, p 815). Following the restrictions on hold-over relief under TCGA 1992 s 165 (and s 260) introduced by FA 2004 s 116 and Sch 21, care will be needed when determining whether the relief is available if any individual who has (or may acquire) an interest in the employee trust has ever contributed property to it (see further **[25.21]** ff).

When dealing with trusts, IHT is an additional tax consideration. To qualify for favoured treatment, an employee trust must satisfy the conditions set out in IHTA 1984 s 86, especially the requirement that *all or most* of the employees of the establishing employer *must be* within the class of potential beneficiaries. If the trust falls outside s 86, or s 13 or s 28 are not satisfied, contributions to the trust may be transfers of value for IHT purposes (eg if the employer is a close company). Further, if s 86 does not apply the trust will be subject to an IHT charge on each ten-year anniversary (s 64) and to an exit charge when capital is distributed (s 65). Even if the trust falls within s 86, an exit charge may, in certain circumstances, arise under s 72 if a transfer of property is made to an excluded person where the transfer is not classed as income.                                                                    **[9.112]**

## 2   Employee share ownership plans

FA 1989 introduced the concept of qualifying employee share ownership plans (QUESTs). The main advantage that a QUEST had over a non-statutory employee trust was a guaranteed corporation tax deduction for company contributions. However, to benefit from that statutory deduction, numerous conditions had to be satisfied. As a result, very few QUESTs were established until a change introduced by FA 1996 enabled them to be used in conjunction with SAYE schemes, so that the company could obtain a corporation tax deduction for providing the shares to satisfy the SAYE options. As FA 2003 introduced a more general corporation tax relief, the specific relief for QUESTs is no longer available (see further Section V below). Since this was the *raison d'etre* of most QUESTs, most are now being wound up (FA 2003 s 142(2) (by amending FA 1989 s 69) allowed the assets held by QUESTs on 26 November 2002 to be transferred to a Share Incentive Plan trust): they are not considered further. Readers desiring more information are referred to previous editions.                                                                    **[9.113]**

## 3 Treasury shares

Since 1 December 2003, UK listed companies have been able to hold their shares 'in treasury'. This means that they do not have to cancel shares they purchase from shareholders but are able to retain them. The shares can then later be sold, cancelled or transferred pursuant to an employee share scheme. The introduction of this facility, combined with that of a general corporation tax deduction for shares acquired by employees (see Section V below), may lead listed companies to reconsider whether they need to operate an employee benefit trust. The guidelines on share incentive schemes issued by the Association of British Insurers, however, require the use of treasury shares to count towards the 'headroom' limits contained in scheme rules (see **[9.164]**). As a result, few companies are making use of treasury shares over shares acquired by a trust. **[9.114]–[9.120]**

## V  CORPORATION TAX

### 1  Introduction

*Lowry v Consolidated African Selection Trust Ltd* (1940) established that a company cannot claim a corporation tax deduction for the notional loss it suffers when it issues shares to employees for less than their market value. In order to obtain such a deduction, some companies operating employee share schemes therefore established employee trusts: they contributed cash to the trust which then purchased shares and distributed them via the share scheme.

Prior to FA 2003, a statutory corporation tax deduction was only available for contributions to qualifying employee share ownership trusts (QUESTs) and approved Share Incentive Plans (SIPs). The deductibility of other company contributions to an employee trust depended on the application of general principles. FA 2003 introduced a general statutory corporation tax deduction when certain types of employee share benefits are provided to employees (Sch 23); and prevents or delays any deduction for contributions to trusts to provide other sorts of benefits which would be available under general principles (Sch 24). **[9.121]**

### 2  Deductibility under general principles

Subject to what is said in 3 below, payments by a company to an employee trust are deductible under normal principles if they are of a revenue (income) nature and are wholly and exclusively for the purposes of the trade. In *Mawsley Machinery Ltd v Robinson* (1998), the Special Commissioner disallowed a small company's contributions to a trust on both grounds: the purpose of the payments was to enable the trust to purchase the controlling shareholder's shares when he retired as managing director, which made them both capital in nature and partially for the purpose of enabling him to sell his shares without trouble when he retired (so not exclusively for the purposes of the trade).

Employer contributions to a trust should not be made under a binding legal obligation nor expressed as instalments of a lump sum. The best policy is to make regular payments geared to a variable factor—eg a percentage of profits. Funding by close companies requires special care in view of IHTA 1984 s 13 and TA 1988 s 419. To avoid CGT, employee trusts are often established offshore (see **[9.112]**).

The Special Commissioner's decision in *Waterloo plc v IRC* (2002) acts as a reminder that proper recharging mechanisms must be in place if the transfer-pricing provisions in TA 1988 Sch 28AA are not to apply, if the trust provides benefits to employees of subsidiaries but is funded only by contributions from the parent company.

These general principles will continue to apply when specific statutory provisions do not.                                                                                    **[9.122]**


## 3  Restriction of tax relief

Prior to the introduction of the anti-avoidance legislation in FA 2003 Sch 24, a company could obtain a corporation tax deduction (and other, non-corporate, employers could claim a deduction in computing their Schedule D income tax profits) under general principles when it made a contribution to an employee benefit trust. However, two things could affect the timing of the deduction. The first was FA 1989 s 43 which delayed the deduction if the company paid 'potential emoluments' to an 'intermediary'; the second, the accounting treatment (see **[9.160]**).

In *Dextra Accessories v Macdonald* (2002) the Special Commissioners held that s 43 was not widely enough drawn to prevent a company claiming a corporation tax deduction even though the employees suffered no income tax on the benefits provided by the trustees of an employee benefit trust. Not prepared to wait for the decision of the High Court ((2003)—which did in fact uphold the Commissioners), nor the Court of Appeal ((2004)—which allowed HMRC's appeal), nor the House of Lords ((2005)—which upheld the Court of Appeal decision in favour of HMRC), draft legislation was issued at the time of the 2002 Pre-Budget Report and this became Schedule 24 to FA 2003. This sequence of events explains why the new rules apply to contributions made on or after 27 November 2002. However, they do not apply where the rules in Schedule 23 apply (see 4 below).

Schedule 24 contains anti-avoidance legislation, the main aim of which is to prevent an employer claiming a tax deduction for contributions to an employee benefit trust (and other arrangements—see definition of 'employee benefit scheme' in Schedule 24 para 9), that would potentially be allowable under general principles, unless and until an employee receives 'qualifying benefits'. A deduction for a contribution is allowed only to the extent that it is used to provide 'qualifying benefits' or pay 'qualifying expenses' during the accounting period when the deduction would be allowed under general principles or within nine months from the end of it (para 1(3)); or if it is subsequently used to provide 'qualifying benefits'.

'Qualifying benefits' are defined in paragraph 2 and are basically limited to money or assets which: give rise to both an income tax and NIC charge (or would do so if the employee were resident and ordinarily resident in the UK); are provided on a termination of employment or (from 6 April 2006) are provided under an employer-financed retirement benefit scheme (FA 2004 s 245). Paragraph 8 (as amended by FA 2004 s 245) sets out payments to which Schedule 24 does not apply (for instance, contributions to an accident benefit scheme). What is surprisingly absent is a provision allowing the deduction to be claimed (assuming it is allowable under general principles) if the employee is exempt from income tax for some reason other than non-residence (for instance, because of the nature of the benefit or because of an exemption in ITEPA 2003); or if he would not be subject to NICs even if resident in the UK because of a tax treaty between his home country and the UK. Companies providing share benefits to employees in circumstances which do not qualify for relief under Schedule 23, and all employers providing other types of benefits via a trust, will need to consider the tax and NIC position of their employees carefully before seeking to claim a deduction.

FA 1989 s 43 (as amended by FA 2003 Sch 24 para 10) will continue to apply to delay a deduction until the earnings are actually paid where an employer reserves an amount for earnings in its accounts. **[9.123]**

### 4  Statutory corporation tax relief

a)  *Interaction with other provisions*

FA 2003 Sch 23 introduced a new regime for claiming corporation tax relief for all accounting periods beginning after 31 December 2002. The relief is available if the conditions set out in Sch 23 are satisfied. If they are not, then relief may still be available under general principles but subject to the restrictions set out in FA 2003 Sch 24.

FA 2003 s 141 withdrew the statutory relief under FA 1989 s 67 for contributions to QUESTs in accounting periods beginning after 31 December 2002. However, if a QUEST is used to distribute share benefits directly to employees, relief under Schedule 23 will be available. If previous contributions for which relief has already been given under FA 1989 are used to provide shares to employees in circumstances where a deduction would be available under Schedule 23, that relief will reduce the one claimable under the new rules (Sch 23 para 33). The same will apply if a deduction has previously been claimed under general principles for contributions to other types of employee benefit trust.

If relief can be claimed under Schedule 23 in respect of the cost of providing shares, no other relief can be claimed (para 25), save that the deductions available under TA 1988 Sch 4AA in relation to SIPs (see **[9.70]**) take priority over relief under this Schedule. This provision resulted in a concern arising in relation to the extension of the transfer pricing regime to UK-UK transactions (FA 2004 s 30). A company that operates a share scheme in which employees of its subsidiary participate needs to recharge the subsidiary or be subject to a deemed receipt under TA 1988 Sch 28AA (see *Waterloo plc v IRC* (2002)). In other types of intra-group transaction this receipt by the parent company would be included in its corporation tax calculation, but the subsidiary would receive a corresponding deduction for the payment. However, in the case of a share-based transaction where Schedule 23 applies, para 25 denies the subsidiary the corresponding deduction (although the Schedule 23 deduction outlined below will be available). This issue does not arise for accounting periods after 1 January

2005 as a result of the accounting treatment of share-based payments under IFRS 2/FRS 20. HMRC has issued guidance which states that, as any recharge (or transfer pricing adjustment) relating to a grant or award is now accounted for within reserves by the parent company (see **[9.160]**), this element is treated as 'capital' and, therefore, not subject to corporation tax. This effectively avoids the double tax problem, reinstating the position prior to FA 2004.

It remains possible to claim relief under general principles for other costs, such as fees and stamp duty.                                    **[9.124]**

### b)   *Availability of relief*

The availability of the relief depends upon the tax position of the employee and the type of shares being acquired.

#### i)   *Tax position of employee*

The basic idea behind the legislation is that a company can claim a corporation tax deduction for the value of shares received by its employees but only if and when the employee is taxed thereon. This is subject to two caveats. Firstly, the deduction is available even if the employee is not taxed because either the shares were acquired on exercise of an approved or EMI option (para 14) or he is not resident and ordinarily resident (paras 7,14 and 20). Secondly, not all income tax charges under ITEPA 2003 Part 7 count for these purposes. Schedule 23 Part 2 gives relief where there is an income tax charge in respect of the *award* of shares; Part 3 where there is a charge in relation to the exercise of an option; Part 4 where there is a charge on acquisition of restricted securities or where there is a chargeable event under Part 7 Chapter 2; and Part 4A in relation to convertible shares. Therefore, no corporation tax relief can be claimed when the employee is taxed under ITEPA 2003 Part 7 Chapters 3A, 3B, 3C, 3D and 4 (see **[9.26]–[9.29]**).

#### ii)   *Type of shares*

Schedule 23 only gives relief where *shares* are acquired—not when the range of securities covered by ITEPA 2003 Part 7 are acquired. Only certain types of shares qualify (Sch 23 paras 4, 6, 12): in essence, these are the same type that can be used for approved SAYE Option Schemes and Company Share Option Plans (see **[9.62]** (1)), although the rules relating to consortium companies are slightly different. The most notable absence is shares in an unlisted subsidiary of an unlisted parent—if such a company wants to distribute its own shares to employees, it will still have to rely on general principles to claim a deduction and will be subject to Schedule 24.                **[9.125]**

### c)   *Amount and timing of relief*

The employing company (not, if different, the company whose shares are acquired) will obtain a corporation tax deduction equal to the amount on which the employee is (or would be) taxed if the conditions in **[9.125]** are satisfied. The relief will be claimable for the accounting period in which the employee is (or would be) taxed. Thus, except in the case of SIPs (as to which see [9.70]), approved (including EMI) options and non-residents, there will be symmetry between the employing company's corporation tax deduction and the employee's tax charge. FA 2006 s 93 amends Schedule 23 to correct an oversight in drafting in relation to discounted EMI options over restricted or convertible shares. Schedule 23 is amended to bring EMI gains in line with other options, allowing the employing company a deduction for full gain realised by the employee and not solely for the amount of the upfront discount on which the employee is taxed (see [9.75]).          [9.126]

d)   *Arbitrage receipts rules*

The arbitrage receipts rules were introduced by F (No 2) A 2005 s 26 to counter tax arbitrage where a UK-resident company receives a benefit from a payment that is not fully taxable as income or gains, but where the payee has received a tax deduction. The legislation allows HMRC to issue the UK company with a 'notice' requiring the company to compute its income or gains for tax purposes as if it had received taxable income equal to any untaxed amount.

   HMRC does not expect the arbitrage receipts rules to apply generally to recharge payments from the employing company to its UK parent where shares are provided by the parent company to its employees, provided that the amount of any tax deduction available to the employing company (the payer) is based on the economic value of what is provided (the shares or options).

   Any recharge arrangements made on the basis of the transfer pricing provisions referred to above (see [9.124]) would not, therefore, be caught, nor would recharge arrangements between two UK companies, as a result of the operation of Schedule 23. However, an example of where the arbitrage receipts rules may apply is where a non-UK employing company is required to makes a payment (which is tax deductible) to a UK company in respect of the 'spread' at the time of exercise (the difference between the exercise price and the market value of the shares acquired), and this exceeds the fair value of the options at the time of grant.          [9.127]–[9.150]

## VI   CHOICE OF SCHEME

### 1   Non-tax aspects

Whenever any commercial transaction is considered it is vital to look at the tax implications from all angles. However, no transaction can or should be entirely tax-driven. Thus, an employer should first decide what commercial objective he is seeking by his scheme of employee participation. Set out below is a list of the likely objectives, together with a note of the schemes (approved and non-approved) that may go some way towards achieving them.
          [9.151]

a)   *Tax-efficient bonus scheme*

Approved schemes are the most efficient schemes to operate. In some cases, the selectivity offered by EMIs and Company Share Option Plans may be the deciding factor (see [9.159])).          [9.152]

b)   *Performance-related incentives*

Unapproved schemes are better in this regard because targets can be changed and directly related to individual performance. With all approved schemes, targets must be fixed at the outset (although the decision in *IRC v Burton Group plc* (1990) affords some flexibility). If looking to the profitability of the company, rather than individual employees, an employee trust may be preferred, since this enables the amount passing into the trust for the benefit of the employees to be directly related to the company's performance.   **[9.153]**

c)   *Reward for growth in share value*

Share incentive schemes or share options may be used and, again, the selectivity of EMIs and Company Share Option Plans may make them the more attractive of the approved schemes. However, if there are difficulties with institutional investors (see **[9.164]**), an employee trust arrangement might be appropriate.   **[9.154]**

d)   *Retention of employees*

Long-running schemes are required. Most schemes will be appropriate where they operate over a long period and are made subject to the employee remaining with the company. Unapproved share incentives with restrictions on sale could also be used.   **[9.155]**

e)   *Creation of 'friendly' shareholdings*

Shares may be sold immediately after exercise of options and it is therefore better to use an employee trust or a SIP to create a friendly block holding of shares. This has the added benefit of the shares of the employees being 'co-ordinated' through trustees. Alternatively, SAYE schemes tend not to result in an immediate sale because the employee does not need to raise funds to exercise the option.   **[9.156]**

f)   *Creation of market in non-quoted shares*

Any arrangement involving the use of a trust would be ideal as the trust can be funded to acquire shares from employees where no other market exists. Often a private company's articles of association will restrict the sale of shares other than to existing shareholders or to an employee trust.   **[9.157]**

g)   *Generation of sense of identity between employees and the company*

Any form of share ownership should promote this and the normal procedure would be to tie this into a long-term commitment as suggested above. The employee trust is particularly useful in this respect. On an all-employee basis, the SIP provides tax benefits whilst aligning the interests of employees with those of the company as they share the risks through their investments. Many employees, however, prefer to participate in option schemes, particularly an SAYE, on the basis that they are not at risk of making a loss—if the share price falls employees do not need to exercise their options and those employees participating in an SAYE are able to recover their contributions and the tax-free bonus. **[9.158]**

h)  *Selective employee participation*

One problem with approved SIPs and SAYE schemes is that they must apply to *all* employees (subject to qualifying periods of employment). EMIs and Company Share Option Plans permit selectivity. Should that type of scheme not be suitable, companies may consider an unapproved scheme that provides *total* flexibility on this matter. **[9.159]**

i)  *Accounting treatment*

There have been moves over the last few years to ensure that a company's accounts adequately reflect all its assets and liabilities. A radical change to the accounting treatment of share-based remuneration came into force for most listed companies on 1 January 2005 as a result of the requirement under the EU International Accounting Standards Regulation (1606/2002) for them to use international standards to prepare their consolidated financial statements. For share incentives, this means accounting under the International Accounting Standards Board's IFRS 2 'Share-based payment' (which is mirrored in the UK by the Accounting Standards Board's (ASB) FRS 20 and applied to all listed companies still following UK GAAP from the same date). For all other companies the new accounting treatment applies from 1 January 2006. The driving force behind the change is the belief that the previous accounting treatment led to corporate profits being overstated.

IFRS 2 and FRS 20 require that an expense be charged in the company's profit and loss account whenever it enters into any share-based obligation. The expense will have to be measured as the 'fair value' of the equity instrument (the share or option) at the grant date and will be derived from the market value of the instrument, where this can be determined (eg for a share) or, in the case of an option, as calculated by using a valuation technique or model. This value will be accrued in the accounts over the performance period: the charge to the profit and loss account will be finalised on vesting depending on the proportion of the shares or option which vest as a result of the application of (non-market based) vesting conditions.

FRS 20 supersedes Abstract 17 issued by the Urgent Issues Task Force of the ASB dealing with the accounting treatment of share benefits for employees, where shares or rights to shares are issued at a discount to employees.

UITF Abstract 13 ('Accounting for ESOP Trusts') and UITF Abstract 32 ('Employee benefit trusts and other intermediate payment arrangements') deal with the accounting treatment of employee trusts, in particular their balance sheet presentation.

UITF Abstract 25 deals with the accounting treatment of employers' NICs on unapproved options. Under it, companies have to make provision for the liability. No provision has to be made, however, if there has been an election to transfer the employer's liability to the employee; if the employee has agreed to reimburse the employer's liability, then that promise will appear as an asset if receipt is virtually certain (see further **[9.35]**). **[9.160]**

## 2　Tax aspects

Having determined what type of scheme can best meet its commercial objectives, the employer will need to look at the relative tax benefits of the various schemes available. Two main questions need to be asked: *first*, do approved schemes offer real tax benefits in comparison with non-approved schemes; and, *secondly*, if they do, which of the approved schemes is most beneficial?　**[9.161]**

### a)　*Approved or unapproved?*

So far as share-based schemes are concerned, it has been explained that the benefits provided under *approved* schemes will usually be subject only to *CGT* in the employee's hands, and that any charge will arise only if and when the relevant shares are *sold*. By contrast, benefits provided for an employee under an *unapproved* scheme will usually be taxed as *income* and charges can arise even *before sale*.

Prior to FA 1988, with a top rate of income tax of 60%, compared with a CGT rate of only 30%, the attractions of approved schemes from an employee's point of view were obvious. Since 1988–89, however, capital gains have been charged at the employee's marginal income tax rate (although there is a small CGT benefit for basic rate taxpayers). Accordingly, for higher rate taxpayers, the rate of CGT has been increased and *the taxation of such gains has to some extent been equated with the treatment of income profits*. To this extent, the distinction between approved and unapproved schemes has become somewhat blurred.

*However, a capital gain rather than an income profit will still be advantageous for the following reasons.*

*First*, the due date for payment of the two taxes differs: earnings under ITEPA 2003 may attract an immediate tax charge under PAYE, whereas any capital gain realised will only fall into charge on 31 January following the tax year in which the disposal occurred, as CGT is collected under self-assessment. *Secondly*, in arriving at the chargeable gain, an individual will be entitled to an annual exemption of (currently) £8,800 and taper relief (particularly advantageous now that employee shareholdings are generally treated as business assets (see **[9.36]**) and even more advantageous for Enterprise Management Incentives since the taper relief period runs from the date of option grant (see **[9.75]**)). *Thirdly*, the taxation of benefits received under approved schemes is only triggered on the disposal of the shares: accordingly, as long as the employee or director intends to retain the shares over a period of years, it may be possible to reduce, or even eliminate, the charge. In due course, that individual may be able to arrange for disposals to occur in different tax years (thereby taking advantage of more than one annual exemption) and for disposals to be channelled through his family.

These advantages are further enhanced by the difference in the treatment of approved and unapproved schemes for national insurance purposes (cf **[9.35]** and **[9.78]**). The real extra cost to employers of operating unapproved schemes has once again introduced a clear distinction between these and approved schemes.　**[9.162]**

b)   *Which approved scheme?*

If the employer decides that his overall objectives fit within the structure of an approved scheme, which scheme should be chosen? This question should be answered by looking at the non-tax aspects of the matter noted above.

The main difference between the various approved share schemes lies in the amount of relief available and whether or not benefits can be given on a selective basis.

If shares are retained in a SIP for the period necessary to avoid an income tax charge and sold immediately on removal, the effect of the 100% CGT base cost uplift will be to make the gain tax-free. Shares may be retained in the SIP trust generally for as long as the employee remains in employment. This is the only way of *ensuring* a tax-free benefit for an employee irrespective of his own tax position. However, in many cases benefits from approved schemes *will be* tax-free as there will be no income tax liability and the gains will be within the recipient's (unused) annual CGT exemption.   **[9.163]**

## 3   **Other shareholders**

The presence of institutional shareholders may be a further factor for a company considering setting up an employee participation scheme to consider. Any listed company will not only have to comply with the Listing, Disclosure and Prospectus Rules but will also usually feel obliged to follow the guidelines issued by committees representing institutional investors. The Listing Rules require prior shareholder approval for any employee share scheme which involves or may involve the issue of new shares or transfer of treasury shares, and for any long-term incentive scheme in which at least one director is eligible to participate. This will cover an employee trust which has the power to subscribe for shares in the company as well as those schemes more obviously involving new issues.

Institutional investor guidelines impose limits ('headroom limits') as to the number of shares that can be issued under employee share schemes and, broadly, set the ceiling at 10% of issued share capital in any ten-year period (or 5% for discretionary schemes). Further, institutional investors generally do not accept the use of shares in subsidiaries for incentive schemes.

Guidelines issued by institutional investors cover matters other than the number of shares that can be used for incentive schemes, in particular the circumstance when executive share options may be exercised. Institutional investors are adamant that this should depend on performance targets being met. The key points are the requirement for 'challenging performance conditions', with awards granted on an annual or other regular basis and subject to lapse if the conditions are not met at the end of a fixed 'performance measurement' period (see Association of British Insurers' guidelines issued 15 December 2005).   **[9.164]**

# 10   Trading income

*Updated by Sarah Deeks LLB FCA*

'... take a gang of burglars. Are they engaged in trade or an adventure in the nature of trade? They have an organisation. They spend money on equipment. They acquire goods by their efforts. They sell the goods. They make a profit. What detail is lacking in their adventure? You may say it lacks legality, but it has been held that legality is not an essential characteristic of a trade. You cannot point to any detail that it lacks. But still it is not a trade, nor an adventure in the nature of trade. And how does it help to ask the question: If it is not a trade, what is it? It is burglary and that is all there is to say about it.'

(Lord Denning in *Griffiths v Harrison* (1963)).

**[10.1]**

## I   INTRODUCTION

The law relating to the taxation of trading income differs according to whether a business is unincorporated or a limited company. For income tax purposes, trading income is dealt with under Part 2 Income Tax (Trading and Other Income) Act 2005 (ITTOIA 2005) from 2005–06 onwards. For corporation tax, trading income is computed under Schedule D Cases I and II, but ITTOIA 2005 applies where relevant, for accounting periods ending after 5 April 2005 (ITTOIA 2005 s 883(1)).

Since this chapter applies to all trading entities, the general description 'trading income' has been adopted throughout rather than the Schedule D terminology, unless the context specifically requires it.                    **[10.2]**

## 1   Income tax

Income tax is charged under the trading income provisions of ITTOIA 2005 Part 2 on the profits of a trade, profession or vocation (ITTOIA 2005 s 5). Accordingly all sole-traders and partnerships have 'trading' income regardless of their business activities. The profits of a trade arising to a UK resident person are chargeable to tax under these provisions irrespective of where in the world the trade is carried on. The trading profits of a non-UK resident person are chargeable to income tax only if they arise from a trade carried on wholly in the UK, or if it is carried on partly in the UK and partly abroad, from the part carried on in the UK (ITTOIA 2005 s 6).

Before 2005–06, income tax was charged under Schedule D Case I for trades, Schedule D Case II for professions and vocations and Schedule D Case V for trades, professions and vocations carried on wholly abroad by a UK resident taxpayer.                                                    **[10.3]**

## 2   Corporation tax

For corporation tax purposes the distinction between Schedule D Case I which taxes trading profits or gains and Schedule D Case II which taxes professional profits remains: see *Kowloon Stock Exchange Ltd v Commr of Inland Revenue* (1984). The distinction is, however, now of little practical significance although certain provisions apply only to trades or to professions. A Schedule D Case I trade or a Schedule D Case II profession must be carried on wholly or partly in the UK by a UK resident company (TA 1988, s 18; ITTOIA 2005 Sch 1 para 9). Trading or professional activities carried on wholly abroad fall within Schedule D Case V.

In this chapter Schedule D Case I includes Schedule D Case II, and trade includes profession, unless otherwise stated.                        **[10.4]–[10.20]**

## II   WHAT IS A TRADE?

### 1   The problems involved

'Trade' is not defined. According to TA 1988 s 832(1) it 'includes every trade, manufacture, adventure, or concern in the nature of a trade'. This provision, although generally unhelpful, indicates that a single adventure may constitute a trade (see eg *Martin v Lowry* (1927) below). In *Ransom v Higgs* (1974) Lord Wilberforce considered that a trading transaction would usually exhibit the following features:

> 'Trade normally involves the exchange of goods or services for reward ... there must be something which the trade offers to provide by way of business. Trade moreover presupposes a customer.'
>
> ([1974] 3 All ER at 964.)

In the absence of a satisfactory statutory definition the meaning of trade must be sought from the voluminous case law. The Final Report of the Royal Commission on the Taxation of Profits and Income (1955: Cmnd 9474) concluded that there could be no single test but suggested certain objective tests ('the badges of trade').

Before considering these 'badges of trade', two general matters should be noted in connection with the case law. *First,* when the case is concerned with whether a taxpayer carried on a trade or not, caution needs to be exercised in citing it as precedent since the findings of the commissioners are decisions of fact which will rarely be overturned on appeal (see *Edwards v Bairstow and Harrison* (1956): at **[4.59]**). The appeal court is often and reluctantly forced to conclude that facts exist to justify the findings of the commissioners. *Secondly,* before the introduction of CGT in 1965, the question whether or not a person engaged in a trade was of fundamental significance. If he was trading, any profit was charged under Case I; if not, income tax was inapplicable so that the (capital) profit escaped tax altogether. Since 1965 the choice is normally between paying income tax and CGT. The taxpayer's preference for one or the other will depend on the availability of the various reliefs, for example losses, taper relief and EIS deferral relief. Capital receipts, although they may suffer CGT, are not charged to income tax as trading income (ITTOIA 2005 s 96), see also **[10.103]**.

HMRC's Business Income Manual BIM20050 should be referred to for their interpretation of 'trading'. **[10.21]**

## 2 The 'badges of trade'

The Royal Commission identified six 'badges' designed to determine whether or not the purchase and sale of property is a trading transaction.
**[10.22]**

### a) *The subject matter of the transaction*

Property that neither yields an income nor gives personal enjoyment to its owner is more likely to form the subject matter of a trading transaction. Other property (typically land, works of art, and shares) may be acquired for the income and/or enjoyment that it provides.

In *Rutledge v IRC* (1929), the taxpayer was a businessman connected with the film industry. Whilst in Berlin he purchased 1 million toilet rolls for £1,000 that he resold in the UK at a profit of approximately £11,000. The Court of Session held that the taxpayer had engaged in an adventure in the nature of a trade so that the profits were assessable under Case I. They stressed that such a quantity of goods must have been intended for resale. Similarly, in *Martin v Lowry* (1927), the gigantic speculation involved in the purchase and sale of 44 million yards of Government surplus aeroplane linen, at a profit of £1,600,000, amounted to a trade largely because of the nature of the subject matter and the commercial methods employed to sell it.

The purchase and sale of land causes more difficulty since owning land in quantity does not raise a presumption that trading is intended. In *IRC v Reinhold* (1953), for instance, despite the taxpayer having bought four houses over two years, admittedly for sale, the Court of Session concluded that 'heritable property is not an uncommon subject of investment' and that the taxpayer was not trading.

Similar difficulties arose in *Taylor v Good* (1974) where the taxpayer was held not to be trading when he sold at a considerable profit, because he had obtained planning permission, a house which he had purchased with the original intention of using it as a residence. The Court of Appeal took the view that a person intending to sell property is entitled to take steps to ensure that he obtains the best possible price for it. In particular, the court decided that the house did not become his trading stock merely because he had applied for planning permission before the sale:

'If you find a trade in the purchase and sale of land, it may not be difficult to find that properties originally owned (for example) by inheritance, or bought for investment only, have been brought into the stock in trade of that trade. But where, as here, there is no question at all of absorption into a trade of dealing in land or lands previously acquired with no thought of dealing, there is no ground at all for holding that activities such as those in the present case, designed only to enhance the value of the land in the market, are to be taken as pointing to, still less as establishing, an adventure in the nature of trade.'

(Russell LJ [1974] STC 148 at 155.)

The definition of a trade was further limited in this area in *Marson v Morton* (1986). The taxpayer was a potato merchant and on advice from an estate agent friend, purchased land suitable for development. He paid £65,000: £35,000 out of his own resources and £30,000 on a mortgage arranged by the estate agent. At the time of the purchase the taxpayer said that he intended to make a medium to long-term investment in the land. However, two months later, on advice from the same estate agent, the land was sold for £100,000. Both the commissioners and Sir Nicolas Browne-Wilkinson V-C held that the taxpayer was not trading and that land could be held as an investment even though it produced no income. The following passage from the judgment is especially worthy of note:

'In 1986 it is not any longer self evident that unless land is producing income it cannot be an investment. The legal principle, of course, cannot change with the passage of time: but life does. Since the arrival of inflation and high rates of tax on income, new approaches to investment have emerged putting the emphasis in investment on the making of capital profit at the expense of income yield. For example, the purchase of short dated stocks giving capital yield on redemption but no income has become commonplace. Similarly, split level investment trusts have been invented which produce capital profits on one type of share and income on another. Again, institutions now purchase works of art by way of investment. In my judgment those are plainly not trading deals; yet no income is produced from them. I can see no reason why land should be any different and the mere fact that land is not income producing should not be decisive or even virtually decisive on the question whether it was bought as an investment.'    **[10.23]**

b)    *Length of ownership*

A quick sale is more consistent with a trading activity rather than an investment that is more likely to be long term. The reason for sale may be special and could rebut such a presumption (see *Wisdom v Chamberlain* (1969), a case involving the purchase and sale of silver bullion, and see also **[10.28]**).    **[10.24]**

c)    *Frequency of similar transactions*

Repeated transactions in the same subject matter point to a trade. Since a single adventure may amount to a trade this 'badge' will be applicable only in circumstances where that would not otherwise be the case. In *Pickford v Quirke* (1927) the court held that although a single purchase and sale by a syndicate of four cotton mills did not amount to trading, the series viewed as a whole did. Note also that later transactions may colour earlier transactions and may trigger a Case I or trading income liability on those earlier transactions (see also *Leach v Pogson* (1962) in which the founding and subsequent sale of 30 driving schools consecutively, was held to be trading).

[10.25]

d) *Work done on the property*

When work is done to the property in order to make it more marketable, or when an organisation is set up to sell the asset, there is some evidence of trading (see *Martin v Lowry* (1927): compare *Taylor v Good* (1974)). In *Cape Brandy Syndicate v IRC* (1921) three individuals engaged in the wine trade who formed a syndicate and purchased some £3,000 casks of Cape brandy which they blended (with French brandy), recasked, and sold in lots over an 18-month period were held to be trading.

[10.26]

e) *Circumstances responsible for the realisation*

A forced sale to raise cash for an emergency raises a presumption that the transaction is not a trade. Sales by executors in the course of winding up the deceased's estate and by liquidators and receivers in the administration of an insolvent company will often fall into this category (see *Cohan's Executors v IRC* (1924) and *IRC v The 'Old Bushmills' Distillery Co Ltd* (1927) and see [10.30]).

[10.27]

f) *Motive*

If the transaction was undertaken in order to realise a profit that is some evidence of trading. The absence of a profit motive does not prevent a commercial operation from amounting to a trade (see, for instance, dividend stripping and for the effect of fiscal motives, *Ensign Tankers (Leasing) Ltd v Stokes* (1992)); conversely, the mere fact that an asset is purchased with the intention of ultimate resale at a profit will not of itself lead to a finding of trading. Often the subject matter involved will be decisive. In *Wisdom v Chamberlain* (1968) the taxpayer (a comedian) who bought £200,000 of silver bullion as a 'hedge' against an expected devaluation of sterling and three months later sold it realising a profit of £50,000 was held to be trading. His claim that he had made no profit, but rather that the pound had fallen in value, was rejected.

[10.28]

3  **Mutual trading**

No man can trade with himself. Thus, when persons join together in an association and jointly contribute to a common fund for their mutual benefit, any surplus received by the members on a division of that fund is tax-free (*New York Life Insurance Co v Styles* (1889)) but equally there is no relief for losses and capital allowances cannot be claimed. If however, the association trades with non-members, the profits attributable to that activity are taxable. In *Carlisle and Silloth Golf Club v Smith* (1913), fees paid by visitors for the use of the club facilities were held to be trading receipts. TA 1988 s 491 prevents the mutual trading rules from being used to avoid tax, by imposing a charge on the return of surplus assets in circumstances when the original contributions were tax deductible. For HMRC's view of mutual trading see Business Income Manual BIM24000.                                                    **[10.29]**

## 4  Trading after a discontinuance

The realisation of assets after the permanent discontinuance of the business is not trading. Hence, in *IRC v Nelson* (1938) income tax under the then Case I was not charged when a whisky broker, who because of ill-health had closed his business, sold the entire business including the stock in trade. By contrast, a sale of stock *with a view to* the cessation of trading (a 'closing-down sale') is chargeable because the trade is still continuing (see *J & R O'Kane & Co Ltd v IRC* (1922)).

Special rules operate for the valuation of trading stock held at the date of cessation of a business (ITTOIA 2005 ss 173–181; TA 1988 s 100, see **[10.112]**).                                                      **[10.30]–[10.40]**

## 5  Meaning of 'profession' and 'vocation'

In common with 'trade', neither 'profession' nor 'vocation' are statutorily defined. 'Profession' has been judicially described as involving 'the idea of an occupation requiring either purely intellectual skill or manual skill controlled by the intellectual skill of the operator' (see Scrutton LJ in *IRC v Maxse* (1919)). This definition can be misleading, because a person exercising an occupation in those terms (such as a solicitor) may be doing so as an employee assessable under ITEPA 2003 (see **[8.22]**). A profession differs from a trade as it involves an element of continuity. Hence, casual profits and fees arising from an isolated professional or vocational transaction are more likely to be taxed as miscellaneous income under ITTOIA 2005 Part 5. For an examination of when an author becomes a publisher, see *Salt v Fernandez* (1997).

'Vocation' has been judicially defined by Denman J in *Partridge v Mallandaine* (1886) as '… the way in which a man passes his life'. This definition is somewhat unhelpful as it would embrace a very wide variety of activities not all of which would be vocations.                                         **[10.41]–[10.60]**

## III  COMPUTATION OF PROFITS

## 1  The accounts

Income tax is charged on the full amount of the trading profits (ITTOIA 2005 s 7). Corporation tax is based on the 'annual profits of the trade, profession or vocation' (TA 1988 s 18). 'Annual' in this context means profits of an income, as opposed to of a recurring, nature (*Martin v Lowry* (1927)).

Accounts prepared for commercial purposes and according to generally accepted accountancy practice (see **[10.62]**) will rarely show the taxable trading profits, although in recent years the accounting and tax profits have become more closely harmonised. Some items that have been deducted in the accounts may not be deductible for tax purposes (such as entertainment expenses: see [**10.138**]). Other items are treated differently for taxation purposes: expenditure on a capital asset, for instance, is written off annually over the life of the asset as depreciation under generally accepted accounting practice but is deductible for income tax and corporation tax only to the extent that it falls within the system of capital allowances (see **Chapter 48**). The taxpayer's trading accounts must therefore be adjusted for tax purposes by adding back deductions that are not allowable and, where appropriate, by making permitted deductions (such as capital allowances). [**10.61**]

## 2 Generally accepted accounting practice (GAAP)

In drawing up accounts for tax purposes, the taxpayer traditionally used one of three bases: the earnings; the cash; or the bills delivered (the cash and bills delivered bases being known as the 'conventional' bases). The conventional bases ignored debtors, creditors, stock and work-in-progress and although case law established that the legal basis for computing profits was the earnings basis (*CIR v Gardner Mountain & D'Ambrumenil Ltd* (1947)), in many cases the conventional bases were acceptable to the then Inland Revenue for unincorporated professions or vocations, but not trades, as long as the profits taking one year with another did not differ materially from the profits computed on the earnings basis. The earnings basis, however, had to be used for the first three accounting years of a new profession. Once the Revenue had assessed the taxpayer on one basis, it could not supplement that assessment by an assessment on an alternative basis (see *Rankine v IRC* (1952)).

For periods of account beginning on or after 7 April 1999, FA 1998 s 42 made it a statutory requirement for trading profits to be computed for tax purposes on an accounting basis that gives a true and fair view subject to any adjustments required under specific legislation. FA 1998 s 42 was amended by FA 2002 s 103(5), FA 2004 s 50 and ITTOIA 2005 s 25 to provide from 24 July 2002 that trading profits must be computed in accordance with generally accepted accounting practice (GAAP). For any entity this means that their accounts must be prepared in accordance with UK and international accounting standards, or adjusted for tax purposes to reflect these requirements (see [**10.64**]).

Compliance with GAAP requires all trading profits to be computed on the earnings basis. This requires the accounts for sole-traders, partnerships and companies to reflect debtors, creditors, stock and work-in-progress. Compliance with GAAP does not for these purposes require the accounts to be audited or to be disclosed under either the Companies Acts and accounting standards. The conventional bases may no longer be employed for tax purposes, with a limited exception for barristers and advocates in ITTOIA 2005 s 160 (see [**10.73**]). [**10.62**]

## 3 Accounting principles

### a) *Introduction*

Historically, in computing trading profits, the starting point is the profit as shown by the accounts drawn up in accordance with the principles of commercial accounting and taking into account the specific provisions of tax law (*Heather v P-E Consulting Group Ltd* (1972)). This concept was established by case law long before it was given statutory effect, (*Lothian Chemical Co Ltd v Rogers* (1926), *Odeon Associated Theatres Ltd v Jones* (1972); *Threlfall v Jones* (1993), *Lloyds UDT Finance Ltd v Chartered Finance Trust Holdings and ors (Britax Int. GmbH and anor)* (2002)). It is now enshrined in the principle that trading profits must be computed in accordance with generally acceptable accounting practice (GAAP) (see **[10.62]**).                                    **[10.63]**

b)   *Accounting standards*

Generally accepted accounting practice has no legal definition in the UK. It encompasses the principles set out in the accounting standards and other statements issued by the Accounting Standards Board (ASB) but goes beyond this to include the requirements of company law, industry-specific requirements, regulatory factors and pronouncements by HMRC. When considering compliance with GAAP, the relevant question to ask is 'how would accountants present the trading profit in practice?'

All entities, regardless of whether they are incorporated or not, must take into account the following statements when computing their trading profits:

● Financial Reporting Standards (FRSs);
● Statements of Standard Accounting Practice (SSAPs);
● Urgent Issue Task Force (UITF) Abstracts;
● Statements of Recommended Practice (SORPs);
● Financial Reporting Exposure Drafts (FREDs); and
● other statements by the ASB.

Accounting standards are continually evolving and as new ones are published they will need to be taken into account. A full list of current statements is available on www.frc.org.uk/asb/technical/index.cfm.

Small entities can apply the principles in the Financial Reporting Standard for Smaller Entities (FRSSE effective 2005) instead of the other statements. 'Small' in accordance with the Companies Act definition means turnover of less than £5.6m, assets below £2.8m and not more than 50 employees.

Listed companies, for accounting periods beginning on or after 1 January 2005, must draw up their consolidated accounts in accordance with international accounting standards (IAS), international financial reporting standards (IFRS) and the related interpretations (SIC-IFRIC interpretations) (The European Union Regulation (Regulation (EC) No 1606/2002). Companies affected by this requirement must account in accordance with IFRS to ensure compliance with GAAP (FA 2004 s 50). Finance Acts 2004–2006 have included legislation to ensure that companies using international accounting standards are taxed in an equivalent way to companies using UK GAAP. HMRC have produced a summary of the UK tax implications of international accounting standards: see www.hmrc.gov.uk/practitioners/int_accounting.htm.

The following accounting standards are considered in this chapter: FRS5 and UITF 40 **[10.72]** and **[10.112]**; FRS 12 **[10.67]**; FRS18 **[10.66]**; SSAP 9 **[10.111]** and SSAP 17 **[10.76]**.                                    **[10.64]**

c) *Materiality*

Materiality is an accounting concept and is relevant to the preparation of accounts which form the starting point for the computation of taxable trading profits. An item is material if its misstatement or omission would affect a reader's view of the accounts. The extent to which materiality impacts on the accounts is a matter of judgement but a certain level of materiality should not be assumed. Materiality does not sit comfortably with HMRC's view of the tax legislation which requires accuracy, ultimately to be determined by the Commissioners. HMRC permit some relaxation in the requirement for complete accuracy in large businesses where rounding to £1,000 is permitted in some circumstances, see Statement of Practice (SP 15/93).

**[10.65]**

d) *Accounting policies*

All entities must comply with FRS 18 'Accounting Policies' which requires businesses to identify and adopt the most appropriate accounting policies to their circumstances, changing them over time as necessary to produce reliable accounts that reflect the substance of their transactions. A key feature is comparability with previous accounts produced by the same entity and with other similar trades (see **[10.72]**). FRS 18 replaced the now withdrawn SSAP 2 which set out four fundamental accounting concepts – going concern, accruals, consistency and prudence. In order to comply with GAAP, accounts must be prepared on an accruals and a going concern basis unless the business has ceased trading. Consistency and prudence are regarded as factors to be considered in assessing the appropriateness of an entity's accounting policies. *Herbert Smith v Honour* (1999) provided support for the practical application of the prudence concept. In this case the taxpayer provided for the net future rent payable (some £5.5m) on business premises that had become surplus to requirements. The High Court held that this was acceptable if there was just one acceptable accounting practice. Such a provision must now comply with FRS 12 in order to be tax deductible: see **[10.67]**.

The accounting policies adopted must have sufficient regard to the facts. In *Minister of National Revenue v Anaconda American Brass Ltd* (1956), it was held that the stock valuation policy that the company adopted in its statutory accounts was based on a theoretical pattern of stock use, 'last in first out' (LIFO), which disregarded the facts. The Privy Council concluded that the basis to be used for tax purposes was 'first in first out' (FIFO): see also **[10.111]**.

HMRC considers that FRS18 reduces the opportunity for there to be conflict about the choice of accounting policy, as where more than one policy could be selected, the policy chosen must be *the most* suitable. Revenue accountants may review how the decision to adopt a particular policy was reached. Providing, however, that the accounts are prepared on a tenable basis under FRS 18, HMRC will not challenge them, nor seek to substitute an alternative policy.

**[10.66]**

e) *Provisions*

FRS 12 'Provisions, contingent liabilities and contingent assets' governs the inclusion of provisions in accounts. The cases of *Owen v Southern Railway of*

*Peru Ltd* (1957) and *IRC v The Titaghur Jute Factory Co Ltd* (1978) established that a deduction may be allowed for a contingent liability provided that:

(1)　the profit would not be adequately stated if the obligation was not taken into account; and

(2)　it has been possible to arrive at a sufficiently reliable figure.

The admissibility of provisions was also considered in *Johnston v Britannia Airways Ltd* (1994), *Jenners Princes Street (Edinburgh) v IRC* (1998) (provision for refurbishment expenditure) and *Herbert Smith v Honour* (1999) (provision for onerous leases). As accounting profits must now accord with GAAP, accounting in accordance with FRS 12 is mandatory and this negates the effect of much of the previous case law.

Under FRS 12 provisions can only be made where there is a present obligation as the result of a past event, and it is probable that expenditure (for which a reliable estimate can be made) will be required to settle the obligation. In consequence, provisions for future repairs are not permitted so *Johnston v Britannia Airways Ltd* (1994) no longer applies and provisions cannot be made for future operating losses (*Meat Traders v Cushing* (1997). Provisions for future restructuring costs can, however, be made where the entity has a detailed development plan and provisions for onerous contracts are permitted provided that a reliable estimate can be made of the costs: *Herbert Smith v Honour* (1999). **[10.67]–[10.71]**

f)　*Change of accounting basis*

The need for consistency in accounts was recognised by the courts in *Ostime v Duple Motor Bodies Ltd* (1961) and *Pearce v Woodall Duckham Ltd* (1978).These cases established the principle that where:

(1)　there has been a change, from one valid accounting basis to another; and

(2)　as a result a profit or loss is recognised in the period in which the change is made (usually by being shown as a prior year adjustment in the accounts),

then the profit or loss should be included in the computation of the assessable profit of the period in which the change was made. The legislation regarding a change of accounting basis was originally reflected in FA 1998 s 44 and Sch 6 and is now encompassed in ITTOIA 2005 ss 226–240 and FA 2002 s 64 and Sch 22.

A change occurs where there is, from one period of account to the next, a change of basis in computing taxable trading profits, the old basis accorded with the law or practice applicable in relation to the period of account before the change, and the new basis accords with the law and practice applicable to the period of account following the change.

A change of basis for these purposes consists of either a change of accounting principle or practice in accordance with generally accepted accounting practice giving rise to a prior period adjustment, or a change resulting from a change of view as to application of the statute. This includes:

● 　the change from the conventional to the earnings basis in 1998 (see **[10.62]**);

● 　the adoption of international accounting standards; and

● 　changes to revenue recognition and the valuation of work-in-progress as a result of Application Note G to FRS 5 and UITF 40.

Where a change of accounting basis gives rise to a positive adjustment, tax is charged on the full amount of any adjustment (subject to spreading relief outlined below). For income tax, the adjustment income is charged separately from the trading profits and, before 2005–06, was chargeable under Schedule D Case VI. A negative adjustment is treated as a trading expense. There are exceptions from this rule where expenses are spread over more than one period of account after the change, where an adjustment is not required until an asset is realised or written off and on a change from realisation basis to mark to market.

Following the change from conventional to earnings basis, a positive adjustment in respect of a profession or vocation could be spread over 10 years (FA 1998 Sch 6). In the first nine years tax was charged on 10% of the adjustment charge or (if less) of assessable profits, with the balance being taxed in year ten irrespective of that year's profits. The taxpayer has the right to elect to pay tax on more than the adjustment figure, for example to utilise losses.

Changes due to the implementation of international accounting standards are considered to be a change of accounting basis but do not qualify for spreading relief. Furthermore the adjustment is treated not as arising on the last day of the first period of account after the change, but for periods of account beginning on or after 1 January 2005, the first day of the first period of account after the change. This measure is to ensure there is no deferral in taxing the increase in profits or in reducing loss relief (FA 2005 s 81 amending FA 2002 s 64(3) and Sch 22).

Changes due to UITF 40 (see [10.112]) do, however, qualify for spreading relief (FA 2006 s 102 and Sch 15). Broadly, any uplift from a change in revenue recognition on a service contract will be apportioned over between three and six tax years starting with the tax year for which the first period of account ending on or after 22 June 2005 is the basis period. For each year, the amount chargeable will be the lesser of one-third of the uplift and one-sixth of the taxable profit for that year; but in the sixth year, any part of the uplift not yet taxed will be charged. No relief is available for businesses that voluntarily adopted the new accounting treatment in periods ended before 22 June 2005. **[10.72]**

## 4  The cash basis

Although the general rule is that accounts must be prepared on an earnings basis to comply with generally accepted accounting practice (see **[10.62]**), barristers and advocates in independent practice can account on a cash or bills delivered basis for periods of account ending not more than seven years after they first hold themselves out as available for fee-earning work provided that the basis adopted is applied consistently (ITTOIA 2005 s 160).

### EXAMPLE 10.1

Justinian, a barrister, makes up his accounts to 31 December each year. For 2005 he received fees of £42,000 and is owed a further £50,000; and he has paid bills of £12,000, but owes a further £5,000. On a cash basis his accounts show a profit as follows:

| | | |
|---|---|---:|
| Cash receipts | | 42,000 |
| Cash payments | | 12,000 |
| Profit | | £30,000 |

This profit would be reduced to £25,000 were he to pay off all his outstanding liabilities on 31 December.

If his accounts were made up on the earnings basis his profits would be:

| | | | |
|---|---|---:|---:|
| Fees rendered: | received | | 42,000 |
| | outstanding | | 50,000 |
| | | | 92,000 |
| Expenses: | paid | 12,000 | |
| | outstanding | 5,000 | |
| | | | 17,000 |
| Profits | | | £75,000 |

**[10.73]**

## 5    Expenditure

a)    *Deductibility*

Expenditure cannot be deducted in computing the profits of a business if it falls within the scope of any of the prohibitions specified in the Taxes Acts or ITTOIA 2005, or it violates a rule of tax law derived by the courts (ITTOIA 2005 s 7; TA 1988 s 9).            **[10.74]**

b)    *Capital or revenue*

Capital expenditure is not allowable as a deduction in computing the profits of a trade (ITTOIA 2005 s 33; ICTA 1988 s 74(1)(f)(g)).

Whether expenditure is of a capital nature is ultimately a question of law to be determined in the light of the facts of an individual case. There is no single test to be applied in distinguishing capital from revenue expenditure. For determining profits for accountancy purposes, the important issue is whether expenditure is 'consumed', ie used up, and, therefore, when it must be charged to the profit and loss account or whether the expenditure brings into existence an asset or advantage for the enduring benefit of the trade: see *Atherton v British Insulation Helsby Cables Ltd* (1925). Other more recent cases which considered this issue include *Lawson v Johnson Matthey* (1992) and *Halifax plc v Davidson* (SpC 239 2000).            **[10.75]**

c)    *Date at which allowable*

Expenditure included in the commercial accounts of a trader is generally deductible for tax purposes in the accounting period covered by the accounts if they have been prepared in accordance with generally acceptable accounting practice including the benefit of hindsight to the extent permissible by SSAP 17, 'Post Balance Sheet Events'.            **[10.76]–[10.79]**

## 6  Post-cessation receipts and expenses

### a)  *Receipts*

Sums received in respect of a trade after its discontinuance which would not otherwise be charged to tax because the source of the income no longer exists, are taxed as trading income (ITTOIA 2005 ss 242–253) or under Schedule D Case VI (TA 1988 ss 103–110). For this purpose, a debt released after a discontinuance is treated as a receipt (ITTOIA 2005 s 249; TA 1988 s 103(4)). Certain sums are excluded; in particular, receipts on the transfer of stock or work-in-progress in order to avoid an overlap with ITTOIA 2005 ss 173–186; TA 1988 ss 100 and 102 (see ITTOIA 2005 s 252; TA 1988 s 103(3) and [10.113]).

Where profits were assessed on the cash basis (see [10.73]), TA 1988 s 104 imposes a similar charge to tax on post-cessation receipts, except that sums received for the transfer of work-in-progress after a discontinuance are brought within the charge.

Post-cessation receipts are generally taxed in the year of receipt or, if an unincorporated taxpayer elects, in the year of discontinuance so long as that discontinuance has not occurred more than six years before the receipt (ITTOIA 2005 s 257).                                                  [10.80]

### b)  *Expenses*

Expenditure that would have been deductible if the trade had not discontinued may be offset against post-cessation receipts (ITTOIA 2005 s 254; TA 1988 s 105). Relief against total income is available for certain payments made within seven years after cessation. Relief is given for the year in which the payment is made and unused relief cannot be carried forward (ITTOIA 2005 s 250; TA 1988 s 109A). Payments qualifying for relief are those made wholly and exclusively to remedy defective work done, goods supplied or services rendered or by way of damages for defective work; to meet legal and professional fees in connection with a claim for defective work; to insure against claims and to collect debts of the former trade.

The expenditure provisions also apply to debts of the business which are, after discontinuance, shown to be bad. The relief must be claimed and is given against income of the year of assessment in which the expenditure is incurred although the taxpayer may claim for the excess to be treated as an allowable capital loss of the same year if there is insufficient income in that year (ITTOIA 2005 s 248; TA 1988 s 109A).          [10.81]–[10.100]

## IV  TRADING RECEIPTS

To be a 'trading receipt' a sum must possess two characteristics:
- it must be derived from the trade; and
- it must not be capital.                                           [10.101]

## 1  The sum must be derived from the trade

If the payment is in return for services or goods it is a trading receipt, whereas if it is made voluntarily in recognition of some personal quality of the taxpayer it is not (compare this with the rules for employment income at [**8.62**]). In *Murray v Goodhews* (1976), for instance, Watneys took back tied tenancies (mainly pubs) from their tenant traders as they fell vacant and made *ex gratia* lump sum payments to the traders which were held not to be trading receipts; they were paid voluntarily by Watneys to acknowledge the good relationship with the traders and to maintain their good name. (As to whether the payments were deductible expenditure of the payer, see [**10.132**].) By contrast, in *McGowan v Brown and Cousins* (1977) the taxpayer, an estate agent, found sites for a company for which he was paid a low fee because it was expected that he would handle the subsequent lettings for the company. The company, however, found another agent to do the letting and 'paid off' the taxpayer with £2,500. This was held to be a trading receipt: it was a reward for services even though paid in pursuance of a moral rather than a legal obligation.

In *Higgs v Olivier* (1952) Laurence Olivier was paid £15,000 by a film company not to appear in any other film for a period of 18 months. The amount was held not to be a receipt of his profession but compensation for not exercising that profession and it therefore escaped tax. Such a receipt would now be taxed as income from an employment under ITEPA 2003 ss 225–226 (see [**8.133**]).

A receipt which is not in return for services or goods may nevertheless be a trading receipt if it is intended to be used in the taxpayer's business. Thus, in *Poulter v Gayjon Processes Ltd* (1985), a Government subsidy paid to encourage a shoe manufacturer to retain persons in employment was held to be a taxable trading receipt (see also *Ryan v Crabtree Denims Ltd* (1987)). In *Donald Fisher (Ealing) Ltd v Spencer* (1989), compensation paid by an agent whose negligence had resulted in the taxpayer becoming liable to pay substantially increased rent on its business premises was held to be a trading receipt. In the course of his judgment, subsequently upheld in the Court of Appeal, Walton J stated that:

> 'If compensation is received which is in substance payable in respect of either the non-receipt of what ought to have been received or the extra expense which would not have been incurred if all had gone properly, it seems to me that the principle is exactly the same.'                    [**10.102**]

## 2    The sum must be income not capital

The difficulty of determining whether payments are income receipts or capital receipts was forcibly expressed by Greene MR in *IRC v British Salmson Aero Engines Ltd* (1938):

> '... in many cases it is almost true to say that the spin of a coin would decide the matter almost as satisfactorily as an attempt to find reasons'.

A number of tests have been suggested. The classic test is the distinction between a sale of the fixed capital of the business and of its circulating capital. Sale of the circulating capital produces income receipts. The defect with this test is that the classification of the asset (is it fixed or circulating?) depends upon the particular trade.

**EXAMPLE 10.2**

(1)   Koob, a bookseller, owns a bookshop in Covent Garden. The books are his circulating capital (his stock in trade) so that the sale proceeds are trade receipts. The shop premises represent his fixed capital, the sale of which would give rise to a CGT liability.

(2)   Seisin buys vacant premises in Covent Garden which he renovates and sells as shops. He is trading in the sale of shops that are his circulating capital so that the receipts are income receipts.

Other tests are but variations on the original theme and contain the same defect. For example, whether or not the expenditure brings into existence an enduring asset for the benefit of the trade (see **[10.75]**), and the 'trees and fruit' test (the tree is the capital producing the fruit which is income).

The case law is considerable and characterised by subtle distinctions. Many involve compensation receipts where the question is whether the receipt is for the loss of a permanent asset (capital), or is in lieu of trading profits (income) (see also *Tapemaze Ltd v Melluish* (2000)). In *London and Thames Haven Oil Wharves Ltd v Attwooll* (1967), the taxpayer owned jetties used by oil tankers. A tanker crashed into and badly damaged a jetty. The taxpayer received compensation of £100,000, £80,000 to rebuild the jetty (capital) and £20,000 to compensate him for lost tanker fees (income). In *Lang v Rice* (1984) the taxpayer ran two clubs in Belfast until they were destroyed by bombings. He did not resume trading thereafter and received compensation from the Northern Ireland Office for 'consequential loss'. The then Revenue argued that the payment was a once and for all capital payment to compensate the taxpayer for the permanent loss of his business. The Northern Ireland Court of Appeal held that the payment was designed to compensate the taxpayer for loss of profit during the period that would elapse before business could be resumed. Accordingly, the fact that business did not recommence had no effect on the nature of the payment. An air of some unreality pervades this decision since, as the premises had been totally destroyed and the taxpayer held only a short lease, there was never any question of the business being resumed.   **[10.103]**

The decided cases will be considered under six headings:

*Restrictions on activity:* If, as part of his trading arrangements, the taxpayer agrees to restrict his activities in return for payments made to him, the payments are trade receipts. In *Thompson v Magnesium Elektron Ltd* (1944), the taxpayers manufactured magnesium that required chlorine, a by-product of which is caustic soda. ICI agreed to supply the chlorine at below market value and paid the taxpayers a lump sum to prevent them from making their own chlorine and caustic soda, sales of which would compete with those of ICI. The sum was a taxable receipt paid as compensation for profits that the taxpayers would have made on the sale of caustic soda. In *IRC v Biggar* (1982), a payment to a farmer, under EC regulations, to compensate him for changing from milk to meat farming was a trade receipt, being compensation for lost profits.   **[10.104]**

*Sterilisation of an asset:* A payment for the permanent restriction on the use of an asset is capital even though the sum is computed by reference to loss of profits. In *Glenboig Union Fireclay Co Ltd v IRC* (1922), fireclay manufacturers who received compensation for the permanent loss of their right to work fireclay under neighbouring land were held to have received a capital sum. If the compensation is for the temporary loss of an asset, however, it is a trade receipt. Hence, in *Burmah Steamship Co Ltd v IRC* (1931), repairers of a vessel over-ran the contractual date for completion of the work and paid compensation for the lost profits of the owners. The payments were trade receipts.

[10.105]

*Cancellation of a business contract or connection:* When a taxpayer receives compensation for the cancellation of a contract, the nature of the receipt depends upon the significance of the cancelled contract to the business. If it relates to the whole structure of the profit making apparatus, the compensation is capital. Thus in *Van den Berghs Ltd v Clark* (1935) a Dutch and an English company (both manufacturing margarine) had contracted to trade in different areas so as to avoid competition. The Dutch company cancelled the contract, which had 13 years to run, and paid £450,000 in compensation. It was held to be a capital receipt because the contract had provided the means whereby profits were produced; the English company had lost the equivalent of a fixed asset of the business (see also *Whitehead v Tubbs Elastics Ltd* (1984)).

However, if the contract is merely one of many and of short duration, the compensation received is income. In *Kelsall Parsons & Co v IRC* (1938) the taxpayer was a manufacturers' agent who had contracts with different manufacturers and received commission on a sale of their products. One such contract was terminated a year early and the manufacturer paid £15,000 compensation. It was held to be a trade receipt. The contract was the source of profits and the compensation equalled the estimated profit that the taxpayer would have made. Likewise in *Rolfe v Nagel* (1982) a payment to compensate a diamond broker for a client transferring his business elsewhere was taxable as a payment in lieu of profits.

[10.106]

*Appropriation of unclaimed deposits and advances:* Sums are often received from customers as deposits to be used later in part payment towards the price of goods supplied. If they can be forfeited, because of the customer's failure to take delivery of the goods, they are trade receipts in the year of payment (*Elson v Price's Tailors Ltd* (1962)). If at the time of receipt, a deposit is not a trade receipt, it does not later become one by appropriation, unless its nature has been changed by statute. Thus in *Morley v Tattersall* (1938), deposits taken by auctioneers remained clients' money and were not trading receipts even though unclaimed and appropriated by the auctioneers. Contrast *Jays the Jewellers Ltd v IRC* (1947) where pawnbrokers' pledges, although originally customers' money, became trading receipts when rendered irrecoverable by statute. See also *Anise Ltd v Hammond* (2003) where unclaimed overpayments written off to the profit and loss account were not taxable receipts; they were not received as part of the trading activities before they were written off and writing them off did not make them taxable.

[10.107]

*Sale of information ('know-how'):* Where a trader disposes of know-how but continues to trade, any receipt is a trading receipt (ITTOIA 2005 ss 193–194; TA 1988 s 531), but where he disposes of know-how as one of the assets of his business which he is selling as an entity, it is treated as a sale of goodwill. In the latter case liability will be to CGT, unless the trader elects to treat the sum as a trading receipt. Any sum received as consideration for a restriction on the vendor's freedom of activity (following a sale of know-how) is treated as a payment for know-how (ITTOIA 2005 s 192; TA 1988 s 531(8)). **[10.108]**

*Release of debts:* A debt owed by the trader which has been deducted as a trade expense and later released, becomes a trade receipt in the year of its release (ITTOIA 2005 s 97; TA 1988 s 94). HMRC's view is that the writing back of a trade debt in the accounts will be treated as a trading receipt whether it is formally released or not (*Tax Bulletin*, 56, December 2001).TA 1988 s 94 does not apply to debts released as part of a voluntary arrangement under the Insolvency Act 1986 Part I (ie such debts are *not* treated as receipts of the debtor's trade).

**EXAMPLE 10.3**

Bill, a greengrocer, obtains lettuces from his brother Ben who runs a market garden. In 2003–2004 he incurs debts of £10,000 to Ben which is a trading expense. In 2005–06 Ben agrees to forgo the debt because of the critical state of Bill's business; £10,000 will be a trading receipt in Bill's 2005–06 accounts.
**[10.109]**

## 3 Valuation of trading stock

### a) *Why value stock?*

Taxpayers must value their unsold stock at the end of the accounting period, otherwise the business could spend all its receipts on the purchase of new stock, thereby increasing its deductible expenses and reducing the taxable profits to nil. The same principle applies to work-in-progress.

**EXAMPLE 10.4**

In year 1 Zac, a trader, buys 10,000 units of stock at £1 each. During the year he sells 5,000 units at £2 each.

| **Stock not valued** | £ |
|---|---|
| Receipts (sales) | 10,000 |
| *Less:* Expenses (purchases) | 10,000 |
| Result | £Nil |

The trader appears to have made no profit whereas, in fact, his profit is £5,000. At the end of the accounting year, the cost of his unsold (closing) stock must be deducted from the cost of his total purchases. Hence, the profit becomes:

| **Stock valued** | £ | £ |
|---|---|---|
| Sales | | 10,000 |
| Purchases | 10,000 | |
| *Less:* closing stock | 5,000 | |
| Cost of sales | | 5,000 |
| Profit | | £5,000 |

At the start of the next accounting period the stock-in-hand (opening stock) must be entered into the accounts for that year at the same figure (ie £5,000 from *Example 10.4*). **[10.110]**

**EXAMPLE 10.5**

Continuing *Example 10.4*, in year 2, Zac has opening stock of 5,000 units at a cost of £1 each. His purchases during the year are 15,000 units of stock at £1 each and he sells 10,000 units at £2 each.

|  | £ | £ |
|---|---|---|
| Sales |  | 20,000 |
| Opening stock | 5,000 |  |
| Purchases | 15,000 |  |
| *Less*: closing stock | (10,000) |  |
| Cost of sales |  | 10,000 |
| Profit |  | £10,000 |

b)    *Method of stock valuation*

The method of stock valuation is not provided for in statute except on a discontinuance of the trade (see **[10.113]**). SSAP 9 provides for each item of unsold stock to be valued at the lower of its cost price and market value (see **[10.64]**). This principle was originally established in *IRC v Cock Russell & Co Ltd* (1949) and, in effect, allows losses but not profits to be anticipated, ie the trader can apply 'cost' to items that have increased in value and 'market value' to items that have fallen in value. Cost is the original acquisition price. This should include not only the cost of materials and direct labour but overheads (*Duple Motor Bodies v Ostime* (1961)). Market value means the best price obtainable in the market in which the trader sells—for instance, a retailer in the retail and a wholesaler in the wholesale market (*BSC Footwear v Ridgway* (1972)).

Cost is more difficult to calculate where the price of stock has altered during the accounting period so that it is necessary to identify which stock is left. There are a number of methods of valuing stock including: the trader treats the stock sold as the stock first bought (first in first out, ie FIFO); and the opposite, last in first out (LIFO). HMRC take the view that any stock valuation can be acceptable if the accounts are prepared in accordance with generally accepted accounting practice (see **[10.62]**) and the most suitable accounting policy for valuing the stock of the particular circumstances of the business in question has been used (see **[10.66]**). **[10.111]**

c)    *Method of valuing work-in-progress*

The basis of valuing work-in-progress is not provided for in statute except when a trade is discontinued (see **[10.113]**). This has resulted in different types of work-in-progress being valued in different ways.

Long-term contracts (for example civil engineering contracts) are valued in accordance with SSAP 9. This provides for income to be recorded in the accounts as the contract progresses and means that where the outcome of a contract can be predicted with reasonable certainty, some of the profit on the contract will be included in the accounts before the contract is completed.

Professional work-in-progress (for example a solicitor's unbilled work) on the other hand has historically been valued at cost. As principals' and partners' time is an appropriation of a firm's profits not a cost this means that only employees' salaries, overheads relating to fee-earners and a proportion of general overheads are included in the value of work-in-progress.

For accounting periods ending on or after 22 June 2005 all businesses must include the value of ongoing work in their accounts as income. The valuation must be based on the proportion of the work completed at the accounting date in a similar way to the valuation of work-in-progress for long-term contracts. This means that the profit on the contract will be included as it progresses rather than at the end when the work is billed (Application Note G 'Revenue recognition' to FRS 5 'Reporting the substance of transactions' interpreted by UITF 40 'Revenue recognition and service contracts' issued on 10 March 2005). This change is likely to result in a one-off increase in profits for which spreading relief can be obtained (see [10.72]).      [10.112]

d)   *Valuation on a discontinuance*

On discontinuance of a trade (which includes a deemed discontinuance under TA 1988 s 337) the rule in *IRC v Cock Russell* does not apply and trading stock unsold must be entered into the final accounts at the amount realised on its sale or transfer or at market value (ITTOIA 2005 ss 173–181; TA 1988 s 100) and *Moore v R J Mackenzie & Sons Ltd* (1972)). A similar rule applies to work-in-progress (ITTOIA 2005 ss 182–186; TA 1988 s 101). These provisions are designed to prevent tax avoidance by the taxpayer discontinuing his business, entering his unsold stock or work-in-progress at cost in the final accounts and then selling it privately at a tax-free profit.

Where the stock is sold to another UK trader for valuable consideration so that it will appear in his accounts for tax purposes anyway, tax could be avoided by a manipulation of the price. Typically where the parties are connected an undervalue might be agreed in order to ensure a loss for the vendor which could be relieved against past profits of his business. Alternatively the sale could be at overvalue in order to absorb losses of the vendor and, in effect, to pass losses to the purchaser. At the very least, it could be used as a way of deferring the tax liability into the next accounting period. ITTOIA 2005 s 177 and s 184; TA 1988 s 100 and s 101 provide that disposals between connected persons (the basic definition in TA 1988 s 839 being widened for these purposes) will be taken to be for the amount which would have been realised if the sale had been at arm's length. This 'arm's length rule' can be excluded by joint election of the parties if the arm's length value exceeds both (a) the actual price paid, and (b) the acquisition value of the stock. If an election is made arm's length value will be replaced by the greater of (a) and (b).      [10.113]

**EXAMPLE 10.6**

Aldo ceases trading and sells his stock of CDs to his great rival Baldo and his stock of 'vinyls' to his son Caldo. Both Baldo and Caldo carry on business in the UK and so far as the sale to Baldo (an unconnected person) is concerned, the actual sale price will be taken. The arm's length rule will apply to the Caldo sale unless that produces a figure that is higher than both the actual sale price and Aldo's acquisition costs in which case the joint election referred to above may be made.

## 4    Gifts and dispositions for less than market value

A trader has no duty to make the maximum profit and normally tax is assessed according to the actual sum received on a disposal of his stock. There are, however, certain exceptions to this rule.                          **[10.114]**

### a)    *Transfer pricing*

TA 1988 s 770A and Sch 28AA apply to prevent certain companies including multi-nationals, and partnerships from obtaining a tax advantage. Prior to 1 April 2004, it was restricted to cross-border transactions that are not undertaken at arm's length prices. From 1 April 2004, the rules apply to all transactions—cross-border or domestic. There is, however, a let-out for many small and medium-sized enterprises and some dormant companies (based on the EU definition).                          **[10.115]**

### b)    *Rule in Sharkey v Wernher (1956)*

If an item of trading stock is disposed of otherwise than in the ordinary course of the taxpayer's trade, it must be brought into account as a trading receipt at its market value at the date of the disposal. In *Sharkey v Wernher* (1956) the taxpayer carried on the trade of a stud farm. She also raced horses for pleasure and she transferred five horses from the stud farm to the racing stable. The House of Lords held that the market value as opposed to the cost price of the horses at the date when they left the stud farm must be entered in the accounts of the trade as a receipt. Interestingly, the rule in *Sharkey v Wernher*, was not incorporated into the ITTOIA 2005 as there was no consensus that it was accepted as a rule of law. It had been decided when generally accepted accounting practice was in its infancy and accounting expert evidence had not been taken.

In many cases *Sharkey v Wernher* will not apply and instead of the accounts including a trading receipt at market value, the expenditure concerned will be disallowed under the 'wholly and exclusively' rule (ITTOIA 2005 s 34; TA 1988 s 74(1)(b)). This particularly applies to services rendered to the trader personally or to his household, the value of meals provided for proprietors of hotels, pubs, restaurants and members of their families, and expenditure incurred by a trader on the construction of an asset which is to be used as a fixed asset in the trade (Statement of Practice A32).                          **[10.116]**

**EXAMPLE 10.7**

(1)    Rex is a diamond merchant and on the occasion of his daughter's wedding he gives her a diamond which cost him £80,000 and has a market value of

£110,000. As the disposal is not a trading transaction, the market value (£110,000) is a trading receipt. The result is that Rex is treated as making a taxable profit of £30,000 on the stone. There is no distinction between the trader using the goods himself and giving them away to a friend or relative: see *Petrotim Securities Ltd v Ayres* (1964).

(2) Company A sells an asset forming part of its trading stock for which it had paid £400,000 to an associated UK trading company (company B) for £200,000. The asset then had a market value of £800,000. The following points should be noted:

   (i) TA 1988 s 770A is inapplicable since the purchaser company is a UK-resident trading company and there is no tax advantage (TA 1988 Sch 28AA para 5).

   (ii) The sale will be caught by the rule in *Sharkey v Wernher* (see comments above) which applies to both gifts of trading stock and to sales at undervalue (see *Petrotim v Ayres* (1964) and also TCGA 1992 s 161).

   (iii) The recipient of trading stock caught by the rule in *Sharkey v Wernher* is treated as receiving the goods for their market value. Hence, company B is treated as having paid £800,000 for the securities (see *Ridge Securities Ltd v IRC* (1964)).

   (iv) In extreme cases both the purchase and the resale may be expunged from the accounts of the trader if neither constitutes a genuine trading transaction (see the Y transaction in *Petrotim v Ayres* (1964)).

The market value rule is subject to two major qualifications. *First*, it is only appropriate when the disposal of stock is not a genuine trading transaction. So long as the disposal can be justified on commercial grounds the general principle remains that a trader is free to charge what he likes for his goods.

**[10.117]**

#### EXAMPLE 10.8

Cutthroat runs a business selling sound systems. In an attempt to encourage custom he gives away an i-pod (market value £100) to any customer who purchases goods costing more than £2,000. The gift is a commercial disposition and outside the scope of *Sharkey v Wernher*. Accordingly, Cutthroat is not required to enter the market value of the player as a trading receipt. There may, however, be a VAT liability on the 'gift' (see **[38.23]**).

*Secondly*, the rule does not apply to professional persons. In *Mason v Innes* (1967), Hammond Innes, the novelist, began writing *The Doomed Oasis* in 1958 and incurred deductible travelling expenses in obtaining background material. When the manuscript was completed in 1960 he assigned it to his father in consideration of natural love and affection when it had a market value of about £15,000. Innes was taxed under Case II and rendered accounts on the cash basis. When the then Revenue sought to tax the market value of the copyright as a receipt of his profession the Court of Appeal held that the market value rule was limited to traders and to dispositions of trading stock. In rejecting the Revenue's argument, Lord Denning MR said:

'Suppose an artist paints a picture of his mother and gives it to her. He does not receive a penny for it. Is he to pay tax on the value of it? It is unthinkable. Suppose he paints a picture which he does not like when he has finished it and destroys it. Is he liable to pay tax on the value of it? Clearly not. These instances … show that … *Sharkey v Wernher* does not apply to professional men.' **[10.118]–[10.129]**

**EXAMPLE 10.9**

Lex is a partner in the solicitors' firm of Lex, Lax & Lazy and he purchases a house in Chelsea. All the conveyancing work is done by his firm free of charge. The rule in *Sharkey v Wernher* does not apply but the costs of undertaking the work may, however, not be deductible as a business expense (ITTOIA 2005 s 34; TA 1988 s 74(1)(b)).

## V   DEDUCTIBLE EXPENSES

### 1   Basic principles

An expense will be deductible in arriving at the taxpayer's trading profits only if:
(1)   It is an income and not a capital expense (see **[10.75]**).
(2)   It is incurred wholly and exclusively for the purpose of the trade (ITTOIA 2005 s 34; TA 1988 s 74).
(3)   Its deduction is not prohibited by statute (see generally ITTOIA 2005 s 34; TA 1988 s 74).

Expenses are only deductible from trading income by implication from the charging sections which impose tax on 'profits' (see **[10.61]**) and from ITTOIA 2005 Part 2 and TA 1988 s 74 which contains a list of prohibited deductions. These rules are more generous than under the employment income provisions in ITEPA 2003 (see **[8.171]**).

A distinction is drawn between expenses incurred in earning the profits (which may be deductible) and expenses incurred after the profits have been earned, which are not deductible. For example, the payment of income tax is an application of profit which has been earned and is, therefore, not deductible (*Ashton Gas Co v A-G* (1906)). Other taxes, such as rates and stamp duty, may be paid in the course of earning the profits and so may be deductible.

The professional costs involved in drawing up the trader's accounts and fees paid for tax advice are, in practice, deductible, but expenses involved in contesting a tax assessment are not. In *Smith's Potato Estates Ltd v Bolland* (1948), Viscount Simonds stated that:

> 'His [the trader's] profit is no more affected by the eligibility to tax than a man's temperature altered by the purchase of a thermometer, even though he starts by haggling about the price of it.'    **[10.130]**

### 2   The expense must be income not capital

#### a)   *General*

Similar tests are applied for classifying expenditure as income or capital as those for deciding whether a receipt is income or capital (see **[10.103]**). Hence, a distinction is drawn between the fixed and the circulating capital of the business. A payment is capital if it is made to bring into existence an asset for the enduring advantage of the trade (see *British Insulated and Helsby Cables v Atherton* (1926)). The asset may be intangible as in *Walker v Joint Credit*

*Card Co Ltd* (1982) where a payment by a credit card company to preserve its goodwill was held to be a capital payment.

A once and for all payment, even though it brings no enduring asset into existence, is more likely to be of a capital nature than a recurring expense. In *Watney Combe Reid & Co Ltd v Pike* (1982), *ex gratia* payments made by Watneys (the brewers) to tenants of tied houses to compensate them for the termination of their tenancies were held to be capital, because their purpose was to render capital assets (the premises) more valuable (and see the Special Commissioners' decision in *Dhendsa v Richardson* (1997) where an introductory payment paid to Post Office Counters Ltd by a new sub-postmaster was considered capital).                                                    **[10.131]**

b)  *Employee payments*

These are generally deductible in computing the profits of the employer, so long as they are paid for the purposes of the business. In *Mitchell v B W Noble Ltd* (1927), a company deducted the sum of £19,500 paid to a director to induce him to resign. It was held to be in the interests of the company to get rid of him and to avoid undesirable publicity by encouraging him to 'go quietly'. For similar reasons, the House of Lords in *Lawson v Johnson Matthey plc* (1992) decided that the sum of £50m was a deductible revenue expense being paid to save its business (by removing an obstacle to successful trading). It was not, as the lower courts had concluded, a sum paid to get rid of a burdensome capital asset (which would itself have been capital).

Problems may arise when the payments in question are linked to the cessation of the business; in particular, such payments may not satisfy the 'wholly and exclusively' test (discussed below at **[10.137]**). In *O'Keeffe v Southport Printers Ltd* (1984) payments made to employees in lieu of notice were deductible by the employer since they were incurred as part of the orderly conduct of the business prior to its termination (see also on severance payments, *IRC v Cosmotron Manufacturing Co Ltd* (1997)).

No deduction is allowed for an amount charged in the accounts in respect of employees' remuneration unless it is paid no later than nine months after the end of the period of account. Remuneration paid at a later time is deductible when it is paid (FA 1989 s 43).                                     **[10.132]**

c)  *Employee trusts*

In *Heather v PE Consulting Group* (1978) payments made by a company to a trust created in order to acquire shares in that company for the benefit of employees and to prevent outside interference in the affairs of the company were deductible expenses because, *inter alia*, they encouraged the recruitment of well-qualified staff (see also *Jeffs v Ringtons Ltd* (1985)). However, in *Mawsley Machinery Ltd v Robinson* (1998) it was held that the objective of the payment to the trust was to provide the shareholder/vendor with a means to dispose of his shareholding. It was thus a capital payment. In *MacDonald v Dextra Accessories Ltd* (2005), at the High Court, contributions made to an employee benefit trust were allowed on the grounds that they were made to motivate the company's employees. Various awards were made out of the trust to employees, some of which gave rise to tax, but others (such as loans) did not. The then Inland Revenue argued that FA 1989 s 43 prevented the deduction of the payments until such time as the employees were taxed on the amounts as emoluments. Their view was upheld in the Court of Appeal and House of Lords.

ITTOIA 2005 ss 38–44; Finance Act 2003 Sch 24 now denies relief for payments to an employee benefit trust unless the employee is taxed on 'qualifying benefits' received within nine months of the accounting period: see generally **[9.124]**.                                          **[10.133]**

d)    *Restrictive covenants*

*Associated Portland Cement Manufacturers Ltd v Kerr* (1946) involved payments to two retiring directors in return for covenants that they would not compete with the company for the rest of their lives. The payments were held not to be deductible as they were a capital expenditure being payments to enhance the company's goodwill. Had the covenant been for a shorter period the expenditure might have been of an income nature and therefore deductible. To prevent the making of restrictive covenant payments instead of salary increases (which could result in the deduction of the payment by the employer even though it was not fully taxed in the hands of the employee), ITTOIA 2005 s 69; FA 1988 s 73(2) now provide that such payments are tax deductible by the employer and taxed in the hands of the employee where the payments are within ITEPA 2003 ss 225–226 (see **[8.133]**).        **[10.134]**

e)    *Capital allowances*

Capital expenditure is not generally deductible and provisions for depreciation are not allowable (ITTOIA 2005 s 33). Tax relief may, however, be given in accordance with the rules governing capital allowances (see **Chapter 48**). If 100% first year allowances can be claimed it does not matter whether a particular item of expenditure is of an income or of a capital nature. Where allowances on plant and machinery can only be claimed at a lower rate, the taxpayer will prefer to claim that the expense is of an income nature so that it can immediately be deducted in full.                         **[10.135]**

f)    *Depreciation in stock and work in progress*

Sometimes the depreciation charge in the trading and profit and loss account is reduced by capitalising part of it and including it in the balance sheet in the stock valuation. Where this occurs, it has been held that the depreciation to be added back in the tax computation as a disallowable expense must be the gross depreciation ie the depreciation before it is reduced by the sum capitalised in stock (*Small v Mars UK Ltd* (2005) and *William Grant & Sons Distillers Ltd v CIR* (2005)).        **[10.136]**

3    **Expense must have been incurred 'wholly and exclusively' for business purposes**

The courts have generally interpreted the requirement strictly, so that the *sole* reason for the expenditure must be a business purpose. In *Bentleys, Stokes & Lowless v Beeson* (1952), Romer LJ explained the requirements that have to be satisfied for an expense to be deductible as follows:

'it is quite clear that the purpose must be the sole purpose. The paragraph says so in clear terms. If the activity be undertaken with the object both of promoting business and also with some other purpose, for example, with the object of indulging an independent wish of entertaining a friend or stranger or of supporting a charitable or benevolent object, then the paragraph is not satisfied though in the mind of the actor the business motive may predominate. For the statute so prescribes. Per contra, if, in truth, the sole object is business promotion, the expenditure is not disqualified because the nature of the activity necessarily involves some other result, or the attainment or furtherance of some other objective, since the latter result or objective is necessarily inherent in the act.'

Dual purpose expenditure is not deductible and there are numerous cases where this rule has been strictly applied. In *Caillebotte v Quinn* (1975) a self-employed carpenter worked on sites 40 miles from home. He ate lunch at a nearby café which cost him 40p per day instead of the usual 10p which it cost him at home. His claim to deduct the extra 30p per day as an expense was disallowed on the grounds that he ate to live as well as to work so that the expenditure was incurred for dual purposes. Similarly, in *Prince v Mapp* (1970) a guitarist in a pop group could not deduct the cost of an operation on his little finger because he played the guitar partly for business, but partly for pleasure (but contrast *McKnight v Sheppard* (1997) in which legal expenses incurred at disciplinary hearings of the taxpayer—a stockbroker—were held deductible). In *Mallalieu v Drummond* (1983) the House of Lords held that expenditure on clothing to be worn in court by a female barrister was not deductible. Although she only wore the clothes for business purposes and that was her sole conscious purpose when she purchased the garments, Lord Brightman concluded that 'she needed the clothes to travel to work and clothes to wear at work ... it is inescapable that one object though not a conscious motive, was the provision of the clothing that she needed as a human being'. In practice, the cost of protective clothing is deductible where the 'wholly and exclusively' test is met.

The same test for deductible expenditure is applied whether the business is run as a sole trade or partnership. In *MacKinlay v Arthur Young McClelland Moores & Co* (1990) the Court of Appeal had allowed a partnership to deduct removal costs paid to encourage two partners to move house: in one case from London to Southampton, in the other from Newcastle to Bristol. In both cases the move was desirable from the point of view of the firm's business and neither partner would have agreed to move had his relocation expenses not been borne by the firm. This decision was not easy to reconcile with earlier authorities and its reversal by the House of Lords was scarcely surprising. Their Lordships restated the principles underlying the rules governing deductible expenditure and stressed that the same rules applied to individuals and to unincorporated partnerships.

The 'dual purpose' cases show that it is not possible to split a purpose: ie if the taxpayer incurs the expenditure for two purposes, one business and the other personal, none of the expenditure is deductible. It may, however, be possible to split a payment into a portion which is incurred for business purposes and a portion which is not. This approach was apparent in *Copeman v Flood* (1941) where the son and daughter of the managing director of a small private company were employed as directors at salaries of £2,600 each pa. The son was aged 24 and had some business experience; the daughter was only 17. Although both performed duties for the company, the then Revenue claimed that the entire salary was not an expense incurred by the company 'wholly and exclusively' for business purposes. Lawrence J remitted the case to the commissioners for them to decide, as a question of fact, to what extent the payments were deductible expenses of the trade. He accepted that the expenditure could be apportioned into allowable and non-allowable parts (see also *Earlspring Properties Ltd v Guest* (1994) and contrast *Abbott v IRC* (1996)). This approach is now enshrined in ITTOIA 2005 s 34(2) which provides that if an expense is incurred for more than one purpose a deduction can be made for any identifiable part or identifiable proportion of the expense which is incurred wholly and exclusively for the purposes of the trade. In practice, payments are regularly split in this fashion when a car is used both for business and private use and when a business is run from the taxpayer's home and he claims to deduct a proportion of the overheads of the house. If the 'wholly and exclusively' test is satisfied there is no further test—based on the expenditure being 'sufficiently connected' with the business—to be satisfied (*McKnight v Sheppard* (1997)).    **[10.137]**

### 4   Deduction of the expense must not be prohibited by statute

The deduction of expenses against trading income is permitted by implication. ITTOIA 2005 Part 2 includes details of non-deductible expenses and expenditure where a limitation deduction is permitted and TA 1988 s 74 contains a list of expenses which are stated not to be deductible. For instance, under s 74(1) no deduction is allowed for any sum 'recoverable under an insurance or contract of indemnity' whilst expenditure incurred for private as opposed to business purposes is made non-deductible by ITTOIA 2005 s 34.

The deduction of business gifts and entertainment expenses is severely curtailed by ITTOIA 2005 s 45; TA 1988 s 577. The legislation is widely drafted although a number of exceptions are permitted (ITTOIA 2005 ss 46–47; TA 1988 s 577) and see *Fleming v Associated Newspapers Ltd* (1972).
**[10.138]**

### 5   Illustrations of deductible expenditure

Expenditure on heating and lighting business premises, rates on those premises and the wages paid to employees are obvious examples of allowable expenditure. Other expenditure may be more problematic, as the examples considered below show.    **[10.139]**

### a)   *Rent paid for business premises*

TA 1988 s 74(c) accepts that rent is deductible and it may be apportioned if part of the premises is used for non-business activities. An individual's private house may, of course, be used in part for business purposes and a portion of the overheads may be claimed as allowable expenditure. So long as no part of the house is used exclusively for business purposes the full CGT main residence exemption will still be available.

When the taxpayer pays a premium in return for the grant of a lease, a portion of the premium (corresponding to the portion that is taxed under the property income provisions of ITTOIA 2005 Part 3 or Schedule A in the case of companies; see **[12.85]**) may be deducted as an expense (ITTOIA 2005 ss 60–67; TA 1988 s 87). **[10.140]**

### b) *Sale and leaseback arrangements*

Specific provisions were enacted to deal with the problems caused by sale and leaseback, and surrender and leaseback arrangements. The attraction of such schemes stemmed from booming land values which encouraged the owner of the land (or of an interest therein) to sell (or surrender) it, thereby realising a capital sum, and immediately to take a leaseback of the same property. TA 1988 s 779 prohibits the deduction of rent in excess of a commercial level and in certain circumstances TA 1988 s 780 imposes a tax charge on a capital sum received in return for surrendering a lease which has less than 50 years to run, when a leaseback for a term not exceeding 15 years is taken. **[10.141]**

### c) *Repairs and improvements*

Sums expended on the repair of business assets are deductible (TA 1988 s 74(d)). The Special Commissioners held that the wording in s 74(d) did not restrict the deductions to the cash expended—a provision accurately made was sufficient (*Jenners Princes Street (Edinburgh) v IRC* (1998)). Provisions must now comply with FRS 12 (see **[10.68]**) in order to be deductible.

The cost of improvement or reconstruction is not, however, allowable being capital expenditure (ITTOIA 2005 s 33; TA 1988 s 74(g)). The borderline between the two is a difficult factual question which depends upon the nature of the asset and the importance of the work in relation to it (see *Lurcott v Wakely and Wheeler* (1911) on the duty to repair and *O'Grady v Markham Main Colliery Ltd* (1932)).

The cost incurred on initial repairs carried out to a business asset may cause difficulties. In *Law Shipping Co Ltd v IRC* (1924), a vessel purchased for £97,000 was in such a state of disrepair that a further £51,000 had to be spent before it could obtain its Lloyd's Certificate. The Court of Session disallowed most of the subsequent expenditure; as Lord Cullen stated:

'It is in substance the equivalent of an addition to the price. If the ship had not been in need of the repairs in question when bought, the appellants would have had to pay a correspondingly larger price.'

By way of contrast, in *Odeon Associated Theatres Ltd v Jones* (1972) subsequent repair work on a cinema, which had been purchased in a run-down condition after the war, was allowed. There are three points of distinction from the *Law Shipping* case: *first*, the cinema was a profit-earning asset when purchased despite its disrepair; *secondly*, the purchase price was not reduced because of that disrepair; and *thirdly*, the Court of Appeal accepted that the expenses were deductible in accordance with the principles of proper commercial accounting. **[10.142]**

d)    *Pre-trading expenditure*

Under ITTOIA 2005 s 57; TA 1988 s 401 income expenditure incurred in the seven years before a trade, profession or vocation commences is treated as incurred on the day on which the business commences.    **[10.143]**

e)    *Bad debts*

Bad debts are deducted when shown to be bad (ITTOIA 2005 s 35; TA 1988 s 74(j)); if later paid they are treated as a trading receipt for that later year. These rules have been amended in the case of voluntary arrangements under the Insolvency Act 1986 Part I. The release of a trade debt in such circumstances is fully deductible by the creditor (even if the debt could not be shown to be 'bad') and does not give rise to a taxable receipt in the hands of the debtor.    **[10.144]**

f)    *Damages and losses*

In *Strong & Co of Romsey Ltd v Woodifield* (1906) damages paid to an hotel guest injured by the fall of a chimney from the building were not deductible. Lord Loreburn, somewhat unsympathetically, observed that 'the loss sustained by the appellants ... fell upon them in their character not of traders but of householders' whilst Lord Davey rejected the claim because 'the expense must be incurred for the purpose of earning the profits'. Had the guest suffered food poisoning from the hotel restaurant any compensation would have been deductible! In practice, the *Strong v Woodifield* case will be avoided by the trader carrying insurance to cover compensation claims; further, the premiums that he pays for such insurance will be deductible.

Theft by employees causes particular difficulties. Petty theft by subordinates, so that money never finds its way into the till, will result in reduced profits for tax purposes, but defalcations by directors will not be similarly allowable (*Curtis v Oldfield* (1933); *Bamford v ATA Advertising* (1972)).    **[10.145]**

g)    *Work training and outplacement counselling*

The costs of training an employee in skills relating to present or future duties of his job are deductible. In addition, the costs of retraining an employee or former employee for a new job with another employer (or for self-employment) are in certain circumstances deductible (see further **[8.173]**: ITTOIA 2005 s 74; TA 1988 s 588). Training costs incurred by a self-employed person are deductible in computing his profits, provided the costs are incurred wholly and exclusively for the purposes of his trade or profession (ITTOIA 2005 s 34; TA 1988 s 74). The provision of outplacement counselling services to employees who are made redundant is not a taxable benefit for that employee and the costs are deductible by the employer (ITTOIA 2005 s 73; TA 1988 ss 589A and B).    **[10.146]**

h)    *Expenditure involving crime*

A payment (such as a bribe) which involves the commission of a crime in the UK (or if paid overseas would amount to a crime if it were paid in the UK) is not deductible and nor is a payment made as a result of blackmail (such as a payment made under duress to terrorist groups): ITTOIA 2005 s 55; TA 1988 s 577A.                                                                            **[10.147]**

i)   *Travelling expenses*

The cases establish two general propositions. *First*, that the cost of travelling to the place of business is not deductible; and, *secondly*, that the cost of travelling in the course of the business is deductible. In *Horton v Young* (1971), for instance, a labour-only sub-contractor who operated from his home was entitled to deduct expenses incurred in collecting his team of bricklayers and travelling to the building site. Contrast this with *Jackman v Powell* (2004) in which a milkman was not allowed to deduct the cost of travelling between his home and the depot from which he collected his supplies.                                                                     **[10.148]**

**EXAMPLE 10.10**

Wig is a barrister who travels into chambers each day from his home in Isleworth. He also travels from chambers to courts in the London area.
(1)   The cost of travelling from Isleworth to chambers is not deductible because chambers is his base. It does not matter that he does a substantial amount of work at home and that he claims a deduction for a portion of the expenses of the house (see *Newsom v Robertson* (1953)).
(2)   Expenses in travelling from chambers to court are deductible (contrast *Horton v Young* (1971): travelling between two centres of work).
(3)   If he were regularly to go from Isleworth to a case at Bow Street Magistrates' Court and then on to chambers could he deduct all the travelling expenses? The difficult case of *Sargent v Barnes* (1978) in which a dental surgeon was unable to deduct travelling expenses to collect false teeth from a laboratory on his way to work, suggests that the answer is no, although it should be noted that the laboratory was not a place of work whereas the court is. A claim for travelling from the court to chambers might succeed. (See also HMRC leaflet IR 490 (2005)).

The 'dual purpose' rule (see **[10.137]**) will cause the disallowance of the entire cost of a journey with a material private purpose. A solicitor's expenses incurred in travelling abroad partly for a holiday and partly to attend professional conferences were disallowed: *Bowden v Russell & Russell* (1965). Contrast this with the expenses incurred by an accountant in attending a professional conference abroad which were allowed: *Edwards v Warmsley, Henshall & Co* (1967).                                                       **[10.149]**

j)   *National insurance contributions*

Contributions paid by an employer in respect of his employees are a deductible business expense.                                      **[10.150]–[10.170]**

## VI   RELIEF FOR FLUCTUATING PROFITS

The profits earned from certain businesses are so irregular that it would be unfair to tax them all in the year of receipt. Instead, they are deemed to have been received over a longer period ('averaged').                      **[10.171]**

## 1   Farmers, market gardeners and creative artists

ITTOIA ss 221–225 allows farmers, market gardeners and creative artists etc to compare the profits of two consecutive years of assessment and, if the profits of either year are nil or one is less than 70% of the other, the profits of both years are equalised. ('Profit' means profit before deducting loss relief and capital allowances.) The relief is tapered where the profits in one year are between 70% and 75% of the other. The trader must claim the relief within two years of the end of the second year of assessment and he may not claim it for his opening or closing years.                              **[10.172]**

### EXAMPLE 10.11

A farmer's profits in year 1 are £600 and in year 2 £16,000. £600 is less than 70% of £16,000. Therefore profits are averaged and in years 1 and 2 he is taxed on profits of £8,300 (£16,600 ÷ 2).

## 2   Inventors

Similar provisions apply to lump sums received by inventors for the exploitation of their patents. By ITTOIA 2005 ss 587–592; TA 1988 s 524, a sum received in return for patent rights is spread over the year of receipt and the next five years. By TA 1988 s 527, sums received for the use of a patent for a period of at least six years may be spread back over six years.        **[10.173]–[10.191]**

## VII   BASIS OF ASSESSMENT (SOLE-TRADERS AND PARTNERSHIPS)

## 1   Background

A taxpayer can commence or cease his business at any time and adopt an accounting date of his choosing. It is not necessary that this date coincide with the tax year. In the first and closing years and upon a change of accounting date the accounts may not necessarily be of 12 months duration. This flexibility about accounting gives rise to two difficulties in some cases:

(1)   the actual profits made in a year of assessment may only be arrived at by splitting two accounting years and taking the proportions which fall into the assessment year;

(2)   the calculation of the taxpayer's liability has to await the completion of the accounts. For this reason many traders choose to prepare their accounts to coincide with the tax year (or 31 March) which is treated as if it were the same date as 5 April.

Tax is assessed and calculated on a current year basis under ITTOIA 2005 ss 197–220. There are special rules for the opening and closing years of a business and upon a change of accounting date.                              **[10.192]**

## 2 How the current year basis operates

### a) *The position of a continuing business*

**EXAMPLE 10.12**

Bob makes his accounts up to 30 April each year. For the accounting year ending 30 April 2005 his profits are £50,000. As that accounting period ends in the tax year 2005–06, those profits will be assessed to tax in that year. The tax is payable in three instalments: two being estimated on the basis of the previous year's tax on 31 January 2006 and 31 July 2006 with a balancing payment (or refund) on submission of the tax return on 31 January 2007. **[10.193]**

### b) *Opening years of a new business*

**EXAMPLE 10.13**

Assume that Thelma begins her millinery business on 1 July 2003 making up her accounts to the following 30 June. Her profits are as follows:

|  | £ |
|---|---|
| y/e 30.6.2004 | 6,000 |
| y/e 30.6.2005 | 9,500 |
| y/e 30.6.2006 | 12,650 |

For the *first tax year* of the business (2003–04) Thelma is taxed on her profits from the date of commencement (1 July 2003) to the following 5 April, ie:
    $\frac{9}{12} \times £6,000 = £4,500$

For the *second year* (2004–05) the current year basis applies so that the first year's profit of £6,000 is subject to tax.

When the accounting date chosen is not 5 April (as in *Example 10.13*) the first year's profits are used as the basis for part of the tax charge in both the first and second years (in this case £4,500). This is contrary to the principle that profits taxed must equal profits earned and accordingly a limited relief is available for these doubly taxed profits (*'overlap relief'*: see **[10.201]**), ITTOIA 2005 s 204. If there is an accounting date in the second year which falls less than 12 months after the commencement, the basis period for this year is the profits of the first 12 months of trading. For the third (and subsequent) years of assessment tax is calculated on a current year basis. **[10.194]**

### c) *The closing years of a business*

In the final tax year, profits from the end of the basis period of the preceding year until the date of cessation are taxed.

**EXAMPLE 10.14**

Assume that Louise, who has previously made up her accounts to 30 April, ceases trading on 30 September 2005. Her final accounts are as follows:

|  | £ |
|---|---|
| to 30.4.04 | 10,000 |
| to 30.4.05 | 4,500 |
| to 30.9.05 | 1,500 |

Her tax position is as follows:

| *Tax year* | *Taxed profits* (£) |
|---|---|
| 2004–05 | 10,000 (current year basis) |
| 2005–06 | 6,000 (final period) |

Note that Louise may be entitled to 'overlap relief' (see *Example 10.13* above); this will reduce the taxable profit in her final tax year, ITTOIA 2005 s 205 (see also **[10.201]**).

If the business ceases in its second tax year, the assessment is on profit from the end of the commencement year until cessation. If the business starts and finishes in the same tax year, the basis period is the actual profits earned.

**[10.195]**

## 3   Accounting dates

A taxpayer is free to choose whatever accounting date he wishes. There are, however, statutory provisions concerning changes of accounting date, ITTOIA 2005 s 214–220.

*First,* a change of accounting date in the second or third year of a business is permitted without restriction thereby enabling a business to make suitable adjustments when the original date turns out to be impractical.

*Secondly,* in all other cases a change will only have a fiscal effect if certain prescribed conditions are satisfied. Otherwise the change is disregarded and tax computations continue on the basis of the old date (thereby necessitating apportionments). There are four conditions: both conditions I and II must be satisfied together with either condition III or condition IV.

*Condition I:* The first accounting period ending on the new (changed) date must not exceed 18 months.

*Condition II:* Notice of the change must be given to HMRC by 31 January following the year of change . The 'year of change' is the first year in which accounts are made up to the new date or, if there is a year without an accounting date, it is that year.

*Condition III:* Either no accounting date change occurred in any of the five preceding tax years *or* any such change was fiscally ineffective (ie because these conditions were not met).

*Condition IV:* The notice under condition II must set out the reasons for the change and HMRC then has 60 days to decide whether they are satisfied that the change is for '*bona fide* commercial reasons'. If they are not so satisfied they must give the taxpayer notice of the fact: if he or she does not respond at all within this period the change is effective. The taxpayer can appeal against HMRC's notice of dissatisfaction within 30 days and the commissioners then have to decide if there are *bona fide* commercial reasons for the change. 'Obtaining a tax advantage' is *not* regarded as a *bona fide* commercial reason for a change (ITTOIA 2005 s 218(6)) and HMRC has indicated that this includes the obtaining of a cashflow benefit as well as a reduction in liability. Bearing in mind, however, that condition IV is irrelevant if condition III is satisfied, so it is possible to make one change for purely fiscal *reasons* every five years.

How are effective changes of date treated for income tax purposes? Consider the following situations. **[10.196]**

*Situation 1* If the accounting period of change is under 12 months (or the change occurs in the second year of business) the basis period is 12 months to the new accounting date. **[10.197]**

**EXAMPLE 10.15**

Hank's business, having made up its accounts to 31 October, changes its accounting date to 30 April in 2005. Its profits are as follows:

|  | £ |
|---|---|
| y/e 31.10.04 | 8,500 |
| p/e 30.4.05 | 4,500 |
| y/e 30.4 06 | 10,500 |

The tax assessments are:

| Tax year | Accounting period | £ |
|---|---|---|
| 2004–05 | y/e 31.10.04 | 8,500 |
| 2005–06 | y/e to 30.4.05 | |
| | (ie six months' accounts | 8,750 |
| | to 30.4.05 + $^6/_{12}$ of | |
| | profit to 31.10.04) | |
| 2006–07 | y/e 30.4.06 | 10,500 |

*Situation 2* If, as a result of the change, no account ends in the next financial year, this is the year in which the change is deemed to take effect and the basis period is 12 months to the new accounting date. **[10.198]**

**EXAMPLE 10.16**

If Hank had prepared an 18-month account to 30 April 2006 the position would be:

|  | £ |
|---|---|
| y/e 31.10.04 | 8,500 |
| p/e 30.4.06 | 15,000 |

and the tax assessment would be:

| Tax year | Accounting period | £ |
|---|---|---|
| 2004–05 | y/e 31.10.04 | 8,500 |
| 2005–06 | 12-month period to | |
| | 30.4.05 (ie $^6/_{12}$ of | 9,250 |
| | £8,500 (as before) + | |
| | $^6/_{18}$ of £15,000) | |
| 2006–07 | 12-month period to | 10,000 |
| | 30.4.06 (ie $^{12}/_{18}$ of £15,000) | |

*Situation 3* If the accounting period exceeds 12 months but ends in the next tax year, profits of that accounting period are assessed. If, for instance, Hank had made up accounts to 31 December 2005, profits of the period from 31 October 2004 to that date would be taxed in the tax year 2005–06.
**[10.199]**

*Situation 4* If the new period is a short one so that there are two accounting periods ending in the same tax year, the two are treated as a single period ending on the new date.                                    **[10.200]**

## 4   Overlap relief

This is given where the same profits are used twice as the basis of assessment (as for instance in *Example 10.13*). The relief for the overlap, which is calculated in money terms and is not index-linked, is given on the earlier of:
(1)   a change of accounting date which results in an assessment for a period of *more than* 12 months; or
(2)   a cessation of the trade or business.
    If none or not all the overlap is used in (1) above, then it can be carried forward for use in (2).                                    **[10.201]**

## 5   Taxing partners and the position of partners joining the firm

Taxable profits or losses are allocated amongst partners according to their interest in the partnership during the accounting period not according to the shares in the tax year for which that period is the basis period. Each partner is treated as carrying on a notional sole trade which begins when he becomes a partner and ends when he ceases to be a partner. As a result initial overlap relief can be given on leaving and terminal loss relief is likewise available on leaving the partnership even though the business itself may continue.          **[10.202]**

### EXAMPLE 10.17

Firm ABC makes up accounts to 30 June each year. On 1 January 2006 D joined the firm. Assume profits always split equally.
    (1)   *Tax year 2005–06*
    ABC taxed on profits of the accounts to 30 June 2005: profits divided equally.
    D taxed on his share of the profits when he became a partner (1 January 2006) to following 5 April. Hence profits for the year ended 30 June 2006 must be divided as follows:
(a)   1 July 2005 to 31 December 2005 (6/12) divided equally between ABC and taxed in the year 2006–07.
(b)   1 January 2006 to 5 April 2006 (3/12) divided equally between ABCD and D's share taxed in the year 2005–06.
    (2)   *Tax year 2006–07*
    ABC taxed on their profit share for year to 30 June 2006: being one-third each to 31 December 2005 and thereafter one-quarter each.
    D will be taxed on his share of the profits to 30 June 2006 (being one half of one-quarter) and in addition on his share of the profit for the following six months to 31 December 2006 (this will be one half of one-quarter of the profits to 30 June 2007). These accounts will require speedy completion in order for D to meet the tax return filing date.

(3)   *D's position*
(a)   He will receive credit for profits doubly taxed on commencement, ie on his profit of the year to 30 June 2006 (taxed in 2005–06) plus a six-month share of profits for the year to 30 June 2007 (since those profits will be taxed in full in the year 2007–08).
He will receive overlap relief on the earlier of:
  (i)   when he leaves the firm;
  (ii)  when the firm's business ceases;
  (iii) on a change to a later accounting date (relief may only be partial).
(b)   For D no accounting period fell within the period of 12 months from the date when his notional trade began hence he only reaches the current year basis in the third tax year (being 2007–08).

## 6   Partners leaving the firm

Given that each partner is treated as carrying on a notional sole trade, the usual principles apply.                                                                    **[10.203]**

### EXAMPLE 10.18

XYZ make up their accounts to 30 June each year. Profits are divided equally. On 31 December 2006 Z retires and X and Y continue the business splitting the profits equally.
*Position of Z*
He is taxed on the basis of his share of the profits from the end of the basis period of the preceding year until 31 December 2006, ie profits from 30 June 2005 to 31 December 2006 (18 months).
Overlap relief will be due from when he joined the firm on 1 January 2001. This will amount to approximately nine months. In theory therefore he is taxed on retirement on the nine-month period from 5 April to 31 December 2006 (but note that there is no necessary link between profits at the start and at the end and there is no index-linking of overlap relief).

## 7   Partnership changes

When there is a change in the persons carrying on a trade and at least one person was a member of the firm before and after the change, there is a continuing partnership, ie there is no deemed discontinuance and recommencement. Accordingly, it is only *actual* discontinuances which have tax consequences. These occur when:
(1)   all the partners sell out;
(2)   on the death of a sole trader;
(3)   on an actual discontinuance: for instance on a merger (or demerger) when there results a change in the nature of the business carried on by the two firms engaged in the merger (or demerger): see for instance *George Humphries Ltd v Cook* (1934); Statement of Practice SP 9/86.
                                                                    **[10.204]–[10.250]**

# 11   Losses

*Updated by Sarah Laing, CTA, Chartered Tax Advisor, CPE Consulting Ltd*

## I   INTRODUCTORY

### 1   General

Whenever an individual or partnership makes a loss (ie where allowable expenses in an accounting period exceed taxable receipts) there are two repercussions.

*First*, any year of assessment using that accounting period as its basis period will have a nil tax assessment.

*Secondly*, the loss may be used to reduce tax assessments of that or other years of assessment so that the taxpayer will either pay less tax or be able to reclaim tax that he has previously paid. Losses are, however, personal to the taxpayer. They are not in any sense an asset that can be bought and sold.

A draft of the fourth Bill (the Income Tax Bill) produced by the Tax Law Rewrite project was published in March 2006. The new Bill includes provisions dealing with relief for losses. The text of the draft Bill (with and without origins), draft explanatory notes and a separate table of origins and destinations are all available on the HMRC website at www.hmrc.gov.uk/rewrite.

[**11.1**]

### 2   Companies

Companies are subject to a separate regime governing the use of losses—see [**41.60**].

As a matter of planning, it should be noted that when the loss is made by a trading company it is not available for use by individual shareholders (even in a 'one man' company). Hence, when it is proposed to start a business and early losses are anticipated the advantages of income tax relief for the losses must be weighed against the protection of limited liability. This is particularly the case now that it is possible to use a limited liability partnership in order to obtain the benefits of limited liability whilst retaining the transparency of a partnership (see **[45.11]**). To prevent companies with accumulated losses being sold to a purchaser who wishes to use the losses to shelter his own profits (by injecting income or profits into the company) TA 1988 s 768 imposes a series of conditions for the utilisation of the losses. In broad terms, where during a period of three years there is a change in the ownership of the company and a major change in the nature or conduct of the company's trade, the brought-forward losses will not be available for relief (see **[41.63]**).

**[11.2]**

### 3  Loss relief on income from property

The loss reliefs available for the landlord are discussed at **[12.44]**. It should be noted, however, that losses under the income from property provisions of ITTOIA 2005 (formerly Schedule A) are 'ring fenced', ie they can only be set against profits from the property business (unless attributable to certain capital allowances or in relation to an agricultural estate as defined in TA 1988 s 379A).                                                           **[11.3]**

### 4  Losses in a trade profession and vocation

This chapter concentrates on the loss reliefs available against profits from trades, professions or vocations. When seeking to apply relief under these provisions it is important to realise that the loss may be eligible for relief under more than one provision and that the choice will usually rest with the taxpayer. The reliefs apply, with some modification, to members of a partnership in respect of their share of any business losses.      **[11.4]–[11.20]**

### II  RELIEF UNDER TA 1988 s 385: CARRY-FORWARD

A loss that is sustained in carrying on a trade, profession or vocation can be carried forward under s 385 and set off against the first available profits of the same trade, profession or vocation without time limit. The loss must be deducted as far as possible from the earliest subsequent profits with the result that the taxpayer may not be able to make use of his personal allowance.

**EXAMPLE 11.1**

Scrooge's accounts are as follows:

| *Accounting period* | £ |
|---|---|
| Year to 31 December 2002 | 2,000 profit |
| Year to 31 December 2003 | (6,000) loss |
| Year to 31 December 2004 | 1,600 profit |
| Year to 31 December 2005 | 3,600 profit |
| Year to 31 December 2006 | 4,000 profit |

The income tax assessments are:

| Tax year | Taxable profit (loss) |
|---|---|
| | £ |
| 2002–03 | 2,000 |
| 2003–04 | (6,000) |
| 2004–05 | nil (1,600–6,000 loss) |
| 2005–06 | nil (3,600–4,400 loss) |
| 2006–07 | 3,200 (4,000–800 loss) |

Scrooge would lose the benefit of his personal allowance in 2003–04, 2004–05 and 2005–06 if he had no other income against which to set it.

In calculating the loss to be carried forward under s 385, certain items may be treated as losses. For instance, by s 387 an annual payment which is made wholly and exclusively for the purpose of the business and assessed under TA 1988 s 349 (because the taxpayer has no income) and which cannot be relieved because there are no profits against which to set it, may be treated as a loss for s 385. The same principle applies to unrelieved interest payments (TA 1988 s 390).

**EXAMPLE 11.2**

Oliver makes a loss of £10,000 in his accounting year ended 31 July 2005 and is expected to make a loss in the year to 31 July 2006. He makes an annual payment each year on 1 June of £1,000. In 2005–06 there will be a nil assessment on his business profits, but under TA 1988 s 349 HMRC requires Oliver to pay basic rate income tax on £1,000 at 22% (£220). As he made a loss of £10,000 and has paid out £1,000 in total, Oliver's loss to be carried forward under s 385 is £11,000.

Losses can only be carried forward under s 385 against future profits from the *same* business. Thus, if the nature of the business changes in a future year, there can be no carry-forward of losses. In *Gordon and Blair Ltd v IRC* (1962) brewing losses could not be carried forward against bottling profits. Similarly, if the business ceases, there can be no carry-forward.

There are two major drawbacks to loss relief under s 385. *First*, it is only available against profits from the same business and not against any other income of the taxpayer. *Secondly*, the relief is not immediate. Even assuming that the business makes profits in the future, full loss relief may not be obtained for some years (see *Example 11.1*). In inflationary times, this delay renders the loss relief less valuable in real terms (cp TA 1988 s 380).

The time limit for making a claim under s 385 is laid down in TMA 1970 s 43 (ie five years and ten months from the end of the year in which the loss arose): once an effective claim has been made the loss will then be carried forward and utilised each year until extinguished without the need for any further claim. **[11.21]–[11.40]**

## III RELIEF UNDER TA 1988 s 380: CARRY-ACROSS

Under s 380(1)(a) trading losses may be set against the taxpayer's total income of the year in which the loss arises and (see s 380(1)(b)) of the *preceding year.* It is possible to choose the year in which the loss is to be set off—for instance, the claim may indicate that the loss is to be allowed in the preceding year. If the claim is for relief in both years, the claim for relief in the current year takes precedence over that for the preceding year (s 380(2)); claims for relief must generally be made within 12 months from 31 January following the end of the tax year in which the loss arose.

### EXAMPLE 11.3

Confused makes his account up to 5 October each year. For the year to 5 October 2006 a loss of £24,000 is suffered; for the previous year a loss of £18,000.
   (i)   *The loss of £18,000*
   Given that these accounts are the basis period for tax year 2005–06, loss relief may be claimed as follows:
   (a)   against Confused's other income for 2005–06 under s 380(1)(a); or
   (b)   against his income for 2004–05 (under s 380(1)(b)).
   He may choose the year in which relief is given in the claim: namely by stipulating that the loss is to be relieved in (or as far as possible in) 2005–06.
   (ii)   *The loss of £24,000*
   The rules are the same with the qualification that if relief is claimed for both a loss in the current year and a loss in the preceding year, the current year is given priority. Accordingly if relief was claimed for the £18,000 loss in 2005–2006 that would take priority over a claim to relief for the £24,000 loss in that year.

Certain restrictions are placed on the availability of s 380 relief in order to prevent a taxpayer indulging in a 'hobby' trade. TA 1988 s 384 denies the relief unless the taxpayer can show that the loss-making business was run on a commercial basis with a view to profit (although a reasonable expectation of profit is conclusive evidence of this: for a recent illustration, see *Wannell v Rothwell* (1996)). By TA 1988 s 397, a farmer or market gardener will automatically lose the relief if he incurs a loss in each of the preceding five years unless he can show that any competent farmer or market gardener would have made the same losses. The moral here is 'let your losses be those of the reasonable man or make a profit every sixth year!'     **[11.41]–[11.60]**

## IV   RELIEF AGAINST CAPITAL GAINS (FA 1991 S 72)

The manner in which CGT is charged does not involve a joining together of the taxes themselves. The taxes remain distinct so that income losses cannot generally be offset against chargeable gains and nor can capital losses be offset against income. The position is slightly different for companies – see **[41.62]**.

Trading losses of an individual can be offset against his capital gains in the tax year when the loss arises and in one preceding year. The following matters are particularly worthy of note concerning this relief:
(1)   The relief depends upon an election being made by the taxpayer and this claim for relief may only be made if a claim is also submitted under TA 1988 s 380 (ie to set the loss against the taxpayer's other income). Capital gains may only be used to the extent that the trading loss cannot be used against the taxpayer's other income for the year (this is 'the relevant amount').

(2) Relief is obtained by setting the trading loss against the amount which would otherwise be subject to a CGT charge—ie after deducting current year and losses carried forward—but *disregarding for this purpose the taxpayer's annual exemption* (this is referred to as 'the maximum amount'). For these purposes the trading losses are treated as an allowable capital loss made in that year.

(3) To the extent that full relief is not available in the year when the trading loss is incurred, any unrelieved balance may then be carried back and set against gains in the immediately preceding tax year in accordance with the s 380 procedure.  **[11.61]–[11.80]**

**EXAMPLE 11.4**

Curious' tax position for 2006–07 is as follows:

|  |  | £ |
|---|---|---|
| Taxable income |  | 50,000 |
| Trading losses |  | 75,000 |
| Chargeable gains |  | 120,000 |
| Allowable capital losses | (current year) | 30,000 |
|  | (brought forward) | 25,000 |

He makes claims under s 380(1)(a) and s 72(1) in respect of the trading loss.

(1) *Assessable income:* reduced to nil (hence a loss of personal allowances) and the 'relevant amount' for s 72 is £25,000.

(2) *The 'maximum amount':* £120,000 − (£30,000 + £25,000) = £65,000. Accordingly relief is not restricted.

Hence £25,000 of trading losses are treated as allowable (capital) losses. Curious' gains for the year are therefore £40,000.

## V  RELIEF FOR LOSSES IN THE EARLY YEARS

### 1  TA 1988 s 381: initial loss relief

A business will often make losses in its early years and TA 1988 s 381 provides relief where a loss is sustained in the year of assessment in which the business is first carried on, or in any of the next three years of assessment, as an alternative to relief under TA 1988 ss 380, 385 and FA 1991 s 72.

The relief is obtained by a set-off against the taxpayer's total income of the three years of assessment preceding the year of loss. The set-off is against earlier years before later years (the loss can, of course, only be relieved once: see *Gamble v Rowe* (1998)). The effect of the relief is to revise earlier income tax computations and to obtain a tax refund. Section 381 is available to individuals (including partners) for a maximum of four years only and is not available to a limited company. Therefore, where early losses are envisaged, it may be worth starting as a sole trader (or partnership) and at a later stage incorporating the business.

Section 381 relief requires a specific election by 31 January in the second tax year following the year of assessment in which the loss is sustained. Relief is denied unless it can be shown that the business was conducted on a commercial basis with a view to profit (TA 1988 s 381(4)). The relief cannot be extended by the taxpayer transferring the business to his spouse after the first four years (TA 1988 s 381(5)).                                    **[11.81]**

### EXAMPLE 11.5

Fergus began business as a sole practitioner on 1 July 2005. His results for the first 12 months showed a loss of £36,000. This is apportioned as follows:
    2005–06: loss £27,000 (ie 1 July 2005–5 April 2006)
    2006–07: loss £9,000.
    Before beginning his own business, Fergus was employed as an assistant solicitor. He worked increasingly part-time as he prepared to launch his business. Salary from his job was as follows:

|          | Salary   |
|----------|----------|
| 2002–03  | £20,000  |
| 2003–04  | £15,000  |
| 2004–05  | £10,000  |

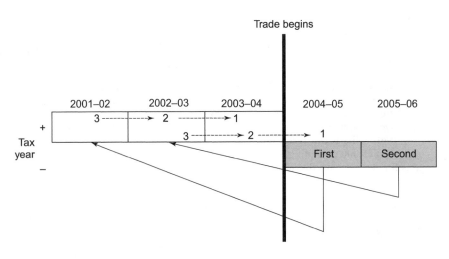

The position is as follows:

| *2002–2003*                              | £        |
|------------------------------------------|----------|
| Salary                                   | 20,000   |
| Less: 2005–06 loss carried back (part)   | (20,000) |
| Revised liability                        | NIL      |

| *2003–04*                                      |        |
|------------------------------------------------|--------|
| Salary                                         | 15,000 |
| Less: 2005–06 loss carried back (remaining)    | (7,000)|
|                                                | 8,000  |
| Less: 2006–07 loss carried back (part)         | 8,000  |
| Revised liability                              | NIL    |

*2004–05*

| | |
|---|---:|
| Salary | 10,000 |
| Less: 2006–07 loss (remaining) | 1,000 |
| Revised liability | £9,000 |

## 2 Relationship of s 381 with ss 380 and 385

As with s 380, relief under s 381 requires a specific election. The election need only be made for one year of loss, but, once made, that loss must be carried back against the taxpayer's income in the earlier years without limit, which may result in a loss of personal allowances.

Sections 381 and 380 are alternatives so that the same portion of any loss cannot be relieved under both sections (ie twice). Where, however, relief has been given as far as possible under one section, any surplus loss remaining can be relieved by a specific election under the other section (see *Butt v Haxby* (1983)). Any surplus loss still unrelieved will then be carried forward under s 385.

### EXAMPLE 11.6

Angus begins trading on 1 August 2006 and in the period to 5 April 2007 makes a loss of £15,000. His income in the preceding three years (2003–04 onwards) amounted to £10,000. If Angus elects for s 381 relief he will have wasted his personal allowances in the preceding years. He will be left with an unrelieved loss of £5,000 which can be relieved under s 380 against any other income which he may have in 2006–07. To the extent that relief is not given under s 380, the surplus loss will be carried forward under s 385.

Which relief the taxpayer chooses will depend upon his circumstances. Section 381 relief is advantageous when the taxpayer has a large pre-trading income, since it will ensure a cash refund. Alternatively, if his other income/ gains in the year(s) of loss is large, relief under TA 1988 s 380/FA 1991 s 72 may be more attractive. Changes in income tax rates are also an important factor to bear in mind. **[11.82]–[11.100]**

## VI RELIEF FOR LOSSES IN THE FINAL YEARS

### 1 TA 1988 s 386: transfer of a business to a company

The general rule is that loss relief is personal to the taxpayer who sustains the loss; it cannot be 'sold' with the business or otherwise transferred. Thus, if a business is incorporated, any unabsorbed loss of the old business that ceases to trade cannot be carried forward under s 385 by the company. However, TA 1988 s 386 provides that where the business of a sole trader or a partnership is transferred to a company and the whole or main consideration for the transfer is the allotment of shares to the former proprietor, he can set his unrelieved losses against income which he receives from the company for any year throughout which he owns the shares allotted to him and during which the company continues to trade. The set-off must be used first against direct assessments (eg on director's fees, etc) with any balance set against dividends, etc from the company. HMRC have confirmed that even if the vending agreement refers to a cash consideration, provided that shares are taken relief is available (IM 3551) and that this relief will be allowed provided that the taxpayer keeps shares which represent more than 80% of the consideration received for the business (BIM 75500).

**EXAMPLE 11.7**

Evans sells his business to a company in return for an allotment of shares on 30 September 2005. His unused losses from the trade amount to £4,200.

In the period from 1 October 2005 to 5 April 2006, he receives a salary of £3,000 and dividends (gross) of £400 from the company. In 2006–07 he receives a salary of £5,000 and dividends of £600. Evans obtains relief under s 386 as follows:

|  | Total income | Losses |
|---|---|---|
|  | £ | £ |
| *2005–06* |  |  |
| Unabsorbed trading loss |  | (4,200) |
| Salary | 3,000 |  |
| Dividends | 400 |  |
|  | 3,400 |  |
| *Less* s 386 relief | (3,400) | 3,400 |
|  | Nil | (800) |
| *2006–07* |  |  |
| Salary | 5,000 |  |
| *Less* s 386 relief | (800) | 800 |
|  | 4,200 |  |
| Dividends | 600 |  |
|  | £4,800 |  |

Relief under s 386 is given automatically (as an extension of s 385) as if the original business had not ceased and as if the income derived from the company were profits of that business. However, for all other purposes the business has discontinued and, if the taxpayer wants relief for his business loss in the year of discontinuance under s 380(1), or terminal relief under s 388 (see **[11.102]**), he must make a specific election to that effect. Section 386 relief is, of course, given to the individual taxpayer who sustains the loss and affords no relief for losses made by the newly formed company.

**[11.101]**

## 2    TA 1988 s 388: terminal loss relief

If a loss is sustained in the last 12 months of a business, the unrelieved loss of that period, so far as not otherwise relieved (eg under TA 1988 s 380/FA 1991 s 72, in the year of discontinuance), may be relieved by set-off against the business profits in the year of cessation and the three preceding years of assessment. Relief is given as far as possible against later rather than earlier years. A terminal loss is defined as one sustained in the year of assessment in which the trade discontinued together with such proportion of any loss sustained in the previous year beginning 12 months before the discontinuance (if in either case there was a profit then nil is entered in calculating the terminal loss).

The loss includes: (1) any annual payments charged under TA 1988 s 349; and (2) any unrelieved interest payments so long as they are incurred wholly and exclusively for the purposes of the business.

If profits of a preceding year are insufficient to absorb the loss, dividends and interest taxed at source in that year (and which are received in the course of carrying on the business) are treated as profits for the purposes of obtaining a repayment of income tax (TA 1988 s 385(4)).

Relief may be claimed under TA 1988 s 388 as an alternative to relief under TA 1988 s 386 (transfer to a company) and any unused loss can be relieved under s 386.                                                    **[11.102]–[11.120]**

**EXAMPLE 11.8**

Dolly closes down her hairdressing business on 5 June 2006. Her results for the four years ending 5 December 2005 and for her final six months of business were:

| Accounting period | Profit/loss | Tax years | Original assessments |
|---|---|---|---|
| Year to 5 December 2002 | £11,000 profit | 2002–03 | £11,000 |
| Year to 5 December 2003 | £7,000 profit | 2003–04 | £7,000 |
| Year to 5 December 2004 | £3,000 profit | 2004–05 | £3,000 |
| Year to 5 December 2005 | £1,000 profit | 2005–06 | £1,000 |
| Six months to 5 June 2006 | £(12,000) loss | 2006–07 | nil |

The terminal loss is calculated as:
(i)  loss in year of discontinuance:
     $\frac{2}{6} \times £(12,000) = £(4,000)$
*plus*
(ii)  loss in preceding year of assessment:
     $\frac{4}{6} \times £(12,000) = £(8,000)$
*plus*
     $\frac{6}{12} \times £1,000 = $ nil
*ie £12,000 terminal loss*
     That loss is relieved as follows:

| Tax year | Fiscal assessment |
|---|---|
| 2006–07 | Nil |

| 2005–06 | |
| 2004–05 | profits for these years (starting with 2003–04) reduced by the terminal loss of £12,000. |
| 2003–04 | |

## VII INVESTMENT IN UNQUOTED CORPORATE TRADES (TA 1988 ss 573–576)

As a general rule, a person who subscribes for shares in a company and later disposes of them at a loss can only claim CGT relief for his loss. In an attempt to stimulate investment in corporate trades, TA 1988 s 574 enables an individual to obtain income tax relief for his loss in certain circumstances. Broadly, the section allows an individual who has made a loss on the disposal of shares in an 'eligible trading company' to deduct the loss from his total income in the year of assessment in which the loss is incurred or against total income of the preceding year (s 574(1)(b) and see *Hobart v Williams* (1997)). This relief contains a number of restrictions:

(1) It is available only to an individual who subscribes for shares in a company for money or money's worth, including one who acquires the shares from a subscribing spouse; it is not available to a subsequent purchaser of the shares.

(2) The disposal giving rise to the loss must be a sale at arm's length for full consideration; or a distribution from the company on a dissolution or a winding up; or a deemed disposal under TCGA 1992 s 24(1) (entire loss, destruction, dissipation or extinction of asset); or a deemed disposal under TCGA 1992 s 24(2) where the shares have become of negligible value.

(3) The company must satisfy the complex requirements of s 576(4)–(5). Basically, it must be an eligible trading company, carrying on its business wholly or mainly in the UK, which does not trade in certain prohibited items such as land or shares and which is not a building society, or a registered industrial and provident society. An eligible company is, broadly, one that satisfies the requirements to be a qualifying company for the purposes of the Enterprise Investment Scheme. The company must be unquoted at the time of issue and no arrangements must then exist for it to cease to be unquoted. However, there is no requirement that the company remain unquoted.

If these conditions are satisfied, the allowable loss is calculated on CGT principles and is deducted in priority to relief under TA 1988 s 380 or s 381.

The deduction is given in accordance with the s 380 rules, ie against income of the year of assessment in which the loss arises and income of the previous year. A claim must be made by notice given within 12 months from 31 January of the tax year following the disposal. Relief may be claimed against either or both of the income tax years: to the extent that part of the loss is unrelieved the capital gains tax rules apply (see **[19.61]**).

To prevent the taxpayer from obtaining double tax relief on his investment, any income tax relief he received on the acquisition of the shares under the Enterprise Investment Scheme must be deducted from the base value of the shares when calculating an allowable loss for CGT and, therefore, for s 574.                                                   **[11.121]**

## VIII ANTI-AVOIDANCE

FA 2004 introduced measures to prevent the use of losses in avoidance schemes. The provisions relate to:

(*a*) *Partnership losses: non-active partners.* Loss relief under TA 1988 s 380 or s 381 (and interest relief under TA 1988, s 353) is restricted in the case of an individual partner who does not devote 'a significant amount of time' to the trade (professions are not affected). The relief available is restricted to the amount of the partner's 'contribution to the trade' as at the end of the tax year in which the loss is sustained. The restriction applies to losses sustained in the tax year in which the partner first carries on the trade and in any of the next three tax years. The restricted losses may be carried forward and used against profits of the same trade, or used against general income or chargeable gains to the extent that the partner makes a further contribution to the trade.

(*b*) *Partnership losses from exploiting a licence: non-active partners.* This measure is designed to tackle schemes used by partners to reduce the tax charge on income from a licence or similar agreement. The schemes aim to generate trading losses followed by a disposal of the licence or related income rights for a sum not otherwise chargeable to income tax. The legislation ensures that the disposal of income rights is charged to income tax, but only in relation to a partner who does not devote 'a significant amount of time' to the trade (professions are not affected) at the time the losses are generated.

(*c*) *Partnership losses derived from exploiting films: non-active partners.* Relief under TA 1988, s 380 or s 381 for trading losses derived from exploiting films is restricted in certain circumstances in the case of an individual partner who does not devote 'a significant amount of time' to the trade. Such relief can be given only against income consisting of profits from the trade in question and not against other income or against chargeable gains. The restriction applies to losses sustained in the tax year in which the partner first carries on the trade and in any of the next three tax years. FA 2004 provisions have been further extended by FA 2005. The HMRC now have the power (FA 2005 s 79) to set out in regulations details of the kind of contributions that are excluded in computing the amount of the partner's contribution to the trade for this purpose. The new provisions apply from 2 December 2004.

(*d*) *Film-related losses: disposal of a right to profits.* There is a potential exit charge where an individual has claimed loss relief under TA 1988, s 380 or s 381 for a trade that has benefited from the special reliefs available for certain films (see F(No 2)A 1992 s 40A–40C, 41–43 and F(No 2)A 1997 s 48) and subsequently disposes of a right to profits arising from the trade. A charge may also arise where the losses claimed exceed the individual's capital contribution to the trade.

(e) FA 2005 ss 73–78 add to the anti-avoidance legislation introduced in FA 2004. Broadly, the new provisions remove restrictions on the amount of interest relief that an individual can claim in respect of a loan to buy into a partnership. The provisions also disregard such interest relief in computing any restrictions on the amount of loss relief that an individual partner can set off against their other income or capital gains. The new measures apply to interest paid by a partner on or after 2 December 2004 and to restrictions on the amount of loss relief that a partner can set off in respect of trading losses sustained in periods beginning on or after 2 December 2004.

As stated in (a) above, such claims to loss relief are restricted to the amount of the partner's contribution to the trade as capital. The new rules give HMRC power to set out in regulations details of the kind of contributions that are excluded in computing the amount of the individual's contribution to the trade for this purpose. Partners whose loss relief may be restricted in this way are limited partners, members of a limited liability partnership and other partners who do not spend a significant amount of time personally engaged in carrying on the trade.

Under the provisions outlined above, excess relief will be recovered if, after loss relief has been claimed, the partner's capital contribution is reduced by the exclusion of amounts under the provisions outlined above. Excess relief is recovered by means of an income tax charge on the partner. The chargeable amount is computed under FA 2005 s 75 and is taxable as income of the partner arising otherwise than from the trade (under Schedule D Case VI for tax years before 2005–06) for the tax year in which the relevant decrease in the partner's capital contribution occurred. Partners whose excess loss relief may be recovered in this way are those who have claimed relief for trading losses sustained in periods beginning on or after 2 December 2004 during which they were limited partners, members of a limited liability partnership, or did not spend a significant amount of time personally engaged in carrying on the trade.

For the treatment of partnership losses generally, see **[44.9]**, and for other statutory provisions to counter tax avoidance, see **[42.71]**.           **[11.122]**

# 12  Land

*Updated by Sarah Laing, CTA, Chartered Tax Advisor, CPE Consulting Ltd*

---

| | |
|---|---|
| I | Application of trading principles [**12.1**] |
| II | Chargeable persons and computation [**12.41**] |
| III | Furnished holiday lettings [**12.61**] |
| IV | The taxation of premiums and rent factoring [**12.81**] |
| V | TA 1988 s 776 and the development of land [**12.101**] |

---

## I  APPLICATION OF TRADING PRINCIPLES

### 1  Ambit of income from property rules

ITTOIA 2005 Part 3 (formerly Schedule A) charges *profits of a business of letting property* which include isolated or casual lettings, income from furnished lettings and certain lease premiums. ITTOIA 2005 s 264 provides: 'A person's UK property business consists of every business which the person carries on for generating income from land in the United Kingdom, and every transaction which the person enters into for that purpose otherwise than in the course of such a business.' The following matters should be noted.

*First*, the tax is not levied by reference to income produced from individual properties but instead looks at *all* properties owned by the individual under the umbrella of a 'property income business'.

*Secondly*, that business includes isolated transactions provided that they are entered into 'for generating income from land'. (Insofar as the term 'a business' implies continuous activities, it is, therefore, something of a misnomer.)

*Thirdly*, rents from furnished lettings that were formerly taxed under Schedule D Case VI are also now within the ITTOIA 2005 Part 3 net.

*Finally*, 'other receipts', not just rent, are caught by the ITTOIA 2005 provisions although given that the charge is on *annual* profits or gains, it is only receipts of an *income* nature that are caught (subject to the special rules in ITTOIA 2005 Part 3 Chapter 4 (TA 1998 ss 34–36 prior to 2005–06) governing lease premiums: see [**12.81**] ff). [**12.1**]–[**12.21**]

#### EXAMPLE 12.1

(1) Rustic sells turves from his land: he falls within ITTOIA 2005 Part 3 and the payments are of an income nature being received for the exploitation of

rights in UK land (*Lowe v J W Ashmore Ltd* (1971)). Contrast the position of Campo who received a 'one-off' payment in return for a licence to tip. This payment is of a capital nature and, therefore, outside the income from property business rules; see *McClure v Petre* (1988) in which Sir Nicolas Browne-Wilkinson V-C concluded that:

'The substance of the present matter is that the payments were received by the taxpayer as consideration for a once and for all disposal of a right or advantage appurtenant to the land; namely the right or advantage of using it for dumping. Immediately before the licence was granted, the value of the land itself included the value of the right to turn it to advantage by using it for dumping. After the licence that right or advantage had gone forever in return for a lump sum. True the acreage of land and the taxpayer's interest remain the same; but it was shorn of this valuable advantage. It was in truth a realisation of part of the value of the freehold. That strikes me as a disposal of a capital nature ...'

(2)    Junius lets flats and the tenants pay a service charge aimed at recouping Junius's costs of maintenance, insurance and repairs. These payments fall within ITTOIA 2005 Part 3 (see ITTOIA 2005 s 266(2)). Contrast the position if Junius provided other services, such as a caretaker, when he would be carrying on a trade and so payments made in return for such services would be assessed under ITTOIA 2005 Part 2 (formerly Schedule D Case I).

## 2    The income is unearned

The concept of the 'property income business' is limited in that, although the tax charge is computed on normal trading principles, the income is not itself treated as earned income. As a result income tax benefits associated with earned income (notably pension entitlement) and the CGT business reliefs do not apply. Special rules, however, apply to 'furnished holiday lettings' in the UK (see **[12.61]**). Whether property lettings qualify for IHT business property relief is considered elsewhere.                                    **[12.22]**

## 3    Lettings outside trading provisions

The changes have not affected a line of cases decided in the early 1980s, such as *Webb v Conelee Properties Ltd* (1982), in which the court held that there was no such trade as 'the letting of properties producing a rent'. That is precisely what is charged to tax under (former) Schedule A and the taxpayer had conducted no other activities which could have amounted to a trade. Similarly, in *Griffiths v Jackson* (1983), income from letting furnished flats or bedsitting rooms to students was held to be income from land and not assessable under (former) Schedule D Case I (see also *Gittos v Barclay* (1982)). Unless a landlord can establish that either he is running an hotel or guest house or can bring himself within the holiday letting provisions, then all his income from land (apart from charges for ancillary services constituting a trade, such as caretaking) will be taxed as the unearned income of a property income business.                                                        **[12.23]**

## 4    Exclusions from the property income charge

ITTOIA 2005 s 267 expressly excludes certain income from the property income charge: namely, profits from the occupation of land; profits and gains arising from mines, quarries and certain other concerns such as markets, tolls, bridges and ferries (which by ITTOIA 2005 s 12 are taxed under ITTOIA 2005 Part 2 Chapter 2 (Trades and Trade Profits)); mineral rent and royalties (taxed half as income from trade and half as capital) and miscellaneous receipts such as income from wayleaves or tolls, which is received after basic rate income tax has been deducted at source by the payer under ITTOIA 2005 s 335 (and see ITTOIA 2005 s 344 in relation to payment for wayleaves for electricity cables, telephone lines, etc).

Rental income from land outside the UK is charged to tax under ITTOIA 2005 s 265. Specifically, s 265 states that: 'a person's overseas property business consists of every business which the person carries on for generating income from land outside the United Kingdom, and every transaction which the person enters into for that purpose otherwise than in the course of such a business.'

Letting property abroad is treated as a separate trade with the same rules for computing receipts and expenses. The lease premium rules also apply to property outside the UK (see [12.37]).

Profits from the occupation of land such as farming are taxed as a trade under ITTOIA 2005 s 9. There is a specific exemption from this charge in the case of 'the occupation of land which comprises woodlands or is being prepared for use for forestry purposes' (ITTOIA 2005 s 10–11) but in *Jaggers (t/a Shide Trees) v Ellis* (1997) this was held not to cover the planting and cultivating of conifers for Christmas. This activity was taxable as a trade.

[12.24]–[12.40]

## II CHARGEABLE PERSONS AND COMPUTATION

### 1 Chargeable persons

ITTOIA 2005 s 271 provides for the tax to be charged on and paid by 'the person receiving or entitled to the profits', whilst s 270(1) provides for the tax to be computed on 'the full amount of the profits arising in the tax year'.

In the application of these rules to settlements comprising land HMRC considers that it will normally be the trustees who are carrying on the business save where there is an old style strict settlement or where the trustees have delegated their management powers to the life tenant under TLATA 1996 s 9. In both these cases the business will be carried on by the beneficiary. This distinction will be significant in cases where a life tenant personally owns land on which he makes a loss. Only in these two exceptional cases does HMRC consider that he is entitled to set his loss against the property income in the settlement. [12.41]

### 2 Computation: accountancy practice

So far as computation is concerned, ITTOIA 2005 s 272 states that: 'profits of a property business are calculated in the same way as the profits of a trade'.

As a result, property business profits must be computed on the basis of generally accepted accountancy practice that will, in the absence of express statutory provision, decide what is a taxable receipt and what is an allowable expense. The trade and trade receipts principles are applicable (see **[10.61]** et seq) so that deduction is available for items of expenditure incurred wholly and exclusively for the purpose of the property business provided that the particular type of expenditure is not prohibited by the statute (eg capital expenditure incurred in the making of improvements or acquiring the premises: ITTOIA 2005 s 33.                                                    **[12.42]**

### EXAMPLE 12.2

Julia acquires a Fulham flat for letting. It is in a rundown condition and she expends substantial sums restoring it to its former glory. These sums will be deductible expenses provided that the property was capable of letting without repair works having to be carried out. Otherwise they would be capital and disallowable under ITTOIA 2005 s 33 (see generally the cases of *Law Shipping Co Ltd v IRC* (1924) and *Odeon Associated Theatres Ltd v Jones* (1972) discussed at **[10.142]**).

### 3    Interest payments

A deduction is permitted for interest paid on loans where the money borrowed is 'wholly and exclusively' incurred for the purposes of the property business. Linking interest payments to rent from a particular property is unnecessary: indeed the particular property acquired by means of the relevant loan may be sold but it may be that relief will continue provided that the property business continues (in this connection consider, however, *Wharf Properties v IRC* (1997)).                                      **[12.43]**

### EXAMPLE 12.3

Jennie borrows substantial sums to acquire property A, to renovate property B and to re-roof property C. During the year, despite her best endeavours, property A remains unlet whilst property C is sold. Property B is let throughout the year. Jennie is carrying on a property business and all the interest payments are deductible in computing her profit.

### 4    Losses

The general principle is that losses incurred in a property business can only be offset against future profits of that business (TA 1988 s 379A). Relief against other income is only available in two cases—*first*, losses resulting from claims to capital allowances and, *secondly*, for 'agricultural expenses' incurred in connection with the management of an agricultural estate. There is no right to carry back unrelieved property business losses. The trade rules for bad debts and pre-business expenditure apply.                              **[12.44]**

### 5    Capital allowances

Capital allowances for machinery and plant used in the management of property will be given as a property business expense, as part of the profit calculation. Capital allowances are not available for plant or machinery let in a dwelling house (CAA 2001 s 35) so the renewals basis or the wear and tear allowances for furnished lettings are given instead (see ESC B47). Under the renewals basis the entire cost of replacing furniture, furnishings and chattels (excluding any additions or improvements) may be deducted in arriving at the profits from the lettings in the year when that expense is incurred. The alternative method, the allowance for depreciation, permits the deduction of (usually) 10% of the gross rent less water rates each tax year that the premises are let. In addition to this 10% allowance, the landlord may claim the cost of renewing fixtures such as baths, washbasins and toilets. Once a taxpayer has claimed allowances on one of these two bases, the practice is for that basis to continue.

From 6 April 2004, a landlord may claim up to £1,500 per building per tax year for expenditure incurred in respect of energy-saving items (such as loft and cavity wall insulation), where the expenditure is incurred in the course of a property income business. The scope of the Landlord's Energy Saving Allowance (LESA) was extended from 6 April 2006 to include draught proofing and insulation for hot water systems. Where more than one person has an interest in the building concerned, the allowance may be apportioned accordingly (ITTOIA 2005 s 312). [12.45]

**EXAMPLE 12.4**

Rakeman is the landlord of furnished premises the rent from which is £10,000 in 2006–07. During that tax year, his total expenses comprising the costs of managing, maintaining and repairing the premises (including the decoration of two rooms and water rates of £800) amount to £6,000. His profit is, therefore, £4,000. In addition, however, Rakeman spent £6,500 on refurbishments (buying new carpets and furniture). If Rakeman claims the renewals basis he has further deductible expenditure in 2006–07 of £6,500 leaving him with no property business taxable income, but instead a loss of £2,500 (£10,000 – (£6,000 + £6,500)) which he can set against other property business income in that year or in future tax years. Alternatively, under the depreciation basis, Rakeman can claim a 10% deduction of £920 calculated on gross rent less water rates (ie 10% × (£10,000 – £800)) that he can treat as a further deductible expense to leave him with a taxable profit for 2006–07 of £3,080 (£10,000 – (£6,000 + £920)). Under this basis, he will continue to claim a 10% deduction in each tax year during which the premises are let.

6 **Rent-a-room relief (ITTOIA 2005 Part 7 Chapter 1)**

Designed as a tax incentive to encourage owner-occupiers and tenants who have a spare room in their home to let it out, gross annual rents not exceeding £4,250 are exempt from income tax. The following conditions must be satisfied:
(1)   relief is available to *individuals* on a letting of *furnished* accommodation;
(2)   the individual does not derive any taxable income other than rent-a-room receipts from a relevant trade, letting or agreement;
(3)   the letting must be in the individual's *'only or main residence'* in the *'basis period'* (ie in the current year: letting for office accommodation does not qualify);

(4)   the gross income limit of £4,250 will be halved if more than one person lets rooms in the same house. A husband and wife may so arrange matters that the income is either wholly the wife's or wholly the husband's;

(5)   the individual can elect for this exemption not to apply (he may wish to do so, for instance, in order to claim loss relief for the relevant period);

(6)   if gross annual receipts exceed £4,250, the individual can choose either to pay tax in the normal way (on gross receipts less actual expenses) or, alternatively, on gross receipts less £4,250 (this is termed 'the alternative basis'). An election must be made on or before the first anniversary of the 31 January next following the year of assessment for which it is made (or such later date as the Board may allow) if the alternative basis is to apply. Such election remains in force until withdrawn.

**[12.46]–[12.60]**

### III   FURNISHED HOLIDAY LETTINGS

ITTOIA 2005 s 323 provides that income from furnished holiday lettings in the UK is to be treated as trading income and for the CGT business reliefs to be available (including business assets taper relief). The provisions apply to lettings by individuals and by companies. The property business rules do not affect these provisions and owners of property suitable for letting as holiday accommodation are advised to satisfy the conditions of s 323 wherever possible so that full (rather than restricted) loss relief is available; the income qualifies as earned for pension purposes and the CGT reliefs are available.

**[12.61]**

### 1   Definition

The accommodation must be available for letting to the public commercially as furnished holiday accommodation for at least 140 days in the tax year and must be actually let for at least 70 days. These periods need not be continuous and accordingly both winter and summer holiday accommodation may qualify. To ensure a 'genuine' holiday letting, it must not 'normally' (undefined) be let to the same person continuously in any seven months of the year (but including the 70-day period above) for more than 31 days. In the remaining five months of the tax year, therefore, the landlord may do what he wishes with the property, eg let it continuously; keep it empty; go into occupation himself. The above requirements will normally exclude student accommodation. The letting of caravans is included, insofar as it is not taxed as a trade under the trading income provisions, but not the letting of sites (taxed under former Schedule A) nor residential caravans for long-term occupation (IR Press Release [1984] STI 386).

The term 'holiday' accommodation is undefined; if the above conditions are satisfied, it will be deemed to be a holiday letting (see eg *Gittos v Barclay* (1982) where these requirements were satisfied). 'Letting' means occupation by a person other than the landlord and includes granting a licence to occupy.

Whether the accommodation qualifies as a holiday let in any tax year is judged on the facts of that year (for company landlords, the financial year).

However, where the letting begins in a tax year (eg on 1 August 2006), it may qualify as a holiday let for that year if it satisfies the above requirements within the following 12 months (ie between 1 August 2006 and 31 July 2007). Likewise, a letting that ends in a tax year must satisfy the necessary conditions during the previous 12 months. **[12.62]**

## 2   Tax treatment

The income profits for the whole year are assessed under ITTOIA 2005. However, they are treated as trading profits for the purposes specified in ITTOIA 2005 s 323 and, therefore, receive most of the benefits of an assessment under the income from trade provisions. Thus, the income is earned income. The tax is usually payable in two equal instalments in January and July each year.

For CGT purposes the letting is treated as a trade in any year when it satisfies the above conditions or would do so but for the fact that the property is under construction or repair. Thus, roll-over (replacement of business assets) relief (TCGA 1992 ss 152 ff) and hold-over relief on a gift of business assets (TCGA 1992 s 165) may be available on a disposal. However, a landlord who claims roll-over relief and occupies the property himself may not claim the main residence exemption against the entire gain on a subsequent disposal. In such a case the rolled-over gain is chargeable and the exemption applies only to any remaining gain. No special relief is given from IHT and property lettings do not generally qualify for business property relief.

### EXAMPLE 12.5

'Seaview' is purchased for £40,000 in 1993 and let as furnished holiday accommodation until 2000. It is then sold for £60,000 and the proceeds used in the purchase of 'Belvedere' for £85,000 that is similarly let. In 2002 the landlord takes possession and lives there until 2006 when he sells it for £145,000.

In 2000, the gain on 'Seaview' is rolled over into the purchase of 'Belvedere' giving it a base cost for CGT of £65,000. On the sale of 'Belvedere' in 2006 the gain is £80,000 of which £20,000 (rolled over from 'Seaview') is chargeable. The remaining gain is apportioned between the period of occupation that is exempt (ie 4/6 = £40,000) and the let period (ie 2/6 = £20,000) that is chargeable.

Where the same landlord lets several 'qualifying' properties, they are taxed as one trade. Should one or more properties qualify as furnished holiday lettings in the tax year and others not, because they fail to satisfy the 70-day requirement, the landlord can claim, within two years of the end of the relevant tax year, for the days of letting to be averaged between all or any of the properties thereby enabling all the properties to qualify. Thus, if property A had been let in 2006–07 for 90 days and properties B and C for 50 days each respectively, A and B or A and C can be averaged so that two properties qualify; there are insufficient letting days for all three to qualify. **[12.63]–[12.80]**

## IV   THE TAXATION OF PREMIUMS AND RENT FACTORING

### 1   Introductory

A premium is a capital sum paid by a tenant to a landlord in connection with the grant of a lease. To understand the income tax treatment of premiums, it should be remembered that the original Schedule A was introduced before CGT so that a landlord could have avoided paying any tax by extracting a capital sum from the tenant instead of rent. Accordingly, certain premiums are deemed to be income and so chargeable to income tax. Insofar as a premium is not chargeable as income it may be subject to CGT. As CGT is charged at income tax rates, the importance of the distinction between the taxes is not large but it does exist and can be used to advantage. For instance, when a landlord is entitled to substantial interest relief or has incurred deductible expenditure, he may prefer any premium to be taxed as rent. The rules on taxing a premium are something of a minefield (see the remarks of Lightman J in *Hurlingham Estates Ltd v Wilde & Partners* (1997):

> '... I would expect any reasonably competent solicitor practising in the field of conveyancing or commercial law to be aware of this concealed trap for the unwary. It is a matter he should have in mind for any transaction involving the grant of a lease and a related payment by the lessee to the lessor.')    **[12.81]**

## 2   The charge (ITTOIA 2005 s 277)

If a lease is granted for a period not exceeding 50 years and the consideration includes a premium, a proportion of that premium is treated as additional rent taxable under ITTOIA 2005. This proportion is the amount that is left after deducting 2% of the premium for each complete year of the lease other than the first. The effect of the 2% discount is that the amount of premium charged to income tax falls with the length of the lease. For a 1-year lease all the premium is taxed and for a 50-year lease 2%.

### EXAMPLE 12.6

Lease 16 years; premium £3,000.
  Discount 2% of £3,000 over 15 years = £3,000 × $\frac{2}{100}$ × 15 = £900
  Chargeable slice: £3,000 − £900 = £2,100

The grant of a sub-lease of 50 years or less will, as a general rule, be taxed in the same way as the grant of a head lease. If, however, a premium on the grant of the head lease was taxed under the property business rules, this is taken into account when taxing any premium on the grant of the sub-lease.    **[12.82]**

## 3   Anti-avoidance provisions

There are elaborate provisions designed to prevent the charge to income tax on premiums from being circumvented.

*First*, a landlord cannot avoid the ITTOIA 2005 s 277 charge by disguising the length of the lease. If its length can be shortened by an option to surrender or to terminate, the option will be taken into account only insofar as it is likely to be exercised (ITTOIA 2005 s 303).

### EXAMPLE 12.7

L grants a lease to T for 60 years at a premium of £20,000 and a rent of £1,000 pa for the first ten years and thereafter at an annual rent of ten times the then market rent. T has an option to surrender the lease after ten years. For income tax purposes this is treated as a ten-year lease since the tenant is likely to exercise the option to surrender in view of the penal increase in the rent after ten years.

*Secondly*, where a landlord, instead of taking a premium on the grant of a lease for 50 years or less, requires the tenant to make improvements to the premises, the amount by which the value of the landlord's reversion is increased as a result of those improvements is treated as a premium (ITTOIA 2005 s 278). This provision does not, however, apply if the tenant is required to make improvements to another property of the landlord; if the obligation is not imposed by the lease or if the expenditure would have been a deductible expense of the landlord.

**EXAMPLE 12.8**

Property is let from 1 June 2005, for seven years. Under the terms of the lease the tenant is required to carry out certain structural alterations as a result of which the value of the landlord's interest in the premises is increased by £2,000.

| | |
|---|---:|
| Increase: | £2,000 |
| *Less:* discount: $\frac{2}{100} \times £2,000 \times 6$: | £240 |
| Included in 2005–06 property business profits: | £1,760 |

*Thirdly*, ITTOIA 2005 ss 279–281 charge 'delayed premiums' as income. If a premium becomes payable at some date during the currency of the lease or the tenant has to pay a sum for the waiver or variation of any terms of the lease, the sum is treated as a premium and in both cases the premium is taxed in the year of receipt as a premium for the then unexpired period of the lease. If a tenant has to pay a sum for the surrender of a lease it is taxed as a premium on a lease running from the date of commencement to the date of surrender.

*Fourthly*, the assignment of a lease, which has been granted at an under-value is charged under ITTOIA 2005 s 282. The charge under s 277 could be circumvented by a landlord granting a lease to, say, his spouse or to a company that he owns. No premium would be charged on the grant but the lease could then be assigned to the intended tenant and a premium taken. Section 277 only applies to a premium paid on the grant of a lease not on its assignment. However, s 282 provides that, when a lease is granted for less than its market premium, tax is charged under the property business provisions on assignors of the lease up to the amount of premium forgone by the landlord and to the extent that such assignors have made a profit on that assignment.

**EXAMPLE 12.9**

A grants B a 21-year lease at a premium of £2,000 although he could have charged £3,000. Therefore, the 'amount forgone' is £1,000. A is chargeable on the premium that he actually receives.

Two years later B assigns the lease to C charging a premium of £2,800. B receives £800 more than he paid; that is within the 'amount forgone'.

B is, therefore, chargeable on:

£800 − ($\frac{2}{100} \times 20 \times £800$) = £480

Notice that the 'amount forgone' still outstanding is £200 and that the period of the lease remains at the original length (namely 21 years) for the purpose of discounting. Two years later C assigns the lease to D charging a premium of £3,200. He has received £400 more than he paid but only £200 of that is caught under ITTOIA 2005 s 282 since that exhausts the 'amount forgone' by A. C is chargeable, therefore, on:

$$£200 - (\tfrac{2}{100} \times 20 \times £200) = £120$$

An assignee should, therefore, ensure (so far as possible) that the lease was not granted at an undervalue, and if necessary should take advantage of the clearance procedure under ITTOIA 2005 s 300.

The *final* anti-avoidance provision prevents the grant of a lease from being disguised as a sale (ITTOIA 2005 s 284). If D sells land (freehold or leasehold) to E with a right to have the property reconveyed to him in the future, any difference between the price paid by E and the reconveyance price payable by D is treated as a premium on a lease for the period between the sale and the reconveyance and is taxed accordingly.

ITTOIA 2005 s 285 extends ITTOIA 2005 s 284 so that if D sells land to E with a right for him (or a person connected with him) to take a leaseback of the property in the future, any difference between the price paid by E and the aggregate of the premium (if any) payable on the grant of a lease by E, together with the value of the reversion in E's hands, is treated as a premium on a lease for the period between the sale and leaseback and is taxed under the property business provisions. So as not to prejudice a commercial sale and leaseback, this provision does not apply where the leaseback is within one month of the sale.    **[12.83]**

### EXAMPLE 12.10

D sells land to E for £40,000 with a right to take a 20-year lease of the property after 11 years for a premium of £8,000. The value of E's reversionary interest subject to the lease is £2,000. There is a deemed premium under ITTOIA 2005 s 285 of £30,000 (£40,000 − (£8,000 + £2,000)) on a lease of 11 years. D is chargeable on:

$$£30,000 - (\tfrac{2}{100} \times £30,000 \times 10) = £24,000$$

## 4  Premium payable in instalments

If a premium is payable in instalments, the taxpayer may opt to pay the tax in such instalments as the Revenue may allow (ITTOIA 2005 s 299). The instalment period may not exceed eight years, and must end not later than the time the last instalment of the premium is payable.    **[12.84]**

## 5  Relief for traders paying a premium on trading premises (ITTOIA 2005 s 60)

Rent is an allowable deduction from the trading income of a trader (ITTOIA 2005 s 34). If a trader is granted a lease of business premises for 50 years or less at a premium, he can treat a portion of the premium as an annual rent and deduct it from his trading income (ITTOIA 2005 s 60). This portion is the amount of the premium that is charged to income tax in the landlord's hands under the property business provisions divided by the unexpired term of the lease. The rest of the premium is a capital expense.

A premium paid by a trader who takes an assignment of a lease is not allowable as a deduction from trading income unless the premium is caught by s 282.                                                                                     **[12.85]**

#### EXAMPLE 12.11

L grants T a lease of business premises for 10 years at an annual rent of £100 and a premium of £10,000.

   L is chargeable under ITTOIA 2005 on £8,200 of the premium (see ITTOIA 2005 s 277). The yearly equivalent of this sum, £820 (£8,200 ÷ 10), can be treated by T as additional rent so that each year he can deduct rent of £920 (£820 + £100) from his trading receipts.

### 6   Position of trusts

Lease premiums received by trustees are a capital receipt as a matter of general law. Hence whilst the trustees will run a property income business so that basic rate income tax will be charged on the income deemed to arise from the premium, that deemed income will not be subject to the 'surcharge' under ITTOIA 2005 s 568 and, in the case of interest in possession trusts, will not lead to a higher rate liability in the hands of the life tenant. And, of course, the sum received will form part of the trust capital.        **[12.86]**

### 7   Reverse premiums (**ITTOIA 2005 Sch 2 paras 28 and 71**)

A reverse premium is a sum paid by a landlord to a prospective tenant as an inducement to enter into a lease. In *IRC v Wattie* (1998) the Judicial Committee of the Privy Council held that although the premium was linked to an increased rent payable by the tenant it was a capital sum. As a result the premium would be subject to neither income tax nor capital gains tax. FA 1999 reversed this decision by treating them as income receipts taxable under former Schedule A or, in the case of a trader, etc under former Schedule D Case I or II. Note the following:
(1)   the definition of a reverse premium for these purposes is 'an induce-ment in connection with a transaction being entered into' by the recipient or a connected person. It is not thought that the paying of a sum to cover fitting-out costs would fall within this definition;
(2)   if the premium is taken into account to reduce the amount qualifying for capital allowances it is not taxed as an income receipt under these rules (thereby avoiding an effective double charge).        **[12.87]**

### 8   Rent factoring (**TA 1988 ss 43A–43G**)

#### EXAMPLE 12.12

(1)   Dumb Ltd borrows £100,000 for the purposes of its property business. The interest is tax deductible in arriving at the profits of the company but repayments of capital are not.

(2)    Smart Ltd disposes of its right to receive the rents of its portfolio properties for seven years in consideration for the payment of a lump sum (in effect a loan which will be repaid — as to both principal and interest — out of future rents) which the company then argues is chargeable to corporation tax as capital gains and which is therefore offset by available losses and reliefs (see *IRC v John Lewis Properties plc* (2003)).

Legislation introduced by FA 2000 prevents Smart Ltd from obtaining these benefits by providing that the sums received (ie the capital sum) is to be taxed as income. There are detailed rules to ensure that there is no double taxation where the sum forms part of a company's trading profits or falls within other specific property business legislation. The legislation applies to a 'rent factoring transaction' that is identified by reference to its correct accounting treatment in the accounts of Smart. It does not apply to rent factoring arrangements entered into by partnerships or individuals nor to factoring agreements that exceed 15 years.                    **[12.88]–[12.100]**

## V    TA 1988 s 776 AND THE DEVELOPMENT OF LAND

### 1    Transactions in land and s 776

The section was formerly headed 'Artificial Transactions in Land' and s 776(1) states that it was enacted to prevent the avoidance of tax by persons concerned with land or its development. However, the relevant transaction need not be *artificial* and a tax avoidance motive is not an essential precondition for liability (*Page v Lowther* (1983): see **[12.108]**). The basic requirement for the section is that land (or property deriving its value from land) is acquired with the sole or main object of realising a gain of a capital nature from its disposal.                    **[12.101]**

### 2    Trading transactions

Section 776 does not apply to trading transactions which are chargeable to income tax under ITTOIA 2005 Part 2. The definition of a trade has been restrictively interpreted in *Marson v Morton* (1986) in which the judge stated that:

'the mere fact that land is not income producing should not be decisive or even virtually decisive on the question whether it was bought as an investment'.

However, land originally acquired for a non-trading purpose (eg investment) may subsequently be appropriated to trading stock. At this point a CGT charge may arise under TCGA 1992 s 161 although this can be avoided by the election to transfer the land at no gain/no loss. In *Taylor v Good* (1974), discussed at **[10.23]**, the house in question did not become trading stock merely because the taxpayer had applied for planning permission before the sale:

'If you find a trade in the purchase and sale of land, it may not be difficult to find that properties originally owned (for example) by inheritance, or bought for investment only, have been brought into the stock in trade of that trade. But where, as here, there is no question at all of absorption into a trade of dealing in land or lands previously acquired with no thought of dealing, there is no ground at all for holding that activities such as those in the present case, designed only to enhance the value of the land in the market, are to be taken as pointing to, still less as establishing, an adventure in the nature of trade.' (Russell LJ)

By contrast, in *Pilkington v Randall* (1966) land was held in a will trust for a brother and sister absolutely. It was sold at different times and roads and drains were constructed prior to the sales. Furthermore, the brother bought parcels of the land from his sister. He was held to be trading. At first instance, Cross J stated:

'I do not think that one can lay down hard and fast rules, such as that the construction of roads and sewers and the installation of services can never be enough to make the case one of embarking upon a trade. One has to look at the whole picture and say whether the amount of money spent on the development before sale and the objects for which and the circumstances in which the money was spent are such as to make it reasonable to say that what was inherited has changed its character and become part of the raw material or stock in trade of a business.'

In the Court of Appeal, Danckwerts LJ likewise stated that there was no general proposition of law to the effect that whenever a property owner develops his land by making roads and laying sewers and selling plots he can never be carrying on a trade:

'This would be opening the door very wide to modern property developers. I think the highest it can be put is that usually in such circumstances the property owner is not carrying on a trade, but whether in the particular case he is or is not doing so must depend on the facts of the particular case. It is essentially a question of fact and degree.'

It is apparent from the forgoing cases that how the land came to be owned by the taxpayer is an important factor in determining whether he is trading. If it is acquired by *inheritance* or *gift* HMRC will have to show that it has at some point been appropriated to trading stock (in such cases it may also be argued that the land has not been 'acquired' as required by s 776(2)(a)). On the other hand, if acquired *by purchase* the taxpayer's motive at that time will be relevant. If it is clear that it was acquired as an investment, again the burden will be on HMRC to show that at a subsequent stage it was appropriated to trading stock. Furthermore, if land was originally acquired as an investment, the mere act of obtaining planning permission prior to a sale will not by itself result in an appropriation of the land to trading stock. Generally the taxpayer is entitled to get the best possible price for the land (*Taylor v Good*, above).

Care needs to be exercised if, as a prelude to sale to a developer, the taxpayer decides to acquire adjacent parcels of land. Such extra parcels will have been acquired purely for resale and there is a risk therefore that the taxpayer will be treated as a trader (and not just in relation to those portions but also in relation to the previously owned land). The purchase of small areas of land need not necessarily create problems: the taxpayer may merely be taking steps to obtain the best possible price for his existing land as in

*Taylor v Good*. However, it would naturally be advisable, whenever practicable, to arrange for the developer to acquire any extra land that will be needed for the development.                                                        **[12.102]**

### 3   The effect of falling within s 776

The section converts a gain that would otherwise be of a capital nature (and therefore in the case of an individual subject to CGT) into an income profit subject to income tax for the chargeable period in which that gain is realised (s 776(3)). The gain is to be computed by such method as is 'just and reasonable' in all the circumstances (s 776(6)) so that CGT computational rules will not necessarily apply.

The effect of taxing the gain as income is that for an *individual* the maximum rate of charge is 40%. The lower rates applicable to corporation tax may make it advantageous to shelter the gain in a company. If the gain is realised by *trustees*, income tax will be charged at basic rate. If there is an interest in possession, as a matter of trust law the capital sum will not belong to the life tenant and it is not thought that the amount charged on the trustees by reason of s 776 can be treated as the income of the beneficiary. In general, therefore, gains realised through the medium of a trust will escape income tax at the top rate of 40% (subject to an exception where the trust income is deemed under the tax legislation to be that of the settlor: see further **Chapter 16**).

There remains a danger that trusts falling within TA 1988 s 686 will be subject to tax at 'the rate applicable to trusts' (40% for 2006–07). That section applies in two situations. *First*, to 'income which is to be accumulated'. These words are not thought appropriate to catch a sum that remains, for trust purposes, capital. *Secondly*, the section applies to income 'which is payable at the discretion of the trustees' and it is arguable that a sum treated as income by s 776 could fall within these words if the trustees of a settlement have a power to pay or advance capital to beneficiaries. Accordingly, there is a danger of an income tax charge in such cases at the 40% rate on s 776 gains. As against this construction of s 686, it is thought that the word 'income' is used throughout the provision in a purely trust sense and will not apply to capital sums deemed to be income under the tax legislation. HMRC are not known to have taken the point that payments caught by s 776 fall within the provisions of s 686.

The gain is taxed as unearned income so that, although it may be reduced by other unearned income losses, it cannot be reduced by pension contributions nor by trading losses.                                                        **[12.103]**

### 4   When does s 776 apply?

The following requirements must be satisfied:
(1)  *Requirement I*—either:
    (a)   the land or property deriving its value from land is acquired with the sole or main object of realising a gain from disposing of the land (s 776(2)(a)); or
    (b)   land is held as trading stock (s 776(2)(b)); or

      (c)   the land held is developed with the sole or main object of realising a gain from disposing of the land when developed (s 776(2)(c)).

(2)   *Requirement II*—a gain of a capital nature is obtained.

(3)   *Requirement III*—the gain is obtained from a disposal of the land.

(4)   *Requirement IV*—that gain must be obtained either:

      (a)   by the person who acquired, held or developed the land or any connected person(s); or

      (b)   as a result of a scheme or arrangement which has allowed a gain to be realised by an indirect method by any person who is a party to or concerned in the arrangements or the scheme.   **[12.104]**

## 5   Comments on Requirement I

If land is held as trading stock or obtained with the main purpose of selling at a profit, that profit will be subject to tax under the trading income provisions of ITTOIA 2005 in the majority of cases (see **[12.102]**). However, a disposal of land is widened in s 776(4) to include transactions, arrangements, and schemes concerning the land or property deriving its value from the land as a result of which there is a disposal of the land or control over the land. Hence, it is likely that s 776(2)(a) will apply in cases where the land (or more likely property deriving its value from the land) is acquired with the intent of transferring control over the land by some indirect means.

An owner-occupier who decides to develop his land will naturally fall within s 776(2)(c). It is provided in s 776(7) that the relevant gain is that arising after the intention to develop is formed. Apart from the difficulties of determining when this occurs, the formation of this intention may result in the land becoming trading stock, with the result that any charge will arise under ITTOIA 2005 Part 2 (former Case I) (see also s 777(11)). The owner-occupier who sells his land for development by a third party will not normally fall within this provision unless he stipulates for some future payment linked to the value of the land after it has been developed (see **[12.108]**).   **[12.105]**

## 6   Comments on Requirement II

As the gain must be of a capital nature, the section does not catch trading profits nor other gains of an income nature. Hence, if land is let there will be no charge under s 776 if rent only (assessable under the property business rules) is payable. Thus s 777(13) provides that a 'capital amount' means a sum that (apart from these provisions) does not fall to be included in the calculation of a person's income for the purposes of the Taxes Acts. A trading profit made by an overseas trust or company and not subject to UK tax under the Taxes Acts may, therefore, amount to a gain of a capital nature for these purposes (see *Yuill v Wilson* (1980) at **[12.110]**).   **[12.106]**

## 7   Comments on Requirement III

For a charge under s 776 to arise there must be a disposal of land. 'Disposal' is not defined but it may include the disposal of shares in a land company and an interest in a company, partnership or trust which is wound up.

Land is also deemed to be disposed of if, as a result of arrangements and schemes falling within s 776(4), there is an effective disposal of the land itself or control over the land. It is a moot point whether the letting of land at a rack rent is a disposal. Given that the value of the property in the hands of the taxpayer is unchanged, it may be argued that such a lease does not involve any disposal of land despite the fact that such a letting does confer rights in land on the tenant.

For tax to be imposed it is also necessary for a gain to be *realised*. Under s 777(13) this will only occur when a person can effectively enjoy or dispose of money or money's worth. In the case of the right to future sums the question is, therefore, whether such sums can be valued and treated as part of the disposal proceeds (see *Yuill v Wilson* (1980)). A further disposal for the purposes of s 776 will occur when sums become quantifiable (see *Yuill v Fletcher* (1984)).                                          **[12.107]**

## 8   Comments on Requirement IV

The person who holds or develops the land may be caught as may a person connected with him (for 'connected persons', see TA 1988 s 839). In addition, a gain realised through a scheme or arrangement by an indirect method, or as a result of a series of transactions, will lead to a s 776 charge on any person concerned in that scheme or arrangement. In such cases, tax is imposed to the extent of the gain realised by the particular individual as can be seen by the case of *Winterton v Edwards* (1980). In that case L was the prime mover in a complicated tax avoidance scheme and owned all the shares in the relevant property company except for two small holdings owned by W and B. He acquired two sites outside the company for development and when W and B protested at this he arranged to give them a share in any sale proceeds from the land. Section 776 assessments on W and B were upheld because, although they were not parties to L's various transactions, they were *concerned in* the transactions as a result of their small interests in the proceeds of sale. Hence, if one person intends to realise a gain within s 776 (in this case both acquiring and developing land with the intention of realising a gain on its disposal) other persons may then be caught, even though they lack that intention, if they participate in the arrangement.

The phrase 'scheme or arrangement' is wide enough to catch a vendor or landowner who retains a share of the ultimate development profits. In *Page v Lowther* (1983), trustees owned four houses forming a site suitable for redevelopment. They granted a 99-year lease to the developers who in turn granted underleases of new dwellings when constructed at premiums payable partly to the trustees and partly to the developers. In all, the trustees received premiums totalling £1.2m. On these facts, the Court of Appeal held that the expression 'an arrangement or scheme' had no sinister overtones so that the grant of the lease by the trustees to the developers was such an arrangement. Further, the grant of the underlease was a disposal (albeit not by the trustees) in return for a capital sum so that the trustees were held liable on their share under s 776. The Court of Appeal did not accept that the duty of the trustees to obtain the best possible price afforded any defence to them. The case is authority for the proposition that the section is not limited to artificial transactions nor need tax avoidance be a motive on the part of the taxpayer (see **[12.101]**). For the rate of tax charged on the trustees, see **[12.103]**.

**[12.108]**

### 9 Shares in landholding companies

There is a disposal of land if control over it is disposed of (s 776(4)). Hence the disposal of a controlling shareholding in a landowning company is treated as a disposal of the land.

The further requirement, that a gain of a capital nature must be obtained from the disposal by a person owning that land *or by any connected person,* may be satisfied when shares in a landowning company are sold if the vendor controls that company. In such a case he will then be a connected person (s 839(6)). If two or more shareholders act together their interests may be aggregated in order to determine whether they have control for these purposes: the agreement of a number of minority shareholders to sell their shares may amount to an 'arrangement' under s 776(4).

There is an exemption from charge under s 776(10) when land is held as trading stock by a company and there is a disposal of the shares in that company *provided* that the land is subsequently disposed of by the company in the normal course of its trade in order to ensure that all opportunity of profit in respect of that land arises to the company. To take advantage of this exemption it is normal when selling a property dealing company to obtain from the purchaser a warranty that the trading stock (ie the land) will be sold in the normal course of the trade. However, it is obviously difficult to draft such warranties and the vendor remains very much in the hands of the purchaser. It should also be noted that this exemption does not furnish any defence when a scheme or arrangement has been entered into.     **[12.109]**

### 10 Providing an opportunity

A gain may be obtained for another person (eg under s 776(7) trusts are treated as distinct entities from the beneficiaries). In general, a gain is obtained in such circumstances if the opportunity of making that gain is transmitted by premature sale or otherwise (s 776(5)): eg if B allows value to pass out of his land into A's land whereupon A makes a gain falling within the section, all or part of that gain may be attributed to B (s 776(8)). In such cases B is given a right of recovery against A for the tax that he suffers (under s 777(8)(a)) although this may prove to be worthless if A is a non-resident.

The opportunity of making a gain is not presumably transmitted merely because land is sold even when it is possible that a gain will be made in the future. As the following case illustrates, however, it is no defence to claim under this section that the land was transferred for full consideration.

In *Yuill v Wilson* (1980), Mr Yuill, who controlled various UK companies, arranged for land to be sold to Guernsey companies who thereupon obtained planning consent for redevelopment and sold the land back to a Yuill UK company at a substantial profit. This profit constituted a gain of a capital nature (see **[12.106]**) and Mr Yuill was treated as a person who indirectly furnished the opportunity for the making of that gain. It was Yuill personally who was subject to charge not the companies which he controlled and which actually transferred the land to the Guernsey company. Note also that all these transactions were at market value. It is somewhat surprising that sales at full value can be regarded as a transfer of an opportunity to make a gain simply because at some later date the market value of the land increases.

Does an outright sale of land with the benefit of planning permission constitute the transmission of an opportunity? It is generally thought that the answer to this question is no, so long as the sale is a genuine transaction to an unconnected person for which full consideration is paid.          **[12.110]**

## 11  Typical situations

*First*, a landowner may sell his land for a capital sum at a time when there is obviously development potential. That sale will not usually be a trading transaction (assuming that there are no other trading factors present) and s 776 will also be inapplicable assuming that it is on arm's length terms to an unconnected person (see **[12.110]**).

*Secondly*, the landowner may obtain planning permission and then sell the land. This is not usually trading (see *Taylor v Good*, **[12.102]**) and s 776 will not apply if the sale is at arm's length etc (see **[12.110]**).

*Thirdly*, the landowner may develop his own land. On an eventual disposal of the land or an interest therein he will be subject to an income tax charge either as a trader or under s 776. In both cases his gain will be computed from the time when the intention to develop was formed. If a landowner buys extra land with a view to developing the enlarged site he may then become a trader (see **[12.102]**). Similarly, there is a risk of trading if agreements are entered into with an adjacent landowner (such agreements may even result in the formation of a trading partnership) although a mere agreement to find a single purchaser for two parcels of land should not have this result.

*Finally*, a vendor or landowner who intends to sell but who wishes to obtain a slice of any future development profits runs the risk of falling within *Page v Lowther* (see **[12.108]**). In this case the courts proposed a fairly general test for the applicability of s 776: for instance 'has a gain of a capital nature been derived from the relevant disposal?' (which will usually be the leasing of the developed site) and 'did the (original landowner) obtain any gain from the disposals effected by the under-leases?'          **[12.111]**

## 12  Possible ways of avoiding s 776 but still obtaining 'a slice of the action'

A vendor could insert a covenant against development into the contract of sale and subsequently agree to release this in return for a capital sum. Although this arrangement may offer advantages when there is no immediate prospect of the purchaser wishing to develop the land it is impractical if that is his immediate intention. Furthermore, such restrictions may not be commercially acceptable to the purchaser.

Alternatively, provision could be made in the original sale agreement for a further sum to be payable based on a proportion of the market value of the land after it has been developed. Arguably this does not constitute a gain of a capital nature derived from a disposal of land falling within s 776(2)(c) and the other subsections ((a) and (b)) are inapplicable. Further, even if this sum is calculated by reference to rents achieved, it is thought that the capital sum is still not derived from a *particular disposal.*

There are two major objections to this arrangement. *First,* the developer may find it unacceptable since it imposes an obligation on him to pay a capital sum unrelated to moneys received for letting the developed site. (Thus it will be payable even if he fails to let or sell that site.) *Secondly,* this may be a scheme or arrangement sufficient to be caught on the reasoning in *Page v Lowther* (see [12.108]). *Thirdly,* it has been suggested that the arrangement involves the landowner in trading. This view may be doubted: if it is correct it is difficult to see why *Page v Lowther* was argued under s 776 since the arrangements in that case would be trading transactions.

A further possibility is to shelter the gain by transferring the land to a trading company. This operation should be carried out before any development is undertaken and the result will then be that the land is held as trading stock so that any profit from the development will be an income receipt of that company (but taxed, at most, at 30%) and therefore a gain of a capital nature will not have been obtained. This arrangement depends upon the existence of a suitable company and there is obviously a risk of a s 776 charge if the shares in that company are subsequently sold for a capital sum (see [12.109]).

As an alternative sheltering device, ensure that any gain is realised by trustees. Only the basic rate of tax (22%) will be payable unless s 686 can be invoked by HMRC (see [12.103]).

Finally, ensure that a capital sum is not received from a disposal of the developed land. Assume, for instance, that the purchaser/developer agrees that he would only take a rack rent (not premiums) on lettings of the developed site. For s 776 to apply in this case, a capital sum received by the taxpayer would have to fall within sub-s (2)(c). Under that provision it is necessary for land to be developed 'with the sole or main object of realising a gain from disposing of the land when developed'. It is arguable that the grant of leases at a rack rent is not a disposal (see [12.107]) and furthermore, that the receipt of rents will not amount to the realisation of a *gain* for the purpose of the subsection. The difficulties with this arrangement are, *first,* will the purchaser agree to accept only a rental return? And *secondly,* the original vendor remains entitled on the properties being let to a capital sum based upon a multiple of the rental value. Thus, it is arguable that *Page v Lowther* may apply since he will then have obtained a capital sum from a disposal of the developed land, albeit that that sum was paid by the original purchaser not the sub-lessee.                                          [12.112]

## 13   Other matters

Although there is a clearance procedure under s 776(11), opinions vary as to whether it should be used. In *Page v Lowther,* for instance, clearance was refused, the scheme went ahead and was then challenged. There are those who feel that applying for clearance merely puts the Revenue on notice. Unlike the other clearance procedures (eg under TA 1988 s 707 and TCGA 1992 s 138) the application must be made to the local tax office: ie the matter is considered at a much lower level where there is obviously a temptation simply to issue a blanket refusal giving no reasons.

Section 776 applies to non-UK residents if all or any part of the land is situated in the UK (s 776(13)). When the person entitled to the consideration is not resident in the UK the Revenue can require the payer to deduct income tax at the basic rate from the consideration and pay it over to the Revenue (s 777(9) and see *Pardoe v Entergy Power Development Corp* (2000)). This can apply even if the recipient is not the taxable person but the Revenue obviously needs to know about the transaction in advance and this will not normally be the case. Section 776 does not apply to a gain arising to an individual on the disposal of his principal private residence which is exempt from CGT (TCGA 1992 ss 222 ff), or (generously) which would be exempt from CGT were it not that the property was acquired with the intention of making a gain on its disposal (TCGA 1992 s 223(3)).          **[12.113]**

# 13 Miscellaneous income

*Written by Rupert Shiers, Associate, McGrigors*

## I SCOPE

With effect from tax year 2005–06, the rules on miscellaneous income are expressed differently for income tax and corporation tax, and found in different Acts. However, the new income tax rules (in ITTOIA 2005) are broadly a rewrite of the old rules (described here as 'Case VI'), and for corporation tax purposes those old rules continue to apply just as they did before the rules were split. Therefore, although there are technical differences, the scope of the charge is similar. It is expected that this twin system will remain in place until the corporation tax rules have also been rewritten.

The first role of Case VI is as a residual or 'sweeping-up' case. The rules are in Schedule D Case VI, the last case of Schedule D, set out at the very end of TA 1988 s 18(3). This provides that tax shall be charged under Case VI on 'any annual profits or gains not falling under any other case of Schedule D and not charged by virtue of Schedule A ...'. For income tax, the corresponding rules are found in ITTOIA 2005 Part 5 Chapters 7–8, which charge tax on any annual payments that are not charged to income tax under any other provision (s 683) and any income from any source (ie, excluding annual payments) that is not charged to income tax under any other provision (s 687). Much of the discussion in this chapter deals with the principles surrounding this 'residual' or 'sweeping-up' role.

However, neither Case VI nor the corresponding ITTOIA concept of miscellaneous income is just a default head of charge. Various specific corporation tax charges (and income tax charges not yet rewritten by the Tax Law Rewrite Committee) throughout the Taxes Acts are expressly made under Case VI, and ITTOIA 2005 Part 5 contains five specific charges to tax under the 'miscellaneous' heading, in addition to the catch-all provisions in ss 683 and 687. This chapter contains an outline discussion of these charges. As noted below, many of these charges are also discussed in more detail elsewhere in this book.

Further, in appropriate corporation tax circumstances HMRC can choose which Case of Schedule D to apply to particular profits. Although this principle has now been heavily restricted in practice, it is still a key tenet in one very significant area (the taxation of life assurance companies); that whole area proceeds on the basis that profits which might otherwise be taxed as trading profits will normally be taxed instead under Case VI. This is also discussed in outline below.

The concluding section of this chapter also deals with certain procedural aspects of Case VI and the catch-all ITTOIA provisions.               **[13.1]**

## II   THE VARIOUS CHARGES

### 1   The general charge (TA 1988 s 18(3), ITTOIA 2005 ss 683, 687)

Prior to the split of the 'miscellaneous income' rules, the starting point for the student of Case VI in its 'sweeping-up' capacity was the statement by Lord Blackburn in *Attorney-General v Black* (1871). He said that the expression 'annual profits or gains' in Case VI is to be construed *ejusdem generis* with the profits and gains specified in the other Cases of Schedule D. In practice, this means that profits are only caught if they are of an income nature and arise from a taxable source. If those two conditions are satisfied, the profits will be taxable as income; the only question that remains is whether they are caught by another Case of Schedule D, or fall into the residual Case VI.

Of course, those rules now apply in terms only to corporation tax, but this same principle has now been spelt out in the corresponding provisions of ITTOIA (ss 683 and 687). These both expressly tax only income and both catch only income from a 'source' (for s 683 annual payments, for s 687 any other source). It is considered that the Case VI case law can be used to interpret these terms. 'Income' in ITTOIA must mean exactly the same as 'annual profits and gains' in Case VI. Further, as no guidance appears on the meaning of the word 'source' here, it can be safely assumed that the case law analysis should continue to apply. Therefore, the discussion below applies equally to income tax (under the residual ITTOIA charges) and corporation tax (under Case (VI) itself).               **[13.2]**

### a)   *Of an income nature?*

The use of the word 'annual' in s 18(3) means only that (as with the other Cases of Schedule D) profits must be of an income nature to be chargeable under Schedule D Case VI. For income tax purposes, this same rule is codified in ss 683 and 687 ITTOIA 2005 by the use of the word 'income'. Therefore, the principles discussed in **[10.103]** on the boundary between income and capital will apply equally here. In particular, there is absolutely no rule that profits must recur each year to be taxable as miscellaneous income. In brief, where profits are derived from the provision of services, or the exploitation of a capital asset, then those profits will be treated as having an income quality. However, where profits are derived instead from the disposal of a capital asset, or a sufficiently substantial interest in a capital asset, they will be treated as of a capital nature and so are not taxable as income at all (but only as chargeable gains). A high proportion of the reported cases on Case VI turned on this issue. Therefore, in *Hobbs v Hussey* (1942) where a solicitor's clerk (who was not an author by vocation) contracted with a newspaper to write his memoirs, the payment that he received was taxable under Schedule D Case VI as a payment for services. In *Benson v Counsell* (1942), the sale of stud rights in a stallion in which the taxpayer had a part-share was also held to be an activity taxable under Case VI, being the exploitation of the taxpayer's rights arising under a capital asset: the interest in the stallion itself. In contrast, in *Trustees of Earl Haig v IRC* (1939), the trustees of Earl Haig's estate allowed an author to use Earl Haig's diaries for the purposes of writing a biography. It was held that the sums they received were capital in nature, being the sale price for the part-disposal of a pre-existing capital asset (the copyright in the diaries). It was clear that this was a disposal of a sufficiently important interest in that asset; three of the four members of the Court of Session expressly noted that this transaction largely exhausted the publication value of the diaries.

In certain circumstances, an activity may have aspects of both the provision of services and the sale of a capital asset. In this case, it is important to determine whether the profits are to be treated as income, or capital, or to be split between the two. In *Hobbs v Hussey* (1942), the taxpayer not only provided services to the newspaper, but also assigned (or at least licenced) the copyright in his words to them. However, on the facts, the court found that the assignment of copyright was of little importance. It characterised the transaction as one that involved, in substance, the provision of services, and imposed a tax treatment accordingly. By contrast, in *Hale v Shea* (1964) the court sought to apportion the taxpayer's profits between two separate aspects (even though this was not possible on the facts). The cases do not provide a clear test for when one aspect of a mixed transaction is to be subsumed within the other. However, it is considered that, in an appropriate case, the very helpful test set out by the ECJ in another context in the case of *Card Protection Plan Ltd v Customs and Excise Commissioners* (1999) (see **[30.71]**, **[37.25]** and **[40.36]**) could well be of assistance. **[13.3]**

b)   *A taxable source?*

Even if profits are of an income nature, they will only be taxable as income if they arise from a taxable source. The requirement for a taxable source does not fall to be considered in the other cases of Schedule D or (for income tax) the other ITTOIA charges, because those cases and charges are defined often so as only to cover profits arising from a particular source. However, the general principle is clearly established in the context of Case VI and (as noted above) has now been codified for the corresponding ITTOIA charges.

Authoritative statements on the need for a source ('the source doctrine') can be found in relation to many areas of the tax code. In the employment tax case of *Bray v Best* (1989) (see **[8.13]**–**[8.20]**) the House of Lords held that particular income was non-taxable as there was no source in the relevant period. In *Ryall v Hoare* (1923), Rowlatt J said that gambling winnings, gifts and items obtained by finding are generally not taxable: his reasoning is based on the proposition that such receipts have no relevant source. Therefore, in *Graham v Green* (1925), the profits of a professional gambler were held not to be subject to tax under Case VI (or, indeed, any other Case of Schedule D) as they then applied to income tax. It should be noted though that 'gambling' is to be narrowly construed, and it does not necessarily extend to profits on speculative transactions in financial instruments (see

*Coogan v Stubbs* (1925), below). More recently, in *Anise v Hammond* (2003) sums were held not to be taxable income because they had been received (broadly) by chance.

Broadly speaking, unless arising from a 'trade', 'profession' or 'vocation', income profits will only be taxable if they arise from the provision of services (as, in for instance, *Hobbs v Hussey* (1942)) or the exploitation of an asset. For income tax purposes prior to the introduction of ITTOIA it appeared that, for non-residents, the profits will only be taxable if the source is cited in the UK (*Alloway v Phillips* (1980)); this was presumably on the basis of the introductory words of Schedule D, though they were not as clear (at least in relation to services) as they might be. The position under ITTOIA is less clear.

Any services can amount to a source. However, there are two qualifications to bear in mind. First, it appears that only services which are more than minimal can only be a source: in *Dickinson v Abel* (1969) an 'introduction fee' was held to be a mere gift and escaped tax under Schedule D Case VI (and should now do so under ITTOIA s 687) because the taxpayer had provided no substantial services (in addition, there was no binding contract which could have been treated as a source). Further, the services must have been motivated at least in part by the prospect of a reward: in *Bloom v Kinder* (1958), a fee paid to a solicitor who had provided his services with no expectation of reward was held to be a mere gift.

Similarly, and as will be clear from cases referred to above, almost any asset can be a source for these purposes. The concept even extends to cover bare rights under a binding agreement (*Brocklesby v Merricks* (1934)). However, *Alloway v Phillips* (1980) seems to stand for the proposition that mere information does not count.   **[13.4]**

c)   *Caught by another head of charge?*

As noted above, even if profits are of an income nature and from a taxable source, they will not be taxable as miscellaneous income (ie under Case VI or ss 683 and 687) if they are taxed under another head. For Case VI purposes, the principal challenge is (and always has been) to determine whether profits are really trading profits or profits of a profession (ie some other Case of Schedule D). For ITTOIA purposes, the same question applies, but the technical question is whether they are caught by Part II. Although such profits will not be taxable as miscellaneous income if caught by another part of the legislation (say, Schedule A or F or, for income tax purposes, their ITTOIA equivalents or as employment income under ITEPA 2003), the need to compare the miscellaneous category and these other heads of charge does not arise frequently in practice, and so this is not dealt with in detail here.   **[13.5]**

*Case I—trading profits (ITTOIA Part 2: trading income)* Certain quasi-trading profits will not be caught by Case I or ITTOIA Part 2, and so will be taxable under Case VI (or ITTOIA s 687) instead.

Transactions carried out otherwise than with a profit motive will not be treated as trading transactions. Profits from such transactions will often be caught by Case VI (or ITTOIA s 687). In *Ryall v Hoare* (1923), Rowlatt J held that a fee paid to company directors for guaranteeing the company's overdraft was taxable under Schedule D Case VI, relying on the fact that the directors had given the guarantee only by way of a favour. Similarly, in *Clarke v British Telecom Pension Scheme Trustees* (2000), fees paid to the taxpayer for providing certain services were held to fall within Case VI on the basis that the taxpayer had provided the services not with a view to profit, but so as to protect the value of other investments. In *CIR v Forth Conservancy Board No 2* (1931) the House of Lords held that fees paid to a statutory body were taxable under Case VI rather than Case I, as it was not constituted as a profit-making body.

In addition, there are cases where profit-motivated quasi-trading activities have been taxed under Case VI on the basis that they do not amount to trade. In *Benson v Counsell* (above) profits from the sale of stud rights were held to be taxable under Case VI. In *Cooper v Stubbs* (1925) and *Townsend v Grundy* (1933), profits from transactions in cotton futures were held to be capable of being taxed under Case VI (and the profits in question in those cases were taxed in that way). It is notable, in particular, that these were not considered to be gambling profits. These decisions have now been reversed on their facts by TA 1988 s 128 (and now, for income tax purposes, ITTOIA 2005 s 779), which provide that dealings in commodity and financial futures, traded options and financial options which are not part of a trade and so to be taxed as such, or (for corporation tax purposes) caught by TA 1988 Sch 5AA, are to be charged to CGT rather than under Schedule D Case VI or ITTOIA Part 5 Chapter 8. However, *Cooper v Stubbs*, like *Benson v Counsell*, still stands as authority for the proposition that certain items of quasi-trading income will be taxable under Case VI or Chapter 8. It is necessary in such instances simply to consider whether the taxpayer can truly be said to be trading, which will be a question of fact in each case (see **[10.22]–[10.40]**).

However, it is necessary to avoid one widely-prevailing misconception. Despite the authorities cited above, it is often said that 'annual profits', if they arise from a quasi-trading transaction, will inevitably be taxable under Case I rather than Case VI. This is not the law. Authority for this mistaken proposition is usually taken from *Leeming v Jones* (1930). In that case, the taxpayer acquired rubber estates for resale at a profit, and then resold them at the hoped-for profit. The General Commissioners found that the taxpayer had not been trading, and the Revenue then sought to argue that the profit was assessable under Schedule D Case VI. The House of Lords held for the taxpayer, relying in part on the definition of 'trade' now found in TA 1988 s 832(1) which encompasses 'an adventure in the nature of a trade'. They said that either this transaction was 'an adventure in the nature of a trade' in which case the profit was a trading receipt taxable under Schedule D Case I (see **[10.22]–[10.40]**), or a capital transaction. Either way, Case VI was not applicable. However, it is quite clear from the speeches in the House of Lords that this is very much a decision on its own facts. Their Lordships had no doubt that the purchase of assets for resale is either a trading activity or a capital activity, and they held that, in this case, it was a capital activity. *Leeming v Jones* says nothing whatsoever about whether a particular activity producing profits of an income character might be something different from a trade, and so taxable as miscellaneous income (as it was in *Cooper v Stubbs*).

*Case II—profits from a profession or vocation*  Very many of the cases where profits have been taxed under Case VI involve profits realised from the performance of casual services. Neither 'profession' nor 'vocation'—the terms which made up the old Schedule D Case II—is extended in the way that 'trade' is extended by TA 1988 s 832(1) (which definition, by virtue of Schedule 4, is carried over into ITTOIA 2005) to include an adventure in the nature of a 'trade'. Accordingly, the profits of one-off quasi-professional or quasi-vocational transactions have historically fallen outside Schedule D Case II, and if annual profits fell into Case VI. With the introduction of ITTOIA 2005, the idea of 'Case II' as a stand-alone item is now effectively defunct (a number of provisions, including particularly ss 24 and 241, make clear that for ITTOIA 2005 purposes the rules are folded into Part 2 which deals with trades, and Case II has never had significant scope in the corporation tax context) but the rules continue to apply in the same way.

The 'profession' or 'vocation' at stake in many of the reported cases (such as *Hobbs v Hussey* (1942) and *Alloway v Phillips* (1980), noted above) has been that of author. However, the cases do not provide much in the way of guidance as to how frequently a particular activity must be pursued in order for it to become a profession or vocation in that way. It appears that this is to be considered a question of fact in each case.                    **[13.6]**

*Cases III, IV and V—other profits*    It has always been quite clear, in any given case, whether a particular item of income falls within one of Cases III, IV and V, or falls instead within Case VI. Each of Cases III, IV and V is defined by reference to a readily identifiable source (broadly, money or certain securities, non-UK securities and non-UK possessions, respectively). There is one exception: following *Colquhoun v Brooks* (1889), the concept of 'possession' for the purposes of Case V includes a trade, and accordingly there may be questions as to whether a non-UK activity is a trade so that its profits are taxable under Case V, or not so that its profits are taxed instead under Case VI. However, in those circumstances, by virtue of the general words in TA 1988 s 18(1), the profits of that activity may not be amenable to Schedule D tax in any event.

For income tax purposes under ITTOIA 2005, the point of principle remains the same (though the application will be somewhat different, particularly as Cases IV and V no longer exist, their effect being recreated by bolting on special non-UK-source rules to the normal code dealing with trading, property, and savings income). To identify whether income is taxable under Part 5 Chapter 8 it is simply necessary to clarify whether it is caught instead by another section (for its residual character see, in particular, ITTOIA 2005 ss 575 and 576). Subject to points of detail that will only be clarified as ITTOIA 2005 comes to be operated and tested in practice, it can reasonably be expected that income from money and securities will be caught by Part 4, and from other property will be caught by Part 5.    **[13.7]**

## 2   Various specific provisions

As noted above, there are a significant number of specific charging provisions that bring items into charge as Case VI profits. In particular, for corporation tax purposes the charge under TA 1988 s 703 to effectively cancel any tax advantage arising from certain 'transactions in securities' (TA 1988 ss 703–709; see **[42.100]**) is a charge under Case VI. An exhaustive analysis of each such provision is beyond the scope of this work. However, other items specifically charged as Case VI profits include:

(1) Payments received for 'know-how' if not taxed as a trade receipt or as a capital gain:
For individuals: ITTOIA 2005 ss 583
For corporations: TA 1988 s 531(4); see **[10.108]**.

(2) Certain receipts after a change of accounting basis or cessation of a trade:
For individuals: ITTOIA 2005 s 242
For corporations: TA 1988 ss 103–104; see **[10.80]**.

(3) Various profits of life assurance companies:
corporations only: (principally, TA 1988 ss 431–458A and FA 1989).

(4) Income from certain settlements that is taxed as that of the settlor:
For individuals: eg under ITTOIA 2005 ss 619–648 and Sch 2 para 132; see **[12.101]**.

(5) Disposal proceeds of interests in offshore 'roll-up' funds:
For individuals and corporations: TA 1988 ss 757–764.

(6) Capital gains arising from certain transactions in land:
For individuals and corporations: TA 1988 s 776; see **[12.101]**.

(7) Capital gains from securities transactions intended to produce a guaranteed return:
For individuals: ITTOIA 2005 ss 555–569 and Sch 1 para 434 and Sch 2 para 95
For corporations: TA 1988 Sch 5AA para 1(1).

(8) The profits of theatre backers (by ESC A94).

(9) The entry charge and anti-avoidance charge for companies that elect to be taxed under the Real Estate Investment Trust Regime (FA 2006, ss 112 and 117)

In addition to ss 683 and 687, Part V of ITTOIA charges income tax on:

(1) receipts from intellectual property (ss 579 and 587: see also s 583 in relation to know-how as referred to in (1) above);

(2) films and sound recordings (otherwise than from a trade) (see s 609);

(3) telecommunications rights (otherwise than from a trade) (see s 614);

(4) settlement income where it is treated as income of the settlor (ss 619–648, and see (4) above);

(5) beneficiaries' income from estates in administration (s 649).     **[13.8]**


## 3  Taxation under Case VI by Revenue election

As noted in **[6.42]** above, it has been clear since the case of *London and Liverpool and Globe Insurance Co v Bennett* (1913) that (as Lord Shaw of Dunfermline said in that case) 'if a sufficient warrant be found in the Statute for taxation under alternate heads, the alternative lies with the taxing authority'. However, as a matter of the Schedular system, this position only applies as between different Cases in a single Schedule: *Fry v Salisbury House Estate Ltd* (1930) makes clear that there is no scope for overlap between the Schedules themselves. Following the introduction of ITTOIA 2005, it is quite clear that Part 8 can only be invoked in the income tax context where no other head of charge is available.

Even prior to ITTOIA 2005, the importance of the rule in *London and Liverpool* was probably diminishing; it appears from FA 1998 Sch 18 para 84 that it was thought, practically, only to apply in one or two situations. However, one of those situations—which still applies, arising as it does in a corporation tax context—is very significant, as it relates to the taxation of life assurance companies. This is a very complex subject, far beyond the scope of this work. However, it is not possible to sensibly discuss Schedule D Case VI without at least a reference to the topic. In particular, life assurance companies almost certainly pay more tax under Case VI than all other taxpayers combined.

In briefest outline, the business of writing life assurance policies involves the collection of premiums, investment of those premiums, and then, as appropriate, payment to the policyholder of a lump sum after a certain amount of time has expired or a particular event has occurred (typically, the death of the policyholder). However, the policy terms will very frequently provide that the lump sum will depend somewhat on the value of the investments held by the life assurance company. Therefore, a part of any profit that the company may make from investment of premiums will be matched by a corresponding increase in the company's liabilities to policy-holders.

When computing its trading profits under Schedule D Case I for any given year, a life assurance company can claim a deduction for any increase in its liability to policyholders (following *Scottish Union and National Insurance Co v Smiles and Northern Assurance Co v Russell* (1889)). However, that right to a deduction does not apply to the calculation of profits under any other Case of Schedule D. It is axiomatic that, except where specifically prohibited by the legislation, HMRC can choose instead to tax those investment profits under Schedule D Case VI. Because the life assurance company can claim no deduction under Case VI in respect of liabilities to policyholders, if HMRC choose to tax under Case VI then tax is charged not only the life assurance company's share of the investment profits, but also on the profits which will ultimately pass to the policyholders when they receive payment on their policies.

Taxation of the global amount of investment profits in this way is known as the 'income less expenses' or 'I minus E' basis of taxation. Extremely detailed rules for its operation are set out in the Taxes Acts, principally in TA 1988 ss 431–458A and FA 1989. For further analysis of this area, reference should be made to a specialist work.

As noted above, it is thought that HMRC do not now exercise any right to choose between Cases in many other situations. In relation to Case VI, the author is certainly not aware of any such situations in practice.    **[13.9]**


## III  PROCEDURAL ASPECTS

For corporation tax purposes, tax is calculated under Schedule D Case VI on the full amount of the profits or gains arising in the period in question (TA 1988 ss 69, 70). However, there is authority for the proposition that profits are taxable when received, rather than when they become due *Grey v Tiley* (1932). It is thought at least possible that the courts would no longer uphold this position, but there is no contrary authority as yet. There are no express rules for deductible expenses, but it is considered that the words 'profits or gains' imply a surplus of income after deducting expenses (see, for instance, *CIR v Forth Conservancy Board* (above)). There seems to be a technical argument that the restrictions in TA 1988, s 74 **[10.138]** on deductions which are allowable in computing profits for Case I and II purposes do not apply to Case VI profits. However, it is not considered that much is made of this in practice. Any corporation tax loss arising on Schedule D Case VI transactions can only be used against profits from other Case VI transactions in the same tax year or in future years (TA 1988 s 396). However, there is no general right to set losses against other income or gains (unlike the position for losses arising under Schedule D Cases I and II **[10.131]**).

From an income tax perspective ITTOIA 2005 fails to clarify many of these issues; it can be assumed that the case law noted above will continue to apply. Income is still charged on income 'arising' in the period (ss 684 and 688), and bar some specific deductions in s 688(2) there is no express rule on the deductibility of expenses (for s 687—there is obviously no question of deducting expenses in respect of s 683 income). Prior to the introduction of ITTOIA 2005, Case VI losses could be set off against Case VI profits and also pension income under ITEPA 2003 Pt 9 (TA 1988 s 392); that provision remains in force and is considered to apply equally to losses arising under transactions which, if profitable, would incur tax under s 687.        **[13.10]**

# 14 Annual payments and savings income

*Written and updated by Natalie Lee, Barrister, Senior Lecturer in Law, University of Southampton*

## I GENERAL

### 1 Introduction

Schedule D Case III which, until 6 April 2005, charged to tax interest, annuities and other annual payments, has been abolished for income tax purposes, and is replaced by provisions in the Income Tax (Trading and Other Income) Act 2005 (ITTOIA) (the provisions of the TA 1988 remain in force for corporation tax). As with the two previous pieces of rewritten tax legislation (see **[1.22]**), this new Act does not change the *substance* of the law but, rather, endeavours to set it out in a clearer fashion. Thus, the form has changed considerably.                                              **[14.1]**

### 2 Ambit of charge to tax on annual payments and savings income

ITTOIA 2005 Part 5 imposes a charge to tax on miscellaneous income, which includes annual payments not otherwise charged to tax. Part 4 of the new Act provides for 'savings and investment income'. This includes, amongst other things, charges to tax on interest, purchased life annuities, discounted securities and distributions from unauthorised unit trusts. All of these will be discussed in this chapter. Other heads of charge include dividends from resident and non-UK resident companies (see **Chapter 42**), loans to participators in a close company which are waived (see **[7.25]**), gains from contracts for life insurance, etc (see **[15.2]**), transactions in deposits, disposals of futures and options involving guaranteed returns (see **[14.6]**) and sales of foreign dividend coupons (see **Chapter 18**).

Income discussed in this chapter is often termed 'pure income' because it is not normally reduced by any deductible expenses; it is pure profit. Annual payments are sometimes referred to as settlements of income since they can operate to reduce the income of the payer and increase that of the payee. Hence, the payer may be seen as settling an income sum on the payee. **[14.2]**

## 3    The tax is on income arising

Income tax is charged under ITTOIA 2005 Part 4 in respect of annual payments and on the person receiving or entitled to receive the income in question (in the case of payment by cheque the sum is received when it is credited to the account of the recipient; see *Parkside Leasing Ltd v Smith* (1985)). If the payment is not made at all, there is no liability to tax (*Woodhouse v IRC* (1936)). However, if it is paid late, the rate of tax deducted, and the time limits for a repayment claim, are determined in the case of a payment falling under TA 1988 s 348 by reference to the year when the payment fell due (*IRC v Crawley* (1987)).

In *MacPherson v Bond* (1985) a bank held a charge on the taxpayer's deposit account as security for a loan to a company. The taxpayer had not personally guaranteed this loan and accordingly interest earned on the deposit account and which was credited to it could not be said to reduce his personal liability. In the event, the company debt finally absorbed the whole of the deposit account plus interest but as Vinelott J explained:

> 'Even before the liability of the company to the bank had been finally determined ... the taxpayer's only prospect was that he would in time become entitled to repayment of so much of the deposit as was not required to meet the company's liability to the bank and to interest on that part of the deposit. The crediting of interest on the whole of the deposit could therefore be aptly described as a mere book entry: a matter of convenience of accounting for the bank.'

On the facts of this case, because the taxpayer was not entitled to the interest, he was not subject to any tax charge thereon. See also *Cooker v Foss* (1998) that involved a form of 'set-off' and *Girvan v Orange Personal Communications Services Ltd* (1998) where, due to a renegotiated agreement between the taxpayer and its bank, interest on deposit accounts was compounded quarterly and not paid until the accounts were closed. Since the compounded interest was retained by the bank, it was not income which arose until it was actually paid to the taxpayer on closure of the relevant accounts. Nor was the decision altered by the fact that the agreement had been renegotiated in order to gain a tax advantage. By contrast, if the security is backed up by a personal guarantee, interest credited to the account is not then a mere book entry but can be seen as reducing the sum payable by the taxpayer under the guarantee. It will, therefore, be subject to income tax in the hands of the taxpayer as it arises even though he does not actually receive it! (*Dunmore v McGowan* (1978); *Peracha v Miley* (1990) and on the general position of receipts and payments under guarantees, see *Taxation*, 1992, p 157.)) **[14.3]**

## 4  Basis of assessment

Income assessable under Part 4 and in respect of annual payments in Part 5 is charged to tax on the actual income of the fiscal year.                              **[14.4]**

## 5  Companies

Special rules apply for corporation tax purposes: see 'loan relationships' and TA 1988 s 18(3A) inserted by FA 1996 and modified and amended by FA 2002 and FA 2004.                              **[14.5]**

## II  TERMINOLOGY

## 1  Interest

Apart from payments treated as interest for certain purposes (ITTOIA 2005 s 369(2) and see FA 2005 ss 46–57 which provide that the same rules that apply for interest will apply to alternative finance arrangements) and specified exemptions (ITTOIA 2005 s 369(3)), the term 'interest' is not statutorily defined. It has been described as 'payment by time for the use of money' (*per* Rowlatt J in *Bennett v Ogston* (1930)). More precisely, interest:

> 'may be regarded either as representing the profit the lender might have made if he had had the use of the money, or conversely, the loss he suffered because he had not that use. The general idea is that he is entitled to compensation for the deprivation' (*per* Lord Wright in *Riches v Westminster Bank Ltd* (1947) 28 TC 159 at 189).

Interest generally presupposes the idea of a debt to be repaid (see, for instance, *Re Euro Hotel (Belgravia) Ltd* (1975)). The *Riches* case established that interest awarded by the court under the Law Reform (Miscellaneous Provisions) Act 1934 fell within the then Schedule D Case III charge, now ITTOIA 2005 s 369 (today the award is under either the Supreme Court Act 1981 s 35A or the County Courts Act 1984 s 69, but note that interest on damages paid for personal injuries or death is not taxed (ITTOIA 2005 ss 732–734)).

**EXAMPLE 14.1**

> Bigco Ltd executes a debenture deed in favour of Mr Big who has made a secured loan to the company of £10,000. The deed provides for repayment of the loan together with a 'premium' of £2,000 by the end of 2006 and interest at 10% pa on the full redemption figure (£12,000) until 2006. The interest falls within ITTOIA 2005 s 369 and the repayment of £10,000 is a capital sum. The so-called 'premium' may be seen as deferred interest or, alternatively, as a capital sum paid as compensation for the capital risk taken by Mr Big.

The true nature of the payment is a matter of fact and the terms used by the parties are not conclusive (see *Lomax v Peter Dixon & Son Ltd* (1943) and *Davies v Premier Investment Co Ltd* (1945)). So long as the rate of interest charged is commercial, it is likely that the sum on which the interest is calculated will be treated as capital and will escape both income tax and CGT unless the debt is a 'debt on a security' within the meaning of TCGA 1992 s 132 (see TCGA 1992 s 251 and **[22.44]**).

Finally, it should be noted that if the principal debtor defaults so that the moneys are paid under a contract of indemnity the sum will still be taxed as interest; if paid by a guarantor, the position is unclear (see *Re Hawkins, Hawkins v Hawkins* (1972) on indemnities and contrast *Holder v IRC* (1932) on guarantors).                                                      **[14.6]**

## 2    Purchased life annuities

Annuities fall into two broad categories. *First,* a purchased annuity usually arising from a contract with an insurance company under which a capital sum is paid in return for a right to income (an annuity) for a stated period of time (see **[14.41]**). *Secondly,* annuities payable under an instrument, such as an annuity provided for in a will. The changes made by FA 1988 in the treatment of annual payments (see **[14.13]**) did not affect annuities, and such annuities fall within the ambit of annual payments.                        **[14.7]**

## 3    Annual payments not otherwise charged to tax

Despite the fact that most annual payments have been taken outside the tax net altogether (see **[14.13]**), it is still important to be able to identify a certain sum of money as an annual payment. If such a sum is an annual payment, it cannot then fall within any other head of charge and be classified, for example, as trading or earned income; it will simply remain outside of the tax net. As the name suggests, annual payments not otherwise charged to tax comprise a residual category, although the term is wide enough to include an annuity. Hence, all annuities may be described as annual payments but not all annual payments as annuities. The main features of annual payments were laid down by Jenkins LJ in *IRC v Whitworth Park Coal Co Ltd* (1958):

'(1)    To come within the rule as an "other annual payment" the payment in question must be *ejusdem generis* with the specific instances given in the shape of interest of money and annuities ...

(2)    The payment in question must fall to be made under some binding legal obligation as distinct from being a mere voluntary payment ...

(3)    The fact that the obligation to pay is imposed by an order of the court and does not arise by virtue of a contract does not exclude the payment ...

(4)    The payment in question must possess the essential quality of recurrence implied by the description "annual" ... A payment is annual if it is recurrent or is capable of recurrence. Payments made at intervals of less than a year will still be "annual" provided that they may continue beyond a year. Only payments that are income in the hands of the recipient are included. Payments may, therefore, be annual income payments; or they may represent instalments of a capital sum; or they may represent part income and part capital (in the latter case the income element will usually be interest on a debt which is being repaid in instalments). ... In considering whether payments constitute capital and/or income, the form of the document drawn up by the parties is not conclusive and a payment may represent a capital expenditure of the payer, but an income receipt for the payee and, presumably, *vice versa.*

(5) The payment in question must be in the nature of a "pure income" profit in the hands of the recipient. Accordingly, the recipient must not have incurred allowable expenditure in return for the payment. This proposition prevents any attempt to disguise trading receipts as annual payments (see Scrutton LJ in *Howe v IRC* (1919)).'

**EXAMPLE 14.2**

Denis wants to sell his dental practice (which is worth £30,000) to Flossie and retire. The contract could be drawn up in a variety of different forms, eg:

(1) Flossie is to pay the purchase price of £30,000 over five years, at £6,000 pa. Each payment is a capital sum (see generally *IRC v Ramsay* (1935)).

(2) Flossie is to pay by instalments as in (1) above, but is to pay five instalments of £6,250 (so that the total sum to be paid will be £31,250). Each payment probably represents a capital and an income element and must accordingly be dissected. £6,000 is an instalment of capital and £250 interest on the unpaid balance (see *Secretary of State in Council of India v Scoble* (1903)).

(3) Denis agrees to be paid by Flossie either 15% of the profits of the business each year for the rest of his life or £1,000 pa whichever is the higher. Denis is in effect purchasing a life annuity so that the payments each year will be income in his hands (see *IRC v Church Comrs for England* (1977): ITTOIA s 717 (see **[14.41]**) does not apply by reason of s 423(1)); Flossie's payments are instalments of capital (see *IRC v Land Securities Investment Trust Ltd* (1969)). **[14.8]–[14.10]**

## III  THE TAXATION OF ANNUAL PAYMENTS

### 1  Annual payments in a modern context

a)  *The former attractions of annual payments*

One of the key features of annual payments has always been the way in which tax is collected, namely by deduction of basic rate income tax at source (see **[14.21]**), thus forging a distinction between the person on whom the burden of taxation falls on the one hand and, on the other, the person from which it is actually collected. In the case of annuities and annual payments, historically the payer was looked upon as having alienated that part of his income representing the annuity or annual payment. This resulted in such payments being deductible in computing the total income of the payer with the burden of both basic and higher rate tax thereby falling on the payee (but with basic rate tax being collected from the payer). As a consequence, annual payments were used over the years for the purposes of avoiding or minimising tax. A taxpayer, subject to the higher rates of tax, would assign a part of his income, eg by deed of covenant, to a taxpayer who paid no income tax, such as charity, or to one who paid at the lower rates of tax. In *IRC v Duke of Westminster* (1936), for instance, gardeners were paid by the Duke, their employer, by means of a deed of covenant in lieu of wages, with the advantageous tax result that the Duke escaped paying higher rate taxes on the covenanted sums. **[14.11]**

b)   *The growth of anti-avoidance legislation*

The ability to avoid tax in this way was reduced over the years by the enactment of provisions (now found in ITTOIA Part 5 Chapter 5 (see **[16.91]** ff) designed to prevent income tax benefits being obtained by:

(1)   short-term covenants not capable of lasting for more than six—or in the case of charities, three—years;

(2)   revocable settlements (including covenants);

(3)   an assignment of income to the infant unmarried child of the settlor (see **Chapter 16**);

(4)   covenants to trustees who do not distribute income.

Other annual payments not caught by these provisions were nevertheless limited in their effect by a provision that the taxpayer should be subject to excess liability (ie the difference between the higher rate and the basic rate of income tax) on the payment. So, if in 1987 a taxpayer had executed a seven-year covenant in favour of, say, his niece, while the recipient, the niece, would bear the burden of basic rate tax (collected at source from the payer), the taxpayer would be liable for any excess liability on the covenanted sum. Despite these endeavours of the legislature, annual payments continued to be used for tax avoidance purposes, notably covenants by grandparents in favour of their grandchildren for the payment of school fees, and by parents in favour of their adult children to support them during their time at college or university.                                                                          **[14.12]**

c)   *The 1988 and subsequent changes*

The process culminated in the enactment of FA 1988 s 36 (now ITTOIA 2005 s 727(1)) which had the dramatic effect of taking most annual payments by individuals outside the tax net altogether. Two further categories of annual payment have been removed from the tax net by more recent legislation. *First*, by virtue of FA 1999, relief for maintenance payments under a court order or agreement made prior to 15 March 1988 was withdrawn, generally from 6 April 2000 (see **[52.6]**). *Secondly*, FA 2000, took covenanted payments to charity outside of the charge under the former Schedule D Case III and incorporated them into the Gift Aid rules. As a result TA 1988, ss 348 and 349 (which provide for deduction of tax at source: see **[14.21]**), along with the anti-avoidance provisions in TA 1988 Part XV, have lost much of their impact.
**[14.13]**

2   **The charge to tax**

ITTOIA 2005 s 683(1) imposes a charge to tax on annual payments not otherwise charged to income tax. Section 683(4) provides for exemptions to the charge, including certain annual payments by individuals, but to this there are also exceptions (ss 727–730). In effect, what this means is that most individuals in receipt of annual payments will not suffer a charge under s 683. The payment will have been made out of the taxed income of the payer. There are exceptional cases, however, where the annual payment remains effective (see **[14.15]**–**[14.16]**) and in respect of which tax will continue to be collected at source under TA 1988 ss 348 and 349 (see

**[14.21]**), with the anti-avoidance rules remaining of importance. It should also be borne in mind that the ITTOIA 2005 Part 5 Chapter 5 provisions are concerned with capital as well as income settlements. This breadth of coverage is inevitable since, if it is desired to stop a particular income settlement from attracting fiscal benefit, it is necessary to cover a settlement of income-producing assets (ie capital) that might otherwise achieve the same result. The provisions in the context of capital settlements are considered in **Chapter 16**.

ITTOIA 2005 s 727 provides that:

'(1) No liability to income tax arises under Part 5 (s 683) in respect of an annual payment if it—

(a)    is made by an individual, and
(b)    arises in the United Kingdom.'

As already stated, the majority of annual payments now fall wholly outside the tax system. The section is, however, subject to the following exceptions.
**[14.14]**

a)    *The annual payment must be made by an individual*

ITTOIA 2005 s 727(1) is limited to annual payments made by individuals. Annuities, whether purchased or payable out of a deceased's estate, are therefore unaffected and, similarly, the beneficiary of a discretionary trust who receives income payments from the trustees will be charged to tax under s 683. **[14.15]**

b)    *Bona fide commercial payments*

Annual payments made for *bona fide* commercial reasons in connection with a trade, profession or vocation continue to fall within s 683. The main examples are annuities payable under partnership agreements to outgoing partners. **[14.16]**

c)    *The payment of interest*

These changes made over the years only applied to annual payments: the tax treatment of interest has continued unchanged (see **[14.31]**).
**[14.17]–[14.20]**

IV   THE MACHINERY OF TAX COLLECTION FOR ANNUAL PAYMENTS (TA 1988 ss 348–350)

1   **Deduction of tax at source**

One of the characteristic features of annual payments, although not applicable to all such payments, has always been that basic rate income tax is not directly assessed on the recipient but, rather, is deducted and collected at source from the payer by virtue of TA 1988 ss 348 and 349 (and s 3). Both s 348 and s 349 are designed to achieve the same objective: under both, the

Revenue collects basic rate income tax from the payer on the annual payment and the payer is permitted to deduct that sum from the amount paid to the payee. Generally, therefore, the payee will receive a net sum together with a credit for the basic rate income tax which has been deducted at source and paid to the Revenue on his behalf (note that TA 1988 s 3 specifically provides that deduction from annuities (other than purchased life annuities) and annual payments is made at the basic rate: this is unaffected by the existence of the lower rate: contrast, however, payments of interest and the income element of purchased life annuities from which the 20% rate is deducted). If he is not liable to pay income tax (because his income is below the taxable threshold) he will be entitled to repayment by the Revenue of the basic rate tax already paid on his behalf. The payee will be assessed directly to higher rate tax, if that is appropriate in the circumstances. It follows that he is not entitled to claim that he has been underpaid because of the deduction at source by the payer (TA 1988 ss 348(1)(d) and 349(1)). The scheme of deduction at source used also to apply to payments of yearly interest as well as to annuities and other annual payments. Nowadays, most payments of interest are outside the scheme (see further **[14.31]**).    **[14.21]**

## 2   Operation of TA 1988 s 348 for the payer

ITTOIA 2005 s 686 provides that income tax deducted under s 348(1)(b) is treated as income tax paid by the recipient. Section 348 applies where any annual payment charged with tax under Part 5, not being interest, is payable wholly out of profits or gains brought into charge to income tax. It is, therefore, confined to the payer who has income ('profits and gains') on which he is subject to income tax. It cannot apply to companies as they do not pay income tax. When the payer satisfies these requirements, it is presumed (in the absence of contrary evidence) that the payment is made out of his income.

**EXAMPLE 14.3**

Under a partnership agreement Wilbur, with an income of £10,000 pa from investments, pays to his former partner, Oscar, an annuity of £1,000 pa.
*Step 1:* Wilbur is permitted under s 348(1)(c) to deduct from the £1,000 a sum equal to the basic rate tax thereon. Hence, at present rates, Wilbur can deduct £220 (22% × £1,000). He will, therefore, give Oscar £780 together with a certificate showing that tax has been deducted (TA 1988 s 352; the appropriate form is IR 185).
*Step 2:* Wilbur's income is reduced from £10,000 to £9,000 because the annuity operates as a charge on his income. It, therefore, follows that his 'total income' is £9,000 (TA 1988 s 835) and that he can set his personal allowances only against that sum (TA 1988 s 276). Wilbur's own tax will, therefore, be calculated on the taxable income that is left.
*Step 3:* In addition, Wilbur is also charged on the annuity at the basic rate of income tax (see TA 1988 s 3).
The result is that the total cost of the covenant to Wilbur is £1,000 since he handed £780 to Oscar at *Step 1* and £220 to the Revenue at *Step 3*.

As Viscount Simon explained in *Allchin v Coulthard* (1943), by deducting the tax from the covenant at source (*Step 1*) 'the payer recoups himself for the tax which he has paid or will pay on the annual payment'. It is, therefore, in the interests of the payer to make the deduction of tax and does not directly concern the Revenue since it will collect the basic rate tax under TA 1988 s 3 at *Step 3* in any event. Hence, s 348(1)(c) *permits* the payer to make the deduction, but does not compel deduction. The whole process in *Example 14.3* may be represented diagrammatically thus:

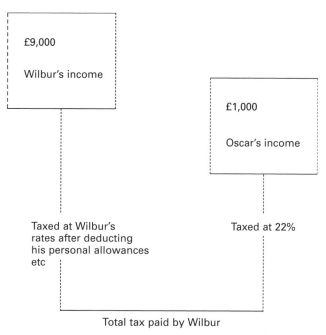

If Wilbur's taxable income had been such that he was liable to higher rate income tax, because the annual payment was made in connection with his trade, profession or vocation, he would not be liable to higher tax on that sum. **[14.22]**

### 3 Operation of TA 1988 s 349 for the payer

TA 1988 s 349 provides that where any annual payment, not being interest, charged with tax under Part 5 is not payable, or not wholly payable, out of profits or gains brought into charge to income tax, the person by or through whom any payment is made must deduct from it a sum representing the amount of income tax thereon. The income tax thereby deducted is treated as income tax paid by the recipient (ITTOIA 2005 s 686(1)).

Section 349 will apply when the payer has no income or insufficient income to cover the amount of the annual payment and when he is not subject to income tax. Annual payments made by companies are, therefore, payable subject to the deduction of income tax under s 349. Unlike under TA 1988 s 348, deduction from the covenanted sum is compulsory.

As soon as a relevant annual payment is made there is an obligation on the payer to notify the Revenue who will then assess him to basic rate income tax on the annual payment. The annual payment net of basic rate income tax is made to the recipient who receives a certificate of tax deducted on Form IR 185.

Under s 349 tax may be collected from agents of the payer (on the dangers of being held liable as an agent see *Rye and Eyre v IRC* (1935)). This difference in collection machinery from that under s 348 is necessary because the payer will not normally be subject to income tax when a s 349 payment is made. It will not, therefore, be possible to collect the basic rate tax on the annual payment at the same time as the rest of his income tax.

**[14.23]**

### EXAMPLE 14.4

Wilbur (see *Example 14.3*) falls on hard times and receives no income. He remains bound to pay the annuity to Oscar. When he makes the next annual payment:

*Step 1:* Wilbur should deduct the basic rate tax (£220) on that annual sum and pay Oscar £780 only.

*Step 2:* In accordance with s 350(1) Wilbur should notify the Revenue that the payment has been made. He will, therefore, be liable to pay income tax of £220.

The total cost of the covenant is, therefore, £1,000, made up of £780 paid to Oscar and £220 to the Revenue.

### 4   Position of the recipient

The position of the recipient of an annual payment falling under s 683 is broadly the same whether that payment is made under TA 1988 s 348 or s 349. He will have income under s 683 equivalent to the gross value of the payment (not just of the sum that he actually receives) and will be given a tax credit equal to the basic rate income tax deducted at source by the payer. Accordingly, he may be entitled to reclaim that tax (eg if the recipient has unused personal allowances); or, the tax may exactly discharge his tax liability; or, he may be liable to extra income tax at the higher rate. This third possibility (more tax owed by the recipient) is comparatively rare and is only likely to arise in respect of annual payments made for *bona fide* commercial reasons in connection with a trade, profession or vocation (see **[14.16]**).

**[14.24]**

### EXAMPLE 14.5

Watson received £780 from Holmes in respect of an annuity of £1,000 payable under a partnership agreement on his retirement. He is also given an IR 185 certificate of tax deducted.

Watson's income under s 683 is £1,000 and he has a credit for income tax paid of £220. Therefore, his tax position will be as follows:

(1)   If he is subject to tax at the basic rate (ie if he has no unused allowances or charges and has used up his lower rate band), there is no further liability to tax and no question of a refund.

(2)   If he has no other income and so has available personal allowances he can reclaim the £220 tax paid on his behalf by Holmes. If he had (say) £200 of unused allowances he would have taxable income of £800 (£1,000 − £200) on which tax at 10% would be £80. As the tax credit of £220 exceeds his tax liability by £140, he can obtain a refund of £140 of the tax deducted at source.

(3)   If he has other income so that he is paying income tax at the top rate (currently 40%), he will be liable to excess liability on the annuity, ie the difference between the higher and basic rates of tax. On present rates, such excess liability would be 18% × £1,000.

## 5   Principal problems arising in connection with the deduction of tax at source

a)   *Effect of failure to deduct tax at source*

The payer of an annual payment falling within the charge to tax under s 683 is allowed to deduct tax from the payment under s 348 and bound to do so under s 349. Failure to do so will not lead to any penalty. It will not generally concern the Revenue when the payment is made under s 348 since it will assess the payer to tax on the whole of his income without distinguishing the annual payment and if it fails to recover tax from the payer in a case where s 348 applies, the payee may be assessed.

Where there is a failure to pay the tax under s 349, however, the Revenue will seek to recover the sum either from the payer or by direct assessment from the payee. When an assessment is made upon the recipient, the burden is on him to show that he was only paid a net sum. If he discharges that burden he cannot be assessed to tax (see eg *Hume v Asquith* (1969)).

Failure to deduct tax will of course affect the parties *inter se.* In general, if the payee has been overpaid, that overpayment cannot be reclaimed or corrected from later payments; it is a payment made under a mistake of law and the excess is treated as a perfected gift which cannot be undone (*Re Hatch* (1919)). There are a few exceptions to this general principle: if the mistake is one of fact, recovery is possible (*Turvey v Dentons (1923) Ltd* (1953)); if the basic rate of tax increases after the payment, the excess can be recovered (TA 1988 s 821 as amended), but it appears that under-deductions cannot be recouped from later payments made in that tax year (*Johnson v Johnson* (1946) explaining *Taylor v Taylor* (1938) and see *Tenbry Investments Ltd v Peugeot Talbot Motor Co Ltd* (1992)). There is of course nothing to stop a recipient who has been overpaid from reimbursing the payer!        **[14.25]**

### EXAMPLE 14.6

Wilton has income of £5,000 for the tax year 2006–07. He pays to Twist an annuity of £1,000 under a partnership agreement on his retirement from which he fails to deduct basic rate income tax.
(1)   The Revenue may assess Wilton under the s 348 machinery.
(2)   If Wilton fails to pay, the Revenue may assess Twist. Note that in the event of Wilton paying the tax, Twist's income is £1,000 with a credit for £220 tax paid. The extra £220 that Twist has received is ignored; it is a tax-free gift.

b)   *Use of formulae*

TMA 1970 s 106(2) provides that 'every agreement for payment of interest … or other annual payment in full without allowing any such deduction shall be void'. The parties may not, therefore, agree not to operate ss 348 and 349. If s 106(2) is infringed, the instrument is void only as to the provision seeking to oust the deduction machinery. The section is also limited in that it only applies to 'agreements', so that payments under court orders and wills are outside its terms (see **Chapter 17**).

Despite s 106, the parties will often wish to ensure that a fixed sum is paid each year to the recipient regardless of fluctuations in the basic rate of income tax. Say, for instance, that Felix is paying an annuity to Hope, his former partner, under the terms of the partnership agreement, and wants to ensure that it receives £780 each year. Whilst the basic rate is 22%, a covenant to pay £1,000 pa would achieve this result. Were the basic rate to rise to 35%, however, Hope would only receive £650. As it is not possible to agree to pay £780 and not to deduct tax, the only way of achieving what Felix wants is to use a formula in the covenant. The standard formula would be that 'Felix agrees to pay Hope such sum as will after deduction of income tax at the basic rate for the time being in force leave £780'. This takes effect as an undertaking to pay the gross sum which after deducting the appropriate income·tax leaves Hope with £780. What Hope receives is, therefore, constant; what will vary with the rate of tax is the sum paid to the Revenue and, therefore, the total cost of the annuity to Felix.

An alternative formula would be to agree to pay Hope £780 'free of tax', which takes effect as an undertaking to pay such sum as after deduction of income tax leaves £780 (*Ferguson v IRC* (1969)). One danger if such a formula is employed is that it is arguable that a promise to pay £780 free of tax means that the recipient should in any event end up with neither more nor less than £780. It follows that if the recipient is liable to higher rate income tax on the annual payment the payer must reimburse him for that tax, whilst conversely, any repayment of tax should be returned to the payer (the rule in *Re Pettit* (1922)).

If a covenant were made in favour of a charity after 5 April 2000 (the charge upon which has now been removed: see **[14.13]**), it should no longer use a formula of the type just described. Since such a covenant will be subject to the Gift Aid rules if tax relief is to be available and, if a formula were to be used, the payer would be liable to pay the whole of the grossed-up value, which would then be further grossed up under FA 1990 s 25(6).     **[14.26]**

c)   *Which section applies: TA 1988 s 348 or s 349?*

Difficulties will arise, for instance, if an annual payment falls due in a year when the payer has no income, and is finally paid in a year when he does have taxable income and *vice versa* (see generally *Luipaard's Vlei Estate and Gold Mining Co Ltd v IRC* (1930) and ESC A16). Which section applies is of considerable significance; it will, for instance, determine the ownership of the sum deducted from the annual payment since, under s 348, it belongs to the payer whereas under s 349 it should be handed to the Revenue. In general, if the payer has taxable income for the appropriate year, it is presumed that the payment is made out of that income. This provision is normally advantageous to the taxpayer as the following example illustrates.

**EXAMPLE 14.7**

Hank has taxable income of £10,000 for 2006–07 and pays an annuity of £1,000 under a partnership agreement.

(1)　*If s 348 operates* Hank will be assessed to income tax on £2150 at 10% (£215) and £6,850 at 22% (£1,507), and in addition to 22% on £1,000 (£220). (£9,000 is Hank's income and £1,000 is that of the recipient.) The total sum payable to the Revenue will be £1,942.

(2)　*If s 349 operates* Hank will be assessed on £2,150 at 10% (£215) and £7,850 at 22% (£1,727) together with £1,000 at 22% (£220). The total sum payable to the Revenue will be £2,162.

The presumption that s 348 applies if income is available is displaced when the payer has secured some fiscal or other advantage from charging the payment to capital (as in *Birmingham Corpn v IRC* (1930)), or where he has made a deliberate decision to charge the sum to capital (see, for instance, *Chancery Lane Safe Deposit and Offices Co Ltd v IRC* (1966)). In such cases, despite the availability of income profits, s 349 will be applied.

In making an annual payment under TA 1988 s 348 the payer should deduct tax at the basic rate in force when the payment fell due and not at the rate when it was actually paid. Accordingly, in calculating the income of the payee, the covenanted sum will be treated as his income of the tax year in which it fell due and not of that in which the payment was made (if the two are different). In *IRC v Crawley* (1987) payments under a charitable covenant were made in arrears and, although the charity made a claim for repayment of tax deducted under TA 1988 s 348 within six years of the payment being made, the claim was refused because it was made more than six years after the date when the payments had fallen due. Vinelott J agreed with the Revenue's argument in the case that:

> 'the payer on making an annual payment deducts tax at the rate in force at the date when the payment became due or at the date of payment according to whether the payment is or is not made out of profits or gains brought into charge to tax. In estimating the total income of the payee the income is deemed to be the income of the year by reference to which the tax was deducted.'　　　**[14.27]**

## 6　Payments outside the tax net—ITTOIA 2005 s 727(1)

The result of the majority of annual payments being outside the tax system is illustrated in the following example:　　　　　　　　　　**[14.28]–[14.30]**

### EXAMPLE 14.8

On 20 June 2006 Toby, with an income of £50,000, entered into a deed of covenant to pay £1,000 pa to his nephew, Jacques. Jacques has no income. The sum falls outside the charge under s 683 with the following result:

(1)　Toby is taxed on £50,000 without any deduction for the annual payment. As the payment has to be discharged out of taxed income, the gross cost to Toby (in 2006–07) is, therefore, £1,667.

(2)　The sum of £1,000 is paid over to Jacques and is not taxed in his hands.

(3)　Jacques has no income so that his personal allowances remain unused.

## V　TAXATION OF INTEREST PAYMENTS

### 1　Tax relief for payment of interest

Tax relief for the payment of interest is only given in certain limited cases. Formerly, to attract such relief interest had either to be 'annual' chargeable to tax under the former Schedule D Case III or, alternatively, payable in the UK or Eire on an advance from a bank carrying on business in those countries. These restrictions were removed by FA 1994 s 81 (amending TA 1988 s 353) and this change was of particular assistance to non-UK residents with foreign borrowings. Accordingly and depending upon the purpose for which the loan was taken out, interest is accorded different tax treatment:

(1)  payment of interest in respect of, eg a bank overdraft or credit card interest, receives no tax relief;

(2)  payment of interest made, eg for the purposes of a trade, receives relief by allowing the payment as a deduction in computing the profits of that trade under Schedule D Case I (similar rules apply to a landlord: see **Chapter 12**). Interest relief on loans to buy land, etc was repealed by FA 1999 with effect from 6 April 2000.                           **[14.31]**

## 2  Deduction of tax at source

For the deduction of tax at the lower rate for interest paid by building societies and banks, see **[7.26]–[7.28]**. TA 1988 ss 348 and 349 do not generally apply to interest payments. It is only in the relatively few cases falling within TA 1988 s 349(2) that lower rate tax must be deducted at source and, in accordance with TA 1988 s 349(2), the payer is put under a duty to notify the Revenue that the payment has been made. This subsection covers the payment of yearly interest chargeable to tax under ITTOIA 2005 s 369 and which is paid either:

(1)  by a company or local authority otherwise than in a fiduciary or representative capacity, eg debenture interest; or

(2)  by or on behalf of a partnership of which a company is a member; or

(3)  by any person to another person whose usual place of abode is outside the UK.

Generally, interest must be 'yearly' if these provisions are to operate. The distinction between 'yearly' and 'short' interest depends upon the degree of permanence of the loan. The crucial question is whether it is stated, or expected, that the loan will last, or is capable of lasting for 12 months or longer and in this connection the intention of the parties is crucial (see *Tax Journal*, 30 March 1995, p 14).

Even if the payment falls within one of the three categories of interest payments listed in s 349(2), it must still be paid gross if it is:

(1)  paid in a representative or fiduciary capacity;

(2)  payable on an advance from a bank if the person beneficially entitled to the interest is within the charge to corporation tax on that interest (TA 1988 s 349(3)(A)) and, in relation to payments made on or after 1 April 2001 to interest payments between companies where the recipient is within the charge to corporation tax as regards that income (see TA 1988 ss 349A–D inserted by FA 2001);

(3)  is interest paid on direction from FICO consistent with terms of a double tax treaty;

(4)  is interest paid by a UK company (or a UK permanent establishment of an EU company) to an EU company (or a non-UK permanent establishment of such a company), provided that the Revenue has first issued an 'exemption notice' following a request by the recipient of a payment

(see ITTOIA 2005 ss 758–762). Where a person entitled to exemption from tax on interest payments receives them under deduction of tax, he can claim repayment of the tax deducted (see FA 2004 s 102). As from 1 January 2004, these provisions will enable UK companies to make payments to associated companies in EU Member States without deduction of tax, where previously existing double tax treaties did not eliminate UK withholding;

(5)  is payable under a group election under TA 1988 s 247.

FA 2000 ss 111–112 introduced new deduction rules for public revenue dividends and Eurobonds. [14.32]

### 3  Source of the interest

The availability of tax relief for payments of interest (and the existence of an obligation to deduct tax at source from the payments) depends on whether the interest falls within the charge under ITTOIA 2005 s 369 since, falling within Part 4 of the Act, there is required to be a UK source. Section 369 may apply whether or not the recipient is UK resident and in cases where the payment is made abroad (and hence ss 348 and 349 will apply). Factors to be considered in deciding whether this is the case were discussed in *Westminster Bank Executor & Trustee Co (Channel Islands) Ltd v National Bank of Greece SA* (1968) and subsequently enumerated by the Inland Revenue in the *Tax Bulletin*, November 1993, at p 100 as follows:

'The factors considered relevant in that case (leading to the conclusion that the income involved did not have a UK source) were

- there was an obligation undertaken by a principal debtor which was a foreign corporation
- the obligation was guaranteed by another foreign corporation with no place of business in the UK
- the obligation was secured on lands and public revenues outside the UK
- funds for payments by the principal debtor of principal or interest to residents outside Greece would have been provided either by a remittance from Greece or funds remitted by debtors from abroad (even though a cheque might be drawn in London).

Although the Greek Bank case was concerned with income which turned out not to have a UK source, inferences can be drawn from that case about the factors which would support the existence of a UK source and we regard the most important as

- the residence of the debtor, ie the place in which the debt will be enforced
- the source from which interest is paid
- where the interest is paid, and
- the nature and location of the security for the debt.

If all of these are located in the UK then it is likely that the interest will have a UK source.' [14.33]

### 4  Interest on legacies

For the tax treatment of interest paid by PRs on pecuniary legacies left in a will, see **Chapter 17**. [14.34]–[14.40]

## VI   OTHER SAVINGS INCOME

### 1   **Purchased life annuities (ITTOIA 2005 s 717)**

Purchased life annuities were formerly taxed as income with no allowance being given for their capital cost. ITTOIA 2005 ss 717, 719 (formerly TA 1988 s 656) permits the amount of any annuity payment which falls within its scope to be dissected into an income and a capital amount. The capital amount in each payment is found by dividing the cost of the annuity by the life expectancy of the annuitant at that time, calculated according to Government mortality tables. The balance is treated as income taxable under the rules of ITTOIA 2005 s 422, with income tax deductible under either s 348 or s 349. It is necessary to distinguish between a purchased life annuity on the one hand and, on the other, an investment of capital, with annual payments being in the nature of a return of that capital. In *Sugden v Kent* (2001), the taxpayer invested £200,000 with an insurance company and, at the commencement of the policy, he decided to effect annual partial surrenders of about £20,000. He argued that these annual amounts were of a capital nature, and so were partial surrenders within the provisions of ITTOIA 2005 Part 4 Chapter 9 (see **Chapter 7**). The Revenue took the view that each payment was an annuity, and probably a purchased life annuity under TA 1988 s 656 (now ITTOIA 2005 s 717), with it then being open to the taxpayer to make a claim under that section. In holding for the taxpayer, the Special Commissioner distinguished an annuity on the grounds that, *first*, in this case, the initial investment did not cease to exist; the amount that the taxpayer would receive over the term of the contract was £200,000, plus or minus the value of the units in the linked fund. If he died before receiving the full value, the value of the remaining units would be payable to his trustees. This is not be the case where income is purchased with a sum of money that then ceases to exist; and, *secondly*, there was no possibility that the insurance company in the present case would have a liability greater than the amount of the initial investment, however long the taxpayer should live.

Generally, s 717 does not apply if the annuity has already been given tax relief (as is the case with purchased annuities for a fixed term of years which have always been dissected); or, if the annuity was not purchased by the annuitant but by a third party (eg if it was purchased as the result of a direction in a will); or, if the premiums qualified for tax relief under TA 1988 s 266, s 273 or s 619 when they were paid or if the annuity is payable under approved personal pension arrangements (ITTOIA 2005 s 718).

For 2004–05 and subsequent tax years, the rate at which tax must be deducted at source on the payment of a purchased life annuity is the lower rate of 20% (TA 1988 ss 4(1A), 1A(2)(a), 1A(7), 1A(1B). In respect of other annuities (apart from those to which PAYE applies), the rate is 22%. **[14.41]**

### 2   **Deeply discounted securities**

Income tax is charged on the profits on the disposal of 'deeply discounted securities' (ITTOIA 2005 s 427). In simple terms, a deeply discounted security is one where the amount that would (or might) be payable on redemption exceeds the issue price by a particular percentage. A profit may be realised in the year of disposal (defined as: (i) the redemption of the deeply discounted security; (ii) its transfer by way of any sale, gift, exchange 'or otherwise'; and (iii) to its conversion into shares in a company or other securities (unless covered by (i) or (ii)) (ITTOIA 2005 s 437(1)). It is specifically provided that, on death, the individual is treated as transferring the security for market value immediately before death (ITTOIA 2005 s 437(3)). The taxed profit is the proceeds of transfer or redemption less the amount paid on acquisition. Only incidental expenses incurred before 27 March 2003 are allowable (ITTOIA 2005 s 439(1)(4)).                      **[14.42]**

### 3 Unauthorised unit trusts

Unit trusts provide a form of pooled investment and, being trusts in the strict legal sense, operate according to the terms of the trust deed. Unit trusts that are now authorised by the Financial Services Authority (FSA) were first introduced as vehicles for investment by individuals, and the tax rules were designed to ensure that tax-paying individuals fared no worse by investing via an authorised unit trust than would have been the case had they invested in a company directly. Those rules involve treating authorised unit trusts like companies for taxation purposes. In contrast, by definition, unauthorised unit trusts are unit trusts not authorised by the FSA, and are taxed as trusts. This means that when trustees receive income from a unit trust, they are liable to pay income tax on it at the basic rate of tax (TA 1988 s 469(2)). Distributions of income to unit holders are deemed to have been paid as annual payments under deduction of income tax at the basic rate (TA 1988 s 469(3)).                      **[14.43]**

## VII   MISCELLANEOUS MATTERS

### 1 Patents and copyrights

Patent royalties are payable subject to the deduction of basic rate tax (22% for 2005–06) under the provisions of TA 1988 ss 348 and 349. Such payments may be annual payments, but will usually fall within ITTOIA 2005 Part as receipts of a trade or profession. There are 'spreading provisions' in certain cases where lump sums are received (ITTOIA 2005 ss 587, 590, see **[10.173]**). With effect from 1 January 2004, payments of royalties by a UK company (or a UK permanent establishment of an EU company) to an EU company (or a non-UK permanent establishment of such a company) may be made without deduction of income tax at source (see FA 2004 s 101). No advance approval needs to be obtained by HMRC; it is sufficient that the payer had a reasonable belief that the recipient will be entitled to receive the payment gross.

Copyright royalties do not fall within ss 348 and 349 and are payable without deduction of tax. The recipient will be taxed under either ITTOIA 2005 Part 2 (if a professional author) or otherwise under ITTOIA 2005 s 687 (income not otherwise charged to tax). Again, spreading provisions are available for certain of these lump sum payments (TA 1988 ss 534 and 535 (as amended); see **[10.172]**).                      **[14.44]**

# 15 Tax shelters and insurance products

*Updated by Natalie Lee, Barrister, Senior Lecturer in Law, University of Southampton and David Brookes FCA, Tax Partner, BDO Stoy Hayward LLP*

---

I     Insurance products [15.1]
II    Investment and savings products [15.21]
III   Enterprise investment scheme (EIS) [15.51]
IV    CGT reinvestment and deferral relief [15.81]
V     Venture capital trusts [15.121]

---

## I  INSURANCE PRODUCTS

### 1  Life assurance policies

#### a)  *Treatment of qualifying policies*

Tax relief is available for premiums paid by a UK resident on a 'qualifying' life assurance policy made *before* 14 March 1984 (TA 1988 ss 266–267 and, for the definition of a 'qualifying policy', Sch 15 as amended by ITTOIA 2005). The relief is given by allowing the policyholder to deduct and retain 12½% of the premium, provided that the total annual premiums payable do not exceed the greater of £1,500 and one-sixth of his total income. The insurer reclaims the deduction from the Revenue. The relief is not available for policies made after 13 March 1984, nor for those made before that date where the holder subsequently alters the policy to increase the benefits secured or to extend the term. In such cases premiums will be paid without the 12½% deduction.

   The proceeds of a qualifying policy are not normally subject to income tax.
[15.1]

#### b)  *Non-qualifying policies (TA 1988 ss 539–554 now see ITTOIA 2005 s 461 et seq.)*

The typical example of a non-qualifying policy is the single premium insurance bond or with-profits investment bond. Not only is no relief available on the sum invested, but any gain realised by the policyholder, net of premiums paid, on the occasion of a 'chargeable event' (eg on surrender or death) may be subject to income tax at higher rate (but tax at the lower rate, or, for years prior to 2004–05 at the basic rate, is deemed to have been paid) subject to top slicing relief. Annual tax-free withdrawals are allowed up to the value of the original investment so long as they do not exceed 5% of the premium paid for each year of the policy (ie the tax-free withdrawals cease after 20 years). Single premium bonds therefore provide shelter for income in the case of higher rate taxpayers. However, for non-taxpayers they are not necessarily the most tax efficient investments since the underlying assets held by the life insurance company are subject to tax (see **[15.3]**).

**[15.2]**

c)   *Taxation of insurance companies*

The rate of corporation tax on the relevant profits (both income and capital) of a life assurance company is equal to the lower rate of income tax (20% in 2004–05). The policyholder is not charged on these accumulating profits.

**[15.3]**

d)   *FA 1998 changes*

FA 1998 contained measures aimed at preventing 'avoidance loopholes', ie:
(1)   in the case of policies held in trust it was possible to avoid any charge by the 'dead settlor trick' (see **[15.7]**). From 6 April 1998 this is prevented by gains being taxed on the trustees or beneficiaries who receive benefits;
(2)   special rules for 'personal portfolio bonds' (ie a life policy where benefits are linked to a portfolio of assets that is personal to the policyholder). In such cases an annual tax charge on the basis of deemed gains is imposed;
(3)   compliance rules aimed at non-UK insurance companies who sell insurance in the UK and special rules for overseas life assurance business if the policyholder becomes UK resident.   **[15.4]**

## 2   General treatment of non-qualifying insurance policies

Gains arising from dealings in non-qualifying policies are subject to higher rate tax if there is a chargeable event. Lower rate tax (basic rate for years prior to 2004–05) is deemed to have been paid but is not recoverable.

A chargeable event occurs when there is a surrender, a death giving rise to benefits under the policy, maturity or assignment for consideration.

**EXAMPLE 15.1**

Elizabeth, a higher rate taxpayer, takes out a non-qualifying single premium life contract in June 1997 for £20,000. She withdraws 5% each year from June 1998 until June 2000, ie a total of £2,000. She takes no further amounts.

In June 2006 she surrenders the policy for, say, £24,000.

The total withdrawals are £26,000, ie £2,000 plus surrender proceeds of £24,000.

Deduct premium paid of £20,000. No gains previously charged, so no further deduction. Chargeable gains are £6,000 top sliced over nine years.

By concession (ESC B53) individuals who are non-UK resident throughout a year of assessment are not liable to UK tax on gains on chargeable events even on UK non-qualifying policies. If the policy has been assigned by that individual to a trust the position is usually more adverse.   **[15.5]**

a) *Offshore policies*

A policy issued by an offshore life office that does not trade in the UK is not subject to tax on the income and gains from the investments underlying the policy. The chargeable events legislation still applies so that gains realised when the policy matures, is surrendered, or assigned for consideration will be taxable. **[15.6]**

b) *Trusts*

Any gain on the policy is taxed as the income of an individual if immediately before the chargeable event he or a trust created by him owns the policy. Note that there is still a charge on the settlor even if he cannot benefit from the trust although he has a right of reimbursement. Therefore trustees should be careful before taking out policies where the settlor is still alive.

If the settlor has died or is non resident, then the gain on the policy is chargeable at the rate for trusts and assessed on the trustees.

However, if the trust had taken out a policy with funds left by a settlor who died prior to 17 March 1998 and the policy was issued before 17 March 1998 and has not subsequently been varied, then there is no tax payable. (see FA 1998 Sch 14 para 7). This is the so-called dead settlor trick. **[15.7]**

c) *FA 2003 changes*

FA 2003 introduced a number of changes to prevent marketed tax avoidance schemes in relation to life insurance policies and deferred annuity contracts. TCGA 1992 s 210 is amended with effect from 9 April 2003 in order to prevent capital losses being generated which exceed the amount of any economic loss and also prevent gains escaping a charge to tax simply because the person making the disposal has received the policy or contract by way of gift. **[15.8]**

**EXAMPLE 15.2**

Miss X takes out a new life insurance policy paying a single premium of £500,000. The policy is one liable to income tax on a chargeable event gain. She sells it to Mr Y for £525,000, Mr Y surrenders the policy back to the insurance company and receives £502,000 in cash. Mr Y is treated as making a chargeable event gain of £2,000 on which he is liable to income tax (£502,000 less the amount of the premium paid of £500,000). Under the old rules for capital gains tax he was treated as receiving £502,000 but this was taken into account in calculating his chargeable gain so was disregarded for capital gains tax purposes. His cost of acquiring the policy of £525,000 was not taken into account in the income tax calculations so it is not disregarded for capital gains tax purposes. Therefore under the old legislation he made an allowable loss of £525,000. Following amended section 210 the income tax position is unchanged but his allowable loss is restricted to £23,000, ie £525,000 less the amount he received on surrender of the policy of £502,000.

**EXAMPLE 15.3**

Mrs Z buys a second-hand life insurance policy for £20,000. It is not a policy which attracts liability to income tax but she is liable to capital gains tax on any gain because she is not the original owner and she paid cash to acquire it. Just before maturity she gives the policy to her husband and he receives £36,000 from the insurance company. Mr Z does not have an income tax liability but makes a gain of £16,000. Under the old rules this gain was not liable to capital gains tax because Mr Z did not give any actual consideration to acquire the policy. Under new section 210 neither of them will have any income tax liability but Mr Z is now treated as having made a gain of £16,000 liable to capital gains tax because, although he gave nothing to acquire the property, his spouse has given actual consideration to acquire the policy.

d) *FA 2004 changes*

FA 2004 s 140 seeks to close an avoidance opportunity by limiting the amount of the deficiency relief that can be set off against the income of the individual in circumstances where there is a deficiency when the insurance policy, life annuity contract or capital redemption policy comes to an end. FA 2004 s 140 amends ICTA 1988 s 549. As a result of the amendment, the amount of the relief to which the individual is entitled cannot be greater than the total amounts of earlier gains made on the insurance policy, life annuity contract or capital redemption policy which formed part of the individual's income in an earlier year of assessment. Earlier gains may have arisen as a result of earlier part surrenders of the policy or contract.

This amendment has effect from 3 March 2004 in relation to all new life insurance policies, capital redemption policies and life annuity contracts. It also applies to life insurance policies, capital redemption policies and life annuity contracts that existed at 3 March 2004 if:

a)   the life insurance policies, capital redemption policies or life annuity contracts are varied on or after 3 March 2004 so as to increase the benefits secured;

b)   all or part of the rights conferred by the life insurance policies, capital redemption policies or life annuity contracts are assigned on or after 3 March 2004; or

c)   all or part of the right conferred by the life insurance policies, capital redemption policies or life annuity contracts come to be held as security in relation to a debt on or after 3 March 2004.

e) *ITTOIA 2005 changes*

As part of the Tax Law Rewrite project, many of the provisions relating to the taxation of insurance policies have been rewritten and are now found in ITTOIA 2005 Chapter 9. These rewritten provisions deal with all three types of contracts/policies while at the same time attempting to preserve the different rules that relate to each specific type of contract/policy.

## 3   Group life policies

Many partnerships have inadequate life cover in the event that one of their partners dies in service before retirement. The occupational death in service approved life insurance options are not open to them because they are self-employed and each partner has therefore traditionally had to take out life cover individually on his own life for the benefit of his dependants.

Increasingly, partnerships instead want to take out some form of group life cover that insures the lives of all their partners and pays benefits on more than one death. This can be obtained more cheaply on a group rather than an individual basis.

Following changes in FA 2003, the income tax situation has been improved because, provided a group life policy qualifies as an excepted group life policy within TA 1988 s 539A (now ITTOIA 2005 ss 481–482), it is now outside the scope of the income tax charge if there is a chargeable event such as a death. Previously there was an income tax charge on the second and subsequent deaths. If structured properly the group life assurance scheme can also be held in trust to pay out benefits to the dependants of the deceased partner on a discretionary basis in order to obtain maximum inheritance tax advantages. In order to qualify as an excepted group life policy a number of conditions must be satisfied.

Condition 1 provides that under the policy, sums or other benefits of a capital nature must be payable on the death of each of the individuals insured under the policy but only if the individual dies before reaching his or her 75th birthday. The same method of calculation must be used for calculating each of the death benefits payable under the policy. Generally no sums or benefits may be paid or conferred under the policy other than on death. The recipients of the death benefits paid must be individuals or charities so, if the death benefits have been written in trust, care will be needed on payment out of those benefits to ensure that the payments are made outright rather than on trusts to the partners' dependants. This could cause problems if such dependants are minor children. It is not possible to allow another partner who has survived the deceased partner to receive any benefits on payment out unless such other partner receives the death benefits for another reason—for example, they are the spouse of an insured person who has died.                                         **[15.9]–[15.20]**

## II   INVESTMENT AND SAVINGS PRODUCTS

### 1   Investment products and IHT planning

There are a number of insurance products or 'schemes' currently in the marketplace which centre round the idea of the investor giving a cash sum into trust but continuing to benefit from the funds, allegedly without inheritance or other tax problems.

These products generally involve some type of single premium non-qualifying endowment policy written in some form of trust.

The initial minimum premiums invested are often quite high—£50,000 is not atypical. The idea is that the investor is limited to his 5% 'tax-free' withdrawal. If withdrawals exceed 5% of the premium paid, there is the usual higher rate income tax charge on the excess subject to top-slicing relief. In addition, the life assurance company, unless based abroad, usually pays tax on the relevant underlying profits currently at the rate of 20%. However, provided the 5% limits are not exceeded, the investor is not charged to any income tax or gains even though the trust is settlor interested because the trust holds all its assets in the wrapper of the bond. Thus the underlying gains (if any) realised within the bond itself are not taxable on the settlor.

The types of scheme are described below. It should be noted, however, that FA 2006 will have a profound effect on new trust arrangements for life assurance based products, which will be subject to the new inheritance tax regime for trusts (see [33.35]). For pre-22 March 2006 interest-in-possession trusts holding pre-22 March 2006 contracts of life assurance, even where premiums are paid on or after that date, measures exist in FA 2006 which effectively exclude them from the new regime for the inheritance taxation of interest-in-possession trusts (see **Chapter 33**). Nor will ongoing premium payments affect the transitional provisions applicable to pre-22 March accumulation and maintenance trusts (see **Chapter 34**).                [15.21]

a)  *Spousal interest trust*

Such trusts are no longer possible to set up from 20 June 2003 due to FA 2003 s 185. Under the 'old scheme', the donor, eg the husband, effected a capital investment bond which was written on interest-in-possession trusts under which his wife was entitled to the interest in possession. The settlor was among the class of potential beneficiaries. Say six months later the trustees exercised their powers of appointment to terminate her interest in possession in favour of the settlor's children who would take interests in possession. The wife would no longer benefit and was treated as having made a PET when her interest in possession was ended by the trustees. If she survived seven years the initial value of the bond fell outside her estate for inheritance tax purposes. The idea was that any later growth in the bond should also fall outside the couple's estate for inheritance tax purposes whether or not she survived seven years.

The husband continued to benefit and from time to time the trustees could use their 5% withdrawal facility to make partial encashments from the bond and appoint such capital out to the settlor. Provided the encashments did not exceed 5%, there was no income tax charge on the settlor.

The idea behind this scheme was that the gifts with reservation (GWR) provisions were avoided due to the initial gift being to the settlor's spouse. Therefore FA 1986 s 102(5)(a) arguably applied which says that to the extent any gift is covered by the spouse exemption then no GWR will occur.

The Revenue did not accept this analysis and argued that there was a reservation of benefit. The point went to the High Court and then the Court of Appeal in the context of family homes—see *IRC v Eversden* (2003) considered at [29.138]).

The scheme was effectively stopped by FA 2003 s 185. For further details on this section see [29.139]. Insurance bonds taken out and settled prior to 20 June 2003 are not affected by the FA 2003 changes.                [15.22]

b)  *Gift and loan scheme*

The investor as settlor sets up a trust for the benefit of his children. He cannot benefit from the trust. The settlor then makes an interest-free loan repayable on demand to the trustees who use this money to invest in a bond normally written on the lives of the named beneficiaries under the trust. The idea is that the loan is not a diminution in the settlor's estate and therefore effectively no transfer of value has been made under this arrangement.

From time to time, the settlor demands repayment of part of the loan and to finance this the trustees will make a part surrender of the bond within their 5% entitlement. Normally repayment of loans to a settlor can cause income tax problems for the settlor, but as before the idea is that the trust 'income' is restricted to the 5% withdrawal, at least while the settlor is alive.

As the settlor receives loan repayments and spends them, his taxable estate will reduce and the growth in value of the bond will be outside his estate. He can ask for the whole of the loan back at any time although this may trigger income tax charges if the bond has grown in value since the trustees will be forced to encash it.

The trust and loan documentation has to be drafted carefully to ensure that it does not breach any anti-avoidance legislation. And this is of course only an estate freezing exercise. There is no immediate inheritance tax benefit because the loan still forms part of the settlor's estate. It is the growth in value of the investment product which will be outside his estate.

The inheritance tax planning is rather inflexible. The settlor may not in fact need repayment of the entire loan but it will still form part of his estate. Alternatively, he may end up needing some of the capital growth in the bond as well but cannot get access to this. Or he may want to be repaid on the loan at a greater rate than 5% of the initial premium each year. Calling for repayment at a greater rate than 5% could, as noted above, generate income tax charges. Many clients might also feel unhappy in this economic climate about basing their inheritance tax planning on the idea that investment products they take out really will grow in value in the future!

If the settlor dies shortly after the product is taken out then some thought needs to be given as to what happens regarding this loan. It will be necessary to avoid a situation where the loan is automatically called in by his executors because this will result in the trustees being forced to encash the bond early. This could be expensive in terms of tax and commission charges. To avoid this, the settlor could leave his right to receive loan repayments to another beneficiary under his will, eg his spouse. If he leaves the benefit of the loan back to the trust then this will be a chargeable transfer under the terms of his will and (even if it does not jeopardise the inheritance tax planning) may result in unnecessary tax charges if his nil rate band has already been exhausted.                                                                    **[15.23]**

c)   *Trust carve out*

There are many varieties of the carve out idea. In some the settlor takes out a cluster of single premium non-qualifying endowment life assurance policies maturing at regular intervals. The policies are assigned by the settlor to a trust. The terms of the trust provide that the settlor can take if living at the maturity date, but otherwise he has no interest in the policy. He cannot benefit in any other circumstances. The trustees but not the settlor have the option of deferring the maturity date and can surrender the policies at any time. In either event the settlor receives nothing. He can only benefit if the policy actually matures.

The beneficiaries of the trust are usually his children who take immediate vested interests in possession. The idea is that if the settlor requires some income, then the trustees will let a policy mature and he will take the proceeds. If he does not require income, the policy is extended by the trustees and the settlor receives nothing. The argument is that the settlor has 'carved out' or retained a reversionary interest under the trust, but this interest is liable to be defeated in a number of ways by the exercise of powers vested in the trustees. Therefore although the retained reversionary interest is not excluded property (see IHTA 1984 s 48(1)(b)), it has little or no value. The beneficiaries take the benefit of an insurance policy which is shorn of a reversionary interest retained by the settlor.

The Revenue appears to accept that the retention by the settlor of a reversionary interest under a trust is not a reservation of benefit (see letter to the Law Society dated 18 May 1987). The settlor has retained actual property rather than reserved a benefit in the policy gifted. There is some question as to whether the Revenue may argue that the effecting of the bond, the assignment into trust and the extension of the maturity date are associated operations giving rise to a chargeable transfer at the date of the last operation, ie the extension date.

In addition, there is a potential double inheritance tax charge if the settlor dies within seven years of settling the property but in that time has received the policy proceeds back on maturity. The Double Charges Regulations (see **Chapter 34**) would not appear strictly to give relief in this situation.  **[15.24]**

d)  *Discounted gift schemes*

There are also a number of schemes combining a carve out with a discounted gift. Under this route, the settlor broadly retains from the outset certain rights in the trust which add up to more than just a reversionary interest.

The trust is often split into two defined parts with certain rights (eg the right to withdraw a specified amount each year) belonging to the settlor outright and the other part being called the residuary fund and held on trust for the residuary beneficiaries. These persons do not include the settlor. When the settlor makes the investment he is retaining certain rights under the trust (eg the right to withdraw a specified amount each year) and therefore the loss to his estate is not the full capital value of the bond. The gift of the residuary fund is treated as less than the face value. The discount depends on the donor's life expectancy. The longer he is likely to live and draw on the benefits, the greater the discount on the gift.

All of these schemes involve complex provisions, have certain disadvantages and risks and may only be suitable in very limited circumstances. Specialist advice should always be sought.  **[15.25]**

## 2   ISAs, PEPs, TESSAs and SAYE

a)  *Individual Savings Accounts (ISAs)*

These were announced by the Government in the July 1997 Budget: the intention being to 'build on' the experience of TESSAs and PEPs (see below) and for the new account to provide a tax-favoured environment for savings. The scheme came into effect on 6 April 1999 when the rules permitting tax credits to be repaid to individuals in respect of company distributions ceased. The basic features of the scheme are as follows:
(1)   the account may comprise two elements: cash (including National Savings), and stocks and shares;

(2)    individuals over 18 who are resident and ordinarily resident in the UK will be able to subscribe;

(3)    subscription levels will be £7,000 per tax year of which no more than £3,000 may go in cash. Both husband and wife are entitled to a full allowance;

(4)    accounts will be administered by a manager;

(5)    the tax relief provided is:

    (a)    an exemption from income tax and CGT on the investments;

    (b)    payment of a 10% tax credit until April 2004 in respect of dividends on UK equities.

Withdrawals can be made without forfeiting tax relief.                    **[15.26]**

b)    *Personal Equity Plans (PEPs)*

PEPs are no longer available. However, existing PEPs continue to qualify for the tax reliefs and may be transferred from one manager to another. PEPs were a tax incentive aimed at encouraging saving through the purchase of shares and unit trusts. They permitted resident individuals to invest up to £6,000 pa with an authorised PEP manager. The resulting fund could be invested in equities listed on a UK stock exchange or dealt in on AIM or similar shares in EU companies, in corporate bonds; convertibles; preference shares in sterling eurobonds issued by qualifying companies and (subject to certain restrictions) placed in unit trusts. To qualify for the full £6,000 general PEP limit, unit and investment trusts had to hold at least half their assets in UK ordinary shares and similar shares in EU companies. Unit and investment trusts not satisfying this requirement ('non-qualifying trusts') qualified for an annual PEP investment of up to £1,500 if they held at least half their assets in UK ordinary shares or similar shares listed on a stock exchange anywhere in the world, provided that the exchange was recognised by the Revenue.

Although the initial investment in a PEP attracted no tax relief (contrast EIS and VCTs), the following tax advantages are conferred.

*First,* no income tax is charged on income arising from the investment (eg dividends).

*Secondly,* no CGT is charged on the disposal of the investment nor on a switch of investments within the PEP. Given the relatively small sums that could be invested in the PEP, relief from CGT was the major attraction for taxpayers although with an annual exemption of £8,200 for 2004–05 only individuals who have already exhausted that exemption will benefit. It should be remembered that PEP fund managers will continue to deduct a management charge (usually about 3% of the sum invested, but it may be nominal or even nil if the fund comprises units in a unit trust or shares in an investment trust).

Up to £3,000 pa could be invested in a single company PEP ('a corporate PEP') as well as investing £6,000 in one or more other companies ('the general PEP'). Accordingly, up to £9,000 pa was available for PEP investment.

No subscriptions to PEPs may be made after 5 April 1999 when the new savings account ('ISA': see **[15.26]**) was introduced. However, existing PEPs may continue to be held outside an ISA, the 10% tax credit on dividends from UK companies continued to be paid until 2004 and PEPs may be transferred from one manager to another.                    **[15.27]**

c)    *Tax exempt special savings accounts (TESSAs)*

New TESSAs are no longer available. The relative success of PEPs encouraged the introduction of tax exempt special savings accounts (FA 1990 s 28). The intention was to stimulate savings in (largely risk-free) interest bearing accounts with banks and building societies (now including 'European Authorised Institutions'). Adult individuals, and for this purpose husband and wife were separate individuals, could open one TESSA account with either a bank or building society in which interest earned on the sum deposited would be free from income tax *provided that* the savings were left in the account for five years. Maximum permitted savings over the five-year period were £9,000 but this figure could be arrived at in a variety of ways since the scheme was intended to be flexible. For instance, the individual could make regular savings of up to £150 per month or, alternatively, deposit up to £3,000 in the TESSA in year 1 with up to £1,800 in each of the following three years and then up to £600 in year 5.

The sums involved were hardly startling—for a basic rate taxpayer the saving was less than £100 pa. Once the five-year time period ended the account ceased to qualify for tax relief with the result that interest subsequently earned became subject to tax in the normal way.

An advantage of TESSA was that although the capital had to remain frozen in the account during the five-year period, interest earned in any one year (less a sum equivalent to the basic rate income tax for that year) could be withdrawn. Assume, for instance, that interest of £200 was credited to the account in June 1998: £160 could then be withdrawn without giving rise to any tax penalty.

As noted above, like PEPs, no new TESSAs can be taken out after 5 April 1999. TESSAs already taken out will, however, be able to run their full course and the capital (but not interest) may be transferred to an ISA account (ie a TESSA only ISA) when the TESSA matures (without affecting the amount that can be subscribed to the new account).                    **[15.28]**

d)    *Save As You Earn (SAYE)*

SAYE contracts were first introduced in 1969 and allowed a fixed monthly saving of between (only!) £1 and £20 for five years (for SAYE share option schemes the monthly investment permitted is £250). As compared with TESSA investments, the sum invested (maximum £1,200 over five years) was relatively derisory and no interest could be withdrawn during the five-year period. Instead the investor received at the end a tax-free bonus equivalent to the interest earned over the period and this bonus was doubled if the sum was not withdrawn for a further two years. With the intention of simplifying the tax incentives for reliefs given that SAYE has largely been superseded by other schemes (especially TESSA), 'ordinary' schemes were abolished as from 29 November 1994. Existing contracts will continue with full tax relief and tax relief will still be available for SAYE sharesave schemes (ie contracts linked to approved employee share option schemes).          **[15.29]–[15.50]**

III   ENTERPRISE INVESTMENT SCHEME (EIS)

The Business Expansion Scheme (BES) came to an end on 31 December 1993; the Enterprise Investment Scheme (EIS) was in a sense a replacement although the tax relief that it afforded was less generous and the scheme was more closely targeted in an attempt to avoid some of the pitfalls which had affected BES. FA 1998 fused EIS with CGT reinvestment relief as well as introducing both an increased level of relief and restrictions aimed at targeting the relief for subscriptions of cash into trading companies. (See FA 1994 s 137 and Sch 15 amended by FA 1995 reviving TA 1988 ss 289–312, as further amended by FA 1998.)                                                         **[15.51]**

1   **The relief**

EIS applies to new eligible shares issued in qualifying companies and provides income tax relief at 20% (only) on qualifying investments of up to £400,000 (for 2006–07 onwards, previously £200,000) in any tax year. To calculate the available relief, an individual's taxable income is arrived at by deducting charges on income and other allowances which afford relief at the highest rate (ie the personal allowance and the blind person's allowance). EIS relief is then given *after* venture capital relief (see **[15.122]**) but *before* those allowances attracting relief at only 10%. The relief can only be utilised to the extent that the investors income tax liability is reduced to nil; the relief cannot be used to create a tax refund.

Any gain made by an investor on the eventual disposal of his qualifying shares, provided that these are held for three years (five years for shares issued before 6 April 2000), is exempt from CGT. If the shares are sold at a loss (on cost) the cost of the shares is treated as reduced by the EIS relief given (TCGA 1992 s 150A). Subject to that, if the loss cannot be offset against CGT gains, relief may be obtained under TA 1988 s 574 (see **[7.121]**) against the taxpayer's income.

**EXAMPLE 15.4**

Eddy Investor puts £150,000 into an EIS investment in June 1998. In the tax year 2006–07 he sells the shares for either (a) £200,000 or (b) £100,000. His tax position is as follows:
(1)   *The original investment:* EIS relief at 20% was available so that Eddy's net investment cost was £120,000.
(2)   *The sale for £200,000:* Given that the shares have been owned for more than five years the gain is tax free.
(3)   *The sale for £100,000:* A capital loss of £50,000 minus £30,000 (being the EIS relief) is available for offset against Eddy's chargeable gains in 2006–07 failing which against his income under TA 1988 s 574.

A form of carry-back relief is available for shares issued before 6 October in the tax year. This enables the lower of, one half of the investment or £50,000 (£25,000 if the shares were issued before 6 April 2006) to qualify for relief in the preceding tax year subject to the limits for that year not being exceeded.
                                                                                    **[15.52]**

**EXAMPLE 15.5**

Argent makes the following investments:

| | | |
|---|---|---|
| 9 December 2005 | X Ltd | £120,000 |
| 9 July 2006 | Y Ltd | £150,000 |
| 1 October 2006 | Z Ltd | £100,000 |

His tax position is as follows:

*Tax year 2005–06:* Relief is available for investments of up to £200,000 pa. Accordingly the December investment qualifies for EIS relief at 20% and Argent can carry back relief of £50,000 for his investment in Y Ltd. This will then attract 20% EIS relief in 2005–06.

*Tax year 2006–07:* Assuming that £50,000 of the Y Ltd investment is carried back to 2005–06, EIS relief is available on the remainder of the Y Ltd investment and all of the investment in Z Ltd (£200,000).

## 2    Qualifying individuals

EIS Income Tax relief is available to individual investors (and not therefore trustees or companies) who are liable for UK income tax, whether or not they are actually resident in the UK, who are not connected with the company (contrast CGT deferral: see **[15.89]**). Broadly an individual is so connected if he, or an associate of his, is an employee or paid director of the company; or if he and his associates possess more than 30% of the capital (including loan capital) or voting power of the company (see ICTA 1988 s 291B(5A) dealing with subscriber shares). For these purposes, an associate excludes brothers and sisters but otherwise has a close company meaning **[41.121]** whilst a director is not debarred from the relief if the only payments that he receives from the company are for travelling and other tax deductible expenses. Relief will not therefore be available in the case of management or employee buy-outs (see generally TA 1988 s 291). Certain individuals (commonly called 'business angels') will, however, qualify for the tax relief even though they are connected with the company by being paid directors. (They must not, however, be connected with a company or its trade at any time *before* the shares were issued.) Precisely how these rules on business angels are intended to operate is far from clear: the drafting in FA 1994 leaves much to be desired. *IR 137* (a booklet published in the Inland Revenue's Business Series) comments that:

> 'the "business angel" must have subscribed for and been issued with the shares on which income tax relief is to be claimed before the first day for which he or she receives payment as a director ... the remuneration must be reasonable for the services ... perform[ed]. What qualifies as reasonable remuneration in any particular case depends on the facts. The level of remuneration will not be challenged unless there are grounds for supposing that it is excessive in the circumstances.'

**[15.53]**

## 3    Qualifying company

The relevant company must be unquoted at the time of issue; it must not be controlled by another company and must not control any company that is not a qualifying subsidiary. It can be a qualifying holding company only if its subsidiaries qualify. It need not be UK resident but the trade must be mainly carried on mainly in the UK. The company must exist wholly for the purpose of carrying on one or more qualifying trades and generally must do so for three years from the date of issue of the shares or from the commencement of the qualifying activity (whichever is later).

FA 1998 introduced a 'gross assets' test whereby a company does not qualify unless the value of its gross assets immediately before an issue of eligible shares is no more than £15m and no more than £16m immediately thereafter. FA 2006 reduced the gross asset limits for shares issued after 5 April 2006 to £7m and £8m respectively. If there are qualifying subsidiaries, the gross assets of the company and those subsidiaries must be aggregated for these purposes.

FA 2004 s 93 and Sch 18 introduced some changes to the EIS regime. Among these changes is the removal of the 'active company' requirement. Henceforth, the company issuing the EIS shares ('the qualifying company') or a qualifying directly held 90% subsidiary of that qualifying company must, during the relevant period, carry on the qualifying activity which is funded by the money raised by the EIS share issue. It is no longer necessary that the qualifying activity must be carried on by the same company at all times during the relevant period.

Further, a company can be a qualifying subsidiary if it is a 51% subsidiary of an EIS company. This rule does not apply to a company that actually carries on the trade or research and development in question nor to a company which is a property management company. In order for such companies to be qualifying subsidiaries, they must be 90% subsidiaries.

Another change effected by FA 2004 Sch 18 is that, as a result of the relaxation of the rules governing the repayment of loans made to an EIS company, it should now be easier for investors to make short-term loans to an EIS company without jeopardising future income tax relief on further investments in that EIS company.                                      [15.54]

## 4   Eligible shares

These must be new shares issued on or after 1 January 1994 and during three years (five years for shares issued prior to 6 April 2000) from the date of the issue there can be no preferential rights to dividends or to the company's assets on a winding up, and there must be no right to redeem the shares (s 289(7)). The shares must be subscribed for wholly in cash and be fully paid up at the time of subscription (other than, for shares issued after 16 March 2004, any of them which are bonus shares) and all shares comprised in that issue (once again, other than bonus shares) must be issued in order to raise money for a 'qualifying business activity' (see s 289(2)).             [15.55]

## 5   Qualifying activities

Although the company need not be incorporated or resident in the UK, it must carry on trading or research and development activities wholly or mainly in the UK if it is to qualify. Those activities must either be carried on, or intended to be carried on and actually carried on, within two years of the date of issue of the shares. Certain trading activities are prohibited including dealing in shares, securities or land; dealing in goods otherwise than in the course of an ordinary trade or wholesale or retail distribution; banking or other financial activities; provision of legal or accountancy services and leasing. FA 1998 (predictably) extended the list to include:

(a)    property development;
(b)    farming and market gardening;
(c)    forestry and timber production;
(d)    hotelkeeping, guest houses etc (but see s 297(3A));
(e)    the operation and management of nursing or residential care homes (but see s 297(3A)).

Not for the first time the purpose is to exclude asset-backed trades. The Press Release referred to sharpening 'the focus of the schemes and (to) ensure that the funds they raise are used to benefit activities which carry an appropriate degree of risk ...'. It is ironical that the relief would therefore be excluded for investment in a contract farming business which carried on activities on land occupied under short-term arrangements.          **[15.56]**


## 6    Anti-avoidance and pre-arranged exits

TA 1988 s 289(6) contains an anti-avoidance rule founded on the experience of BES. It provides that relief is not given to an individual in respect of any shares unless those shares are subscribed for and issued for *bona fide* commercial purposes and not as part of a scheme or arrangement the main purpose of which (or one of the main purposes of which) is the avoidance of tax. FA 1998 added provisions denying EIS relief on investments affording the investor undue protection in the form of:

(1)    arrangements providing the investor with an exit route;
(2)    predetermined plans for the disposal of the underlying trade;
(3)    third party guarantees or assurances;
(4)    sub-contracting the activities to a third party with which any of the preceding arrangements have been made. See generally s 299B (inserted by FA 1998).          **[15.57]–[15.80]**


## IV    CGT REINVESTMENT AND DEFERRAL RELIEF

FA 1993 introduced what, at first glance, looked like a valuable new category of roll-over relief, designed to encourage individuals to reinvest in a qualifying company ('entrepreneurial relief'). The relief operated to defer a potential charge on a gain arising on a disposal of shares in a company where the gain was rolled over into qualifying replacement shares. The provisions blended elements of retirement relief, roll-over relief and BES, but the relief given was quite distinct from these other forms of relief. Whilst appearing generous, the legislation contained a number of formidable hurdles that had to be overcome before relief was available, and was criticised as being of Byzantine complexity. In the event, FA 1994 extended the relief (the enhanced relief being known as 'reinvestment relief') and improvements were subsequently made by FA 1995. Further changes made by FA 1997 were restrictive in nature. Following announcements in the July 1997 Budget speech and in the November pre-Budget statement indicating future reform of the Enterprise Investment Scheme (EIS) and Venture Capital Trusts (VCT), reinvestment relief was abolished in relation to acquisitions made after 6 April 1998. It was replaced by the effective merger of the EIS and reinvestment relief regimes under the guise of a new EIS, aimed at encouraging investment in new shares in qualifying trading companies, whilst excluding so-called low-risk, guaranteed-return investments. This section will consider both reinvestment relief (in relation to acquisitions prior to 6 April 1998) and the new EIS insofar as it is concerned with the CGT rules for EIS shares and the effective integration of the reinvestment relief rules with those already providing for the deferral of gains on the disposal of EIS shares. Eligibility for EIS relief generally as is above (see **[15.52]**). It should be noted that relief under EIS is significantly restricted in that the list of non-qualifying trades has been increased to cover most 'property-based' activities. The new relief may also be seen as something of a mess involving an attempt to weld together the old EIS and reinvestment relief systems: note, however, that it remains possible to claim CGT deferral in cases where income tax relief is not available (eg trustees can only benefit from the CGT relief) and that a connection with the company does not matter so far as CGT is concerned.

The more restricted entrepreneurial relief applied to disposals in the period from 16 March 1993 to 29 November 1993 and is not considered further. **[15.81]**

## 1 Reinvestment relief (TCGA 1992 ss 164A–164N)

The position for acquisitions *prior to 6 April 1998* is that to obtain relief a *chargeable gain* must accrue to an individual (or to trustees) on a *disposal of* (*any*) *assets*, and that person must then reinvest in a *qualifying investment* in the *qualifying period* and make the appropriate claim for relief. **[15.82]**

### a) *A disposal of assets*

Reinvestment relief permitted *any* chargeable gain to be rolled into a qualifying investment. This was achieved by allowing for the disposal of *any asset*, in contrast to the previous position which required a 'material disposal' involving the disposal by an individual of shares in his personal company of which he was a full-time working officer or employee. Relief was available on a chargeable gain arising on the disposal of a Qualifying Corporate Bond (see s 164A(2A) and **[22.45]**). The relief could also be claimed by trustees in respect of all forms of trust *provided that* the beneficiaries were either individuals or charities (see further *Tax Journal*, 10 March 1994). **[15.83]**

### b) *A qualifying investment*

Relief was available only if within a one-year period before, or the three-year period following, the disposal ('the qualifying period') ordinary shares were acquired in a qualifying company. That acquisition could be by subscription for new ordinary shares in a new or existing company or by the purchase of existing ordinary shares (but not by receipt of a gift or inheritance). FA 1994 had removed the requirement that at least 5% of the voting shares must be acquired; the only restrictions were that:

(1)   the asset *disposed of* must not be shares in the qualifying company or shares in a member of the same group as the qualifying company; and

(2)   where a share acquisition is by subscription, the company or one of its subsidiaries must intend to use the money wholly for the purpose of a qualifying trade (see below).

There was no requirement that the person must work in that company so that a pure investment sufficed. However, a major restriction was that the company itself was 'qualifying' and the basic definition of such a company, largely lifted from the BES/EIS legislation (see [15.51]), was 'an unquoted company which exists wholly for the purpose of carrying on one or more qualifying trades or which so exists apart from purposes capable of having no significant effect ... on the extent of the company's activities'. The following were *excluded* trades: dealing in land, commodities, futures, shares, securities or other financial instruments; dealing in goods other than wholesale or retail distributions; banking, insurance, money lending, debt factoring, hire purchase, financing or other financial activities; leasing or receiving royalties or licence fees; providing legal or accountancy services. FA 1995 removed the previous restrictions on property development and farming companies, whilst FA 1997 inserted the requirement that the trade must be carried on wholly or mainly in the UK.

Formerly reinvestment was also prohibited in a company if more than half the value of the company's assets was represented by land and buildings. This restriction was also abolished by FA 1995 (as it was for the purpose of the then EIS relief).                                                              **[15.84]**

c)   *Corporate groups*

Formerly, a company with subsidiaries could only be a *qualifying company* if *all* the subsidiaries were directly owned and were either occupied in the carrying on of a qualifying trade or in the holding and managing of group property. FA 1997 (inserting new s 164G) provided that a company qualified if it was the unquoted parent of a trading group; and a company was a parent company if it was the principal company of the group within the meaning of the CGT group rules and the activities of the group were substantially trading. In determining whether a group's business was substantially trading, certain activities were disregarded. These were holdings in, and loans to, group companies and properties owned for the purpose of group trading activities.

It should be noted: (1) that the parent company could only control a company or otherwise have a subsidiary if such company was a *qualifying subsidiary* (a qualifying subsidiary had to be a 75% subsidiary); (2) for the purposes of reinvestment relief, a company could be in a CGT group even if it was registered or resident outside the UK.                              **[15.85]**

d)   *The relief*

The familiar principle of roll-over, which allows CGT to be deferred, applied so that the disposal consideration and the consideration for the reacquisition were both reduced.

The amount of the reduction was the *lowest* of:

(1) the chargeable gain on the disposal;
(2) the consideration paid (or market value) for the reinvestment;
(3) the amount specified in the claim.

Crucially therefore, and unlike roll-over relief, the gain was the first part of the proceeds reinvested: accordingly *CGT could be avoided by reinvesting only the gain.* It was possible to claim relief for part only of the gain and this was desirable if the remainder was covered by the taxpayer's annual exemption and/or retirement relief. **[15.86]**

## EXAMPLE 15.6

Eddie, aged 65, realised a gain of £1m on the sale of his widget company. He reinvested £100,000 12 months later (but before 6 April 1998) in the acquisition of ordinary shares in Nuts & Bolts Ltd (a qualifying trading company).

|  |  | £ | £ |
|---|---|---:|---:|
| (i) | Chargeable gain | | 1,000,000 |
| (ii) | Deduct retirement relief | 625,000 | |
| (iii) | Deduct annual exemption | 5,800 | 630,800 |
| (iv) | Maximum reinvestment relief | | 100,000 |
| | Remaining chargeable gain | | £269,200 |

*Note:*
The claim for reinvestment relief must be made within six years of the end of the tax year to which the claim relates. The Revenue will now not usually accept a claim for postponement of tax based only on an intention to acquire a new asset, but the new asset actually has to be acquired.

e) *Anti-avoidance*

FA 1995 contained provisions to ensure that a tax deferral was not converted (at least in part) into an exemption. Under these provisions, the amount of any gains which could be rolled over into a qualifying investment was restricted to the *acquisition cost* of the qualifying reinvestment. **[15.87]**

## EXAMPLE 15.7

Frank realised a chargeable gain of £140,000 on a disposal of assets. He acquired (before 6 April 1998) shares in a qualifying company for £10,000 from his wife, Constance. She had acquired them in 1993 for £60,000.

|  | £ |
|---|---:|
| Chargeable gain | 140,000 |
| Reinvestment relief (restricted to cost of | |
| acquisition by Frank, ie acquisition by one spouse | |
| from another is at disponor spouse's base cost: | |
| TGCA 1992 s 58) | 60,000 |
| Remaining chargeable gain | £80,000 |

*Notes:*
(1)    But for these provisions, Frank could have claimed maximum reinvestment relief of £100,000. This would have exceeded his acquisition cost, deemed under TCGA 1992 s 58 to be £60,000. Since the acquisition cost could not be reduced to less than zero, the excess of £40,000 would have escaped tax altogether on a subsequent disposal of the shares.
(2)    The provisions also prevented the same result as in (1) above where the taxpayer rolled the gain on more than one disposal into the acquisition of a single qualifying investment, in which case it was possible for the total amount of rolled-over gains to exceed the acquisition cost of the qualifying investment.

f)    *Clawback of gain*

Relief may be lost for two reasons. *First,* the held-over gain may crystallise early if certain events occur within three years of the investment: for instance, if the acquired shares cease to be eligible shares (ie ordinary shares) or the company in which the reinvestment is made ceases to be a qualifying company (although relief is not withdrawn if it obtains a Stock Exchange listing) or if the person who acquired the holding emigrates (although there are certain exceptions if they work full-time abroad). In addition there are complex rules to prevent the investor receiving any return of value during the three-year period, eg excessive dividends or remuneration. If there is *any* return of value, then the *entire* relief is forfeited. The period of clawback is, however, limited to three years following the date of reinvestment—after that clawback cannot occur so that the tax deferral will then only be terminated on a disposal. A clawed-back gain can be rolled into a qualifying investment under the new EIS provided that the new holding is acquired within the one-year period before, or three-year period after, the occurrence of the event which triggered the clawback, or such extended period as the Revenue may agree. The deferred gain crystallises in full immediately before the clawback event but is not retrospective to the date of reinvestment.

*Secondly,* there will be a clawback of the gain where money is raised by subscription and was: (1) intended for use in an existing trade and the money is not used within one year; (2) raised for the purposes of a trade not yet carried on and the trade started up within two years, but the money is not used within one year of the start-up date; and (3) the trade does not start up at all, and the money is not used within one year. In cases (1) and (3), clawback will be awarded if the money is in fact used for the purposes of that *or another* qualifying trade within one year. Where clawback occurs in these circumstances, the deferred gain is treated as accruing to the reinvestor at the expiry of the appropriate time limit. Unlike the return of value provisions, the clawback is only to the extent that the money is not used. **[15.88]**

## 2    Deferral relief under the Enterprise Investment Scheme (TCGA 1992 s 150C and Sch 5B)

a)    *The two codes*

There are now two separate codes in operation:
(1)    Income tax and CGT exemption: these rules are considered at **[15.52]**;

(2)  CGT deferral relief (see **[15.90]**). It is important to appreciate that for the purpose of deferral there is no prohibition on the investor being connected with the company and the £400,000 pa subscription limit does not apply. **[15.89]**

b)  *The relief*

The deferral relief operates to defer a CGT charge on a gain arising on disposals by an individual (the investor) where that gain is rolled over into a qualifying investment within the qualifying time. There is no limit on the amount of gains that may be sheltered (but see the gross assets test described in **[15.54]**). **[15.90]**

c)  *A disposal*

The gain must accrue to the investor (which may include a trustee—see **[15.98]**) on the disposal of *any* asset, or upon the occurrence of a chargeable event in respect of gains previously deferred by an investment in EIS shares or VCT shares or where, in respect of shares acquired prior to 6 April 1998 as a qualifying investment for reinvestment relief, there has been a clawback of the reinvestment relief. **[15.91]**

d)  *Qualifying investment*

Relief is available only if within *the qualifying time*, that is, a one-year period before or the three-year period following the disposal upon which the gain has arisen (*the accrual time*) a *qualifying investment* is made. A qualifying investment is made where:
(1)  the investor subscribes wholly in cash (other than, for shares issued after 16 March 2004, any bonus shares) for eligible shares (ie ordinary, non-preferential shares; there is no requirement that they should be shares to which EIS income tax relief is attributable);
(2)  the company issuing the shares is a company which is a qualifying company for the purposes of EIS income tax relief (see **[15.54]**) in relation to those shares. For instance, the company's gross assets before the issue of new shares after 5 April 2006 must be no more than £7m and after the issue no more than £8m;
(3)  the shares on which relief is claimed are subscribed for wholly in cash and are fully paid up at issue (other than, for shares issued after 16 March 2004, any of them which are bonus shares). An undertaking to pay cash at a future date will not qualify the shares as fully paid up;
(4)  where the investment is made before the accrual time, the shares are still held by the investor at accrual time;
(5)  the company issuing the shares or its qualifying subsidiary must carry on the qualifying trade or research and development (see **[15.54]** and **[15.56]**);
(6)  all shares (other than bonus shares, as above) are issued in order to fund a 'qualifying business activity' carried on by the issuing company or its directly held 90% subsidiary (see below and at **[15.56]**);
(7)  at least 80% of the proceeds of the issue are applied wholly (or practically wholly) for that activity within the period required for income tax purposes;

(8)    the subscription and issue are made for *bona fide* commercial purposes and not as part of a tax avoidance scheme.

It is not a requirement that the investor must not be connected with the company in which the investment is being made (contrast income tax relief: see [15.52]). The main limitation in respect of the relief is in the exclusion of certain trade activities. Some of these were already excluded under the previous legislation, but some were added. Crucially, these comprise property development, farming and market gardening and forestry and timber production. Also excluded are hotel-keeping and the management of nursing or residential care homes, but only where the person operating such an establishment has either a property interest in it or is in occupation of it. Certain financial activities such as insurance and money-lending are excluded, but not the giving of financial advice.

FA 2004 has introduced some changes to the deferral relief rules in order to bring them into line with the changes made for income tax purposes. These amendments are found at FA 2004 Sch 18 para 12 et seq. Broadly, deferral relief can be obtained by trustees of some trusts and by individuals who have a pre-existing connection with the company.    **[15.92]**

e)    *Taper relief and EIS investments*

Prior to FA 1999, where an individual disposed of an investment in a company qualifying for EIS relief and reinvested the proceeds in another company qualifying for EIS relief, whilst the gain on the disposal could be deferred, the holding period for taper relief would be limited to the period for which the investor held the original shares.

However, where shares in the first EIS company were issued after 5 April 1998 and are disposed of after 5 April 1999, individuals will be able to benefit from taper relief on a cumulative basis. The amount of the deferred gain which becomes chargeable to tax when the shares in the second EIS company are sold will be calculated for taper relief purposes as though the holding period began when the shares in the first company were acquired and ended when the shares in the second company were sold.    **[15.93]**

**EXAMPLE 15.8**

Jack invested £100,000 in the acquisition of ordinary shares in Gorgeous Gear Ltd (a qualifying EIS investment) in June 1998. He disposed of these shares in September 2000, realising a gain of £20,000, which is then invested in May 2001 in the acquisition of shares in Super Swimwear Ltd (another qualifying investment). Jack sold these shares in July 2006, realising a gain of £6,000. Neither investment was of business assets.

|  | £ |
|---|---|
| Gain arising on disposal of shares in second EIS | 6,000 |
| *But*: exempt because held for five full years | |
| Deferred gain | 20,000 |
| Taper relief for asset held for seven whole years: 75% × £20,000 | 15,000 |

The following matters should be noted:
(1)    The period between the disposal of shares in the first EIS company and the acquisition of the shares in the second EIS company will not count towards the taper relief holding period.

(2) A taxpayer cannot aggregate periods of ownership in shares in EIS companies for the purpose of satisfying the five-year period after which gains arising on the disposal of shares in an EIS company would be exempt from capital gains tax under TCGA 1992 s 150A.

(3) No relief is afforded for a deferred gain which is invested in an EIS company: the relief is for successive EIS gains only.

## f) *Withdrawal of relief*

Shares cease to be eligible and deferral relief may be withdrawn in the following circumstances:

(1) where, during the qualifying period, the company is no longer a qualifying company;

(2) where, during the qualifying period, the qualifying trade or research and development is not being carried on by the qualifying company or a qualifying 90% subsidiary;

(3) where less than 80% of the proceeds of the issue have been applied towards a qualifying business activity within one year and the balance within the following year;

(4) where not all the shares (other than, for shares issued after 16 March 2004, any of them which are bonus shares) were issued in order to fund a qualifying business.

In cases (1)–(3), shares cease to be eligible at the time of the relevant event; in (4), deferral relief is deemed never to have been available.

Relief can only be withdrawn where the company concerned has given notice to the inspector where required to do so, or where the inspector has given notice to the company that, in his opinion, relief should be withdrawn.

**[15.94]**

## g) *Appeals*

A notice from an inspector is treated as a decision to refuse a claim by the investee company and provides grounds for an appeal. If an appeal has been determined in respect of the parallel income tax provisions, that determination is decisive in relation to the same issue on a CGT appeal and *vice versa*.

**[15.95]**

## h) *Clawback of gain*

A chargeable event, giving rise to a chargeable gain, may be triggered *first*, when the investor disposes of the EIS shares otherwise than by way of an inter-spouse transfer; *secondly*, when shares issued cease to be eligible shares (see **[15.94]**); *thirdly*, when either the investor or the investor's spouse who has acquired the shares from the investor becomes non-resident less than five years from the date of issue of the shares; and *fourthly* where the investor (or any associate of the investor) receives any value from the company (or any person connected with it) at any time during the 'period of restriction', namely, the period beginning one year prior to the share issue and ending on the termination date relating to the shares. The rules that determine the amount of the value received correspond to the rules for EIS income tax relief. Receipts of 'insignificant value' will not trigger a chargeable event unless there have been a number of such receipts in the period of restriction in question and a receipt of their aggregate value would not be construed as insignificant. The rules for determining whether a receipt is of insignificant value are broadly the same as those for EIS income tax relief, with one exception. Where the amount received exceeds £1,000, for deferral relief purposes the amount received is compared with the total amount of any gains deferred in respect of the subscription for the shares.

The identification of share rules that apply on disposals that may give rise to a chargeable gain after a chargeable event are aligned with the identification rules for EIS income tax purposes.                                    **[15.96]**

### i)    *Anti-avoidance*

A number of rules exist to prevent, *inter alia, first,* the obtaining of deferral relief in respect of a gain from shares or securities where the reinvestment is in the same company as that in which the shares or securities disposed of subsisted or in a company in the same group and, *secondly,* obtaining deferral relief where the investor takes little or no risk in making the investment due to a guaranteed exit route (see **[15.57]**).                                **[15.97]**

### j)    *Trustees*

Trustees may obtain deferral relief on the disposal of trust assets where either:
(1)    the trust is a discretionary trust, provided that all those who may benefit are individuals or charities; or
(2)    the trust is an interest-in-possession trust (which, for these purposes, excludes an interest for a fixed term) where any of the beneficiaries is an individual or a charity. Where not all of the beneficiaries are individuals or charities, then only the 'relevant proportion' of the gain may qualify for relief. The 'relevant proportion' is the proportion that the income accruing to beneficiaries who are individuals or charities bears to the total income of the trust.                                **[15.98]**

### k)    *Claims*

The procedure for claiming relief is the same as for EIS income tax relief.
**[15.99]–[15.120]**

## V    VENTURE CAPITAL TRUSTS

### 1    Background

The then Chancellor (Kenneth Clarke) announced in his 1993 November Budget that he proposed, subject to consultation, to introduce a further measure to assist small business by channelling investment into unlisted trading companies (the definition of which mirrors that in the EIS legislation). His proposal was to establish a new type of quoted investment company (called a venture capital trust: 'VCT'). Investors' dividends and gains on shares held in the VCT (which would be quoted on The Stock

Exchange) would be free of income tax and CGT. The intention of using a VCT was to enable the investors' risk to be spread across a number of different companies. The original Consultation Document (published in March 1994) was not well received. **[15.121]**

## 2   The provisions in outline

In the light of the adverse reaction the Chancellor announced substantial improvements to the original proposals in his 1994 Budget speech. As a result tax reliefs are as follows (see TA 1988 s 332A and Schs 15B and 28B as amended by ITTOIA 2005 s 882 Sch 1 para 140; TCGA 1992 ss 151A, B; Sch 5C all inserted by FA 1995 s 71 as amended by FA 1998 and ITTOIA s 882(1) Sch 1 paras 426, 437).

a)   *Income tax*

Individual investors are exempt from tax on dividends received from shares in a VCT (whether the shares have been acquired by subscription or purchase) and are also entitled to relief at 30% (40% for 2004–05 and 2005–06 only – for earlier years relief was at 20%) for investment in *new* ordinary shares in a VCT (this relief is limited to investments of up to £200,000 in any tax year (£100,000 for 2003–04 and earlier tax years) and requires the shares to be retained for five years). The investment relief is given in priority to other deductions and reliefs available to the taxpayer which are given in terms of a tax offset (such as EIS relief). To the extent that full relief is not available it is not possible to carry forward any unused portion. **[15.122]**

b)   *Capital gains*

The individual investor is exempt from CGT on disposals of ordinary shares in a VCT (whether the shares were acquired by subscription or purchase and so that losses will equally not be allowable) so long as the VCT was and has remained approved by the Revenue throughout. In addition reinvestment relief was available to an individual who after 5 April 1995 had crystallised a chargeable gain. That gain could be deferred either in whole or part by matching it against a subscription for eligible shares in a VCT subject to the permitted maximum limit: that investment must take place within a qualifying period of 12 months before and 12 months after the chargeable event. This two-year period may straddle three tax years so that it was possible to shelter a gain of up to £300,000. However, deferral relief was abolished with effect in relation to VCT shares issued after 5 April 2004. **[15.123]**

## 3   The venture capital trust

A VCT must be quoted on The Stock Exchange and, in general, will enjoy the same exemption from corporation tax on its capital gains as investment trusts (TCGA 1992 s 100(1)). At least 70% of the investments of VCTs must be in unquoted trading companies ('qualifying holdings' as defined in Sch 28B which exclude securities relating to a guaranteed loan) with not more than

15% in any one company or group of companies. At least 10% of the total investment in any one company must be in ordinary non-preference shares. The investments may include both equity and loans with a minimum term of five years but at least 30% of the investments must be in new ordinary shares. VCTs will initially have up to three years to meet the 70% unquoted trading company and 30% ordinary share requirements: investments in unquoted trading companies held by VCTs at a time when such companies become quoted may be treated as investments in unquoted trading companies for up to a further five years. Finally, there are requirements about the size of the companies in which VCTs may invest to qualify for tax relief: broadly speaking the value of the relevant company's gross assets (for this purpose the gross assets of a group of companies would be taken) immediately before the issue of the relevant holding must not exceed £15m where the VCT raised the funds it invests before 6 April 2006. Following changes introduced by FA 2006, funds raised by a VCT after 5 April 2006 can only be used to invest in unquoted trading companies that have gross assets of up to £7m immediately before the share issue and £8m immediately afterwards.

The following example illustrates how the VCT rules operate.    **[15.124]**

**EXAMPLE 15.9**

Mr Smith acquires existing VCT shares for the value of £30,000 on 1 May 2004. He is entitled to relief on distributions and CGT relief on disposals of those shares. He also subscribes £200,000 for new VCT shares issued on 1 October 2004. He is entitled to relief on distributions and relief on disposals for £170,000 of that subscription. He can claim income tax investment relief on the full £200,000 subscription.

## 4   CGT aspects

a)   *The trust itself*

Chargeable gains realised by the trust are exempt provided that it has not lost its approval (TCGA 1992 s 151A(1) as amended).    **[15.125]**

b)   *Relief on disposals by investors*

An individual (aged 18 or over) is exempt from CGT on gains arising from a disposal of ordinary shares in a VCT (whether or not acquired as a new issue) provided that it retains approval until the date of disposal and the shares disposed of were not acquired in excess of the permitted maximum (ie investments not exceeding £200,000 in any tax year from 2004–05 onwards—see **[15.122]**). Capital losses are not allowable.    **[15.126]**

c)   *Deferred CGT relief on reinvestment in a VCT*

Deferral relief was abolished with effect in relation to shares issued after 5 April 2004. Prior to abolition, the relief worked as follows (FA 2004 Sch 19 Part 2).

An individual may claim a deferral of a chargeable gain to the extent that the gain is matched against a qualifying investment in a VCT (which must be a new issue of shares) made within a period of 12 months prior to the chargeable event giving rise to the gain (but not before 6 April 1995) and 12 months after the chargeable event (TCGA 1992 Sch 5C(1)(3)(a)). The maximum amount of the gain that can be deferred is the amount of the qualifying investments (TCGA 1992 Sch 5C(2)). This is a further species of reinvestment relief (see **[15.81]**).

The deferred gain will become chargeable on the happening of certain events, most notably on a disposal of the shares other than to a spouse (TCGA 1992 Sch 5C(3)(1)(a)–(f)) and is assessed for the year in which that chargeable event occurs. Where the investor, or a person who acquired the shares on a disposal within marriage, becomes non-resident while holding the shares, normally the deferred gain becomes chargeable. However, no charge will crystallise if that investor or person becomes non-UK resident more than five years after making the qualifying investment. Apart from this particular instance, there is no time limitation on the deferred gain becoming chargeable. **[15.127]**

**EXAMPLE 15.10**

Alex subscribes £50,000 for shares in an approved VCT on 10 May 2001. On 19 June 2002 he realises a chargeable gain of £70,000 accruing from a disposal of chargeable assets, and he subscribes a further £50,000 for new ordinary shares in an approved VCT on 10 March 2003.

Alex is entitled to CGT relief in respect of disposals of *all* the acquired shares (they are within the permitted maximum). In addition, he can claim deferral relief of *£50,000* in respect of his subscription for new shares on 10 March 2003, being a reinvestment made within 12 months after the event causing the chargeable gain.

# 16 Trusts and settlements

*Updated by Natalie Lee, Barrister, Senior Lecturer in Law, University of Southampton*

## I  INTRODUCTION – TRUST MODERNISATION

Following the publication of a series of discussion papers in December 2003, a subsequent consultation document in August 2004 and a further discussion paper in March 2005, provisions were included in the Finance Acts of 2004, 2005 and 2006 aimed at 'trust modernisation' for income and capital gains tax purposes. In addition to the stated aim of simplifying the tax regime for UK trusts, the main thrust behind the proposals contained in the various discussion papers and the new provisions is to move towards a more 'tax neutral' system, in which the amount of income or capital gains tax chargeable should not vary to any great extent depending on whether the property upon which it arises is held under a trust or directly by an individual. In achieving this goal, the Government sought to strike a balance between a system that does not provide artificial incentives to set up a trust, and one that avoids artificial obstacles to the use of trusts where significant non-tax benefits could be gained. Reform began with the Finance Act 2004, which increased the rate applicable to trusts (RAT) (**[16.21]**ff) to bring it in line with the higher rate of income tax. In order to mitigate the possible harsh effects of this measure on smaller trusts and trusts with vulnerable beneficiaries, the Finance Act 2005 introduced a standard rate band for all trusts that pay tax at the dividend rate or the RAT (**[16.21]**), and a new regime for trusts with vulnerable beneficiaries (**[16.74]**ff). The latest stage in the process of reform, provided for in the Finance Act 2006 and aimed at reducing the burden of administering the taxation of trusts, is an attempt to bring the main trust-related definitions for tax on income and chargeable gains into line with each other, along with an increase in the standard rate band for trustees.

HMRC have stated (HMRC Guidance Note, March 2006) that 'the simplification measure' in the Finance Act 2006 that reduces the age limit at which, for inheritance tax purposes, eligible children should become entitled to the assets of a trust from 25 to 18 (**[34.91]**), aligns the age limit for inheritance tax with those for income tax and capital gains tax, and that this age limit was part of the public consultation on modernising the tax system for trusts. Interestingly, nothing in the relevant documents suggest that this was the case and, moreover, there is no mention of this measure in the Regulatory Impact Assessment for Trust Modernisation (8 March 2006). This is an important measure, and will have an enormous impact on the use of the A&M trust as it has hitherto been structured.                                           **[16.1]**


## II  DEFINITIONS

### 1.  What is a settlement?

Although the term settlement is not statutorily defined, the idea behind the provisions in FA 2006 is the alignment of what is treated as a settlement for the general purposes of income tax and tax on chargeable gains. This is achieved through a common definition of 'settled property', being any property held in trust other than property held by one person as nominee for another, or as a trustee for another who, but for being an infant or under some disability, is absolutely entitled against the trustee (TA 1988 s 685A). This definition mirrors the equivalent capital gains tax provisions (**[25.2]**– **[25.4]**).                                                                 **[16.2]**


### 2.  The settlor

A person is a settlor in relation to a settlement if the settlement was made, or is treated as having been made, by that person. A person is treated as having made a settlement if he has made or directly or indirectly entered into it, if he has provided, or undertaken to provide, property directly or indirectly for the purposes of the settlement, or if the settlement arose on his death and any of the settled property is, or is derived from, property of which he was competent to dispose immediately before his death (TA 1988 s 685B). Once again, the provisions are almost identical to their capital gains tax counterparts (**[25.21]**–**[25.40]**).                                             **[16.3]**


### 3.  The trustees

TA 1988 s 685E provides that the trustees of a settlement are to be treated as a single person, meaning that the trustees are distinct from the persons who may from time to time be trustees of the settlement. It also provides a common test to determine whether the trustees of a settlement are resident in the UK (**[18.13]**–**[18.15]**).                                              **[16.4]**

## III   GENERAL PRINCIPLES

### 1   Trustees' liability at basic rate

Trustees are subject to basic rate income tax under the appropriate statutory provisions on all the income produced by the fund regardless of their own personal tax position and that of the beneficiary. For this reason, they are not allowed to deduct their personal allowances (the trust income is, after all, not their property) nor those of any beneficiary (see *Trusts, Settlements and Estates Manual* (*TSEM*) para 3610, which indicates that the basis for taxing trustees under ITTOIA 2005 (encompassing the former Schedules A and D) is that although not *beneficially* entitled to the income, the charge is on 'persons receiving or entitled to' (the income)). Trustees are 'persons' but not individuals—hence their liability is normally limited to tax at the basic rate and they have no personal allowances. A beneficiary, entitled to the income under the terms of the trust, enjoys a credit for the tax paid by the trustees—see **[16.62]**.

Expenses incurred in administering the fund may not be deducted in computing the tax liability of the trustees and are, therefore, paid out of taxed income (see *Trust Management Expenses Guidance* (HMRC, January 2006)).                                                                    **[16.5]**

#### EXAMPLE 16.1

(1)   The trustees of the Jenkinson family trust run a bakery. The profits of that business will be calculated in accordance with the normal rules applicable to trading income under ITTOIA 2005 and be subject to basic rate income tax in the trustees' hands (but note that the profits of a business carried on by trustees are not 'earned income': see *Fry v Shiels' Trustees* (1915)).

(2)   A and B, trustees of the Joel family settlement, farm trust land in partnership with Sir Joel (head of the family) who owns adjacent land. Normal rules of partnership taxation apply and as the trustees have entered the partnership agreement *qua* trustees any change in their composition will not lead to a cessation of a trade carried on by that retiring trustee. In the event of losses arising the relevant proportion may be set against other trust income.

### 2   Trust returns, direct assessment and deduction at source

Where trustees, for example, carry on a trade or engage in a letting of land, assessment to income tax at the basic rate is made upon them directly; where, however, they receive investment income arising, for example, under ITTOIA 2005 Parts 4 and 5 (formerly Schedule F and Schedule D Case III), tax will have been deducted at source (for the taxation of savings income, see **[7.23]**). The tax deducted will satisfy the trustees' liability to pay tax at the basic rate.

Dividends and other distributions paid by UK companies carry a tax credit of only 10%: this, however, is treated as satisfying the trustees' liability to pay basic rate tax.

The normal self-assessment rules apply to trustees, but note that every person who was a trustee when the income arose or who subsequently becomes one is responsible for making trust returns etc (TMA 1970 s 7(9)).

However anything done by one trustee satisfies the liability of all and penalties can only be recovered once (from a person who was a trustee when the penalty was triggered). Trustees are generally required to complete the trust and estate tax return: there is, however, no requirement on bare trustees to complete a self-assessment tax return or to make any payment on account (see (1997) SWTI, 88).                                      **[16.6]**

## 3    Exceptional cases

In exceptional cases trustees do not have to complete a return. The main situation is where professional trustees are acting; there is no untaxed income or any such income is mandated directly to a beneficiary; it is clear because of the small value of the fund that CGT will not arise and the trustees undertake to notify the Revenue of any change in their circumstances. A similar rule is applied where the sole or main asset is a residential property which is occupied rent free by a beneficiary under the terms of the trust. In cases not falling within the above but where the payment of untaxed income is made directly to a beneficiary under the authority of the trustee, then a trust return is required but the beneficiary will be directly assessed on that income (see TSEM 3040). Further to FA 2005 s 14 (see **[16.21]**) as amended by FA 2006, trustees whose income does not exceed £1,000 (for 2006–7 and subsequent years) and is made up of net interest and UK dividends, may need to make a return only periodically (*Tax Bulletin*, August 2005, pp 1217–1218; *Regulatory Impact Assessment for Trust Modernisation* (March 2006)).
                                                                        **[16.7]**

## 4    Trustees' remuneration

If a trust instrument authorises the remuneration of a trustee the payment will be regarded as an annual payment falling within TA 1988 ss 348–349 (see **[14.21]**) but is nonetheless treated as earned income in the trustees' hands (*Dale v IRC* (1954) and see TM para 3130).                              **[16.8]**

## 5    Other matters

The UK treatment of non-resident trustees is discussed at **[18.79]**; and the treatment of foreign source income received by trustees at **[18.38]**.
                                                                   **[16.9]–[16.20]**

## IV    TRUSTS WHERE THE TRUSTEES ARE LIABLE TO 'THE RATE APPLICABLE TO TRUSTS' (TA 1988 ss 686–687)

## 1    The charge imposed by TA 1988 s 686

### a)    *The 'rate applicable to trusts' (RAT)*

Trustees are not liable to income tax at the higher rate because they are not individuals. Trustees of settlements falling within s 686(2) are, however, liable to pay income tax at a single flat rate. Until 2004–05, this rate stood at 34%, chargeable on all income (with the exception of dividends and company distributions) which they receive. For the tax year 2004–05 and subsequent years, this rate is increased to 40%, thereby equating it with the higher rate of tax for individuals. The rate applicable to trusts in respect of dividends and company distributions is also increased for 2004–05 and subsequent years from 25% to 32.5%, the same as the higher rate applicable to dividend income (see [**42.76**]). The general effect of these increases is, in some cases, to remove the advantages that previously could have been gained by using trusts falling within s 686(2). The following matters should be noted:

(1)    in the case of savings income which has suffered a deduction of tax at 20% at source the result is an additional tax charge at a rate of 20%;

(2)    although the charge is levied on *income* arising to trustees of a settlement, TA 1998 s 686A (inserted by FA 2006) provides for certain payments of a capital nature to be treated as income for the purposes of s 686. These include lease premiums, which prior to 2006–07, were not subject to the additional rate and only suffered tax at the basic rate: see further [**16.28**];

(3)    the charge is on net income, ie income after the deduction of permitted expenses (see further [**16.23**]).

For 2006–07 and subsequent years, the first £1,000 of income taxable at the RAT will, depending upon the source of the income, instead be taxed at either the basic, lower or dividend ordinary rate (the standard rate band) (TA 1988 s 686D inserted by FA 2005 s 14 and amended by FA 2006). The standard rate band applies equally to payments of a capital nature that are deemed to be income by virtue of s 686A ([**16.28**]). Although not specified in the provision:

(a)    the standard rate band should apply after deduction of allowable trust management expenses (see [**16.23**]);

(b)    the tax deducted from payments of bank or building society interest should satisfy the tax liability of the trustees up to the £1,000 threshold; similarly, where dividend income is received, the associated tax credit should meet the trustees' tax liability and they would have no further tax to pay; and

(c)    where the trustees have annual income above £1,000, the excess should be chargeable at the RAT, but the standard rate band should apply to the first £1,000 of the income.

(For the effect of the standard rate band on TA 1988 s 687, see *Examples 16.4* and *16.5*).                                                    [**16.21**]

b)    *Which trusts are caught?*

TA 1988 s 686(2) provides as follows:

'This section applies to income arising to trustees of a settlement in any year of assessment so far as it—

(a)    is income which is to be accumulated or which is payable at the discretion of the trustees or any other person (whether or not the trustees have power to accumulate it); and

(b)    is not, before being distributed either—

(i)    the income of any person other than the trustees, or

(ii)   treated for any of the purposes of the Income Tax Acts as the income of a settlor; and

(c)   is not income arising under a trust established for charitable purposes only ...'

Settlements containing a power for trustees to accumulate income, and those which give the trustees a discretion over the distribution of the income are caught (a typical example would be the A&M settlement, which, until the changes provided by FA 2006, was largely established for its IHT advantages: see [34.91]). The result is not only to increase the cost of accumulating income in such settlements but, with the new rate applicable to trusts standing at 40%, the effect in some cases is to remove altogether any tax advantage that might otherwise have been enjoyed.

### EXAMPLE 16.2

Magnus is a wealthy individual who pays income tax at the highest rate (currently 40%). He creates a settlement of income-producing assets on discretionary trusts for his children giving the trustees power to accumulate the income for 21 years. Under the general principles discussed above, the income which was accumulated would suffer tax at only 20% (if it was savings income (other than dividend income for which there are special rules)) or 22% (instead of 40% in Magnus' hands) and would subsequently be paid out as capital and so be free from any further income tax. As a result of s 686, however, the trustees have to pay an extra 20% or 18% rate of tax respectively (making a 40% rate in all) so that the attractions of the settlement to Magnus are wholly removed.

The ambit of s 686(2)(a) was considered in *IRC v Berrill* (1982) where the settlor's son was entitled to the income from the fund unless the trustees exercised a power to accumulate it. Vinelott J held that the section applied since the income was 'income ... which is payable at the discretion of the trustees'. 'Discretion' is wide enough to cover a discretion or power to withhold income. The phrase 'income which is to be accumulated' in para (a) presumably refers to income which the trustees are under a positive duty to accumulate. A mere power to accumulate is not sufficient, although it will usually mean that the income 'is payable at the discretion of the trustees' within para (a).                                                                          **[16.22]**

c)   *Management expenses*

Expenses which are properly chargeable to income by statute or case law (which includes, for instance, the cost of preparing trust accounts) are not deductible against the trustees' liability to tax at the basic rate but may be deducted in arriving at the amount of income chargeable at the rate applicable to trusts (TA 1988 s 686(2AA) (2A) (2B)).

In *Carver v Duncan* (1985) trustees paid premiums on policies of life assurance out of the income of the fund as they were permitted to do under the trust deed. The House of Lords held that the payments did not fall to be deducted under s 686(2)(d) (forerunner of s 686(2AA)) which was limited to expenses which were properly chargeable to income under the general law. As the life assurance premiums were for the benefit of capital they should, as a matter of principle, be borne by capital and accordingly, the express authority in the instrument did not bring the sums within the section.

It should, of course, be remembered that most management expenses are referable to the capital of the trust fund: examples of income expenses include the costs of collecting and distributing the income and (by concession) the costs of preparing the trust accounts (see *TSEM* para 3515). Against which sources of income should allowable expenses be met? The order is:

(1)   against dividend income (ITTOIA 2005 Part 4 (formerly Schedule F);
(2)   against foreign dividends (as defined in TA 1988 s 1A(3)(b));
(3)   against savings income; and finally
(4)   against other income.

See further *Example 16.4* below and *Trust Management Expenses Guidance* (HMRC, January 2006).                                                                 **[16.23]**

### d)   *Income of a person other than the trustees*

The rate applicable to trusts will not apply to income that is treated as that of any person other than the trustees. This will be the case, as explained in RI 162 December 1996, where the beneficiary has 'a complete right' to receive the capital without having to satisfy any conditions, ie where the beneficiary has 'an indefeasibly vested interest in capital'. Any income arising to the trust in such circumstances is to be treated as the beneficiary's income so long as he is alive or unless and until the trustees exercise an overriding power of appointment in respect of that income in favour of another. This will also be the case where a beneficiary has a vested interest in the income (eg a life tenant). These cases must be contrasted with the *Pilkington* settlement, in which the income of a life tenant could be taken from him after it had arisen by the exercise of a power to accumulate it. Accordingly, it would be subject to the surcharge as the income still 'belongs' to the trustees.         **[16.24]**

### e)   *Income taxed on the settlor*

The trust rate does not apply to settlements where the anti-avoidance provisions of ITTOIA 2005 Part 5 Chapter 5 (formerly TA 1988 Part XV) operate to deem the income to be that of the settlor (see **[16.91]**). Prior to 6 April 1995, this exception applied to *all of the income* so deemed. Section 686(2)(b) now provides that it applies only to income so treated *before it is distributed*. Under the rules in ITTOIA s 629 (see **[16.95]**–**[16.97]**), income will only be treated as that of the settlor for income tax purposes if it is actually paid to or for the benefit of the settlor's unmarried minor child. In the event of a distribution out of a discretionary or accumulation trust in favour of such a child, TA 1988 s 687, as amended by FA 1995, provides that it will be treated as a payment net of the additional and basic rate tax. **[16.25]**

### f)   *Will trusts*

TA 1988 s 686 does not apply to the income of an estate of a deceased person during administration: of course if distributed to the trustees by the PRs it will then be subject to the 40% rate (with a credit for tax suffered by the PRs).                                                                                           **[16.26]**

g)    *Deduction of tax at source from relevant deposits*

TA 1988 s 480A provides for the deduction at source of income tax at 20% from bank interest on deposits. If the trustees make a declaration that they are not resident in the UK and have no reasonable grounds for believing that any beneficiary of the trust is either an individual who is ordinarily resident in the UK, or a company which is resident in the UK, bank interest may be paid gross (see TA 1988 s 480B and s 482(5A) and **[7.28]**). Concern has been expressed over the width of the definition of 'beneficiary' for these purposes. The view of HMRC as stated by the Financial Secretary to the Treasury, is that the term 'beneficiary' will extend only to those identified as beneficiaries under the terms of the relevant trust deed *at the time of the declaration*. It will not include somebody who might become a beneficiary at a later date under a power to add to the class of beneficiaries and who might be a UK resident.

**[16.27]**

h)    *What is 'income' for s 686 purposes?*

Although the section only applies to income in a trust sense, and generally would not apply to capital sums treated as income under a provision in ITTOIA 2005, however, TA 686A provides specifically that certain payments will be treated as income for the purposes of s 686. Thus it is that the payment of a lease premium (treated as an income receipt under ITTOIA 2005 s 277) on or after 6 April 2006 will also be treated as income for the purposes of s 686. This has not always been the case. Further examples include certain deemed income receipts of employee share ownership trusts, profits or gains from the disposal of interests in certain offshore funds and gains from contracts for life insurance. It should be noted that the standard rate band applies equally to such deemed income (**[16.21]**).          **[16.28]**

**EXAMPLE 16.3**

Discretionary trustees granted a lease for 35 years over a commercial property taking a premium on the grant of £100,000. For income tax purposes a part of that premium is taxed as income (see ITTOIA 2005 s 277 **[12.82]**). For 2005–06, the trustees would accordingly have suffered income tax at the basic rate (22%) on that sum (£22,000). They would not, however, have suffered a further charge under s 686 since the sum would have been viewed as a capital receipt. (Contrast the position of an individual taxpayer who may suffer tax at 40% on the chargeable slice of the premium.) For 2006–07 and subsequent years, the receipt is now treated as income for s 686 purposes, with the result that the trustees will suffer a further charge. Thus, assuming the trustees receive no other income during 2006–07, their liability would be as follows:

|  |  | £ |
|---|---|---|
| Deemed income |  | 100,000 |
| Tax at standard rate | £1,000 at 22%= | £220 |
| Tax at the RAT | £99,000 at 40% = | £39,600 |
| Tax liability |  | 39,820 |

## 2 Dividends and the s 686 charge

a) *The 6 April 1999 changes*

Prior to 6 April 1999 distributions of UK companies were paid with a tax credit of 20%. From that date the tax credit has been reduced to 10% and is irrecoverable. To ensure that these changes did not increase the tax payable by trustees under s 686 the tax rate on such dividends (until 2004–05) was reduced to 25%. The following table shows that the position remains broadly the same:

| *Dividends pre-6 April 1999* | £ | *Position from 6 April 1999* | £ |
|---|---|---|---|
| Dividend | 80 | | 80.00 |
| Tax credit (20%) | 20 | (10%) | 8.89 |
| Income | 100 | | 88.89 |
| s 686 tax (34%) | 34 | (25%) | 22.22 |
| After tax income | £66 | | £66.67 |

However, along with the increase of the rate applicable to trusts on all other income to 40%, for the tax year 2004–05 and subsequent years, the tax rate on dividends is increased to 32.5%. The effect of this change with reference to the previous table is illustrated below.

Position from 6 April 2004

| | £ |
|---|---|
| Dividend | 80.00 |
| Tax credit (10%) | 8.89 |
| Income | 88.89 |
| S 686 tax (32.25) | 28.89 |
| After tax income | £60.00 |

The increase in the rate applicable to trusts, which will clearly result in the trustees paying much more income tax, will be considered in the context of the change made in FA 2005 s 14 (see [16.21]) and the reform of the taxation of trusts, discussed at both the beginning and end of this chapter [16.1] and [16.108]). [16.29]


b) *The tax credit*

It is important to note that from 6 April 1999 the tax credit at 10% does not enter the trust tax pool (the 'tax pool' is considered at [16.32]). This is to ensure that the principle that the credit is irrecoverable will not be breached by the dividend being paid through a s 686 trust. Management expenses have been considered at [16.23] where the order of set-off against different types of trust income was noted: these rules, together with the use of the standard rate band, can be illustrated in the following example. [16.30]

**EXAMPLE 16.4**

(a)    *Facts*

| Income | Gross (£) | Tax (£) | Net (£) |
|---|---|---|---|
| Untaxed interest | 692 | | |
| Taxed investment income | 226 | 45.20 (a) | 180.80 |
| Foreign income | 82 | 16.40 (b) | 65.60 |
| Dividends | 8,717 | 871.70 | 7,845.30 |
| | £9,717 | | |

| | | |
|---|---|---|
| *Trust management expenses* | £1,251 | |

(b)    *Tax calculation*

(*i*) *Basic rate of untaxed interest*

| Income (£) | Rate of Tax | Tax due (£) | |
|---|---|---|---|
| 692 | @ 20% | 138.40 | (c) |

(*ii*) *Excess due to the RAT*

| Income (£) | Rate of Tax | Tax due (£) | |
|---|---|---|---|
| 692 (within standard rate band and no further tax liability) | | | |
| 226 (within standard rate band and no further liability) | | | |
| 82 (within standard rate band and no further liability) | | | |
| 8,717 – 1,390* = 7,327 | @ 10% (notional) | 732.70 | (d) |
| 8,717 – 1,390* = 7,327 | @ 22.5% | 1,648.58 | (e) |
| | | 2,519.68 | |

| | £ |
|---|---|
| Less: already paid | |
| | 732.70 |
| *Charge on trustees* | £1,786.98 |

*£1,390 = Trust management expenses £1,251 grossed up @ 10%, ie £1,251 × 100/90.

(c)    *Income available for distribution*

To establish the income available to distribute it will be necessary to make two separate calculations, one for the dividend income and another for the non-dividend income. These figures will then need to be added together on the form R185 (the charge imposed on trustees under TA 1988 s 687 when distributions are made to beneficiaries is considered at **[17.31]** and readers may wish to read this before considering the rest of this example).

(d)  *Non-dividend income*

Tax entering the tax pool and available to frank payments (a) + (b) + (c) = 200.*

Available to pay out to the beneficiary[ies] 200 × 100/40 = 500

| Gross (£) | Tax (£) | Net (£) |
|---|---|---|
| 1000 | 200 | 800 |

\* Tax charged at the basic or lower rate under s 686D (standard rate band) enters the tax pool (TA 1988, s 687(3)).

(e)  *Dividend income*

Tax entering the tax pool available to frank payments is £8,717 less gross expenses of £1,390 @ 22.5% = £1,648.58.

| Gross (£) | Tax (£) | Net (£) |
|---|---|---|
| 4,121.45 | 1,648.58 | 2,472.87 |

The above only shows the amount of income available to distribute on which the tax payable will not exceed the tax pool (ie so that no additional tax is payable under s 687).

(f)  *Maximum income distribution without use of capital*

To establish how much income is available to distribute it is necessary to multiply the dividend distribution received less net trust management expenses tax due (£7,845.30 – £1,251 = £6,594.30: this is the income actually held by the trustee) by 60%, ie £6,594.30 × 60% = £3,956.58, which is the net income available to pay out to the beneficiary without using capital to satisfy any tax charged on the trustees under s 687. The figures to be included on the R185 are as follows:

| Gross (£) | Tax (£) | Net (£) |
|---|---|---|
| 6,594.30 | 2,637.72 | 3,956.58 |

To satisfy the tax shown above, the trustee will be charged under s 687 for the difference between the tax included on the R185 of £2,637.72 and the tax entering the tax pool of £1,648.58 = £989.14.

Total distribution of both non-dividend and dividend income is as follows:

| Gross (£) | Tax (£) | Net (£) |
|---|---|---|
| 6,594.30 | 2,637.72 | 3,956.58 |
| 1,000.00 | 200.00 | 800.00 |
| *R185 figures* | | |
| 7,594.30 | 2,837.72 | 4,756.58 |

Therefore the tax paid by the trustees (not including the notional tax of £871.70) is:

|  | £ |  |
|---|---|---|
|  |  |  |
| s 686 | 1,786.98 |  |
| Tax deducted at source | 61.60 | (45.20 + 16.40) |
| s 687 | 989.14 |  |
|  | £2,837.72 |  |

(g)    *Summary*

This can be balanced by the following computations:

|  | £ |
|---|---|
| Dividend distribution | 7,845.30 |
| Notional tax | 871.70 |
|  | 8,717.00 |
| Other gross income | 1,000.00 |
|  | 9,717.00 |
| *Less:* gross trust management expenses | 1,390.00 |
|  | £8,327.00 |

|  | £ |
|---|---|
| Notional tax | 732.70 |
| Tax @ 20% on 1,000 | 200.00 |
| Tax @ 22.5% on dividends | 1,648.58 |
| s 687 charge | 989.14 |
| Net distribution to beneficiary | 4756.58 |
|  | £8,327.00 |

## 3    The charge imposed by TA 1988 s 687

a)    *The charge*

Section 687 imposes a charge to income tax on income payments made at the trustees' discretion. Section 687(2) provides that:

> 'The payment shall be treated as a net amount corresponding to a gross amount from which tax has been deducted at the rate applicable to trusts for the year in which the payment is made; and the sum treated as so deducted shall be treated—
>
> (a)    as income tax paid by the person to whom the payment is made or, as the case may be, the settlor; and
> (b)    so far as not set off under the following provisions of this section, as income tax assessable on the trustees.'    **[16.31]**

b)    *'The tax pool'*

The 'set-off' referred to enables trustees to deduct from the tax credit the amount comprising the 'tax pool'. This is the sum of the tax suffered by the trustees on income that has been taxed under s 686 and s 686D (less, of course, any amount already used to 'frank' the s 687 charge). The tax pool includes tax actually paid by the trustees together with recoverable tax credits and for many trusts (which have accumulated income) the tax pool will be substantial. Apart from dividend income, which is considered below, the fact that, from 2006–07, the first £1,000 of income liable to the RAT is subject to a new and lower rate band (see [16.21]), means that where income is received and distributed within the same tax year, the tax due under s 686 will no longer be equivalent to the s 687 set-off. The result is then the same as that where income is received in one tax year, but distributed in another when the tax rate has increased. [16.32]

**EXAMPLE 16.5**

**SCENARIO 1**

In 2004–05 trustees of the newly established Jenkins family discretionary trust receive rental income of £2,000 that is (in the same tax year) distributed to Gilly Jenkins. The tax position of the trustees was as follows:
(1)  Under s 686 they will be liable to pay tax at 40% = £800.
(2)  On distributing the net income remaining to Gilly Jenkins (£1,200) they are taxed under s 687 on the sum distributed grossed up at 40% (so that £1,200 is grossed up to £2,000) with tax at 40% being charged on the gross sum. The tax charge under s 687 is therefore £800 which can be reduced by sums standing in the 'tax pool'. Given that £800 is in the pool, tax under s 687 is reduced to zero (and the pool—assuming no previous credits—reduced to zero).
(3)  Assume now that the distribution of £1,200 was made in a later tax year when the rate of tax suffered by discretionary trustees had increased to 50%. The gross sum treated as distributed is accordingly £2,400 on which tax of £1,200 is payable under s 687 but from which can be deducted the tax pool of £800 leaving the trustees with a liability of £400.

**SCENARIO 2**

Assume the same facts as in scenario 1, but they occur in 2006–07. The tax position of the trustees is as follows:
(1)  Under s 686 and s 686D, they will be liable to pay tax at:
     (a)  22% (the basic rate) on the first £1,000 = £220; and
     (b)  40% on £1,000 (the excess over £1,000) = £400.
(2)  On distributing the net income remaining to Gilly Jenkins (£1,380) they are taxed under s 687 on the sum distributed grossed up at 40% (so that £1,380 is grossed up to £2,300) with tax at 40% being charged on the gross sum. The tax charge under s 687 is, therefore, £920 that can be reduced by sums standing in the 'tax pool'. Given that £620 is in the pool, tax under s 687 is reduced to £300 (and the pool—assuming no previous credits—reduced to zero).

c)  *Dividends and the s 687 charge*

As already discussed, dividends from UK companies: (a) are taxed under s 686 at a reduced rate of 32.5%; but (b) carry a tax credit of only 10% which is irrecoverable. It is important to realise that if distributed to beneficiaries the net sum must still be grossed up at 40% (because such a payment is treated as an annual payment under ITTOIA 2005 Part 5 Chapter 7, with the result that by passing through the trust the sum has lost its character as a dividend) and that the tax pool will not include the irrecoverable 10% tax credit. [16.33]–[16.60]

**EXAMPLE 16.6**

In 2006–07 trustees of the Roberts Trusts receive dividend payments of £9,000 with irrecoverable tax credits of £1,000. They propose to distribute the entire trust income. Their income tax position is as follows

(1)    Under s 686 the gross income of £10,000 is taxed as follows:

      (a)    10% (the dividend ordinary rate) on the first £1,000 = £100

      (b)    32.5% on the remaining £9,000 = £2,925

      (c)    *less* a reduction for the tax credit of £1,000. The trustees must, therefore, pay £2,025. They are left with net income of £6,975.

(2)    Under s 687 tax is charged on the income distributed grossed up at 40%. Accordingly, if the trustees wish the tax to be met out of the net income received, they should only distribute 60% of the cash dividend received.

|  | £ |
|---|---:|
| Distribution to beneficiary (£9,000 × 60%) | 5,400 |
| Addition for tax at 40% under s 687 | 3,600 |
| Gross distribution | £9,000 |

|  | £ |
|---|---:|
| Tax due under s 687 | 3,600 |
| *Less:* credit in tax pool | 2,025 |
| Balance payable | £1,575 |

The net income left in the trustees' hands after the s 686 charge ((1) above) has been used therefrom:

(a)    to distribute £5,400 to the beneficiary and

(b)    to pay the s 687 tax of £1,575.

    In these cases the trust can distribute 60% of the net dividend (£9,000) since:

(i)    the beneficiary receives £5,400;

(ii)    the Revenue receives (under a combination of s 686 and s 687) £3,600.

## V   THE TAXATION OF BENEFICIARIES

### 1   Taxing a beneficiary who is entitled to trust income

a)   *General rule*

A beneficiary who is entitled to the income of a trust as it arises (or is entitled to have it applied for his benefit) is subject to income tax for the year of assessment in which that income arises, even if none of the money is paid to him during that year (*Baker v Archer-Shee* (1927)). The sum to which the beneficiary is entitled is that which is left in the trustees' hands after they have paid administration expenses and discharged their income tax liability. The beneficiary is, as a result, entitled to a net sum which must be grossed up at the basic rate of income tax in order to find the sum which enters his total income computation and to a credit for some of the income tax paid by the trustees; not, it should be noted, for the full amount in cases where management expenses have been deducted (*Macfarlane v IRC* (1929)).

**[16.61]**

b) *Calculating tax (reclaim) of the beneficiary*

Depending upon his other income and allowances, a beneficiary may be entitled to reclaim all or some of the tax paid by the trustees (although not, of course, the irrecoverable credit on company distributions). Alternatively, he may be liable for tax at the higher rate. The income that he receives from the trust will be unearned even if it arises from a trade run by the trustees (see *Fry v Shiels' Trustees* (1915) and TA 1988 s 833(4) but note also *Baker v Archer-Shee* (1927) which indicates that if a beneficiary is entitled to the income as it arises, he will be taxed according to the rules of the statutory provision appropriate to that source of income). **[16.62]**

EXAMPLE 16.7

(1) Zac is entitled to the income of a trust fund. In 2006–07 £6,000 of property business (formerly Schedule A) income is produced and the trustees incur administrative expenses (properly chargeable against income: see **[16.23]**) of £1,000. The trustees are taxed at 22% on the income of £6,000. The balance of the income available for Zac will be:

|  | £ | £ |
|---|---|---|
| Gross income |  | 6,000 |
| *Less:* tax | 1,320 |  |
| expenses | 1,000 | 2,320 |
|  |  | £3,680 |

Zac, is, therefore, taxed on £3,680 grossed up by tax at 22%, ie:

$$\frac{£3,680 \times 100}{78} = £4,717.95$$

He will be given a credit for that portion of the basic rate tax paid by the trustees which is attributable to £4,717.95, ie £1,038, but does not receive a credit for the rest of the tax paid by the trustees (£1,320 – £1,038 = £282) and the result is that management expenses have been paid out of taxed income so that the total cost of these expenses is £1,282.

(2) Trustees received dividend income of £900 (plus a tax credit of £100 that discharges their liability to pay basic rate income tax). Zac, the life tenant, is taxed on a gross income of £1,000 and, if a basic rate taxpayer, will suffer no further tax charge; if a non taxpayer, he will not be able to obtain a repayment of the £100 credit; if a higher rate taxpayer, he will be taxed at 32.5% (the higher rate applicable to dividend income: see **[42.76]**) on an income of £1,000 and may deduct the credit of £100. He suffers additional tax of £225.

c) *What is income?*

'Income' for these purposes will not (in the absence of an express provision to the contrary) include items which are capital profits under trust law although income tax may have been charged on them in the hands of the trustees: see **[16.28]**. **[16.63]**

**EXAMPLE 16.8**

The Wonker Trust is a cash fund. The trustees are offered a run-down city centre property in Liverpool which they purchase for £1m (being the entire trust fund). At the time of purchase they were already in negotiations to sell the site to Norwest Developers and the sale is completed the next day for £10m. The trustees have realised a profit of £9m that will be taxed as follows:

(1)    in the *trustees' hands* as a trading receipt on which they will suffer income tax at basic rate (see **Chapter 10** for a consideration of 'one-off' trading transactions);

(2)    so far as the *beneficiaries* are concerned the £10m is trust capital and the profit of £9m will not be distributed to the Wonker life tenant.

## 2    Taxing an annuitant

An annuitant under a trust is not entitled to income of the trust as it arises; he is taxed under ITTOIA 2005 Part 5 Chapter 7 (formerly Schedule D Case III) on the income that he receives. As basic rate income tax will be deducted from the annuity by the trustees under TA 1988 s 348, an assessment for basic rate tax on the beneficiary will be precluded. He has a tax credit for the basic rate tax deducted at source in the usual way.    **[16.64]**

## 3    Taxing a discretionary beneficiary

### a)    *General rules*

A discretionary beneficiary has no right to a specific amount of income but is merely entitled to be considered. The Revenue therefore considers that any payments that he receives will be charged as his income under ITTOIA 2005 s 683 (presumably they are annual payments since they may recur) and he will receive a credit for the tax paid by the trustees under TA 1988 s 687 which is attributable to that payment. The effect is to encourage trustees to distribute income to beneficiaries who are subject to income tax at less than 40% so that all or a part of the surcharge can be repaid. If, however, the payment is received from a settlor-interested trust, it will not be charged to tax in the hands of the beneficiary (ITTOIA 2005 s 685A and see **[16.98]**ff)

Once an irrevocable decision has been taken by the trustees to retain income as a part of the capital of the fund, the sum accumulated loses its character as income and is treated in the same way as the original fund, ie as capital. It follows, therefore, that the income tax suffered by that income (at 40%) is irrecoverable and that no further income tax will be charged on the accumulations when they are eventually paid out to the beneficiaries as capital (although such distributions may have CGT and IHT consequences). In deciding whether it is more advantageous to accumulate income or to pay it out to beneficiaries under their discretionary powers, trustees need to consider, *inter alia*, the tax position of the individual beneficiaries.    **[16.65]**

**EXAMPLE 16.9**

Trustees are proposing to distribute £6,000 (net) of trust income. There are three discretionary beneficiaries, Ding, Dang and Dong. Ding has no other income and has an unused personal allowance; Dang is a basic rate taxpayer; and Dong is subject to tax at a marginal rate of 40%. The trustees are deciding whether to pay income to any one or more of the beneficiaries or whether to accumulate it. The following tax consequences will ensue:

(1) The trustees have paid 40% tax on the trust income (ie £4,000 tax) since none of the income is from dividends (TA 1988 s 686D is ignored for the purposes of this example).

(2) If the trustees decide to pay all the income to Ding (who has no other income) he will be entitled to a partial repayment of tax as follows:

|  | £ |
|---|---|
| Income (ITTOIA 2005 s 683) | 10,000 |
| *Less:* personal allowance | 5,035 |
| Total income | £4,965 |
| *Income tax* | |
| £0–£2,150 at 10% | 215.00 |
| £2815 at 22% | 619.30 |
| | 834.30 |
| *Less:* tax credit | 4,000.00 |
| Tax refund | £(3165.70) |

(3) If the trustees pay the income to Dang (the basic rate taxpayer), he will not be entitled to a refund of any basic rate tax, but, depending upon the amount of his other income, he may obtain a refund of such part of the rate applicable to trusts as exceeds the basic rate of tax.

(4) If the trustees pay the income to Dong (the higher rate taxpayer), no extra tax will be levied since the rate of tax on the trust income (40%) is the same as his own marginal rate.

(5) If the trustees accumulate the income, the £4,000 tax paid will be irrecoverable and the net income of £6,000 will be converted into capital.

Ideally, the trustees will avoid payments to Dong (since there will be no advantage whatever), will consider appointing all or part of the income to Ding and Dang and accumulate any balance.

b) *Dividends and other company distributions*

The tax treatment of dividends (and other company distributions) in the hands of the trustees has been considered at **[16.29]**. If the net sum is retained by the trustees as an accumulation, the position is, broadly speaking, no different from that which applies to other trust income. In many cases, however, the trusts will either be required or will wish to distribute that income to their beneficiaries (eg in the case of a discretionary trust, the power to accumulate may have ended, whilst in A&M trusts it may be required for the education of the beneficiaries). If this occurs, two major problems arise as a result of which the income suffers a further substantial tax charge. *First,* because what is distributed is considered to be a new source of income (and not therefore dividends), a 40% rate of charge is imposed under s 687 and, *secondly,* the 'tax pool' does not include the tax credit of 10%. **[16.66]**

**EXAMPLE 16.10**

Continuing *Example 16.9* above, assume that the trustees distribute £1,800 of dividend income (with a credit for 40% tax paid under s 687 of £1,200) to each of three beneficiaries as follows:

(1)    *To Ding a non taxpayer* He will recover all the tax paid by the trustees on the sum that he receives and so ends up with £3,000. He is in no worse a position than an individual shareholder in a company who receives a cash dividend of £3,000 with an irrecoverable tax credit of £333. Current A&M trusts which pay school fees for, eg the settlor's grandchildren may, therefore, not be adversely affected by these rules given that the sums involved will fall within the beneficiaries' personal allowances.

(2)    *To Dang a basic rate taxpayer* He recovers £540 (the difference between 22% and 40%) of the tax deducted by the trustees. This, however, means that he receives in total £2,340, which compares unfavourably with a basic rate taxpayer who directly owns shares in the company (and who would be left with £3,000).

(3)    *To Dong a higher rate taxpayer* Since the rate applicable to trusts is the same as an individual's higher rate, he suffers no further tax charge. However, he is worse off than a higher rate individual shareholder, who will only be liable for tax at the dividend upper rate of 32.5% (see **[42.76]**).

*Notes*:

(a)    For some (old) trusts these problems will be alleviated by a substantial tax pool.

(b)    Consider whether the problems can be overcome by accumulating income and making only capital payments to beneficiaries (see **[16.67]**).

(c)    Does mandating the income avoid the problem? See *Taxation*, 15 April 1999, and subsequent correspondence.

(d)    Given that these rules only apply to dividend income, trustees may consider switching their investments but need to beware of the CGT costs involved.


## 4    The dangers of supplementing income out of capital

a)    *The problem*

Capital payments will not generally be subject to income tax. However, if a beneficiary is given a fixed amount of income each year and is entitled to have that sum made up out of capital should the trust fail to produce the requisite amount of income, such 'topping up' payments will be taxed as income in the hands of the beneficiary (see *Brodie's Will Trustees v IRC* (1933) and *Cunard's Trustees v IRC* (1946)).                                         **[16.67]**


**EXAMPLE 16.11**

(1)    The settlor's widow is given an annuity of £4,000 pa; the trustees have a discretion to pay it out of the capital of the fund if the income is insufficient. The widow will be assessed to income tax on the payments that she receives whether paid out of income or capital since they will be annual payments (TA 1988 s 349 will apply to the extent that there is insufficient income in the trust and they are paid out of capital).

(2)    The settlor's widow is given an annuity of £4,000 pa and, in addition, the trustees have the power 'to apply capital for the benefit of the widow in such manner as they shall in their absolute discretion think fit'. Any supplements

out of capital will now escape income tax since the widow has an interest in both income and capital, and payments out of capital will, therefore, be treated as advances of capital rather than as income payments.

b)   *Stevenson v Wishart*

At one time the Revenue sought to argue that payments made out of trust capital could be taxed as income in the hands of the recipient beneficiary even when the payments were not paid in augmentation of an income interest. This argument was based on its view that the income nature of the payment in the hands of the recipient could be discovered by looking at the size, recurrence, and purpose of the payments. *Stevenson v Wishart* (1987) provided a test case for this view since the discretionary trust income was there paid out in full each year to a charity and capital sums were then paid to one of the beneficiaries who had suffered a heart attack. The purpose of the payments was to cover medical expenses and the cost of living in a nursing home. The Revenue's view that these sums were paid out for an income purpose and were therefore subject to income tax was rejected both at first instance and by the Court of Appeal. Fox LJ stated that:

> 'There is nothing in the present case which indicates that the payments were of an income nature except their recurrence. I do not think that is sufficient. The trustees were disposing of capital in exercise of a power over capital. They did not create a recurring interest in property. If, in exercise of a power over capital, they chose to make at their discretion regular payments of capital to deal with the specific problems of the beneficiary's last years rather than release a single sum to her of a large amount, that does not seem to me to create an income interest. Their power was to appoint capital. What they appointed remained capital.'

The Court of Appeal did stress the exceptional nature of nursing home payments. Fox LJ, for instance, stated that such expenditure, although involving day-to-day maintenance, was emergency expenditure of very substantial amounts that would usually fall outside normal income resources. It may be, therefore, that if the expenditure was not of an emergency nature the court would consider the payments to be income. A typical example is the payment of school fees out of a trust fund where the Revenue argued for a number of years that lump sum payments could be taxed as the income of the recipient beneficiary in the year when that payment was made.   **[16.68]**

c)   *Current position*

It is understood that the Revenue currently treats advances or appointments out of trust capital as capital in the hands of the recipient beneficiary unless the payments in question fall within one of the following three categories. *First*, when they are designed to augment income as in the *Brodie* case; *secondly*, if the trust instrument contains a provision authorising the use of capital to maintain a beneficiary in the same degree of comfort as had been the case in the past (the *Cunard* case); and, *finally*, if the capital payment in question really amounts to an annuity (see *Jackson's Trustees v IRC* (1942)).   **[16.69]**

## 5   **The effects of Trustee Act 1925 s 31**

This section is concerned with trustees' powers of maintenance. It can be excluded by the trust instrument: in practice it is commonly amended. The section can have both a vesting and a divesting effect on the income of beneficiaries.                                                                        **[16.70]**

### a)   *Divesting effect*

A beneficiary with a vested interest in income (not, notice, in capital) is treated as enjoying a contingent interest only until attaining the age of 18. This is illustrated in *Example 16.12(1)*: see *Stanley v IRC* (1944).        **[16.71]**

### b)   *Vesting effects*

By contrast, a beneficiary who is contingently entitled to the capital of the settlement at an age greater than 18 (in the situation where no prior interest exists) is treated as entitled to the income at age 18. This vesting effect of the section is illustrated in *Example 16.12(2)*. This provision is particularly significant in current A&M trusts where capital entitlement may be postponed to (say) 25 but the beneficiary takes income at an earlier age (usually under s 31 at 18) Note that the use of A&M trusts in the future will be severely limited by reason of the changes made in the FA 2006 to the treatment of them for IHT purposes (see *Example 16.12* and **[33.28]**). **[16.72]**

### c)   *Tax treatment*

When entitlement to income is postponed (the divesting effect) TA 1988 s 686 will apply to the income. When income vests in a beneficiary at 18 that section ceases to apply.

> **EXAMPLE 16.12**
>
> (1)   Property in a settlement is held on trust for Barbara (aged six) for life with remainder to her Uncle Silas. As Barbara, the life tenant, has only a vested interest in income and s 31 has not been modified in the trust deed, the trustees will be liable for tax at 40%. Barbara will not be subject to tax on the income and will not, therefore, be able to reclaim any of the tax paid by the trustees, except to the extent that income is applied for her maintenance (this illustrates the divesting effect of the section).
>
> (2)   Tilley is entitled to the Biggins Trust Fund when she becomes 30. On attaining 18 she will be entitled to income under TA 1925 s 31: as a result TA 1988 s 686 will cease to apply to that income (which will now be taxed at basic rate in the trustees' hands and at higher rate (if appropriate) on Tilley). Note also the consequences for capital taxes, and compare the difference of treatment before and after FA 2006:
>
> *Before FA 2006:*
> (a)   *at 18* Tilley enjoys an interest in possession for IHT purposes;
> (b)   *at 30* When she becomes entitled to the capital—there will be a deemed disposal under TCGA 1992 s 71 for CGT purposes (see **[25.47]** and **[33.28]**).

*After FA 2006*, unless the terms on which this trust are held are modified to ensure that Tilley becomes absolutely entitled to the property at 18 (when the current IHT treatment will continue and hold-over relief under TCGA 1992 s 260(2)(d) will be available), the trust property will become subject to a 4.2% IHT charge in respect of the period between Tilley's 18th and 25th birthdays.

New post-22 March 2006 A&M trusts will only qualify for special IHT treatment if created by a parent for the benefit of a minor child who will become absolutely entitled to the assets at the age of 18. This means that special treatment will no longer be accorded to an A&M trust established by a grandparent, when its creation will incur an immediate IHT charge (at 20% unless the value transferred is within the settlor's nil rate band).

**[16.73]**

## VI   TRUSTS WITH VULNERABLE BENEFICIARIES

### 1   Background

It is unusual (and undesirable) that the whole of the income arising in any one year under trusts established for the long-term benefit of the disabled and for the benefit of minors who have lost a parent (or both parents) should be paid out to those beneficiaries. The result is that for income tax purposes, the retained income suffers income tax at the RAT. With the increase in the RAT to 40% and the dividend trust rate to 32.5%, the Government has acknowledged that this could have an adverse impact on such trusts. Accordingly, FA 2005 provides for special tax treatment for qualifying trusts with vulnerable beneficiaries, the effect of which are backdated to 6 April 2004.

**[16.74]**

### 2   Who are vulnerable beneficiaries?

Vulnerable beneficiaries fall into two categories:
(1)   *Disabled persons.* These are defined as persons who are incapable of administering their property or managing their affairs because they have a mental disorder within the meaning of the Mental Health Act 1983 and persons in receipt of an attendance allowance or of a disability living allowance by virtue of entitlement to the care component at the highest or middle rate. In addition, a person may be treated as being in receipt of an attendance allowance or disability living allowance provided that they would be entitled to receive the relevant allowances if they were to meet the necessary residence requirements.
(2)   *Relevant minors.* These are young persons who have not yet reached the age of 18 and who have lost at least one parent.   **[16.75]**

### 3   What are qualifying trusts?

In the case of a disabled person, trusts will be qualifying trusts provided that, during the disabled person's lifetime or until the earlier termination of the trusts, any property applied for the benefit of a beneficiary must be applied for the benefit of the disabled person *and* either the disabled person is entitled to all of the income (if there is any) or the income may not be applied for the benefit of any other person. Trusts for relevant minors qualify, subject to conditions, if either they were established under the will of a deceased parent of the minor or under the Criminal Injuries Compensation Scheme, or are statutory trusts arising under the Administration of Trusts Act 1925 in favour of a minor whose parent (or parents) has died intestate. The conditions are: (i) that the minor will, on reaching 18, become absolutely entitled to the property, any income arising from it and any income accumulated for his or her benefit before that time; (ii) until that time, any of the property that is applied during the minor's lifetime must be applied for his or her benefit; and (iii) until that time, and while the minor is alive, either the minor must be entitled to all of the income (if any) arising from any of the property, or no such income may be applied for the benefit of any other person.                                                        **[16.76]**

## 4   Special treatment of income arising under trusts for vulnerable persons

The trustees and the vulnerable person may make a joint and irrevocable election that the trustees' tax liability will be brought into line with what the beneficiary's tax liability would have been had he or she received the income directly and relief is given by way of a reduction in the trustees' liability. The amount of the relief is the difference between the total tax paid by the trustees and the vulnerable beneficiary without the special treatment, and the amount that would be paid if the trust income was deemed to be that of the vulnerable beneficiary. The amount of income tax paid should be reduced considerably since the trustees will be able to take into account the beneficiary's personal allowances and starting and basic rate income tax bands (similar provisions apply for chargeable gains: see **Chapter 27**). The following example shows how the relief is given.

**EXAMPLE 16.13**

Under the terms of her father's will, property is held on trust for Anastasia on attaining the age of 18. Anastasia, who is ten years of age, lost both of her parents in a car accident in 2003. During the tax year 2006–07, the trustees received dividend income amounting to £15,000, which they decided to accumulate since Anastasia received other income of £10,000 from a trust established for her benefit by her grandfather.

A joint election is made for special treatment and this will be given by way of a reduction in the income tax liability of the trustees. The amount of the reduction is calculated by deducting the vulnerable person's liability (b) from the liability that the trustees would suffer without the special treatment (a). The vulnerable person's liability is calculated by deducting the total tax liability of the vulnerable person (d) from the income tax to which the vulnerable person would be liable if the special treatment applied (c).

| Trustees liability (the s 686 charge): | | £ | £ |
|---|---|---|---|
| Income | | | 15,000.00 |
| Liability to RAT: | £1,000@ 10% | 100.00 | |
| | £14,000@ 32.5% | 4,550.00 | |
| | | | 4,650.00 (a) |
| Anastasia's liability if the special treatment applied: | | | |
| Income | | | 25,000.00 |
| *Less* personal allowance | | | 5,035.00 |
| | | | 19,965.00 |
| Income tax | £ 2,150 @ 10% | 215.00 | |
| Liability | £17,815 @ 22% | 3,919.30 | |
| | | | 4,134.30 (c) |
| Anastasia's tax liability without special treatment: | | | |
| Income | | | 10,000.00 |
| *Less* personal allowance | | | 5,035.00 |
| | | | 4,965.00 |
| Income tax | £2,150 @ 10% | 215.00 | |
| Liability | £2,815 @ 22% | 619.30 | |
| | | | 834.30 (d) |
| Vulnerable person's liability: (c–d) | | | 3,300.00 (b) |
| Relief : (a—b) | | | 1,350 |

The trustees liability to income tax will be reduced by £1,350.

*Note.*

In calculating the beneficiary's liability to tax in (c) and (d), no account is taken of:

(i)  any distribution to the vulnerable beneficiary of income that has arisen to the trustees in that year; and

(ii)  any income tax relief which is given by way of a reduction in the income tax payable by the vulnerable beneficiary (eg, the married couple's allowance).

**[16.77]–[16.90]**

## VII    THE ANTI-AVOIDANCE PROVISIONS (ITTOIA PART 5 CHAPTER 5)

### 1    Introductory

a)    *Background*

Prior to 15 March 1988, a wealthy individual paying income tax at a top rate of 60% who wished to transfer a part of his income, eg to a grandchild, could have done so in one of two ways. *First,* by entering into a deed of covenant (ie an income settlement); or, *secondly,* by transferring capital assets that produce the required amount of income to trustees to hold for the benefit of the chosen grandchild for a stated period. Inevitably, the legislation that sought to restrict the efficacy of covenants was also drafted so as to deal with capital settlements. Income settlements were generally rendered tax ineffective by TA 1988 s 347A (as amended) (see **[14.12]**) so that the choice open to the wealthy taxpayer was whether or not to create a capital settlement.

**[16.91]**

b)    *Effect of the rules applying*

When the anti-avoidance rules apply they generally deem the income of a capital settlement to be that of the settlor and enable him to recover from the trustees any tax that he suffers on that income in excess of the basic rate.

**[16.92]**

c)    *What is a 'settlement' for these purposes?*

The term '*settlement*' is widely defined for these purposes to include any 'disposition, trust, covenant, agreement, arrangement or transfer of assets', and 'settlor' has a similarly wide meaning as well as including reciprocal settlors (ITTOIA 2005 s 620(1)). Although as a matter of general law a settlement can be established even though created for consideration, according to cases such as *IRC v Plummer* (1979), liability under Part 5 Chapter 5 depends upon there being some element of bounty. In the recent case of *Jones v Garnett*, the taxpayer, an information technology specialist, and his wife each owned one share in a company that earned profits by providing the taxpayer's personal services to clients. He drew a comparatively small salary so that the company earned profits, which were then distributed as dividends. His wife, the company secretary, received half. HMRC contended that the 'arrangement' amounted to a settlement within ITTOIA 2005 s 625 (formerly TA 1988 s 660A) and that, accordingly, dividends paid to his wife were to be treated as his income for tax purposes. The Court of Appeal held that there could be no arrangement because there was no bounty; that, although there were subsequent bounteous elements, such as the declaration of dividends in the wife's favour, these could not be included in the original arrangement because they were not arranged in advance. The view was that intention alone could not be an arrangement or part of an arrangement (see **[51.50]**). This essentially commercial organisation of the taxpayer's business is very different from the arrangement in *Example 16.4,* although an appeal by HMRC to the House of Lords is, however, pending.(HMRC's further contention that ITTOIA 2005 s 626, which excludes from the effect of s 625 outright gifts by one spouse to the other, did not apply in this case, is discussed at **[16.102]**.)                                                                                                   **[16.93]**

**EXAMPLE 16.14**

Sirius establishes a company (SE Ltd) of which he is the managing director. He takes £100 1 shares and his four infant children subscribe for the remaining 400 issued shares. The subscription moneys are given to the children by their grand-parents. Thanks to Sirius's enterprise and skill the company is profitable and dividends (equal to their personal allowances) are paid to the children. Sirius has created a settlement in favour of his infant children and the income will be taxed as his (see ITTOIA 2005 s 629 considered at **[16.95]–[16.97]** and *Butler v Wildin* (1989); see also *Young v Pearce*; *Young v Scrutton* (1996) and *Jones v Garnett* (2005) considered at **[16.102]**).

d)   *The charge to tax*

The charge to tax (formerly found in TA 1988 Part XV) is imposed by ITTOIA 2005 s 619 and covers:
(1)   rules which apply where the unmarried minor children of the settlor receive a benefit from the settlement (**[16.95]–[16.97]**);
(2)   rules which apply where the settlor or his spouse has retained an interest in the settlement or where the settlor transfers income not capital (**[16.98]**); and
(3)   rules which apply where the settlor or his spouse or minor child have received a capital payment or benefit from the settlement (**[16.106]**).
                                                                                                   **[16.94]**

## 2   Benefits received by unmarried infant children from parental settlements (**ITTOIA 2005 s 629**)

a)   *Basic rule*

Payments of income made to or for the benefit of the settlor's own unmar-ried infant child will be treated as the income of the settlor. The rule applies to settlements whenever made, but where the total income paid to the child under such a settlement does not exceed £100 in any year, it will not be treated as that of the settlor. If income is accumulated under a capital settlement in favour of unmarried infant children, the income is not treated as that of the settlor until paid out, eg to maintain the child, although note that payments of capital out of the fund will be treated as the income of the settlor to the extent that they can be matched against any available undistrib-uted income.

There will be taken to be available retained or accumulated income so long as the total amount of settlement income arising since the settlement was made is more than the aggregate of:
(1)   the amounts treated as income of the settlor;
(2)   payments treated as the income of other beneficiaries;
(3)   payments of expenses properly charged to income (ITTOIA 2005 s 631).                                                                        **[16.95]**

**EXAMPLE 16.15**

Darien settles property for the benefit of his three children: Amien, Darien Jr and Arres in equal shares contingent upon them attaining the age of 21. They are all infants and unmarried. If the income of the fund is £10,000 pa the income tax position is as follows:

(1)  The trustees will be liable for income tax at the standard rate band (depending upon the source of the income) on the first £1,000 and a rate of 40% on the remaining income (TA 1988 ss 686, 686D).

(2)  If the balance of the income (after the payment of tax) is accumulated, it will not be treated as the income of the settlor. Hence, so long as the income is retained in the trust no further income tax is payable.

(3)  If any of the income is paid to a child, it is treated as income of Darien. Say, for instance, that £1,200 is paid to, or for the benefit of, Amien. The result will be that Darien's income is increased by £2,000 (£1,200 grossed up at 40%). He has a tax credit for the £800 tax paid by the trustees (TA 1988 s 687). Since the rate applicable to trusts is now the same as an individual's higher rate, he will not be charged to further income tax on that sum.

(4)  TA 1988 s 687 did not allow for the settlor of a *non-resident* trust to claim credit against his income tax liability arising under ITTOIA 2005 s 629 for income tax paid by the trustees. That position was changed by ESC A93.

(5)  If all the net income (£6,000) is distributed amongst the three beneficiaries it is treated as Darien's income. Once the income treated as that of the settlor (together with any payments becoming the income of other beneficiaries and payment of expenses properly charged to income) exceeds the aggregate amount of income which has arisen under the settlement since it was made, any further distributions to the beneficiaries will be capital advancements and thus *not* treated as the income of the settlor.

(6)  This settlement is currently an A&M trust for IHT purposes; but this does not bestow any income tax advantages. It will continue to enjoy IHT advantages after 6 April 2008 only if it is modified by that date so that the beneficiaries will become entitled to the trust assets *at the age of 18*. If it is not, the trust property will become subject to a 4.2% IHT charge in respect of the period between each beneficiary's 18th and 21st birthdays.

(7)  It should be noted that references to 'payments' include payments in money *or money's worth*. Thus a non-cash distribution *in specie* will be caught (ITTOIA 2005 s 629(7)).

b)   *Vulnerable beneficiaries*

Discretionary income payments made on or after 6 April 2006 to unmarried minor children of a settlor, where that child is a vulnerable person for the purposes of FA 2005 and the trustees have made a successful claim under FA 2005 s 25 for special income tax treatment (**[16.74]**ff), do not give rise to a charge to tax on the settlor under ITTOIA 2005 s 629.

c)   *Other points*

Four other general matters should be noted. *First*, that income covenants by the settlor/parent in favour of trustees will be ineffective annual payments in accordance with the rules discussed in **Chapter 14**. *Secondly*, 'child' is widely defined to include 'a stepchild, an adopted child, and an illegitimate child' (ITTOIA 2005 s 629(7)), but does not include a foster child. *Thirdly*, the definition of settlement includes a transfer of assets (ITTOIA 2005 s 620(1));

and see *Thomas v Marshall* (1953)). *Finally,* if the settlor is not the parent of the infant beneficiary, ITTOIA 2005 s 629 is not applicable; grandparental settlements may, therefore, be advantageous from an income tax point of view.                                                                    **[16.96]**

d)  *Bare trusts for infants*

Prior to 9 March 1999 there were advantages for parents who established a bare trust for their infant child (a bare trust is one in which the child is absolutely entitled to the assets or income and only prevented from claiming them because of infancy). The position is illustrated in the following example:

**EXAMPLE 16.16**

Dad's marginal rate of income tax is 40%. In 1996 he settled property, which produced an income of £1,000 gross, upon trust for his infant daughter, Daisy, absolutely. The income is retained by the trustees (Daisy cannot, of course, give a good receipt for the income).
(1)    If Dad had received the income, the income tax payable would have been £400, so that he would have been left with £600.
(2)    As the income is settled upon trust for Daisy absolutely, the income was treated as belonging to her so long as it was not used for her benefit but retained by the trustees. As a result, she was able to set her allowances against the income that resulted in no income tax being charged. (The rate applicable to trusts did not apply because the income belonged to a beneficiary.) If the settlor did not want the assets to become the absolute property of the child (bearing in mind that once Daisy became 18 she could call for the assets), similar income tax advantages were obtained if the child was given a vested income entitlement only (which involved the exclusion of Trustee Act 1925 s 31(2)). At 18 she was merely entitled to sums representing accrued income but the capital remained in trust.

These arrangements are now prevented by legislation originating in FA 1999 s 64 and the position as a result is:
(1)    bare trusts already in existence are not affected although no further property should be added;
(2)    income produced by such trusts established on or after 9 March 1999 is taxed on the settlor as it arises.                                              **[16.97]**

3    **Settlements in which the settlor retains an interest**

a)  *Basics*

The charging rules are to be found in ITTOIA 2005 ss 624–628. In outline, these sections provide that where during the life of a settlor any property subject to a settlement, or any 'derived property', can become payable to, or applicable for the benefit of, the settlor or spouse or civil partner of the settlor in any circumstances whatsoever, the income of the settlement is treated as the settlor's income for all income tax purposes. ITTOIA 2005 s 685A seeks to ensure that discretionary income payments to beneficiaries from a settlement where the settlor is chargeable to tax under s 624 are not also chargeable in the hands of the beneficiaries. In effect, such payments are treated as gifts of income from the settlor to the beneficiary.          **[16.98]**

b)    *Other taxes*

There are similar CGT rules for UK settlements (see TCGA 1992 ss 77–79: **[19.85]** and more wide-ranging CGT rules for offshore trusts (see **[27.94]**). In some circumstances the retention of a benefit may result in the settlor being caught, for IHT purposes, by the reservation of benefit rules (see **Chapter 29**).          **[16.99]**

c)    *Inter-relationship with the former rules*

For a discussion of a comparison between the rules that existed prior to the tax year 1995–96 and the existing rules, see earlier editions of this book. The important points to note are: (i) the current rules apply to settlements *whenever made*, (ii) under the existing provisions, the income is treated as that of the settlor's for *all* income tax purposes, although the settlor may claim reimbursement from the trustees of any tax paid in respect of that income. Settlors are under an obligation to notify their tax office of any liability under these provisions even if they do not normally receive a tax return.    **[16.100]**

d)    *Retention of benefit*

ITTOIA 2005 s 625 provides that if property or any related property is, or will or may become, payable to or applicable for the benefit of the settlor or his spouse or civil partner in any circumstances, then the income from that property is taxed as his for all income tax purposes.          **[16.101]**

**EXAMPLE 16.17**

Jasper wishes to make provision for his son, Jonas, who is going up to Cambridge to read law. A covenant to pay Jonas £1,000 pa so long as he is studying law is, since FA 1988, ineffective for tax purposes. Accordingly, Jasper proposes to settle ICI shares on trust for Jonas for so long as he is reading law at Cambridge with a provision that thereafter the shares will revert to him. Because the property will revert to the settlor on the ending of Jonas' university career, Jasper will be taxed on the income. The section does not apply in cases where there has been an absolute divesting: hence, were the property to pass on Jonas finishing his law studies to, eg Jasper's adult daughter, the income would then fall outside the provision and be taxed as that of Jonas so long as he was studying law. Where Jasper has retained an interest but subsequently ceases to do so for whatever reason, ITTOIA 2005 s 625 will then cease to treat the income of the settled property as his for income tax purposes.

e)    *Benefit to spouse or civil partner*

The settlor is treated as having an interest in settled property if his spouse or civil partner is capable of benefiting from it (ITTOIA 2005 s 625 as amended, unless that benefit derives from an outright gift made to the spouse or civil partner (ITTOIA 2005 s 626 as amended). Section 626 will only apply if the gift of property carries a right to the whole of the income and the property is not wholly or substantially a right to the income.

**EXAMPLE 16.18**

In January 2002 Popeye settled property on trust for his wife, Olive, for life, with remainder to his children. Because a benefit from the settlement is being received by the spouse of the settlor (and there is no outright gift to that person) the income will be taxed as Popeye's under ITTOIA 2005 s 625.

In *Young v Pearce, Young v Scrutton* (1996) the spouses of two directors who ran a tooling company were allocated preference shares in the company by special resolution. This arrangement constituted a 'settlement' (for the wide meaning of 'settlement', see [16.93]). In the subsequent three years, they received dividends amounting to more than 30% of the net profits of the company. The spouses had no voting powers and, apart from the preferential rights to dividends, their only other entitlement was to repayment of the sums subscribed for the preference shares in a liquidation of the company. Accordingly, although the allotment of the preference shares did amount to an outright gift to the spouses, it was property which was 'wholly or substantially a right to income', and Vinelott J concluded that the dividends on the shares were caught by the anti-avoidance provisions. The key point in the decision was the absence of rights, apart from the right to income, attaching to the preference shares. He observed, '[A]s a matter of strict legal principle, the preference shares were assets distinct from the income derived from them ... '. However, he concluded that 'in reality they could never have been realised'. The decision has to be read in the context of this particular anti-avoidance legislation and, for a similar scheme to succeed, it will be necessary to ensure that greater rights attach to the shares, eg by making the preference shares convertible or by giving a right to participate in capital on a winding up of the company. The issue was considered further in *Jones v Garnett* (2005) (see [16.93]), in which case, concluding that this was not an arrangement giving rise to a settlement within s 625, the Court of Appeal went on to express the, necessarily *obiter*, view that, if this did amount to an outright gift (which their Lordships did not believe it to be), it was not 'wholly or substantially a right to income'. As an item of property, Mrs Jones' share carried with it exactly the same rights as that of her husband's, those rights being more than just a right to income. In the light of the pending appeal by HMRC to the House of Lords, it would seem prudent in the meantime to pay market value salaries if they are capable of being calculated (see further *Tax Bulletin*, April 2003, *Tax Bulletin*, December 2003, *Taxation*, 31 July 2003, p 477 and TSEM4350).

ITTOIA 2005 s 625(4) restricts the definition of a spouse or civil partner of the settlor. It does not include a widow or widower or survivor of a civil partnership, so that a possibility of benefit for the widow or widower or surviving civil partner of the settlor will not cause the income of the settled property to be taxable as the settlor's (and see *Lord Vestey's Executors v IRC* (1949)). In a similar fashion, s 625(4)(d) excludes a prospective spouse or civil partner, and s 625(4)(a) and (b) a separated spouse or civil partner. An exception for settlements made by one party to a marriage or civil partnership to provide for the other after divorce, termination of a civil partnership or separation, where the income is being paid to that other, is to be found in ITTOIA 2005 s 627(1). So, on the break-up of a marriage, one party to the marriage can make a settlement to provide for the other under which the income is paid to that other, but under which the settled property may revert to the settlor, without the income being taxed as the settlor's.        **[16.102]**

### f)    *Benefit to charity*

There is no charge on the settlor in relation to income of the trust that is given to a charity in the year of assessment in which it arises or which is income to which the charity is entitled under the terms of the trust. **[16.103]**

### g)    *When the settlor is not to be regarded as retaining an interest*

Further exceptions are provided by ITTOIA 2005 s 625(2). These deal with the possibility of a settlor becoming entitled to settled property on a disposition, bankruptcy or death by or of beneficiaries, or on the death of his own child or children over the age of 25 where the child has, for example, a life interest. Moreover, the settlor will not be regarded as retaining an interest while there is a living beneficiary under the age of 25 during whose life the settled property cannot be paid to or applied for the benefit of the settlor except in the events mentioned above (ITTOIA 2005 s 625(3)).        **[16.104]**

> **EXAMPLE 16.19**
>
> Tybalt settles property upon trust for such of his three children as attain the age of 25 and if more than one in equal shares absolutely and subject thereto for the benefit of the settlor.
>     As a result of s 625(3) Tybalt is not treated as having retained an interest in the fund. Even if the children took only life interests so that the property would revert to Tybalt on death, he is not taxed on the income (ITTOIA 2005 s 625(2)(e)).

### h)    *Non-domiciled settlors*

A non-domiciled settlor cannot be taxed on foreign income accumulated overseas even if he had an interest in the settlement. *However,* it is provided that if such income is subsequently remitted to the UK in a year of assessment in which the settlor is resident in the UK, it is to be treated as income arising *in that year* and chargeable to tax as the settlor's income. This means that although the income might have arisen in a year when the settlor had *no* connection with the UK, it will be taxed if there is a remittance after the settlor has acquired such a connection (ITTOIA 2005 s 648(2)–(5) and *Tax Journal,* 30 March 1995, p 9).        **[16.105]**

## 4    Receipt of capital benefits (ITTOIA 2005 ss 633–643)

These provisions prevent the settlor obtaining any benefit of a capital nature from a settlement in which the income may be taxed at a lower rate than that which would have applied had the settlor retained the income. In effect, capital payments to the settlor (or his spouse) from the fund are matched with undistributed income of the fund and taxed as the settlor's income under ITTOIA 2005 s 619. The sum is grossed up at the rate applicable to trusts but the settlor is entitled to a credit for tax paid by the trustees—although not to any repayment! There are no provisions enabling the settlor to recover any tax that he may have to pay.

A 'capital sum' covers any sum paid by way of loan or repayment of a loan and any sum paid otherwise than as income and which is not paid for full consideration in money or money's worth (ITTOIA 2005 s 634(1)–(4)(7)). A capital sum is treated as paid to the settlor if it is paid at his direction, or as a result of his assignment, to a third party (ITTOIA 2005 s 634(4)–(6)).

The capital sum will only be caught by s 633 to the extent that it is less than, or equals, the income available in the settlement; this means the undistributed income of the fund from any relevant year: ie any year of assessment after 1937–38. Any excess will not be charged in the year of receipt but it may be charged later if income becomes available in any of the next 11 years (ITTOIA 2005 s 633(3)–(4)).

**EXAMPLE 16.20**

The undistributed net income of a settlement is as follows:

| | |
|---|---|
| Year 1 | £10,000 |
| Year 2 | £2,500 |
| Year 3 | £15,000 |
| Year 4 | £6,000 |
| Year 5 | £7,000 |

In year 3, the trustees lend the settlor £45,000. That loan is a capital sum and, therefore, the settlor is charged to income tax in year 3 on that sum to the extent that it represents available income. As the available income is £27,500 (years 1–3) he will be taxed on £27,500 grossed up at 40%—ie on £45,833.33. He will not be subject to basic or additional rate tax on that income, and if his marginal rate is 40% he will be charged no further tax.

The remaining £17,500 is carried forward to be taxed in succeeding years when income becomes available; in year 4, for instance, £6,000 is available. If the loan is repaid, there will be no further charge on available income in subsequent years, but any tax paid during the loan period cannot be recovered (s 638(1)–(3)).

Section 633 ff also applies to a capital sum received by the settlor from a body corporate connected with the settlement. Generally, a company will be connected with a settlement if it is a close company and the participators include the trustees of the settlement (ITTOIA 2005 s 637(8)). The width of s 633 ff and its somewhat capricious nature (see eg *De Vigier v IRC* (1964)) means that settlements will often contain a clause prohibiting the payment of capital sums to the settlor or his spouse. **[16.106]**

## 5 General conclusions

(1) With the demise of the income settlement, the transfer of income-producing capital assets has assumed greater importance. So long as the settlor is prepared to sever all interest in the property settled, the anti-avoidance provisions considered above need not cause problems in the majority of cases. Particularly attractive settlements include those

made by grandparents on their infant grandchildren through which use is made of the grandchild's personal allowance to ensure that income in the settlement is effectively tax free. By contrast, parental settlements in favour of the settlor's own infant unmarried children are less attractive since the income must be retained in the trust if it is not to attract tax at the settlor's rate. Normally, the settlement income will now suffer an irrecoverable 40% charge and, given a top rate of income tax of 40%, there is no longer anything to justify the expenses involved in creating and running the relevant trust. Note, however, the changes to the taxation of trusts for the purposes of IHT, giving no special treatment to inter-vivos A&M trusts and those made by grandparents; indeed if this type of trust is set up on or after 22 March 2006, the settlor will incur an immediate IHT charge at 20%, unless he is still able to utilise his nil rate band.

(2)    The increase in the rates applicable to trusts (40% on ordinary income and 32.5% on dividends and other company distributions) will largely affect those, typically, smaller trusts with beneficiaries who either pay no tax at all, or who are liable at lower rates on income and gains received by them in their non-beneficial capacity. However, it has been suggested that, with the introduction of the standard rate band on the first £1,000 of income taxable at the RAT, around one-third of all trusts currently liable to tax at the RAT will no longer pay the RAT on any of their income because their total income falls below this threshold. Moreover, that percentage might be higher given that the standard rate band applies after deduction for allowable trust management expenses.

(3)    The Part 5 Chapter 5 provisions involve 'looking through' a settlement and treating the income as that of the settlor: similar provisions are found in the CGT treatment of UK resident trusts and more draconian provisions in the case of non-resident trusts.

(4)    Part 5 Chapter 5 is capable of applying to foreign as well as UK trusts. For instance, in a case where assets are transferred to non-resident trustees, these provisions need to be considered as, of course, does TA 1988 s 739 (see **[18.111]** ff). Unlike the latter provision, Part 5 Chapter 5 is, however, only concerned with the income of the settlement and does not catch income retained in a company that is owned by the settlement.                                                        **[16.107]**

## VIII    REFORM

Much of the reform proposed in the various discussion and consultation documents since December 2003 has now been implemented. This embraces increasing the rate applicable to tax for both dividends and all other income, the introduction of a standard rate band for the first £1,000 (for 2006–07 and subsequent years) of income taxable at the RAT, legislation providing for special treatment of trusts for the most vulnerable beneficiaries and the harmonisation of the main definitions and tests for trusts and trustees used in the taxation of UK personal resident trusts. Other measures which were discussed, including income streaming, are not currently being taken forward.                                                        **[16.108]**

# 17  Estates in the course
# of administration

*Updated by Jonathan Cooke, ACIB, TEP, Partner, Humphrey & Co (Chartered Accountants)*

---

---

Personal representatives (PRs, meaning both executors and administrators) are under a duty to administer a deceased's estate. From the point of view of taxation this involves:

(1)  Settling the deceased's outstanding tax liabilities to the date of death. Although this chapter is concerned primarily with income tax, notice that there may also be an outstanding CGT liability (see **Chapter 21**) and that the PRs cannot obtain a grant of probate until any IHT, payable on their application for a grant, has been accounted for (see **Chapter 30**).

(2)  Liability to income tax on any income produced during the administration period. In addition, the PRs may incur a CGT liability (see **Chapter 21**) and the original IHT bill may require adjustment as a result of events happening after the death (see **[30.63]**).

Apart from considering the PRs' liability to pay income tax, this chapter also considers the liability of beneficiaries to tax on any income distributed to them from the estate.                                           **[17.1]**

## I  THE DECEASED'S INCOME

The PRs are accountable for any income tax owed by the deceased (TMA 1970 s 74(1)). They should report the death to the appropriate inspector of taxes and complete an ordinary income tax return on behalf of the deceased for the period from 6 April preceding his death to the date of death, and for earlier tax years (if necessary!). In computing the income tax of the deceased, normal principles operate and full personal allowances are available for the year of death.

Any outstanding income tax is a debt of the estate thereby reducing the value of that estate for IHT purposes. Conversely, any repayment of income tax will swell the assets of the estate and may increase the IHT bill on death. The Revenue can assess the PRs, at any time within three years after

31 January following the year of assessment in which he died, for any tax that is owing for a period ending within six years of the date of death (TMA 1970 s 40). An assessment is made for these purposes when the inspector authorised to make assessments signs the certificate contained in the assessment books kept at the relevant district (*Honig v Sarsfield* (1986) and see [**4.40**]).

[**17.2**]

### EXAMPLE 17.1

A died on 28 September 2005 (tax year 2005–06). If the Revenue assesses his PRs on 2 January 2007 they can recover back tax to the tax year 2000–01 but no further.

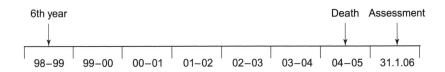

### 1   Dividends

Dividends received before the deceased's death form part of the deceased's income. For IHT purposes the quoted securities in the deceased's estate must be valued at death; if that quotation was *ex div* (ie it did not include the value of a declared dividend) the dividend that is to be paid must be added to the value of the security. This problem does not arise when the shares were valued at death *cum div* since the quotation includes any accruing dividend to date.

If the dividend is paid after the death but relates to a period partly before and partly after death, it may have to be apportioned (Apportionment Act 1870 s 2) for succession purposes.

However, whether or not the dividend is apportioned for succession purposes any dividend paid after the deceased's death is treated as the *income of the estate and not of the deceased* and must not be included in the deceased's tax return (*IRC v Henderson's Executors* (1931)). This rule follows from the fact that as the dividends were never owed to the deceased they never became a part of his income. Only in cases where a dividend is declared due before death, but paid after that death will it be taxed as the deceased's income (see, for instance, *Re Sebright* (1944) and contrast *Potel v IRC* (1971)). Similarly, certain other investment income paid after death but relating to the period before death (eg bank deposit interest) should be apportioned for succession purposes, but included as estate income for tax purposes. This may lead to some double taxation in that the income which is deemed for succession purposes to accrue before death is charged both to IHT (as part of the deceased's estate on death) and also to income tax in the hands of the PRs and beneficiaries. ITTOIA 2005 s 669 affords some relief against such double taxation but only to an absolutely entitled residuary beneficiary who is a higher rate taxpayer (see [**16.54**]).

[**17.3**]

**EXAMPLE 17.2**

T died on 30 May 2005 leaving his residuary estate (including 1,000 shares in Z Ltd) to his brother B absolutely. On 15 June 2005 Z Ltd declared a dividend on those shares of £450 in respect of the year ending on 30 June. The dividend was paid on 28 July 2005.

Of this dividend 11/12 (£412.50) is deemed to have accrued before T's death and will be reflected in the value of the shares in T's estate which will have been valued *cum div*. It will thus be taxed as part of the capital in T's estate.

However, for income tax purposes the whole dividend is taxed as the income of the estate, albeit with some relief for double taxation against any higher rate liability of B under ITTOIA 2005 s 669.

## 2 Trust income

Where the deceased was a life tenant under a trust, any income that was received by the trustees before his death is treated as his income and must be included in the PRs' tax return to the date of death. If income was paid to the trustees after the death but is attributable in part to the period before death, tax is payable according to the actual apportionment. Any income that is apportioned to the deceased life tenant is taxed as the income of the estate—and not of the deceased (*Wood v Owen* (1941)).

Income that is apportioned to the deceased life tenant forms an asset of his estate, thereby increasing his IHT liability. This could result in an element of double IHT because the apportioned income will affect the value of the trust assets on which the trustees pay IHT on the life tenant's death. This double taxation is avoided by deducting the apportioned income from the value of the settled assets.

**EXAMPLE 17.3**

T who died on 30 June 2005 was life tenant of a trust. Included in the settled assets was debenture stock in Blank Ltd. On 31 December 2005 B Ltd paid the trustees the annual interest of £80 (£100 gross). This interest was apportioned by the trustees as to half (£40) to T and half (£40) to the remainderman X. The £40 apportioned to the deceased is estate income. Notice, also, that the £40 besides forming an additional asset of T's estate for IHT purposes also swells the value of the trust fund on which the trustees pay IHT at T's rates (see **[33.23]**). To avoid the £40 being charged twice to IHT, it is deducted from the value of the settled assets. (If T's free estate passed to a residuary beneficiary absolutely, the latter may be entitled to relief under ITTOIA 2005 s 669 above.)

If the Apportionment Act 1870 is excluded so that all the income is paid to either a subsequent life tenant or a remainderman, income tax follows the actual payment made. That income, therefore, is not taxed as part of the deceased's estate. **[17.4]**

## 3 Sole traders and partners

A sole trader's business is discontinued as a result of death: tax for the year of death is based on profits for the previous basis period to the date of death less any overlap profits (see generally **[10.201]**). Unused losses or capital allowances are not available for use by the PRs but can be carried back as a terminal loss (see [11.102]). If the business is carried on by the surviving spouse capital allowances are given on the basis that the spouse acquired the assets at probate value. If the deceased had been a member of a partnership his death is treated as the discontinuance of the separate trade carried on by him alone.                                                          [17.5]–[17.20]

## II   THE ADMINISTRATION PERIOD

### 1   Duration of administration

The administration period is the period from the date of death until the date when the residue is ascertained and ready for distribution. Until that time no beneficiary is entitled to the income or to any property comprised in the estate and, accordingly, is generally not liable to income tax unless income is actually distributed to him. Identifying precisely when completion of the administration of the estate occurs can present problems: for the position in Scotland see ITTOIA 2005 s 653(2) and for the position elsewhere see, for instance, *IRC v Pilkington* (1941) and *Prest v Bettinson* (1980) and the IR Manual CG 30840.                                                        [17.21]

### 2   Taxing PRs during administration

During the administration period, the PRs are liable, in a representative capacity, to income tax on all the income of the estate computed in the usual way. This liability is to pay tax at either the lower rate (20%) or basic rate (22%). Savings income generally, which includes sums equivalent to interest paid in respect of a solicitor's undesignated client account, is therefore taxed at the 20% rate whilst rents, royalties and profits from trading are taxed at basic rate. Dividend income is taxed at 10% that is met by the 10% tax credit.

Some income received by the PRs will already have borne tax: in those cases the PRs have no further tax to pay. Generally such income falls into three categories:
(1)   income which has borne tax at basic rate;
(2)   income which has borne tax at the lower rate (eg interest paid by banks and building societies); and
(3)   income with non-repayable tax credits (eg dividend income).

The main examples of income on which PRs are directly assessed are:
(a)   rents from property;
(b)   foreign source income;
(c)   interest (eg from National Savings) which is paid gross; and
(d)   royalties.                                                          [17.22]

### 3   Interest relief

Tax relief is available, for one year from the making of the loan, for interest on a loan raised to pay the IHT payable on delivery of the PRs' account, which is attributable to personal property owned beneficially by the deceased and which vests in his PRs, provided that the loan is on a loan account not merely by way of overdraft (TA 1988 s 364). Relief is given against the income of the estate for the year in which the interest is paid but where that income is insufficient relief may be given against income of the preceding year and then against the future income of the estate. In practice this is normally the only deduction that can be made against the estate income: expenses incurred by the PRs in administering the estate are not deductible.   **[17.23]**

## 4  Trading

When the PRs carry on a business after the death of a sole trader in order to sell it as a going concern or to transfer it to a beneficiary, they must pay basic rate tax on any profits calculated in the usual way. Hence, they can deduct business expenses and claim loss relief in the usual way.   **[17.24]**

## 5  Letting

Similarly, any expenses incurred directly in connection with the letting of freehold or leasehold property may be deducted in arriving at the net income liable to tax.   **[17.25]**

## 6  Apportionments

Dividends and certain other income received by the PRs after the death in respect of a period wholly or partly before death is taxed as the income of the estate whether or not it is apportioned for succession purposes. Similarly, trust income received by the trustees after the deceased life tenant's death and apportioned to him is taxed as the income of the estate (see **[16.4]**).

When property which produces no income is left to persons in succession (eg to A for life, remainder to B), part of the capital sum realised on the sale of that property may be treated for trust purposes as income, eg the rules in *Howe v Dartmouth* (1802) and *Re Earl of Chesterfield's Trusts* (1883) since, otherwise, the life tenant would receive nothing. Income apportioned to the life tenant may be liable to basic rate tax if it is of a recurring nature as in the case of a *Howe v Dartmouth* apportionment, but if it is paid as a one-off lump sum from capital by way of compensation as in the case of a *Re Chesterfield* apportionment it is not liable to tax.   **[17.26]–[17.40]**

## III  TAXATION OF DISTRIBUTIONS TO BENEFICIARIES

### 1  The basic principles

Income received by the PRs suffers the equivalent of basic or lower rate tax either by deduction at source or by direct assessment in their hands. From this taxed income the PRs deduct administration expenses chargeable against income, leaving a net sum available for distribution to beneficiaries entitled to the income from the estate. In the days when income was taxed at basic and higher rate only the position was straightforward. As already explained, however, the current position offers a variety of possibilities with

PRs receiving savings income with a credit of only 20% whilst dividends have non-reclaimable tax credits. These different types of income fall to be divided between beneficiaries as is just and reasonable having regard to their different interests (ITTOIA 2005 ss 663 and 670). Which type of income are administration expenses deducted against? The legislation leaves the matter open, but the best approach will normally be to set expenses first against income carrying a non-reclaimable credit, then against income bearing tax at lower rate and finally against basic rate income (this order is accepted by HMRC).

If the PRs have a discretion whether to deduct administration expenses from income or capital they may consider the tax position of a beneficiary (if any) absolutely entitled to the residue of the estate. When that beneficiary has a large income, they may deduct their expenses from income so as to reduce his income and, therefore, his tax bill. Conversely, if the beneficiary has only a small income or is a charity, they may deduct expenses from capital so as not to prejudice any claim that he may have for a repayment of income tax.                                                                                    **[17.41]**

## 2   General legatees

A general legatee is a person who is entitled to a sum of money (a pecuniary legacy) not charged on any particular fund. This sum is capital and the legatee is generally not entitled to any interest unless:
(1)   the will directs the PRs to pay him interest; or
(2)   the legacy remains unpaid at the end of the executor's year, in which case he is entitled to interest at the basic rate payable on funds in court in the absence of a contrary direction; or
(3)   the legacy is a 'statutory legacy' arising on intestacy (eg to a surviving spouse) in which case he is similarly entitled to interest at the rate indicated above from the date of death to the date of payment.

Interest is paid gross by the PRs and the legatee is assessed directly to tax under ITTOIA 2005 s 369 on the interest (unless the interest is paid to a person whose usual place of abode is outside the UK when basic rate tax must be deducted by the PRs: see TA s 349(2)). If that interest is neither claimed nor paid, there is no income to be assessed in the beneficiary's hands (*Dewar v IRC* (1935)). Once a sum has been set aside to pay the legacy it may, however, be too late to disclaim any income (*Spens v IRC* (1970)). For the PRs, interest is ignored in computing their tax liability and so does not appear on their tax returns: this follows from the basic principle that the payment of interest does not attract tax relief (see further **[7.43]**). Such interest may, however, be treated as an administration expense and properly be deducted from the net income that is available for allocation and vouching to the residuary beneficiaries (ITTOIA 2005 s 666).     **[17.42]**

## 3   Specific legatees

A specific legatee is entitled to a particular item of property and to any income produced by it as from the date of death. Therefore, once the PRs vest the asset in the beneficiary, any income from it that arose during the administration period is related back and taxed as the legatee's income for the tax year(s) when it arose (*IRC v Hawley* (1928)). It will have suffered tax either through deduction at source or as a result of direct assessment on the PRs. Accordingly, the net income will be passed to the beneficiary together with a tax deduction certificate completed by the PRs. **[17.43]**

**EXAMPLE 17.4**

A died in September 2005 leaving his 1,000 shares in B Ltd to his nephew T. A dividend of £90 is paid in respect of the shares in January 2006. The administration is completed and the shares vested in T in May 2006 together with the dividend and tax credit for the £10 tax that has been deducted. T must include the £100 in his income tax return for the tax year 2005–06 (when the dividend was paid) and not 2006–07(when T received it).

## 4  Annuitants

### a)  *Definition*

An annuity is a pecuniary legacy payable by instalments. The payments are income from which the PRs must deduct basic rate income tax (ITTOIA 2005 s 426). The net sum will be paid to the annuitant who will be given a certificate of tax deducted.

Modern wills rarely provide for the payment of an annuity. **[17.44]**

### b)  *Use of formula*

A testator may want the annuitant to receive a constant sum despite fluctuations in the tax rates. The two methods most commonly employed are:
(1)  The testator provides for the payment of 'such sum as will after deduction of income tax at the basic rate for the time being in force leave (say) £78 pa'.
 The PRs must pay £78 grossed up at the current basic rate, but they are not liable to indemnify the annuitant against any higher rate income tax for which he may be liable. Conversely, if the annuitant can reclaim all or any of the basic rate tax paid, he need not account for it to the PRs.
(2)  If the testator provides for the payment of '£78 pa free from income tax' this imposes an obligation on the PRs to pay such sum as after deducting basic rate income tax leaves £78. However, it also means that the annuitant can recover from the PRs any higher rate tax that he may have to pay on the annuity and any basic rate tax that he reclaims must be repaid to the PRs. In effect, he will never be left with more nor with less than £78 (see *Re Pettit, Le Fevre v Pettit* (1922)). **[17.45]**

### c)  *Setting aside a capital sum and purchased life annuities*

An annuitant can insist on a capital sum being set aside to provide for his annuity (thereby creating an interest in possession trust for IHT purposes: see **Chapter 32**). If the capital in the estate is insufficient he can demand that the actuarial value of the annuity be paid to him, abated if necessary (*IRC v Lady Castlemaine* (1943)). This capitalised annuity is not subject to income tax either in the PRs' or in the annuitant's hands.

If the will directs the PRs to purchase an annuity for the beneficiary, he will be charged to income tax on the full amount of each annual payment and cannot claim relief under ITTOIA 2005 s 717 which taxes only the income element. The beneficiary should, therefore, request that the PRs give him the appropriate capital sum so that he can buy the annuity himself and claim a s 717 relief.                                                      **[17.46]**

### d)   *Beware top-ups!*

Where there is insufficient income in the estate to pay the annuity in full, the will may direct the PRs to make up the income from capital. If they do so, that capital is treated as income from which basic rate tax must be deducted (*Brodie's Will Trusts v IRC* (1933)). The unfortunate result of such 'top-up' provisions is to convert capital into income and it is, therefore, better to give the PRs a discretion to make good any shortfall in the annuity by capital advances (see **[16.68]**).                                              **[17.47]**

## 5   **Residuary beneficiaries**

A beneficiary may have a limited or an absolute interest in residue. A limited interest exists where he is entitled to income only, eg if the will leaves residue to 'my wife for life, remainder to my children', the wife is entitled only to income from the estate. An absolute interest exists when the beneficiary is entitled to both the income and capital of the residue, as where the residue is left to 'my wife absolutely'.                                          **[17.48]**

### a)   *Beneficiary with a limited interest in residue*

Any income paid to the beneficiary during the administration period will be paid net of tax deducted by the PRs. The beneficiary must gross up these sums, at the tax rate applicable in the year of *payment* to that category of income, as part of his total income in the year of receipt for the purposes of his excess liability or to obtain a repayment of tax (as appropriate). Where any sum remains payable on completion of administration, it is treated as being the income of the beneficiary in the tax year in which the administration ends (ITTOIA 2005 ss 654–655).                          **[17.49]–[17.51]**

**EXAMPLE 17.5**

Mandy died on 6 March 2004 leaving her residuary estate to Shirley for life remainder to Jemima. The net income of the estate was:

| Tax year | | Amount |
|---|---|---|
| | | (£) |
| 2003–04 | | 3,000 |
| 2004–05 | | 10,000 |
| 2005–06 | | 1,000 |
| | Total | £14,000 |

Payments made to Shirley were:

| Tax year | Amount |
| --- | ---: |
| | (£) |
| 2003–04 | nil |
| 2004–05 | 9,000 |
| 2005–06 | 5,000 |
| Total | £14,000 |

Shirley is taxed on the payments in the tax years of receipt, ie in 2004–05 and 2005–06.

*Note:* If at the end of administration there is an undistributed income balance it is deemed to have been paid to the beneficiary in the tax year when the administration ended (this being the one exception to the receipts basis). For instance, if the administration of Mandy's estate had been complete on 4 April 2005 the undistributed income balance of £5,000 would be taxed on Shirley in 2004–05 even though she did not receive it until the following tax year.

b) *Beneficiary with an absolute interest in residue*

Such a beneficiary is entitled to receive both income and capital from the estate. He can, of course, only be charged to income tax insofar as any payments that he receives represent income. The position is that:

(1) payments during administration are taxed as income up to the amount of the aggregated income entitlement of the beneficiary for the year of assessment in which the sum is paid (see ITTOIA 2005 s 652): '*aggregated income entitlement*' means the net income to which the beneficiary is entitled);

(2) if on completion of administration the beneficiary has not received his full aggregate entitlement to income, the shortfall is treated as having been paid to him immediately before the end of the administration period; and

(3) the beneficiary must gross up the sums treated as income, at the tax rate applicable in the year of *payment* to that category of income, as part of his total income in the year of receipt for the purposes of his excess liability or to obtain a repayment of tax (as appropriate).        **[17.52]**

**EXAMPLE 17.6**

Simple Simon died on 6 March 2004 leaving his entire estate to Dorothy. Net income arising to the estate was as follows:

| Tax year | Net income |
| --- | ---: |
| | (£) |
| 2003–04 | 3,000 |
| 2004–05 | 10,000 |
| 2005–06 | 1,000 |
| Total | £14,000 |

(1)    *Tax year 2003–04* Assuming that no payment is made to Dorothy £3,000 is carried forward to 2004–05. As at 5 April 2004 Dorothy's aggregated income entitlement is £3,000.

(2)    *Tax year 2004–05* At 5 April 2005 Dorothy's aggregated income entitlement assuming no payment in 2003–04 is £13,000. As a result, if a payment of £63,000 is made to her in this year the first £13,000 is treated as income.

*Notes:*

(a)    The timing of the payment in the tax year is irrelevant: it could for instance occur on 6 April 2004 but nonetheless it is Dorothy's aggregated income entitlement at 5 April 2005 that is crucial.

(b)    The rules apply to the payment of 'any sum': it is not possible for the PRs to specify that the payment is 'of capital'. Furthermore, HMRC considers that for these purposes the payment of 'any sum' includes a transfer of assets. It will therefore treat the value of such assets as income up to the amount of the beneficiary's aggregated income entitlement (ITTOIA 2005 s 681).

*Position when a multiplicity of beneficiaries* In this situation income arising during administration must be split between beneficiaries in the same proportion as their capital shares (see ITTOIA 2005 s 667) referring to a 'proportionate part' of the residuary income). A further complexity arises from the different types of estate income: this too needs to be split proportionately between the beneficiaries (see ITTOIA 2005 ss 656 and 679). Payments are made first from income bearing tax at basic rate before income bearing tax at lower rate and income carrying non-reclaimable credits.

**[17.53]**

**EXAMPLE 17.7**

Betty's estate is to be divided between Adam (50%); Claude (25%) and Cecil (25%). In 2005–06 the net income of the estate was £13,900 made up of:

dividends                £10,000 (credit for 10% non-reclaimable)

rent income            £3,900 (credit for 22%)

(*i*)    *Aggregated income entitlement for 2003–04*

| Type of income | Adam (50%) | Claude (25%) | Cecil (25%) |
|---|---|---|---|
| Basic rate | 1,950 | 975.0 | 975.0 |
| Non-reclaimable dividend rate | 5,000 | 2,500.0 | 2,500.0 |
| £13,900 | £6,950 | £3,475 | £3,475 |

(*ii*)    *Treatment of income distribution in the year*

Assuming that each beneficiary received one half of his aggregated income entitlement for the year, the position would be:

| | Adam (£) | Claude (£) | Cecil (£) |
|---|---|---|---|
| Receipt | 3,475 | 1,737.5 | 1,737.5 |
| made up of: | | | |
| Basic rate income | 1,950.0 | 975.0 | 975.0 |
| Non-reclaimable dividend rate | 1,525 | 762.5 | 762.5 |

*Notes:*
(1)  Each beneficiary would carry forward an aggregated income entitlement to the next tax year: in Adam's case this would be £3,475 being comprised of non-reclaimable dividend income.
(2)  What if tax rates change between receipt of income by PRs and its distribution? ITTOIA 2005 ss 663 and 670 provide for income to be paid with the appropriate credit for rates of tax current in the year of payment not in the year of receipt by PRs.
(3)  Each beneficiary is considered separately and a distribution to one beneficiary may not be matched by an equivalent distribution to another in that tax year. For instance, the PRs may distribute income to Claude but not to Adam or Cecil in 2005–06. Of course, ultimately income of the estate must be split in the ratio 50:25:25 and so the other beneficiaries shares must be made good in the future.

*Relief against a double charge* Income which accrued before death, but is received by the PRs after death, is included in the value of the deceased's estate for IHT purposes and is also taxed as the income of the estate (see **[16.3]**). Some relief against this double taxation is provided by ITTOIA 2005 s 669 that allows a reduction in the residuary income for the purposes of any liability to higher rate tax of a residuary beneficiary absolutely entitled to residue. The reduction is of an amount equal to the IHT chargeable on that income at the estate rate and the resultant sum is then grossed up at the basic rate of income tax (or, on savings income, the lower rate or dividend ordinary rate) for the tax year in which the charge to higher rate arises.

**[17.54]**

**EXAMPLE 17.8**

X died on 30 April 2005. He left his residuary estate including 1,000 debentures in B Ltd to his daughter D. His PRs received interest of £160 (£200 gross) from B Ltd in November 2005 in respect of that company's accounting year ending 31 October 2005. The whole interest is taxed as the income of the estate but, as half the interest accrued before death, that portion is included in X's estate for IHT purposes. Under ITTOIA 2005 s 669 if D is a higher rate taxpayer one half of the interest is eligible for relief. Assume that the estate rate of IHT is 20%.

|  | £ |
|---|---|
| Interest (gross) | £200 |
| Sum accrued before death | 100 |
| *Less:* income tax for year of death | 20 |
|  | £80 |
| The relief is calculated as: | £ |
| £80 × 20% (IHT estate rate) | 16 |
| Grossed-up (at 20%) amount that can be deducted from the residuary income to reduce D's liability to higher rate income tax only | £20 |

## 6   **Conclusions**

### a)   *Position of PRs*

The payments basis of assessment for residuary beneficiaries means that the dates of payment or conclusion of administration are critical: if all payments are bunched in a single tax year this may push the beneficiary into the higher rate of income tax.

When deciding upon the timing of distributions, therefore, PRs should consider whether the bunching or spreading of income over the administration best suits the tax position of the beneficiaries. However, to do this the PRs will need to know the circumstances of each beneficiary. **[17.55]–[17.56]**

### b)   *Successive interests in residue*

ITTOIA 2005 ss 671–675 provide for the situation where an interest in the whole or part of the residue is held successively by different persons during the course of administration. In the case of instruments of variation (as to which see **[30.153]**) the result is that provided no distributions have been made to the original beneficiary before the variation all income will be assessed on the new beneficiary. The same applies to a change of beneficiary as the result of an exercise by the PRs of a power of appointment. In the case of a beneficiary with a limited interest in residue, eg a life tenant, dying during the course of the administration, however, any income that would otherwise be due to that beneficiary up to and including the day he died is payable (in the absence of a contrary indication in the will) to his own PRs and assessable on them accordingly.                              **[17.57]**

# 18 The overseas dimension

*Updated by Peter Vaines, Squire, Sanders & Dempsey*

'The [UK resident] is taxed because (whether he be a British subject or not) he enjoys the benefit of our laws for the protection of his person and his property. The [non-UK resident] is taxed because in respect of his property in the United Kingdom he enjoys the benefit of our laws for the protection of that property.'

(*Whitney v IRC* (1926) 10 TC 88 at 112.)

The territorial scope of any tax raises both theoretical and practical questions. A strong element of practical reality inevitably permeates this area: theoretically the UK could impose a tax on the Chinese income of a Chinaman resident in China but little revenue would be raised from that source! The practical constraints upon tax collection and enforcement are well illustrated in the House of Lords' speeches in *Clark v Oceanic Contractors Inc* (1983): see **[18.51]**—but see also *Agassi v HMIT* (2006).

The 'connecting factors' that determine the extent to which the individual should be subject to income tax are residence, ordinary residence and domicile and the meaning of these terms will be considered in this chapter. This discussion will also be relevant when the territorial scope of CGT, IHT and corporation tax are considered (in **Chapter 41**).

As a general rule, a UK resident is subject to UK income tax on all his income worldwide wherever its source, whereas a foreign resident is only liable to UK income tax on income arising to him in the UK. However, a foreign domiciled but UK resident individual will generally be taxed on foreign income only if it is remitted to the UK.                                                                 **[18.1]**

## I  RESIDENCE, ORDINARY RESIDENCE AND DOMICILE

### 1  Residence

Neither 'residence' nor 'ordinary residence' is statutorily defined and the meaning of these terms has to be sought from decisions of the courts. The practice of HMRC is set out at length in its booklet, 'Residents and Non-Residents': IR 20, December 1999. The dictionary definition of these words has usually been adopted but for taxation purposes questions of residence do not generally depend upon any mental element (unlike domicile). Hence, the American who finds himself stuck in the UK because of a strike or other extra work commitments and other difficulties may become resident here although his intention is to return to America as soon as the strike etc is over.

A person can be resident in more than one country at the same time so that the individual who spends the winter months in Manchester and the summer in the Costa del Sol could be resident both in the UK and in Spain. Alternatively, an individual may not be resident anywhere as in the case of the travel writer who spends two years exploring North and South America by bus and is, therefore, continually on the move, but see **[18.7]** for the concept of occasional residence which can affect the liability to income tax. In this sense, residence contrasts with domicile since a person must always have a country of domicile.

A permanent abode is not necessary for residence in a country so that the individual who moves from UK hotel to UK hotel may be resident here. This proposition can be illustrated as follows:

> 'Take the case of a homeless tramp, who shelters tonight under a bridge, tomorrow in the greenwood and as the unwelcome occupant of a farm outhouse the night after. He wanders in this way all over the United Kingdom. But will anyone say that he does not live in the United Kingdom?—and will anyone regard it as a misuse of language to say he resides in the United Kingdom?'
>
> (Lord President Clyde in *Reid v IRC* (1926).)

Residence and ordinary residence are not decided in a vacuum but in relation to particular tax years. It is not possible to split tax years into periods of residence and non-residence and the individual who is resident for any part of a tax year is treated as being resident for the whole of that year. It is therefore probably unnecessary for the CGT legislation expressly to provide in TCGA 1992 s 2(1) that CGT is levied if the individual is resident in the UK during *any part* of the tax year.

### EXAMPLE 18.1

Alan, resident and ordinarily resident in the UK, goes to live abroad from June 2004 to March 2006. He will be treated as retaining his UK residence in 2003–04 and 2004–05 for both income tax and CGT purposes (see IR 20 at pp 11–12).

As a matter of practice, in certain cases the tax year may be split for income tax purposes into a period of residence and non-residence (ESC A11). This applies when an individual leaves the UK for permanent residence abroad and likewise when an individual comes to the UK for permanent residence or to stay for at least two years. In the former case, UK residence ceases on the day following the day of departure from the UK: in the latter, UK residence is acquired from the day of arrival. A similar splitting of the tax year occurs when an individual leaves the UK to take up full-time employment abroad or to work full time in a trade or profession.

The position for CGT is slightly different. There is a corresponding concession (ESC D2) which provides for the tax year to be split in a similar fashion, but only where the individual leaving the UK has not been resident or ordinarily resident for at least four out of the seven years preceding the year of departure. For individuals coming to the UK, to benefit from split year treatment they must have been non-resident for at least five years prior to the year of arrival.                                                           **[18.2]**

## 2   Who is a UK resident?

In the following situations an individual will be taxed as a resident in the UK.
                                                                                      **[18.3]**

a)   *The '183-day' rule*

If he spends more than six months here in the tax year an individual will invariably be resident in the UK. This rule is derived from TA 1988 s 336 and six months is interpreted by the Revenue to mean 183 days (even in a leap year). It is possible to count hours and minutes in determining whether the 183-day limit has been breached: see *Wilkie v IRC* (1952). However, it is normal practice to ignore days of arrival and departure (IR 20 para 1.2).
                                                                                      **[18.4]**

b)   *The '91-day' rule*

A person who has left the UK for permanent residence abroad is regarded as continuing to be resident here if his visits to the UK average 91 days or more per tax year. In addition a regular visitor to the UK becomes resident after four years if his visits during those years average at least 91 days per year. In cases where it is clear that the taxpayer intends to make such visits he is treated as resident either from the year of his arrival or from the year when he forms that intention (if later). In IR 20 he is referred to as a 'longer term visitor'. For this purpose SP 2/91 provides that 'any days spent in the UK because of *exceptional circumstances beyond an individual's control* (such as illness) are excluded from the calculation'. This SP does not apply for the purpose of computing the six-month (or 183-day) period.          **[18.5]**

> **EXAMPLE 18.2**
>
> (1)   Barry comes to England from America to study law at London University. The course is to last three years. As Barry will be present in the UK for more than six months in each of those tax years he is UK resident from the date of his arrival.
> (2)   Ellie regularly comes to the UK on holiday from America. Her visits do not exceed two months per annum. She will not be treated as UK resident.

c)   *Available accommodation*

The individual who had UK accommodation available for his use and who merely set foot in this country (even if he did not visit that accommodation) used to be treated as UK resident.

In 1993 the 'available accommodation' test was abolished. The current position is that in determining whether an individual is in the UK for some temporary purpose only, and not with a view to establishing his residence there, no regard shall be paid to living accommodation available for that person's use in the UK (see TA 1988 s 336(3)).    **[18.6]**

**EXAMPLE 18.3**

Toki, an international playboy, comes to London each year for 'the season'. If he acquires a flat in London, that will not by itself make him UK resident and, provided that he does not remain in the UK for 91 days in any tax year, he will not become so resident (but for the use of accommodation in deciding whether the individual is a long-term visitor, see IR 20, p 18).

d)    *Occasional Residence Abroad*

The absence of a person from the UK *throughout* a tax year provides strong evidence that he is not resident in that year.

By TA 1988 s 334, a Commonwealth citizen who has been ordinarily resident in the UK and who leaves for *occasional residence* abroad will continue to be liable to income tax the same way as a UK resident. In *Reed v Clark* (1985), it was held that s 334 was a charging provision and was not limited to persons who were out of the UK for part only of a tax year but could equally apply to persons living abroad throughout a year of assessment. In that case, the taxpayer (the pop star Dave Clark) left the UK with the deliberate intention of living and working abroad for a limited period in excess of one tax year and then returning to the UK. The judge held that his absence could not be described as for the purpose of merely occasional residence abroad so that he was not treated as UK resident under s 334. Occasional residence under this section was to be contrasted with ordinary or settled residence.

> 'The presence of a tax avoidance intention may help to show, for instance, why a person went abroad at all or at the particular time he did, how long he intended to remain away, or where his home in fact was in the year of assessment. But residence abroad for a carefully chosen limited period of work there ... is no less residence abroad for that period because the major reason for it was the avoidance of tax. Likewise with ordinary residence.'
>
> (Nicholls J, at 346.)

Crucially there was a 'distinct break' with the UK in this case: where the individual has *not* become resident or ordinarily resident elsewhere it may be difficult to rebut the presumption that he remains UK resident. For the tax treatment of mobile workers (those who come to the UK during the week to work and live elsewhere, or those who live in the UK but spend the working week abroad) see *Tax Bulletin*, April 2001, p 836 and *Taxation*, 26 April 2001, p 81. See also *Shepherd v HMRC* (2005) where the Special Commissioner summarised the principles to be adopted in determining residence.    **[18.7]**

3    **Acquiring and losing resident status**

An individual who comes to the UK with the intention of taking up permanent residence will by concession be regarded as both resident and ordinarily resident from the date of his arrival. By contrast, a short-term visitor will not become UK resident unless he falls within the 91-day rule. The casual UK resident (eg one who spends an isolated six months here) will lose his resident status simply by returning abroad.

An individual may go abroad for full-time service under a contract of employment that requires all the duties of his employment to be performed abroad (with any UK duties being merely incidental). Providing his absence from the UK lasts for a complete tax year with interim visits to the UK not exceeding six months in any tax year (or an average of 91 days per tax year for four years), he is normally regarded as neither resident nor ordinarily resident in the UK from the day following the date of his departure. (For the meaning of 'incidental duties', see *Robson v Dixon* (1972).) **[18.8]**

## 4 Ordinary residence

Ordinary residence has been held to mean a choice of abode adopted voluntarily and which is a settled purpose and forms part of the regular order of an individual's life (see, in particular, *R v Barnet London Borough Council, ex p Nilish Shah* (1983)). A person may be resident without being ordinarily resident in the UK and probably *vice versa*. (IR 20 states: 'If you are resident in the UK year after year, you are treated as ordinarily resident here' and see IM 36.) In *Nessa v Chief Adjudication Officer* (2000) the House of Lords considered the meaning of 'habitual residence' in the context of the Income Support Regulations and concluded that a mere intention to live in a place was insufficient: there must be actual residence for a period which showed that it had become habitual. A similar construction is likely to be put on ordinary residence which might cast doubt on the Revenue's view that a person who comes to the UK permanently is both resident and ordinarily resident from his date of arrival (see IR 20 para 3.1).

### EXAMPLE 18.4

(1) Bonzo has lived in Hackney for many years. He sells his terraced house in February 2005 and goes on a world cruise for 18 months. He would cease to be UK resident (see **[18.7]**) but he would probably remain ordinarily resident.

(2) Claude, a French journalist, visits the UK for six months in the 2005–06 tax year to study the eating habits of the natives. He becomes UK resident but is not ordinarily resident.

In some cases liability to UK tax is *only* imposed on individuals who are ordinarily resident (for example under TA 1988 ss 739–740) whilst, in other cases, liability arises if the individual is *either* resident *or* ordinarily resident, eg CGT liability under TCGA 1992 s 2(1).

When a person comes to the UK with the intention of visiting the UK regularly for at least four tax years (so that his visits will average 91 days or more per tax year) ordinary residence will be presumed from the outset. If there is no such intention, SP 17/91 indicates that ordinary residence will commence from the beginning of the tax year after the individual has visited the UK over four years (averaging 91 days per year) provided that he originally came with no definite plans about the extent of his future visits.

**[18.9]**

## 5  Corporations

Prior to 15 March 1988, a company was resident in the UK (and therefore subject to corporation tax on its worldwide profits) if its central management and control was located in the UK. Central management and control was considered to be located at the place where board meetings were held and not necessarily where the company was incorporated or registered (see *De Beers Consolidated Mines v Howe* (1906) and SP 1/90).

### EXAMPLE 18.5

The directors of a Kenyan subsidiary company always held meetings in Kenya but in fact the company was managed, in breach of its articles, by its UK parent company. The company was therefore held to be resident in England since the question was where the actual control and management was located (see *Unit Construction Co Ltd v Bullock* (1959) but see *Untelrab Ltd v McGregor* (1996) in which the Revenue failed to prove that a subsidiary was managed and controlled by its UK parent company and more recently *Wood v Holden* (2005)).

From 15 March 1988 this control and management test has been supplemented by a further test based on the place of company incorporation. Companies incorporated in the UK will remain UK resident even if control and management is exercised abroad unless under the terms of a 'tie-breaker' article in a double tax treaty they would be treated as resident in the other treaty country. Foreign incorporated companies may become resident, as before, if their central management and control is situated in the UK.

**[18.10]**

## 6  Partnerships

### a)  *Non-resident partnerships*

A similar central management and control test applies to partnerships. If the management and control of the business is exercised abroad, the firm is deemed to be non-resident even though individual partners may be resident in the UK. Conversely, a firm established abroad will be treated as resident in the UK if managed and controlled here. However, as a partnership is not normally taxed as a separate entity, the residence of the individual partners is much more important: ITTOIA 2005 s 849.

It appears that the forerunner of s 849 was aimed at clarifying the source classification of income from foreign controlled partnerships rather than altering the liability to tax of the individual partners. In practice, a foreign source is attributed to profits from foreign trading operations even when the firm also trades in the UK (this being treated as a UK source). This departs from the normal analysis of a trade as a single indivisible source.    **[18.11]**

### b)  *Fiscal transparency*

HMRC will look through a partnership to the residence of its individual members for the purpose of determining the tax liability of that person. So far as *UK source* income is concerned, individual members of a partnership will be subject to income tax at all rates whether UK resident or not. So far as *non-UK source* income is concerned, UK residents will be subject to tax in the UK whereas partners who are non-UK resident will not, although they may be taxable in the country where the profits are earned or, alternatively, in the country of their residence. In the case of a trading partnership which is itself managed and controlled in the UK, it is highly unlikely that a trade carried on, for instance, in France would be treated as being carried on wholly outside the UK and therefore the profits will attract tax under ITTOIA 2005 Part 9 (*Colquhoun v Brooks* (1889)). **[18.12]**

## 7 Trustees and personal representatives

a) *Residence of trustees*

The residence of a trust for income tax purposes is determined by FA 1989 s 110. Where the trustees of a settlement include one UK-resident and one non-UK resident (a 'mixed' trust), the trustees will be treated as UK-resident *unless* the settlor was neither resident, ordinarily resident, nor domiciled in the UK when he set up the trust or at a later time when he provided funds for the trust. Assessments may be made in the name of any one or more of the trustees. **[18.13]–[18.14]**

### EXAMPLE 18.6

(1) The de Vere family trust was set up in 1990 when the settlor had no connection with the UK. All the trustees are non-UK resident and therefore the trust will be liable to UK income tax on UK source income *only.*

(2) The Walpole trust was set up by a UK-resident unmarried settlor who is excluded from any benefit under the trust. It has since been exported and currently all the trustees are non-UK resident and there is no UK source income. There is no liability to UK income tax.

(3) As in (2) except that there is now one UK-resident trustee. The trust's worldwide income is subject to UK income tax that can be assessed on the UK-resident trustee.

b) *Tax status of trusts*

For income tax purposes the position is complicated by the division between trusts where the beneficiary has an immediate entitlement to the income (where the trustees are only liable for UK income tax at the basic rate) and other trusts (discretionary and accumulation) where liability to UK tax may be imposed in full on the trustees. Where the settlor and his spouse are incapable of benefiting from the trust it is only in the case of such 'other trusts' that the residence of trustees is of critical importance and in this connection it should be borne in mind that income arising in the UK is always subject to UK tax subject only to specific exemptions (for instance, income arising on FOTRA ('Free of Tax to Residents Abroad') securities under FA 1996 s 154). Non-resident trustees do not qualify for 'excluded income' treatment (see **[18.71]**) if a relevant beneficiary is UK ordinarily resident (FA 1995 s 128(5)).

Some trusts have a protector who may be UK resident. Save in exceptional circumstances (when the protector is given—or exercises—wider powers than normal) this will not cause the trust to be UK resident. The powers of a protector are fiduciary in nature (see *IRC v Schroder* (1983)).

For capital gains tax the residence of a trust is determined differently. A trust will be treated as resident and ordinarily resident in the UK unless the general administration of the trusts is ordinarily carried on outside the UK and the trustees, or a majority of them for the time being, are not resident or not ordinarily resident in the UK (see TCGA 1992 s 69). However, a special rule applies for this purpose (see TCGA 1992 s 69(2) which treats a UK-resident trustee to be non-resident if he carries on a business which consists of or includes the management of trusts and acting as trustee of a trust in the course of that business—providing the settlor is not domiciled, resident or ordinarily resident in the UK). From 6 April 2007 the residence of trusts for CGT purposes will be aligned with the income tax rules and the above distinctions will disappear.                                              **[18.15]**

c)    *Personal representatives*

FA 1989 s 111 extended the residence rules for trustees to personal representatives and in so doing created an apparent injustice. Assume, for instance, that Dan Dare is an American domiciliary who comes to the UK to work or to start up a business. As it is envisaged that he will stay in this country for a number of years he acquires a house and other assets here and, accordingly, is advised to make a UK will (with UK personal representatives) disposing of this property. The bulk of his assets remain in America and a separate American will disposing of this property is also made. Assume then that Dan dies without having altered these arrangements. Under s 111, UK tax will be imposed on *all the income produced by his estate* passing under *both* wills since under his English will UK resident personal representatives have been appointed. As Dan is resident in the UK the conditions laid down for the operation of the section are satisfied given that the definition of personal representatives includes not just the UK appointees but also (in relation to another country) 'the persons having under its law any functions corresponding to the functions for administration purposes of personal representatives'. The end result appears unjust: surely UK tax should only be charged on UK source income arising under his UK estate? In practice, although no formal statement has been made, it is understood that HMRC apply the legislation in this way.                                              **[18.16]**

8   **Double tax treaties**

A person may be resident in more than one country at the same time so most double tax treaties contain a provision to determine in which of the contracting countries a person is to be treated as resident (sometimes referred to as 'tie-breaker' clauses). It is important to realise that although the treaty may therefore lead to the person being treated as resident in one of the two countries, this will only apply for the purposes of the taxes and types of income and gains covered by the relevant treaty. For other purposes, the individual may still be treated as resident in the other country (see generally IR 20 Chapter 9).                                              **[18.17]**

## 9 Domicile

### a) *Introduction*

The concept of domicile is extremely important having regard to the tax advantages that are allowed to individuals with a foreign domicile. A foreign domiciled individual resident in the UK is chargeable to UK tax on his foreign income and capital gains on the remittance basis, ie if the income or gains are actually brought to the UK. There are other provisions that provide valuable reliefs for CGT and inheritance tax.

Domicile is not the same as residence or nationality and should not be confused with either of them. An individual's domicile is generally the country that he regards as his home. It is where he has his closest ties and when he is away, the place to which he intends to return—although maybe not for some time.

There is a great deal talked about giving up clubs, changing nationality, selling property or even arranging to be buried in a foreign country. Whilst these things are relevant, they really do not matter very much except in marginal cases. Where an individual leaves the UK to live in another country, the maintenance of these connections could indicate some continuity of association with the UK that can be taken into account in deciding whether an expressed intention to stay abroad is real or imaginary. In most cases, however, it will not be necessary to suffer the personal inconvenience and possibly the financial disadvantage of giving up these things. The UK might be a good place to invest, so investing money here should not necessarily indicate an intention to return (or a lack of intention to stay away). Many foreign domiciled individuals are members of clubs in the UK because when they visit the UK they can be assured of the use of the clubs' facilities. The ability to just turn up at a familiar club without making prior arrangements is obviously very convenient—all the more so if he is settled in another country and does not visit the UK very often.

Domicile is not specifically defined for tax purposes but takes its meaning from the general law which has developed over a very long period. There are various types of domicile and they all have different characteristics. **[18.18]**

### b) *Domicile of origin*

The most important type of domicile is the domicile of origin which is acquired by an individual at birth usually by reference to the domicile of his father at the time of his birth—where he was actually born has little or nothing to do with it. Accordingly if an individual is claiming to have a foreign domicile of origin, the circumstances of his parents at the time of his birth must be investigated—and account must also be taken of what he has done and where he has lived since that date, particularly since he was 16 which is the age when an individual is able to acquire an independent domicile.

A domicile of origin is retained unless and until it is abandoned by the acquisition of a domicile of choice. In that event the domicile of origin goes into a kind of limbo, able to be revived if the domicile of choice is later abandoned without the acquisition of a further domicile of choice. An individual can never be without a domicile so if he were unable to satisfy the conditions for a domicile of choice, his domicile of origin would revive, even if he has no continuing connection with that country. The strange effects of this rule are explained in more detail below.                    **[18.19]**

c)    *Domicile of choice*

A domicile of choice is acquired by satisfying two tests:
(1)    physical residence in the chosen territory; and
(2)    an intention of permanent or indefinite residence in that territory.

It is virtually impossible to acquire a domicile of choice in a country without actually residing there—so an individual cannot claim a foreign domicile of choice unless he has at least established a residence in that country.

It is also necessary to show an intention of permanent or indefinite residence in that country. Intention is a subjective matter and is therefore difficult to prove. It is not enough just to claim the necessary intention; HMRC will require positive proof and actions speak louder than words. It is obviously fatal to a claim for a domicile of choice in some foreign territory if there is an intention to return to the country of origin or indeed if there is an intention to leave and live somewhere else. If such an intention does exist the domicile of origin will continue. The actual conduct must therefore support the expressed intention to reside there permanently. If a person has a home in one country and visits it occasionally but spends most of their time somewhere else, it may be difficult to argue that there is sufficient commitment to that country to demonstrate an intention of permanent residence.

The individual may want to avoid acquiring a domicile of choice. Many people coming to live in the UK would prefer not to acquire a UK domicile of choice because of the substantial tax privileges that would immediately be lost. For those individuals it will be necessary to demonstrate that their period in the UK is for a specific or limited purpose and that their long-term intention is to leave the UK and either return to their country of origin, or to live somewhere else. Note that to avoid the acquisition of a UK domicile it is not necessary to show an intention to return to your country of origin; an intention to live anywhere but the UK, or indeed no intention at all, will do. The test is a positive one, ie to intend to reside permanently or indefinitely in the UK. However, again actions speak louder than words and after a long period of UK residence HMRC may well take the view that the expressed intentions of leaving are a mere hope or aspiration and the reality is that the taxpayer is intending to stay. It is therefore necessary either to preserve ties in the country of origin or develop ties elsewhere, both of which would indicate a lack of commitment to the UK. (For an example of a claim to a domicile of choice and a summary of all the main issues see *Civil Engineer v IRC* (2002) and *Personal Tax Planning Review* Volume 8 Issue 3.)                    **[18.20]**

d)    *Losing a domicile of choice*

It can be just as important for someone who has acquired a domicile of choice, not to lose it before they want to. This would be particularly important to those individuals who for example have a UK domicile of origin but acquired a domicile of choice in (say) Hong Kong by reason of being permanently settled there for many years. If they were to leave, they might

find that their Hong Kong domicile disappears. The test is very specific. A domicile of choice is lost by the combination of:
(1)   ceasing to reside in the country in question; and
(2)   ceasing to intend to reside there permanently or indefinitely,
but not otherwise.

Note that there are two different conditions—and both need to be satisfied if the domicile of choice is to be lost. Ceasing to reside sounds like a plain question of fact, but it may not be quite as simple as that. The individual might leave Hong Kong to live in the UK but retain some residential accommodation for occasional visits for social or business purposes. Will this mean he continues to reside in Hong Kong? Possibly, but it may not matter because there is the other condition to consider as well. Has he ceased to intend to reside in Hong Kong? If he retains residential accommodation there and visits regularly, this would be very supportive of a claim that he had not ceased to intend to reside there permanently; he is just away for a while. Even if he does not retain any ties or accommodation there, this does not mean that he had necessarily ceased to intend to reside there permanently. He may intend to return, for example when his children are settled in school or have finished their education. It is only when he has decided not to return, or his actions indicate that resuming residence there is not a reality, that his domicile of choice will be lost. On that occasion, either the domicile of origin will revive or he will acquire a new domicile of choice. If therefore his domicile of origin is not the UK but (say) Australia, the loss of a Hong Kong domicile by taking up residence in the UK is more likely to mean the revival of the Australian domicile of origin than the acquisition of a UK domicile of choice.                                    **[18.21]**

e)   *Special situations*

If an individual with a foreign domicile of origin intends to come to the UK to take up permanent residence he may become UK domiciled as soon as he arrives. That is possible if when he arrives he comes with the settled intention of residing in the UK on a permanent basis. However in many cases this will be an over-simplification. It is more likely that a domicile of choice in the UK will not be acquired until he has been in the UK for some time and is sure that he has made the right decision. Before he arrives the foreign domiciled individual cannot possibly become UK domiciled because he would not satisfy the requirement of physical residence in this country.

Some people have ties in a number of different countries and this can create confusion about their domicile.

**EXAMPLE 18.7**

A had a domicile of origin in the UK but subsequently acquired a domicile of choice in Singapore. He decides to leave Singapore and retire to France. He will spend five months every year in France, three months in Italy and the rest of the year in other parts of the world. Where does this leave his domicile?

When A leaves Singapore, he ceases to reside there and ceases to intend to reside there permanently, so his Singapore domicile of choice will be abandoned. He cannot be without a domicile so either his Singapore domicile of choice will be replaced by a new domicile of choice, or his domicile of origin will revive. If it is his intention to reside permanently (although not exclusively) in France, and he has sufficient knowledge and experience of France to be able to make an informed judgment on the matter, he may acquire a French domicile immediately he arrives in France. If however his intentions are less clear and he merely wants to divide his time between a number of different countries and enjoy his retirement, he may not have the necessary firmness of intention to acquire a French domicile of choice. In the absence of any other suitable territory his UK domicile of origin will revive—even though he has no intention of returning to the UK permanently; indeed even if he was determined never to set foot in the UK again.

He may think that if he is never going to live in the UK and will not be resident there, he need not worry about UK tax. That is true for income tax and CGT but it could still be a problem for IHT and it is clearly something to be avoided, or at the very least prepared for by action before it happens. It would be a mistake to think that HMRC would be unable to collect any IHT. If he had any property in the UK, HMRC would have no difficulty in getting its hands on it in satisfaction of the tax. Even if he had no UK property but those who will inherit his estate live in the UK, HMRC would be able to collect the tax from them.

It is important to appreciate the crucial distinction in *Example 18.7* above between a domicile of origin and a domicile of choice. A domicile of origin is extremely adhesive and will be retained unless and until positive steps are taken to acquire a domicile of choice. An individual can leave his country of origin vowing never to return but he will keep his domicile of origin until a domicile of choice is acquired elsewhere. There is a clear contrast here with a domicile of choice that can be much more easily abandoned.          **[18.22]**

f)    *Deemed domicile*

A special rule applies for IHT (and only for IHT) which is that an individual will be deemed to be domiciled in the UK if he has been resident for tax purposes for 17 out of the preceding 20 years. (However, in calculating the years of residence there is no requirement to count any year in which residence occurred only by reason of the existence of available accommodation.) In these circumstances the real domicile is disregarded and liability to IHT is determined as if he were UK domiciled. This means that he becomes chargeable to IHT on the whole of his worldwide assets.

There is a further rule for IHT, which only partly follows the 17-year rule, that a person with a UK domicile who leaves the UK and acquires a domicile in another country will continue to be regarded as UK domiciled (and therefore within the charge to IHT) for three years following the acquisition of his new domicile. (see further **[35.4]**).          **[18.23]**

g)    *Married women*

The domicile of a married woman is not entirely straightforward. Where the marriage took place before January 1974 the wife took her husband's domicile automatically at the time of her marriage. If the marriage took place on or after 1 January 1974 the domicile of a married woman is determined independently of her husband and is based on her own intentions and circumstances (see the Domicile and Matrimonial Proceedings Act 1973 s 1). However, this does not mean that marriage is wholly irrelevant to her domicile. Whilst the ceremony of marriage itself is no longer capable of causing a change in her domicile, the fact of getting married can do so. She may not acquire the domicile of her husband, but a decision to marry may represent a sufficient indication of her intentions to enable a domicile of choice to be acquired on general principles. If a woman marries a man who lives in the UK and continues to do so, her decision to reside in the UK with him (being a necessary consequence of her marriage) may well be sufficient evidence for the acquisition of a UK domicile of choice under the normal rules.

For a woman who was married before 1 January 1974, her domicile did not necessarily change on that date—it just changed its nature from a domicile of dependence to a domicile of choice (see Domicile and Matrimonial Proceedings Act 1973 s 1(2)). This is a strange rule because the wife of a UK domiciled husband might never have set foot in the UK and could not therefore have acquired a UK domicile of choice under general principles (see **[18.20]**); she will nevertheless have acquired a UK domicile of choice on 1 January 1974. This gives rise to some complex implications but it is fair to say that a married woman who acquired a domicile of choice on 1 January 1974 and has continued to live abroad since that time, will almost certainly have abandoned this domicile of choice either immediately or shortly after it was imposed upon her (see *IRC v Duchess of Portland* (1982) and *Taxation*, 17 January 1988). **[18.24]**

h)  *Proposals for change*

It has often been suggested that the tax privileges allowed to foreign domiciled individuals are too generous. The 1987 Law Commission's report on the subject recommended various changes. (This is not to be confused with a document issued by the UK Inland Revenue in 1988, which reviewed the operation of the rules relating to domicile and residence and how they affected liability to tax.) On 17 October 1991, the Attorney-General stated that the government had decided to accept the recommendations and would introduce legislation when a suitable opportunity arises. On 27 May 1993 the government stated that it had 'no immediate plans to introduce legislation on the subject'. Nothing further was heard on the subject despite the change in government until Budget 2002 on 17 April 2002. In his speech the Chancellor said that the subject of residence and domicile were to be reviewed and that the result of this review would be available in time for the Pre Budget Report in November 2002. However, it was not until 9 April 2003 that a discussion paper was published which reviewed the subject generally and set out a number of objectives that any changes should be able to fulfil. These were mainly that the rules should be fair, support the competitiveness of the UK economy and be clear and simple to apply with minimal opportunities for exploitation. Nothing has happened since.

Unlike the 1988 Consultation Document, no specific proposals are made and there is no indication when, if and how any changes may be made to the taxation of foreign domiciled individuals. **[18.25]–[18.30]**

## II   TAXATION OF FOREIGN INCOME

### 1   Revision of Schedule D Cases IV and V

Before 6 April 2005 Case IV charged income arising from foreign securities and Case V charged income arising from foreign possessions but the distinction has now been abolished by ITTOIA 2005 and both types of income are now described as 'relevant foreign income'. 'Foreign possessions' had been given the widest meaning and includes land, shares, interests in foreign partnerships and interests under non-resident discretionary trusts.
                                                                                    **[18.31]**

### 2   Calculation of liability

A current year basis applies in respect of unearned income (ie on the whole amount arising or received in the tax year). In the case of a trade carried on abroad the assessment is by reference to the accounting period (see **[10.192]** ff).                                                               **[18.32]**

Deductible expenses (including travelling expenses if, broadly, the same conditions are met as in the case of an employee working abroad (see below)), capital allowances and losses are calculated in the normal way but loss relief is only given against other foreign income. Where, despite the endeavours of the taxpayer, income cannot be remitted to the UK because of foreign laws, executive action abroad, or the non-availability of foreign currency, the payment of tax may be postponed until that problem passes (ITTOIA 2005 s 841).                                             **[18.33]**

### 3   The remittance basis

If the taxpayer is not UK domiciled or, being a citizen of the Commonwealth or the Republic of Ireland, not ordinarily resident in the UK, tax is only charged on the remittance basis: ie on sums received in the UK (ITTOIA ss 831 and 832). Unless income is actually brought to the UK there is therefore no tax charge. It follows that a remittance of capital cannot be treated as a remittance of the income. Such a taxpayer may therefore arrange for income to be reinvested or spent abroad. If assets are bought out of income and then sold, a remittance of the proceeds of sale is treated as a remittance of the original income (see *Timpson's Executors v Yerbury* (1936)). ITTOIA 2005 introduces the concept of a UK linked debt that broadly corresponds to the previous concept of a constructive remittance. A remittance occurs if the taxpayer applies income outside the UK in or towards the satisfaction of any of the following:
(1)   the principal or interest on any loan made to him in the UK;
(2)   the principal of any loan made to him outside the UK, the proceeds of which are brought to or received in the UK (note that this provision does not cover the payment of interest on such a loan); or
(3)   the principal of any loan made to satisfy any debt within (1) or (2) above.
      The opportunity noted in (2) above is often exploited: the individual borrows money abroad, spends it in the UK, pays interest on the loan out of

foreign income and eventually clears the loan either out of capital or when he has ceased to be UK resident. Such loans may be secured on foreign *situs* assets provided that these have not been purchased out of foreign income.

A remittance does not occur if, when the income reaches the UK, the taxpayer is no longer entitled to it (*Carter v Sharon* (1936), and also *Grimm v Newman* (2002)) nor does it occur in respect of relevant foreign income if an asset bought abroad out of income is brought to the UK *in specie*, because no 'sum' will have been received in the UK. However, a remittance will occur if the asset is sold while in the UK (*Scottish Provident Institution v Farmer* (1912)).

The remittance rules operate on the basis of the income that is received in the UK in the year of assessment (see IM 1655). Accordingly, if the source of the income does not exist in the year of remittance there can be no liability to charge (but see Part 5 for the position with employment income). However, once a liability exists the measure may be income which arose in a period when the taxpayer was not liable to tax, whether by reason of non-residence or otherwise (see IR 20 para 6.20).

The remittance basis provides a valuable element in tax planning for non-domiciled UK residents.

**EXAMPLE 18.8**

(1) Jacques, domiciled and ordinarily resident in France, but resident in England carries on his business in France. Out of the profits of his business he buys a Picasso painting in France that he brings to England. This is not a sum and not a remittance. Were he to sell the Picasso in the UK, he would be taxable under ITTOIA 2005 s 831.

(2) Diego, resident but not domiciled in the UK, retains his savings abroad. Should he need to remit foreign moneys he will still avoid UK income tax if the remitted sum is capital. He may be able to arrange this by operating a number of separate overseas bank accounts. Assume, for instance, that all the income is paid into one account and that receipts from disposal of capital assets are paid into a separate account. Remittances from the latter are capital (and not subject to UK income tax though a CGT charge may arise. Diego can compensate for the reduction in this account by arranging for sums in the other (income) account to be invested, for example, in the purchase of replacement capital assets abroad (see generally on how non-UK domiciliaries should bring money into the UK, *Taxation*, 1992, p 441).

If the taxpayer acquires a UK domicile he can no longer take advantage of the remittance basis but previously unremitted foreign income can be remitted without charge to tax (see *Taxation Practitioner*, December 1992, p 541). This treatment does not apply to CGT.                    [18.34]

## 4  Particular categories of income

### a)  *Profits of a trade, profession or vocation*

A UK resident is assessed as trading on professional income on all his profits arising from a trade, profession or vocation ('trade') carried on by him in the UK, despite some of the profits being attributable to overseas business: ITTOIA 2005 s 6.

For a trader to be assessed on the income as foreign income, he must be resident in the UK, but the trade must be carried on *wholly* abroad. This is a question of fact, and for the sole trader who is resident in the UK and who has the sole right to manage and control the business it will be difficult to argue that the trade is wholly carried on abroad (*Ogilvie v Kitton* (1908)).

A UK resident company may, however, be able to show that it is trading wholly abroad (*Mitchell v Egyptian Hotels Ltd* (1915)). Where the company establishes a foreign subsidiary (as opposed to a branch) it is a question of fact whether that subsidiary is carrying on its own trade or acting merely as agent for the parent company. To avoid the risk of the subsidiary being treated as UK resident it is prudent to ensure that UK resident directors are not in a majority on the subsidiary's board; that the non-resident directors of the subsidiary are men of substance who are capable of independent thought and judgment; and that board meetings (where 'real' decisions and not just 'rubber stampings' occur) should be held outside the UK (see **[41.153]** and *Untelrab v McGregor* (1996) and *Wood v Holden* (2005)).

Where a partner is a UK-resident individual the profits of the firm are calculated as if the firm were a UK resident individual; the opposite applies in the case of non-UK resident individuals: ITTOIA 2005 s 849.

**EXAMPLE 18.9**

Wino and Co, a French partnership, have one partner resident in London who arranges for sales of their wine in the UK. In deciding whether the firm is trading in the UK the precise mechanics of the wine sales are important. If contracts are made in the UK it is likely that a business in the UK is being carried on, whereas if the orders are merely solicited here and the actual contracts are made in France, the firm may be trading with the UK so that any assessment to UK tax will be as foreign income (see generally the problem of when non-UK residents trade within the UK discussed at **[17.72]**).

Although 'trade' is used here to include professions and vocations, in practice, profits arising from a profession will rarely be taxed as foreign income because the individual exercising his profession wholly abroad is unlikely to be a UK resident and hence will not be chargeable to UK income tax at all (see *Davies v Braithwaite* (1931)).                              **[18.35]**

b)   *Distributions from companies*

Distributions are charged to tax as savings and investment income. The distribution will only be taxable if it is income. This is decided by applying the local law to see whether or not the *corpus* of the asset is left intact after the distribution: if it is, the payment will be taxed as income; if not, it is capital (*IRC v Reid's Trustees* (1949); *IRC v Burrell*; *Rae v Lazard Investment Co Ltd* (1963) and *Courtaulds Investments Ltd v Fleming* (1969)).

Dividends received from a foreign company are subject to UK tax at *10%* *only* ('the dividend ordinary rate') until the dividend (treated as a top slice of income) brings the recipient into the 32.5% ('the dividend upper rate') band (TA 1988 s 1A(3): for the treatment of dividends generally, see **Chapter 42**).                              **[18.36]**

**EXAMPLE 18.10**

Fergus has employment income of £8,000 and dividends from a Bermudian company (no tax deducted at source) of £30,000 in 2006–07. His tax position is:

|  | £ |
|---|---|
| Total income | 40,000 |
| *Less:* personal allowance | 5035 |
|  | £34965 |

The tax charge is as follows:

| employment income (£2965) | £ |
|---|---|
| £2,150 at 10% (lower rate) | 215.00 |
| £815 at 22% (basic rate) | 179.30 |
|  |  |
| £30335 at 10% | 3033.50 |
| £1665 at 32.5% | 541.12 |
|  | £3968.92 |

*Notes*:
(1)   The taxation of foreign dividends at the ordinary and upper rates does not apply to income charged on the remittance basis. Accordingly, in particular cases there may be attractions in ensuring that the remittance basis does not apply to the income (see *Taxation*, 15 February 2001, p 460).
(2)   If a foreign dividend has suffered withholding tax, credit will be given for that foreign tax against any liability to UK tax.
(3)   The dividend may have borne tax at two levels: *first* the company's profits may have suffered tax and, *secondly*, the dividend itself may have been taxed. Relief from the former ('underlying tax') may be given to UK corporate shareholders (TA 1988 s 790(6)) but not to individual shareholders unless provided by a double tax treaty.

c)   *Income from land and unsecured loans*

This income is taxable overseas property income and is computed in accordance with the rules relating to property income (ITTOIA 2005 Part 3 Chapter 11)). The same deductions in arriving at profits will be made and lease premiums and analogous receipts will also be taxed (interest paid on a loan to acquire the property may for instance be deducted in arriving at the income). However a UK property income business is wholly separate thereby preventing losses on one being offset against the other (see **[12.24]**). **[18.37]**

d)   *Income from a foreign trust*

If a UK resident beneficiary has an absolute right to all or part of the income of the foreign trust (one where the trustees are non-UK resident and the assets are abroad), he is taxed on the foreign income as it arises and whether or not he receives it (*Williams v Singer* (1921)). Similar principles apply to a discretionary beneficiary in whose favour the trustees have exercised their discretion to appoint income (see further **[18.79]**).

In appropriate cases income tax may be charged on a UK settlor under the settlement provisions (see **[16.61]**); under TA 1988 s 739 (see **[18.111]**) or on the beneficiary under TA 1988 s 740 in respect of benefits received from the trust.                                                                                                                                   **[18.38]**

e)    *Income from a foreign partnership*

In *Padmore v IRC* (1987) it was held that a UK resident partner was not subject to income tax on his share of the profits of an overseas partnership as foreign income because of the Jersey double tax treaty. The decision was reversed retrospectively and the present position is that such treaties do not affect the taxation of a UK partner's share of overseas profits or gains (see ITTOIA 2005 s 858).                                                                                          **[18.39]**

f)    *Offshore 'roll-up' funds*

The tax treatment of a UK investor is considered in **Chapter 13**.      **[18.40]**

g)    *Miscellany*

Certain pensions (see **[18.50]**) and alimony ordered by a foreign court are taxed as foreign income.                                                                              **[18.41]**

h)    *Coming to the UK*

In cases where an individual becomes UK resident and ordinarily resident during the course of a tax year there are complex rules that identify the overseas investment income that thereupon becomes subject to UK tax. Arrangements should be made *before* becoming UK resident to maximise the amount of income arising in the non-resident period (see generally IR 20 paras 6.17 ff).                                                                                        **[18.42]**

## 5    **Employment income**

The three Cases of Schedule E have been swept away and the taxation of employment income since 6 April 2003 is covered by ITEPA 2003. The general principle still applies that earnings of an individual who is resident and ordinarily resident in the UK are chargeable to income tax wherever earned or received, whether in respect of that year or an earlier year and whether or not the employment is held at the time the earnings are received, (ITEPA 2003 s 15).

The useful expression 'foreign emoluments' which under TA 1988 s 192 meant the emoluments of an individual not domiciled in the UK whose employer was not UK resident, has been eliminated and not replaced by a similar phrase. We now have earnings and amounts treated as earnings where the employee is not domiciled in the UK and the employment is with a foreign employer. A foreign employer is defined in ITEPA 2003 s 721 as meaning:

'(a)    in the case of an employee resident in the UK, an individual partnership or body of person resident outside the UK and not resident in the UK or Eire; and

(b) in the case of an employee not resident in the UK an individual, partnership or body or persons resident outside the UK and not resident in the UK.'

Such earnings are taxable on a remittance basis and so are earnings of an individual who is resident but not ordinarily resident in the UK (see ITEPA 2003 s 25).

For earnings to be chargeable on the remittance basis, it is necessary to establish, *first*, that the duties of the office are performed wholly outside the UK; *secondly*, that the employment is with a foreign employer; and, *thirdly*, that the individual is not domiciled in the UK. In the case of an individual who needs to work both abroad and in the UK, it is sensible to ensure that the overseas duties are carried out under a separate contract of employment. Care needs to be taken in drafting the terms of any such contract because HMRC has power to ensure that the emoluments are not artificially weighted in favour of the overseas contract (see ITEPA 2003 s 24). See also *Tax Bulletin 76* (April 2005) for the latest HMRC approach to dual contracts where they explain their intention to scrutinise such contracts to identify whether there is in fact only one contract. **[18.43]**

a) *Individual resident and ordinarily resident:*

Where a person is resident and ordinarily resident in the UK, but is required by his employment to perform duties wholly or partly outside the UK, he is taxed on all his earnings from the employment. **[18.44]–[18.45]**

b) *Emoluments for duties performed in the UK:*

Where a person is resident, but not ordinarily resident in the UK, or is neither resident nor ordinarily resident, he is taxed only on the earnings in respect of duties performed in the UK (see ITEPA 2003 s 25). **[18.46]**

c) *The remittance basis*

Remittances, for the purposes of the charge on earnings, are governed by ITEPA 2003 s 33 and have a wider scope than for savings and investment income (see **[18.34]**) to include earnings 'paid, used or enjoyed in the UK or transmitted or brought to the UK, in any manner or form'. Remittances of earnings are assessed on a current year basis and will be subject to tax even if the emoluments were for some previous year or the employment has ceased.

Prior to 6 April 2003, where an employee, resident but not ordinarily resident, in the UK was potentially liable under both Cases II and III in respect of emoluments paid partly in the UK and partly abroad from a single employment performed inside and outside the UK, any emoluments paid in, enjoyed in, or remitted to the UK were only be taxed under Case III to the extent that they exceed the Case II emoluments for the year (SP 5/84). The emoluments assessable under Case II had to be computed 'in a reasonable manner', eg on a time basis by reference to working days. It is expected that this concession will continue in the new system on charging earnings (see also *Tax Bulletin* 63, February 2003.) **[18.47]**

d)    *Place of work*

In deciding whether the duties of an employment are in substance performed wholly abroad, merely incidental duties performed in the UK are ignored (ITEPA 2003 s 39 and see *Robson v Dixon* (1972)).

By ITEPA 2003 s 40 some duties are deemed to be performed in the UK. Generally, crews of ships and aircraft will be treated as performing their duties abroad in respect of any part of a voyage that does not begin *and* end in the UK. Areas designated under the Continental Shelf Act 1964 are regarded as part of the UK (eg workers on oil rigs in the UK sector of the North Sea are deemed to work in the UK).                [18.48]


e)    *Deductible expenses*

The general rule is that a deduction from earnings is allowed for expenditure which the employee is obliged to incur and pay as the holder of the employment and the amount is incurred wholly, exclusively and necessarily in the performance of the duties of the employment (ITEPA 2003 s 336). An identical rule applies for deductions in respect of travel expenses (ITEPA 2003 s 337).

Non-UK residents and seafarers entitled to the long absence deduction will not suffer UK tax on reimbursements by their employer for travelling expenses incurred during those periods. A UK resident individual who is wholly employed abroad, will still be liable to tax on such expenses (and reimbursements) (because they will not be 'necessarily' incurred in the performance of the duties). ITEPA 2003 s 370, therefore, provides that he can deduct his costs of travelling to and from the UK to take up or leave the employment. If the expenses of board and lodging incurred in carrying out the duties abroad are paid or reimbursed by the employer, the employee will be entitled to a deduction so that those payments will not be emoluments. In addition, s 371 provides that where he spends 60 or more continuous days outside the UK, the expenses of travel of his spouse and children under 18 are not taxable if met by his employer (limited to two trips in each year of assessment). Any number of other journeys made by the employee between the place of work and the UK can be paid for by the employer without such payments being taxed as emoluments (though notice that the employee cannot deduct the costs of such journeys where he pays for them).

The travelling expenses available to non-UK domiciled employees working in the UK broadly mirror the provisions discussed above for UK residents who work abroad. Accordingly, so long as the employer bears the cost of (any number of) journeys undertaken between the employee's usual place of abode and the UK such sums will not be taxed as earnings and there are similar provisions to those already discussed for visits by spouses and children. However, for foreign domiciled employees who perform duties in the UK, a relaxed interpretation exists in respect of the continuous period of 60 days; for such employees it is sufficient to spend two-thirds of their working days in the UK over a period of 60 days provided they are present in the UK at the beginning and end of the period (see *Tax Bulletin* 56, December 2001). It should be noted that the reliefs for expatriates are limited to a period of two years from the date of the expatriate's arrival in the UK.         [18.49]

## f)  *Foreign pensions and annuities*

Foreign pensions and annuities are taxed on 90% of the income arising (ITEPA 2003 s 575). However, such income will be taxable under ITEPA 2003 if it is payable in the UK through a department or agent of a Commonwealth government. **[18.50]**

## g)  *Collection of tax*

Tax on earnings is generally collected at source from the employer under the PAYE system (see **Chapter 8**). Accordingly where an employer is resident in the UK he must as a general rule operate PAYE in respect of all his employees assessable earnings.

The application of PAYE to a non-resident employer, was considered in *Clark v Oceanic Contractors Inc* (1983). In that case a non-resident company made payments abroad to employees engaged in performing duties in the UK sector of the North Sea and so within the UK for the purpose of liability to tax on earnings. The House of Lords held that PAYE applied to the employer company so that it should have deducted tax from the payments. The only limit on the territorial scope of s 203 is whether it can effectively be enforced. It will, therefore, apply to the non-resident employer who maintains a 'trading presence' in the UK. This was so in the *Oceanic* case: the company carried on activities in the UK and in the UK sector of the North Sea; was liable to corporation tax on its profits; and had an address for service in the UK (see further **Chapter 8**). See also *Agassi v HMIT* (2006).

**[18.51]–[18.70]**

## III  TAXATION OF THE FOREIGN TAXPAYER

The following general rules apply to an individual who is not resident in the UK:
(1)  He is not charged to UK income tax on foreign source income.
(2)  So far as *earned income* is concerned, tax is charged on UK pensions and employments where the duties are carried on in the UK (see ITEPA 2003 ss 25 and 27: **[18.73]**). Tax is also charged on the profits of a trade or profession which is not carried on wholly outside the UK (see **[18.72]**).
(3)  For *investment income*, with the exception of UK rental income (as to which see **[18.75]**), the general rule is that the tax is limited to the amount (if any) deducted at source ('excluded income': see FA 1995 s 128). Note:
   (a)  If the taxpayer has other fully taxed UK source income any personal allowances to which he is entitled (as to which, see below) will be first set against excluded income (although not so as to result in any tax refund).
   (b)  If the taxpayer is resident in a country with which the UK has a double tax treaty, then he may be entitled to exemption or relief from tax on UK investment income (although not on income from land).

(c)    These rules do not apply to non-resident trustees when a 'relevant beneficiary' (broadly speaking, one who is or may be entitled to income) is ordinarily resident in the UK (FA 1995 s 128(5), (6)).

Non-residents are entitled to personal allowances in the circumstances set out in TA 1988 s 278 generally to Commonwealth citizens: citizens of a state within the European Economic Area and residents of the Isle of Man or Channel Islands.                                                        **[18.71]**

## 1    Profits of a trade, profession or vocation

As an application of the source doctrine, the foreign resident taxpayer will be taxable as trading or professional income on the profits of any trade carried on *within* as opposed to *with* the UK. For these purposes, however, maintaining an administrative or representative office as opposed to a branch in the UK will not *per se* constitute trading within the UK. The same principle applies to the exercise of a profession or vocation although the exercise of either in the UK would normally render the taxpayer UK resident.

The majority of cases in this area have been concerned with the sale of goods by a non-resident to a person in the UK. The courts have tended to say that the trade is carried on in the place where, under English law, the contract is made. This is the place where acceptance of the offer is communicated. In general terms, acceptance by post occurs at the place of posting, whereas acceptance by any other form occurs at the place where acceptance is received. Accordingly, the non-resident who faxes his acceptance of an order to a UK customer is in danger of trading within the UK, whereas the non-resident who posts his acceptance to such a customer from outside the UK would appear to be merely trading with the UK. However, the place where contracts are made is only one (albeit important) factor to be considered and is of greater significance where the trade consists simply in the purchase and resale of goods. The better test is probably whether the trading operations that give rise to the profits take place in the UK (*Firestone Tyre and Rubber Co Ltd v Lewellin* (1957). It is likely, for instance, that if land in the UK is acquired, developed and then sold the trade will take place in the UK irrespective of where the contract of sale was entered into.

When a trade is carried on within the UK, the profits are computed under the normal rules under ITTOIA 2005 Part 2 Chapter 2 . The tax charge is limited to the profits from the part of the trade carried on in the UK measured on an arm's length basis.

When a foreign taxpayer is assessed to tax on trading income, the tax can be levied on the branch or agency within the UK through which the trade is being carried on although certain agents, eg independent brokers, are excepted from this provision (FA 1995 ss 126–127, Sch 23 and see *Willson v Hooker* (1995)).

So far as non-resident companies are concerned, even if they are trading within the UK, there will be no liability to UK corporation tax unless that trade is carried on through a permanent establishment in the UK. If that is not the case the liability will be to income tax at basic rate not corporation tax (TA 1988 s 6(2)(b)). In the latter case, as the company will not have any UK presence, HMRC may be presented with problems of tax collection.
                                                                **[18.72]**

## 2 Employment income

The foreign resident taxpayer is chargeable under ITEPA 2003 s 25 on emoluments he receives for duties performed in the UK. This provision has the effect of treating the UK duties as a source of income that would otherwise escape tax completely. **[18.73]**

## 3 Non-resident entertainers and sportsmen

The UK has encountered difficulties (also experienced by other countries) in securing tax payments from non-resident entertainers and sportsmen and women (eg tennis players, golfers, actors and pop stars) who only pay short visits to the country and who have often left before tax can be assessed and collected. Accordingly, a withholding tax was introduced by TA 1988 ss 555–558; SI 1987/530. In general, the payer of the moneys is obliged to make returns to HMRC at quarterly intervals and to account for basic rate income tax that he should deduct from the payment made to the entertainer. There is a *de minimis* provision that ensures that these rules do not operate if the total payments made in the tax year to an entertainer do not exceed £1,000. (See also *Agassi v HMIT* (2006) in respect of payments to third parties.) **[18.74]**

## 4 Income from land in the UK (TA 1988 s 42A; SI 1995/2902)

Profits from letting property in the UK are subject to income tax at basic and higher rate as appropriate.

(1) *Position of the landlord*: A non-resident landlord (including a person whose usual place of abode is outside the UK) can apply to the Financial Intermediaries and Claims Office (FICO) for confirmation that the rental income can be paid gross. FICO must be satisfied that his tax affairs are up to date; or that he has never had UK tax obligations; or that he does not expect to be subject to UK tax (see further IR booklet 150).

(2) *Position of tenants and agents*: In the absence of any agreement with FICO for the rent to be paid gross overseas, a tenant paying rent direct to his landlord should deduct tax at the basic rate and account for the tax to the Revenue.

The burden is on the tenant to know the landlord's usual place of abode: if the tenant fails to deduct tax from an instalment of rent the right to deduct is lost and cannot be made good out of later rent payments (*Tenbry Investments Ltd v Peugeot Talbot Motor Co Ltd* (1992)). A repayment to the landlord may be made in the event of the tax deducted exceeding the landlord's liability (for example, because of deductible expenses).

In cases where an agent is employed to collect the rent, the agent is responsible for making a tax return and then liable to pay the relevant tax after taking into account all allowable deductions.

(3) *Deductible expenses*: Letting agents must pay tax at basic rate on rental income less deductible expenses: by contrast tenants must account for basic rate tax on all rent directly paid to the landlord together with

basic rate tax on rental income paid to third parties which is not a deductible expense. In general an expense can only be deducted when the letting agent/tenant can reasonably be satisfied that it is allowable in computing the profits of the landlord's letting business (SI 1995/2902 regs 9(4), 8(2)). Note also that deduction is only permitted if the expense is borne by the tenant/letting agent and not if it is directly paid by the landlord.

(4)   *Assessment on the landlord*: The tax deducted at source by the tenant or letting agent will usually not represent the correct liability of the landlord so an adjustment will be needed. For instance, letting agents cannot deduct expenses paid by the landlord and landlords who are individuals may be subject to the higher rate of income tax whilst discretionary trustees may suffer the additional rate of tax for trusts. A non-resident company is normally subject to income tax at basic rate on its profits from UK lettings because it will not be chargeable to corporation tax in the absence of any trade carried on in the UK through a permanent establishment.                                      **[18.75]**

## 5   Interest from UK banks and building societies

Interest can be paid gross provided that an appropriate declaration is made that the taxpayer is not ordinarily resident in the UK (TA 1988 s 481(5)(k)).
**[18.76]**

## 6   UK government securities

Tax is not chargeable on certain government securities owned by persons not ordinarily resident in the UK (FOTRA securities: ITTOIA 2005 s 713).
**[18.77]**

## 7   Dividends paid by UK companies

A non-UK resident is not entitled to a tax credit in respect of a qualifying distribution unless he is entitled to personal allowances under TA 1988 s 278(2) (see **[18.71]** and TA 1988 s 231(1)). This position may be altered by a double tax treaty which may provide for part of the tax credit to be payable to a non-resident. Typically:

(1)   the UK may grant a payment to overseas 'direct investors' (ie a company controlling at least 10% of the voting rights in the paying company) of half the tax credit less 5% (or eg in the case of Canada and Norway, 10%) of the aggregate of the dividend plus the half tax credit;

(2)   in other cases (ie for 'portfolio investors') the tax credit less 15% of the sum of the dividend and the tax credit.

   Since 6 April 1999, portfolio investors and direct investors resident in Canada and Norway are not entitled to any payment of tax credit whilst a small payment may be due to direct investors in Belgium, Italy, Luxembourg, the Netherlands, Sweden, Switzerland and the USA (see *Tax Bulletin*, February 1999, p 626).                                      **[18.78]**

**EXAMPLE 18.11 (DIRECT INVESTOR UNDER US/UK TREATY)**

|  | £ |
|---|---|
| Dividend declared by subsidiary | 90.00 |
| Half tax credit (10 ÷ 2) | 5.00 |
| Aggregate | 95.00 |
| Deduction (5% × 95) | 4.75 |
| Received by shareholder | £90.25 |

## 8  Non-resident discretionary trusts

Non-resident trusts that fall within ITTOIA 2005 s 568 are liable to the rate applicable to trusts in respect of UK source income (*IRC v Regent Trust Co Ltd* (1979)). Of course, HMRC may face enforcement problems in such cases and, in this connection, ESC B18 should be studied. A UK beneficiary receiving payments out of such a trust may claim credit for tax actually paid by the trustees on the income out of which the payment is made (as if the payment came from a UK trust and fell within s 687(1)) but only if the trustees have made tax returns and paid all relevant tax. It may be inferred from this concession that HMRC accepts that s 687 (see **[16.29]**) does not apply to payments out of non-resident trusts. **[18.79]–[18.90]**

## IV  DOUBLE TAXATION RELIEF

Overseas income may be taxed in its country of origin and if UK tax is also chargeable on the same income, the taxpayer is entitled to relief in one of three ways.

*First,* under the double tax treaty with the other country. The treaties differ in detail but generally provide that certain categories of income will be taxed in only one of the countries concerned (usually where the taxpayer is resident). Other income will be taxable in both countries, but with a credit for one amount of tax against the other (the application of a treaty to income (or gains) covered by a 'deeming' provision needs careful consideration: see *Bricom Holdings v IRC* (1997)).

*Secondly,* if there is no treaty in force, 'unilateral relief' is given under TA 1988 s 790. This takes the form of a credit against the UK tax equal to the foreign tax paid (see SP 7/91). Whereas a double tax treaty specifies the taxes which are covered by the agreement, s 790 relief is limited to taxes which are similar to UK taxes against which the relief is claimed (see, for instance, *Yates v GCA International Ltd* (1991) and SP 7/91).

*Thirdly,* if neither of the above applies, unilateral relief may be given under TA 1988 s 811 by way of deduction (from the foreign income which is assessable to UK tax) of the amount of foreign tax paid. Relief by deduction is less advantageous to the taxpayer than relief by credit. **[18.91]–[18.110]**

## V   ANTI-AVOIDANCE LEGISLATION: TRANSFER OF ASSETS ABROAD (TA 1988 ss 739–746)

### 1   General

#### a)   *The mischief*

A person who is neither resident nor ordinarily resident in the UK cannot be assessed to UK income tax on income that arises from a source outside the UK. Accordingly, an individual resident in the UK could seek to avoid UK income tax by transferring income-producing assets to a non-UK resident who is not subject to UK income tax. The relevant wording in TA 1988 s 739(1) is as follows:

> '... the following provisions of this section shall have effect for the purpose of preventing the avoiding by individuals ordinarily resident in the United Kingdom of liability to income tax by means of transfer of assets by virtue or in consequence of which, either alone or in conjunction with associated operations, income becomes payable to persons resident or domiciled outside the United Kingdom.'

#### EXAMPLE 18.12

(1)   Toby, who is ordinarily resident in the UK, owns land in Barbados that produces a substantial income. He transfers it to a non-UK resident company in return for an allotment of shares.

(2)   Toby also owns shares in a German company which he transfers to a non-UK resident trust in which he is one of the beneficiaries.

To prevent such arrangements being effective in avoiding tax, these sections operate to treat the income of the company in (1) or the trust in (2) above as Toby's income. TA 1988 s 739 provides that if an individual transfers assets and as a result of that transfer, or of associated operations, income becomes payable to any person resident or domiciled outside the UK and the transferor has either power to enjoy that income (TA 1988 s 739(2)) or receives a capital sum (TA 1988 s 739(3)), the income of the non resident person is taxed as that of the transferor. The scope of the legislation was restricted as a result of the House of Lords decision in *Vestey v IRC* (1980) to the original transferor of the assets or his spouse. As a result, fresh legislation (now s 740) was introduced to bring into charge those individuals (other than the transferor) who receive benefits as a result of the arrangements.

**[18.111]**

#### b)   *'Individuals ordinarily resident in the UK'*

The legislation applies even if the transfer occurred at a time when the individual was not ordinarily resident in the UK. (See FA 1997 s 81 reversing the decision of the House of Lords in *IRC v Willoughby* (1997).)    **[18.112]**

#### c)   *Purpose*

An individual will avoid liability under these sections if he can satisfy HMRC *either* that the transfer or associated operation was not made for the purpose of avoiding any tax (s 741(a)) *or* that it was a *bona fide* commercial transaction the purpose of which was not to avoid tax (s 741(b); see *Tax Bulletin*, April 1999, p 651 and *Carvill v IRC* (2000)). There is no clearance procedure and the onus of proof is on the taxpayer. In *IRC v Willoughby* (1997) the court accepted that if the overall objective was not tax avoidance the motive defence could apply even if the objective was achieved in a tax-efficient manner. In the course of rejecting HMRC's submission that a tax avoidance motive must attach to an individual who invested in a personal portfolio bond with a non-resident life office, Lord Nolan commented:

'it would be absurd in the context of s 741 to describe as tax avoidance the acceptance of an offer of freedom from tax which Parliament has deliberately made. Tax avoidance within the meaning of s 741 is a course of action designed to conflict with or defeat the evident intention of Parliament'

If a purpose of the taxpayer is to avoid any UK tax, the defence will not apply: by contrast, avoiding foreign tax falls within the *bona fide* commercial transaction defence! (*IRC v Herdman* (1969) and, putting the matter beyond doubt, s 739(1A)(b).)

**EXAMPLE 18.13**

G was domiciled and resident in Japan and opened a substantial sterling bank account in London for the benefit of his granddaughter. For IHT reasons he transferred the moneys to the Channel Islands and then established a Channel Islands trust (into which the money was paid) for the benefit of his granddaughter. The Special Commissioners concluded that avoiding a liability to tax was not the purpose, or one of the purposes, for which the transfer was effected. The test to be applied was subjective and the creation of the settlement was prompted by a wish to ensure the financial independence of his granddaughter. There was no evidence that on this matter he had sought UK tax advice (see *A Beneficiary v IRC* (1999) and *Carvill v IRC* (2000) confirming the subjective nature of the test).

The defence under s 741 only applies if the individual 'shows in writing or otherwise to the satisfaction of the Board' that its conditions are fulfilled. It cannot simply be assumed. See *Tax Bulletin* 40, April 1999, on the view of the Revenue on disclosure for this purpose:

'Taxpayers are required to disclose clearly in their self assessment return if there is any income or benefit assessable under Section 739 or 740, and whether reliance is being placed on Section 741 to exclude income or benefit from assessment. Where such a disclosure has been made and exemption under Section 741 claimed, the Revenue will make any necessary enquiries about that exemption in the statutory period allowed, and will not seek to reopen that year's return on discovery grounds if the Section 741 exemption has to be reconsidered in later years.'

New legislation was published in draft at the time of the Pre-Budget Report on 5 December 2005 to turn the test in s 741 to an objective test. Now the application of s 739 will only be avoided if it would not be reasonable to draw the conclusion that the avoidance of tax was one of the purposes behind the relevant transactions; alternatively if the transactions were genuine commercial transactions where it would be reasonable to conclude that avoiding liability to tax was no more than incidental: s 741A as inserted by Finance Act 2006 Sch 7.                                                    **[18.113]**

## 2   Liability of the transferor (TA 1988 s 739)

a)   *General*

There are two preconditions.

*First*, there must be a transfer of assets by an individual. This means a transfer of property or rights of any kind but also includes the creation of those rights so that the incorporation of a company or formation of a partnership will be caught. In *IRC v Brackett* (1986), the taxpayer, by entering into a contract of employment with a Jersey company, fell within the section since rights created under that contract were assets and, as 'transfer' included the creation of rights, those assets were transferred to a non-UK resident person. The assets need not be situated in the UK.

*Secondly*, as a result of the transfer, either alone or together with associated operations, income must become payable to a non-UK resident or non-UK domiciled person. 'Person' includes a company and, for these purposes, a company incorporated outside the UK is always considered non-resident even if it is in fact resident in the UK (TA 1988 s 742(8) and, for the implications of this deeming, see *R v Dimsey; R v Allen* (1999)).

'Associated operations' is widely defined in s 742(1). Basically, any operation (except death) which is carried out by any person (not necessarily the transferor) is capable of being an associated operation, provided only that, together with the transfer, it results in income becoming payable to a person resident or domiciled outside the UK; (for cases where this did not happen see *Fynn v IRC* (1958) and *Carvill v IRC* (2000)). Whether the operation has this result is judged objectively without regard to the intention of the person effecting the operation.                                          **[18.114]**

### EXAMPLE 18.14

(1)   Sam settles overseas property on a UK trust under which he can benefit. Subsequently overseas trustees are appointed so that the trust becomes non-UK resident. Income produced in the trust may be taxed as Sam's under s 739 (note that there may be an overlap in such cases with TA 1988 Part XV: when this is the case the Revenue practice is to apply Part XV not s 739).

(2)   A transfers assets to a UK resident company which happens to have been incorporated abroad. The company is liable to corporation tax on its income in the normal way as a UK resident company. A is also liable to income tax on the same income because the company is deemed for s 739 purposes to be non-resident (see *R v Dimsey; R v Allen* (1999) although the Revenue has confirmed it will not in practice seek to tax the same income twice).

(3)   A transfers assets to a UK resident company, B Ltd, in consideration for an allotment of shares. Some years later B Ltd sells the assets to a non-resident company, C Ltd, in return for shares in C Ltd. The transfer by B Ltd to C Ltd is associated with the transfer of assets from A to B Ltd although the operations were not contemplated as part of a single scheme at the time of the transfer (*Corbett's Executors v IRC* (1943)).

(4)   A sells foreign investments to an overseas company in return for shares in that company. He makes a will leaving the shares to a non-resident trust for the benefit of his daughter. The making of the will, although not the death, is an operation associated with the transfer of the assets abroad. Hence, on the death of A the daughter is within the scope of s 740 in respect of any benefits received from the trust.

b) *The liability is that of the transferor*

Once there has been a transfer of assets resulting in income becoming payable to a non-UK resident, s 739 will then apply if the transferor has the power to enjoy the income (s 739(2)) *or* receives or is entitled to receive a capital sum (s 739(3)).

Who is a transferor? The key cases are *Congreve v IRC* (1948), *Pratt v IRC* (1982) and *Carvill v IRC* (2000) which show that the term may include a person who acts through an agent as well as a person who owns all or practically all the share capital of the company which makes the transfer (see *Example 18.14(2)* above).

In *Pratt*, Walton J commented on *Congreve* as follows:

> 'The only authority dealing with quasi-transferors so far as a company is concerned—or indeed, at all—is *Congreve's case*, and what that case does is, whilst recognising that a transfer by an individual, even one holding 99.9 per cent of the shares of the company, is not the same as a transfer by the company, to hold that a transfer by the company "procured" by a quasi-transferor holding the vast majority of the shares in the company is to be regarded as having been made by the quasi-transferor himself.'

In *Carvill* the Special Commissioner stressed that cases where an individual had such influence over another that he should be regarded as the transferor of that other's shares were 'exceptional': the majority shareholder in that case was not to be treated as the transferor of the minority shareholders' shares.

As was pointed out in *Pratt* joint assessments are not possible under s 739 and there can only be a single transferor to consider at a time. Given that no apportionments are provided for, it must follow that for the section to apply an identifiable part of the asset transferred must be attributed to a particular transferor. For this reason it is not considered that discretionary beneficiaries can be transferors. **[18.115]**

c) *Section 739(2)*

A tax charge will only apply if, given that the above conditions are satisfied, an individual ordinarily resident in the UK has 'power to enjoy the income of a person resident or domiciled outside the UK' (for a recent illustration of when a settlor was considered to have such a power, see *IRC v Botnar* (1999)). The income caught by the section need not be derived directly from the assets transferred, but the power of enjoyment must be held by the transferor or his spouse (*Vestey v IRC* (1980); TA 1988 s 742(9)(a)). An individual has the power to enjoy income if any of the five circumstances in s 742(2) are satisfied. Generally, they apply to any situation whereby the transferor receives, or is entitled to receive, any benefit in any form from the income:

(1) The income is dealt with by any person so that it will at some time benefit the individual in some manner.

**EXAMPLE 18.15**

A non-resident company accumulates its profits for the purpose of redeeming the debentures of the transferor. This is a benefit within (1) because it results from a use of the income (*Latilla v IRC* (1943)).

(2)   Where assets that he holds, or which are held for his benefit, increase in value as a result of the income becoming payable to the non-UK resident.

### EXAMPLE 18.16

(a)   X Ltd, a non-resident company, is in debt to A, a UK resident. When income becomes payable to X Ltd, A's *chose in action* (the debt) increases in value (unless X Ltd had sufficient funds to repay the debt) because X Ltd is more likely to be able to honour its obligations (*Lord Howard de Walden v IRC* (1942)).

(b)   As in (a) save that A also owned shares in X Ltd which he transferred to a discretionary trust for the benefit of himself and his family. The section applies because the value of the shares is increased and they are assets held for his benefit.

(3)   Where he receives, or is entitled to receive, a benefit from the income or the assets representing the income.

### EXAMPLE 18.17

(a)   C, who is ordinarily resident in the UK, holds 90% of the issued shares of a non-UK resident company, B Ltd, which gives him the right to a dividend when declared. C is entitled to receive a benefit within (3) (*Lee v IRC* (1941)). Similarly, if, after he has transferred his shares, the directors make a gift to him, C has then received a benefit and it does not matter that the directors were acting *ultra vires*.

(b)   Trustees of a non-UK resident trust exercise their discretion to pay income to a UK resident settlor B. B has received a benefit within (3) above.

(4)   Where he is or may become entitled to some of the income as a result of the exercise of discretions by any persons. Even if the discretions are never exercised so that the transferor never benefits, he is still within (4). Thus, in *Example 18.17(b)*, B has power to enjoy the income whether or not he receives a benefit. This paragraph also catches revocable settlements and settlements where trustees have power to appoint absolute or income interests back to the settlor as well as settlements where the settlor is within the class of discretionary beneficiary—although in those cases TA 1988 Part XV is also likely to apply.

(5)   Where he can control the application of the income in any way, not necessarily for his own benefit. This does not include a right to direct the investments nor a power of appointment that is concerned with capital rather than income payments (*Lord Vestey's Executors v IRC* (1949)). Thus, in *Example 18.17(a)*, C has power to enjoy B Ltd's income through his ability to replace the existing directors by virtue of his 90% shareholding (contrast the power to appoint trustees; *IRC v Schroder* (1983)).

When applying these tests regard must be had to the substantial result and effect of the transfer and any associated operations (TA 1988 s 742(3)).   **[18.116]**

d)   *Section 739(3)*

Section 739(3) applies where, in connection with a transfer of assets abroad, the transferor or his spouse receives or is entitled to receive a capital sum, whether before or after the relevant transfer. 'Capital sum' is defined as a sum paid or payable by way of loan or repayment of a loan; or any sum (not being income) which is paid or payable otherwise than for full consideration in money or money's worth.                                                        **[18.117]**

### EXAMPLE 18.18

B, who is ordinarily resident in the UK, has transferred income-producing assets to a non-UK resident trust. A loan is made to his wife. B falls within s 739(3).

e)    *Computation of the income chargeable under TA 1988 s 739(2) and (3)*

When a transferor is caught by s 739(2), he will be assessed to income tax on the non-resident's income to the extent that it arose by virtue or in consequence of the relevant transfer of assets and any associated operation(s) (see *Tax Bulletin*, April 1999, p 651). Hence, the purchase of an existing offshore company with an existing income stream is not within the section.

If s 739(3) applies, the assessment is not limited to the amount of the capital sum and includes income arising in the year when the capital sum was paid or payable and *all* such income arising thereafter (see *Private Client Business*, 1995, p 209).

Should the Revenue assess both the transferor and his spouse under either subsection, it cannot tax the same income twice (TA 1988 s 744(1)), but must charge it in such proportions as it considers 'just and reasonable'.

In computing the income of the non-resident which is chargeable under s 739(2) or (3), the transferor is only entitled to such deductions and reliefs as he would have been allowed had he, and not the non-resident, actually received the income (see *Lord Chetwode v IRC* (1977); management charges of a non-resident company were not deductible by a UK resident individual, and see TA 1988 s 743(2). If, however, the income has already suffered basic rate tax, this will not be collected again from the UK resident (TA 1988 s 743).                                                                    **[18.118]**

f)    *Remittance basis for non-domiciliaries*

Section 743(3) provides that a non-UK domiciliary is not chargeable 'in respect of any income ... if he would not, by reason of his being so domiciled, have been chargeable to tax in respect of it if it had in fact been his income'. The wording may be tortuous, but the effect is to preserve the remittance basis to income caught by s 739.                                              **[18.119]**

## 3   Liability of non-transferors: s 740

a)    *Ambit*

This provision was designed to fill the gaps in the legislation revealed by the *Vestey* case. The section has effect where:

'(a)   By virtue or in consequence of a transfer of assets, either alone or in conjunction with associated operations, income becomes payable to a person resident or domiciled outside the UK; and

(b)   An individual ordinarily resident in the UK who is not liable to tax under s 739 by reference to the transfer receives a benefit provided out of assets which are available for the purpose by virtue or in consequence of the transfer or of any associated operations' (s 740(1)).          **[18.120]**

b)   *A receipts basis*

The important limitation in s 740 is that such an individual is only assessed to income tax *to the extent of any benefit that he receives*. It should be realised therefore that the section leaves open planning opportunities (and it may be noted that the CGT rules are now far more restrictive given the definition of a 'defined person'. An overseas settlement (in which the settlor and his spouse do not have power to enjoy the income) in which the income is accumulated will be free from UK income tax unless and until benefits are conferred on a beneficiary (so at the very least there will be a deferment of UK tax).          **[18.121]**

c)   *What is a 'benefit'?*

The term 'benefit' is not defined except only that it includes a payment of any kind (TA 1988 s 742(9)). A cash advance or the transfer of an asset *in specie* will be caught and HMRC also considers that the free use of property constitutes a benefit. In general, tax is charged even if the benefit is received and kept abroad. This is subject to limited protection for non-domiciliaries under TA 1988 s 740(5) who will remain taxable in such cases unless the benefit is received outside the UK and all the relevant income is foreign source income which has not been remitted to the UK. If some of the relevant income is UK source income or is remitted, then the benefit is taxable to the extent of such income.          **[18.122]**

d)   *'Relevant income'*

The benefit is taxed as the income of the UK resident in the year of receipt to the extent that it does not exceed the 'relevant income' of the non-resident in the tax years up to and including the year when the benefit is paid. Insofar as it exceeds the relevant income of those years, any excess is carried forward and set against the first available relevant income of future years until it is finally absorbed. HMRC consider that the tax charge cannot be relieved by double tax relief.

'Relevant income' means, in relation to an individual, income arising in any year of assessment to the non-resident and which, as a result of the transfer of assets, can be used to provide a benefit to that individual (s 740(3)).          **[18.123]**

e)   *Apportionment of liability*

The same income cannot be charged to tax twice (s 744). Therefore, where several beneficiaries receive benefits, the relevant income is allocated amongst them by HMRC in such proportions as may be just and reasonable (in the first instance they will seek to agree the division of liability with the taxpayer). The taxpayer may appeal against the apportionment to the Special Commissioners.          **[18.124]**

**EXAMPLE 18.19**

A non-resident discretionary trust has relevant income in three consecutive years of £6,000, £6,000 and £12,000 respectively. It makes payments to two UK resident beneficiaries in *Year* 2. It is assumed that the apportionment provisions would be applied *pro rata* and not according to the order in which the payments are made.
The benefits are taxed as follows:

|  |  |  | A £ | B £ |
|---|---|---|---|---|
| *Year 1* | | | | |
| Benefits paid | | | Nil | Nil |
| | Relevant income £6,000 (unapportioned) | | | |
| *Year 2* | | | | |
| Benefits | | | 6,000 | 12,000 |
| Relevant income | £6,000 | | | |
| *Plus* income brought forward | £6,000 | | | |
| | £12,000 | appor-tioned | 4,000 | 8,000 |
| Untaxed benefit carried forward | | | 2,000 | 4,000 |
| *Year 3* | | | | |
| Benefits paid | | | Nil | Nil |
| Relevant income | £12,000 | | | |
| | £6,000 | appor-tioned | 2,000 | 4,000 |
| Relevant income carried forward | £6,000 | | Nil | Nil |

In *Year* 2 A and B are assessed to income tax on £4,000 and £8,000 of their respective benefits. The balance is assessed in *Year* 3.

f)   *CGT tie-in*

If the benefit is of a capital nature and results from a capital gain made by the non-resident, the same sum is not charged to both income tax under s 740 and CGT under TCGA 1992 s 87. To the extent that the benefit exceeds relevant income it is charged to CGT, in which case, it cannot be treated as income in a subsequent year under s 740 (TA 1988 s 740(6)).          **[18.125]**

## 4   **Powers of the Revenue to obtain information (TA 1988 s 745)**

The Revenue has wide investigatory powers for the purposes of this section which are exercisable against a taxpayer, and also against his advisers. It can demand, at 28 days' notice, such particulars as it deems necessary.
   A solicitor is exempt from these powers and can only be compelled to state that he was acting on his client's behalf and to give the client's name and

address. However, he is only exempt to the extent that he is acting *qua* solicitor. Thus, a solicitor would not be able to claim the exemption in respect of his own affairs.

A bank is also exempt from providing details of ordinary banking transactions (s 745(5)), except to the extent that it has acted for a customer in connection with either the formation and management of a non-resident company which would be close if resident in the UK and is not a trading company, or the creation or execution of a trust which may be used for schemes under these provisions. The banks' exemption was narrowly construed in *Royal Bank of Canada v IRC* (1972) and in *Clinch v IRC* (1973) where a 'fishing expedition' was upheld in the courts. Other advisers, eg barristers and accountants, have no exemption from s 745.                    **[18.126]**

## 5   The legislation—an overview

A joint working group of HMRC and professional experts set up to review the legislation on the transfer of assets abroad produced a report in 1997. The legislation has now been redrawn by the Tax Rewrite Committee and is contained in Chapter 2 of the Income Tax Bill (Bill 4) which will no doubt emerge into an Act of Parliament in due course.

It is interesting to note that a UK domiciliary may still employ an offshore trust to obtain an income tax advantage for his family without falling within s 739 although s 740 will still apply to benefits received by beneficiaries. The following factors should be borne in mind:

(1)   the trust must be in discretionary; all trustees must be non-resident and income must be foreign source;

(2)   the settlor and his spouse must be excluded from all benefit; they must not receive any benefit; nor be entitled to control the application of the income;

(3)   UK tax is avoided provided that the income is accumulated and distributions are made only to non-residents.

(4)   The inheritance tax and capital gains tax implications of such a transfer need also to be considered particularly following the changes in FA 2006 to the application of inheritance to trusts.                    **[18.127]**

# Section 3    Capital gains tax

**Chapters**

# 19 CGT—basic principles

*Updated by Andrew Farley, Partner, Wilsons*

---

---

'It is impossible to draw an unambiguous distinction between "capital" gains and "income" gains and the attempt to do so necessarily results in great uncertainty for the taxpayer because a particular transaction may or may not be found by the courts to fall on one side of the line or the other'

(Carter Commission, Canada, 1966).

**[19.1]**

## I INTRODUCTION

### 1 Background

Capital gains tax (CGT) was introduced in FA 1965 and was first consolidated in the Capital Gains Tax Act 1979 (CGTA 1979) and then in the Taxation of Chargeable Gains Act 1992 (TCGA 1992). It was largely introduced to tax profits left untaxed by income tax. Income tax, in the much quoted dictum of Lord Macnaghten, was and is a tax on income. Thus, it does not (save in exceptional cases where capital is deemed to be income) tax the profit made on a disposal of a capital asset. However, since 1965, the taxpayer may be charged to CGT on any capital gains after deducting any available exemptions and reliefs.

The then Chancellor of the Exchequer, Mr James Callaghan, in his 1965 Budget speech introducing CGT, explained:

'Yield is not my main purpose ... The failure to tax capital gains is ... the greatest blot on our system of direct taxation. There is little dispute nowadays that capital gains confer much the same kind of benefit on the recipient as taxed earnings more hardly won. Yet earnings pay tax in full while capital gains go free ... This new tax will provide a background of equity and fair play ... ' **[19.2]**

a) *Overlap with income tax*

CGT aims to tax only what is untaxed by income tax and, normally, there will be no CGT on a transaction that is chargeable to income tax. Hence, in the case of certain transactions which might attract both taxes, CGT is chargeable on only so much of the transaction as is not charged to income tax, as, for instance, on the purchase and sale of assets which qualify for capital allowances (see **[19.66]**) and the grant of leases at a premium where part of the premium is assessable to income tax under the income from property business rules (formerly Schedule A): see **[12.81]**).

There is, however, no general rule against double taxation that prevents the same sum from being subject to two different taxes and in *Bye v Coren* (1986) Scott J (whose judgment was upheld in the Court of Appeal) held that 'whether it is so subject is a matter of construction of the statute or statutes which have imposed the taxes'. TCGA 1992 s 37 will provide relief in most cases since it states that once an income tax assessment has become final in respect of a sum of money the same person cannot be subject to a CGT assessment on that same sum. There is, of course, nothing to prevent the Revenue from raising alternative assessments (eg to income tax and CGT) on the same sum of money (*Bye v Coren*, above and *IRC v Wilkinson* (1992)).

For the use of trading losses to reduce chargeable gains, see FA 1991 s 72 which is discussed at **[11.61]**                                                      **[19.3]**

b)  *The changing face of CGT*

The scope of the tax has fluctuated since its introduction in 1965. The charge on death was removed in 1971 and criticism that the tax was levied on inflationary gains was largely removed by the introduction of an indexation allowance in 1982 and by the rebasing of the tax to 1982 (introduced in FA 1988). This trend towards limiting the scope of the tax was, however, reversed by changes made in FA 1989. These concerned lifetime gifts where the position from 1980 had been that in most cases tax could be postponed by the exercise of a hold-over election (provided for in FA 1980 s 79 as subsequently amended). It is now only possible to make such an election in a limited number of cases (see **Chapter 24**). As a result, CGT may be charged and on a gift of assets where hold-over relief is not available so that the curious position is that a tax aimed at catching profits will often apply to gifts (deemed profits) whereas the tax intended to catch all gifts (CTT now IHT) will only apply to lifetime gifts which are not potentially exempt transfers (albeit the extent of such gifts has increased considerably with the enactment of FA 2006) or which are made in the period of seven years before the death of the donor!

The yield from CGT is under 1% of the total revenue raised in direct taxes. In his 1984 Budget Speech the Rt Hon Nigel Lawson MP acknowledged the 'unfairness and complexity' of the CGT legislation. In his 1985 Budget Speech he declared that the right way to reform the tax was to improve the indexation allowance thereby ensuring that a charge was levied only on real and not inflationary gains. As a result of a number of changes that he then introduced he felt able to conclude that 'the tax is now on a broadly acceptable and sustainable basis'. Three years later, his views had altered, and a further reform (rebasing the tax from 1982 instead of 1965) was introduced in FA 1988 to remedy the 'manifest injustice' of taxing 'paper profits resulting from the rampant inflation of the 1970s'. Gordon Brown has inherited the mantle and after a widespread consultation process FA 1998 introduced far-reaching reforms of the tax for individuals, trustees and PRs (but not for companies) in the form of taper relief. The Press Release of 17 March 1998 announced:

> 'The reform will help investment through encouraging longer-term holding of assets by reducing the effective rate of CGT ... It will stimulate entrepreneurial activity by rewarding longer term investment in businesses. The changes will lead to simplification of the CGT system by progressively removing indexation, a major complicating feature.'

Not surprisingly, the system has in fact become more complex and taper relief itself has been subject to major revisions in FA 2000, FA 2001, and FA 2002, with further amendments in FA 2003. In 'Enterprise for All—the challenge for the next Parliament' (18 June 2001) there is the following:

> 'The Government will also consult whether there are worthwhile and good value for money options to simplify capital gains tax within the existing policy framework.'

Unfortunately, the problem of complexity has proved rather more intractable than anticipated.                                        **[19.4]**

## 2  Basic principles

CGT is charged on any gain resulting when a chargeable person makes a chargeable disposal of a chargeable asset. Tax is charged on so much of the gain as is left after taking into account any exemptions or reliefs and after deducting any allowable losses. The tax is payable on 31 January following the year of assessment (which is on a current year basis: TCGA 1992 s 7). It is, therefore, sensible to make disposals early in a tax year in order to achieve the greatest delay in the payment of tax—provided, of course, that all other things are equal (it is never advisable to let tax considerations dictate investment decisions).

The tax was introduced in 1965 and was not retrospective. Accordingly, it only taxed gains arising after 6 April in that year. Thus, where an individual acquired an asset in 1960 for £10,000 and sold it in 1970 for £20,000, thereby realising a gain of £10,000, only such part of the gain as accrued after 6 April 1965 was charged (see **[19.37]**). For assets owned on 31 March 1982, the chargeable gain may be computed on the basis that the asset in question had been acquired in March 1982 at its then market value (TCGA 1992 s 35). This rebasing of the tax is discussed in detail at **[19.38]** and means that gains accruing between 1965 to 1982 have now been removed from the tax charge.

**[19.5]**

### a)  *Who is a chargeable person? (TCGA 1992 s 2)*

Chargeable persons include individuals who are resident or ordinarily resident in the UK; trustees, PRs and partners. In the case of partners, each partner is charged separately in respect of his share of the partnership gains (TCGA 1992 s 59, see **Chapter 44**). Although companies are not chargeable persons for CGT purposes, the corporation tax to which they are subject is levied on corporate profits that include chargeable gains. Non-residents are—in general—not taxed on a disposal of UK *situs* assets (see **Chapter 27**).

[**19.6**]

b)    *What is a chargeable asset? (TCGA 1992 s 21(1))*

A number of assets are not chargeable to CGT and the gain on the disposal of certain other assets is exempt from charge (for details see **Chapter 22**). Apart from these exclusions, however, all forms of property are assets for CGT purposes including options, debts, incorporeal property, any currency (other than sterling), milk quota (*Cottle v Coldicott* (1995)) and property that is created by the person disposing of it (eg goodwill which is built up from nothing by a trader).

An asset which cannot be transferred by sale or gift may be within the tax charge. In *O'Brien v Benson's Hosiery (Holdings) Ltd* (1979), for instance, a director under a seven-year service contract paid his employer £50,000 to be released from his obligations. The employer was charged to CGT on the basis that the contract, despite being non-assignable, was an asset under s 21(1) so that the release of those rights resulted in 'a capital sum being received in return for the forfeiture or surrender of rights' (TCGA 1992 s 22(1)(c); see further [**19.112**]).

In *Marren v Ingles* (1980) shares in a private company were sold for £750 per share, payable at the time of the sale, plus a further sum if the company obtained a Stock Exchange quotation and the market value of the shares at that time was in excess of £750 per share. Two years later a quotation was obtained and a further £2,825 per share was paid. The House of Lords held that the taxpayers were initially liable to CGT calculated on the original sale price of £750 per share plus the value of the contingent right to receive a further sum (their Lordships did not attempt to put a value on it; was it nominal?). That right was a *chose in action* (a separate asset) which was disposed of for £2,825 per share two years later, leading to a further CGT liability (see [**19.26**]).

A 'right' may be used in both a colloquial and a legal sense. In its wider colloquial sense a right is not an asset for CGT purposes: it must be legally enforceable and capable of being turned into money. In *Kirby v Thorn EMI plc* (1988) the Revenue initially argued that the right to engage in commercial activity was an asset for CGT purposes with the result that if the taxpayers agreed to restrict their commercial activities in return for a capital payment, that sum would be brought into charge to tax. This argument was rejected on the basis that freedom to indulge in commercial activity was not a legal right constituting an asset for CGT purposes. On appeal, the Revenue produced an alternative argument that the taxpayers had derived a capital sum from the firm's goodwill and that therefore the payment in question was chargeable to CGT. In this argument it was successful.

[**19.7**]

c)    *What is a chargeable disposal?*

This topic is considered at [**19.111**] ff. 'Disposal' is extended to include cases where a capital sum is derived from an asset (for instance, insurance money paid for the damage or destruction of an asset). [**19.8**]–[**19.20**]

## II CALCULATION OF THE GAIN

The chargeable gain is found by taking the disposal consideration of the asset and deducting from that figure allowable expenditure (often called the '*base cost*'). The disponer's acquisition cost is usually the main item of expenditure. If the allowable expenditure exceeds the disposal consideration, the disponer has made a loss for CGT purposes which may be used to reduce the chargeable gains that he has made on disposals of other assets (see TCGA 1992 s 2(2) and **[19.61]**).

**EXAMPLE 19.1**

A sells a painting for £20,000 (the disposal consideration). He bought it six months ago for £14,000 (the acquisition cost) and has incurred no other deductible expenses. His chargeable gain is £6,000. If A sold the picture for £10,000 he would have an allowable loss of £4,000.

Inevitably, the calculation of disposal consideration and allowable expenditure is not always as simple as in *Example 19.1*: for instance, the chargeable gain may be reduced by taper relief (see **Chapter 20**).

The onus is on the taxpayer to establish what (if any) part of the disposal consideration is not within the charge to CGT (see *Neely v Rourke* (1987)).

**[19.21]**

### 1 What is the consideration for the disposal?

a) *General*

When the disposal is by way of a sale at arm's length, the consideration for the disposal will be the proceeds of sale. For disposals between husband and wife the disposal consideration is deemed to be of such a sum that neither gain nor loss results (TCGA 1992 s 58: a 'no gain/no loss' disposal), irrespective of the actual consideration given. It should also be noted that the Civil Partnership Act 2004 (CPA 2004), which gives legal recognition to same-sex couples, became law in November 2004 and comes into effect on 5 December 2005. Broadly, the Act allows same-sex couples to make a formal legal commitment to each other by entering into a civil partnership through a registration process. A range of important rights and responsibilities flows from this, including legal rights and protections. For tax purposes, registered same-sex couples will be treated the same as opposite-sex couples—disposals between registered same-sex couples will be deemed to be 'no gain/no loss' disposals. Where the disposal is not at arm's length, however, the consideration for the disposal is taken to be the market value of the asset at that date. This applies to gifts, to disposals between 'connected persons' (where the disposal is always *deemed* to be otherwise than by bargain at arm's length), to transfers of assets by a settlor into a settlement and to certain distributions by a company in respect of shares (TCGA 1992 s 17(1)(a)). In the case of disposals by excluded persons who are exempt from CGT (including charities, friendly societies, approved pension funds, and non-residents), the recipient is taken to acquire the asset at market value.

**EXAMPLE 19.2**

(1)    Sarah gives her husband a Richard Eurich painting for which she had paid £10,000. He acquires the picture for such sum as ensures neither gain nor loss results to Sarah, ie for £10,000 plus an indexation allowance to April 1998 (if appropriate): see further **[19.32]** and for the taper relief position **[20.33]**).

(2)    A gives a Ming vase worth £40,000 to the milkman. The consideration for the disposal is taken to be £40,000. If, instead, A sold the vase to his son B for £10,000 (or, indeed, for £60,000), B is a 'connected person' and the consideration for the disposal is taken to be £40,000.

(3)    Anna, a long-term resident of Peru, gives a house in Mayfair worth £1.5m, which she had acquired in 1989 for £20,000, to her son Paddington who is a UK resident. Anna is not chargeable to CGT on her gain because she is an excluded person and Paddington acquires the property at a value of £1.5m.

The market value of the asset is taken to be the disposal consideration whenever the actual consideration cannot be valued or the consideration is services (TCGA 1992 s 17(1)(b) but note that this provision does not apply to the exercise of an option: see **[19.118]**).

**EXAMPLE 19.3**

A, an antiques dealer, gives B, a fellow dealer, his country cottage worth £40,000 in consideration of B entering into a restrictive covenant with A, whereby he (B) agrees not to open an antique shop in competition with A. The consideration for the disposal is taken to be £40,000.

This market value rule can work to a taxpayer's advantage by giving the recipient a high acquisition cost for any future disposal in a transaction where the disponer is not charged to CGT on the gain (known as '*reverse Nairn Williamson*' arrangements). To some extent this is prevented by TCGA 1992 s 17(2) which provides that, where there is an acquisition without a disposal (eg the issue of shares by a company) and *either* no consideration is given for the asset, *or* the consideration is less than its market value, the actual consideration (if any) given prevails.                    **[19.22]**

**EXAMPLE 19.4**

A Ltd issues 1,000 £1 ordinary shares to B at par when their market value is £2 per share. The issue of shares by a company is not a disposal. This is, therefore, an acquisition of a chargeable asset by B without a disposal. Were it not for s 17(2), B's acquisition cost of the shares would be £2,000. As it is, B's acquisition cost is what he actually paid for the shares: ie £1,000.

b)    *Connected persons*

'Connected persons' for CGT purposes fall into four categories (TCGA 1992 s 286).

(1)    An individual is connected with his spouse, his or her relatives and their spouses. Relatives include siblings, direct ancestors (parents, grandparents), and lineal descendants (children, grandchildren) but not

lateral relatives (uncles, aunts, nephews and nieces). Marriage continues for these purposes until final divorce (see *Aspden v Hildesley* (1982)).

(2)   A company is connected with another company if both are under common control. A company is connected with another person if he (either alone or with other persons connected with him) controls that company.

(3)   A partner is connected with a fellow partner and his spouse and their relatives except in relation to acquisitions and disposals of partnership assets under *bona fide* commercial arrangements (eg where a new partner is given a share of the assets).

(4)   A trustee is connected with the settlor, any person connected with the settlor and any close company in which the trustee or any beneficiary under the settlement is a participator (for the definition of *close company* and *participator*, see **Chapter 41**). He is not connected with a beneficiary as such and, once the settlor dies, ceases to be connected with persons connected with the settlor (see RI 38, February 1993).          **[19.23]**

### EXAMPLE 19.5

A would like to 'unlock' the unrealised losses on a number of his assets. He disposes of the assets into a trust in which he enjoys a life interest. The result is to crystallise the loss but, because of the connected persons rule, that loss will only be available to set against gains on disposals *between the same parties* (see **[19.62]**). Accordingly, A disposes of assets showing a gain to the same trustees. Now the loss can be offset against that gain and, if those assets are immediately sold by the trustees, no chargeable gain will result to them.

c)   *The market value of assets*

Market value is the price for which the asset could be sold on the open market with no reduction for the fact that this may involve assuming that several assets are to be sold at the same time (TCGA 1992 s 272).

The market value of shares and securities listed in The Stock Exchange Daily Official List is taken as the lesser of:

(1)   the lower of the two prices quoted for that security in the Daily Official List, plus one quarter of the difference between the two prices (quarter-up);

(2)   half way between the highest and lowest prices at which bargains were recorded in that security on the relevant date excluding bargains at special prices (mid-price).

Unquoted shares and securities are valued on a number of criteria including the size of the holding and, therefore, the degree of control of the company.

TCGA 1992 s 19 modifies the basic rule: it applies when assets are fragmented (ie when one transferor makes two or more transfers to connected persons and the transfers occur within six years of each other).

### EXAMPLE 19.6

Alf owned a pair of Ming vases which as a pair were worth £100,000 but separately each was worth only £40,000. In January 2003 he gave one to his daughter and in the following July the other to his son.

(1)    The disposal to his daughter was for an original market value of £40,000. However, as it is linked to the later disposal to his son, the assets disposed of by the two disposals are valued as if they were disposed of by one disposal and the value attributed to each disposal is the appropriate proportion of that value. The market value of the two vases is £100,000 and the appropriate proportion is £50,000. (Notice that this revaluation of an earlier transaction will lead to an adjusted CGT assessment.)

(2)    The later disposal, occurring within six years, is a linked transaction. Again the original market value (£40,000) is replaced by the appropriate proportion (£50,000).

(3)    Compare the CGT rules on a disposal of sets of chattels (see [**22.23**]) and the IHT associated operations provisions (see [**28.101**]).

(4)    With the removal of general hold-over relief in the case of disposals by way of gift these rules are of increased importance.

Disposals to a spouse (and registered same-sex couples from 5 December 2005) are treated as giving rise to neither gain nor loss (TCGA 1992 s 58: [**19.22**]) but may form part of a series in order to determine the value of any of the other transactions in that series.                                                    [**19.24**]

### d)    *Deferred consideration*

Where the consideration for the disposal is known at the date of the disposal (which will normally be the date of contract: TCGA 1992 s 28 and see [**19.126**]) but is payable in instalments (TCGA 1992 s 280) or is subject to a contingency (TCGA 1992 s 48), the disponer is taxed on a gain calculated by reference to the full amount of the consideration receivable with no discount for the fact that payment is postponed. If, in fact, he never receives the full consideration his original CGT assessment is adjusted.                       [**19.25**]

**EXAMPLE 19.7**

(1)    A bought land two years ago for £50,000. He sells it today for £100,000 payable in two years' time. A is taxed now on a gain of £50,000 despite the fact that he has received nothing and with no discount for the fact that the right to £100,000 in two years' time is not worth £100,000 today. If A had been 'connected' with his purchaser, market value would be substituted for the actual consideration under s 17 thereby enabling a 'discount' to be taken into account. (For the CGT position when the purchase price is paid in instalments, see [**19.94**].)

(2)    Mucky sells four oil rigs for a consideration of $38.6m payable by instalments over nine years. At exchange rates prevailing at the date of disposal this produced a gain of £6.7m. Taking rates at the time when each instalment was paid, however, Mucky realised a loss of £2.7m. The basic CGT rule for foreign currency transactions is that the gain is to be computed by taking the exchange rate equivalent of the allowable expenditure at the time when it was incurred and the rate equivalent of the disposal consideration at the date of disposal (see *Capcount Trading v Evans* (1993)). Accepting this position, will Mucky succeed in arguing that because of the change in exchange rates part of his consideration was irrecoverable under TCGA 1992 s 48? Not according to the Court of Appeal who held that 'consideration' meant what was promised (ie dollars) rather than any sterling equivalent (see *Loffland Bros North Sea Inc v Goodbrand* (1998)).

e)   *Marren v Ingles*

It may be that the deferred consideration cannot be valued because it is dependent on some future contingency. In *Marren v Ingles* (1980) (see [**19.7**]) part of the payment for the disposal of shares was to be calculated by reference to the price of the shares if and when the company obtained a Stock Exchange listing. The taxpayer's gain at the time of the disposal of the shares could not be calculated by reference to such unquantifiable consideration. Accordingly he was treated as making two separate disposals. The first was the disposal of the shares. The consideration for this was the payment that the taxpayer actually received plus the value (if any) of the right to receive the future deferred sum (a *chose in action*). The value of the *chose in action* then formed the acquisition cost of that asset. Hence, once the deferred consideration became payable, the taxpayer was treated as making a second disposal, this time of the *chose in action*. He was, therefore, chargeable on the difference between the consideration received and whatever was the acquisition cost of that asset.

The House of Lords did not attempt to value the *chose in action*. In all probability its value would have been nominal, with the result that on the first disposal (of the shares) the gain would have been calculated by reference only to the cash received, whilst on the second disposal (of the *chose in action*) the entire consideration received would constitute a gain. There is no element of double taxation involved in the *Marren v Ingles* situation. Instead, the CGT is collected (in effect) in two instalments with the result that the taxpayer may be better off than A, in *Example 19.7(1)*, above, who is taxed on money years before receiving it. Of course, taper relief will often not be available on the disposal of the *chose in action* but in the event that the *chose* is subsequently sold at a loss, relief may be available against the gain on the disposal of the original asset (see TCGA 1992 s 279A–D inserted by FA 2003).

[**19.26**]

## 2   What expenditure is deductible?

Once the disposal consideration is known, the chargeable gain (or allowable loss) can be calculated by deducting allowable expenditure. This is defined in TCGA 1992 s 38 as 'expenditure incurred wholly and exclusively' in: [**19.27**]

a)   *Acquiring the asset*

The purchase price or market value, including any allowed incidental costs (such as stamp duty), or where the asset was created rather than acquired (eg a painting), the cost of creating or providing it, may be deducted (TCGA 1992 s 38(1)(a)). In certain circumstances a deemed acquisition cost will be deducted. This is the case, for instance, when an asset is acquired by inheritance (probate value being the acquisition cost) and when the 1982 rebasing rules apply (market value in 1982 being the acquisition cost: see TCGA 1992 s 35(2)).

[**19.28**]

b)   *Enhancing the value of the asset*

Expenditure on *improvements* must be reflected in the state or nature of the asset at the time of its disposal (TCGA 1992 s 38(1)(b)). It is presupposed that the asset is in existence when the expenditure is incurred (*Garner v Pounds Shipowners and Shipbreakers Ltd* (2000)). Thus, in the case of land, the costs of an application for planning permission which is never granted are not deductible, whereas the costs of building an extension are. Also deductible under this head are the costs of *establishing, preserving* or *defending* title to the asset (eg the costs of a boundary dispute and, in the case of PRs, a proportion of probate expenses—see also *Lee v Jewitt* (2000) where the costs of a partnership dispute were incurred in defending the taxpayer's title to goodwill).

In *Chaney v Watkis* (1986) the taxpayer agreed to pay his mother-in-law a cash sum (£9,400) if she surrendered up vacant possession of a house which he wished to sell. Between exchange of contracts on the property and completion this agreement was varied by mutual consent. Instead of the cash sum, the taxpayer agreed to build an extension onto his own home and allow her to occupy it rent-free for life. It was held that the cash sum would have been deductible in arriving at his gain on sale of the house if it had been paid (since vacant possession enhanced the value of the house). The same principle applied to a consideration in money's worth (the rent-free accommodation) and the case was remitted to the Commissioners for them to determine the value of this consideration. Two matters are worthy of note: *first*, that expenditure incurred post-contract but pre-completion was taken into account and the phrase 'at the time of the disposal' in s 38(1)(b) must be construed accordingly; and, *secondly*, that the taxpayer's mother-in-law was a protected tenant of the property (and had been before he purchased the house) and hence the agreement with her was a commercial arrangement.

**[19.29]**

c)   *Disposing of the asset*

The incidental costs of disposal that are deductible include professional fees paid to a surveyor, valuer, auctioneer, accountant, agent or legal adviser; costs of the transfer or conveyance; costs of advertising to find a buyer and any costs incurred in making a valuation or apportionment necessary for CGT (TCGA 1992 s 38(1)(c)). Expenses incurred in making a valuation and in ascertaining market value include the costs of an initial valuation to enable a tax return to be submitted but do not include costs of negotiating that value with the Revenue nor costs of appealing an assessment (*Caton's Administrators v Couch* (1997)). Other taxes, such as IHT on a gift, are not deductible.

The requirement in TCGA 1992 s 38 that expenditure must be 'wholly and exclusively' incurred makes use of the same test for allowable expenditure as that found for income tax under ITTOIA 2005 s 34 (see **[10.137]**). For CGT purposes, however, the words have been interpreted relatively liberally. In *IRC v Richards' Executors* (1971), PRs who sold shares at a profit claimed to deduct from the sale proceeds the cost of valuing the relevant part of the deceased's estate for probate. The House of Lords held that they could do so even though the valuation was for the purposes of estate duty as well as for establishing title (ie even though the costs were 'dual purpose expenditure').

'Expenditure' within TCGA 1992 s 38 must be something that reduces the taxpayer's estate in some quantifiable way. Thus in *Oram v Johnson* (1980) the taxpayer who bought a second home for £2,500, renovated it himself and later sold it for £11,500 could not deduct the notional cost of his own labour.

On a deemed disposal and reacquisition (see **[19.47]**) notional expenses are not deductible (TCGA 1992 s 38(4)), but actual expenses are. Thus, in *IRC v Chubb's Settlement Trustees* (1971), where the life tenant and the remainderman ended a settlement by dividing the capital between them so that there was a deemed disposal under (now) TCGA 1992 s 71, the costs of preparing the deed of variation of the settlement were deductible (the result of this case is to leave TCGA 1992 s 38(4) as a prohibition on the deduction of imaginary expenses!). **[19.30]**

d) *Disallowed expenditure*

The deduction of certain items of expenditure is specifically prohibited. For instance, interest on a loan to acquire the asset (TCGA 1992 s 38(3)); premiums paid under a policy of insurance against risks of loss of, or damage to, an asset; and, most important, any sums that a person can deduct in calculating his income for income tax. Additionally, no sum is deductible for CGT purposes which would be deductible for income tax, if the disponer were in fact using the relevant asset in a trade; in effect therefore, no items of an income, as opposed to a capital, nature will be deductible. For example, the cost of repair (as opposed to improvement) or of insurance of a chargeable asset, both of which are of an income nature, are disallowed as deductions for CGT. **[19.31]**

**EXAMPLE 19.8**

A buys a country cottage in 1997 for £200,000 to rent to high net worth individuals. He spends £30,000 in installing a gold plated bathroom and £14,000 on mending the leaking roof. Over the following five years he spends a further £500 on repairing leaking radiators and £400 on general maintenance. He pays a total of £3,000 on property insurance. He sells it in 2005 for £650,000.

His chargeable gain (ignoring indexation and taper) is:

|  | £ | £ |
|---|---|---|
| Sale proceeds |  | 650,000 |
| *Less:* |  |  |
| Acquisition cost | 200,000 |  |
| Cost of improvements | 30,000 | 230,000 |
|  |  | £420,000 |

The cost of repairs, maintenance and insurance are not deductible for CGT because they are deductible in computing his income under the property income rules of ITTOIA 2005 (formerly Schedule A). The insurance premiums are specifically disallowed under TCGA 1992 s 205.

If A had bought the cottage as a second home, his gain on sale would still be £420,000; the other items are disallowed as deductions for CGT because they are of an income nature.

## 3   The indexation of allowable expenditure

a)   *Rationale for an indexation allowance*

Before 1982 CGT made no allowance for the effects of inflation on the value of chargeable assets and, accordingly, it taxed both real and paper profits. FA 1982 afforded a measure of relief by introducing an indexation allowance for disposals of assets on or after 6 April 1982 (1 April in the case of companies); FA 1985 made major improvements to that allowance in respect of disposals on or after 6 April 1985 (or 1 April) but FA 1994 introduced restrictions to prevent the allowance from creating a loss. Generally items of allowable expenditure were index-linked (to rises in the RPI), so that the eventual gain on disposal should represent only 'real' profits (see TCGA 1992 ss 53–57).

**[19.32]**

b)   *The changes of FA 1998*

The allowance has been abolished for months after April 1998 in the case of individuals, PRs and trustees. It continues, however, to apply in calculating the chargeable gains of companies (TCGA 1992 s 53(1A)). In its place an entirely new relief, taper relief, was introduced (see **Chapter 20**). The current position for individuals, etc is, therefore, as follows:
(1)   assets acquired before April 1998 will continue to benefit from an indexation allowance but only for the period ending with that month;
(2)   assets acquired in April 1998 or at a later time will not benefit from indexation. Eventually, therefore, this allowance will wither away, but the process will occupy many years.

**EXAMPLE 19.9**

Roy has run his family business for 20 years since inheriting it from his father. He sells it in May 2005. In calculating Roy's gain he will benefit from:
(1)   indexation relief until April 1998 on (presumably) the 1982 value of the business (see **[19.38]**); and
(2)   business asset taper relief (see **[20.20]**).

The ending of indexation was presented as a simplifying measure:

'The calculation of the allowance is a major complicating feature of the present CGT system and its eventual withdrawal, together with the withdrawal of retirement relief, will lead to significant simplification.'

(Press Release, 17 March 1998)
**[19.33]**

c)   *Basic rules of indexation*

It is calculated by comparing the RPI for the month in which the allowable expenditure was incurred (ie due and payable) with the index for the 'relevant month' which (except for companies) is April 1998 (TCGA 1992 s 54(1A)). Assuming that the RPI has increased, the allowable expenditure is multiplied by the fraction

$$\frac{RD-RI}{RI}$$

where RD is the index for the relevant month and RI is the index for the month in which the item of expenditure was incurred or March 1982 if later (this fraction, calculated to three decimal places, produces the 'indexed rise' decimal which is published by the Revenue each month). The resultant figure (known as the 'indexation allowance') is a further allowable deduction in arriving at the chargeable gain on disposal of the asset.

As the allowance is linked to allowable expenditure, it follows that, where an asset has a nil base cost (for instance, goodwill built up by the taxpayer) there can be no indexation allowance.

ESC D42 makes provision for the situation where a leaseholder acquires a superior interest in the land so that his interests merge and the inferior interest is extinguished. Strictly, the indexation allowance on the total costs of the two acquisitions (as wasted, if appropriate: see **[19.49]**) should be calculated only from the date of the later acquisition of the superior interest but by concession the allowance on the acquisition cost of the earlier, inferior, interest can be calculated from the date of its acquisition.  **[19.34]**

**EXAMPLE 19.10**

A painting was bought for £20,000 on 10 April 1991 and sold for £100,000 on 30 June 2005. RPI for April 1991 is (say) 300; RPI for April 1998 is (say) 500. The indexed rise is:

$$\frac{(500-300)}{300} \text{ :ie } 0.667 \text{ (correct to three decimal places).}$$

Indexation allowance is: £20,000 × 0.667 = £13,340
Therefore, the chargeable gain is:

|  | £ | £ |
|---|---|---|
| Sale proceeds |  | 100,000 |
| *Less:* |  |  |
| Acquisition cost | 20,000 |  |
| Indexation allowance | 13,340 | 33,340 |
| Chargeable gain |  | £66,660 |

Assume that the painting was restored on 12 November 1994 for £2,000. RPI for November 1994 is (say) 400. Indexation allowance is £13,340, as above, plus:

$$£2,000 \times \frac{(500-400)}{400} = £500$$

Therefore, the chargeable gain is £64,160 (£66,660 − £2,000 − £500). Taper relief on the basis that the picture was not a business asset will be available (see **Chapter 20**).

d)   *The indexation allowance and capital losses*

The indexation allowance cannot create or increase a capital loss: it only operates to reduce or extinguish capital gains (TCGA 1992 s 53(1) (2A)).

**[19.35]**

**EXAMPLE 19.11**

Alain acquired an asset for £100,000. He disposes of it for £110,000 and his indexation allowance is £15,000. Alain can use £10,000 of the indexation allowance (*only*) thereby wiping out his gain. If he had sold the asset for £90,000 none of the allowance would be used. If he had sold it for £125,000 then the full allowance would be available to reduce the gain to £10,000.

**4   Taper relief (TCGA 1992 s 2A; Sch A1 inserted by FA 1998 and amended by FAs 2000–2003)**

These provisions are considered in detail in the next chapter.       **[19.36]**

**5   Calculation of gains for assets acquired before 6 April 1965**

Only gains after 6 April 1965 are chargeable (TCGA 1992 s 35(9)). Accordingly, for assets acquired before 6 April 1965, the legislation contains rules determining how much gain is deemed to have accrued since that date. Generally, the gain is deemed to accrue evenly over the whole period of ownership (the so-called straight-line method: TCGA 1992 Sch 2 para 16(3)). The chargeable gain is, therefore, a proportion of the gross gain calculated by the formula:

$$\text{Gross gain} \times \frac{\text{period of ownership since 6 April 1965}}{\text{total period of ownership}} = \text{chargeable gain}$$

**EXAMPLE 19.12**

(The indexation allowance, 1982 rebasing and taper relief have been ignored.)

|  | £ |
|---|---:|
| A bought a picture on 6 April 1964 for | 5,000 |
| He sells it on 6 April 2005 for | 19,000 |
| His gain is | £14,000 |

His chargeable gain is: £14,000 × $^{40}/_{41}$ = £13,658

In applying this formula, the ownership of the asset can never be treated as beginning earlier than 6 April 1945 (TCGA 1992 Sch 2 para 11(6)) so that if it was acquired before that date it is deemed to have been acquired on that date.

In *Smith v Schofield* (1993) the taxpayer inherited a Chinese cabinet and French mirror (combined value £250) on the death of her father in 1952.

She sold both items early in 1987 for a price that, after deducting incidental costs of sale and the deemed acquisition cost, left a net gain of £14,088. That figure had to be further reduced for CGT charging purposes by (1) the indexation allowance which would be calculated on the value of the assets in March 1982, and (2) by the straight-line allowance for chargeable assets owned on 6 April 1965. The House of Lords decided that the indexation allowance must be deducted first, and then time apportionment applied with the result that the chargeable gain was £7,189. Had time apportionment been applied first, thereby reducing the gain to £8,864, and then the indexation allowance deducted in full, the chargeable gain would have been only £6,224. Commenting on the decision, Lord Jauncey had some regrets:

> 'I reached this decision with regret because its effect is that an allowance which was given to offset the effect of inflation on gains accruing from and after 1982 is in part being attributed to notional non-chargeable gains accruing prior to 6 April 1965, a situation which cannot occur where an election of valuation on that date is made. In the present case the effective value of the indexation allowance will be reduced by more than one-third ... I should be surprised if Parliament had intended such a result.'

These rules are of limited importance in view of the rebasing provisions.
**[19.37]**

## 6 Calculation of gains on assets owned on 31 March 1982 (rebasing)

The following rules apply to disposals of assets that were owned on 31 March 1982 by the person making the disposal. **[19.38]**

### a) *Basic rule*

Assets that the taxpayer owned on 31 March 1982 are deemed to have been sold by that person and immediately reacquired by him at market value on that date. Rebasing involves the taxpayer in incurring expenses in agreeing with the Revenue a valuation figure for the relevant asset in March 1982 (TCGA 1992 s 35). **[19.39]**

**EXAMPLE 19.13**

Jacques' valuable collection of porcelain cost £12,000 in 1970; it was worth £100,000 on 31 March 1982 and has just been sold for £175,000. In computing Jacques' capital gain arising from his disposal, rebasing to March 1982 will result in a reduction in the gain from £163,000 to £75,000 (before considering the indexation allowance and taper relief).

### b) *Qualifications*

In cases where a computation based on the actual costs and ignoring 1982 values would produce a smaller gain or loss, rebasing will not generally apply so that it is that smaller gain or loss which will be relevant. In cases where one computation would produce a gain and the other a loss, there is deemed to be neither. **[19.40]**

**EXAMPLE 19.14**

(1)   Assume that under rebasing the disposal of an asset would show a loss of £60,000 whereas ignoring 1982 values the loss would be only £35,000. In this case the £35,000 loss will be taken.

(2)   Alternatively, assume that the disposal would show a gain of £25,000 if rebasing applied but only £15,000 if it did not. The smaller gain (£15,000) will be taxed.

(3)   Under the rebasing calculation there is a gain of £50,000 on the disposal of a chargeable asset: on the alternative calculation ignoring 1982 values, however, there is a loss of £2,000. In this case there is deemed to be neither gain nor loss. (Similarly if the loss had been produced by rebasing and the gain under the alternative calculation.)

(4)   Assume that there is a loss of £6,000 if the asset is rebased to 1982 but, on the alternative calculation, a loss of £20,000. In this case mandatory rebasing will occur with the result that the loss is restricted to £6,000.

c)   *The election*

Because the qualifications discussed above require the taxpayer to keep pre-1982 records and will usually involve alternative calculations, the taxpayer is given an election for rebasing to apply to all disposals of assets which he held on 31 March 1982. This election may be made at any time before 6 April 1990 or (if no election has been made by that time) within two years from the end of the tax year in which the first relevant disposal (ie of assets owned at 31 March 1982) occurs or within such longer period as the Board may allow (see SP 4/92). The election is irrevocable and will apply to all disposals of assets owned on 31 March 1982 by the particular taxpayer (TCGA 1992 s 35(5)). In SP 2/89 the Revenue indicated that it will always exercise its discretion to extend the election time limit to (at least) the date on which the statutory time limit would expire (ie five years after 31 January following the year of disposal) if the first relevant disposal was one on which the gain would not be chargeable (eg a disposal of private cars; chattels which are wasting assets; gilt-edged securities).                                                   **[19.41]**

d)   *Technical matters*

A crucial feature of the rebasing rules is the determination of when an asset was acquired by the taxpayer. In exceptional cases, the ownership period of another person can be included in deciding whether the asset was owned on 31 March 1982. These are situations where the disponer acquired the asset as a result of a no gain/no loss disposal that took place after 31 March 1982 and was made by a transferor who had owned the asset before that date.

**EXAMPLE 19.15**

(The indexation allowance on the no gain/no loss disposal has been ignored.)
    Doris inherited a gold snuff box on the death of her father in 1977. Its probate value was £10,000. In 1983 she gave it to her husband, Sid, on their wedding anniversary. In March 1982, the box was worth £25,000 and in 1983 £28,000. Sid has just sold the box for £35,000.

(1)   The 1983 transfer between spouses was made at no gain/no loss so that Sid is treated as having acquired the box for £10,000.

(2)  In calculating the gain on sale, Sid is treated as having held the asset on 31 March 1982 so that the market value at that date (£25,000) will be his allowable base cost.

In certain other situations ownership of an asset may be related back to an earlier date: generally these are cases where the asset is treated as forming part of or replacing an earlier asset. This, for instance, is the case where securities are issued as the consideration for a company takeover under TCGA 1992 ss 135–137 (see **Chapter 26**).

Rebasing of the acquisition cost to market value on 31 March 1982 was introduced by FA 1988 in relation to disposals on and after 6 April 1988. Accordingly, where an asset held on 31 March 1982 had been disposed of before 6 April 1988 no rebasing would have applied; but FA 1988 (now TCGA 1992 Sch 4) provides that where the gain on such a disposal has been held-over or rolled-over the gain ultimately realised is relieved by deducting half that held-over or rolled-over gain. This was a rough-and-ready substitute for recomputing the held-over or rolled-over gain so as to give effect to March 1982 rebasing.                                                   **[19.42]**

### EXAMPLE 19.16

Simpkin, who has been a partner in an estate agency business, sells his interest in goodwill in 1983. The acquisition cost of the goodwill was nil: its value in 1982 was estimated at £85,000. When he sold the goodwill in 1983 he obtained £100,000 that he then rolled over into a farm purchased in 1985 at a total cost of £210,000. As a result of roll-over relief (see **[22.72]**), the base cost of the farm in Simpkin's hands was reduced to £110,000. As the farm was acquired in 1985 there is no question of March 1982 rebasing. However, on the eventual sale of the farm, one half of the rolled-over gain will be relieved so that Simpkin's base cost will be £110,000 + £50,000 (one half of the rolled-over gain) = £160,000.

## 7   Part disposals

### a)   *General rule*

The term 'disposal' includes a part disposal, so that whenever part of an asset or an interest in an asset is disposed of it is necessary to calculate the original cost of the part sold before any gain on it can be computed (TCGA 1992 s 42). This applies, for instance, to a sale of part of a landholding or to the grant of a lease (for leases, see **[19.47]**).

The formula used for calculating the deductible cost of the part sold is:

$$C \times \frac{A}{A+B}$$

Where
C = all the deductible expenditure on the whole asset
A = sale proceeds of the part of the asset sold
B = market value of part retained (at the time when the part is sold).

The indexation provisions applied in the same way for part disposals as for disposals of the whole, except that only the apportioned expenditure was index-linked.                                                   **[19.43]**

**EXAMPLE 19.17**

Ten acres of land were bought for £10,000 on 1 January 1991. Four acres of land were sold for £12,000 on 1 October 2005 (the remaining six acres were then worth £24,000). RPI for January 1991 is (say) 250. RPI for April 1998 is (say) 340.

Acquisition cost of the four acres sold is:

$$£10,000 \times \frac{£12,000}{£36,000} = £3,333$$

Indexation allowance is: £3,333 × 0.360 = £1,200
Therefore the chargeable gain is:

|  | £ | £ |
|---|---|---|
| Sale proceeds | | 12,000 |
| *Less:* | | |
| Acquisition cost | 4,000 | |
| Indexation allowance | 1,200 | 5,200 |
| | | £6,800 |

(The amount of taper relief will depend on whether the land was a business asset: see **Chapter 14.**)

b)    *Cases when the formula is not used*

The part disposal formula need not be used (thereby removing the need to value the part of the asset not disposed of) when the cost of the part disposed of can easily be calculated. In particular, there are special rules relating to a part disposal of shares of the same class in the same company (see Chapter 21 Part III).

Further the rules will not be applied to small part disposals of land (TCGA 1992 s 242) if the taxpayer so elects. Where the consideration received is 20% or less of the value of the entire holding and does not exceed £20,000 (or is 'small' in the case of a disposal to an authority with compulsory powers of acquisition: see s 243) the transaction need not be treated as a disposal. Instead, the taxpayer can elect to deduct the consideration received from the allowable expenditure applicable to the whole of the land.

Similar principles apply to small capital distributions made by companies (see **[26.21]** and for the meaning of 'small', see *Tax Bulletin*, February 1997).

**[19.44]**

8    **Wasting assets (TCGA 1992 ss 44–47)**

a)    *Definition*

A wasting asset is one with a predictable useful life not exceeding 50 years. If the asset is a wasting chattel (ie an item of tangible movable property such as a television or washing machine), there is a general exemption from CGT (see **[22.21]**). In the case of plant and machinery qualifying for capital allowances there are special rules (see **[19.66]**). Short leases of land are likewise subject to their own rules (see **[19.47]**ff); freehold land, needless to say, can never be a wasting asset. The main types of asset subject to the ordinary wasting asset rules are:

(1) tangible movable property with the exception of commodities dealt with on a terminal market (TCGA 1992 s 45(4));

(2) options with the exception of quoted options to subscribe for shares in a company; traded options quoted on a recognised stock exchange or recognised futures exchange; financial options and options to acquire assets for use in a business (TCGA 1992 s 146);

(3) purchased life interests in settled property where the predictable life expectation of the life tenant is 50 years or less (TCGA 1992 s 44(1)(d));

(4) patent rights;

(5) copyrights in certain circumstances; and

(6) leases for 50 years or less (for leases of land, see **[19.47]**). **[19.45]**

### b) *Calculation of gain on disposal*

On disposal of any of the above assets any gain is calculated on the basis that the allowable expenditure on the asset is written down at a uniform rate over its expected useful life so that any claim for loss relief will be limited. Consistent with the general principles that apply to such assets, it was only the written down expenditure that was entitled to the indexation allowance. **[19.46]**

**EXAMPLE 19.18**

Copyright (19 years unexpired) of a novel was bought for £2,800 on 1 April 1991. The copyright is sold for £2,600 on 1 April 2005. Assume the RPI for March 1982 is 250; RPI for April 1998 is 350. The gain on disposal is calculated as follows:

Calculate written down acquisition cost:

$$£2,800 - \left( £2,800 \times \frac{14 \text{ years}}{19 \text{ years}} \right) = £737$$

The indexation allowance is:
£737 × 0.4 = £294
Therefore the chargeable gain is:

|  | £ | £ |
|---|---|---|
| Sale proceeds |  | 2,600 |
| *Less:* |  |  |
| Acquisition cost | 737 |  |
| Indexation allowance | 294 | 1,031 |
| Chargeable gain (subject to taper relief) |  | £1,569 |

## 9    Rules for leases of land (TCGA 1992 s 240, Sch 8)

a)    *Basic rules*

The grant of a lease out of a freehold or superior lease is a part disposal. The grant of a lease for a 'rack rent' and no premium will not attract any CGT charge: sums charged to income tax are excluded from the consideration in computing the gain for CGT (TCGA 1992 s 37(1)).                    **[19.47]**

b)    *CGT on premiums*

The gain is computed by deducting from the disposal consideration (ie the premium) the cost of the part disposed of, calculated as for any part disposal (see **[19.43]**). Included in the denominator of the formula as a part of the market value of the land undisposed of is the value of any right to receive rent under the lease. In *Clarke v United Real (Moorgate) Ltd* (1988), the court held that a premium included any *sum* paid by a tenant to his landlord in consideration for the grant of a lease and therefore caught payments to the landlord covering past and future development costs. The definition of 'premium' in TCGA 1992 Sch 8 para 10(2) does not address the giving of consideration other than by payment of a sum, eg where a lease is granted in consideration of the tenant undertaking works of improvement to the demised or other premises. This is in contrast to the position for income tax where the value (to the landlord) of an undertaking by the tenant to carry out development or improvement works to the demised premises (though not to other premises of the landlord) is treated as a premium (ITTOIA 2005 s 278 and see **[8.83]**). On general principles the value of a tenant's undertaking to carry out development or improvement works would constitute consideration for the lease; and in so far as this notional premium is not subject to income tax (for example, because the works relate to other premises of the landlord) it would be taken into account in computing the landlord's chargeable gain (or allowable loss) on the part-disposal arising from the grant of the lease.                    **[19.48]**

c)    *The wasting asset rules for leases*

A lease which has 50 or less years to run is a wasting asset. It does not depreciate evenly over time, however, so that on any assignment of it, its cost is written down, not as described in **[19.46]**, but according to a special table in TCGA 1992 Sch 8 (on the duration of a lease, see *Lewis v Walters* (1992) deciding that the possibility of extending the term under the Leasehold Reform Act 1967 should be ignored).

Where a sub-lease is granted out of a lease that is a wasting asset, the ordinary part disposal formula is not applied. Instead, any gain is calculated by deducting from the consideration received for the sub-lease, that part of the allowable expenditure on the head lease that will waste away over the period of the sub-lease.                    **[19.49]**

**EXAMPLE 19.19**

A acquires a lease of premises for 40 years for £5,000 (that lease is, therefore, a wasting asset). After ten years he grants a sub-lease to B for ten years at a premium of £1,000.

A's gain is calculated by deducting from the consideration on the part disposal (ie £1,000), such part of £5,000 as will waste away (in accordance with TCGA 1992 Sch 8 para 1) on a lease dropping from 30 years to 20 years.

d)   *Income tax overlap*

Any part of a premium that is chargeable to income tax under the property income provisions of ITTOIA 2005 (formerly Schedule A) (see **Chapter 12**) is not charged to CGT. Thus, on the grant of a short lease out of an interest that is not a wasting asset (eg the freehold) there must be deducted from the premium received such part of it as is taxed under ITTOIA 2005. The part disposal formula is then applied (see **[19.43]**) but in the numerator (though not in the denominator) the sum representing the sale proceeds of the part disposal is the premium received *less* that part taxed under ITTOIA 2005.

[19.50]

**EXAMPLE 19.20**

A buys freehold premises for £200,000. He grants a lease of the premises for 21 years at a premium of £100,000 and a rent. The value of the freehold subject to the lease and including the right to receive rent is now £150,000.

Of the premium of £100,000, £60,000 is taxed under ITTOIA 2005 (ie the premium less 2% x 20 ie less 40%: see **[12.82]**).

A's chargeable gain is, therefore:

|  | £ |
|---|---|
| Consideration received | 100,000 |
| *Less:* amount taxed under ITTOIA 2005 | 60,000 |
|  | 40,000 |
| *Less:* cost of the part disposed of | 32,000 |
| $£200,000 \times \dfrac{£40,000}{£100,000+£150,000}$: |  |
| Chargeable gain (ignoring indexation and taper) | £8,000 |

e)   *Tenants and lease surrenders/regrants*

For the position of a tenant who extends his lease, often by surrendering the old lease in return for the grant on a new long lease and payment of a premium, see ESC D39 (**[19.124]**); for the calculation of his indexation allowance ESC D42. A reverse premium received by a tenant as an inducement to enter into the lease will not normally attract a CGT charge: see CG 70833 and for the income tax rules, see **[12.87]**.                **[19.51]–[19.60]**

## III    LOSSES FOR CGT

### 1    When does a loss arise?

A loss arises whenever the consideration for the disposal of a chargeable asset is less than the allowable expenditure incurred by the taxpayer (but excluding any indexation allowance). Losses are not tapered (see [**19.63**]).

#### EXAMPLE 19.21

If an antique desk was bought for £12,000, restored for £1,000 and then sold for £11,000, a loss of £2,000 would result.

Although the disposal of a debt (other than a debt on a security) is usually exempt from CGT, a loss that is made on a qualifying loan to a trader may be treated as a capital loss (see TCGA 1992 s 253 and [**22.43**]).

If an asset is destroyed or extinguished; abandoned, in the case of options that are not wasting assets ([**19.118**]); or if its value has become negligible (see [**19.117**]), the taxpayer may claim to have incurred an allowable loss.

[**19.61**]

### 2    Use of losses

Losses must be relieved primarily against gains of the taxpayer in the same year, but any surplus loss can be carried forward and set against his first available gain in future years without time limit.

Losses cannot be carried back and set against gains of previous years except for the net losses incurred by an individual in the year of his death (TCGA 1992 s 62(2) and [**21.41**]). Capital losses cannot generally be set against the taxpayer's income for tax purposes. The only exception is for losses arising as a result of investment in a corporate trade under TA 1988 s 574 (see [**11.121**]). Similarly, income losses cannot generally be set against an individual's capital gains: although this rule is also subject to an important exception whereby trading losses which cannot be relieved against the taxpayer's income may be set against his chargeable gains for both the year when the loss was incurred and one preceding tax year (see FA 1991 s 72 and [**11.61**]) and as a result of changes in FA 2000 payments under the Gift Aid scheme may be covered by tax on chargeable gains (see [**53.82**]).

A loss that is incurred on a disposal to a connected person can only be set against any gains on subsequent disposals to the same person (TCGA 1992 s 18(3) and see [**19.22**]).

For the exceptional relief when a loss arises on the disposal of certain rights to unascertainable consideration (as in *Marren v Ingles* situations) see TCGA 1992 s 279A–D inserted by FA 2003.    [**19.62**]

### 3    Losses and taper relief

a)    *Basic principles*

Unlike gains, losses are not tapered. Relief for losses is therefore available for the full amount of the loss and this is obviously of benefit to taxpayers:

curiously therefore, if an asset has been owned for the maximum period only 25% (business assets) or 60% (non-business assets) of any gain is chargeable, but all of any loss is allowable! However, the use of losses is not straightforward and the following points should be noted:

(1)    Losses must be deducted from gains *before* those gains are tapered. In effect, therefore, part of the loss relief may be lost by being attributed to that portion of the gain that would not, in any event, be taxed: TCGA 1992 s 2(2) and s 2A(2).

(2)    Losses may be set off against gains in the way that is most advantageous to the taxpayer (TCGA 1992 s 2A(6)).                                    **[19.63]**

**EXAMPLE 19.22**

Zee realises gains on two separate assets in the same year of assessment.

*Asset 1* is a business asset and the gain before taper is £10,000. The period for which the asset has been held (the taper period) is four years.

*Asset 2* is a non-business asset and the gain before taper is £8,000; taper period seven years.

In the same year he makes a loss of £5,000 on the sale of a third asset.

For the purposes of computing the taper relief, the loss is set against the gain which qualifies for the least taper relief so that the tax reduction provided by the taper is the maximum. The loss is therefore set against the gain on asset 2 because as a non-business asset it qualifies for reduction to only 75% of the untapered amount, whereas the gain on asset 1 will be reduced to 25%.

So of the net gain of £3,000 (£8,000 – loss of £5,000), 75% is chargeable, ie £2,250.

Of the gain of £10,000 on asset 1, 25% is chargeable, ie £2,500.

The gains chargeable, subject to Zee's annual exemption, total £4,750.

b)    *Attributed gains*

There are three situations in which trust gains may be attributed to an individual, namely:

(1)    under TCGA 1992 s 77 (see **[19.85]**).

(2)    under TCGA 1992 s 86 (see **[27.94]**).

(3)    under TCGA 1992 s 87 (see **[27.111]**).

When taper relief was introduced in 1998 it was provided that these attributed gains were to be the trust gains after taper but they could not then be reduced by personal losses of the individual. Although unfortunate for taxpayers, the logic was that the attributed gains had already benefited from taper (on the basis of the trustees' ownership period) so that further relief was not due.

FA 2002 has changed the position for gains attributed to settlors in 2003–04 *et seq* by virtue of (1) and (2) above (and settlors can also elect for this treatment for all or any of the tax years 2000–01, 2001–02 and 2002–03). Under the new provisions the mechanics are as follows:

(1)    gains are attributed to the settlor *before* deduction of any taper relief;

(2)    the settlor may then offset his personal losses against those gains to the extent that those losses cannot be relieved against his personal chargeable gains;

(3)    taper relief will then apply to the net gains at the trustees' rate of relief.

The following example contrasts the 'old' and 'new' rules.                **[19.64]**

**EXAMPLE 19.23**

| | Old rules | New rules |
|---|---|---|
| *Trust* | £100,000 | £100,000 |
| *Less* trust losses | –£20,000 | –£20,000 |
| Net trust gains | £80,000 | £80,000 |
| Gain after taper relief: | £20,000 | No taper relief applied |
| | (in this example 25% of the gain is charged to tax) | |
| Gain attributed to settlor | £20,000 | £80,000 |

| | | |
|---|---|---|
| *Settlor* | | |
| Personal gains | £50,000 | £50,000 |
| Attributed gain | £20,000 | £80,000 |
| *Less* personal losses | –£60,000 | –£60,000 |
| | (deducted from personal gains only—£10,000 carried forward for possible use if the individual has gains in a later year) | (deducted first from personal gains, then from attributed gain) |
| Net gains | £20,000 | £70,000 |
| Gain after taper relief | No taper relief on attributed gain | £17,500 |
| | | (applied to attributed gain at the rate at which the trustees would have applied it—so in this example 25% of the gain is charged to tax) |
| Deduct annual exemption | –£8,200 | –£8,200 |
| Chargeable to CGT | £11,800 | £9,300 |
| Tax paid (at 40%) | £4,720 | £3,720 |
| Reimbursement from the trust | £4,720 | £3,720 |

c)   *Link up with annual exemption*

The position of losses and the annual exemption is considered at **[19.86]** ff.

**[19.65]**

## 4   Restriction of losses: capital allowances

Generally, chattels that are wasting assets are exempt from CGT (see **[22.21]**). That exemption does not, however, extend to an item of plant or machinery if throughout the taxpayer's period of ownership it has been used in a trade and the taxpayer has claimed (or could have claimed) capital allowances in respect of any expenditure on the asset. It follows that if capital allowances are not available, eg because the asset is never brought into use in the business, the CGT exemption will apply: see *Burman v Westminster Press Ltd* (1987). Other assets that qualify for capital allowances, such as industrial buildings, are chargeable assets because they are not wasting.

A gain that is charged to income tax will not be charged to CGT; and a loss will not be allowable for CGT if it is deductible for income tax. Thus, for CGT purposes the gain or loss on a disposal of plant and machinery and other assets qualifying for capital allowances is calculated in the usual way (and not written down in the case of wasting assets) and any gain is charged to CGT only to the extent that it exceeds the original cost of the asset.

**EXAMPLE 19.24**

|  | £ |
|---|---|
| *Year 1:* Machine bought for | 10,000 |
| WDA at 25% | 2,500 |
| *Year 2:* Machine sold for | 12,000 |

There is a balancing charge for income tax of £2,500 (ie to the extent of the capital allowance given—see further **Chapter 41**). The excess of the sale price over the acquisition cost (£2,000) is chargeable to CGT.

However, it is rare for plant and machinery to be sold at a gain; it is more likely to be sold at a loss, in which case the loss is not allowable for CGT to the extent that it is covered by capital allowances. Capital allowances may reduce a loss to nil, but they cannot produce a gain.           **[19.66]–[19.80]**

**EXAMPLE 19.25**

|  | £ |
|---|---|
| Machine bought for | 4,000 |
| Sold later for | 2,000 |
| Capital allowance given of | 2,000 |
| *Loss for CGT is:* | |
| Disposal proceeds | 2,000 |
| *Less:* acquisition cost | 4,000 |
| Capital loss | (2,000) |
| Credit for capital allowances | 2,000 |
| Allowable loss | £Nil |

## IV   CALCULATING THE TAX PAYABLE

### 1   **Rates (TCGA 1992 s 4)**

a)   *Fusion with income tax*

CGT was formerly charged at a flat rate of 30%. Changes in FA 1988, however, resulted in the abandonment of this single rate and the appropriate rate now depends upon the identity and circumstances of the disponor. In his 1988 Budget Speech, the then Chancellor (Nigel Lawson) explained these changes as follows:

> 'In principle, there is little economic difference between income and capital gains, and many people effectively have the option of choosing to a significant extent which to receive. And, insofar as there is a difference, it is by no means clear why one should be taxed more heavily than the other. Taxing them at different rates distorts investment decisions and inevitably creates a major tax avoidance industry ... I therefore propose a fundamental reform ... I propose in future to apply the same rate of tax to income and capital gains alike ... Taxing capital gains at income tax rates makes for greater neutrality in the tax system. It is what we now do for companies. And it is also the practice in the United States, with the big difference that there they have neither indexation relief nor a separate capital gains tax threshold.'                                                    **[19.81]**

b)   *Individuals*

CGT is taxed at the rate of income tax applicable to the taxpayer, which will be either:
(1)   the starting rate (10% for 2006–07); or
(2)   the lower rate (20% for 2006–07); or
(3)   the higher rate (40% for 2006–07).
     These terms are considered at **[7.120]**.
     CGT is charged at the taxpayer's marginal income tax rate (TCGA 1992 s 4, as amended). Accordingly, capital gains realised in a particular tax year may push the individual into the higher rate that will apply to that gain.
     The following diagram illustrates the position and shows that gains from non-resident trusts attributed to settlors are treated as the highest slice of a taxpayer's gains:

| CAPITAL GAINS | Offshore trust gains attributed under TCGA 1992 s 86 |
|---|---|
| | Other gains |
| INCOME | Dividends |
| | Savings income |

Other income (eg earned and rental income)

For many taxpayers linking the rates of income tax and CGT resulted in an increase in the rate of tax applicable to capital gains from 30% (in 1987–88) to 40%.                                                    **[19.82]**

**EXAMPLE 19.26**

(1)  Bill has no income in the tax year 2006–07 but realises chargeable capital gains of £10,000. His rate of tax on those gains is 10% on the first £2,150 and thereafter 20%: note that he cannot reduce the gain by deducting his unused personal allowance.

(2)  Had Bill's gain been £33,500, CGT would be charged as follows:
first £2,150 at 10%
next £31,150 at 20%
final £200 at 40%.

c)  *Companies*

Companies are subject to corporation tax, not CGT, but that tax is charged on corporate profits including chargeable gains. The rate of tax charged on such gains in the financial year to 31 March 2007 is therefore either 19% (small company rate) or 30%.                                          **[19.83]**

d)  *Personal representatives*

PRs are subject to tax at 40%. Given that this rate may be higher than the beneficiaries' rates care should be exercised if assets in the estate showing a gain on probate value are to be sold (see **[21.81]**).                    **[19.84]**

e)  *Trustees*

Trustees are taxed at 40% with effect from tax year 2004–2005, except where the settlor or his spouse has an interest in the settlement when tax is assessed on the settlor as if the gains had been realised by him and not by the trustees (TCGA 1992 ss 77–78).

A settlor retains an interest for these purposes if there are any circumstances in which the settled property, or any derived property, is payable to, or applicable for the benefit of, the settlor or the settlor's spouse or civil partner, or may become so payable or applicable in the future.

As can be appreciated these provisions are widely drawn so that they could catch, for instance, a situation where money was lent to the settlor by his trustees. Compare the income tax rules in ITTOIA 2005 Part 5 Chapter 5: see **[16.98]**.

With effect from 6 April 2006, a settlor also retains an interest in the settlement if any settled property is, will or may become payable to any unmarried minor child or step-child of his ('a dependent child'). A settlor will not, however, be regarded as having an interest in the settlement:

(a)  in respect of any time during which he has no living dependent children even if such children are capable of benefiting under the terms of the settlement, or

(b)  in the tax year during which he ceases to have dependent children.

A settlor caught by the settlor-interested provisions has the right to recover the CGT from the trustees on production of a certificate from his Inspector certifying the CGT attributable to the trust gains.                          **[19.85]**

## 2  The annual exemption

The amount of the annual exemption depends on the capacity in which the
person makes the gain.                                                    **[19.86]**

### a)  *Individuals*

The first £8,800 (for 2006–07) of the total gains in a tax year are exempt from
CGT (TCGA 1992 s 3).

**EXAMPLE 19.27**

|                                                                   | £      | £       |
| ----------------------------------------------------------------- | ------ | ------- |
| A sells a painting in July 2006 for                               |        | 23,150  |
| Original cost of painting in 1996                                 | 8,700  |         |
| Indexation allowance to April 1998 (say)                          | 1,000  | 9,700   |
| Chargeable gain                                                   |        | 13,450  |
| *Less* 35% taper (non-business asset rate, including the bonus year) |      | 8,742   |
| *Less:* annual exemption for 2006–07                              |        | 8,800   |
| Gain charged to CGT                                               |        | £(nil)  |

If the exemption is unused in a tax year it is lost since there is no provision
to carry it forward (contrast the IHT annual exemption). It applies to gains
after any reduction attributable to taper relief.                          **[19.87]**

### b)  *Personal representatives*

In the tax year of the deceased's death and the two following tax years, PRs
have the same annual exemption as an individual. In the third and following
tax years they have no annual exemption and so are charged to CGT on all
chargeable gains they make (see **[21.64]**).                              **[19.88]**

### c)  *Trustees*

Trustees generally enjoy only half the annual exemption available to an
individual, ie £4,400 (for 2006–07). Where the same settlor has created more
than one settlement since 6 June 1978 the annual exemption is divided
equally between them. Four post-June 1978 settlements, for instance, would
each have an exemption of £1,100. This is subject to a minimum exemption
per trust of one-tenth of the individual's annual exemption, ie £880 (for
2006–07). Thus, if a settlor creates 12 settlements they will each have an
exemption of £880.

Where the settlement is for the mentally or physically disabled, the trustees
have the same exemption as an individual, ie £8,800 (for 2006–07) (subject
to similar rules for groups of settlements).                               **[19.89]**

d) *Husband and wife and registered same-sex couples*

Husband and wife are both entitled to a full exemption (see further **Chapter 51**). Any unused annual exemption cannot be transferred to the other spouse.

CPA 2004, which gives legal recognition to same-sex couples, became law in November 2004 and comes into effect on 5 December 2005. Broadly, the Act allows same-sex couples to make a formal legal commitment to each other by entering into a civil partnership through a registration process. A range of important rights and responsibilities flows from this, including legal rights and protections. For tax purposes, registered same-sex couples will be treated the same as opposite-sex couples—disposals between registered same-sex couples will be deemed to be 'no gain/no loss' disposals.　　**[19.90]**

## 3　Order of set-off of capital losses

Current year losses must be deducted from current year gains in full.

### EXAMPLE 19.28

A makes chargeable gains of £4,000 and incurs allowable losses of £3,000 in the tax year. His gain is reduced to £1,000 and is further reduced to zero by £1,000 of his annual exemption. He is forced to set his loss against gains for the year which would in any event have escaped tax because of the annual exemption.

Unrelieved losses in any tax year can be carried forward to future tax years without time limit though they must be deducted from the first available gains. However, the loss need only be used to reduce later gains to the amount covered by the annual exemption and not to zero. Losses carried back from the year of death are treated in the same way (TCGA 1992 s 62(2)). Losses of one spouse can only be used to reduce the gains of that spouse—they cannot be set against gains of the other spouse.　　**[19.91]**

### EXAMPLE 19.29

A makes the following gains and losses:

| Tax year | Gain | Loss |
|---|---|---|
| | £ | £ |
| 2004–05 | 4,000 | 9,000 |
| 2005–06 | 7,500 | 3,000 |
| 2006–07 | 13,000 | Nil |

In *Year 1* A pays no CGT and carries forward an unused loss of £5,000. His annual exemption for that year is wasted. In *Year 2* A's gain is reduced to £4,500 and he pays no CGT as this is covered by his annual exemption. The £5,000 loss from *Year 1* does not reduce his gain to zero. It is carried forward to *Year 3*. In *Year 3* £4,500 of the £5,000 loss carried forward from *Year 1* is used to reduce his gain to £8,500. He has £500 of loss remaining to carry forward.

## 4　Use of trading losses

The relief enabling trading losses to be offset against capital gains under FA 1991 s 72 is considered at **[11.61]**.　　**[19.92]**

## 5    When is CGT payable?

### a)    *General rule*

CGT is assessed on a current year basis and is normally payable in full on 31 January following the year of assessment unless a return is issued after 31 October following the year of assessment and there has been no failure to notify chargeability under TMA 1970 s 7 when the date becomes three months from the issue of the return (TMA 1970 s 59B). Interest is charged on tax remaining unpaid after the due date.                    **[19.93]**

### b)    *Payment by instalments*

CGT may be paid in instalments in two cases. *First*, when the consideration for the disposal is paid in instalments over a period exceeding 18 months running from the date of the disposal or later and the taxpayer elects to pay by instalments. The instalments of tax can be spread (in the discretion of the Board) over a maximum of eight years provided that the final instalment of tax is not payable after the final instalment of the disposal consideration has been received (TCGA 1992 s 280).

*Secondly*, CGT may be paid by 10 annual instalments when there is a gift of any of the following assets and if hold-over relief is not available on the disposal:
- land;
- a controlling shareholding in any company;
- a minority holding in an unquoted company (TCGA 1992 s 281).

In these cases, the outstanding instalments carry interest and all outstanding instalments plus interest become payable in full if the gifted asset is sold (even if sold by someone other than the donee) unless the gift was made to a donee who was not 'connected with' the donor.

*Finally*, in a *Marren v Ingles* type case (see **[19.26]**) an incidental result of two disposals having occurred is that tax on the overall gain of the disponor will be paid in two or more stages. Of course, when the deferred consideration is received it will only attract taper relief if it arises after the third anniversary of the original disposal at the non-business asset rate.    **[19.94]**

### c)    *Reporting requirements (TCGA 1992 s 3A)*

Individuals do not normally have to complete the CGT section of their tax return if:
  (i)   their chargeable gains for the year do not exceed the annual exemption; and
  (ii)  the total proceeds from their chargeable disposals in the year do not exceed four times the annual exemption (this is 'the disposal proceeds limit').

There are corresponding provisions for PRs and trustees. So far as (i) is concerned, 'chargeable gains' means chargeable gains after taper relief *unless* there are allowable losses in which case the expression means the chargeable gains before both losses and taper relief.    **[19.95]–[19.110]**

## V  MEANING OF 'DISPOSAL'

### 1  General

A 'disposal' is not defined for CGT. Giving the word its natural meaning, there will be a disposal of an asset whenever its ownership changes or whenever an owner divests himself of rights in, or interests over, an asset (eg by sale, gift or exchange). Additionally, the term is extended by the legislation to cover certain transactions which would not fall within its commonsense meaning. Thus, in certain circumstances, trustees of a settlement are treated as disposing of and immediately reacquiring settlement assets at their market value (deemed disposals: see **[19.41]**).

A part disposal of an asset is charged as a disposal according to the rules considered earlier (**[19.44]**). Death does not involve a disposal (see **Chapter 21**).                                                            **[19.111]**

### 2  Capital sums derived from assets (TCGA 1992 s 22)

When a capital sum is derived from an asset there is a disposal for CGT. This is so whether or not the person who pays the capital sum receives anything in return for his payment (see *Marren v Ingles* (1980)).

All legal rights that can be turned to account by the extraction of a capital sum are assets for CGT purposes. The test is whether such rights can be converted into money or money's worth and the mere fact that they are non-assignable does not matter so long as consideration can be obtained in some other way (for instance, by surrendering the right). This is apparent from the case of *O'Brien v Benson's Hosiery (Holdings) Ltd* (1979) (see **[19.7]**). In *Marren v Ingles* (1980) (see **[19.26]**) the right to receive an unquantifiable sum in the future was considered to be an asset, a *chose in action*, from which a capital sum was derived when the right matured.

The rights must, however, be legally enforceable. Thus, the receipt of a sum by a person in return for his agreement eg to restrict his future activities is not a disposal because it is not a disposal of an asset (the right to work is not a legal right, although it may be a right of man!). The position is different, however, if the restrictive agreement means that a capital sum has been derived from the goodwill (an asset) of the taxpayer's business. In this case there will be a disposal under s 22 (see *Kirby v Thorn EMI plc* (1988)).

Four specific instances of disposals are given in s 22:

(1)  where a capital sum is received by way of compensation for the loss of, or damage to, an asset (for instance, the receipt of damages for the destruction of an asset). It should be noted that there is only a disposal where a capital sum is received and so if the receipt is of an income nature, it is charged to income tax and not to CGT: an example is compensation received by a trader for loss of trading profits—see, for instance, *London and Thames Haven Oil Wharves Ltd v Attwooll* (1967) and *Lang v Rice* (1984): **[10.103]**. For compensation payments made under the Foreign Compensation Act 1950 and similar payments, see ESC D50;

(2)  where a capital sum is received under an insurance policy for loss of or damage to an asset;

(3) where a capital sum is received in return for the forfeiture or surrender of rights. This category includes payments received in return for releasing another person from a contract (*O'Brien v Benson's Hosiery (Holdings) Ltd* (1979)); or from a restrictive covenant; but not a statutory payment on the termination of a business tenancy since that sum is not derived from the lease (*Drummond v Austin Brown* (1984));

(4) where a capital sum is received for the use or exploitation of assets, eg for the right to exploit a copyright or for the right to use goodwill created by another person. In *Chaloner v Pellipar Investments Ltd* (1996) Rattee J commented of this provision 'those words are apt to include capital sums received as consideration for the use or exploitation of assets title to which remains unaffected in their owner (eg by the grant of a licence) but are not apt to include capital sums received as consideration for a grant of the owner's title to the assets, whether in perpetuity or for a term of years. He therefore held that the subsection did not catch consideration for the grant of a lease which took the form of the agreement by a developer to develop other land owned by the lessor (see [19.48]).

In the case of disposals falling within (1)–(4) above the time of disposal is when the capital sum is received, not when the contract (if any) was made (see [19.126]).

The receipt of a capital sum from an asset under categories (1) and (2) above need not be treated as a disposal or part disposal if the asset has not been totally lost or destroyed. Instead, the taxpayer can elect to deduct the capital sum from the acquisition cost of the asset thereby postponing a charge to CGT until the eventual disposal of the asset (TCGA 1992 s 23). However, this relief is only available if one of three conditions is satisfied:

● the capital sum is wholly used to restore the asset; or
● if the full amount of the capital sum is not used to restore the asset, the amount unused does not exceed 5% of the sum received. Where the sum unused exceeds 5% the asset is treated as being partly disposed of for a consideration equivalent to the unused sum; or
● the capital sum is 'small' compared with the value of the asset (for the meaning of 'small' see *Tax Bulletin*, February 1997 and [26.21]).

Restoration relief is modified in its application to wasting assets.  [19.112]

**EXAMPLE 19.30**

A buys a picture for £20,000 that is now worth £30,000. It is damaged by rain from a leaking roof and A receives £8,000 compensation with which he restores the picture. The £8,000 received is deducted from the cost of the asset (reducing £20,000 to £12,000), but its expenditure on restoration qualifies as allowable expenditure on a future disposal so that for CGT the cost of the asset remains £20,000 and A is in the same position as if the damage had never occurred.

Assume, however, that A restores the picture for £7,600. The £400 unused does not exceed 5% of £8,000. It is, therefore, deducted from the total allowable expenditure that is reduced to £19,600.

Alternatively, if A received compensation of £1,500 which he does not use to restore the picture, A need not treat this receipt as a part disposal (since the amount is 'small'). Instead, he can elect to deduct £1,500 from his acquisition cost, so that the picture has a base value of £18,500 on a subsequent disposal.

### 3 Total loss or destruction of an asset (TCGA 1992 s 24(1))

Total loss or destruction of an asset is a disposal for CGT purposes and, where the owner of the asset receives no compensation, it may give rise to an allowable loss equal to the base costs of the taxpayer. Where the asset is tangible movable property, however, the owner is deemed to dispose of it for £6,000 thereby restricting his loss relief (TCGA 1992 s 262(3)). This limitation derives from the fact that gains on such assets are exempt from CGT insofar as the consideration does not exceed £6,000 (see [22.22]). As a corollary, therefore, loss relief on the disposal of these assets is not available to the extent that the consideration received is less than £6,000.

#### EXAMPLE 19.31

A buys a picture for £10,000 which is destroyed by fire; A is uninsured. Although the picture is now worthless, A's allowable loss is restricted to £4,000.

Land and the buildings on it are treated as separate assets for these purposes. Where the building is totally destroyed both assets are separately deemed to have been disposed of and reacquired, and it is the overall gain or loss which is taken into account.

Where the taxpayer later receives compensation or insurance moneys for an asset which is totally lost or destroyed, this would appear to be a further disposal for CGT purposes under TCGA 1992 s 22 since it is a capital sum derived from an asset (the right under the insurance contract). In practice, however, the Revenue treats both disposals (ie the entire loss of the asset and the receipt of capital moneys) as one transaction (see also the discussion of this problem by Hoffmann J in *Powlson v Welbeck Securities Ltd* (1986)). If the taxpayer uses the capital sum within one year of receipt to acquire a replacement asset, he may claim to roll over any gain made on the disposal of the destroyed asset against the cost of the replacement asset; this relief does not apply to wasting assets. If only part of the capital sum is used in replacement, only partial roll-over is available (TCGA 1992 s 23(4), (5) and (6)).

#### EXAMPLE 19.32

A buys a picture for £6,000 that is destroyed when its value is £10,000. He receives insurance money of £10,000 and uses it towards the purchase of a similar picture for £12,000. A has made a gain of £4,000 on the original picture (£10,000 – £6,000) on which he need not pay CGT. Instead he may deduct the gain from the cost of the new picture so that his base cost becomes £8,000 (£12,000 – £4,000).

Assume that A buys the new picture for only £7,000 and claims roll-over relief.

Amount of insurance money not applied in replacement = £3,000 (£10,000 – £7,000).

£3,000 is therefore A's chargeable gain, instead of the £4,000 he made on the picture. The relief is limited to £1,000 which is given by reducing A's base value for the new picture from £7,000 to £6,000.

The same relief applies where the asset destroyed is a building. The gain on the old building can be rolled over against the cost of the new building. Any gain deemed to have been made on the land cannot, however, be so treated and will, therefore, be chargeable. **[19.113]**

## 4    Compensation, damages and Zim Properties

### a)    *The Zim case*

In *Zim Properties v Proctor* (1985) a firm of solicitors acting for the taxpayer in a conveyancing transaction were allegedly negligent, with the result that a sale of three properties owned by the taxpayer fell through. An action in negligence against the solicitors was eventually compromised and compensation of £69,000 was paid to the taxpayer. Undoubtedly, this was a capital sum, but was it derived from the disposal of an asset? Warner J held that it arose from the right of action against the solicitors that, as it could be turned into a capital sum by negotiating a compromise, was an asset for CGT purposes. Although the ownership of the properties put the taxpayer in the position to enjoy that right of action, the sum was not derived from the properties themselves, because, after receipt of that sum, the taxpayer still owned the properties.                                              **[19.114]**

### b)    *The difficulties created by the Zim decision*

*First,* not all rights to payment or compensation are themselves 'assets' for CGT purposes. Warner J cited as an example the right of a seller of property to payment of the price. The relevant asset in such a case must be the property itself (contrast, however, *Marren v Ingles,* discussed at **[19.26]**). A further example is shown by *Drummond v Austin Brown* (1984) where a tenant's right to statutory compensation on the termination of his lease under the Landlord and Tenant Act 1954 was not subject to CGT; it was neither compensation for loss of the lease, nor was it derived from that lease (contrast *Davenport v Chilver* (1983) where the right to statutory compensation for confiscated property was held to be an asset). There are also a number of statutory exemptions: eg for damages following personal injury.

*Secondly,* the date of acquisition of the right of action will in many cases be unclear. In *Zim* Warner J held that the asset was acquired at the time when the taxpayer acted upon the allegedly negligent advice – entered into the sale contracts – although this matter is not free from doubt (see the House of Lords judgments in *Pirelli v Oscar Faber* (1983)).

*Thirdly,* the question of how to calculate the acquisition cost of this asset, namely the taxpayer's right to sue, was left unclear (see also *Marren v Ingles* and *O'Brien v Benson's Hosiery*). Arguably, it was acquired otherwise than by bargain at arm's length, so that the market value (if any) of the right should be taken at the moment of its acquisition (see TCGA 1992 s 17(1), discussed at **[19.22]**: it may be doubted, however, whether the taxpayer is able to satisfy the requirements in s 17(2)(b) and failure to do so would result in a nil acquisition cost).

*Finally,* as the purpose of damages is to compensate the claimant, the award in such cases would need to be grossed up if the damages themselves are to be reduced by taxation.                                              **[19.115]**

### c)    *ESC D33*

Some of the difficulties resulting from the *Zim* case have been solved by ESC D33 that affords relief from CGT in two ways.

*First,* 'where the right of action arises by reason of the total or partial loss or destruction of or damage to a form of property which is an asset for CGT purposes, or because the claimant suffered some loss or disadvantage in connection with such a form of property, any gain or loss on the disposal of the right of action may by concession be computed as if the compensation derived from that asset and not from the right of action'. As a consequence, part of the acquisition cost of the chargeable asset may be deducted from the gain in accordance with the usual part-disposal rules (see [**19.43**]).

### EXAMPLE 19.33

(1) Because of the negligence of his land agent, Lord Q's sale of a plot of land to Out of Town Supermarkets Ltd falls through. The agent is forced to pay £70,000 in compensation to Lord Q. Instead of treating this sum as consideration on the disposal of a separate *chose in action* it may be treated as arising on a part disposal of the land itself. Accordingly, part of the expenditure attributable to that land may be deducted in arriving at Lord Q's chargeable gain.

(2) Zara, because of the negligence of her solicitor, ends up with less money from the sale of her main residence than would otherwise have been the case. Because the underlying asset (her main residence) is exempt from CGT (see **Chapter 23**) any compensation paid by the solicitor will likewise escape tax.

*Secondly,* if there is no underlying asset. In this case, any gain accruing on the disposal of the right of action will be exempt from CGT.

### EXAMPLE 19.34

Zappy, a wealthy taxpayer, suffers a massive income tax liability because his professional adviser negligently fails to shelter that income from tax by arranging for Zappy to invest in an EIS and in an industrial building in an enterprise zone. Substantial compensation is therefore paid to Zappy and because there is no underlying property that is an asset for CGT purposes, the sum is not subject to charge.

The logic behind this is that as the compensation merely puts the taxpayer into the position he would have been in but for the negligence, there should be no tax charge since the benefit which he was entitled to (a lesser income tax liability) is not itself subject to charge. It should be noted that the *Zim* case has no application to compensation payments that attract an income tax charge (see, for instance, *London and Thames Haven Oil Wharves Ltd v Attwooll* (1967) at [**10.103**]) whilst its application in the context of warranties and indemnities on a company takeover is discussed in **Chapter 47**.     [**19.116**]

## 5   Assets becoming of negligible value (TCGA 1992 s 24(2))

Where an asset becomes of negligible value (eg shares and securities in an insolvent company) the taxpayer is deemed to have disposed of and immediately reacquired the asset at its market value (nil) thus enabling him to claim loss relief. This disposal is deemed to occur in the tax year in which the Revenue accepts the claim or at any earlier time specified in the claim provided that: (a) the taxpayer owned the asset at that earlier time; (b) the asset had become of negligible value at that earlier time; and (c) that earlier time was not more than two years before the beginning of the year of assessment in which the claim is made (*Williams v Bullivant* (1983) and see *Larner v Warrington* (1985)). The Revenue considers that 'negligible' means considerably less than 5% of the original cost (or March 1982 value).

Should the value of the asset subsequently increase, the result of claiming relief under s 24(2) will be that on a later disposal the base value will be nil so that all the consideration received will be treated as a gain and there will be no question of claiming any indexation allowance.                    **[19.117]**

## 6   Options (TCGA 1992 ss 144–147)

The grant of an option (whether to buy or to sell an asset) is a disposal, not of a part of the asset that is subject to the option, but of a separate asset, namely, the option itself at the date of the grant. The gain will be the consideration paid for the grant of the option less any incidental expenses (see *Strange v Openshaw* (1983)). In *Garner v Pounds Shipowners and Shipbreakers Ltd* (2000) P Ltd granted an option to M to purchase its land which included a term that P Ltd was to use its best endeavours to obtain the release of restrictive covenants and would only receive the option fee if it was successful. In the event the covenants were released in return for a payment of £90,000 by P Ltd and the option was never exercised so that the option fee (£399,750) was retained by P Ltd. The House of Lords held that P Ltd's obligations regarding the release of the covenants, even though involving the probable payment of sums to third parties, did not affect the amount of consideration received for the grant of the option (ie the option fee), nor were the sums paid by P Ltd deductible under TCGA 1992 s 38(1): the expenditure was not incurred in *providing* the asset disposed of (the option), nor was the expenditure reflected in the state or nature of the option at the time it was granted (see **[19.28]** and **[19.29]**).

### EXAMPLE 19.35

(1)   A grants to B for £3,000 an option to buy A's country cottage in two years' time for £30,000 which is its current market value. A has made a gain of £3,000 from which he can deduct any incidental expenses involved in granting the option. (This is an option to buy.)

(2)   A pays B £3,000 in return for an option from B enabling A to sell that country cottage to B in two years' time for £30,000. (This is an option to sell.) B has made a gain of £3,000 less any incidental expenses.

If the option is exercised, the grant and the exercise are treated as a single transaction for both grantor and grantee. In the case of an option to buy (ie binding the grantor to sell) the consideration received for the grant of the option is treated as part of the consideration for the sale. Any CGT that has been charged on the grant itself will be either set off or repaid.

In the case of an option to sell (ie binding the grantor to buy) the consideration received for the option is deducted from the acquisition cost of the asset to the grantor.

**EXAMPLE 19.36**

As in *Example 19.35*, assuming that A had deductible expenses of £15,000:
(1)   when B exercises the option and pays A £30,000 for the house, A's gain is:

|  | £ |
|---|---|
| Proceeds from sale of house | 30,000 |
| Consideration for option | 3,000 |
|  | 33,000 |
| *Less:* deductible expenses | 15,000 |
| Chargeable gain | £18,000 |

B's acquisition cost is £30,000 plus the cost of the option, ie £33,000 (both items may, in appropriate cases, be index-linked from the dates when the expenditure was incurred).
(2)   when A exercises the option and sells the house to B for £30,000, A's gain is:

|  | £ | £ |
|---|---|---|
| Proceeds of sale |  | 30,000 |
| *Less:*   cost of option | 3,000 |  |
|              deductible expenses | 15,000 | 18,000 |
| Chargeable gain |  | £12,000 |

B's acquisition cost of the cottage is only £27,000 (ie £30,000 reduced by the amount that he received for the option).

The date of acquisition for taper relief is the time when the option is exercised (or 6 April 1998 if later), not when the option is granted.

The Revenue (now HMRC) took the view that the market value rule in TCGA 1992 s 17 (see **[19.22]**) did not normally apply to shares acquired as a result of the exercise of an option but this view was not upheld by the Court of Appeal in *Mansworth v Jelley* (2003). As a consequence the taxpayer's acquisition of the shares on exercising the option was deemed to be at market value so that on his immediate disposal of the shares no gain arose. TCGA 1992 s 144ZA, inserted by FA 2003, reversed the effect of *Mansworth v Jelley* and, broadly speaking, disapplies the market value rule (in cases where it would otherwise apply) in relation to options exercised after 9 April 2003. In *Mansworth v Jelley*-type circumstances the taxpayer's gain is now calculated by deducting the sum actually paid on exercise, not the (higher) market value of the asset acquired.

An option is a chargeable asset so that, if disposed of other than by exercise or abandonment (see below), there may be a chargeable gain or allowable loss on ordinary principles. In particular, an option which has a predictable life of 50 years or less will be a wasting asset unless it is an option to subscribe for shares that is listed on a recognised stock exchange; a traded option; a financial option; or it is an option to acquire assets to be used in a trade. Consequently the cost of acquiring the option will be written down over its predictable life on a straight-line basis (see **[19.46]**).

The abandonment of an option that is a wasting asset is not a disposal (but notice that a capital sum received for relinquishing an option will be chargeable under TCGA 1992 s 22(3): see *Golding v Kaufman* (1985); BTR, 1985, p 124 and CG 12340).                                    **[19.118]**

## 7   Appropriations to and from a trader's stock in trade (TCGA 1992 s 161)

There are two cases to consider. *First*, where a trader acquires an asset for private use and later appropriates it to his trade. As a general rule, this is a disposal and CGT is payable on the difference between the market value of the asset at the date of appropriation and its original cost.

### EXAMPLE 19.37

A owns a picture gallery. He buys a picture for private use for £5,000 and transfers it to the gallery when it is worth £15,000. He has made a chargeable gain of £10,000. Later he sells the picture to a customer for £30,000. The profit on sale of £15,000 (£30,000 – £15,000) is chargeable to income tax under ITTOIA 2005 (former Schedule D Case I).

However, the trader can elect to avoid paying CGT at the date of appropriation by transferring the asset into his business at a no gain/no loss value (see s 161(3A) for time limits in making the election). When the asset is eventually sold, the total profit will be charged to income tax as a trading receipt. So, in the above example, were A to make the election he would pay no CGT, but instead he would be liable to income tax on a profit of £25,000 (£30,000 – £5,000). Because the gross gain is deferred and charged to income tax by the election any taper relief accrued will be permanently lost.

Whether the election should be exercised or not must depend upon the particular facts of each case. CGT may be more attractive as a choice of evils with its annual exemption, but income tax, on the other hand, will be paid later (on eventual sale) and the profit so made may be offset against personal allowances or unused capital allowances.

*Secondly*, where an asset originally acquired as trading stock is taken out for the trader's private use. In this case, there is no election and the transfer is treated as a sale at market value for income tax purposes (see *Sharkey v Wernher* (1956) at **[10.115]**). The taxpayer will have market value as his CGT base cost.                                                    **[19.119]**

### EXAMPLE 19.38

One of the pictures in A's gallery cost him £6,000. He removes it to hang it in his dining room when its market value is £16,000. He later sells it privately for £30,000.

On the appropriation out of trading stock, A is treated as selling the picture for its market value (£16,000) and the profit (£10,000) is assessed to income tax. The gain on the subsequent sale (£30,000 – £16,000 = £14,000) is chargeable to CGT.

## 8   Miscellaneous cases

### a)   *Hire-purchase agreements (TCGA 1992 s 27)*

Although the hirer does not own the asset until he pays all the instalments, the owner is treated as having disposed of the asset at the date when the hirer is first able to use it (usually the date of the contract). The consideration for the disposal is the cash price payable under the contract. These transactions rarely give rise to a CGT charge, however, either because the asset is exempt (eg a private car or a chattel worth less than £6,000) or because it is a wasting asset. Further, the contract will normally be a trading transaction falling within the income tax charge (for an illustration where these provisions were held to apply to the sale of a taxi-driver's licences, see *Lyon v Pettigrew* (1985)).

In the rare case where there is a CGT charge and the hire term ends without title passing (eg because the hirer defaults) tax is adjusted, or discharged, according to the amount the owner actually received. **[19.120]**

b) *Mortgages and charges (TCGA 1992 s 26)*

Neither the grant nor the redemption of a mortgage is a disposal. Where the property is sold by a mortgagee or his receiver, the sale is treated as a disposal by the mortgagor. **[19.121]**

c) *Settled property*

On the happening of certain events the trustees are deemed to have disposed of the trust assets and immediately reacquired them (see **Chapter 19**). **[19.122]**

d) *Value shifting (TCGA 1992 ss 29–34)*

There are anti-avoidance provisions intended to charge a person who passes value to another without actually making a disposal (see **[26.61]**). **[19.123]**

e) *Lease extensions (ESC D39)*

The ESC provides that a tenant who surrenders his lease in return for the grant of a new lease over the same premises does not make a disposal or part disposal of the old lease provided that the terms of the new lease (other than its duration and the amount of rent) are the same as those of the old lease. It does not address the position of the landlord. The concession can apply to transactions between connected persons provided that the terms of the transaction are equivalent to those that would have been made between unconnected parties bargaining at arm's length. **[19.124]**

f) *Relief for exchanges of joint interests in land (ESC D26)*

Roll-over relief along the lines of that in TCGA 1992 ss 247–248 in the case of compulsory acquisitions (see **[22.82]**) is available when a joint holding of land is partitioned (so that each joint owner becomes a sole owner of part of the land) or when a number of separate joint holdings are partitioned. **[19.125]**

## 9 Time of disposal

a) *Timing—the general rule*

A disposal under a contract of sale takes place for CGT purposes at the date of the contract, not completion, with an adjustment of tax if completion never occurs (TCGA 1992 s 28(1): contrast s 38(1)(b)—see **[19.29]**). By contrast, a disposal arising from the receipt of a capital sum under TCGA 1992 s 22 is treated as taking place when the capital sum is received (see **[19.112]**).

See *Jerome v Kelly* (2003) for authority for the proposition that TCGA 1992 s 28 not only serves to fix the time of a disposal but also the identity of the person making the disposal for CGT purposes.                    **[19.126]**

b)    *Conditional contracts*

If the contract is conditional, the disposal takes place when the condition is fulfilled (s 28(2) and see *Hatt v Newman* (2000)). The subsection specifically provides that when a contract is conditional on the exercise of an option (eg a put or call option) the disposal occurs when that option is exercised. In order to decide whether a contract is conditional for these purposes the contract in question has to be construed in order to determine whether any conditions stipulated therein are truly conditions precedent to any legal liability or whether they are merely conditions precedent to completion. In the former case there is a conditional contract for CGT purposes: in the latter, the contract is unconditional (*Eastham v Leigh London and Provincial Properties Ltd* (1971)).

**EXAMPLE 19.39**

Lord W agrees to grant a lease to Concrete (Development Company) Ltd if they obtain satisfactory planning permission to develop the relevant land as a business park. The contract to grant the lease is conditional on satisfactory permission being obtained and so the relevant part disposal will occur only if and when that happens.

Where a local authority compulsorily acquires land (other than under a contract), the disposal occurs when the compensation is agreed or when the authority enters the land (if earlier). In the case of gifts, disposal occurs when the ownership of the asset passes to the donee (usually the date of the gift). Where a capital sum is derived from an asset, the disposal occurs when the sum is received (TCGA 1992 s 22(2) and see *Chaloner v Pellipar Investments Ltd* (1996)).                    **[19.127]–[19.140]**

VI    CAPITAL GAIN OR INCOME PROFIT?

With the linking of the rates of CGT to the income tax rates of the taxpayer, much conventional tax planning designed to ensure that capital profits rather than income were received by a taxpayer, was rendered redundant. A number of anti-avoidance sections, notably TA 1988 s 776, became of reduced importance. The distinction between capital and income receipts remains important, however, and the following are some of the factors to bear in mind. As will be apparent the facts of each individual case will largely determine whether the taxpayer is better off receiving a sum as capital or income. (See *Hitch v Stone* (2001) for an example of agreements being entered into with the object of converting capital sums into income. The agreements were dismissed by the Court of Appeal as shams.)                    **[19.141]**

## 1 Consequences of realising a capital gain

Tax on the gain will not be due until 31 January of the following tax year and in computing the chargeable gain not only may an indexation allowance to April 1998 and taper relief be available, but in addition the annual exemption may be deducted. Income profits are commonly taxed in the year of receipt without any allowance for indexation or an annual exemption. It is also important to remember that CGT is only levied when a disposal has occurred and therefore it may be possible to arrange disposals in the most advantageous tax year. There is the ability to defer the gain from CGT by rolling it over into a qualifying investment under the amended EIS provisions (see **[50.89]**ff.).                                                    **[19.142]**

## 2 Taxation of income profits

Receiving a profit as income may be advantageous for the taxpayer in that the sum may be reduced by personal allowances, charges on income, unused losses, and there is the possibility of obtaining limited income tax relief by investing in an EIS (see **[50.52]**).                                                    **[19.143]**

# 20 Taper relief

*Written and updated by Emma Chamberlain, BA Hons (Oxon), CTA (Fellow), LRAM, Barrister, 5 Stone Buildings, Lincoln's Inn*

I     Introduction [**20.1**]
II     General principles [**20.20**]
III    Comments and conclusions [**20.62**]

## I INTRODUCTION

Taper relief came into effect in respect of disposals made on or after 6 April 1998 and affords relief on the surplus of chargeable gains over allowable losses in a tax year. Losses must, therefore, be deducted *before* the relief, but they are set off against gains in the way that is generally most advantageous for the taxpayer (see *Examples 21.1* and *21.2*). Gains are, however, only eligible for taper relief if the relevant asset has been owned for a minimum qualifying period which in the case of business assets is one year: for other assets it is three years. The relief applies to individuals, trustees and PRs but not to companies. [**20.1**]

### EXAMPLE 20.1

Mr D sells ICI shares in 2006 acquired in 2002 realising a gain of £10,000 after deduction of the base cost and he has separately realised a loss of £4,000. The net gain is therefore £6,000. The ICI shares are non-business assets since Mr D owns less than 5% voting shares and is not an employee of ICI.

The ICI shares have been owned for four complete years. The percentage of gain chargeable is 90% (see the non-business assets Table at [**20.21**]). The chargeable gain is 90% of £6,000 not 90% of £10,000. The losses are deducted first before any taper relief. This result is less favourable to the taxpayer.

If Mr D was also selling shares that qualified for business assets taper relief (BATR) in the same year he would be allowed to deduct the loss against the ICI shares first and not from the shares that qualify for BATR. This is more favourable to him since he is not then wasting business assets taper relief. However, if he sold assets that qualified for BATR in 2006 and sold the ICI shares in a later tax year, he would have to use the loss of £4,000 against the gain realised on the business asset before being able to deduct BATR. He cannot carry the loss forward to deduct against the ICI shares sold in the later tax year.

Thus a taxpayer should ensure that in a year he makes a disposal of assets which qualify for full BATR, any losses already realized or brought forward from previous years are used against disposals of assets qualifying for non-BATR in the same tax year.

If there are unused trading losses the excess losses may be treated as capital losses and can therefore be offset against the individual's chargeable gains for the year of the loss and/or the previous year (see FA 1991 s 72). For excess trading losses in 2004–05 and later years the maximum amount of trading losses which can be relieved under FA 1991 s 72 is computed before, not after, the deduction of taper relief. This is more favourable to the taxpayer. (For worked example and more detailed explanation see Tolleys Tax Digest Issue 41 page 9 Maximising Taper Relief by Robert Jamieson.)

Taper relief is one of the most complex areas of capital gains tax in relation to individuals partly because the rules changed in almost every year between 1998 and 2003. Since each set of new rules was generally only effective from the date of the change and taper relief depends on qualifying over a continuing period of ownership, great care must be taken to check that the asset qualifies under both the old and new rules.          **[20.2]–[20.19]**

## II   GENERAL PRINCIPLES

### 1   How is the relief given?

For disposals made between 6 April 1998 and 5 April 2000 the gain was multiplied by the percentage in the table in TCGA 1992 s 2A(5) that is set out below. This means that the gain on an asset sold with maximum business assets taper relief is effectively taxed at 10% for a higher rate taxpayer while the gain on an asset which qualifies for maximum non-business assets taper relief is effectively taxed at 24% – a marked difference. There is no suggestion that the regime governing taxation of non-business assets will be relaxed.

| *Gains on disposals of business assets* | | *Gains on disposals of non-business assets* | |
| --- | --- | --- | --- |
| *Number of whole years in qualifying period* | *Percentage of gain chargeable* | *Number of whole years in qualifying period* | *Percentage of gain chargeable* |
| 1 | 92.5 | — | — |
| 2 | 85 | — | — |
| 3 | 77.5 | 3 | 95 |
| 4 | 70 | 4 | 90 |
| 5 | 62.5 | 5 | 85 |
| 6 | 55 | 6 | 80 |
| 7 | 47.5 | 7 | 75 |
| 8 | 40 | 8 | 70 |
| 9 | 32.5 | 9 | 65 |
| 10 or more | 25 | 10 or more | 60 |

For disposals after 5 April 2000 and before 6 April 2002 relief on a disposal of a *business* asset was substantially improved by the introduction of the following amended table:

| Period business asset held (years) | Percentage of gain chargeable | Equivalent rate for higher rate CGT payer (%) |
|:---:|:---:|:---:|
| 0–1 | 100 | 40 |
| 1–2 | 87.5 | 35 |
| 2–3 | 75 | 30 |
| 3–4 | 50 | 20 |
| >4 | 25 | 10 |

From 6 April 2002, the relief on a disposal of business assets was further improved as follows:

| Period business asset held (years) | Percentage of gain chargeable |
|:---:|:---:|
| 0–1 | 100 |
| 1–2 | 50 |
| >2 | 25 |

The effect of the relief is to reduce the 'percentage of gain chargeable': ie taper relief wipes out part of the chargeable gain.

TCGA 1992 s 2(2) provides for the calculation of the pre-taper gain that is arrived at by deducting from the disposal consideration:
(1)   items of allowable expenditure (including when appropriate an indexation allowance);
(2)   retirement relief (if relevant); and
(3)   current year and brought forward losses (see *Example 20.1*).

It is the resultant gain that may attract taper relief. See *Example 20.2* for basic application of the rules.                                                                     **[20.20]**


## 2   The qualifying holding period

As can be seen from the table above, while relief on business assets is now given once the asset has been owned for only one year, for a non-business asset a three-year period is required. Because the relief depends on the number of 'whole years' in the qualifying holding period, for assets already owned on 6 April 1998 that period is measured in terms of tax years, but for later acquired assets it is the 12 months running from the date of acquisition (TCGA 1992 s 2A(8)). Relief on business assets is substantially greater: under the original table the level of relief was 7.5% pa (as compared with 5% for non-business assets). For disposals on or after 6 April 2002, however, full business taper (at 75%) is available after only two years' ownership and after one year, relief at 50% will be given. Note, however, the important and curious effect of the apportionment rules which mean that someone holding an asset which did not qualify as a business asset until 6 April 2000 will not qualify for full taper relief until 6 April 2010—see *Example 20.6* and *Example 20.7*.

When the relief was introduced in 1998, taxpayers who owned the relevant asset on 17 March 1998 (which was Budget Day) were credited with a 'bonus year' of ownership: the bonus year remains for non-business assets but was abolished for disposals after 6 April 2000 of business assets. However, where an asset qualifies as both a business and non-business asset during the period of ownership the bonus year is still relevant when apportioning the gain—see *Example 20.6.*

In summary, a taxpayer disposing of a business asset now which they acquired two years ago and was a business asset throughout that period will pay capital gains tax at an effective rate of 10%. A taxpayer disposing of a non-business asset in say May 2007 which was owned prior to 17 March 1998 and has been a non-business asset throughout that period, will pay capital gains tax at an effective rate of 24%—the lowest rate that can be paid on a non-business asset.                                                                **[20.21]**


**EXAMPLE 20.2**

Bob has run an electrical business since acquiring all the shares from a distant relative in June 1994. He paid £600,000 for the shares that are now worth £1.5m. In May 1999 he acquired a Mark Gertler picture ('Still Life with Pomegranates') for £20,000 for which he has received an offer of £35,000.

(1)    If he sold the business for £1.5m at any time *during the tax year 1999–2000* his gain would have been calculated as follows:

       *Step 1* deduct from sale proceeds (a) acquisition cost: £600,000; (b) indexation allowance to April 1998: (say) £50,000. Net gain = £850,000.

       *Step 2* apply taper relief to £850,000. The shares are a business asset and because they were owned on 17 March 1998 attract two years' relief (ie the bonus year and 1998–99 tax year). Accordingly 85% of the gain is chargeable = £722,500.

       *Note:* It is assumed that Bob did not qualify for retirement relief: had he done so it would have been deducted at *step 1.*

(2)    If Bob were to sell the Gertler *during the tax year 1999–2000:*

    (i)    he does not benefit from any indexation allowance (which ceased before he bought the picture);

    (ii)   nor will he benefit from taper relief (as a non-business asset he would need to retain it for three whole years (ie until May 2002) in order to obtain a 5% reduction in his chargeable gain).

       The £15,000 gain is, therefore, taxed in full.

       *Note:*

    (a)    If Bob realised losses, these are set against the gains in the order which is most beneficial to the taxpayer—Bob will therefore set them against the gain on the Gertler in order to maximise the taper relief on his shares (the use of losses is considered at **[20.63]**.

    (b)    Bob's annual exemption is set against the total gains after relief, ie £722,500 + £15,000.

(3)    If Bob were to sell both assets *during the tax year 2000–01*, the revised business assets rules apply to the shares:

       At *step 2* instead of three-year taper (including the bonus year) he is only credited with two years' taper giving a reduction of 25% *but this is better than three years at the old rates* (which would have reduced the gain by only 22.5%). The treatment of the Gertler would be unaltered.

(4)    If Bob were to sell both assets *during the tax year 2001–02*, there would still be no relief on the Gertler but relief on the business is now at 50%.

(5)    Finally, if the sale is *in the tax year 2002–03*, relief on the business asset is now at 75% (the maximum) and the Gertler now attracts relief at 5% (from May 2002).

## 3   Timing points

Because relief is given on the basis of whole years in the qualifying holding period:

(1)   in the case of assets owned on 5 April 1998 whole years in the qualifying holding period expire on 5 April (ie are calculated by reference to tax years). It may, therefore, be advantageous to sell early in the tax year rather than late in the previous year;

(2)   for assets acquired after 5 April 1998, years are calculated from the date of acquisition to the date of disposal;

(3)   will there be an incentive in the case of non-business assets—to retain the asset for longer than would otherwise be the case in order to benefit from enhanced taper? In the case of business assets it may be preferable to sell the asset early if it ceases to qualify for relief in order to prevent the rate of tax going up—see *Example 20.5*;

(4)   there is no restriction in the relief if the value of an asset is enhanced by subsequent expenditure. Assume, for instance, that A purchased a piece of land for £1,000 in Year 1: in Year 10 he constructed a house on it at a cost of £100,000 and in Year 11 he sold the property for £500,000. The entire gain benefits from full taper relief (on the basis of a non-business asset). This can be relevant to jointly held property – see *Examples 20.3 and 4*;

(5)   similarly, where an asset is derived from another asset in the same ownership it is treated as acquired when the original asset was acquired. An asset is derived from another asset where assets have merged, an asset has divided or has otherwise changed its nature or different rights of interest in or over any asset have been created or extinguished at any stage and the value of any asset disposed of is thus derived from one or another assets previously acquired into the same ownership. See Sch A1 para 14(1);

(6)   It is sensible to ensure that losses are only crystallised in years when there are gains attracting little or no taper relief. Otherwise taper relief is wasted. It may be possible to convert a capital loss to an income loss by making a s 574 TA 1988 claim (relief for losses on unlisted shares in trading companies) if it could only otherwise be set against a tapered gain.

### EXAMPLE 20.3

Joe owns the leasehold interest in Goblins Palace acquired in April 1998. He later buys the freehold in April 1999 (thereby extinguishing the lease). Joe is deemed to have acquired the entire land in April 1998 for taper relief purposes.

### EXAMPLE 20.4

A, B and C hold land as tenants in common inherited on the death of their mother in April 1997. A dies in 2003 leaving his share to B who then buys out C in 2004. B sells in 2006. What is his taper relief position?

   As tenant in common B held a fractional share in the whole asset, ie the freehold. When he increased his fractional share this was a merger of assets within s 43. Schedule A1, para 14 means that B will qualify for non-business assets taper relief on his entire gain based on a period of ownership since April 1997 (with the bonus year therefore available.) In calculating the gain B will take as his acquisition cost one third of the probate value of the land in April 1997, the probate value of the one third held by A at his death and the purchase price he pays C for his one third share.

(6)    the 'relevant period of ownership' is the shorter of:
    (a)    the holding period; and
    (b)    the last ten years of the qualifying holding period (but the bonus year is ignored for these purposes).

    This period determines how much of a gain attracts business assets taper, and is therefore relevant when the taxpayer's use of the asset changes from business to non-business and *vice versa* (see *Examples 21.4 and 21.5* for apportionment rules).

(7)    The gain is never tapered to zero. In the case of business assets qualifying for the maximum relief, the effective capital gains tax rate after taper is:
    (a)    for individuals: 10% (40% × 25) if they are higher rate taxpayers or 5% (20% × 25) if they are basic rate taxpayers or 2.5% (10% × 25) if they have no other taxable income or gains;
    (b)    trustees (and PRs) 10% (Note this increased with effect from 2004–05 because the rate of capital gains tax for trustees increased from 34% to 40% pre-taper relief). (Despite the Trusts Modernisation programme (see Schs 12 and 13 Finance Act 2006) this remains unchanged unless an election has been made for the trust to be taxed under the vulnerable persons provisions (see FA 2005 s 37) or it is settlor interested in which case gains realised by the trustees are taxed on the settlor at his rates under TCGA 1992 s 77.

It is important, however, to be aware that if an asset was owned prior to April 2000 it needs to qualify as a business asset under both old and new rules if the full business assets taper relief is to be obtained. (see *Example 20.5*).    **[20.22]**


## 4    **What is a business asset?**

The relevant definitions are in TCGA 1992 Sch A1 (and see *Tax Bulletin*, Issue 53, June 2001 and *Tax Bulletin*, Issue 62, December 2002 for the meaning of a 'trading company' which is discussed later). The rules distinguish between shares and other assets.    **[20.23]**


### a)    *Qualifying companies*

Shares can qualify for business assets taper relief if the company is a trading company or the holding company of a trading group and the taxpayer is an individual, the trustees of a settlement or PRs (a 'qualifying company').

Shares in foreign trading companies can also qualify but note TCGA 1992 s 13 may tax gains realised by certain foreign 'close' companies and any gains realised by the company (as opposed to gains on the shares themselves) will not qualify for taper relief but only for indexation relief. In this section, references to trading company should be taken to mean a company that is a trading company for business assets taper relief purposes. The rules are generally tighter than those for inheritance tax, so shares in a company may qualify for business property relief under the inheritance tax legislation but not for business assets taper relief under the capital gains tax legislation.

**[20.24]**

b) *When is BATR available on shareholdings in trading companies?*

For periods of ownership up to 6 April 2000, in order to qualify for BATR at least 25% of the voting rights in the trading company had to be exercisable by the taxpayer: alternatively, the shares qualified if at least 5% of the voting rights were exercisable by the taxpayer who was a full-time officer or employee of the company. In the case of a trust, the alternative 5% test was only appropriate if there was an eligible beneficiary (defined broadly as one who had an interest in possession in the whole of the settled property) who was a full-time officer or employee. These old rules are still relevant if the taxpayer owned the asset before 6 April 2000 even if there are disposals after that date and it must always be checked to ascertain if the taxpayer qualified under the old rules. There was no difference in the rules between unlisted and listed trading companies—the same minimum voting requirements of 5% if full-time employee or 25% if not were required. As from 6 April 2000 a distinction was drawn between unlisted and listed companies. The thresholds for shareholdings in unlisted and listed trading companies of 5% for full-time employees and 25% for others were removed so that the following shareholdings now qualify as business assets:

(1) all shareholdings in unlisted trading companies (no minimum voting requirement or work required);
(2) all shareholdings held by officers or employees in listed trading companies; (in the case of trusts the eligible beneficiary needs to be the employee – see post) and
(3) shareholdings in a listed trading company where the holder is not an employee but can exercise at least 5% of the voting rights.

For the position of shares in non-trading companies, see **[20.31]**.

All employees including (since April 2000) part-time employees of the listed trading company in which they hold shares (or any group company, etc) will qualify. Officers of a trading company are treated in the same way as employees. The changes in 2000 and 2002 were not retrospective: consequently a shareholding in a qualifying trading company owned before 6 April 2000 might have been a non-business asset if the minimum voting requirements were not met but could become a business asset from that date thereby producing apportionment problems on sale (see *Examples 21.4* and *21.5*).

The company must exist for the purpose of trading commercially and for profit but subject to that, provided it satisfies the definition of a trading company for taper relief (see **[20.27]** ff), there is no restriction if non-business assets, such as investment property, are also owned by the company. Compare in this respect holdover relief under TCGA 1992 s 165 where the company has to be a qualifying trading company for BATR purposes (from 6 April 2003) but relief can also be restricted by reference to the underlying assets in the company—see also **[22.72]**).

Listed companies are those quoted on a recognised stock exchange. HMRC publish an updated list of such exchanges on its website. NASDAQ is a recognised stock exchange. AIM listed companies are not treated as listed companies for these purposes and therefore any shareholding in such a qualifying trading company will now be eligible for BATR irrespective of the percentage owned or whether the shareholder works in the business. **[20.25]**

**EXAMPLE 20.5**

Harry owns 5% of shares in a qualifying unlisted trading company Makepiece Ltd. He has held the shares since 1995 and has never worked in the business. He sells the shares in April 2004. Up until April 1998 his base cost can be indexed. From April 1998 to 6 April 2000 he can claim non-BATR and has the benefit of the bonus year since the shares were owned pre-17 March 1998. From 6 April 2000 to the date of sale the shares qualify for BATR. Of the total gain, 2/6 will qualify for non-BATR with the benefit of the bonus year and 4/6 will qualify for full BATR. Obviously if he holds the shares beyond 2004 the adverse effect of the non-business asset qualifying period will be diluted.

For the taper relief position on trustees and beneficiaries holding shares and other assets see **[20.38]**).

c)   *Other business assets*

The asset must be owned by an individual, a partnership, the trustees of a settlement or PRs and generally used in a trade carried on by the owner or by a qualifying company, although note changes in FA 2003 s 160 discussed below which extend BATR to let property used for trading purposes by third parties in certain circumstances. Assets used partly for trading purposes are subject to an apportionment. Relief is also given if the asset is used by an employee for the purpose of his employment with a trader.

A trade for these purposes means 'anything which is a trade, profession or vocation within the meaning of the Income Tax Acts' (TCGA 1992 Sch A1 para 22(1)). Hence farming, property development and furnished holiday lettings are a trade, but the activities of a commercial or residential landlord are not.                                                                                   **[20.26]**

**EXAMPLE 20.6**

(1)   Tim acquires shares in an AIM company in 2000. In 2004 he discovers that it is about to get a full listing. When that happens the shares will cease to be business assets. He does not work in the business.

(2)   Tara has worked for a listed company, Supamarket plc, for many years and has built up a small shareholding in the company. She is sacked in June 2002. Her shareholding was not a business asset until 6 April 2000, but was a business asset from 6 April 2000 to June 2002. After she is sacked her shares cease to be business assets.

(3)   On 16 March 1998 the 'Laundry Discretionary Trust' was established by Mr Clean to hold 20% of the shares in Clean It Ltd.
      (a)   Until 6 April 2000 the shares did not qualify as business assets.
      (b)   From 6 April 2000 they became business assets.
      (c)   Assume that the trustees sell the shares on 6 April 2004. Their gain must be apportioned on a time basis:
            (i)   the business asset period runs from 6 April 2000 to 6 April 2004 and is 48 months long;

    (ii)   the non-business period runs from 6 April 1998 to 6 April 2000 and is 24 months long;

    (iii)   the total period of ownership is 72 months or six years.

    *Hence* one-third of the gains (24/72) receives non-business taper over the period 6 April 1998 to 6 April 2004 (six years ownership plus the bonus) so that 75% of one-third of the gain is taxed;

       *and* two-thirds of the gain receives business assets taper over the same period (six years—no bonus) so that only 25% of two thirds of the gain is taxed.

*Note:* An apportionment will be required if the disposal by the trustees occurs at any time before 6 April 2010: only after that date can the non-business period of ownership be ignored. The apportionment is done on the basis of months, not complete years, so if the trustees had sold in June 2004 a further two months' business assets relief would have been available (50/74).

(4)    The apportionment rules lead to anomalies. For example, Ray acquires 3,000 shares (3%) in Sellwell—an unlisted trading company—in February 1998. The purchase price was £3,000. He buys a further 10,000 (10%) shares from a retiring director in April 2000. The purchase price was still £1 a share = £10,000.

He and the other shareholders have now received an offer to buy the company for £1m and Ray wants to know his CGT rate if he sells on, say, 10 April 2002. He will receive 13% of the sale price = £130,000.

The gain (ignoring the minimal indexation on the first 3,000 shares) is £117,000.

The 10,000 shares he acquired in April 2000 will qualify for full business assets taper relief at 25% and therefore he pays tax at an effective rate of 10% on these shares.

For half the relevant period until April 2000 the other 3,000 shares were not business assets. Therefore half the gain on these qualifies for non-business assets taper relief (with the bonus year) and half the gain qualifies for business assets taper relief. The overall rate of tax is about 22% on those shares.

If he had acquired all his shares in April 2000 he would have qualified for the 10% rate on all his shares. Until 5 December 2003 it had been common to try and lose a non-business assets taper relief period by transferring the shares to an interest in possession trust for the settlor and claiming holdover relief (see para **[20.39]**). After that date such an approach is no longer possible since holdover relief is not possible on transfers to settlor interested trusts. In any event, such a transfer post 21 March 2006 could also result in an inheritance tax charge since it will be treated as a chargeable transfer (see FA 2006 Sch 20 and IHTA 1984 s 5(1)(a) as amended: an inter vivos interest in possession trust for the settlor is no longer treated as part of the settlor's estate and therefore he makes a transfer of value).

## 5  What is a trading company?

### a)  *Pre-FA 2002 position*

A trading company was defined pre-FA 2002 in TCGA 1992 Sch A1 para 22 as a company 'existing wholly for the purpose of carrying on one or more trades or a company that so exists apart from any purposes capable of having no substantial effect on the extent of the company's activities'. The company could be non-UK resident and the trade did not need to be carried on in the UK.

Compare the definition of relevant business property for the purposes of inheritance tax relief (IHTA 1984 s 105(3)) where shares are not relevant business property if the business consists wholly or mainly of one or more of the following, that is to say, dealing in securities, land or buildings or making or holding investments. There is no purpose test and the test is 'wholly' or 'mainly' not 'substantially' (see [31.47].

*Tax Bulletin* No 53, June 2001, set out the Revenue's views of what the Revenue considered the terms 'trading company' and 'holding company of a trading group' to mean in the context of taper relief under the pre-FA 2002 legislation and, since FA 2002 was not designed to produce any changes in practice, this interpretation should still be referred to. It was confirmed that only actual activities, not the scope of the company's powers under its memorandum, were to be taken into account. In other words, the Revenue would judge a company not from its objects clause but from its behaviour.

However, it should be noted that the Revenue indicated: 'Purposes ... can only be established by looking at the intentions of the directors at a particular moment as well as looking at the transactions themselves. This is important because similar transactions by different companies (eg buying shares) may be for different purposes.'

In the situation where a company retains funds that it invests (so receiving investment income), the Revenue does not automatically consider that such a company's purpose is no longer wholly trading:

'Whether the generation of income from investments is or is not evidence of a non-trading purpose must ultimately depend on the nature of the company's trade and whether the holding of the investment is closely related to the conduct of that trade. If it can be shown that holding any investment is integral to the conduct of the trade or is a short-term lodgement of surplus funds held to meet demonstrable trading liabilities, then this is unlikely to be taken as evidence of non-trading purposes. For example, if a company has surplus funds which it intends to use for an expansion of the trading business in the near future, and it invests these in equities in the short term, then it may be that the company's purpose continues to be wholly trading during the period those equities are held.'

The Revenue comments on the common problem where property held by a company is surplus to its immediate business requirements:

'We would not ... regard the following as necessarily indicating non-trading purposes: letting part of the trading premises; letting properties that are no longer required for the purposes of the trade, where the objective is to sell those properties; subletting property where it would be impractical or uneconomic in terms of the trade to assign or surrender the lease ... the acquisition of property where it can be shown that the intention is that it will be brought into use for the purposes of the trade.'

Minutes of the directors' meetings may be relevant here as evidencing future intentions. The test is not dissimilar to the one used for excepted assets in IHTA 1984 s 112 and see also *Barclays Bank Trust Co Ltd v IRC* [1998] STC (SCD) 125.

Even if the investments cannot be considered to be integral to the trade, a company will continue to be a 'qualifying company' if its purposes are trading 'apart from any purposes capable of having *no substantial effect* on the extent of the company's activities'. The Revenue considers that 'substantial' means more than 20% and, in considering whether any company's non-trading purposes are capable of having a substantial effect it takes into account the following:

(1) turnover receivable from non-trading activities;
(2) the asset base of the company;
(3) expenses incurred or time spent by officers and employees of the company in undertaking its activities;
(4) the historical context of the company.

The Revenue considers that the basis for measurement will vary according to the facts in each case. For example, 'holding on to an asset which has increased in value may indicate non-trading purposes if the company lacks liquid resources to develop it or too much time is spent looking after it—the historical context of the company may be relevant.'

Compare the factors identified for the purposes of IHT business property relief by the Special Commissioner in *Farmer v IRC* (1999). This decision was approved by the Court of Appeal in *IRC v George* [2004] and it is felt by some that HMRC's summary of the various factors to be taken into account in both Tax Bulletins 52 and 62 for periods pre- and post-16 April 2002 do not give full weight to this decision. In *Farmer* the Commissioner considered profits to be a critical factor insofar as business property relief was concerned but HMRC refer to turnover rather than profits and in Tax Bulletin 62 refer to 'receipts' in the context of 'income from non-trading activities'. Is this a reference to turnover or profits? Similarly it is not clear whether the reference to 'asset base of the company' is a reference to net or gross assets, although HMRC in practice apply a gross assets test. **[20.27]**

b) *The definition of trading company and holding company post-16 April 2002*

Finance Act 2002 Sch 10 adopted a new definition of trading company and holding company for business assets taper relief purposes, based on the substantial shareholding exemption (see **[41.75]**).

Trading company now means 'a company carrying on trading activities whose activities do not include to a substantial extent activities other than trading activities (para 22A(1))'.

Trading activities is then defined and includes preparatory activities and the acquisition of an interest in a company that becomes a trading subsidiary.

The new definition is not retrospective but only applies for periods of ownership and disposals on or after 17 April 2002. Therefore the old rules will still need to be examined to ascertain the position in respect of earlier periods of ownership even if disposals take place after 5 April 2002. However, in *Tax Bulletin* 62 the Revenue noted: 'For taper relief, the changes to the wording of the definitions of trading company and trading group align the statute with existing practice. They are not intended to alter the substance of the original definitions, or to have different meanings before and on or after 17 April 2002'. The emphasis on activities rather than purposes is generally helpful to the taxpayer. However, see article by Mark McLaughlin in *Taxation*, 14 July 2005 for problems in HMRC practice in determining trading company status.

There are other problems where the company has organised its activities in a group structure. A holding company of a trading group was defined pre-17 April 2002 as a company whose business (disregarding any trade carried on by it) consisted wholly or mainly of the holding of shares in one or more companies which are its 51% subsidiaries. This meant that where a holding company also carried out some trading activities and some property investment activities the trading activities had to be ignored in assessing whether it was wholly or mainly holding shares but the investment activities could not be ignored. Intra-group activities were generally ignored (eg the holding company letting property to a trading subsidiary).

The definition has now been amended with effect from 17 April 2002 so that holding company simply means a company that has one or more 51% subsidiaries irrespective of its other activities. In *Tax Bulletin 62*, December 2002, the Revenue shed further light on the definitions of trading company and group.

It will now at a company's request after the end of an accounting period 'respond positively' by expressing a view on the company's taper relief status for that period. This can be useful for clients who are selling shares and taking loan notes or shares in another company where they may have a material interest (see below) or if they do not work in the company and wish to know whether or not the company is a trading company. If the company shares do not qualify for business assets taper relief then any sale may need to be structured quite differently (for example, using a pre-sale dividend). For those wanting a Revenue ruling on whether a company is qualifying, the company should write to its Inspector setting out:

- the reason why it is seeking the Inspector's opinion and the period over which the company wants the Inspector to consider its status;
- all the facts that the company considers relevant in measuring the extent of its trading and non-trading activities and, where appropriate, the assumptions it has made in describing what it expects its activities to comprise over the part of the period falling after the latest point for which data is available;
- why the company considers that there is uncertainty as to its status;
- the company's conclusion as to its status, and why it considers, if applicable, that the measures that point in that direction outweigh those pointing in the opposite direction; and
- what disposal is being contemplated and when it is expected that the transaction will be completed.

The Inspector will offer his or her opinion whenever this is practicable and, if this differs from the company's view, explain the reasons for that difference. It appears that it has not always been easy to obtain consistent rulings from HMRC. For further information on COP10 rulings see para CG17953r of the Capital Gains Manual.

It should be noted that in relation to 'unused' cash balances which appear to represent more than 20% of the company's gross assets, the problem may in fact disappear if the other balance sheet assets are shown at their current market values. HMRC also seem to consider that the source of the cash reserves is relevant. If the cash represents undrawn trading profits they are apparently more relaxed than if the cash represents the sale proceeds of an investment from some years ago. (See Tolley's Tax Digest Issue 41 – Maximising Taper Relief by Robert Jamieson.)    **[20.28]**

## 6  Relief for joint venture companies

### a)  *The original relief*

TCGA 1992 Sch A1 para 23 introduced, with effect from 6 April 2000, the concept of 'qualifying shareholdings' in 'joint venture companies'. The amendment was designed to extend the benefit of business assets taper relief to certain cases where companies took part in joint ventures and held shares in companies that were not 51% subsidiaries.

Therefore, before 6 April 2000, if A held shares in Newco 1 which owned 50% of Newco 2, a trading company, no business assets taper relief was available for A. Newco 1 had to own at least 51% of Newco 2 and therefore be a holding company of a trading group.

The first effect of Sch A1 para 23 is that a share of the activities of the joint venture companies in which a company participates can now be taken into account in assessing whether the 'investing company' or group is trading.

The second effect of the changes is that employees of a joint venture company who own shares in the *listed* parent trading company owning the joint venture company will be entitled to business assets taper relief regardless of the level of their interest. They do not need to hold 5% of the voting rights.

Note, however, that the joint venture company (in the above example Newco 2) had to have 75% or more of its ordinary share capital held by not more than five companies. In addition Newco 1 (again following the above example) had to hold *more than* 30% of the ordinary share capital of Newco 2. **[20.29]**

### b)  *FA 2002 improvements*

FA 2002 eased these conditions with effect for periods of ownership post-5 April 2002. The investing company (Newco 1) only needs to hold 10% or more in Newco 2 instead of 'more than 30%'. In addition the requirement is that 75% of Newco 2's share capital needs to be held by not more than five *persons* rather than by not more than five *companies*. The difficulty is that these improvements have not been made retrospective in effect, so again one needs to examine the position pre- and post-April 2002. In addition, loans made by a trading company (in the above example Newco 1) to a joint venture company (Newco 2 above) could cause problems to the status of Newco 1 so the financing of a joint venture must be examined carefully. **[20.30]**

## 7  Relief for employee shareholdings in non-trading companies (TCGA 1992 Sch A1 para 6 as amended by FA 2001)

These changes, effected by FA 2001, were backdated to disposals after 5 April 2000. Under the amended rules an individual is entitled to business assets taper relief on shares in any company in which he is employed as an officer or employee (or if he is employed in a company having a relevant connection with that company) *provided that* neither he nor a person connected with him has a material interest in that company or, if it is controlled by another company, in that other company. Note therefore that:

(1)    employees of property investment companies (for instance) may now qualify for business assets taper: of course, if the relevant shares were held before 6 April 2000 an apportionment calculation will be required on any disposal (see *Example 20.6(3)*);

(2)    'connected person' bears the normal CGT meaning: see TCGA 1992 s 286 and **[19.23]**;

(3)    a 'material interest' is defined in para 6A as possession or control of more than 10% of any of the issued shares; of any class of issued shares; of voting rights; of the right to profits available for distribution; or of rights to assets on a liquidation;

(4)    in the case of trusts an 'eligible beneficiary' must be the officer or employee: hence discretionary trusts cannot benefit from this extended business taper relief. Note that an eligible beneficiary can be an interest in possession beneficiary without necessarily having a qualifying interest in possession under the new inheritance tax rules. See **[20.44]**.  **[20.31]**

## 8   Relief for property let to a qualifying company or used for trading purposes

A new apportionment provision and therefore a further complication was introduced by FA 2003 s 160 with effect from 6 April 2004, presumably as a result of extensive lobbying from the property industry.

Formerly let property (broadly) only qualified for business assets taper relief on a disposal by an individual if:

(a)    it was furnished holiday accommodation; or

(b)    it was used for the purposes of a trade carried on by a partnership of which the property owner was a partner; or

(c)    it was used for the purposes of a trade carried on by a qualifying company. Prior to 6 April 2000 it was necessary for the owner of the land either to be a full-time employee and own 5% of the shares or to hold 25% of the shares. Post-6 April 2000 a listed company is qualifying in relation to an individual if the person is an employee whether or not full-time or the individual owns 5% or more voting shares; lettings of land to an unlisted trading company can now qualify for full business assets taper relief post-5 April 2000 even if there is no minimum ownership and the landowner is not an employee.

(d)    It was used for the purposes of any office or employment held by an individual with a person carrying on a trade such as an unlisted trading company or a listed trading company where the owner was an employee or owned 5% voting shares. (Full-time employment is no longer required after 5 April 2000.)                                    **[20.32]**

### EXAMPLE 20.7

Assume that Archer is a farmer and that he lets agricultural land (a) to Tom Cobbler a neighbouring farmer or (b) to Dan Gurner Ltd (an unquoted farming company). In the first situation the land was a non-business asset in Archer's hands until April 2004 (see below) but in (b) because Dan Gurner Ltd is a qualifying company (see TCGA 1992 Sch A1 para 6(1)(b)) business assets taper is available from April 2000 (see TCGA 1992 Sch A1 para 5(2)(b)).

This was probably an accident of drafting resulting from the definition of qualifying company. However, the Government has now extended the relief so that from 6 April 2004 business assets taper relief is available on almost all disposals of land let for trading purposes.

FA 2003 provides that all assets used for the purposes of a trade carried on by individuals, trustees, personal representatives, partnerships whose members include such persons or qualifying companies will qualify for business assets taper relief *irrespective of whether the asset owner is involved in the carrying on of the trade*. The new provisions will only take effect for periods of ownership from *6 April 2004* and the intention is that the landlord's letting decision should now be neutral as between incorporated and unincorporated businesses.

*Note:*

- Interestingly, it is only necessary that the property is used for trading purposes. If, for example, a piece of land is let to a solicitors' firm who then sublets the premises to another partnership which uses it for trading, business assets taper relief can still be obtained on the whole provided all the premises are used for trading purposes.
- What happens if there is a period, say, of fitting out the premises prior to starting the trade? HMRC appear to accept that this qualifies for BATR.
- What if some of the premises are not used for trading purposes and some are? Arguably para 9 providing for apportionment does not work adequately since an asset is a business asset *if it is used wholly or partly* for the qualifying purposes. There is no need then to look at the actual purposes for which the whole land is used and full relief is available! HMRC do not accept this interpretation.
- Note the difficulties that can arise where there is one building, part of which is used for trading purposes and part is not. See CG Manual 17959 and *Taxation* article, 14 July 2005 'Flatly Incredible' by Mike Truman. **[20.33]**

#### EXAMPLE 20.8

An individual A owns a business park divided into separate units and lets out five of the units. All lettings commenced after 6 April 1998 but before 6 April 2004. Unit 1 is let to individual B who uses it for her trade. Unit 2 is let to a partnership C whose membership consists of companies, one of which is an unlisted trading company. The partnership uses the unit for the purposes of its trade. Unit 3 is let to a listed trading company that uses it for the purposes of its trade. A is not employed by this company and does not own 5% of the shares in it. Unit 4 is let to a partnership D whose members are all individuals (one of whom is A) but the premises are not used for the purposes of a trade. Unit 5 is let to an unlisted trading company that uses it for its trade and A owns no shares in the company.

For periods of ownership *before 6 April 2004* while the units are let as described, the business assets status of those units for taper relief purposes in relation to individual A will be as follows:

- **Unit 1** – will not qualify as a business asset because, although it is being used for the purposes of a trade carried on by an individual, that individual is not individual A.
- **Unit 2** – will not qualify as a business asset as although the partnership uses the asset for the purposes of its trade, individual A is not a member of the partnership.

- **Unit 3** – will not qualify as a business asset as the listed trading company is not a qualifying company by reference to individual A.
- **Unit 4** – will not qualify as a business asset because it is not being used for a trade even though A is a partner.
- **Unit 5** – will qualify for BATR from 6 April 2000 but not for the period of letting before 6 April 2000, as prior to this date, the unlisted trading company was not a qualifying company by reference to individual A for the purposes of its trade.

For periods of ownership from *6 April 2004* while the units are let as described, the business assets status of those units for taper relief purposes in relation to individual A will be as follows:

- **Unit 1** – will qualify as a business asset as it is being used by an individual for the purposes of her trade even though individual A is not the trader.
- **Unit 2** – will qualify as a business asset as at least one member of the partnership (the unlisted trading company) is a qualifying company by reference to individual A and the partnership is using the premises for the purposes of its trade.
- **Unit 3** – will not qualify as a business asset as the listed trading company is not a qualifying company by reference to individual A.
- **Unit 4** – will not qualify as a business asset because the partnership does not use the unit for the purposes of a trade.
- **Unit 5** – will qualify as a business asset as it is being used by a company that is a qualifying company by reference to individual A for the purposes of its trade.

On balance it is preferable for A to consider letting to partnerships or sole traders provided they use the asset for trading purposes because then she is not required to consider the qualifying status of the company and whether or not it is a trading company for business assets taper relief purposes. She also avoids the worry then of the unlisted trading company becoming listed and then ceasing to be a qualifying company in relation to A (see Unit 3 in example above).

## 9    Incorporation

a)    *The rules pre-6 April 2002*

On the incorporation of an unincorporated business, the transfer of the business assets to the company is a disposal for CGT purposes. In order to ensure that CGT is not a bar to the act of incorporation, relief under TCGA 1992 s 162 provides for any net chargeable gains on the disposal of such assets to be rolled over against the acquisition cost of shares in the new company. This defers the charge to tax on the rolled over gain until the shares themselves are disposed of (see **[22.100]**).

Unlike roll-over relief under s 152, incorporation relief under TCGA 1992 s 162 was, until FA 2002, mandatory if the relevant conditions were satisfied. This could be unfortunate if incorporation was followed shortly afterwards by the sale of shares in the company, given that the rolled over gain did not attract taper relief and that the taper relief clock was reset to start afresh.

**[20.34]**

b)    *Flexibility in FA 2002*

FA 2002 s 48 now provides a facility for individuals and trustees to elect (with effect for transfers of a business on or after 6 April 2002) for s 162 *not* to apply in relation to the transfer of an unincorporated business to a company. This is helpful if, for example, there is an unexpected offer to buy the business shortly after incorporation.

Similarly this flexibility will help to ease the process in cases where an individual has incorporated as part of the sale of the business but where the sale subsequently falls through. Previously, a well-advised taxpayer would have structured the deal so as to fall out of incorporation relief in order to maximise his taper entitlement and would then be faced with an immediate tax charge. One of the effects of this new measure is that he can now go ahead and structure the transaction so as to obtain relief under TCGA 1992 s 162 but opt out of relief if the sale goes ahead as planned (see further *Example 22.15*).

The time limits for making the necessary election are as follows:

(1) The second anniversary of 31 January next following the tax year in which the incorporation took place. So if the business is incorporated in March 2003, the election must be made by January 2006; *or*

(2) if the shares acquired at the time of the incorporation have all been disposed of by the end of the tax year following that in which the transfer of the business took place, the election must be made no later than the first anniversary of the 31 January next following the tax year in which that transfer took place. So if incorporation takes place in March 2003 (2002–03) and the shares are all sold or given away in 2003/4, the election must be made by 31 January 2005 (ie within the normal time limits for amending a self-assessment return).

If the shares acquired at the time of the incorporation have not all been disposed of by the end of the tax year following that in which the transfer of the business took place, the deadline for the election is extended by one year. The time limits therefore effectively give a two-year wait and see window.

Any transfer of shares between husband and wife will not be treated as a disposal for the purpose of triggering the shorter time limit.

Following the incorporation of a partnership, each partner has a separate entitlement to make the election—the fact that one partner makes the election does not require his fellow partners to do the same. **[20.35]**

## 10 Replacement of business assets—roll-over relief

Until the advent of taper relief, the rules for roll-over relief meant that there was generally no fiscal disincentive stopping businesses *replacing* their business assets (for example, premises) as opposed to *enhancing* existing assets.

However, the introduction of taper relief means that it can now be preferable to enhance rather than replace an existing asset in order to preserve existing taper relief. See *Example 20.9*. **[20.36]**

**EXAMPLE 20.9**

Suppose that brother and sister Emma and John run their own businesses. They both acquired their factories in April 1998 paying £100,000. Suppose that in April 2004, Emma sells her premises for £200,000 and buys new premises for £400,000. At the same time, John spends £200,000 enhancing his existing premises.

Suppose that on eventual sale in April 2005 both factories are worth £600,000 and Emma and John wish to calculate the capital gains tax that would be payable if they sold up. The net cash flows are the same but the tax effects can differ considerably.

In John's case, the calculation would be as follows:

|  | £ |
|---|---|
| Proceeds | 600,000 |
| Less: | |
| Original cost | (100,000) |
| Enhancement cost | (200,000) |
| Untapered gain | 300,000 |

As the factory has been owned for more than two years, 75% taper relief is available reducing the chargeable gain to £75,000. The fact that he enhanced the value of the asset only one year before does not matter. The tax payable is £30,000.

Emma can either claim rollover relief or not but in both cases will be worse off than John.

Suppose a rollover relief claim is made:

|  | £ | £ |
|---|---|---|
| Proceeds | | 600,000 |
| Less: original cost | 400,000 | |
| Less: rolled over gain | (100,000) | |
| | | (300,000) |
| Untapered gain | | 300,000 |

However, since the replacement premises were acquired less than two years previously, the taper relief available is only 50% and can therefore only reduce the gain to £150,000. This will mean that Emma's tax is twice that of John's.

Suppose Emma does not make a claim for roll-over relief. She is better off than before but still has to pay more capital gains tax and earlier than John.

She would have to pay capital gains tax on the gain from the first disposal of £100,000. That disposal on 6 April 2004 would have been subject to 75% taper relief—leaving £25,000 chargeable = £10,000 capital gains tax payable in January 2006.

She makes a further gain in 2005 (£200,000) which qualifies for 50% taper relief so has to pay capital gains tax of £40,000 on £100,000. Total tax liability = £50,000.

It will often be sensible for the trader (in the above case Emma) to make a provisional rollover relief claim under s 153A which at a later date she can replace with a formal claim under TCGA 1992 s152 or else withdraw once she has had a chance to consider likely future events. This will allow her a longer time to revoke the claim than if she made a s 152 formal claim from the start.

## 11   Holdover relief

Similar points arise in relation to gifts although, as with roll-over relief, the problem is less acute now that full BATR is available after only two years. Any gift or sale ends the taper relief period and the donee cannot take over the donor's period of ownership (see generally **Chapter 24**).          **[20.37]**

**EXAMPLE 20.10**

Mrs Goodfellow qualifies for full 75% BATR on the shares in her successful golf business worth £20 million. She decides to do some inheritance tax planning and gives half her shares to her daughter. She claims holdover relief under s165 in order to avoid paying CGT on the gain of say £10 million. Six months later there is a sale of the company for £25 million. Mrs Goodfellow pays 10% tax on her gain of £12.5 million.

The daughter does not qualify for any taper relief and will pay 40% CGT on the full gain of £12.5 million including the gain held over. It would be better then for Mrs Goodfellow not to make a holdover claim (or revoke it within the necessary time limits) and pay immediate CGT of £1 million on the gift. Then at least the daughter acquires the shares at the high cost of £10 million and will pay 40% CGT on only £2.5 million and not on £12.5 million. Note, however, that the position is still worse than if Mrs Goodfellow had given no shares away at all since in that case she would have paid 10% on the entire gain of £25 million.

The fact that the donee does not take on the donor's period of ownership for taper relief purposes used to be helpful in washing out the effect of the apportionment provisions described in *Example 20.5* above.                    **[20.38]**

**EXAMPLE 20.11**

Assume the facts are the same as in *Example 20.5* but instead Harry decides to settle shares in Makepiece Ltd on an interest in possession trust for his children in 2001. He claims holdover relief under TCGA 1992 s 165. When the company is sold in 2006 the entire gain in the hands of the trustees qualifies for full BATR and the trustees will pay CGT at an effective rate of 10%. Note that the earlier non-BATR period has effectively been washed out. Until 10 December 2003 it was possible to use this device and wash out gains by gifting to a settlor interested trust. However, holdover relief is no longer available on gifts to settlor interested trusts and therefore Harry could no longer wash out the 'tainted period' and settle the shares on interest in possession trusts for himself or his spouse post December 2003 or (in respect of disposals from 6 April 2006) for his minor children and claim holdover relief. See FA 2004 Sch 21 and FA 2006 schedule 12 para 3 amending s 77 TCGA 1992 so that trusts for minor children are now settlor interested.

Note also that an inter vivos interest in possession trust set up on or after 22 March 2006 will be treated as a relevant property settlement and will be an immediate chargeable transfer by Harry although it may be possible to claim business property relief. Hence such planning is likely to be rare now although it is possible that assets held within a trust for some years may have a tainted taper relief period that the trustees wish to wash out. Note there is no restriction on holdover relief in respect of disposals *out of* settlor interested trusts.

**EXAMPLE 20.12**

Harry set up a trust for himself and his wife in 2000. The trust is discretionary. The assets in the trust comprise let land (to a sole trader farmer) which only qualifies for business assets taper relief from 6 April 2004. Prior to that date the let land was a non-business asset. The plan is to sell the land in April 2008. The trustees decide to advance the land back to the settlor, holding over the gain. Note that there may be an exit charge for inheritance tax purposes since the transfer is out of a discretionary trust. Holdover relief is still available under s 260 even though the transfer is back to the settlor. The settlor then holds the land which is let to the sole trader farmer for a further two years prior to selling it and claiming full business assets taper relief untainted by the pre-2004 period.

It is possible to revoke a holdover claim (which might be desirable in the above example if there was an unexpected sale of the property shortly after advancement to the settlor). HMRC allow revocation of a claim before the expiry of the normal time limits for enquiries into tax returns.

If Harry emigrates within six years from the end of the tax year of the advancement, the held over gain is clawed back under TCGA 1992 s 168. In these circumstances it appears that the held over gain clawed back is the chargeable gain *without the benefit of the trustees' taper relief* although presumably, since a chargeable gain is deemed to accrue to the donee in the year of emigration, taper relief can be claimed on the clawed back gain by reference to the holding period of the donee (Harry) rather than the donor (the trustees).

If this sort of device is used, care is needed on implementation. Has the gift been effected properly (in terms of following the formalities on transfer of shares laid out in the articles)? Are the trustees (or the beneficiary) registered as the new owners?                    **[20.39]**

## 12   Foreign assets

TCGA 1992 s 12(1) provides that where a non-domiciled person disposes of a foreign asset, chargeable gains are taxed in the year (or years) in which the gains are remitted to the UK. Para 16(4) ensures that in this situation taper relief is calculated by reference to the actual period of ownership of the asset and not the period up until when the gain is remitted. The same provision applies where TCGA 1992 s 279(2) applies to defer liability where the taxpayer is unable to remit the proceeds to the UK because of the laws of the country where the gain accrued, or actions of its government.          **[20.40]**

### EXAMPLE 20.13

In June 2000 a non-domiciled UK resident taxpayer acquired shares in a foreign company that do not qualify for business assets taper relief and disposed of them in June 2004. The gain is remitted to the UK in June 2005. There will be four and not five whole years in the qualifying period for taper relief in respect of the gain that accrued in January 2005, which runs from June 2000 to June 2004. The delay in remitting the gain does not affect the length of the qualifying holding period.

### Non-resident companies

Taper relief does not apply to gains that are attributed to members of non-resident companies under TCGA 1992 s 13. Although such gains are chargeable to capital gains tax they are computed according to the rules applicable for gains chargeable to corporation tax and hence indexation continues to be available.

### EXAMPLE 20.14

A, a UK resident and UK domiciled person, owns 100% of a Jersey investment company that realises indexed gains of £100,000. Such gains are attributed to him under s 13. No taper relief is available. If A later sold the shares in the Jerseyco then taper relief would be available on those shares.

## 13   Spouses—interaction of taper relief and the identification rules

The rules on transfers of shares and other assets between spouses and (from 5 December 2005) civil partners, are complex: see *Tax Bulletin* 54, August 2001, where the Revenue set out its view on the way taper relief works when shares have been transferred from one spouse to another before sale. These views do not find universal acceptance in relation to disposals of part shareholdings—see articles in *Taxation* 18 October 2001 by Mike Thexton and in 22 November 2001 by Maurice Parry Wingfield. The problem highlighted in the *Tax Bulletin* will arise where the shares being transferred by the donor were not all acquired on the same day and the transferee spouse disposes of only some of them later.

As a general rule the transferee spouse—for taper relief purposes only, not for identification purposes—is treated as having acquired the asset when the transferor spouse did and the no gain no loss rule in TCGA 1992 s 58 continues to apply. Thus when the asset is eventually disposed of by the transferee spouse, the periods of ownership of the spouses are aggregated, both to decide the number of complete years of ownership and to determine the extent to which the asset was a business asset during that period. In the case of shares, for identification purposes the transferee spouse is treated as acquiring them at the actual date of acquisition. This may enable the annual exemption to be used or losses preserved (see *Example 20.15*).     **[20.41]**

**EXAMPLE 20.15**

Michael has 1,000 shares in ICA, a listed company, 500 acquired in 1990 and 500 acquired in 1999. Each holding is worth £1,000. The 1990 holding shows a gain. The 1999 holding is breaking even. If he sells 500 shares now he does not realise a gain since the sale is identified with the 1999 holding. If he wants to use his annual exemption he has failed. But if instead he gives 500 shares to his wife Susan these are treated as being out of the 1999 holding (LIFO) and if he then sells his remaining shares he has realised a gain and used his annual exemption. If Susan sells later she is treated as holding the shares since 1999.

For shares in a company to qualify as a business asset it is necessary to determine whether the company was the qualifying company of the *transferee* spouse throughout the whole of the period of ownership falling after 5 April 1998. If the company was not the qualifying company of the transferee spouse throughout the whole period of ownership, the gain must be apportioned.     **[20.42]**

**EXAMPLE 20.16**

Michael acquires 500 shares in ICA in 1990. He works in ICA but gives them all to Susan in April 2002 because he wants her to have the dividends. She sells the holding in April 2006. Susan does not work for the company and so the shares qualify for effectively nine years' non-business assets taper relief (with the bonus year) with 65% of the gain being chargeable. No business assets taper relief is available. Susan does not work in the listed company and owns under 5%.

If Michael had sold the shares in 2006 and made no gift then business assets taper relief would have been available from the period after 5 April 2000 because he does work in the listed company. By giving them to Susan all business assets taper relief has been lost.

Where an asset other than shares is transferred between spouses the rule is different. The asset can qualify for business assets taper relief depending on the extent to which the asset satisfies the business use tests during the combined period of ownership. However, in this case it is necessary to review both the period during which the asset was held by the transferee spouse and the period during which the asset was held by the transferring spouse.

For the period after the gift, the asset will be a business asset at any time if the conditions are satisfied by the transferee spouse. For the period before the gift, the asset will be a business asset at any time if the conditions are satisfied by either of the spouses.                    **[20.43]**


**EXAMPLE 20.17**

Michael farms land that is owned by Susan. Susan transfers the farmland to Michael. If Michael then sells it will be a business asset throughout the period of ownership because of his business use.

If Michael farms and owns the land and then gives it to Susan who does not farm, there is no business assets taper relief after the date of the gift. Some business assets taper relief is still available for Michael's period of ownership.


14   **Taper relief and trusts**

Trustees qualify for taper relief in the same way as individuals, wherever they are resident. However, in considering whether an asset owned by a trust qualifies for business or non-BATR one must have regard not only to the trustees' position but also to the position of the beneficiaries (in relation to interest in possession trusts).

As noted earlier, from 6 April 2000, all trusts holding shares in unlisted trading companies will qualify for BATR whatever their level of holding and irrespective of the type of trust. However, trusts holding shares in listed trading companies will only qualify if the trustees hold more than 5% of the voting shares or an eligible beneficiary is an officer or employee (not necessarily full time) in the company or its subsidiary. An eligible beneficiary is one who has a relevant interest in possession (defined as an interest in possession not being an annuity or fixed-term entitlement unless the beneficiary will become absolutely entitled to the property at the end of the fixed term). Schedule 20 amended the definition of qualifying interest in possession for inheritance tax purposes and introduced certain amendments to the capital gains tax legislation in relation to the deaths of those holding interests in possession which arose post 21 March 2006. No amendment was made to the definition of relevant interest in possession for taper relief purposes. Hence it would appear that a beneficiary who is an employee and has an entitlement to income which arose post 21 March 2006 is still an eligible beneficiary for the purposes of the taper relief legislation even though his interest is not a qualifying interest in possession for inheritance tax purposes.

Where there are multiple settlors of the same trust the shares cannot be cumulated so as to create a single umbrella settlement that would then qualify for relief.                    **[20.44]**

**EXAMPLE 20.18**

A, B and C each own 3% in ICA, a listed trading company. They cannot transfer their respective holdings into a single trust in order to get over the 5% threshold. The trust now owns 9% of the shares in ICA but for taper relief purposes it is as if the shares are held in three separate settlements.

Trustees who trade on their own account or in partnership, or own assets used in a trade by an 'eligible' beneficiary or a qualifying company, will also qualify for BATR. (Note, however, that for trustees in partnership BATR is arguably only available on the asset in question from April 2000–see para 5(3)(a).)

If the beneficiary has an interest in part only of the trust, he is an eligible beneficiary in relation to an asset if the asset is included within the part of the trust assets in which he has an interest in possession. Where the trust holds unlisted shares this will no longer matter but in relation to listed shares or in respect of periods pre-6 April 2000 the rate of taper relief could alter depending on which fund held the shares.

**EXAMPLE 20.19**

Suppose Chris sets up a trust for his two children Joe and Dot each with an interest in possession in half the trust. He settles 10% shares in his unlisted company Timeshare in February 1998 and some cash that is used to buy a house now rented out. Dot works in Timeshare full time. Joe mends old cars in his own business. The trustees do not appropriate the assets to any particular fund and therefore although Dot is an eligible beneficiary for the entire period from April 1998 only part of the shares will qualify for BATR up to April 2000 since Joe is not an eligible beneficiary. The gain on a later disposal will need to be apportioned. After April 2000 the trustees qualify in their own right anyway since the shares are unlisted.

If instead Chris had specifically given all the shares to Dot's fund and the cash to Joe's fund, all the shares would have qualified for full BATR.

It was possible prior to 22 March 2006 to dilute the effect of the apportionment rules by the trustees appointing the shares out to a new trust for Joe and Dot depending on whether holdover relief is available without restriction (see *Example 20.11*). There are now a variety of problems with this. First the restrictions in FA 2004 Sch 21 and FA 2006 Sch 12 limit holdover relief if the new trust is settlor interested or becomes so within the clawback period (six years from the end of the tax year of the disposal). That definition has been extended from 6 April 2006 to include minor children. Moreover if a beneficiary adds to the trust within the clawback period it becomes settlor interested and the original held over gain can be clawed back. Therefore, Joe and Dot should not add to such a trust from which they can benefit within the clawback period. Even though the shares did not originate from them, holdover relief can still be clawed back if the second trust becomes settlor interested.

Second, a transfer of assets from one trust to another may cause inheritance tax problems. In the above example, Joe and Dot have interests in possession. If they take interests in possession under the new trust then prior to 22 March 2006 this would have been a non-event for inheritance tax purposes. If the transfer to the new trust takes place post-21 March 2006, the interests in possession taken by Joe and Dot are not qualifying interests under the transitional serial interest provisions. Hence they end up making chargeable transfers for inheritance tax purposes and putting the assets comprised in the new trust within the relevant property regime!                    **[20.45]**

Taper relief and private residence relief

The availability of principal private residence relief usually means that taper relief is irrelevant on disposals of houses that qualify for relief under TCGA 1992 s 223. However, there is a difficulty where there is a disposal of residential property that had some exclusive business use.

If part of a dwelling house is used exclusively for the purposes of a trade or business the gain must be apportioned and no principal private residence relief is due on that part of the gain. Unfortunately such gain does not then qualify for full business assets taper relief and therefore the rate of tax is not 10% as might otherwise be expected. This is because Sch A1 para 9 provides that where the asset is used for both business and non-business purposes the chargeable gain must be apportioned on a pro rata basis into a business and non-business gain prior to the application of taper relief.

**EXAMPLE 20.20**

John works as a dentist from his home. One quarter of the rooms are used exclusively for the purposes of his business. On sale in 2006 (after owning the home for seven years) he makes a gain of £100,000. Given that the gain arises wholly in respect of business use, he might expect that the computation will be as below:

| | |
|---|---:|
| Gain | 100,000 |
| Exempt as main residence | 75,000 |
| Chargeable gain before taper | 25,000 |
| Business taper relief 75% | 18,750 |
| Chargeable | 6,250 |

In fact, this is wrong in principle: the computation must reflect the fact that the whole of the chargeable gain arises on a single asset which has been used as to only one-quarter for business purposes. The correct computation is as below:

| | |
|---|---:|
| Gain | 100,000 |
| Exempt as main residence | 75,000 |
| Chargeable gain before taper | 25,000 |
| Business taper relief (at 75%) on 25% of gain | 4,687 |
| Non-business taper relief (at 25%) on 75% of gain | 4,687 |
| Chargeable | 15,625 |

**[20.46]**

## 15   Anti-avoidance provisions

a)   *Relevant changes of activity*

TCGA 1992 Sch A1 para 11 provided that, on a disposal of shares in a close company, taper relief was restricted if, after 5 April 1998, the company had started to trade or started, or had significantly increased the size of, a business of holding investments. Any such event was known as a 'relevant change of activity'. If there was a 'relevant change of activity' the taper relief clock was reset to zero and any accrued taper relief was forfeited. The provision caught a number of innocent transactions but could fairly easily be circumvented.

Paragraph 11 was repealed by FA 2002 in relation to disposals of shares on or after 17 April 2002. A new para 11A was inserted, which operates from 17 April 2002 onwards in respect of disposals, but affects earlier periods of ownership.

The replacement rule provides that any period after 5 April 1998 does not count for taper relief purposes (either business or non-business) if the company is a close company and is not 'active'. Any company that is carrying on a business, preparing to carry on a business or winding up the affairs of a business will be treated as active. However, holding small amounts of cash on deposit or shares in non-active companies may not be regarded as active. See *Tax Bulletin*, October 2002.

The new rule is much simpler although the definition of 'active' may still lead to some anomalies. The Revenue explained in the Treasury Explanatory Notes to the Finance Bill 2002 the aim of the new provisions. One of the aims was to provide protection against transactions seeking excessive taper relief. For example, an individual could set up a company in year 1, do nothing with it for several years, in year 8 use it to acquire an asset and in year 10 sell the company. Without this provision the individual could effectively obtain ten years' non-business assets taper relief on the gain on an asset held for only two years. Note though that disallowing the first eight years would only be a disadvantage for the individual if when the company became active it was not a trading but an investment company. The rules prevent him claiming 10 years non-business assets taper relief.

The rule also aims to prevent individuals from being accidentally disadvantaged if they use a long-held dormant company to start up a trade. In the above example, if the company was trading between year 8 and 10 the individual might expect to get full business assets taper relief. Instead without this provision ignoring periods when the company is inactive the individual would find that part of the gain on disposal was a gain on a non-business asset and part on a business asset. **[20.47]**

b)  *Value freezing*

In some cases it may be sensible to try and postpone the disposal date for CGT purposes in order to maximise business assets taper relief but still endeavour to fix the deal now commercially. The classic mechanism for achieving this is through use of put and call options. The time of disposal of any asset disposed of under an option is the time of exercise of the option and not when the option was granted: see TCGA 1992 Sch A1 para 13. However, such cross-options may breach the anti-avoidance provisions in para 10 which prevent taper relief continuing to accrue where the owner is not exposed to the risk of loss or the possibility of profit to any substantial extent. Substantial in this context means more than 20%. However, note that provided the owner of the asset continues to be exposed to a substantial extent to the possibility of either profit or loss then the anti-avoidance provisions do not apply. Hence bank guaranteed loan notes issued on a takeover of a company's shares do not bring para 10 into play because it only provides protection from downward, not upward, movements in the value.

**[20.48]**

c)   *Value shifting*

There are two types of value shifting provisions found in the legislation. The first provision, TCGA 1992 s 29, is discussed at **[26.61]** but Sch A1 para 12 only applies to disposals of shares or securities in a close company (as defined in TA 1988 s 414).

Under the normal capital gains value shifting rules in s 29 the concern arises where value is moved out of existing assets and that then creates a deemed taxable deemed disposal to the extent of the value reduction. By contrast, the taper relief value shifting rules do not themselves *create* a deemed disposal but rather penalise the recipient of the shift by causing a resetting of the taper relief clock. If para 12 applies the effect is penal because all taper relief built up is lost. If there is 'a relevant shift of value' into shares in the close company from other shares, any period before the time of the later shift in value will not count for taper relief.

The relevant shift of value is defined in para 12(3) as taking place whenever a person who has control of a close company exercises his control so that value passes out of that holding into the shares which are later disposed of. However, if the value passing into the shares from the relevant holding is insignificant, or when the shift of value takes place the qualifying holding period for the relevant holding is at least as long as the qualifying holding period for the shares into which the value is shifted, then para 12(4) excludes the provisions.                                              **[20.49]–[20.60]**

**EXAMPLE 20.21**

A owns shares in two companies: he owns 900 shares in X Limited acquired for £900 in 2002 which are now worth £9,000 and 100 shares in Y Limited acquired for £100,000 in 2010 and now worth £991,000. He receives an offer to sell the shares in Y Limited. Before disposing of the shares in Y Limited, A arranges that X Limited acquires all of the shares in Y Limited in consideration of X Limited issuing 100 shares. The revised holding of X Limited is now 1,000 shares worth £1m. 900 of these were acquired in 2002 and the remaining 100 shares would be deemed to have been acquired in 2010 and are worth at most £100,000 (10% of the whole). There has been a value shift into the 900 shares that are now worth £900,000. Thus when the 1,000 shares are sold the gain on the 900 shares would (apart from para 12) qualify for more taper relief having the benefit of a longer qualifying holding period.

In those circumstances, for the 900 shares the period up to the date of transfer of value is treated as a period that does not count for taper relief. The qualifying holding period of the 100 shares deemed to have been acquired in 2010 will run from 2010. The qualifying period of the 900 shares is effectively nil. Taper relief before the shift of value is completely ignored.

Value shifts before 5 April 1998 are ignored for taper relief purposes. There is no motive test and, therefore, paragraph 12 can inadvertently apply.

**EXAMPLE 20.22**

Suppose two siblings Chris and Kate own two companies A Limited and B Limited. Chris owns 100% of A Limited and Kate owns 100% of B Limited. Chris has carried on his business in the company for 20 years. Kate has only just started the business.

Chris and Kate decide that they would be better off amalgamating the businesses. Kate decides to sell her shares to Chris for a fixed sum but HMRC determine that this is less than market value. There has been a shift of value into Chris' shares as the company A Limited has acquired B Limited at an undervalue. All Chris' accrued taper relief is lost.

Similar problems can arise if there is an alteration of any *rights* attaching to shares that can affect the value of those shares. Reclassification of shares that then give different dividend rights will need some care.

Curiously there is no value shift where an asset is gifted to a company and the gain held over under s 165 because there is no diminution in value in any other shareholding.

## 16  Miscellaneous—postponed gains

In certain cases, where gains are postponed or held over but eventually crystallise, the taper relief is not calculated by reference to the date on which such gains crystallise but by reference to the **original** period of ownership. For example, where gains are realised when someone is not resident or ordinarily resident here they are not chargeable then. However, if that person becomes UK-resident within five years of leaving then (unless double tax treaty relief is available or the assets were acquired when he was non-resident—see **Chapter 27**) the gains then crystallise in the tax year of return. The taper relief is, however, calculated by reference to the date when the assets were originally sold not by reference to the date of return.

Similarly if gains are deferred by taking QCBs in exchange for shares on a sale of the company (s 116) or investing in a company qualifying for EIS relief (TCGA 1992 Sch 5B), when the QCBs or EIS shares are sold, taper relief on the deferred gain is calculated by reference to the holding period of the original asset disposed of. The subsequent holding period of the QCB or EIS shares is irrelevant. (Note though that if capital gains tax exemption is not available on the EIS shares, nevertheless gains arising from increases in value of the EIS shares over the EIS period of ownership do qualify for further taper relief.)                                              **[20.61]**

**EXAMPLE 20.23**

A sells some shares which qualify for 30% taper relief. The gain before taper is £100,000. He decides not to pay any capital gains tax and reinvests £100,000 in an EIS company, claiming deferral relief. Note that in order to avoid a capital gains tax charge he has to invest the gross gain before, not after, calculating his taper relief. He owns more than 30% in the company so can only claim deferral relief not income tax relief.

Five years later his shares in the EIS company are sold for £150,000. £100,000 of this represents the gain deferred and will still only qualify for 30% taper relief. The five-year period of ownership is ignored. The other £50,000 represents the gain during the EIS period and will qualify for 75% business assets taper relief.

Earn outs can pose particular problems given that the earn out right is a separate chose in action.

**EXAMPLE 20.24**

B sells some shares which qualify for full business assets taper relief. He receives cash of £1m plus an earn out based on defined profits for the next two years. That earn out right is valued at £500,000. He is taxed on the sale of shares as if he received consideration of £1.5m with business assets taper relief. However, if he receives the earn out consideration two years later which is (say) £750,000 he is treated as making a gain of £250,000 which will not qualify for any taper relief because the earn out right is a non-business asset and he has held it for less than three years.

## III    COMMENTS AND CONCLUSIONS

(1)  Taper relief may discourage the making of lifetime gifts: see **[24.29]**.
(2)  The phasing out of retirement relief will not in all cases be compensated for by the introduction of taper relief: see **[22.85]**.
(3)  For the use of losses, see **[19.63]** and for the relationship with the annual exemption, see **[19.87]**.
(4)  Trustees with effect from 6 April 2004 suffer CGT at 40% so that they no longer benefit from the 34% rate of tax. However, trusts are still useful as an umbrella to hold assets, permitting the interests of beneficiaries to be changed whilst the trust qualifies for full taper relief and the period of ownership is unbroken.
(5)  Taper relief as it affects PRs is considered at **[21.63]**.
(6)  For the impact of taper relief on the payment of pre-sale dividends, see **[47.36]** and on company sales involving loan notes and consideration see **[47.40]**.
(7)  In the case of EMI share option schemes (see FA 2000 Sch 14 para 57 and see **[9.71]**) taper relief on a disposal is calculated as if the shares had been acquired when the original option was granted. (Contrast the general practice under TCGA 1992 Sch A1 para 13.)
(8)  The provisions on let property introduced in FA 2003 with effect from 6 April 2004 further complicate the apportionment provisions. The result is that commercial lettings qualify for much more favourable capital gains tax relief than inheritance tax business property relief.
(9)  For HMRC's view on certain taper relief aspects of partnerships (particularly in relation to goodwill), see *Tax Bulletin*, October 2002.
(10) The abolition of holdover relief on gifts into settlor interested trusts has made the resetting of the taper relief clock more problematic and in any event such trusts are no longer tax neutral following the 2006 Budget changes.
(11) The taper relief regime should become simpler as time passes because the old pre-April 2000 and April 2002 rules will gradually become redundant.                                                                      **[20.62]**

# 21 CGT—death

*Updated by Emma Chamberlain, BA Hons (Oxon), CTA (Fellow), LRAM, Barrister, 5 Stone Buildings, Lincoln's Inn*

---

| | |
|---|---|
| I | General [21.1] |
| II | Valuation of chargeable assets at death [21.21] |
| III | CGT losses of the deceased [21.41] |
| IV | Sale of deceased's assets by PRs [21.61] |
| V | Losses of the PRs [21.81] |
| VI | Transfers to legatees (TCGA 1992 s 62(4)) [21.101] |
| VII | Disclaimers and variations (TCGA 1992 s 62(6)) [21.121] |

---

## I GENERAL

On death the assets of the deceased of which he was competent to dispose are deemed to be acquired by the personal representatives (PRs) at their market value at death. There is an acquisition without a disposal: an uplift in the value of the assets but no charge to CGT (TCGA 1992 s 62(1)). Hence, death generally wipes out capital gains.

**EXAMPLE 21.1**

Included in T's estate on his death in October 2004 is a rare first edition of *Ulysses* that T had acquired in 1990 for £10,000. It is worth £100,000 at death. The gain of £90,000 is not chargeable on T's death. Instead his PRs acquire the asset at a new base value of £100,000. Note however, that held over gains in a trust are not wiped out on the death of the life tenant although gains on assets accruing over the trust's period of ownership which are subject to a 'qualifying'interest in possession (see post) are generally wiped out on the death of life tenant provided the property then does not revert to the original 'disponer' or settlor (see TCGA 1992 ss 72–73).

**EXAMPLE 21.2**

Suppose T was the life tenant of a pre-22 March 2006 interest in possession trust and the book had been given to the trust by his mother in, say, 1982 with the benefit of a holdover claim. The gain held over was £20,000. On T's death, the held over gain of £20,000 gain becomes chargeable then and only the balance of the gain (£70,000) is wiped out on death (see TCGA 1992 s 74). (Ignore for the moment issues on rebasing discussed in **Chapter 19**.) It may be possible to make another holdover claim to avoid paying tax on the £20,000 if T's death is a chargeable transfer.

Contrast the position if mother had given T the book outright rather than into trust and claimed holdover relief. In these circumstances there is no clawback of the held over gain on T's death.

Note that FA Act 2006 has amended TCGA 1992 ss 72 and 73 so that if the interest in possession arises on or after 22 March 2006 there is no deemed disposal or base cost uplift to market value on the death of the life tenant unless:

(a)    the interest is an immediate post-death interest (IPDI); or
(b)    a transitional serial interest (TSI); or
(c)    a disabled person's interest within s 89B(1)(c) or (d) IHTA; or
(d)    an 18–25 trust where the person dies under 18; or
(e)    a bereaved minor trust.

The effects of all this can be summarised as follows:

### EXAMPLE 21.3

Husband dies leaving his assets on interest in possession trusts for his wife or a child in his will. (Section 31 is excluded if the child is a minor so they take immediate entitlement to income.) In either case this is an IPDI. On the death inheritance tax will be chargeable and capital gains tax base cost uplift is available.

If the wife or child's interest is terminated during her lifetime and the beneficiaries take absolutely this is a PET and a disposal for capital gains tax purposes at market value. No holdover relief is available.

### EXAMPLE 21.4

Husband has an interest in possession on a pre-March 2006 trust. He dies in 2009 and his wife takes an interest in possession. This is a transitional serial interest under IHTA s 49BB and on both husband and wife's deaths there is a base cost uplift for capital gains tax purposes.

### EXAMPLE 21.5

Father dies leaving his estate on a bereaved minor trust for his two children, Amy and John. They are each given entitlement to income before they are 18 and Amy dies at 17. There is no inheritance tax charge (IHTA s 71B(2)(b)) but a base cost uplift for capital gains tax purposes. (TCGA s 72(1B)) (Contrast the pre-Budget position.)

### EXAMPLE 21.6

Mother dies leaving her estate on trust for her only child Mary at 25. Mary is made entitled to the income from the age of 16 with capital at 25. If she dies under 18 then a base cost uplift for capital gains tax purposes is available under s 72(1A)(b) even if the property remains settled. There is no inheritance tax charge. (IHTA s 71E(2)(b))

If Mary dies after reaching 18 but before 25 there is no base cost uplift for capital gains tax purposes but there is an inheritance tax exit charge even though the trust continues. (IHTA s 71F(2))

If the 18–25 trust is extended so that Mary does not take outright at 25 there is an inheritance tax charge then. If she later dies after 25 retaining her interest in possession there is no inheritance tax charge then unless the trust ends (in which case there is an exit charge at maximum 6%) and no capital gains tax uplift since the property is within the relevant property regime.

**EXAMPLE 21.7**

If mother had left her estate on trust for Mary at 30 with Mary taking entitlement to income at 18, note that even though she has an interest in possession it is not qualifying for inheritance tax purposes and this is not an 18–25 trust. On Mary's death there is no inheritance tax payable unless the trust ends (in which case there is an exit charge at 6% maximum) and no base cost uplift for capital gains tax purposes. If the trust does end on Mary's death holdover relief would be available.

**EXAMPLE 21.8**

H sets up a trust during his lifetime giving his adult child an immediate interest in possession. Prior to 22 March 2006 the child took a qualifying interest in possession. Unless the child is disabled this is no longer the case. On the death of the child there is no base cost uplift for capital gains tax purposes but no inheritance tax charge unless the trust ends in which case there is an exit charge but the property is not taxed at 40% as part of the child's estate.

PRs are deemed to have the same residence, ordinary residence and domicile status as the deceased had at the date of death but the remittance basis—which is available to a UK-resident but non-domiciled individual in respect of a disposal of non-UK *situs* assets—does not apply to PRs: see TCGA 1992 s 62(3); s 65(2) and **[27.1]**. Note that PRs are also charged on the gains of non-resident companies apportioned under TCGA 1992 s 13. The exclusion for non-domiciliaries only applies to individuals.

Like trustees, PRs are treated as a single and continuing body of persons and liability is imposed on any PR: HMRC will, therefore, assess UK PRs on the estate's worldwide gains even though those PRs may have no control over foreign assets which are vested in foreign PRs. Any one of them is assessable and chargeable on behalf of the body as a whole.

Because PRs are deemed to take the deceased's residence status, UK personal representatives of a non-resident deceased are outside the charge to capital gains tax. However, this exemption only applies while they are acting in their capacity as PRs; once they become trustees (eg assets are assented to them as trustees) they are taxed as UK residents. **[21.1]–[21.20]**

## II VALUATION OF CHARGEABLE ASSETS AT DEATH

### 1 Basic rule

The assets of the deceased are valued at their open market value at the date of death. If an asset has been valued at that time for the purpose of calculating a charge to inheritance tax that figure will constitute the CGT acquisition cost of the deceased's PRs (TCGA 1992 s 274). When the IHT-related property rules apply the resultant figure may be artificially high (see **[28.70]**). **[21.21]**

## 2   Relevance of s 274

Section 274 refers to the value of an asset being 'ascertained for the purpose of that [ie IHT] tax'. In cases where the deceased's estate does not attract IHT (eg because it is wholly left to a surviving spouse or where the property qualifies for 100% agricultural or business relief) the value will not have been ascertained and so the figure returned on the IHT account will not fix the CGT value (see *Tax Bulletin*, April 1995, p 209). There is no reduction in the CGT cost because business or agricultural property relief reduces the value transferred for IHT purposes.                                    [21.22]

## 3   IHT revaluations

Where property valued on death as 'related property' is sold within three years after the death, or land is sold within four years of death, or listed securities within one year, for less than the death valuation, the PRs may substitute a lower figure for the death valuation and so obtain a reduction in the IHT paid on death (see [30.7]). Not surprisingly, this lower figure will also form the death value for CGT so that the PRs cannot claim CGT loss relief. As an alternative to reducing the estate valuation, the PRs may prefer to claim a CGT loss on the disposal. This would be advantageous where they have made chargeable gains on disposals of other assets in the estate and where no repayment of IHT would result from amending the value of the death estate. Note, though, *Stonor (executors of Dickinson) v IRC* 2001 STC (SCD) 199 where it was held that the executors could not substitute the higher sale price for probate value where the estate was left to charity because no values had been ascertained for inheritance tax purposes. Presumably the executors had wanted to do this in order to avoid a capital gains tax problem on a sale when the assets had increased in value from probate.       [21.23]

## 4   General conclusion

Ideally, for CGT purposes, the PRs want a high value for the assets because of the tax-free uplift, whereas in the case of estates where IHT is payable they want as low a value as possible. Generally since IHT will be levied on the entire value not just on the gain, a low valuation is usually desirable unless the assets in question qualify for business property relief or agricultural property relief.                                    [21.24]–[21.40]

## III   CGT LOSSES OF THE DECEASED

Losses of the deceased in the tax year of his death must be set against gains of that year. Any surplus loss at the end of the year of death can be carried back and set against chargeable gains of the deceased in the three tax years preceding the year of death, taking the most recent year first (TCGA 1992 s 62(2): for the treatment of such losses in calculating taper relief, see [19.63]). Any tax thus reclaimed will, of course, fall into the deceased's estate for IHT purposes! Losses are not set against the gains of any year if and to the extent that they would cause the basic annual capital gains tax exemptions to be wasted.                                    [21.41]–[21.60]

## IV SALE OF DECEASED'S ASSETS BY PRS

### 1 **Rate of tax**

A sale of the deceased's chargeable assets by his PRs is a disposal for CGT purposes and will be subject to CGT on the difference between the sale consideration and the market value at death (less any available taper relief accrued since death). PRs paid tax at a rate of 34% until 6 April 2004. For disposals on or after that date, the rate of tax has been increased to 40%. These rules apply even if the beneficiaries under the will would not themselves be subject to CGT (typically UK charities). In appropriate cases, therefore, assets should be vested in the beneficiary before sale (see **[21.105]**). In December 2003 four discussion papers were issued by the Revenue intended to prompt debate about the tax regime for trusts and estates.

As a result of the responses received, a consultation document was published in August 2004 making more definite proposals. Various changes to the way in which chargeable gains of estates are taxed (a subject which is discussed further at **[21.105]** below) were suggested. In the discussion papers issued in December 2003, one idea had been to stream gains through to beneficiaries where the proceeds of the sale were passed on to them within a reasonable period but this proposal was abandoned as too complex. The second idea was to allow PRs to make an election to be treated as though the asset disposed of had been transferred to the beneficiary immediately before the disposal. This would be very useful if the PRs needed to retain some assets or their net sale proceeds in order to pay inheritance tax liabilities but nevertheless wanted a beneficiary to be able to take advantage of his or her exempt tax status or personal reliefs.

This idea was also abandoned by the Government. Instead the last proposal was that for the year of death and the subsequent two tax years, there would be a capital gains tax rate of 20% up to a capped limit for PRs combined with the individual annual exempt amount. The 20% rate would often be lower than a beneficiary's personal rate of tax but it would not help PRs deal with exempt residuary beneficiaries such as charities (see below). The proposals were thought likely to come into effect from 6 April 2006 but, in fact, while most of the other trust modernisation changes have been implemented in FA 2006 the proposals for deceased estates have been put on hold. **[21.61]**

### 2 **Deductions and allowances**

#### a) *Incidental expenses*

The normal deductions for the incidental expenses of sale are available and PRs can deduct an appropriate proportion of the cost of valuation of the estate for probate purposes (*IRC v Richards' Executors* (1971) and see *Administrators of the Estate of Caton v Couch* (1997)). Although HMRC publish a scale of allowable expenses for the cost of establishing title (see SP 8/94), PRs may claim to deduct more than the 'scale' figure when higher expenses have been incurred. **[21.62]**

b)  *Indexation and taper*

For deaths before April 1998, the PRs enjoyed the benefit of the indexation allowance. As with individuals that relief has now been replaced with taper relief (see **Chapter 20**) and the position for PRs is as follows:

(1)  On the *sale* of an asset business taper will be available provided that it was used for the purposes of a trade carried on by the PRs or by a qualifying company (TCGA 1992 Sch A1 para 5(4)). In the case of disposals before 6 April 2000, shares were business assets if the company was a trading company and the PRs had 25% of the voting rights. With the changes in the definition of business assets in FA 2000 all shareholdings in unlisted trading companies are now business assets (TCGA 1992 Sch A1 para 6(3)).

(2)  On a *disposal by a legatee* for the purposes of calculating his period of ownership he is treated as acquiring the asset at the date of death (TCGA 1992 s 62(4)(b)) thus extending his qualifying holding period. For taper relief purposes, the period of ownership by the PRs can be incorporated within the legatee's period so as to increase the amount of business taper available if the PRs would have qualified for business assets taper relief in their own right. (TCGA 1992 Sch A1 paras 4(5)) and 5(5)). However, the legatee's rate of taper can be adversely affected if the PRs do not qualify for taper relief.                    **[21.63]**

**EXAMPLE 21.9**

In 1999 Marx left 10% of the shares in CP Ltd to the managing director, Engels. The shares are vested in Engels two years after Marx's death and he promptly sells them. Although Engel's ownership period is related back to Marx's death and despite the fact that in his hands the shares would have qualified for business taper, for Engels to get business taper the PRs would have needed to qualify during the two-year administration and before April 2000 because they held less than 25% of the shares in Marx Ltd they did not qualify. From April 2000 the shares were business assets: accordingly this is a case where Marx's gain will need to be apportioned between business and non-business periods of ownership (see further *Example 20.5 for effect of apportionment rules* and *Capital Gains Tax Reform: The FA 1998*—published in November 1998 by the Inland Revenue—at para 2.86).

c)  *Annual exemption*

PRs enjoy an annual exemption from CGT of £8,800 in the tax year of death (for 2006–07) and in each of the two following tax years they receive the annual CGT exemption applicable to individuals. Thereafter they have no exemption, so that if it is intended to sell property in the estate and that sale will result in a chargeable gain, it may be advantageous to vest the asset in the appropriate beneficiary for him to sell. This will ensure that the beneficiary's annual exemption and personal losses (if any) will be available to reduce the chargeable gain. Now that the rate for disposals by PRs is 40% rather than 34% there may be little advantage in their making the disposal unless they have significant losses. The facts of each case have to be examined.  **[21.64]**

**EXAMPLE 21.10**

(1)  Dougall died in May 2001. In June 2005 a valuable Ming vase then worth £100,000 (probate value in 2001 £40,000) is to be sold. Administration of the

estate has not been completed. The proceeds of sale will be split equally between Dougall's four children. The following possibilities should be considered:

(a)  the PRs could first appropriate the vase to the four children who could then sell it taking advantage of four CGT annual exemptions (£34,000 in all being £8,500 each in 2005–06). The resultant gain (say £26,000) is attributed equally (£6,500 per child) and taxed at the appropriate rate on the child which may be less than 40% if they are not higher rate taxpayers. *Accordingly, maximum total tax bill will be £10,400;* or

(b)  the PRs could themselves sell the vase and realise gains of £60,000. No annual exemption will be available and the rate of CGT will be 40%. *Accordingly, the maximum tax bill will be £24,000.*

(2)  Continuing *Example 21.1*, if the PRs sell the book in March 2005 for £130,000, they have made a gross gain of £30,000 from which they can deduct their annual exemption for 2005–06 of £8,500 (if unused), the incidental expenses of sale and a proportionate part of the cost of valuing the estate for probate in November 2003. No taper relief will be available.

(3)  Different issues arise when an asset is to be sold and the residuary beneficiary who will be entitled to all or the bulk of the proceeds of sale is not subject to CGT (eg because they are a UK charity or non-UK-resident): see **[21.105]** and **[53.41]**.

## 3   The principal private residence

Where PRs dispose of a private dwelling house which, both before and after the death, was occupied by a person who is entitled on death to the whole, or substantially the whole, of the proceeds of sale from the house, either absolutely or for life, PRs were by concession given the benefit of the private residence exemption from CGT (ESC D5 and for principal private residence exemption, see **Chapter 23**). The concession addressed the sort of situation where a house-owner died and his widow and perhaps some children occupied the house. 'Substantially the whole' meant 75% of the proceeds. The concession did not cover disposals of part of the house or an interest in the house or grounds. Nor did it help the child who moved into the house after the death of the mother.

FA 2004 now gives statutory force to the ESC and ensures that the position for PRs is more consistent with the capital gains tax exemption available to trustees under TCGA 1992 s 225. Schedule 22 provides that relief is available if the people who occupied the house immediately before and after the death are together entitled to at least 75% of the net proceeds of disposal. Disposals of part are covered.                                                    **[21.65]–[21.80]**

### EXAMPLE 21.11

Bill and his brother Ben live in Bill's house. On his death Bill leaves the house to Ben who goes on living in it. The property has to be sold by the PRs to pay for Bill's funeral. Any gain will be exempt.

## V   LOSSES OF THE PRS

Losses made by the PRs on disposals of chargeable assets during administration can be set off against chargeable gains on other sales made by them. Any surplus losses at the end of the administration period cannot be transferred to beneficiaries (*contrast* losses made by trustees on a deemed disposal under TCGA 1992 s 71 which can in certain limited circumstances be passed to a beneficiary when the trust ends: **[25.45]**). Accordingly, when PRs anticipate that a loss will not be relieved, they may prefer to transfer the loss-making asset to the relevant beneficiary so that he can sell it and obtain the loss relief. If PRs do realise losses then they should ensure that they sell an asset that shows a gain before the administration of the estate is complete in order to fully utilise the loss relief. Even if the asset has not been formally assented to a beneficiary, if the administration of the estate is complete and residue ascertained, HMRC may argue that the loss is not allowable against the gain realised later on the basis that the disposal is being done by the PRs as bare trustees for the beneficiaries and at their direction. See *HMRC Capital Gains Manual* 30730.                                   **[21.81]–[21.100]**

## VI   TRANSFERS TO LEGATEES (TCGA 1992 s 62(4))

### 1   Basic rule

On the transfer of an asset to a legatee, the PRs make neither a gain nor loss for CGT purposes and the legatee acquires the asset at the PRs' base value together with the expenses of transferring the asset to him. The base cost will in appropriate cases be a fraction of the probate value: for instance, if a 60% shareholding (valued at death as a majority holding) was split between the deceased's four sons each would receive a 15% holding with a base cost equal to one-quarter of the probate valuation of the 60% holding.        **[21.101]**

#### EXAMPLE 21.12

The PRs transfer the book (see *Example 21.1*) to the legatee (L) under the will in March 2006 when it is worth £130,000. The cost of valuing the book as a part of the whole estate in November 2005 was £1,000 and the PRs incurred incidental expenses involved in the transfer of the book in March 2006 of £150. L sells the book in July 2006 for £140,000. On the transfer by the PRs to L, no chargeable gain accrues to the PRs and L's base cost is:

|  | £ |
|---|---|
| Market value at death | 100,000 |
| Valuation cost | 1,000 |
| Expenses of transfer | 150 |
| Base cost of L | £101,150 |

When L sells the book in July 2006 for £140,000 he is charged to CGT on his gain that is £38,850 (£140,000 – £101,150) as reduced by any allowable expenditure that he has incurred or available annual CGT exemption. (No taper relief will be available given that the PRs and L have not together owned the book for three years.)

### 2   Who is a legatee?

A legatee is defined in TCGA 1992 s 64(2) as any person taking under a testamentary disposition or on intestacy or partial intestacy, whether beneficially or as a trustee. This definition covers only property passing under the will or on an intestacy to a beneficiary so that to the extent that a beneficiary contracts with the PRs to purchase a particular asset or to obtain a greater share in an asset he is not taking that asset *qua* legatee. In *CG Manual* 30772 HMRC cite *Passant v Jackson* (1986) as authority for the view that, where a residuary legatee pays some balancing sum to the executors in order to acquire a property in the deceased's estate, he does not acquire the asset *qua* legatee. However, in the author's opinion, *Passant* is not authority for this view. In that case, a residuary legatee wished to retain a property worth more than the net value of the estate. He paid the executors a balancing payment to cover the shortfall and they executed an assent in his favour. On a subsequent disposal, the legatee sought to include both the probate value of the property and the sum he paid to the executors in his acquisition cost but this claim was rejected. However, the court said nothing to suggest that on the original acquisition by him from the executors he did not acquire *qua* legatee. He was not allowed to include the cash sum he paid the executors to reduce the overall gain on the later sale, but that is a very different point. The HMRC Manual seems incorrect on this point: see CG30772.

A *donatio mortis causa* is treated for these purposes as a testamentary disposition and not as a gift, so that the donee acquires the asset at its market value on the donor's death and the donor is not treated as having made a chargeable gain. **[21.102]**

## 3  Taking under a will trust

Difficult questions may arise when a person receives assets under a trust created by will or under the intestacy rules. Does he receive them as a legatee (in which case there is no charge to CGT) or as a beneficiary absolutely entitled as against the trustee, in which case there is a deemed disposal under TCGA 1992 s 71 which may be chargeable if the property has increased in value (see **Chapter 25**)? The answer depends upon the status of the PRs (have they turned into trustees at the relevant time?) and the terms of the will (see *Cochrane's Executors v IRC* (1974) and *IRC v Matthew's Executors* (1984)).

During the course of administration PRs are the sole owners of the deceased's assets, albeit in a fiduciary capacity (*Stamp Duties Comr (Queensland) v Livingston* (1965)) so that there is no trust of particular assets at that time (although the beneficiaries will own a *chose in action*). Accordingly, if, before the completion of administration or the vesting of assets in themselves as trustees (whichever first occurs), the property ceases to be settled for CGT purposes, when it is transferred to the relevant beneficiary he will take *qua* legatee (see *Example 21.13(2)* below and *Marshall v Kerr* (1994) at **[21.124]**). **[21.103]**

**EXAMPLE 21.13**

(1)  T dies leaving his house to executors on trust for his three children all of whom are over 18, in equal shares absolutely. Whether the children receive the assets before the administration is completed or after the executors have assented to themselves as trustees does not matter since they take as legatees.

For CGT purposes joint ownership does not result in the property being settled (TCGA 1992 s 60: see further **Chapter 25**).

(2)    T dies in 2006 leaving his property to executors on trust for his widow for life and then for his three children absolutely, all of whom are over 18. If the widow dies *before the executors become trustees*, any distributions to the children will be received by them as legatees since, for CGT purposes, the trust ended on the widow's death. If, however, the widow dies *after* the executors have become trustees, the property is settled, so that the children receive assets as persons absolutely entitled as against the trustees with a consequent deemed disposal under TCGA 1992 s 71 (there will be no charge in this case because the event leading to their entitlement was the death of the life tenant: contrast the position if the interest had terminated *inter vivos*—see **Chapter 25**).

(3)    Z leaves his residuary estate on discretionary trusts. Within two years of his death the assets are distributed amongst his children so that:

(a)    for IHT purposes, IHTA 1984 s 144 ensures that the distributions are 'read back' into Z's will (see **[30.145]**);

(b)    although holdover relief under TCGA 1992 s 260 will not be available (see **[24.61]**), provided that the children become entitled during the administration period and the assets are not vested in the trustees first, HMRC accept that the children will take *qua* legatees. Furthermore HMRC's view is that such appointment is not a disposal of a chose in action of the legatee (which would be disastrous since such chose would have a nil base cost). *See Taxation Practitioner,* September 1995, p 23.

## 4    The deceased's main residence

When the former matrimonial home of the deceased passes to his surviving spouse there is an uplift in the base value of the property on death in the usual way. On a subsequent disposal by that spouse, any gain since death will be exempt from CGT if the house has been occupied as that spouse's main residence. Even if it has not, by virtue of TCGA 1992 s 222(7), the deceased's period of ownership is deemed to be that of the surviving spouse in deciding what proportion of the gain (if any) is chargeable (see **[23.82]**).    **[21.104]**

**EXAMPLE 21.14**

T bought a house in 1996 for £50,000. It was his main residence until his death in 2000 when it was worth £150,000. His wife (W) whom he married just before his death never lived there with him, but became entitled to the house on his intestacy. T's administrators transferred the house to W in 2001. She occupied it as her main residence since T's death until 2002 and then went abroad until 2006 when she returned and sold the house for £250,000.

For the purpose of the main residence exemption, W can claim that she has occupied the house as her main residence for nine out of the ten years that it has been in the ownership of herself or T, ie:

| | |
|---|---|
| 1996–2000 (4 years) | Occupied by T as his main residence |
| 2000–02 (2 years) | Occupation by W. |
| 2002–2006 (4 years) | Abroad from 2002 but last three years of ownership disregarded (TCGA 1992 s 223(1)) |

W is, therefore, charged on a proportion of the gain:

(1)  Sale consideration (£250,000) – base cost (£150,000) = £100,000 (assuming no other allowable expenses).
(2)  Fraction chargeable: £100,000 × ¹⁄₁₀ = £10,000.

Were it not for s 222(7), she would be charged on a larger proportion of the gain, ie:

$$£100,000 \times \frac{1}{6 \text{ (length of her ownership)}} = £16,667$$

Of course if the husband had not occupied it during his period of ownership then s 222(7) could prove disadvantageous to the wife because then her period of ownership would be 10 years of which only half would qualify for principal private residence relief.

## 5  Exempt legatees

Assume that the estate includes land which is showing a substantial gain over probate value and which is to be sold. The relevant beneficiary is a UK charity. If the PRs sell the land in the course of the administration, tax at a rate of 40% will be payable: by contrast if the land is assented to the charity which sells it no CGT will be payable (see TCGA 1992 s 256). In cases where the estate is to be divided amongst several charities the PRs may appropriate the assets in partial satisfaction of the charities' entitlement and hold it as bare trustees for those charities. The sale will then be taxed on the basis that it was by the charities so that the s 256 exemption will apply (for the CGT treatment of bare trusts, see **[25.3]**). Note also the following:

(1)  similar considerations apply if the legatee is non-UK-resident and so outside the CGT net;
(2)  what if the PRs need part of the sale proceeds (eg to pay administration costs). Consider vesting the asset in the charity (eg by declaration of trust) but subject to a lien in favour of the PRs. Does this mean the sale proceeds are not entirely applied for charitable purposes so that the capital gains tax exemption under s 256 is denied? It is suggested that the PRs may want to ensure that, where the estate comprises a variety of assets, some are advanced separately to the charities and only these are made subject to the lien with the balance being taken by the charities free of any lien. That at least minimises the risk.

If the assets are vested in the charity, HMRC require evidence that the charity has approved the sale and complied with the provisions of the Charities Act 1993.

There are other options but none are straightforward and unfortunately HMRC appear to have abandoned the idea of allowing PRs to elect for disposals to be taxed as if made by legatees.  **[21.105]–[21.120]**

## VII  DISCLAIMERS AND VARIATIONS (TCGA 1992 s 62(6))

## 1  Basic rule

Subject to conditions, which are the same as for IHT (see **[30.153]**), any variation of the deceased's will or of the intestacy rules, or any disclaimer, made in both cases within two years of the deceased's death may be treated:

(1)    as if it were not a disposal (s 62(6)(a)); and
(2)    as if it had been effected by the deceased or, in the case of a disclaimer, as if the disclaimed benefit had never been conferred (s 62(6)(b)).

As with inheritance tax, the instrument must be made in writing within two years of the death and the variation (or disclaimer) must not be made for consideration in money or money's worth other than consideration consisting of the making of a variation or disclaimer in respect of another of the dispositions. The variation can be made regardless of whether the administration of the estate is complete or whether the property has already been distributed in accordance with the original disposition. The same property cannot be subject to more than one variation.                                      **[21.121]**

### EXAMPLE 21.15

A dies leaving a house Blackacre to B and a house Whiteacre to C. B would rather have Whiteacre and C would rather have Blackacre. They enter into a deed of variation such that A is deemed to have left Whiteacre to B and Blackacre to C. Although each one does the variation in consideration of the other beneficiary also varying his interest, this does not prevent reading back.

### EXAMPLE 21.16

Facts as in *Example 21.1.* L is entitled under T's will to the book worth £100,000. Within two years of T's death L varies the will so that the book (now worth £140,000) passes to his brother B. Provided that the appropriate statement for reading back (formerly election) is made (see **[21.122]**) this will be treated as if T's will had provided for the book to pass to B. Accordingly, B acquires the asset at its market value at death (£100,000) as legatee plus any additional expenses of the PRs.

## 2    'Reading back' (TCGA 1992 s 62(7) as amended)

### a)    *The 'reading back' decision*

Prior to 1 August 2002 the above treatment did not apply to a variation unless the person or persons making the instrument so elected within six months of the instrument (or such longer period as the Board may allow). From that date the requirement for a separate election was abolished: if 'reading back' is desired the instrument of variation itself must now so provide.      **[21.122]**

### b)    *To read back or not*

In many cases, it will be desirable that the variation is read back for both CGT and IHT purposes. This is not necessary, however, since the decisions are independent of each other with the result that a taxpayer may decide to read back for IHT purposes without doing so for CGT and *vice versa.* Careful thought should be given to this problem. Consider the following:      **[21.123]**

### EXAMPLE 21.17

(1)    A will leaves quoted shares worth £100,000 to the testator's daughter. She transfers the shares within two years to her mother (the testator's surviving spouse). The shares are then worth £106,000.

*For IHT* reading back will be desirable as the result will be to reduce the testator's chargeable estate at death by £100,000 since the shares are now an exempt transfer to a surviving spouse.

*For CGT* the election to read the disposal back should *not* be made since, if the daughter makes a chargeable disposal, her gain will be £106,000 – £100,000 = £6,000 which will be more than covered by her annual CGT exemption. Her mother will then acquire the shares at the higher base cost of £106,000.

(2) A will leaves quoted shares worth £100,000 to the testator's surviving spouse. After they have risen in value to £140,000 she decides (within the permitted time limit) to vary the will in favour of her daughter.

*For IHT* it is debatable whether the disposition should be read back. If it is, £100,000 will constitute a chargeable death transfer so that, assuming that the nil rate band has already been exhausted, tax will be charged at 40%. If it is not, the widow will make a lifetime gift of £140,000 that, if she survives by seven years, will be free of all tax. On the other hand, if it is likely that she will only survive her husband by a few weeks, then it will be necessary to consider whether it is better for £100,000 to be taxed as part of her dead husband's estate or for £140,000 to be taxed on her death.

*For CGT* the disposal should be read back into the will since otherwise there will be a chargeable gain of £140,000 – £100,000 = £40,000. Generally reading back is desirable for capital gains tax purposes when the administration of the estate is not completed in order to avoid certain 'chose in action' problems. See *HMRC Capital Gains Manual* 31900 onwards for a somewhat puzzling interpretation of the position.

## 3 Marshall v Kerr (1994)

### a) *The issue*

The testator died in 1977 domiciled in Jersey and Mrs Kerr (UK-resident and domiciled) became entitled to one half of the residuary estate. By a deed of family arrangement executed in January 1978 made before the administration of the estate had been completed, her half share was to be retained by the PRs (a Jersey resident company) as trustees for, *inter alia*, Mrs Kerr. In due course gains were realised by those trustees and capital advanced to Mrs Kerr. If the settlement had been created by Mrs Kerr then the rules of TCGA 1992 s 87 applied and capital payments made to her attracted a CGT charge (see chapter 27). Given that she had transferred property to trustees, on general principles she would be treated as the settlor of that trust: but was this conclusion displaced by the deeming provision in s 62(6) whereby if a variation is made within two years of death—provided that the appropriate election is made—it takes effect 'as if the variation had been effected by the deceased'? **[21.124]**

The Inland Revenue successfully argued in the House of Lords that Mrs Kerr rather than the deceased was the settlor for capital gains tax purposes. **[21.125]**

#### EXAMPLE 21.18

Boris, domiciled in France, leaves his villa in Tuscany and moneys in his Swiss bank account to his son Gaspard, UK-resident and domiciled. By a variation of the terms of his will made within two years of Boris' death, the property is settled on discretionary trusts where the trustees are resident in Jersey for the benefit of Gaspard and his family.

*For IHT* purposes, reading back ensures that the settlement is of excluded property. Hence on Gaspard's death the trust is not subject to UK tax and there is no ten-year anniversary or exit charge provided that no UK situs assets are held on those dates (see [35.5]).

*For CGT* purposes, the settlement has been created by Gaspard, a UK-resident domiciliary, so that the charging provisions in TCGA 1992 s 86 ff (see **Chapter 27**) will apply given that he and other defined persons can benefit from the trust.

For *income tax* purposes, the settlement has been created by Gaspard and as he and his wife can benefit all trust income will be taxed on him wherever the trustees are resident or the assets are sited.

Note that there is no need for the Trustees to be non-resident to obtain continuing favourable inheritance tax treatment—the requirements for excluded property for inheritance tax purposes are simply that Boris the settlor must not be UK domiciled or deemed domiciled at his death (when he is treated as establishing the trust) and that the assets are non-UK situs. Hence for capital gains tax reasons it may be easier to have UK-resident trustees in order to avoid any offshore tax implications although Gaspard will still be subject to capital gains tax on any trust gains and to income tax on trust income, this time under TCGA 1992 s 77 and ITTOIA 2005 s 625 respectively.

The case does not affect the IHT treatment of instruments of variation and disclaimer: see RI 101 (February 1995).

In any event the whole question of who is the settlor has now been put on a statutory footing. Schedule 12 of the Finance Act 2006 introduces statutory provisions on identification of the settlor where there is a variation of a will or intestacy – see s 68C TCGA 1992 as amended. If property becomes settled property as a result of the variation, the person making the variation is treated as the settlor. If property was already settled under the will or intestacy and then becomes comprised in another trust as a result of the variation, the deceased person, not the person making the variation, is treated as the settlor for capital gains tax purposes. This is presumably on the basis that if several persons act to vary their entitlements under a will trust and settle the assets in a new trust, it would be difficult to establish who is the settlor. The position is unclear where a variation merely amends or varies a will trust rather than transferring the property to a new settlement or where the person making the variation, eg the life tenant, simply varies their own interest under the settlement. Does the settled property then become comprised in a new trust? Is the life tenant the settlor of the new trust? Suppose the life tenant assigns her interest to a discretionary trust under which income is rolled up. If the trustees then make gains, it would appear that she is not taxed on those gains even though she may be a beneficiary under the trust.

The drafting is in so-called plain English and, as frequently seems to be the case, leaves something to be desired in terms of clarity.          [21.126]

# 22 CGT—exemptions and reliefs

*Written (in part) and updated by Natalie Lee, Barrister, Senior Lecturer in Law, University of Southampton*

In many cases a gain on the disposal of an asset will not be chargeable either because the gain itself is exempt or because the asset is not chargeable. Even if a gain is chargeable, there are various reliefs whereby the tax can be minimised or deferred indefinitely. As already noted at [**19.87**], there is an annual exemption for an individual whose gains do not exceed £8,800 (for 2006–07) in the tax year; trustees are generally entitled to half of the exemption available to individuals: ie £4,400 unless they are trustees of settlements for the disabled when they enjoy the same exempt amount as individuals (see [**19.89**]). The principal private residence relief is considered in **Chapter 23**.                                                      [**22.1**]

## I  MISCELLANEOUS EXEMPTIONS

*Exempt assets* Certain assets are not chargeable to CGT. The taxpayer, therefore, realises no chargeable gain or, often more significantly, no allowable loss on their disposal.

Non-chargeable assets include sterling (TCGA 1992 s 21), National Savings Certificates, Premium Bonds and Save As You Earn deposits (s 121), and private motor vehicles (s 263). Gains and losses arising on the disposal of investments in a Personal Equity Plan and an Individual Savings Account are disregarded.                                                            [**22.2**]

*Exempt gains* The following gains are exempt from CGT:
(1)  damages for personal injuries and betting winnings (s 51 and see ESC D33);
(2)  gains on the disposal of decorations for valour unless the decoration was acquired for money or money's worth (s 268);
(3)  gains on the disposal of foreign currency obtained for private use (s 269). A foreign currency bank account is a chargeable asset (a debt) unless the sum in that account was obtained for the personal expenditure of an individual or his family outside the UK (s 252). Where several accounts in a particular foreign currency are owned by the same

taxpayer he may treat them as one account so that direct transfers between the accounts will not be chargeable disposals (SP 10/84);

(4)   gains on the disposal of gilt-edged securities (s 115): the exemption also applies to futures and options in these instruments;

(5)   gains on the disposal of ordinary shares in a venture capital trust are exempt from CGT (see **Chapter 15**). There is also a qualified exemption for shares acquired under the complementary Enterprise Investment Scheme (EIS) (see **Chapter 15**). See TCGA 1992 ss 150A, 150B;

(6)   the disposal of pension rights, annuity rights and annual payments will not generally give rise to a chargeable gain (s 237);

(7)   any gain on the disposal of a life policy, a deferred annuity policy, or any rights under such policies, unless the disposal is by someone other than the original beneficial owner and *that person* acquired the interest or right for money or money's worth (s 210 and see *Taxation*, 17 November 1994, p 153); and

(8)   gains are exempt if made by such bodies as authorised unit trusts and investment trusts (s 100); and charities, provided that the gain is applied for charitable purposes (s 256).                                        **[22.3]**

*Charities* Disposals to charities and to certain national institutions are treated as made on a no gain/no loss basis (s 257 and see **[53.89]**).                **[22.4]**

*Heritage property and woodlands* The exemptions for heritage property are basically the same as for IHT (see **Chapter 31**).

*First,* where property of national interest is given (or sold by private treaty) to a non-profit making body (including a charity or other national institution mentioned in s 256) any gain will be exempt from CGT (s 258(2)) provided that the Treasury so directs (see IHTA 1984 ss 23, 25). *Secondly,* any gain on a disposal of such property may be conditionally exempt from CGT in the same way as for IHT (s 258(3)(4): see IHTA 1984 ss 30, 31). The changes made to strengthen the conditions for the IHT exemption for undertakings given on or after 31 July 1998 apply equally where relief from CGT is sought (see **[31.79]**). *Thirdly,* the gain on any property that is accepted by the Treasury in satisfaction of IHT is exempt from CGT (s 258(2)(b)).

Consideration received for a disposal of trees (or saleable underwood) is excluded from any CGT computation provided that the disposer is the occupier who manages the woodlands on a commercial basis with a view to profit (s 113).                                                         **[22.5]–[22.20]**

## II   CHATTELS

### 1   Chattels that are wasting assets

A gain on the disposal of a chattel that is a wasting asset is generally exempt from CGT, the rationale being that since the taxpayer has enjoyed the use of the chattel, he should not be entitled to claim any loss in respect of it. A wasting asset is one with a predictable useful life of 50 years or less and includes yachts, caravans, washing machines, animals and all plant and machinery, the latter term to include, in the Revenue's view, such assets as antique clocks and watches, certain vintage cars and (generally) shotguns (see TCGA 1992 s 44; *Tax Bulletin,* October 1994 and February 2000; and [**19.45**]).                                                                                    [**22.21**]

## 2   Non-wasting chattels

In the case of non-wasting chattels (eg items of jewellery, fine wine, antiques etc), if the disposal consideration is £6,000 or less, any gain is exempt and so does not enter the computation of the taxpayer's total gains in a tax year, leaving the annual exemption to be set against other gains (TCGA 1992 s 262(1)). CGT is as a result easier and less costly to administer as there is no need to calculate gains and losses on assets of relatively low value. Insofar as the disposal consideration exceeds £6,000, the chargeable gain is limited to 5/3 of the excess of that consideration over £6,000.

   Where a loss is made on the disposal of a chattel and the disposal consideration is *less than* £6,000, the sum of £6,000 is substituted for that consideration so as to limit a claim for loss relief.                                [**22.22**]

### EXAMPLE 22.1

(1)   A bought a necklace for £4,600 and later sold it for £7,200 so making a total gain of £2,600. The chargeable gain is reduced to 5/3 × £1,200 (£7,200 − £6,000) = £2,000.

(2)   A bought a brooch for £8,000 and sold it for £4,600 so making an actual loss of £3,400. He is deemed to have sold it for £6,000 so that his allowable loss is restricted to £2,000 (£8,000 − £6,000).

   *Note:* For the purpose of this example, incidental costs of disposal, the indexation allowance and taper relief have been ignored: they should, of course, be taken into account in computing the chargeable gain which is subject to reduction.

## 3   Chattels comprising a set

The taxpayer cannot dispose of a set of articles to the same person by a series of separate transactions so as to take advantage of the £6,000 exemption on each disposal. Whether the disposals are to the same person or to connected persons (albeit on different occasions) they are regarded as a single transaction (see also TCGA 1992 s 19 and [**19.24**]). The meaning of 'a set' is not always obvious: a valuable collection of lead toy soldiers, for instance, is arguably not a set. Whether bottles of fine wine amount to a set would appear to be a question of fact depending on (a) whether the bottles are 'similar and complementary', requiring them to have been produced from the same vineyard in the same vintage year; and (b) whether the bottles are of greater worth when sold collectively than when sold individually (*Tax Bulletin,* August 1999 and February 2000, which considers the treatment of a pair of shotguns). More generally, the wording of s 262(4) suggests that at least three articles are required for a set: the Revenue, however, consider (incorrectly it is felt) that two items can comprise a set (see CG 76632).   [**22.23**]–[**22.40**]

### EXAMPLE 22.2

A owns three Rousseau paintings which, as a set, have a market value of £30,000. He paid £4,000 for each of the paintings that individually are now worth £6,000.

He sells all three paintings at different times to his sister B for £6,000 each. He thereby appears to fall within the chattel exemption on each disposal. The Revenue can, however, treat the three disposals as a single disposal of an asset worth £30,000 with a base value of £12,000 so that A has made a gain of £18,000.

## III   DEBTS

### 1   What is a debt?

A debt is a chargeable asset (TCGA 1992 s 21). It is not defined and bears the common law meaning of 'a sum payable in respect of a liquidated money demand recoverable by action' (*Rawley v Rawley* (1876)). It can include a right to receive a sum of money that is not yet ascertained (*O'Driscoll v Manchester Insurance Committee* (1915)) or a contingent right to receive a definite sum (*Mortimore v IRC* (1864)). However, for the purposes of CGT, it cannot include a right to receive an uncertain sum at an unascertained date; there must be a liability, either present or contingent, to pay a sum which is ascertained or capable of being ascertained at the time of disposal (*Marren v Ingles* (1980): see [19.26]).                                         [22.41]

### EXAMPLE 22.3

Barry agrees to sell his Ming vase to Bruce for £15,000 plus one half of any profits that Bruce realises if he resells the vase in the next ten years. The disposal consideration received for the vase is £15,000 plus the value of a *chose in action*. As that *chose* is both contingent (on resale occurring) and for an unascertained sum (half of any profits) it is not a debt. The *chose in action* is a separate asset and a CGT charge may arise on its disposal (see [19.26] and note that if that disposal results in a loss, relief may be available against gains of earlier years: see TCGA 1992 s 279A–D inserted by FA 2003).

### 2   The general principle

A disposal of a debt by the original creditor, his personal representatives or legatee is exempt from CGT unless it is a debt on a security (see [21.44]). 'Disposal' includes repayment of the debt (TCGA 1992 s 251). Since a contractual debt will normally give a creditor merely the right to repayment of the sum lent, together with interest, the disposal of a debt will rarely generate a gain and the aim of s 251 is to exclude the more likely claim for loss relief, particularly where the debt is never repaid. This provision only applies to the original creditor so that an assignee of a debt can claim an allowable loss if the debtor defaults, unless the assignee and the creditor are connected persons (s 251(4)).

If the debt is satisfied by a transfer of property, that property is acquired by the creditor at its market value. Since this could operate harshly for an original creditor who can claim no allowable loss, s 251(3) provides that on a subsequent disposal of the property, its base value is taken as the value of the debt.                                                                            [22.42]

**EXAMPLE 22.4**

A owes B £30,000 and in full satisfaction of the debt he gives B a painting worth £22,000. B does not have an allowable loss of £8,000. However, if B later sells the painting for £40,000 he is taxed on a gain of £10,000 only (£40,000 − £30,000).

## 3   Loans to traders

The harshness of TCGA 1992 s 251 is mitigated by s 253, allowing original creditors to claim loss relief in respect of a qualifying loan. The loan must have become irrecoverable and the creditor must not have assigned his rights. Creditor and debtor must not be married to each other nor be companies in the same group. A 'qualifying loan' must be used by a UK-resident borrower *wholly for the purpose of a trade* (not being moneylending) carried on by him and the debt must not be 'on a security'. The relief is extended to include a loss arising from the guaranteeing of a 'qualifying loan' (see s 253(4) and *Leisureking Ltd v Cushing* (1993)).                    **[22.43]**

## 4   Debt on a security

The legislation distinguishes between debts that can normally only decrease in value and those which may be disposed of at a profit. It, therefore, provides that a 'debt on a security' is chargeable to CGT even in the hands of the original creditor (TCGA 1992 s 251).

The term 'debt on a security' lacks both statutory and satisfactory judicial interpretation despite a number of cases (for instance, *Cleveleys Investment Trust Co v IRC* (1971); *Aberdeen Construction Group Ltd v IRC* (1978); *W T Ramsay Ltd v IRC* (1981)). It has a limited and technical meaning and '[it] is not a synonym for a secured debt' *per* Lord Wilberforce in *Aberdeen Construction Group Ltd v IRC* above. The word 'security' is defined in TCGA 1992 s 132(3) as including 'any loan stock or similar security whether of the Government of the UK or elsewhere, or of any company, and whether secured or unsecured'. Despite the word '*including*' the Revenue has stated that it regards the definition as exhaustive (see CCAB June 1969 although this is not referred to in CG 53421 which refers to this definition as being 'of limited use').

In *Taylor Clark International Ltd v Lewis* (1998) Robert Walker J, whose views were upheld by the Court of Appeal, concluded that the basic requirements for a debt on security were:
(1)   the debt had to be capable of being assigned;
(2)   it had to carry interest;
(3)   to have a structure of permanence; and
(4)   to provide proprietary security.

Relief was denied in this case which involved an interest-bearing loan with security from a parent company to its subsidiary. The loan was essentially impermanent and not intended to be marketable or dealt in even though it was assignable. However, the fact that it was in a foreign currency was not significant.

For the Revenue's views on the meaning of a 'debt on security', see CG 53425 and note that for taper relief purposes shares include securities, see TCGA 1992 Sch A1 para 22(1) and see **[47.40]**.

With the introduction of a new regime for the taxation of company loan relationships most debt held by companies has been removed from the capital gains charge: instead profits and losses on such debt together with interest are charged or allowed as income.                                    **[22.44]**

## 5  Qualifying corporate bonds

Gains on the disposal of a 'qualifying corporate bond' (which includes most company debentures) are exempt from CGT under TCGA 1992 s 117 (see **[41.92]**).                                                                 **[22.45]–[22.70]**

## IV  BUSINESS RELIEFS

### 1  The problems and the taxes

A number of CGT reliefs relate to businesses both incorporated and unincorporated. Their aim is to enable businesses to be carried on and transferred without being threatened by taxation. This chapter is concerned only with CGT reliefs: bear in mind a disposal of a business will normally involve other taxes.

The disposal may be by way of gift (including death) or by sale. If by way of *gift*, the relevant taxes will be CGT, income tax and IHT. For CGT, hold-over relief under TCGA 1992 s 165 (as amended) may be available on a lifetime gift; on a death, there will be no CGT (see Chapter 19). Where the transfer is a *sale*, income tax and CGT may apply.

The CGT business reliefs may apply to a disposal of:
(1)   a sole trade/profession;
(2)   a part of a trade/profession (eg a partnership share);
(3)   shares in a company; and
(4)   assets used by a company or partnership in which the owner of the assets either owns shares or is a partner.

In a number of cases relief is given by a deferment of the CGT charge and this is usually done by deducting the otherwise chargeable gain from the acquisition cost of a new or replacement asset (roll-over or hold-over relief). For the Revenue's views on the order of reliefs, see CG 60210. Careful note should be taken of the impact on taper relief when roll-over or hold-over relief applies.                                                              **[22.71]**

## 2  Roll-over (replacement of business assets) (TCGA 1992 ss 152–159)

#### a)  *Basic conditions for relief*

Where certain assets of a business are sold and the proceeds of sale wholly reinvested in acquiring a 'new' asset to be used in a business, the taxpayer can elect to roll over the gain and deduct it from the acquisition cost of the new asset. Tax is, therefore, postponed until that asset is sold and no replacement qualifying asset purchased. The new asset must be bought within one year *before* or three years *after* the disposal of the old one, and once it is acquired, it must 'on the acquisition' be taken into use for the purposes of the taxpayer's trade. The Revenue has the power to extend this time limit and, whilst the exercise of the power can be challenged by judicial review, the Commissioners cannot themselves exercise it (*Steibelt v Paling* (1999)). This point was reiterated in *R (on the application of Barnett) v IRC* (2004), in which case, it was made clear that, although the Board was under a duty to take into account relevant findings by the Commissioners, the issue of whether the taxpayer had been prevented from re-investing in further property by circumstances beyond his control was a question for the Revenue and it was entitled to conclude that such circumstances did not exist. A gap between the time of acquisition and the time when it is used in the trade will mean that the exemption will not be available (see *Campbell Connelly Co Ltd v Barnett* (1993) and *Milton v Chivers* (1996) holding that while 'on the acquisition' did not imply immediacy, it did exclude dilatoriness: see also *Joseph Carter & Sons v Baird* (1999)).                    **[22.72]**

**EXAMPLE 22.5**

A makes a gain of £50,000 on the sale of factory 1, but he immediately buys factory 2 for £120,000. He can roll the gain of £50,000 into the purchase price of factory 2 thereby reducing it to £70,000 (actual cost £120,000 minus rolled-over gain of £50,000). Note that the gain that is rolled over takes no account of any taper relief that would have been available to A. This important matter is considered further at **[21.79]**.

b)  *Prior acquisitions of replacement assets*

It will be appreciated that the 'new' asset can be acquired before the disposal of the old asset—the Revenue accepts that the requirements are met if 'the old assets, or the proceeds of the old assets, are part of the resources available to the taxpayer when the new assets are acquired'. An important limitation on the relief was, however, confirmed by the Court of Appeal in *Watton v Tippett* (1997) where the taxpayer, having purchased certain freehold land and buildings (unit 1) for a single unapportioned consideration, within 12 months of that purchase sold part of the same land and buildings (unit 1A) and claimed to roll over the gain made on that disposal into the land and buildings retained by him (unit 1B). Rejecting this claim the court held that it was critical to identify the asset acquired and disposed of and unit 1B had not been acquired as such. The position would have been different if two separate properties had been purchased albeit for a single unapportioned consideration given that this could be apportioned under TCGA 1992 s 52(4).                    **[22.73]**

**EXAMPLE 22.6**

If A acquires factory 1 (as in the above example), but almost immediately sells part of it, he cannot roll any gain over into the acquisition cost of the remainder of the factory retained by him. It is a part disposal of a single asset; the consideration for that single asset cannot, according to *Watton v Tippett* (above), be apportioned.

If A acquires two adjacent factories (1 and 2) at the same time but under separate contracts, and immediately sells factory 2, A can roll over any gain into the acquisition cost of factory 1: this is *not* a part disposal of a single asset, but rather a disposal of a severable part of the taxpayer's assets, with separate consideration attributable to the 'old' asset (factory 2) and 'other' assets (factory 1). *Note* that s 152 does not as such require 'new' assets to be acquired; rather it refers to the consideration being applied in acquiring *other* assets (and see, for instance, ESC D22 permitting expenditure on improvement to existing assets).

c)    *Qualifying assets*

The assets must be comprised in the list of business assets in TCGA 1992 s 155. These are land and buildings; fixed plant and machinery; ships; aircraft; hovercraft; goodwill (for a discussion of whether part of a taxpayer's chargeable gains related to the sale of goodwill, see the Special Commissioners decision in *Balloon Promotions Ltd v Wilson* (2006)); satellites, space stations and spacecraft; milk and potato quotas, fish quota, the EU quotas for the premium given to producers of ewes and suckler cows and payment entitlements under 'the single payment scheme' (a new system of support for farmers under the EU Common Agricultural Policy). This list can be added to by Treasury Order. The old and new assets need not be of the same type, however, eg a gain on the sale of an aircraft can be rolled over into the purchase of a hovercraft. Further, although the old asset must have been used in the taxpayer's trade during the whole time that he owned it (otherwise only partial roll-over is allowed), it could have been used in successive trades provided that the gap between them did not exceed three years.                                                                                    **[22.74]**

**EXAMPLE 22.7**

A inherited a freehold shop in 1989 when its value was £36,000. The shop was kept empty until 1993 when he started a fish and chip shop. He sold the shop in 2006 for £60,000 and purchased new premises for £75,000.

His total gain in 2006 (excluding indexation) is £24,000 and the premises have been used for business purposes during twelve-sixteenths of the ownership period. Hence £18,000 of the gain is rolled over but the balance (£6,000) is taxed.

d)    *Occupation for business purposes*

The assets that are sold must be occupied as well as used for the purposes of the taxpayer's business. If the property is occupied by his partner or employee, he must be able to show that their occupation is *representative* (ie attributed to him) to obtain the relief. For occupation to be representative it must *either* (1) be essential for the partner or employee to occupy the property to perform his duties; *or* (2) be an express term of the employment contract (or partnership agreement) that he should do so, and the occupation must enable him to perform his duties better. If either of these conditions is proved, the Revenue accepts that the property is used for the purpose of the owner's trade (see *Anderton v Lamb* (1981)).

The new asset need not be used in the same trade as the old but can be used in another trade carried on by the taxpayer simultaneously or successively, provided in the latter case that there is not more than a three-year gap between the ceasing of one trade and the start of another (see SP 8/81). There is nothing to prevent the taxpayer from rolling his gain into the purchase of more than one asset or to require him to continue to use the new asset in a trade throughout his period of ownership. ESC D22–25 extend the relief, *inter alia*, to cover improvements to, or capital expenditure to enhance the value of, existing assets; the acquisition of a further interest in an asset already used for the purposes of the trade; and the partition of land on the dissolution of a partnership. **[22.75]**

### e) *Non residents and foreign assets*

Relief is not available to a non-UK resident who sells a chargeable asset (ie one used in a trade carried on through a UK branch or agency) and then purchases a new asset that is not chargeable because it is situated outside the UK (TCGA 1992 s 159). Relief is, however, available if he acquires further UK branch or agency assets and is also given to a UK resident who rolls over into the acquisition of a qualifying asset wherever situated (and even though he may be non resident at the time of acquisition: see CG 60253). **[22.76]**

### f) *Partnerships, companies and employees*

This relief is available to partnerships and to companies and it can be claimed for an asset that is owned by an individual and used by his partnership or personal company. In such cases, however, the relief is only available to the individual and the replacement asset can not be purchased by the partnership or company (*Cassell v Crutchfield (No 2)* (1997)). Employees may claim the relief for assets owned by them so long as the assets are used (or, in the case of land and buildings, occupied) only for the purposes of the employment. (Note, however, that it is not necessary for the asset to be used *exclusively* by the employee in the course of his employment so that relief may apply even if the asset is provided for the general use of the employer: see SP 5/86.) **[22.77]**

### g) *Restrictions on the relief*

There are certain restrictions on the relief.

*First,* if the new asset is a depreciating asset (defined as a 'wasting asset'—see **[19.45]**—or one which will become a wasting asset within ten years, such as a lease with 60 years unexpired) the gain on the old asset cannot be deducted from the cost of the new. Instead, tax on the gain is postponed until the earliest of the three following events:

(1)   ten years elapse from the date of the purchase of the new asset; or
(2)   the taxpayer disposes of the new asset; or
(3)   the taxpayer ceases to use the new asset for the purposes of a trade.

ESC D45 exempts from tax gains arising when the new asset ceases to be used in a trade because of the death of the taxpayer.

If, before the deferred gain becomes chargeable, a new asset is acquired (whether the depreciating asset is sold or not), the deferred gain may be rolled into the new asset (see TCGA 1992 s 154).

#### EXAMPLE 22.8

Sam sells his freehold fish and chip shop for £25,000 thereby making a gain of £12,000. One year later he buys a 55-year lease on new premises for £27,000 and seven years after that acquires a further freehold shop for £35,000.

(1)    Purchase of 55-year lease: this lease is a depreciating asset. The gain of £12,000 on the sale of the original shop is, therefore, held in suspense for ten years.

(2)    Purchase of the freehold shop: as the purchase occurs within ten years of the gain, roll-over relief is available so that the purchase price is reduced to £23,000.

*Secondly*, if the whole of the proceeds of sale are not reinvested in acquiring the new asset there is a chargeable gain equivalent to the amount not reinvested and it is only the balance that is rolled over. Accordingly, if the purchase price of the new asset does not exceed the acquisition cost of the old, all the gain is chargeable and there is nothing to roll over (contrast 'reinvestment relief' which required the gain *only* to be reinvested: see the reinvestment provisions of the Enterprise Investment Scheme (EIS): **Chapter 15**). TCGA 1992 s 50 that excludes from the computation of the gain expenditure on the acquisition of an asset met by a public authority, is only applicable in computing any gain arising on a future disposal of the asset. It does not have the effect of reducing the cost of acquisition of the asset with the effect of limiting any hold-over relief available (*Wardhaugh v Penrith Rugby Union Football Club* (2002)). The new asset must, of course, be purchased for use in a business so that if there is an element of non-business user relief will be restricted accordingly.

### EXAMPLE 22.9

A buys factory 1 for £50,000 and sells it for £100,000 thereby making a gain of £50,000. A buys factory 2 for £80,000. The amount not reinvested (£20,000, ie £100,000 – £80,000) is chargeable. The balance of the gain (£30,000) is rolled over so that the acquisition cost of factory 2 is £50,000. If factory 2 had only cost £50,000 the amount not reinvested would equal the gain (ie £50,000) and be chargeable.

In *Tod v Mudd* (1987) the taxpayer sold his accountancy practice and with his wife bought premises to carry on business as hoteliers in partnership. The premises were bought as tenants in common with a 75% interest being held by Mr Mudd and 25% by his wife and it was agreed that they would be used as to 75% for business purposes and 25% for private purposes. The partnership agreement stated that the business of the partnership should be conducted on that portion of the premises attributable to Mr Mudd's share. The court held that roll-over relief should be given to Mr Mudd but only on 75% of 75% of the purchase price because his interest as a tenant in common constituted a share in the whole property and not in a distinct 75% portion thereof. Accordingly, because of the way in which this arrangement had been structured, roll-over relief was restricted. There are a number of ways in which matters could have been organised so that full relief would have been given to Mr Mudd. *First*, he could have bought the whole of the new premises for business use and then given 25% to his wife. *Secondly*, he could have purchased an identified and separate portion of the premises (75% thereof) in his sole name and for business use leaving his wife to purchase the remaining portion for private purposes. Finally, the defective arrangement could have been cured had Mr Mudd bought out Mrs Mudd's 25% share within three years of the disposal of his accountancy practice.

If the taxpayer knows that the price of the new asset will be too low to enable him to claim roll-over (or full roll-over) relief and he is married, it may be advantageous to transfer a share in the old asset to his wife before it is sold although this ruse could be challenged under the *Ramsay* principle (**Chapter 42**). [**22.78**]

### EXAMPLE 22.10

H buys factory 1 for £50,000 and transfers 2/5 of it to his wife W. The factory is sold for £100,000. H's gain is £30,000 ([3/5 × £100,000]–[3/5 × £50,000]). W's gain is £20,000 ([2/5 × £100,000]–[2/5 × £50,000]).

H's share of the proceeds of sale is £60,000. H then buys factory 2 for £50,000. The proceeds of sale are not wholly reinvested in factory 2 and, therefore, H is charged to CGT on £10,000 (£60,000 – £50,000). The balance of his gain £20,000 (£30,000 – £10,000) can be rolled over, leaving him with a base value for factory 2 of £30,000. H and W between them are taxed on a gain of £30,000 instead of (as in *Example 22.9*) H being taxed on a gain of £50,000.

### h)   *Problems if the relief is claimed*

Roll-over relief should not be claimed where the taxpayer makes an allowable loss on the sale of the old asset since he cannot add this loss to the base value of the new asset. Nor should he claim the relief where the gain does not exceed his annual exemption. Even if his gain does exceed the exempt limit, it may not be worth claiming the relief, as the claim cannot be to hold over only a part of the gain and the effect of rolling over a gain is a loss of accrued taper relief. [**22.79**]

### EXAMPLE 22.11

Unlucky acquires land and buildings for his trade in 1994 at a cost of £200,000. In February 1998 because of pressure on space he disposes of this property for £500,000, acquiring replacement premises in April 1998 for £750,000. The gain he elects to roll over. A similar situation arises in July 2004: the sale proceeds are £1.2m which are ploughed back into new premises costing £1.5m. In May 2006 Unlucky retires selling the premises for £2m. The CGT computations are as follows:

*Scenario 1*

a)      *Sale in February 1998*

|  | £ | £ |
|---|---|---|
| Proceeds |  | 500,000 |
| Cost | 200,000 |  |
| Indexation (say) | 20,000 | (220,000) |
| Gain to roll over |  | 280,000 |

b)      *Sale in July 2004*

|  | £ | £ |
|---|---|---|
| Proceeds |  | 1,200,000 |
| Cost | 750,000 |  |
| *Less:* rolled-over gain | 280,000 | 470,000 |
| Gain to roll over |  | 730,000 |

c)    *Final sale in May 2006*

|  | £ | £ |
|---|---|---|
| Proceeds |  | 2,000,000 |
| Cost | 1,500,000 |  |
| *Less:* rolled-over gain | 730,000 | 770,000 |
| Chargeable gain |  | 1,230,000 |

Taper relief by reference to period of ownership of 'new asset' ONLY—one year.

|  | £ |
|---|---|
| 1,230,000 × 50% | (615,000) |
| Gain charged | £615,000 |

*Notes:*
(1)    Note that no allowance is made for the period April 1998–July 2004 in the taper relief calculation. Accrued taper is lost on a roll-over (a similar situation occurs on a held-over gain on a gift of business assets (see **[24.29]**)).
(2)    Contrast the position if instead of moving, Unlucky had expanded his existing site (eg by building an extension). No loss of taper results: the gain would become:

*Scenario 2*

|  | £ | £ |
|---|---|---|
| Proceeds |  | 2,000,000 |
| Cost | 200,000 |  |
| Indexation | 20,000 |  |
| Enhancement (1) | 250,000 |  |
| Enhancement (2) | 300,000 | 770,000 |
| Chargeable gain |  | 1,230,000 |

Taper relief (April 1998–May 2005)—7 years

|  | £ |
|---|---|
| 1,230,000 × 75% | (922,500) |
| Gain charged | £307,500 |

(3)    This problem is either less acute, or may not exist at all, with respect to a disposal of business assets on or after 6 April 2002, when maximum taper relief is available after a holding period of only two years. Accordingly, in *scenario 1*, had Unlucky retired and disposed of the premises just two months later (in July 2006) the gain, calculated as follows, would be identical to that in *scenario 2*.

|  | £ | £ |
|---|---|---|
| Proceeds |  | 2,000,000 |
| Cost | 1,500,000 |  |
| *Less:* rolled-over gain | 730,000 | 770,000 |

| | |
|---|---:|
| Chargeable gain | 1,230,000 |
| Taper relief by reference to period of ownership of new asset | |
| ONLY—two years.   1,230,000 × 75% | 922,500 |
| Gain charged | £307,500 |

i) *Self-assessment and provisional relief where an intention to reinvest*

TCGA 1992 s 153A allows taxpayers to obtain provisional relief in advance of the reinvestment of the proceeds from the sale of the assets. At such time as the conditions for the granting of the relief have been satisfied, the provisional relief will be replaced by that actual relief. **[22.80]**

j) *Intellectual property roll-over for companies (FA 2002 Sch 29)*

The Government introduced a new code for taxing intellectual property, goodwill and other intangible assets with effect from 1 April 2002. These rules apply only to companies. Under this regime, gains in respect of intangible fixed assets are chargeable to corporation tax as income with relief for the costs of acquiring and enhancing such assets. Included in the provisions is a new reinvestment relief, closely based on CGT roll-over relief (Sch 29 Part 7). Tax on the profits of the disposal of intangible assets within the code are deferred if the proceeds are reinvested in new assets (that are also within the code) within one year before or three years after the disposal of the original asset.

Conditions for relief are:

(1) The old assets must have been used throughout the period of ownership by the company selling them as fixed assets for trading or business purposes. An asset may meet this condition where it was an asset for only part of that period, provided that it was a chargeable intangible asset at the time of realisation *and* for a substantial part of the period it was held. A 'reasonable' apportionment then produces a separate asset meeting the condition.

(2) The 'new' intangibles must be within the code, and must be similarly used.

(3) The proceeds of disposal of the old assets must exceed their cost. This requirement will always be satisfied on the realisation of assets, such as internally generated goodwill, which have no cost for tax purposes.

Full deferral will only be available when the entire proceeds of the sale of the 'old' intangibles are reinvested; where this is not the case, the profit eligible for relief will be reduced by the amount not reinvested. Where there is a part disposal, eg where a licence is granted to exploit a patent for a period of time, the cost of the asset to be taken into account is reduced to the 'appropriate proportion'. The appropriate proportion is the cost reduced in the ratio that the reduction in the 'accounting value' (net book value) of the asset on the part disposal bears to the accounting value immediately before the disposal. Where there is a disposal of what is left of an asset following an earlier part disposal, the cost is the 'adjusted cost', which is obtained by deducting the appropriate proportion of the cost taken into account on the previous part disposal from the original cost.   **[22.81]**

**EXAMPLE 22.12**

Tech Gear Ltd acquired for £100,000 the patent to TDNA, a by-product of DNA, which the company believes will revolutionise computer technology over the coming years. In September 2005, Tech Gear granted a licence for £80,000 to Quick Systems Ltd for the exploitation of the patent for a period of five years. In July 2006, Tech Gear assigned the patent to the computer giants JCN plc for £200,000.

*The part disposal to Quick Systems Ltd*

|  | £ | £ |
|---|---|---|
| Proceeds of part disposal |  | 80,000 |
| Cost for tax purposes of old asset | 100,000 |  |
| Book value immediately prior to disposal | 40,000 |  |
| Book value immediately after disposal | 30,000 |  |
| Appropriate proportion: |  |  |
| $\dfrac{£100,000 \times (£40,000 - £30,000)}{£40,000} \quad =$ |  | 25,000 |
| Gain |  | 55,000 |

If expenditure on a new asset exceeds the proceeds from the partial disposal of the old asset (£80,000), full reinvestment relief in respect of the gain of £55,000 may be claimed. If, however, expenditure is less than £80,000 but is more than £25,000 (the appropriate proportion), partial relief may be available.

*The disposal of the remainder of the asset to JCN plc*

|  | £ |
|---|---|
| Proceeds of disposal | 200,00 |
| Adjusted cost: £100,000 – £25,000 | 75,000 |
| Gain | £125,000 |

## 3   Roll-over relief on compulsory acquisition of land (TCGA 1992 s 247)

This form of roll-over relief is limited to the disposal of land (or an interest in land) to an authority exercising or able to exercise compulsory purchase powers. Any gain arising can be rolled over into the cost of acquiring replacement land. Similar restrictions to those which apply to the replacement of business assets roll-over relief (see **[21.72]**) apply: for instance, the replacement asset must not have a limited life expectancy and, for full relief, all the disposal consideration must be reinvested. Further, reinvestment into property qualifying for the main residence relief is not allowed.   **[22.82]**

## 4 Extensions of TCGA 1992 s 247

The Revenue allows s 247 relief to be claimed by landlords when leasehold tenants exercise their statutory rights to acquire the freehold reversion (see revised SP 13/93 and *Tax Bulletin*, June 1999, p 672) and, by concession, when two or more persons sever their joint interests in land (or in milk or potato quotas: ESC D26). No charge arises irrespective of the s 247 concession when persons pool their resources and subsequently extract their shares from the pool. (See *Example 25.3(2)* and the cases there cited.) **[22.83]**

## 5 Retirement relief

Following a five-year period of phased withdrawal, retirement relief is no longer available for 2003–04 and subsequent years. For details of the relief, reference should be made to earlier editions of this book. **[22.84]**

Whilst retirement relief has been replaced by taper relief (see **Chapter 20**), it should be noted that there are cases where the latter will never adequately compensate for the loss of retirement relief. For example, the taxpayer who sold his business in 2002–03 realising a gain of £50,000 would have paid no tax had he satisfied the necessary conditions for retirement relief; however, if he were to sell in 2003–04 or later years, maximum taper relief would merely reduce his chargeable gain to £12,500. In order to avoid that scenario, some taxpayers crystallised retirement relief, eg by settling the business on life interest trusts (a disposal which would have triggered retirement relief) under which the taxpayer was a beneficiary (typically the life tenant) and continued to run the business. **[22.85]**

One matter that is worthy of note is that where there is an unconditional contract to sell a business entered into before 5 April 2003 (when retirement relief was still available) but not completed until after that date (when relief is no longer available), the operation of ESC D31 will deny retirement relief since the date of completion is treated as the date of disposal. **[22.86]–[22.98]**

## 6 Postponement of CGT on gifts and undervalue disposals (TCGA 1992 s 165)

This provision is considered in detail in **Chapter 24**. **[22.99]**

## 7 Roll-over relief on the incorporation of a business (TCGA 1992 s 162 and s 162A)

### a) *The relief*

This relief takes the form of a postponement of, rather than an exemption from, CGT. It applies when there is a disposal of an unincorporated business (whether by a sole trader, a partnership, or trustees but *not* by an unincorporated association) to a company and that disposal is wholly or partly in return for shares in that company. Any gains made on the disposal of chargeable business assets will be deducted from the value of the shares received (the gain is 'rolled into' the shares) and the relevant assets are acquired by the company at market value (ie there is a 'step-up' in their value). (Note that a similar relief is available for companies which transfer a trade carried on outside the UK to a non-resident company: see TCGA 1992 s 140.) **[22.100]**

b)   *Conditions to be satisfied*

The business must be transferred as a going concern; a mere transfer of assets is insufficient. Further, all the assets of the business (excluding only cash) must be transferred to the company. As only a gain on business assets can be held over, it will be advisable to take investment assets out of the business before incorporation. The Revenue accepts that 'business' has a wider meaning than 'trade': managing a landed estate would, for instance, qualify as a business (see CG 65712).

**EXAMPLE 22.13**

On the incorporation of a business in consideration for the issue of fully paid shares, there is a gain on business assets of £50,000. The market value of the shares is £150,000. The gain is rolled over by deducting it from the value of the shares so that the acquisition cost of the shares becomes £100,000 (£150,000 – £50,000). The assets are acquired by the company at market value of (say) £150,000.

Where only a part of the total consideration given by the company is in shares (the rest being in cash or debentures), only a corresponding part of the chargeable gain can be rolled forward and deducted from the value of the shares. That part is found by applying the formula:

$$\text{Gain rolled forward} = \text{total gain} \times \frac{\text{market value of shares}}{\text{total consideration for transfer}}$$

In practice, the assumption of liabilities by the company is not treated as consideration for this purpose (see CG 65746 and ESC D32).

**EXAMPLE 22.14**

A transfers his hotel business to Strong Ltd in return for £160,000, consisting of £10,000 shares (market value £120,000) and £40,000 cash. The chargeable business assets transferred are the premises (market value £130,000), the goodwill (market value £10,000) and furniture, fixtures etc (market value £20,000). On the premises and the goodwill A makes chargeable gains of £35,000 and £5,000 respectively.

$$£40,000 - \left( £40,000 \times \frac{£120,000}{£160,000} \right) = £40,000 - £30,000 = £10,000$$

and the acquisition cost of the shares is £120,000 – £30,000 = £90,000 (ie £9 per share).

Taper relief may be available on a subsequent disposal of the shares if the relevant conditions are satisfied. **[22.101]**

c) *Deferring tax on the sale of an unincorporated business*

If it is desired to sell an unincorporated business s 162 may be used to defer any CGT liability on the sale. The business is first incorporated and s 162 ensures that the vendors will not be subject to CGT until they dispose of their shares in that company. As the company acquires the business assets at market value, however (under TCGA 1992 s 17: see **[19.22]**), the trade can immediately be resold to the intended purchaser without any CGT charge (see *Gordon v IRC* (1991)). **[22.102]**

d) *Election to disapply the s 162 roll-over relief*

FA 2002 inserted a new s 162A into TCGA 1992 that applies to transfers of a business after 5 April 2002. Provided that the relevant conditions are met the roll-over relief under s 162 had always been mandatory: it is the purpose of s 162A to enable a taxpayer to opt out of that relief. In two cases, in particular, this may be beneficial:

(1) Sid incorporates his business and before two years have elapsed (ie before he has become entitled to full business assets taper he receives an unexpected offer for the business which he accepts).

(2) Sad agrees to sell his business and as part of the arrangement first incorporates. The sale then falls through. To maximise taper relief prior to 6 April 2002 Sad would have ensured that the conditions of s 162 were *not* met in order to preserve his entitlement to business assets taper. With the loss of the sale, Sad would be exposed to a CGT charge in the incorporation.

In both cases the arrangements may now be structured so that s 162 relief is given on the incorporation, but the taxpayers may opt out of that relief if this becomes desirable (see also **[20.32]**).

**EXAMPLE 22.15**

On 25 April 2006, B incorporates his trade as Y Ltd. He transfers all the assets of the business to the company in consideration for all the shares of Y Ltd. CGT incorporation relief applies.

*Incorporation of business*

| | | |
|---|---|---|
| Value of shares received in consideration | | £650,000 |
| Acquisition cost of assets used in the business (6 April 1998) | *Less* | £200,000 |
| Net chargeable gains on disposal of business assets (rolled-over into deemed acquisition cost of shares) | | £450,000 |

On 20 May 2006, B receives an unexpected offer to sell his shares in Y Ltd.

*Sale of shares*

| | | |
|---|---|---|
| Consideration | | £700,000 |
| Acquisition cost of shares | £650,000 | |
| less net chargeable gain rolled | | |
| Over | £450,000 | |
| | £200,000 | |

| | | |
|---|---|---|
| Deemed acquisition cost | *less* | £200,000 |
| Gain chargeable to tax (after less than one year no taper relief: 100% of gain chargeable) | | £500,000 |

Instead B elects on 31 October 2006 for incorporation relief not to apply. Therefore the two disposals above are recalculated as follows.

*Transfer of unincorporated business*

| | | |
|---|---|---|
| Value of shares received in | | |
| Consideration | | £650,000 |
| Acquisition cost of assets of | | |
| business (6 April 1998) | *less* | £200,000 |
| Net chargeable gains on disposal | | |
| of business assets | | £450,000 |
| Untapered gain chargeable to tax | | £450,000 |
| Gains chargeable (after two years | | £112,000 |

business asset taper relief: 25% of gain chargeable)

*Sale of shares*

| | | |
|---|---|---|
| Consideration | | £700,000 |
| Acquisition cost of shares | *less* | £650,000 |
| Untapered gain chargeable to tax | | £50,000 |

(after less than one year no taper relief: 100% of gain chargeable)

| | | |
|---|---|---|
| Total gains chargeable to tax | | £162,500 |

The time limits for opting out of s 162 relief are as follows:

(1) If all the shares acquired on incorporation have been disposed of before the end of the tax year following incorporation the election must be made no later than 31 January following the end of the later tax year. (Hence if incorporation is in 2005–06 and the sale occurs in 2006–07, the election has to be made at the latest on 31 January 2008).

(2) In other cases the deadline is extended by one year, ie for an incorporation in 2005–06 to 31 January 2009. This may be attractive because if the shares are sold in 2006–07 full business taper relief may not be available.                                                                 **[22.103]**

## 8   Relief on company reconstructions, amalgamations and takeovers

The relief afforded by TCGA 1992 ss 135–137 in respect of 'paper for paper exchanges' is considered in **Chapter 47**.

If there is a bonus or rights issue so that the existing shareholders are allotted shares or debentures in proportion to that existing holding, the new securities are treated as acquired when the original shares were acquired. The price for this combined holding will then be the sum originally paid for the original shares plus whatever is paid for the new securities (TCGA 1992 ss 127–130). Altering the rights attached to a class of shares or the conversion of securities can similarly be achieved without an immediate charge to CGT (TCGA 1992 ss 133–135). **[22.104]**

# 23 CGT—The main residence

*Updated by Natalie Lee, Barrister, Senior Lecturer in Law, University of Southampton*

## I WHEN IS THE EXEMPTION AVAILABLE?

The most important exemption from CGT for the individual taxpayer, and the one which probably affects more taxpayers than does any other, is from any gain made on the disposal of the principal private residence (TCGA 1992 ss 222–226). There is no similar relief for IHT purposes; only if the house is a qualifying farmhouse will APR be available on the 'agricultural value' whilst BPR will be given on part of any property used 'exclusively' for business purposes.

The CGT exemption is available for any gain arising on the disposal by gift or sale by a taxpayer of his only or main residence, including grounds of up to half an hectare or such larger area as is required for the reasonable enjoyment of the dwelling house (TCGA 1992 s 222). **[23.1]–[23.20]**

## II MEANING OF 'DWELLING HOUSE' AND 'RESIDENCE'

### 1 Meaning of a 'dwelling house'

What qualifies as a dwelling house is a question of fact. In *Makins v Elson* (1977) the taxpayer bought land intending to build a house on it. In the meantime, he lived there in a caravan. He never built the house and later sold both land and caravan at a profit. The caravan was held, on the facts, to be a dwelling house; the most significant of these facts being that it was connected to the mains services as well as to the telephone system and that it was resting on bricks so that it was not movable. In contrast, in *Moore v Thompson* (1986) the court held that since there was no supply of water or electricity, the caravan in question was not a dwelling house. **[23.21]**

## 2   'Residence': a degree of permanence

Although permanent residence is not a *condition* for the application of relief, a distinction has to be drawn between a permanent residence and temporary accommodation. In *Goodwin v Curtis* (1998), the taxpayer agreed to purchase (by way of sub-sale) a farmhouse from a company with which he was connected. The purchase by the company was completed on 7 March and the taxpayer put the property on the market at that time, only completing his purchase on 1 April. The taxpayer then occupied the property living there seven days a week and had a telephone connected. On 3 April, however, he completed the purchase of a small cottage to which he moved when he sold the farmhouse on 3 May 1985. The taxpayer paid £70,000 for the farmhouse and sold it for £177,000! The Court of Appeal confirmed the findings of the commissioners that relief was not available notwithstanding the taxpayer's occupation of the property. There was not the required 'degree of permanence, continuity and the expectation of continuity' (to use the language of Vinelott J in the High Court) for the occupation to amount to a residence. According to Millett LJ, the nature of the taxpayer's personal circumstances together with the size of the house indicated that his occupation was a 'stop gap measure' (in passing it may be suggested that size of the house should not be a factor of any significance: a single person should qualify for relief on an eight-bedroom mansion!). This case demonstrates that the intention of the taxpayer at the time of acquisition is central to the availability of the relief. Where there is a clear intention to reside permanently in a dwelling house, relief will be available even if that intention is thwarted after only a brief period of occupation. However, even actual occupation for a reasonable period may be insufficient to attract the relief where no continuity of occupation is intended. **[23.22]**

## 3   A 'residence': the entity test

So far as the term 'a residence' is concerned, a major problem is whether, in any given situation, two or more units can constitute a single residence. Selling a house with additional accommodation available either for staff or aged relatives is not unusual and there now exists a substantial body of case law, but from which no clear or satisfactory guidelines have emerged. In *Batey v Wakefield* (1982), the first in the series of cases, a separate bungalow within the grounds of the taxpayer's house and found by the General Commissioner as fact to have been used by a caretaker to enable him to perform the duties of his employment with the taxpayer, was considered by the Court of Appeal to be exempt from CGT on its sale. The court concluded that it was necessary to identify the entity that could properly be described as constituting the residence (the 'entity' test). Fox LJ commented:

> 'in the ordinary use of English, a dwelling house, or a residence, can comprise several dwellings which are not physically joined at all'.

In his view, the fact that the bungalow was physically separate from the main dwelling house was 'irrelevant'.

This was followed by Vinelott J in *Williams v Merrylees* (1987) who echoed the words of Fox LJ when he summarised the approach to be taken:

'what one is looking for is an entity which can be sensibly described as being a dwelling house though split into different buildings performing different functions'. **[23.23]**


## 4   The curtilage test

However, in *Markey v Sanders* (1987), Walton J, ignoring the entity test, indicated that two conditions had to be satisfied: *first*, that occupation of the 'secondary' building had to increase the taxpayer's enjoyment of the main house and, *secondly*, that the other building had to be 'very closely adjacent' to the main building. He decided that a staff bungalow some 130 metres distant from the main residence and standing in its own grounds did not satisfy the second of the two conditions and so could not be treated as part of a single residence, with the result that, on its disposal, CGT was chargeable.

The Court of Appeal had the opportunity to review these decisions in *Lewis v Rook* (1992) which concerned the sale of a cottage some 200 yards from the main house and which had been occupied by the taxpayer's gardener. Giving the judgment of the court, Balcombe LJ concluded that no building could form part of a dwelling house that included the main house unless the building was 'appurtenant to, and within the curtilage of the main house' (the 'curtilage' test). In applying what he believed to be 'well-recognised legal concepts' in the interpretation of the term 'dwelling house' or 'residence' and rejecting the previous approach of treating the matter as a question of fact, Balcombe LJ concluded that the main residence exemption was inapplicable.

It is a cause for concern that the word 'curtilage' appears nowhere in the CGT legislation, although in other contexts it has been held to mean 'a small area about a building', and that the court appears to be preferring the restrictive approach in *Markey v Sanders* to the flexibility of *Batey v Wakefield* and *Williams v Merrylees*.

*Honour v Norris* (1992) largely turned on its own facts with the judge rejecting as an 'affront to common sense' the suggestion that a number of separate flats in a square could constitute a single dwelling house.

Revenue thinking in this area was set out in RI 75 August 1994 where it is stated:

'Where more dispersed groups of buildings have a clear relationship with each other they will fall within a single curtilage if they constitute an integral whole. In the Leasehold Reform Act case of *Methuen-Campbell v Walters,* quoted with approval in *Lewis v Rook*, the Court held that "for one corporeal hereditament to fall within the curtilage of another, the former must be so intimately associated with the latter as to lead to the conclusion that the former in truth forms part and parcel of the latter". Whether one building is part and parcel of another will depend primarily on whether there is a close geographical relationship between them. Furthermore, because the test is to identify an integral whole, a wall or fence separating two buildings will normally be sufficient to establish that they are not within the same curtilage. Similarly, a public road or stretch of tidal water will set a limit to the curtilage of the building. Buildings which are within the curtilage of a main house will normally pass automatically on a conveyance of that house without having to be specifically mentioned. There is a distinction between the curtilage of a main house and the curtilage of an estate as a whole and the fact that the whole estate may be contained within a single boundary does not mean that the buildings on the estate should be regarded as within the curtilage of a main house.' (See also CG 64245.)                                                        **[23.24]–[23.40]**

## III   HOW MANY RESIDENCES CAN QUALIFY FOR THE EXEMPTION?

### 1   Property owned by the taxpayer but used as a residence by a dependent relative

Prior to 6 April 1988, a maximum of two houses qualified for exemption; the only or main residence and a property owned by the taxpayer but used as a residence by a dependent relative rent free and for no other consideration.

This exemption for dependent relatives does not apply to disposals on or after 6 April 1988 (when mortgage interest relief was similarly withdrawn from dependent relative accommodation, see **[7.52]**). However, transitional relief continues to be available so long as the dependent relative conditions were satisfied either on 5 April 1988 or at any earlier time. Where this relief is claimed, ESC D20 permits payment by the relative of rates and of the costs of repairs to the dwelling house attributable to normal wear and tear without prejudicing the condition that the dwelling house must have been provided free and without consideration. In contrast, any payments made by the occupier towards repayment of a mortgage would lead to a loss of relief.

If qualifying occupation ceased before 6 April 1988 or ceases thereafter, the subsequent re-occupation of the property by a dependent relative will not be included in calculating the amount of any gain which, when the property is sold, is exempt from CGT.                                                    **[23.41]**

#### EXAMPLE 23.1

Thoughtful's widowed mother-in-law has lived since 1980 rent free in a bijou cottage owned by Thoughtful. He does not provide similar accommodation for any other dependent relative.

(1)    As an existing arrangement, Thoughtful will continue to be entitled to the CGT exemption on any disposal of the cottage so long as his mother-in-law continues to live there on the same terms.

(2)    If the cottage is sold after 6 April 1988 and a small flat purchased as a replacement, no CGT will be charged on the sale but the flat will not qualify for CGT relief.

(3)    If, instead, Thoughtful's mother-in-law ceases to occupy the cottage as her main residence either before or after 6 April 1988 but at some stage thereafter resumes occupation, no CGT exemption will be available to Thoughtful in respect of the gain attributable to his mother-in-law's later period of occupation.

### 2   Husband and wife

Husband and wife and civil partners (see generally **[51.130]** and **[23.42]**) can have only one main residence whilst they are living together (TCGA 1992 s 222(6)). For the operation of the election (which is considered below) when a couple marry or enter into a civil partnership, see CG 64525. **[23.42]**

## 3   Where the taxpayer has more than one residence

The question of whether a particular property is a taxpayer's only or main residence is sometimes a difficult one to answer. If only one property is occupied by him as a residence the exemption *prima facie* applies to that property. Where the taxpayer has two residences, only the residence which is his main residence can qualify for relief. Any problems that might arise in deciding which of two residences is the main residence are obviated since the taxpayer can elect for one to be treated as his main residence (TCGA 1992 s 222(5)). Of course, the election is only available in respect of 'residences' and cannot be used to convert a dwelling house which is not in use as a residence into one for the purpose of obtaining relief (see CG 64486). The election can be backdated for up to two years to the date when the second residence was acquired and can be varied at any time, the variation also being effective for the two previous years. In *Griffin v Craig-Harvey* (1993), the taxpayer's argument that an election could be made at any time during the period of ownership of a dwelling house to take effect for a period of up to two years prior to the date of the notice, was rejected. Vinelott J held that an election could only be made within two years of the acquisition of a second or subsequent residence. This decision has practical implications for taxpayers owning more than one residence who may find themselves out of time to make the necessary election.

Failure to make an election means that the self-assessment return of the taxpayer has to resolve the question on the basis of the facts and this may be decided not simply by the periods of time spent in each residence.

An election can and should be made if a taxpayer occupies a property as a residence under a tenancy agreement (but not under a licence, where the occupier has only a personal, and not a proprietary, interest) whilst at the same time owning a second property (see further ESC D21). **[23.43]–[23.60]**

**EXAMPLE 23.2**

Barber having lived in Spitalfields for many years acquires a luxury flat on the Essex coast in June 2004. At the same time he puts the Spitalfields house up for sale. When the house is sold he intends to rent a *pied-à-terre* in London.

(1)   By June 2006 he should elect whether Spitalfields or the flat is his main residence in respect of the period from June 2004.

(2)   The last three years of ownership are ignored in applying the main residence exemption (see **[23.83]**) and so if Spitalfields is sold by June 2007 or if he expects it to sell within the following year he should elect for the flat to be his main residence.

(3)   When he acquires the rented property in London he will again have two residences and should therefore elect within two years for the Essex flat to be his main residence.

(4)   If, instead of renting a property in London, he moves into job-related accommodation under a service occupancy, an election *cannot* be made and relief will remain available for the Essex flat. This is because his rights, which derive from the contract of service, are personal only and create no proprietary rights in his favour (for residences occupied under licence, see RI 89, October 1994).

## IV MISCELLANEOUS PROBLEMS

### 1 Land used with the house

Land of up to half an hectare (or permitted larger area) is exempt only if it is being used for the taxpayer's own occupation and for the enjoyment of his residence. In *Longson v Baker* (2001), the court had to determine whether 7.56 hectares (18.6 acres) of land should be included with a sizeable farmhouse and stabling for the purpose of obtaining the relief. It was held that the issue of whether a larger area of land was 'required' for the reasonable enjoyment of the dwelling house was a matter of fact. Further, it was held that bearing in mind that the commissioners were to have regard to 'the size and character of the dwelling house', the particular requirements of the owner of the house (in the present case, the grazing of horses) were irrelevant. Evans-Lombe J commented as follows:

> 'In my judgment it cannot be correct that the dwelling house at a farm *requires* an area of land amounting to more than 18 acres in order to ensure its reasonable enjoyment as a residence, having regard to its size and character.
>
> I have come to the conclusion that it may have been desirable or convenient for the taxpayer to have a total area of 7.56 hectares to enjoy with the farm, but such an area is not in my judgment required for the reasonable enjoyment of the farm as a residence having regard to its size and character.'

(For a criticism of the case, see *Taxation*, 8 February 2001, p 429.)

It should be noted that the legislation as it relates to the *land* (in contrast to the *dwelling house*) refers to the position at the date of disposal. Thus, a gain made on a disposal of land will not be exempt if the residence has already been sold. In *Varty v Lynes* (1976) the taxpayer sold his house and part of the garden. Later he sold the remaining part of the garden with the benefit of planning permission. It was held that this second disposal was chargeable and the whole gain, including that which had accrued whilst the garden land was occupied by the taxpayer along with the house, was taxed. Had the taxpayer sold the garden before or at the same time as the house, any gain would have been exempt. Brightman J suggested that his construction of s 222(1)(b) created an anomaly in that 'if the taxpayer goes out of occupation of the dwelling house a month before he sells it, the exemption will be lost in respect of the garden'. However, the current Revenue practice as explained in *Tax Bulletin*, August 1994, p 148 is not to apply arguments based upon that *dictum*, so that contemporaneous sales of the house and the garden (even if for development) benefit from the exemption.

What constitutes land for the enjoyment of a principal private residence was considered in *Wakeling v Pearce* (1995). In that case, the taxpayer had cultivated a garden and maintained a washing-line in a field which was separated from her residence by another property not owned by her. The use of the field declined over the years, but it continued in a reduced form until its eventual sale as two building plots. The Special Commissioner held that the field was enjoyed with the residence and that there was no statutory requirement that the land should adjoin or be contiguous with the residence. Following its decision not to appeal against this decision because of the particular circumstances of the taxpayer, the Revenue published its interpretation of the legislation (RI 119, August 1995). Attributing to the terms 'garden' and 'grounds' their normal, everyday meaning, the Revenue regards a garden as land devoted to cultivation of flowers, fruit or vegetables but that grounds cover 'enclosed land serving chiefly for ornament or recreation surrounding or attached to the dwelling house or other building'. So where land surrounds the residence and both are in the same ownership, the land qualifies for relief unless it is used for other purposes such as trade or agriculture. Relief will not be lost by reason only of the fact that the land is not used exclusively for recreational purposes or if there is a building on the land, provided that it is not being used for business purposes. Where land is physically separated from the residence, relief cannot be claimed merely by reason of the fact that it is used as a garden and that the two are in common ownership; by the same token, mere separation is not by itself sufficient to deny relief. The practice of the Revenue is to allow a claim in respect of land which can be shown to be 'naturally and traditionally the garden of the residence, so that it would normally be offered to a prospective purchaser as part of the residence'. **[23.61]**

**EXAMPLE 23.3**

(1) Bill is the owner of a village house that he purchased along with a small garden across the road from the residence. He later bought a further area of land upon which he built a tennis court. This land is separated from his house by the neighbouring property, and is reached by means of an informal path. Bill has recently sold all of his land, whilst retaining his residence.

It is common in villages for a garden to be across the road from the residence. If it can be shown that this was such a village, then Bill is entitled to relief under TCGA 1992 s 222(1)(b) for this part of his garden, even though separated from his residence, on the ground that it is a garden that would 'normally be offered to prospective purchasers as part of the residence'. The land upon which the tennis court stands is unlikely to qualify for relief. Although Bill may regard it as part of the garden, it was bought because the existing garden was inadequate for a tennis court, and could not be viewed as being 'naturally and traditionally' the garden of the residence.

(2) Assume that Sally owns a property with 7 hectares of land. It is accepted that some 6 hectares of the land does not attract the principal private residence relief and the relief is given on the land 'which, if the remainder were separately occupied, would be the most suitable for occupation and enjoyment with the residence' (see TCGA 1992 s 222(4)). Difficult valuation issues may arise: for instance the non-qualifying land may well have no permitted access. Is this a factor to be taken into account in apportioning the sale consideration if the whole property is sold?

## 2 Houses held in trust

Where trustees dispose of a house that is the residence of a beneficiary who is entitled to occupy it by the terms of the settlement the relief applies (TCGA 1992 s 225: it does not matter that the beneficiary pays rent to the trustees). For disposals after 10 December 2003, relief is only available where an actual claim for it is made by the trustees. *Sansom v Peay* (1976) decided that the section applied both where the relevant beneficiary enjoyed an interest in possession in the property and where the trust was discretionary so that occupation was entirely a matter for the discretion of the trustees. The decision in this case has repercussions for IHT since the Revenue will argue that the beneficiary in whose favour the discretion has been exercised thereby acquires an interest in possession in the settlement (see SP 10/79).

**[23.62]**

### EXAMPLE 23.4

'Westwinds' is held in trust for Julian for life remainder to his children on attaining 40. In exercise of their overriding powers the trustees advance £10 on trust for the children with separate trustees and then grant those trustees a reversionary lease over Westwinds to commence in ten years time when Julian will be aged 90.

**Notes:**
   (i)   It is not considered that this arrangement creates reservation of benefit problems for IHT purposes. Although Julian makes a transfer of value he does not make a gift.
  (ii)   If the house were to be sold during Julian's life it is considered that the trustees would benefit from the full principal private residence exemption (subject to a claim for it being made) albeit that Julian's residence was by virtue of the encumbered freehold interest. This is because the settlement is treated as a single composite settlement for CGT purposes and because the wording of s 225 merely requires occupation of trust property by a beneficiary as his main residence.

## 3   Use of a house for a business

If part of the house is used exclusively for business purposes, a proportionate part of the gain on a disposal of the property becomes chargeable (TCGA 1992 s 224 and for IHT BPR, see IHTA 1984 s 112(4)). However, as long as no part is used *exclusively* for business purposes no part of the exemption will be lost. Doctors and dentists who have a surgery in their house are advised to hold a party in that surgery at least once a year (and to invite their tax inspector!).                                                              **[23.63]**

## 4   Letting part of the property

Where the whole or part of the property has been let as residential accommodation, this may result in a partial loss of exemption. However, the gain attributable to the letting (calculated according to how much was let and for how long) will be exempt from CGT up to the lesser of £40,000 and the exemption attributable to the owner's occupation. This relief does not apply if the let portion forms a separate dwelling (TCGA 1992 s 223(4)). The Revenue has stated that the taking of lodgers will not result in a loss of any of the exemption provided that the lodger lives as part of the family and shares living accommodation (SP 14/80).

In *Owen v Elliott* (1990) the taxpayer carried on the business of a private hotel or boarding house on premises which he also occupied as his main residence and argued that he was entitled to relief since taking in hotel guests amounted to 'residential accommodation'. The Court of Appeal accepted this and rejected the argument that the occupation had to be by persons making their home in the premises let as opposed to paying guests staying overnight or on holiday. Leggatt LJ stated that:

> 'The expression "residential accommodation" does not directly or by association mean premises likely to be occupied as a home. It means living accommodation, by contrast, for example, with office accommodation. I regard as wholly artificial attempts to distinguish between a letting by the owner and a letting to the occupant; and between letting to a lodger and letting to a guest in a boarding house; and between a letting that is likely to be used by the occupant as his home and one that is not.' **[23.64]**

### EXAMPLE 23.5

A sells his house which he has owned for 20 years realising a gain of £120,000. He occupied the entire house during the first ten years. For the next six years he let one-third of it and for the final four years the entire property.

|  |  | £ | £ |
|---|---|---:|---:|
| Total gain | | | 120,000 |
| *Less:* exemptions | | | |
| (i) | 10 years' occupation | 60,000 | |
| (ii) | 6 years' occupation of | | |
| | 2/3 (£60,000 × 2/3 × 6/10) | 24,000 | |
| (iii) | final 3 years' ownership | | |
| | (£60,000 × 3/10) | 18,000 | 102,000 |
| Gain attributable to letting | | | 18,000 |
| *Less:* exemption (part) | | | 18,000 |
| Chargeable portion | | | £NIL |

## 5  Disposals by PRs

Statutory effect has now been given to an extra-statutory concession (ESC D5), giving the benefit of the principal private residence exemption to PRs on their disposal of a private dwelling house which, both before and after the death, was the only or main residence of one or more individuals who, on the death of the testator, are entitled to 75% of the net proceeds of sale from the house, either absolutely or for life (TCGA 1992 s 225A, inserted by FA 2004: see **[21.104]**). The new provision will supersede the concession with effect for disposals on or after 10 December 2003, from which time the relief will only be available where a claim for it is actually made by the personal representatives. **[23.65]**

## 6  Disposals by legatees

A spouse who inherits a dwelling house on the death of the other spouse also inherits the other spouse's period of ownership for the purpose of calculating the relief (TCGA 1992 s 222(7)(a); and see TCGA 1992 s 62; RI 75,

August 1994). In other cases the beneficial period of ownership begins on the date of death and if the beneficiary does not become resident until a later date, the period prior to becoming resident will not qualify for relief (unless falling within the final 36-month period prior to disposal): see RI 75, August 1994.                                                              **[23.66]–[23.80]**

## V   EFFECT OF PERIODS OF ABSENCE

### 1   General rule

To qualify for the exemption, the taxpayer must occupy the property as his only or main residence throughout the period of his ownership: for these purposes only the period of ownership after 31 March 1982 counts (TCGA 1992 s 223(7)). As a general rule, therefore, the effect of periods of absence is that on the disposal of the residence a proportion of any gain will be charged. That proportion is calculated by the formula:

$$\text{Total gain} \times \frac{\text{period of absence}}{\text{period of ownership}}$$

**[23.81]**

### 2   Husband and wife, and same-sex couples

Special rules operate for husband and wife and same-sex couples who have entered into a civil partnership (see **[51.130]**) since in deciding whether a house has been occupied as a main residence throughout the period of ownership one spouse can take advantage of a period of ownership of the other (TCGA 1992 s 222(7)(a): see **[21.104]** for an illustration of this rule).

**[23.82]**

### 3   Permitted absences

Despite the general rule that absences render part of the gain chargeable, certain permitted absences are ignored. These include, by concession, the first 12 months of ownership in cases where occupation was delayed because the house was being built or altered, or up to a period of two years where there are good reasons for exceptional delay (SP D4). More important, the last three years of ownership are likewise ignored (TCGA 1992 s 203(1)) and this may prove helpful on a matrimonial breakdown. It also means that a taxpayer owning two houses can, by careful use of his election, obtain a tax advantage, subject, of course, to the necessity of making the election within two years of the second or subsequent acquisition.                           **[23.83]**

#### EXAMPLE 23.6

Janet acquires a property in Raynes Park in June 2004 that she lets until June 2006. She then occupies the property as her main residence until selling it in April 2007. Because she has occupied the property as her residence there is no CGT charge on any gain arising during her final three years of ownership.

## 4   Periods allowed under s 223

TCGA 1992 s 223(3) allows other periods of absence to be ignored provided that the owner had no other residence available for the exemption during these periods and that as a matter of fact he resided in the house *before and after* the absence in question. These periods are:
(1)   any period or periods of absence not exceeding three years altogether;
(2)   any period when the taxpayer was employed abroad; and
(3)   a maximum period of four years where the owner could not occupy the property because he was employed elsewhere.
The proviso for residing in the house before and after an absence does not require that it should be immediate.                                    **[23.84]**

## 5   Absence because of employment

The Revenue accepts that if the absence exceeds the permitted period in (1)–(3) above it is only the excess which does not qualify for the exemption.

The requirement that the taxpayer should reside after the period of absence will not apply in (2) and (3) if that is prevented by the terms of his employment (ESC D4). If he is required either by the nature of his employment or as the result of his trade or profession to live in another accommodation ('job-related accommodation') he will obtain the exemption if he buys a house intending to use it in the future as a main residence. It does not matter that he never occupies it and that it is let throughout, provided that he can show that he intended to live there. He should, of course, be advised to make the main residence election since he is occupying other (job-related) property (unless this occupation derives from his contract of service).                                    **[23.85]–[23.100]**

## VI   EXPENDITURE WITH A PROFIT-MAKING MOTIVE

The principal private residence exemption does not apply if the house was acquired wholly or partly for the purpose of realising a gain, nor to a gain attributable to any expenditure that was incurred wholly or partly for the purpose of realising a gain (TCGA 1992 s 224(3)). The acquisition of a freehold reversion by a tenant with a view to selling an absolute title to the property would appear to fall within this provision. If so, the portion of the gain attributable to the reversion would be assessable. The Revenue has, however, indicated that expenditure incurred in obtaining planning permission or obtaining the release of a restrictive covenant would be ignored for the purpose of s 224(3). The requirement of motive makes this provision difficult to apply, but the Revenue view is that only where the *primary purpose* of the acquisition was an early disposal at a profit will it be invoked (RI 75, August 1994). In *Jones v Wilcock* (1996) the taxpayer and his wife had lived in their home for nearly five years. In trying to establish an allowable loss, he argued that the exemption should not apply since he had acquired his home with the object of selling it at a profit. The Special Commissioner rejected this argument, saying that the word 'intention' did not always equate with 'purpose' and that the taxpayer had bought the property in order to provide himself and his wife with a home. An eventual gain was a hope, possibly an expectation, but it was not a 'purpose' within s 224(3).    **[23.101]–[23.120]**

## VII   SECOND HOMES

Principal private residence relief is not available on second homes and taxpayers will commonly find that on the disposal of such properties a substantial chargeable gain is produced. It is not possible for husband and wife to have separate main residences and the Revenue will resist any suggestions that a minor child has acquired a main residence separate from his parents. Further, by virtue of FA 2004, principal private residence relief is no longer available for disposals on or after the 10 December 2003 if the gain includes a gain that was held over on one or more previous disposals, for example, on the house being transferred into trust (TCGA 1992 s 226A). If, however, one or more of such disposals were made before 10 December 2003, the relief will continue to apply to that part of the gain referable to the period prior to the 10 December 2003. Because of the operation of these transitional provisions, it is advisable to trigger a disposal of the property sooner rather than later.                                              **[23.121]–[23.140]**

> **EXAMPLE 23.7**
>
> Mr Wealthy wished to give his seaside cottage (then valued at £200,000) to his son Oliver, but was concerned to postpone the payment of any CGT on its disposal (which would have realised a gain of £120,000 before any taper relief). Accordingly, on 1 February 2003, he settled the property on discretionary trusts. No IHT was payable since the transfer fell within Mr Wealthy's available nil rate band, and CGT hold-over relief was successfully claimed. The trustees permitted Oliver to occupy the cottage as his only residence from 1 May 2003 to November 2006. On 10 December 2006, the trustees sell the cottage for £220,000 (net of incidental costs). The trustees have a gain of £140,000. TCGA 1992 226A denies the availability of principal private residence relief to the whole gain although, because the gifts related to a transfer before 10 December 2003, the transitional rule applies so that the trustees are entitled to the relief in respect of the period from the 1 February 2003 to 9 December 2003 (312 days). Their total period of ownership was 1408 days. Accordingly, they are entitled to principal private residence relief of £ 31,022.73 (£140,000 X 312/ 1408). They remain chargeable on a gain of £ 108,977.30. *Note* that even though the period between 10 December 2003 and 10 December 2006 is part of the final three years of the trustees' ownership of the property, principal private residence relief is not available: the transitional provisions specifically prevent any period on or after 10 December 2003 from qualifying for relief as part of the final three years of ownership.

## VIII   LINK UP WITH IHT SCHEMES

A number of arrangements have been entered into in recent years with a view to mitigating IHT on main residences. For instance:

(i)   *'Ingram arrangements'* Under these arrangements the taxpayer reserved a lease for (say) 20 years and gifted the freehold interest to his children.

(ii)  *Reversionary leases*: In practical terms a similar arrangement to (i) but conceptually quite distinct. The taxpayer grants a long lease (commonly 999 years) to his children to take effect in (say) 21 years. He continues to occupy the property as a result of his retained freehold interest.

(iii) On the death of Mr H his will provides for the IHT nil rate sum to be held on discretionary trusts with the residue passing to Mrs H (his wife). Mr H's share in the main residence (he will frequently be a tenant in common as to a 50% beneficial share) will often be held by the trustees of the nil rate trust.

In these cases whilst IHT saving is the goal it is important that the arrangements do not ignore any potential CGT liability. Thus if in due course the property will be sold (typically by the children on the death of the parents) then in all these cases there is likely to be a chargeable gain given that the children will not acquire the property for market value on the death of their parents. There is, therefore, a risk that IHT savings will be offset (at least in part) by subsequent CGT liabilities.                     **[23.141]**

# 24 CGT—gifts and sales at undervalue

*Updated by Andrew Farley, Partner, Wilsons*

---

---

'Mr Turner has really argued his case on broader lines than I have so far indicated, and has used language, though moderate and reasonably temperate, as to the ways of Parliament in misusing language and in effect "deeming" him into a position which on any ordinary use of the words "capital gains" was impossible to assert. He in effect says "Here is a discreditable manipulation of words. The Statute is not truthful. Words ought to mean what they say".'

> (Russell LJ in *Turner v Follett* (1973) 48 TC 614 at 621.)
> **[24.1]**

## I INTRODUCTORY

### 1 A gift as a disposal at market value

A disposal of an asset, otherwise than by way of a bargain at arm's length, is treated as a disposal at the open market value (TCGA 1992 s 17). A donor is, therefore, deemed to receive the market value of the property that he has given away even though he has in fact received nothing (*Turner v Follett* (1973)). A disposal between connected persons is treated as a transaction 'otherwise than by way of bargain at arm's length' (and hence taxed as a disposal at market value: see TCGA 1992 s 18(2); for the definition of connected persons see **[19.23]**).          **[24.2]**

#### EXAMPLE 24.1

Jackson sells a valuable Ming vase to his son Pollock for £10,000 which is the price that he had paid for it ten years before. The market value of the vase at the date of sale is £45,000. This disposal between connected persons is deemed to be made otherwise than by way of bargain at arm's length so that market value is substituted for the price actually paid and Jackson is deemed to have received £45,000. Pollock is treated as acquiring the vase for a cost price of £45,000.

## 2  IHT overlap

In addition to being treated as a disposal at market value for CGT purposes, a gift of assets may be chargeable (or potentially chargeable) to IHT. Only limited relief is available against this double charge (see further [24.32]).

*First*, in calculating the fall in value of the transferor's estate for IHT purposes, his CGT liability is ignored. IHT is not, therefore, charged on CGT paid by a donor (see [28.63]).

*Secondly*, if the CGT is paid not by the transferor but by the transferee, the amount of that tax will reduce the value transferred for IHT purposes (IHTA 1984 s 165(1)). Normally CGT is paid by the transferor but there is nothing to stop the parties from agreeing that the burden shall be discharged by the transferee.

### EXAMPLE 24.2

Mr Big transfers a freehold office block to his daughter Martha Big. Assume that the value of the freehold (ignoring IHT business relief) is £750,000 and that the CGT amounts to £250,000.
(1)    If the CGT is paid by Mr Big the diminution in his estate for IHT purposes is £750,000 (ie it is *not* £750,000 + £250,000).
(2)    If the CGT is paid by Martha the diminution in Mr Big's estate is reduced to £500,000 (ie £750,000 – £250,000).

In certain situations CGT on a lifetime gift may be postponed if a holdover election is made and these are considered in the following sections.

**[24.3]–[24.20]**

## II  GIFTS OF BUSINESS ASSETS (TCGA 1992 ss 165–169; Sch 7)

### 1  When does s 165 apply?

There must be a disposal by *an individual* although this is extended to trustees (see TCGA 1992 Sch 7 para 2—this includes the deemed disposal made by trustees under TCGA 1992 s 71 on the termination of a trust: see [25.47]). The disposal must be 'otherwise than under a bargain at arm's length' and therefore includes both gifts and undervalue sales. In general the recipient can be any 'person', a term which embraces not just individuals but also trustees and companies. However, relief is not available when shares or securities are transferred to a company (s 165(3)(ba): note that all other business assets attract the relief if gifted to a company).    **[24.21]**

### 2  What property is included?

The section is limited to gifts of business assets, defined as follows (s 165(2)):

'an asset is within this sub-section if—

(a)    it is, or is an interest in, an asset used for the purposes of a trade, profession or vocation carried on by—
    (i)   the transferor, or

    (ii)   his personal company, or

    (iii)   a member of a trading group of which the holding company is his personal company, or

  (b)   it consists of shares or securities of a trading company, or of the holding company of a trading group, where—

    (i)   the shares or securities are not listed on a recognised stock exchange, or

    (ii)   the trading company or holding company is the transferor's personal company.'

Accordingly, under s 165(2)(b)(i), AIM shares can benefit from the relief but the disposal of a qualifying corporate bond (QCB) does not attract relief (see **[41.93]**). **[24.22]**

### a)   *Which assets qualify?*

It should be noted that *any* asset is included provided only that it is used for the purposes of a trade, profession or vocation (contrast, for instance, roll-over reinvestment relief (see **[22.72]**) which is limited to certain categories of asset). A mere disposal of assets suffices: it is not necessary for the disposal to be of part of the business.

Non-business assets do not attract relief. Similarly, if the assets disposed of are shares, the amount of the gain eligible for hold-over relief may be restricted if the company owns chargeable assets other than business assets. This restriction only applies if the transferor has had a significant interest in the company within the 12-month period before the disposal, ie if the company has been his 'personal company' at some time within this period or, in the case of trustees, if they have owned at least 25% of the voting rights at some time within this period. Where the restriction applies the proportion of the gain eligible for the relief is the proportion which the market value of the company's business assets bears to the market value of the company's total chargeable assets: TCGA 1992 Sch 7 para 7. **[24.23]**

### b)   *Used for the purposes of a trade*

Whether an asset is used for the purposes of a trade may be a moot point: for instance, would the relief be available on a gift of a valuable Munch oil painting (*The Sick Corpse*) which has adorned the offices of a funeral parlour for many years?

Where the asset has been used for a trade for only part of the period of ownership or, in the case of a building, where only part of the building has been used for a trade, the gain eligible for the relief is, in each case, reduced proportionately: TCGA 1992 Sch 7 paras 5 and 6. **[24.24]**

### c)   *APR land*

Land qualifying (or which would qualify on a chargeable transfer being made) for 100% or 50% IHT agricultural property relief is specifically included as a business asset for these purposes (TCGA 1992 Sch 7: for APR, see [31.61] ff). Accordingly let land may qualify for the relief.    [24.25]

### EXAMPLE 24.3

Let agricultural land is owned by the trustees of the Milford Grandchildren's Trust. The trust was established in 1981; in 2002 Debbie becomes entitled to an interest in possession in the entire trust fund on becoming 21. In 2006 when she is 25 the trust ends.

*For IHT purposes* The ending of the trust in 2006 is not an occasion of charge (see IHTA 1984 s 53(2)).

*For CGT purposes* the ending of the trust results in a deemed disposal under TCGA 1992 s 71 (see [25.47]) and hold-over relief under s 165 *will not be available*. This is because the land would not attract APR: although the land has been owned by the trustees for more than the required seven years, in 2002—when Debbie became entitled to an interest in possession—a new ownership period began and, of course, *she* has only owned the land for four years.

*Note:* As a result of the changes to the IHT treatment of trusts introduced by FA 2006 the acquisition of an interest in possession in most trusts after 21 March 2006 will not now trigger a new ownership period for IHT.

### d)    *Meaning of 'personal company' and 'trading company'*

An individual's 'personal company' is defined as one in which the individual owns not less than 5% of the voting rights (TCGA 1992 s 165(8)(a)). 'Trading company' has the same meaning as for taper relief (see [20.28]).
                                                                                        [24.26]

### e)    *Trustees*

These definitions and requirements are modified in the case of business assets owned by trustees. Broadly, in the case of assets, the relevant 'trade, profession or vocation' must either be that of the trustees or of a beneficiary with an interest in possession in the settled property; and in the case of shares in a trading company, unless the shares qualify as being not listed on a recognised stock exchange, at least 25% of the voting rights at the company's general meeting must be exercisable by the trustees.    [24.27]

## 3    The election

Hold-over relief under the section will only be given on a claim being made in the prescribed form by both transferor and transferee (save where the transferee is a trustee when only the transferor need elect: TCGA 1992 s 165(1)). The donor is treated as disposing and the donee as acquiring the asset for its market value at the date of the gift *minus* the chargeable gain which is held over. This postponement of tax continues until the donee disposes of the asset although, if the donee in turn makes a gift of the asset, a further hold-over election may be available. In the event of the donee dying still owning the asset, the entire gain is wiped out by the death uplift in value.

Since the election is to hold over a gain which would otherwise be chargeable, in principle it is necessary to agree the amount of that gain with the Revenue so that the election should be accompanied by relevant valuations. In SP 8/92, however, the Inland Revenue published a revised statement of practice whereby computation of the gain (and hence formal valuation of the asset) is in many cases not required. Both transferor and transferee must request this treatment in writing and provide full details of the asset transferred (the date of its acquisition and the allowable expenditure) or, alternatively, a calculation of the gain based on informally estimated valuations. Once such a request has been accepted it cannot subsequently be withdrawn. In the majority of cases, taxpayers will be only too happy to avoid the time and trouble (not to mention the expense) involved in agreeing valuations with the Revenue.

**EXAMPLE 24.4**

(1)   Sim gives his ironmonger's business to his daughter Sammy in 2005. For CGT purposes any gain resulting from this gift of chargeable business assets may be held over on the joint election of Sim and Sammy.
(2)   Jim settles his ironmonger's business on trust for his son Jack absolutely contingent on becoming 30 (Jack is aged 10). As in (1) above, s 165 will apply: however in this case only Jim need elect. When the trust ends, eg on Jack becoming absolutely entitled to the business, a further hold-over election may then be made by the trustees and Jack to postpone payment of tax which would otherwise arise under TCGA 1992 s 71.
(3)   Oliver is the sole shareholder and director of a computer company (ACC Ltd) and owns the freehold site used by the company. He gives away his shares to his four daughters equally and the freehold to his son. Section 165 relief is available to postpone tax on all five gifts since ACC is Oliver's personal company.

When the election is made:

'(a)   the amount of any chargeable gain which, apart from this section, would accrue to the transferor on the disposal, and
(b)    the amount of the consideration for which, apart from this section, the transferee would be regarded for the purposes of CGT as having acquired the asset or, as the case may be, the shares or securities,
shall each be reduced by an amount equal to the held-over gain on the disposal.'

**EXAMPLE 24.5**

Smiley gives Karla shares in his family company worth £35,000. Smiley's allowable expenditure for CGT purposes (including any indexation allowance until April 1998) is £10,000. They make a joint election under s 165 so that Smiley's chargeable gain (£35,000 – £10,000 = £25,000) is reduced to nil. Smiley is effectively treated as disposing of the shares for £10,000 and, as his expenses are £10,000, he has made neither gain nor loss. Karla is treated as acquiring the shares for the market value consideration (£35,000) less the held-over gain (£25,000) ie for £10,000.

Assume that within 12 months of the gift Karla sells the shares for £41,000 incurring deductible expenses of £2,000. He will be assessed to CGT on a gain calculated as follows:

|  | £ | £ |
|---|---|---|
| Sale proceeds | | 41,000 |
| *Less:* | | |
| Acquisition costs | 10,000 | |
| Deductible expenses | 2,000 | |
| | | 12,000 |
| Chargeable gain | | £29,000 |

*Notes:*
(1)    Of this gain, £4,000 is attributable to Karla's period of ownership (£29,000 – £25,000) and £25,000 represents the gain held over on the gift from Smiley.
(2)    Karla's deemed acquisition costs will include the value of Smiley's indexation allowance until April 1998 (if any) but any taper relief built up by Smiley will be lost (see **[24.29]**).

No time limit for making this election is prescribed in the section and hence the general rule laid down in TMA 1970 s 43 applies: namely the claim must be made within five years from 31 January in the tax year following that in which the disposal occurred (ie a period of some five years and ten months). There is a standard claim form which *must* be used in all cases (although photocopies of the form will be accepted).                    **[24.28]**

## 4    The effect of taper relief

Taper relief reduces the amount of gain on which tax is charged; it does not affect the calculation of the gain itself. By contrast, indexation (which taper replaced) operated as a further deduction in computing the gain. This contrast is significant when calculating the gain that is to be held over under either s 165 or s 260. Moreover, unlike indexation the donee receives no credit for the accrued taper relief of the donor: his taper relief is calculated by reference only to the period for which he personally owned the asset.
                                                                                            **[24.29]**

**EXAMPLE 24.6**

Calculus acquired a farm for £1m on 6 April 1998. On 1 January 2005 he gives the farm to his son when its value has increased to £10m. As he has owned the farm for more than two years only 25% of Calculus' gain of £9m will be taxed (tax of £900,000 at a 40% rate). If they elect to hold over the gain, however, the son's base cost is *only £1m*. If he were immediately to sell the farm therefore he would suffer tax of £3.6m (40% × £9m). *In cases when a would-be donor has substantial accrued taper there is a disincentive to making a gift of the asset.* Note the following points:
(a)    with the reduction of the business asset taper period to two years the disincentive is not as great as when taper was first introduced in 1998;
(b)    the parties may delay claiming hold-over relief in case the son sells the farm before he has built up 75% relief.

## 5    The annual exemption and retirement relief

The legislation does not permit CGT *annual exemption* (see **[19.86]**) to be combined with an election under s 165, ie it is not possible to set off the annual exemption against part of a chargeable gain and apply hold-over relief to the balance. Either the whole chargeable gain must be held over or it must be subject to CGT but with the benefit of the annual exemption. Where any gain will not exceed the annual exemption, the s 165 election should not be made: and even if the gain just exceeds the exemption it may be preferable to pay a small CGT charge. In appropriate cases it will be possible to obtain the best of both worlds, ie to make two disposals, the first of an asset where the gain is covered by the annual exemption and the second of other business assets where hold-over relief under s 165 is claimed.

Unlike the annual exemption, *retirement relief* operated by reducing the gross gain made by a taxpayer on the disposal of a business or part of a business so that only the balance (if any) remaining was chargeable gain (TCGA 1992 Sch 6 para 6; and see **Chapter 22**). (Retirement relief was abolished from tax year 2003–04). **[24.30]**

## 6 Sales at undervalue

Although s 165 applies both to gifts and sales at undervalue, if the actual consideration paid on a disposal exceeds the allowable CGT deductions of the transferor, that excess is subject to charge. It is only the balance of any gain (ie the amount by which the consideration is less than the full value of the business asset) which may be held over under s 165. For the Revenue's attitude when assets are transferred on a divorce, see *Tax Bulletin* August 2003, p 1051.

### EXAMPLE 24.7

Julius sells shares in his family company worth £25,000 to his brother Jason for £16,500. Julius has allowable deductions for CGT purposes of £11,500. The CGT position is:
(1) Total gain on disposal: £25,000 – £11,500 = £13,500.
(2) Excess of actual consideration over allowable deductions:
£16,500 – £11,500 = £5,000.
(3) Gain subject to CGT ((2) above) is £5,000, as reduced by any taper relief. After deducting Julius' annual exemption the tax payable will be nil.
(4) Balance of gain, £8,500 (ie (1) – (2)) can be held over under s 165.

If the partial consideration is less than the allowable deductions it is ignored so that a CGT loss cannot be created. **[24.31]**

### EXAMPLE 24.8

Assume in *Example 24.7* that the sale price was £11,500 and the allowable deductions £16,500 instead of the other way around. The total gain of £8,500 could be held-over under s 165. The sale price of £11,500 would be ignored: Julius would not have made a loss for CGT even though he sold the shares for an amount less than his allowable deductions; and Jason's initial base cost would still be £16,500 (market value less held-over gain) and would be unaffected by the actual consideration paid by him.

## 7 The inter-relationsip between hold-over relief and IHT

The overlap between CGT and IHT in the area of lifetime gifts and gratuitous undervalue transfers has already been noted (see **[24.3]**).

When chargeable gains are held over under s 165 the transferee can add to his CGT acquisition costs all or part of the IHT paid on the value of the gift. This principle applies whoever pays the IHT.

**EXAMPLE 24.9**

Wendy gives shares in her family cookery company ('Cook-Inn & Co') to her daughter, Kim. The chargeable gain arising of £100,000 is held over under s 165 and Kim therefore acquires the shares at a value of £75,000. For IHT purposes the gift by Wendy is a PET when made and therefore no tax is payable at that stage. Assume, however, that Wendy dies within seven years so that the gift then becomes chargeable and that IHT of £20,000 is paid. Kim can add that sum to her base cost for CGT purposes which therefore becomes £95,000 (£75,000 + £20,000).

*Notes:*

(1)   A similar principle applies in the case of lifetime gifts which are subject to an immediate IHT charge. The IHT payable on the lifetime chargeable transfer, including the increased amount payable if the transferor dies within the following seven years, can be added to the transferee's base cost for CGT.

(2)   Although the IHT paid is added to Kim's base cost in order to reduce her gain on a subsequent disposal of the shares, this sum is not an item of deductible expenditure for CGT purposes *and therefore did not benefit from the indexation allowance.*

(3)   It may be that Kim has already disposed of the shares before the death of her mother. Nevertheless she is entitled to have her allowable expenditure increased by the IHT resulting from Wendy's death and therefore an adjustment will be made to any CGT paid on the disposal of the shares.

There are two limits on the amount of IHT that can be added to the donee's CGT base cost.

*First,* the maximum amount permissible is the IHT *attributable to the gift.* This means that if IHT had been paid by the transferor on a chargeable lifetime gift so that 'grossing-up' applied, it is only the IHT charged on the value of the gift received by the donee which can be used (grossing-up is discussed at **[28.124]**).

*Secondly,* IHT which is added to the transferee's base cost cannot be used to create a CGT loss on a later disposal by the transferee. Accordingly, in *Example 24.9* above, if Kim were to sell the shares after the death of Wendy for £90,000 she would only be able to use £15,000 of the IHT payable on Wendy's death since this could have the effect of wiping out any chargeable gain and she cannot use the remaining £5,000 to create a CGT loss (TCGA 1992 s 165(10)). **[24.32]**

## 8   Non-UK residents

### a)   *Individuals*

Section 165 hold-over relief is not available if the transferee is neither resident nor ordinarily resident in the UK (TCGA 1992 s 166). This limitation is necessary since disposals by such a person are outside the CGT net! In addition, any held-over gain will be triggered if, whilst still owning the asset in question, the transferee emigrates before six complete tax years have expired after the tax year of the disposal to him: TCGA 1992 s 168.

**EXAMPLE 24.10**

In 1998 Imelda's father gave her shares in the family company. A gain of £80,000 was held over so that she had an acquisition cost of £10,000. In 2005 she took up permanent residence in Spain. The held-over gain of £80,000 becomes chargeable 'immediately before' she ceased to be UK resident at the rates in force in the tax year of emigration.

If the shares had increased in value to £130,000 by 2005, there is no question of charging that increase which is attributable to her period of ownership; any loss would likewise be ignored.

The CGT in such cases is payable primarily by the transferee, but if tax remains unpaid 12 months after the due date it can be recovered from the transferor (TCGA 1992 s 168(7)). In such an event the transferor is given a right to recover a corresponding sum from the transferee (TCGA 1992 s 168(9)) although, if the Revenue has not obtained payment from the transferee, the transferor is unlikely to succeed!

The emigration charge will not apply if the transferee leaves the UK because of work connected with his office or employment and performs all the duties of that office or employment outside the UK, provided he does not dispose of the asset whilst outside the UK (if so the gain is taxed unless the disposal is to a spouse) and resumes UK residence within three years of his initial departure; otherwise the gain is taxed (TCGA 1992 s 168(5)).

It will obviously be unnecessary to invoke this emigration charge if, before becoming non-resident, the transferee had made a disposal of the asset (TCGA 1992 s 168(1)(b)). That disposal will either have triggered the held-over gain or, if it was by way of gift and a s 165 election had been made, the asset pregnant with gain will now be owned by another UK resident, so that the Revenue is not threatened with a loss of tax. If that prior disposal was merely a part disposal, so triggering only a part of the held-over gain, the balance will be chargeable on emigration.

An exception to the provision that the transferee who emigrates after the disposal of the asset will not be subject to a charge is when that prior disposal is to the emigrating transferee's spouse. If that spouse had also disposed of the asset, however, resulting in a CGT charge on the gain originally held over, that further disposal will be treated as if it had been by the transferee so that the emigration charge will not apply (TCGA 1992 s 168(3)).          **[24.33]**

b)  *Companies*

Section 167 deals with gifts to foreign controlled companies and prevents hold-over relief from being available: a company is foreign controlled for these purposes if it is controlled by a person or persons who are neither resident nor ordinarily resident in the UK and who are connected with the disponer (for the meaning of control, see TA 1988 s 416: **[41.123]**).   **[24.34]**

**EXAMPLE 24.11**

Z, a UK resident, transfers his business to Q Ltd, a company which is owned as to 51% by Z and as to 49% by an offshore structure. Hold-over relief under s 165 will be available.

*Notes*:

(1)    If Z is non-UK domiciled there will be attractions in Q Ltd being incorporated outside the UK (so that its shares will be non-UK situs assets which is significant both for CGT and IHT purposes given Z's non-domiciled status) but which is UK resident by virtue of its management being situated in the UK (**[18.10]**).

(2)    There is no trigger of the held-over gain if in the future further shares in Q Ltd are issued to non-resident shareholders.

(3)    The restriction noted at **[24.21]** prevents hold-over relief being available on a disposal of *shares* to Q Ltd.

## 9   Other triggering events

Apart from the emigration of the transferee, a gain held over on creation of a settlement will become chargeable on the death of the life tenant (this matter is discussed at **[25.51]**). A subsequent sale of the property by the donee will also result in the held-over gain becoming taxable and it should be noted that, because rebasing was not available when the gift was made between 1982 and 1988, in such cases there will be a 50% reduction in the amount of the held-over gain which is taxed (see also **[19.42]**).

### EXAMPLE 24.12

Diane acquired a business for £10,000 in 1980. By 31 March 1982 its value had increased to £25,000. In June 1986 she gave it to her niece when its value was £40,000 and both entered into a hold-over election. In July 2005 the niece sold the business for £50,000. Ignoring the indexation allowance, taper relief and any incidental expenditure and assuming that the business comprises only chargeable business assets, the CGT position is as follows:

(1)    In 1986 the niece acquired the assets at a base cost of £10,000 (ie £40,000 minus the held-over gain of £30,000).

(2)    In 2005 her gain on disposal is £40,000 but one half of the gain held over in 1986 (ie £15,000) is not subject to charge so that the chargeable gain is £25,000 (£40,000 – £15,000).

*Note:* The mechanism of TCGA 1992 Sch 4 para 1 means that it is the niece's acquisition cost in 1986 which is increased by £15,000 (to £25,000). This beneficially affects the calculation of the indexation allowance.

A subsequent gift of the property will not trigger a charge provided that a further election is made: on the death of the transferee any held-over gain is wiped out (though note the special rules when a gain is held over on creation of a settlement and the interest in possession beneficiary subsequently dies: see **[25.51]**).                                                   **[24.35]**

### EXAMPLE 24.13

Boy Sam settled his family trading company shares on trusts for his companion Justin for life, remainder to his mother, Iris. Under a power in the settlement the trustees subsequently advanced the shares to Justin. No CGT arose on the creation of the settlement provided that Boy Sam so elected (in this case an election by the settlor alone sufficed) nor on the deemed disposal under TCGA 1992 s 71(1) resulting from the termination of the settlement when the property was advanced *in specie* to Justin (provided that the trustees and Justin so elected). As in the case of outright gifts, therefore, CGT may be postponed until the assets are sold.

## 10 Anti-avoidance

There are anti-avoidance provisions denying hold-over relief (under both TCGA 1992 s 165 and s 260 – see **25.65**) on a transfer to a settlor-interested settlement (TCGA 1992 ss 169B – 169G). For this purpose a settlor has an interest in a settlement where any property in the settlement (or any property derived from that property) may be, or is, used for the benefit of the settlor or his spouse *or any minor unmarried child of his (who is not in a civil partnership)*. 'Child' includes step-child. The extension to cover minor unmarried children applies to all settlements, whenever created, from 6 April 2006 (FA 2006) and many settlements which have not been settlor-interested for CGT purposes will automatically become so on 6 April 2006 as a result of this provision.

The legislation is designed to prevent a gain being, in effect, transferred to trustees who are in a position to realise the gain at less tax cost (because of available reliefs or losses) than the settlor, with the settlor then able to benefit directly or indirectly from the resulting funds.

The obvious counter of transferring property to a settlement that is not a settlor-interested settlement but which subsequently becomes settlor-interested is prevented by means of a clawback of hold-over relief (and a corresponding increase in the trustees' base cost). This occurs if the settlement becomes settlor-interested within six years of the end of the tax year in which the gift was made. One effect of the FA 2006 legislation is that a settlement could become settlor-interested inadvertently eg if a settlor makes a settlement for the benefit of his children, all whom are adult at the time the settlement is made, and he then acquires minor step-children on re-marriage. But a saving provision applies for pre- 6 April 2006 disposals to a settlement from which the settlor's minor children could, and still can, benefit: if hold-over relief under s 165 was claimed on the disposal there will not be an immediate clawback of the relief as a result of the extended meaning now given to settlor-interested settlements.

*Note:* If held-over gains are clawed back and charged to CGT there will be no taper relief on those gains even though taper relief would have been available if the settlor had chosen to pay the CGT and not elect for hold-over relief. **[24.36]–[24.60]**

## III GIFTS OF ASSETS ATTRACTING AN IMMEDIATE IHT CHARGE (TCGA 1992 s 260(2)(A))

The second situation where hold-over relief is available on a gift or under-value sale, is if the relevant disposal 'is a chargeable transfer within the meaning of the IHTA 1984' or would be such a transfer but for the availability of the annual exemption. A chargeable transfer of business or agricultural property qualifying for 100% relief from IHT is eligible for relief under this provision notwithstanding that no IHT will actually be due.

A gain arising on the disposal of a qualifying corporate bond (QCB) cannot be held over under this section. **[24.61]**

## 1 When is there an immediate IHT charge on inter vivos gifts?

Lifetime transfers which are PETs (now reduced in scope considerably by FA 2006) do not attract an immediate IHT charge: accordingly, in such cases hold-over relief under this section is not available and this applies *even if* the PET subsequently becomes chargeable because of the death of the transferor within seven years.

The circumstances in which s 260(2)(a) hold-over relief is available have been considerably enlarged as a consequence of the changes to the IHT treatment of trusts introduced by FA 2006, with most disposals into, and out of, settlements now being chargeable transfers for IHT. Relief under s260(2)(a) is available in the following cases with effect from 22 March 2006:

(1) on the lifetime disposal of assets *to* all new trusts made on or after 22 March 2006 (except where the trust is a disabled trust under IHTA 1984 ss 89 or 89A: most disposals to such trusts will be PETs);

(2) on the lifetime disposal of assets on or after 22 March 2006 *to* all pre-existing trusts (whether discretionary, interest in possession or accumulation and maintenance);

(3) on the disposal of assets by trustees *out of* all new trusts made on or after 22 March 2006, except where the disposal is made on the lifetime termination of an immediate post-death interest (see [33.4]) in favour of a beneficiary absolutely entitled (such a disposal will be a PET) *Note:* disposals to minors from trusts under IHTA 1984 ss 71A or 71D are not chargeable transfers for IHT but nevertheless qualify for hold-over relief under new paragraphs of s 260(2) inserted by FA 2006: see [24.91]–[24.110];

(4) on the disposal of assets by trustees *out of:*
   - pre-existing discretionary trusts
   - pre-existing interest in possession trusts, except where the disposal is made on the lifetime termination of the pre-existing interest in possession, or of a transitional serial interest (see [33.4]), in favour of a beneficiary absolutely entitled (such a disposal will be a PET)
   - pre-existing accumulation and maintenance trusts which enter the IHT relevant property regime on 6 April 2008 or on an interest in possession arising before that date. (For hold-over relief on disposals from such trusts prior to them entering the relevant property regime see [24.91]–[24.110]).

In addition, relief under s 260(2)(a) is available:

(5) On a gift between individuals or on the creation of a disabled trust in circumstances where such gifts fall outside the definition of a PET. Such cases are rare: see [28.41].

Because s 260 specifies that to come within its terms the disposal must be to and by either an individual or the trustees of a settlement, gifts to and by companies do not attract hold-over relief even though they are not PETs. (Unless, of course, the gift to a company is of a business asset other than shares when relief may be available under s 165 as discussed at [24.21].)

[24.62]

## 2 The relief

The relief afforded by s 260 is broadly the same as that given under s 165. Relief under s 260 does, however, take precedence over the s 165 relief (TCGA 1992 s 165(3)(d)) and this may have attractions when what is contemplated is a transfer of shares in a family company which owns non-business assets since there is no apportionment requirement under s 260 (contrast s 165 at **[24.27]** and see *Capital Taxes*, 1990, p 52).

An election is required in the same terms as under s 165; the effect of holding over the gain is the same (ie the asset is disposed of and acquired at market value less held-over gain); the transferee must be either UK resident or ordinarily resident and subsequent emigration may trigger the charge. Unlike s 165 there is, however, no restriction on the type of asset for which relief may be claimed.                                   **[24.63]**

## 3 Practical uses of s 260(2)(a)

To date the main situations where hold-over relief under s 260(2)(a) has been employed have been when a discretionary trust has been either created or ended. These have been the principal occasions on which an immediate IHT charge has arisen and hence a gain on a chargeable asset entering or leaving a trust has been held-over. The following example illustrates the various permutations that are now available for s 260(2)(a) hold-over relief following the considerable extension of IHT lifetime chargeable transfers by FA 2006.                                   **[24.64]**

**EXAMPLE 24.14**

(1)  In May 2006, Jake transfers his portfolio of stocks and shares (worth £500,000) into a new trust for the benefit of his adult children; the transfer results in an immediate IHT charge and therefore any gain on the investments can be held over if Jake (alone) elects under s 260(2)(a). Note that any IHT paid by Jake (ignoring grossing-up) can be deducted by the trustees in arriving at the CGT charge on a subsequent disposal of the shares (and this sum may be increased should an extra tax charge result from the death of Jake within seven years of establishing his trust: see **[24.32]**).

(2)  Joseph establishes a new trust by transferring land worth £255,000 to the trustees. As his first chargeable transfer, IHT will not be payable since it falls within Joseph's nil rate band. Despite this, hold-over relief under s 260(2)(a) is available since the transfer by Joseph is chargeable to IHT albeit at a nil rate. This gives the best of all worlds: no IHT but CGT hold-over. (Note that s 260(2)(a) also applies if a transfer of value which would otherwise attract an immediate IHT charge is covered by the transferor's annual exemption.)

(3)  Were the trustees of Joseph's trust subsequently (eg six months later) to appoint the cottage to a beneficiary outright, there should still be no IHT charge but again CGT hold-over relief will be available.

(4)  Thal and Thad, trustees of the Mallard discretionary trust, appoint chargeable assets to Billy Beneficiary. This being a trust of 'relevant property' for IHT (see **[28.1]–[28.20]**), an 'exit' charge will arise (see **[34.23]**) and therefore any chargeable gain can be held over on the joint election of Thal, Thad and Billy. Note, however, that an appointment out of a relevant property trust *within three months of its creation* does not give rise to any IHT charge (see **[34.25]**) and that appointments out of a relevant property trust

established by will made within two years of the testator's death are 'read back' into that will (see **[30.145]**). Therefore CGT hold-over is not available in either case.

(5)     Trustees Tom and Ted, in exercise of powers conferred on them by the settlement, resettle the trust property (non-business assets) into a new settlement. This is a deemed disposal under s 71(1) for CGT purposes but any resulting gain may only be held over if it is also a chargeable event for IHT. With many inter-settlement transfers after 22 March 2006 this will not be the case since the property will have moved from one 'relevant property' settlement to another and no IHT 'exit' charge will arise due to the operation of IHTA 1984 s 81 (see **[34.32]**) which deems the property to remain comprised in the transferring settlement. If, by contrast, trustees exercise their powers so as to appoint new trusts of the *same* settlement (eg by terminating a pre-22 March 2006 life interest and appointing fresh discretionary trusts) then although this will give rise to a lifetime chargeable transfer for IHT there will be no deemed disposal at all for CGT purposes since the trust assets will not have left the settlement (and so hold-over relief will not need to be considered).

(6)     In 1990 Seth made an accumulation and maintenance settlement in favour of his infant grandchildren, Gus and Zac, by which each would acquire a life interest in an equal half share on reaching 25. In fact Gus acquired an interest in possession in his share under Trustee Act 1925 s 31 on reaching 18 in January 2005 and he was then treated as becoming the beneficial owner of his share for IHT under IHTA 1984 s 49(1). Zac, however, does not acquire an interest in possession in his share until reaching 18 in November 2006 and, as a result of FA 2006 IHTA 1984, s 49(1), does not apply to his share at that point, and the share enters the IHT relevant property regime instead. After some deliberation the trustees consider both Gus and Zac to be financially responsible and, in order to curtail the IHT charges on Zac's share, they decide in March 2007 to exercise their powers of advancement by terminating the settlement in its entirety and transferring the assets out to Gus and Zac. Many of the assets are standing at a substantial gain.
The disposal of assets to Gus will not be a chargeable transfer for IHT since he is already deemed to be the beneficial owner of his share. Accordingly hold-over relief under s 260(2)(a) will not be available for the disposal to him. The disposal of assets to Zac, however, will result in a small IHT 'exit' charge, and therefore hold-over relief under s 260(2)(a) will be available on the disposal of assets to him. *Note:* Assuming they have the necessary power the trustees might consider appropriating the chargeable assets showing the large gains to Zac's share with the chargeable assets showing no gains and the non-chargeable assets such as cash and gilts being appropriated as necessary to achieve equality.

(7)     In May 1990 property was settled on A & M trusts for Sid by which he will acquire a life interest in the trust fund on attaining the age of 25. Sid will reach 25 in June 2010 and, because of the trustees' express power to accumulate the income until that time, he has not become entitled to an interest in possession under Trustee Act 1925 s 31 even though he is now over 18. To reduce future IHT charges to acceptable proportions the trustees decide to alter the terms of the trust with effect from 6 April 2008 so that Sid will become absolutely entitled to the capital on reaching 25 and the trust also satisfies the other conditions of IHTA 1984 s 71D. The special charge prospectively payable under s 71E on transfers to the beneficiary between the ages of 18 and 25 is considered an acceptable price to pay in order to avoid the heavier 10-yearly anniversary charge that would otherwise be due under the relevant property regime in May 2010 shortly before Sid

reaches 25. The trustees exercise their power of advancement to transfer some of the trust assets to Sid over the period from April 2008 and the remainder are transferred to him when he becomes absolutely entitled on attaining age 25. Each such transfer to Sid will be a chargeable transfer for IHT (by virtue of s 71E) and will therefore qualify for hold-over relief under s260(2)(a).

*Note:* care should be taken in arranging transfers from a s 71D trust shortly after the beneficiary has reached 18 because the special charge under s 71E does not apply to transfers to the beneficiary during the first three months after his/her 18th birthday. Accordingly hold-over relief under s 260(2)(a) will not be available on disposals during this brief period.

## 4  Anti-avoidance

The anti-avoidance measures described at **[24.36]** in relation to transfers to settlor-interested settlements apply equally to hold-over relief under s 260. However, hold-over under s 260 is subject to an additional anti-avoidance provision in relation to main residence relief (see TCGA 1992 s 226A; and for main residence relief see chapter 18). Where gifts relief has been claimed under s 260, private residence relief is denied. The legislation was designed to prevent arrangements such as that in the following example.     **[24.65]**

### EXAMPLE 24.15

Tarquin owns a house that is not his only or main residence. It has a market value of £500,000 and would realise a chargeable gain of £400,000 (before taper relief) if he sold it. Tarquin would like to sell the house and give the proceeds to his adult son, Torquil.

Tarquin therefore gifts the house into a discretionary trust, claiming relief under s 260(2)(a) (note that if the settlement were settlor-interested, the anti-avoidance described at **[24.36]** would be in point). Under the terms of the settlement, the trustees allow Torquil to occupy the house as his main residence. A few months later, Torquil leaves the house, and the trustees sell it for £510,000. The resultant gain of £410,000 is not chargeable because of main residence relief (see **[24.62]**). The trustees can then distribute the proceeds to Torquil.

The anti-avoidance provisions (introduced by FA 2004) operate to deny main residence relief in these circumstances.

Because of the time allowed to make a hold-over election (see **[24.28]**) it may be that the trustees' disposal takes place before a hold-over claim has been made, so that the anti-avoidance rule would not be in point. If a claim is made subsequent to the trustees' disposal, main residence relief will be withdrawn and all necessary tax adjustments made.

Conversely, if a hold-over election is in place, and it is desired to make main residence relief available, the claim may be revoked.     **[24.66]–[24.90]**

## IV  DISPOSALS FROM ACCUMULATION AND MAINTENANCE TRUSTS AND CHILDREN'S TRUSTS (TCGA 1992 s 260(2)(D), (DA) AND (DB))

Accumulation and maintenance (A & M) trusts were the creature of the IHT legislation where they were accorded privileged treatment and kept out of the relevant property regime with its anniversary and 'exit' charges. With effect from 22 March 2006 A & M trusts can no longer be created and the privileged IHT treatment for existing ones will end on 6 April 2008 at the latest unless their terms are changed before that date so that the beneficiaries become absolutely entitled to the capital by the time they reach 18.

The hold-over position under s 260(2)(a) on disposals *to* existing A & M trusts is dealt with in [**24.62**].

Whilst the trust still qualifies as an A & M trust the disposal of assets to beneficiaries – whether on the termination of the trust or on an advance to a beneficiary – will qualify for hold-over relief even though this will not be a chargeable transfer for IHT. This is by virtue of the special hold-over relief that has applied to disposals from A & M trusts under TCGA s 260(2)(d). It should be noted that relief under s 260(2)(d) is not available if the beneficiary acquired an interest in possession before 22 March 2006, since the trust will have ceased to qualify as an A & M trust at that time: see (6) in *Example 24.14.* (A beneficiary under an A & M trust often acquires an interest in possession at age 18 or 21 even though the trust deed gives him a life or absolute interest only on reaching 25.)

As a result of the IHT changes introduced by FA 2006 the acquisition by a beneficiary of an interest in possession on or after 22 March 2006 will cause the trust to enter the IHT relevant property regime. In any event the trust will enter the regime on 6 April 2008 at the latest unless their terms are changed before that date in the manner indicated above. Once the trust has entered the relevant property regime disposals of the trust assets will qualify for hold-over relief under s 260(2)(a) (see again (6) in *Example 24.14*).

[**24.91**]

**EXAMPLE 24.16**

(1)   Property is settled on an A&M trust for Floyd on attaining 18. Floyd reaches 18 in January 2007 and becomes absolutely entitled to the assets; the A&M trust ends, and a hold-over election is possible under s 260(s)(d) (whatever the nature of the trust assets).

(2)   Assume in (7) in *Example 24.14* that the trustees, instead of converting the A & M trust to a s 71D trust, calculate that less IHT will be payable if they allow the trust to enter the relevant property regime on 6 April 2008 but transfer several of the trust assets out to Sid in March 2008, just before the trust ceases to qualify as an A & M trust and enters the relevant property regime. Such transfers to Sid will be free of IHT but hold-over relief under s 260(2)(d) will be available on the disposals (whatever the nature of the trust assets).

FA 2006 has established two successors to A & M trusts:

(1)   Trusts for minors under IHTA 1984 s 71A (see [**34.118**]). These can be set up by will or intestacy or under the Criminal Injuries Compensation Scheme. The main condition is that the minor has to be entitled to the capital on attaining the age of 18 (or earlier).

(2)   Trusts under IHTA 1984 s 71D (see [**34.118**]). The main condition here is that the beneficiary has to be entitled to the capital on attaining the age of 25 (or earlier). Trusts under s 71D can come into existence in one of two ways. Firstly, like s 71A trusts, they can be created by will or intestacy or under the Criminal Injuries Compensation Scheme. Secondly, they can be created out of an existing A & M trust by the trustees

altering the terms of the trust so that it satisfies the s 71D conditions immediately it ceases to qualify as an A & M trust (which will be on 6 April 2008 at the latest).

Both s 71A and s 71D trusts are outside the IHT relevant property regime of anniversary and 'exit' charges, and the special charge imposed on transfers out of s 71D trusts applies only on transfers when the beneficiary is aged between 18 and 25. Accordingly transfers from a s 71A or s 71D trust to the beneficiary up to (or on) his/her 18th birthday are not chargeable transfers for IHT but, as with disposals from A & M trusts, a special hold-over relief is accorded to such disposals: TCGA s 260(2)(da) and (db).

**[24.92]–[24.110]**

**EXAMPLE 24.17**

In 2000 property was settled on A & M trusts for Harry, then aged 2, by which he would obtain an interest in possession in the trust fund on reaching 25. In March 2008, just before the trust loses its A & M status on 6 April 2008 and would otherwise enter the IHT relevant property regime, the trustees exercise their powers so that the trust will satisfy the s 71D conditions with effect from 6 April 2008 including the principal requirement that Harry will become entitled to the capital at 25. Shortly before Harry reaches 18 in 2016 the trustees decide to avoid all IHT charges and end the trust by advancing all the trust assets out to Harry on the occasion of his 18th birthday. The transfers will be free of IHT and the disposals will qualify for hold-over relief under s 260(2)(db). See *Note* to (7) in *Example 24.14* for the trap if the disposals to Harry were made immediately *after* his 18th birthday.

## V MISCELLANEOUS CASES

Hold-over relief under s 260(2) is also available in the following situations where the relevant transfer is exempt from any IHT charge:
(1) transfers to political parties under IHTA 1984 s 24;
(2) transfers to maintenance funds for historic buildings under IHTA 1984 s 27 and for disposals out of settlement to such funds;
(3) transfers of designated property under IHTA 1984 s 30;
(4) transfers of works of art under IHTA 1984 s 78.

It may also be noted that there are other provisions in the CGT legislation which result in a postponement of tax. Share exchanges under TCGA 1992 ss 135–137 (considered at **[26.3]**) and relief on the incorporation of a business under s 162 (discussed at **[22.100]**) are examples whilst disposals between husband and wife are always taxed on a no gain/no loss basis irrespective of any actual consideration paid (**[19.22]**). **[24.111]–[24.130]**

## VI PAYMENT OF TAX BY INSTALMENTS

### 1 General rule

CGT must generally be paid on 31 January following the tax year when the disposal occurs and, even if the disponer receives payment in instalments, there is no general right to pay the tax by instalments (see TCGA 1992 s 7 and **[19.93]**). **[24.131]**

## 2  **Payment by instalments**

Section 281 qualifies this general principle in the case of gifts of certain property (but not, apparently, for sales at undervalue) and also in the case of deemed disposals of settled property. Even in these cases, however, the ability to pay by instalments will broadly be available only if the relevant chargeable gain could not have been held over under either s 165 or s 260 (notice, therefore, that failure to make the election will not give the right to pay tax by instalments).

The property on which tax may be paid by instalments is land (including any estate or interest in land); a controlling shareholding; and a minority shareholding in a company neither listed on a recognised stock exchange nor dealt in on the Unlisted Securities Market.

The person paying the CGT must give notice if he wishes to pay by instalments: tax is then paid by ten equal yearly instalments starting on the usual payment date (ie 31 January following the tax year of the disposal). Interest is charged on the unpaid CGT and is added to each instalment. The outstanding tax can be paid off at any time and must be paid off if the gift was to a connected person or was a deemed disposal of settled property and the relevant assets are subsequently sold for valuable consideration. **[24.132]**

### EXAMPLE 24.17

In July 2005 Bob gives his seaside cottage to his daughter Thelma. The resulting CGT of £50,000 may be paid by ten equal annual instalments on the appropriate notice being given by Bob (who is to pay that tax). The first instalment of £5,000 falls due on 31 January 2007 and subsequent instalments will carry interest on the unpaid balance of the CGT.

## 3  **Payment by a donee**

TCGA 1992 s 282 provides that if a donor fails to pay the tax referable to the gift the Revenue may look to the donee for payment (for a criticism of the drafting of this provision see *PTPR* (*Personal Tax Planning Review*), vol 4, p 107).   **[24.133]**

# 25 CGT—settlements

*Updated by Sarah Laing, CTA, Chartered Tax Advisor, CPE Consulting Ltd*

The legislation distinguishes between UK-resident trusts and non-resident trusts. The latter are considered in **Chapter 27**. So far as the former are concerned, the legislation generally seeks to tax gains that arise (or are deemed to arise) on property comprised in the trust fund and not on a disposal of the interests of the beneficiaries. Actual disposals by the trustees and certain deemed disposals may trigger a charge, but disposals of beneficial interests will normally be exempt.                              [**25.1**]

## I   WHAT IS A SETTLEMENT?

### 1   Definition

A 'settlement' is sometimes referred to as a trust, implying that they share the same meaning. However, a settlement can include any disposition, trust, covenant, agreement, arrangement or transfer of assets.

Finance Act 2006, Schs 12 and 13 contain provisions to redefine settled property from 6 April 2006 as any property held in trust other than property held as nominee, bare trustee for a person absolutely entitled, an infant or disabled person (TCGA 1992 s 60). References in the legislation to a settlement are construed as references to settled property and the meaning of settlement is determined by case law. This measure effectively aligns what is treated as a settlement for the general purposes of income tax and tax on chargeable gains. The effect is that income tax will be charged on income arising to the trustees of a 'settlement' with the definition of settlement being derived from existing trust law and case law, and 'settled property' being defined in the tax legislation (TCGA 1992 s 68A).                    [**25.2**]

## 2   Nominees and bare trusts

Property is not settled where 'assets are held by a person as nominee for another person, or as trustee for another person absolutely entitled as against the trustee'. The provision covers nomineeships and bare or simple trusts.

**[25.3]**

### EXAMPLE 25.1

Tim and Tom hold 1,000 shares in DNC Ltd on trust for Bertram, aged 26, absolutely. This is a bare trust since Bertram is solely entitled to the shares and can at any time bring the trust to an end (see *Saunders v Vautier* (1841)). The shares are treated as belonging to Bertram so that a disposal of those shares by the trustees is treated as being by Bertram and any transfer from the trustees to Bertram is ignored.

## 3   Beneficiaries under a disability

Where the property is held on trust 'for any person who would be [absolutely] entitled but for being an infant or other person under a disability' it is not settled.   **[25.4]**

### EXAMPLE 25.2

(1)   Topsy and Tim hold property for Alex absolutely, aged nine. Because of his age Alex cannot demand the property from the trustees and the trust is not simple or bare. Alex is, however, a person who would be absolutely entitled but for his infancy and he is (for CGT purposes) treated as owning the assets in the fund.

(2)   Teddy and Tiger hold property on trust for Noddy, aged nine, contingent upon his attaining the age of 18. At first sight it would seem that there is no material difference between this settlement and that considered in (1) above since, in both, the beneficiary would be absolutely entitled were it not for his infancy. Noddy, however, is not entitled to claim the fund from the trustees. Unlike (1) above, Noddy's entitlement is contingent upon living to a certain age, so that, were he to ask the trustees to give him the property, they would refuse because he has not satisfied the contingency. This distinction would be more obvious if the settlement provided that the contingency to be satisfied by Noddy was the attaining of (say) 21 (see *Tomlinson v Glyns Executor and Trustee Co* (1970)). The property in this example is, therefore, settled for the purposes of CGT.

## 4   Concurrent interests

Where property is held for 'two or more persons who are or would be jointly [absolutely] entitled' the property is not settled. The word 'jointly' is not limited to the interests of joint tenants, applying to concurrent ownership generally. It does not, however, apply to interests that are successive, but only covers more than one beneficiary concurrently entitled 'in the same interest' (see *Kidson v MacDonald* (1974); *Booth v Ellard* (1980); and *IRC v Matthew's Executors* (1984)).   **[25.5]**

**EXAMPLE 25.3**

(1) Bill and Ben purchase Blackacre as tenants in common in equal shares. The land is held on a trust of land, but for the purposes of CGT the property is not settled and is treated as belonging to Bill and Ben equally (*Kidson v MacDonald* (1974)).

(2) Mr T and his family hold 72% of the issued share capital in T Ltd (their family company). They enter into a written agreement as a result of which the shares are transferred to trustees and detailed restrictions, akin to pre-emption provisions in private company articles, are imposed. The beneficial interests of Mr T and his family are not, however, affected. Subsequently the shares are transferred out again to the various settlors. In such a 'pooling arrangement' the shares will be treated as nominee property with the result that there is no disposal for CGT purposes on the creation of the trust nor on its termination (cp *Booth v Ellard* (1980) and see *Jenkins v Brown* and *Warrington v Sterland* (1989) in which a similar result was arrived at (surprisingly?) in the case of a pooling of family farms. See further **[22.83]**).

(3) Thal and Tal hold property on trust for Simon for life, remainder to Karl absolutely. Both are adult. Although Simon and Karl are, in common parlance, jointly entitled to claim the fund from the trustees, they are not 'jointly absolutely entitled' within the meaning of s 60. The property is settled for CGT purposes.

## 5 Meaning of absolute entitlement

It is the concept of being 'absolutely entitled as against the trustee' which lies at the root of the three cases mentioned in s 60. Section 60(2) provides that:

'It is hereby declared that references in this Act to any asset held by a person as trustee for another person absolutely entitled as against the trustee are references to a case where that other person has the exclusive right, subject only to satisfying any outstanding charge, lien or other right of the trustees to resort to the asset for payment of duty, taxes, costs or other outgoings, to direct how that asset shall be dealt with.'

The various rights against the property possessed by trustees and mentioned in s 60(2) refer to personal rights of indemnity; they do not cover other beneficial interests under the settlement.

**EXAMPLE 25.4**

Jackson is entitled to an annuity of £1,000 pa payable out of a settled fund which is held in trust for Xerxes absolutely. The property is settled for CGT purposes (*Stephenson v Barclays Bank Trust Co Ltd* (1975) and contrast *X v A* (2000) where in exercise of their lien trustees retained trust property against a beneficiary absolutely entitled—it is considered that in this case the property had ceased to be settled for CGT purposes).

A person can become absolutely entitled to assets without being 'beneficially' entitled (see **[25.81]**). **[25.6]**

## 6 Crowe v Appleby and trustee appropriations

Section 60(2) does not offer any guidance on the question of when a beneficiary has 'the exclusive right ... to direct how [the] asset in [the settlement] shall be dealt with'. Under general trust law beneficiaries will not be able to issue such directions unless they have the right to end the trust by demanding their share of the property (see eg *Re Brockbank* (1948)). Difficulties may arise where one of a number of beneficiaries is entitled to a portion of the fund.

**EXAMPLE 25.5**

A trust fund is held for the three daughters of the settlor (Jane, June and Joy) contingent upon attaining 21 and, if more than one, in equal shares absolutely. Jane, the eldest, is 21 and is, therefore, entitled to one-third of the assets. Whether she is absolutely entitled as against the trustees to that share depends upon the type of property held by the trustees and the terms of the settlement. The general principle is that she will be entitled to claim her one-third share, but not if the effect of distributing that slice of the fund would be to damage the interests of the other beneficiaries and nor if the trustees are given an express power of appropriation.

(1)    If Jane is absolutely entitled to her share that portion of the fund ceases to be settled (even though Jane leaves her share in the hands of the trustees).

(2)    But, if the fund consists of land, Jane will not be absolutely entitled (see *Crowe v Appleby* (1975)). Hence, the settlement will continue until all three daughters either satisfy the contingency or die before 21. Only then will the fund cease to be settled since one or more persons will, at that point, become jointly absolutely entitled. (For problems that can arise on a division of a controlling shareholding see *Lloyds Bank plc v Duker* (1987).)

What assets other than land are subject to a similar rule? HMRC (at CG 37560) comment as follows:

'In *Stephenson v Barclays Bank Trust Co Ltd* Walton J said that as regards shares in a private company in very special circumstances, and possibly mortgage debts, the person with a vested interest in a share of the property might have to wait for sale before he could call upon the trustees to account to him for his share. The principle of *Crowe v Appleby* therefore may apply to other indivisible assets. A good example would be an Old Master painting or valuable antique, or indeed a single share in a company.'

If the trustees have an express power to appropriate assets in satisfaction of the share of a beneficiary, HMRC's view is:

(1)    that any gain on the deemed disposal is calculated on the assets actually appropriated and not on a proportion of the total gain on all assets in the settlement; and

(2)    pending the trustees making an appropriation, tax is not charged.

**[25.7]**

### 7    Class closing

In deciding whether the class of beneficiaries has closed so that those in existence (who have satisfied any relevant contingency) have become absolutely entitled the medical impossibility of further beneficiaries being born to a living person is ignored. Hence a settlement on the children of A who attain 21 and if more than one in equal shares will remain settled property until the death of A even though he may have become incapable of having further children before that time (*Figg v Clarke* (1996)).    **[25.8]–[25.20]**

## II THE CREATION OF A SETTLEMENT

### 1 General rule

The creation of a settlement is a disposal of assets by the settlor whether the settlement is revocable or irrevocable, and whether or not the settlor or his spouse is a beneficiary (TCGA 1992 s 70). If chargeable assets are settled, a chargeable gain or allowable loss will result unless holdover relief is available (as to which see **Chapter 24**).                                         **[25.21]**

### 2 The 'connected persons' rule

As the settlor and his trustees are connected persons (TCGA 1992 s 18(3): see **[19.23]**), any loss resulting from the transfer will only be deductible from a gain realised on a subsequent disposal by the settlor to those trustees. Apart from being connected with the settlor, trustees will also be connected with persons connected with the settlor who will often be beneficiaries. However, it has been confirmed by HMRC that:

'if the settlor dies the connection with the trustees and relatives and spouse of the settlor is broken. Therefore if, for instance, the beneficiaries of the settlement are the children of the late settlor, the trustees are not connected with those beneficiaries, even if one or more of the children are trustees' (RI 38, February 1993).                                                   **[25.22]–[25.40]**

#### EXAMPLE 25.6

(1) Roger settles his Van Gogh sketch 'Peasant with Pig' worth £200,000. His allowable expenditure totals £50,000. He also settles his main residence. The beneficiaries are his wife Rena for life with remainder to their two children, Robina and Rybina. For CGT purposes, the following rules apply:
   (a) *Main residence* This is exempt from CGT.
   (b) *The Van Gogh* This is treated as disposed of for its market value (£200,000) and, hence, Roger has made a gain of £150,000.
(2) Robin wishes to sell his share portfolio but that will realise a substantial gain. He owns real property (which he wishes to retain) that would realise a loss if sold. Robin transfers both assets to trustees on a life interest trust for himself. This triggers the gain on the investments that will be offset by the loss on the land. The trustees immediately sell the portfolio (in due course the trustees may under a power in the settlement return the assets to Robin). Robin has therefore sheltered his gain.

## III ACTUAL AND DEEMED DISPOSALS BY TRUSTEES

A charge to CGT may arise as a result of either actual or deemed disposals of property by the trustees. Trustees are taxed at the rate applicable to trusts (40% for 2004–05 onwards) irrespective of the type of trust involved: the only exception is where the settlor has reserved an interest in his trusts under TCGA 1992 ss 77–79 when the gains are attributed to him (see **[19.85]**). From 6 April 2005 a standard rate band of £500 was introduced for all trusts paying tax at the rate applicable to trusts (ICTA 1988 s 686D(3), inserted by

FA 2005 s 14). The standard rate band has been increased to £1,000 from 6 April 2006 (FA 2006 s 89 Sch 13 para 4(1)(b)). The introduction of this rate band is designed to ensure that trusts with small amounts of taxed income have no further liability and no longer have to submit a self-assessment return each year. Note that where a settlor has made more than one settlement, the band is restricted to the lesser of £200 or £1,000 divided by the number of settlements made (ICTA 1988 s 686E, inserted by FA 2006 s 89 Sch 13 para 4(2)).                    **[25.41]**

## 1    Transfers of property on a change of trustees

When the property is transferred from old to new trustees this is not treated as a CGT disposal since trustees are treated as a single and continuing body (TCGA 1992 s 69(1)). Note, in particular:
(1)    the position when UK resident trustees are replaced by non-residents (see **[27.57]**);
(2)    if part only of the trust property is appointed into trusts administered by non-resident trustees, given that there is a single composite settlement for CGT purposes the continuing UK trustees will be accountable for gains realised offshore (see *Roome v Edwards* (1981) and **[25.82]**).
                    **[25.42]**

## 2    Actual disposals and trust losses

When chargeable assets are sold by trustees, normal principles apply in calculating the gain (or loss) of the trustees. If the disposal generates a loss it may be set off against gains of the same year or of future years made by the trustees.                    **[25.43]**

## 3    Use of trust losses by a beneficiary

### a)    *The Old Rule*

Prior to 16 June 1999, if a beneficiary became absolutely entitled to trust property, any loss which had accrued to the trustees in respect of that property (including a carried forward loss) and which could not be offset against trustee gains for that year occurring prior to the beneficiary becoming so entitled was transferred to that beneficiary. If more than one beneficiary became so entitled, the loss was apportioned between them (TCGA 1992 s 71(2) and see **[25.48]**)). (Note that a trust loss was therefore more favourably treated than losses made by PRs: see **[21.81]**.)                    **[25.44]**

### b)    *Restricted use of losses by beneficiaries*

As a result of these rules being abused the availability of losses to a beneficiary was then severely restricted. Only on the occasion when a beneficiary becomes absolutely entitled to trust assets (so that the trustees make a deemed disposal which produces a loss: see **[25.48]**) may that loss be passed to a beneficiary and then only to be offset against a future gain on a disposal of the property that he received from the trust (TCGA 1992 s 71(2)).

[**25.45**]

**EXAMPLE 25.7**

In May 2006 Daisy becomes absolutely entitled to one half of the assets in her grandmother's trust. At that time the trustees have unused capital losses of £25,000 and the assets to which Daisy becomes entitled are worth £30,000 less than when acquired by the trustees.
(1) None of the realised losses of £25,000 accrue to Daisy: they remain available for use by the trustees against future disposals of trust property.
(2) The loss that occurs on the s 71 deemed disposal is, however, available to Daisy but only to be set against future gains on a disposal of that trust property. (*Note:* This loss would not be available to Daisy if the trustees could use it either against gains realised earlier in the tax year 2006–07 or against gains arising on the s 71 deemed disposal.)

c) *Adding property to the trust*

**EXAMPLE 25.8**

The Jokey Trust has unused realised capital losses. Bill purchases an interest in the trust; adds assets to the trust which are pregnant with gain (claiming holdover); those assets are sold by the trustees thereby utilising the trust losses and the cash is paid out to Bill.

TCGA 1992 s 79A provides that in the circumstances of *Example 25.8* the trustees' losses may not be set against the gain. Note that for this section to apply:
(1) a transferor must add assets to the settlement claiming holdover relief; *and*
(2) that person (or someone connected with him) must purchase an interest in the settlement.
Accordingly an original beneficiary may add property to use the trust losses.

[**25.46**]

## 4  The exit charge: TCGA 1992 s 71(1)

a) *The general rule*

Section 71(1) provides for a deemed disposal of the chargeable assets in the trust fund, whenever a person becomes absolutely entitled to any portion of the settled property (an 'exit charge'). The section is a 'deeming' provision and treats the assets in the fund as being sold by the trustees (so that it is the trustee rate of CGT which is relevant) for their market value at that date and immediately reacquired for the same value, thereby ensuring that any increase in value in the chargeable assets is taxed (except in the situation discussed below). The deemed reacquisition by the trustees is treated as the act of the person who is absolutely entitled to the fund as against the trustees (see TCGA 1992 s 60(1)).

[**25.47**]

**EXAMPLE 25.9**

Shares in Dovecot Ltd are held by trustees for Simone absolutely, contingent upon her attaining the age of 25. She has just become 25 and the shares are worth £100,000. The trustees' allowable expenditure is £25,000. She is now absolutely entitled to the fund and the trustees are deemed to sell the shares (for £100,000) and to reacquire them (for £100,000). On that deemed disposal they have realised a chargeable gain of £75,000 (£100,000 – £25,000) that may benefit from taper relief in the normal way. The shares are now treated as Simone's property so that if she directs their sale in the future and £107,000 is raised she will have a chargeable gain of £7,000 (£107,000 – £100,000).

b)   *Losses*

A loss arising on the deemed disposal which occurs under s 71 will be deducted from 'pre-entitlement gains', defined as gains accruing to the trustees in that same tax year (but before the s 71 deemed disposal) or accruing on the deemed disposal. Subject to that, the loss is passed to the beneficiary under s 71(2) as discussed in **[25.45]**. How is this rule affected by the existence or otherwise of connected persons? The Revenue has confirmed that the beneficiaries' entitlement to the loss under s 71 is *not* affected by this rule. Indeed, it seems odd that there was ever any doubt about the matter bearing in mind that the utilisation of losses is only restricted if the relevant disposal is to a connected person. On the termination of a trust the legislation provides not for a disposal of the settled property to the relevant beneficiary but rather for a deemed disposal by the trustees (see RI 38, February 1993).                                                           **[25.48]**

c)   *Deemed disposal triggered by the death of a beneficiary entitled to an interest in possession: TCGA 1992 s 73*

The termination of an interest in possession because of the death of the beneficiary may result in a deemed disposal by the trustees under s 71(1) if on that occasion the settlement ends (ie a person becomes absolutely entitled to the trust assets). Although there is a deemed disposal and reacquisition, no CGT (or loss relief) is charged (or allowed) on any resultant gain (loss): see **[25.54]** for the definition of an interest in possession. This corresponds to the normal CGT principle that on death there is an uplift in value but no charge to tax (see **Chapter 21**; and, for the IHT consequences, **Chapter 33**).

**EXAMPLE 25.10**

Property consisting of shares in Zac Ltd is held on trust for Irene for life, or until remarriage and thereafter to Dominic absolutely.
(1)   *If Irene dies* There will be a deemed disposal and reacquisition of the shares at market value by the trustees (TCGA 1992 s 71(1)), but CGT will not be charged. The property henceforth belongs to Dominic.
(2)   *If Irene remarries* The life interest will cease with the same consequences as in (1), save that CGT may be chargeable.

If the interest is in a part only of the fund, the death of the beneficiary will result in an uplift in the appropriate portion of each asset in the fund without any CGT charge thereon (TCGA 1992 s 73(2)) although assets may be appropriated by the trustees in satisfaction of that share in which case the uplift is in respect of those assets only (see [25.7]).

The above treatment also applies to interests in possession which are not life interests but which came to an end on death. For instance, if the income of a trust fund was settled on A until the age of 40 and thereafter the entire fund passed to B and A died aged 35 (see, for the definition of an interest in possession, [25.54]).                                                                    [25.49]

### d)   *Reverter to settlor*

If the death causes the property to revert to the settlor, the 'reverter to disponer' exception applies (see TCGA 1992 s 73(1)(b) and [33.34]). The death of the beneficiary in these circumstances does not lead to a charge to IHT and, hence, the normal tax-free uplift provisions are modified to ensure that there is no double benefit. For CGT therefore the death will cause a deemed disposal and reacquisition, but for such a sum as will ensure that neither gain nor loss accrues to the trustees (a no gain/no loss disposal). Curiously, the position is different if property reverts to the settlor as life tenant. In this case a full uplift is given.                                      [25.50]

#### EXAMPLE 25.11

In 1999 Sue settled property on trust for Samantha for life. In 2006 Samantha dies whereupon the property reverts to Sue and the acquisition value and allowable expenses of the trustees are then £15,000 (value at the death of Samantha is £25,000). There is a deemed disposal and reacquisition by the trustees for £15,000 (to ensure neither gain nor loss). Contrast, however, the position if on Samantha's death the property reverted to Sue on a life interest trust. Despite the IHT exemption still applying, for CGT purposes the usual death uplift applies (see [25.54]).

### e)   *Holdover relief and the tax-free death uplift*

Normally, a tax-free uplift occurs when the death of the interest in possession beneficiary gives rise to a s 71(1) disposal. However, if the settlor had made an election to holdover his gain when he created the settlement, that held-over gain is not wiped out on the subsequent death of the life tenant but instead is chargeable at that time (TCGA 1992 s 74: for holdover relief, see generally **Chapter 24**).

Following the imposition of the inheritance tax regime for discretionary trusts on other types of trust in the Finance Act 2006, holdover relief for CGT purposes now applies to certain other types of transfer. Transfers into and out of a trust that come within the IHT relevant property rules will automatically be eligible for holdover relief under TCGA 1992 s 260(2)A. It should be noted, however, that changes to the holdover regime generally remove the ability to elect for this relief to apply where a settlement is created for the benefit of a settlor's minor children. Where assets remain in trust following the death of life tenant, there will be no CGT-free uplift on death unless a succeeding interest in possession meets the new IHT rules.

**EXAMPLE 25.12**

Property was settled on trust for Frank for life with remainder to Brian absolutely. The settlor elected to holdover the gain of £12,000 when he created the settlement. When Frank dies, the *total* gain on the deemed disposal made by the trustees under s 71 is £40,000. The CGT position is:

(1)    There will be a tax-free uplift on the death of Frank, but only for gains arising since the creation of the settlement. Of the total gain of £40,000, £28,000 is, therefore, free of CGT.

(2)    The remaining £12,000 gain (the gain held over by the settlor) is subject to tax on Frank's death (unless a further claim for holdover relief is made at that time).

The result of s 74 is a partial revival of the CGT charge on death that is explicable as an anti-avoidance measure. Assume that Bertha wished to give her daughter Brenda an asset on which there was a large unrealised capital gain and on a gift of which a holdover election was available. They could have elected for holdover relief, but that would have resulted in Brenda taking over the gain. As an alternative, therefore, Bertha could have settled the asset on an aged life tenant, who was expected to die imminently, and given the remainder interest to Brenda. No CGT would have arisen on the creation of that settlement if Bertha elected for holdover relief and, were it not for s 74, the death of the life tenant would have wiped out all gains leaving Brenda with the asset valued at its then market value.    **[25.51]**

f)    *The anti flip-flop legislation*

FA 2000 inserted provisions (TCGA 1992 s 76B and Sch 4B) aimed at 'flip-flop' arrangements which were widely employed in non-UK resident trusts. The legislation is, however, drafted sufficiently widely to catch UK trusts where the only benefit of the scheme was a 6% tax saving. Where these anti-avoidance rules apply, the trustees are deemed to dispose of and to reacquire trust assets at market value. The provisions are considered at **[27.93]**.    **[25.52]**

g)    *Allowable expenditure on a deemed disposal*

By its very nature a deemed disposal will rarely lead to any expenditure. TCGA 1992 s 38(4) (which prohibits notional expenditure) seems somewhat redundant, especially in the light of *IRC v Chubb's Settlement Trustees* (1971) which permitted the deduction of *actual* expenses incurred upon the partition of a fund (see **[19.30]**).    **[25.53]**

5    **The termination of an interest in possession on the death of the beneficiary, the settlement continuing (TCGA 1992 s 72)**

The death of a beneficiary entitled to an interest in possession, in cases where the settlement continues thereafter (ie where TCGA 1992 s 71(1) does not operate), results in a deemed disposal and reacquisition of the assets in the fund by the trustees at their then market value (TCGA 1992 s 72). CGT will not normally be imposed, and the purpose of s 72 is the familiar one of ensuring a tax-free uplift.

The termination of an interest in a part of the fund, where the settlement continues thereafter, results in a proportionate uplift in the value of all the assets.

An interest in possession for these purposes includes an annuity—the relevant provisions in s 72 are as follows:

'(3) This section shall apply on the death of the person entitled to any annuity payable out of or charged on, settled property or the income of settled property as it applies on the death of a person whose interest in possession in the whole or any part of settled property terminates on his death.

(4) Where, in the case of any entitlement to an annuity created by a settlement some of the settled property is appropriated by the trustees as a fund out of which the annuity is payable, and there is no right of recourse to, or to the income of, settled property not so appropriated, then without prejudice to subsection (5) below, the settled property so appropriated shall, while the annuity is payable, and on the occasion of the death of the person entitled to the annuity, be treated for the purposes of this section as being settled property under a separate settlement.'

**EXAMPLE 25.13**

Property is held on trust for Walter for life and thereafter for his son Vivian contingently on attaining 25. Walter dies when Vivian is 24. The CGT consequences are:
(1)    *Death of Walter*: There is a deemed disposal of the property under TCGA 1992 s 72; there is a tax-free uplift. The settlement continues because Vivian is not yet 25.
(2)    *Vivian becomes 25*: There is a further deemed disposal under s 71(1) and CGT may be charged on any increase in value of the assets since Walter's death.

As with deemed disposals under s 71(1) (see **[25.51]**) on the death of a life tenant the full tax-free uplift on death does not apply to a gain held over on the creation of a settlement which becomes chargeable. The uplift does, however, apply if the property becomes held on an interest in possession trust for the settlor ('reverter to settlor' no gain/no loss treatment (s 73(1)(b), see **[25.50]**) is limited to the s 71 charge).                                    **[25.54]**

## 6    Conclusions on deemed disposals under TCGA 1992 ss 71 and 72

The ending of general holdover relief in 1989 had important consequences for settlements. In particular, if it is no longer possible to postpone payment of the tax, the termination of a trust may result in a substantial tax liability. For instance, in the case of a life interest settlement rather than bringing the settlement to an end (whether by agreement between the beneficiaries or by exercise of overriding trustee powers), it may be preferable to wait for the death of the life tenant. In the case of discretionary trusts, because there will normally be a chargeable transfer for IHT on the settlement ending, it remains possible to holdover any capital gains.

Resettlements of property (considered at **[25.81]**) should normally be avoided since the act of resettlement will (in most cases) itself trigger a CGT charge. Note, however, that not every change in beneficial interests results in a deemed disposal: for instance, if a life interest terminates, for a reason other than the death of the beneficiary and the settlement continues, there is no deemed disposal for CGT purposes. This is also the case when a beneficiary merely acquires a right to the income of the trust.

**[25.55]–[25.80]**

**EXAMPLE 25.14**

Property is settled upon trust for Belinda for life or until remarriage, and thereafter for Roger contingent upon his attaining 25. If Belinda remarries when Roger is ten, the CGT position is:
(1)    *The remarriage of Belinda*: Belinda's remarriage terminates her life interest, but there is no deemed disposal as Roger is not at that time absolutely entitled to the fund. Hence, there are no CGT consequences.
(2)    *When Roger attains 18*: He will become entitled to the income from the fund as a result of the Trustee Act 1925 s 31. There is no CGT consequence.
(3)    *When Roger attains 25*: There is a deemed disposal under s 71(1), and (unless the property comprises business assets) holdover relief will not be available.

## IV    RESETTLEMENTS AND SEPARATE FUNDS

### 1    Basic rule

From 6 April 2006, where property is transferred from the trustees of one settlement to another, the settlor of the property disposed of by the trustees of the first settlement will be treated from the time of the disposal as having made the second. Property which was provided for the purposes of the first settlement, or which is derived from it, will be treated from the time of the disposal as having been provided for the purposes of the second settlement (TCGA 1992, s 68B).

When property is transferred from one settlement into another, different, settlement a CGT charge may arise under TCGA 1992 s 71(1) because the trustees of the second settlement (who may be the same persons as the trustees of the original settlement) become absolutely entitled to that property as against the original trustees (see *Hoare Trustees v Gardner* (1978)).

**[25.81]**

### 2    When does property become comprised in a separate settlement?

Exactly when a resettlement occurs as the result of the exercise by trustees of dispositive powers (eg of appointment and advancement) contained within the trust deed is still a matter of uncertainty (see especially *Roome v Edwards* (1981); *Bond v Pickford* (1983); and *Swires v Renton* (1991)). In *Roome v Edwards*, Lord Wilberforce stressed that the question should be approached 'in a practical and common sense manner' and suggested that relevant indicia included separate and defined property, separate trusts and separate trustees, although he emphasised that such factors were helpful but not decisive and that the matter ultimately depended upon the particular facts of each case. He contrasted special powers of appointment which, when exercised, will usually not result in a resettlement of property, with wider powers (eg of advancement) which permit property to be removed from the original settlement.

In *Bond v Pickford* (1983), the Court of Appeal distinguished between two types of power:

(1)  a power *in the narrower form* (such as a power of appointment); and

(2)  a power *in the wider form* (typically a power of advancement).

The distinction depends on whether the trustees are permitted to free settled property from the original settlement and transfer it into a new settlement. In the absence of an express provision enabling them to do this such action would be prohibited because of the principle that trustees cannot delegate.

Powers in the narrower form cannot create a new settlement: so far as powers in the wider form are concerned *their exercise will not necessarily* create a new settlement. In *Swires v Renton* (1991), Hoffmann J stressed that the classic case involving a new settlement would be where particular assets were segregated, new trustees appointed, and fresh trusts created exhausting the beneficial interest in the assets and providing full administrative powers so that further reference back to the original settlement became redundant. The absence of one or more of these features leaves open the question whether a new settlement has arisen: the question then has to be decided on the basis of intention. In the *Renton* case, for instance, despite exhaustive beneficial trusts, the administrative powers of the original settlement were retained and the appointment made other references to it thereby indicating that a new settlement had not been created. SP 7/84 generally conforms to the recent cases and indicates that the exercise of a power in the wider form will *not* create a new settlement if it is revocable, non-exhaustive, or if the trustees of the original settlement still have duties in relation to the advanced fund.

In order to provide maximum flexibility, settlements should have dispositive powers which are in the narrower and wider form so that the trustees can then decide whether it is their wish to create a new settlement or not. **[25.82]**

## 3  Separate funds within a single settlement

It is common for settlements (and especially A&M trusts) to split into separate funds that often have separate trustees managing assets which have been appropriated to that fund. Because these funds are treated as part of a single settlement (a 'composite settlement') for CGT purposes various difficulties arise as illustrated in the following example.     **[25.83]–[25.110]**

**EXAMPLE 25.15**

The Bladcomb family trust was created in discretionary form in 1965 since when 90% of the assets have been irrevocably appointed on various interest in possession trusts with the remaining 10% being appointed on A&M trusts for infant beneficiaries. The various funds are administered by the original trustees of the 1965 discretionary trust. On these facts the property has remained comprised in the original settlement for CGT purposes. Accordingly:

(1)  Even if separate trustees are appointed for part of the assets held on interest in possession trusts, the trustees of the original 1965 trust will remain liable for any CGT attributable to that portion of the assets.

(2)  Only one annual exemption is available for gains realised in any part of the settled fund.

(3)   A loss made in one fund will be used to offset a gain in another (because the settlement is a single entity). Should some form of 'compensation' be paid to the fund losing the benefit of the loss (but, if so, how is this calculated?)

## V   DISPOSAL OF BENEFICIAL INTERESTS

### 1   **The basic rule**

The basic rule is that there is no charge to CGT when a beneficiary disposes of his interest (TCGA 1992 s 76(1): contrast the disposal of an interest in an unadministered estate). The rationale is that gains in the trust are taxed (see above) so that to charge tax on the disposal of the interest of a beneficiary would be a form of double taxation. There is, however, a growing list of exceptions—which is added to each year as tax avoidance schemes seek to exploit the basic exemption. And, of course, if a trust is viewed as akin to a company, in which not only are corporate gains taxed but also disposals of shares are chargeable, it may be thought that the rationale behind the general rule is misconceived.                                           **[25.111]**

### 2   **Position of a purchaser**

Once a beneficial interest has been purchased for money or money's worth, a future disposal of that interest will be chargeable to CGT. The consideration does not have to be 'full' or 'adequate': ie any consideration however small will turn the interest into a chargeable asset. An exchange of interests by two beneficiaries under a settlement is not, however, treated as a purchase so that a later disposal of either interest will not be chargeable.

When a life interest has been sold, the wasting asset rules (see **[19.45]**) may apply on a subsequent disposal of that interest by the purchaser.     **[25.112]**

#### EXAMPLE 25.16

Ron is the remainderman under a settlement created by his father. He sells his interest to his friend Algy for £25,000. No CGT is charged. If Algy resells the remainder interest to Ginger for £31,000, Algy has made a chargeable gain of £6,000 (£31,000 – £25,000).

### 3   **Purchaser becoming absolutely entitled to any part of the settled property**

The termination of the settlement may result in the property passing to a purchaser of the remainder interest (of course, he may also become entitled to such property in other situations, eg if an advancement is made in his favour). As a result, that purchaser will dispose of his interest in return for receiving the property in the settlement (TCGA 1992 s 76(2)). The resultant charge that he suffers does not affect the deemed disposal by the trustees (and the possible CGT charge) under s 71(1).                          **[25.113]**

#### EXAMPLE 25.17

Assume, in *Example 25.16*, that Ginger becomes entitled to the settled fund which is worth £80,000. He has realised a chargeable gain of £49,000 (£80,000 – £31,000). In addition, the usual deemed disposal rules under s 71(1) operate.

## 4 Disposal of an interest in a non-resident settlement

TCGA 1992 s 85(1) provides that the disposal of an interest in a non-resident settlement is chargeable: the basic exemption conferred by s 76(1) is therefore excluded in such cases although it is expressly provided that no charge arises under s 76(2) if the beneficiary becomes absolutely entitled to any part of the trust fund (this charge is therefore restricted to a purchaser of the interest). When the trust was originally UK resident the appointment of non-resident trustees triggers an exit charge (see [27.57]) and some protection against a double charge if a beneficial interest is subsequently sold is provided by s 85(3):

> 'in calculating any chargeable gain accruing on the disposal of the interest the person disposing of it shall be treated as having:
>
> (a)    disposed of it immediately before the relevant time, and
> (b)    immediately reacquired it, at its market value at that time.'

Although not happily drafted, the purpose of the subsection is to fix the acquisition cost of the disponor at the date when the trustees emigrated (ie his acquisition cost will take into account the gains then realised and subject to UK tax). On first reading, the provision might be thought to impose a second charge at that time but this is not thought to be the case.

An infelicity in the drafting is that the provision is said to be relevant for the purpose of calculating the chargeable gain of the disponor: it should also be relevant in arriving at any allowable loss which he may have suffered!

**EXAMPLE 25.18**

The Halibut trust was set up in 1988 with Jason Halibut being entitled to the residue of the trust on the death of his sister, Rose. The trustees became non-UK resident in 2006 and Jason sold his remainder interest shortly afterwards for £150,000.

*Analysis:*
(1)    Jason has made a chargeable disposal (TCGA 1992 s 85(1));
(2)    in order to compute his chargeable gain (if any) the market value of his interest when the trust became non-resident needs to be ascertained.

FA 2000 amended s 85 to prevent what might be termed 'the in and out scheme'. Assume that a non-resident trust has stockpiled gains (for the meaning of this term, see [27.112]) and is now a cash fund. UK trustees are appointed so that the trust becomes resident and subsequently it is exported (by the appointment of further non-resident trustees). On the latter event s 85(3) would operate to increase the base costs of all the beneficial interests but, given that the assets in the trust are sterling, there will be no exit charge. Accordingly a beneficiary could sell his interest (effectively extracting stockpiled gains) tax free. From 21 March 2000 the disposal of a beneficial interest in a settlement that had stockpiled gains at 'the material time' (ie when it ceased to be UK resident) will not benefit from the uplift in value under s 85(3).                                                                          **[25.114]**

### 5   Disposal of an interest in a settlement that had at any time been non-resident (TCGA 1992 s 76(1A), (1B) and (3))

This provision was introduced by FA 1998 and was something of a panic measure aimed at various schemes intended to avoid any charge on gains which had accrued in foreign trusts by repatriating the trust and a beneficiary then disposing of his interest. Various points should be noted about this provision:

(1)   it catches the disposal of an interest if the settlement had at any time been non-resident or if it had received property from a non-resident settlement;

(2)   like s 85(1) there is no charge if (or to the extent that) the beneficiary becomes entitled to the trust property;

(3)   it would seem to overlap with s 85 and, in effect, makes that provision redundant.                                                                           **[25.115]**

### 6   Sale of an interest in a 'settlor interested' trust (TCGA 1992 s 76A and Sch 4A)

a)   *Basic rule*

These rules took effect from 21 March 2000 and when they apply the trustees, provided that they are UK resident, are treated as disposing and reacquiring trust assets at market value (ie there is a deemed disposal). Tax is then calculated at either the settlor rate (if the settlor still has an interest in the trust) or at the rate applicable to trusts and may be recovered by the trustees from the beneficiary who sold the interest.                               **[25.116]**

b)   *When is a settlor interested in his trust?*

The normal provisions of TCGA 1992 s 77(2) apply: see **[19.85]**. For a charge to apply the trust must either have been a settlor interested trust at any time in the previous two years or must contain property derived from a trust which had been settlor interested at any time in the previous two years. Notice that the disposal can be by *any* beneficiary: the legislation is not limited to disposals by the settlor. The settlor must, however, be either resident or ordinarily resident in the UK.

   Finance Act 2006, Sch 12 amends TCGA 1992 s 77 from 6 April 2006 to extend the definition of a settlor-interested trust to include accumulation and maintenance trusts set up by parents. The legislation provides that a settlor has an interest in a settlement where property is or may be comprised in a settlement, or may become payable for the benefit of the settlor's dependent child, or the child derives any benefit from it whatsoever either directly or indirectly.                                                   **[25.117]**

c)   *The mischief under attack*

The intention is to prevent exploiting the s 76(1) exemption by individuals who place assets in trusts (instead of selling the assets) and retain an interest that is sold. However, the scope of the legislation is not so limited and may catch the wholly innocent.                                        **[25.118]–[25.140]**

**EXAMPLE 25.19**

(1) Dodgy put assets into a trust making a holdover election to avoid the payment of any CGT. He is absolutely entitled to those assets on attaining 35 (which is, say, in three months time). He sells this interest to Tug and Thug, trustees of a settlement with realised capital losses.

    (a) under general principles the sale by Dodgy will not attract a CGT charge (TCGA 1992 s 76(1));

    (b) when Tug and Thug become absolutely entitled a further holdover election is available and when they dispose of the assets they can offset the resultant gain by their unused trust losses.

In these circumstances s 76A provides that when Dodgy sells his interest the trustees make a deemed disposal of the trust property and the tax charge (at Dodgy's rates) will be borne by him.

(2) The Tinkerbell estate was resettled in 1990 and Teddy, the current life tenant, will therefore be considered to be a settlor. His son, Syd, is the remainderman but is tired of waiting for his inheritance and so sells his interest. Section 76A will apply and Syd will suffer a wholly undeserved CGT charge!

## VI RELIEF FROM, AND PAYMENT OF, CGT

### 1 Payment

CGT attributable to both actual and deemed disposals of settled property is assessed on the trustees at a rate of 40%: in exceptional cases the settlor's rate will apply, see [**19.85**]. If the tax is not paid within six months of the due date for payment, it may be recovered from a beneficiary who has become absolutely entitled to the asset (or proceeds of sale therefrom) in respect of which the tax is chargeable. The beneficiary may be assessed in the trustees' name for a period of two years after the date when the tax became payable (TCGA 1992 s 69(4)). **[25.141]**

### 2 Exemptions and reliefs

Exemptions and reliefs from CGT have been discussed in **Chapter 22**, but note the following matters in the context of settled property:

*Main residence exemption* May be available in the case of a house settled on both discretionary and on interest in possession trusts (see *Sansom v Peay* (1976) and [**52.62**]). However, there are restrictions where holdover relief is claimed on the property entering the trust (see [**25.65**]). **[25.142]**

*The annual exemption* Trustees are generally allowed half of the exemption appropriate to an individual (for 2006–07, half of £8,800 = £4,400). **[25.143]**

*Death exemption* As already discussed, the tax-free uplift will be available for most trusts. **[25.144]**

*Roll-over relief* Available only if the trustees are carrying on an unincorporated business. **[25.145]** **Trust rate band. From 6 April 2006 a £1,000 rate band is available to all trusts paying tax at the rate applicable to trusts.** **[25.146]**

*Deferral relief for chargeable gains* Available if the beneficiaries are either individuals or charities. **[25.147]**

### 3   Taper and trusts

Taper relief replaced the indexation allowance for trustees as it did for individuals from April 1998 (see generally **Chapter 20**). The following points may be noted about the application of taper to trusts:

(1)   Before 6 April 2000 discretionary trustees only qualified for business taper on company shares if they owned at least 25% of the shares. With the change from that date it may be necessary to apportion gains between business and non-business periods of ownership when the disposal occurs (see *Example 20.2(3)*);

(2)   Trusts may be used as an umbrella to obtain a full taper period (see **[20.62]**).

(3)   Assume that trustees wish to let farmland forming part of the trust fund. If it is let to the adjoining farmer (a sole trader) the land is a non-business asset for taper purposes. By contrast if let to the neighbour's family farming company then because this is a 'qualifying company' for taper purposes the asset will attract business assets taper. This quirk in the legislation has been corrected in FA 2003 but only in respect of disposals after 5 April 2004 and to periods of ownership after that date. Time apportionment problems may therefore arise. **[25.148]**

## VII   TRUSTS WITH VULNERABLE BENEFICIARY

### 1   Introduction

FA 2005 introduced new rules, backdated to 6 April 2004, so that trusts set up for the most vulnerable, for example, for the disabled, are taxed as if the beneficiary had received the income and gains directly. (The income tax aspects of the new rules are dealt with in **Chapter 16**.). CGT aspects are summarised in the following paragraphs.

FA 2005 ss 23–45, create a new tax regime for certain trusts with vulnerable beneficiaries (defined by s 23 as disabled persons or relevant minors). They determine which trusts and beneficiaries will be able to elect into the regime and where a claim for special tax treatment is made for a tax year, provide for no more tax to be paid in respect of the relevant income and gains of the trust for that year than would be paid had the income and gains accrued directly to the beneficiary.

A claim for special tax treatment for a tax year may be made by trustees if (FA 2005 s 25):

> '(a) in the tax year they hold property on qualifying trusts for the benefit of a vulnerable person; and
>
> (b) a vulnerable person election has effect for all or part of the tax year in relation to those trusts and that person.'   **[25.149]**

### 2   Qualifying trust gains: special capital gains tax treatment

The provisions relating to trust gains are set out in FA 2005 s 30. This section applies to a tax year if:

(a)  in the tax year chargeable gains accrue to the trustees of a settlement from the disposal of settled property which is held on qualifying trusts for the benefit of a vulnerable person ('the qualifying trusts gains');

(b)  the trustees would (if not for the new regime) be chargeable to capital gains tax in respect of those gains;

(c)  the trustees are either resident or ordinarily resident in the UK during any part of the tax year; and

(d)  a claim for special tax treatment under s 30 for the tax year is made by the trustees.

It is worth noting that a claim cannot be made if the vulnerable person dies during the year in question (FA 2005 s 30(3)).  **[25.150]**

### 3  UK-resident vulnerable persons: s 77 treatment

Under the new regime, a charge to CGT on the settlor with an interest in the settlement (TCGA 1992 s 77(1)) will apply in relation to the qualifying trusts gains as if:

(a)  the vulnerable person were a settlor in relation to the settlement;

(b)  the settled property disposed of, and any other settled property disposed of at any time when it was relevant settled property, originated from him; and

(c)  he had an interest in the settlement during the tax year.

Property is 'relevant settled property' at any time when it is property held on the qualifying trusts for the benefit of the vulnerable person, and the trustees would (if not for these new rules) be chargeable to CGT in respect of any chargeable gains accruing to them on a disposal of it.  **[25.151]**

### 4  Non-UK resident vulnerable persons: amount of relief

The trustees' liability to CGT for the tax year will be reduced by an amount equal to:

TQTG –VQTG

Where:

TQTG is the amount of CGT to which the trustees would (if not for these new rules) be liable for the tax year in respect of the qualifying trusts gains, and

VQTG is calculated using the formula TLVA –TLVB

Where:

TLVB is the total tax liability of the vulnerable person (see below), and

TLVA is what the total tax liability of the vulnerable person would be if it included tax in respect of notional s 77 gains).

TLVB is the total amount of income tax and capital gains tax to which the vulnerable person would be liable for the tax year:

(a)  if his income for the tax year were equal to the sum of his actual income for the tax year (if any) and the amount of the trustees' specially taxed income (if any) for the tax year; and

(b)  if his taxable amount for the tax year (under TCGA 1992 s 3) were equal to his deemed CGT taxable amount for the tax year (if any).

TLVA is what TLVB would be if the vulnerable person's taxable amount for the tax year (under TCGA 1992 s 3) were equal to the sum of the amount mentioned in (b) above and his notional s 77 gains for the tax year. **[25.152]**

# 26 CGT—companies and shareholders

*Updated by Peter Vaines, Squire, Sanders & Dempsey*

---

---

## I  CGT PROBLEMS INVOLVING COMPANIES

### 1  CGT and corporation tax

Companies and unincorporated associations are not subject to CGT; instead chargeable gains are assessed to corporation tax. Broadly, and with the important exception of taper relief, the principles involved in computing the chargeable gain (or allowable loss) are the same as for individuals.

Disposals from one company in a group (as defined) to another will generally be treated as taking place at a value giving rise to neither gain nor loss (TCGA 1992 s 171). Any gain is deferred until the asset is sold outside the group or if the company owning the asset leaves the group within six years of the transfer (TCGA 1992 s 179).                                    **[26.1]**

### 2  Company reorganisations

The basic principle is that there is neither a disposal of the original shares nor the acquisition of a new holding: instead, the original shares and new holding are treated as a single asset acquired when the original shares were acquired. When new consideration is given on a reorganisation (for instance, on a rights issue), that is added to the base cost of the original shares and treated as having been given when they were acquired (TCGA 1992 ss 126–131).                                                                   **[26.2]**

### 3  Company takeovers and demergers

If the takeover is by means of an issue of shares or debentures by the purchasing company (a 'paper for paper exchange'), CGT on the gain made by the disposing shareholder may generally be postponed until the consideration shares are sold (TCGA 1992 ss 135–137). If the consideration for the acquisition is partly shares and partly cash, the cash element is treated as a part disposal of the shareholding and s 135 will apply to the balance. The purchaser must obtain more than 25% of the shares in the target company subject to a number of conditions. Furthermore the transaction must be effected for *bona fide* commercial reasons and not form part of any scheme or arrangement of which the main purpose or one of the main purposes is to avoid a liability to CGT or corporation tax. An advance clearance may be sought (TCGA 1992 s 138).

Where the assets of the target company are acquired for a cash consideration, any chargeable gain arising on those assets will be chargeable on the target company. An exemption might apply, such as the substantial shareholdings exemption, see **[41.75]** or a deferral such as roll-over relief under TCGA 1992 ss 152–159 (see **[22.72]**). From the point of view of the target's shareholders, they may be left with the problem of what to do with a 'cash shell' company see **Chapter 47**.

TCGA 1992 s 192 contains provisions aimed at facilitating arrangements whereby trading activities of a single company or group are split up in order to be carried on either by two or more companies or by separate groups of companies, see **Chapter 47**.                                             **[26.3]**

### 4   Incorporation of an existing business

TCGA 1992 s 162 provides relief in cases where an unincorporated business is transferred to a company as a going concern in return for the issue of shares in the company. The relief enables the gains on the business assets transferred to the company to be rolled over into the acquisition of the shares. (For detailed examination of the rules see **[22.100]**.)          **[26.4]–[26.20]**

## II   CAPITAL DISTRIBUTIONS PAID TO SHAREHOLDERS

A capital distribution (whether in cash or assets) is treated in the hands of a shareholder as a disposal or part disposal of the shares in respect of which the distribution is received (TCGA 1992 s 122(1)). 'Capital distribution' is restrictively defined to exclude any distribution that is subject to income tax in the hands of the recipient (s 122(5)(b)). As the definition of a distribution is extremely wide (see **[42.1]**) the CGT charge is confined to repayments of share capital and to distributions in the course of winding up.

**EXAMPLE 26.1**

(1)   Prunella buys shares in Zaba Ltd for £40,000. Some years later the company repays to her £12,000 on a reduction of share capital. The value of Prunella's shares immediately after that reduction is £84,000.

The company has made a capital distribution for CGT purposes and Prunella has disposed of an interest in her shares in return for that payment. The part disposal rules must, therefore, be applied as follows:

(i)   consideration for part disposal: £12,000

(ii)   allocation of base cost of shares:

$$£40,000 \times \frac{A}{A+B} = £40,000 \times \frac{£12,000}{£12,000+£84,000} = £5,000$$

(iii)　gain on part disposal: £12,000 – £5,000 = £7,000.

(2)　Stanley buys shares in Monley Ltd for £60,000. The company is wound up and Stanley is paid £75,000 in the liquidation. Stanley has disposed of his shares in return for the payment by the liquidator and, therefore, has a chargeable gain of £15,000 (£75,000 – £60,000).

If the company had been insolvent so that the shares were worthless, Stanley should claim loss relief on the grounds that his shares had become of negligible value (see TCGA 1992 s 24(2); *Williams v Bullivant* (1983); and **[19.117]**). He has an allowable loss of £60,000. Income tax relief may be available for this loss under TA 1988 s 574 (see **[11.121]**).

These rules are also applied when a shareholder disposes of a right to acquire further shares in the company (TCGA 1992 s 123). The consideration received on the disposal is treated as if it were a capital distribution received from the company in respect of the shares held.

Under s 122(2), if the inspector is satisfied that the amount distributed is small, the part disposal rules are not applied but the capital distribution is deducted from the allowable expenditure on the shares. The result is to increase a subsequent gain on the sale of the shares (in effect the provision operates as a postponement of CGT). For these purposes, a capital distribution is treated as small if it amounts to no more than 5% of the value of the shares in respect of which it is made. However, a revised approach was announced in *Tax Bulletin* 27 in February 1997 as a result of *dicta* in *O'Rourke v Binks* (1992) which noted that the purpose of the legislation was to avoid the need for an assessment in trivial cases, an approach that would have regard to the likely costs of carrying out the part disposal computation and the likely tax consequences in each case. As a result, in addition to the 5% test, HMRC now considers that s 122(2) can apply in cases where the distribution is £3,000 or less (see CG 57836).

Under s 122(4) where the allowable expenditure is *less than* the amount distributed the taxpayer may elect that the part disposal rules shall not apply and that the expenditure shall be deducted from the amount distributed. In *O'Rourke v Binks* (1992), the Court of Appeal held that the capital distribution must be small for the purpose of this subsection and that what was 'small' was a question of fact for the Commissioners.

On a liquidation there will often be a number of payments made prior to the final winding up and each is a part disposal of shares (subject to the relief for small distributions) so that the shares will need to be valued each time a distribution is made (see SP 1/72).

**EXAMPLE 26.2**

Mark purchased 5,000 shares in Rothko Ltd for £5,000. The company has now made a 1:5 rights issue at £1.25 per share. Mark is, therefore, entitled to a further 1,000 shares but, having no spare money, sells his rights to David for £250. At that time his 5,000 shares were worth £7,500. As the capital distribution (£250) is less than 5% of £7,500 the part disposal rules will not apply. Therefore, £250 will be deducted from Mark's £5,000 base cost. (NB Mark may prefer the part disposal rules to apply since any gain resulting may be covered by his annual exemption.)

**[26.21]–[26.40]**

## III   THE DISPOSAL OF SHARES

### 1   Introduction

a)   *Pre-FA 1982 system*

Before FA 1982, the CGT rules were relatively straightforward and involved treating identical shares as a single asset. This 'pooling' system involved a cumulative total of shares with sales being treated as part disposals from the pool and not as a disposal of a particular parcel of shares. Special rules applied where all or part of a shareholding was acquired before 6 April 1965.

**[26.41]**

b)   *FA 1982 regime—operative from 6 April 1982 to 6 April 1985*

Shares of the same class acquired after 5 April 1982 and before 6 April 1985 were not pooled. Instead, each acquisition was treated as the acquisition of a separate asset. A disposal of shares was then matched with a particular acquisition in accordance with detailed identification rules that applied even where the shares were distinguishable from each other by, for instance, being individually numbered. Shares were therefore treated as a 'fungible' asset. These rules were introduced because of the indexation allowance which made it necessary to know whether the shares disposed of had been acquired within 12 months (when no allowance was available) or, in other cases, to calculate the indexation allowance by reference to the original expenditure.

**[26.42]**

c)   *The 1985 regime—operative from 6 April 1985 to 6 April 1998*

Major changes in the indexation allowance in 1985 enabled a form of pooling to be re-introduced. Shares of the same class acquired after 5 April 1982 and still owned by the taxpayer on 6 April 1985 were treated as one asset and further acquisitions of the shares after that date formed part of this single holding (TCGA 1992 s 104). There was an indexed pool of expenditure for each class of share and, if shares in the pool were acquired between 1982 and 1985, the initial value of this pool on 6 April 1985 comprised the acquisition costs of the relevant shares together with the indexation allowance (including an allowance for the first 12 months of ownership) that would have been given had the shares been sold on 5 April 1985.

If identical shares were acquired after 6 April 1985 they were added to the share pool with the cost of their acquisition increasing the indexed pool of expenditure (a similar result occurred if a rights issue was taken up).

**EXAMPLE 26.3**

Silver acquired 10,000 ordinary shares in Mines Ltd for £10,000 in August 1982 and a further 5,000 shares (cost £7,500) in November 1984. Assume 'indexed rise' from August 1982 to April 1985 was 0.25 and from November 1984 to April 1985 was 0.01.

The value of qualifying expenditure and of the indexed pool of expenditure on 5 April 1985 was as follows:

| (1) | *Qualifying expenditure* | £ |
|---|---|---|
| | (i)  1982 purchase | 10,000 |
| | (ii)  1984 purchase | 7,500 |
| | | £17,500 |

| (2) | *Indexed pool of expenditure* | £ |
|---|---|---|
| | (i)  at 0.25 on 1982 purchase | 2,500 |
| | (ii)  at 0.01 on 1984 purchase | 75 |
| | (iii)  add acquisition costs | 17,500 |
| | | £20,075 |

When some of the shares were sold the part disposal rules were applied to both the qualifying expenditure and the indexed pool of expenditure. The indexation allowance was then found by deducting a proportion of the qualifying expenditure from a proportion of the indexed pool. The allowance could only be used to reduce a gain—not to create or increase a loss.

**[26.43]**

**EXAMPLE 26.4**

In March 1997 Silver sold 7,500 of the shares for £18,750 (the value of his remaining holding was £18,750). Indexation from April 1985 to March 1997 was 0.15.

(1)  *Proportion of qualifying expenditure*

$$\frac{18,750}{37,500} \times £17,500 = £8,750$$

(2)  *Proportion of indexed pool*
Indexed pool at March 1997:
£20,075 × 1.15 = £23,086.25

$$\frac{18,750}{37,500} \times £23,086.25 = £11,543.125$$

(3)  *Indexation allowance available*
£11,543.125 − £8,750 = £2,793.125

(4)  *Gain*
£18,750 − (£8,750 + £2,793.125) = £7,206.875

## 2  The regime introduced by FA 1998

### a)  *Basic rule*

With the introduction of taper relief, which depends upon the length of ownership of an asset, the government decided to end pooling for individuals, PRs and trustees. As a result:

(1) acquisitions of shares on or after 6 April 1998 are not pooled (except for reorganisations being rights or bonus issues under TCGA 1992 s 127 (see [26.2]));

(2) pools at 5 April 1998 are preserved as a single asset (a 's 104 holding').

[26.44]

Where shares of the same class are acquired on the same day they are treated as having been acquired by a single transaction unless some of the shares are 'approved scheme shares' and the appropriate election is made: see TCGA 1992 s 105A and [9.42].

b)   *The new identification rules*

Each acquisition of shares is treated as a separate asset and so new acquisition rules prescribe the order of disposals on the basis of 'last in first out' (LIFO). The order of disposals is therefore as follows (subject to what is said in the next section about bed and breakfasting):

(1) the most recently acquired unpooled shares;

(2) shares from a s 104 holding (this is treated as a single asset when the pool first came into being);

(3) 1982 pools (see [26.47]);

(4) shares held on 6 April 1965 (see [26.48]);

(5) later acquired shares.                                                            [26.45]

c)   *Bed and breakfasting*

In simple terms, bed and breakfasting involved the disposal of shares on day one and their repurchase on day two: a transaction that was commonly employed to realise a loss on the shares for relief against other gains, or to realise a gain to enable the annual exemption to be utilised.

**EXAMPLE 26.5**

Alberich has unused CGT losses. He owns shares which have an unrealised gain and which he wishes to retain. He sells the shares at close of business one day and repurchases them at the start of business the next.

TCGA 1992 s 105 was introduced to match securities bought and sold on the same day but was able to be avoided by buying back the following day. FA 1998 introduced a more widespread provision aimed at stopping bed and breakfasting by providing that disposals are to be matched with acquisitions in the following 30-day period (matching with the first securities acquired during this period): see TCGA 1992 s 106A(5). This brought an end to traditional bed and breakfasting whilst leaving some continuing opportunities: for instance, A sells his shares and his wife purchases an identical shareholding; or the disposal is triggered by the transfer to a trust for A. These simple arrangements are not caught by this provision but any transfers into trust must now take into account the inheritance tax implications following the FA 2006.

The '30-day rule' may produce surprising results, see the example below.

[26.46]

**EXAMPLE 26.6**

(1)   Rover is returning to the UK after a period of non-residence. He 'bed and breakfasts' his investment portfolio with the intention that on his return to the UK his base cost will be market value. The 30-day rule will apply and needs to be taken into consideration by Rover (see *Tax Bulletin*, April 2001, p 839).

(2)   With effect from 22 March 2006 the rules are amended so that they do not apply where the person acquiring the shares is neither resident nor ordinarily resident in the UK. This follows the case of *Davies v Hicks* (2005) which highlighted the mismatch of the bed and breakfast rules with the exit charge arising when a trust ceases to be resident and ordinarily resident in the UK. In that case the trustees successfully argued that the exit charge under s 80 TCGA 1992 involved a deemed disposal and reacquisition of the shares by trust. However, under TCGA 1992 s 106A(5), the bed and breakfast rules applied to eliminate the gain on the deemed disposal. To correct this anomaly s 106A(5) will not apply to any acquisition on or after 22 March 2006 by a person who is neither resident nor ordinarily resident, nor a person who is resident but is treated as non-resident by reason of a Double Taxation Agreement: s 106A(5A).

## 3   Shares acquired after 5 April 1965 and before 6 April 1982

Shares and securities of the same class acquired after 5 April 1965 and before 6 April 1982 are treated as a single asset with a single pool of expenditure (hence, they must *not* be aggregated with identical shares subsequently acquired). For the purpose of the indexation allowance and the rebasing rules the market value of the shares on 31 March 1982 will generally be treated as the taxpayer's acquisition cost (TCGA 1992 s 109).          **[26.47]**

## 4   Shares acquired before 6 April 1965

For unquoted shares any gain is deemed to accrue evenly (the 'straight-line method') and it is only the portion of the gain since 6 April 1965 that is chargeable. The disposer may elect to have the gain computed by reference to the value of the shares on 6 April 1965. This election may only reduce a gain; it cannot increase a loss or replace a gain by a loss. Where different shares are disposed of on different dates the general rule of identification is last in, first out (LIFO) (TCGA 1992 Sch 2 paras 18–19).

For listed shares and securities the general principle is that a gain is calculated by reference to their market value on 6 April 1965 (the rules for ascertaining the market value are laid down in TCGA 1992 Sch 2 paras 1–6). If, however, a computation based upon the original cost of the shares produces a smaller gain or loss, it is the smaller gain or loss that is taken. If one calculation produces a gain, and one a loss, there is deemed to be neither.

As an alternative to the above procedure, the taxpayer may elect to be charged by reference to the market value of either all his shares or all his securities or both on 6 April 1965 (ie pooling on 6 April 1965). The original cost becomes wholly irrelevant and can neither reduce a gain; nor reduce a loss; nor result in neither gain nor loss (TCGA 1992 Sch 2 para 4).

Section 109(4) permits this election to be made within two years after the end of the year in which the first disposal of such securities occurs after 5 April 1985 (31 March for companies). If the election is made, pre-1965 shares are treated either as part of the taxpayer's 1965–82 pool or as forming a separate 1965–82 pool (see [**25.47**]).                    [**26.48**]–[**26.60**]

## IV   VALUE-SHIFTING

Complex provisions designed to prevent 'value-shifting' are found in TCGA 1992 ss 29–34. Although the sections are not limited to shares, the commonest examples of value-shifting involve shares.

Under s 29 three types of transaction are treated as disposals of an asset for CGT purposes, despite the absence of any consideration, so long as the person making the disposal could have obtained consideration. The disposal is deemed not to be at arm's length and the market value of the asset is the consideration actually received plus the value of the 'consideration foregone'. Instances of value-shifting are to be found in the following paragraphs.
                                                                   [**26.61**]

### 1   Controlling shareholdings (see CG 58853)

Section 29(2) applies when a person having control (defined in TA 1988 s 416) of a company exercises that control so that value passes out of shares (or out of rights over the company) in a company owned by him, or by a person connected with him, into other shares in the company or into other rights over the company. In *Floor v Davis* (1979) the House of Lords decided that the provision could apply where more than one person exercised collective control over the company, and that it covered inertia as well as positive acts.                                              [**26.62**]

> **EXAMPLE 26.7**
>
> Ron owns 9,900 ordinary 1 shares in Wronk Ltd and his son, Ray, owns 100. Each share is worth £40. A further 10,000 shares are offered by the company to the existing shareholders at their par value (a 1:1 rights issue). Ron declines to take up his quota and all the shares are subscribed by Ray. Value has passed out of Ron's shares as he now holds a minority of the issued shares. He is treated as making a disposal of his shares by reason of s 29(2).

### 2   Leases

Section 29(4) provides as follows:

> 'If, after a transaction which results in the owner of land or of any other description of property becoming the lessee of the property, there is any adjustment of the rights and liabilities under the lease, whether or not involving the grant of a new lease, which is as a whole favourable to the lessor, there shall be a disposal by the lessee of an interest in the property.' (And see CG 58860.) [**26.63**]

**EXAMPLE 26.8**

Andrew conveys property to Edward by way of gift, but reserves to himself in the conveyance a long lease at a low rent. As the lease is valuable, the part disposal will give rise to a relatively small gain. Andrew later agrees to pay a rack rent so that the value of Edward's freehold is increased. When the rent is increased tax is charged on the consideration that could have been obtained for Andrew agreeing to pay that increased sum.

## 3 Tax-free benefits resulting from an arrangement

In contrast to s 29, s 30 applies only if there is an actual disposal of an asset. It strikes at schemes or arrangements, whether made before or after that disposal, as a result of which the value of the asset in question (or a 'relevant asset', as defined) has been reduced and 'a tax-free benefit has been or will be conferred on the person making the disposal or a person with whom he is connected; or on any other person'. When it applies, the inspector is given power to adjust, as may be just and reasonable, the amount of gain or loss shown by the disposal (s 30(4)). This widely drafted provision will not operate if the taxpayer shows that the avoidance of tax was not the main purpose, or one of the main purposes, of the arrangement or scheme. Further, it does not catch disposals between husband and wife (within TCGA 1992 s 58); disposals between PRs and legatees; or disposals between companies that are members of a group. TCGA 1992 s 31 extends the scope of these provisions to circumstances where a distribution is made out of profits created by an intra group transfer to reduce the value of a shareholding prior to sale.

**EXAMPLE 26.9**

H Ltd has two subsidiaries, A Ltd and B Ltd. A Ltd is to be sold for a gain of £1 million. A Ltd has distributable profits of only £300,000 but it has a valuable property which it sells intra group to B Ltd for a profit of £700,000. No tax arises on this transfer by reason of TCGA 1992 s 171 but A Ltd still increases its distributable profits.

A Ltd pays a dividend of £1 million to H Ltd and A Ltd is then sold for a nominal sum. The idea is for the tax on the £1 million to be avoided.

Section 31 applies here to bring s 30 into play, allowing HMRC to make a just and reasonable adjustment to the capital gain to counteract the tax-free benefit intended to be obtained from these arrangements. **[26.64]**

# 27 CGT—The foreign element

*Written and updated by Emma Chamberlain, BA Hons (Oxon), CTA (Fellow), Barrister, 5 Stone Buildings, Lincoln's Inn*

## I   GENERAL

### 1   Territorial scope: residence as the connecting factor

a)   *UK residents*

An individual who is resident or ordinarily resident in the UK during any part of a year of assessment is taxed on his worldwide chargeable gains made during that year: 'resident' and 'ordinarily resident' have their income tax meanings (TCGA 1992 s 2(1): s 9(1) and see [**18.2**]). There are two qualifications to this general proposition.

*First*, where the gain is on overseas assets and cannot be remitted to the UK because of local legal restrictions, executive action by the foreign government or the unavailability of the local currency, CGT will only be charged when those difficulties cease (TCGA 1992 s 279).

*Secondly*, an individual who is resident, but not domiciled, in the UK is liable only to CGT on such gains on overseas assets as are remitted to the UK. For the location of assets, see TCGA 1992 s 275 and note that a non-sterling bank account belonging to a non-UK domiciliary is located overseas (TCGA 1992 s 275(1)). Accordingly, the remittance basis is applicable to the account. Note also that non-domiciliaries are not entitled to loss relief in respect of the disposal of assets situated outside the UK (TCGA 1992 s 16(4)). Hence offshore gains cannot be reduced by offshore losses in such cases. See *Example 27.4.*                                                                         [**27.1**]

b)   *Non-residents*

A person who is neither resident nor ordinarily resident in the UK is generally not liable to CGT on gains even if resulting from a disposal of assets situated in the UK (but see **[27.41]**). A trust is not UK-resident if a majority of the trustees are non-resident *and* the trust is administered outside the UK. As a result of changes made by FA 1998 as amended by FA (no 2) 2005, an individual who is 'temporarily non-resident' (as defined) is taxed on certain gains realised whilst non-resident on his return to the UK (see further **[27.3]**).                                                                                       **[27.2]**

## 2    The temporary non-resident individual (TCGA 1992 s 10A)

As CGT is only charged on individuals either resident or ordinarily resident in the UK it could be avoided by the simple expedient of becoming resident and ordinarily resident outside the UK and then disposing of the asset. **[27.3]**

### a)    *Position before 17 March 1998*

'Residence' and 'ordinary residence' are interpreted in the same way as for income tax (see **[18.2]**). Absence for three complete tax years ensures that the individual is neither resident nor ordinarily resident in the UK. In addition there is a long-established practice whereby an individual going abroad for full-time employment is regarded as neither resident nor ordinarily resident from the date of his departure until the date of his return provided that absence abroad extended over at least one complete tax year. See IR 20 for a full statement of HMRC's position in this area. As a taxpayer's residence is determined for a complete tax year, an individual resident in the UK *at any time during that year* is taxed on gains realised at any time during the year (TCGA 1992 s 2). It is only by concession that the year may be split into periods of residence and non-residence (see amended ESC D2: **[27.6]**).
                                                                                       **[27.4]**

### b)    *TCGA 1992 s 10A—position on or after 17 March 1998*

The basic rules on whether an individual is resident in the UK have not been altered although, with effect from 17 March 1998, ESC D2 has been substantially amended to limit the circumstances when the year may be split.

   If the following conditions are satisfied an individual who becomes non-resident is taxed on his return to the UK on gains realised during the period of non-residence:
(1)    The individual was UK resident or ordinarily resident for at least some part of four of the seven tax years preceding the year of departure.
(2)    The individual becomes non-UK resident for *less than five complete tax years.*
(3)    During his period of absence he disposes of assets which he had owned when he left the UK *or* he receives capital payments from an offshore trust (see TCGA 1992 s 87: **[27.111]**); *or* a trust of which he was the settlor realises a gain in circumstances where he would be taxed on those gains on an arising basis if he were UK resident and domiciled (TCGA 1992 s 86: see **[27.91]**); or gains from an offshore company are attributed to him under TCGA 1992 s 13 (see **[27.43]**). In all these situations the individual is taxed *as if the gains accrued to him in the year of return to the UK.* Because no distinction is made between one interven-

ing year and another it follows that the annual exempt amount is only available for the year of return (that being the year in which the gains are deemed to accrue) and that losses realised in later intervening years may be offset against gains from earlier years deemed to accrue in the year of return.

A number of further points should be noted about this provision:

(1)  it applies to losses as well as gains;
(2)  it does not (with certain exceptions) apply to disposals of assets which the taxpayer acquired at a time when he was non-resident (s 10A(3)) ('the after-acquired assets rule');
(3)  the normal limitation period for CGT assessments is extended to two years after 31 January next following the year of return in order to catch gains made in the year of departure;
(4)  gains (and losses) are calculated in the normal way at the time when the asset is disposed of, as if the taxpayer were then UK resident. Tax will, however, be charged at rates current in the year of return;
(5)  there are special rules to prevent a possible double charge under TCGA 1992 ss 86 and 87 (see **[27.91]** and **[27.111]**);
(6)  until Budget 2005 it was thought that the charge could be neutralised by relief under a double tax treaty (see s 10A(10)). HMRC have now said that they do not accept this view (see **[27.20]**);
(7)  the taper relief rules on return to the UK are set out at **[20.61]**. **[27.5]**

**EXAMPLE 27.1**

Don was born and bred in the UK but on 30 March 1999 he leaves the UK to take up a three-year contract of employment in Belgium. His broker liquidates his portfolio on 3 April and during his absence Don sells his country cottage and a valuable Ming vase given to him by his wife as a leaving present. He returns to the UK in March 2004 having extended his original contract. The CGT position is as follows:

(1)  Don remains resident in the UK in the tax year 1998–99 so that the disposal of shares on 3 April is chargeable (note that ESC D2 does not apply: see **[27.6]**).
(2)  Because Don returns in March 2004 he has not been out of the UK for five complete tax years so that the disposal of the country cottage is *prima facie* brought into charge in tax year 2003–04 (his year of return). Likewise the sale of the Ming vase that, because it was acquired from a spouse, is not excluded under the after-acquired assets rule. Don may try to claim protection under the double tax treaty with Belgium so that his gain on the Ming vase will be exempt from CGT (although the gain on the real property could never be protected under the double tax treaty). It was thought by practitioners that although the gain is deemed to accrue to the taxpayer in the year of return (when he becomes UK-resident) HMRC accepted that if the gain was actually realised at a time when he was resident in Belgium, treaty relief could apply. This view has now been rejected—see **[27.8]**.
(3)  If Don acquires an asset such as a picture in the tax year after departure ie while non-resident (and not relying on the split year) and sells the picture in the tax year before he returns to the UK then any gain is not chargeable on him. Equally any loss would not be allowable.
(4)  If Don had gone abroad on or before 16 March 1998 he will not be chargeable on gains made while not resident or ordinarily resident on any of the assets even though he may return within five years.

## 3   Splitting the tax year (ESC D2 as amended)

As already indicated, CGT is charged on individuals resident or ordinarily resident at any time during a tax year on gains made during the course of that year. Heavily amended ESC D2 enables the year to be split so that gains arising after someone ceases to be resident are untaxed whilst gains arising before someone becomes resident here are similarly outside the tax net. Observe the following restrictions, however:

(1)   the concession does not apply to trustees;
(2)   like any concession it will not apply 'if any attempt is made to use it for tax avoidance' (see *R v IRC, ex p Fulford-Dobson* (1987));
(3)   in the case of an individual becoming UK resident on or after 6 April 1998 split-year treatment will only apply if he has satisfied the s 10A five-year test (see [**27.5**]). An individual leaving the UK on or after 17 March 1998 will only benefit from split-year treatment if he was not resident in the four out of seven years of assessment referred to in s 10A (see [**27.5**]). Therefore, in *Example 27.1* Don could not benefit from split-year treatment for gains realised in the year of departure even if he leaves the UK permanently and therefore for more than five years.

[**27.6**]

## 4   Other matters

Two other matters should be noticed. *First*, any CGT losses should be realised prior to departure; and, *second*, care should be taken to ensure that arrangements with a potential purchaser, made before going non-resident, do not amount to a disposal at that time. Accordingly, careful thought is required before a conditional contract is concluded or put and call options granted. See *CG Manual 25800* onwards for HMRC's view on this.

HMRC comment as follows:

'There are three circumstances where Capital Gains Tax liability may arise where the date of disposal appears to be after the date of emigration. These are where it can be shown that

1   there was a binding agreement or contract for sale on or before the date of emigration
2   a business was carried on in the UK through a branch or agency in the period from the date of emigration to the date of disposal
3   an attempt has been made to use ESC D2 for tax avoidance.'

As already noted, ESC D2 does not apply to trustees nor to gains realised on the disposal of assets of a business carried on in the UK through a branch or agency and has limited applicability since most people emigrating will have to make the disposal in the tax year after departure in order to ensure that the gain is realised when they are not resident or ordinarily resident in the UK for the complete tax year.

HMRC may argue that a binding contract has been reached particularly where there is a sale of shares. Put and call options should be used with care. HMRC accept that there can be no binding agreement for the disposal of land unless the contract is in writing.

If shares in a company have been sold in consideration of receiving shares or loan notes issued by the purchasing company, HMRC may argue that s 135 does not apply (see example 27.2). Even if a clearance has been obtained under s 138 this will be invalidated if the taxpayer had definite plans to go abroad at the time of the sale and he did not disclose this in the clearance. See *Snell v HMRC* Sp 532 2006 where a company was sold for a mixture of shares and loan notes. The main shareholder subsequently became non-resident and disposed of his loan notes free of capital gains tax. HMRC successfully argued that the arrangements for the issue of loan notes in exchange for shares had a tax avoidance motive and therefore no deferral relief was available. The Special Commissioner held that the paper for paper provisions were not intended to be an exemption mechanism for somebody who wished to use them as a prelude to becoming non-resident: 'We find that he had the purpose of becoming non-resident before redeeming the loan notes and accordingly that one of his main purposes, indeed the only main purpose of effecting the arrangement, was the avoidance of capital gains tax.'

[27.7]

**EXAMPLE 27.2**

Luke owns all the shares in a food distribution company S Limited. He receives an offer from a rival company FD Limited to buy S Limited for £20 million cash. Luke and the purchaser reach an informal agreement on terms in February 2003. Luke emigrates in March 2003 and the actual agreement is signed on 6 April 2003. HMRC may ask to see the papers surrounding the sale in order to establish whether a binding oral agreement had been reached in February before Luke left the UK.

Alternatively Luke sells the company in March just before emigration in consideration of receiving guaranteed loan notes from the purchaser which he cashes in six months after the sale in October 2003 after he has left the UK intending to stay away for five complete tax years. In the light of *Snell*, HMRC may well successfully argue on the above facts that there was a disposal in March 2003 and not in October 2003 when the loan notes were encashed and that TCGA 1992 s 137(1) applies so that there is no s 135 relief.

5   **Finance (No 2) Act 2005**

The capital gains tax rules on non-residence have been tightened up further. As noted above, the general rule in TCGA 1992 s 2 is that gains accruing on the disposal of an asset only attach to taxpayers who are either resident or ordinarily resident in the UK in the tax year of disposal. TCGA 1992 s 10A provides for an exception: where a UK resident becomes non-resident but resumes UK residence within five tax years then any gains in the intervening years of non-residence on disposals of assets acquired before becoming non-resident become chargeable to capital gains tax as if such gains 'were gains ... accruing to the taxpayer in the year of return'. However, s 10A was stated to be 'without prejudice to any right to claim relief in accordance with any double taxation relief arrangements' (s 10A(10)).

Hence it had been assumed that a capital gains article in a standard double tax treaty (such as between Belgium and the UK) which gave sole taxing rights on disposals of most assets to the country where the alienator was resident at the time of disposal, would apply to prevent a charge under s 10A in the year of return. This also appeared to be HMRC's stated view—see *CG Manual* 26290: 'although section 10A requires gains accruing in the intervening years between UK departure and return to be assessed to tax there is no intention that this charging provision should override the terms of any double taxation agreement. This will mean any exemption agreement specifically given under an agreement between the UK and another taxing state should be taken into account in arriving at any UK liability.'

On this basis Don in *Example 27.1* above would have been protected under the Belgium treaty from a capital gains tax charge on the Ming vase even if not the country cottage. (The double tax treaties do not usually protect gains realised on land situated in the UK.)

HMRC now state that, while they originally accepted the view that a DTA can override a charge under s 10A, this is no longer the case. F(No 2)A 2005 s 32(6) simply omits s 10A(10). The change has effect in any case in which the year of departure is 2005–06 onwards. However, the explanatory notes state 'the reason it is being removed is that it is considered unnecessary: its continuing presence in s 10A might cause doubt to be cast on the effects of other tax provisions which do not contain a corresponding statement.' HMRC suggest that the only double taxation relief is that the individual is allowed to obtain a credit for the foreign tax he has paid (if any)!

It is doubtful whether HMRC's present view is correct or that this view can be altered in respect of past arrangements in this way. If chargeable gains or losses are treated as accruing in the year of return it is surely those **same** gains that are protected by double taxation agreements and which arose during the year of disposal when the disponer was non-resident. Such gains are just taxed at a different time under s 10A.

The HMRC view also leaves taxpayers who have already come back to the UK having relied on a double tax treaty and not spent the full five years out of the UK since March 1998 in a position of some uncertainty.

There have been some changes for taxpayers who became dual resident. Section 32 also deals with persons who are dual resident but are treated under the tie-breaker provisions as resident in the foreign state, so are treaty non-resident. Such persons were never within the scope of s 10A at all because, although treaty non-resident, they never ceased to be resident or ordinarily non-resident in the UK. Hence they did not need to rely on a five-year absence provided they maintained residence in both states and under the tie-breaker provisions could be treated as resident in the foreign state.

Whenever a person becomes treaty non-resident on or after 2005–06 they will in future be treated as non-resident for the purposes of s 10A. Hence they will need to do their full five years abroad in order to avoid a capital gains tax charge on disposals of assets. However, as with non-residents under general law, assets acquired and disposed of while treaty non-resident will not be subject to the five-year rule.

Although a treaty non-resident taxpayer will now be treated as non-resident for the purposes of s 10A, gains attributed to him under the ss 86–87 offshore settlement regime and TCGA 1992 s 13 will not be postponed until the tax year of arrival back in the UK. In effect gains attributed under such provisions will continue to be taxed as at present, ie on the basis that the taxpayer is treated as resident in the UK throughout the time.

If HMRC's view is correct, prior to 16 March 2005, persons who were genuinely non-resident in a jurisdiction where there was a double tax treaty protecting them from gains are worse off than persons who remained UK-resident under general law who were merely treaty non-resident! On HMRC's view, the former have had to stay out for five years throughout the period since March 1998. The latter have not had to unless their departure is on or after 16 March 2005. (See *Example 27.3*.) **[27.8]–[27.20]**

**EXAMPLE 27.3**

Assume the facts are as in *Example 27.1* but Don never loses his UK residence (eg he spends at least 120 days here each year). However, he has a permanent home in Belgium and no such home in the UK. Under the tie-breaker tests he is treated as resident in Belgium and should not be chargeable on his return in March 2004 on the Ming vase.

## II REMITTANCE OF GAINS BY A NON-UK DOMICILIARY (SEE HMRC MANUAL CG 25350 FF)

An individual who is resident or ordinarily resident, but not domiciled, in the UK is chargeable to CGT only on the remitted gains from overseas assets, with no relief for any overseas losses. The definition of remittance is wide and catches a sum resulting from the gain which is paid, used or enjoyed in the UK or brought or sent to the UK in any form (TCGA 1992 s 12(2)) and a transfer to the UK of the proceeds of sale of assets purchased from the gain. Anti-avoidance provisions in ITTOIA 2005 ss 833–834 (formerly TA 1988 s 65) designed to catch disguised remittances are extended to CGT. The section applies, for example, where a loan (whether or not made in the UK so long as the moneys are remitted to the UK) is repaid out of the overseas gain (see **[18.34]**).

Use of losses on foreign-sited assets against remitted gains or gains realised on UK situated assets is not possible for the non-UK domiciliary.     **[27.21]**

**EXAMPLE 27.4**

Freda is resident but not domiciled here. She has a second home in Cornwall that shows a large capital gain. She wishes to sell the home. She has realised substantial losses from the disposal of her foreign investments managed by a broker in Switzerland. She cannot set those losses against the gains on the Cornish home. Nor can she set the losses against the gains from any other foreign or UK investments. If Freda remits some of the gains from her foreign investments she will pay tax on the gains at the rates prevailing at the time of remittance.

It is not possible to 'divide up' the gain from the original capital and remit only the original capital. The position is different from a separation of the income and capital (see *Example 27.5*).

**EXAMPLE 27.5**

Freda has invested £1 million in shares in a German bio-tech company BTI Limited. These produce £20,000 dividends each year that she receives into her overseas income account. She eventually sells BTI shares for £2 million. She remits £1 million to the UK. She cannot argue that the £1 million represents the original capital and that the gain has not been remitted even if the sale proceeds have been split up. HMRC will tax her on half the remittance on the basis that remittances are treated as taxable gain in the proportion that the gains bear to the total amount in the account—see *CG Manual* 25401. However, the dividend income that has been paid to the overseas income account is not taxable unless remitted here.

A foreign domiciled taxpayer who is UK-resident would be better holding all foreign assets which are likely to show a gain through a trust in order to bypass the remittance rules on capital gains and indeed avoid capital gains tax even on UK-situated assets.

### EXAMPLE 27.6

Freda buys £1 million worth of shares in BTI Limited. She settles the shares in an offshore trust from which she can benefit. There is no deemed remittance and the trust acquires the shares at market value of £1 million. The trustees sell the shares two years later realising a gain of £0.5 million. The trustees then pay some of the capital to Freda in the UK. There is no taxable remittance on Freda since neither ss 86 or 87 apply (see below) and s 12 is not applicable. (Note that in certain circumstances if the trust has accumulated income there may be an income tax charge on Freda.) Even if the shares settled were UK situated and the trustees sold the shares at a gain and distributed the proceeds to her in the UK, there would still be no tax chargeable on Freda—the remittance basis does not apply.

(See **[20.40]** for taper relief position of remittances on foreign assets.)

Review on domicile

During the course of 2003–04 the Government conducted a review of the status of foreign domiciliaries and consulted on whether the rules should be changed. It appeared likely that changes would be made not only to the remittance basis but also to the residence rules. In particular there were fears that the generally favourable capital gains tax regime for non-UK domiciliaries involving offshore trusts would end. However, it appeared the Government could reach no firm conclusion on what should be done. At the end of 2003 they said they 'will move forward with a formal consultation paper on possible approaches to reform' but in paragraph 5.103 of the *Budget Red Book* stated:

> "The Government is continuing to review the residence and domicile rules as they affect the taxation of individuals and is considering various aspects of this issue in the light of the responses to the paper published at Budget 2003. The Government remains determined to proceed on the basis of evidence and in keeping with its key principles. It would welcome further contributions to the debate which would then be taken forward by the publication of the consultation paper setting out possible approaches to reform."

Something similar was said in 2004. In the 2006 Budget the Government said it was keeping the matter under review and will proceed on the basis of evidence and in keeping with its principles. Hence the matter has not been dropped although it appears that nothing very definite is being contemplated at the moment! The inheritance tax changes contained in BN25 do affect foreign domiciliaries adversely in various ways.

F(No 2)A 2005 did introduce changes to the situs of assets for capital gains tax purposes and extend the statutory code set out under TCGA 1992 s 275. These changes will affect foreign domiciliaries who are resident here and rely on the remittance basis to avoid a charge to CGT. They do not affect persons who are resident, ordinarily resident and domiciled here.

Changes to TCGA 1992 s 275 mean that the situs of any intangible asset will be treated as being in the UK if any right or interest comprised in the asset is governed by, exercisable in or enforceable under or is subject to the law of the UK. The same is true of futures or options over such intangibles. The situs of such futures or options will be governed by the situs of the underlying asset.

Furthermore all shares in and debentures of UK incorporated companies whether registered or not will be treated as situated in the UK. Foreign domiciliaries will now need to operate through foreign incorporated holding companies that wholly own UK incorporated and resident companies with the holdco preferably held through an offshore trust for greater CGT safety and to avoid the remittance basis. Alternatively the UK-resident company will need to be foreign incorporated (but watch TA 1988 s 739).

Those foreign domiciliaries who restructured their holdings in UK incorporated companies so as to dispose of bearer shares, hoping to sell at a time when the bearer instrument is held abroad and thereby take advantage of the remittance basis, will no longer be protected from a CGT charge unless the bearer shares were also placed in an offshore trust.

Note that for IHT purposes no statutory changes to the situs of bearer shares have been made. When analysing the situs of any asset one now has to consider the statutory code on situs for capital gains tax purposes, inheritance tax purposes and in the absence of any express statutory provisions, the common law rules. Double tax treaties can also change the situs of particular assets for certain tax purposes.                                **[27.22]–[27.40]**

## III   CGT LIABILITY OF NON-RESIDENTS

### 1   Individuals

A non-resident individual (excluding the 'temporary non-resident' whose position has been considered above) escapes tax even on disposals of assets situated in the UK *except* where he carries on a trade, profession or vocation in the UK through a branch or agency (TCGA 1992 s 10(1)). In such cases he is taxed on any gain that arises on a disposal of assets used or previously used for the business or held or acquired for that branch or agency (eg a lease of premises). The charge under s 10 cannot be avoided by removing assets from the UK or by ceasing to trade in the UK. In both cases a deemed disposal at market value will occur (compare the deemed disposal which results from the migration of a foreign company). Further, ESC D2 does not apply when disposals of assets used by a branch or agency are made during the year of emigration. Such disposals will therefore continue to be made by a UK resident and to attract a tax charge: in the following tax year disposals will fall under the s 10 charge with a deemed disposal arising on the final cessation of the trade.                                        **[27.41]**

## 2   **Companies**

### a)   *General rule*

A non-resident company is excluded from liability to CGT except when it trades in the UK through a branch or an agency. Thus, a non-resident investment company is never liable to CGT.                                    **[27.42]**

### b)   *Anti-avoidance*

There are provisions designed to prevent UK-resident and domiciled individuals from using these rules to avoid the payment of CGT by the formation of non-resident companies. Note that there is no motive test. The legislation, in TCGA 1992 s 13, was substantially amended as a result of increasing evidence that its provisions could be circumvented, for instance by the use of guarantee companies. The recast section applies in the following circumstances:

(1)   Chargeable gains must accrue to a company which is not resident in the UK but which would be a close company if it were so resident (note that such gains are calculated by reference to a continuing indexation allowance: for the definition of a close company, see **[41.122]**).

(2)   The gain is attributed to a 'participator's' interest in the company to the extent of that interest and there is an attribution process that involves looking through multiple layers of intermediate holdings with final attribution being on a just and reasonable basis. 'Participator' has the TA 1988 s 417 meaning as further amplified and will catch all interests in shares as well as the interest of loan creditors. Trustees can be participators but the provisions do not 'look through' to their beneficiaries (ie the gains are attributed to the trust but further provisions may then charge the gain on the settlor (see TCGA 1992 s 86) or to beneficiaries (see TCGA 1992 s 87)).

(3)   No assessment is made if the participator's interest in the company is less than 10% (increased from 5% by FA 2001).

(4)   Gains made on the disposal of most assets of a trading company that are used in the trade are not apportioned (TCGA 1992 s 13(5)). Thus, problems really arise only for the shareholder of a non-resident investment or holding company.

(5)   Losses made by the non-resident company cannot be used to reduce its gains before apportionment, nor can the losses as such be apportioned except to the extent that a shareholder has had a gain apportioned to him in that tax year and the apportioned loss would eliminate or reduce the gain. See *Example 27.7*.

(6)   A shareholder can be reimbursed by the company for tax paid on apportioned gains without a further charge. Otherwise, he can deduct the tax paid from any gain made on a subsequent disposal of the shares. In calculating the gain realised by the company and assessed under s 13, indexation relief is applied: taper relief (see **Chapter 20**) does not apply although taper relief will apply to the gain realised by the taxpayer on a disposal of the shares of the company itself.

(7)   Under the former provisions an assessment was discharged if, within two years of the relevant disposal, the gain was distributed by way of

dividend; distribution of capital or on a winding up of the offshore company. That position has now been altered so that on a subsequent distribution the s 13 assessment stands but any tax paid thereon is allowed as a credit against any liability arising on the distribution. That disposition must occur before the earlier of:

(a) three years from the end of the period of account in which the gain accrued; and

(b) four years from the date on which the gain accrued.

(8) If the non-resident company is situated in a country with which the UK has a double tax treaty, gains realised by the company may be protected by the treaty and so be outside s 13 (see *Bricom Holdings v IRC* (1997)). FA 2000 has altered this position in the case of trustee shareholders by providing that 'nothing in any double taxation relief arrangements' shall prevent the attribution of gains to trustees under s 13 (see TCGA 1992 s 79B inserted by FA 2000). Individuals remain protected by treaty relief in these circumstances!

(9) Section 13 does not apply if the UK-resident participator is not domiciled here. **[27.43]**

### EXAMPLE 27.7

Xcon Limited is a Guernsey company owned as to 90% by two non-UK residents and 10% by Eddie, a UK resident and domiciled person. Xcon Limited holds equities. Eddie will suffer a charge under s 13 on 10% of the indexed gains realised by Xcon.

In 2003–04 Xcon realises losses of £2 million and gains of £1 million from the disposal of some equities. The losses can be set off against the gains made by Xcon Limited in the same tax year and can be used against gains made in the same *tax year* by other non-resident companies in which Eddie has an interest and which have been apportioned to Eddie under s 13. However, Eddie cannot use the surplus losses in Xcon Limited against his personal gains nor can those Xcon losses be carried forward to use against future gains Xcon may make in later tax years. If not used in 2003–04 they are lost forever.

### EXAMPLE 27.8

In the early 1980s the Wonka family set up a Jersey trust that owned all the shares in a Netherlands Antilles ('NA') company that in turn owned all the issued share capital of a Californian corporation (CC). Assume that the latter company owned substantial property interests around Los Angeles that have just been sold showing a substantial gain. The settlor is deceased.

(1) That gain realised by CC may be apportioned to NA: see TCGA 1992 s 13(9).

(2) In turn, the apportioned gain may be further apportioned to the Jersey trust (TCGA 1992 s 13(10)) and to the extent that the trust makes capital payments to UK beneficiaries, those apportioned gains may attract a UK tax charge.

Notice that the provisions whereby the profits of a 'controlled foreign company', including an investment company, may be apportioned to its UK resident corporate members do not apply to its chargeable gains (see TA 1988 s 747(6): and see **[41.161]**). **[27.44]**

## IV  NON-RESIDENT TRUSTEES

### 1  **Background**

The CGT treatment of offshore trusts has undergone a number of radical changes of which the following is a brief summary.                    **[27.45]**

a)  *From 1965 to 1981*

FA 1965 s 42 imposed a charging system for non-UK-resident trusts that led to major difficulties and was ultimately abandoned in 1981.            **[27.46]**

b)  *From 1981 to 1998*

FA 1981 s 80 introduced a charging system based on capital distributions received by UK domiciled and resident beneficiaries provided that the trust had been established by a UK settlor. One consequence was that offshore trusts could be used to defer indefinitely the payment of CGT and, in addition, there was no exit charge when a UK trust migrated. Section 80 (now TCGA 1992 s 87) was supplemented by changes introduced in FA 1991 and FA 1998.                                                    **[27.47]**

*An exit charge* From 19 March 1991 an exit charge has been levied on UK trusts which migrate: see TCGA 1992 ss 80–84 and *Example 27.11*.    **[27.48]**

*Settlor charge* In cases where a 'defined person' can benefit under the trust, gains realised by non-UK-resident trustees result in a CGT charge on the UK-resident and domiciled settlor: TCGA 1992 s 86 and Sch 5.        **[27.49]**

*The 'interest' charge* An interest charge supplements the s 87 charge in cases where capital distributions are not made promptly out of a non-resident trust in which the trustees have realised gains (TCGA 1992 ss 91–97). The effect can be that higher rate taxpayers will pay at rates of up to 64% on gains realised by offshore trusts. See also **[27.119]** and *Examples 27.20* and *27.21*.
                                                                    **[27.50]**

c)  *FA 1998 changes*

These amounted to a further tightening of the screws involving:
(1)    an extension of the settlor charge to settlements created before the 1991 changes (before 1998 the settlor charge was only relevant to settlements created or 'tainted' on or after 19 March 1991);
(2)    including 'grandchildren' in the class of 'defined person' for the purpose of that charge if the trust was established or tainted after 16 March 1998;
(3)    extending the capital payments charge to trusts where the settlor was not domiciled or resident in the UK;
(4)    widening the tax charge on disposals of beneficial interests in a settlement;
(5)    new rules to deal with the charge when the settlor or beneficiary is temporarily non-resident.

This process was continued by anti-avoidance measures in FA 2000, FA 2003 and F(N0 2)A 2005.                                              **[27.51]**

## 2   Exporting a UK trust

a)   *Why export?*

Moving a trust offshore has usually been undertaken in order to obtain all or some of the following benefits: protection from a reintroduction of exchange control; deferment of CGT; and deferment of income tax. So long as the settlor and any spouse are excluded from benefit, UK income tax will be avoided unless beneficiaries ordinarily resident in the UK receive a benefit and the trust produces 'relevant income' (TA 1988 ss 739–740 and see **[18.111]**). For CGT, provided that the settlor charge does not apply, TCGA 1992 s 87 will not lead to any UK tax charge so long as capital payments are not made to UK domiciled and resident beneficiaries. Because of the wide definition of 'defined person' (and hence of the settlor charge), however, it is now relatively uncommon for UK domiciled residents to set up new offshore trusts or to export existing trusts.

Even if the settlor is dead, the penalty charge referred to in **[27.119]** may make the tax advantages very marginal unless it is intended that no UK-resident and domiciled beneficiary is to receive capital payments from the trust.                                              **[27.52]**

(b)   *When is a trust non-resident?*

The rules changed in FA 2006 with effect from 6 April 2007. Prior to 6 April 2007, a trust is non-resident for CGT purposes when a majority of the trustees are neither resident nor ordinarily resident in the UK *and* the general administration of that trust is ordinarily carried on outside the UK (TCGA 1992 s 69(1)). There is a proviso to s 69(1) for professional trustees. Where a person who is resident in the UK carries on a business consisting of or including the management of trusts and is acting as a trustee in the course of that business he is treated in relation to the trust *for capital gains tax purposes only* as non-resident if the whole of the settled property consists of or derives from property that was provided by someone not at the time of making that provision domiciled, resident or ordinarily resident in the UK. Note, however, that this let-out does not apply for income tax purposes and therefore is of limited use if the intention is to keep the trust non-resident for income tax purposes. See **Chapter 18**.

FA 2006 Sch 12 amends s 69 so that from 6 April 2007 the test for residence of trustees will be the same for income tax and capital gains tax purposes. The rules have been aligned to the existing income tax rules. From 6 April 2007, where a trust is created by a settlor who is resident, ordinarily resident and domiciled in the UK, all the trustees must be resident outside the UK if the trust is to be non-resident. If the settlor is non-resident and not domiciled in the UK it is only necessary that there is one non-resident trustee for the trust to be treated as non-resident for both income tax and capital gains tax purposes. If the settlor is not UK domiciled but is UK resident at the date of setting up or funding the trust, all trustees must be non-resident. Note that the place where the administration of the trust is carried out will no longer be relevant for capital gains tax purposes. Despite representations from the various professional bodies, the exemption for professional trustees will be abolished on the basis that it constitutes 'state aid'. Note that if the trust property is transferred from one trust to another, the residence of the settlor has to be tested both at the time the original trust was funded and at the time of the transfer. See s 68B and s 69(2C) TCGA 1992.

**EXAMPLE 27.9**

Mr A was not resident or domiciled here when he died leaving assets in trust. The trustees comprise two friends resident in the UK and one non-resident. The trust is non-resident for income tax purposes but currently resident for capital gains tax purposes unless one of them is a professional. From 6 April 2007 it will no longer be resident here for capital gains tax purposes.

By contrast:

**EXAMPLE 27.10**

Mr A was resident but not domiciled here when he died leaving assets in trust. The trustees comprise one UK resident and two non-UK residents and the general administration is carried on abroad. The trust is currently resident here for income tax purposes and non-resident for capital gains tax purposes. From 6 April 2007 it will become UK resident for capital gains tax purposes and income tax purposes.

ESC D2 (see **[27.6]**) does not apply to trustees and hence the tax year is not split so that the UK trustees may be taxed on gains realised later in the tax year after foreign-resident trustees have been appointed.            **[27.53]**

c)   *Can UK trusts be exported?*

Many trusts start off abroad but where a trust is to be moved abroad, what is the position where the trust is originally UK and all the beneficiaries are resident here? The equitable rules on the appointment of overseas trustees were set out by Pennycuick VC in *Re Whitehead's Will Trusts* (1971) as follows:

'The law has been quite well established for upwards of a century that there is no absolute bar to the appointment of persons resident abroad as trustees of an English trust. I say "no absolute bar" in the sense that such an appointment would be prohibited by law and would consequently be invalid. On the other hand, apart from exceptional circumstances, it is not proper to make such an appointment, that is to say, the court would not, apart from exceptional circumstances, make such an appointment; nor would it be right for the donees of such a power to make an appointment out of court. If they did, presumably the court would be likely to interfere at the instance of beneficiaries. There do, however, exist exceptional circumstances in which such an appointment can properly be made. The most obvious are those in which the beneficiaries have settled permanently in some country outside the UK and what is proposed to be done is to appoint new trustees in that country.'

This *dictum* would suggest that appointing non-resident trustees is acceptable but usually 'improper'. (Trustee Act 1925 s 36(1) might imply that residence outside the UK for more than 12 months is unacceptable for a trustee whilst s 37(1)(c) may create difficulties for emigrations pre-1 January 1997 given that a non-UK corporate trustee cannot be a 'trust corporation': see *Adam & Co International Trustees Ltd v Theodore Goddard* (2000).) However, since *Re Whitehead's Will Trusts* judicial attitudes have changed so that provided that the export can be shown to be for the beneficiaries' advantage (eg in saving tax) the courts are not likely to interfere (see *Richard v Hon A B Mackay* (1987)).

HMRC may not be able to object to the appointment since they do not have *locus standi* but any UK trustee should consider taking indemnities from the new overseas trustees in case beneficiaries at some future date allege that breaches of trust have been committed and seek to set aside the appointment. It is also sensible to include in any trust instrument an express power for the existing trustees to retire in favour of non-resident trustees.   **[27.54]**

### d)   *The CGT export charge (TCGA 1992 s 80(2))*

When trustees of a UK settlement become neither resident nor ordinarily resident in the UK, they are deemed to have disposed of assets in that settlement and immediately to have reacquired those same assets. This deemed disposal is closely modelled on that which applies when a person becomes absolutely entitled to settled property (see **[25.47]**) and on the exit charge which is levied when a non-UK incorporated company ceases to be UK-resident (TCGA 1992 ss 185: see **[41.154]**).

Imposing the exit charge gives rise to a number of problems. When, for instance, does the charge come into effect? Section 80(1) defines the phrase 'relevant time' as meaning any occasion when trustees become non-UK-resident provided that *the relevant time falls on or after 19 March 1991.*

A second problem is when do trustees become non-UK-resident? A simple view would be that this would occur whenever UK trustees (Alan and Ben) are replaced by, say, two Jersey trustees (Cedric and Desmond). Certainly, if s 80 stood alone, such a simple change in the trusteeship would be 'the relevant time'. However, the section must be read in the light of the rest of the CGT legislation and under s 69(1) it is provided that:

> 'The trustees of the settlement shall for the purposes of this Act be treated as being a single and continuing body of persons ... and that body shall be treated as being resident and ordinarily resident in the United Kingdom *unless the general administration of the trusts is ordinarily carried on outside the United Kingdom and the trustees or a majority of them for the time being are not resident or not ordinarily resident in the United Kingdom.'*

Replacing A and B with C and D will satisfy part of s 69(1) but there is a 'frequently overlooked' second limb in that provision: namely that the administration of the trust must be conducted outside the UK. Until that occurs, the trustees remain UK-resident.

So far as timing is concerned, the deemed disposal is said to take place 'immediately before' the relevant time: accordingly the disponors are the retiring UK trustees who, given that the CGT year cannot generally be split, also remain liable for gains realised by the new trustees in the tax year in which they are appointed (SP 5/92 para 2).   **[27.55]**

**EXAMPLE 27.11**

Trustees of the Fisher Trust hold valuable land. The settlor is dead. The land shows a substantial gain. They decide that they wish to sell the land. If they sell the land they realise a gain taxed at 40%. They, therefore, decide instead to retire in favour of Jersey trustees in February 2005 and in May 2005 the Jersey trustees sell the land.

The effect of s 80 is that there is a deemed disposal of the land in February 2005 and therefore that the original trustees of the Fisher Trust realise a gain at that point. They pay tax at 40% and will need to ask the Jersey trustees for funds if the UK trustees have not made a sufficient retention to pay this tax.

Who is liable to pay the export charge? Because the deemed disposal is by the retiring UK trustees they are primarily responsible. It is therefore important that they retain sufficient assets to cover this liability. TCGA 1992 s 82 further provides that if tax is not paid by those trustees within six months of the due date, any former trustees of that settlement who held office during the 'relevant period' can be made accountable. The relevant period (broadly) means the 12-month period that ends with the emigration (although not backdated before 19 March 1991). Assume, for instance, that A and B, two professional trustees, retire on 1 January 1999 in favour of two family members. Those family trustees subsequently (on 1 July 1999) retire in favour of two non-UK-resident trustees, C and D, such retirement being without the prior knowledge of A and B. On these facts, the appointment of C and D constitutes the 'relevant time' for s 80 purposes and any gain arising as a result of the deemed disposal will therefore be payable on 31 January in the following tax year (ie on 31 January 2001). If not paid within six months of that date HMRC may demand that tax from all or any of A, B and the family trustees. However, a former trustee can escape liability if he shows that 'when he ceased to be a trustee of the settlement there was no proposal that the trustees might become neither resident nor ordinarily resident in the UK' (s 82(3) and SP 5/92 para 5). It is advisable to put a suitable clause in all deeds of retirement (where appropriate) to demonstrate that emigration was not in mind at the date the trustee stepped down.

The deemed disposal is of 'defined assets' which (predictably) includes all the assets that constitute the settled property at the relevant time. The term does not include UK assets used for the purpose of a trade carried on by the trustees through a UK branch or agency. This is because such assets remain within the UK tax net even after the trustees become non-resident: hence there is no need to subject them to the deemed disposal (see **[27.41]**).

Section 81 deals with involuntary exports and imports. Assume that the trustees of a settlement are Adam (UK-resident) and Cedric (a Jersey-resident accountant) who does all the paperwork and performs the administrative tasks for the trustees. Adam dies with the result that the conditions laid down in s 69(1) are satisfied and the trust ceases to be UK resident. On these facts, there was no intention to export the trust. Imposing an exit charge in such a case would be unjust and hence s 81 prevents the charge arising *provided that* within six months of Adam's death the trustees of the settlement become again UK resident. Not surprisingly, the exit charge remains in force for those defined assets that are disposed of during the period of non-UK residency (ie between the death and the resumption of residence).

Finally, the converse situation (a non-resident settlement becoming UK resident because of the death of a trustee) is provided for in sub-ss (5)–(7). Reverting to non-resident status within six months of the death will not generally trigger the s 80 exit charge subject only to an exception where the period of UK residence has been used to add assets to the settlement claiming holdover relief on that transfer. Resuming non-resident status will result in a deemed disposal at market value of such assets. See also *Green v Cobham* (2002) for the difficulties that can arise where a trustee who was professional retires hence ceasing to be a professional, and the trust inadvertently becomes UK-resident for capital gains tax purposes. **[27.56]**

### EXAMPLE 27.12

Suppose that in *Example 27.11* above the asset held by the Fisher Trust was not land but instead the trustees held shares in a listed company RZX Limited. HMRC's view was that this made no difference and s 80 still applied to impose a charge. See *IR Tax Bulletin*, April 2001 and their example 2 for further details.

However, this view was rejected in *Davies v Hicks* 2005 STC 850. The case related to the interaction of the bed and breakfast rules with the exit charge on the export of a settlement. It enabled UK-resident trusts to be exported without a tax charge through use of the identification provisions and then do a round the world scheme—see below.

The bed and breakfast provisions are designed to prevent the establishment of a capital loss by the sale and subsequent repurchase of the same assets. TCGA s 106A provides that where securities are sold they must be identified with securities of the same class acquired by the same person in the period of 30 days. This eliminates any loss assuming that the values remain similar. The argument successfully run in *Hicks* was therefore that when UK trustees sold shares, retired in favour of non-UK trustees who reacquired the shares within 30 days, s 106A required the security disposed of to be identified with the securities reacquired, thereby eliminating any gain which would otherwise have arisen under general principles (unless in that short period the shares had increased in value). Did s 106A(5)(a) deem the shares to remain in trustee ownership throughout as the Revenue maintained or did the trust emigrate with cash? Park J held the latter applied. There was nothing in s 106A that deemed the trustees still to hold shares at the date of export:

'I cannot accept in this case that a provision which was intended to identify which shares acquired by a particular taxpayer should be matched with shares sold by the same taxpayer can be deemed to have had effects going far beyond that and requiring it to be imagined, for a quite different statutory purpose, that the assets held by the taxpayer at a different time did not consist of the actual assets then held by him, but rather consisted of different assets altogether.'

(There is some analysis of how far deeming provisions should be taken generally in para 26 of the judgment. Arguably the same analysis could apply to avoid capital gains tax on export of a trust where there is no actual sale and reacquisition but merely a deemed disposal and reacquisition of securities by virtue of s 106A itself!)

This loophole was often combined with what was commonly known as 'a round the world' scheme.

This involved trustees resident in, say, Jersey retiring in favour of trustees resident in a foreign jurisdiction with a suitable treaty. While in that country (eg New Zealand) the new non-resident trustees sold an asset but before the end of the same tax year, UK-resident trustees were appointed. The aim was to avoid ss 86–87 by avoiding any time when there was a single and continuing body of trustees with dual-resident status. The analysis was that ss 86–87 would be inapplicable because of the trustees being resident in the UK at some time in the year of assessment but at a *different* time from the disposal. Arguably s 77 would not apply because the treaty would protect the gain.

It could be argued that a treaty cannot protect against either a s 77 or s 86 charge—see *Bricom* (1979) STC 1179. If it is not as such the gains realised by the trustees that are deemed to be the gains taxable on the settlor but a notional sum equal to such gains then no relief is due. The argument that a double tax treaty can protect against s 77 but not s 86 gains is based on the idea that under s 86 there has to be determined the gains that would accrue to the trustees if the trustees were resident in the UK throughout the year. By contrast s 77 uses a different wording and requires a calculation first of what gains the trustees would actually be taxable upon in the UK in the absence of s 77 before then attributing such gains to the settlor. The trustees arguably would not be taxable upon any gains that are protected by a treaty. The scheme was also used in respect of non-settlor interested trusts.

In 2003 the Revenue amended the Mauritius and Canada treaties to stop trusts emigrating there. Last year the New Zealand treaty was amended. Now more radical action has been taken and the whole scheme stopped.

Under F(No 2)A 2005 s 33 a new TCGA 1992 s 83A was inserted so that nothing in any double tax treaty precluded a charge to capital gains tax arising when:

(a)    the trustees were, at some time in the year of claim, resident in the UK; and

(b)    were not resident in the UK at the time of disposal.

The new measure applied to disposals of settled property on or after 16 March 2005. The idea is to ensure that either the settlor is chargeable if the trust is settlor interested within s 77 or that the trustees are chargeable if the trust is not settlor interested.

However, until FA 2006, TCGA 1992 ss 105 and 106A could still be used to nullify the effect of s 80 on shares if the UK trust emigrated because no amendment had been made to these sections. This could be helpful if the settlor was also likely to go non-UK resident for five years and wanted to export his trust.

FA 2006 s 74 amends TCGA 1992 s 106A and will apply in respect of acquisitions of shares made on or after 22 March 2006 irrespective of when the disposal was made. The bed and breakfasting rules are disapplied where the person making the disposal of securities acquires them at a time when he is non-resident or treaty non-resident.

The position of beneficiaries who dispose of their interests in a trust after it has been exported is considered at [27.120].                    [27.57]–[27.90]

V  TAXING THE UK SETTLOR ON TRUST GAINS (TCGA 1992 s 86, Sch 5)

## 1  Introduction

These provisions resemble (although they are more severe!) those in TCGA 1992 s 77 which deals with UK-resident trusts: see **[19.85]**. When they apply, gains realised by the trustees, which would have attracted a UK CGT charge had the trustees been resident, are taxed as gains of the settlor and form the top slice of his taxable gains for that year (although such gains can now be reduced by the 'personal' losses of the settlor— see **[27.98]**). As in the s 77 rules, the gains are not reduced by a trustee annual exemption whilst losses realised by the trustees (although available to set against future gains which they may make) are not treated as losses of the settlor. The settlor is given a statutory right to recover any tax that he suffers from his trustees, but the extent to which this right may be enforced in a foreign jurisdiction is uncertain (see *Example 27.15* and also see CG 38321). It is not, however, thought that a right of reimbursement is the same as the enforcement of foreign revenue laws: see Lord Mackay of Clashfern in *Williams & Humbert Ltd v W & H Trade Marks (Jersey) Ltd* (1986) where he commented that 'the existence of (an) unsatisfied claim to the satisfaction of which the proceeds of the action will be applied appears to me to be an essential feature of the principle (that foreign revenue laws will not be enforced)'. The proper law of the settlement may also be relevant here. Where the settlement is English law, in practice reimbursement may be easier to enforce. See discussion in *Trusts and Estates Law and Tax Journal*, July/August 2004, p 5.

Two key questions need to be answered. *First,* which settlements are caught and, *secondly,* when does a settlor retain an interest for these purposes? The answers to both questions were affected by changes made by FA 1998. **[27.91]**

## 2  'Qualifying settlements'

So far as the first question is concerned, the original rules applied to 'qualifying settlements' which were defined in Sch 5 para 9 as settlements created 'on or after 19 March 1991' which could benefit defined persons (see 29.95). Old settlements were therefore generally outside the scope of the rules (and were known as '*golden trusts*') *but* para 9(2) provided that in four situations such settlements could *become* qualifying settlements (see further SP 5/92): this is known as '*tainting*').                                    **[27.92]**

### EXAMPLE 27.13

(1) The Jonas Family UK Trust was set up in 1982. In 1996 the trustees become non-UK-resident. Not only did that event trigger an exit charge but, in addition, because the settlement was exported after 18 March 1991 it became a 'qualifying settlement'.

(2) The Popeye Settlement had been resident in Liechtenstein since 1989. In 1996:
    (a) A court order was obtained in Vaduz whereby the beneficial class was widened to include the settlor. This had the effect of turning the trust

into 'a qualifying settlement'. By contrast, in settlements where the trustees have always had the power to *add* beneficiaries and exercised that power to add a 'defined person' after March 1991 it was not thought that the terms of the trust had been varied so that it became a 'qualifying settlement'. (In SP 5/92 it is stated that 'where the terms of the trust include a power to appoint anyone within a specified range to be a beneficiary, exercise of that power after 19 March 1991 will not be regarded as a variation of the settlement'. When the trust has a general power to add *anyone* the position remains unclear.)

(b)    The trustees distributed funds to the settlor's spouse who was not a beneficiary. The effect of what was a breach of trust was to convert the trust into 'a qualifying settlement' since she was now a person who had enjoyed a benefit (and was a 'defined person') and she was not a person who might have been expected to have enjoyed such a benefit from the settlement after 18 March 1991.

(c)    On 1 March 1992 Julian Popeye added property to his father's trust. Such an addition, whether by the settlor or another, had the effect of turning the trust into a 'qualifying settlement' and Julian would be taxable under s 86 in respect only of gains realised from property added by Julian. This provision had to be watched carefully: it did not apply in cases where there was an accretion to settlement funds (eg where the trust received dividends or bonus shares from a company in which it had investments) nor if the settlor added property to discharge the administrative expenses of the trust (not the company) to the extent that such expenses could not be discharged out of trust income. (On the meaning of 'administrative expenses' and further details on tainting see the important SP 5/92 para 26).

## 3    The 1998 changes to 'qualifying settlements'

From 6 April 1999, pre-19 March 1991 settlements capable of benefiting a 'defined person' (see [27.95]) were brought within the tax charge on the settlor, ie gains realised on or after that date by the trustees are taxed on him (FA 1998 s 132). The following matters are worthy of note:

(1)    From 17 March 1998 to 6 April 1999 there was a 'transitional period'. During this time the trust could, for instance, have become UK-resident, been wound up, or been converted into a 'protected settlement' (considered below). However, if the trust remained off-shore and was not converted into a protected settlement gains realised during this period were also taxed on the settlor (unless it did not benefit defined persons) but they were deemed to accrue in the following tax year, ie on 6 April 1999.

(2)    The settlor charge could have been avoided if during the transitional period all 'defined persons' were excluded from benefit. Alternatively, the charge was avoided if the beneficiaries were limited to infant children of the settlor; to grandchildren; to unborn persons, to future spouses etc, albeit that these persons would be within the class of 'defined persons'. Such a trust is known as a *'protected settlement'*: see TGCA 1992 Sch 5 para 9(10A). A settlement cannot be made protected after 6 April 1999.

(3)    A settlement which is currently qualifying because it benefits defined persons can be made non-qualifying at any time and the settlor will

then escape the s 86 charge on future trust gains provided the trust is non-qualifying for the **entire** tax year when the gain is made. The rules for making a settlement non-qualifying differ depending on whether the trust was set up pre-17 March 1998—see **[27.95]**.

### EXAMPLE 27.14

The Larg Jersey Trust was set up in 1988. The settlor, Joseph, is life tenant with remainder to his infant children. With the introduction of the 1998 changes, the trustees immediately and in the exercise of powers under the settlement:

(1) appointed half the fund to Joseph absolutely. This was a deemed disposal by the trustees on which Joseph was subject to CGT both on the gains realised by the trustees from the disposal and on stockpiled gains realised prior to March 1998 since he had received a capital payment (see **[27.111]**);

(2) the trustees then (and before 6 April 1999) excluded Joseph from all future benefit in the trust with the result that as the only beneficiaries were his infant children the settlement became a 'protected settlement'. So long as it retains this status, future gains will not be taxed on the settlor.

(4) Protected settlement treatment is lost if the settlement is tainted (see **[27.92]**). In addition, privileged treatment ceases in a year where the conditions are not satisfied: notably in the tax year following a beneficiary attaining 18 (in *Example 27.14* above, the year after the first child of Joseph Larg becomes 18).

(5) The 1998 changes may have catastrophic results for settlors given that they may not be able to recover tax from the trust.

### EXAMPLE 27.15

On his divorce in 1990, Joseph K set up a Jersey trust for the benefit of his children under which he was prohibited from benefiting. He is estranged from his children. In 2000 the children become absolutely entitled to the trust fund leading to a gain of £2m. Joseph is taxed on this gain with no prospect of recovering tax either from the trustees or his children. (Given that the trust is governed by Jersey law it is far from certain that courts in that country will recognise Joseph's right to reimbursement even if it does not amount to the enforcement of a foreign revenue debt.) See, however, the Jersey case of *Re the T Settlement* (2002) 4 ITLR 820 where the settlor was expressly excluded from benefit but the Court nevertheless permitted a variation of the trust in order to allow the trustees to reimburse her the capital gains tax due under s 86. It was held that the variation would be for the benefit of unborn beneficiaries in that it included the discharge of certain moral obligations on their behalf. If the trust is made UK-resident, future gains realised will not be taxable on Joseph since it will no longer be a settlor-interested trust.

Capital gains tax problems are now likely to arise on divorce as a result of the inheritance tax changes in FA 2006.

### EXAMPLE 27.16

John and Carolyn decide to divorce in 2007. They are both resident and domiciled in the UK. John's main asset is the offshore trust which he set up in 1991 and in which he has an interest in possession. It has £1m s 87 gains and £0.5 m unrealised gains. The trust is worth £4m. The main wealth of the family is contained in the trust and it is agreed that Carolyn should get half of this. However, if a payment of £2m is made to her or John outright, there will be s 87 gains attributed to the recipient of £1m since these are treated as coming out first plus the payment may trigger unrealised gains which are now taxed on John. The parties decide to split the trust assets but retain them in a trust structure. Pre-22 March 2006 half the trust fund could have been appointed over to a UK-resident interest in possession trust for wife with the husband excluded. Although this may have triggered s 86 gains on the settlor (and posed certain s 87 risks for the wife if the transfer could be regarded as a capital payment to her) at least going forward John was not taxed on the future gains of the new trust assuming minor children of the settlor were excluded. £0.5m of the s 87 gains would be transferred to the new trust under s 90 (ie half the gains equal to half the sum appointed across). The two trusts could then operate independently.

Any new post-21 March 2006 trust will no longer qualify as an interest in possession trust for Carolyn but will instead fall within the relevant property regime. In addition there is an upfront 20% inheritance tax since IHTA s 10 does not apply to transfers out of trusts. Hence it will be necessary to keep the funds within the existing trust and have one fund held on interest in possession trusts for Carolyn (which will qualify as a transitional serial interest if set up pre-6 April 2008) and one fund retained on interest in possession trusts for John. The difficulty is that even though John is excluded from Carolyn's share, he still suffers capital gains tax on all future unrealised gains even if the trust is brought back to the UK (s 77 would then operate). The problem could be avoided if a sub-fund election was made under FA 2006 Sch 12 but the conditions necessary for sub-fund elections make it unlikely to be workable. John will need to consider how he is reimbursed for capital gains tax arising on future disposals out of Carolyn's fund if he is excluded from benefit on her part.

(6)   TCGA 1992 s 76B and Sch 4B (inserted by FA 2000) were introduced to prevent the settlor charge being avoided by a 'flip-flop' arrangement (see **[27.96]**).                                                            **[27.93]**

## 4   Which settlors are caught by the offshore trust provisions?

Apart from the settlement needing to 'qualify', the legislation under which gains realised by offshore trusts are taxed on the settlor only applies in years when the settlor is *both* domiciled and either resident or ordinarily resident in the UK. Gains realised in other years are not taxed as the settlor's and nor are gains realised in the tax year when the settlor dies. Thus s 86 does not apply to offshore trusts provided the settlor is not domiciled here. However, note that if in the future there is a change to the current domicile rules or the legislation changes, offshore trusts set up by non-UK domiciliaries could be caught in the future.                                                           **[27.94]**

### EXAMPLE 27.17

Red (domicile of origin New Zealand) is the settlor and life tenant of an offshore trust that realises substantial gains. He is aged 90 and until now has successfully claimed he is not UK domiciled even though he has lived in the UK for many years. He does not pay tax on any gains realised by the trustees even if such gains are remitted to him or they are UK situated assets. (See also *Example 27.6* above.) In 2005–06, HMRC successfully determine that he is domiciled here because he now has no intention to leave the UK. He will be taxed on an arising basis under s 86 on all gains realised by the trustees after that date, whether or not they make capital payments to him. Even if no changes are made to the law of domicile as such or Red's New Zealand domicile continues, it is easy to envisage the Government changing the current legislation so that gains realised by an offshore trust are taxable on a foreign domiciliary who is resident in the UK if remitted here or gains from UK-situated assets realised by trusts are taxable on foreign domiciliaries who are settlors of such trusts.

## 5   Meaning of a 'defined person'

Gains will be taxed on the settlor only if a 'defined person' benefits or will or may become entitled to a benefit in either the income or the capital of the settlement. When the rules were introduced in 1991 a 'defined person' was identified as follows:

'(a)   the settlor;
(b)   the settlor's spouse;
(c)   any child of the settlor or of the settlor's spouse [no age limit];
(d)   the spouse of any such child;
(e)   a company controlled by a person or persons falling within paragraphs (a) to (d) above;
(f)   a company associated with a company falling within paragraph (e) above.'

The list was formidable (contrast the provisions of s 77(3) in relation to UK trusts) and it was particularly worthy of note that children (including step-children) *of whatever age* were included. A deliberate policy decision was taken not to apply the provisions of s 77 to offshore trusts but to include a far wider class of persons. Note the trap that exists for a settlor in cases where a UK trust has been created in favour of his children which is then exported. Although the settlor is otherwise excluded from all benefit under the rules of the trust, the effect of the export is to create a qualifying settlement with the result that gains will be taxed as the settlor's since defined persons (his children—even if they are geriatric adults) will or may benefit.

The only exclusion of real significance from the above list of defined persons was grandchildren and this omission was rectified by FA 1998. In respect of offshore trusts created on or after 17 March 1998 the list of defined persons is extended to catch:

(a)   any grandchild of the settlor or his spouse;
(b)   the spouse of any such grandchild; and
(c)   companies controlled by such persons and companies associated with such companies.

Note, however, that grandchildren trusts established before 17 March 1998 are not brought within the settlor charge unless the trust is tainted (eg by the addition of further property). Therefore, if the settlor wishes to avoid a s 86 charge a trust established before 17 March 1998 can be made exclusively for the benefit of the grandchildren and their issue at any time thereafter provided it is not tainted.                                                          **[27.95]**

### EXAMPLE 27.18

Johnny set up an offshore trust for himself and his issue and his brothers and sisters and their issue in 1990. The trust has realised no gains since 1998. It has not been added to or tainted. In 2003–04 the trustees want to realise a substantial gain from the sale of a piece of land. Provided that Johnny, his spouse, children and their spouses and any company controlled by them are permanently excluded from any benefit in the tax year before the disposal: ie in 2002–03, then any gains realised by the trustees in the following tax year will not be taxed on Johnny. The only beneficiaries will then be his siblings, their issue and his grandchildren and remoter issue. None of these are defined persons in respect of settlements established before 17 March 1998. Note that the settlement is not a protected settlement and therefore the change in beneficiaries does not need to be done prior to April 1999 but can be done at any point provided the trust is not tainted after 16 March 1998. If no change to the class of beneficiaries is made in 2002–03, any gains realised in 2003–04 by the trustees will be taxed on Johnny under s 86 unless he dies in that year.

## 6    Anti-flip-flop legislation

TCGA 1992 s 76B and Sch 4B (inserted by FA 2000) were introduced to prevent the settlor charge under s 86 being avoided by a 'flip-flop' arrangement. These provisions have been supplemented by further changes in FA 2003 although these changes do not increase the s 86 charge but affect the s 87 pool (see [27.122]).                                            [27.96]

**EXAMPLE 27.19**

*Year 1*: Trustees of the A Trust, which has no stockpiled gains and only unrealised gains, borrow against the security of the trust assets and advance the cash to the B Trust (which includes eg the settlor as a beneficiary); they then exclude 'defined persons' from the A Trust.

*Year 2*: A Trust disposes of assets to pay off loan, whilst the cash is advanced out of B Trust to the settlor in *Year 2*.

Under this arrangement no gains were read through to the B Trust (because there were no stockpiled gains which had been realised before *Year 2*) so that the distribution (in *Year 2*) from B Trust was tax free: the only disposal in the A Trust occurs at a time when the settlor charge does not apply.

The amending legislation introduced by FA 2000 applies if three conditions are satisfied:

(a)    the trustees make a transfer of value (as defined: for instance, the transfer of moneys, to B Trust);

(b)    in the year of transfer s 86 (the settlor charge), s 87 (the capital payments charge) or s 77 (UK trusts settlor charge) apply to the trust;

(c)    that transfer of value is linked with trustee borrowing.

If these conditions are satisfied, then if a transfer of value occurs on or after 21 March 2000, the trustees are deemed to dispose of the assets in A Trust and immediately reacquire them at market value. In a case where s 86 applies the resultant gain will be taxed on the settlor in the normal way. See also [27.122] for the effect of FA 2000 and FA 2003 on beneficiaries of non-settlor interested offshore trusts and on the s 87 pool of gains.

## 7    Attributed trust gains and personal capital losses (FA 2002 s 51)

### a)    *Background*

Although capital losses are not themselves tapered, TCGA 1992 s 2A(1) states that losses must be deducted from gains before the application of taper. This is the case both for current year losses and for those brought forward from earlier years (see [20.20]).

The gains of settlor-interested trusts are attributed to settlors under TCGA 1992 ss 77 and 86. The original rule was that, where there are attributed gains, taper relief would already have been taken into account in computing the figures; therefore, it was not permitted for settlors to deduct their personal (untapered) lossses from the tapered trust gains attributed to them. Equally trust losses cannot generally be deducted from personal gains.

An individual who had large personal capital losses brought forward and whose only chargeable assets were held in a settlor-interested trust could not, from 1998–99 onwards, make any further use of those losses as and when his trust realised gains.                                                                 **[27.97]**

### b)   *FA 2002 changes*

FA 2002 provides that the gains attributed to settlors for 2003–04 onwards will be the amount of the trust gains before the deduction of taper relief. If the settlor has personal capital losses, he must set them against his own chargeable gains first, but they can then be deducted from the gains attributed to him under TCGA 1992 ss 77 and 86. Taper relief is then applied.

The settlor is assessed to tax on these tapered gains and he is still entitled to claim from the trustees of the settlement reimbursement of the tax paid in respect of the attributed gains.

Note that there is no election procedure from 2003–04. The relief is mandatory. The settlor cannot choose to set personal losses against attributed trust gains in priority to personal gains even if that gives a better taper relief position.

Although this regime did not come into force until 6 April 2003, a settlor could *elect* for these new arrangements to apply for the tax years 2000–01, 2001–02 and 2002–03. Elections could be made for one, two or all three of these years. This means that there is a need to review past tax returns already submitted where there have been personal losses and settlor-interested trust gains.

Elections must be made no later than 31 January 2005. Note that trust losses of settlor-interested trusts cannot be set against personal gains of the settlor.                                                                                       **[27.98]**

### c)   *The section 87 beneficiary*

Contrast the position of s 87 gains imputed to UK-resident and domicilied beneficiaries of offshore trusts following the receipt of a capital payment. Personal losses of the beneficiary cannot be set against such attributed gains taxed under s 87.                                                           **[27.99]–[27.110]**

## VI   TAXING UK BENEFICIARIES OF A NON-RESIDENT TRUST (TCGA 1992 ss 87 ff)

### 1   **Basic rules**

Subject to the settlor charge which may apply if a 'defined person' has an interest in a qualifying settlement (see **[27.92]**), TCGA 1992 ss 87 ff apply to non-resident trusts in respect of gains made from 1981–82 onwards where the trustees are not resident nor ordinarily resident in the UK during the tax year. Prior to 17 March 1998 for the section to apply the settlor had to be domiciled *and* either resident or ordinarily resident in the UK at some time during the tax year or when the settlement was made. Hence, if the settlor was UK domiciled and resident at the date of the trust's creation the rules of s 87 *always* applied. If the settlement was originally created by a non-domiciled settlor, who subsequently became a UK domiciliary, it was caught by these rules only for those years when the settlor was UK resident and ceased to be caught on his death. Trusts set up by non-resident but UK domiciled settlors were also not caught by s 87 until the settlor became resident here.

As a result of disquiet caused by the 'Robinson trust', in the case of gains realised in an offshore trust and capital payments received by UK resident and domiciled beneficiaries on or after 17 March 1998 the residence and domicile of the settlor became irrelevant. Section 87, therefore, now extends to all non-resident trusts irrespective of when set up and whether or not the avoidance of UK tax was one of the motives of the settlor. However, it will only attribute trust gains realised post 16 March 1998. (Contrast the provisions of TA 1988 ss 739–740 which are subject to a 'purpose' defence in s 741: see **[18.113].**)

'Settlement' and 'settlor' are defined as for income tax (see ITOIA 2005 s 620(1)) and settlor includes the testator or intestate when the settlement arises under a will or intestacy (TCGA 1992 s 87(9)).

**EXAMPLE 27.20**

(1)   Sergei, domiciled and resident in France, has settled his holiday home in Nice on an overseas trust for his daughter, Nina, who is domiciled and resident in England. As a result of the new rules introduced by FA 1998 capital payments (including (it may be: see below) the use of the property by Nina) are within the CGT net. Assuming that no gains are realised in the trust, any tax charge will be postponed until, for instance a beneficiary becomes entitled to the property or it is sold (note (1) that the property may benefit from main residence relief and (2) that Nina's beneficial interest is a chargeable asset: see **[27.120]**).

(2)   John Kaput moved to the West Indies in 1920 and settled his island paradise on trust for his Scottish descendants who become absolutely entitled to the property in 2005 when the trust period ends. On this occasion a tax charge will arise and, since the beneficiaries receive a capital payment on absolute entitlement, it will be necessary for beneficiaries to include in their tax returns a calculation showing gains realised by the trust since 17 March 1998!

(3)   The trustees of a non-UK settlement set up by Irek, a Russian actor now deceased, hold the trust property for Irek's four grandchildren; two of whom, Adam and Ivan, are now resident and domiciled in the UK. Any capital payments made by the trustees to Adam and Ivan prior to 17 March 1998 are not taxable on them even if gains are realised post-17 March 1998. Gains and losses accruing to the trustees before 17 March 1998 and capital payments received before 17 March 1998 are wholly ignored. However, if the trustees now realise gains in 2003–04, any capital payments Adam and Ivan have received after 16 March 1998 can be taxed on them (see section 2 below— operation of the s 87 charge). There may be some possibility of washing out gains by payments first to the non-UK beneficiaries if such

payments are made in an earlier tax year before payments to UK-domiciled and resident beneficiaries although note at **[27.122]** the changes in FA 2003 which can limit this.

Section 87 is now the catch-all charge: first consider if gains are taxed on the settlor (if they are, that is the end of the matter) but if they are not, then the s 87 rules must be applied.                                                     **[27.111]**

## 2   Operation of the section 87 charge

The charging system operates as follows:

### a)   *Trust gains ('stockpiled gains')*

The trust gains for each year must be calculated ('the amount on which the trustees would have been chargeable to tax ... if they had been resident and ordinarily resident in the UK in the year'). Non-resident trustees are *not* entitled to the benefit of a CGT annual exemption, but the normal uplift in value in the settled assets will occur on the death of a life tenant in possession (see **[25.49]**); the principal private residence exemption may apply (see **Chapter 23**); and taper relief is applied to reduce the gain. In computing this total, gains made in offshore companies may be attributed to the trustees (see TCGA 1992 s 13(10)). The anti 'flip-flop' rules introduced by FA 2000 (see **[27.122]**) provide for a separate pool of stockpiled gains is to be drawn on when the normal gains have been exhausted (TCGA 1992 s 85A, Sch 4C).
                                                                        **[27.112]**

### b)   *Capital payments*

The gains realised by the trustees will be attributed to beneficiaries and subject to CGT to the extent that they receive 'capital payments' unless otherwise taxed as income. A 'capital payment' is widely defined (see TCGA 1992 s 97(1) and (2)) to include, *inter alia*, the situation where a beneficiary becomes absolutely entitled to the trust property as well as to 'the conferring of any other benefit'.

This can include, for example, rent-free occupation of houses owned by a trust, use of pictures owned by a trust as well as loans to beneficiaries.

In *Billingham v Cooper; Edwards v Fisher* (2001) it was decided that the provision of an interest-free loan which was repayable on demand conferred a benefit on the borrower (a beneficiary of the trust) every day for which the loan was left outstanding. That benefit was a 'payment' within s 97(2) and a capital payment by virtue of s 97(1). The value of the benefit could be quantified retrospectively and the legislation would be applied year by year. Two other matters are worthy of note:

(1) It was accepted that a fixed period loan (eg for ten years) conferred a benefit once and for all at the date of the loan and that there was no subsequent conferment of a benefit.

(2) The Court of Appeal rejected the argument that no benefit was received (or its value was nil) on the basis that if interest had been charged it would have gone to the beneficiary (who was life tenant of

the settlement). The following extract from the judgment of Lloyd J at First Instance was expressly approved by the appeal court:

'It seems to me that the legislation does not call for or permit a comparison of the position that the recipient might have been in if a different transaction had been undertaken by the trustees. There are too many different possible comparisons for that to be a tenable approach. The proper comparison is with the position of the recipient if the actual loan had not been made rather than if some other transaction had been entered into. The recipient of the actual loan, if it had not been made, would not have had the use of the money lent.

It seems to me that this is particularly clear from the fact that the sections are directed to attributing gains not only to beneficiaries but also among beneficiaries in circumstances in which more than one beneficiary has received a capital payment, which of course is not true of either of these cases.

I accept it is not sensible to suppose that the person entitled to income has a special status which exempts him from this treatment or requires him to be treated more favourably than other beneficiaries.'

More controversially HMRC argue that a settled advance by the trustees in favour of a particular beneficiary can be a capital payment within s 97. Suppose the trustees of an accumulation and maintenance offshore trust with a dead settlor decide that they wish to defer Michael's absolute entitlement to capital at 25? He would otherwise become entitled to one third of the trust fund and be subject to capital gains tax on the stockpiled gains. (Since he is the eldest child he will have the disadvantage of being taxed on all the stockpiled gains so far realised and effectively then 'wash out' the gains to the benefit of the others.)

They have no overriding powers of appointment. They do have a wide power of advancement and, therefore, exercise this power so as to make a settled advance for the benefit of Michael perhaps by way of resettlement of one third of the trust fund (say £2 million) so that he does not become absolutely entitled. Is this a capital payment? Even if he has no right to demand the capital can HMRC argue that he has received a capital payment up to the value of the assets advanced? Michael may only have a revocable life interest—in these circumstances can he really be taxed on the whole capital value?

The difficulty is that there is essentially a conflict between ss 90 and 97. TCGA 1992 s 90 provides that a proportion of outstanding trust gains are carried forward to the transferee settlement when a transfer of assets is made between settlements. However, s 97(2) provides that a payment includes the conferring of any benefit and s 97(5)(b) then states that a payment is received by the beneficiary if it is paid or 'applied for his benefit'.

The power of advancement can by definition only be exercised if it is for the benefit of a beneficiary. HMRC apparently take the view that the precise terms of the settlement under which a child takes is irrelevant and the value of that interest is also immaterial because if the application is for his benefit it is squarely within s 97(5)(b). The alternative view is that s 97(5)(b) is concerned with payments made to a third party **but where the beneficiary still receives full value**. For example, payments made to the school in settlement of fees that are a parent's liability on behalf of a child could be classed as payments applied for the benefit of a parent.

In the above example Michael had not in reality received anything like £2 million since the actual value of his settled interest is far less than this. If HMRC's view is right and the 64% rate applies, then he would have to find tax of over £1 million out of his personal funds! **[27.113]–[27.114]**

c)  *Method of attribution*

Trust gains are attributed to *all* beneficiaries who receive capital payments as follows. The first beneficiary to receive a payment has (unless he is not resident here and the trust is caught by the FA 2003 changes—see **[27.122]**) attributed to him all the gains then realised by the trustees to the extent of the benefit which he receives. This can produce unfair results: assume, for instance, that Bill and Ben become absolutely entitled to an overseas trust fund worth £200,000 in equal shares when they become 25. The trust fund has realised gains of £100,000 when Ben becomes 25 (Bill will become 25 in a following tax year). *All the gains are attributed to Ben.*

When more than one capital payment is made in a single tax year, gains are attributed to the payments *pro rata* (TCGA 1992 s 87(5)). If a capital payment is made at a time when there are no trust gains, subsequent gains may be attributed to that beneficiary (s 87(4)). Finally, if no capital payments are made, trust gains are carried forward indefinitely until such a payment occurs (s 87(2)). (For the position of a non-UK domiciled or resident beneficiary who receives capital payments, see **[27.117]**.)  **[27.115]**

**EXAMPLE 27.21**

A non-resident discretionary settlement has four beneficiaries, two of whom (A and B) are UK domiciled. Over three years the fund has no income and makes the following net gains and capital payments. No capital payments have been made to the non-UK-resident or domiciled beneficiaries.

|  |  | A | B |
| --- | --- | --- | --- |
| *Year 1* | £ | £ | £ |
| Capital payments |  | 10,000 | 5,000 |
| Net gains £6,000 apportioned |  | 4,000 | 2,000 |
| Capital payments c/f |  | 6,000 | 3,000 |
|  |  | A | B |
| *Year 2* | £ | £ | £ |
| Capital payments |  | 3,000 | 6,000 |
| Including payments b/f |  | 9,000 | 9,000 |
| Trust gains | 20,000 |  |  |
| Amount apportioned | 18,000 | 9,000 | 9,000 |
| Gains c/f | £2,000 |  |  |

|  |  | A | B |
|---|---|---|---|
| *Year 3* | £ | £ | £ |
| Capital payments | | 15,000 | 5,000 |
| Trust gains | 10,000 | | |
| Gains b/f | 2,000 | | |
| Amount apportioned | £12,000 | 9,000 | 3,000 |
| Capital payments c/f | | £6,000 | £2,000 |

d)    *Section 740 tie-in*

A capital payment made by trustees may be treated as income in the hands of the beneficiary under TA 1988 s 740 (see **Chapter 18**). Such payments are charged to income tax up to the trust income for that year; income from previous years is included to the extent that such income has not already been charged to a beneficiary. It is only the excess that is treated as a capital payment for the purpose of the apportionment of trust gains.        **[27.116]**

**EXAMPLE 27.22**

The same settlement as in *Example 27.21*, except that the following payments made to A and B over three years are first treated as income under TA 1988 s 740.

|  |  | A | B |
|---|---|---|---|
| *Year 1* | £ | £ | £ |
| Trust payments | | 20,000 | 10,000 |
| Trust income | £12,000 | | |
| Charged to income tax on A and B | | 8,000 | 4,000 |
| | | 12,000 | 6,000 |
| Trust gains | £15,000 | | |
| Apportioned for CGT | | 10,000 | 5,000 |
| Payments c/f | | £2,000 | £1,000 |

|  |  | A | B |
|---|---|---|---|
| *Year 2* | £ | £ | £ |
| Payments b/f | | 2,000 | 1,000 |
| Payments made | | 10,000 | 11,000 |
| | | 12,000 | 12,000 |
| Trust income | 30,000 | | |
| Charged to income tax on A and B | 24,000 | 12,000 | 12,000 |
| Income c/f | £6,000 | — | — |
| Trust gains made in Year 2 and c/f | £12,000 | | |

| | | A | B |
|---|---|---|---|
| *Year 3* | £ | £ | £ |
| Trust payments | | 10,000 | 10,000 |
| Trust income | 8,000 | | |
| Trust income b/f from year 2 | 6,000 | | |
| Charged to income tax on A and B | £14,000 | 7,000 | 7,000 |
| | | 3,000 | 3,000 |
| Trust gains | 4,000 | | |
| Trust gains b/f from year 2 | 12,000 | | |
| | 16,000 | | |
| Apportioned for CGT | 6,000 | 3,000 | 3,000 |
| Trust gains c/f | £10,000 | | |

### e) The non-UK beneficiary

A beneficiary who receives a capital payment is subject to CGT on the attributed gains *provided that* he is UK domiciled and resident (TCGA 1992 s 87(7)). Accordingly, a non-UK-resident may have trust gains attributed to him (subject to FA 2003—see **[27.122]**) *but will not suffer any tax on those gains.* The UK beneficiary cannot deduct his personal losses from the gain attributed to him (contrast the position of a settlor beneficiary and s 86 gains and losses) but may deduct his annual exemption and the balance will then attract tax at 10%, 20% or 40% as appropriate. In calculating his liability offshore gains will be treated as the *lowest part* of his total gains for the year (thereby enabling him to benefit from the beneficiary's annual exemption and, in appropriate cases, reducing any surcharge: see **[27.119]** and see CG 38321 in the context of the charge on the settlor). **[27.117]**

### f) Offshore losses

If non-resident trustees make losses these will be set off against future gains made by those trustees in the normal way for the purposes of calculating s 87 gains attributable to a beneficiary. Note, however, important qualifications to the general provisions dealing with losses:
(1) Such losses do not pass to a beneficiary who becomes absolutely entitled to the trust assets (see TCGA 1992 s 16(3) and s 97(6)).
(2) If losses have been realised in the trust prior to when it became 'qualifying' and the trust gains then fall within the s 86 charge being realised after it became qualifying (eg in the case of a 'pre-1991 trust'), the existing realised losses cannot be used to reduce future gains which are taxed on the settlor. Such gains may be reduced by losses that are also realised during the period of the settlor charge). The existing losses from the period when the trust was non-qualifying may be used against future trust gains arising after the settlor charge has ceased to apply, eg when the settlor has died or the trust is imported.

(3)    Losses which have arisen during a period of settlor charge cannot be used by the trustees against future gains that may otherwise be taxed under s 87.

(4)    Gains attributed to a beneficiary under s 87 cannot be reduced by that beneficiary setting such gains off against personal losses.

**EXAMPLE 27.23**

Bonzo (now dead) created a non-UK-resident settlement in the mid 1980s. Capital payments have not so far been made by the trustees and the gains (losses) of the settlement are as follows:

| Tax year | Gain (loss) |
|---|---|
| 1986–87 | 250,000 |
| 1987–88 | (75,000) |

Assume further that the Bonzo family now wish to import this trust and that there are some assets in the fund showing an unrealised gain and some showing an unrealised loss.

(1)    The trust can be imported by the appointment of a majority of UK resident trustees. Future gains will be taxed at 40% with effect from 2004–05. Note that the stockpiled gains realised in the past will still remain on the clock until such time as capital payments are made.

(2)    The trust has realised gains of £250,000 from 1986–87 that will remain on the settlement 'clock' and so attract a tax charge as and when capital payments are made to UK beneficiaries.

(3)    The loss of £75,000 in 1987–88 may be offset against future trust gains including gains realised by UK resident trustees.

(4)    If, however, Bonzo was still alive and was domiciled and resident here, and the trust is within s 86 if non-UK resident or s 77 if UK-resident, the loss realised in 1987–88 could not be used against gains realised by the trust now.

A charge under s 87 can be deferred so long as the trustees avoid making capital payments. The charge can be avoided altogether if such payments are made to a non-UK-resident or non-UK-domiciled beneficiary or distributions are made to UK-resident and domiciled beneficiaries which do not exceed their annual capital gains tax exemptions. Gains may, therefore, be washed out of the trust by the making of such payments in the tax year prior to distributions to UK-resident and domiciled beneficiaries provided the trust is not caught by FA 2003—see **[27.122]**.

Following the introduction of 'temporary non-residents' by FA 1998, difficulties may arise if a settlor—who would otherwise be subject to the s 86 charge—ceased to be UK-resident. As a result the capital payment rules in s 87 will apply, but if the settlor returns to the UK within five years of his departure gains during his absence will be attributed to him on his return (see **[27.5]**). To prevent a double charge such gains will not include capital payments made to UK-resident and domiciled beneficiaries (although note that no deduction is made for payments to non-resident beneficiaries: see TCGA 1992 s 86A).                                              **[27.118]**

## 3    The supplementary (interest) charge

A 'supplementary' charge may apply to beneficiaries who receive capital payments on or after 6 April 1992. Because it is intended to be supplementary to the s 87 charge, this extra levy will *not* apply if the recipient beneficiary is non-resident or non-domiciled (TCGA 1992 ss 91–95).

The charge operates as an interest charge on the delayed payment of CGT following a disposal of chargeable assets by non-resident trustees. It is, however, limited to a six-year period and, therefore, the time covered by the charge begins on the *later* of (a) 1 December in the tax year following the year in which the disposal occurred, and (b) 1 December six years before 1 December in the year of assessment following that in which the capital payment was made. It ends in November of the year of assessment following that in which the capital payment is made. The rate of charge is 10% pa of the tax payable on the capital payment (this percentage may be amended by statutory instrument). The minimum period is two years so the minimum charge is 20%. For a higher rate taxpayer, the effective maximum rate is 64%.

**EXAMPLE 27.24**

The Moisie Liechtenstein Trust realises capital gains in the tax year 1998–99 and a capital payment is made to a UK domiciled and resident Moisie beneficiary on 1 July 2004.
(1)   That beneficiary will be assessed to CGT on the capital payment received (at current rates at, say, 40%).
(2)   The interest charge will apply for the period from 1 December 1999 to 30 November 2005 at 4% per annum so that the interest charge continues to run after the capital payment has been made. In all, six years will be subject to the additional charge (being 24%) thereby giving a capital gains tax rate of of 64% 40 + 24) Note that if the beneficiary does not suffer a CGT charge—for instance because he is able to set his annual exemption against the gains attributed to him—there is no interest charge.

The precise mechanics governing the supplementary charge are complex, with capital payments being matched first with total trust gains at 6 April 1991 and then on a first-in first-out basis. By way of concession, however, trustees are given at least 12 months in which to distribute gains since the interest charge does *not* apply to gains realised in the same or immediately preceding year of assessment.

**EXAMPLE 27.25**

In 1996–97 the Cohen Offshore Settlement has accumulated trust gains of £100,000. Although the interest charge begins to run on 1 December 1997 no charge is levied on capital distributions made before 6 April 1998.

To what extent has the charge encouraged the break-up of existing offshore trusts? Much turns on the facts of individual cases but it should be remembered that one way of avoiding the s 87 charge—distributing to non-residents—generally still remains available to 'wash-out' all the potential tax including this interest charge provided the trust is not caught by the FA 2003 provisions. For the wealthy family, who view their trust as a roll-up fund that they do not need to dip into, a 10% charge may be seen as a relatively small impost, given that the deferred tax may be an insignificant percentage of the total offshore fund.

Finally, remember that because income from offshore trusts may be taxed less heavily (at a maximum rate of 40%) trustees should, in appropriate cases, ensure that income rather than capital is distributed.    **[27.119]**

## 4    Disposal of a beneficial interest in an offshore trust

The basic rule is that disposals of beneficial interests in non-resident trusts are subject to charge (TCGA 1992 s 85(1) disapplying s 76(1)). The following points should be noted about this section.

*First,* what happens if the interest of a beneficiary terminates not as a result of any voluntary action on his part but by act of the trustees: eg where a life interest is terminated by the trustees under a power reserved to them in the settlement? In this case it is thought that the termination will not amount to a disposal for CGT purposes since whilst it is true that under the legislation certain involuntary disposals (eg a sale under a compulsory purchase order) are subject to charge (so that a voluntary act on the part of the disponor is not always required) even in these cases there is a transfer of assets as opposed to a mere forfeiture of rights. So far as a forfeiture of rights is concerned there is no disposal unless a capital sum is paid or deemed to be paid on that event (TCGA 1992 ss 22–24). If the trustees, therefore, exercise overriding powers of appointment and, say, terminate the settlor's life interest in favour of trusts for his children, there should be no tax charge on the settlor because he has made no disposal of his beneficial interest as such. If the trustees can exercise their overriding powers but only with the consent of the settlor, is there any disposal in these circumstances? The better view is that the giving of consent by the settlor in relation to an offshore trust is not a disposal within s 85 although HMRC's view is not entirely clear on this point. In the past HMRC have indicated that if no consideration is given to the consent there is no disposal by the beneficiary. The beneficiary in question may be able to release the requirement for his consent before any appointment by the trustees is actually contemplated.

Note that if the consent is treated as some sort of disposal of a chose in action asset for capital gains tax purposes, variations of any settlement whether UK-resident or not, where the beneficiary has to consent might be problematic!

*Second,* note that the effect of s 85 may mean that even if the settlor wants to be excluded from the trust (along with all defined persons) in order to avoid the s 86 charge, it may not be possible to do this easily without triggering a s 85 charge because the terms of the trust are such that the settlor can only be excluded if he positively surrenders his life interest. This would be regarded as a deemed disposal on which the settlor would be liable to capital gains tax (since the life interest is likely to have a low or nil base cost.) The only alternative to avoiding the s 86 charge is to wait until the death of the settlor before realising gains or to import the trust (although the settlor and spouse would still need to be excluded in order to avoid a s 77 charge and again this may prove difficult to engineer without a s 76/s 85 charge and see point 5 below). For this reason it is generally sensible to ensure that all offshore trustees have wide powers of appointment, exclusion etc in order to be able to rearrange the beneficial interests without triggering unexpected charges under s 85.

*Third*, the section makes it clear that although a disposal of such an interest is subject to charge this does not apply when the beneficiary becomes absolutely entitled as against the trustees in respect of any property (eg if an advance is made to him or on the deemed disposal occurring on the termination of the trust).

*Fourth*, if a UK-resident trust is exported thereby triggering a deemed disposal of the settled property (**[27.57]**) a beneficiary is treated as disposing of his interest at that time for the purpose of providing him with a market value at that date which will be used in calculating his gain on a subsequent disposal of the interest (see **[25.113]**]. This provision was used to avoid tax as illustrated in the following example:

**EXAMPLE 27.26**

The Itchyfoot Settlement has substantial stockpiled gains and is a cash fund. The trust is imported and then exported. The beneficiaries then disposed of their interests at no gain and the s 87 charge was avoided.

FA 2000 amended s 85 so that from 21 March 2000 there is no uplift in the value of the interests of the beneficiaries if a settlement is exported at a time when it has stockpiled gains.

*Fifth*, note that disposals of beneficial interests in a trust which was *at any time* non-UK-resident (or which had received property from such a trust) were brought into charge in respect of disposals occurring on or after 6 March 1998. This matter is considered further at **[25.115]**.

**[27.120]–[27.121]**

## 5   Anti-flip flop legislation—FA 2000 and FA 2003

As noted earlier, FA 2000 attempted to stop flip flop schemes by introducing Schedules 4B and 4C. Essentially where Trust A borrows and does not apply the borrowing for 'normal trust purposes' (narrowly defined) but makes a 'transfer of value' (widely defined to include capital transfers, loans on commercial terms etc) there is a deemed disposal of all the trust assets remaining in Trust A (resultant gains fall into the 'Schedule 4C pool'). FA 2000 prevented the use of old-style flip flop schemes which had effectively worked by delaying the realisation of gains until a later year. The pre-2000 flip flop schemes generally involved settlor interested trusts where the intention was to avoid a s 86 charge on future gains (see *Example 27.19*). However FA 2000 introduced a loophole that was exploited where trustees wished to reduce or eliminate the future pile of stockpiled gains that could be attributed to beneficiaries on future capital payments. See *Example 27.27*.

The FA 2000 provisions have created a number of problems: there is no motive test so perfectly innocent transactions which involved no tax avoidance and no diminution in the trust assets could be caught. For example a trust that borrowed from one underlying company and lent funds to another wholly-owned company to enable that company to make an investment would be caught. The safest course for offshore trusts (and indeed UK-resident trusts which had s 87 gains or were within s 77) was to avoid trustee borrowing at all, although curiously, companies wholly owned by trustees could borrow and were not caught by the legislation (see *Tax Bulletin*, issue 66 p 1048).

The loophole referred to above was contained in s 90(5)(a) which prevented s 87 gains from being carried across to the transferee settlement (trust B) to the extent that the transfer was (under Schedule 4B) linked with trustee borrowing. The legislation that had aimed to stop s 86 avoidance thus opened up extensive opportunities for s 87 tax avoidance as illustrated in the following example.                                              **[27.122]**

### EXAMPLE 27.27

Offshore Trust A has £1m stockpiled gains and is worth £1m. It holds mostly cash or assets showing no gain. It borrows £1m and in 2002 appoints all the borrowed funds of £1 million to Trust B. On a simple reading under the pre-FA 2003 legislation, since there was a transfer of value linked to trustee borrowing, s 90(5)(a) provided that the stockpiled gains of £1m did not pass across into Trust B. Trust B took £1m free of the stockpiled gains. There was a deemed disposal of the assets remaining in Trust A but since these showed no gains this did not matter. There was nothing to go into the Schedule 4C pool.

Such 'section 90' schemes were widely used in an attempt to get rid of the stockpiled gains which could not easily be washed out where all the beneficiaries were UK-resident. Often the penalty charge meant that if any capital payments were made to beneficiaries these would be taxed at 64%. Therefore the incentive to get rid of the stockpiled gains was high.

The Government response to the s 90 avoidance scheme has been aggressive. FA 2003 s 163 introduced further changes to Schedule 4C. These changes are complex but the effects can be summarised as follows:

(a)  FA 2003 changes are relevant wherever trustees of a settlement have made a transfer of value linked to trustee borrowing after 20 March 2000 even if the original settlement (Trust A in the above example) has ceased to exist. Since, as noted above, a transfer of value linked to trustee borrowing can occur in a number of unexpected instances where there is no avoidance motive, the position must be checked wherever trustees have borrowed.

(b)  The provisions in FA 2003 do not affect beneficiaries who have received capital payments from Trust 2 prior to 9 April 2003. Thus in *Example 27.27* if Trust B had distributed the entire £1m to the relevant beneficiaries by 9 April 2003, such beneficiaries are not caught by the FA 2003 legislation and such payments are tax free if the s 90 scheme works (although the scheme may fail for other reasons eg if Trust B was a sham).

(c)  FA 2003 now provides that the Schedule 4C pool comprises not only the Schedule 4B gains realised on the deemed disposal but also any outstanding s 87 gains in the transferor settlement at the end of the tax year in which the transfer was made. Thus in *Example 27.27*, Trust B no longer takes £1m cash free of the s 87 gains. All those s 87 gains fall into the Schedule 4C pool (along with any deemed Schedule 4B gains) and can be allocated to any future payments made to beneficiaries of either Trusts A or B.

(d)  The fact that (as in *Example 27.27*) no gains may be realised on the deemed disposal under Schedule 4B is irrelevant. If there is a transfer of value linked to trustee borrowing then the anti-avoidance legislation is triggered and a Schedule 4C pool is formed comprising the Schedule 4B trust gains plus the s 87 stockpiled gains.

(e)   For the purposes of calculating the Schedule 4C pool, the outstanding s 87 gains are calculated ignoring payments to non-resident or exempt beneficiaries in the tax year of the transfer of value (or subsequently) although payments to non-resident beneficiaries that took place prior to 9 April 2003 can reduce the s 87 stockpile.

(f)   The old s 87 stockpile in Trust A is reduced to nil. There is just one Schedule 4C pool overhanging both trusts.                                    **[27.123]**

### EXAMPLE 27.28

In 2003–04, Trust A borrows £2 million and appoints the cash to Trust B in June 2003. There is a deemed disposal of all the assets remaining in Trust A as at June 2003 (say shares in RS Limited worth £0.6 million with a base cost of £0.1 million) which disposal, therefore, realises a Schedule 4B gain of £0.5 million ignoring taper relief. The level of stockpiled s 87 gains in Trust A at the end of 2003–04 is £1 million. The Schedule 4C pool is therefore £1.5 million and can be attributed to future capital payments made to beneficiaries out of either Trust.

Trust B then makes distributions of £1.5 million to Eric and John, both not domiciled in the UK. The following tax year Trust B distributes the balance of the fund, being £0.5 million to Fiona who is resident and domiciled here. The distributions to Eric and John do not reduce the Schedule 4C pool of gains (which remains at £1.5m) although Eric and John do not suffer a CGT charge. Fiona pays tax on the entire £0.5 million distributed to her. Similarly, if Trust A makes any distributions to Eric and John, such distributions will not reduce the Schedule 4C pool hanging over Trust A and future capital payments to UK-resident and domiciled beneficiaries will be taxed.

(g)   Thus the risk of triggering a transfer of value is not only that one creates a deemed disposal of the remaining assets in the original settlement but also that one has also lost the opportunity to structure future capital payments tax efficiently—gains cannot be 'washed out' by making distributions to non-chargeable beneficiaries.

(h)   The deemed disposal of the remaining assets in the original settlement means that those assets are rebased for all future purposes.          **[27.124]**

### EXAMPLE 27.29

Facts as in *Example 27.28* except that Trust A actually sold RS shares 11 months later in May 2004 for £0.7 million. The gain realised then would be £0.1 million (which gain would not fall into the Schedule 4C pool unless a further transfer of value is made) not £0.6 million.

(i)   Presumably in *Example 27.28* taper relief is available on the deemed disposal in June 2003 calculated on a period of ownership from the date of acquisition up to June 2003. No further taper relief is available on the actual disposal in May 2004 because the shares have not been held for 12 months. The actual gain of £0.1 million realised on a later actual disposal of RS shares is a s 87 gain which is not attributed to Trust B and can still be washed out on future payments by Trust A to non-resident or non-domiciled beneficiaries. It is only the Schedule 4C gains that cannot be washed out.

(j)    The interest charge can also apply to Schedule 4C gains and, to maximise the adverse effects, the legislation provides that Schedule 4C gains of earlier years are attributed to beneficiaries before gains of later years.

(k)    When there are both s 87 and Sch 4C gains the earliest gains of either type are attributed to beneficiaries first. Where the s 87 and Sch 4C gains are of the same year, the Sch 4C gains are attributed first. This maximises the penalty charge.

(l)    There are wide anti-avoidance provisions catching further transfers to other trusts. Thus if in *Example 27.27* any of Trusts A, B or C later makes a further transfer of value creating a further Schedule 4C pool then that pool can be visited on any of the beneficiaries who receive capital payments from Trusts A, B or C even if say, the beneficiaries are excluded from the Trust which made the further transfer of value.

**[27.125]**

**EXAMPLE 27.30**

The facts are as in *Example 27.28* except that Trust B makes no distributions to Eric and John. Instead Trust B transfers one-third of its fund to Trust C for the benefit of Eric and his issue and one-third to Trust D for the benefit of John and his issue and retains the remaining one-third for the benefit of Fiona and her issue. John and Eric are excluded from Trust B; Fiona and John are excluded from Trust C and Fiona and Eric are excluded from Trust D. Trust C realises further s 87 gains of say £1 million in later tax years (which cannot at that point be attributed back to Trusts A, B or D) and eventually in 2009–10 makes a further transfer of value linked to trustee borrowing. The Schedule 4C pool that then arises is £1.2 million. Since all the settlements remain relevant settlements for the purposes of Schedule 4C due to the first transfer of value made in 2003–04, that £1.2 million pool can now be attributed to any capital payments made to any of the beneficiaries of Trusts A to D. Each trust's original pool of Schedule 4C gains has been retrospectively increased. In this case, the only person who would be concerned is Fiona since the other beneficiaries are not domiciled here, but she has no control over what Trust C does. There is also no obvious way in which she or indeed Trust B can require the trustees of Trust C to provide the necessary information to the trustees of Trust B regarding the calculation of the Schedule 4C pool.

Thus once a transfer of value linked to trustee borrowing has been made, each transferor and transferee settlement will need to keep monitoring any future transfers of value linked to trustee borrowing as well as the capital payments each trust makes and to whom, in order to establish whether the Schedule 4C pool has been reduced. Trustees of transferee and transferor settlements should ensure that in these circumstances they make suitable provision in the documentation to require all trustees to provide the relevant information in the future.    **[27.126]**

## 6    Offshore trusts: information (TCGA 1992 s 98A, Sch 5A)

FA 1994 widened the information provisions to catch all non-resident trusts, not just those in which a defined person retains an interest. Accordingly, they apply to additions to an existing trust; to the establishment by a UK settlor of a foreign settlement and indeed to a foreign settlement created by a non-UK-resident and domiciliary who subsequently becomes resident and domiciled and, finally, to the export of a UK trust. In all cases details of the date when the settlement was created; name and address of persons delivering the return and details of the trustees must be provided.          **[27.127]**

# Section 4    Inheritance tax

**Chapters**

# Introduction—from estate duty to inheritance tax

*Updated by Natalie Lee, Barrister, Senior Lecturer in Law, University of Southampton and Aparna Nathan, LLB Hons, LLM, Barrister, Gray's Inn Tax Chambers*

Most countries impose some kind of wealth tax. It usually takes the form of a death duty either levied on property inherited or on the value of a deceased's estate on death. In the UK estate duty was introduced in 1894 as a tax on a deceased's property whether passing under a will or on intestacy. Over its long life the tax was extended from its originally narrow fiscal base (property passing on death) to catch certain gifts made in the period before death and at the time of its replacement by capital transfer tax (CTT) it extended to gifts made in the seven years before death. By the 1970s estate duty was, however, widely condemned as an unsatisfactory tax. 'A voluntary tax'; 'a tax on vice: the vice of clinging to one's property until the last possible moment'—were typical descriptions.

In 1972 the Conservative Government considered replacing estate duty with an inheritance tax (Cmnd 4930). The idea was that a beneficiary would keep a cumulative account of all gifts that he received on death and pay tax accordingly. Nothing came of this proposal, largely because such a tax would have been too costly to administer and because the Conservative government fell from office.

The Labour government, which came to power in 1974, was committed to achieving a major redistribution of wealth. As a first stage (without any prior consultation) it introduced CTT in the 1974 Budget. This tax had '… as its main purpose to make the estate duty not a voluntary tax, but a compulsory tax, as it was always intended to be' (Mr Healey, the then Chancellor of the Exchequer). A proposed wealth tax (Cmnd 5074) was never introduced. In reality CTT, substantially altered during its passage through Parliament in 1974–75, never achieved its espoused redistributive purpose. There was no doubt, however, that in concept it was a brilliantly simple tax which removed the arbitrariness of the old estate duty. All gifts of property, whether made *inter vivos* or on death, were cumulated with earlier gifts and progressive rates of tax applied to that cumulative total.

The advent of Conservative governments in 1979 saw a steady erosion of the principles underlying CTT. The idea of a fully comprehensive cradle to grave gifts tax was abandoned in 1981 in favour of ten-year cumulation, thresholds were raised, and a new relief introduced for agricultural landlords. By 1986, as a percentage of GNP, CTT yielded less than one-third of the revenue formerly produced by estate duty.

To some extent, the changes made by FA 1986 merely completed this process. Ten-year cumulation was reduced to seven years and the majority of lifetime gifts made more than seven years before death were removed from charge. As in the days of estate duty, therefore, tax is now levied on death gifts and gifts made within seven years of death. In an attempt to prevent schemes whereby taxpayers could 'have their cake and eat it' (ie give property away but continue to enjoy the benefits from it) there was a further echo from estate duty in the reintroduction of rules taxing gifts with a reservation of benefit. These changes did not amount to a replacement of CTT by estate duty but did represent a welding of certain estate duty rules onto the already battered corpse of CTT. The end result is simply a mess and to call this amalgam an inheritance tax is to confuse matters further since the tax is not levied on beneficiaries in proportion to what they receive from an estate and neither is it a true tax on inheritances since certain lifetime transfers are subject to charge. 'There has been no attempt at reform. The Chancellor has merely given us some reasons for making a shabby handout to the very rich. Not only has he reverted to the old estate duty, he has falsified the label' (Cedric Sandford, *Financial Times*, 26 March 1986).

Capital transfer tax was rechristened inheritance tax as from 25 July 1986 and the former legislation (the Capital Transfer Tax Act 1984) *may* be cited as the Inheritance Tax Act 1984 from that date (FA 1986 s 100). Despite the permissive nature of this provision the new title for this Act will be used in this book and inheritance tax abbreviated to IHT. All references to CTT take effect as references to IHT and, as all references to estate duty became references to CTT in 1975, they subsequently became references to IHT.

As a further curiosity it may be noted that the removal of a general hold-over election for CGT in the 1989 Budget was justified by the then Chancellor (Nigel Lawson) on a somewhat inaccurate view of the current scope of IHT. In his Budget Speech, he stated that:

> 'the general hold-over relief for gifts was introduced by my predecessor in 1980, when there was still Capital Transfer Tax on lifetime gifts, in order to avoid a form of double taxation. But the tax on lifetime giving has since been abolished, and the relief is increasingly used as a simple form of tax avoidance.'

The bizarre position has now been reached whereby what was intended as a general tax on gifts has been limited (in the main) to gifts on or within seven years of death whilst a tax intended to catch capital profits may now operate to impose a tax charge on any gain deemed to be realised when a lifetime gift is made!

The last Conservative Government under John Major promised to abolish IHT when it could afford to do so. Not surprisingly, this theme was not one that successive Labour governments since 1997 warmed to but, it has to be said, until March 2006, they did little to the tax save for a general updating of some of the administrative provisions and targeted legislation aimed at closing loopholes revealed by the *Ingram, Melville* and *Eversden* cases. However, substantial changes to the inheritance taxation of trusts announced out of the blue and without prior consultation in the 2006 Budget, and now incorporated in the FA 2006, clearly seek to thwart the efforts to minimise IHT of those who are perceived to be wealthy. Whilst government amendments were made to the Bill during its passage through Parliament, the main thrust of the government's original proposals remains substantially the same and, although this cannot be said to amount to full-scale reform, it is perhaps an indication that the government has IHT in its sights, and that there might be more changes yet to come.

# 28   IHT—lifetime transfers

*Updated by Natalie Lee, Barrister, Senior Lecturer in Law, University of Southampton and Aparna Nathan, LLB Hons, LLM, Barrister, Gray's Inn Tax Chambers*

For a charge to IHT to arise there must be a *chargeable transfer*. Whether tax is levied on that transfer then depends upon whether it is:

(1)   *potentially exempt* in which case IHT will only be charged if the donor dies within seven years of that transfer: otherwise it is exempt.

(2)   *chargeable immediately* at 'lifetime rates' but so that if the transferor dies within seven years a supplemental charge to IHT may arise.     [**28.1**]

## I   DEFINITION OF A 'CHARGEABLE TRANSFER'

IHTA 1984 s 1 states that 'IHT shall be charged on the value transferred by a chargeable transfer'. A chargeable transfer is then defined in IHTA 1984 s 2(1) as having three elements: a transfer of value; made by an individual; which is not exempt.     [**28.2**]

### 1   A transfer of value

A *transfer of value* is defined in IHTA 1984 s 3(1) as any disposition which reduces the value of the transferor's estate. It includes certain deemed transfers of value ('events on the happening of which tax is chargeable *as if* a transfer of value had been made': see IHTA 1984 s 3(4)). Examples of deemed transfers of value include death (see **Chapter 30**); the termination of an interest in possession in settled property (see **Chapter 33**) and transfers of value made by a close company which are apportioned amongst its participators (see [**28.152**]).

*'Disposition'* is not defined, but the ordinary meaning is wide and includes any transfer of property whether by sale or gift; the creation of a settlement; and the release, discharge or surrender of a debt but not, it is thought, a consent (eg to an advancement of trust property). It includes a disposition effected by associated operations, a matter recently considered in the *Rysaffe* case (see [28.104]).                                                                        [28.3]

## 2  Omissions

By IHTA 1984 s 3(3), a disposition includes an omission to exercise a right. The right must be a legal right and the omission must satisfy three requirements:

(1)    The estate of the person who fails to exercise the right must be reduced in value.

(2)    Another person's estate (or a discretionary trust) must be increased in value.

(3)    The omission must be deliberate, which is presumed to be the case in the absence of contrary evidence.

Examples of omissions include failure to sue on a debt which becomes statute-barred; failure to exercise an option either to sell or purchase property on favourable terms; and failure by a landlord to exercise his right to increase rent under a rent review clause. The omission will constitute a transfer of value at the latest time when it was possible to exercise the right, unless the taxpayer can show (1) that the omission was not deliberate but was a mistake of fact (eg he forgot) or of law (eg failure to realise that the debt had become statute- barred) or (2) that it was the result of a reasonable commercial decision involving no element of bounty (eg failure to sue a debtor who was bankrupt).                                                               [28.4]

## 3  Examples of transfers of value

(1)    A gives his house worth £60,000 to his son B.

(2)    A sells his car worth £4,000 to his daughter C for £2,000.

(3)    A grants a lease of his factory to his nephew D at a peppercorn rent. The factory was worth £100,000; the freehold reversion after granting the lease is worth only £60,000. A's transfer of value is of £40,000.

(4)    A is owed £1,000 by a colleague E. A releases the debt so that his estate falls in value and E's estate is increased in value.          [28.5]

## 4  Transfers of value and gifts contrasted

It will be noted that IHT is based on the concept of a 'transfer of value': curiously, however, the reservation of benefit rules—introduced in 1986—only come into play if an individual makes a 'gift' (this term is not defined). Whilst the two concepts generally overlap (all the examples of transfers of value in [28.5] are also gifts) there will be exceptional cases where, for instance, there will be a deemed transfer of value which will not involve the individual making a gift (see generally [29.41].              [28.6]–[28.20]

## II WHAT DISPOSITIONS ARE NOT CHARGEABLE TRANSFERS?

### 1 Commercial transactions (IHTA 1984 s 10(1))

A disposition is not a transfer of value and, therefore, is not chargeable if the taxpayer can show that he did not intend to confer a gratuitous benefit on another. This excludes from charge commercial transactions which turn out to be bad bargains. The transferor must not have intended to confer a gratuitous benefit on *any* person. Hence any disposition reducing the value of the transferor's estate may trigger a liability to IHT (by analogy to a crime the disposition may be seen as the *actus reus*) unless the taxpayer can show that he did not have the necessary *mens rea* for the liability to arise, ie that he had no gratuitous intent.

#### EXAMPLE 28.1

A purchases a holiday in the Bahamas in the name of C. A must show that he had no intention to confer a gratuitous benefit on C which he may succeed in doing if, for instance, C was a valued employee.

In order for a disposition between two *unconnected* persons not to be a transfer of value, the transferor must show that he had no gratuitous intent and that the transaction was made at arm's length. In the case of a disposition to a *connected* person, in addition to proving no gratuitous intent, the taxpayer must show that the transaction was a commercial one such as strangers might make. A 'connected person' is defined as for CGT (IHTA 1984 s 270: see TCGA 1992 s 286 and **Chapter 19**) and includes:
(1) spouses, civil partners and relatives, extended for IHT to include uncle, aunt, nephew and niece;
(2) trustees, where the terms 'settlement', 'settlor' and 'trustees' have their IHT meaning (IHTA 1984 ss 43–45, see **Chapter 32**);
(3) partners (for certain purposes only); and
(4) certain close companies.

#### EXAMPLE 28.2

(1) T sells his house valued at £70,000 to his daughter for £60,000. T will not escape a potential liability to IHT unless he can show that he never intended to confer a gratuitous benefit on his daughter and that the sale at an undervalue was the sort of transaction that he might have made with a stranger (eg that he needed money urgently and, therefore, was prepared to sell to anyone at a reduced price).
(2) Z sells his lease to his son Y subject to an obligation on Y to grant Z a leaseback for 20 years at a peppercorn rent. (This period has been arrived at on the basis of Z's life expectancy.) The price paid by Y reflects the existence of the lease and hence is substantially discounted.

**Note:**
    (a) There will be a substantial loss in Z's estate (namely, a loss of 'marriage value') which, provided that s 10 applies, is not a PET.
    (b) HMRC apparently accepts that in a case like this a lease for life can be granted to Z but this practice is open to question since, unless the lease is granted for full consideration, it will be treated for IHT as a

settlement with Z enjoying an interest in possession (see **Chapter 32**). Hence it is considered safer to select a suitable term of years.

(c)    In Z's hands the lease is a wasting asset and so this arrangement may be especially attractive when Z is elderly and unlikely to survive a PET by seven years.

In *IRC v Spencer-Nairn* (1991) the taxpayer owned an estate in Scotland. He had little experience of farming and estate management and relied heavily on the family's adviser, a chartered accountant and actuary. In 1975 one of the farms was leased to a Jersey resident company at a rent which was largely absorbed in the costs of repairs and maintenance. The Jersey company almost immediately demanded that the piggery buildings on the farm be replaced at the taxpayer's expense. The adviser obtained a professional report which estimated the cost at in the region of £80,000. As the taxpayer could not afford this the adviser recommended that the farm should be sold. He handled all matters connected with the sale and eventually it was sold for £101,350 to a second Jersey company. The farm was never advertised for sale and the taxpayer accepted this offer on the recommendation of his adviser: interestingly, neither the taxpayer nor the adviser were aware at the time that the company was a 'connected person'.

For CGT purposes the Lands Tribunal for Scotland determined the market value of the farm at £199,000 on the basis that, contrary to the adviser's view, the taxpayer was not liable to pay for the improvements demanded by the tenant. In due course (not surprisingly!) the Revenue raised a CTT assessment on the basis of a transfer of value of £94,000. It was generally accepted that the taxpayer did not have a gratuitous intention: but the Revenue argued that the transfer was not such as the taxpayer would have made in an arm's length transaction with an unconnected person.

For s 10 to be relevant the transferor must be shown to have entered into a disposition as a result of which his estate has been diminished, and, once that is shown, the taxpayer is then forced into the position of having to prove that he did not intend to make any gift *and* that what he did would satisfy the test of an objective commercial arrangement. The Revenue had taken a restricted view (some would say a minimalistic view!) of the section. In effect it had argued that if there was a substantial fall in the transferor's estate that was the end of the matter. In *Spencer-Nairn* the Lord President dismissed arguments of this nature in summary fashion:

'The fact that the transaction was for less than the open market value cannot be conclusive of the issues at this stage, otherwise the section would be deprived of its content. The gratuitous element in the transaction becomes therefore no more than a factor, which must be weighed in the balance with all the other facts and circumstances to see whether the onus which is on the transferor has been discharged.'

The case is a curiosity in that a substantially higher value had been determined by the Lands Tribunal, largely because of the view it took of the relevant Scottish agricultural holdings legislation. It had concluded that under that legislation the landlord was not obliged to erect the new piggery buildings. Clearly, had this burden rested on the landlord the actual sale price which he received would not have been unreasonable.

In applying s 10 it was accepted by the Revenue that the vendor had no intention of conferring a gratuitous benefit on anyone so that the sole question for the court was whether the sale was such as would have been made with a third party at arm's length. In applying this test, although it is basically drafted in objective terms, they found it necessary to incorporate subjective ingredients. The hypothetical vendor must be assumed to have held the belief of the landlord that the value of the property was diminished by his obligation to rebuild the piggeries. A wholly unreasonable (and in the event mistaken) belief will not presumably be relevant.

The *Spencer–Nairn* case is unusual in that the parties did not know that they were connected: in a sense therefore they were negotiating *as if* they were third parties on the open market.

> 'A good way of testing the question whether the sale was such as might be expected to be made in a transaction between persons not connected with each other is to see what persons who were unaware that they were connected with each other actually did' (Lord President Hope).

The following conclusions are suggested:
(1)  whether the transferor has a gratuitous intent is entirely subjective;
(2)  there can be a sale at arm's length for the purposes of the second limb of s 10 even though the price realised is not approximately the same as the 'market value';
(3)  in considering what amounts to an 'arm's length' sale, features of the actual sale (such as the reasonably held beliefs of the vendor) must be taken into account—this limb is not a wholly objective test.  **[28.21]**

There are special rules in the following cases:

a)  *Reversionary interests*

A beneficiary under a settlement who purchases for value any reversionary interest in the same settlement may be subject to IHT on the price that he pays for the interest and s 10(1) cannot apply to the transaction (IHTA 1984 s 55(2): for the rationale of this rule see **Chapter 33**).  **[28.22]**

> **EXAMPLE 28.3**
>
> Property is settled on A for life, remainder to B absolutely. B has a reversionary interest. A buys B's interest for its commercial value of £50,000. A has made a potentially exempt transfer of £50,000.

b)  *Transfer of unquoted shares and debentures*

A transferor of unquoted shares and securities must show, in addition to lack of gratuitous intent, *either* that the sale was at a price freely negotiated at that time, *or* at such a price as might have been freely negotiated at that time (IHTA 1984 s 10(2)). In practice, such shares are rarely sold on an open market. Instead the company's articles will give existing shareholders a right of pre-emption if any shareholder wishes to sell. Provided that the right does not fix a price at which the shares must be offered to the remaining shareholders, but leaves it open to negotiation or professional valuation at the time of sale, HMRC will usually accept that the sale is a *bona fide* commercial transaction satisfying the requirements of IHTA 1984 s 10(1).

**[28.23]**

#### EXAMPLE 28.4

The articles of two private companies make the following provisions for share transfers:

(1)   *ABC Ltd:* the shares shall be offered *pro rata* to the other shareholders who have an option to purchase at a price either freely negotiated or, in the event of any dispute, as fixed by an expert valuer.

(2)   *DEF Ltd:* the shares shall be purchased at par value by the other shareholders.

*Position of shareholders in ABC Ltd:* they will be able to take advantage of IHTA 1984 s 10(1) since the price is open to negotiation at the time of sale.

*Position of shareholders in DEF Ltd:* s 10(1) will not be available with the result that if the estate of a transferor falls in value (if, for instance, 1 shares have a market value of 1.50 at the time of transfer) IHT may be charged *even in the absence of gratuitous intent.* (Note that articles like those of DEF Ltd may also cause problems for business property relief, see **[31.52]** and that valuing shares in such circumstances is subject to an artificial rule, see **[27.72]**.)

c)   *Partnerships*

Partners are not connected persons for the purpose of transferring partnership assets from one to another.

**[28.24]**

#### EXAMPLE 28.5

A and B are partners sharing profits and owning assets in the ratio 50:50. They agree to alter their asset sharing ratio to 25:75 because A intends to devote less time to the business in the future. Although A's estate falls (he has transferred half of his partnership share to B), he will escape any liability to IHT if there is a lack of gratuitous intent. Assuming that A and B are not connected otherwise than as partners, lack of gratuitous intent will be presumed, since such transactions are part of the commercial arrangements between partners.

### 2   Other non-chargeable dispositions

*Excluded property (IHTA 1984 s 6)* No IHT is charged on excluded property (see **Chapter 35**). The most important categories are property sited outside the UK owned by someone domiciled outside the UK and reversionary interests under a trust. Although not excluded property, business or agricultural property which qualifies for 100% relief will not attract any IHT charge (see **Chapter 31**).

**[28.25]**

*Exempt transfers (IHTA 1984 Part II)* Exempt transfers are not chargeable transfers and hence are not subject to charge (see **Chapter 31**). Examples are:

(1)   transfers between spouses and civil partners, whether *inter vivos* or on death;

(2)  transfers up to £3,000 in value each tax year;

(3)  outright gifts of up to £250 pa to any number of different persons.

**[28.26]**

*Waiver of remuneration and dividends (IHTA 1984 ss 14, 15)* A waiver or repayment of salaries and other remuneration assessable as employment income by a director or employee is not a chargeable transfer; the remuneration is formally waived (by deed) or if paid, repaid to the employer who adjusts his profits or losses to take account of the waiver or repayment. It should be noted that HMRC take the view that the waiver must occur before the salary is paid to or put at the disposal of the employee – see Revenue Manual EIM 42705.

A person may, in the 12 months before the right accrued (which time is identified in accordance with usual company law rules), waive a dividend on shares without liability to IHT. A general waiver of all future dividends is only effective for dividends payable for up to 12 months after the waiver and should, therefore, be renewed each year. **[28.27]**

*Voidable transfers (IHTA 1984 s 150)* Where a transfer is voidable (eg for duress or undue influence or under the rule in *Hastings-Bass*) and is set aside, it is treated for IHT purposes as if it had never been made, provided that a claim is made by the taxpayer. As a result any IHT paid on the transfer may be reclaimed. Tax on chargeable transfers made after the voidable transfer, but before it was avoided, must be recalculated and IHT refunded, if necessary. **[28.28]–[28.40]**

III   WHEN ARE LIFETIME TRANSFERS SUBJECT TO IHT? THE POTENTIALLY EXEMPT TRANSFER (PET)

If the taxpayer makes an *inter vivos* transfer, IHT may be charged at once: alternatively the transfer may be potentially exempt (a PET). In the latter case, IHT is only levied if the taxpayer dies within seven years of the transfer: otherwise the transfer is exempt. During the 'limbo' period (being the period of seven years following the transfer or, if shorter, the period ending with the transferor's death) the PET is treated *as if it were exempt* (IHTA 1984 s 3A(5)) so that despite the legislation calling the transfer potentially exempt it would be more accurate to refer to it as potentially chargeable. With the exception of transfers involving discretionary trusts and transfers to companies (and by close companies), the majority of lifetime transfers are PETs.

**[28.41]**

What is a PET?

a)   *Gifts made by individuals prior to 22 March 2006*

A PET is defined in IHTA 1984 s 3A(1). Prior to the changes made by FA 2006, Sch 20 which, in effect, alters fundamentally its definition, a PET had to satisfy two preliminary requirements: *first*, it must have been made by an individual on or after 18 March 1986; and *secondly*, the transfer must, apart from this section, have been a chargeable transfer (hence exemptions—such as the annual £3,000 exemption—are deducted first). If these preconditions for gifts made prior to 22 March 2006 are satisfied, the following transfers then fall within the definition:                                                    **[28.42]**

### i)    *Outright gifts to individuals*

A transfer which is a gift to another individual is a PET so long as *either* the property transferred becomes comprised in the donee's estate *or*, by virtue of that transfer, the estate of the donee is increased (s 3A(2)).          **[28.43]**

#### EXAMPLE 28.6

(1)    Adam gives Bertram a gold hunter watch worth £5,000: this is a PET.

(2)    Claude pays Debussy's wine bill of £10,000. Although property is not transferred into the estate of Debussy, the result is to increase Debussy's estate by paying off his debt. Accordingly this also is a PET.

(3)    Edgar who owned 51% of the shares in Frome Ltd transfers 2% of the company's shares to Grace who had previously owned no shares in the company. Edgar suffers a substantial drop in the value of his estate (since he loses control of Frome Ltd) which exceeds the benefit received by Grace. The whole transfer is a PET.

### ii)    *Creation of accumulation and maintenance trusts or trusts for the disabled*

These trusts are discussed in **Chapter 34**. In both cases until the Finance Act 2006, the transfer which established the trust was treated as a PET *to the extent that the value transferred was attributable to property which by virtue of the transfer becomes settled.* Whilst the tax treatment for trusts for the disabled remains the same for post-22 March 2006 trusts, that for accumulation and maintenance trusts ('A&M trusts') has changed (see **Chapter 34** below).

**[28.44]**

#### EXAMPLE 28.7

In November 2005:

(1)    A settles £100,000 in favour of his infant grandchildren on A&M trusts. This transfer is a PET.

(2)    B settles an insurance policy, taken out on his own life, on A&M trusts. (This transfer is a PET.) He subsequently pays premiums on that policy and, although the payments are transfers of value, they do not increase the property in the settlement and are not, therefore, PETs. B should, therefore, consider making a gift of that sum each year to the trustees to enable them to pay the premiums on the policy (alternatively the problem will be avoided if B's payments are exempt from IHT as normal expenditure out of income: see **[31.3]**).

### iii)    *Interest in possession settlements*

As will be seen in **Chapter 33**, a beneficiary entitled to an interest in possession is treated as owning (for IHT purposes) the capital of the trust in which that interest subsists. Hence, the *inter vivos* creation of such a trust is treated as a transfer of value to that person and the *inter vivos* termination of his interest as a transfer of value by him to the person or persons next entitled. In *Example 28.8(1)* below, for instance, Willie is treated as if he had made a gift to Wilma (the next life tenant). Taking different facts, if on the termination of the relevant interest in possession the settled property is then held on discretionary trusts, the lifetime termination of his interest cannot be a PET, since the PET definition excludes the creation of trusts without interests in possession (see **[28.46]**).                                        **[28.45]**

**EXAMPLE 28.8**

In December 2005, Wilbur Wacker settles £100,000 on trust for his brother Willie for life, thereafter to his sister Wilma for life, with remainder to his godson Wilberforce. Wilbur's transfer is a PET. In February 2006, he settles a life insurance policy on the same trusts and continues to pay the premiums to the insurance company (as in *Example 28.7(2)*, above). The premiums (if not already exempt) will be PETs since the more restrictive definition of a PET in the context of an A&M trust does not apply to interest in possession trusts. Assume also that the following events occur:
(1)  Willie surrenders his life interest on 10 March 2006, his fiftieth birthday: this deemed transfer of the property in the trust is a PET made by Willie.
(2)  Wilma purchases Wilberforce's remainder interest on 19 March 2006 for £60,000 (see *Example 28.3*, above); this transfer by Wilma is a PET.

*iv)  The limits of PETs for pre-22 March 2006 gifts*

Although the majority of lifetime transfers made prior to 22 March 2006 are PETs, there are two main types of transfer which were immediately chargeable and, because of the wording of s 3A, there are a number of traps which may have caught other transfers. Those traps which also affect post-22 March 2006 gifts are dealt with below (see **[28. 48]**).
(1)  The creation of no interest in possession trusts. Hence, a charge was levied on the creation of, eg discretionary trusts and, in addition, ten-year anniversary and exit charges may occur during the life of the trust (see **Chapter 34**).
(2)  'Where, under any provision of this Act other than s 52, tax is in any circumstances to be charged *as if* a transfer of value had been made, that transfer shall be taken to be a transfer which is not a PET.'
This provision ensures that PETs are limited to lifetime gifts because it excludes the transfer deemed to take place immediately before death and it also means that tax charges will arise when close companies are used to obtain an IHT advantage (see **[28.151]**).
(3)  In the case of A&M and disabled trusts property must have been transferred directly into the settlement if the PET definition is to be satisfied (see *Example 28.7(2)*).                                        **[28.46]**

b)  *Gifts by individuals made on or after 22 March 2006*

The result of the changes made by FA 2006 Sch 20 is that, whilst gifts made before 22 March 2006 remain subject to the regime that operated prior to the changes, a gift made by an individual on or after 22 March 2006 can only be a PET if (i) it is an outright gift to another individual or (ii) it is a gift into a disabled trust (see [32.22] for the definition of a disabled trust).    **[28.47]**

**EXAMPLE 28.9**

If, in example 28.8, Wilbur Wacker settles the £100,000 on 24 November 2006, this no longer qualifies as a PET, but gives rise to an immediate chargeable transfer.

c)   *The limits of PETs generally*

For gifts made either before or after 22 March 2006, the following traps should be noted:
(1)  Jack pays the school fees of his infant grandson Jude *or* Simon buys a holiday for his uncle Albert. In neither case does property become comprised in the estate of another by virtue of the transfer, and neither Jude's nor Albert's estate is increased as a result of the transfer. Accordingly, both Jack and Simon have made immediately chargeable transfers of value (by contrast, a direct gift to each donee would ensure that the transfers were PETs).
(2)  The reservation of benefit provisions are analysed in **Chapter 29** and it should be noted that, when they apply, property which has been given away is brought back into the donor's estate at death. The original gift will normally have been a PET (provided that, if it was made on or after 22 March 2006, it was either an outright gift to an individual or a gift into a disabled trust) and, therefore, there is a possibility of a double charge to IHT should the donor die within seven years of that gift at a time when property is still subject to a reservation. (This double charge will normally be relieved by regulations discussed in **Chapter 36**.)
[28.48]

d)   *CGT tie-in*

CGT hold-over relief continues to be available in cases where a gift falls outside the PET definition (ie is an immediately chargeable transfer) provided that it is made *by* an individual or trustees to an individual or trustees (TCGA 1992 s 260). Both the creation and termination of a discretionary trust will generally satisfy this wording so that the CGT that would otherwise be levied on the chargeable assets involved may be held over. By contrast, gifts to close companies do not involve gifts between individuals and trustees so that, unless the property given away is business property within the definition in TCGA 1992 s 165, hold-over relief will not be available (for the CGT position on gifts generally, see **Chapter 24** and note that hold-over relief is no longer available on gifts of shares to companies).          [28.49]

e)   *The taxation of PETs*

As already noted there is no charge to tax at the time when a PET is made and that transfer is treated as exempt unless the transferor dies within the following seven years. *There is, therefore, no duty to inform HMRC that a PET has been made and for cumulation purposes it is ignored.* All of this, however, changes if the donor dies within the following seven years: the former PET then becomes chargeable; must be reported; and the transfer must be entered into the taxpayer's cumulative total *at the time when it was made*. As a result, IHT on subsequent chargeable lifetime transfers may need to be recalculated (these transfers may in any event attract a supplementary charge). These consequences are illustrated in *Example 28.10* and explained further in **Chapter 30**. [28.50]–[28.60]

#### EXAMPLE 28.10

(1) On 1 May 1999 Ian gave £3,000 to Joyce.
(2) On 1 May 2000 he settled £500,000 on discretionary trusts in favour of his family.
(3) On 1 May 2001 he gave £60,000 to his daughter.
(4) On 1 May 2006 he died.

Ian died within seven years of all three transfers. The transfer in 1999 ((1) above) is, however, exempt since it is covered by his annual exemption (see [31.3]).

*Transfer (2)* was a chargeable lifetime transfer and attracted an IHT charge when made. Because of Ian's death within seven years a supplementary IHT charge will arise (the calculation of this additional IHT caused by death is explained in **Chapter 30**).

*Transfer (3)* was a PET. Because of Ian's death it is rendered chargeable and is subject to IHT. Further, Ian's cumulative total of chargeable transfers made in the seven years before death becomes (if we assume the non-availability of the £3,000 annual exemption in both 2000 and 2001) £560,000. Had Ian lived until 1 May 2007 this PET would have become an exempt transfer (ie free from all IHT).

### IV ON WHAT VALUE IS IHT CALCULATED?

### 1 What is the cost of the gift?

a) *General*

When an individual makes a chargeable disposition (including a PET rendered chargeable by death within seven years) IHT is charged on the amount by which his estate has fallen in value as a result of the transfer. A person's estate is the aggregate of all the property to which he is beneficially entitled (IHTA 1984 s 5(1)). [28.61]

b) *Meaning of 'property' (IHTA 1984 s 272)*

Property 'includes rights and interests of any description'. It includes property (other than settled property) over which an individual has a general power of appointment (IHTA 1984 s 5(2), because he could appoint the property to himself), but not property owned in a fiduciary or representative capacity: eg as trustee or PR. *Melville v IRC* (2001) decided that a general power exercisable over settled property amounted to a 'right or interest' and was property within the definition in s 272 (see further on this case [32.52]) but FA 2002 reversed this decision by adding to s 272 the words 'but does not include a settlement power' and a settlement power is then defined in IHTA 1984 s 47A as 'any power over, or exercisable (whether directly or indirectly) in relation to settled property or a settlement'. [28.62]

#### EXAMPLE 28.11

Mac transfers property worth £500,000 into a discretionary trust. He retains a power to revoke the trust after (say) three months. Although Mac can recover the entire £500,000 by exercise of this power his estate falls in value by the full £500,000. The power to revoke is a 'settlement power' and so not 'property' for IHT purposes. (Similarly a reversionary interest acquired in the circumstances set out in s 55 does not form part of the taxpayer's estate: see [28.22].)

c)   *Calculating the fall in value of an estate*

In theory the transferor's estate must be valued both before and after the transfer and the difference taxed. In practice, this is normally unnecessary since the transferor's estate will only fall by the value of the gift (and, as discussed in *Example 28.12* below, by the costs of making the gift). However, in unusual cases the cost to the transferor of the gift may be more than the value of the property handed over (see *Example 28.14*).

**EXAMPLE 28.12**

A gives £500,000 to a discretionary trust. His estate falls in value by £500,000 *plus* the IHT that he has to pay, ie £500,000 must be grossed up at the appropriate rate of IHT to discover the full cost of the gift to A (see [28.124]).

   Were he to give the trust land worth £500,000 his estate falls in value by the value of the property (£500,000) and by any CGT and costs of transfer (such as conveyancing fees) that A pays. It will also fall by the IHT payable.

However, IHTA 1984 s 5(4) provides that, for the purpose of calculating the cost of the gift, the transferor's estate is deemed to drop by the value of the property plus the IHT paid by the transferor but *not* by any other tax nor by any incidental costs of transfer. Thus, in *Example 28.12*, A's estate falls only by the value of the land and by the IHT that he pays.

   Where the donees (the trustees in the above example) agree to pay the IHT, the overall cost of the gift is reduced since A's estate will fall only by the value of the property transferred. The trustees will be taxed on that fall in value.                                                                                        [28.63]

**EXAMPLE 28.13**

A gives property worth £50,000 to the trustees. If A pays the IHT, the £50,000 is a net gift and if A is charged to IHT at 20% (rates of tax are considered at [28.122]: for the purpose of this example it is assumed that A has used up his nil rate band and annual exemption for the year) then that rate of tax is chargeable on the larger (gross) figure (here £62,500) which after payment of IHT at 20% leaves £50,000 in the trustees' hands.

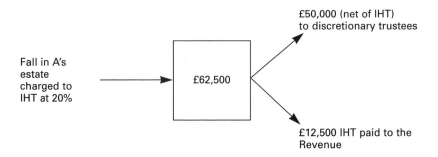

If, in this example, the trustees paid the IHT the result would be:

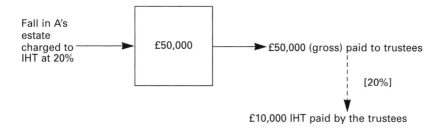

Fall in A's estate charged to IHT at 20% → £50,000 → £50,000 (gross) paid to trustees

[20%]

£10,000 IHT paid by the trustees

d) *Relationship between the fall in value of the donor's estate and the increase in value of the donee's estate*

IHT is generally calculated on the fall in value of the transferor's estate not on the increase in value of the transferee's estate. This can work to the taxpayer's advantage, or disadvantage.

**EXAMPLE 28.14**

*Compare*
(1)    A gives B a single Picasso plate value £20,000; B agrees to pay any IHT that may fall due. B owns the remaining plates in the set (currently worth £150,000) and the acquisition of this final plate will give B's set a market value of £200,000. Although B's estate has increased in value by £50,000, IHT will only be charged on the fall in value in A's estate (£20,000).
(2)    A owns 51% of the shares in A Ltd. This controlling interest is worth £100,000. He gives 2% of the shares to B who holds no other shares. 2% of the shares are worth (say) 2 but A, having lost control, will find that his estate has fallen by far more than 2—say to £80,000. It will be the loss to A (£20,000) not the gain to B (2) which is taxed.

Note that for an omission to exercise a right to be chargeable another person's estate must be increased in value (see s 3(3) and **[28.4]**).      **[28.64]**

## 2   Problems in valuing an estate

Any calculation of IHT will require a valuation of the property transferred (see generally IHTA 1984 Part VI Chapter 25). As a general rule it is valued at the price that it would fetch on the open market. No reduction is made for the fact that the sale of a large quantity of a particular asset might cause the price to fall (IHTA 1984 s 160).      **[28.65]**

a) *Examples of the value transferred*

*Liabilities* Except in the case of a liability imposed by law, a liability incurred by a transferor will only reduce the value of his estate if it was incurred for a consideration in money or money's worth (IHTA 1984 s 5(5)) and even in this case artificial debts are non-deductible (FA 1986 s 103 see **[30.14]**).
      **[28.66]**

**EXAMPLE 28.15**

A gives his house to his son B. The market value of the house is £80,000, but it is subject to a mortgage to building society of £25,000 which B agrees to discharge. Hence, the property is valued for IHT purposes at £55,000. This position will commonly arise when a death gift of a house is made since, in the absence of a contrary intention stated in the will, the Administration of Estates Act 1925 s 35 provides that debts charged on property by the deceased must be borne by the legatee or donee of that property. Note also the stamp duty consequences when a debt is taken over by a donee.

*Co-ownership of property* If land worth £100,000 is owned equally by A and B, it might be assumed that the value of both half shares is £50,000. In fact the shares will be worth less than £50,000 since it will be difficult to sell such an interest on the open market (see the Lands Tribunal cases of *Wight v IRC* (1984) and *Charkham v IRC* (2000)). Whoever purchases will have to share the property with the other co-owner and in practice a discount of 10–15% is reasonable. Because of the related property rules—see **[28.70]**—there will, however, be no discount when the co-owners are husband and wife. Co-ownership of chattels poses other problems and it may be argued that because of the difficulty of enforcing a sale a larger discount is in order.
**[28.67]**

*Shares and securities* When listed shares and securities are transferred, their value is taken (as for CGT; see **Chapter 19**) as the lesser of the 'quarter-up' and 'mid-price' calculation.

Valuation of unquoted shares and securities is a complex topic. A number of factors are taken into account, eg the company's profit record, its prospects, its assets and its liabilities. The percentage of shares which is being valued is a major factor. A majority shareholding of ordinary voting shares carries certain powers to control the affairs of the company (it will, for instance, give the owner the power to pass an ordinary resolution). A shareholding representing more than 75% confers greater powers, notably the power to pass special resolutions. Correspondingly, a shareholder who owns 50% or less of the voting power (and, even more so, a shareholding of 25% or less) has far fewer powers (he is a minority shareholder). In valuing majority and substantial minority holdings HMRC takes a net asset valuation as the starting point and then applies a discount (between 10–15%) in the case of minority holdings.

When shares are subject to a restriction on their transfer (eg pre-emption rights) they are valued on the assumption of a sale on the open market with the purchaser being permitted to purchase the shares, but then being subject to the restrictions (*IRC v Crossman* (1937) and see **[28.72]**).
**[28.68]**

b)   *Special rules*

IHTA 1984 Part VI Chapter 1 contains special valuation rules designed to counter tax avoidance.
**[28.69]**

*Related property* (*IHTA 1984 s 161*) IHT savings could be engineered by splitting the ownership of certain assets (typically shares, sets of chattels, and interests in land) amongst two or more taxpayers. The saving would occur when the total value of the individual assets resulting from the split was less than the value of the original (undivided) asset. A pair of Ming vases, for instance, would be worth more as a pair than the combined values of the two individual vases. When it is desired to split the ownership of such assets, however, it should be remembered that the transfer needed to achieve this result will normally be potentially chargeable and, as any tax will be charged on the fall in value of the transferor's estate, no tax saving may result. Inter-spouse transfers are, however, free of IHT and hence, were it not for the related property provisions, could be used to achieve substantial savings by asset splitting. To frustrate such schemes the related property rules provide that, in appropriate circumstances, an asset must be valued together with other related property and a proportion of that total value is then attributed to the asset (compare the CGT provisions on asset splitting: **[19.24]**).

**EXAMPLE 28.16**

X Ltd is a private company which has a share capital of £100 divided into 100 £1 shares. Assume that shares giving control (ie more than 50%) are worth £100 each and minority shareholdings £20 per share. If Alf owns 51% of the shares the value of his holding is £5,100 (£100 per share). Assume that Alf and Bess are married. Alf transfers 26% of the company's shares to Bess. Alf becomes a minority shareholder with shares worth £500 but pays no IHT because transfers between spouses are exempt. Bess also has a minority holding worth £520. If Alf and Bess then each transfer their respective holdings to their son Fred, they may be liable to pay IHT on a value of £1,020, whereas if Alf had transferred his 51% holding to Fred directly he would be potentially liable to tax on £5,100.

To prevent this IHT saving Alf and Bess's holdings are valued together as a majority holding worth £5,100. Accordingly, when Alf transfers his 25% holding to Fred this is 25/51 of the combined holding and is valued, therefore, at £2,500 (ie 25/51 of £5,100). Once Alf has disposed of his holding, Bess's 26% holding is then valued in the normal way on a subsequent transfer: ie as a minority holding worth £520 (in certain cases the associated operations rule or the '*Ramsay* principle' might be invoked; see **[28.101]**).

Inter-spouse/civil partner transfers are the main instance of transfers which attract the related property provisions. However, the rules also catch other exempt transfers (eg to a charity or political party) in circumstances where the transferor could otherwise obtain a similar tax advantage.

**EXAMPLE 28.17**

As *Example 28.16*, Alf owns 51% of the shares in X Ltd. He transfers 2% to a charity paying no IHT because the transfer is exempt. He then transfers the remaining 49% to Fred. Alf is a minority shareholder and the loss to his estate is only £980 compared with £5,100 if he had transferred the entire 51% holding directly to Fred. Some time later Fred might purchase the 2% holding from the charity for its market value of £40. Unless the two transfers (ie to the charity and to Fred) are more than five years apart, the charity's holding is related to Alf's so that his 49% holding is valued at £4,900 on the transfer to Fred.

The related property rules apply to the deemed transfer on death subject to the proviso that if the property is sold within three years after the death for a price lower than the related property valuation, it may be revalued on death ignoring the related property rules (see **Chapter 30**). **[28.70]**

*Property subject to an option* (*IHTA 1984 s 163*) When property is transferred as a result of the exercise of an option or other similar right created for full consideration, there is no liability to IHT.

Where an option is granted for less than full consideration, however, there will be a chargeable transfer or a PET at that time and there may be a further charge when the option is exercised. A credit will be given against the value of the property transferred, when the option is exercised, for any consideration actually received and for any value that was charged to IHT on the grant of the option.                                                    [28.71]

#### EXAMPLE 28.18

(1)    Harold grants Daisy an option to purchase his house in three years' time for its present value of £120,000. Daisy pays £30,000 for the option which represents full consideration. When Daisy exercises the option three years later the house is worth £250,000.
Harold has not made a transfer of value and is not liable to IHT since (as the option was granted for full consideration) the house is only worth £120,000 to him.

(2)    Assume instead that Daisy gives no consideration for the option which is worth £30,000. IHT may, therefore, be chargeable on that sum. On the exercise of the option IHT may be payable on £100,000 ((£250,000—£120,000) minus the sum that was chargeable on the grant of the option (£30,000)).

*Property subject to restrictions on transfer* In *IRC v Crossman* (1937) the testator owned shares in a private company the articles of which imposed restrictions on alienation and transfer. By a bare majority the House of Lords held that in valuing those shares for estate duty purposes the basis to be taken was the price which they would fetch on the open market on the terms that a purchaser would be registered as the owner of the shares but would in turn be subject to the restrictions contained in the company's articles of association. The view contended for by the executors would have resulted in property which could not be sold in the open market escaping the tax net altogether. The *Crossman* case was subsequently followed by the House of Lords in *Lynall v IRC* (1972) and has been adopted in a series of cases concerning IHT. For instance, in *Alexander v IRC* (1991) a Barbican flat was purchased under the 'right to buy' provisions of the Housing Act 1980. All or part of the discount under that legislation had to be repaid in the event of the flat being sold within five years of its purchase. The taxpayer, however, died in the first year. The Court of Appeal—following *Crossman*—held that for valuation purposes an open market value must be taken and the flat was to be valued on the basis of what a purchaser would pay to stand in the deceased's shoes: ie taking over the liability to repay the discount should he sell the property within the prescribed period. It is inherent in this approach that the valuation thereby obtained may result in a higher figure than would actually be the case if the property were sold by the executors (and it appears that such a sale, even if occurring within four years of death, will not result in revaluation relief under IHTA 1984 s 190: see **Chapter 30**).        [28.72]

*Non-assignable agricultural tenancies* The vexed question of whether a non-assignable agricultural tenancy had any value was decided in the affirmative by the Lands Tribunal for Scotland on *Crossman* principles (see generally [**31.72**]). Once it was accepted that *Crossman* applied, the issue is one of fixing the correct value. In the Scottish case, *Baird's Executors v IRC* (1991), this matter was not argued and the 'robust approach' of the District Valuer in taking 25% of the open market value was accepted. The Court of Appeal decision in *Walton v IRC* (1996), confirmed that there can be no hard and fast valuation rule in such cases. The tenancy will not automatically be valued on the basis of a percentage of the freehold value on the assumption that the landlord will always be a special purchaser: in *Walton*, for instance, the freeholder had no interest in acquiring the tenancy. Evans LJ commented that 'the sale has to take place "in the real world" and account must be taken of the actual persons as well as of the actual property involved'.          [**28.73**]

*Life assurance policies* Life assurance policies normally involve the payment of annual premiums in return for an eventual lump sum payable either on retirement or on death. Special valuation rules, which do not apply on death (see **Chapter 30**), are provided by IHTA 1984 s 167 to prevent a tax saving when the benefit of such a policy is assigned.          [**28.74**]–[**28.100**]

> **EXAMPLE 28.19**
>
> A gives the benefit of a whole life policy effected on his own life to B when its open market value is £10,000. A has paid five annual premiums of £5,000, so that the cost of providing the policy is £25,000 to date. For IHT purposes the policy is valued at the higher of its market value or the cost of providing the policy. As a result tax may be charged on £25,000.

## V  'ASSOCIATED OPERATIONS' (IHTA 1984 s 268)

The legislation contains complex provisions to prevent a taxpayer from reducing the value of a gift or the IHT chargeable by a series of associated operations.

'Associated operations' are defined in IHTA 1984 s 268 as:

'(1)    ... any two or more operations of any kind, being—

(a)    operations which affect the same property, or one of which affects some property and the other or others of which affect property which represents, whether directly or indirectly, that property, or income arising from that property, or any property representing accumulations of any such income; or

(b)    any two operations of which one is effected with reference to the other, or with a view to enabling the other to be effected or facilitating its being effected, and any further operation having a like relation to any of those two, and so on; whether those operations are effected by the same person or different persons, and whether or not they are simultaneous; and "operation" includes an omission.

(2)    The granting of a lease for full consideration in money or money's worth shall not be taken to be associated with any operation effected more than three years after the grant, and no operation effected on or after 27 March 1974 shall be taken to be associated with any operation effected before that date.

(3)   Where a transfer of value is made by associated operations carried out at different times it shall be treated as made at the time of the last of them; but where any one or more of the earlier operations also constitute a transfer of value made by the same transferor, the value transferred by the earlier operations shall be treated as reducing the value transferred by all the operations taken together, except to the extent that the transfer constituted by the earlier operations but not that made by all the operations taken together is exempt under s 18 (spouse exemption).'   **[28.101]**

In a series of cases the courts have imposed restrictions on this widely drafted section.

### 1   Macpherson, Reynaud and 'relevant' associated operations

In *IRC v Macpherson* (1989) trustees entered into an agreement which reduced the value of the settled property and subsequently appointed that property in favour of a beneficiary. The House of Lords held that the two transactions were associated operations, which formed part of an arrangement designed to confer a gratuitous benefit, this benefit being conferred by the appointment (see further **Chapter 31**). Lord Jauncey (in a speech with which the other Law Lords concurred) identified the boundaries of the associated operations provisions as follows:

'If an individual took steps which devalued his property on a Monday with a view to making a gift thereof on Tuesday, he would fail to satisfy the requirements of s 20(4) (now s 10(1)) because the act of devaluation and the gift would be considered together ... The definition in s 44 (now s 268) is extremely wide and is capable of covering a multitude of events affecting the same property which might have little or no apparent connection between them. It might be tempting to assume that any event which fell within this wide definition should be taken into account in determining what constituted a transaction for the purposes of s 268. However, counsel for the Crown accepted, rightly in my view, that some limitation must be imposed. Counsel for the trustees informed your Lordships that there was no authority on the meaning of the words "associated operations" in the context of capital transfer tax legislation but he referred to a decision of the Court of Appeal in Northern Ireland, *Herdman v IRC* (1967) in which the tax avoidance provisions of ss 412 and 413 of the Income Tax Act 1952 had been considered [now TA 1988 s 739: see **[18.111]**]. Lord MacDermott CJ upheld a submission by the taxpayer that the only associated operations which were relevant to the subsection were those by means of which, in conjunction with the transfer, a taxpayer could enjoy the income and did not include associated operations taking place after the transfer had conferred upon the taxpayer the power to enjoy income. If the extended meaning of "transaction" is read into the opening words of s 20(4) the wording becomes:

"A disposition is not a transfer of value if it is shown that it was not intended, and was not made in a transaction including a series of transactions and any associated operations intended, to confer any gratuitous benefit ..."

So read it is clear that the intention to confer gratuitous benefit qualifies both transactions and associated operations. If an associated operation is not intended to confer such a benefit it is not relevant for the purpose of the subsection. That is not to say that it must necessarily *per se* confer a benefit but it must form a part of and contribute to a scheme which does confer such a benefit.'

In *Reynaud v IRC* (1999) brothers transferred shares into trusts from which they were wholly excluded: the following day the company bought back those shares from the trustees. The Special Commissioners held that, although both operations were associated, no disposition had been effected by associated operations since the value of the brothers' estates had been diminished by the gift into settlement alone:

'the purchase of own shares contributed nothing to the diminution which had already occurred and was not therefore a relevant associated operation.' **[28.102]**

## 2 The Hatton case

*Hatton v IRC* (1992) involved a tax avoidance scheme. Within the space of 24 hours two settlements were created. In the first, the settlor (Mrs C) reserved a short-term life interest; in the second, the reversionary interest in the first settlement was itself settled (by Mrs H) on Mrs C for a further 24-hour period with the property then being held absolutely for Mrs H. The creation of the original settlement by Mrs C involved no loss to her estate (under the relevant legislation she was treated as still owning the property by virtue of her interest in possession: see **Chapter 33**). The creation of the second settlement was likewise tax free since it involved the settlement by Mrs H of excluded property (the reversionary interest: see now IHTA 1984 s 48 and **Chapter 33**). Because the termination of Mrs C's first interest in possession was immediately succeeded by an interest in possession in the second settlement it attracted no tax charge (see now IHTA 1984 s 52(2)). Finally, the termination of that second interest in possession was also tax free since the settled property thereupon resulted to Mrs H, the settlor of that second settlement (see FA 1975 Sch 5 para 4(2): amended to prevent such schemes by FA 1981 s 104(1), now enacted as IHTA 1984 s 53(5)(b): see **Chapter 33**).

So far as the associated operations provisions were concerned, the judge concluded that the first settlement was made with a view to enabling or facilitating the making of the second (see IHTA 1984 s 268(1)(b)). Accordingly there was a disposition by associated operations which was treated as a single disposition of property from Mrs C into the second settlement of which she therefore became a settlor (see the definition of a settlement in IHTA 1984 s 43(2): **Chapter 32**).

It is not unusual for there to be two or more settlors of a single settlement. For instance, A and B could both transfer identified assets into a single trust. Under the IHT legislation, when circumstances require, that property may be treated as comprised in two separate settlements (see s 44(2)). For instance, A might settle £100 and B £50 and the resulting settlement fund could, when appropriate, be split into A's settlement (as to two-thirds) and B's settlement (as to one-third). Chadwick J concluded, however, that there could be circumstances where a division of the settlement property in this way was impractical and so, given that more than one settlor existed, the legislation must, in appropriate circumstances, treat each settlor as having created a separate settlement comprising, in each case, *the whole of the settled property*. This position can be illustrated in the *Hatton* case itself where Mrs C was, by dint of the associated operation rules (and, according to the Special Commissioners, because she was a person who had provided funds directly or indirectly), a person who had settled all the property in the second settlement. Mrs H was also a settlor; she was named as the settlor and had provided property in the shape of her reversionary interest in the first settlement. Given the nature of the property settled by these two settlors, Chadwick J was forced to conclude that each had created a separate settlement of the entirety of the property in the second settlement. Under the settlement created by Mrs C, the reverter to settlor rules did not apply.

This approach (treating each settlor as having established a separate settlement of the entirety of the settled property) would, the judge suggested, also apply to reciprocal settlements. In a simple case A would settle property on X for a limited interest in possession and as a *quid pro quo* B would settle property on Y for a similar interest. In both cases the reverter to settlor provisions would, at first sight, apply on the termination of X and Y's respective interests. Once it is accepted, however, that A is also a settlor of B's trust and *vice versa* (see s 44(1)) that analysis does not hold good. Instead, because B is a settlor of 'A's settlement' on the termination of X's limited interest an IHT charge may arise. The judge viewed the situation as one in which A and B were settlors of two separate settlements rather than accepting the view propounded by the Revenue that B should be seen as 'a dominant settlor' of A's trust.

Presumably the judge's approach would not be applied in cases where a full tax charge would, in any event, arise. Take, for instance, the situation where A as part of a reciprocal arrangement settles property on B's son for life with remainder to B's daughter and B creates a similar trust in favour of A's son and daughter. Although there are reciprocal settlements, on the death of (say) B's son a full tax charge would then arise on the property in 'A's settlement' so that even though the analysis may be that B is also a settlor of the whole of the property in that trust there can surely be no question of imposing a further tax charge on the ending of B's son's interest in possession.

Finally, the analysis is not easy to apply in cases where property is settled on trusts lacking an interest in possession by two settlors, one who has made chargeable lifetime transfers and one who has not. Will HMRC be able to argue, in appropriate cases, that the former is to be treated as the settlor of the entirety so that in arriving at the IHT charge on the settlement his previous chargeable transfers will be taken into account?    **[28.103]**

## 3    The problem of multiple settlements

In *Rysaffe Trustee Co (CI) Ltd v IRC* (2003) a taxpayer established five 'mirror' discretionary settlements: ie in each case the beneficiaries and trustees were the same; each comprised an initial sum of £10 and private company shares were subsequently added to each trust. The settlements were dated on different days. The Revenue sought to impose tax on the basis that the taxpayer had made only a single settlement since the various transfers were associated and so amounted to a single disposition (see further **Chapter 34**). Park J (and a unanimous Court of Appeal) rejected the Revenue's arguments as follows:

(1)    'the practical operation of the associated operations provisions is comparatively limited. It is not some sort of catch-all anti-avoidance

provision which can be invoked to nullify the effectiveness of any scheme or structure which can be said to have involved more than one operation and which was intended to avoid or reduce IHT ... section 268 is not an operative provision which of itself imposes IHT liabilities. It is a definition of an expression (associated operations) which is used elsewhere. The definition only comes into effect so far as the expression "associated operations" is used elsewhere, and then only if the expression in another provision is relevant to the way in which that other provision applies to the facts of the particular case.'

(2)     although a 'disposition' in s 272 can include a disposition effected by associated operations, associated operations are, however, only relevant if in substance there is a single disposition which has been divided into a number of separate 'operations'.

In addition, Park J made two further points:

(1)     the transfers of the shares to the five trusts were not effected with reference to each other (s 268(1)(b)):

'It is true that each transfer was a part of one plan or scheme, but the transfer of parcel 1 to settlement 1 made no reference to the transfer of parcel 2 to settlement 2; and vice versa. Each transfer was effected in the knowledge that the other was being effected as well, but that does not seem to me to be the equivalent of saying that each transfer was effected "with reference to the other".'

(2)     the five parcels of shares did not amount to the same property (see s 268(1)(a)).                                                          [28.104]


## 4   The effects of s 268 applying

It enables HMRC to tax as one transaction any number of separate transactions (including omissions) which, when looked at together, reduce the value of the taxpayer's estate. The transactions need not be carried out by the same person nor need they be simultaneous. Apparently the lifetime act of making a will can amount to an associated operation although the subsequent death will not! (*Bambridge v IRC* (1955)). Intestacy is covered by the reference to an omission.

*Section 268(1)(a)* is concerned with the channelling of gifts, in particular between spouses (where the transfers are exempt). In such dispositions the transferor is deemed to have made a transfer equivalent to the value of all the operations at the time when the last of them is made. If one of the operations involved a transfer of value by the same transferor, he is entitled to a credit for that value against the aggregate value of the whole operation unless the transfer was anyway exempt because it was made to a spouse (IHTA 1984 s 268(3)).

### EXAMPLE 28.20

It is certain that H will die shortly whereas his wife is in good health. Any transfer H makes to his son (S), although a PET, will, therefore, be made chargeable by his death. Accordingly, he transfers £20,000 to his wife (W). W then passes the £20,000 to the son. Under IHTA 1984 s 268(1)(a) HMRC could argue that the transfers (H to W and W to S) are 'associated'. H is deemed to have made a transfer of value equivalent to the value transferred by all the associated operations, ie £40,000, £20,000 (H to W) and £20,000 (W to S). However, on his death, IHT is only chargeable on £20,000 as his transfer of £20,000 to W is exempt as an inter-spouse transfer. It is unclear whether under s 268(3) IHT could also be charged on her gift of £20,000 to S. The preferable view is no since the one charge on H should cover all the relevant transfers; but assume that H also gives £3,000 to his son which is exempt by his annual exemption (but see the *Hatton* case [**28.103**]). All three transfers (H to S, H to W and W to S) are associated at the time of the last of them (W to S). Under IHTA 1984 s 268(3) on H's death IHT is not charged on the aggregate value of all three transfers (ie £43,000) but on £20,000 only because he has a credit for any previous (associated) transfers of value (the £3,000 transfer to S) and the inter-spouse transfer of £20,000.

Commenting upon the associated operation provisions, Mr Joel Barnett (then Chief Secretary to the Treasury) stated that they would only be used to attack inter-spouse transfers in blatant tax avoidance cases:

'... where the transfer by a husband to a wife was made on condition that the wife should at once use the money to make gifts to others, a charge on a gift by the husband might arise under [s 268].'
(Official Report, Standing Committee A (13 February 1975) col 1596.)

Thus, spouses may channel gifts in order to utilise the poorer spouse's exemptions, eg the £3,000 annual exemption and the exemption for gifts on marriage of up to £5,000, and to obtain income tax and CGT benefits resulting from the independent taxation of spouses.

**EXAMPLE 28.21**

H is wealthy, his wife, W, is poor. Both wish to use up their full IHT exemptions and to provide for their son who is getting married. It would be sensible for the following arrangement to be adopted:

*Stage 1* H transfers £11,000 to W which is exempt as an inter-spouse transfer. This will enable W to utilise two years' annual exemption of £3,000 plus the £5,000 marriage exemption.

*Stage 2* Both spouses then each give £11,000 to the son.

Section 268 will not be invoked provided that the gift to W is not made on condition that she pass the property to S.

*Section 268(1)(b)* also enables HMRC to put two separate transactions together.

**EXAMPLE 28.22**

(1)    A owns two paintings which together are worth £60,000, but individually are worth £20,000. A sells one picture for £20,000. This is a commercial transaction (s 10(1)) and, therefore, not subject to IHT. A then sells the second picture, also for £20,000, to the same purchaser.
As a result of the two transactions, the purchaser has paid only £40,000 but received value of £60,000 and A's estate has fallen in value by £20,000. The effect of s 268(1)(b) is that HMRC can put the two transactions together and in appropriate cases tax the loss to his estate (ie £20,000) provided there is a gratuitous intent. Where the transactions are with a connected person the presumption of gratuitous intent will be hard to rebut. If both sales were to a commercial art gallery, however, it is likely that, despite s 268, no tax would be chargeable.

*Contrast:* assume as above that A owns two paintings but wishes to give one to his son. Accordingly, he settles that picture on trust for himself for life, remainder to his son. Provided that the settlement commenced prior to 22 March 2006, no IHT would have been charged on creation of that settlement since A would have been treated as owning the picture (see **Chapter 33**). A then surrenders his life interest and as a result tax appears to be chargeable on the value of the picture in the settlement: ie on £20,000 only (IHTA 1984 s 52(1)). Could it be argued by an application of s 268 that A has directly disposed of the picture to his son so that £40,000 is subject to IHT? (Alternatively, might the *Ramsay* principle apply to produce that result?) Note that for interest in possession trusts (apart from disabled trusts) created during the settlor's lifetime on or after 22 March 2006, there is an immediate IHT charge.

(2)   A owns freehold premises worth £200,000. A gives the property to his nephew (N) in two stages. He grants a tenancy of the premises to N at a full market rent thereby incurring no potential liability to IHT. Two years later, he gives the freehold to N which being subject to a lease is worth only £100,000. Hence, there is a potential liability for IHT on £100,000 only, although A has given away property worth £200,000.

Under IHTA 1984 s 268(1)(b) HMRC can tax the overall loss to his estate. IHTA 1984 s 268(2), however, provides an exemption where more than three years have elapsed between the grant of the lease for full consideration and the gift or sale of the reversion.

(3)   A wants to give his annual exemption of £3,000 to B each year. Although he has no spare cash, he owns a house worth £30,000. Accordingly, A sells the house to B for £30,000 which is left outstanding as a loan repayable on demand. Each year A releases as much of the outstanding loan as is covered by his annual exemption. After ten years the loan is written off. The house is then worth £40,000 (the scheme is generally known as a 'sale and mortgage back'). A loan which is repayable on demand is not chargeable to IHT (see **[28.131]**) and the release of part of the loan each year, although a transfer of value, is covered by A's annual exemption.

These may be associated operations under IHTA 1984 s 268(1)(b). HMRC has intimated that it *might* regard the overall transaction as a transfer of value by A of the asset at its market value (£40,000) at the date when the loan is written off. A would have a credit for his previous transfers of value, ie £30,000 (s 268(3)), and there would, therefore, be a potential charge to IHT on the capital appreciation element only, ie £10,000.

For HMRC's view in *Example 28.22(3)* to be upheld it would have to show that the donor retained ownership of the house throughout the period of ten years. In support, it could be argued that the transferor's estate must be valued immediately after the disposition and that in the case of a disposition effected by associated operations that means at the time of the last of those operations (see IHTA 1984 ss 3(1), 268(3)). The counter-argument is that the value transferred is the difference between the value of the house immediately before the first stage in the operation (ie £30,000) and the value of the debt after the last operation (nil) so that the loss to the transferor is £30,000, all of which is covered by the annual exemptions.

**[28.105]–[28.120]**

## VI   HOW IS IHT CALCULATED?

### 1   **Cumulation and rates of tax**

a)   *Cumulation*

Each individual must keep a cumulative account of all the chargeable transfers made by him because IHT is levied not at a flat rate but at progressively higher rates according to that total. It is the cumulative amount that fixes the rate of IHT for each subsequent chargeable transfer. From 18 March 1986 cumulation has only been required over a seven-year period. This restricted period contrasts with the original CTT legislation that had provided for unlimited cumulation (a ten-year period was introduced in 1981).                                                                      **[28.121]**

b)   *Rates of tax*

From 6 April 2006 IHT rates are as follows:

| Portion of value | | Rate of tax |
| --- | --- | --- |
| *Lower limit* | *Upper limit* | *Per cent* |
| £ | £ | Nil* |
| 0 | 285,000 | 40* |
| 285,000 | — | |

* Chargeable lifetime transfers (for instance into a discretionary trust) are charged at half rates (ie at 0% or 20%).

**[28.122]**

**EXAMPLE 28.23**

(Ignoring exemptions, reliefs and assuming that current IHT rates apply through-out.) A makes the following chargeable transfers (ie none of the transfers is a PET):
(1)   *June 1995* £100,000
        Applying the half rates of IHT the £100,000 falls within the nil rate band.
(2)   *June 2001* £195,000
        The starting point in using the table is £100,000 which was the point reached by the gift in 1995 and IHT is charged at rates applicable to transfers from £100,000 to £295,000:
        ie first £285,000 at nil%
        the final £10,000 at 20%.
(3)   *July 2002* £55,000
        The 1995 gift of £100,000 drops out of the account as it was made more than seven years before. IHT is, therefore, charged at rates applicable to transfers from £195,000 to £250,000 (ie at 0%).

c)   *Taxing PETs*

PETs are presumed to be exempt *unless and until* the transferor dies within seven years of the transfer. If the donor does die within seven years the PET becomes a chargeable transfer (thereby necessitating the payment of IHT). In cases where the deceased taxpayer had made a mixture of chargeable transfers and PETs in the seven years before death, tax paid on the chargeable transfers may have to be recalculated, *first* because the PETs are converted into chargeable transfers from the date when they were made and, *secondly*, because of the death within seven years of making the chargeable transfer.

**EXAMPLE 28.24**

T makes the following transfers of value:
  *Year 1* PET of £75,000
  *Year 2* chargeable transfer of £250,000
  *Year 4* T dies.
  IHT charged on the chargeable transfer in *Year 2* will have been calculated ignoring the PET made in *Year 1*. Accordingly it will have proceeded on the basis that T had made no prior chargeable transfers. As a result of his death in *Year 4*, however, the PET of £75,000 is chargeable in *Year 1* so that IHT on the Year 2 transfer must be recalculated on the basis that when it was made T had made a prior chargeable transfer of £75,000. Hence it is recalculated using the IHT rates applicable in *Year 2* from £75,000 to £325,000.

The effect of death on chargeable lifetime transfers and PETs is considered more fully in **Chapter 30**.                                                      [28.123]

## 2   Grossing-up

As already stated IHT is charged on the fall in value in the transferor's estate. Accordingly, tax is charged on the value of the gift *and* on the IHT on that gift, when the tax is paid by the transferor. To understand this principle, take the example of A, who has made no previous chargeable transfers and who settles £298,000 on discretionary trusts. IHT payable by A can be calculated as follows:

*Step 1* Deduct from the transfer any part of it that is exempt. A has an available annual exemption of £3,000 (see further [31.3]): there is, therefore, a chargeable transfer of £295,000.

*Step 2* Calculate the rate(s) of IHT applicable to the chargeable transfer. The first £285,000 falls within the nil rate band and, therefore, IHT is payable only on the balance of £10,000 at 20%.

*Step 3* If A pays the IHT on the gift, his estate falls in value by £295,000 plus the IHT payable on the £10,000, ie A is charged on the cost of the gift by treating the £295,000 as a gift net of tax.

Therefore, the part of the gift on which IHT is payable (here £10,000) must be 'grossed up' to reflect the amount of tax payable on the gift by using the formula:

$$\frac{100}{100-R}$$

where R is the rate of IHT applicable to the sum in question. In A's case the calculation is:

£10,000 × $^{100}/_{80}$ = £12,500 gross.

As a result:

(1)    *Position of A:* Gift to trust (£298,000) plus IHT liability (£2,500) means a total cost of £300,500;

(2)    *Position of the trust:* Receives from A £298,000.

Once the taxpayer's cumulative total exceeds the nil rate band (currently £285,000) tax is levied (because of the grossing-up computation) at 25% on the excess. For instance, if A gives £50,000 to his close company (a chargeable lifetime transfer) at a time when his cumulative total exceeds £285,000, tax on that transfer, if paid by A, will be 25% × £50,000 = £12,500.   **[28.124]**

### 3    Effect of the tax being paid by a person other than the transferor

Grossing-up establishes the cost to a donor of making a gift where the donor is paying the IHT. There is no grossing-up, however, if the tax is paid by any other person. Accordingly, as most lifetime transfers will be PETs, any IHT that is eventually charged will be due after the transferor's death from the donee and it will not, therefore, be necessary to gross up. In such cases the transferee is charged on the gift that he receives (strictly, on the fall in value of the transferor's estate) and the tax will be calculated according to the previous chargeable transfers of the donor.   **[28.125]**

#### EXAMPLE 28.25

(1)    A has made no previous chargeable transfers but has used up his annual exemption. He gives £295,000 to discretionary trustees who agree to pay the IHT due on the chargeable transfer. A has made a chargeable transfer of £295,000, on £10,000 of which IHT is payable at the rate of 20%. If the trustees pay, A's estate falls in value by only £295,000. The trustees are charged to IHT at A's rates. The trustees, therefore, pay IHT at 20% on £10,000 (ie £2,000) so that £500 less tax is paid than if A had paid (he would have paid tax at a rate of 25% on £10,000 = £2,500). However, the trust ends up with less property than if A had paid the IHT: £293,000, instead of £295,000. A further result of the trustees paying the tax is that A's cumulative total of gross chargeable transfers is lower for the purposes of future chargeable transfers, ie £295,000, rather than £297,500.

*Compare*

(2)    If the trustees are to pay the IHT on A's gift to them and A wants them to retain a net sum of £295,000 after paying the tax, A must give a larger sum (£297,500) to enable them to pay the tax of £2,500. The result is that whether donor or donee pays the IHT, HMRC will receive £2,500 tax and the total cost to A will be the same.

### 4    Transferring non-cash assets the cheapest way

When the gift is of a non-cash asset such as land, IHT is calculated as before, but the question of who pays the tax and how much has to be paid will be of critical importance since neither party may have sufficient cash to pay the IHT without selling the asset. If the donor pays the IHT, the value of the gift must be grossed up. In addition, the tax must be paid in one lump sum. If, however, the donee (normally trustees on a chargeable lifetime transfer) pays the tax, there is no grossing-up so that the transfer attracts less IHT. Additionally, in the case of certain assets the tax can be paid by the donee in ten yearly instalments (IHTA 1984 s 227). If the asset is income producing, the donee may have income out of which to pay, or contribute towards, the instalments. Alternatively, the donor can fund the instalments paid by the donee by gifts utilising his annual exemption. The assets on which IHT may be paid by instalments are:

(1)  land, whether freehold or leasehold;
(2)  a controlling shareholding of either quoted or unquoted shares;
(3)  a minority shareholding of unquoted shares in certain circumstances (see [**30.54**]);
(4)  a business or part of a business, eg a share in a partnership.

However, in the case of a transfer of land ((1) above), interest on the outstanding tax is charged when payment is made by instalments.    [**28.126**]

### EXAMPLE 28.26

A wants to settle his landed estate which is valued at £ 535,000 on discretionary trusts. A has made no previous chargeable transfers. If A pays the tax (ignoring exemptions and reliefs) the gift (£ 535,000) must be grossed up so that the total cost to A is £ 597,500 and the IHT payable is £62,500; A must pay this in one lump sum. If the trust pays the tax, the £ 535,000 is a gross gift on which the IHT at A's rates is £50,000. Thus, there is a tax saving of £12,500. Further, the trust can pay the tax in instalments out of income from the estate.

## 5   Problem areas

### a)   *Transfers of value by instalments (IHTA 1984 s 262)*

Where a person buys property at a price greater than its market value, the excess paid will be a transfer of value (assuming that donative intent is present). If the price is payable by instalments, part of each is deemed to be a transfer of value. That part is the proportion that the overall gift element bears to the price paid.    [**28.127**]

### EXAMPLE 28.27

A transfers property worth £40,000 to B for £80,000 payable by B in eight equal yearly instalments of £10,000. Hence, after eight years there will be a transfer of value of £40,000 divided between each instalment as follows:

$$\text{Annual instalment} \times \frac{\text{value of gift}}{\text{price payable}} = £10,000 \times \frac{£40,000}{£80,000} = £5,000.$$

### b)   *Transfers made on the same day (IHTA 1984 s 266)*

If a person makes more than one chargeable transfer on the same day and the order in which the transfers are made affects the overall amount of IHT payable, they are treated as made in the order which results in the least amount of IHT being payable (IHTA 1984 s 266(2)). This will be relevant where the transfers taken together straddle different rate bands and the donor does not pay the tax on all the transfers. Where this is the case the overall IHT will be less if the grossed-up gift is made first. In other cases an average rate of tax is calculated and applied to both transfers. When a PET made on the same day as a chargeable transfer is rendered chargeable by the donor's death within seven years these rules apply.                    **[28.128]**

c)    *Transfers reported late (IHTA 1984 s 264)*

When a transfer is reported late (for the due date for reporting transfers, see **[28.172]**) after IHT has been paid on a subsequent transfer, tax must be paid on the earlier transfer and an adjustment may have to be made to the tax bill on the later transfer. The tax payable on the earlier transfer is calculated as at the date of that transfer and interest is payable on the outstanding tax as from the date that it was due. If there is more than seven years between the earlier and the later transfers, no adjustment need be made in respect of the later transfer since the seven-year limit on cumulation means that the later transfer is unaffected by the earlier transfer. When there is less than seven years between the two transfers the extra tax charged on the later transfer is levied on the earlier transfer in addition to the tax already due on that transfer. The recalculation problems that arise when PETs become charge-able are considered in **Chapter 30**.                    **[28.129]**

d)    *Order of making lifetime transfers*

If the taxpayer wishes to make both a chargeable transfer (eg the creation of a discretionary trust) and a PET (eg a gift to a child) the chargeable transfer should be made *before* the PET so that if the latter becomes chargeable it will not necessitate a recomputation of tax on the chargeable transfer (nor, in the case of a discretionary trust, have an effect on the subsequent calculation of tax charged on the settlement: see **Chapter 34**).                    **[28.130]**

e)    *Non-commercial loans*

There are no special charging provisions for loans of property and accord-ingly (subject only to IHTA 1984 s 29 which ensures that the usual exemp-tions and reliefs are available) tax will be charged, if at all, under general principles (ie has the loan resulted in a fall in value of the lender's estate?). In the case of money loans it is necessary to distinguish between interest-free loans repayable after a fixed term and loans repayable on demand. If A lends B £20,000 repayable in five years' time at no interest, A's estate is reduced in value because of the delay in repayment and (assuming gratuitous intent) A makes a PET equal to the difference between £20,000 and the value of the right to receive £20,000 in five years' time.

If, instead, A lent B £20,000 repayable on demand with no interest charged, A's estate either does not fall in value because it includes the immediate right to £20,000 or, alternatively, any fall is likely to be *de minimis*. Accordingly, A has not made a transfer of value and there is no question of any charge to IHT. Loans repayable on demand may be employed so that the use of property, and any future increase in its value, is transferred free from IHT to another.

If a commercial rate of interest is charged on a loan, the transaction is not a chargeable transfer since the estate of the lender will not have fallen in value. Further, any interest may (normally) be waived without any charge to IHT by using the exemption for regular payments out of income (see **Chapter 31**).                                              **[28.131]**

**EXAMPLE 28.28**

Jasmine benefits her children without attracting a potential liability to IHT as follows:
(1)    She lends her daughter £100,000 repayable on demand. The money is invested in a small terraced house in Fulham which quickly trebles in value. That increase in value belongs to the daughter who is merely obliged to repay the original sum loaned if and when Jasmine demands it.
(2)    She allows her son to occupy her London flat rent free. The son enjoys the benefit of living there during the winter and lets the property to wealthy summer visitors. As there is no loss to Jasmine's estate the son's benefits are not subject to IHT (but note in such cases the possibility of an income tax charge under Settlement Provisions in Income Tax (Trading and Other Income) Act (ITTOIA 2005)): see **Chapter 16**).

f)    *Relief against a double charge to IHT*

In a number of situations there is the possibility of a double charge to IHT:

**EXAMPLE 28.29**

Gustavus gives Adolphus his rare Swedish bible (a PET). Two years later the bible is given back to Gustavus who dies shortly afterwards. As a result of his death within seven years the original gift of the bible is chargeable and, in addition, Gustavus' estate on death, which is subject to IHT, includes the bible.

Regulations made under FA 1986 s 104 provide a measure of relief and are discussed in **Chapter 36**.                                    **[28.132]–[28.150]**

VII   SPECIAL RULES FOR CLOSE COMPANIES

Only transfers of value made by *individuals* are chargeable to IHT (IHTA 1984 s 2(1)). An individual could, therefore, avoid IHT by forming a close company and using that company to make a gift to the intended donee, or a controlling shareholder in a close company could alter the capital structure of the company or the rights attached to his shares, so as to reduce the value of his shareholding in favour of the intended donee.

**EXAMPLE 28.30**

(1)    A transfers assets worth £100,000 to A Ltd in return for shares worth £100,000. A's estate does not fall in value so that there is no liability to IHT. The company then gives one of the assets (worth £50,000) to A's son B. The company and not A has made a transfer of value.

(2)    A Ltd has an issued share capital of £100 all in ordinary £1 shares owned by A. The company is worth £100,000. The company resolves:

   (i)    to convert A's shares into non-voting preference shares carrying only the right to a repayment of nominal value on a winding up;

   (ii)   to issue to B a further 100 £1 ordinary shares at par value.

The result is that the value has passed out of A's shares without any disposition by A.

IHTA 1984 Part IV contains (*inter alia*) provisions designed to prevent an individual from using a close company to obtain a tax advantage in either of these ways. For these purposes 'close company' and 'participator' have their corporation tax meaning (see **Chapter 41**) except that a close company includes a non-UK resident company which would be close if it was resident in the UK and participator does not include a loan creditor (IHTA 1984 s 102).    **[28.151]**

### 1    Transfers of value by close companies (IHTA 1984 s 94)

When a close company makes a transfer of value, it is apportioned amongst the participators in proportion to their interests in the company, so that they are treated as having made the transfer ('lifting the veil') (IHTA 1984 s 94(1)). Thus, in *Example 28.30(1)* above, A is treated as having made a transfer of value of £50,000. For s 94(1) to apply the company must have made a transfer of value, ie its assets must fall in value by virtue of a non-commercial transaction (IHTA 1984 s 10(1)). The value apportioned to each participator is treated as a net amount which must be grossed up at the participator's rate of IHT. Any participator whose estate has increased in value as a result of that transfer can deduct the increase from the net amount (ignoring the effect that the transfer may have had on his rights in the company). The transfer in these circumstances is a deemed transfer of value and cannot be a PET (see **[28.46]**). IHT is therefore chargeable.

**EXAMPLE 28.31**

A Ltd is owned as to 75% of the shares by A and 25% by B. It transfers land worth £100,000 to A. By IHTA 1984 s 94, A and B are treated as having made net transfers of value of £75,000 and £25,000 respectively. B will be charged to IHT on £25,000 grossed up at his rate of IHT. A, however, can deduct the increase in his estate (£100,000) from the net amount of the apportionment (£75,000), so that he pays no IHT. If A's shares (and B's) have diminished in value, that decrease is ignored.

Apportionment is not always as obvious as it may seem. For instance, in calculating a participator's interest in the company, the ownership of preference shares is usually disregarded (IHTA 1984 s 96). Further, where trustees are participators and the interest in the company is held in an interest in possession settlement (see **Chapter 33**) the apportioned amount is taxed as a reduction in the value of the life tenant's estate (IHTA 1984 s 99(2)(a)). In non-interest in possession trusts the apportioned amount is taxed as a payment out of the settled property by the trustees (IHTA 1984 s 99(2)(b)). Finally, where a close company is itself a participator in another close company any apportionment is then sub-apportioned to its own participators (IHTA 1984 s 95).

In two cases no apportionment occurs. *First*, if the transfer is charged to income tax or corporation tax in the donee's hands, there is no IHT liability (IHTA 1984 s 94(2)(a)). *Secondly*, where a participator is domiciled abroad, any apportionment made to him as a result of a transfer by a close company of property situated abroad is not charged to IHT (IHTA 1984 s 94(2)(b)).

**EXAMPLE 28.32**

(1)    A Ltd (whose shares are owned 50% by A and 50% by B) pays a dividend. The dividend is not chargeable to IHT in A or B's hands because income tax is charged on that sum under ITTOIA 2005 Part 4 Chapter 3 (tax on dividends and other distributions).

(2)    A Ltd in (1) above provides A with free living accommodation and pays all the outgoings on the property. If A is a director or employee of A Ltd, these items are benefits in kind on which A pays income tax under ITEPA 2003 (earnings income) (see **Chapter 8**). If A is merely a shareholder in the company these payments are treated as a distribution by A Ltd and are charged to income tax in A's hands under ITTOIA 2005 Part 4 Chapter 3 (tax on dividends and other distributions). However, if A was not a member of A Ltd, there would be no income tax liability, so that the participator, B, would be treated for IHT purposes as having made a chargeable transfer of value under IHTA 1984 s 94(1).

(3)    An English company, A Ltd, in which B and C each own 50% of the shares, gives a factory in France worth £100,000 to B, who is domiciled in the UK. C is domiciled in France and, therefore, the amount apportioned to him (£50,000) is not chargeable under IHTA 1984 s 94(1).

Participators can reduce their IHT liability on sums apportioned by the usual lifetime exemptions with the exception of the small gifts exemption and the exemption for gifts on marriage. Insofar as the transfer by the company is to a charity or political party it is exempt. Participators are also entitled to 100% business relief if the close company transfers part of its business or shares in a trading subsidiary.

The company is primarily liable for the tax. If it fails to pay, secondary liability rests concurrently with the participators and beneficiaries of the transfer. A participator's liability is limited to tax on the amount apportioned to him; for a non-participator beneficiary it is limited to the increase in value of his estate.                                                                                    **[28.152]**

## 2    Deemed dispositions by participators (IHTA 1984 s 98)

When value is drained out of shares in a close company by an alteration (including extinguishment) of the share capital or by an alteration in the rights attached to shares, this is treated as a deemed disposition by the participators although the section does not deem a transfer of value to have been made. When such a transfer occurs, liability under IHTA 1984 s 98 rests solely on the participators and not on the company. There is no deemed transfer of value under s 98, but such transfers are expressly prevented from being PETs by IHTA 1984 s 98(3) (see *Example 28.33(3)*, below).

**[28.153]–[28.170]**

**EXAMPLE 28.33**

(1)   Taking the facts of *Example 28.30(2)* above there is no actual transfer of value by A or A Ltd. However, under IHTA 1984 s 98 there is a deemed disposition by A equivalent to the fall in value of his shareholding. From owning all the shares and effectively all the assets he is left with a holding of 100 shares worth (probably) only their face value.

(2)   A owns 60% and B 40% of the shares in A Ltd. Each share carries one vote. The articles of association of the company are altered so that A's shares continue to carry one vote, but B's shares are to carry three votes each. There is a deemed disposition by A to B equivalent to the drop in value in A's estate resulting from his loss of control of A Ltd.

(3)   Zebadee, the sole shareholder in Zebadee Ltd, arranges for a bonus issue of fully paid preference shares which carry the right to a fixed dividend. He retains the shares but gives his valuable ordinary shares to his daughter. This familiar tax planning rearrangement depends in part upon the gift of the ordinary shares being a PET. Under s 98(1) the alteration in the share structure is treated as a disposition by Zebadee but as the bonus shares are at that stage issued to him, he does not then make any transfer of value. Accordingly, the subsequent gift of the ordinary shares will be a PET. It is thought that HMRC will not normally seek to argue that the bonus issue and later gift are associated operations falling within s 98(1) as an extended reorganisation (so that the gift of the shares is not prevented from being a PET by s 98(3)).

## VIII   LIABILITY, ACCOUNTABILITY AND BURDEN

### 1   Liability for IHT (IHTA 1984 Part VII)

The person primarily liable for IHT on a chargeable lifetime transfer is the transferor (IHTA 1984 s 199), although in certain cases, his spouse may be held liable as a transferor to prevent him from divesting himself of property to that spouse so that he is then unable to meet an IHT bill (IHTA 1984 s 203).

**EXAMPLE 28.34**

H makes a gross chargeable transfer to a discretionary trust of £1m and fails to pay IHT. He later transfers property worth £50,000 to his wife W which is exempt (inter-spouse). W can be held liable for H's IHT not exceeding £50,000.

If HMRC cannot collect the tax from the transferor (or his spouse) it can then claim it, subject to specified limits, from one of the following:

(1)   The transferee, ie any person whose estate has increased in value as a result of the transfer. Liability is restricted to tax (at the transferor's rates) on the value of the gross transfer after deducting any unpaid tax.

**EXAMPLE 28.35**

A makes a *gross* chargeable transfer to discretionary trustees of £40,000 on which IHT at A's rate of 20% is £8,000. A emigrates without paying the tax. HMRC can only claim £6,400 in tax from the trustees, ie:

|  | £ |
|---|---|
| Gross chargeable transfer by A | 40,000 |
| *Less:* unpaid tax | 8,000 |
| Revised value transferred | £32,000 |
| Trustees are liable for IHT at 20% | £6,400 |

(2)   Any person in whom the property has become vested after the transfer. This category includes a person to whom the transferee has in turn transferred the property; or, if the property has been settled, the trustees of the settlement and any beneficiary with an interest in possession in it; or a purchaser of the property unless he is a *bona fide* purchaser for money or money's worth and the property is not subject to an HMRC charge. The liability of these persons is limited to tax on the net transfer only and liability is further limited, in the case of trustees and beneficiaries, to the value of the settled property and, in the case of a purchaser, to the value of the property. Also included within this category is any person who meddles with property so as to constitute himself a *trustee de son tort* and any person who manages the property on behalf of a person under a disability.

(3)   A beneficiary under a discretionary trust of the property to the extent that he receives income or any benefit from the trust. Liability is limited to the amount of his benefit after payment of any income tax.

The liability to pay additional IHT on a gift because of the transferor's death within seven years, and liability to tax on a PET which becomes a chargeable transfer is considered in **Chapter 30**.

Quite apart from those persons from whom they can claim tax, HMRC has a charge for unpaid tax on the property transferred and on settled property where the liability arose on the making of the settlement or on a chargeable transfer of it (IHTA 1984 s 237). The charge takes effect in the same way as on death (see **Chapter 30**) except that for lifetime transfers it extends to personal property also. It will not bind a purchaser of land unless the charge is registered and in the case of personal property unless the purchaser has notice of the facts giving rise to the charge (IHTA 1984 s 238).

Once IHT on a chargeable transfer has been paid and accepted by HMRC, liability for any further tax ceases six years after the later of the date when the tax was paid or the date when it became due (IHTA 1984 s 240(2)). However, if HMRC can prove fraud, wilful default or neglect by a person liable for the tax (or by the settlor which results in an underpayment of tax by discretionary trustees), this six-year period only starts to run once HMRC knows of the fraud, wilful default or neglect, as the case may be (IHTA 1984 s 240(3)). When HMRC is satisfied that tax has been or will be paid, it may, at the request of a person liable for the tax, issue a certificate discharging persons and/or property from further liability (IHTA 1984 s 239).   **[28.171]**

## 2   **Accountability and payment**

a)   *Duty to account*

An account should only be delivered in respect of a chargeable transfer which is not a PET: in the case of PETs an account is only required if the transferor dies within seven years (IHTA 1984 s 216). Thus, HMRC need not be notified of a transfer of excluded property or of a transfer that is wholly exempt (eg within the annual exemption or inter-spouse), with the exception of an exempt transfer of settled property which must normally be notified.

In addition, in two situations chargeable transfers are 'excepted' from the duty to account (SI 2002/1731). *First*, where the gift is by an individual and, together with other chargeable transfers in the same tax year, does not exceed £10,000 so long as the gift and other chargeable transfers in the previous seven years do not exceed £40,000 in total; and, *secondly*, where the value transferred on the termination of an interest in possession in settled property is extinguished by the beneficiary's annual or marriage gifts exemption (see IHTA 1984 s 57 and **Chapter 33**). (There are also exempting regulations for 'excepted settlements': see SI 2002/1732 and **[34.21]**.)

As a general rule, the person who is primarily liable for the IHT must deliver the account (ie the transferee in the case of a lifetime gift, but note that FA 1999 expressly extended the obligation to PRs in respect of gifts made within seven years before death). This obligation to deliver an account under IHTA 1984 s 216 is removed where regulations made under IHTA 1984 s 256 provide otherwise. Under the current regulations (SI 2002/1733), there is no need to deliver an account where, broadly, the estate is simple and valued less than £240,000. The aim of the FA 2004 changes is to apply the simpler reporting procedures to estates which are non-taxpaying but which do not currently qualify for the simpler procedures eg estates which are greater than the current nil rate band but where no IHT is payable because the bequests are exempt such as to a spouse or to charity.

When the transfer is by a close company, nobody is under a duty to account, but in practice the company should do so in order to avoid a charge to interest on unpaid tax.

The account must be delivered within 12 months from the end of the month when the transfer was made or within three months from the date when that person first became liable to pay IHT (if later). In practice the account should be delivered earlier, since the tax is due before this date. Form IHT 100 is used for all lifetime transfers including transfers of settled property on life or death with an interest in possession. Anyone who fails to deliver an account, make a return, or provide information when required may be subject to penalties and HMRC has a wide general power to obtain information from 'any' person (IHTA 1984 s 219 and ss 219A–B) by means of a notice. HMRC cannot use the s 219 power to compel a solicitor or barrister to disclose privileged information concerning a client, but can use it to obtain the name and address of a client. The s 219A power (requiring information from persons obliged to submit accounts), however, contains no exclusion for professionally privileged information.                **[28.172]**

b) *Payment of tax*

For all lifetime chargeable transfers of settled or unsettled property made between 6 April and 30 September, the tax is due on 30 April following and for transfers made between 1 October and 5 April it is due six months from the end of the month when the transfer was made (IHTA 1984 s 226). The optimum date to make a chargeable transfer is therefore 6 April which gives a 12-month delay before tax is due. **[28.173]**

*Payment by instalments* Generally IHT must be paid in one lump sum. IHTA 1984 s 212 provides that any person liable for the tax (except the transferor and his spouse) can sell, mortgage or charge the property even if it is not vested in him, so that if, for instance, A gives property to B who settles it on C for life, either B, the trustees, or C (if called upon to pay the tax) can sell, mortgage or charge the property in order to do so.

As an exception to the general rule, if the transferee pays the IHT he can elect in the case of certain assets to pay the tax in ten yearly instalments; the first becoming due when the tax is due (IHTA 1984 s 227). This lifetime instalment option is available for the same assets as on death (see **Chapter 30**), except for the transfer of a minority holding of unquoted shares or securities within category (4) (relief when the IHT on instalment property amounts to 20% of the total bill). Trustees or beneficiaries who are liable for the tax on transfers of settled property can elect to pay in instalments provided that the property falls within one of the specified classes. Despite this election, the outstanding tax (and any interest due) may be paid at any time and if the relevant property is sold or transferred by a chargeable transfer the tax must be paid at once (IHTA 1984 s 227(4)). **[28.174]**

*Interest* Interest is charged on any tax which is not paid by the due date (IHTA 1984 s 233). Where the tax is to be paid by instalments, interest is charged on overdue instalments only, except in the case of land where interest is charged on all the outstanding tax. **[28.175]**

*Satisfaction of tax* HMRC has a discretion to accept certain property in satisfaction of tax (see IHTA 1984 s 230 and **Chapter 31**). **[28.176]**

*Adjustments to the tax bill* Subject to a six-year limitation (see **[28.202]**) if HMRC proves that too little tax was paid in respect of a chargeable transfer, tax underpaid is payable together with interest. Conversely, if too much tax was paid, HMRC must refund the excess together with interest, which is free of income tax in the recipient's hands (IHTA 1984 s 235). **[28.177]**

3 **Burden of tax**

The question of who, as between the transferor and the transferee, should bear the tax on a lifetime transfer is a matter for the parties to decide as discussed above. The decision may affect the amount of tax payable (see **[28.125]**). The parties can agree at any time before the tax becomes due and HMRC will accept their decision so long as the tax is paid. However, the agreement does not affect the liability of the parties, so that if the tax remains unpaid, HMRC can collect it from persons liable under Part VII of the legislation (see [28.171]).                                    [28.178]–[28.200]


IX   ADMINISTRATION AND APPEALS

1   **Calculation of liability**

IHT is not assessed by reference to the tax year. Instead, when HMRC is informed of a chargeable transfer of value it raises an assessment called a determination (IHTA 1984 s 221). If it is not satisfied with an account or if none is delivered when it suspects that a chargeable transfer has occurred, it can raise a 'best of judgment' or estimated determination of the tax due. A determination of IHT liability is conclusive against the transferor and for all subsequent transfers, failing a written agreement with HMRC to the contrary or an appeal.

If the taxpayer disputes the determination he can appeal to the Special Commissioners within 30 days of it (IHTA 1984 s 222). The appeal procedure is basically the same as under TMA 1970 for income tax, corporation tax and CGT, except that an appeal can be made direct to the High Court, thereby bypassing the commissioners, either by agreement with HMRC or on application to the High Court (as, for instance, occurred in *Bennett v IRC* (1995): see **Chapter 31**). In this case, the appeal is not limited to points of law. Appeal then lies in the usual way to the Court of Appeal and, with leave, to the House of Lords (or by the 'leap frog' procedure direct to the House of Lords). The disputed tax is not payable at the first stage of the appeal (IHTA 1984 s 242). However, if there is a further appeal, the tax becomes payable; if this appeal is then successful, the tax must be repaid with interest.   [28.201]


2   **Penalties**

FA 1999 tightened up the IHT penalty provisions by introducing new sections, ss 245 and 245A, into IHTA 1984 and by amending s 247. If a person is fraudulent (including wilful default) in producing accounts and other information, the penalty is £3,000 plus the difference between the liability calculated on the true and false bases. For negligence, the penalty is £1,500 plus that difference (IHTA 1984 s 247 as amended: for a consideration of this provision in the context of estimated valuations, see *Robertson v IRC* (2002) discussed in [30.43]). Solicitors and other agents who fraudulently produce incorrect information are liable to a maximum penalty of £3,000 reduced to £1,500 in cases of neglect (IHTA 1984 s 247(3)(4) as amended).

FA 2004 s 295 contains provisions that are aimed at bringing the current IHT penalty procedure more into line with the procedures applicable to income tax and capital gains tax. For instance, there is no longer a penalty charge where no additional IHT becomes payable as a result of fraudulent or negligent information/material submitted to HMRC. Further, the reasonable excuse provisions will apply to all failures to provide information and to deliver accounts. Further still, a penalty of £3000 is introduced for continuing failure to deliver an account or notify tax payable.

Proceedings for these penalties may be taken before the Special Commissioners or the High Court within three years of the determination of the correct tax due (IHTA 1984 ss 249–250).

Assessments to recover IHT lost through fraud, wilful default and neglect of a person liable for the tax (which for these purposes includes the settlor in the case of discretionary trusts) may be made up to six years from the discovery of the fraud, etc (IHTA 1984 s 240).          **[28.202]–[28.220]**

# 29 IHT—reservation of benefit

*Updated by Natalie Lee, Barrister, Senior Lecturer in Law, University of Southampton and Aparna Nathan, LLB Hons, LLM, Barrister, Gray's Inn Tax Chambers*

## I  LEGISLATIVE HISTORY

It was possible, under the CTT regime, for taxpayers to give away property but at the same time retain the benefit and control of it. Typical arrangements included:

**EXAMPLE 29.1**

(1)  Joe creates a discretionary trust and includes himself amongst the beneficiaries.

(2)  Arty owns a fine Constable landscape. He transfers legal ownership to his daughter by deed of gift but the picture remains firmly hanging up in his house until his death.

(3)  Sam gives his Norfolk farm to his son and continues to live in the farmhouse.

These arrangements were ideal for the moderately wealthy since, although the original transfer might attract tax (to the extent that it was not covered by the annual exemption and the nil rate band) future increases in value of the gifted property occurred outside the transferor's estate whilst, should the need arise (and especially if the property was settled as in *Example 29.1(1)*), the property could be recovered by the transferor. The widespread use of such arrangements made it likely that they would be attacked by legislation and the switch from CTT to IHT, which included the introduction of PETs, made this inevitable. Accordingly, provisions were introduced to deal with property subject to a reservation (see FA 1986 s 102 and Sch 20) which apply to lifetime gifts made on or after 18 March 1986.

The legislation is closely based on earlier estate duty provisions and the estate duty authorities remain relevant in construing the legislation (as was confirmed in the *Ingram* case which is considered below).     **[29.1]–[29.20]**

## II    IHT CONSEQUENCES IF PROPERTY IS SUBJECT TO A RESERVATION

A gift of property subject to a reservation is treated, so far as the donor is concerned, as a partial nullity for IHT purposes. This is because he is deemed to remain beneficially entitled to the gifted property immediately before his death. It is clear from the wording of s 102(3) that the property only returns into the estate of the donor at this moment although, if the benefit reserved ceases during the lifetime of the donor, he is treated as making a PET of the property at that time (a deemed PET). No advantage therefore flows from releasing any reserved benefit just before death. Possible double charges to IHT in this area are dealt with in the regulations discussed in **Chapter 36**. It should be remembered that the reservation of benefit rules only apply to the donor for the purposes of IHT; accordingly, although the property may be taxed as part of the death estate of the donor, there is no question of such property benefiting from the CGT uplift on death. Further, the property is also comprised in the estate of the donee so that IHT charges can arise on his death.

The legislation is widely drafted to catch a benefit reserved in the gifted property itself and a 'collateral advantage' (defined in s 102(1)(b) as 'any benefit to [the donor] by contract or otherwise').

**EXAMPLE 29.2**

(1)    In 1998 A gives his daughter his country cottage (then worth £50,000) in return for an annuity of £500 pa payable for the next four years. The annuity ends in 2002 and A dies in 2003. By stipulating for the payment of an annuity A reserved a benefit.

    (i)    *The original transfer:* In 1998 was a PET. The value transferred was reduced because of A's annuity entitlement.

    (ii)    *On the ending of the annuity in 2002:* A made a PET equal to the then value of the cottage. (Note that because this was a 'deemed' PET the value transferred is not reduced by A's annual exemption.)

    (iii)    *With his death in 2003* both the earlier transfers became chargeable.

(2)    Had A died in 2000 the reservation would have been operative at his death so that, in addition to the 1998 PET being chargeable, the value of the cottage in 2000 would have formed part of his death estate.

    For relief against a double IHT charge, see **Chapter 36**.

(3)    Zac gives his house to Jim and they live in it together. The gift is caught by the reservation of benefit rules so that:

    (a)    on Zac's death the house will be taxed as part of his estate. There will be no CGT death uplift;

    (b)    on Jim's death, because he owns the house, it will be taxed as part of his estate with the usual CGT uplift.

As a result of including the property in the deceased's estate immediately before death, it is necessary to value it at that time (and not at the time of the gift). Hence, where a transferor makes a gift with reservation there is no 'asset freezing' advantage. It also follows, of course, that as the value of the property swells the size of the estate, it may increase the estate rate of IHT (see **[30.28]** for 'estate rate') that is charged on the rest of the estate. Primary liability to pay the IHT attributable to reservation property lies with the donee (who should submit an account within 12 months of the end of the month of death) although the donor's PRs are liable if tax remains unpaid at the end of 12 months from the death. PRs who have made a final distribution of the assets in the estate may therefore be faced with a wholly unexpected claim for more IHT and this matter is considered in detail at **[30.49]**. As already noted, although the gifted property is included in the estate for IHT purposes it does *not* form part of the estate otherwise and hence does not benefit from the CGT uplift on death with the result that the donee may be faced with a substantial CGT liability on selling the property. **[29.21]–[29.40]**

## III   WHEN DO THE RESERVATION RULES APPLY?

### 1   There must be disposal of property by way of gift

To base liability on the making of a gift does not fit in with the general scheme of the IHT legislation which bases the tax charge upon chargeable transfers of value (see **[28.2]**). The resultant difficulties perfectly illustrate the problems of attempting to weld legislation from estate duty onto the CTT structure. Obviously, the gift must have been completed (and it should be remembered that the courts have no general power to perfect an uncompleted gift: see *Milroy v Lord* (1862)) but it may be assumed that the reservation provisions apply not just to pure gifts but also to the situation where, although partial consideration is furnished, there is still an element of bounty (see *A-G v Johnson* (1903)). A bad bargain, on the other hand, lacks any element of gift. The distinction between a gift (the basis of the reservation rules) and a transfer of value (the basis for IHT liability) is illustrated in the following example:                                                                  **[29.41]**

### EXAMPLE 29.3

(1)   Adam owns a pair of Constable watercolours and sells one to his daughter, Jemima. He retains possession of the picture. Each picture is worth £10,000: as a pair they are worth £35,000. Jemima pays Adam £10,000 for the picture.

  (i)   There is a *transfer of value* of £15,000 (drop in value of Adam's estate). This transfer is a PET (see **[28.43]**).

  (ii)   Is there a *gift* of property so that the reservation rules apply? As Jemima has paid full value for the picture that she has acquired there is no element of gift, so the rules are inapplicable.

(2)   Sam settles property on trust retaining the right to income until he is aged 50 with the remainder being settled on discretionary trusts for his family (including Sam). Assume that the trustees have the power to terminate Sam's life interest which they exercise six months after the creation of the trust.

  (i)   There is no *transfer of value* when Sam creates the settlement since he is the life tenant (IHTA 1984 s 49(1)).

  (ii)   Does Sam, however, make a gift at the time when he sets up the trust? Arguably, on general principles, he does: after all he has given property to trustees reserving only a life interest. If this is correct then once that life interest ends he will be caught by the reservation rules given that he is one of the discretionary beneficiaries.

  (iii)   When his life interest terminates Sam makes a chargeable *transfer of value* but does not make a *gift* (contrast the position if he had voluntarily surrendered his interest). With the cessation of the life interest the fund is now held on discretionary trusts and (see (ii) above) may be property subject to a reservation (FA 1986 Sch 20 para 5(1)).

## 2    Possession and enjoyment of the property by the donee

The reservation rules apply if full possession and enjoyment of the gifted property is not enjoyed by the donee either at or before the beginning of the *relevant period*. For this purpose the relevant period is the period ending with the donor's death and beginning either seven years before that date or (if later) on the date of the gift.                                              **[29.42]**

### EXAMPLE 29.4

(1)    By deed of gift A gives B the family silver but he retains it locked in a cupboard till his death; *or*

(2)    A gives full possession and enjoyment of the family silver to B and dies two years later; *or*

(3)    Assume in (1) above that the deed of gift was made in 1990 but that A only hands over the silver in 1993 and dies in 2003; *or*

(4)    A gives the family silver to B in 1988 but borrows it back just before his death in 2003.

In (*1*) possession of the silver is never enjoyed by B so that there is a gift with reservation and the silver forms part of A's estate on death.

In (*2*) full possession and enjoyment is obtained at the beginning of the relevant period. (Hence no reservation although there is, of course, a failed PET.)

In (*3*) full possession and enjoyment is obtained more than seven years before death. (No reservation.)

In (*4*) although full possession and enjoyment was given to B, the return of the silver to A is fatal because of the next requirement.

## 3    Exclusion of donor from benefit

The reservation rules apply if the donor has not been excluded from benefit *at any time* during the relevant period. In *Example 29.4(4)* the return of the silver shortly before the donor's death results in the property being subject to a reservation at A's death and, accordingly, it is subject to IHT.       **[29.43]**

### EXAMPLE 29.5

In 1924 the taxpayer created a settlement for the benefit of his infant daughter contingent upon her attaining 30. He was wholly excluded from benefit. In 1938 (just before she became 30) he arranged with her to borrow the income from the trust fund in order to reduce his overdraft. Until 1943 he borrowed virtually all the income: he finally died in 1946 (see *Stamp Duties Comr of New South Wales v Permanent Trustee Co* (1956)). On these facts the Privy Council held that a benefit had been reserved for estate duty purposes and the same would be true for IHT. Notice that the settlor had no enforceable right to the income: he merely made an arrangement with his daughter that she could have revoked at any time.

## 4    The two limbs

The requirement that the donor must be excluded from all benefit during the relevant period is comprised in two alternative limbs. Limb I requires his exclusion from the gifted property, whilst Limb II stipulates that he should not have received any benefit 'by contract or otherwise'.

So far as Limb I is concerned, in order to determine whether the donor has been entirely excluded from the gifted property, it is necessary to decide what that property comprises. There is a distinction of some subtlety between keeping back rights in the property (ie making only a partial gift) and giving the entire property but receiving a subsequent benefit therein from the donee (but note the limitations on this principle in the case of land resulting from FA 1999: see **[29.130]**). Once the gift is correctly identified, the donor must be entirely excluded both in law and in fact (see *Example 29.5*).

**EXAMPLE 29.6**

A father owned two properties on which an informal farming partnership was carried on with his son. Profits were split two-thirds to the father, one-third to the son. The father gave one of the properties to his son, free of all conditions, so that the son could have farmed it independently. In fact both continued to farm the property sharing the profits equally. It was held that the father had not been entirely excluded from the gifted property (*Stamp Duties Comr of New South Wales v Owens* (1953)).

Limb II, that the donor must be excluded from any benefit by contract or otherwise, is sufficiently widely drafted to catch collateral benefits that do not take effect out of the gifted property.

**EXAMPLE 29.7**

(1) Charlie gives land in Sussex to his son Jasper who covenants, at the same time, to pay Charlie an annuity of £500 pa for the rest of his life. The land is property subject to a reservation (cp *A-G v Worrall* (1895): '… it is not necessary that the benefit to the donor should be by way of reservation' *per* Lopes LJ).

(2) Adam sells his farm to Bertram for £100,000 when its true value is £500,000. As a sale at undervalue there is an element of gift. However, it is not easy to see how there can be a benefit reserved. The estate duty cases do not go this far and even if it is accepted that there is a reserved benefit, it presumably ceases at the moment when the £100,000 is paid to Adam with the result that there may be a deemed PET on that date. Accordingly, the somewhat absurd result is that on the same day there would be a PET of £400,000 (value of farm less consideration received) and a further PET of £500,000 (value of property in which the reservation has ceased). It is understood that HMRC will *not* argue that on these facts there is a benefit reserved.

(3) Claude wishes to give his farm to his son Dada subject to Dada taking over the existing mortgage thereon. If the arrangement is structured in this manner, the provision for the discharge of his mortgage would appear to result in Claude reserving a benefit. However, the Revenue has commented, with reference to this example, that 'the gift would be the farm subject to the mortgage and it would be an outright gift'. Were he to sell the farm for the amount of the outstanding mortgage that sale for partial consideration is not thought to involve a reservation (see (2) above); Dada could raise a mortgage on the security of the land; Claude would pay off his existing mortgage and any capital gain resulting from the consideration received (the gift element is subject to the hold-over election under TCGA 1992 s 165) might be covered by taper relief. Note also the stamp duty land tax

implications: see FA 2003 Sch 4 para 8.

Although the benefit need not come from the gifted property itself, it must be reserved as part of a linked transaction: a purely accidental benefit in no way connected with an earlier gift is ignored. In determining whether there is such a connection, account must be taken of any associated operations (see FA 1986 Sch 20 para 6(1)(c) incorporating for these purposes IHTA 1984 s 268: see **[28.101]**).

Limb II is concerned with benefits reserved 'by contract *or otherwise*'. According to estate duty authority these words should be construed *eiusdem generis* with contract and, therefore, as requiring a legally enforceable obligation (see the unsatisfactory case of *A-G v Seccombe* (1911)). It seems most unlikely that courts today—in the era of *Ramsay*—would permit obligations binding in honour only to slip through this net, however, and the statutory associated operations rule (discussed above) is couched in terms of conduct (ie what actually happened) not of legal obligation. Not surprisingly, the Revenue has confirmed that 'for IHT purposes [the words 'or otherwise'] should be given a wider meaning than they had for estate duty'.    **[29.44]–[29.70]**

## IV   EXCEPTIONS—WHEN THE RULES DO NOT APPLY

### 1   De minimis

Certain benefits to the donor are specifically ignored. FA 1986 s 102(1) requires the entire exclusion or *virtually* the entire exclusion of the donor from the gifted property. 'Virtually the entire exclusion' had no predecessor in the estate duty legislation and is apparently designed to cover, for instance, occasional visits by the donor to a house which he had earlier given away (including short holidays! For the Revenue's views on this matter see *Tax Bulletin*, November 1993).    **[29.71]**

### 2   Full consideration

A second exclusion is available where the donor furnishes full consideration for the benefit enjoyed (FA 1986 Sch 20 para 6(1)(a) and ss 102A(3), 102B(3)(b)). The consideration must be 'full' throughout the donor's period of use—hence rent review clauses should be included in any letting agreement. The gifted property, however, must be an interest in land or a chattel and to come within the exclusion actual occupation, enjoyment or possession of that property must have been resumed by the donor (see *Example 29.8*).    **[29.72]**

### EXAMPLE 29.8

(1)    Gift of land but donor is subsequently given shooting/fishing rights or rights to take timber. So long as full (not partial) consideration is furnished there is *no reservation* of benefit.

(2)    Gift of Ming vase—returned to donor in return for the payment of full rent. *No reservation*.

(3)   As in (1) save that donor sub-lets his rights. *Outside Sch 20 para 6(1)(a)* since actual enjoyment is not resumed and therefore there is a reservation of benefit.

(4)   Gift of shares: donor continues to enjoy dividends and pays full value for that right. *Outside Sch 20 para 6(1)(a)* since the property in question is neither land nor chattels. Hence a benefit is reserved.

### 3   Hardship

Additionally, a benefit may be ignored on hardship grounds but this provision is restrictive and is concerned solely with the occupation of gifted land by a donor whose circumstances have changed since the original gift and who has become unable to maintain himself for reasons of old age or infirmity. Further, the donee must be related to the donor (or his spouse) and the provision of occupation must represent reasonable provision for the care and maintenance of the donor (FA 1986 Sch 20 para 6(1)(b) and see s 102C(3)).

**[29.73]–[29.100]**

## V   IDENTIFYING PROPERTY SUBJECT TO A RESERVATION

FA 1986 Sch 20 paras 1–5 contains complex rules for identifying property subject to a reservation and makes provision, in particular, for what happens if the donee ceases to have possession and enjoyment of the property whether by sale or gift; for the effect of changes in the structure of bodies corporate when the original gift was of shares or securities; for the position if the donee predeceases the donor; and finally for the effect of changes in the nature of the property when the original gift was settled. The rules distinguish between settled and unsettled gifts and in the latter case there appears to be a defect in the legislation in relation to cash.

When property subject to the reservation qualified for agricultural or business relief at the date of the gift that relief may also be available if IHT would otherwise be charged because of the retained benefit (see **[31.60]**).

The recent case of *Sillars v IRC* [2004] SSCD 180 concerned a deposit account held in the joint names of the deceased and her two daughters. The daughters each regarded one third of the balance in the account as theirs. When the deceased died, the deceased's share in the account was returned as a one-third share. The Revenue contended that the whole balance of the account fell within the deceased's estate because the account was property where the deceased had a general power or authority enabling her to appoint or dispose of the property as she thought fit (IHTA 1984 s 5(2)). Alternatively, that the deceased had reserved a benefit in the account because the daughters did not have possession and enjoyment of the account and because the deceased was excluded from benefit. The Special Commissioner held that deceased did have a general power to dispose of the balance of the account as she thought fit. The property was therefore within her estate for IHTA 1094 s 5(2) purposes. Alternatively, the deceased had reserved a benefit in the account because the deceased was not excluded from benefiting from the account and the daughters had not assumed possession or enjoyment of the account. The Deceased's gift was a gift of a chose in action of the whole account and not just of two-thirds of the initial balance. This case was followed in *Perry v IRC* [2005] SSCD 474 (joint bank account).

[29.101]–[29.120]

## VI   RESERVING BENEFITS AFTER FA 1986

### 1   General matters

The avowed purpose behind the provisions of FA 1986 was to prevent the 'cake and eat it' arrangements that had flourished in the CTT era. To what extent do the new rules achieve their purpose? When it is necessary to identify the property given away, it may be that there is a defect in the rules of FA 1986 Sch 20 with regard to gifts of cash. Such gifts are expressly excluded from the rules and it is arguable that once the money is spent by the donee there is no property in which a benefit can be reserved (a similar principle applies if property originally given was turned into cash by the donee and that cash was either dissipated or used to purchase a replacement asset). A further loophole related to inter-spouse gifts (apparently closed in the wake of the *Eversden* case: see **[29.138]**) whilst the rules do not prevent the retention of control over the property given (see **[29.134]**).          [29.121]

### 2   Drafting: reservation or partial gift ('shearing')

'[By retaining] something which he has never given, a donor does not bring himself within the mischief of [the statutory provisions] … In the simplest analysis, if A gives to B all his estates in Wiltshire except Blackacre, he does not except Blackacre out of what he has given; he just does not give Blackacre' (Lord Simonds in *St Aubyn v A-G* (1952)).

**EXAMPLE 29.9**

(1)   A owned freehold land. In 1909, a sheep farming business was carried on in partnership with his six children on it.
*1913*: he gave the land to his children. The partnership continued.
*1929*: A died.
*What had he given away in 1913?* Only his interest in the land subject to the rights of the partnership. Accordingly there was no property subject to a reservation of benefit (see *Munro v Stamp Duties Comr* (1934)). It is thought that the FA 1999 changes would now result in a reserved benefit (see **[29.130]**).

(2)   In 1934 a father made an absolute gift of grazing land to his son. In 1935 that land was bought into a partnership with, *inter alia*, the father. On the death of the father in 1952 it was held that he had reserved a benefit in the land because of his interest in the partnership. (See *Chick v Stamp Duties Comr* (1958): contrast (1) above in that interest of the father arose *after* the absolute gift.)

(3)   T owns Whiteacre. He grants a lease to a nominee, assigns the freehold reversion to his daughter, and continues to occupy the property. Has T made a partial gift (of the reversion) so that the reservation of benefit rules do not apply?

It should be noted that in *Munro* (*Example 29.9(1)*, above) not only was there a substantial time gap between the grant of the lease and the gift of the freehold but, at the time when the lease was granted, the donor had no intention of making a gift of the freehold: ie it was both prior and demonstrably independent.

Doubts about shearing operations that involved the use of a nominee were caused by *Kildrummy (Jersey) Ltd v IRC* (1990), a case decided in the Scottish Court of Session and concerning a stamp duty avoidance scheme. Attempting to avoid duty, the taxpayers formed a Jersey company to which they granted a lease over property that they owned outright: the Kildrummy estate. That Jersey company executed a declaration that the lease was held 'in trust and as nominee for' the taxpayers. Just over one month later the freehold was disposed of to a second Jersey company. The Court of Session decided, unanimously, that the grant of the lease to the nominee company was null and void. Lord Sutherland commented as follows:

> 'There is no doubt that it is perfectly competent for a person to enter into a contract with his nominee but such a contract would normally be of an administrative nature to regulate the relationship between the parties and to describe the matters which the nominees are empowered to do by their principal. A contract of lease, however, is in my opinion of an entirely different nature. It involves the creation of mutual rights and obligations which can only be given any meaning if the contract is between two independent parties.'

The whole question of 'shearing operations' of this type was considered by the courts in the *Ingram* litigation.                                **[29.122]**

### 3   Ingram v IRC

#### a)   *The facts*

In *Ingram v IRC* (1999), Lady Jane Ingram transferred landed property to a nominee in 1987; the following day (on her directions) he granted her a 20-year rent-free lease in the property and on the next day transferred the property (subject to the lease) to trustees who immediately executed declarations of trust whereby the property settled was held for the benefit of certain individuals, excluding Lady Jane. The arrangements, all part of a pre-planned scheme, amounted to a classic carve-out or shearing operation. Lady Jane died in 1989 and the Revenue issued a determination that, because of the reservation of benefit rules, the gifted property still formed part of her estate at her death.                                **[29.123]**

#### b)   *The Revenue's claim*

The Revenue argued that the grant of a lease by a nominee in favour of his principal was a nullity with the result that, although it was accepted that the trustees took the property subject to the interest of Lady Jane (as per the abortive lease), that interest took effect by way of a leaseback. Hence Lady Jane's interest could only arise contemporaneously with the gift made to the trustees, thereby resulting in a reservation of benefit. Alternatively, and even if the nominee lease was effective, the same result would follow as a result of applying the *Ramsay* principle.                                **[29.124]**

c)    *The approach of the House of Lords*

Lord Hoffmann referred to the long history of the legislation in this area and noted that the decided cases showed that although its provisions prevent a donor from 'having his cake and eating it', there is nothing to stop him from 'carefully dividing up the cake, eating part and having the rest'. He decided the appeal on the assumption that the lease granted by the nominee was a nullity, ie on the basis that the leasehold interest came into existence only at the time when the freehold was acquired by the trustees. The consequences of such a 'contemporaneous carve-out' involved a consideration of the estate duty case of *Nichols v IRC* (1975) which had concerned a gift by Sir Philip Nichols of his country house and estate to his son, Francis, subject to Francis granting him an immediate leaseback. Goff J, giving the judgment of the Court of Appeal, concluded that such an arrangement involved a reservation of benefit by Sir Philip:

> '... we think that a grant of the fee simple, subject to and with the benefit of a lease-back, where such a grant is made by a person who owns the whole of the freehold free from any lease, is a grant of the whole fee simple with something reserved out of it, and not a gift of a partial interest leaving something in the hands of the grantor which he has not given. It is not like a reservation or remainder expectant on a prior interest. It gives an immediate right to the rent, together with a right to distrain for it, and, if there be a proviso for re-entry, a right to forfeit the lease. Of course, where, as in *Munro v Commissioner of Stamp Duties (NSW)* (1934) the lease, or, as it then may have been, a licence coupled with an interest, arises under a prior independent transaction, no question can arise because the donor then gives all that he has, but where it is a condition of the gift that a lease-back shall be created, we think that must, on a true analysis, be a reservation of benefit out of the gift and not something not given at all.'

In the event the *Nichols* case fell to be decided on the basis of the covenants given by the son in the lease in which he assumed the burden of repairs and the payment of tithe redemption duty, which covenants themselves amounted to a reservation. The wider statement of Goff J quoted above to the effect that a leaseback must *by itself* involve a reservation constituted the main authority relied upon by the Revenue (and the comment that the *Munro* case involved a 'prior independent transaction' had subsequently been widely debated).

Lord Hoffmann unequivocally rejected this approach:

> 'It is a curious feature of the debate in this case that both sides claim that their views reflect the reality, not the mere form of the transaction, but the Revenue's version of reality seems entirely dependent upon the *scintilla temporis* which must elapse between the conveyance of the freehold to the donee and the creation of the leasehold in favour of the donor. For my part I do not think that a theory based on the notion of a *scintilla temporis* can have a very powerful grasp on reality ... If one looks at the real nature of the transaction, there seems to me no doubt that Ferris J was right in saying that the trustees and beneficiaries never at any time acquired the land free of Lady Ingram's leasehold interest.'    **[29.125]**

d)    *The nominee lease*

Given that no reservation was involved even if the nominee lease was a nullity, it was not strictly necessary for their Lordships to express any view on the validity of such an arrangement. Lord Hoffmann, however, indicated that he was of the opinion that such a lease was valid as a matter of English law for reasons given by Millet LJ in the Court of Appeal. (Nominee leases are in fact widely used in practice.) It should, however, be appreciated that nothing in the speeches affects the proposition that a man cannot grant a lease to himself (see *Rye v Rye* (1962)) nor the position under Scots law (see *Kildrummy (Jersey) Ltd v IRC* (1990)).                        **[29.126]**

e)   *Ramsay*

Given the conclusion that a leaseback did not involve any reservation of benefit, the question of the *Ramsay* principle being used to nullify the nominee lease did not arise, and neither Lord Hoffmann nor Lord Hutton expressed any views on this matter.                        **[29.127]**

f)   *The meaning of 'property' in FA 1986 s 102*

Lord Hoffmann pointed out that s 102 is concerned with a gift of 'property' and that term does not necessarily refer to something that has a physical existence such as a house, but is used in a technical sense and requires a careful analysis of the nature of what has been gifted. A landowner may, for instance, gift an unencumbered freehold interest in his house in which case were he to continue to occupy that property (in the absence of a payment of full consideration and assuming that such occupation was more than on a *de minimis* level) then he would reserve a benefit. By contrast, he might retain a leasehold interest and only give away the encumbered freehold interest, in which case no benefit would be reserved in the property gifted (which would be the encumbered freehold). Of course, if the donor in the latter situation continued to occupy the house after the expiry of the retained lease, then that would (subject to what is said above about full consideration and *de minimis*) amount to a benefit retained in the freehold interest gifted. As Lord Hoffmann concluded, section 102 'requires people to define precisely the interest which they are giving away and the interest, if any, which they are retaining'.                        **[29.128]**

g)   *The use of shearing arrangements*

The speeches demolished the argument that the creation of the lease and the gift of the encumbered freehold had to be independent transactions. The lease could be carved out contemporaneously with the gift. Accordingly a prior nominee arrangement is not necessary; the arrangement could be structured as a gift and leaseback. However, it was essential that all the relevant terms of the lease were agreed before the freehold gift was made so that it is clear that the proprietary interest retained was defined with the necessary precision.                        **[29.129]**

## 4   FA 1999 s 104 (inserting new ss 102A–C into FA 1986)

Unsurprisingly the *Ingram* decision was reversed in respect of gifts of interests in land made after 8 March 1999, but the reversing legislation is narrowly targeted and, it would seem, does not otherwise change the reservation of benefit rules. If the following conditions are met the donor is treated as reserving a benefit in the gifted property with the normal consequences:

(1)    There must be a gift of an interest in land (other assets are not included). Note that as with the original legislation the trigger is a gift.

(2)    The donor must retain 'a significant right or interest ... in relation to the land' (in certain circumstances it will be sufficient if this is retained by his spouse) or be party to a significant arrangement in relation to the land. A right or interest is not 'significant' if the donor pays full consideration for it nor if the interest was obtained at least seven years before the gift (hence it is possible to grant a lease; wait seven years and then gift the freehold interest without falling foul of these rules).

It is not thought that these rules apply where a property is divided (eg lodge/main house) and one is gifted, one retained.                    **[29.130]**

### EXAMPLE 29.10

(1)    *In 2003 A carves out a lease (using a nominee arrangement) and gifts the encumbered freehold interest to his daughter.* Because A has given away an interest in land and retained an interest in the same land, the gifted interest is caught by the reservation rules: hence it will form part of A's estate on his death (s 102A(2));

(2)    *As above except that having carved out the lease A waits seven years before giving away the freehold.*
The reservation rules do not apply to the gifted freehold interest (s 102A(5)).

(3)    *A is the life tenant of a settlement created by his grandfather and which owns his main residence. The trustees exercise overriding powers to appoint an encumbered freehold interest on continuing trusts for A's children leaving a leasehold interest in the life interest fund.*
Although A makes a transfer of value (to the extent of the freehold interest ceasing to be subject to his life interest) he does not make a gift and so the reservation rules will not apply.

## 5   Reversionary leases

### EXAMPLE 29.11

Tom owns the Red House. He grants a 350-year lease to his son at a peppercorn rent to begin in 21 years' time. Meanwhile he continues to occupy the property.

*Analysis:* This is an alternative 'shearing' arrangement: the gift is of the leasehold interest whilst Tom's continued occupation is attributable to his retained freehold interest. In the light of the speeches in *Ingram* it would seem likely that such arrangements are outside the original reservation rules and they do not seem to be affected by the 1999 legislation *provided that* the freehold interest was acquired at least seven years before the deferred lease was granted. (It is understood that HMRC does not accept this on the basis that there is a 'significant arrangement' that is not protected by the seven-year provision in s 102A(5).) Alternatively, the rules may not apply if the freehold was acquired for full consideration. **[29.131]**

## 6   Settlements

### a)   *Retaining an interest*

If the settlor reserves an interest for himself under his settlement, whether he does so expressly or whether his interest arises by operation of law, there is no reservation of benefit and he is treated as making a partial gift (see *Re Cochrane* (1906) which involved a reversionary interest).                **[29.132]**

### b)   *The object of a discretionary trust*

The position with regard to discretionary trusts is more problematic. If the settlor is one of the beneficiaries he is not entirely excluded from the property with the result that the entire fund will be included as part of his estate. In view of the limited nature of a discretionary beneficiary's rights (see *Gartside v IRC* (1968)), he cannot be treated as making a partial gift (see *IRC v Eversden* (2003)). If the donor could be added as a beneficiary under a power to add contained in the settlement it is thought that again the property is subject to a reservation.                **[29.133]**

### c)   *The settlor as paid trustee*

A danger arises if the settlor is one of the trustees and is entitled to remuneration as trustee. According to the estate duty case of *Oakes v Stamp Duties Comr* (1954) he has reserved a benefit (although at present HMRC does not follow this case). In any event there is no problem if the settlor/trustee is not entitled to remuneration and so it is possible for a donor to retain control over the settled property without infringing the reservation of benefit rules.                **[29.134]**

### d)   *The termination of an interest in possession*

Where an individual either became entitled to an interest in possession before 22 March 2006 or, if after that time, the interest was an immediate post-death interest, a transitional serial interest or a disabled person's interest (for definitions, see **Chapter 32**), and is accordingly treated as owning the property itself (see **Chapter 33**), a termination of the interest in the individual's lifetime on or after 22 March 2006, where the property continues to be settled after that termination, will be treated as a gift for the purposes of the gift with reservation rules. Thus, if such an individual retains the use of the settled property after their interest in it ends, it will remain chargeable in their hands.                **[29.135]**

#### EXAMPLE 29.12

In November 2000, Cliff settled his country house on trust for Richie for life or until he should re-marry, thereafter to Richie's ex-wife Maddie for life, with remainder to his niece, Saphron. Richie re-married in September 2006 and, since Maddie had settled in France, the trustees permitted Richie to remain living in the house. Should Richie die in, say, December 2008, the value of the house will form part of his estate for IHT purposes in the same way as if he had formerly owned it outright.

## 7    Benefits that are permitted

a)    *Statutory 'get outs'*

It is only necessary for the property to be enjoyed *virtually* to the entire exclusion of the donor, thereby permitting the occasional visit or holiday (see [29.71]). More important is the exception where the donor provides full consideration for the benefit retained.                                    **[29.136]**

**EXAMPLE 29.13**

Dad gives his farm to Phil but continues to reside in the farmhouse under a lease which requires him to pay a full rent. Dad's continued use of a part of the gifted property does not bring the reservation rules into play.

b)    *Co-ownership*

The following situation was considered by ministers at the time when the rules were introduced in 1986.

'Elderly parents make unconditional gifts of a share in their house to their children (so that the children become tenants in common with the parents). Assuming that they all reside in the house and each bears his share of the running costs, it appears that the parents' continued occupation or enjoyment of that part of the house which they have given away is in return for similar enjoyment by the children of the other part of the property. Accordingly, the parents' occupation is for full consideration' (Standing Committee G: Hansard, 10 June 1986, col 425).

The restrictive nature of this statement is all too obvious: it is assumed, for instance, that the children are occupying the house with their parents. If they lived elsewhere would their *right* to occupy be sufficient to lead to the same result? (Furthermore, if they never lived in the house after the making of the gift can they be said to have assumed 'full possession and enjoyment' of the gifted property?) It appears implicit in the statement that ownership of the house is divided equally between the various tenants in common (or that less than 50% is given away) since otherwise the full consideration argument would seem inapplicable.

Perhaps the major difficulty with the views expressed in the statement is that they proceed upon the premise that the house is divided into 'parts' so that the parents use the children's 'part' in return for letting the children use their 'part'. In reality, of course, the interest of a tenant in common is in the whole property: *he is the owner of an undivided share.* Accordingly, the right of such a tenant to occupy the entire property is derived from the interest retained. As it does not amount to a reservation in the gifted share the full consideration argument becomes irrelevant. If this view is correct, it would follow that the precise interest of a tenant in common (eg does he have a 50% share or only 1%?) becomes irrelevant since whatever the size of the interest it confers a right to occupy the entirety.

FA 1986 s 102B (inserted by FA 1999) was introduced to deal with gifts of a share in land and is couched in significantly wider terms than the 1986 Ministerial Statement. Accordingly, that Statement should, in relation to events occurring after 8 March 1999, be regarded as wholly superseded. Under the legislation, there will be no reservation of benefit if:

(1)   there is a gift of a share in land;
(2)   both donor and donee occupy the land;
(3)   the donee does not receive any benefit other than a negligible one which is provided by the donee for some reason connected with the gift.

The abandonment of any reference to 'full consideration' should be noted which indicates that the gift may be of (say) a 90% interest in the property. Note also that the donor can, if he wishes, continue to pay all the running costs of the property.                    **[29.137]**

#### EXAMPLE 29.14

Sally owns a five-bedroom property at the seaside and is regularly visited by her daughter and two children (who live in Tooting). She gives a 50% beneficial interest in the house to the daughter who comes and goes as she pleases and leaves possessions in the rooms of the house (eg her bedroom). Although it is not the daughter's main residence and is not her 'family home' it is nevertheless felt that s 102B(4) applies so that Sally has not reserved any benefit in the gifted share. The daughter is 'in occupation' in much the same way as owners of a country cottage would be in occupation. Take care in relation to the division of expenses: Sally must not receive any benefit from the daughter in any way connected with the gift. She should, for instance, continue to bear her own day-to-day living expenses and her proportionate share (she could pay all!) of the property expenses.

## 8   Reservation and spouses: the Eversden case

a)   *General principles*

The reservation of benefit rules do not apply in the case of an inter-spouse gift (see FA 1986 s 102(5)).                    **[29.138]**

#### EXAMPLE 29.15

(1)   S creates a discretionary trust. He is the unpaid trustee, his wife is one of the beneficiaries. S has not reserved any benefit although it appears that *if* his wife benefits under the trust and *if* he shares that benefit HMRC will argue that he has not been excluded from enjoyment or benefit in the gifted property.

(2)   H settles a bond on his wife, W, for life but subject to an overriding power of appointment in favour of a class of beneficiaries including H. Her life interest is terminated after (say) six months by the trustees whereupon the bond is held in an interest in possession trust for H's daughter (but still subject to the power of appointment which could be exercised in favour of H). Because the original gift made by H was spouse exempt the Court of Appeal decided in *Eversden* that the reservation of benefit rules could not apply to the subsequent trusts affecting the property.

b)   *The Eversden case*

Slightly simplifying the facts, in 1988 the settlor conveyed her house to a trust under which she reserved a 5% absolute beneficial share with the remaining

95% being held for her husband for life and subject thereto on discretionary trusts for a class of beneficiaries including the settlor. The husband and settlor occupied the property: on the husband's death in 1992 IHT was payable on the termination of his life interest and the wife continued to occupy the property until her death in 1998. The Court of Appeal decided:

(1) that the original settlement involved a gift by the settlor which was covered by the spouse exemption;

(2) accordingly there was no room for the application of the reservation of benefit rules.

The Revenue argued that although the gift of the life interest was spouse exempt, the gift on discretionary trusts was not and because the settlor was a beneficiary of those trusts she had reserved a benefit.

Concluding that the spouse exemption in s 102(5)(a) was wide enough to cover gifts of even a determinable life interest to a spouse, Carnwath LJ in the Court of Appeal commented as follows:

> 'However the problem if it exists derives from s 49, which treats the acquisition of an interest in possession as equivalent to the acquisition of the property itself. That has the result that, in the present case, the estate of the settlor's husband is taxed on the property, but that of the settlor is not. There is nothing in s 102 to modify that aspect of the scheme of the 1984 Act. If that is of concern to the Revenue, they must look for correction to Parliament, not to the courts.'    **[29.139]**

c)   *Amending legislation (FA 2003 s 185)*

The so-called '*Eversden* loophole' was closed by legislation effective in relation to disposals made on or after 20 June 2003. The effect of this can be illustrated as follows:

(i)   Assume that on 1 August 2003 Adam settles property on a revocable life interest trust for his wife Eve.

That disposal will be spouse exempt and even if Adam continues to benefit from the property there will be no reservation of benefit;

(ii)  On 1 April 2004 the trustees exercise their overriding powers to end Eve's life interest whereupon the property is held on discretionary trusts under which Adam is capable of benefiting.

The termination of Eve's life interest will be a chargeable transfer by her. So far as Adam is concerned, the new s 102(5B) provides that it is as if Adam's original disposal by way of gift 'had been made immediately after (Eve's) ... interest in possession came to an end'. The reservation rules therefore apply at that point to catch Adam's gift.

As can be seen the effect of the change (a) is not to effect the treatment of outright spouse gifts—nor indeed of life interest gifts which are enlarged into absolute ownership—but (b) in other cases limits the spouse exemption to the period during which the spouse retains an interest in possession in the property.    **[29.140]**

## 9   Post-death variations

Instruments of variation and disclaimer provide an ideal way of transferring wealth without resulting in any IHT or CGT liability and permit the disponor to reserve a benefit in the property (see generally **[30.153]**).    **[29.141]**

**EXAMPLE 29.16**

(1)  Father dies leaving his country cottage to his daughter. She continues to use it for regular holidays and at all bank holidays but transfers it to her son by instrument of variation made within two years of father's death and read back into his will.

   The crucial point is that the variation is treated as made by father for *all* IHT purposes so that his daughter has not made a gift of property capable of falling within the reservation of benefit provisions.

(2)  On H's death property (including the second home) is left to his wife on a terminable life interest, remainder to the son. The trustees terminate the spouse's life interest in the country cottage but the son permits her to continue to use it on a regular basis. The reservation of benefit rules do not apply because the termination of the interest in possession, although a transfer of value (a PET) by the spouse, is not a gift (see **[29.41]**).

## 10  Pre-owned assets

FA 2004 s 84 and Sch 15 introduce an income tax charge where disponors enjoy benefits from pre-owned assets. The rules will apply from 2005/06. As the name suggests, 'pre-owned assets' are assets previously owned by the disponor and disposed of by him since March 1986. the disposition may be of a part or the whole of the pre-owned asset.

In relation to land, an charge to income tax under these provisions will arise in respect of a 'chargeable amount' where an individual ('the chargeable person') occupies any land ('the relevant land'), whether alone or together with or her persons and either the disposal condition or the contribution condition is met as respects the land.

The disposal condition is met where at any time after 17 March 1986, the chargeable person owned an interest in the relevant land or other property the proceeds on the disposal of which were applied (directly or indirectly) by another person in acquiring the relevant land and the chargeable person has disposed of all or part of his interest in the relevant land otherwise than by an excluded transaction. Excluded transactions are set out at FA 2004 Sch 15 para 10(1) and include transfers to the spouse of the chargeable person, arms' length transactions, gifts by virtue of which the relevant property became settled property in which the spouse or former spouse has an interest in possession, and transfers falling within the exemptions set out at IHTA 1984 ss 11, 19 and 20.

The contribution condition is, broadly, satisfied where the chargeable person has funded some other person, otherwise than by an excluded transaction, to acquire an interest in the relevant property. Excluded transactions for these purposes are set out at FA 2004 Sch 15 para 10(2) and include acquisitions by the spouse of the chargeable person, or where the spouse becomes entitled to an interest in possession in the relevant property on its acquisition, where the consideration provided by the chargeable person was by way of outright gift and was made at least seven years before the chargeable person occupied the relevant land, the consideration provided by the chargeable person falls within IHTA 1984 ss 11, 19 or 20.

The chargeable amount for any taxable period is the appropriate rental value less the amount of any payments which, in pursuance of any legal obligation, are made by the chargeable person during period to the owner of the relevant landing respect of the occupation by the chargeable person of the relevant land.

There are equivalent provisions for chattels. These are found at FA 2004 Sch 15 paras 6–7. There are similar provisions in relation to intangible assets.

Exemptions from charge under FA 2004 Sch 15 are set out at para 11. These include situations where the chargeable person's estate includes the relevant property or other property that derives its value from the relevant property and its value is not substantially less than the value of the relevant property.

FA 2004 Sch 15 does not apply in any year where the former owner is not UK resident. If the chargeable person is UK-resident but non-domiciled, then the charge only applies in relation to UK situs property. The charge does not apply to disposals of property by persons who were non-domiciled at the time of the disposal but who have since acquired UK domicile.

There is a de minimis amount set of £2,500. Benefits falling below this figure will not be changeable under FA 2004 Sch 15.

Where post-death variations have been effected, the persons who owned the property which is the subject of the variation are not treated for the purposes of FA 2004 Sch 15 as having previously owned the property (FA 2004 Sch 15 para 16).                                        **[29.142]**

# 30 IHT—death

*Updated by Natalie Lee, Barrister, Senior Lecturer in Law, University of Southampton and Aparna Nathan, LLB Hons, LLM, Barrister, Gray's Inn Tax Chambers*

I  GENERAL

IHTA 1984 s 4(1) provides that:

> 'on the death of any person tax shall be charged as if immediately before his death he had made a transfer of value and the value transferred by it had been equal to the value of his estate immediately before his death ...'.

Accordingly, there is a deemed transfer of value that occurs immediately before the death and which must be cumulated with chargeable transfers made by the deceased in the preceding seven years. In addition to causing a charge on his estate at death, death also has the effect of making chargeable potentially exempt transfers made in the seven years before death and it may lead to a supplementary IHT charge on chargeable transfers made in that same period. It should be noted that, following the changes made by FA 2006 Sch 20 to the inheritance taxation of trusts, whereby inter vivos interest in possession trusts (apart from disabled trusts) created on or after 22 March 2006 will incur an immediate charge to tax rather than qualify as PETs (see **[28.42]**), there are likely to be fewer PETs and more chargeable transfers. The complex tax computations that may result in either case are considered in **[30.21]** ff.                                                      **[30.1]**

## 1  Meaning of 'estate'

The definition of 'estate' has already been considered in connection with lifetime transfers (IHTA 1984 s 5(1); see **[28.61]**. For a recent decision confirming that rights under an intestacy are 'property' for IHT purposes and hence form part of a taxpayer's estate, see *Daffodil v IRC* (2002). On death, the estate does not include excluded property (see **[35.20]** for the meaning of excluded property) although it does include property, given away by the deceased, in which he had reserved a benefit at the time of his death (see **Chapter 29**). Property owned by the deceased in a fiduciary capacity, for instance as 'treasurer' for his family, does not form part of his estate (*Anand v IRC* (1997)). The person opening a joint bank account may be found, on the facts, to be the beneficial owner of the moneys in that account at the date of his death (*O'Neill v IRC* (1998)). As the transfer is deemed to occur immediately before the death, the estate includes the share of the deceased in jointly owned property that passes by operation of law (*jus accrescendi*) at the moment of death.

#### EXAMPLE 30.1

Bill and his sister Bertha own their home as beneficial joint tenants so that on the death of either that share will pass automatically to the survivor and will not be transferred by will. For IHT purposes the half share in the house will be included in their respective death estates and will be subject to charge (for the valuation of the half share, see **[28.64]**).

The estate at death also includes a gift made before death in anticipation of death and conditional upon it occurring (a *donatio mortis causa*). Hence, although dominion over the property will have been handed over, it is still taxed as part of the deceased's estate at death.                    **[30.2]**

### 2  Valuation

a)   *A hypothetical sale*

(See also **[28.62]** ff.)

In general, assets must be valued at 'the price which the property might reasonably be expected to fetch if sold in the open market at that time'. No reduction is allowed for the fact that all the property is put on the market at the same time (IHTA 1984 s 160). This hypothetical sale occurs immediately before the death and if the value is ascertained for IHT purposes it becomes the value at death for CGT purposes and, hence, the legatee's base cost (TCGA 1992 s 274: see **[21.21]**). Reliefs that reduce the IHT value (notably business property relief) are ignored for CGT purposes. For IHT, low values ensure the least tax payable but will give the legatee a low base cost and so a higher capital gain when he disposes of the asset.                    **[30.3]**

b)   *Lotting and the Fox decision*

In valuing an estate at death, 'lotting' requires a valuation on the basis that 'the vendor must be supposed to have' taken the course which would get the largest price for the combined holding 'subject to the caveat ... that it does not entail undue expenditure of time and effort'. For instance, if a taxpayer dies possessed of a valuable collection of lead toy soldiers they will not be valued individually but rather as a collection (see *Duke of Buccleuch v IRC* (1967)).

In *IRC v Gray* (1994) the deceased (Lady Fox) had farmed the Croxton Park Estate in partnership with two others and the land was subject to tenancies that Lady Fox, as freeholder, had granted to the partnership. The Revenue sought to aggregate (or lot) the freehold in the land with her partnership share as a single unit of property so that the value of Lady Fox's freehold reversion was an appropriate proportion of the aggregate value of that reversion and her partnership interest treated as a single item of property (in effect therefore the reversion was being valued on a vacant possession basis with an allowance for the partnership interests of the other partners). It may be noted that under the partnership deed she was entitled to 921/2% of profits (and bore virtually all the losses). The Court of Appeal reversed the Lands Tribunal, holding that lotting was appropriate since that was the course that a prudent hypothetical vendor would take to obtain the best price. The fact that the two interests could not be described as forming a 'natural unit of property' was irrelevant. Hoffmann LJ commented that:

> 'The principle is that the hypothetical vendor must be supposed to have "taken the course which would get the largest price" provided that this does not entail "undue expenditure of time and effort". In some cases this may involve the sale of an aggregate which could not reasonably be described as a "natural unit" ... The share in the farming partnership with or without other property, was plainly not a "natural" item of commerce. Few people would want to buy the right to farm in partnership with strangers. Nevertheless [s 160] requires one to suppose that it was sold. The question for the Tribunal was whether, on this assumption, it would have been more advantageous to sell it with the land.'

In many ways this was not a typical case involving the fragmentation of farm land within a family and therefore it should not be assumed that this judgment will apply in all such cases: see *Private Client Business* (1994) p 210.

**[30.4]**

### c) *Funeral expenses*

Although the general rule is that assets must be valued immediately before death, IHTA 1984 Part VI permits values to be amended in certain circumstances, eg reasonable funeral expenses can be deducted including a reasonable sum for mourning for family and servants and the cost of a tombstone or gravestone: see SP 7/87. The Revenue have indicated that 'what is reasonable in one estate may not be reasonable in another and regard has to be had to the deceased's position in life and to the size of the estate. Each case has to be treated on its own merits'. **[30.5]**

### d) *Changes in value resulting from the death*

In certain cases, a change in the value of assets caused by the death is taken into account. **[30.6]**

#### EXAMPLE 30.2

(1) A took out a whole life insurance policy for £100,000 on his own life. Its value immediately before death would be equal to the surrender figure. As a

result of A's death £100,000 will accrue to A's estate and hence the value of the policy for IHT purposes is treated as that figure (IHTA 1984 s 167(2)).

(2)    A and B were joint tenants in equity of a freehold house worth £100,000. Immediately before A's death his joint interest would be worth in the region of £50,000. As a result of death that asset passes to B by survivorship (ie its value is nil to A's estate). In this case it is not possible to alter the pre-death valuation (IHTA 1984 s 171(2)).

e)    *Post-death sales*

In three cases the pre-death valuation can be altered if the asset is sold within a short period of death for less than that valuation. Relief is not given merely because the asset falls in value after death; *only if it is sold by bargain at arm's length is the relief available.* Normally the sale proceeds will be substituted as the death valuation figure if an election is made by the person liable for the IHT on that asset (in practice this will be the PRs who should elect if IHT would thereby be reduced). Where such revaluations occur, not only must the IHT bill (and estate rate) on death be recalculated but also, for CGT purposes, the death valuation is correspondingly reduced so as to prevent any claim for loss relief. The three cases when this relief is available are:                              **[30.7]**

*Related property sold within three years of death (IHTA 1984 s 176)* The meaning of related property has already been discussed (see **[28.67]**). So long as a 'qualifying sale' (as defined) occurs, the property on death can be revalued ignoring the related property rules (ie as an asset on its own). Although the sale proceeds need not be the same as the death value, if the sale occurs within a short time of death the proceeds received will offer some evidence of that value.                                                                                                      **[30.8]**

**EXAMPLE 30.3**

Sebastian's estate on death includes one of a pair of Constable watercolours of Suffolk sunsets. He leaves it to his son; the other is owned by his widow, Jemima. As a pair, the pictures are worth £200,000. Applying the related property provisions, the watercolour is valued at £100,000 on Sebastian's death. If it were to be sold at Sotheby's some eight months after his death for £65,000, the death value could, if a claim were made, be recalculated ignoring the related property rules. It would be necessary to arrive at the value of the picture immediately before the death.

*Quoted shares and securities sold within 12 months of death (IHTA 1984 ss 178 ff)* If sold for less than the death valuation the sale proceeds can be substituted for that figure. It should be noted that if this relief is claimed it will affect *all* such investments sold within the 12-month period; hence, the aggregate of the consideration received on such sales is substituted for the death values. Special rules operate if investments of the same description are repurchased. The shares or securities must be listed on the Stock Exchange so that the provisions do not apply to private company shares. Relief is also available in cases where the investments are either cancelled without replacement within 12 months of death or suspended within 12 months of death and remain suspended on that anniversary. In the former case, there is deemed sale for a nominal consideration of 1 at the time of cancellation; in the latter a deemed sale of the suspended investments immediately before the anniversary at their then value. With recent falls in the Stock Market this is a valuable relief and PRs may be criticised if they fail to take advantage of it to reduce the IHT bill. **[30.9]**

*Land sold within four years of death* (*IHTA 1984 ss 190 ff*) The relief extends to all interests in land and is similar to that available for quoted securities although it enables a higher as well as a lower figure to be substituted. Hence, all sales within the four-year period are included in any election. Note, however, that in the fourth year the election is not available if the sale value would exceed the probate value (IHTA 1984 s 197A). Exchange of contracts is not a 'sale': see *Jones (Balls' Administrators) v IRC* (1997). **[30.10]**

*The 'appropriate person'* In the case of both quoted shares and land, the election to substitute the sale proceeds must be made by the appropriate person who is defined in the legislation as 'the person liable for inheritance tax attributable to (the property)'. This will be the PRs. Obviously the election in such cases will commonly be made if the property is sold for less than its probate value, but the section dealing with land is not so limited and therefore the election may appear attractive in the sort of case illustrated in *Example 30.4* where substituting a higher probate value would wipe out a CGT liability. **[30.11]**

---

**EXAMPLE 30.4**

MacLeod left his entire estate to his wife Tammy on his death in 2000; it included land valued at death at £10,000. As a result of new regional development plans, the land now has hope value and is worth in the region of £100,000. Accordingly, it is now to be sold. An election to substitute the sale proceeds for the probate value would be beneficial in CGT terms. However, because there is no appropriate person (since IHT is not payable on MacLeod's death), that election cannot be made. Had the land been left to MacLeod's son, Ronnie, and fallen within MacLeod's unused nil rate band an election would then be possible (and desirable if the increased value would still attract IHT at 0%!) (and see *Stonor v IRC* (2001)).

---

f) *Provisional valuations*

The valuation of certain assets (notably private company shares) may take some time and the PRs may wish to obtain a grant immediately. In such cases it is possible to submit a provisional estimate for the value of the property that must then be corrected as soon as the formal valuation has been obtained (see IHTA 1984 s 216(3A) and the *Robertson* case, considered at **[30.43]**). **[30.12]**

---

3 **Liabilities**

a) *General rule*

Liabilities only reduce the value of an estate if incurred for consideration in money or money's worth, eg an outstanding mortgage and the deceased's unpaid tax liability (IHTA 1984 s 5(5)). **[30.13]**

b)    *Artificial debts*

FA 1986 s 103 introduced further restrictions on the deductibility from an estate at death of debts and incumbrances created by the deceased. These provisions supplement s 5(5) in relation to debts or incumbrances created after 17 March 1986. Broadly, their aim is to prevent the deduction of 'artificial' debts, ie those where the creditor had received gifts from the deceased as in the following example:

**EXAMPLE 30.5**

Berta gives a picture to her daughter Bertina in 1998. In 2000 she buys it back, leaving the purchase price outstanding until the date of her death.
(1)    The gift is a PET and escapes IHT if Berta survives seven years.
(2)    The debt owed to Bertina is incurred for full consideration and hence satisfies the requirements of IHTA 1984 s 5(5). Deduction is, however, prevented by FA 1986 s 103.

Section 103(1) provides that debts must be abated in whole or in part if any portion of the consideration for the debt was *either* derived from the deceased *or* was given by *any* person to whose resources the deceased had contributed. In the latter case contributions of the deceased are ignored, however, if it is shown (ie by the taxpayer) that the contribution was not made with reference to or to enable or facilitate the giving of that consideration.

Accordingly, unless property derived from the deceased furnished the consideration for the debt, a causal link is necessary between the property of the deceased and the subsequent debt transaction.

**EXAMPLE 30.6**

(1)    In *Example 30.5* the consideration for the debt is property derived from the deceased and therefore the debt may not be deducted in arriving at the value of her estate. (NB: it does not matter that the gift of the deceased occurred before 17 March 1986 so long as *the debt* was incurred after that date.)
(2)    In 1974 Jake gave a diamond brooch to his daughter (Liz). In 1984 she in turn gave the brooch to her sister Sam. In 1996 Sam lends £50,000 to Jake who subsequently dies leaving that debt still outstanding.
The consideration for the debt was not derived from property of the deceased and Sam would (presumably) be able to show that, although she received property from a person whose resources had been increased by the gift of deceased, the disposition of that property by the deceased was not linked to the subsequent transaction. Had Jake bought the brooch back from Liz in 1996 (leaving the price outstanding as a debt) the consideration for the debt would then be property derived from him so that the debt would not be deductible.

When a debt, which would otherwise not be deductible on death because of s 103(1), is repaid *inter vivos* the repayment is treated as a PET (a deemed PET). This provision is essential since otherwise such debts could be repaid immediately before death without any IHT penalty. However, the application of this rule when a taxpayer repurchases property that he had earlier given away is a matter of some uncertainty. Take, for instance, the not uncommon case where A, having made a gift of a valuable chattel, subsequently decides that he cannot live without it. Accordingly, he repurchases that chattel paying full market value to the donee. Has A made a notional PET under s 103(5) at the time when he pays over the purchase price or, if the money is paid as part and parcel of the repurchase agreement, did A never incur any debt or incumbrance falling within the section? It is thought that the latter view is correct since if the purchase price is paid at once a debt will never arise.

An element of multiple charging could arise from the artificial debt rule (in *Example 30.5*, for instance, the PET is made chargeable if Berta dies before 2005; the debt is non-deductible and the picture forms part of Berta's estate). However, the regulations discussed in **Chapter 36** prevent the multiple imposition of IHT in such cases.

Finally, although a debt may not be deducted in order to arrive at the value of the deceased's estate for IHT purposes, it must still be paid by the PRs and it is, therefore, treated as a specific gift by the deceased (see further [**30.56**]).

[**30.14**]–[**30.20**]

**EXAMPLE 30.7**

(1)   S settled property on discretionary trusts in 1980. In 1990 the trustees lend him £6,000. This debt is non-deductible. NB: it does not matter when the trust was created.

(2)   Terry-Testator borrows £50,000 from the Midshire bank which he gives to his son. The debt that he owes to the bank is deductible on his death: in no sense is this an 'artificial debt'.

(3)   Terry-Testator lends £50,000 to his daughter (interest free; repayable on demand). She buys a house with the money that increases in value. There is no transfer of value by Terry; the debt provisions are irrelevant, and Terry has not reserved any benefit in the property purchased with the loan.

## II   HOW TO CALCULATE THE IHT BILL ON DEATH

Tax is calculated according to the rates set out in the following table:

| *Gross cumulative transfer* (£) | *Rate* (%)—*Death* | *Rate* (%)—*Life* |
|---|---|---|
| 0–285,000 | 0 | 0 |
| Above 285,000 | 40 | 40 |

These rates (which came into force on 6 April 2005) are applied to the estate at death and, in addition, when that death occurs within seven years of a chargeable lifetime transfer or PET made by the deceased the following results occur:

(1)   In the case of a *chargeable transfer*, IHT must be recalculated either in accordance with the rates of tax in force at the donor's death if these are less than the rates at the time of the transfer or, alternatively, by using full rates at the time of the transfer. Subject to taper relief, extra tax may then be payable (IHTA 1984 s 7(4), Sch 2 para 2).

(2)   In the case of a PET, the transfer is treated as a chargeable transfer so that *first*, IHT must be calculated (subject to taper relief) at the rates

current at the donor's death (again provided that these rates are less than those in force at the time when the transfer occurred: otherwise the latter apply: see Sch 2 para 1A), and *secondly*, the PET must now be included in the total transfers of the taxpayer for cumulation purposes which may necessitate a recalculation of the tax charged on other chargeable transfers made by the donor and, where a discretionary trust is involved, the recalculation of any exit charge.

These problems will be considered in order, looking first at the effect of death upon the chargeable lifetime transfers of the deceased and then at the taxation of the death estate. The consequences for discretionary trusts are considered at **[34.22]**.                                                  **[30.21]**

## 1    Chargeable transfers of the deceased made within seven years of his death

As already explained (see **[28.122]**) IHT will have been charged, at half the then death rate, at the time when the transfer was made. In computing that tax, chargeable transfers in the seven preceding years will have been included in the cumulative total of the transferor. As a result of his death within the following seven years IHT must be recalculated on the original value transferred at the full rate of IHT in force at the date of death. After deducting the tax originally paid, extra tax may be payable.          **[30.22]**

a)    *Taper relief (IHTA 1984 s 7(4))*

If death occurs more than three years after the gift, taper relief ensures that only a percentage of the death rate is charged. The tapering percentages are as follows:
(1)    where the transfer is made more than three but not more than four years before the death, 80%;
(2)    where the transfer is made more than four but not more than five years before the death, 60%;
(3)    where the transfer is made more than five but not more than six years before the death, 40%; and
(4)    where the transfer is made more than six but not more than seven years before the death, 20%.

### EXAMPLE 30.8

Danaos settles £335,000 on discretionary trusts in July 2003 (IHT is paid by the trustees). He dies:
(1) on 1 January 2005
*or*      (2) on 1 January 2009
*or*      (3) on 1 January 2011.
    The *original transfer* in 2003 was subject to IHT at one half of rates in force for 2003–04 (see Table at **[30.21]**).
    *In (1)* he dies within three years of the gift: accordingly, a charge at the full tax rates for 2004–05 must be calculated, tax paid in 2003 deducted, and any balance is then payable.
    *In (2)* he dies more than five but less than six years after the gift: therefore only 40% of the full amount of tax on death is to be calculated, the tax paid in 2003 deducted, and the balance (if any) is then payable.

*In* (3) death occurs more than seven years after the transfer and therefore no supplementary tax is payable.

If it is assumed that the current rates of IHT apply throughout this period, the actual tax computations are as follows (assuming that the 2003 transfer was the first chargeable transfer of Danaos):

(a) *IHT on the 2003 chargeable transfer is as follows:*

| | | |
|---|---|---|
| first £ 285,000 | — | nil |
| Remaining £ 50,000 at 20% | — | £ 10,000 |

total IHT payable by the trustees is therefore £10,000.

(b) *If death occurs within three years:* tax on a transfer of £ 335,000 at the then death rates is:

| | | |
|---|---|---|
| first £285,000 | — | nil |
| remaining £50,000 at 40% | — | £ 20,000 |

Total IHT is therefore £20,000 which after deducting the sum paid in 2003 (£10,000), leaves a further £10,000 to be paid.

(c) *If death occurs in 2009* the calculation is as follows:
  (i)   full IHT at death rates £20,000 (as in (b) above)
  (ii)  take 40% (taper relief) of that tax: £20,000 × 40% = £8,000
  (iii) as that sum is less than the tax actually paid in 2003 *there is no extra IHT to pay.*

It should be noted in *Example 30.8* that even though the result of taper relief may be to ensure that extra IHT is not payable because of the death, it does not lead to any refund of the original IHT paid when the chargeable transfer was made: in such cases the taper relief is inapplicable, see IHTA 1984 s 7(5). (The assumption in *Example 30.8* that rates of tax remain unchanged is, of course, unrealistic since the IHT rate bands are linked to rises in the RPI.) Taper relief is moreover of no benefit if the gift fell within the donor's nil rate band since, although using up all or part of that band, no tax is actually paid and taper relief operates by reducing the tax payable (contrast taper relief for CGT purposes: see **Chapter 20**). [30.23]

b) *Fall in value of gifted property*

If the property given falls in value by the date of death, the extra IHT is calculated on that reduced value (IHTA 1984 s 131). This relief is not available in the case of tangible movables that are wasting assets and there are special rules for leases with less than 50 years unexpired.

**EXAMPLE 30.9**

In Year 1 Dougal gave a Matisse figure drawing worth £335,000 to his discretionary trustees (who paid the IHT). He died in Year 3 when the Matisse was worth only £292,000.

(1) Assuming it was Dougal's first chargeable transfer, IHT paid on the Year 1 gift was £10,000 (£335,000 – £285,000) x 20%.

(2) IHT on death (assume rates unchanged) is calculated on £292,000 = £2,800. Hence extra IHT payable is nil.

Had the property been sold by the trustees before Dougal's death for £43,000 less than its value when given away by Dougal the extra (death) IHT would be charged on the sale proceeds with the same result as above. If, however, the property had been given away by the trustees before Dougal's death, even though its value might at that time have fallen by £43,000 since Dougal's original gift, no relief is given, with the result that the extra charge caused by Dougal's death will be levied on the full £335,000.

The *value* of a chargeable lifetime transfer for cumulation purposes is not reduced in the seven-year period since s 131 merely reduces the value that is taxed (not the value cumulated) whilst taper relief is given in terms of the rate of IHT to be charged on that transfer. Hence the full value of the life transfer remains in the cumulative total of the transferor and there is no reduction in the tax charged on his death estate.                    **[30.24]**

## 2   PETs made within seven years of death

The PET becomes a chargeable transfer and is subject to IHT in accordance with the taxpayer's cumulative total *at the date when it was made* (ie taking into account chargeable transfers in the preceding seven years). The value transferred is frozen at the date of transfer unless the property has fallen in value by the date of death in which case the lower value is charged (the rules concerning the fall in value of assets are the same as those considered at **[30.24]**). Despite these provisions, which look back to the actual date of the transfer of value, the IHT is calculated by reference to the rates in force at the date of death unless those rates have increased in which case the rates at the time of the transfer are taken (subject to taper relief, as above).   **[30.25]**

### EXAMPLE 30.10

In October 2002 Zanda gave a valuable doll (then worth £310,000) to her granddaughter Cressida. She died in July 2006 when the value of the doll was £287,000. Assuming that Zanda had made no other transfers of value during her life, ignoring exemptions and reliefs, the IHT consequences are:
(1)   The 2002 transfer was potentially exempt. However, as Zanda dies within seven years it is made chargeable.
(2)   As the asset has fallen in value by the date of death IHT is charged on the reduced value, ie on £287,000.
(3)   IHT at the rates current when Zanda died is:
first £285,000 = nil
next £2,000 at 40% = £800
Total IHT = £800.
(4)   Taper relief is, however, available since Zanda died more than three years after the gift. Therefore:
£800 × 80% (taper relief) = £640.
*Note:* Although IHT is calculated by reference to the reduced value of the asset, for cumulation purposes (and for CGT purposes) the original value transferred (£310,000) is retained.

## 3   Position where a combination of PETs and chargeable transfers have been made within seven years of death

PETs are treated as exempt transfers unless the transferor dies within the following seven-year period. Accordingly, they are not cumulated in calculating IHT on subsequent chargeable transfers. Consider the following illustration:

**EXAMPLE 30.11**

In July 1999 Planer gives shares worth £287,000 to his son.

In April 2003 he settles land worth £295,000 on discretionary trusts and pays the IHT himself (so that grossing-up applies: see **[28.124]**).

He dies in February 2004. (Assume no other transfers of value were made by Planer; ignore exemptions and reliefs; current IHT rates apply throughout.)

(1)   The transfer in 1999 was a PET.

(2)   In calculating the IHT on the chargeable transfer in 2003 the PET is ignored and IHT is £2,000 ([£295,000–£285,000] × 20%).

The chargeable transfer in 2003 is therefore £297,000 (£295,000 + £2,000).

(3)   As a result of his death within seven years the PET is made chargeable and the IHT calculation is as follows:

(a)   *On the 1999 transfer* IHT at the rates when Planer died is subject to 60% taper relief (gifts more than four, less than five years before death). Hence IHT at death rates is:

first £285,000 — nil

next, £2,000 (£287,000 – £285,000) at 40% = £800

Taper relief at 60%:

£800 × 60% = £480 (tax due on 1999 transfer)

*Note:* Primary liability for this tax falls upon the donee (see **[30.27]**). Grossing-up does not apply when IHT is charged, or additional tax is payable, because of death.

(b)   *On the 2003 transfer* IHT must be recalculated on this transfer since the transferor has died within seven years, and the former PET must be included in the cumulative total of Planer at the time when this transfer was made. Hence:

(i)   cumulative transfers of Planer in 2003 = £287,000

(ii)   value transferred in 2003 = £297,000

(iii)   IHT at death rates on transfers between £287,000 and £584,000 is £297,000 × 40% = £118,800

Taper relief is not available on this transfer since Planer dies within three years.

*Therefore:*

deduct IHT paid in 2003:

£118,800–£2,000 = £116,800

*Additional IHT payable on the 2003 transfer is £116,800*

*Note:* The cumulative total of transfers made by Planer at his death (which will affect the IHT payable on his death estate) is £584,000.

The following diagram illustrates how seven-year cumulation operates for PETs and chargeable transfers (CTs) made within seven years of a death occurring on 1 June 2003:

When a PET is made after an earlier chargeable transfer and the transferor dies in the following seven years, tax on that PET will be calculated by including the earlier transfer in his cumulative total. In this sense the making of the PET means that there is no reduction in his cumulative total for a further seven years and the result is that IHT could eventually turn out to be higher than if the PET had never been made ('the PET trap'!).      **[30.26]**

**EXAMPLE 30.12**

Yvonne made a chargeable transfer of £285,000 on 1 May 1995 and on 1 May 2001 made a gift of £330,000 to take advantage of the PET regime. Unfortunately, she dies after 1 May 2002 (when the 1995 transfer drops out of cumulation) but before 1 May 2004 (when taper relief begins to operate on the PET).

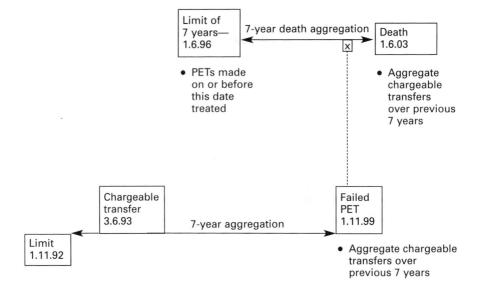

(1)    IHT on the former PET (at current rates) is £134,000 since the 1995 transfer forms part of Yvonne's cumulative total at the time when the PET was made in 2001. Tax on the death estate will then be calculated by including the 2001 transfer (the former PET) in Yvonne's cumulative total.

(2)    Had Yvonne not made the 2001 PET so that £330,000 formed part of her death estate, tax thereon (ignoring the 1995 transfer that has dropped out of cumulation) is £18,000.

Extra IHT resulting from the making of the PET is therefore £134,000 – £18,000 = £116,000

## 4   Accountability and liability for IHT on lifetime transfers made within seven years of death

The donee of a PET which becomes chargeable by virtue of the subsequent death of the transferor must deliver an account to HMRC within 12 months of the end of the month of death (IHTA 1984 s 216(1)(bb): PRs of the deceased must also report such transfers, see s 216(3)(b)). Tax itself is payable six months after the end of the month of death and interest on unpaid IHT runs from that date. There is no question of interest being charged from the date of the PET. Primary liability for the tax is placed upon the transferee although HMRC may also claim the IHT from any person in whom the property is vested, whether beneficially or not, excluding, however, a purchaser of that property (unless it was subject to an HMRC charge for the tax owing: see generally **[28.171]**).

To the extent that the above persons are not liable for the IHT *or* to the extent that any tax remains unpaid for 12 months after the death, the deceased's PRs may be held liable (IHTA 1984 s 199(2)). An application for a certificate of discharge in respect of IHT that may be payable on a PET may not be made before the expiration of two years from the death of the transferor (except where the Board exercises its discretion to receive an earlier application). If the property transferred qualified for the instalment option (see **[28.174]**) the tax resulting from death within seven years may be paid in instalments if the donee so elects and provided that he still owns qualifying property at the date of death (IHTA 1984 s 227(1A)).

So far as additional tax on chargeable lifetime transfers is concerned the same liability rules apply. Primary liability rests upon the donee although the deceased's PRs can be forced to pay the tax in the circumstances discussed above.

The problems posed for PRs by this contingent liability for IHT on PETs and *inter vivos* chargeable transfers are considered at **[30.49]**.          **[30.27]**


## 5   Calculating IHT on the death estate

Having considered the treatment of PETs and the additional IHT on lifetime transfers that may result from the death of the transferor, it is now necessary to consider the taxation of the death estate (which includes property subject to a reservation and settled property in which the deceased was the life tenant). To calculate the IHT the following procedure should be adopted:

*Step 1* Calculate total chargeable death estate; ignore, therefore, exempt transfers (eg to a spouse) and apply any available reliefs (eg reduce the value of relevant business property by the appropriate percentage).

*Step 2* Join the IHT table at the point reached by the deceased as a result of chargeable transfers made in the seven years before death. This cumulative total must include both transfers that were charged *ab initio* and PETs brought into charge as a result of the death.

*Step 3* Calculate death IHT bill.

*Step 4* Convert the tax to an average or estate rate—ie divide IHT (*Step 3*) by total chargeable estate (arrived at in *Step 1*) and multiply by 100 to obtain a percentage rate. It is then possible to say how much IHT each asset bears. This is necessary in cases where the IHT is not a testamentary expense but is borne by the legatee or by trustees of a settlement or by the donee of property subject to a reservation (see **[30.47]**). If the deceased had exhausted his nil rate band as a result of lifetime transfers made in the seven years before death, his death estate will be subject to tax at a rate of 40% which will be the estate rate.


### EXAMPLE 30.13

Dougal has just died leaving an estate valued after payment of all debts etc at £285,000. A picture worth £10,000 is left to his daughter Diana (the will states that it is to bear its own IHT) and the rest of the estate is left to his son Dalgleish. Dougal made chargeable transfers in the seven years preceding his death of £100,000. To calculate the IHT on death:

(1)    Join the death table at £100,000 (lifetime cumulative total).

(2)    Calculate IHT on an estate of £285,000:

|  | £ |
|---|---:|
| £100,000 × 0% | 0 |
| £100,000 × 40% | 40,000 |
|  | £40,000 |

(3)    Calculate the estate rate:

$$\frac{\text{£40,000 (IHT)}}{\text{£285,000 (Estate)}} \times 100 = 14.04$$

(4)    Apply estate rate to picture (ie 14.04% × £10,000) = £1,404. This sum is payable by Diana.

(5)    Residue (£275,000) is taxed at 14.04% = £38,610. The balance is paid to Dalgleish.

Property subject to a reservation and settled property in which the deceased had enjoyed an interest in possession at the date of death is included in the estate in order to calculate the estate rate of tax. The appropriate tax is, however, primarily the responsibility of the donee and the trustees. The IHT position on death can be represented as follows:

**[30.28]–[30.40]**

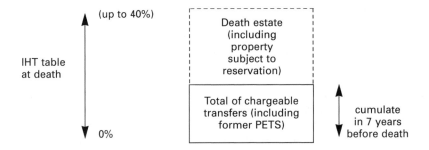

## III    PAYMENT OF IHT—INCIDENCE AND BURDEN

If the deceased was domiciled in the UK at the time of his death, IHT is chargeable on all the property comprised in his estate whether situated in the UK or abroad. If he was domiciled elsewhere, IHT is only chargeable on his property situated in the UK. (For the meaning of domicile in this context, see **[35.4]**.)                                                                 **[30.41]**

### 1    Who pays the IHT on death?

#### a)    *Duty to account*

The deceased's PRs are under a duty to deliver to HMRC within 12 months of the end of the month of the death an account specifying all the property that formed part of the deceased's estate immediately before his death and including property:

(1)    in which the deceased had a beneficial interest in possession (eg where the deceased was the life tenant under a settlement); and

(2)    property over which he had a general power of appointment (this property is included since such a power enabled the deceased to appoint himself the owner so that in effect the property is indistinguishable from property owned by him absolutely).

In practice, the PRs will deliver their account as soon as possible because they cannot obtain probate and, therefore, administer the estate until an account has been delivered and the IHT paid; further, they must pay interest on any IHT payable on death and which is unpaid by the end of the sixth month after the end of the month in which the deceased died (for instance, a death in January would mean that IHT is due before 1 August and, thereafter, interest is payable).                                                   **[30.42]**

b)   *Estimated values and penalties: the Robertson case*

The practice of sending in provisional valuations in order to obtain a grant of representation has been noted at **[30.12]**. IHTA 1984 s 216(3A) is in the following terms:

> 'If the personal representatives, after making the fullest enquiries that are reasonably practicable in the circumstances, are unable to ascertain the exact value of any particular property, their account shall in the first instance be sufficient as regards that property if it contains—
>
> (a)   a statement to that effect;
> (b)   a provisional estimate of the value of the property; and
> (c)   an undertaking to deliver a further account of it as soon as its value is ascertained.'

In *Robertson v IRC* (2002) the executor wished to obtain an early grant of representation in order to sell the deceased's house in Scotland. In his IHT calculation he estimated a value for the deceased's personal chattels at £5,000 (subsequently valued at £24,845) and for a property in England at £50,000 (subsequently valued at £315,000). The Revenue considered that the return had been prepared negligently and that a penalty of £9,000 was due (see IHTA 1984 s 247). Corrective valuations were submitted within six months of the deceased's death so this was not a case where there had been any loss of tax and nor was any interest payable. A Special Commissioner decided that no penalty was payable and the following matters may be noted:

(1)   The executor had acted in accordance with standard practice and with common sense.

(2)   The values were clearly marked as estimates and corrective accounts submitted.

(3)   There was a need to obtain the grant as a matter of urgency.

(4)   A penalty is only payable if an incorrect account has been negligently produced and the exeeutor had not been negligent.

(5)   In the subsequent decision, *Robertson v IRC (No 2)* (2002), the costs of the Commissioners' hearing were awarded against the Revenue on the basis that it had acted 'wholly unreasonably' in connection with the hearing.

In cases where a grant is required urgently and the PRs are in difficulties in completing the IHT account, a helpline is available and HMRC may then confirm its acceptance of estimated values.                                            **[30.43]**

c)   *'Excepted estates'* (*SI 2002/1733 amended by SI 2003/1658*)

No account need be delivered in the case of an 'excepted estate'.

The taxpayer must die domiciled in the UK; must have made no charge-able lifetime transfers other than 'specified transfers' where the value did not exceed £75,000; must not have been a life tenant under a settlement; his death estate must not include property subject to a reservation and he must not have owned at death foreign property amounting to more than £50,000. Subject thereto the estate will be excepted if the *gross* value at death does not exceed £240,000. This figure takes account of all property passing under the will or intestacy; of nominated property; and, in cases where the deceased had been a joint tenant of property, the value of the deceased's share in that property.

HMRC reserves the right to call for an account (on Form 204) within 35 days of the issue of a grant of probate, but if it does not do so, the PRs are then automatically discharged from further liability.                **[30.44]**

### d)   *IHT form*

In cases other than c) above, to obtain a grant the PRs must submit an HMRC account (an IHT Form).

From 2 May 2000 a new HMRC account for estates was introduced comprising a basic eight-page form together with supplementary pages that will only need to be completed if they are relevant to that estate. The new form replaced old Forms 200, 201 and 202.                **[30.45]**

### e)   *Liability for IHT (IHTA 1984 Part VII)*

*Personal representatives* PRs must pay the IHT on assets owned beneficially by the deceased at the time of death and on land comprised in a settlement which vests in them as PRs. Their liability is personal, but limited to assets which they received as PRs or might have received but for their own neglect or default (IHTA 1984 s 204 and see *IRC v Stannard* (1984) which establishes that overseas PRs or trustees may find that their personal UK assets are seized to meet that liability).                **[30.46]**

*Other Persons* If the PRs fail to pay the IHT other persons are concurrently liable, namely:
(1) Executors *de son tort*, ie persons who interfere with the deceased's property so as to constitute themselves executors. Their liability is limited to the assets in their hands (see *IRC v Stype Investments (Jersey) Ltd* (1982)).
(2) Beneficiaries entitled under the will or on intestacy in whom the property becomes vested after death. Their liability is limited to the property that they receive.
(3) A purchaser of real property if an HMRC charge is registered against that property. His liability is limited to the value of the charge.
(4) Any beneficiary entitled to an interest in possession in the property after the death. Liability is generally limited to the value of that property.                **[30.47]**

*Trustees* Where the deceased had an interest in possession in settled property at the date of his death, it is the trustees of the settlement who are liable for any IHT on the settled property to the extent that they received or could have received assets as trustees. Should the trustees not pay the tax, the persons set out in (3) and (4) above are concurrently liable.          **[30.48]**

*Contingent liability of PRs* In three cases PRs may incur liability to IHT if the persons primarily liable (the donees of the property) have reached the limits of their liability to pay or if the tax remains unpaid for 12 months after the death. These occasions are, *first*, when a lifetime chargeable transfer is subject to additional IHT because of the death; *secondly*, if a PET is brought into charge because of the death; and *thirdly* if the estate includes property subject to a reservation. The following example illustrates the type of problem that may arise:

**EXAMPLE 30.14**

Mort dies leaving an estate (fully taxed) of £635,000. The PRs are unaware of any lifetime gifts and, therefore, pay IHT of £140,000 and distribute the remainder of the estate. Consider the following alternatives:

(1) After some years a lifetime gift by Mort of £275,000, which had been made six years before his death and was potentially exempt when made, is discovered. Although no IHT is chargeable on that gift the PRs are accountable for extra IHT on the death estate of £110,000; or

(2) A gift of £1,000,000 made one year before Mort's death is discovered. In this case not only will the PRs be accountable for extra IHT of £110,000 as above but in addition if the donee fails to pay IHT on the £1,000,000 gift the PRs will be liable to pay that IHT (limited to the net assets in the estate which have passed through their hands).

Contingent liabilities present major problems for PRs and the following matters should be noted:

(1) Their liability may arise long after the estate has been fully administered and distributed (eg a PET may be discovered which is not only itself taxable but also affects the charge on subsequent lifetime chargeable transfers and on the death estate). It may therefore be desirable for PRs to obtain suitable indemnities from the residuary beneficiary before distributing the estate although such personal indemnities are of course always vulnerable (eg in the event of the bankruptcy of that beneficiary).

(2) The liability of PRs is limited to the value of the estate (as discussed above). However, even if IHT has been paid on the estate and a certificate of discharge obtained they are still liable to pay the further tax that may arise in these situations.

(3) If PRs pay IHT no right of recovery is given in IHTA 1984 against donees who were primarily liable except in the case of reservation of benefit property (in this situation s 211(3) affords a right of recovery), although such a right may exist as a matter of general law (see *Private Client Business* (1998) p 58). There is, of course, nothing to stop a donor taking an indemnity from his donee to pay any future IHT as a condition of making the PET. Such an arrangement would be expressed as an indemnity in favour of his estate and does not involve any reservation of benefit in the gifted property. As noted above,

personal indemnities are, of course, vulnerable in the event of the bankruptcy or emigration of the donee.

(4)    It will not be satisfactory for PRs to retain estate assets to cover the danger of a future tax liability. Apart from being unpopular with beneficiaries there is no guarantee that PRs will retain an adequate sum to cover tax liability on a PET which they did not know had been made: only by retaining all the assets in the estate will they be wholly protected!

(5)    Insurance would seem to be the obvious answer to these problems. PRs should give full information on matters within their knowledge and then seek cover (up to the limit of their liability) in respect of an unforeseen IHT liability arising. It would seem reasonable for testators to give expressly a power to insure against these risks. It is understood that cover can be arranged on an individual basis in such cases.

Limited comfort to PRs is afforded by a letter from the Inland Revenue to the Law Society dated 11 February 1991 which states:

'The Capital Taxes Office will not usually pursue for inheritance tax personal representatives who

— after making the fullest enquiries that are reasonably practicable in the circumstances to discover lifetime transfers, and so
— having done all in their power to make full disclosure of them to the Board of Inland Revenue
— have obtained a certificate of discharge and distributed the estate before a chargeable lifetime transfer comes to light.

This statement ... is made without prejudice to the application in an appropriate case of s 199(2) Inheritance Tax Act 1984.'    **[30.49]**

*Land* In addition to persons who are liable for IHT on death, real property (including a share in land under a trust for sale) is automatically subject to an HMRC charge from the date of death until the date when the IHT is paid (IHTA 1984 s 237(1)(a) and see *Howarth's Executors v IRC* (1997)).    **[30.50]**

f)    *Payment of tax: the instalment option* (*IHTA 1984 ss 227, 8*)

To obtain a grant of representation, PRs must pay all the IHT for which they are liable when they deliver their account to HMRC.

However, in the case of certain property the tax may, at the option of the PRs, be paid in ten-yearly instalments with the first instalment falling due six months after the end of the month of death. The object of this facility is to prevent the particular assets from having to be sold by the PRs in order to raise the necessary IHT.

The instalment option is available on the following assets:

(1)    land, freehold or leasehold, wherever situate;

(2)    shares or securities in a company which gave the deceased control of that company ('control' is defined as voting control on all questions affecting the company as a whole);

(3)    a non-controlling holding of shares or securities in an unquoted company (ie a company which is not quoted on a recognised Stock Exchange) where HMRC is satisfied that payment of the tax in one lump sum would cause 'undue hardship';

(4)   a non-controlling holding as in (3) above where the tax on the shares or securities and on other property carrying the instalment option comprises at least 20% of the tax due from that particular person (in the same capacity);

(5)   other non-controlling shareholdings in unquoted companies, where the value of the shares exceeds £20,000 and either their nominal value is at least 10% of the nominal value of all the issued shares in the company, or the shares are ordinary shares whose nominal value is at least 10% of the nominal value of all ordinary shares in the company; and

(6)   a business or a share in a business, eg a partnership share.

An added attraction of paying by instalments is that, generally, no interest is charged so long as each instalment is paid on the due date. In the event of late payment the interest charge is merely on the outstanding instalment. Interest is, however, charged on the total outstanding IHT liability (even if the instalments are paid on time) in the case of land that is not a business asset and shares in investment companies. If the asset subject to the instalment option is sold, the outstanding instalments of IHT become payable at once. Note that the definition of 'qualifying property' for these purposes is not subject to the same limitations as business property relief with regard to investment businesses and excepted assets: see **[31.58]**.          **[30.51]**

*Exercising the option: cashflow benefit* If the instalment option is exercised the first instalment is, as already mentioned, payable six months after the month of death. Hence, PRs will normally exercise the option *in order to pay as little IHT as possible before obtaining the grant.* Once the grant has been obtained they may then discharge the IHT on the instalment property in one lump sum. PRs should, however, bear in mind that some IHT will usually be payable before the grant. The necessary cash may be obtained from the deceased's account at either a bank or a building society (building societies, in particular, will commonly issue cheques to cover the initial inheritance tax payable); from the sale of property for which a grant is not necessary; or by means of a personal loan from a beneficiary. If a loan has to be raised commercially, the interest thereon will qualify for income tax relief for 12 months from the making of the loan so long as it is on a loan account (not by way of overdraft) and is used to pay the tax attributable to personal property (including leaseholds and land held on trust for sale: TA 1988 s 364).

After the grant has been obtained, if the remaining tax is not paid off at once, PRs may vest the asset in the relevant beneficiary on the understanding that he will discharge the unpaid instalments of tax. Adequate security should, however, be taken in such cases because if the beneficiary defaults, the PRs remain liable for the outstanding IHT (see *Howarth's Executors v IRC* (1997)). In the case of a specific gift which bears its own IHT and that qualifies for the instalment option, the decision whether to discharge the entire IHT bill once probate has been obtained should be left to the legatee. PRs should not make a unilateral decision (see further **[30.56]**).          **[30.52]**

*Certificates of discharge* Once PRs have paid all the outstanding IHT they are entitled to a certificate of discharge under IHTA 1984 s 239(2).          **[30.53]**

*Instalments on chargeable lifetime transfers* As already discussed, the instalment option may also be available when a chargeable *inter vivos* transfer is made (see **[28.174]**) and when IHT becomes payable on a PET or additional IHT on a chargeable transfer. In these situations, however, further requirements must be satisfied before the option can be claimed. The donee must have retained the original property or, if it has been sold, have used the proceeds to purchase qualifying replacement property (for a discussion of these requirements in the context of business relief see **[31.59]**). Further, when the property consisted of unquoted shares or securities those assets must remain unquoted from the date of transfer to the date of death (IHTA 1984 s 227(1A)).                                                            **[30.54]**

### 2    Allocating the burden of IHT

a)    *The general rule*

HMRC is satisfied once the IHT due on the estate has been paid. As far as the PRs and beneficiaries under the will are concerned, the further question arises as to how the tax should be borne as between the beneficiaries: eg should the tax attributable to a specific legacy be paid out of the residue as a testamentary expense or is it charged on the property (the specific legacy)? The answer is particularly important when specific legacies are combined with exempt or partially exempt residue, since, if the IHT is to be paid out of that residue, the grossing-up calculation under IHTA 1984 s 38 (see **[30.96]**) will be necessary and will result in more IHT being payable.            **[30.55]**

b)    *Impact on will drafting*

As a general rule, a testator can, and should, stipulate expressly in his will where the IHT on a specific bequest is to fall. If the will makes no provision for the burden of tax, the general principle is that IHT on UK unsettled property is a testamentary expense payable from residue. Under the estate duty regime land had, in such cases, borne its own duty, but the Scottish case of *Re Dougal* (1981) decided that the IHT legislation drew no distinction between realty and personalty and the matter was put beyond doubt by IHTA 1984 s 211.

#### EXAMPLE 30.15

In Lyslie's will his landed estate is left to his son and his stocks and shares to his daughter. The residue is left to his surviving spouse. In addition he owned a country cottage jointly with his brother, Ernie.
(1)    IHT on the specific gifts of the land and securities is borne by the residue in the absence of any provision to the contrary in Lyslie's will. Note that the spouse exemption therefore only applies to exempt from charge what is left after the payment of IHT on the specific gifts.
(2)    IHT on the joint property is paid by the PRs who are given the right to recover that tax from the other joint tenant(s): IHTA 1984 s 211(3).

In drafting wills and administering estates the following matters should be borne in mind:

(1) When drafting a new will, expressly state whether bequests are tax-bearing or are free of tax.

(2) Old wills which have been drawn up but are not yet in force should be checked to ensure that provision has been made for the payment of IHT on gifts of realty. The will may have been drafted on the assumption that such gifts bear their own tax in which case amendments will be necessary.

(3) IHT on foreign property and joint property will always be borne by the beneficiary unless the will provides to the contrary. If the will provides for a legacy to be 'tax free' these words are likely to be limited to UK tax: accordingly if it is intended that the estate should also pay any foreign taxes an express statement to that effect needs to be included (see *re Norbury* (1939)).

Assuming that the will contains a specific tax-bearing legacy, how will the IHT, in practice, be paid on it? As the PRs are primarily liable to HMRC for the IHT, they will pay that tax in order to obtain probate and either deduct it from the legacy (eg if it is a pecuniary legacy) or recover it from the legatee. For specific legacies of other property (eg land or chattels), the PRs have the power to sell, mortgage or charge the property in order to recover the tax. If they instead (usually at the legatee's request) propose to transfer the asset to him, they should ensure that they are given sufficient guarantees that the tax will be refunded to them. Where the PRs pay IHT that is not a testamentary expense (ie on all tax-bearing gifts; joint property and foreign property), they have a right to recover that sum from the person in whom the property is vested (IHTA 1984 s 211(3)). **[30.56]**

### c) *IHTA 1984 s 41; Re Benham's Will Trusts and Re Ratcliffe*

*IHTA 1984 s 41* As a qualification to the general rules stated above, a chargeable share of residue must always bear its own tax so that the burden of tax cannot be placed on an exempt slice of residue and any provision to the contrary in a will is void (IHTA 1984 s 41). **[30.57]**

*The Benham case* The implications of IHTA 1984 s 41 in the context of a will containing both chargeable and exempt gifts of residue were considered in *Re Benham's Will Trusts, Lockhart v Harker, Read and the Royal National Lifeboat Institution* (1995) in which residue was left as follows:

(1) upon trust to pay debts, funeral and testamentary expenses;

(2) subject thereto 'to pay the same to those beneficiaries as are living at my death and who are listed in List A and List B hereunder written in such proportions as will bring about the result that the aforesaid beneficiaries named in List A shall receive 3.2 times as much as the aforesaid beneficiaries named in List B and in each case for their own absolute and beneficial use and disposal'.

List A contained one charity and a number of non-charitable beneficiaries; and List B contained a number of charities and non-charitable beneficiaries.

By an originating summons, the executor asked whether, in view of IHTA 1984 s 41 and the terms of the will, the non-charitable beneficiaries should receive their shares subject to IHT, or whether their shares should be grossed up.

On this question, there were three theoretical possibilities:

(1)   the non-charitable beneficiaries received their respective shares subject to IHT, which would mean that they would receive less than the charities; *or*

(2)   the non-charitable beneficiaries should have their respective shares grossed up, so that they received the same net sum as the charities; *or*

(3)   the IHT was paid as part of the testamentary expenses under clause 3(A), so that the balance was distributed equally between the non-charitable beneficiaries and the charities.

The court agreed that the third possibility was precluded by s 41. However, it did not agree that the charities should receive more than the non-charitable beneficiaries. The plain intention of the testatrix was that each beneficiary, whether charitable or non-charitable, should receive the same as the other beneficiaries on the relevant list. The court therefore concluded that the non-charitable beneficiaries' shares should be grossed up.    **[30.58]**

*The available options* In analysing the effect of this case, consider an estate of £100,000 to be divided between wife and daughter (although remember that the problem arises whenever residue is divided between exempt and chargeable beneficiaries: for instance, between relatives on the one hand and a charity on the other).

**EXAMPLE 30.16**

Net residue of £100,000 to be divided equally between surviving spouse and daughter. Estate rate 40%.

(1)   *Option 1*: deduct tax on £50,000 and divide balance (£80,000) equally: prohibited by s 41.

(2)   *Option 2*: divide equally so that spouse gets £50,000 and daughter's £50,000 then bears tax so that she ends up with £30,000.

(3)   *Option 3*: gross up daughter's share so that both end up with the same:
      ie $x + (^{100}\!/_{60})\ x = £100,000$
      $x = £37,500$
      Both receive £37,500; gross value of daughter's share is £62,500.

|          | Spouse (£) | Daughter (£) | Tax man (£) |
|----------|------------|--------------|-------------|
| Option 1 | 40,000     | 40,000       | 20,000      |
| Option 2 | 50,000     | 30,000       | 20,000      |
| Option 3 | 37,500     | 37,500       | 25,000      |

The difficulty posed by *Benham* lies in the court's assertion that:

'the plain intention of the testatrix is that at the end of the day each beneficiary, whether charitable or non-charitable, should receive the same as the other beneficiaries ...'.

On one view the case therefore depends upon its own facts and, in particular, on the wishes of the testatrix. However, the ready inclusion (as a matter of construction) of a grossing-up clause in all cases where:

(1)   the residue is left to exempt and non-exempt beneficiaries;

(2)   the will provides for them to take in equal shares and there is no evidence that the testator did not intend *Benham* to apply; and

(3) the value of the estate is such that IHT is payable on the chargeable portion of residue;

would have gone against the existing practice which had been to apply s 41 (*Option 2*, in *Example 30.16* above) in such cases. **[30.59]**

*Will drafting after Benham* It is important that the whole matter is explained to the testator (with a suitable example to illustrate the fiscal and other consequences of the grossing-up route) and that the will is then drafted *either* to provide for a division of residue into shares before imposing the tax liability *or* to incorporate a grossing-up clause. The drafting should make it clear whether *Option 2* or *Option 3* is being adopted. **[30.60]**

*The Ratcliffe case Re Ratcliffe* (1999) was brought as a test case to resolve the problems which had resulted from the *Benham* decision. The testatrix left some £2.2m to be divided in accordance with the following residue clause:

'4 I give devise and bequeath all my real and personal estate whatsoever and wheresoever not hereby otherwise disposed of unto my Trustees upon trust to sell and convert the same into money with power at their absolute discretion to postpone any such sale and conversion for so long as they shall think fit without being answerable for any loss and after payment thereout of my debts and funeral and testamentary expenses to stand possessed of the residue as to one-half part thereof for John Hugh McMullan and Edward Brownlow McMullan (the sons of my cousin Helen McMullan) in equal shares absolutely ... and as to the remainder of my estate upon trust for the following Charities in equal shares ...'

If *Option 2* in *Example 30.16* above were followed the charities would receive £1.12m; the chargeable beneficiaries £720,000 and tax payable would be £400,000; if *Option 3*, the charities and chargeable beneficiaries would each share £870,000 and the IHT would rise to £500,000.

Blackburne J indicated that the matter turned on a true construction of the will that, in this case, pointed to the intention to divide equally the residuary estate including the tax attributable to the chargeable beneficiaries' share (ie the *Option 2* approach). He accepted that a will could result in grossing-up the chargeable beneficiaries' share (ie *Option 3*) but 'much clearer wording would be needed than the common form wording' actually used'. He dismissed the decision (and comments of the judge) in *Benham* as follows:

'If I had thought that *Re Benham's Will Trusts* laid down some principle, then, unless convinced that it was wrong, I would have felt that I should follow it. I am not able to find that it does and, accordingly, I do not feel bound to follow it'.

Although the case was set down for appeal, a compromise was agreed. **[30.61]**

*Administering estates after Ratcliffe* In cases where the will does not put the matter beyond doubt practitioners are now faced with two conflicting decisions, *Benham* and *Ratcliffe*. Of the two, the latter is to be preferred given that the judge carefully reviewed all the authorities including *Benham*: that case had involved, of course, a most obscurely drafted will and the wide *dicta* on grossing-up were not relevant to the case itself. **[30.62]**

## 3   Cases where IHT has to be recalculated

In a limited number of instances IHT paid on a deceased's estate will need to be recalculated.                                                                                        **[30.63]**
*Cases where sale proceeds are substituted for the death valuation* (see **[30.7]**.) **[30.64]**

*As the result of a variation or disclaimer* Such instruments, if made within two years of the death, may be read back into the original will which *may* necessitate a recalculation of the tax payable (see **[30.153]**).                 **[30.65]**

*Discretionary will trusts* If the conditions of IHTA 1984 s 144 are satisfied, tax is calculated as if the testator had provided in his will for the dispositions of the trustees (see **[30.145]**).                                                         **[30.66]**

*Orders under the Inheritance (Provision for Family and Dependants) Act 1975* When the court exercises its powers under s 2 of the 1975 Act to order financial provision out of the deceased's estate for his family and dependants, the order is treated as made by the deceased and may result in there having been an under- or overpayment of IHT on death. Any application under this Act should normally be made within six months of the testator's death, so that the PRs will have some warning that adjustments to the IHT bill may have to be made. Further adjustments to the tax bill may be required if the court makes an order under s 10 of the Act reclaiming property given away by the deceased in the six years prior to his death with the intention of defeating a claim for financial provision under the Act. In this case, the deceased's cumulative total of chargeable lifetime transfers is reduced by the gift reclaimed. This, of itself, may affect the rate at which tax is charged on the deceased's estate on death. Also the value of the reclaimed property and any tax repaid on it falls into the deceased's estate thus necessitating a recalculation of the IHT payable on death.

These rules are bolstered up by a somewhat obscure anti-avoidance provision in IHTA 1984 s 29A. It is relevant when there is an exempt transfer on death (eg to the surviving spouse) and that beneficiary then, in satisfaction of a claim against the estate of the deceased, disposes of property 'not derived from the death transfer'.                                         **[30.67]–[30.90]**

**EXAMPLE 30.17**

A dies leaving everything to Mrs A. Dependant B has a claim against A's estate but is 'bought off' by Mrs A making a payment (out of her own resources) of £150,000.
(1)   *In the absence of specific legislation:* the arrangement would probably be a PET by Mrs A to B and so free from IHT provided that Mrs A survived by seven years. Alternatively it could be argued that there was no transfer of value since the compromise was a commercial arrangement under IHTA 1984 s 10. No IHT was, of course, charged on A's death.
(2)   *Position under s 29A:* A's will is deemed amended to include a specific gift of £150,000 to B with the remainder (only) passing to Mrs A. Accordingly a recalculation will be necessary and an immediate IHT charge will arise.

## IV PROBLEMS CREATED BY THE PARTIALLY EXEMPT TRANSFER

### 1  When do ss 36–42 apply?

In many cases the calculation of the IHT bill on death will be straightforward. Difficulties may, however, arise when a particular combination of dispositions is made in a will. IHTA 1984 ss 36–42 provide machinery for resolving these problems with a method of calculating the gross value of the gifts involved and, accordingly, the IHT payable. Consider, first, a number of instances where the calculation of the IHT on death poses no special difficulties:
[**30.91**]

*Where all the gifts are taxable* A leaves all his property to be divided equally amongst his four children. In this case the whole of A's estate is charged to IHT.
[**30.92**]

*Where all the gifts are exempt* eg A leaves all his property to a spouse and/or a charity. In this case the estate is untaxed.
[**30.93**]

*Where specific gifts are exempt and the residue is chargeable* eg A leaves £100,000 to his spouse and the residue of £500,000 to his children. Here the gift to the spouse is exempt, but IHT is charged on the residue of £500,000 so that only the balance will be paid to the children.
[**30.94**]

*Where specific gifts are chargeable and bear their own tax under the terms of the will and the residue is exempt:* eg A leaves a specific tax-bearing gift of £300,000 to his niece and the residue to his spouse. The spouse receives the residue after deduction of the £300,000 gift; IHT is calculated on the £300,000 and is borne by the niece.
[**30.95**]

*Where there are no specific gifts and part of the residue is exempt, part chargeable* eg A leaves his estate to be divided equally between his son and his spouse. As already discussed the chargeable portion of residue must always bear its own tax; any provision in the will to the contrary is void (IHTA 1984 s 41: see [**30.57**]).

There are bequests where the calculation of the IHT is not so obvious and it becomes necessary to apply the rules in ss 36–42. Taking the simplest illustration, consider a will containing a specific gift which is chargeable but does not bear its own IHT and residue which is exempt, eg A's estate on death is valued at £630,000 and he leaves £345,000 to his daughter with remainder to his surviving spouse. As previously explained, the specific gift of £345,000 will be tax-free unless the will provides to the contrary. The problem that arises is to decide how much IHT should be charged on the specific gift and this involves grossing-up that gift. With the simplified IHT rate structure, grossing-up has become relatively straightforward and, in the tax year 2006–07, the IHT payable will be two-thirds of the amount by which the chargeable legacies exceed the available nil rate band. Hence, assuming that A has an unused nil rate band of £285,000, tax payable on the daughter's legacy will be two-thirds of £345,000 – £285,000: ie £40,000. As a result:

(1) The gross value of the legacy becomes £385,000 and the daughter receives the correct net sum of £345,000 after deducting IHT at 40% on the amount by which the gross legacy exceeds the available nil rate band.

(2) The £40,000 tax is paid out of the residue leaving the surviving spouse with £245,000. **[30.96]**

*Business and agricultural property* When business property is specifically given to a beneficiary that person will benefit from the appropriate relief but in other cases the benefit of the relief is apportioned between the exempt and chargeable parts of the estate (IHTA 1984 s 39A). **[30.97]**

### EXAMPLE 30.18

Deceased's estate is valued at £1m and includes business property (qualifying for 50% relief) worth £600,000. He left a £600,000 legacy to his widow and the residue to his daughter.

|  | £ |
|---|---|
| Estate | 1,000,000 |
| *Less:* 50% relief on business property | 300,000 |
| Value transferred | 700,000 |

(1) Legacy of £600,000 to widow is multiplied by

$$\frac{R \ (\text{value transferred})}{U \ (\text{estate before relief})} = \frac{£700,000}{£1,000,000} = £420,000$$

(2) Accordingly the value attributed to the residue (given to the daughter) is:

$$400,000 \times \frac{R \ (£700,000)}{U \ (£1,000,000)} = £280,000$$

(3) IHT is therefore charged on £280,000.

*Notes:*

(1) Had relief at 100% been available the taxable sum would have been £160,000.

(2) The lowest tax bill results if the agricultural or business property is specifically given to a non-exempt beneficiary. 'Specific gift' is inadequately defined in

IHTA 1984 s 42(1) and the following points may be noted:

(i) an appropriation of business property in satisfaction of a pecuniary legacy does not count as a specific gift;

(ii) a direction to pay a pecuniary legacy 'out of' business property is likewise not a specific gift of business property (IHTA 1984 s 39A(6));

(iii) it is possible to employ a formula to leave business property equal in value to the testator's nil rate band *after* relief at 50%;

(iv) a defectively drafted will may be cured by an instrument of variation whereby a specific gift of business property is 'read back' into the will.

(3) Difficulties can be caused if a nil rate band clause is used in a will and the estate includes business or agricultural property as illustrated in the following example.

**EXAMPLE 30.19**

(1) Jill leaves an estate valued at £1m that includes a shareholding in a private company (qualifying for 100% business property relief (BPR)) valued at £570,000.

If she leaves the shares to her son Paul by way of specific gift and residue to her husband Jack, no tax is payable.

If she leaves a cash gift of £570,000 to son Paul (this gift to bear its own tax) and residue to husband, the son's gift will attract relief at 50% (being the appropriate part of the business property relief) so its value will reduce to £285,000. After deduction of the nil rate band the taxable value is nil.

(2) Jill instead leaves a will which provides that her son will take 'a cash sum which is the largest amount that can be given without any Inheritance Tax being payable on the transfer of value of my estate which I am deemed to make immediately before my death'. She had anticipated that her son would take £285,000 (being the amount of the nil rate band legacy) although she was aware that if she made chargeable lifetime gifts within seven years of her death, the amount her son would take under the will on her death would be reduced.

With 100% BPR, however, the amount which her son will take, assuming her nil rate band is unused on death, is £570,000 (which will be reduced by its share of BPR to £285,000, the amount of the nil rate band). The consequence will be that Jill's husband Jack will receive far less than his wife had anticipated when the will was drafted. The effect would be even more dramatic if business property in the estate was worth, say, £800,000. In this case, the cash gift that Paul could take without payment of tax would leave Jack with nothing!

(3) This unintentional result would have been avoided if the will had stated that her son should take:

'a cash sum which is the lesser of:

(i) the largest amount that can be given without any Inheritance Tax being payable on the transfer of value of my estate which I am deemed to make immediately before my death, and

(ii) the upper limit of the nil rate band in the table of rates of tax applicable on my death in Schedule 1 to the Inheritance Tax Act 1984.'

## 2   Effect of previous chargeable transfers on the ss 36–42 calculation

In considering the application of ss 36–42, it has so far been assumed that the deceased had made no previous chargeable lifetime transfers in the seven years before his death. If he has, any specific gift on death must be grossed up taking account of those cumulative lifetime transfers because they may affect the rate at which tax is charged on the estate on death.                **[30.98]**

**EXAMPLE 30.20**

A's estate on death is valued at £250,000 and he leaves £90,000 tax-free to his son and the residue to a charity. A had made gross lifetime transfers in the previous seven years of £285,000.

The lifetime gifts have wiped out A's nil rate band and therefore IHT on the specific legacy of £90,000 is two-thirds of £90,000 = £60,000. Accordingly, the gross legacy is £150,000 so that the charity is left with £100,000.

## 3   Double grossing-up

IHTA 1984 ss 36–42 also deal with the more complex problems that arise if specific tax-free gifts are combined with chargeable gifts bearing their own tax, and an exempt residue.                                                    **[30.99]**

### a)   *The problem*

Assume that B makes a specific bequest of £300,000 tax free to his son, and leaves a gift of £90,000 bearing its own tax to his daughter with residue of £400,000 (before deducting any IHT chargeable to residue) going to his spouse. To gross up the specific tax-free gift of £300,000 as if it were the only chargeable estate would produce insufficient IHT bearing in mind that there is an additional chargeable legacy of £90,000. On the other hand, if the £300,000 were grossed up at the estate rate applicable to £415,000 (ie the two gifts of £300,000 and £90,000) the resulting tax would be too high because the £90,000 gift should not be grossed up. Further, to gross up £300,000 at the estate rate applicable to the whole estate including the exempt residue would produce too much tax because this assumes, wrongly, that the residue is taxable.                                                              **[30.100]**

### b)   *The solution*

The solution provided in ss 36–42 is to gross up the specific tax-free gift at the estate rate applicable to a hypothetical chargeable estate consisting of the grossed-up specific tax-free gift and the gifts bearing their own tax. The procedure, known as double grossing-up, is as follows:

*Step 1* Gross up the specific tax-free gift of £300,000 by multiplying excess over nil rate band by ⅗: £15,000 × ⅗ = £25,000
£25,000 + £300,000 = £325,000

*Step 2* Add to this figure the tax-bearing gift of £90,000 making a hypothetical chargeable estate of £415,000.

*Step 3* Calculate IHT on £415,000 using the death table = £52,000. Then convert to an estate rate: namely

$$\frac{52,000}{415,000} \times 100 = 12.53\%$$

*Step 4* Gross up the specific tax-free gift a second time at this rate of 12.53%:

$$£300,000 \times \frac{100}{100 - 12.53} = £342,974.73$$

*Step 5* The chargeable part of the estate now consists of the grossed-up specific gift (£342,974.73) and the gift bearing its own tax (£90,000) = £432,974.73.

*Step 6* On the figure of £432,974.73, IHT is recalculated at £59,189.89

$$\frac{59,189.89}{432,974.73} \times 100 = 13.67\%$$

*Step 7* The grossed-up specific tax-free gift (£342,974.73) is then charged at this rate (13.67%) = tax of £46,886.39.

It should be noted that the IHT on specific tax-free gifts must always be paid from the residue and it is only the balance that is exempt so that the surviving spouse will receive £400,000–£46,886.39 = £353,113.61. The tax-bearing gift of £90,000 will of course be taxed at 13.67%, but the tax (ie £12,303) will be borne by the daughter. **[30.101]**

c) *Conclusion*

Sections 36–42 are relevant whenever a tax-free specific gift is mixed with an exempt residue, and, if tax-bearing gifts are also included in the will, then a double grossing-up calculation is required. Logically, to gross up only twice is indefensible since the estate rate established at *Step 6* should then be used to gross up further the £300,000 (ie repeat *Step 4*) and so on and so on! Thankfully, the statute only requires the grossing-up calculation to be done twice with the consequence that a small saving in IHT results! **[30.102]**

## 4 Problems where part of residue is exempt, part chargeable

So far we have been concerned with a wholly exempt residue. What, however, happens if part of the residue is chargeable? For example, A, whose estate is worth £500,000, leaves a specific tax-free gift of £300,000 to his son; a tax-bearing gift of £90,000 to his daughter; and the residue equally to his widow and his nephew.

The method of calculating the IHT is basically the same as in the double grossing-up example above in that the chargeable portion of the residue (half to nephew) must be added to the hypothetical chargeable estate in *Step 2* to calculate the assumed estate rate. The difficulty is caused because, although IHT on grossed-up gifts is payable before the division of residue into chargeable and non-chargeable portions, the IHT on the nephew's portion of the residue must be deducted from his share of residue after it has been divided (IHTA 1984 s 41). To take account of this, the method for calculating the IHT payable in such cases is amended as follows:

*Step 1* Gross up the specific tax-free gift of £300,000 to £325,000.

*Step 2* Calculate the hypothetical chargeable estate by adding to the grossed-up gift of £325,000: (1) the tax-bearing gift of £90,000 and (2) the chargeable residue:

|  | £ | £ |
|---|---|---|
| Estate |  | 500,000 |
| Less: grossed-up gift | 325,000 |  |
| tax-bearing gift | 90,000 | 415,000 |
|  |  | 85,000 |

The nephew's share (the chargeable residue) is half of £85,000 = £42,500.
This results in a hypothetical chargeable estate of:
£325,000 + £42,500 + £90,000 = £457,500
*Step 3* Calculate the 'assumed estate rate' on £457,500:
IHT on £457,500 = £68,800

Estate rate is

$$\frac{68,800}{457,500} \times 100 = 15.04\%$$

*Step 4* Gross up the specific tax-free gift at this rate of 15.04%:

$$£300,000 \times \frac{100}{100 - 15.04} = £353,107.32$$

*Step 5* The chargeable part of the estate now consists of:

|  | £ | £ |
|---|---|---|
| Estate |  | 500,000 |
| *Less:* grossed-up gift | 353,107.32 |  |
| tax-bearing gift | 90,000.00 | 443,107.32 |
|  |  | 56,892.68 |

Nephew's share is ½ × £56,892.68 = £28,446.34
Therefore, chargeable estate is
£28,446.34 + £90,000 + £353,107.32 = £471,553.66
*Step 6* Calculate the estate rate on the chargeable estate of £471,553,66:
IHT on £471,553.66 = £74,621.46
Estate rate is

$$\frac{74,621.46}{471,553.66} \times 100 = 15.82\%$$

*Step 7* The grossed-up specific tax-free gift of £353,107.32 is taxed at the rate of 15.82% = £55,877.79.

*Step 8* The tax-bearing gift of £90,000 is taxed at 15.82% = £14,238. This tax is paid by the daughter.

*Step 9* The residue remaining is £500,000 − (£300,000 + £55,877.79 + £90,000) = £54,122.21. This is then divided:

Half residue to spouse = £27,061.11

Half residue to nephew = £27,061.11 less IHT calculated at a rate of 15.82% on £28,446.34 (ie the nephew's share of the residue at *Step 5*, above). Therefore, the tax on the nephew's share is £4,500.21 so that the nephew receives £22,561.                                    **[30.103]–[30.120]**

V   ABATEMENT

Although ss 36–42 are mainly concerned with calculating the chargeable estate in cases where there is an exempt residue, they also deal with certain related matters:

*Allocating relief where gifts exceed an exempt limit* A transfer may be partly exempt only because it includes gifts which together exceed an exempt limit, eg a transfer to a non-UK domiciled spouse which exceeds £55,000. To deal with such cases IHTA 1984 s 38(2) provides for the exemption to be allocated between the various gifts as follows:

(1) Specific tax-bearing gifts take precedence over other gifts.
(2) Specific tax-free gifts receive relief in the proportion that their values bear to each other.
(3) All specific gifts take precedence over gifts of residue. **[30.121]**

*Abatement of gifts* If a transferor makes gifts in his will which exceed the value of his estate, those gifts must be abated in accordance with IHTA 1984 s 37. There are two cases to consider:

(1) Where the gifts exceed the transferor's estate without regard to any tax payable, the gifts abate according to the rules contained in the Administration of Estates Act 1925 and tax is charged on the abated gifts.

### EXAMPLE 30.21

A testator's net estate is worth £300,000. He left his house worth £100,000 to his nephew, the gift to bear its own tax, and a general tax-free legacy of £300,000 to a charity. Under IHTA 1984 s 37(1) the legacy must abate to £200,000 to be paid to the charity free of tax. The house will bear its own tax.

(2) Where the transferor's estate is only insufficient to meet the gifts as grossed up under the rules in ss 36–42, abatement is governed by IHTA 1984 s 37(2). The order in which the gifts are abated depends on the general law. **[30.122]–[30.140]**

## VI SPECIFIC PROBLEMS ON DEATH

### 1 Commorientes

#### a) *The problem*

Where A and B leave their property to each other and are both killed in a common catastrophe or otherwise die in circumstances such that it is not clear in what order they died, LPA 1925 s 184 stipulates that the younger is deemed to have survived the elder. Hence, if A was the elder, he is presumed to have died first so that his property passes to B and IHT will be chargeable. B's will leaving everything to A will not take effect because of the prior death of A so that his assets (including his inheritance from A) will pass on intestacy. IHT would *prima facie* be chargeable. The result is that property bequeathed by the elder would (subject to quick succession relief) be charged to IHT twice. **[30.141]**

#### b) *The IHT solution*

To prevent this double charge, IHTA 1984 s 4(2) provides that A and B 'shall be assumed to have died at the same instant'. Hence, A's estate is charged only once—on his death; it is not taxed a second time on B's death since the gift is treated as lapsing. LPA 1925 s 184 is, therefore, ousted in order to avoid a double charge to IHT, but it still governs the actual destination of the property bequeathed by A and the question of whether the transfer on A's death is chargeable. This may produce bizarre results: **[30.142]**

**EXAMPLE 30.22**

(1)   Fred (aged 60) and his wife Wilma (aged 55) are both killed in a car crash. Fred had left all his property to Wilma, Wilma had left all her property to their son Barnie. According to LPA 1925 s 184, the order of deaths is Fred then Wilma and Fred's property, therefore, passes to Wilma and thence to Barnie. However, the effect of IHTA 1984 s 4(2) is to impose IHT on Fred's death only; ie on the transfer to Wilma which is exempt from IHT, so that Barnie acquires Fred's property free from IHT.

*Compare:*

(2)   Assume that Fred and Barnie are killed in the same crash and that Fred had left his property to Barnie who in turn had left his estate to charity. Although the property passes on Fred's death through Barnie's estate to the charity (which is exempt from IHT), there is a chargeable transfer on Fred's death to Barnie.

## 2   Survivorship clauses

To inherit property on a death it is necessary only to survive the testator so that if the beneficiary dies immediately after inheriting the property, the two deaths could mean two IHT charges. Some relief is provided by quick succession relief (see **[30.144]**, but the prudent testator may provide in his will for the property to pass to the desired beneficiary only if that person survives him for a stated period. Such provisions are referred to as survivorship clauses and IHTA 1984 s 92 states that provided the clause does not exceed six months there will be (at most) only a single IHT charge.

**EXAMPLE 30.23**

T leaves £100,000 to A 'if he survives me by six months. If he does not the money is to go to B'.

The effect of IHTA 1984 s 92 is to leave matters in suspense for up to six months and then to read the will in the light of what has happened. Hence, if A survives for six months it is as if the will had provided '£100,000 to A'; if he dies before the end of that period, it is as if the will had provided for £100,000 to go to B. Accordingly, two charges to IHT are avoided; there will merely be the one chargeable occasion when the testator dies.

In principle, it is good will drafting to include survivorship clauses. The danger of choosing a period in excess of six months is that IHTA 1984 s 92 will not apply so that the bequest will be settled property to which ordinary charging principles will apply. If a longer period is essential, insert a two-year discretionary trust into the will (see **[30.145]**).          **[30.143]**

## 3   Quick succession relief (IHTA 1984 s 141)

Quick succession relief offers a measure of relief against two charges to IHT when two chargeable events occur within five years of each other.

For unsettled property quick succession relief is only given on a death where the value of the deceased's estate had been increased by a chargeable transfer (*inter vivos* or on death) to the deceased made within the previous five years. It is not necessary for the property then transferred to be part of the deceased's estate when he dies.

In the case of settled property the relief is only available (and necessary) for interest in possession trusts. It is given whenever an interest in possession terminates and hence can be deliberately activated by the life tenant assigning or surrendering his interest. The earlier transfer in the case of settled property will be either the creation of the settlement or the termination of a prior life interest.

**EXAMPLE 30.24**

S, who had settled property by will on A for life, B for life, C absolutely, died in 2004. In 2005 A dies and in 2006 B surrenders his life interest.

2004  IHT will be chargeable.

2005  Quick succession relief is available on A's death. The chargeable transfer in the previous five years was the creation of the settlement in 2002.

2006  Quick succession relief is available on the surrender of B's life interest. The chargeable transfer in the previous five years was the termination of A's life interest.

The relief reduces the IHT on the second chargeable occasion. IHT is calculated in the usual way and then reduced by a sum dependent upon two factors. First, how long has elapsed since the first chargeable transfer was made. The percentage of relief is available as follows:

100% if previous transfer one year or less before death
80%  if previous transfer one–two years before death
60%  if previous transfer two–three years before death
40%  if previous transfer three–four years before death
20%  if previous transfer four–five years before death.

The second factor is the amount of IHT paid on the first transfer. IHTA 1984 s 141(3) states that the relief is 'a percentage determined as above of the tax charged on so much of the value transferred by the first transfer as is attributable to the increase in the estate of the second transferor'. Hence, if A had left £275,000 to B who died within one year of that gift, the appropriate percentage will be 100% of the tax charged on the transfer from A to B and if the transfer by A had been his only chargeable transfer and had fallen into his nil rate band the relief is 100% × 0!                                        **[30.144]**

**EXAMPLE 30.25 (ASSUMING CURRENT RATES OF IHT THROUGHOUT)**

(1)  *Tax-free legacy/death:* A, who has made no previous chargeable transfers, dies leaving an estate of £570,000 out of which he leaves a tax-free legacy of £285,000 to B. B dies 18 months later leaving an estate of £410,000.

| | | |
|---|---|---|
| (a) | IHT on A's estate | = £114,000 |
| | Proportion paid in respect of tax-free legacy (50%) | = £57,000 |
| (b) | Quick succession relief 80% × £57,000 | = £45,600 |
| | | £ |
| (c) | IHT on B's estate ((£410,000 – £285,000) × 40%) | 50,000 |
| | *Less:* Quick succession relief | 45,600 |
| | IHT payable | 4,400 |

(2)  Diego gives £25,000 to Madonna in October 1999 (a PET). Madonna dies in July 2001 and Diego in January 2002. As a result of Diego's death, the PET is chargeable and IHT of (say) £5,000 is paid by Madonna's estate.

(a)    Quick succession relief (QSR) at 80% is available—on the tax attributable to the increase in the donee's estate.

(b)    The increase in Madonna's estate is £25,000 – £5,000 = £20,000. IHT attributable to that increase is:

$$\frac{20,000}{25,000} \times £5,000 = £4,000$$

(c)    QSR available on Madonna's death is 80% × £4,000 = £3,200.

## 4    Flexible will drafting (IHTA 1984 s 144)

If a testator, who dies before 22 March 2006, created, by his will, a trust without an interest in possession, so long as an event occurs on which tax is chargeable (ie a conventional 'exit' charge, see **[34.23]**) *within two years* of his death, the IHT that would normally arise under the discretionary trust charging rules 'shall not be charged but the Act shall have effect as if the will had provided that on the testator's death the property should be held as it is held after the event' (s 144(2)). In other words the dispositions of the trustees are 'read back' into the will. Where the testator dies on or after 22 March 2006, the provisions will apply equally to will trusts with an interest in possession, except where that interest is an immediate post-death interest or a disabled person's interest (IHTA 1984 s 144(1A) inserted by FA 2006 Sch 20 para 27). Such a trust enables wills to be drafted with some flexibility and is advantageous where, for example, the testator is dying and desires his estate to be divided between his four children, but is not sure of the proportions. By inserting the two-year trust a decision about the final distribution of the estate can be postponed for a further two years. **[30.145]**

### a)    *IHT consequences*

IHT will be charged at the estate rate on the property settled at death but if the ultimate distributions made by the trustees are 'read back' into the will that IHT may need to be recalculated. In *Example 30.26(1)*, for instance, a discretionary trust is ended in favour of the testator's surviving spouse and the reading back provisions result in a repayment of any IHT charged on the death estate. *Example 30.26(2)* reveals an important restriction in the relief afforded by s 144 that only applies if the transfer out of the discretionary trust *would otherwise attract a tax charge*. However, by virtue of FA 2006 Sch 20, both pre- and post-22 March 2006 appointments of immediate post-death interests, trusts for bereaved minors or age18-to-25 trusts (which would not otherwise be the occasion of a charge – for definitions, see **Chapter 32**), may be made without an IHT charge and back-dated to the death.        **[30.146]**

### EXAMPLE 30.26

A creates a flexible trust in his will and the trustees:
(1)    Six months after death appoint the property to A's widow. This appointment is read back to A's death: ie it takes effect as an exempt spouse gift so that there is a resulting IHT repayment.

(2)    As in (1) but the appointment is made two months after death. Now there is no question of reading back since there is no charge imposed on events occurring within three months of the creation of a discretionary trust (IHTA 1984 s 64(4), see [**34.25**]). As a result, the original will remains intact, IHT is charged on the entire estate and the spouse exemption is unused. Although, this result was probably never intended the position has been confirmed by the Court of Appeal in *Frankland v IRC* (1996).

(3)    Six months after A's death on 1 February 2006 appoint the property to a trust for a bereaved minor (see **Chapter 32**). Although no charge is imposed when property is put into this kind of trust (IHTA 1984 s 71A, inserted by FA 2006 Sch 20), the appointment may nevertheless be read back into the will (IHTA 1984 s 144(5) inserted by FA 2006 Sch 20 para 27).

b)   *Theoretical problems and practical uses of s 144*

Because at the date of death property is left on a discretionary trust or, for deaths on or after 22 March 2006, an interest in possession trust that is not an immediate post-death interest or a disabled person's interest, that property is subject to IHT and, in normal circumstances, tax will need to be paid before the PRs can obtain a grant of probate. In cases where the trust is ended (as in *Example 30.26(1)*) by appointment to a surviving spouse there will then be a refund of the tax paid, but nonetheless the estate may have been put at a cashflow disadvantage. In *Fitzwilliam v IRC* (1993) the testator's residuary estate was settled on trusts that gave the trustees power in the 23 months following the death to appoint amongst a discretionary class of beneficiaries. After the expiration of that period the trustees were to pay the income to the testator's widow for the remainder of her life. The executors indicated that they intended to appoint the property to the surviving spouse and the Winchester District Probate Registry therefore accepted that the estate was spouse exempt. This conduct was criticised by the Revenue but Vinelott J did not join in that criticism and pointed out that because the estate was largely composed of agricultural land and chattels it would have been very difficult for the executors to have paid such a bill. This matter was not raised in the higher courts.    **[30.147]**

c)   *Vesting of property issue*

The operation of s 144 was for a time bedevilled by traps. In particular, the Revenue took the view that an appointment could only be made out of a trust that had been properly constituted with the vesting of property in trustees. That by itself was unexceptionable but the Revenue originally considered that this involved either the completion of the administration of the estate or, alternatively, an express assent of property by the PRs to the trustees before any appointment could be made. Helpfully, the Revenue has now abandoned this position and accepts that such trusts are immediately constituted at the date of the testator's death: see further *Capital Taxes News*, July 1990, p 98.
    **[30.148]**

d)   *CGT tie-in*

There is one remaining disadvantage: namely that if an appointment is made out of such a trust which is duly read back under s 144 there can be no question of CGT hold-over relief being available unless the property in the trust qualifies as business assets. There is no equivalent relief to s 144 permitting reading back in CGT legislation. If the estate is not fully administered at the relevant time HMRC does, however, accept that the beneficiaries take *qua* legatees at probate value (see **[21.103]**).                    **[30.149]**

e)   *Uses*

This trust can be used as an alternative to a survivorship clause. Say, for instance, that the testator wants Eric to get the property if he survives him by 18 months failing which Ernie is to receive it. This cannot be achieved by a conventional IHT survivorship clause (which must be limited to six months; see **[30.143]**). If Eric and Ernie are made beneficiaries of a discretionary trust, however, and the trustees know the testator's wishes concerning the distribution of the fund, there is no risk of a double IHT charge in carrying out his wishes.

Such a trust is also attractive as compared with variations and disclaimers. If there is any doubt about who should be given the deceased's estate, it is better to use a trust than to rely upon an appointed legatee voluntarily renouncing a benefit under the will. All the most convincing fiscal arguments will often fail to persuade people to give up property and they cannot be compelled to vary or to disclaim!

Finally, if the estate includes business property which *may* attract IHT relief at 100%, consider leaving that property on discretionary trusts for beneficial class including surviving spouse and issue. If it turns out that relief is *not* available the trustees can appoint the business to the spouse with reading back under s 144. Hence any IHT charge has been avoided.        **[30.150]**

f)   *Precatory trusts*

Instead of imposing a trust, the deceased may be content to leave property subject to a non-binding memorandum of wishes. Such 'precatory trusts' are dealt with by IHTA 1984 s 143 (which provides that if the legatee carries out the wishes within two years of the testator's death there is reading back) and should not be confused with the s 144 'two-year' trust (see *Harding (Loveday's Executors) v IRC* (1997)).                    **[30.151]**

## 5   Channelling through a surviving spouse

In cases where the testator is survived by his spouse, prior to the substantial changes introduced by FA 2006, there was another attractive way of drafting a will in flexible form. Consider the following illustration.

Lord and Lady Y were both possessed of 'serious money'. Lord Y left his property by will as follows:
(1)   as to any unused proportion of his nil rate band on A&M trusts for his collection of grandchildren;
(2)   as to the residue of his estate on a life interest trust for Lady Y with the trustees having the power to terminate that interest (in whole or in part) at any time once (say) six months have elapsed from the date of Lord Y's death. Although there is a power to advance capital it is

understood between Lord and Lady Y that the trustees will in practice exercise their power of termination (probably at different times) and when that happens the property passes into the A&M trust.

Lord Y's will was in standard form: first, he exhausted his nil rate band and then left all his assets to his surviving spouse. On his death, therefore, no IHT would be charged. The intention, however, was that the trustees would revoke the interest in possession of Lady Y either in whole or in part. Restricting the power of revocation until, say, six months had elapsed from death was commonly done in order to avoid any suggestion that Lady Y's interest lacked 'materiality' and so could be ignored. In *Fitzwilliam*, the House of Lords refused to excise an interest in possession lasting one month (compare *Hatton v IRC* (1992) at **[28.103]**). To some extent therefore the six-month period was an arbitrary choice: some draftsmen preferred a 12-month period whilst others were content with a lesser period.

When Lady Y's interest was terminated, she was treated as making a PET (see **[28.45]**). Provided that she survived for seven years IHT would be wholly avoided. Of course, if she had died within that time an IHT charge would then have resulted but it should be stressed that this would not have worsened the position of the couple. Such a tax charge levied at the full rate of 40% would in any event have arisen if Lord Y had directly left the property to his grandchildren. Accordingly, there was no downside to this arrangement and, moreover, the reservation of benefit rules would have no application if, after her life interest was terminated, Lady Y continued to benefit from the property.

The attractions as compared with the s 144 trust are obvious. Had this property been left on a discretionary trust with the beneficiaries including Lady Y and the grandchildren and appointed out to the grandchildren within two years, reading back would have resulted in a tax charge to Lord Y's rates.

The changes introduced by FA 2006 will not only ring the death knell for such arrangements in the future, but will also have an impact on existing arrangements:

(1) Where Lord Y died prior to 22 March 2006, and the A&M trust remains in existence, relief from the relevant property regime (see **Chapter 34**) will continue to be given on or after 6 April 2008 provided only from that date the grandchildren will become absolutely entitled to the settled property (not just an interest in it) by the age of 18 (IHTA 1984 s 71(1)(a) as amended by FA 2006 Sch 20, para 3 (1) and (2)) .

(2) Were Lord Y to die on or after 22 March 2006, then the arrangement would no longer be attractive for two reasons. *First*, the occasion of the termination of Lady Y's interest in possession would no longer qualify as a PET (the circumstances in which the termination of an interest in possession will continue to be a PET are limited to where the successor interest is absolute, a transitional serial interest, a disabled person's interest or a trust for a bereaved minor. These terms are discussed in **Chapter 32**). This in itself would not be a disaster (see above). *Secondly*, A&M trusts created on or after 22 March 2006 no longer enjoy relief from the relevant property regime (unless they are classed as trusts for disabled minors (see **Chapter 32** for a definition), and this depends upon the trust being established under the will of a *parent*). Moreover,

where, on or after 22 March 2006, a beneficiary whose life interest is terminated continues to enjoy the property, the reservation of benefit rules will apply (see [**29.135**]).

Accordingly, a simple alternative would be for the property to be left to Lady Y absolutely and to rely upon her to then make PETs. However, wealthy male testators may be reluctant to leave matters in the control of the surviving spouse.　　　　　　　　　　　　　　　　　　　　　　　　　　　**[30.152]**

## 6　Disclaimers and variations (post mortem tax planning)

It will often be desirable to effect changes in a will after the death of the testator, for instance, to rearrange the dispositions with a view to saving tax (and especially IHT) or to provide for someone who is omitted from the will or who is inadequately provided for. In these cases, persons named in the original will reject a portion of their inheritance; hence, they will (usually) be making a gift. Similar problems arise on an intestacy—indeed the statutory intestacy provisions will often prove even less satisfactory than a will.

So far as both IHT and CGT are concerned certain changes to a will, or to the intestacy rules, are permitted, if made within two years of death, to take effect as if they had been provided for in the original will or intestacy (for IHT, see IHTA 1984 s 142; for CGT, TCGA 1992 s 62(6)–(9): the CGT rules are considered at [**21.121**]). The effect of 'reading back' these changes into the will or amending the intestacy rules is to avoid the possibility of a second charge to IHT and to require a recalculation of the IHT charged on death.

**EXAMPLE 30.27**

T by will leaves property to his three daughters equally. He omits his son with whom he had quarrelled bitterly. The daughters agree to vary the will by providing that the four children take equally and, for the capital taxes, T's original will can be varied to make the desired provision. Provided that the rearrangement is made in writing within two years of T's death no daughter will be taxed on the gift of a part of her share to her brother. Instead tax will be charged as if T had left his estate to his four children equally (so that the IHT liability will be unchanged).

To take advantage of these provisions there must be a voluntary alteration of the testamentary provisions; in the case of enforced alterations: eg as a result of applications under the Inheritance (Provision for Family and Dependants) Act 1975, different provisions apply, see [**30.67**].

No specific alterations were made to IHTA 1984 s 142 by FA 2006. Accordingly, where a testator died prior to 22 March 2006, and a variation to the will has been made on or after that date giving rise to an interest in possession, it will be treated as an interest in possession in existence prior to 22 March 2006 and subject to the former regime applying to interests in possession (see **Chapter 33**). Where the death occurs on or after 22 March 2006, followed by a variation, the new interest in possession will be an immediate post-death interest. This means that it remains possible to take advantage of the spouse/civil partner exemption for interests in possession created by deed of variation within s 142 whenever the deceased died.

Where an A&M trust is created under a variation made on or after 22 March 2006, and is deemed to arise on the testator's death prior to that date, for the purposes of the new regime under FA 2006, it will be treated as in existence on that date and, provided the beneficiaries will become entitled to the trust property itself by the age of 18, then it will receive relief from the relevant property regime (IHTA 1984 s 71(1)(a) as amended by FA 2006 Sch 20, para 3). **[30.153]**

a)   *Permitted ways of altering the will or intestacy*

There are two methods of altering the dispositions of a will or intestacy; by disclaimer or by variation. A *disclaimer* operates as a refusal to accept property and, hence, to be valid, should be made before any act of acceptance has occurred (such as receiving any benefit). When a disclaimer is effected the property passes according to fixed rules of law. It is not possible to disclaim in favour of a particular person. Hence, if a specific bequest is disclaimed the property falls into the residue of the will; if it is the residue itself which is disclaimed the property will pass as on an intestacy. Property can also be disclaimed on intestacy. A disclaimer is, therefore, an all or nothing event; it is not possible to retain part and disclaim the rest of a single gift. If, however, both a specific bequest and a share of residue are left to the same person, the benefit of one could be accepted and the other disclaimed. For a consideration of when a disclaimer can be implied by conduct, see *Cook (exor of Watkins Dec'd) v IRC* (2002).

In a *variation*, the deceased's provisions are altered at the choice of the person effecting the alteration so that the gift is redirected and the fact that some benefit had already accrued before the change (and that the estate had been fully administered) is irrelevant. Any part of a gift can be redirected. Unlike a beneficiary who disclaims, the person who makes the variation has owned an interest in the property of the deceased from the death up to the variation. **[30.154]**

b)   *The IHT rules on variations and disclaimers*

If the following conditions are satisfied the variation or disclaimer is not itself a transfer of value but instead takes effect as if the original will or intestacy had so provided:
(1)   The variation or disclaimer must occur within two years of death. In the case of disclaimers it is likely that action will need to be taken soon after the death otherwise the benefit will have been accepted.
(2)   The variation or disclaimer must be effected by an instrument in writing (in practice a deed should be used), executed by the person who would otherwise benefit.
(3)   In the case of variations, where it is desired to 'read them back' into the original will, it was formerly the case that an election in writing to that effect had to be made to the Revenue (within six months of the variation). This election should have referred to the appropriate statutory provisions and was made by the person making the variation and, where the effect of that election would be to increase the IHT chargeable on the death, also by the PRs. PRs could only refuse to join in the election, however, if they had insufficient assets in their hands to discharge the extra IHT bill (for instance, where administration of the estate had been completed and the assets distributed). No election was

necessary in the case of a disclaimer that, assuming that the other requirements are satisfied, is automatically 'read back' into the will. The separate election required when it was desired to 'read back' the effect of an instrument of variation was abolished for instruments executed after 31 July 2002. To obtain reading back it is now essential that the instrument itself contains a statement to that effect. For many practitioners this change was of limited significance given that they had always included the relevant election in the instrument itself.

(4)    A variation or disclaimer cannot be for money or money's worth, except where there are reciprocal disclaimers or other beneficiaries also disclaim for the ultimate benefit of a third person.

(5)    All property comprised in the deceased's estate immediately before death can be redirected under these provisions *except for* property which the deceased was treated as owning by virtue of an interest in possession in a settlement (although in this case relief may be afforded by IHTA 1984 s 93) and property included in the estate at death because of the reservation of benefit rules.

**EXAMPLE 30.28**

(1)    A and T were beneficial joint tenants of the house they lived in. On the death of T, A can redirect the half share of the property that he acquired by right of survivorship taking advantage of IHTA 1984 s 142 (expressly confirmed in *Tax Bulletin*, October 1995, p 254).

(2)    T by will created a settlement giving C a life interest. C can redirect that interest under IHTA 1984 s 142 (but see below for the position if after C's death it is desired to effect the variation).

(3)    T was the life tenant of a fund—the property now vests in D absolutely. D cannot take advantage of IHTA 1984 s 142 to assign his interest in the settled property. (Notice, however, that IHTA 1984 s 93 permits a beneficiary to disclaim an interest in settled property without that disclaimer being subject to IHT.)

(4)    Mort had been life tenant of a trust fund and on his death the assets passed to his sister Mildred absolutely. He left his free estate equally to his widow and daughter. By a post-death variation the widow gave her half share to the daughter. Assuming that this variation is read back for IHT purposes the extra tax charged on Mort's death will adversely affect the trustees who are not required to consent to the election and are not protected by a deed of discharge (IHTA 1984 s 239(4)).

(5)    Father leaves £100,000 shares in J Sainsbury plc to his daughter. She gives those shares to her son, within two years of his death, but continues to be paid the dividends. She elects to read the gift back into the will of her father and as her gift thereupon takes effect *for all IHT purposes* as if it had been made by the deceased the reservation of benefit rules are inapplicable (see **[29.141]**).

(6)    Boris, domiciled in France, leaves his villa in Tuscany and moneys in his Swiss bank account to his son Gaspard, a UK resident. By a variation of the terms of his will made within two years of Boris' death, the property is settled on discretionary Liechtenstein trusts for the benefit of Gaspard's family. For IHT, reading back ensures that the settlement is excluded property (see **[35.20]**). For the CGT position, see *Example 22.10*.

In the case of variations, the choice to elect or not to elect is with the taxpayer. A similar election operates for CGT but it is not necessary to exercise both IHT and CGT elections; either can be exercised (see **[21.123]**).

PRs of deceased beneficiaries can enter into variations and disclaimers which can be read back into the original will. Further, the estate of a beneficiary alive at the testator's death can be increased by such a variation or disclaimer (see *Tax Bulletin*, February 1995, p 194). **[30.155]**

**EXAMPLE 30.29**

(1) T leaves property to his wealthy brother. The brother wishes to redirect it to grandchildren. An election for IHT purposes is advisable since (a) it will not increase the IHT charged on T's death and (b) it will avoid a second charge at the brother's rates if the brother were to die within seven years of the gift (for which quick succession relief would not be available—see **[30.144]**).

(2) T leaves residue to his widow. She wishes to redirect a portion to her daughter. If the election is made, the IHT on T's death may be increased because an exempt bequest is being replaced with one that is chargeable. If the election is not made, on T's death the residue remains spouse exempt but the widow will make a PET. If she survives by seven years, no IHT will be payable: if she survives by three years, tapering relief will apply. Even if the PET becomes chargeable, any IHT may be reduced by the widow's annual exemption (in the year when the transfer is made) and the chargeable transfer may fall within her nil rate band. In cases like this, it will be advantageous to ensure that T's nil rate band is fully used up by a reading back election but, once that has been done, given a single rate of tax (40%), there is no advantage in reading back the variation since the rate of tax on the death of the widow will be the same and, moreover, tax will not be charged at once.

(3) In examples like (2) above a variation may be employed to redirect a posthumous increase in the value of the estate without any IHT charge. Assume for instance that the death estate of £200,000 has increased in value to £325,000. T's widow could vary the will (electing to read the charge back) to provide for a specific legacy of £200,000 to herself with the residue to her daughter. Under the provisions of IHTA 1984 ss 36–42 the death estate (£200,000) is attributed to the exempt legacy.

(4) H leaves £1m to his only daughter, D. His widow, W, dies soon afterwards leaving a small estate to D. D should consider varying H's will so that (say) she retains £275,000 (to use up the nil rate band) and the remainder is left to W. D will then receive that sum from W's estate.

*Note:* In (4) above the variation may be considered artificial since it is designed solely to reduce the total IHT bill. D is left with all the property. Accordingly it may be vulnerable to attack either under the *Ramsay* principle or on the basis that the dispositions of H's will have not been varied (although it is understood that the Capital Taxes Office does not at present take this point). Were D to redirect the benefit to her own children it would be more difficult to view the arrangement as wholly artificial.

c) *Other taxes*

So far as *stamp duty* is concerned variations in writing made within two years after the death are not subject to *ad valorem* duty provided that the appropriately worded certificate is included (normally Category L, see **Chapter 49**). No duty is payable on disclaimers which are treated as a refusal to accept, not a disposition of, property. No stamp duty land tax charge arises in respect of post-death variations made within two years of the death (FA 2003 Sch 3 para 4). A variation is not a notifiable transaction for stamp duty land tax purposes (FA 2003 s 77(3)).

There are no specific relieving income tax provisions for variations and disclaimers. Accordingly, income arising between the date of death and the date of a variation will be taxed in accordance with the terms of the will and the rules governing the treatment of estate income (as to which see **Chapter 17**). Of course, residuary income is taxed only when actually paid to the beneficiary: consequently if no income has been paid to a beneficiary who effects a variation of his residuary entitlement, income tax will be charged only on future distributions to the 'new' beneficiary. To this extent a form of reading back can apply for income tax purposes.

So far as a disclaimer is concerned HMRC apparently considers that the basic income tax position is the same as for a variation, since the beneficiary's interest under the will remains intact up to the date of the disclaimer (see further (1984) 5 *CTT News* 142: it may be doubted whether this view is consistent with a disclaimer operating as a refusal to accept property).

A variation made by a beneficiary in favour of his own infant unmarried child creates a settlement for income tax purposes within the settlement provisions in ITTOIA 2005 s 619 et seq (see **[16.95]**). Hence, income arising from the redirected property will be assessed as that of the parent (unless accumulated in a capital settlement). A disclaimer will escape these problems, if it is accepted that the property has never been owned by the disclaiming beneficiary.                                                           **[30.156]**

d)    *Technical difficulties and traps*

A number of technical problems have arisen in connection with instruments of variation.

First, it was argued by the Revenue that for a variation to fall within the IHT relieving provision (IHTA 1984 s 142), the operative clause in the instrument of variation had to state that the transfer of property took effect as a variation to the provisions of a will or intestacy in order to avoid it being construed as a lifetime gift. Accordingly it was suggested that any variation should follow the wording of that section and provide as follows:

> 'The dispositions of property comprised in the estate of the testator (intestate) immediately before his death, shall be varied as follows ...'

After further advice the Revenue apparently abandoned this view (see *Law Society's Gazette*, 1985, p 1454), but will, nevertheless, require the variation to indicate clearly the dispositions that are subject to it and vary their destination from that provided in the will or under the intestacy rules. The notice of election must refer to the appropriate statutory provisions. Further, as the Revenue considers that the instrument *itself* must vary the dispositions the use of a deed would appear to be necessary (although a written instrument is sufficient to transfer an existing equitable interest under LPA 1925 s 53(1)(c)).

Secondly, multiple variations had been employed (before 1985) in an attempt to avoid *ad valorem* stamp duty. Although this is no longer necessary it resulted in the Revenue interpreting IHTA 1984 s 142 as permitting only one variation per beneficiary. Again this is a position from which it has retreated, at least in part (see *Law Society's Gazette*, 1985, p 1454); it now considers that an election, once made, is irrevocable and that s 142 will not apply to an instrument redirecting any item or part of any item that had already been redirected under an earlier instrument. Variations covering a number of items should ideally be made in one instrument 'to avoid any uncertainty', although the Revenue accepts that multiple variations by a single beneficiary are not, as such, prohibited.

**EXAMPLE 30.30**

Under Eric's will £50,000 is left to his brother Wally and £100,000 to his surviving spouse Berta. The following events then occur within two years of Eric's death:
(1)　Wally executes a deed of variation in favour of his own children.
(2)　Berta executes a deed varying £2,500 in favour of her sister Jennie and subsequently a second variation of £47,500 to Jennie.
(3)　Jennie executes a deed of variation of £25,000 in favour of her boyfriend Jonnie.
　　The variations in (1) and (2) satisfy the requirements of IHTA 1984 s 142 as interpreted by HMRC and so may be read back into Eric's will, whereas the variation in (3) will not be so treated and, accordingly, will be a PET by Jennie.

The decision of *Russell v IRC* (1988) confirmed that a redirection of property already varied does not fall within s 142. The deceased had died in 1983 survived by his wife and four daughters. His estate included business assets (Lloyd's underwriting interests) that qualified for business property relief. Under his will, most of the estate passed to his widow and was not therefore subject to a tax charge. As a corollary, however, business property relief was wasted as was the deceased's nil rate band. Not surprisingly, therefore, the family decided to vary the dispositions of his will by providing for each daughter to receive a pecuniary legacy of £25,000 to be raised out of the business property. They hoped that by giving away the business property worth £100,000 that would qualify for a reduction in value of 50%, some £50,000 of the testator's nil rate band would thereby be utilised. The Revenue, however, took the view that these legacies were gifts of cash not of qualifying business assets with the result that as no 50% relief was available a tax charge would arise since part of each legacy would then fall outside the nil rate band. Although the family did not accept this, they tried again in 1985 by executing a fresh deed of variation whereby each daughter was to receive instead of a cash legacy a proportionate share of the business assets worth £25,000.

Knox J had to decide whether this second deed was effective to carry out the family's intentions and, if not, whether the Revenue was correct in its interpretation of the 1983 deed. He decided that under the relevant statutory provision a benefit which had already been redirected once could not be further redirected and read back into the testator's will.

'My principal reason for accepting the Crown's submission that the hypothesis contained in s 142(1) should not be applied to that subsection itself is that this involves taking the hypothesis further than is necessary. No authority was cited to me of a statutory hypothesis being applied to the very provision which enacts the hypothesis. Such a tortuous process would merit a specific reference in the enactment to itself ...' (Knox J).

Accordingly, as there had already been a valid variation in 1983, the further amendment in 1985 could not be read back. Having so decided he then concluded, however, that the Revenue's arguments that the 1983 variation did not have the effect of varying interests in business property was misconceived. He pointed out that the relevant cash gifts could only be satisfied (in this particular case) by resorting to business assets and therefore he was of the opinion that a division of that property by reference to a cash sum should be treated in the same way as a division by reference to a fraction of the assets.

In *Lake v Lake* (1989) Mervyn Davis J held that a deed of variation can be rectified by the court if words mistakenly used mean that it does not give effect to the parties' joint intention. It does not matter that the rectification achieves a tax advantage nor that it is made more than two years after the death. The courts must, however, be satisfied that the deed as executed contains errors: in this case the variation was designed to give legacies to children of the deceased but as the result of a clerical error such gifts were expressed to be 'free of tax'. As residue passed to an exempt beneficiary (the surviving spouse), grossing-up was therefore necessary (see **[30.96]**). The order for rectification substituted 'such gifts to bear their own tax' for 'free of tax' (see also *Matthews v Martin* (1991) and *Schnieder v Mills* (1993)).

Thirdly, s 142(4) contains a trap for the unwary by providing that if a variation results in property being held for a person 'for a period which ends not more than two years after the death' the interest of that person is ignored in applying the section.

### EXAMPLE 30.31

Dan died on 1 January 2001 leaving all his estate to his daughter Delia. By a deed of variation dated 1 January 2002 she gave her mother a six-month interest in possession in that property remainder to her children and made the necessary election. As the mother's interest ends before 1 January 2003 it will be ignored under s 142(4) and IHT calculated as if Dan had left his estate directly to his grandchildren.

*Finally*, in December 2001 the Revenue announced a change of policy based on the somewhat curious idea that variations had to operate in the real world!                                                                            **[30.157]**

### EXAMPLE 30.32

Sid died on 6 April 2003 leaving his estate of £275,000 to his wife Mabel for life with remainder to their only child, Doris. Grief-stricken Mabel died soon afterwards and her entire estate (worth £275,000) then passes to Doris.

(1)  *The current position*: On Mabel's death IHT payable will be £110,000 on the basis that she left a chargeable free estate of £275,000 and had enjoyed a life interest in a trust fund also worth £275,000. Doris would be advised to consider using s 142 to amend Sid's will: specifically to get rid of the gift to Mabel.

(2)  *Disclaimer of the life interest*: It may be that Mabel's PRs can disclaim the benefit of this life interest and HMRC accepts that if this is done the tax on Sid's death will be recalculated on the basis that the property passes to Doris. Full use will therefore have been made of Sid's IHT nil rate band and on Doris'

death her estate is within her nil rate band. Of course, a disclaimer will not be possible if benefits have been received.

(3) *Varying Sid's will:* Prior to the 2001 statement, variations were accepted in such cases: typically Sid's will would be varied to delete Mabel's life interest. HMRC now considers, however, that because Mabel's life interest has ended there is no property that can form the subject matter of such a variation. It is considered that this view is misconceived since what is being redirected is *the property passing under Sid's will* so that the death of Mabel is irrelevant (see also *Soutter's Executry v IRC* (2002), a Scottish Special Commissioners case which affords some support for the Revenue's views).

## 7  IHT and estate duty

Up to 13 March 1975 the estate duty regime operated. The various transitional provisions for estate duty are beyond the scope of this book although mention should be made of IHTA 1984 Sch 6 para 2 that preserves for IHT purposes the estate duty surviving spouse exemption. This exemption provided that where property was left to a surviving spouse in such circumstances that the spouse was not competent to dispose of it (for instance was given a life interest therein) estate duty would be charged on the first death but not again on the death of the survivor. This exemption was continued into the CTT (and now IHT) era by IHTA 1984 Sch 6 para 2 which excludes such property from charge whether the limited interest is terminated *inter vivos* or by the death of the surviving spouse. All too often this valuable exemption may be overlooked and an over-emphasis on the attractions of making PETs may have unfortunate results.                                              **[30.158]**

### EXAMPLE 30.33

(1) On his death in 1973, Samson left his wife Delilah a life interest in his share portfolio. She is still alive and in robust health and the trustees have a power to advance capital to her. Estate duty was charged on Samson's death but because of IHTA 1984 Sch 6 para 2 there will be no charge to IHT when Delilah's interest comes to an end. At first sight, there appear to be advantages if the trustees advance capital to Delilah which she then transfers by means of a PET. However, this arrangement carries with it the risk of that capital being subject to an IHT charge if Delilah dies within seven years of her gift. Accordingly, an interest which is tax free is being replaced by a potentially chargeable transfer.

(2) Terminating Delilah's interest during her life may, however, have other attractions. In particular, the exemption from charge in IHTA 1984 Sch 6 para 2 is limited to the value of the property in which the limited interest subsists but that property may, by forming part of Delilah's estate, affect the value of other assets in that estate. Assume, for instance, that Delilah owns 30% of the shares in a private company (Galilee Ltd) in her own name and that a further 30% are subject to the life interest trust. When she dies she will be treated as owning 60% of the shares: a controlling holding which will be valued as such. Although one half of the value of that holding will be free from charge under para 2, the remaining portion will be taxed. Accordingly, it may be better in such cases for her life interest to be surrendered *inter vivos* even if that operation is only carried out on her deathbed.

# 31 IHT—exemptions and reliefs

*Updated by Natalie Lee, Senior Lecturer in Law, University of Southampton and Aparna Nathan, LLB Hons, LLM, Barrister, Gray's Inn Tax Chambers*

I   Lifetime exemptions and reliefs [**31.3**]
II  Death exemptions and reliefs [**31.21**]
III Exemptions for lifetime and death transfers [**31.41**]

## 1 Policy issues

Predictably, although in marked contrast to CGT, whole categories of property are not exempted from the IHT net. Hence, *excluded property*, which is ignored if transferred *inter vivos* and not taxed as part of the death estate, is restrictively defined in IHTA 1984 s 6 (see [**35.20**]).

Exemptions and reliefs apply in a number of situations: some for lifetime transfers only; some for death only; and some for all transfers, whether in lifetime or on death.

The exemptions may be justified on the grounds of necessity—some gifts must be permitted (eg Christmas and wedding presents); or, in the case of reliefs applicable to particular property, because it is desirable that the property should be preserved and not sold to pay the tax bill (eg business and agricultural property where relief up to 100% of the value is available).

[**31.1**]

## 2 The nil rate band

The nil rate band (currently £275,000) is not an exempt transfer since transfers within this band are chargeable transfers, albeit taxed at 0%. Accordingly, exemptions and reliefs should be exhausted first so that the taxpayer's nil rate band is retained intact as long as possible. [**31.2**]

## I LIFETIME EXEMPTIONS AND RELIEFS

### 1 Transfers not exceeding £3,000 pa (IHTA 1984 s 19)

Up to £3,000 can be transferred free from IHT each tax year (6 April to 5 April). To the extent that this relief is unused in any one year it can be rolled forward for one tax year only. There is no general roll-forward since only where the value transferred in any year exceeds £3,000 is the shortfall from the previous year's £3,000 used.

**EXAMPLE 31.1**

A makes chargeable transfers of £2,500 in 2004–05; £2,800 in 2005–06; and £3,700 in 2006–07.

*For 2004–05:* no IHT (£3,000 exemption) and £500 is carried forward.

*For 2005–06:* no IHT (£3,000 exemption) and £200 only is carried forward. The £500 from 2004–05 could only have been used to the extent that the transfer in 2005–06 exceeded £3,000.

*For 2006–07:* IHT on £500 (£3,200 is exempt).

The relief can operate by deducting £3,000 from a larger gift. Where several chargeable gifts are made in the same tax year, earlier gifts will be given the relief first; if several gifts are made on the same day there is a *pro rata* apportionment of the relief irrespective of the actual order of gifts. The relief applies also to settlements with interests in possession although in this case it will only be given if the life tenant so elects (see **[33.35]**).

The relationship between the annual exemption and the PET depends on the definition of a PET in IHTA 1984 s 3A:

'a transfer of value ... which, apart from this section, would be a chargeable transfer (or to the extent which, apart from this section, it would be such a transfer) ... '.

The position can therefore be stated in two propositions:

(1)   a transfer of value which is wholly covered by the annual exemption is not a PET but *an exempt transfer in its own right;*

(2)   a transfer of value which exceeds the annual exempt amount is *to that extent a PET.*

**EXAMPLE 31.2**

(1)   In 2006–07 Peta gives her father £2,500. This gift is an exempt transfer.

(2)   In the same tax year Beta, who made no gifts in the previous year, gives her mother £6,500. Two annual exemptions mean that £6,000 is exempt: £500 is a PET.

(3)   Cheeta intends to set up a discretionary trust for his family and to make an outright gift to his sister. He should make the discretionary trust first thereby using up his annual exemption and on a subsequent day make a PET to his sister.

What should a would-be donor do who does not wish to transfer assets/ money to the value of £3,000, but at the same time is reluctant to see the exemption lost? One solution is to vest an interest in property in the donee whilst retaining control of the asset (although great care must be taken to ensure that a benefit is not retained in the portion given since a transfer falling within the annual exemption is still a gift for the reservation of benefit rules: see **Chapter 29**). Selling the asset with the purchase price outstanding and releasing part of the debt each year equal to the annual exemption may fall foul of the associated operations rules (see **[28.101]**).                 **[31.3]**

**EXAMPLE 31.3**

On 21 December the Deceased wrote a cheque for £6,000 in favour of his son who paid it into his bank account on the same day. The Deceased died on 22 December and the bank agreed to honour the cheque which was cleared on 27 December. There was no completed gift in the Deceased's lifetime (since the cheque had not cleared) and the cheque was not a liability in the Deceased's estate (since it had not been incurred for full consideration). The Deceased had therefore failed to use his annual exemption (see *Curnock (PR of Curnock Dec'd) v IRC* (2003)).

## 2   Normal expenditure out of income (IHTA 1984 s 21)

Section 21 provides as follows:

'a transfer of value is an exempt transfer if, or to the extent that, it is shown—

(a)   that it was made as part of the normal expenditure of the transferor,
(b)   that (taking one year with another) it was made out of his income, and
(c)   that, after allowing for all transfers of value forming part of his normal expenditure, the transferor is left with sufficient income to maintain his usual standard of living.'

The legislation does not define (nor indeed seek to explain) 'usual standard of living' but HMRC accepts that the gifts do not have to be of cash: regular gifts of shares will, for instance, suffice. Particular difficulties are presented by requirement (a): what evidence is required to prove that payments (or any payment) constitute normal expenditure? A pattern of payments is presumably required and this is most easily shown where the taxpayer is committed to making a series of payments as, for instance, where he enters into a deed of covenant. In other cases (eg where there is no legal commitment to make a series of payments) it has usually been assumed that a number of payments would have to be made before there was sufficient evidence of regularity.

*Bennett v IRC* (1995) casts some light on this problem. Mrs Bennett was the life tenant of a will trust established by her late husband, the gross annual income from which was, until 1987, £300 pa. In that year, as a result of the sale of the trust assets, the income of the trust increased enormously and Mrs Bennett (a lady of settled habits) indicated to the trustees that she wished her sons to have surplus trust income above what was needed to satisfy her relatively modest needs. Accordingly in 1989 each of the three sons received a distribution of £9,300 and in the following year £60,000. Mrs Bennett then unexpectedly died. The Inland Revenue contended that the 1989 and 1990 payments were failed PETs: the executors argued that they were exempt under s 21. The court acknowledged that requirements (b) and (c) were satisfied and so the matter turned on the meaning of 'normal expenditure'. This was explained by Lightman J as follows:

'the term "normal expenditure" connotes expenditure which at the time it took place accorded with the settled pattern of expenditure adopted by the transferor.

The existence of the settled pattern may be established in two ways. First, an examination of the expenditure by the transferor over a period of time may throw into relief a pattern, eg a payment each year of 10% of all income to charity or members of the individual's family or a payment of a fixed sum or a sum rising with inflation as a pension to a former employee. Second, the individual may be shown to have assumed a commitment, or adopted a firm resolution, regarding his future expenditure and thereafter complied with it. The commitment may be legal (eg a deed of covenant), religious (eg a vow to give all earnings beyond the sum needed for subsistence to those in need) or moral (eg to support aged parents or invalid relatives). The commitment or resolution need have none of these characteristics but nonetheless be likewise effective as establishing a pattern, eg to pay the annual premiums on a life insurance qualifying policy gifted to a third party or to give a pre-determined part of his income to his children.

For expenditure to be "normal" there is no fixed minimum period during which the expenditure should have occurred. All that is necessary is that on the totality of the evidence the pattern of actual or intended regular payment shall have been established and that the item in question conforms with that pattern. If the prior commitment or resolution can be shown, a single payment implementing the commitment or resolution may be sufficient. On the other hand if no such commitment or resolution can be shown, a series of payments may be required before the existence of the necessary pattern will emerge. The pattern need not be immutable; it must, however, be established that the pattern was intended to remain in place for more than a nominal period and indeed for a sufficient period (barring unforeseen circumstances) in order for any payment fairly to be regarded as a regular feature of the transferor's annual expenditure. Thus a "deathbed" resolution to make periodic payments "for life" and a payment made in accordance with such a determination will not suffice.

The amount of the expenditure need not be fixed in amount nor indeed the individual recipient be the same. As regards quantum, it is sufficient that a formula or standard has been adopted by application of which the payment (which may be of a fluctuating amount) can be quantified eg 10% of any earnings whatever they may be, or the costs of a sick or elderly dependant's residence at a nursing home.'

On the basis of this analysis he concluded that the two payments were exempted under s 21. In the later case of *Nadin v IRC* (1997) not only did the payments exceed the taxpayer's income for the year but there was no evidence of a prior commitment or resolution and the payments did not form part of any pattern of expenditure.

In *McDowall v IRC* [2004] SSCD 22 an attorney under a power of attorney purported to make lifetime gifts in keeping with the taxpayer's established practice of making gifts to his children, their spouses and grandchildren. The power of attorney contained no express power for gifts to be made. The Special Commissioners held that the gifts were invalid because the attorney was not permitted by the power of attorney to make gifts. However, had the gifts been valid, they would have been exempt under IHTA 1984 s 21 because there was a settled pattern of making gifts and the gifts were made out of income.

**EXAMPLE 31.4**

A takes out a life insurance policy on his own life for £60,000 with the benefit of that policy being held on a trust for his grandchildren. A pays the premiums on the policy of £3,500 pa. He makes a transfer of value of £3,500 pa but he can make use of the normal expenditure exemption to avoid IHT so long as all the requirements for that exemption are satisfied. Alternatively, the £3,000 annual exemption would relieve most of the annual premium. (It is thought that even if the first premium was paid *before* the policy was settled, the normal expenditure exemption would apply to the value of the policy settled.)

Anti-avoidance rules provide that:
(1) The normal expenditure exemption will not cover a life insurance premium unless the transferor can show that the life cover was not facilitated by and associated with an annuity purchased on his own life (IHTA 1984 s 21(2)).
(2) Under IHTA 1984 s 263 (unless the transferor can disprove the presumption of associated transactions, as above) an IHT charge can arise when the benefit of the life policy is vested in the donee. In general, if a charge arises, the sum assured by the life policy is treated as a transfer of value.

These special rules exist to prevent tax saving by the use of back-to-back insurance policies, as in the following example:

**EXAMPLE 31.5**

Tony pays an insurance company £50,000 in return for an annuity of £7,000 pa for the rest of his life. At the same time he enters into a life insurance contract on his own life for £50,000 written in favour of his brother Ted. The potential advantages are that on the death of Tony the sum of £50,000 is no longer part of his estate and the annuity has no value when he dies but can be used during his life to pay the premiums on the life insurance contract. The insurance proceeds will not attract IHT because they do not form part of his estate and Tony could claim that the premiums amounted to regular payments out of his income and so were free of IHT. HMRC accepts that such arrangements are effective so long as the policies are not linked and, ideally, are taken out with different companies.

As with the annual exemption, this exemption does not prevent a gift from being caught by the reservation of benefit rules.                     **[31.4]**

## 3  Small gifts (IHTA 1984 s 20)

Any number of £250 gifts can be made in any tax year by a donor provided that the gifts are to different donees. It must be an outright gift (not a gift into settlement) and the sum cannot be severed from a larger gift. The section provides that the transfers of value made to any one person in any one year must not exceed £250: accordingly, it is not possible to combine this small gifts exemption with the annual £3,000 exemption. A gift of £3,250 would, therefore, be exempt as to £3,000 (assuming that exemption was available) but the excess of £250 would not fall under s 20 even if the gift had been structured by means of two separate cheques.               **[31.5]**

## 4  Gifts in consideration of marriage (IHTA 1984 s 22)

The gift must be made before or contemporaneously with the marriage and only after marriage if in satisfaction of a prior legal obligation. It must be conditional upon the marriage taking place so that should the marriage not occur the donor must have the right to recover the gift (if this right is not exercised, there may be an IHT charge on the failure to exercise that right under IHTA 1984 s 3(3)). A particular marriage must be in contemplation; it will not suffice, for instance, for a father to make a gift to his two-year-old daughter expressed to be conditional upon her marriage on the fatalistic assumption that she is bound to get married eventually!

The exemption can be used to settle property, but only if the beneficiaries are limited to (generally) the couple, any issue, and spouses of such issue (see IHTA 1984 s 22(4)). Hence, a marriage cannot be used to effect a general settlement of assets within the family.

The sum exempt from IHT is:

(1)   £5,000, if the donor is a parent of either party to the marriage. Thus, each of four parents can give £5,000 to the couple.

(2)   £2,500, if the transferor is a remoter ancestor of either party to the marriage (eg a grandparent or great-grandparent) or if the transferor is a party to the marriage. The latter is designed to cover ante nuptial gifts since after marriage transfers between spouses are normally exempt without limit (see [**31.41**]).

(3)   £1,000, in the case of any other transferors (eg a wedding guest).

When a gift of property is an exempt transfer because it was made in consideration of marriage, the reservation of benefit provisions do not apply.

[**31.6**]

### EXAMPLE 31.6

(1)   Father gives son a Matisse sculpture on the occasion of the son's marriage. It is worth £5,000. Possession of the piece is retained by the father but as the transfer is covered by the marriage exemption his continued possession does not fall within the reservation rules (FA 1986 s 102(5)).

(2)   Mum gives daughter an interest in her house equal to £5,000 when the daughter marries. Although Mum continues to live in the house the reservation rules do not apply.

## 5   Dispositions for maintenance etc (IHTA 1984 s 11)

Dispositions listed in IHTA 1984 s 11 are not transfers of value and so are ignored for IHT purposes. HMRC takes the view that this exemption only applies to *inter vivos* dispositions, because 'disposition' does not cover the deemed disposition on death.                                                    [**31.7**]

### a)   *Maintenance of a former spouse (IHTA 1984 s 11(1)(a))*

Even without this provision such payments would in many cases escape IHT. If made before decree absolute, the exemption for gifts between spouses (see [**31.41**]) would operate and even after divorce they might escape IHT as regular payments out of income; or fall within the annual exemption; or be non-gratuitous transfers. What s 11 does is to put the matter beyond all doubt.

Two problems may be mentioned. *First*, maintenance is not defined, so that whether it would cover the transfer of capital assets (eg the former matrimonial home) is uncertain. *Secondly*, if the payer dies but payment is to continue for the lifetime of the recipient, the position is unclear in the light of HMRC's view that this exemption is limited to *inter vivos* dispositions. **[31.8]**

b)  *Maintenance of children*

Provision for the maintenance, education or training of a child of either party to a marriage (including stepchildren and adopted children) is not a transfer of value (IHTA 1984 s 11(1)(b): HMRC accepts that 'party to a marriage' includes a widow or widower). The maintenance can continue beyond the age of 18 if the child is in full-time education. Thus, school fees paid by parents escape IHT. Similar principles operate where the disposition is for the maintenance of a parent's illegitimate child (IHTA 1984 s 11(4)). Relief is also given for the maintenance of other people's children if the child is an infant and not in the care of either parent; once the child is 18, not only must he be undergoing full-time education, but also the disponer must (in effect) have been *in loco parentis* to the child during his minority (IHTA 1984 s 11(2)). Hence, payment of school and college fees by grandparents will seldom escape IHT under this provision. **[31.9]**

c)  *Care or maintenance of a dependent relative*

The provision of maintenance whether direct or indirect must be reasonable and the relative (as defined in IHTA 1984 s 11(6)) must be incapacitated by old age or infirmity from maintaining himself (although mothers and mothers-in-law who are widowed or separated are always dependent relatives). **[31.10]–[31.20]**

## II  DEATH EXEMPTIONS AND RELIEFS

### 1  Woodlands (IHTA 1984 ss 125–130)

This relief takes effect by deferring IHT on growing trees and underwood forming part of the deceased's estate. Their value is left out of account on the death. An election must be made for the relief by written notice given (normally) within two years after the death (s 125(3)). It is not available where the woodlands qualify for agricultural relief (see **[31.62]**) and commercial woodlands will commonly qualify for business property relief ('BPR') (see **[31.42]**): with the introduction of 100% BPR in 1992 for 'relevant business property', woodland relief has become less important).

To prevent deathbed IHT saving schemes the land must not have been purchased by the deceased in the five years before his death (note, however, that the relief is available if the woodlands were obtained by gift or inheritance within the five-year period). If the timber is transferred on a second death no tax is chargeable on later disposals by reference to the first death (s 126). The relief does not apply to the land itself, but any IHT charged as a result of death can be paid in instalments. The deferred tax on the timber may become chargeable as follows: **[31.21]**

a)  *Sale of the timber with or without the land*

IHT will be charged on the net proceeds of sale, but deductions can be made for costs of selling the timber and also for the costs of replanting. The net proceeds are taxed according to full IHT rates at the date of the disposal and the tax is calculated by treating those proceeds as forming the highest part of the deceased's estate. Business property relief (at 50%) may be available where the trees or underwood formed a business asset at the date of death and, but for the deferment election, would have qualified for that relief at that time (see s 127 and [31.42]). In such cases the relief is given against the net proceeds of sale (IHTA 1984 s 127).                                              [31.22]

b)   *A gift of the timber*

Not only is the deferred charge triggered by a gift of the timber, but also the gift itself may be subject to IHT subject to the availability of BPR. In calculating the tax payable on the lifetime gift the value transferred is reduced by the triggered IHT charged on the death and the tax can be paid by interest-free instalments (whoever pays the IHT) spread over ten years (IHTA 1984 s 229).                                                               [31.23]

**EXAMPLE 31.7**

(1)   Wally Wood dies in January 1991 with a death estate of £200,000. In addition, he owns at death woodlands with the growing timber valued at £40,000 and the land etc valued at £30,000. The woodlands exemption is claimed by his daughter Wilma. In 1998 she sells the timber; the net proceeds of sale are £50,000.
  (i)   *Position on Wally's death:* The timber is left out of account. The value of the rest of the business (£30,000) attracts 50% business relief (the relevant level of relief in 1991: see (3) below), so that only £15,000 will be added to the £200,000 chargeable estate.
  (ii)  *Position on Wilma's sale:* The IHT charge is triggered. The net proceeds are reduced by 50% business relief to £25,000 which will be taxed according to the rates of IHT in force in 1998 for transfers between £215,000 (ie Wally's total chargeable death estate) and £240,000.
(2)   As in (1), above except that Wilma settles the timber on her brother Woad in 1998 when its net value is £50,000. The deferred charge will be triggered as in para (ii) of (1), above. IHT on Wilma's gift will be calculated according to IHT rates in force for 1998. She can deduct from the net value of the timber the deferred tax ((1), above) and any IHT can be paid by instalments whether it is paid by her or by Woad.
(3)   With the increase in the level of BPR to 100% in 1992, the woodlands election should not be made if the woodlands form part of a qualifying business: instead of a partial deferment of charge the business is wholly tax free.

c)   *PETs and estate duty*

Estate duty was not charged on the value of timber, trees, wood or under-wood growing on land comprised in an estate at death. Instead, tax was deferred until such time as the woodlands were sold and was then levied at the death estate rate on the net proceeds of sale (subject to the proviso that duty could not exceed tax on the value of the timber at the date of the death). Pending sale, duty was therefore held in suspense and this deferral period only ceased on the happening of a later death when the woodlands again became subject to duty. The introduction of a charge on lifetime gifts with the advent of CTT resulted in this deferral period terminating immediately after the first transfer of value occurring after 12 March 1975 in which the value transferred was determined by reference to the land in question (subject only to an exclusion if that transfer was to the transferor's spouse and therefore exempt from CTT: see FA 1975 s 49(4)). In such cases, the deferred estate duty charge was superseded by a charge to CTT on the transfer value.

With the introduction of the PET it was realised that a transfer of value of woodlands subject to estate duty deferral to another individual would, *prima facie*, be a PET but that the transfer would have the effect of ending the deferral period thereby cancelling any charge to duty without a compensating charge to IHT. Hence, IHTA 1984 Sch 19 para 46 provides that transfers of value which fall within FA 1975 s 49(4) and thereby bring to an end the estate duty deferral period *shall not be PETs*. Accordingly, such transfers remain immediately chargeable to IHT at the transferor's rates (with the possibility of a supplementary charge should he die within the following seven years). **[31.24]**

**EXAMPLE 31.8**

On his death in May 1973 Claude left his landed estate to his son Charles. That estate included woodlands valued, in 1973, at £6,000. Consider the tax position in the following three situations:

(1)  *If Charles sells the timber in 1999 for £16,000.* The net proceeds of sale will be subject to an estate duty charge levied at Claude's estate rate but duty will be limited by reference to the value of the timber in 1973 (ie it will be charged on £6,000).

(2)  *If Charles retains the timber until his death in 1999 when it passes to his daughter.* This transfer of value will end the estate duty deferral period so that the potential charge to duty will be removed. However, the transfer to his daughter will be subject to an IHT charge unless the woodlands deferral election under IHTA 1984, ss 125 ff is claimed.

(3)  *If Charles makes an inter vivos gift of his estate (including the woodlands) in August 1999 to his daughter.* Such a gift will not be potentially exempt because of IHTA 1984 Sch 19 para 46. Accordingly, it will terminate the estate duty suspense period, and will result in an immediate IHT charge levied according to Charles' rates. From the wording of para 46 it is not clear whether any part of this transfer can be potentially exempt or whether the entire value transferred is subject to an immediate charge. Undoubtedly the value of the timber will attract such a charge and likewise it would seem that the value of the land on which the timber is growing will fall outside the definition of a PET (see the wording of FA 1975 s 49(4)). What, however, if the transfer of value made by Charles includes other property, eg other parts of a landed estate which are not afforested? There was a danger that none of the value transferred would be a PET since para 46 is not limited to that part of any transfer of value comprising the woodlands. The injustice is recognised by ESC F15 which states that 'the scope of [para 46] will henceforth be restricted solely to that part of the value transferred which is attributable to the woodlands which are the subject of the deferred charge'.

## 2  Death on active service (IHTA 1984 s 154)

IHTA 1984 s 154 ensures that the estates of persons dying on active service, including members of the UDR and RUC killed by terrorists in Northern

Ireland, are exempt from IHT. This provision has been generously inter-preted to cover a death arising many years after a wound inflicted whilst on active service, so long as that wound was one of the causes of death; it need not have been the only, or even the direct cause (*Barty-King v Ministry of Defence* (1979)). Although a *donatio mortis causa* is covered by the exemption it does not apply to lifetime transfers.                                    **[31.25]–[31.40]**


## III   EXEMPTIONS FOR LIFETIME AND DEATH TRANSFERS

### 1   The inter-spouse/civil partners exemption (IHTA 1984 s 18)

This most valuable exemption from IHT for transfers between spouses is unlimited in amount except where the donor spouse is but the donee spouse is not domiciled in the UK when the amount excluded from IHT is £55,000. In *Holland (Exor of Holland Deceased) v IRC* (2003) the Special Commissioners decided that a couple who had lived together as husband and wife for 31 years did not qualify for the spouse exemption. A spouse for this purpose was a person who was legally married. The Commissioners further expressed the view that this did not involve discrimination against unmarried couples under the HRA 1998 (see **[55.42]**).

The Civil Partnership Act 2004 introduced the concept of 'civil partner-ships' with the aim of putting same-sex couples on a similar footing to married couples. For tax purposes, this has been achieved through FA 2005, and regulations that provide for reliefs applying to married couples to apply equally to civil partners eg the inter-spousal exemption. For the sake of simplicity, references to spouses in the inheritance chapters in this book will generally be deemed to include civil partners.

The use of this exemption is considered in different parts of this book and the following points represent a summary of those sections:

(1)   For tax planning purposes the lowest total IHT bill is produced if both spouses use up their nil rate bands (see **[51.74]**). Particular problems may result on the death of the first to die if the only substantial asset in his estate is the main residence that is needed by his surviving spouse: for a consideration of the *Lloyds Private Banking* case, see **[32.3]**.

(2)   Both should take advantage of the lifetime exemptions. HMRC will normally not invoke the associated operations provisions to challenge a transfer between spouses even if it enables this to occur (**[28.101]**).

(3)   The rules for related property are designed to counter tax saving by splitting assets between spouses (see **[28.70]**).

(4)   IHT on a chargeable transfer by one spouse to a third party may be collected from the other spouse in certain circumstances (see **[28.171]**).                                                                     **[31.41]**


### 2   Business property relief ('BPR': IHTA 1984 ss 103–114)

Business (and agricultural property) relief was introduced in order to ensure that businesses were not broken up by the imposition of an IHT charge. BPR takes effect by a percentage reduction in the value transferred by a transfer of value and, prior to 10 March 1992, that reduction was at either 50% or 30%.

For transfers made on and after that date the levels were increased to 100% and 50% with the result that most family businesses and farms were taken outside the tax net. The relief is given automatically. **[31.42]**

a)   *Meaning of 'relevant business property'*

Business property relief is given in respect of transfers of 'relevant business property' which is defined as any of the following:
(1)   *A business:* For example, that of a sole trader or sole practitioner (s 105(1)(a)). A sole trader who transfers a part of his trade falls within this category and this may include a transfer of settled land (of which he is the life tenant) which is used in the business (*Fetherstonehaugh v IRC* (1984)).
(2)   *An interest in a business:* For example, the share of a partner in either a trading or professional partnership (s 105(1)(a)).
(3)   *Listed shares or securities which gave the transferor control of the company* (s 105(1)(cc)): Control itself does not have to be transferred; the requirement is simply that *at the time of transfer* the transferor should have such control (see **[31.54]**).
(4)   *Unquoted securities which gave the transferor control of the company* (s 105(1)(b)): Similar comments to those in (3) apply: unquoted shares include shares dealt in on the Alternative Investment Market (AIM).
(5)   *Any unquoted shares in a company* (s 105(1)(bb)).
(6)   *Any land or building, plant or machinery which immediately before the transfer was used by a partnership in which the transferor was a partner or by a company of which he had control* (s 105(1)(d)).
   Control for these purposes requires a majority of votes (50%+) on all questions affecting the company as a whole (see (3) and (4), above). Hence, an apparently unjust result is produced if the appropriate asset is used by a company in which the transferor owned a minority of the ordinary shares when no relief will be available, whereas had the asset been used by a partnership, then, irrespective of his profit share, relief would be available. Relief is also available if the asset is held in a trust but is used by a life tenant for his own business or by a company which he controls. The relief is given irrespective of whether a rent is charged for the use of the asset.
   In *Beckman v IRC* (2000) H retired as a partner and her capital account (reflecting capital introduced into the business) was left outstanding as a debt of the business. On H's subsequent death she had ceased to own a share in the business of which she had become a creditor. No relief was therefore available. **[31.43]**

b)   *Relief is on the net value of the business*

Relief is given on the net value of the business and IHTA 1984 s 110(b) states that the net value is:

> ' ... the value of the assets used in the business (including goodwill) reduced by the aggregate amount of any liabilities incurred for the purposes of the business.'

A number of matters are worthy of note in connection with the above definition:

(1)    The definition is limiting—there will be assets and liabilities which are connected with the business but which do not satisfy the wording of s 110(b). Such assets and liabilities will, of course, still form part of the estate of the taxpayer under s 5 but will not benefit from the relief (or, in the case of liabilities, will not reduce the relief).

**EXAMPLE 31.9**

(a)    H was a Lloyd's Name at the time of his death. He had deposited funds at Lloyd's and had borrowed moneys to fund those deposits. At his death he owed amounts on accounts for which a result had not been announced. The Special Commissioner decided that the amounts owed on those accounts were trading losses and did not reduce the assets on which relief was available (although these liabilities did reduce the value of H's estate under s 5(4): see **[31.13]**). It was accepted that the deposited sum and borrowings taken out in connection with it fell within s 110(b) as being assets used in the business and liabilities incurred for the purposes of the business but the losses were trading losses and not liabilities incurred for the purposes of the business. Rather, they arose out of the running of the business: in the language used in a line of income tax cases, they were the fruit (income) produced by the tree (capital) (see, for instance, *Van den Berghs Ltd v Clark* (1935) at **[10.106]**). Of course, in this case the result produced enhanced BPR but the position will often be the opposite since trading receipts will not constitute assets used in the business. The Revenue has indicated that it considers the case to be limited to its own facts but this does not appear to be correct (*Hardcastle v IRC* (2000)).

(b)    Sid acquires Roy's flower business with the aid of a loan from Finance for Flowers (FFF). That debt is not incurred for the purposes of the business and so does not reduce the value of the business assets.

(2)    The value qualifying for BPR cannot be increased by charging business debts on non-business property (contrast *Example 31.19* in the context of APR).

(3)    In *IRC v Mallender* (2001) a Lloyd's underwriter provided a bank guarantee for £100,000 in support of his business. That guarantee was secured by a legal charge on a property worth £1m. The Special Commissioner decided that the £1m property was one of the assets used in the business. Not surprisingly, this was reversed by the High Court: in practice, HMRC accepts that the £100,000 guarantee attracts relief as an asset used in the business (see *Taxation*, 8 August 2002, p 514). **[31.44]**

c)    *Amount of relief*

Relief is given by percentage reduction in the value of the business property transferred. The chargeable transfer will be of that reduced sum. Business property relief is applied before other reliefs (for instance, the £3,000 *inter vivos* annual exemption). The appropriate percentage depends upon which category of business property is involved.

*100% relief* is available for businesses, interests in businesses, and all shareholdings in unquoted companies (ie categories (1), (2), (4) and (5), above).

*50% relief* is available for controlling shareholdings in listed companies (category (3), above) and for assets used by a business (category (6), above).

**[31.45]**

**EXAMPLE 31.10**

Topsy is a partner in the firm of Topsy & Tim (builders). He owns the site of the firm's offices and goods yard. He settles the following property on his daughter Teasy for life: (1) his share of the business (value £500,000) and (2) the site (value £50,000). Business property relief will be available on the business at 100% so that the value transferred is reduced to nil and on the site at 50% so that the value transferred is £25,000.

*Notes:*
(1) Topsy's total transfers amount to £25,000 which may be further reduced if other exemptions are available.
(2) IHT may remain payable on business property after deducting the 50% (and any other) relief(s). Whether the chargeable transfer is made during lifetime or on death, it will usually be possible to pay the tax by interest-free instalments (see **[31.58]** for a discussion of the position when IHT or additional IHT is charged because of death within seven years of a chargeable transfer and for the clawback rules).

d) *The two-year ownership requirement*

In general, relevant business property which has been owned for less than two years attracts no relief (IHTA 1984 s 106). However, the incorporation of a business will not affect the running of the two-year period (IHTA 1984 s 107) and if a transfer of a business is made between spouses on death, the recipient can include the ownership period of the deceased spouse. This is not, however, the case with an *inter vivos* transfer (IHTA 1984 s 108). If the spouse takes the property as the result of a written variation read back into the will under IHTA 1984 s 142 the recipient is treated as being entitled to property on the death of the other spouse. When entitlement results from an appropriation of assets by the PRs this provision would not, however, apply.

**[31.46]**

**EXAMPLE 31.11**

(1) Solomon incorporated his leather business by forming Solomon Ltd in which he holds 100% of the issued shares. For BPR the two-year ownership period begins with the commencement of Solomon's original leather business.
(2) Solomon set up his family company one year before his death and left the shares to his wife in his will. She can include his one-year ownership period towards satisfying the two-year requirement. If he made a lifetime gift to her, aggregation is not possible.
(3) If Mrs Solomon had died within two years of the gift from her husband (whether that gift had been made *inter vivos* or on death) business relief will be available on her death so long as the conditions for relief were satisfied at the time of the earlier transfer by her husband (IHTA 1984 s 109). A similar result follows if the gift from her husband had been by will and she had made a lifetime chargeable transfer of the property within two years of his death (in this case relief could be afforded under s 109 and, if Mr Solomon had not satisfied the two-year requirement, his period of ownership could be aggregated with that of Mrs Solomon under s 108).

e)    *Non qualifying activities: the wholly or mainly test*

'Business' is a word of wide import and a landlord who lets properties with a view to profit may fall within its ambit. IHTA 1984 s 105(3) makes clear, however, that there are certain businesses for which relief is not available ('if the business ... consists *wholly or mainly* of one or more of the following, that is to say, dealing in securities, stocks or shares, land or buildings or making or holding investments'). It was held in *Phillips v R&C Commrs* ((2006) SpC) that a company whose activity was the *making* of loans to related companies was not in the business of *investing* in loans and, accordingly, could not be classed as a company whose business consisted wholly or mainly in the making or holding of investments. However, the Special Commissioner made it clear that it could never be said that the making of loans was never the making of an investment or that it always was; it 'was necessary to have regard to all the facts in the round'). Note that a wholly or mainly test is to be applied and that the legislation does not seek to define this phrase. This means that a taxpayer may conduct, within a single business, two activities one of which may fall on the 'investment' side of the line, eg a trade may have income from managed investments held as a reserve, but the wholly or mainly test may result in that entire business attracting relief. The business must be carried on with a view to making a profit (*Grimwood Taylor v IRC* (1999)).                                                                      **[31.47]**

f)    *Commercial landlords*

An unreported Special Commissioner case decided that a commercial land-lord who maintained a high quality of service to his professional tenants (the services embracing cleaning operations, maintenance and decoration) was entitled to the relief. The taxpayer was considered to be acting as managing agent: his daily activities and his obligations far exceeded those which would normally be placed on the holder of an investment (see *Taxation*, 3 May 1990, p 126: the Special Commissioner has since commented that the facts of this case were 'exceptional': see *Powell v IRC* (1997)). Two later (and reported) Special Commissioner cases have, however, rejected any suggestion that a line can be drawn between 'passive' property investment on the one hand and 'active' management on the other (see *Martin (Executors of Moore) v IRC* (1995); *Burkinyoung (Executor of Burkinyoung) v IRC* (1995)). In the latter case the Special Commissioner commented as follows:

'The construction sought by the taxpayer which seeks to distinguish between the operations of the active and of the passive landlord is too vague and too dependent on degrees of involvement to have been what Parliament contemplated when the relief was designed.

Here the whole gain derived by Mrs Burkinyoung from the property came to her as rent. It all arose from the investment in the property and the leases granted out of it; it all arose from the making or holding investment activities carried on by her. She provided no additional services and so earned nothing from any other sources or activities. The business was, therefore, wholly one of making or holding investments and so is excluded from being "relevant business property" by the words of section 105(3).'                                                                      **[31.48]**

g) *Static caravan sites and residential home parks*

Other cases before the Special Commissioners have considered whether owner/managers of caravan parks qualify for business property relief. In both *Hall (Executors of Hall) v IRC* (1997) and *Powell v IRC* (1997) it was decided that relief was not available because the business 'mainly' involved the making or holding of investments. In the *Hall* case, of the total income of the business (£36,741) the greatest component (amounting to either 84% or 65% depending on how the calculation was performed) was attributable to rents and standing charges. The Special Commissioners concluded therefore that:

> 'In such circumstances we have come to the conclusion that the activities of the business carried on at Tanat Caravan Park consisted mainly of the making or holding investments. Although the receipt of commissions on the sale of caravans forms part of the business we find that it was ancillary to the main business of receiving rents from owners of caravans and lessees of chalets. The business was preponderantly one of the receipt of rents.'

By contrast, in *Furness v IRC* (1999), net profit from caravan sales exceeded the net profit produced by caravan rents and the Special Commissioner decided that s 105(3) was inapplicable. In *Weston v IRC* (2000), another case where the taxpayer lost, the High Court confirmed that whether assets were investments or were held as part of the business and whether the business consisted wholly or mainly of the holding of those investments were questions of fact to be determined by the Commissioners. **[31.49]**

h) *A mixed business: The Farmer case*

It was accepted in this case that there was a single composite business comprising farming and the letting of various former farm buildings. The Special Commissioner concluded that on the application of the 'wholly or mainly' test and taking the business in the round the business consisted mainly of farming. The relevant factors considered by the Commissioner were:
(1) the business property was a landed estate with most of the land being used for farming. Lettings were subsidiary to the farming business and were of short duration;
(2) of the capital employed in the business (£3.5m), £1.25m could be appropriated to the lettings and £2.25m to farming;
(3) the employees and consultants spent more time on the farming activities than on the lettings;
(4) farm turnover exceeded letting turnover in six years out of eight;
(5) in every year the net profit of the lettings exceeded the net profit of the farm.
  Three points should be stressed. *First*, that in all such cases it is necessary to consider the position over a period of time rather than at a particular moment. *Secondly*, that the Revenue's argument that the 'wholly or mainly' test fell to be determined on the basis of net profits was rejected in favour of a test based on the character of the business as a whole. *Thirdly*, there is the tie-in with the test laid down in TCGA 1992 Sch A1 para 22 where a company

is a trading company, so that business asset taper is available on the shares (see *Tax Bulletin*, June 2001). In the context of determining whether a company's non-trading purposes are capable of having a 'substantial' effect on the extent of the Company's activities, the various factors identified in *Farmer* are considered to be relevant (eg turnover from non-trading activities; the assets base of the company; expenses incurred by or time spent by officers and employees in undertaking the activities of the company; the historical context of the company.                                  **[31.50]**

i)    *A mixed business: The Stedman case*

In *IRC v George (Stedman Dec'd)* (2003) the company owned a caravan site and carried on the following activities:

● residential homes park—site fees and connected to sewerage, water, electricity and gas;
● sale of caravans;
● business of buying and selling gas, electricity, water etc at a profit;
● storage of touring caravans when not in use (investment);
● income from letting a warehouse and a grazing agreement (investment);
● a club for residents and non residents.

Laddie J held (confirming *Weston* on this point) that the correct approach in deciding whether business property relief was available was **first** to identify what investments the company had and **then** to decide if the business was mainly one of holding investments. Dealing with this first question he concluded that:

> 'the business of receiving site fees from each of the mobile home owners for the right to place their vehicles on the Company's land ... and the receipt of fees for allowing others to store mobile homes ... constitute exploitation of the Company's proprietary rights in the land. They constitute the business of holding an investment.'

Having so decided, he then concluded that all of the services (the supply of water, electricity and gas) were ancillary to that investment business.

> 'It appears to me that what falls within the investment business "bag" is not only the core holding of the land and the receipt of fees or rent in respect of its use, but also all those activities which, viewed through the eyes of an average businessman, would be regarded as "incidental" to that core activity ... activities which are incidental to the letting of land are not severable from it and take on the investment character of the letting. Activities which have minor commercial justification by themselves are likely to be regarded as part of the business which they support ... the extent to which such subsidiary activity makes a profit will be some indication of whether it is a stand alone business or should be regarded as merely incidental to the business it supports. Put another way, an activity which is incidental to, say, an investment business does not cease to be so because the landlord decides to make an additional profit on it.'

Whilst this concept of 'incidental activities' appears straightforward in the application to (say) let industrial units in respect of compliance and management activities designed to keep up the standard of the investment properties, in other cases it may be difficult to identify the core business to which other activities may then be classified as subsidiary. In the case of caravan/ mobile home parks it is a little difficult to say that the core activity is a simple letting of land given that it is the services provided which are an integral part of the letting. As a not wholly dissimilar example take the business of an hotelier or of providing bed and breakfast, where, although there is an exploitation of land (in the form of the relevant building), the predominant activity is the services provided. The *Furness* case was not mentioned in the judgment: it is perhaps distinguishable on the basis that the most profitable activity involved the selling of caravans and that the site was also used by touring caravans.

Having classified the business as predominantly investment and classified the facilities provided by the company as incidental thereto Laddie J concluded that only the operation of the Country Club and the caravan sales were not investment activities and so the bulk of the gain and net profit flowed from site fees and storage. Hence he concluded that the main activity of the company was the holding of an investment in land so that no business relief was available.

The case came before the Court of Appeal which held that it was difficult to see any reason why an active family business of the kind in this case should be denied business property relief merely because a necessary component of its profits making activity was the use of land. It was further held that IHTA 1984 s 105 did not require the opening of an investment bag into which were placed all the acticities linked to the activity that required the use of land ie the caravan park just because it could be said that such activities were ancillary to the caravan business. Attempting to identify 'the very business' of the company was not required by s 105 nor did it give adequate weight to the hybrid nature of a caravan site business. Further, just because services were provided under the terms of the lease did not mean that they lost their character as services and became part of the investment activity.

This is a welcome decision for the taxpayer because it now means that activities will not be denied relief just because they support or and related to an investment activity. Clearly, whether relief is available in any given case will depend on the facts.

The decision in the *Stedman* case was followed in *Clark (Executors of Clark (decd) v Revenue & Customs Comrs* [2005] (SpC). **[31.51]**

j)  *Excepted assets*

Non-business assets cannot be included as a part of the business in an attempt to take advantage of the relief (IHTA 1984 s 112. Problems commonly arise when surplus cash is retained within the business: relief will only be available if that cash 'was required at the time of transfer for future use for (the purposes of the business)' (see s 112(2)(b) and *Barclays Bank Trust Co Ltd v IRC* (1998)). HMRC may also query sums held in deposits at Lloyd's by Names. **[31.52]**

k)  *Contracts to sell the business and options*

Relief is not available for transfers of the sale proceeds from a business and the relief does not extend to business property subject to a 'buy and sell' agreement. Arrangements are common in partnership agreements and amongst shareholder/directors of companies to provide that if one of the partners or shareholder/directors dies then his PRs are obliged to sell the share(s) and the survivors are obliged to purchase them. As this is a binding contract, the beneficial ownership in the business or shares has passed to the purchaser so that business relief is not available.

**EXAMPLE 31.12**

The shares of Zerzes Ltd are owned equally by the four directors. The articles of association provide that on the death of a shareholder his shares *shall* be sold to the remaining shareholder/directors who *must* purchase them. Business relief is not available on that death. If the other shareholders had merely possessed pre-emption rights or if the arrangement had involved the use of options, as no binding contract of sale exists, the relief would apply.

Particular problems may arise to the context of partnership agreements: professional partnerships, for instance, commonly include automatic accruer clauses whereby the share of a deceased partner passes automatically to the surviving partners with his estate being entitled to payment either on a valuation or in accordance with a formula. After some uncertainty the Revenue now accepts that accruer clauses do not constitute binding contracts for sale and nor do option arrangements (*Law Society's Gazette*, 4 September 1996, p 35). It appears that the section applies only if the contract is to sell a business or part of a business: by contrast a contract to sell assets used in a business is not caught.                                                   **[31.53]**

l)    *Businesses held in settlements*

For interest in possession trusts the relief is given, as one would expect, by reference to the life tenant. (It should be noted that the changes made by FA 2006 in respect of interests in possession do not appear to affect the issue of business property relief as it applies to settled property, because all that is required for the relief to be claimed is for the transferor to have a 'beneficial interest in possession'; the deemed ownership of the underlying capital is not at issue in these circumstances. Whether this was intentional or an oversight remains to be seen). So long as the life tenant satisfies the two-year ownership test, relief will be given at the following rates:
(1)    *100% relief* for all unquoted shares and for businesses belonging to the trust;
(2)    *50% relief* for controlling shareholdings in listed companies held in the trust; and
(3)    *50% relief* for the assets listed in (6) at **[31.43]** which are held in the trust and which are either used by the life tenant for his own business or by a company controlled by him.
*Fetherstonehaugh v IRC* (1984) concerned the availability of relief when land held under a strict settlement was used by the life tenant as part of his farming business (he was a sole trader absolutely entitled to the other business assets). The Court of Appeal held that 100% (then 50%) relief was available under s 105(1)(a) on the land in the settlement with the result that the subsequent introduction of 50% (then 30%) relief is apparently redundant in such cases. HMRC now accepts that in cases similar to *Fetherstonehaugh*

the maximum 100% relief will be available since the land will be treated as an 'asset used in the business' and, as its value is included in the transfer of value, the land will be taxed on the basis that the deceased was the absolute owner of it.

For trusts without interests in possession, relief is given so long as the conditions are satisfied by the trustees. The relief will be given against the anniversary charge and when the business ceases to be relevant property (eg when it leaves the trust) on fulfilment of the normal conditions. **[31.54]**

m) *'Control'*

Control is defined as follows:

> 'a person has control of a company at any time if he then has the control of powers of voting on *all questions* affecting the company as a whole which if exercised would yield a majority of the votes capable of being exercised thereon ...' (IHTA 1984 s 269(1)).

Hence, control of more than 50% of the votes exercisable in general meeting will ensure that the transferor has 'control' for the purposes of BPR. A transfer of his shares in a listed company will attract 50% relief and a transfer of qualifying assets used by a company which the taxpayer controls 50% relief (control is also important in the context of APR: see **[31.67]**). In calculating whether he has control, a life tenant can aggregate shares held by the settlement with shares in his free estate, whilst the related property rules (see **[28.70]**) result in shares of husband and wife being treated as one holding.

In *Walker v IRC* (2001) a Special Commissioner decided that a 50% shareholder, who was the chairman of the company and who had a casting vote at meetings, was able to control a majority of votes at any meeting as required by s 269. In *Walding v IRC* (1996) Knox J decided that all votes had to be taken into account for the purpose of deciding whether the s 269 test was satisfied. The fact that shares were held by a five-year-old child did not therefore mean that those votes could be ignored for this purpose. **[31.55]**

n) *Relief for minority shareholdings in unquoted companies*

For transfers of value made and other events occurring on or after 6 April 1996 relief at 100% is available for all minority shareholdings in unquoted companies (including companies listed on AIM). Prior to that date relief at 100% was only available for substantial minority shareholdings (ie 25% plus) in such companies with smaller shareholdings attracting only 50% relief. As a result of the change all shares in unquoted companies may now attract 100% relief irrespective of the size of holding: the continuing distinction in the legislation between controlling shareholdings and others remains important, however, where assets are owned outside the company. **[31.56]**

o) *Switching control*

It might be assumed that because of the two-year ownership requirement, both the business property (eg the shares) and control must have been owned throughout this period. This, however, does not appear to be the case for relief under s 105(1)(b) since it is only the shares transferred which must have been owned for two years and control is only required immediately before the relevant transfer. Thus the taxpayer may—for instance as the result of a buy-back—obtain control of the company many years after acquiring his shares.

**EXAMPLE 31.13**

Of the 100 issued ordinary shares in Buy-Back Ltd Zack owns 40, Jed 40 and the remaining 20 are split amongst miscellaneous charities. Assume that in July 2002 Buy-Back buys Zack's holding. As those shares are cancelled the issued capital falls to 60 shares of which Jed owns 40. Were he to die in September 2002, his shareholding would fall under s 105(1)(b).

It may be possible for the partners in a quasi-partnership company to ensure that each obtains control for a short period (eg one month) to produce enhanced business relief. **[31.57]**

**EXAMPLE 31.14**

The shares in ABCD Ltd are owned as to 25% each by A, B, C and D. The shares are divided into four classes in December 2002 which will carry control in January, February, March and April 2003 respectively. In January 2003 A transfers his shares.
(1)  As A has control (under s 269(1)) in January 2003 he is entitled to relief at 50% on land which he transfers and which had been used by the company.
(2)  Might temporary shifts of control be nullified under the *Ramsay* principle? It is arguable that, as the legislation expressly requires control at one moment only (namely immediately before the transfer), that is an end to the matter. It is, however, desirable that A should at the time of transfer actually possess control of the business: ie the other shareholders must accept that A could, if he wished, exercise his voting control over the affairs of the company.

p)  *Business relief and the instalment option*

Any value transferred after deduction of BPR may be further reduced by the normal IHT exemptions and reliefs which are deducted *after* business relief so that a lifetime gift, for instance, may be reduced by the £3,000 annual exemption. Further, any tax payable may normally be spread over ten years and paid by annual interest-free instalments (see **[30.51]**). This instalment election is only available, in the case of lifetime gifts, if the IHT is borne by the donee: on death the election should be made by the PRs. Although there is a similarity between assets which attract business relief and assets qualifying for the instalment option, the option may be valuable where there are excepted assets or where the business is disqualified under the s 105(3) test (see **[31.47]**). This is because the definition of 'qualifying property' for the purposes of s 227 (the instalment option) and s 234 (interest-free instalments) is wider than for the purposes of BPR. There are limitations on the availability of instalment relief in the case of a transfer of unquoted shares not giving control (see **[31.54]**), as the following table indicates:

| Relevant business property | Instalment assets |
|---|---|
| (IHTA 1984 Part V Chapter 1) | (IHTA 1984 Part VIII) |
| *s 105( 1) (a)*: a business or an interest in a business | *s 227*: a business or an interest in a business |
| *s 105(1) (b)*: shares etc, giving control | *s 227(2)*: land *s 228(1) (a)*: shares etc, giving control |
| *s 105( 1) (bb)*: unquoted shares | *s 228(1) (b)*: on death, unquoted shares being at least 20%, of the total transfer |
| | *s 228( 1) (c)*: unquoted shares with hardship |
| | *s 228( 1) (d)* and *228(3)*: unquoted shares within the 10% and 20,000 rule |
| | *s 229*: woodlands. |

These limitations on the instalment option have been defended by HMRC on the grounds that 'it has been considered inappropriate for the instalment facility to apply in cases involving less than substantial interests in unquoted companies' (see further (1985) 6 *CTT News* 284). **[31.58]**

### q) *Clawback*

When a transferor makes a lifetime chargeable transfer or a PET and dies within seven years, the IHT or extra IHT payable is calculated on the basis that business relief is not available unless the original (or substituted) property remains owned by the transferee at the death of the transferor (or at the death of the transferee if earlier) and would qualify for business relief immediately before the transferor's death (ignoring, however, the two-year ownership requirement). This 'clawback' of relief is anomalous: relief on death is not similarly withdrawn if the business property is sold after the death. Of course, the instalment option is similarly restricted since it is only available if the original or substituted business property is owned by the transferee at death. Relief is given for substituted property when the entire (net) proceeds of sale of the original property are reinvested within three years (or such longer period as the Board may allow) in replacement qualifying property (for the position where business property is replaced by agricultural property and *vice versa* see *Tax Bulletin*, 1994, p 182 and **[31.74]**).

**EXAMPLE 31.15**

(1)   Sim gave his ironmonger's business to his daughter, Sammy, in 2001 (a PET) and died in 2007. Sammy has continued to run the business. Although the PET became chargeable because of Sim's death within seven years, 100% relief is available (qualifying property retained by donee).

(2)   As in (1) save that Sammy immediately sold the business (or the business was closed down) in 2001.
      No business relief is available on Sim's death. The value of the business in 2001 is taxed and forms part of Sim's cumulative total on death.

(3)   As in (1) save that Sammy had incorporated the business late in 2001 and had continued to run it as the sole shareholder/director.
Business relief is available on Sim's death (substituted qualifying property).

(4)   Sim settled business property on A&M trusts (a PET since the settlement was made prior to 22 March 2006). Before the death of Sim in 2007 a beneficiary either becomes entitled to an interest in possession in the settled property (prior to 22 March 2006) or, alternatively, absolutely entitled. Has the transferee retained business property in these cases so that the original gift continues to qualify for relief? In the former situation (where a life interest has come into being) common sense would suggest the answer is 'yes' since the property is owned throughout the period by the transferee who in this case would be the trustees. HMRC disagrees, however, on the basis that under IHTA 1984 s 49(1) the life tenant is treated as owning the capital assets. In the latter case beneficial title has passed to the beneficiary. Accordingly, *a clawback charge arises in both cases.* If the original settlement had been on interest in possession trusts and by the time of the settlor's death the trustees had advanced the property (under the terms of the trust) to the life tenant there would be no clawback since the life tenant is treated as the 'transferee' throughout.

**EXAMPLE 31.16**

Jock settles his business (then worth £500,000) on discretionary trusts in 1997 (a chargeable lifetime transfer). He dies in 2003 when the business has been sold by the trustees.

(1)   *On the 1997 transfer:* 100% relief is available so that the value transferred is nil.

(2)   *On his death in 2003:* no relief is available so that extra IHT is calculated on a value transferred of £500,000. Note that the result of a withdrawal of relief is that the additional tax is charged on the entire value of the business but this does not alter Jock's cumulative total (*contrast* the effect of loss of relief when the original transfer was a PET: see *Example 31.14(5)*).

There was a technical argument that if the gifted property attracted 100% relief it was an exempt transfer either under IHTA 1984 s 20 (see **[31.5]**) or under s 19 (see **[31.3]**). If so, the transfer could be neither chargeable nor potentially exempt with the result that the clawback rules did not apply! (See *Private Client Business* (1992) p 7.) 'For the removal of doubt' FA 1996 inserted a new subsection (7A) into s 113A which provided that in determining whether there was a PET or chargeable transfer for the purposes of the clawback rules any reduction in value under the BPR rules is ignored. **[31.59]**

r)   *Business property subject to a reservation*

Business property subject to a reservation is treated as comprised in the donor's estate at death (if the reservation is still then subsisting) or, if the reservation ceases *inter vivos*, as forming the subject matter of a deemed PET made at that time (see **Chapter 29**). In both cases business relief may be available to reduce the value of the property subject to charge. Whether the relief is available or not is generally decided by treating the transfer as made by the *donee* who must therefore satisfy the BPR requirements (FA 1986 Sch 20 para 8). However, for these purposes, the period of ownership of the donor can be included with that of the donee in order to satisfy the two-year requirement.

Any question of whether shares or securities qualify for 100% BPR must be decided as if the shares or securities were owned by the *donor* and had been owned by him since the date of the gift. Accordingly, other shares of the donor (or related property of the donor) will be relevant in deciding if these requirements are satisfied. **[31.60]**

**EXAMPLE 31.17**

(1) Wainwright gives his ironmonger's business to his daughter Tina and it is agreed that he shall be paid one half of the net profits from the business each year (a gift with reservation).
  (i) At the time of the original gift (a PET) the property satisfied the requirements for business relief. If the PET becomes chargeable as the result of Wainwright's death within the following seven years, relief continues to be available if Tina has retained the original property or acquired replacement property.
  (ii) The business is also treated as forming part of Wainwright's estate on his death under FA 1986 s 102, but business relief may be available to reduce its value under FA 1986 Sch 20 para 8. Whether relief is available (and if so at what percentage) is decided by treating the transfer of value as made by the *donee*. Accordingly, Tina must satisfy the conditions for relief although she can include the period of ownership/occupation of Wainwright before the gift. (A similar provision applies if the reservation ceases during Wainwright's lifetime so that he is treated as making a PET.)
(2) Assume that Wainwright owns 100% of the shares in Widgett's Ltd and gives 20% of those shares to Tina subject to a reserved benefit. Assuming that he dies within seven years:
  (i) Relief at 100% was originally available under s 105(1)(b) when the gift was made and continues to apply to that chargeable PET if Tina has retained the shares.
  (ii) The shares are treated as forming part of Wainwright's estate because of the reserved benefit. Business relief will be available if Tina satisfies the basic requirements: ie she must have retained the original shares which must still qualify as business property.
*Note*: Where property attracting 100% relief is transferred by outright gift it may be argued that this is an exempt gift under IHTA 1984 s 20 (see **[31.5]**) with the result that the reservation of benefit rules cannot apply (see FA 1986 s 102(5)(b)).

s) *The consequences of relief at 100%*

The introduction of 100% relief has had far-reaching consequences. For instance:
(1) It is more important than ever to ensure that full relief is not lost because of a technicality. Consider, for instance, whether cash reserves will be excepted assets: are they required for use in the business? (see **[31.51]**).
(2) Consideration should be given to the structuring of business activity so that the relief is readily available: simple structures are likely to be best and fragmentation arrangements that have been common in the past may prove disadvantageous.
(3) Relief at 100% is equally available in the case of unquoted companies, sole traders and partnerships.

(4)  In contrast to the relief available for heritage property, there is no clawback of the 100% relief on death if the heir immediately sells the assets: if heritage property is or can be run as a business it would be more attractive to use BPR than the heritage exemption.

(5)  If lifetime gifts are made and the donor dies within seven years, relief may not be available if the donee has already sold the assets (see [31.58]). Because there is no clawback on death, taxpayers may be encouraged to delay passing on property qualifying for 100% relief.

(6)  If it is feared that the new reliefs will be withdrawn in the future, a gift of property on to flexible trusts under which the donor retains control as trustee should be considered (note, however, the trap if it is envisaged that the property will be distributed within the first ten years of the trust: see [34.34]).

(7)  Wills should be reviewed to ensure that, whenever this is practicable, property which is eligible for 100% BPR is left to a person other than a surviving spouse so that BPR is not lost.

**EXAMPLE 31.18**

Assume that X owns a farm worth £1m; farmhouse worth £400,000 and investments worth £1.5m. Mrs X will run the farm on his death and he therefore envisages a will in the following terms:
  (i)   nil rate band (£285,000) to his children;
  (ii)  residue to Mrs X.
  No IHT will be payable on Mr X's death but the position would be much improved if the will had provided:
  (i)   farm and nil rate band to/on trust for children;
  (ii)  residue to Mrs X.
  Again no IHT will be payable but assets passing tax free to the children now total £1,285,000.
  And after X's death Mrs X purchases the farm for £1m—there is no clawback of the APR (see below)/BPR.
  By her will Mrs X leaves everything to the children (including the farm) and provided that she has owned the farm for two years 100% relief is again available.
  *Notes:*
  (a)  In cases where Mrs X cannot afford the purchase price, consider leaving the sum outstanding.
  (b)  To ensure that Mrs X will acquire the farm, consider granting her an option in the will.
  (c)  Stamp duty land tax will be payable on the sale.
  (d)  In cases where the availability of the relief is in doubt (for example, because there is a mixed business) consider leaving the business in a discretionary trust so that if relief turns out not to be available the property can be appointed out to the surviving spouse under IHTA 1984 s 144. Alternatively if relief is available the trust may continue in being or the property can be appointed out to the children.

(8)  Business property relief is intended to benefit businesses as opposed to investments but this objective has not been fully achieved. Investments in limited partnerships may attract 100% relief and an AIM portfolio, qualifying for relief at 100%, may be attractive.

(9)  In some cases it may be worth de-listing: ie turning the fully quoted company back into an unquoted company or one dealt in on AIM because of the higher levels of relief available.                    [31.61]

## 3 Agricultural property relief ('APR': IHTA 1984 ss 115–124)

IHTA 1984 ss 115–124 contains rules, introduced originally in FA 1981, giving relief for transfers of agricultural property. As with BPR, this relief is given automatically. The old (pre-1981) regime will not be considered save for a brief mention of the transitional provisions.　　　　　**[31.62]**

### a) *'Agricultural property'* (*IHTA 1984 s 115(2)*)

Relief is given for transfers of value of *agricultural property*, defined in s 115(2) as follows:

> ' "Agricultural property" means agricultural land or pasture (*part 1*) and includes woodland and any building used in connection with the intensive rearing of livestock or fish if the woodland or building is occupied with agricultural land or pasture and the occupation is ancillary to that of the agricultural land or pasture (*part 2*); and also includes such cottages, farm building and farmhouses, together with the land occupied with them, as are of a character appropriate to the property (*part 3*).'

(The italicised division into parts is adopted from the *Starke* and *Rosser* cases which are considered below and is intended to identify the three separate dimensions of the definition.)

This definition includes habitat land and land used for short rotation coppice (this being a way of producing renewal fuel for bio-mass-fed power stations—in simple terms, willow or other cuttings are planted on farmland and, after the first year, are harvested every three years or so and then made into chips which are used as fuel).

Farm cottages included in the definition of 'agricultural property' must have been occupied for the purposes of agriculture (see s 117(1)); ESC F16 extends relief in such cases to include a cottage occupied by a retired farm employee or his surviving spouse provided that either the occupier is a statutorily protected tenant or the occupation is under a lease granted to the farm employee for his life and that of any surviving spouse as part of his contract of employment by the landlord for agricultural purposes.　　**[31.63]**

### b) *The Starke and Rosser cases*

*Starke v IRC* (1995) concerned the transfer of a 2.5 acre site containing within it a substantial six-bedroomed farmhouse and an assortment of outbuildings together with several small areas of enclosed land which was used as part of a medium-sized farm carrying on mixed farming. The court concluded that the relevant property did not constitute 'agricultural land' within the above definition of 'agricultural property'. The decision is hardly surprising but it does point to the dangers of a farmer giving away the bulk of his farm retaining only the farmhouse and a relatively small area of land. Such retained property will rarely qualify for relief as was emphasised in *Rosser v IRC* (2003) where the deceased having given away 39 acres of land was left owning only a house, barn and two acres of land when she died.　　**[31.64]**

### c) *The 'character appropriate' test: general principles*

When is a farmhouse of a character appropriate to the property? The question arises regularly in practice and the following points may be noted:

(1)    The stakes were dramatically increased in this area as a result of the introduction of 100% relief coupled with rising house prices.

(2)    A farmhouse will be primarily a 'residential' property—hence CGT roll-over relief is not available on it (see **[22.72]**) and nor will business property relief usually be available (save for any part used 'exclusively' for business purposes);

(3)    The general approach of the Revenue has most recently been expressed by Twiddy in *Taxation*, 15 June 2000, p 277.

(4)    In addition to satisfying the character appropriate test, remember that relief is only given on the 'agricultural value' (see **[31.64]**) of the property and that the house must be occupied for purposes of agriculture (see s 117).

(5)    the farmhouse must be of a character appropriate to 'the property': what is meant in this context by 'the property'? In *Rosser* the Special Commissioner had no doubt about the required nexus commenting:

'The nexus between the farm buildings and the property in section 115(2) is that the farm buildings and the property must be in the estate of the person at the time of making the deemed disposition under section 4(1) of the 1984 Act. The alternative view that the farm buildings are in the estate but the property to which they refer is not is untenable. This view would seriously undermine the structure for inheritance tax and create considerable uncertainty about when tax is chargeable and the amount of the value transferred. I would add, however, that *estate* is defined in the 1984 Act as the aggregate of all property to which the person is beneficially entitled. Property is widely defined in the 1984 Act to include rights and interests of any description. It will therefore cover not only tangible property but also equitable rights, debts and other choses in action, and indeed any right capable of being reduced to money value. Thus, under the situation covered in section 115(2) if the person making the deemed disposition at death legally owned the farm buildings and had a legal interest such as a right of profit in the property to which the character of the farm buildings is appropriate then the farm buildings and the property would be part of the estate.'    **[31.65]**

d)    *Case law on the farmhouse and character appropriate test*

The cases (all decided by the Special Commissioners) may be summarised as follows:

In *Dixon v IRC* (2002) the property comprised a cottage, garden and orchard totalling 0.6 acres. Although surplus fruit was sold it was decided that the property was not agricultural land or pasture: rather there was a residential cottage with land.

In *Lloyds TSB (PRs of Antrobus deceased) v IRC* (2002) it was agreed that Cookhill Priory (a listed six-bed country house) was a farmhouse and that the surrounding 125 acres (plus 6.54 acres of tenanted land and buildings including a chapel) were agricultural property. The Special Commissioner decided that the character appropriate test was also satisfied.

In *Higginson's Exors v IRC* (2002) Ballywood Lodge, formerly a nineteenth century hunting lodge of six beds with 63 acres of agricultural land; three acres of formal gardens and 68 acres of woodland and wetland around Ballywood Lake, was considered not to be a farmhouse ('not the style of house in which a typical farmer would live').

Of the three, the most important decision in terms of laying down a guiding principle is the *Antrobus* case in which the Commissioner summed up the factors to be taken into account in applying the character appropriate test as follows:

'Thus the principles which have been established for deciding whether a farmhouse is of a character appropriate to the property may be summarised as: first, one should consider whether the house is appropriate by reference to its size, content and layout, with the farm buildings and the particular area of farmland being farmed (*Korner*); one should consider whether the house is proportionate in size and nature to the requirements of the farming activities conducted on the agricultural land or pasture in question (*Starke*); thirdly, that although one cannot describe a farmhouse which satisfies the "character appropriate" test one knows one when one sees it (*Dixon*); fourthly, one should ask whether the educated rural layman would regard the property as a house with land or a farm (*Dixon*); and, finally, one should consider the historical dimension and ask how long the house in question has been associated with the agricultural property and whether there was a history of agricultural production (*Dixon*).'

No one factor is decisive but the factors are considered in the round and the eventual decision based upon 'the broad picture'. In practice expert evidence (especially evidence of comparables) is of crucial significance.
**[31.66]**


e) *'Agricultural value'* (*IHTA 1984 s 115(3)*)

It is the *'agricultural value'* of such property which is subject to the relief: defined as the value which the property would have if subject to a perpetual covenant prohibiting its use otherwise than as agricultural property. Enhanced value attributable to development potential is not subject to the relief. BPR may apply to this excess value in the case of farmland although not in the case of the farmhouse: in practice the agricultural value is often considered to be around two-thirds of open market value, although in current market conditions a much smaller discount may be appropriate. This point was made by the Special Commissioner in the *Higginson* case when he commented:

'A property may command a high price in the open market because of potential for development; and subsection (3) clearly caters for that situation. But it seems to me that the notional restrictive covenant would have much less of a deprecatory effect in a case where the property has a value greater than ordinary not because of development potential but rather because of what I might call "vanity value" on account of its site, style or the like. In the light of my decision the point is academic.'

The value of agricultural property may be artificially enhanced for the purposes of the relief by charging the costs of acquiring the agricultural property against non-qualifying property (see *Example 31.19*, below; IHTA 1984 ss 5(5), 162(4) and cf BPR, **[31.44]**). Further, it is not necessary to transfer a farming business or part thereof in order to obtain relief which can be given on a mere transfer of assets. **[31.67]**

**EXAMPLE 31.19**

A farmer owns a let farm qualifying for 50% agricultural relief and worth £1m, subject to a mortgage of £500,000. His other main assets are investments worth £500,000. Were he to die, the value of his estate on death would be £1m made up of the investments plus the farm after deducting the mortgage thereon. Agricultural relief at 50% would then be available on the *net* value of the farm (ie on £500,000) which would reduce that to £250,000 leaving a chargeable death estate of £750,000.

Suppose, however, that before his death the farmer arranged with the appropriate creditor to switch the mortgage from the agricultural land to the investments. The result then would be that on death the value of his estate would, as above, be £1m made up of the value of the farm (1m) since the investments now, after deducting the mortgage, are valueless. Accordingly, agricultural relief would be available on the entire value of the farm and amounts to £500,000 leaving a chargeable death estate of £500,000.

f) *The level of relief (IHTA 1984 s 116)*

Section 116 provides (subject to the provisions of s 117 which are considered in [**31.66**]) that the level of APR is 100% where:

'The interest of the transferor in the property immediately before the transfer carries the right to vacant possession or the right to obtain it within the next 12 months.'

This is extended by ESC F17 to cases where the transferor's interest in the property immediately before the transfer *either:*
(1)    carried the right to vacant possession within 24 months of the date of transfer; *or*
(2)    is notwithstanding the terms of the tenancy valued at an amount broadly equivalent to vacant possession value.

The former situation would cover the service of notices under the terms of the Agricultural Holdings Act 1986 and so-called '*Gladstone v Bower* arrangements' while the second situation would be relevant in cases akin to that of *Lady Fox* (discussed below at [**31.71**]).

With the passage of the Agricultural Tenancies Act 1995 100% relief was extended to landlords in cases where property was let on tenancies beginning on or after 1 September 1995. This applies to all tenancies: ie the relevant tenancy does not have to be a new style business tenancy under the 1995 legislation but includes, for instance, statutory succession rights arising on the death of a tenant (see *Private Client Business* (1996) p 2).

Otherwise the level of relief is at 50%.                    [**31.68**]

g) *Ownership and occupation requirements (IHTA 1984 s 117)*

*However*, relief is not available unless the further requirements of s 117 are satisfied:

's 116 does not apply to any agricultural property unless:

(a)    it was *occupied* by the transferor for the purposes of agriculture throughout the period of *two* years ending with the date of the transfer, or

(b)  it was *owned* by him throughout the period of *seven* years ending with that date and was throughout that period occupied (by him *or another*) for the purposes of agriculture.' (See *Harrold v IRC* (1996) for when a farmhouse is 'occupied'.)                                                                        **[31.69]**

### EXAMPLE 31.20

(1)  Dan started farming in 1985 and died in April 2003. As an owner-occupier he was entitled to APR at 100%.

(2)  Bill's farm was tenanted when he acquired it in 1989 but in 2002 the lease was surrendered. In August 2003 Bill died. He was the owner-occupier at death but did not satisfy the requirements of s 117(a); assuming that he has owned the farm for seven years, however, s 117(b) will be satisfied so that he will be entitled to 100% APR.

(3)  Jack acquired his farm as an investment in 1997 and died in 2003. No APR available.

(4)  Tom has owned agricultural land for ten years and has farmed it himself. He wishes to cease the farming operations himself and enters into a share farming arrangement with a neighbouring farmer under which Tom provides the land and the neighbouring farmer provides labour, live and dead stock etc. Tom dies. 100% relief will not be available unless the terms of the share farming agreement are such that Tom could, immediately before his death, serve notice to terminate the arrangements within 12 months.

(5)  Wilf died owning a meadow which had for more than seven years been let under a grazing agreement with a neighbour who had used the land to graze his horses. Relief was not available because the horses had no connection with agriculture and hence the meadow had not been occupied for the purposes of agriculture (*Wheatley (Executors of Wheatley) v IRC* (1998)). Contrast, however, the position if the grazing agreement had related to cattle or sheep, when it is accepted that a farming operation (the sale of grass) is being carried on, provided that it can be shown that the taxpayer is doing something (replanting, maintaining fences, etc) other than just receiving rent. It is not thought that the *Wheatley* decision is correct.

### h)  *Trusts and companies*

The relief (at 100% or 50% as appropriate) is available in three further cases: *first*, where agricultural property is held on discretionary trusts (100% relief, if the trustees have been farming the land themselves); *secondly*, where agricultural property is held on trust for a life tenant under an interest in possession trust; and *finally*, where agricultural property is held by a company in which the transferor of the shares has control. 'Control' has the same meaning as for BPR (see **[31.54]**). To claim the relief the appropriate two- or seven-year period of ownership must be satisfied by the company (*vis-à-vis* the agricultural property) and by the shareholder/transferor (*vis-à-vis* the shares transferred).                                                            **[31.70]**

### EXAMPLE 31.21

Muckspreader dies owning shares in a company owning agricultural land in circumstances when APR is available in respect of the shares. He leaves the shares to his widow. She dies within two years.

On the widow's death no APR is available because she does not get the benefit of Muckspreader's period of ownership of the shares. This is anomalous (compare the position for BPR). The position would have been different if Muckspreader had owned the agricultural land itself and left it to his widow; see IHTA 1984 s 120; cf s 123(1)(b).

### i)    *Technical provisions*

As with BPR there are technical provisions relating to replacement property and clawback (see **[31.58]**), transfers between spouses, and succession from a donor (see **[31.46]**). Similarly, a binding contract for the sale of the property results in APR not being available (see **[31.52]**).                                    **[31.71]**

### j)    *Agricultural tenancies*

The grant of a tenancy of agricultural property is not a transfer of value provided that the grant is for full consideration in money or money's worth (IHTA 1984 s 16). Hence, it is not necessary for the lessor to show (particularly in the case of transfers within the family) that he had no gratuitous intent and that the transaction was such as might be made with a stranger (see IHTA 1984 s 10(1)). For difficulties that may arise in ascertaining the market value of agricultural tenancies, see *Law Society's Gazette*, 1984, p 2749, *Law Society's Gazette*, 1985, pp 420 and 484, *Baird's Executors v IRC* (1991) and *Walton v IRC* (1996) (considered at **[28.73]**).                              **[31.72]**

### k)    *Clawback*

The availability of the relief when extra IHT is payable, or a PET becomes chargeable, because of a death within seven years is subject to the same restrictions as apply for BPR (see **[31.58]**).                                    **[31.73]**

### l)    *Lotting and the Fox decision*

In valuing an estate at death, 'lotting' requires a valuation on the basis that 'the vendor must be supposed to have' taken the course which would get the largest price for the combined holding 'subject to the caveat ... that it does not entail undue expenditure of time and effort' (see further **[30.4]**).

In *IRC v Gray* (1994) the deceased had farmed the Croxton Park Estate in partnership with two others and the land was subject to tenancies which Lady Fox, as freeholder, had granted to the partnership. The Revenue sought to aggregate or lot together the freehold in the land with her partnership share as a single unit of property. It may be noted that under the partnership deed she was entitled to 921/2% of profits (and bore all the losses). The Court of Appeal reversed the Lands Tribunal holding that lotting was appropriate since that was the course which a prudent hypothetical vendor would take to obtain the best price. The fact that the interests could not be described as forming a 'natural unit of property' was irrelevant. The arrangement employed in this case was commonly undertaken (before the introduction of 100% APR) in order to reduce the tax charge on agricultural property. An alternative involved leases being granted to a family farming company and the Revenue seeks to apply this decision to those arrangements. As a result of ESC F17 noted in **[31.65]** transfers in *Fox*-type cases now attract 100% relief.
                                                                          **[31.74]**

m)  *Transitional relief; double discounting*

Under the rules which prevailed up to 1981 APR was available where L let Whiteacre to a partnership consisting of himself and his children M and N. On a transfer of the freehold reversion (valued on a tenanted, not a vacant possession, basis) 50% relief was available. The ingredient of 'double discounting' consisted of first reducing the value of the property by granting the lease and then applying the full (50%) relief to that discounted value. As a *quid pro quo* the Revenue argued that the grant of the lease could be a transfer of value even if for a full commercial rent.

Double discount is not available under the present system of agricultural relief and the grant of the tenancy will not be a chargeable transfer of value if for full consideration (IHTA 1984 s 16). On a transitional basis, however, where land was let, as in the above example, on 10 March 1981 so that any transfer by L immediately before that date would have qualified for relief, on the next transfer of value, that relief will still apply but at the current level of 100%. (Note that the relief was limited to £250,000 of agricultural value (before giving relief) or to £1,000 acres, at the option of the taxpayer.) The transitional relief will not apply in cases where the pre-10 March 1981 tenancy has been surrendered and regranted but similar transitional relief applies where before 10 March 1981 the land was let to a company which the transferor controlled (IHTA 1984 s 116(2)–(5)).                    **[31.75]**

**EXAMPLE 31.22**

For many years Mary has owned agricultural land which has been let to a family farming company in which she owns 100% of the shares. On her death 50% relief only will be available on the land since she is not entitled to obtain vacant possession (the company being a separate legal entity). If, however, the arrangements had been in place before 10 March 1981, Mary may be entitled to 100% relief under the 'Double Discount Rule' (for instance, if she was a director of the company immediately before 10 March 1981). Relief will only be available up to a maximum of 1,000 acres or land which at 10 March 1981 was worth up to £250,000.

n)  *Milk quota*

Following *Cottle v Coldicott* (1995) the Capital Taxes Office now considers that milk quota comprises a separate asset distinct from the land. Accordingly it will not qualify for APR but 'with an owner occupied dairy farm, business relief at the same rate will normally be available in the alternative' (see *Inheritance Tax Manual IHTM 24506*). This treatment appears at odds with the BPR provisions (see *Taxation*, 3 June 1999, p 244).                    **[31.76]**

o)  *Inter-relation of agricultural and business property reliefs*

Although the two reliefs are similar and overlap, the following distinctions are worthy of note:
(1)  APR is given in priority to BPR (IHTA 1984 s 114(1)).
(2)  Differences exist in the treatment of woodlands, crops, livestock, deadstock, plant and machinery, and farmhouses etc. When APR does not apply, consider whether BPR is available.

(3)   APR is only available on property situated in the UK, Channel Islands and Isle of Man whereas BPR is not so restricted.

(4)   In the *Tax Bulletin*, 1994, p 182, the Inland Revenue commented that:

'Where agricultural property which is a farming business is replaced by a non-agricultural business property, the period of ownership of the original property will be relevant for applying the minimum ownership condition to the replacement property. Business property relief will be available on the replacement if all the conditions for that relief were satisfied. Where non-agricultural business property is replaced by a farming business and the latter is not eligible for agricultural property relief, s 114(1) does not exclude business property relief if the conditions for that relief are satisfied.'

'Where the donee of the PET of a farming business sells the business and replaces it with a non-agricultural business the effect of s 124A(1) is to deny agricultural property relief on the value transferred by the PET. Consequently, s 114(1) does not exclude business property relief if the conditions for that relief are satisfied: and, in the reverse situation, the farming business acquired by the donee can be "relevant business property" for the purposes of s 113B(3)(c).'   **[31.77]**

p)   *Relief at 100%*

Many of the comments made at **[31.60]** in the context of BPR apply equally to agricultural property. In addition:

(1)   there is no longer any attraction in the type of fragmentation arrangements illustrated in the *Fox* case (see **[31.71]**). Maximum relief is available for in-hand land;

(2)   in-hand land need not be farmed by the owner himself. He can enter into contract farming arrangements without jeopardising 100% relief provided that these are correctly structured;

(3)   the grant of new tenancies after August 1995 will not jeopardise 100% relief: thought should be given to terminating or amending (eg by adding a small area of extra land) existing tenancies so that a new tenancy resulting in 100% relief for the landlord arises;

(4)   complex structures should no longer be set up but what should be done with existing structures? The costs of unscrambling may be considerable and it is worth reflecting that, assuming that the value of tenanted land is one half of the vacant possession value, the effect of 50% APR is to reduce the tax rate to 10% of vacant possession value and as that tax can be paid in ten instalments, the annual tax charge is a mere 1%.
   **[31.78]**

### 4   Relief for heritage property (IHTA 1984 ss 30–35 as amended)

In certain circumstances an application can be made to postpone the payment of IHT on transfers of value of heritage property. Such claims now have to be made within two years of the transfer of value or relevant death or within such longer period as the Board may allow (IHTA 1984 s 30(3BA) inserted by FA 1998). As tax can be postponed on any number of such transfers, the result is that a liability to IHT can be deferred indefinitely (similar deferral provisions operate for CGT: TCGA 1992 s 258(3)). Tax postponed under these provisions may subsequently become chargeable under IHTA 1984 s 32 on the happening of a 'chargeable event'. If the transfer is potentially exempt, an application for conditional exemption can only be made (and is only necessary) if the PET is rendered chargeable by the donor's death within seven years. HMRC provides a now somewhat out-of-date guide, *Capital Taxation and the National Heritage* (IR 67), and a Guide to the 1998 changes, *Capital Taxes Relief for Heritage Assets* (January 1999). **[31.79]**

a) *Conditions to be satisfied if IHT is to be deferred*

In order to obtain this relief, *first*, the property must fall into one of the categories set out in IHTA 1984 s 31(1):

*Category 1:* any relevant object which appears to the Board to be pre-eminent for its national, scientific, historic or artistic interest (this category was restricted by FA 1998 by the inclusion of the requirement that the object must be pre-eminent): see IHTA 1984 s 31(1)(a).

*Category 2:* land of outstanding scenic, historic, or scientific interest (IHTA 1984 s 31(1)(b)).

*Category 3:* buildings of outstanding or architectural interest and their amenity land (s 31(1)(c), (d)) and chattels historically associated with such buildings (s 31(1)(e)).

*Secondly*, undertakings have to be given with respect to that property to take reasonable steps for its preservation; to secure reasonable access to the public (see *Works of Art: A Basic Guide* published by the Central Office of Information); and (in the case of *Category 1* property) to keep the property in the UK. In appropriate cases of *Category 1* property, it had been sufficient for details of the object and its location to be entered on an official list of such assets and concern had been expressed that proper access for the public was not always available. FA 1998 accordingly provided that the public must have extended access (ie access not confined to access when a prior appointment is made) and for greater disclosure of information about designated items (IHTA 1984 s 31(4FA)(4FB) inserted by FA 1998, see also **[31.78]**).

The undertaking must be given by 'such person as the Treasury think appropriate in the circumstances of the case'. In practice, this will mean a PR, trustee, legatee or donee.

A *third* requirement exists in the case of lifetime transfers of value. The transferor must have owned the asset for the six years immediately preceding the transfer if relief is to be given. Notice, however, that the six-year requirement can be satisfied by aggregating periods of ownership of a husband and wife and that it does not apply in cases where the property has been inherited on a death and the exemption has then been successfully claimed. It is surprising that the six-year requirement is limited to *inter vivos* transfers thereby permitting deathbed schemes. **[31.80]**

b) *Reopening existing undertakings*

With the aim of securing greater public access, FA 1998 provided that in the case of claims for conditional exemption made on or after 31 July 1998 open access (ie other than merely by prior appointment) must be given (s 31(4FA)). Further, the terms of any undertakings must be published. In addition, a procedure was introduced as a result of which existing undertakings (given from 1976 onwards) can be varied by agreement or, in certain circumstances, a variation in their terms might be imposed (s 35A). **[31.81]**

c) *Effect of deferring IHT*

Where relief is given the transfer is a 'conditionally exempt transfer'. So long as the undertakings are observed and the property is not further transferred IHT liability will be postponed. If there is a subsequent transfer, the existing exemption may be renewed and a further exemption claimed.

Three '*chargeable events*' cause the deferred IHT to become payable: *first*, a breach of the undertakings; *secondly*, a sale of the asset; and *thirdly*, a further transfer (*inter vivos* or on death) without a new undertaking. **[31.82]**

d) *Calculation of the deferred IHT charge*

Calculation of the deferred IHT charge will depend upon what triggers the charge. If there is a breach of undertakings, the tax is charged upon the person who would be entitled to the proceeds of sale were the asset then sold. The value of the property at that date will be taxed according to the transferor's rates of IHT. When he is alive, this is by reference to his cumulative total at the time of the triggering event (any PETs that he has made are ignored for these purposes even if they subsequently become chargeable); when he is dead, the property is added to his death estate and charged at the highest rate applicable to that estate but at half the IHT table rates unless the conditionally exempt transfer was made on his death.

**EXAMPLE 31.23**

In 2000 Aloysius settled a Rousseau painting (valued at £500,000) on discretionary trusts. The transfer was conditionally exempt, but, six years later (when the picture is worth £650,000), the trustee breaks the undertakings by refusing to allow the painting to be exhibited in the Primitive Exhibition in London. If Aloysius is still alive in 2006, IHT is calculated on £650,000 at Aloysius' rates according to his cumulative total of chargeable transfers in 2006. Had Aloysius died in 2006 with a death estate of £1,000,000, £650,000 would be charged at half the rates appropriate to the highest part of an estate of £1,650,000. As can be seen from this example, considerable care should be exercised in deciding whether the election should be made. If the relevant asset is likely to increase in value, it may be better to pay off the IHT earlier assuming that sufficient funds are available.

If the deferred charge is triggered by a sale, the above principles operate, save that it is the net sale proceeds that will be subject to the deferred charge. Expenses of sale, including CGT, are deductible. If there is a disposal of *part* of a property which is conditionally exempt the designation of the *whole* is reviewed: if the disposal has not materially affected the heritage entity then the designation for the remainder stays in force and the IHT charge is limited to the part disposal. However, if the part disposal results solely from the leasehold enfranchisement under the Leasehold Reform, Housing and Urban Development Act 1993 (or Leasehold Reform Act 1967) these rules do not apply: instead there is no review of the retained property and the charge is limited to the part sold.

Calculation of the deferred charge is more complex where it is triggered by a gift since two chargeable transfers could occur; the first on the gift and the second by the triggering of the deferred charge. If the gift is a chargeable event (excluding PETs) the tax payable on that gift is credited against the triggered deferred charge. Where the gift is a chargeable transfer, but not a chargeable event, as the triggering charge does not arise the credit will be available against the next chargeable event affecting that property.

**EXAMPLE 31.24**

Eric makes a conditionally exempt transfer to Ernie on his death in 2002. Ernie in turn settles the asset on discretionary trusts in 2006 and (although the asset is pre-eminent) the trustees do not give any undertaking.

*The creation of the settlement* is a chargeable transfer by Ernie. IHT will be calculated at half rates in 2006.

*The triggered charge*: the value of the asset in 2006 will be subject to IHT at Eric's death rates. A tax credit for IHT paid on the 2006 gift which is attributable to the value of the asset is available.

If the trustees had given an appropriate undertaking in 2006 (since Ernie inherited the property on Eric's death, the six-year ownership requirement does not need to be satisfied by Ernie), the trust would be taxed as above. The transfer is not a chargeable event so that no triggering of the conditionally exempt transfer occurs. The tax credit is available if this charge is triggered at a later stage, eg by the trustees selling the asset.

If a conditionally exempt transfer is followed by a PET which is a chargeable event with regard to the property, IHT triggered is allowed as a credit against IHT payable if the PET becomes chargeable.

Where there has been more than one conditionally exempt transfer of the same property, and a chargeable event occurs, HMRC has the right to choose which of the earlier transferors (within 30 years before the chargeable event) shall be used for calculating the sum payable.                    **[31.83]**

**EXAMPLE 31.25**

Z gives a picture to Y who gives it to X who sells it. There have been two conditionally exempt transfers (by Z and Y) and HMRC can choose (subject to the 30-year time limit) whether to levy the deferred IHT charge according to Z or Y's rates.

e)   *Settled property*

Where heritage property is subject to an interest in possession trust created prior to 22 March 2006, or to one of the limited exceptional interest in possession trusts (that is not a trust for a bereaved minor or a disabled person's trust) created on or after that date (see **[33. 4]**), it is treated as belonging to the life tenant and the above rules are applied. The exemption may also be available for heritage property held in a discretionary trust (IHTA 1984 ss 78, 79) and for interest in possession trusts created on or after 22 March 2006 that do not fall within one of the exceptional categories, which are treated in the same way as discretionary trusts.                    **[31.84]**

## f)    *Maintenance funds*

IHTA 1984 ss 27, 57(5) and Sch 4 paras 1–7 provide for no IHT to be charged when property (whether or not heritage property) is settled on trusts to secure the maintenance, repair etc of historic buildings. Such trusts also receive special income tax treatment (TA 1988 ss 690 ff) and, for CGT, the hold-over election under TCGA 1992 s 260 is available.

These funds can be set up with a small sum of money so long as there is an intention to put in further sums later. The introduction of the PET in 1986 has, however, produced a dilemma for an estate owner. He could give away property to his successor as a PET and rely upon living for seven years in order to avoid IHT. Alternatively, he could transfer that property by a conditionally exempt transfer into a maintenance fund. It is not possible to make a gift of the property and then, if the donor dies within seven years, for the donee at that point to avoid the IHT charge by transferring the property into a maintenance fund.

Settled property will be free of IHT on the death of the life tenant if within two years after his death (three years if an application to court is necessary) the terms of the settlement are altered so that the property goes into a heritage maintenance fund (IHTA 1984 s 57A).                    **[31.85]**

## g)    *Private treaty sales and acceptance in lieu*

Heritage property can be given for national purposes or for the public benefit without any IHT or CGT charge arising (IHTA 1984 s 23: see **[31.85]**). Alternatively, the property can be sold by private treaty (not at an auction) to heritage bodies listed in IHTA 1984 s 25(1) and Sch 3. Such a sale can offer substantial financial advantages for the owner. For instance, if conditionally exempt property is sold on the open market, conditional exemption is lost and furthermore a CGT charge may arise. By contrast, a sale by private treaty does not lead to a withdrawal of the exemption or IHT charge, nor is there a liability to CGT. Not surprisingly, because of these fiscal benefits the vendor will have to accept a lower price than if he sold on the open market. The relevant arrangement involves a 'douceur': broadly, the price that he will receive is the net value of the asset (ie market price less prospective tax liability) *plus* 25% of the tax saved in the case of chattels (10% for land).

**EXAMPLE 31.26**

(taken from *Capital Taxation and the National Heritage* (IR 67))
    Calculation of the price, with 'douceur' (usually 25% but subject to negotiation), at which a previously conditionally exempted object can be sold to a public body by private treaty.

| | | |
|---|---|---|
| Agreed current market value (say) | | £100,000 |
| Tax applicable thereto: | | |
| CGT at (say) 30% on gain element, assumed to be £40,000 | £12,000 | |

| | | |
|---|---|---|
| ED, CTT or IHT exemption granted on a previous conditionally exempt transfer now recoverable at (say) 60% on £88,000 (ie market value less CGT) | £52,800 | |
| Total tax | £64,800 | £64,800 |
| Net after full tax | | £35,200 |
| Add back 25% of tax (the 'douceur') | | £16,200 |
| Price payable by a purchaser, all retained by vendor | | £51,400 |

HMRC writes off the total tax of £64,800 (£12,000 + £52,800).

The vendor has £16,200 more than if he had sold the object for £100,000 in the open market and paid the tax. The public body acquires the object for £48,600 less than its open market value.

An asset can be offered to HMRC in lieu of tax (see IHTA 1984 s 230(1)). Acceptance in lieu of tax has similar financial advantages for the vendor to a private treaty sale. The Secretary of State has to agree to accept such assets and it should be noted that the standard of objects which can be so accepted is very much higher than that required for the conditional exemption.

Under these arrangements the offeror obtains the benefit of any rise in the value of property between the date of the offer and its acceptance by HMRC, but he has to pay interest on the unpaid IHT until his offer is accepted. As an alternative, therefore, taxpayers can elect for the value of the property to be taken at the date of the offer (thereby avoiding the payment of any interest but forgoing the benefit of any subsequent rise in the value of the property: F(No 2)A 1987 s 97 and see SP 6/87). [31.86]

## 5 Gifts to political parties (IHTA 1984 s 24)

Such gifts are exempt without limit from IHT, whether made during life or on death. There are detailed provisions which deny relief where the gift is delayed, conditional, made for a limited period, or could be used for other purposes (IHTA 1984 s 24(3) (4)). Any capital gain that would otherwise arise can be held over under TCGA 1992 s 260. [31.87]

## 6 Gifts to charities (IHTA 1984 s 23)

Gifts to charities are exempt without limit. As with gifts to political parties detailed provisions deny the exemption if the vesting of the gift is postponed; if it is conditional; if it is made for a limited period; or if it could be used for non-charitable purposes (on charitable gifts, generally, see **Chapter 53**). Note that relief is not given if the gift is to a foreign charity: for relief to be available the gift must be to a UK charity which carries on its charitable work abroad, or to a UK charity which can then pass the benefit of that gift to a foreign charity. [31.88]

# 32 IHT—settlements: definition and classification

*Updated by Natalie Lee, Senior Lecturer in Law, University of Southampton and Aparna Nathan, LLB Hons, LLM, Barrister, Gray's Inn Tax Chambers*

## I   INTRODUCTORY AND DEFINITIONS

In framing the original IHT rules taxing settled property the objective was to ensure (1) that it is the capital of the settlement which is subject to tax and not just the value of the various beneficial interests and (2) that settled property is taxed neither more nor less heavily than unsettled property. The changes introduced by FA 2006 are a blatant attempt at preventing the wealthy from using trusts to minimise IHT. The measures are, however, unclear and incoherent, and seem to be founded on a misconception of the many and varying reasons for establishing a trust.     [**32.1**]

### 1   What is a settlement?

a)   *Definition*

'Settlement' is defined in IHTA 1984 s 43:

'(2)   "Settlement" means any disposition or dispositions of property, whether effected by instrument, by parole or by operation of law, or partly in one way and partly in another, whereby the property is for the time being—

     (a)   held in trust for persons in succession or for any person subject to a contingency; or

     (b)   held by trustees on trust to accumulate the whole or part of any income of the property or with power to make payments out of that income at the discretion of the trustees or some other person, with or without power to accumulate surplus income; or

(c)   charged or burdened (otherwise than for full consideration in money or money's worth paid for his own use or benefit to the person making the disposition), with the payment of any annuity or other periodical payment payable for a life or any other limited or terminable period;
...

(3)   A lease of property which is for life or lives, or for a period ascertainable only by reference to a death, or which is terminable on, or at a date ascertainable only by reference to, a death, shall be treated as a settlement and the property as settled property, unless the lease was granted for full consideration in money or money's worth, and where a lease not granted as a lease at a rack rent is at any time to become a lease at an increased rent it shall be treated as terminable at that time.'   **[32.2]**

**EXAMPLE 32.1**

(1)   Property is settled on X for life remainder to Y and Z absolutely (a fixed trust; see sub-s (2)(a), above).

(2)   Property is held on trust for 'such of A, B, C, D, E and F as my trustees in their absolute discretion may select' (a discretionary trust; see sub-s (2)(b), above).

(3)   Property is held on trust 'for A contingent on attaining 18' (a contingency settlement; see sub-s (2)(a), above).

(4)   Property is held on trust by A and B as trustees for Z absolutely (a bare trust, although for IHT purposes there is no settlement and the property is treated as belonging to Z).

(5)   A and B jointly purchase Blackacre. Under LPA 1925 ss 34 and 36 (as amended) there is a statutory trust of land with A and B holding the land on trust (as joint tenants) for themselves as either joint tenants or tenants in common in equity. For IHT purposes there is no settlement and the property belongs to A and B equally.

(6)   A grants B a lease of Blackacre for his (B's) life at a peppercorn rent. This is a settlement for IHT purposes and A is the trustee of the property (IHTA 1984 s 45). Under LPA 1925 s 149 the lease is treated as being for a term of 90 years that is determinable on the death of B.

b)   *The Lloyds Bank case*

Mr and Mrs E owned their house as beneficial tenants in common. On her death, Mrs E left her half share on trust providing that:

'While my husband ... remains alive and desires to reside in the property and keeps the same in good repair and insured comprehensively to its full value ... and pays and indemnifies my Trustees against all rates taxes and other outgoings in respect of the property my Trustee shall not make any objection to such residence and shall not disturb or restrict it in any way and shall not take any steps to enforce the trust for sale on which the property is held or to obtain any rent or profit from the property.'

Subject to the above, the property was held on trust for her daughter absolutely. In *IRC v Lloyds Private Banking Ltd* (1998) it was held that the above clause gave Mr E a life interest in the property since it elevated him to the status of a sole occupier of the entirety free from any obligation to pay compensation for excluding the daughter from occupation and free from the risk that an application would be made to court for sale. See also *Woodhall (Woodhall's Personal Representative) v IRC* (2000), *Faulkner (Adam's Trustee) v IRC* (2001) and the comments by Lightman J and the Court of Appeal in *IRC v Eversden* (2002), (2003). **[32.3]**

c) *Associated operations*

In *Rysaffe Trustee Co (CI) Ltd v IRC* (2003) Park J and the Court of Appeal decided that for the purposes of s 43 'dispositions' had its ordinary meaning and was not extended to include a disposition by associated operations. In simple terms therefore provided that a trust lawyer would say that five separate trusts had been established with identical property (in *Rysaffe* it was private company shares) then the IHT legislation must be applied on that basis. The use of the plural 'dispositions' in s 43(2) deals with the situation where property is added to an existing settlement whether by the settlor or by some other person. **[32.4]**

d) *The contrast with income tax: 'bounty'*

Although 'settlement' has a wide definition for income tax purposes it has been restricted to cases where there is an element of bounty (see **[16.61]**): for IHT purposes there is no such restriction and hence commercial arrangements (eg landlord sinking funds) may have IHT ramifications. **[32.5]**

e) *Resettlements*

As discussed in **[25.82]** difficulties have arisen in identifying, for CGT purposes, when property has been resettled (ie when a new settlement has been created out of an existing settlement). Difficulties may also occur when it is necessary to determine whether the settlor has created one or more settlements. There are similar problems in IHT.

In *Minden Trust (Cayman) Ltd v IRC* (1984) an appointment of settled property in favour of overseas beneficiaries was held to amend the terms of the original settlement so that the terms of that appointment read with the original settlement were dispositions of property and, therefore, a settlement. **[32.6]**

**EXAMPLE 32.2**

Each year Sam creates a discretionary trust of £3,000 (thereby utilising his annual exemption) and his wife does likewise. At the end of five years there are ten mini discretionary trusts. As a matter of trust law, and assuming that each settlement is correctly documented, there is no reason why this series should be treated as one settlement. So far as the IHT legislation is concerned the settlements are not made on the same day (see IHTA 1984 s 62); the associated operations provisions (IHTA 1984 s 268) would seem inapplicable (the facts are quite different from those in *Hatton v IRC* (1992) and in no sense is this a series of operations affecting the same property: see the *Rysaffe* case considered above. The *Ramsay* principle, although of uncertain ambit, could only be applied with difficulty to a series of gifts. The separate trusts should be kept apart (there should be no pooling of property) and each settlement should be fully documented.

## 2   Settlors

In the majority of cases it is not difficult to identify the settlor, since there will usually be one settlor who will create a settlement by a 'disposition' of property (which may include a disposition by associated operations; see IHTA 1984 s 272). If that settlor adds further property, this creates no problems in the interest in possession settlement, but difficulties arise if the settlement is discretionary (see [**34.33**]) with further complications if the original property was excluded property and the additional property was not, or *vice versa* (see **Chapter 35** and *Tax Bulletin*, February 1997). A settlement may have more than one settlor:

**EXAMPLE 32.3**

(1)   Bill and Ben create a settlement in favour of their neighbour Barum.
(2)   Bill adds property to a settlement that had been created two years ago by Ben in favour of neighbour Barum.

IHTA 1984 s 44(2) states that:

'Where more than one person is a settlor in relation to a settlement and the circumstances so require, this Part of this Act (except s 48(4)–(6)) shall have effect in relation to it as if the settled property were comprised in separate settlements.'

*Thomas v IRC* (1981) indicates that this provision only applies where an identifiable capital fund has been provided by each settlor. The fund will be treated as two separate settlements in the case of discretionary trusts where both the incidence of the periodic charge and the amount of IHT chargeable may be affected. IHTA 1984 s 44(1) defines settlor (in terms similar to those for income tax purposes) thus:

'In this Act "settlor", in relation to a settlement, includes any person by whom the settlement was made directly or indirectly, and … includes any person who has provided funds directly or indirectly for the purpose of or in connection with the settlements or has made with any other person a reciprocal arrangement for that other person to make the settlement.'                                                   **[32.7]**

## 3   Additions of property

A further problem arises where there is only one settlor who adds property to his settlement; is this for IHT purposes one settlement or two? This question is significant in relation to discretionary trusts (especially with regard to timing and rate of the periodic and inter-periodic charges) and where excluded property is involved in a settlement. As a matter of trust law, there will be a single settlement where funds are held and managed by one set of trustees for one set of beneficiaries, so that such additions will usually not lead to the creation of separate settlements. An article in the *Tax Bulletin*, February 1997 ('Excluded Property Settlements by People Domiciled Overseas') presented a somewhat different view:

'In the light of the definitions of "settlement" and "settled property" in s 43, our view is that a settlement in relation to any particular asset is made at the time when that asset is transferred to the settlement trustees to hold on the declared trusts. Thus, assets added to a settlor's own settlement made at an earlier time when the settlor was domiciled abroad will not be "excluded", wherever they may be situated, if the settlor has a UK domicile at the time of making the addition.'

At first glance it would appear to suggest that in these circumstances each addition of property involves the creation of a separate settlement. This is not, apparently, the Revenue's view, however, and it has subsequently confirmed that there remains a single settlement, but in testing whether that constitutes (in whole) an excluded property settlement, each addition (and the settlor's domicile at that time) needs to be considered. More recently the Revenue has indicated that it is reconsidering the relationship between the reservation of benefit rules and excluded property settlements: at present if X (a non UK domiciliary) establishes a discretionary trust under which he can benefit and subsequently acquires a UK domicile the property remains excluded and the reservation of benefit rules are inapplicable.          **[32.8]**

## 4  Trustees

The ordinary meaning is given to the term 'a trustee', although by IHTA 1984 s 45 it includes any person in whom the settled property or its management is for the time being vested. In cases where a lease for lives is treated as a settlement the lessor is the trustee.          **[32.9]–[32.20]**

## II  CLASSIFICATION OF SETTLEMENTS

The Finance Act 2006 brought about a substantive change in the categorisation of trusts for IHT purposes. Because trusts in existence on 22 March 2006 (Budget day) will, on the whole, continue to be governed by the 'old' regime, both the old and the 'new' regime will be considered in this chapter. Moreover, the term 'interest in possession' continues to be of importance to both regimes, and is considered at some length.

## 1  The categories

### (i)  *The old regime*

Under the former regime, settlements for IHT purposes were divided into two main categories with one sub-category.

*Category 1* A settlement with an interest in possession, eg where the property is held for an adult tenant for life who, by virtue of his interest, is entitled to the income as it arises or, typically in the case of a trust of a residential property, is entitled to the use or occupation of the trust property.

*Category 2* A settlement lacking an interest in possession, eg where trustees are given a discretion over the distribution of the income. At most, beneficiaries have the right to be considered by the trustees; the right to ensure that the fund is properly administered; and the right to join with all the other beneficiaries to bring the settlement to an end.

This category also includes settlements where the property is held on trust for a minor, contingent on his attaining a specified age. As long as the beneficiary is a minor there will be no interest in possession and the settlement will fall into *Category 2*, unless the trust satisfies the requirements for a 'privileged' settlement.

*Sub-category* Into this category fall special or privileged trusts. They lack an interest in possession, but are not subject to the *Category 2* regime. The main example considered in this book is the A&M trust.

To place a particular trust into its correct category is important for two reasons. *First*, because the IHT treatment of each is totally different both as to incidence of tax and as to the amount of tax charged; and *secondly*, because a change from one category to another will normally give rise to an IHT charge. For example, if a life interest ceases, whereupon the fund is held on discretionary trusts, the settlement moves from *Category 1* to *Category 2*, and a chargeable occasion (the ending of a life interest) has occurred.     **[32.21]**

(ii)   *The new regime*

The new regime for the inheritance taxation of trusts introduced by FA 2006 abandons, in effect, the classification of trusts into those with, and those without, an interest in possession and creates a number of new categorisations.

*Category 1* A disabled person's interest. This is an interest in possession to which a disabled person is treated as beneficially entitled (IHTA 1984 s 89B, inserted by FA 2006 Sch 20 para 6). Generally, a disabled person is someone who is either mentally incapable of managing their affairs, or in receipt of an attendance allowance or disability living allowance (IHTA 1984 s 89(4)–(6)).

*Category 2* A settlement with an interest in possession where the settled property forms part of the beneficiary's estate. This category comprises (i) an immediate post-death interest. This is an interest in possession arising immediately on a death on or after 22 March 2006 (for example, on the death of a husband, the wife of whom becomes entitled to a life interest in his property under his will) (IHTA 1984 s 49A inserted by FA 2006 Sch 20 para 5); (ii) a disabled person's interest (see category 1, above); (iii) a transitional serial interest. This includes (a) an interest in possession arising on or after 22 March 2006 but before 6 April 2008 in immediate succession to an interest in possession that was subsisting prior to 22 March 2006 under a trust created before then; and (b) an interest in possession to which a surviving spouse or civil partner becomes entitled on the death on or after 6 April 2008 of his or her late spouse or civil partner, where that late spouse or civil partner's interest in possession had been subsisting prior to 22 March 2006 under a trust created before then.

*Category 3* A settlement with no interest in possession or treated as having no interest in possession. This category comprises not only discretionary trusts (see **[32.21]**, but also trusts with an interest in possession, with the exception of immediate post-death interests, transitional serial interests, and trusts in favour of disabled persons. While trusts for bereaved minors and age 18–25 trusts lack an interest in possession, they are not subject to the *Category 3* regime (see *Category 4*, below).

*Category 4* A settlement for a bereaved minor and age 18–25 trusts. These trusts which, in effect, replace A&M trusts, enjoy similar privileges to those formerly enjoyed by A&M trusts.     **[32.22]**

## 2 The meaning of an 'interest in possession'

Whilst the term 'interest in possession' is not, in itself, as significant under the new regime as it was under the former regime (which continues to apply to those trusts created prior to 22 March 2006), it remains important as the categories in [32.22] above demonstrate. Normally trusts can easily be slotted into their correct category. Trusts falling within the sub-category of the old regime were carefully defined so that any trust not specifically falling into one of those special cases must fall into *Category 2*. Problems were principally caused by the borderline between *Categories 1* and *2* where the division was drawn according to whether the settlement had an interest in possession or not. In the majority of cases no problems arose: at one extreme stood the life interest settlement; at the other the discretionary trust. However, what of a settlement which provides for the income to be paid to Albert, unless the trustees decide to pay it to Bertram, or to accumulate it; or where the property in the trust is enjoyed *in specie* by one beneficiary as the result of the exercise of a discretion (eg a beneficiary living in a dwelling house which was part of a discretionary fund)? To resolve these difficulties, the phrase an 'interest in possession' needs definition. The legislation did not, and still does not, assist; instead, its meaning must be gleaned from a Press Notice of the Revenue and *Re Pilkington (Pearson v IRC)* (1981) which largely endorses the statements in that Press Notice.                                        **[32.23]**

*IR Press Notice (12 February 1976)* This provides as follows:

> 'an interest in settled property exists where the person having the interest has the *immediate entitlement* (subject to any prior claims by the trustees for expenses or other outgoings properly payable out of income) *to any income* produced by that property as the income arises; but ... a discretion or power, in whatever form, which can be exercised *after income arises* so as to withhold it from that person negatives the existence of an interest in possession. For this purpose a power to accumulate income is regarded as a power to withhold it, unless any accumulation must be held solely for the person having the interest or his personal representatives.

> On the other hand the existence of a mere power of revocation or appointment, the exercise of which would determine the interest wholly or in part (but which, so long as it remains unexercised, does not affect the beneficiary's immediate entitlement to income) does not ... prevent the interest from being an interest in possession.'

The first paragraph is concerned with the existence of discretions or powers which might affect the destination of the income after it has arisen and which prevent the existence of any interest in possession (eg a provision enabling the trustees to accumulate income or to divert it for the benefit of other beneficiaries). The second paragraph concerns overriding powers which, if exercised, would terminate the entire interest of the beneficiary, but which do not prevent the existence of an interest in possession (eg the statutory power of advancement). Administrative expenses charged on the income can be ignored in deciding whether there is an interest in possession, so long as such payments are for 'outgoings properly payable out of income'. A clause in the settlement permitting expenses of a capital nature to be so charged is, therefore, not covered and the Revenue has argued that the mere presence of such a clause is fatal to the existence of any interest in possession (see [**32.27**]).                                                                    [**32.24**]

*Re Pilkington (Pearson v IRC)* (1981) The facts of the case were simple. Both capital and income of the fund were held for the settlor's three adult daughters in equal shares subject to three overriding powers exercisable by the trustees: (1) to appoint capital and income amongst the daughters, their spouses and issue; (2) to accumulate so much of the income as they should think fit; and (3) to apply any income towards the payment or discharge of any taxes, costs or other outgoings which would otherwise be payable out of capital. The trustees had regularly exercised their powers to accumulate the income. What caused the disputed IHT assessment (for a mere 444.73) was the irrevocable appointment of some £16,000 from the fund to one of the daughters. There was no doubt that, as a result of the appointment, she obtained an interest in possession in that appointed sum; but did she already have an interest in possession in the fund? If so, no IHT would be chargeable on the appointment (see [**33.28**]); if not, there would be a charge because the appointed funds had passed from a 'no interest in possession' to an 'interest in possession' settlement (*Category 2* to *Category 1*).

The Revenue contended that the existence of the overriding power to accumulate and the provision enabling all expenses to be charged to income deprived the settlement of any interest in possession. It was common ground that whether such powers had been exercised or not was irrelevant in deciding the case. The overriding power of appointment over capital and income did not prevent there from being an interest in possession (see the second paragraph of the Press Notice at [**32.24**] above).

For the bare majority of the House of Lords the presence of the overriding discretion to accumulate the income was fatal to the existence of any interest in possession. 'A present right to present enjoyment' was how an interest in possession was defined and the beneficiary did not have a present right. 'Their enjoyment of any income from the trust fund depended on the trustees' decision as to accumulation of income' (*per* Viscount Dilhorne). No distinction is to be drawn between a trust to pay income to a beneficiary, but with an overriding power to accumulate, and a trust to accumulate, but with a power to pay. Hence, in the following examples there is no interest in possession:
(1)    to A for life but trustees may accumulate the income; and
(2)    on trust to accumulate the income but with a power to make payments to A.

For a recent application of the principles in *Re Pilkington (Pearson v IRC)*, see *Oakley (as Personal Representatives of Jossaume) v IRC [2005]* STC (SCD) 343.
                                                                                       [**32.25**]

3   **Problems remaining after Pilkington**

The test laid down by the majority in the House of Lords established some certainty in a difficult area of law and it is possible to say that the borderline between trusts with and without an interest in possession (under the old regime) is reasonably easy to draw; where there is uncertainty about the entitlement of a beneficiary to income, it is likely that the settlement will fall into the 'no interest in possession' regime.                                    **[32.26]**

The following are some of the difficulties that may affect trusts created prior to 22 March 2006 left in the wake of *Pilkington*:

*Dispositive and administrative powers* For there to be an interest in possession the beneficiary must be entitled to the income as it arises. Were this test to be applied strictly, however, even a trust with a life tenant receiving the income might fail to satisfy the requirement because trustees may deduct management expenses from that income, so that few beneficiaries are entitled to all the income as it arises. This problem was considered by Viscount Dilhorne as follows:

> 'Parliament distinguished between the administration of a trust and the dispositive powers of trustees ... A life tenant has an interest in possession but his interest only extends to the net income of the property, that is to say, after deduction from the gross income of expenses etc properly incurred in the management of the trust by the trustees in the exercise of their powers. A dispositive power is a power to dispose of the net income. Sometimes the line between an administrative and a dispositive power may be difficult to draw but that does not mean that there is not a valid distinction.'

In *Pilkington* the trustees had an overriding discretion to apply income towards the payment of any taxes, costs, or other outgoings which would otherwise be payable out of capital and the Revenue took the view that the *existence* of this overriding power was a further reason for the settlement lacking an interest in possession. Was this power administrative (in which case its presence did not affect the existence of any interest in possession) or dispositive (fatal to the existence of such an interest)? Viscount Dilhorne decided that the power was administrative. Acceptable though this argument may be for management expenses, is it convincing when applied to other expenses and taxes (eg CGT and IHT) which would normally be payable out of the capital of the fund? In *Miller v IRC* (1987) the Court of Session held that a power to employ income to make good depreciation in the capital value of assets in the fund was administrative. It must be stressed that the House of Lords did not have to decide whether the Revenue's contention was correct or not and that Viscount Dilhorne's observations were *obiter dicta*.
                                                                            **[32.27]**

*Power to allow beneficiaries to occupy a dwelling house* This power may exist both in settlements which otherwise have an interest in possession and in those without. The mere existence of such a power is to be ignored; problems will only arise if and when it is exercised. SP 10/79 indicates that if such a power is exercised so as to allow, for a definite or indefinite period, someone other than the life tenant to have exclusive or joint right of residence in a dwelling house as a permanent home, there would be an IHT charge on the partial ending of a life interest. In the case of a fund otherwise lacking an interest in possession, the exercise of the power would result in the creation of such an interest and therefore, an IHT charge would arise. (These consequences do not arise if the trusts grant non-exclusive occupation or a contractual tenancy for full consideration.) Whether this view is correct is arguable; in *Swales v*

*IRC* (1984), for instance, the taxpayer's argument that the mandating of trust income to a beneficiary was equivalent to providing a residence for permanent occupation (and accordingly created an interest in possession) was rejected by the court. In practice, any challenge could prove costly to the taxpayer, and trustees who possess such powers should think carefully before exercising them. In recent years the issue which has arisen is whether on the facts of the case trustees are to *deemed* to have exercised their powers. A particular problem area is where the trustees own a beneficial interest (say 50%) in a residential property occupied by the other co-owner who is also a beneficiary of the trust (see **[32.32]**). **[32.28]**

*Interest-free loans to beneficiaries* It has been suggested that a free loan to a beneficiary would create an interest in possession in the fund. This is thought to be wrong: as the beneficiary becomes a debtor (to the extent of the loan), one wonders in what assets his interest subsists; the moneys loaned would appear to belong absolutely to him and he would not seem to enjoy any such rights in the IOU. **[32.29]**

*Position of the last surviving member of a discretionary class* If the class of beneficiaries has closed, the sole survivor is entitled to the income as it arises so that there is an interest in possession. When the class has not closed, however, trustees have a reasonable time to decide how the accrued income is to be distributed and, if a further beneficiary could come into existence before that period has elapsed, the current beneficiary is not automatically entitled to the income as it arises so that there is no interest in possession (*Moore and Osborne v IRC* (1984)). Likewise, if the class has not closed and the trustees have a power to accumulate income. **[32.30]**

*Trusts of Land and Appointment of Trustees Act 1996* Under s 12 of this Act a beneficiary with an interest in possession is given a right to occupy trust land (provided that various conditions are satisfied). In circumstances where there is more than one such beneficiary the position is regulated by s 13 under which the trustees have power to permit one of the beneficiaries to occupy the land whilst providing for the others to be compensated. **[32.31]**

**EXAMPLE 32.4**

Under the Titmarsh A&M trust the twins Tom and Tim became entitled to interests in possession in 2001 whilst at university. The trust owns a substantial London property (worth £1m) which Tom will now occupy; Tim who plans to travel is happy with the arrangement and does not expect to be paid 'compensation'. In these circumstances the IHT position is far from clear:
(1)   Prior to the 'arrangement' Tom and Tim enjoyed concurrent interests in possession and each would be treated for IHT purposes as entitled to half the value of the property (IHTA 1984 s 50).
(2)   As a result of the arrangement reached, Tom alone is now entitled to occupy and given that Tim has waived any right to compensation, it may be that he has made a PET of the value of his half share to Tom who is now treated as entitled to an interest in possession in the entirety (see *Law Society's Gazette*, 22 January 1997, p 30). The alternative view is that his rights under the settlement are not affected: see *Woodhall (Woodhall's Personal Representative) v IRC* (2000).

*Can an interest in possession be implied?* The question arises in a number of situations:

*Case 1*: Trustees of a discretionary trust exercise their powers to allow a beneficiary to occupy a dwelling house forming part of the trust fund. Occupation is rent free although the beneficiary is responsible for all outgoings and for insuring the property. SP 10/79 indicates that the Revenue would normally consider that an interest in possession has been created (for the CGT main residence relief, see *Sansom v Peay* (1976) at **[23.62]**).

*Case 2*: Trustees of a discretionary trust mandate the income to one of the beneficiaries. This is thought to be an exercise of the trustee's discretionary powers and not to involve the creation of an interest in possession.

*Case 3*: On the death of Mr A his half share in the matrimonial home is settled on discretionary trusts for a class of beneficiaries including Mrs A and the children. Mrs A continues in sole occupation of the house until her death. Has she become entitled to an interest in possession in the beneficial share in the house which was settled on Mr A's death? In this connection, note that:

(1)   Mrs A is the sole legal owner of the property;
(2)   s 12 of the 1996 Act (see **[32.31]**) may apply to give her a protected right of occupation;
(3)   she is entitled to occupy by virtue of her 50% beneficial share.

In these circumstances unless the discretionary trustees exercise their powers to create an interest in possession in favour of Mrs A it is not thought that one will be implied from the simple fact of Mrs A's occupation of the property (see the cases considered at **[32.3]**).

*Case 4*: A slightly different problem is whether a short-lived interest in possession can be treated as a nullity (see the *Hatton* case considered at **[28.103]**). Cautious draftsmen often provide that overriding powers can only be exercised to terminate an interest in possession once it has subsisted for at least (say) 12 months. **[32.32]–[32.50]**

## III   CREATION OF SETTLEMENTS

### 1   IHT on creation

Whereas the creation of a settlement prior to 22 March 2006 *may* have constituted a chargeable transfer of value by the settlor (for instance if the settlement was discretionary or was established by will), a settlement created on or after that date *will* constitute a chargeable transfer unless it is an *inter vivos* trust in favour of a disabled person (IHTA 1984 s 3A as amended by FA 2006 Sch 20 para 9), If the burden of paying the IHT is put upon the trustees of the settlement, HMRC accepts that the settlor of an *inter vivos* trust will not thereby retain an interest in the settlement under the income tax settlement provisions in ITTOIA 2005 s 619 et seq (SP 1/82) (see **[16.91]**).

Further, beneficiaries with life interests in trusts created on or after 22 March 2006 will no longer be treated as owning the capital of the fund itself unless the interest is a disabled person's interest, an immediate post-death interest or a transitional serial interest (see **[32.22]**). The result of this change is illustrated by the following examples, which compare the difference in treatment of pre- and post-22 March 2006 settlements:

**EXAMPLE 32.5**

(1)   In November 2005, S settled £100,000 on trust for himself for life with remainder to his children. The old regime applies. As S, the life tenant, is deemed to own the entire fund (and not simply a life interest in it) his estate has not fallen in value, and no IHT would have been charged. If, instead, this settlement had been made on 22 March 2006, S would no longer be treated as owning the entire fund, just the life interest in it and, to the extent that his estate had fallen in value by an amount representing the difference between the value of the entire fund and the life interest, not being a disabled person's interest and thus not a PET, it would have amounted to a chargeable transfer.

(2)   In December 2005, S settled £100,000 on trust for his wife for life, remainder to his children. S's wife was treated as owning the fund so that S's transfer was an exempt transfer to a spouse (for the position if after the wife's interest the property was held on discretionary trusts under which the settlor could benefit, see the *IRC v Eversden*). Had S settled the property in April, 2006, S's wife would no longer be treated as owning the fund and, accordingly, it would have amounted to a chargeable transfer.

The *inter vivos* creation of a settlement before 22 March 2006 would have been a PET in the following cases:
(1)   If it had created an interest in possession trust.
(2)   If the trust had satisfied the definition of an A&M or disabled trust.

In other cases before 22 March 2006 (and notably when a discretionary trust was created), there was an immediately chargeable transfer. For settlements created before 22 March 2006, even if the settlement as created had contained an interest in possession, the termination of that interest during the lifetime of the settlor and within seven years of the setting up of the trust would have triggered the anti-avoidance rules in IHTA 1984 s 54A if a discretionary trust then arose (see **[33.31]**). The new regime applies for settlements created after 22 March 2006. As a result, the inter-vivos creation of any settlement will trigger an inheritance tax charge. Further, there will be periodic and exit charges to inheritance tax.

No *inter vivos* settlement created on or after 22 March 2006 will qualify as a PET unless it is made in favour of a disabled person. The anti-avoidance rules in s 54A mentioned above will apply in the same fashion on the termination of a disabled person's interest.                                    **[32.51]**

## 2   CGT tie-in and Melville

Whilst general CGT hold-over relief is no longer available it remains possible to defer the payment of tax if the settlor makes a chargeable transfer (eg if he creates a discretionary trust: see TCGA 1992 s 260 and **[24.61]**).

**[32.52]–[32.70]**

**EXAMPLE 32.6**

(1)   Sid puts assets worth £285,000 into a discretionary trust. For *IHT* purposes, the transfer, although chargeable, falls within his nil rate band so that no tax is payable. For *CGT*, hold-over relief is available.

(2)   Hopeful puts assets worth £1m and showing a substantial gain into a discretionary trust which he retains a power to revoke. For *IHT* purposes, a

vexed question was whether he had made a transfer of value at all and, if so, of how much. If he could have revoked the trust as soon as it was created it was argued that he had lost nothing so that he had made no transfer of value and CGT hold-over relief was accordingly unavailable. In *Melville v IRC* (2001) a discretionary settlement included the settlor as a potential beneficiary and gave him (90 days after creation of the trust) the right to direct the trustees to exercise their discretionary powers (for instance by appointing the property to himself). The Court of Appeal held that the right possessed by the settlor was property for IHT purposes which could be exercised to (in effect) revoke the settlement. Therefore, there was a transfer of value (given the 90-day period) but of a relatively small amount. The result of that decision was reversed by FA 2002 which inserted a new provision into IHTA 1984 s 272 restricting the definition of 'property' by excluding settlement powers. Accordingly if Hopeful were to create his settlement today his estate would fall in value by the £1m of assets settled and the power reserved would be ignored. Hence he would suffer a substantial IHT charge. The 2002 legislation was, however, restrictively drafted and Hopeful should consider the following (*Melville Mark II*) variant.

(3) Hopeful puts assets worth £1m into a discretionary trust as above. The difference is that after (say) 100 days he becomes absolutely entitled to the property if he is then alive. This contingent remainder interest is property for IHT purposes and, given that it has a substantial value, restricts the fall in value of his estate. An interest under a settlement is not a 'settlement power' within the 2002 legislation.

## IV PAYMENT OF IHT

Primary liability for IHT arising during the course of the settlement rests upon the settlement's trustees. Their liability is limited to the property which they have received or disposed of or become liable to account for to a beneficiary and such other property which they would have received but for their own neglect or default.

If trustees fail to pay, HMRC can collect tax from any of the following (IHTA 1984 s 201(1)):

(1) Any person entitled to an interest in possession in the settled property. His liability is limited to the value of the trust property, out of which he can claim an indemnity for the tax he has paid.

(2) Any beneficiary under a discretionary trust up to the value of the property that he receives (after paying income tax on it) and with no right to an indemnity for the tax he is called upon to pay.

(3) The settlor, where the trustees are resident outside the UK, since, should the trustees not pay, the Revenue cannot enforce payment abroad. If the settlor pays, he has a right to recover the tax from the trust. **[32.71]–[32.90]**

## V RESERVATION OF BENEFIT

The creation of *inter vivos* settlements can cause problems in the reservation of benefit area and the following matters are especially worthy of note:

(1) *If the settlor appoints himself a trustee of the settlement,* that appointment will not by itself amount to a reserved benefit. If the terms of the settlement

provide for his remuneration, however, there may then be a reservation in the settled property (*Oakes v Stamp Duties Comr* (1954): it appears that this point is not taken by the Capital Taxes Office provided the remuneration is not excessive: see *Inheritance Tax Manual IHTM 14394*). Alternatively, the settlor/trustee could be paid an annuity, since such an arrangement will not constitute a reserved benefit and the ending of that annuity will not lead to any IHT charge (IHTA 1984 s 90). Particular difficulties are caused if the settlor/trustee is a director of a company whose shares are held in the trust fund. The general rule of equity is that a trustee may not profit from his position and this means that he will generally have to account for any director's fees that he may receive. It is standard practice, however, for the trust deed to provide that a trustee need not in such cases account for those fees. When the settlor/trustee is allowed to retain fees under the deed it is arguable that he has reserved a benefit in the trust assets within the ruling in the *Oakes* case. The Revenue has, however, indicated that it will not take this point so long as the director's remuneration is on reasonable commercial terms.

(2)   *If the settlor reserves an interest for himself under his settlement,* whether he does so expressly or whether his interest arises by operation of law, there is no reservation of benefit and he is treated as making a partial gift (see **Chapter 29**).

**EXAMPLE 32.7**

S created a settlement for his infant son, absolutely on attaining 21. No provision was made for what should happen if the son were to die before that age, and therefore there was a resulting trust to the settlor. The settlor died whilst the son was still an infant and was held to have reserved no benefit. Instead, he was treated as making a partial gift: ie a gift of the settled property less the retained remainder interest therein (*Stamp Duties Comr v Perpetual Trustee Co* (1943); and see *Re Cochrane* (1906) where the settlor expressly reserved surplus income).

The position with regard to discretionary trusts in which the settlor is included in the class of beneficiaries has been more problematic. In view of the limited nature of a discretionary beneficiary's rights (see *Gartside v IRC* (1968)) it is unlikely that he can be treated as making a partial gift. HMRC's view is that in all cases where a settlor is a discretionary beneficiary he will be treated as having reserved a benefit in the entire settled fund despite the fact that he may receive no payments or other benefits under the trust. This has now been accepted by the High Court in *IRC v Eversden* (2002) and was agreed between the parties on the appeal. The inclusion of the settlor's spouse as a discretionary beneficiary does not by itself result in a reserved benefit. Were that spouse to receive property from the settlement, however, and that property was then shared with or used for the benefit of the settlor, HMRC may then argue that there is a reserved benefit. Finally, the reservation rules do not apply to an outright exempt gift to a spouse although the FA 2003 amendments mean that reserved benefits can no longer be channelled through a spouse: see **Chapter 29**.                    **[32.91]**

# 33 IHT—settlements with an interest in possession: the old and new regimes

*Updated by Natalie Lee, Senior Lecturer in Law, University of Southampton and Aparna Nathan, LLB Hons, LLM, Barrister, Gray's Inn Tax Chambers*

The Finance Act 2006 introduced substantial changes to the tax treatment of settlements with beneficial interests in possession. Broadly speaking, the tax treatment of settlements created after 22 March 2006 is aligned with the tax treatment of discretionary settlements. Consequently, with limited exceptions, the inter vivos creation of an interest in possession settlement will give rise to an immediate chargeable transfer, and property held within the settlement, which will not be deemed to form part of the life tenant's estate, will be subject to periodic and exit charges. The result of the changes is that, in effect, two sets of rules operate for trusts with interest in possession: one for those where the interest arose prior to 22 March 2006, and the other for those created on or after that date.

## I BASIC PRINCIPLES

### 1 General

#### a) *Charging method*

A person who became entitled to the income of a fund prior to 22 March 2006 (usually the life tenant) and someone who becomes entitled to particular types of interests in possession on or after 22 March 2006 (see [**33.3**]) is treated '*as beneficially entitled to the property in which the interest subsists*' (IHTA 1984 s 49(1)). This rule is, of course, a fiction since a life tenant has no entitlement to capital. Although the section does not expressly provide for the deduction of trust liabilities, in practice it is the *net* value of the trust fund that is attributed to the relevant beneficiary.

As all the capital is treated as being owned by the life tenant, for IHT purposes it forms part of his estate, so that on a chargeable occasion IHT is charged at his rates. The settlement itself is not a taxable entity, although primary liability for IHT falls upon the trustees.

Interest in possession trusts created on or after 22 March 2006 which do not fall within the limited exceptional categories will be treated in the same way as trusts with no interest in possession, which are considered in the next chapter. In short, the IHT levy on these other settlements operates by treating the settlement as a separate chargeable entity and by (generally) imposing a tax charge at regular intervals. Even before the changes made by FA 2006, Carnwath LJ in *IRC v Eversden* (2003) at para 25, suggested that there appeared to be no reason why this method, if it achieves tax 'neutrality', should not be applied across the board. It would appear that FA 2006 sought to do just that, but it is questionable whether there should exist neutrality between two fundamentally different concepts.          **[33.1]**

b)    *Other interests*

As the life tenant of a trust with an interest in possession is treated as owning all the capital in the fund (IHTA 1984 s 49), other beneficiaries with 'reversionary interests' own nothing. IHTA 1984 s 47 defines reversionary interests widely to cover:

> 'a future interest under a settlement, whether it is vested or contingent (including an interest expectant on the termination of an interest in possession which, by virtue of section 50 ... is treated as subsisting in part of any property)'.

Generally, reversionary interests are excluded property and can be transferred without a charge to IHT (see **[33.61]**). Despite the breadth of this definition, the term would not appear to catch the interests of discretionary beneficiaries since such rights as they possess (to compel due administration; to be considered; and jointly to wind up the fund) are present rights. Their interests are neither in possession nor in reversion. 'Settlement powers' (including a power to revoke the settlement) are not 'property' for IHT purposes and hence fall out of charge.          **[33.2]**

## 2    Who is treated as owning the fund?

a)    *Life interests*

The beneficiary who:
   (i)   became entitled to an interest in possession prior to 22 March 2006; or
  (ii)   becomes entitled on or after 22 March 2006 to:
      (a)    an immediate post-death interest; or
      (b)    a disabled person's interest; or
      (c)    a transitional serial interest (see **Chapter 32** for definitions);

      where the interest is not a disabled person's interest or one for a bereaved minor

is treated as being beneficially entitled to the trust property, or to an appropriate part of that property in which the interest subsists (IHTA 1984, s 49(1); if there is more than one beneficiary, it is necessary to apportion the capital in the fund (IHTA 1984 s 50(1)).

### EXAMPLE 33.1

Bill and Ben, beneficiaries under a family settlement created prior to 22 March 2006, jointly occupy 'Snodlands', the ancestral home, which is worth £150,000.

This capital value must be apportioned to Bill and Ben in proportion to the annual value of their respective interests. As their interests are (presumably) equal the apportionment will be as to £75,000 each.

It can be seen from the above that formerly all beneficiaries entitled to an interest in possession were treated in this way. One result of the changes introduced by FA 2006 is that the statutory fiction (that a person with an interest in possession is deemed to be beneficially entitled to the underlying property in which his interest subsists) is disapplied for interests in possession acquired on or after 22 March 2006, with limited exceptions. These exceptions are couched in defined terms (see **Chapter 32**), and are illustrated by the following examples:

(1) Eddie died in September 2006, leaving his entire estate to his wife, Clarrie, for life, with remainder to his son William absolutely. Clarrie's interest is an immediate post-death interest and thus qualifies as an interest in possession for the purposes of IHTA 1984 s 49. On Eddie's death, the transfer to Clarrie is exempt under the spouse exemption (IHTA 1984 s 18; see **[31.41]**); on Clarrie's death, the value of the capital in which her interest in possession subsists will be added to her free estate.

(2) In 1992, Phil left his residuary estate to his wife Jill for life, thereafter to his son David for life with remainder to his grandson Josh absolutely. Jill dies in 2007. David's interest is a transitional serial interest (it arises in immediate succession on or after 22 March 2006 but before 6 April 2008 to an interest in possession subsisting before 22 March 2006 under a trust created before then), and thus qualifies as an interest in possession for the purposes of s 49.

(3) In 1996, Peggy settled her considerable holding of Marks & Spencer shares on her daughter Jenny for life, thereafter to Jenny's husband Brian for life with remainder to Jenny and Brian's children. Jenny dies on 1 May 2008. Brian's interest is a transitional serial interest and thus is an interest in possession for the purposes of s 49. If, rather than dying, Jenny surrenders her interest on 1 May 2008, then Brian's interest would not be a transitional serial interest. If, instead, Jenny surrenders her interest in December 2007, Brian's interest will qualify as a transitional serial interest under (2) above.

Depending upon whether entitlement began before or on or after 22 March 2006, a beneficiary who has the right to the income of the fund for a period shorter than his lifetime (however short the period may be) is still treated as owning the entire settled fund. If the settlement does not produce any income, but instead the beneficiary is entitled to use the capital assets in the fund, IHTA 1984 s 49(1) suggests that he is treated as owning those assets. If the use is enjoyed by more than one beneficiary, the value of the fund is apportioned under IHTA 1984 s 50(5) in accordance with the 'annual value' of their respective interests. Annual value is not defined.

For a recent case on life interests, see *Oakley v IRC* [2005] STC (SCD) 343.

**[33.3]–[33.4]**

b)   *A beneficiary entitled to a fixed amount of income*

Difficulties may arise where one beneficiary is entitled to a fixed amount of income each year (eg an annuity) and any balance is paid to another beneficiary. If the amounts of income paid to the two were compared in the year when a chargeable event occurred, a tax saving could be engineered. Assume, for instance, that the annuity interest terminates so that IHT is charged on its value. The proportion of capital attributable to that interest and, therefore, the IHT would be reduced if the trustees had switched investments into assets producing a high income in that year. A relatively small proportion of the total income would then be payable to the annuitant who would be treated as owning an equivalently small portion of the capital. When a chargeable event affects the interest in the residue of the income (eg through termination) the trustees could switch the assets into low income producers, thereby achieving a similar reduction in IHT.

IHTA 1984 s 50(3) is designed to counter such schemes by providing that the Treasury may prescribe higher and lower income yields which take effect as limits beyond which any fluctuations in the actual income of the fund are ignored (see SI 2000/174).

**EXAMPLE 33.2**

The value of the settlement is £100,000; income £15,000 per annum. A is entitled to an annuity of £5,000 pa; B to the balance of the income. If there is a chargeable transfer affecting the annuity, A is not treated as owning £33,333 of the capital ([£5,000 ÷ £15,000] × £100,000) but instead a proportion of the Treasury 'higher rate' yield. Assume that the higher rate is 8% on the relevant day; the calculation is, therefore:

Notional income = 8% of £100,000 = £8,000.

A's share of capital is, therefore, [£5,000 ÷ £8,000] × £100,000 = £62,500.

This calculation is used whenever the actual income yield exceeds the prescribed higher rate. The calculation cannot lead to a charge in excess of the total value of the fund!

When a chargeable transfer affecting the interest in the balance of the income occurs, if the actual income produced falls below the prescribed lower rate, the calculation proceeds as if the fund yielded that rate. If both interests in the settlement are chargeable on the same occasion, the prescribed rates do not apply because the entire fund is chargeable.          **[33.5]**

c)   *A lease treated as a settlement*

When a lease is treated as a settlement (eg a lease for life or lives: see **[32.2]**), the lessee is treated as owning the whole of the leased property save for any part treated as belonging to the lessor. To calculate the lessor's portion it is necessary to compare what he received when the lease was granted with what would have been a full consideration for the lease at that time (IHTA 1984 ss 50(6), 170).                                              **[33.6]–[33.20]**

**EXAMPLE 33.3**

(1)   Land worth £100,000 is let to A for his life. The lessor receives no consideration so that A is treated as owning the whole of the leased property (ie £100,000). The granting of the lease is a PET by the lessor of £100,000.

(2)    As above, save that full consideration is furnished. The lease is not treated as a settlement (see **[32.2]**). No IHT will be charged on its creation as the lessor's estate does not fall in value.

(3)    Partial consideration (equivalent to 40% of full consideration) is furnished so that the value of the lessor's interest is 40% of £100,000 = £40,000. The value of the lessee's interest is £60,000 and the granting of the lease is a PET of £60,000.

HMRC accepts that if A, the owner of Blackacre, were to sell it for full consideration arrived at on the basis that he reserves a lease for life, then that lease has been granted for full consideration and so does not involve the creation of a settlement. This approach is questionable.

## II   WHEN IS IHT CHARGED?

For interests in possession arising on or after 22 March 2006, with one limited exception, IHT is charged on a transfer of property to the settlement, on 10 year anniversaries and when property leaves the settlement (see **Chapter 34** below). For settlements created prior to 22 March 2006 and in respect of a disabled person's interest created on or after that date, the pre-FA 2006 treatment continues, whereby IHT may be charged on the creation of the settlement and whenever an interest in possession terminates. This event may occur *inter vivos* or on death: whilst there will always be a charge on death (unless the event is subject to an exemption, such as the spouse exemption (IHTA 1984 s 18)), in the former case the settlor or beneficiary (as appropriate) will be treated as making a PET provided that the trust fund is not then held on discretionary trusts. There are anti-avoidance rules to prevent the indirect creation of discretionary trusts via short-lived interests in possession (see **[33.31]**).                                      **[33.21]**

### 1   Creation of interest in possession trusts

If the trust is set up on death the usual IHT charging regime operated (see **Chapter 30**). If created *inter vivos*, whether there is an immediate IHT charge will depend upon when the interest in possession was created. If it was prior to 22 March 2006, the settlor would have made a PET; if it was on or after 22 March 2006, there will be an immediate IHT charge in all cases except where the interest is a disabled person's interest (IHTA 1984 s 3A(1A) inserted by FA 2006 Sch 20, para 9). Where there is a PET, under general rules, a charge to IHT will only occur if the settlor dies within seven years; anti-avoidance rules may, however, trigger a charge by reference to the settlor's circumstances when he created the trust if the life interest ends within seven years, at a time when the settlor is still alive and the property then becomes held on trusts without an interest in possession (see **[33.31]** for a discussion of these rules).                                      **[33.22]**

#### EXAMPLE 33.4

(1)    Sam settles property on his daughter Sally for life, remainder to charity. The creation of the trust, if before 22 March 2006, is a PET by Sam and on Sally's

death the fund will be exempt from charge (see IHTA 1984 s 23 for the charity exemption). If the property had been settled on 23 March 2006, there would have been an immediate chargeable transfer (at half the death rates), unless Sally qualified as a disabled person (see **Chapter 32**).

(2)    Before 22 March 2006, Sid settles property on a stranger, Jake Straw, for life or until such time as the trustees determine and thereafter the property is to be held on discretionary trusts for Sid's family and relatives. The creation of the trust is a PET; a later termination of Jake's life interest will be a chargeable transfer and may trigger the anti-avoidance rules. As with (1) above, had the property been settled on 23 March 2006, there would have been an immediate IHT charge.

(3)    Before 22 March 2006, Sam settles property on Susan, his daughter, for life, remainder to her twins contingently on attaining 21. Susan surrenders her life interest before 22 March 2006 when the twins are (i) 17, (ii) 18, (iii) 21.

The creation of the trust is a PET as is the surrender of Susan's life interest. If it is surrendered at (i), the fund is then held for A&M trusts (a PET); if surrendered at (ii), the transfer is to the twins as interest in possession beneficiaries (a PET); while, if surrendered at (iii), the twins are absolutely entitled and so it will be an outright gift which is a PET. (Note the differing CGT results, see **Chapter 25**). As with (1) and (2) above, if the property had been settled on 23 March 2006, there would have been an immediate IHT charge. Moreover, on the surrender of Susan's life interest (necessarily after 22 March 2006) at either (i), ii) or (iii), there would be an exit charge since her interest is treated in the same way as settlements with no interest in possession (see **Chapter 34**). Furthermore, the relief formerly afforded to A&M trusts is no longer available for trusts created on or after 22 March 2006 (see **Chapter 34**).

## 2  The charge on death

Where an interest in possession was created prior to 22 March 2006, and for a post-22 March disabled person's interest, an immediate post-death interest and a transitional serial interest, as the assets in the settlement are treated as part of the estate of the deceased interest in possession beneficiary at the time of his death, IHT is charged on the settled fund at the estate rate appropriate to his estate. The tax attributable to the settled property must be paid by the trustees. Although the trustees pay this tax, the inclusion of the value of the fund in the deceased's estate may increase the estate rate, thereby causing a higher percentage charge on the deceased's free estate.

[**33.23**]

**EXAMPLE 33.5**

The settlement consists of securities worth £100,000 and is held for Albinoni for life with remainder to Busoni. Albinoni has just died and the value of his free estate is £170,000; he made chargeable lifetime transfers of £105,000. IHT will be calculated as follows:

(1)    Chargeable death estate: £170,000 + £100,000 (the settlement) = £270,000.
(2)    Join table at £105,000 (point reached by lifetime transfers which cumulate).
(3)    Calculate death IHT (£36,000).
(4)    Convert to estate rate:

$$\frac{\text{tax}}{\text{estate}} \times 100 \text{: ie } \times \frac{36,000}{270,000} \times 100 = 13.33\%$$

(5)   IHT attributable to settled property is 13.33% of £100,000 = £3,330.

## 3   Inter vivos terminations

The termination of an interest in possession occurring during the life of the relevant beneficiary is a transfer of value which was, until the Finance Act 2006 changes, a PET provided that the property was, after that event, held for one or more beneficiaries absolutely (so that the settlement was at an end), or for a further interest in possession or on A&M or disabled trusts. IHT was only payable in such cases if the former life tenant died within seven years of the termination. Otherwise (eg where after the termination the fund was held on discretionary trusts), there was an immediate charge to tax.

Following FA 2006, the only post-22 March 2006 termination that will qualify as a PET is the coming to an end during his lifetime of the interest of a person whose interest is an immediate post-death interest when the settled property becomes, at the same time, subject to a trust for a bereaved minor (see **Chapter 32** and **Chapter 34**) (IHTA 1984 s 3A(3A) inserted by FA 2006 Sch 20, para 9).                                                    **[33.24]**

### a)   *Actual terminations*

Any charge will be calculated on the basis that the life tenant had made a transfer of value of the assets comprised in the trust fund when the interest terminates (IHTA 1984 s 52(1)).                                           **[33.25]**

### EXAMPLE 33.6

(1)   £100,000 is held on trust for Albinoni for life or until remarriage and thereafter for Busoni. If Albinoni had remarried before 22 March 2006, his life interest would have terminated and he would have been treated as having made a transfer of value which would have been a PET. Accordingly, should he die within seven years, IHT will be charged on the value of the fund at the time when his interest ended. (The trustees should bear this in mind before making any distribution to Busoni). If his interest had been created prior to 22 March 2006, but he remarries on or after that date, there would be an immediate IHT charge on the termination of his interest. Note, had the interest been a post-22 March 2006 interest, then it would be treated in the same way as trusts with no interest in possession, which are discussed in the next chapter.

If Albinoni never remarried, but consented (before 22 March 2006) to an advancement of £50,000 to Busoni, his interest in that portion of the fund would have ended and he would have made a transfer of value which was a PET of £50,000. Assume that three years later (still prior to 22 March 2006), Albinoni surrendered his life interest in the fund, worth at that time £120,000. This is a further transfer of value which was a PET; IHT may therefore be charged (if he dies in the seven years following the advancement) on £170,000. Notice that in all cases any tax charge is levied on a value transferred which is 'equal to the value of the property in which his interest subsisted' (see s 52(1)). The principle of calculating loss to donor's estate (see **[28.61]**) does not apply. Had the advancement and the surrender occurred on or after 22 March 2006, there would have been an immediate IHT charge.

(2)   Claude owns 49% of the shares in his family investment company, Money Box Ltd, and is the life tenant under a settlement which owns a further 12% of those shares. The remainder beneficiary under the trust is Claude's daughter. No dividends are paid by the company. The tax position if Claude had surrendered his interest in possession prior to 22 March 2006 is as follows:

(a)   The surrender of a beneficial interest in a settlement is generally free from CGT (TCGA 1992 s 76(1)). Assuming that the settlement ends, there will be a deemed disposal under TCGA 1992 s 71(1): see **Chapter 25**.

(b)   For IHT purposes, Claude would have been treated as making a transfer of value which was a PET, but the value transferred is limited to the value of the shares in the settlement (IHTA 1984, s 52(1)). Thus only the value of a 12% minority holding will be subject to tax in the event of Claude's death within seven years.

On Claude's death his estate will then comprise only a 49% minority shareholding (assuming that Claude acquired his interest in the settlement before 22 March 2006 or, if later, the interest was an immediate post-death interest, a disabled person's interest or a transitional serial interest).

The merit of this arrangement was that the substantial loss to Claude's estate resulting from his loss of control of the company did not attract a tax charge: instead, both shareholdings were valued separately. Surrender of the life interest could have occurred on Claude's deathbed but the advantages would not, of course, have been obtained if the life interest had been retained and the 49% holding given away! Had the surrender occurred on or after 22 March 2006, it would have attracted a charge, and the arrangement would thereby lose its merit.

b)   *Deemed terminations*

IHTA 1984 s 51(1) provides that if the beneficiary disposes of his beneficial interest in possession, that disposal '*shall not be a transfer of value but shall be treated as the coming to an end of the interest*'. The absence of gratuitous intent does not prevent an IHT charge on the termination of beneficial interests in possession. As with actual terminations, the life tenant would normally be treated as having made a transfer of value which, before the changes introduced by FA 2006, would have been a PET so that tax will only be charged if he dies within seven years.                               **[33.26]**

**EXAMPLE 33.7**

(1)   Albinoni assigns by way of gift his life interest to Cortot. IHT will be charged as if that life interest had terminated. Cortot becomes a tenant *pur autre vie* and when Albinoni dies Cortot's interest in possession terminates so raising the possibility of a further IHT charge. Assuming that both events occur before 22 March 2006, both Albinoni and Cortot have made PETs (for quick succession relief, see **[33.42]**).

(2)   If, instead of gifting his interest, Albinoni sold it to Cortot for £20,000 (full value) on 1 March 2006 and the trust fund was then worth £100,000, Albinoni's interest would have thereby terminated so that he made a transfer of value of £100,000. However, as he had received £20,000, he made a PET equal to the fall in his estate of £80,000 (£100,000 − £20,000: IHTA 1984 s 52(2)).

c)   *Partition*

A division of the trust fund between life tenant and remainderman causes the interest in possession to terminate and IHT may be charged (in the case of a PET, if the life tenant dies within seven years) on that portion of the fund passing to the remainderman (IHTA 1984 s 53(2)).                          **[33.27]**

> **EXAMPLE 33.8**
>
> On 1 March 2006, Albinoni and Busoni agreed to partition the £100,000 trust fund in the proportions 40:60. Albinoni would have been treated as making a PET of £60,000 (£100,000 – £40,000). Any IHT would have been payable out of the fund which is divided.

d)   *Advancements etc to life tenant*

If all or part of the capital of the fund is paid to the life tenant, or if he becomes absolutely entitled to the capital, his interest in possession will determine *pro tanto*, but no IHT will be charged since there will be no fall in the value of his estate (IHTA 1984 s 53(2)).                          **[33.28]**

e)   *Purchase of a reversionary interest by the life tenant (IHTA 1984 ss 10, 55(1))*

As the life tenant who acquired his interest before 22 March 2006 or, if later, the interest was an immediate post-death interest, a disabled person's interest or a transitional serial interest is treated as owning the fund, his tax bill could be reduced were he to purchase a reversionary interest in that settlement. Assume, for instance, that B has £60,000 in his bank account and is the life tenant of a fund with a capital value of £100,000. For IHT purposes he is treated as owning an estate worth £160,000. If B were to purchase the reversionary interest in the settlement for its market value of £60,000, the result would be as follows: *first*, B's estate has not fallen in value. Originally it included £60,000; after the purchase it includes a reversionary interest worth £60,000 since, although excluded property, the reversionary interest must still be valued. *Secondly*, B's estate now consists of the settlement fund valued at £100,000 and has been depleted by the £60,000 paid for the reversionary interest so that a possible charge to IHT on £60,000 has been avoided.

To prevent this loss of tax, IHTA 1984 s 55(1) provides that the reversionary interest is not to be valued as a part of B's estate at the time of its purchase (thereby ensuring that his estate has fallen in value) whilst IHTA 1984 s 10 (see **[28.21]**) is excluded from applying thereby ensuring that the fall in value may be subject to charge even though there is no donative intent. Hence, by paying £60,000 for the reversionary interest B has made a PET which will be taxed if he dies in the following seven years.          **[33.29]**

f)   *Transactions reducing the value of the property*

When the value of the fund is diminished by a depreciatory transaction entered into between the trustees and a beneficiary (or persons connected with him), tax is charged as if the fall in value were a partial termination of the interest in possession (IHTA 1984 s 52(3)). A commercial transaction lacking gratuitous intent is not caught by this provision.

In *Macpherson v IRC* (1988) the value of pictures held in a trust fund was diminished by an arrangement with a person connected with a beneficiary as a result of which, in return for taking over care, custody and insurance of the pictures, that person was entitled to keep the pictures for his personal enjoyment for some 14 years. Although this arrangement was a commercial transaction, lacking gratuitous intent when looked at in isolation, it was associated with a subsequent operation (the appointment of a protected life interest) which did confer a gratuitous benefit so that the exception in s 10 did not apply and the reduction in value of the fund was subject to charge.

**[33.30]**

### EXAMPLE 33.9

Trustees grant a 50-year lease of a property worth £100,000 at a peppercorn rent to the brother of a reversionary beneficiary. As a result the property left in the settlement is the freehold reversion worth only £20,000. The granting of the lease is a depreciatory transaction which causes the value of the fund to fall by £80,000 and as it is made with a person connected with a beneficiary, IHTA 1984 s 52(3) will apply and IHT may be levied as if the life interest in £80,000 had ended. (Contrast the position if the lease had been granted to the brother on fully commercial terms.)

### 4   Anti-avoidance (**IHTA 1984 s 54A and s 54B**)

Note that whilst these provisions apply in respect of all interest in possession trusts created prior to 22 March 2006, where the beneficiary became entitled to the interest in possession on or after that date, s 54A applies only where that interest is a disabled person's interest or a transitional serial interest (IHTA 1984 s 54A(2) inserted by FA 2006 Sch 20, para 16).

#### a)   *When do the rules apply?*

The three prerequisites are that:
(1)   an interest in possession trust is set up by means of a PET;
(2)   it terminates either as a result of the life tenant dying or by his interest ceasing *inter vivos*; and
(3)   at that time a no interest in possession trust (other than an A&M trust) arises.

   If the termination occurs within seven years of the creation of the original interest in possession trust and at a time when the settlor is still alive, the anti-avoidance rules then apply.   **[33.31]**

#### b)   *Operation of the rules*

The IHT charge on the property at the time when the interest in possession ends is taken to be the higher of two alternative calculations. First, the IHT that would arise under normal charging principles, ie by taxing the fund as if the transfer had been made by the life tenant at the time of termination. The rates of charge will be either half rates (when there is an *inter vivos* termination) or full death rates when termination occurs as a result of the death of the life tenant. The alternative calculation involves deeming the settled property to have been transferred at the time of termination by a hypothetical transferor who in the preceding seven years had made chargeable transfers equal in value to those made by the settlor in the seven years before he created the settlement. For the purpose of this second calculation half rates are used. **[33.32]**

**EXAMPLE 33.10**

In 2003 Sam settled property worth £90,000 on trust for Pam for life or until remarriage and thereafter on discretionary trusts for Sam's relatives and friends. His cumulative total at that time was £200,000 and he had made PETs of £85,000. Pam remarried one year later at a time when she had made chargeable transfers of £50,000, PETs of £45,000; and when the settled property was worth £110,000.

(1) The anti-avoidance provisions are relevant since the conditions for their operation are satisfied.

(2) Normally IHT would have been calculated at Pam's rates, ie on a chargeable transfer from £50,000 to £160,000. Alternatively under these provisions the tax could have been calculated by taking a hypothetical transferor who had Sam's cumulative total at the time when he created the trust; ie the £110,000 would have been taxed as a chargeable transfer from £200,000 to £310,000. In this example the second calculation would have been adopted since a greater amount of IHT results. Tax must be paid by the trustees.

(3) Assume that either Sam or Pam died after the termination of the interest in possession trust. This may result in a recalculation of the IHT liability (in this example PETs made by that person in the seven years before death would become chargeable). So far as the anti-avoidance rules are concerned, however, there is no question of disturbing the basis on which the IHT calculation was made in the first place. Hence, as was shown in (2) above, the greater tax was produced by taking the hypothetical transferor and, therefore, the subsequent death of Pam is irrelevant since it cannot be used to switch the basis of computation to Pam's cumulative total. By contrast, the death of Sam may involve additional IHT liability since his PETs of £85,000 will now become chargeable and thus included in the hypothetical transferor's total when the settlement was created.

c) *How to avoid the rules*

*First,* if the interest in possession continues for seven years these rules do not apply.

*Secondly,* they are not in point if the settlement was created without an immediate interest in possession (eg there was an A&M trust which subsequently became an interest in possession trust), or if the settlement was created by means of an exempt transfer (eg if a life interest was given to the settlor's spouse and that interest was subsequently terminated in favour of a discretionary trust).

*Thirdly,* trustees can prevent the rules from applying if, *within six months* of the ending of the interest in possession, they terminate the discretionary trust either by an absolute appointment or by creating a further life interest.

*Fourthly,* it is always possible to channel property into a discretionary trust by a PET, if an outright gift is made to another individual (a PET) who then settles the gifted property on the appropriate discretionary trusts (a chargeable transfer but taxed at *his* rates). Of course the transferor will have no legal right to force the donee to settle the outright gift.

*Finally*, the rules are only triggered by a PET. Hence a settlement on the settlor's spouse is not caught. **[33.33]**

## 5   Exemptions and reliefs

a)   *Reverter to settlor/spouse (IHTA 1984 s 53(3)–(5))*

If, on the termination of an interest in possession, property reverts to the settlor, there is no charge to IHT unless that interest had been acquired for money or money's worth. This exemption also applies when the property passes to the settlor's spouse or (if the settlor is dead) to his widow or widower so long as that reverter occurs within two years of the settlor's death (for the CGT position, see **Chapter 25**). **[33.34]**

### EXAMPLE 33.11

(1)   In 2004, Janacek created a settlement of £100,000 in favour of K for life (a PET). When K dies and the property reverts to the settlor no IHT will be charged.
*Contrast the position*, if the settlement provided that the fund was to pass to L on the death of K, but the settlor's wife had purchased that remainder interest and given it to her husband as a Christmas present. On the death of the life tenant, although the property will revert to the settlor, the normal charge to IHT will apply. (For the CGT position, see **Chapter 25**.)

(2)   Bert and his wife, Bertha, own their house as tenants in common. On Bert's death in 2004 he left his share to his daughter, Bettina. In 2005, she settled it on trust for her mother (Bertha) for life; remainder to herself (Bettina) for life with remainders over.
*On Bertha's death* in February 2006, Bettina was still alive and the IHT reverter to settlor exception applied. Because Bettina only enjoys a life interest, the CGT uplift on death was available (which it would not have been if Bettina had then become absolutely entitled). The arrangement provides added security for Bertha without forfeiting any IHT benefits (contrast *IRC v Lloyds Private Banking Ltd* (1998) at **[32.3]**).

b)   *Use of the life tenant's exemptions*

The spouse exemption is available on the termination of the interest in possession if the person who then becomes entitled, whether absolutely or to another interest in possession, is the spouse of the former life tenant. In addition, IHTA 1984 s 57 permits the use of the life tenant's annual (£3,000 pa) exemption and the exemption for gifts in consideration of marriage on the *inter vivos* termination of an interest in possession if the life tenant so elects (see IHTA 1984 s 57(3), (4)). The exemptions for small gifts (£250) and normal expenditure out of income cannot be used.

### EXAMPLE 33.12

Orff is the life tenant of the fund. His wife and son are entitled equally in remainder. If he surrenders the life interest, there will be no tax on the half share passing to his wife (spouse exemption). The chargeable half share passing to his son is a PET (provided the surrender occurred prior to 22 March 2006) and, should it become chargeable because of his death within seven years, the annual exemption and, if surrender coincides with the marriage of the son, the £5,000 marriage gift relief will be available.

Although the making of a PET is not reported, the appropriate notice should be given to the trustees by the life tenant indicating that he wishes the transfer to be covered by his relevant exemption (the annual or marriage exemptions) so that it can then be submitted (if needed) to HMRC as required by s 57(4) (and see SI 2002/1731). [33.35]

c) *The surviving spouse exemption*

The carry-over of this estate duty relief is discussed at [30.158]. The first spouse must have died before 13 November 1974 and the relief ensures that IHT is not charged on the termination of the surviving spouse's interest in the property whether that occurs *inter vivos* or on death (IHTA 1984 Sch 6 para 2). [33.36]

d) *Excluded property*

If the settlement contains excluded property, IHT is not charged on that portion of the fund (IHTA 1984 ss 5(1), 53(1)). [33.37]

e) *IHTA 1984 s 11 dispositions*

If the interest in possession is disposed of for the purpose of maintaining the disponer's child or supporting a dependent relative, IHT is not charged (see [31.7]). [33.38]

f) *Charities*

Tax is not charged if on the termination of the interest in possession the property is held on trust for charitable purposes. [33.39]

g) *Protective trusts*

The forfeiture of a protected life interest is not normally treated as the termination of an interest in possession (see [34.117]). [33.40]

h) *Variations and disclaimers*

Dispositions of the deceased may be altered after his death by means of an instrument of variation or disclaimer and treated as if they had been made by the deceased. Disclaimers are possible in the case both of settlements created by the will or intestacy of the deceased (IHTA 1984 s 142) and pre-existing settlements in which the death has resulted in a person becoming entitled to an interest in the settled property (IHTA 1984 s 93). Variations are only permitted for settlements created on the relevant death, not for settlements in which the deceased had been the beneficiary. If an interest in possession is created under a variation made on or after 22 March 2006 and is deemed to arise on the deceased's death pre-22 March 2006, it will be treated as an interest in possession in existence before that date, and so will be subject to the pre-22 March 2006 rules. Where the deceased dies on or after 22 March 2006, the new interest in possession will be an immediate post-death interest and, accordingly, it should still be possible to obtain the spouse/civil partnership exemption for interests in possession created by deed of variation within s 142 whenever the deceased might die.                                  **[33.41]**

**EXAMPLE 33.13**

Poulenc, the life tenant of a settlement created by his father, has just died. His brother Quercus is now the life tenant in possession and if he assigns his interest within two years of Poulenc's death, the normal charging provisions will apply. (*Note:* (1) he could disclaim his interest without any IHT charge (IHTA 1984 s 93); (2) see **[30.155]** for problems caused to trustees when other property of the deceased is varied or disclaimed.)

i)    *Quick succession relief (IHTA 1984 s 141)*

This relief is similar to that for unsettled property (see **[30.144]**). The first chargeable transfer may be either the creation of the settlement or any subsequent termination of an interest in possession (whether that termination occurs *inter vivos* or on death). Hence, it can be voluntarily used (by the life tenant surrendering or assigning his interest) whereas in the case of unsettled property it is only available on a death. The calculation of the relief in cases where there is more than one later transfer is dealt with in IHTA 1984 s 141(4).                                                **[33.42]**

**EXAMPLE 33.14**

(1) A settlement is created in January 2000; (2) the life interest ends in half of the fund in March 2002; (3) the life interest ends in the rest of the fund in February 2003. Assume that both PETs become chargeable because of the death of the life tenant within seven years.

Quick succession relief is available at a rate of 60% on event (2); and again at a rate of 40% on event (3). Generally, relief is given in respect of the earlier transfer first ((2) above). To the extent that the relief given represents less than the whole of the tax charged on the original net transfer ((1) above), further relief can then be given in respect of subsequent transfers ((3) above) until relief equal to the whole of the tax (in (1) above) has been given.

j)    *Business reliefs*

In a settlement containing business property that relief is available to the life tenant provided that he fulfils the conditions for relief (IHTA 1984 ss 103–114). Note that the relief appears to be unaffected by the changes introduced by FA 2006.

**EXAMPLE 33.15**

Satie is the life tenant of the settlement. He holds 30% of the shares in the trading company Teleman Ltd, and the trust holds a further 25%. Further, the trust owns the factory premises which are leased to the company. On the death of Satie, IHT business relief is available as follows:

(1) *On the shares*: the relief (assuming that the two-year ownership condition is satisfied) is at 100% on Satie's shares and on those of the fund. The life tenant is treated as having controlled the company since he held 30% (his own) and is treated as owning a further 25% of the shares.

(2) *On the land*: the relief is at 50% since the asset is used by a company controlled by the life tenant. (But see *Fetherstonehaugh v IRC* (1984).)

Similar rules operate for agricultural relief: ie the life tenant must satisfy the conditions of two years' occupation or seven years' ownership (ownership by the trustees being attributed to the life tenant). Because the interest in possession beneficiary is treated as owning the trust fund (rather than it being owned by the trustees) problems can arise in the case of both APR and BPR when, for instance, a beneficiary under an A&M trust obtains an interest in possession (see, in the context of clawback, *Example 31.15(4)*).

**[33.43]–[33.60]**

## III THE TAXATION OF REVERSIONARY INTERESTS

a) *General rule: excluded property*

Reversionary interests are generally excluded property so that their assignment or transfer does not lead to an IHT charge. (The purchase of a reversionary interest by the life tenant has been considered at **[33.29]**.)

**[33.61]**

**EXAMPLE 33.16**

A fund is settled on trust for A for life (A is currently aged 88); B for life (B is 78); and C absolutely (C, A's son, is 70).

This settlement is likely to be subject to three IHT charges within a fairly short period. The position would be much improved if B and C disposed of their reversionary interests:

(1) B should surrender his interest. Taking into account his age it has little value and is merely an IHT trap.

(2) C should assign his interest to (ideally) a younger person. He might for instance have minor grandchildren and an A&M trust in their favour would be an attractive possibility. (Note the changes made by FA 2006 to such trusts established on or after 22 March 2006: see **Chapter 34**.)

The result of this reorganisation is that the fund is now threatened by only one IHT charge (on A's death) in the immediate future.

b) *Exceptions*

In four cases reversionary interests are not excluded property. This is to prevent their use as a tax avoidance device.

*First*, the sale of a reversionary interest to a beneficiary under the same trust, who is entitled to a prior interest (see **[33.29]**).

*Secondly*, the disposition of a reversionary interest which has at any time, and by any person, been acquired for a consideration in money or money's worth. (For special rules where that interest is situated outside the UK, see **[35.85]**.)

**EXAMPLE 33.17**

Umberto sells his reversionary interest to Vidor (a stranger to the trust) for its market value, £20,000. If the general rules operated the position would be that:
(1)    Umberto is disposing of excluded property so that no IHT is chargeable.
(2)    Vidor has replaced chargeable assets (£20,000) with excluded property so that were he to die or make an *inter vivos* gift IHT would be avoided.
    IHTA 1984 s 48(1)(a) and s 48(3) prevent this result. The reversion ceases to be excluded property once it has been purchased (even for a small consideration) so that a disposition by Vidor may lead to an IHT charge.

*Thirdly*, a disposition of a reversionary interest is chargeable if it is one to which either the settlor or his spouse is, or has been, beneficially entitled (IHTA 1984 s 48(1)(b)).

**EXAMPLE 33.18**

In 2003 Viv settled property worth £100,000 on trust for his father Will for life (Will is 92). Viv retained the reversionary interest which he then gave to his daughter Ursula. If the general rules were not modified the position would be that:
(1)    The creation of the settlement would have been a PET by Viv but the diminution in his estate would have been very small (the difference between £100,000 and the value of a reversionary interest in £100,000 subject only to the termination of the interest of a 92-year-old life tenant!).
(2)    The transfer of the reversion by Viv would have escaped IHT since it is excluded property.
    IHTA 1984 s 48(1)(b) ensures that the transfer of the reversion is a PET so that Viv achieved no tax saving (and, indeed, was left with the danger of a higher IHT bill than if he had never created the settlement since the death of Will is a chargeable event).
    This may be used to the taxpayer's advantage in a *'Melville* type' scheme: namely, where it is desired to create a discretionary trust in order to obtain hold-over relief whilst ensuring that any IHT transfer of value is kept within the nil rate band (see **[32.52]**).

*Fourthly*, the disposition of a reversionary interest is chargeable where that interest is expectant upon the termination of a lease which is treated as a settlement (typically one for life or lives; IHTA 1984 s 48(1)(c)). The lessor's reversion is treated in the same way as a reversionary interest purchased for money or money's worth so that on any disposition of it, IHT may be charged.                                                                    **[33.62]**

# 34 IHT—relevant property: settlements without an interest in possession and those treated as settlements without an interest in possession

*Updated by Aparna Nathan, LLB Hons, LLM, Barrister, Gray's Inn Tax Chambers and Natalie Lee, Barrister, Senior Lecturer in Law, University of Southampton*

## I INTRODUCTION AND TERMINOLOGY

Prior to the changes introduced by FA 2006, relevant property referred to property held in a settlement lacking an interest in possession. The method of charging settlements of this nature is totally different from that for settlements with an interest in possession (see **Chapter 33**). Instead of attributing the fund to one of the beneficiaries, the settlement itself is the taxable entity. Like an individual, a record of chargeable transfers must be kept although, unlike the individual, it will never die and so will only be taxed at half rates. Taking into account the recent changes, this chapter will discuss the rules by reference to relevant property. Until those changes, the discretionary trust was the most significant trust with relevant property. In fact the category is wider than discretionary trusts catching, for instance, the settlement in the *Pilkington* case (**[32.24]**) and trusts where the beneficiaries' interests are contingent. These rules will now also apply to a post-22 March 2006 trust with an interest in possession that is not a transitional serial interest, an immediate post-death interest or disabled person's interest (see **Chapter 33**).

**EXAMPLE 34.1**

(1)   A fund of £100,000 is held upon trust for such of A, B, C, D, E and F as the trustees may in their absolute discretion (which extends over both income and capital) think appropriate. The trust is one without an interest in possession.

(2)   Dad settles property on trust for Sonny absolutely contingent on his attaining 30. Sonny is aged 21 at the date of the settlement and the income is to be accumulated until Sonny attains 30. There is no interest in possession.

(3)   On 1 April 2006, Mum settles property on trust for her daughter Tamsin for life, with remainder to her grandson Victor absolutely. Although there is an interest in possession, it arises post-22 March 2006 and, not being a transitional serial interest, an immediate post-death interest or disabled person's interest (and nor is it a 'special trust' considered in Sections VI and VII of this Chapter), it will be subject to the same regime that applies to settlements where there exists no interest in possession.

IHT is charged on '*relevant property*' (IHTA 1984 s 58(1)) defined, for pre-22 March 2006 trusts, as settled property (other than excluded property) in which there is no qualifying interest in possession, with the exception of property settled on the 'special trusts' considered in Sections V and VI, below.

A 'qualifying interest in possession' was one owned beneficially by an individual or, in restricted circumstances, by a company. If within one settlement there existed an interest in possession in a part only of the settled property, these rules applied to the portion which lacks such an interest. It has already been mentioned that the term 'relevant property' now applies to property settled on a post-22 March 2006 trust giving rise to an interest in possession that is not a transitional serial interest, an immediate post-death interest or disabled person's interest. There continues to be an exception for property on 'special trusts' considered in Sections VI and VII. **[34.1]–[34.20]**

## II   THE METHOD OF CHARGE

The central feature is the *periodic charge* imposed upon relevant property at ten-yearly intervals. The anniversary is calculated from the date on which the trust was created (IHTA 1984 s 61(1)). In the case of settlements initially established with a nominal sum (eg £10) it is from the date when that nominal sum is received by the trustees.

**EXAMPLE 34.2**

(1)   Silas creates a discretionary trust on 1 January 1989. The first anniversary charge will fall on 1 January 1999; the next on 1 January 2009 and so on. If the trust had been created by will and he had died on 31 December 1988, that date marks the creation of the trust (IHTA 1984 s 83). A similar principle applies if the trust was established by an instrument of variation falling within IHTA 1984 s 142 (see **[30.153]**).

(2)   Sebastian creates (in 1988) a settlement in favour of his wife Selina for life; thereafter for such of his three daughters as the trustees may in their absolute discretion select. Selina dies in 1989. For IHT purposes the discretionary trust is created by Selina on her death (IHTA 1984 s 80) although the ten-year anniversary runs from 1988 (IHTA 1984 s 61(2)).

(3)    The first anniversary charge in respect of the trust created by Mum for Tamsin (*Example 34.1(3)*) will fall on 1 April 2016.

Apart from the periodic charge, IHT is also levied (the '*exit charge*') on the happening of certain events. In general, the IHT then charged is a proportion of the last periodic charge. Special charging provisions operate for chargeable events which occur before the first ten-year anniversary. No accounts need be filed by trustees of 'excepted settlements': see SI 2002/1732. In general the assets in the trust must be cash and the value of the settled property at the time of the chargeable event must not exceed £1,000.                                                                              **[34.21]**

## 1   The creation of the settlement

This will, generally, be a chargeable transfer of value by the settlor for IHT purposes. The following matters should be noted: *first*, if the settlement is created *inter vivos*, grossing-up applies unless IHT is paid out of the fund (see **Chapter 28**).

*Secondly*, the cumulative total of chargeable transfers made by the settlor forms part of the cumulative total of the settlement on all future chargeable occasions (ie his transfers never drop out of the cumulative total). Therefore, in order to calculate the correct IHT charge it is essential that the trustees are told the settlor's cumulative total at the date when he created the trust. When as a result of the settlor's fraud, wilful default or neglect there is an underpayment of IHT, HMRC may recover that sum from the trustees outside the normal six-year time limit. In such cases the time limit is six years from the date when the impropriety comes to the notice of HMRC (IHTA 1984 s 240(3)). Obviously a problem would arise for trustees if at the time when the underpayment came to light they held insufficient assets to discharge the extra IHT bill since they could be made personally liable for the tax unpaid. HMRC have, however, previously stated that where the trustees have acted in good faith and hold insufficient settlement assets they will not seek to recover any unpaid tax from them personally (*Law Society's Gazette*, 1984, p 3517).

*Thirdly*, a '*related settlement*' is one created by the same settlor on the same day as the trust with relevant property (other than a charitable trust). Generally such settlements should be avoided (see **[34.27]**). The use of 'pilot' settlements is considered at **[34.35]**.

*Fourthly*, additions of property by the original settlor to his settlement may create problems although it is standard practice in the case of 'pilot' trusts (see **[34.33]**). If property is added by a person other than the original settlor, the addition will be treated as a separate settlement (see **[32.7]**).

Problems may arise for the trustees if the settlor dies within seven years of creating the trust. PETs made *before* the settlement was created and within seven years of his death then become chargeable so that tax on creation of the settlement and the computation of any exit charge made during this period may need to be recalculated. If extra tax becomes payable this is primarily the responsibility of the settlement trustees and their liability is not limited to settlement property in their hands *at that time*. Given this danger it will be prudent for trustees who are distributing property from the trust with relevant property within the first seven years to retain sufficient funds or take suitable indemnities to cover any contingent IHT liability.    **[34.22]**

**EXAMPLE 34.3**

Sumar makes the following transfers of value:

*May 1998*            £200,000 to his sister Sufi (a PET).

*May 1999*            £70,000 to a family discretionary trust.

In May 2000 the trustees distribute the entire fund to the beneficiaries and in May 2003 Sumar dies.

As a result of his death, the 1998 PET is chargeable (the resultant IHT is primarily the responsibility of Sufi) and in addition tax on the creation of the settlement must be recalculated.

When it was set up the PET was ignored so that the transfer fell within Sumar's nil rate band. With his death, however, IHT must be calculated, at the rates in force in May 2003, on transfers from £200,000 to £270,000 (tax is £8,000). In addition it is likely that no IHT will have been charged on the distribution of the fund in 2000 and therefore a recomputation is again necessary with the trustees being liable for the resulting tax.

## 2    Exit charges before the first ten-year anniversary

a)    *When will an exit charge arise?*

A charge is imposed whenever property in the settlement ceases to be 'relevant property' (IHTA 1984 s 65). For instance, if the trustees of a discretionary trust appoint property to a beneficiary or if an interest in possession arises in any portion of the fund, there will be a charge to the extent of the property ceasing to be held on discretionary trusts. Note that if an interest in possession arises on or after 22 March 2006, the property only ceases to be relevant property to the extent that it is a disabled person's interest (by definition, it cannot be an immediate post-death interest or a transitional serial interest). If the resultant IHT is paid out of the property that is left in the discretionary trust, grossing-up will apply. A charge is also imposed if the trustees make a disposition as a result of which the value of relevant property comprised in the settlement falls (a 'depreciatory transaction'; see **[33.30]**: notice that in this case there is no requirement that the transaction must be made with a beneficiary or with a person connected with him).

The exit charge does not apply to a payment of costs or expenses (so long as it is 'fairly attributable' to the relevant property), nor does it catch a payment which is income of any person for the purposes of income tax (IHTA 1984 s 65(5)).    **[34.23]**

b)    *Calculation of the settlement rate*

The calculation of the rate of IHT is based upon half the full IHT rates, even if the trust was set up under the will of the settlor. The rate of tax actually payable is then 30% of those rates applicable to a hypothetical chargeable transfer.

*Step 1* This hypothetical transfer is made up of the sum of the following:

(1) the value of the property in the settlement immediately after it commenced;
(2) the value (at the date of the addition) of any added property; and
(3) the value of property in a related settlement (valued immediately after it commenced (IHTA 1984 s 68(5)).

No account is taken of any rise or fall in the value of the settled fund and the value comprised in the settlement and in any related settlement can include property subject to an interest in possession.

*Step 2* Tax at half rates on this hypothetical transfer is calculated by joining the table at the point reached by the cumulative total of previous chargeable transfers made by the settlor in the seven years before he created the settlement. Other chargeable transfers made on the same day as the settlement are ignored and, therefore, if the settlement was created on death, other gifts made in the will or on intestacy are ignored (IHTA 1984 s 68(4)(b)).

*Step 3* The resultant tax is converted to an average rate (the equivalent of an estate rate) and 30% of that rate is then taken. The resultant rate (the '*settlement rate*') is used as the basis for calculating the exit charge.     **[34.24]**

### EXAMPLE 34.4

Justinian settles £100,000 on discretionary trusts on 6 April 2003. His total chargeable transfers immediately before that date stood at £165,000. He pays the IHT. If an exit charge arises before the first ten-year anniversary of the fund (6 April 2013) the settlement rate would be calculated as follows:

*Step 1* Calculate the hypothetical chargeable transfer. As there is no added property and no related settlement it comprises only the value of the property in the settlement immediately after its creation (ie £100,000).

*Step 2* Cumulate the £100,000 with the previous chargeable transfers of Justinian (ie £165,000). Taking the IHT rates in force in April 2003, tax on transfers between £165,000 and £265,000 is £2,000.

*Step 3* The tax converted to a percentage rate is 2%; 30% of that rate produces a 'settlement rate' of 0.6%.

c)    *The tax charged*

The charge is on the fall in value of the fund. To establish the rate of charge, a further proportion of the settlement rate must be calculated equal to one-fortieth of the settlement rate for each complete successive quarter that has elapsed from the creation of the settlement to the date of the exit charge. That proportion of the settlement rate is applied to the chargeable transfer (the '*effective rate*').

### EXAMPLE 34.5

Assume in *Example 34.4* that on 25 March 2005 there was an exit charge on £20,000 ceasing to be relevant property. The 'effective rate' of IHT is calculated as follows:

*Step 1* Take completed quarters since the settlement was created, ie seven.

*Step 2* Take 7/40ths of the 'settlement rate' (0.6%) to discover the 'effective rate' = 0.105%.

*Step 3* The effective rate is applied to the fall in value of the relevant property. The IHT will, therefore, be 21 if the tax is borne by the beneficiary; or 21.02 if borne by the remaining fund.

There is no charge on events that occur in the first three months after the settlement is created (IHTA 1984 s 65(4)) nor, in certain circumstances when the trust was set up by the settlor on his death, on events occurring within two years of that death (see **[30.145]**).                                          **[34.25]**

### 3    The charge on the first ten-year anniversary

a)    *What property is charged?*

The charge is levied on the value of the *relevant property* comprised in the settlement immediately before the anniversary (IHTA 1984 s 64). Income only becomes relevant property, and thus subject to charge, when it has been accumulated (see SP 8/86). Pending accumulation it is not subject to the anniversary charge and can be distributed free from any exit charge (see **[34.23]**). Note that the income arising in a post-22 March 2006 interest in possession trust that now falls within the definition of relevant property will, by definition, not be accumulated; it will be paid to the beneficiary with an interest in possession. At what moment is income accumulated? Accumulation occurs once an irrevocable decision to that effect has been taken by trustees, and it may also occur after a reasonable time for distribution has passed (but see *Re Locker* (1977) in which income arising between 1965 and 1968 was still available for distribution in 1977). The legislation gives no guidance on what property is treated as being distributed first; ie if an appointment is made by the trustees out of property comprised in the settlement, does it come out of the original capital or out of accumulations of income? As a reduced charge may apply to property which has been added to the trust (such as accumulated income: see **[34.33]**) this is an important omission (for the approach adopted in practice by the Revenue, see *Capital Taxes News*, vol 8, May 1989).

The assets in the fund are valued according to general principles and, if they include business or agricultural property, the reliefs appropriate to that property will apply, subject to satisfaction of the relevant conditions. Any IHT charged on such property may be payable in instalments.                     **[34.26]**

b)    *Calculation of the rate of IHT*

Half rates will be used and, as with the exit charge, the calculation depends upon a hypothetical chargeable transfer.

*Step 1* Calculate the hypothetical chargeable transfer which is made up of the sum of the following:
(1)    the value of relevant property comprised in the settlement immediately before the anniversary;
(2)    the value, immediately after it was created, of property comprised in a 'related settlement'; and
(3)    the value, at the date when the settlement was created, of any non-relevant property then in the settlement which has not subsequently become relevant property.

Normally the hypothetical chargeable transfer will be made up exclusively of property falling within (1) above. (2) and (3), which affect the rate of IHT to be charged without themselves being taxed, are anti-avoidance measures.

Related settlements are included because transfers made on the same day as the creation of the settlement are normally ignored and, therefore, an IHT advantage could be achieved if the settlor were to set up a series of small funds rather than one large fund. Non-relevant property in the settlement is included because the trustees could switch the values between the two portions of the fund.

*Step 2* Calculate tax at half rates on the hypothetical chargeable transfer by joining the table at the point reached by:

(1)  the chargeable transfers of the settlor made in the *seven* years before he created the settlement; and

(2)  chargeable transfers made by the settlement in the first *ten* years. Where a settlement was created after 26 March 1974 and before 9 March 1982, distribution payments (as defined by the IHT charging regime in force between those dates) must also be cumulated (IHTA 1984 s 66(6)).

Settlements with relevant property will, therefore, have their own total of chargeable transfers with transfers over a ten-year period being cumulated (contrast the seven-year period used for individuals). The unique feature of a settlement's cumulation lies in the inclusion (and it never drops out) of chargeable transfers of the settlor in the seven years before the settlement is created.

*Step 3* The IHT is converted to a percentage and 30% of that rate is then taken and charged on the relevant property in the settlement.

The highest rate of IHT is 20% (half of 40%). The highest effective rate (anniversary rate) is, therefore, 30% of 20%, ie 6%. Where the settlement comprises business property qualifying for 50% relief, this effective rate falls to 3% and assuming that the option to pay in instalments is exercised, the annual charge over the ten-year period becomes a mere 0.3%. If the property qualifies for 100% business or agricultural relief there is no charge. **[34.27]**

**EXAMPLE 34.6**

Take the facts of *Example 34.5* (namely, original fund £100,000, exit charge on £20,000; previous transfers of settlor £165,000). In addition, assume Justinian had created a second settlement of £35,000 on 6 April 2003.

The fund is worth £105,000 at the first ten-year anniversary.

(1)  Relevant property to be taxed is £105,000

| (2) | Calculate hypothetical chargeable transfer: | £ |
|---|---|---|
| | Relevant property, as above | 105,000 |
| | Property in related settlement | 35,000 |
| | | £140,000 |

| (3) | Settlement's cumulative IHT total: | £ |
|---|---|---|
| | Settlor's earlier transfers | 165,000 |
| | Chargeable transfers of trustees in preceding ten years | 20,000 |
| | | £185,000 |

(4)  Tax from the IHT table (at half rates) on transfers from £185,000 to £325,000 (£140,000 + £185,000) = £10,000 so that, as a percentage rate IHT is 7.14%.

(5)   The 'effective rate' is 30% of 7.14% = 2.14%.
      Tax payable is £105,000 × 2.14% = £2,250

## 4   Exit charges after the first anniversary charge and between anniversaries

The same events will trigger an exit charge after the first ten-year anniversary as before it. The IHT charge will be levied on the fall in value of the fund with grossing-up, if necessary. The rate of charge is a proportion of the effective rate charged at the first ten-year anniversary. That proportion is one-fortieth for each complete quarter from the date of the first anniversary charge to the date of the exit charge (IHTA 1984 s 69).

**EXAMPLE 34.7**

Continuing *Example 34.6*, exactly 15 months later the trustees appoint £25,000 to a beneficiary. The IHT (assuming no grossing-up) will be:
   £25,000 × 2.14% × 5/40 (five quarters since last ten-year anniversary) = £66.88.

If the rates of IHT have been reduced (including the raising of the rate bands) between the anniversary and exit charges, the lower rates will apply to the exit charge and, therefore, the rate of charge on the first anniversary will have to be recalculated at those rates (IHTA 1984 Sch 2 para 3). So long as the IHT rate bands remain linked to rises in the retail prices index (IHTA 1984 s 8) recalculation will be the norm.

No exit charge is levied if the chargeable event occurs within the first quarter following the anniversary charge.                                **[34.28]**

## 5   Later periodic charges

The principles that applied on the first ten-year anniversary operate on subsequent ten-year anniversaries. So far as the hypothetical chargeable transfer is concerned the same items will be included (so that the value of property in a related settlement and of non-relevant property in the settlement is always included). The cumulative total of the fund will, as before, include the chargeable transfers of the settlor made in the seven years before he created the settlement and the transfers out of the settlement in the ten years immediately preceding the anniversary (earlier transfers by the settlement fall out of the cumulative total). The remaining stages of the calculation are unaltered.                                **[34.29]**

## 6   Technical problems

The basic structure of the charging provisions in IHTA 1984 ss 58–69 is relatively straightforward. The charge to IHT is built on a series of periodic charges with interim charges (where appropriate) which are levied at a fraction of the full periodic charge.                                **[34.30]**

a)   *Reduction in the rate of the anniversary charge*

If property has not been in the settlement for the entire preceding ten years (as will be the case when income is accumulated during that period) there is a proportionate reduction in the charge (IHTA 1984 s 66(2)). The reduction in the periodic rate is calculated by reference to the number of completed quarters that expired before the property became relevant property in the settlement.

**EXAMPLE 34.8**

Assume in *Example 34.6* that £15,000 had become relevant property on 30 April 2009.

The IHT charge on the first ten-year anniversary (on 6 April 2013) would now be calculated as follows:

(1)  £90,000 (£105,000 – £15,000) at 2.14% =£1,926.

(2)  The £15,000 will be charged at a proportion of the periodic charge rate: namely 2.14% reduced by 24/40 since 24 complete quarters elapsed from the creation of the settlement (on 1 April 2003) to the date when the £15,000 became relevant property. As a result the IHT charged is £15,000 × 0.85% (ie 2.14% × 16/40) = £128.40.

This proportionate reduction in the effective rate of the periodic charge will not affect the calculation of IHT on events occurring after the anniversary, ie any exit charge is at the full effective rate.

The legislation does not contain provisions which enable specific property to be identified. Thus, the reduction mentioned above applies to the value of the relevant property in the fund at the ten-year anniversary 'attributable' to property which was not relevant property throughout the preceding ten years. Presumably a proportionate calculation will be necessary where the value of the fund has shown an increase. Furthermore, if accumulated income is caught by the anniversary charge, a separate calculation will have to be made with regard to each separate accumulation (see SP 8/86: **[34.26]**). **[34.31]**

b)  *Transfers between settlements*

IHTA 1984 s 81 prevents a tax advantage from switching property between settlements of relevant property, by providing that such property remains comprised in the first settlement. Accordingly, property cannot be moved out of a discretionary trust to avoid an anniversary charge; property cannot be switched from a fund with a high cumulative total to one with a lower total; and the transfer of property from one discretionary fund to another will not be chargeable. **[34.32]**

c)  *Added property*

Special rules operate if, after the settlement commenced (and after 8 March 1982), the settlor made a chargeable transfer as a result of which the value of the property comprised in the settlement was increased (IHTA 1984 s 67(1)). Note that it is only additions by the settlor that trigger these provisions and that it is the value of the fund which must be increased and not necessarily the amount of property in that fund. Transfers which have the effect of increasing the value of the fund are ignored if they are not primarily intended to have that effect and do not in fact increase the value by more than 5%.

**EXAMPLE 34.9**

Sam, the settlor, creates in 2003 a discretionary trust of stocks and shares in Sham Ltd and the benefit of a life insurance policy on Sam's life.
(1)    Each year Sam adds property to the settlement, equal to his annual IHT exemption.
(2)    Sam continues to pay the premiums on the life policy each year.
(3)    Sam transfers further shares in Sham Ltd.
    The special rules for added property will not apply in either case (1) or (2), since Sam is not making a chargeable transfer; the first transfer is covered by his annual exemption and the second by the exemption for normal expenditure out of income. The transfer of further shares to the fund, however, is caught by the provisions of IHTA 1984 s 67.

If the added property provisions apply, the calculation of the periodic charge which immediately follows the addition will be modified. For the purposes of the hypothetical chargeable transfer, the cumulative total of the settlor's chargeable transfers will be the higher of the totals (1) immediately before creating the settlement plus transfers made by the settlement before the addition; and (2) immediately before transferring the added property, deducting from this latter total the transfer made on creation of the settlement and a transfer to any related settlement. The settlor should normally avoid additions, since they may cause more IHT to be charged at the next anniversary and it will be preferable to create a separate settlement.
**[34.33]**

d)    *The timing of the exit charge*

Assume, for example, that a discretionary trust has been in existence for nearly ten years and that the trustees now wish to distribute all or part of the fund to the beneficiaries. Are they better off doing so just before the ten-year anniversary or should they wait until just after that anniversary? Generally, it will be advantageous to distribute *before* an anniversary because IHT payable will be calculated at rates then in force but on historic values, ie on the value of the fund when it was settled or at the last ten-year anniversary. By contrast, if the trustees delay until after the anniversary, IHT (still at current rates) will then be assessed on the present value of the fund. To this general proposition one major exception exists which may well be the result of defective drafting in the legislation. It relates to a fund consisting of property qualifying for either business relief or agricultural relief at 50%. In this situation trustees *should not* break up the fund immediately before the first anniversary. **[34.34]**

**EXAMPLE 34.10**

A discretionary settlement was created on 1 January 1992. At all times it has consisted of agricultural property which will qualify for 50% relief. Assume no earlier transfers by settlor and that the value of the property is £500,000 throughout. Consider the effect of agricultural property relief if:
(1)    *the trustees distribute the entire fund on 25 December 2001.* The distribution occurs before the first ten-year anniversary. The entire value of the property in the settlement immediately after it commenced must be included in the hypothetical transfer of value since there is no agricultural property relief reduction. Therefore £500,000 must be included (IHTA 1984 s 111(5)(a)).

The rate thus calculated is then applied to the fund as reduced by business relief. Hence, although the amount subject to the charge is only £250,000 (£500,000 minus 50% relief), a higher rate of IHT will apply. (Notice that if 100% relief were to be available in 2001 this trap would not arise.)

(2) *the trustees distribute the entire fund on 3 January 2002.* As the first ten-year anniversary fell on 1 January there will be no exit charge because the distribution is within three months of that anniversary. So far as the anniversary charge is concerned the property subject to the charge will be reduced by 50% relief to £250,000; and for the purpose of calculating the hypothetical chargeable transfer the value of the property is similarly reduced by the relief.

## 7 Using discretionary trusts

Discretionary trusts are likely to remain attractive in the following situations:

(1) Small *inter vivos* discretionary settlements. Notice that two discretionary settlements can be used to create two nil rate band trusts when the transferor is transferring one and a half times his nil rate band.

### EXAMPLE 34.11

A taxpayer transfers agricultural property (qualifying for 50% relief) into two discretionary trusts as follows:

*Into Discretionary Trust 1* property which reduces his estate by £125,000 after 50% agricultural property relief.

*Into Discretionary Trust 2* property which reduces his estate by £62,500 after 50% agricultural property relief.

In both cases, assume that the agricultural property is sold by the trustees. The result is that the first discretionary trust is worth £250,000 and, in working out any IHT charges, the settlor's cumulative total when the trust was created was nil. The second discretionary trust is worth £125,000 and was set up at a time when the cumulative total of the settlor was £125,000. Accordingly, the two trusts are nil rate band trusts, but remember that, to avoid the related settlement rules, they should be created on separate days.

In appropriate cases a settlor can create a number of pilot settlements each with a full nil rate band.

### EXAMPLE 34.12

S wishes to put £400,000 into discretionary trusts. He therefore creates four pilot trusts of £10 each on *different days* (so that they are not 'related settlements') and subsequently but *on the same day* pays £99,990 into each trust thus created. The trusts are not related since they are created on different days and each comprises £100,000. As transfers made on the same day are ignored in computing the settlor's cumulative total, that total is either £10 or £20 or £30 when the relevant addition is made. Notice that although each settlement will enjoy a full nil rate band, the transfer of £400,000 into settlement will attract an immediate IHT charge at half rates. (*Note*: Ensure that each settlement is independent of the others, eg different trustees, beneficial class and see the *Rysaffe* case, [32.4].)

(2) In will drafting, the use of the mini (£275,000) discretionary trust remains attractive for the smaller estate and, for flexibility the 'two-year' trust (see [30.145]).

(3)   Until the FA 2006 changes, it was possible to set up discretionary trusts by channelling property through an A&M trust (ie taking advantage of 'children of straw'). This will not be possible for *inter vivos* trusts created on or after 22 March 2006.                                    **[34.35]–[34.50]**


## III   EXEMPTIONS AND RELIEFS

Many of the exemptions from IHT do not apply to trusts with relevant property, eg the annual exemption, the marriage exemption, and the exemption for normal expenditure out of income. There is no exemption if the settled fund reverts to either the settlor or his spouse (and note that if the settlor is a beneficiary, the reservation of benefit provisions apply, see **Chapter 29**). Business and agricultural property relief may, however, be available, provided that the necessary conditions for the relief are met by the trustees. There is no question of any aggregation with similar property owned by a discretionary or other beneficiary.

Exit charges are not levied in certain cases when property leaves the settlement, eg:
(1)   Property ceasing to be relevant property within three months of the creation of the trust or of an anniversary charge or within two years of creation (if the trust was set up on death and the conditions in IHTA 1984 s 144(1) are satisfied) is not subject to an exit charge (**[30.145]**).
(2)   Property may pass, without attracting an exit charge, to such privileged trusts as employee trusts (IHTA 1984 s 75); maintenance funds for historic buildings (IHTA 1984 Sch 4 para 16); permanent charities (IHTA 1984 s 76(1)); and political parties in accordance with the exemption in IHTA 1984 s 24 (IHTA 1984 s 76(1)(b); and see **Chapter 31**).

If a discretionary fund contains excluded property (and property qualifying for 100% business or agricultural relief) the periodic and exit charges will not apply to that part of the fund.                                    **[34.51]–[34.70]**


## IV   DISCRETIONARY TRUSTS CREATED BEFORE 27 MARCH 1974

Discretionary settlements created before 27 March 1974 are subject to special rules for the calculation of tax which generally result in less tax being charged (see generally IHTA 1984 ss 66–68).                                    **[34.71]**


### 1   Chargeable events occurring before the first ten-year anniversary

The rate of IHT is set out in IHTA 1984 s 68(6). As the settlement is treated as a separate taxable entity only transfers made by the settlement are cumulated. Such chargeable transfers will either be distribution payments (if made under the regime in force from 1974 to 1982) or chargeable events under IHTA 1984 65. Once the cumulative total is known, the rate of tax will be calculated at half rate and the charge will be at 30% of that rate.
                                    **[34.72]**

## 2  The first anniversary charge

No anniversary charge applied before 1 April 1983. Thus, the first trust to suffer this charge was one created on 1 April 1973 (or 1963; 1953; 1943 and so on).

The amount subject to the charge is calculated in the normal way. In calculating the rate of charge, however, it is only chargeable transfers of the settlement in the preceding ten years that are cumulated (as the settlement predates CTT/IHT the settlor has no chargeable transfers to cumulate). Property in a related settlement and non-relevant property in the settlement are ignored. As before, the rate of charge is reduced if property has not been relevant property throughout the decade preceding the first anniversary. The danger of increasing an IHT bill by an addition of property by the settlor (see **[34.33]**) is even greater with these old trusts. If such an addition has been made, the settlor's chargeable transfers in the seven-year period before the addition must be cumulated in calculating the rate of tax on the anniversary charge (IHTA 1984 s 67(4)). The effective rate of charge for the anniversary charge is (as for new trusts) 30% of the rate calculated according to half the table rates. **[34.73]**

## 3  Chargeable events after the first anniversary charge

The position is the same as for new trusts. The charge is based upon the rate charged at the last anniversary. **[34.74]–[34.90]**

### EXAMPLE 34.13

In November 1975 Maggie settled £400,000 on discretionary trusts for her family. The following events have since occurred:

*In May 1981*: a distribution payment of £100,000.

*In May 1984*: trustees distribute a further sum of £85,000 (tax borne by beneficiary).

*In November 1985*: the first ten-year anniversary. The value of relevant property then in the fund is £300,000.

IHT will be charged as follows:

(1)  *May 1984*: The distribution is a chargeable event occurring before the first ten-year anniversary. IHT is calculated by cumulating the chargeable transfer of £85,000 with the earlier transfer made by the settlement (the distribution payment of £100,000).(Notice that there is no proportionate reduction in the effective rate for exit charges levied on old discretionary trusts before the first anniversary.)

(2)  *November 1985*: The anniversary charge will be calculated on the relevant property in the settlement (£100,000). The cumulative total of transfers made by the settlement is £185,000 (£100,000 plus £85,000).

## V  ACCUMULATION AND MAINTENANCE TRUSTS (IHTA 1984 s 71)

*Finance Act 2006*

FA 2006 has made significant changes in the area of A&M trusts. It has effectively put a stop to the creation of new A&M trusts after 22 March 2006, providing that IHTA 1984 s 71 does not apply to any property settled on or after that date. The result is that for A&M trusts subsisting on 22 March 2006 which do not come within the conditions for trusts for bereaved minors (see **[34.102]**), transitional relief is available so that they will continue to be exempt from the relevant property regime if *first,* the trust provides that the beneficiary will become absolutely entitled to the trust property at 18, or the terms are varied before 6 April 2008 to provide for this. If they do not so provide, the trust assets will become relevant property on 6 April 2008, from which time the periodic and exit charges will apply; or *secondly,* the trusts arise under the will of a deceased parent or step-parent in favour of his or her child and, before 6 April 2008, the child will become entitled to an interest in possession (for example, under the Trustee Act 1925, s 31 on attaining the age of 18), and the property is then held for the bereaved minor absolutely on attaining an age no greater than 25, with income and capital being applied only for his benefit in the meantime. What follows is therefore an analysis of the tax treatment of A&M trusts created before 22 March 2006.

## 1    Tax treatment for A&M trusts created pre-22 March 2006

### a)    *Inheritance tax*

Rather than make outright gifts to minor children, it has been fairly common to settle the property in trust (often subject to the satisfaction of a contingency, eg 'attaining the age of 21') for their benefit. The reason for this special treatment was to avoid discriminating between gifts to adults and settled gifts to infants for IHT purposes.

**EXAMPLE 34.14**

Simon makes two gifts: one to his brother, Enrico, and one to his two-month-old granddaughter, Frederica.
(1)    *The gift to Enrico:* The gift is a PET and therefore only subject to IHT if Simon dies within seven years.
(2)    *The gift to Frederica:* In view of her age, it is felt necessary to settle the property on trusts which give the trustees the power to maintain Frederica, but which give her no interest in possession. Under general principles, the creation of that settlement will be a chargeable transfer of value and the discretionary trust charging regime will operate. As a result there would be anniversary charges and, when Frederica obtains either an interest in possession or an absolute interest in the settled fund, an 'exit' charge.

The object of the special provisions was to prevent this double charge. The *inter vivos* creation of an accumulation and maintenance (A&M) settlement was accordingly a PET and thereafter, so long as the property continues to be held on A&M trusts, the ten-year anniversary charge would not apply and there would be no proportionate periodic charge when the property left the trust. As a result, the taxation of gifts to minors was treated in the same way as gifts to adults. For all *inter vivos* trusts created on or after 22 March 2006 and for trusts for minors created by the will of someone other than a parent of the minor (in this case, see **[34.102]**) after that date, discrimination now exists with the removal of these advantages.    **[34.91]**

b)   *Other taxes*

The privileged status of the A&M trust only applies for IHT purposes. So far as the other taxes are concerned, general principles operate. Unless the property settled comprises business assets, CGT hold-over relief is not available on the *inter vivos* creation of the trust and will only be available on its termination if a beneficiary becomes absolutely entitled to the assets on the ending of the accumulation period ([**24.91**]). For income tax, the creation of an A&M trust by a parent on behalf of his own infant unmarried children will result in any income which is distributed being taxed as his under the income tax settlement provisions (see ITTOIA 2005 s 629). The trustees will (generally) suffer income tax at the rate of 40% (TA 1988 s 686).

[**34.92**]

## 2   The requirements of IHTA 1984 s 71

To qualify for privileged IHT treatment, an A&M trust has to satisfy the three requirements considered below. Failure to do so means that the normal charging system (either discretionary trust or interest in possession) applies. When the requirements cease to be satisfied IHT will not be charged save in exceptional cases (see [**34.98**]).                                       [**34.93**]

## 3   Requirement 1

> 'One or more persons (… beneficiaries) will, on or before attaining a specified age not exceeding 25, become entitled to, or to an interest in possession in, the settled property or part of it' (IHTA 1984 s 71).

This is concerned with the age at which a beneficiary becomes entitled either to the income from the fund or to the fund itself. The age of 25 is specified as a maximum age limit and this is generously late when one considers that the justification for these rules is to deal with settlements for infant children.

### EXAMPLE 34.15

(1)   Property is settled (prior to 22 March 2006) upon trust 'for A absolutely, contingent on attaining the age of 18'. A (currently aged 10) will become entitled to both income and capital at that age so that Requirement 1 is satisfied.

(2)   Property is settled in 1982 upon trust 'for B absolutely, contingent upon attaining the age of 30'. At first sight Requirement 1 is broken since B (aged 8) will not acquire the capital in the fund until after the age of 25. However, it will be satisfied if the beneficiary acquires an interest in possession before 25; B will do so, because Trustee Act 1925 s 31 (if not expressly excluded) provides that when a beneficiary with a contingent interest attains 18, that beneficiary shall thereupon be entitled to the income produced by the fund even though he has not yet satisfied the contingency.

The requirement that a beneficiary *'will'* become entitled does not require absolute certainty; death, for instance, can always prevent entitlement. The word causes particular problems when trustees possess overriding powers of advancement and appointment (dispositive powers) which, if exercised, could result in entitlement being postponed beyond 25. So long as the dispositive power can only be exercised amongst the existing beneficiaries (or other persons under the age of 25) and cannot postpone entitlement beyond the age of 25, Requirement 1 is satisfied. Accordingly, a power to vary or determine the respective shares of members of the class, even to the extent of excluding some members altogether, is permissible.

**EXAMPLE 34.16**

Property is held on trust for the three children of A contingent upon their attaining the age of 25 and, if more than one, in equal shares. The trustees are given overriding powers of appointment, exercisable until a beneficiary attains 25, to appoint the fund to one or more of the beneficiaries as they see fit. Requirement 1 is satisfied since the property will vest absolutely in the beneficiaries no later than the age of 25. The existence of the overriding power of appointment is irrelevant since it cannot be exercised other than in favour of the class of beneficiaries and cannot be used to postpone the vesting of the fund until after a beneficiary has attained 25.

The existence of a common form of power of advancement will not prevent Requirement 1 from being satisfied (see *Lord Inglewood v IRC* (1983)). However, such powers can be exercised so as to postpone the vesting of property in a beneficiary beyond the age stated in the trust document and, hence, beyond the age of 25 (see *Pilkington v IRC* (1962)) and they can, in exceptional cases, result in property being paid to a non-beneficiary (as in *Re Clore's Settlement Trusts* (1966) where the payment was to the beneficiary's favourite charity). If the power is so exercised a charge to IHT will result.

The effect of powers of appointment which, if exercised, would break Requirement 1 is illustrated by the following example (and see SP E1):

**EXAMPLE 34.17**

Property is settled in 1983 'for the children of E contingent on their attaining 25'. The trustees are given the following (alternative) overriding powers of appointment.

(1)   *To appoint income and capital to E's sister F:* The mere existence of this power causes the settlement to break Requirement 1. There is no certainty that the fund will pass to E's children since the power might be exercised in favour of F.

(2)   *To appoint income to E's brother G:* The same consequence will follow since the mere existence of this power means that the income could be used for the benefit of G and, hence, break Requirement 2 (for details of this Requirement see below).

(3)   *To appoint capital and income to E's relatives so long as those relatives are no older than 25:* This power does not break Requirement 1 since whoever receives the settled fund, whether E's children or his relatives, will be no older than 25.

It may be difficult to decide whether or not the settlement contains a power of revocation or appointment which will break Requirement 1. In *Lord Inglewood v IRC* (1981), Vinelott J distinguished between events provided for in the trust instrument and events wholly outside the settlor's control:

'the terms of the settlement must be such that one or more of the beneficiaries, if they or one of them survive to the specified age, will be bound to take a vested interest on or before attaining that age ... Of course, a beneficiary may assign his interest, or be deprived of it, by an arrangement, or by bankruptcy, before he attains a vested interest. But he is not then deprived of it under the terms of the settlement, so these possible events, unlike the exercise of a power of revocation or appointment, must be disregarded ...' [1981] STC 318 at 322 (see also Fox LJ, in the Court of Appeal, [1983] STC 133 at 138).

**EXAMPLE 34.18**

Sebag creates a settlement (prior to 22 March 2006) in favour of his second daughter, Juno, under which she will obtain the property if she attains the age of 18. If she marries before that age, however, the property is to pass to Sebag's brother, Sebastian.

This provision in the settlement could operate to deprive Juno of the property in circumstances when, as a matter of general law, she would not be so deprived. The settlement does not satisfy Requirement 1 and so does not qualify for privileged treatment.

Two other matters should be noted in relation to Requirement 1. *First,* even if a trust instrument fails to specify an age at which the beneficiary will become entitled to either the income or capital, so long as it is clear from the terms of that instrument and the known ages of the beneficiaries that one or more persons will in fact become entitled before the age of 25, Requirement 1 will be satisfied (ESC F8).

*Secondly,* for an A&M trust to be created there had to be a living beneficiary at that time. It was possible to set up a trust for a class of persons including some who were unborn ('the grandchildren of the settlor' for instance), but there had to be at least one member of the class in existence at the date of creation (IHTA 1984 s 71(7)). If the single living beneficiary dies, the trust (assuming that it was set up for a class of beneficiaries) will remain an A&M trust until a further member of that class is born. If a further class member is never born, it will eventually pass elsewhere and at that stage an IHT charge may arise. **[34.94]**

## 4 Requirement 2

'No interest in possession subsists in the settled property (or part) and the income from it is to be accumulated so far as it is not applied for the maintenance, education or benefit of such a person' (IHTA 1984 s 71).

There must be no interest in possession and once such an interest arises, the settlement breaks Requirement 2 and ceases to be an A&M trust.

If there is no interest in possession in the income, what is to be done with it? Two possibilities are envisaged; it can either be used for the benefit of a beneficiary (eg under a power of maintenance), or it can be accumulated. There must be a valid power to accumulate: accordingly once the accumulation period ends Requirement 2 will cease to be satisfied and the settlement will no longer be an A&M trust.

**EXAMPLE 34.19**

A trust is set up for Loeb, the child of the settlor, contingent on his attaining the age of 25. So long as he is a minor the trustees will have a power to maintain him out of the income of the fund and a power to accumulate any surplus income (Trustee Act 1925 s 31). When Loeb becomes 18 he will be entitled to the income of the fund so that an interest in possession will arise and the settlement will cease to be an A&M trust. The ending of the trust will not lead to any IHT charge.

Care should be taken in choosing the appropriate period if the intention is to accumulate income beyond the minorities of the beneficiaries. Various periods are permitted under LPA 1925 ss 164 and 165 and under Trustee Act 1925 s 31, but some of them may cause the trust to fall outside the definition of an A&M settlement. In the case of an *inter vivos* trust, for instance, a direction to accumulate 'during the lifetime of the settlor' would mean that an interest in possession might not arise until after the beneficiaries had attained the age of 25; likewise, a provision to accumulate for 21 years when the beneficiaries are over the age of four would be fatal.          **[34.95]**

## 5   Requirement 3

'Either

(i)   not more than 25 years have elapsed since the day on which the settlement was made or (if later) since the time when the settled property (or part) began to satisfy Requirements 1 and 2, or

(ii)  all the persons who are, or have been beneficiaries are, or were, either grandchildren of a common grandparent, or children, widows or widowers of such grandchildren who were themselves beneficiaries but died before becoming entitled as mentioned in [Requirement 1]' (IHTA 1984 s 71).

Requirement 3 was introduced to stop the A&M trust from being used to benefit more than one generation. There are two ways in which it can be satisfied. First, the trust must not last for more than 25 years from the date when the fund became settled on A&M trusts. The second (alternative) limb is satisfied if all the beneficiaries have a common grandparent.

**EXAMPLE 34.20**

(1)   Property is settled for the children and grandchildren of the settlor. As there is no grandparent common to all the beneficiaries, the trust must not last for longer than 25 years if an exit charge to IHT is to be avoided.

(2)   Property is settled for the children of brothers Bill and Ben. As there is a common grandparent the duration of the settlement does not need to be limited to 25 years.

Two generations can be benefited under an A&M trust without the 25-year time limit applying in one case, namely substitution *per stirpes* is permitted where the original beneficiaries had a common grandparent and one of those beneficiaries has died.          **[34.96]**

## 6 Advantages of accumulation and maintenance trusts

An A&M trust created prior to 22 March 2006 and still in existence may continue to enjoy the advantages outlined provided that it falls within one of the two categories discussed in **[34.91]**. For trusts created after 22 March 2006, these advantages will no longer apply. No IHT is charged when property from an A&M trust becomes subject to an interest in possession in favour of one or more of the beneficiaries, nor when any part of the fund is appointed absolutely to such a beneficiary (IHTA 1984 s 71(3), (4)). This exemption, together with the exclusion of the anniversary charge (IHTA 1984 s 58(1)(b)), means that once the property is settled on these trusts there should be no IHT liability whilst the settlement continues in that form and on its termination. Furthermore the *inter vivos* creation of the trust is a PET.

**EXAMPLE 34.21**

'... to A absolutely contingent on attaining 25'. This straightforward trust, created in 1990, will satisfy the Requirements so long as A is an infant. Consider, however, the position:

(1)   *When A attains 18:* he will be entitled to the income from the fund (Trustee Act 1925 s 31) and, therefore, Requirement 2 is broken. No IHT is charged on the arising of the interest in possession.

(2)   *When A attains 25:* ordinary principles for interest in possession settlements apply; A's life interest comes to an end, but no IHT is payable since the life tenant is entitled to all the property (see IHTA 1984 s 53(2)). Note that adverse CGT consequences may occur at this time: see **[24.91]**.

(3)   *If A dies aged 19:* IHT will be assessed on the termination of an interest in possession.

As already discussed, there is nothing to prevent an A&M trust from being created for an open class of beneficiaries, eg 'for all my grandchildren both born and yet to be born'. If such a trust is to be created, it is important to consider whether the class of beneficiaries should close when the eldest obtains a vested interest in either the income or capital. Failure to do so will result in a partial divesting of the beneficiary with the vested interest when a further beneficiary is born, and, as a result, a PET. Class-closing rules may be implied at common law (see *Andrews v Partington* (1791)), but it is safer to insert an express provision to that effect.

IHTA 1984 s 71(4)(b) provides that 'tax shall not be charged ... on the death of a beneficiary before attaining the specified age'. It follows that, if the entire class of beneficiaries is wiped out, an A&M trust will cease on the death of the final member, but, whoever then becomes entitled to the fund, no IHT will be payable. When it is necessary to wait and see if a further beneficiary is born, however, this provision will not operate, since it is not the death of the beneficiary which ends the A&M trust in such a case, but the failure of a further beneficiary to be born within the trust period.

**EXAMPLE 34.22**

(1)   Property is settled upon trust for Zed's grandchild, Yvonne, contingent upon her attaining 18. If she were to die aged 16, the property would (in the absence of any provision to the contrary) revert to Zed and no IHT would be payable.

(2)   Property was settled upon trust for Victor's children contingent upon their attaining 21 and, if more than one, in equal shares absolutely. Victor's one child, Daphne, died in 2000 aged 12 and Victor himself has just died.

No charge to IHT arose on Daphne's death but the property continued to be held on A&M trusts until Victor died when the trust ended with a charge to IHT.

The A&M trust could be drafted to achieve a considerable degree of flexibility. It was common for such a trust to contain the following provisions:

(1)   Primary beneficiaries are present and future grandchildren with a class-closing provision.

(2)   The trustees are given a revocable power of appointment among the beneficiaries (inapplicable once a beneficiary has attained 25).

(3)   The A&M trust will end with beneficiaries being entitled to interests in possession (not absolute interests) and thereafter such a beneficiary is given power to appoint a life interest to his surviving spouse and divide up the capital as he sees fit between his children. However:

(4)   The trustees retain an overriding power to determine the life interest of any beneficiary who has attained (say) 26 and appoint the property in favour of one or more secondary beneficiaries, often called discretionary beneficiaries.

As a result, this kind of settlement includes more than one generation of beneficiaries; has great flexibility; but still qualifies as an A&M trust when set up.                                                                          **[34.97]**

## 7   Occasions when an 'exit charge' will arise

It is rare for property to leave an A&M trust otherwise than by vesting in a qualifying beneficiary and so long as this happens no IHT is chargeable. Provision is, however, made for calculating an 'exit charge' in the following four circumstances (IHTA 1984 ss 70(6), 71(5)):

(1)   When depreciatory transactions entered into by the trustees reduce the value of the fund (IHTA 1984 s 71(3)(b)).

(2)   When the 25-year period provided for in Requirement 3 is exceeded and the beneficiaries do not have a common grandparent.

(3)   When property is advanced to a non-beneficiary or resettled on trusts which do not comply with the three Requirements.

(4)   If the trust ends some time after the final surviving beneficiary has died (see *Example 34.22(2)*).

IHT is calculated in these cases on the value of the fund according to how long the property has been held on the A&M trusts:

0.25%  for each of the first 40 complete successive quarters in the relevant period;

0.20%  for each of the next 40;

0.15%  for each of the next 40;

0.10% for each of the next 40; and

0.05% for each of the next 40.

Hence, on expiry of the permitted 25 years IHT at a rate of 21% will apply to the fund. Thereafter, normal discretionary trust rules will apply, so that five years later there will be an anniversary charge. **[34.98]–[34.100]**

## VI TRUSTS FOR BEREAVED MINORS AND 18–25 TRUSTS

In place of A&M settlements, FA 2006 has introduced two new trust regimes – the 'trust for bereaved minors' and '18–25 Trusts'. The rules governing these trusts are contained in IHTA 1984 s 71A-G (introduced by FA 2006). **[34.101]**

### 1 Trusts for bereaved minors

Broadly, a trust is a 'trust for bereaved minors' if property is held on statutory trusts for minors that arise on intestacy or on trusts established under the will of a deceased parent of the bereaved minor or on trusts established under the Criminal Injuries Compensation Scheme. Trusts of the last two types must fulfil additional conditions. First, the bereaved minor must, on attaining 18 years of age (if not earlier), become absolutely entitled to the settled property, any income arising from such property and any income from such property that has been accumulated before the bereaved minor turned 18. Secondly, while the bereaved minor is under the age of 18, any income or capital payment out of the settled property is provided for the benefit of the bereaved minor. Thirdly, while the bereaved minor is under 18 years of age, either the bereaved minor is entitled to all the income arising from any settled property or no such income may be used to benefit any other person.

Where IHTA 1984 s 71A applies (i.e. there is a trust for bereaved minors) the general rule is that there is a charge to tax where settled property ceases to be property to which s 71A applies ('the exit charge' – the authors' terminology), and where trustees enter into a depreciatory transaction. The exceptions to the general rule are that no charge arises:

- first, when the bereaved minor turns 18 or, if earlier, becomes absolutely entitled to the settled property and any arising or accumulated income;
- secondly, if the bereaved minor dies under the age of 18; or
- thirdly, when the settled property is paid or applied for the benefit of the bereaved minor. **[34.102]**

### 2 Age 18–25 trusts

18–25 trusts are established under IHTA 1984 s 71D, which applies to settled property (including property settled before 22 March 2006) if the property

- is held on trusts for the benefit of a person who is under 25 years of age;
- at least one of the person's parents has died;
- the trusts were established under the will of the deceased parent or under the Criminal Injuries Compensation Scheme; and
- the terms of the trusts satisfy the further conditions that *first*, the bereaved minor must on attaining 25 years of age (if not earlier),

become absolutely entitled to the settled property, any income arising from such property and any income arising from such property which has been accumulated before the bereaved turned 18; *secondly*, while the bereaved minor is under the age of 25, any benefit provided out of the settled property is provided to the bereaved minor; and *finally*, while the bereaved minor is under 25 years of age, either the bereaved minor is entitled to all the income arising from any settled property or no such income may be used to benefit any other person.

It should be noted that s 71D does not apply to any property to which ss 71 and 71A apply or where, if a person has an interest in possession in the settled property, that person became beneficially entitled to the interest in possession before 22 March 2006 or that interest in possession is an immediate post-death interest or a transitional serial interest and the person became entitled to it on or after 22 March 2006.

A charge to tax arises when settled property ceases to be property to which s 71D applies ('the exit charge' – the authors' terminology), or where the trustees enter into depreciatory transactions (IHTA 1984 s 71E (1)). Exceptions from this charge seek broadly to tie in the charge under s 71D with the charge under s 71A (trusts for bereaved minors) (s 71E (2)–(4)). For instance, tax is not charged under s 71E on property ceasing to be property to which s 71D applies where this is the result of the bereaved minor becoming absolutely entitled to the settled property income arising and accumulated income at or under the age of 18, or where the bereaved minor dies under the age of 18.

Property subject to these trusts will be exempt from the relevant property regime, except that there will be a charge when the bereaved minor becomes absolutely entitled to the property on attaining the age of 18 (or if, after attaining the age of 18, the property is applied for his benefit or is by advancement, or if he dies between the ages of 18 and 25), with the maximum rate of charge being 4.2% if absolute entitlement is on attaining the age of 25 (IHTA 1984 s 71G). **[34.103]–[34.110]**

## VII   OTHER SPECIAL TRUSTS

### 1   Charitable trusts

If a trust is perpetually dedicated to charitable purposes, there is no charge to IHT and the fund is not 'relevant property' (IHTA 1984 s 58). Transfers to charities are exempt, whether made by individuals or by trustees of discretionary trusts (IHTA 1984 s 76).

IHTA 1984 s 70 is concerned with temporary charitable trusts defined as 'settled property held for charitable purposes only until the end of a period (whether defined by a date or in some other way)' and ensures that when the fund ceases to be held for such purposes an exit charge will arise. That charge (which is calculated in the same way as for A&M trusts; see above) will never exceed a 30% rate which is reached after 50 years. **[34.111]**

## 2 Trusts for the benefit of mentally disabled persons and persons in receipt of an attendance allowance (IHTA 1984 s 89)

These trusts continue to enjoy their tax advantages even after the changes made by FA 2006.

A qualifying trust for a disabled person is treated as giving that person an interest in possession. As a result, the IHT regime for no interest in possession trusts does not apply. The *inter vivos* creation of this trust by a person other than the relevant beneficiary is a PET. There are no restrictions on the application of *income* which can therefore be used for the benefit of other members of the class of beneficiaries. This can be particularly useful where the application of income to the 'principal' disabled beneficiary could jeopardise his entitlement to state benefits. At least one half of any *capital* benefits must be paid to the 'principal' beneficiary. A charge to IHT will arise on the death of the disabled person whose deemed interest in possession will aggregate with his free estate in the normal way. Although disabled trusts can also obtain CGT advantages (eg a full annual exemption for the trustees), to qualify the disabled beneficiary must be entitled to at least one half of the income or be the sole income beneficiary (see TCGA 1992 Sch 1 para 1 and *Private Client Business* (1993) p 161).                    [34.112]

## 3 Pension funds (IHTA 1984 s 151)

A superannuation scheme or fund approved by HMRC for income tax purposes is not subject to the rules for no interest in possession trusts. This exemption from IHT extends to payments out of the fund within two years of the member's death. It is common practice for the member to settle the 'death benefit' on discretionary trusts: this trust will be subject to normal charging rules although HMRC consider that IHTA 1984 s 81 applies to deem the property to remain comprised in the original fund: eg for the purpose of ten-year anniversary dates (see [34.23]).                    [34.113]

## 4 Employee trusts (IHTA 1984 s 86)

These trusts will not in law be charitable unless they are directed to the relief of poverty amongst employees (see *Oppenheim v Tobacco Securities Trust Co Ltd* (1951)). They may, however, enjoy IHT privileges. Their creation will not involve a transfer of value, whether made by an individual (IHTA 1984 s 28) or by a discretionary trust (IHTA 1984 s 75). Once created, the fund is largely exempted from the IHT provisions governing discretionary trusts, especially from the anniversary charge. To qualify for this treatment, the fund must be held for the benefit of persons employed in a particular trade or profession together with their dependants. These provisions are extended to cover newspaper trusts (see IHTA 1984 s 87); approved profit sharing schemes and the FA 2000 employee share ownership plan.                    [34.114]

## 5 Compensation funds (IHTA 1984 ss 58, 63)

Trusts set up by professional bodies and trade associations for the purpose of indemnifying clients and customers against loss incurred through the default of their members are exempt from the rules for no interest in possession trusts.                    [34.115]

## 6  Maintenance funds for historic buildings (IHTA 1984 s 77, Sch 4)

IHT exemptions are available for maintenance funds where property is settled and the Treasury give a direction under IHTA 1984 Sch 4 para 1. Once the trust ceases, for any reason, to carry out its specialised function, an exit charge, calculated in the same way as for A&M trusts, occurs.    **[34.116]**

## 7  Protective trusts (IHTA 1984 ss 73, 88)

A protective trust may be set up either by using the statutory model provided for by the Trustee Act 1925 (TA) s 33, or by express provisions.

These trusts have always been subject to special IHT rules and, as originally enacted, the rules offered scope for tax avoidance (see IHTA 1984 s 73 and *Thomas v IRC* (1981)). Accordingly, the rules were changed with effect from 11 April 1978 by providing that the life tenant is deemed to continue to have an interest in possession for IHT purposes despite the forfeiture of his interest (IHTA 1984 s 88). It follows that the discretionary trust regime is not applicable to the trust that arises upon such forfeiture. Should the capital be advanced to a person other than the life tenant, a charge to IHT will arise and on the death of the beneficiary the fund will be treated as part of his estate for IHT purposes (*Cholmondeley v IRC* (1986)). As a result of these rules there is the curious anomaly that, after a forfeiture of the life interest, the interest in possession rules apply to a discretionary trust although it should be borne in mind that ordinary rules apply for other taxes. Thus for income tax a 40% rate applies once the life interest is forfeited and there is no CGT uplift on the death of the principal beneficiary.

One cautionary note should be added; this system of charging only applies to protective trusts set up under the TA 1925 s 33 or to trusts 'to the like effect'. Minor variations to the statutory norm are, therefore, allowed; but not the inclusion of different beneficiaries under the discretionary trust (such as the brothers and sisters of the principal beneficiary) nor a provision that enables a forfeited life interest to revive after the lapse of a period of time. In such cases, the normal rules applicable to interest in possession and discretionary trusts apply (see *Law Society's Gazette*, 3 March 1976 and SP E7).
    **[34.117]**

# 35 IHT—excluded property and the foreign element

*Updated by Aparna Nathan, LLB Hons, LLM, Barrister, Gray's Inn Tax Chambers*

## 1 Ambit of IHT

As a general rule, IHT is chargeable on all property situated within the UK regardless of its owner's domicile and on property, wheresoever situate, which is beneficially owned by an individual domiciled in the UK.     [**35.1**]

## 2 Excluded property

Any transfer of 'excluded property' is not chargeable to IHT (IHTA 1984 ss 3(2) and 5(1)). The main example of excluded property is 'property situated outside the UK ... if the person beneficially entitled to it is an individual domiciled outside the UK' (IHTA 1984 s 6(1)). In determining whether property is excluded property relevant factors include not only the domicile of the transferor who is the beneficial owner of the property and the situation of the property (*situs*), but also the nature of the transferred property, since certain property is excluded regardless of its *situs* or the domicile of its owner.     [**35.2**]

## I DOMICILE AND SITUS

### 1 Domicile

#### a) *General rules*

An individual cannot, under English law, be without a domicile which connotes a legal relationship between an individual and a territory. There are three kinds of domicile: domicile of origin, domicile of choice and domicile of dependence.

A person acquires a *domicile of origin* at the moment when he is born. He will usually take the domicile of his father unless he is illegitimate or born after his father's death in which case he takes the domicile of his mother. A domicile of origin is never completely lost, but may be superseded by a domicile of dependence or choice; it will revive if the other type of domicile lapses.

A person cannot acquire a *domicile of choice* until he is 16 or marries under that age. Whether someone has replaced his domicile of origin (or dependence) by a domicile of choice is a question of fact which involves physical presence in the country concerned and evidence of a settled intention to remain there permanently or indefinitely (*animus manendi*).

Unmarried infants under the age of 16 (in England and Wales, younger in Scotland) acquire their father's *domicile by dependence* and women who married before 1 January 1974 acquired their husband's domicile by dependence.    **[35.3]**

### b)   *Deemed domicile*

If a person's domicile under the general law is outside the UK, he may be deemed to be domiciled in the UK, *for IHT purposes only*, in two circumstances (IHTA 1984 s 267).

*First*, if a person was domiciled in the UK on or after 10 December 1974 and within the three years immediately preceding the transfer in question, he will be deemed to be domiciled in the UK at the time of making the transfer (IHTA 1984 s 267(1)(a)). This provision is aimed at the taxpayer who moves his property out of the UK and then emigrates to avoid future IHT liability on transfers of that property. In such a case he will have to wait three years from the acquisition of a new domicile of choice for his property to become excluded property under IHTA 1984 s 6(1) (see *Re Clore (No 2)* (1984)).

*Secondly*, a person will be deemed domiciled in the UK if he was resident for income tax purposes in the UK on or after 10 December 1974 and in not less than 17 out of the 20 income tax years ending with the income tax year in which he made the relevant transfer (IHTA 1984 s 267(1)(b)). This catches the person who has lived in the UK for a long time even though he never became domiciled here under the general law. Residence is used in the income tax sense (see **Chapter 18**), and does not require residence for a period of 17 complete years. This is because the Act is concerned with a person who is resident *in a tax year* and such residence may be acquired if the individual concerned comes to the UK at the very end of that year (eg on 1 April) with the intention of remaining indefinitely in the UK. In such a case, the individual will be resident for the tax year in which he arrived— albeit that it is about to end—and that will count as the first year of residence for the purpose of the 17-year test. Similarly, were he to leave the UK immediately after the commencement of a tax year, he would be treated as resident in the UK in that final tax year. Accordingly, in an extreme case, an individual could arrive in the UK on 1 April in one year, remain for the next 15 years and make a transfer on 10 April in year 17 and yet be caught by the 17-year test, even though only being resident in the UK for a little over 15 years.    **[35.4]**

**EXAMPLE 35.1**

(1) Jack who was domiciled in England moved to New Zealand on 1 July 2001 intending to settle there permanently. He died on 1 January 2003 when according to the general law he had acquired a domicile of choice in New Zealand. However, because Jack had a UK domicile and died within three years of losing it, he is deemed under s 267(1)(a) to have died domiciled in the UK. Accordingly, all his property wherever situated (excluding gilts; see below) is potentially chargeable to IHT. Jack would have had to survive until 1 July 2004 to avoid being caught by this provision.

(2) On 5 June 2003, Jim who is domiciled under the general law in Ruritania and who is a director of BB Ltd (the UK subsidiary of a Ruritanian company) gives a house that he owns in Ruritania to his son. By virtue of his job Jim has been resident for income tax purposes in England since 1 January 1976, but he intends to return to Ruritania when he retires. For IHT purposes Jim is deemed to be domiciled in England under s 267(1)(b); the gift will, therefore, be subject to IHT if Jim dies within seven years.

(3) Boer, resident in the UK but domiciled in South Africa, forms an overseas company to which he transfers the ownership of all his UK property. He has exchanged chargeable assets (UK property) for excluded property (shares in the overseas company). (For the purposes of income tax, this arrangement would fall within the transfer of assets legislation: see **[18.111]**.)

(4) François, a non-UK domiciliary, owns all the shares in a UK property dealing company. He converts that share capital into bearer shares holding the relevant certificates offshore. On his death the assets are not UK *situs* (note the stamp duty charge on an issue of bearer shares: see **Chapter 49**).

## 2 Situs

Subject to contrary provisions in double taxation treaties (and special rules for certain property) the *situs* of property is governed by common law rules and depends on the type of property involved. For instance:

(1) An interest in land (including a leasehold estate or rent charge) is situated where the land is physically located.

(2) Chattels (other than ships and aircraft) are situated at the place where they are kept at the relevant time.

(3) Registered shares and securities are situated where they are registered or, if transferable upon more than one register, where they would normally be dealt with in the ordinary course of business.

(4) Bearer shares and securities, transferable by delivery, are situated where the certificate or other document of title is kept.

(5) A bank account (ie the debt owed by the bank) is situated at the branch that maintains the account. (Special rules apply to non-residents' foreign currency bank accounts: **[35.26]**.) **[35.5]–[35.19]**

## II WHAT IS EXCLUDED PROPERTY?

## 1 Property situated outside the UK and owned beneficially by a non-UK domiciliary (IHTA 1984 s 6(1))

Property falling into this category is excluded regardless of its nature.

Settled property situated abroad will be excluded property only if the settlor was domiciled outside the UK at the time when he made the settlement (IHTA 1984 s 48(3): note that the position of the interest in possession beneficiary is irrelevant in this case). If the settlor retains an interest in possession either for himself or his spouse, and a discretionary trust arises on the termination of that interest, an additional test is imposed in determining whether property is excluded property. This test looks at where the settlor or the spouse (if the interest was reserved for him) was domiciled when that interest in possession ended (IHTA 1984 s 82). As this provision only applies where the property is *initially* settled with a life interest on the settlor or his spouse, it may be circumvented if the trust commences in discretionary form and is then converted into a life interest.          **[35.20]**

**EXAMPLE 35.2**

(1)    Franc, domiciled in Belgium, intends to buy a house in East Anglia costing £500,000. If he buys it in his own name it will be subject to IHT on his death. If he buys it through an overseas company, however, he will then own overseas assets (the company shares) that fall outside the IHT net. Note that if he occupies the house and is a director of the overseas company, HMRC will tax him on an emolument equal to the value of the property each year under the provisions of ITEPA 2003 s 102 (see **[8.116]**). This charge will also arise if Franc is a shadow director of the company: see *R v Allen; R v Dimsey* (2001). As an alternative:

(a)    the company could be owned by an offshore trust (a 'two-tier' structure) or;

(b)    he could buy the property in his own name with a substantial mortgage charged on the house which will have the effect of reducing its IHT value.

The Revenue has confirmed that where a UK-resident individual is provided with rent-free accommodation by an overseas resident company and that company is for the purposes of the transfer pricing legislation (TA 1988 Sch 28AA: see **[41.44]**) under the control of the UK-resident individual, it will not be Revenue practice to impute rental income to the overseas resident company (see *Tax Bulletin*, April 2000, p 742).

(2)    Erik, domiciled in Sweden, settles Swedish property on discretionary trusts for himself and his family. He subsequently acquires an English domicile of choice. The settlement is of excluded property for IHT purposes (IHTA 1984 s 48(3)), although the assets would appear to form part of the settlor's estate when he dies. Because of the reservation of benefit rules in FA 1986 s 102(3), HMRC currently accepts that the property remains excluded so that it will not be subject to any charge (*Law Society's Gazette*, 10 December 1986). The position is, however, different if Erik is excluded from all benefit during his life when a deemed PET occurs under s 102(4).

(3)    Boris, domiciled in France, died in February 2003 and left his villa in Tuscany and moneys in his Swiss bank account to his son Gaspard, a UK resident and domiciliary. By a variation of the terms of his will made within two years of Boris' death the property is settled on discretionary Liechten-stein trusts for the benefit of Gaspard's family. *For IHT*, reading back ensures that the settlement is of excluded property. *For CGT*, however, although the variation is not itself a disposal, Gaspard is treated as the settlor of the trust and hence the provisions in TCGA 1992 s 86 will apply (see **[27.91]** and *Marshall v Kerr* (1994)).

## 2 Property that is exempt despite being situated in the UK

### a) *Government securities*

Certain Government securities (gilts) owned by a person ordinarily resident outside the UK are exempt from IHT (IHTA 1984 s 6(2): see **[18.77]**— FOTRA securities). The domicile of the taxpayer is irrelevant (see *Advanced Instruction Manual* at G33). If these securities are settled they will be excluded property if either the person beneficially entitled to an interest in possession (eg a life tenant) is not ordinarily resident in the UK, or, in the case of a discretionary trust, if none of the beneficiaries are ordinarily resident in the UK (IHTA 1984 s 48(4)).

IHTA 1984 s 48(5) contains anti-avoidance provisions:
(1) If gilts are transferred from one settlement to another they will only be excluded property if the beneficiaries of *both* settlements are non-UK ordinarily resident. This prevents gilts from being channelled from a discretionary trust where they were not excluded property (because some of the beneficiaries were UK ordinarily resident) to a new settlement with non-ordinarily resident beneficiaries only, where they would be excluded property (as was done in *Minden Trust (Cayman) Ltd v IRC* (1984)).
(2) When a close company is a beneficiary of a trust, any gilts owned by the trust will be excluded property only if all participators in the company are non-UK ordinarily resident, irrespective of the company's residence. This aims to prevent individuals from using a company to avoid IHT. **[35.21]**

### b) *Holdings in an authorised unit trust and shares in an open ended investment company*

These securities are excluded property if the person beneficially entitled is an individual domiciled outside the UK (IHTA 1984 s 6(1A) inserted by FA 2003). If held in a settlement these assets will be excluded property unless the settlor was domiciled in the UK at the time when the settlement was made (IHTA 1984 s 48(3A) inserted by FA 2003). **[35.22]**

### c) *Certain property owned by persons domiciled in the Channel Islands or Isle of Man*

Certain savings (eg national savings certificates) are excluded property if they are in the beneficial ownership of a person domiciled and resident in the Channel Islands or the Isle of Man (IHTA 1984 ss 6(3), 267(4)). **[35.23]**

### d) *Visiting forces*

Certain property owned in the UK by visiting forces and staff of allied headquarters is excluded property (IHTA 1984 s 155). **[35.24]**

### e) *Overseas pensions*

Certain overseas pensions (usually payable by ex-colonial governments) are exempt from IHT on the pensioner's death regardless of his domicile (IHTA 1984 s 153). **[35.25]**

## f)    *Non-sterling bank accounts*

On the death of an individual domiciled resident and ordinarily resident outside the UK there is no IHT charge on the balance in any 'qualifying foreign currency account' (IHTA 1984 s 157). This exemption does not apply to *inter vivos* gifts of the money in such an account.

For the inter-relationship of excluded property and settlements, see **[35.81]**.                                                                                  **[35.26]–[35.40]**

## III   DOUBLE TAXATION RELIEF FOR NON-EXCLUDED PROPERTY

Non-excluded property may be exposed to a double charge to tax (especially on the death of the owner); once to IHT in the UK and again to a similar tax imposed by a foreign country. Relief against such double charge may be afforded in one of two ways.

*First*, the UK may have a double taxation treaty with the relevant country when the position is governed by IHTA 1984 s 158. The provisions of the treaty will override all the relevant IHT legislation (e.g. the deemed domicile rule) and common law rules regarding the *situs* of property.

Under these treaties, the country in which the transferor is domiciled is generally entitled to tax all property of which he was the beneficial owner. The other country involved usually has the right to tax some of that property, eg land situated there. In such cases the country of domicile will give relief against the resulting double taxation. Most of these treaties also contain provisions to catch the individual who changes his domicile shortly before death to avoid tax.

*Secondly*, where no double tax treaty exists, unilateral relief is given in the form of a credit for the foreign tax liability against IHT payable in the UK (IHTA 1984 s 159). The amount of the credit depends on where the relevant property is situated; in some cases no credit is available if the overseas tax is not similar to IHT, although some relief is, effectively, given since, in calculating the reduction in the transferor's estate for calculating IHT, the amount of overseas tax paid will be disregarded (IHTA 1984 s 5(3)). This relief is less beneficial than a tax credit.                                              **[35.41]–[35.60]**

## IV   MISCELLANEOUS POINTS

### 1   **Valuation of the estate—allowable deductions**

Certain liabilities of a transferor are deductible when calculating the value of his estate for IHT purposes (see **[30.13]**). However, any liability to a non-UK resident is deductible as far as possible from a transferor's foreign estate before his UK estate. As a result, a foreign domiciliary who is chargeable to IHT on his UK assets cannot usually deduct his foreign liabilities from his UK estate. There are two exceptions to this rule. *First*, if a liability of a non-UK resident has to be discharged in the UK, it is deductible from the UK estate; *secondly*, any liability that encumbers property in the UK, reduces the value of that property.                                                                                   **[35.61]**

**EXAMPLE 35.3**

Adolphus dies domiciled in Ethiopia. His estate includes cash in a London bank account, shares in UK companies and a stud farm in Weybridge that is mortgaged to an Ethiopian glue factory. He owes a UK travel company £500 for a ticket bought to enable his daughter to travel around Texas and £200,000 to a Dallas horse dealer. IHT is chargeable on his UK assets. However, the mortgage debt is deductible from the value of his stud farm and £500 is deductible from the UK estate generally. There is no reduction for the debt of £200,000 assuming that he has sufficient foreign property.

## 2 Expenses of administering property abroad (IHTA 1984 s 173)

Administration expenses are not generally deductible from the value of the deceased's estate. However, the expense of administering or realising property situated abroad on death is deductible from the value of the relevant property up to a limit of 5% of its value. **[35.62]**

## 3 Enforcement of tax abroad

On the death of a foreign domiciliary with UK assets, the deceased's PRs cannot administer his property until they have paid any IHT and obtained a grant of probate. However, the collection of IHT on lifetime transfers by a foreign domiciliary presents a problem if both the transferor and transferee are resident outside the UK and there is no available property in the UK that can be impounded. **[35.63]**

## 4 Foreign assets

If a foreign Government imposes restrictions as a result of which UK executors cannot immediately transfer to this country sufficient of the deceased's foreign assets for the payment of IHT attributable to them, they are given the option of deferring payment until that transfer can be made. If the amount that is finally brought into the UK is less than the IHT, any balance will be waived (see ESC F6). **[35.64]–[35.80]**

## V FOREIGN SETTLEMENTS, REVERSIONARY INTERESTS AND EXCLUDED PROPERTY

## 1 Foreign settlements

As a general rule, settled property which is situated abroad is excluded property if the settlor was domiciled outside the UK when the settlement was made (IHTA 1984 s 48(3) and see *Tax Bulletin*, February 1997). Therefore, the domicile of the individual beneficiaries in such cases is irrelevant, so that even if the beneficiary is domiciled in the UK, there will be no charge to IHT on the termination of his interest in possession nor on any payment made to him from a discretionary trust. **[35.81]**

**EXAMPLE 35.4**

Generous, domiciled in the USA, settles shares in US companies on his nephew, Tom, for life. Tom is domiciled and resident in the UK. The property is excluded property, being property situated abroad settled by a settlor domiciled at that time outside the UK, so that there will be no charge to IHT on the ending of Tom's life interest.

If, however, those shares were exchanged for shares in UK companies, the property would no longer be excluded and there would be a charge to IHT on the termination of Tom's life interest.

If Generous had settled those same US shares on discretionary trusts for his nephews, all of whom were UK domiciled, the property would be, for the same reason, excluded property, so that the normal discretionary trust charges would not apply. (Note the CGT treatment of IHT excluded property settlements as a result of FA 1998 changes: see **[27.111]**.)

## 2   Reversionary interests

### a)   *Definition*

For IHT purposes any future interest in settled property is classified as a reversionary interest (IHTA 1984 s 47). The term, therefore, includes an interest dependent on the termination of an interest in possession, whether that interest is vested or contingent. A contingent interest where the settlement does not have an interest in possession is also a reversionary interest for IHT purposes.

**EXAMPLE 35.5**

Property is settled on the following trusts:
(1)   A for life, remainder to B for life, remainder to C. B and C both have reversionary interests for IHT purposes.
(2)   A for life, remainder to B for life, remainder to C if he survives B. C's contingent remainder is a reversionary interest for IHT purposes.
(3)   To A absolutely contingent upon his attaining the age of 21. A is currently aged six and has a reversionary interest for IHT purposes.

The interest of a discretionary beneficiary is not, however, a 'reversionary interest', being in no sense a future interest. Such a beneficiary has certain present rights, particularly the right to be considered by the trustees when they exercise their discretion and the right to compel due administration of the fund. The value of such an interest is likely to be nil, however, since the beneficiary has no right to any of the income or capital of the settlement. He has merely a hope (*spes*).                    **[35.82]**

### b)   *'Situs' of a reversionary interest*

A reversionary interest under a trust for sale is a *chose in action* rather than an interest in the specific settled assets be they land or personalty (*Re Smyth, Leach v Leach* (1898)). In other cases the position is unclear; but by analogy with estate duty principles it will be a *chose in action* if the settled assets are personalty; but an interest in the settled assets themselves if they are land.

Since a *chose in action* is normally situated in the country in which it is recoverable (*New York Life Insurance Co v Public Trustee* (1924)), in some cases the reversionary interest will not be situated in the same place as the settled assets. [35.83]

c) *Reversionary interests—the general rule*

A reversionary interest is excluded property for IHT (IHTA 1984 s 48(1); see [33.61]) with three exceptions designed to counter tax avoidance:
(1)  Where it was purchased for money or money's worth.

### EXAMPLE 35.6

There is a settlement on A for life, remainder to B. B sells his interest to X who gives it to his brother Y. X has made a transfer of value (a PET) of a reversionary interest (which can be valued by taking into account the value of the settled fund and the life expectancy of A).
(2)  Where it is an interest to which the settlor or his spouse is beneficially entitled.
(3)  Where a lease for life or lives is granted for no or partial consideration, there is a settlement for IHT (IHTA 1984 s 43(3)) and the lessor's interest is a reversionary interest (IHTA 1984 s 47). Such a reversionary interest is only excluded property to the extent that the lessor did not receive full consideration on the grant (see IHTA 1984 s 48(1)(c) for valuation of the lessee's interest in possession and IHTA 1984 s 170 for the valuation of the lessor's interest). [35.84]

### EXAMPLE 35.7

L grants a lease of property worth £30,000 to T for £10,000 for T's life. T is treated for IHT purposes, as having an interest in possession and, therefore, as absolute owner of two-thirds of the property (£30,000 – £10,000). L is treated as the owner of one-third of the property (because he received £10,000). Therefore, one-third of his reversionary interest is not excluded property.

d) *Reversionary interests—the foreign element*

Under IHTA 1984 s 48(1) a reversionary interest (with the three exceptions above) is excluded property regardless of the domicile of the settlor or reversioner or the *situs* of the interest. Where the settled property is in the UK, but the reversionary interest is situated abroad (see [34.83]) and beneficially owned by a foreign domiciliary, the interest probably is excluded property in all cases under the general rule of IHTA 1984 s 6(1).

However, the status of a reversionary interest in settled property situated outside the UK is cast into some doubt by virtue of IHTA 1984 s 48(3) to which s 6(1) is expressly made subject (IHTA 1984 s 48(3)(b)). Section 48(3) states:

'where property comprised in a settlement is situated outside the UK

(a)  the property (but not a reversionary interest in the property) is excluded property unless the settlor was domiciled in the UK at the time the settlement was made; and

(b)    section 6(1) above applies to a reversionary interest in the property, but does not otherwise apply in relation to the property.'

This provision appears to exclude the operation of s 48(1) by saying that a reversionary interest in settled property situated abroad is only excluded property (under the general rule in s 6(1)) if it is itself situated abroad and owned by a foreign domiciliary.

However, it is thought that s 48(3) only prevails over s 48(1) in cases of conflict and that there is no conflict here since the words 'but not a reversionary interest' in s 48(3)(a) mean that whether a reversionary interest is excluded property depends not on the *situs* of the settled property nor on the settlor's domicile, but on the general rule in s 48(1).

In summary, therefore, a reversionary interest is always excluded property regardless of *situs* or domicile with three exceptions (see **[33.61]**). Even if the interest falls within one of the exceptions, it will still be excluded property if the interest (regardless of the whereabouts of the settled property) is situated outside the UK and beneficially owned by a foreign domiciliary (IHTA 1984 s 6(1)); or if the reversionary interest is itself settled property, is situated abroad and was settled by a foreign domiciliary (IHTA 1984 s 6(1) and s 48(3)).                                                                 **[35.85]**

# 36 Relief against double charges to IHT

*Updated by Aparna Nathan, LLB Hons, LLM, Barrister, Gray's Inn Tax Chambers and Natalie Lee, Barrister, Senior Lecturer in Law, University of Southampton*

| | |
|---|---|
| I | Case 1—PETs and death [**36.2**] |
| II | Case 2—Gifts with a reservation and subsequent death [**36.3**] |
| III | Case 3—Artificial debts and death [**36.4**] |
| IV | Case 4—Chargeable transfers and death [**36.5**] |

The risk of a double charge to IHT arises in a number of situations and FA 1986 s 104 enabled the Board to make regulations to give relief to taxpayers in certain cases. The Regulations were made on 30 June 1987 and came into force on 22 July 1987, although the relief is given for transfers of value made, and other events occurring on or after 18 March 1986 (Inheritance Tax (Double Charges Relief) Regulations 1987, SI 1987/1130).                    [**36.1**]

## I   CASE 1—PETS AND DEATH

The first case is concerned with the area of mutual transfers, ie where property is transferred (by a PET which becomes chargeable) but at the death of the donor he has received back property from his donee (either the original property or property which represents it) which is included in the donor's death estate. The position is illustrated in the following example: all the examples in this Appendix are based on illustrations given in the Regulations themselves. It is assumed that current IHT rates apply throughout; grossing-up does not apply to lifetime transfers; and that no exemptions or reliefs are available.

**EXAMPLE 36.1**

| | | |
|---|---|---|
| July 2000 | A makes a gift of a Matthew Smith oil painting (value £100,000) to B (a PET) | |
| July 2001 | A makes a gift into a discretionary trust of £335,000 | IHT paid £10,000 |
| Jan 2002 | A makes a further gift into the same trust of £30,000 | IHT paid £6,000 |
| Jan 2003 | B dies and the Smith picture returns to A | |
| Apr 2004 | A dies. His death estate of £400,000 includes the picture returned to him in 2003 which is still worth £100,000 | |

If no relief were available, A in *Example 36.1* would be subject to IHT on the value of the picture twice: once when it was given away in 2000 (the chargeable PET) and a second time on its value in 2004 (as part of his death estate). In addition A's cumulative total would be increased by the 2000 PET, thereby necessitating a recalculation of the tax charged on the 2001 and 2002 transfers and resulting in a higher charge on his death estate.

Regulation 4 affords relief in this situation and provides for two alternative IHT calculations to be made and for the higher amount of tax produced by those calculations to be payable. The alternative calculations may be illustrated as follows:

**EXAMPLE 36.1 CONTINUED**

*First calculation:*
   Charge the picture as part of A's death estate and ignore the 2000 PET:

| | | | |
|---|---|---|---|
| July 2000 | PET £100,000 ignored | Tax nil | |
| July 2001 | Gift £335,000: tax £20,000<br>*Less:* £10,000 already paid | Tax payable = | £10,000 |
| Jan 2002 | Gift £30,000: tax £12,000<br>*Less:* £6,000 already paid | Tax payable = | £6,000 |
| Apr 2004 | Death estate £400,000 | Tax payable = | £160,000 |
| Total tax due as result of A's death | | | £176,000 |

(*Note:* because the 2000 PET is ignored A's cumulative total is unaltered and a recalculation of tax on the 2001 and 2002 transfers is unnecessary.)

*Second calculation:*
Charge the 2000 PET and ignore the value of the picture on A's death

| | | |
|---|---|---|
| July 2000 | PET £100,000: tax | £nil |
| July 2001 | Gift £335,000: tax £60,000<br>*Less:* £10,000 already paid | £50,000 |
| Jan 2001 | Gift £30,000: tax £12,000<br>*Less:* £6,000 already paid | £6,000 |
| Apr 2003 | Death estate £300,000 | £120,000 |
| Total tax due as result of A's death | | £176,000 |

*Tax payable:* The tax payable is equal in amount under the two calculations: see *Example 36.3* below.

It may be that reg 4 is capable of being exploited to the benefit of the taxpayer as can be seen from the following illustration. Assume that Adam gives property worth £100,000 to his daughter Berta in 2002 and buys the property back for £75,000 (which represents less than full consideration) in 2003. He then dies in 2004. Under reg 4 the value of the property (£100,000) will remain subject to IHT but Adam's estate has been reduced by the £75,000 paid for the property (see especially reg 4(3)(a)).         **[36.2]**

## II   CASE 2—GIFTS WITH A RESERVATION AND SUBSEQUENT DEATH

This case covers the situation where a gift with a reservation (either immediately chargeable or a chargeable PET) is followed by the death of the donor at a time when he still enjoys a reserved benefit or within seven years of that benefit ceasing (ie within seven years of the deemed PET). The situation is illustrated in *Example 36.2*.

**EXAMPLE 36.2**

| | | |
|---|---|---|
| Jan 2000 | A makes a PET of £150,000 to B | |
| Mar 2004 | A makes a gift of a house worth £335,000 into a discretionary trust but continues to live in the property. The gift is of property subject to a reservation | IHT paid £10,000 |
| Feb 2007 | A dies still living in the house. His death estate is valued at £485,000 including the house which is then worth £340,000 | |

Regulation 5 prevents double taxation of the house in this example by providing for two separate IHT calculations to be made as follows:     **[36.3]**

**EXAMPLE 36.2 CONTINUED**

*First calculation:*
Charge the house as part of A's death estate and ignore the gift with reservation:

| | | Tax |
|---|---|---|
| Jan 2000 | PET | Nil |
| Mar 2004 | Gift with reservation ignored | Nil |
| Feb 2007 | Death estate £485,000: tax £80,000 | |
| | *Less*: £10,000 already paid | £70,000 |
| | Total tax due as a result of A's death | £70,000 |

(*Note*: credit for tax already paid on the gift with reservation cannot exceed the amount of death tax attributable to that property. In this example the tax so attributable is £56,082 (ie £80,000 × £340,000/£485,000)—hence credit is given for the full amount of £10,000.)

*Second calculation:*
The gift with reservation is charged and the value of the gifted property is ignored in taxing the death estate:

| | | Tax |
|---|---|---|
| Jan 2000 | PET | Nil |
| Mar 2004 | Gift of house £335,000: tax £20,000 *Less*: £10,000 already paid | £10,000 |
| Feb 2007 | Death estate £145,000 (ignoring house) | £58,000 |
| Total tax due as result of A's death: | | £68,000 |

*Tax payable:* the first calculation yields a higher amount of tax. Therefore the gift of the house in 2004 is ignored and tax on death is charged as in the first calculation giving credit for IHT already paid.

## III   CASE 3—ARTIFICIAL DEBTS AND DEATH

Relief is afforded under reg 6 when a chargeable transfer (or chargeable PET) is followed by the transferor incurring a liability to his transferee which falls within FA 1986 s 103 (the artificial debt rules).

### EXAMPLE 36.3

| Nov 1998 | X makes a PET of cash (£95,000) to Y |
|---|---|
| Dec 1998 | Y makes a loan to X of £95,000 |
| May 1999 | X makes a gift into a discretionary trust of £20,000 |
| Apr 2004 | X dies. His death estate is worth £305,000 but the loan from Y remains outstanding |

Under s 103 the deduction of £95,000 would be disallowed so that the 1997 PET and the disallowed debt would both attract an IHT charge. Relief is provided, however, under reg 6 on the basis of the following alternative calculations:                                                              **[36.4]**

### EXAMPLE 36.3 CONTINUED

*First calculation:*
   Ignore the 1998 gift but do not allow the debt to be deducted in the death estate:

|  |  |  | *Tax* |
|---|---|---|---|
| Nov 1998 | PET ignored |  | Nil |
| May 1999 |  | £20,000 | Nil |
| Apr 2004 | Death estate £295,000 |  | £16,000 |
| Total tax due as result of X's death |  |  | £16,000 |

*Second calculation:*
   Charge the 1998 gift but allow the debt to be deducted from the estate at death.

|  |  | *Tax* |
|---|---|---|
| Nov 1998 | PET £95,000 | Nil |
| May 1999 | Gift £20,000 | Nil |
| Apr 2004 | Death estate (£305,000 – loan of £95,000) | £16,000 |
| Total tax due as result of X's death |  | £16,000 |

*Tax payable:* The total tax chargeable is equal in amount under the two calculations and reg 8 provides that in such cases the first calculation shall be treated as producing a higher amount: accordingly the debt is disallowed against the death estate and the PET of £95,000 is not charged.

## IV CASE 4—CHARGEABLE TRANSFERS AND DEATH

Under FA 1986 s 104(1)(d) regulations can be made to prevent a double charge to IHT in circumstances 'similar' to those dealt with in the first three cases above.

Regulation 7, made in pursuance of this power, applies when an individual makes a chargeable transfer of value to a *person* after 17 March 1986, and dies within seven years of that transfer, at a time when he was beneficially entitled to property which either directly or indirectly represented the property which had been transferred by the original chargeable transfer.

For relief to be given under this regulation it is important to realise that the lifetime transfer must have been chargeable when made. Prior to the changes made by FA 2006, the majority of transfers to individuals would not have fallen within its ambit since they would have been PETs. Since that is no longer the case, the regulation may now be of increased significance and will be of importance in the following cases:

(1) When the chargeable transfer is to a discretionary trust which subsequently returns all or part of the property to settlor.
(2) When the chargeable transfer creates a beneficial interest in favour of the settlor.
(3) When the chargeable transfer is to a company with, again, that property being returned to the transferor.

As with the other cases, relief under reg 7 is given on the basis of two alternative calculations. The first includes the returned property in the death estate but ignores the original chargeable transfer (although there is no question of any refund of tax paid at that time). The second calculation taxes the original chargeable transfer (ie it may be subject to a supplementary charge on death and remains in the taxpayer's cumulative total) but ignores the returned property in taxing the transferor's death estate. **[36.5]**

# Section 5
# VAT

**Chapters**

# 37   VAT—the foundations

*Updated by Sinead Reid, BCL, LLM European Law, Barrister-at-Law, Senior Regulatory Advisor, DLA Piper Rudnick Gray Cary LLP*

## I   HISTORY AND GENERAL PRINCIPLES

### 1   Taxation of value added

Globally, value added tax (VAT) has become a popular means of collecting revenue for governments. It is, in economic terms, intended to be a tax on the value added to the purchases of all raw materials, goods and services and should therefore be economically neutral. Certain transactions are, however, excluded, thus creating distortions. In part this is due to practical considerations (valuation) and in part due to social considerations. Value added can, in theory, be calculated by, broadly, two methods—the additive method or the subtractive method. Further, the tax can be operated as either a direct or an indirect tax. The direct (or accounts) method uses the business profit and loss account as a basis of calculation and represents, in general terms, a combination of a business profits tax and a payroll tax borne by the trader.

The indirect (or invoice) subtractive method is the one used in the European Union: applying general principles, this gives rise to a tax charge on individual sales and a right to deduct the tax charged on expenditure (unless specifically prohibited or restricted—see *Lennartz v Finanzamt Munchen III* (1991) and *Seeling v Finanzamt Starnberg, CJEC* [2003] STC 805. The case of *C & E Comrs v Redrow Group plc* (1999) concerned circumstances where a taxpayer (Redrow) incurred VAT in acquiring services to be provided to a third party—this case has been distinguished in several Tribunal decisions: see Business Brief 27/99, issued on 21 December 1999 in which the Commissioners set out their view that 'the decision only applies ... where there is a claim to input tax credit by a taxable person who has commissioned the goods or services and contracted with the supplier for them', *Ian Flockton Developments Ltd v C & E Comrs* (1987)).                              [**37.1**]

### 2   Uniform basis of assessment

On 11 April 1977, the European Council adopted the Sixth VAT Directive (Directive (EEC) 77/388), which set out the structure of the common system of VAT and the procedures for applying it. The Sixth VAT Directive incorporated the basic structure and procedures previously set out in the Second VAT Directive, which accordingly ceased to have effect in each member state as from the dates on which the provisions of the Sixth VAT Directive were brought into application.

Member States are however permitted to retain taxes, duties or charges that cannot be characterised as turnover taxes.

On 1 January 1993, the text of the Sixth VAT Directive was substantially amended to provide for the introduction of the Single Market and is currently being recast. The structure and contents of the Sixth Directive are important as ultimately domestic legislation is interpreted by reference to that Directive.

**[37.2]**

### 3   Common system of VAT

What is now art 93 of the Treaty on European Union, which replaced EC Treaty, art 99, sets out the basis for the EU's approach towards harmonisation of indirect taxation. It provides:

> 'The Council shall, acting unanimously on a proposal from the Commission and after consulting the European Parliament and the Economic and Social Committee, adopt provisions for the harmonisation of legislation concerning turnover taxes, excise duties and other forms of indirect taxation to the extent that such harmonisation is necessary to ensure the establishment and the functioning of the internal market within the time limit laid down in Article 7a.'        **[37.3]**

### 4   The Single Market

Completing the internal market became a political priority in the early 1980s and this resulted in the Single European Act. The aim of the Community, to establish an area without internal frontiers in which the free movement of goods, persons, services and capital is ensured was achieved with effect from 1 January 1993. However, the VAT system adopted was a compromise and is intended to be transitional. It remains based on a destination rather than origin system of taxation. This transitional system abolished the import procedures in force before 1 January 1993 (thus removing many border controls) for the movement of goods between EU Member States. The provisions with respect to imports and exports are restricted to movements of goods to and from a place outside the Member States. The operation of VAT on supplies between Member States is thus based on:

(1)    zero-rating by the supplier of intra-EU supplies of goods to a registered business in another Member State and the self accounting for VAT on the acquisition of such goods by the registered customer;

(2)    the charging of VAT on intra-EU supplies of goods to non-VAT registered persons by the supplier in the country from which they are supplied.

To prevent distortions which might otherwise arise from cross-border shopping, special rules apply to purchases by non-VAT registered persons above a threshold (which differs between Member States), purchases of new means of transport and goods subject to excise duty, and distance sales (such as mail order) to non-VAT registered persons. In addition, businesses are required to submit regular statistical returns such as intra-EU sales lists and Intrastats.        **[37.4]**

5 **EU Member States**

The EU expanded from 15 Member States to 25 on 1 May 2004.

The VAT territory of the EC consists of

- Austria
- Belgium
- Cyprus (from 1.5.04)
- Czech Republic (from 1.5.04)
- Denmark (not the Faroe Islands and Greenland)
- Estonia (from 1.5.04)
- Finland (not the Aland Islands)
- France (including Monaco but not including Martinique, French Guiana, Guadeloupe, Reunion and St Pierre and Miquelon)
- Germany (not Busingen and the Isle of Heligoland)
- Greece (not Mount Athos (Agion Poros))
- Hungary (from 1.5.04)
- Ireland
- Italy (not the communes of Livigno and Campione d'Italia and the Italian waters of Lake Lugano)
- Latvia (from 1.5.04)
- Lithuania (from 1.5.04)
- Luxembourg
- Malta (from 1.5.04)
- The Netherlands
- Poland (from 1.5.04)
- Portugal (including the Azores and Madeira)
- Slovakia (from 1.5.04)
- Slovenia (from 1.5.04)
- Spain (including the Balearic Islands but not Canary Islands, Ceuta or Melilla)
- Sweden
- United Kingdom (including the Isle of Man but not the Channel Islands or Gibraltar).

The UK comprises England, Scotland and Wales (which together constitute Great Britain) and Northern Ireland. References to the UK in the VAT legislation includes the territorial sea of the UK. Further, the VAT legislation has effect as if the Isle of Man were part of the UK but not the Channel Islands (Jersey, Guernsey etc). This deeming provision is subject to any contrary provisions of specified legislation.                    **[37.5]**

6 **The Sixth Directive (Directive (EEC) 77/388)**

As noted above, the Sixth Directive required Member States to comply with its terms by 1 January 1978, the objective being to make progress towards a common system of VAT. Transitional rules were introduced with the advent of the Single Market in 1993 by Directive (EEC) 91/680. It should be noted that variation from these rules is possible where the language of the directive is permissive rather than mandatory or where Member States are granted a specific derogation under art 27. It is essential that the structure of the Sixth Directive is borne in mind when interpreting domestic legislation. As noted, the Sixth Directive is being recast. In broad outline, and subject to the transitional provisions, the structure and content is:

Article 1      Introductory

Articles 2, 3   Scope of tax      The common system of VAT is to apply,
                and territorial   broadly, to the supply of all goods and serv-
                application       ices effected for consideration throughout
                                  the Member States and for the importation
                                  of goods. Certain exceptions are provided
                                  for in art 3(2).

The common system of VAT is to apply, broadly, to the supply of all goods and services effected for consideration throughout the Member States and for the importation of goods. Certain exceptions are provided for in art 3(2).

Consideration for a supply for VAT purposes must have a direct link with the services supplied and must be capable of being expressed in money. *Staatssecretaris van Financiën v Cooperatieve Vereniging 'Cooperatieve Aardappelenbewaarplaats GA'*, CJEC Case 154/80; [1981].

Article 2(1) of the Sixth Directive effectively excludes from the scope of the tax any person who habitually provides services free of charge, *Staatssecretaris van Financiën v Hong Kong Trade Development Council*, CJEC Case 89/81; [1982]

In two Netherlands cases, the European Court of Justice ('ECJ') held that the illegal sale of drugs such as amphetamines or hashish was not an 'economic activity' and thus not a supply for VAT purposes. While the principle of fiscal neutrality precluded 'a generalised differentiation between lawful and unlawful transactions', supplies of narcotic drugs were outside the scope of this principle, since 'because of their very nature, they are subject to a total prohibition on their being put into circulation in all the Member States, with the exception of strictly controlled economic channels for use for medical and scientific purposes'. *Mol v Inspecteur der Invoerrechten en Accijnzen*, CJEC Case 269/86; [1988]; *Vereniging Happy Family Rustenburgerstrat v Inspecteur der Omzetbelasting*, CJEC Case 289/86; [1988]

In *KapHag Renditefonds v Finanzamt Charlottenburg*, CJEC Case C-442/01, [2003] All ER(D) 362(Jun) (TVC 21.62) a German partnership admitted a new partner. The CJEC ruled that no supply was being made under EC Sixth Directive, Art 2(1) by either the individual partners or the partnership to the incoming partner in return for the capital contribution.

| | | |
|---|---|---|
| Article 4 | Taxable persons | A taxable person is defined as any person who independently carries out in any place any economic activity whatever the purpose or results of that activity. Specific circumstances are also considered.<br><br>A person undertaking acts preparatory to the carrying on of an economic activity qualified as a 'taxable person'. *DA Rompelman & EA Rompelman-van-Deelen v Minister van Financiën*, CJEC Case 268/83; [1985]. |
| Articles 5–7 | Taxable transactions | A supply of goods is defined as the transfer of the right to dispose of tangible property as owner whilst a supply of services is defined as any transaction that is not a supply of goods.<br><br>The CJEC has held that the production of goods from materials supplied by customers only took place where the contractor produced a new article, i.e. one the function of which was different from that of the materials provided. Repairs, however extensive, did not amount to the supply of goods. *Van Dijk's Boekhuis BV v Staatssecretaris van Financiën*, CJEC Case 139/8 |
| Articles 8–9 | Place of supply taxable transactions | For place of supply of services, the primary fiscal point of reference is the place of establishment of the supplier. Where a supplier has a place of establishment and a fixed establishment in two Member States, regard should be had to the establishment from which the service is supplied. Exceptions to the above rule are set out in Art 9(2) which:<br><br>a) specifies services 'connected with immoveable property' and provides that the place of supply of those services is the place where the supplier is established;<br>b) specifies that transport services are supplied where transport takes place;<br>c) specifies services that are supplied where those services are physically carried out;<br>d) deleted;<br>e) specifies services that are supplied where the recipient of the service is established *or* if the recipient has more than one establishment, the establishment to which the service is supplied. |

As is evident from the above, it is necessary to identify the nature of the service that is being provided before the place of supply can be ascertained. *In Azo-Maschinenfabrik Adolf Zimmerman GmbH (No 2)*, [1987], a non-resident company had entered into a contract with a UK company to supply and install a bulk material handling system—the place of supply was held to be the site where the components of the systems were installed and commissioned.

The ECJ ruled that 'an installation for carrying on a commercial activity, such as the operation of gaming machines, on board a ship sailing on the high seas outside the national territory may be regarded as a fixed establishment within the meaning of that provision only if the establishment entails the permanent presence of both the human and technical resources for the provision of those services and it is not appropriate to deem those services to have been provided at the place where the supplier has established his business'. *G Berkholz v Finanzamt Hamburg-Mitte-Altstadt*, CJEC Case 168/84

In *RAL (Channel Islands) v Customs & Excise Comrs* Case 452/03 the CJEC held that the place of supply of gaming machines installed in amusement arcades established in the territory of a Member State was to be regarded as constituting entertainment or similar activities within the meaning of Art 9(2)(c) so that the place of supply of those services was where they were physically carried out.

| Article 10 | Taxable event | Tax is chargeable on the occurrence of a chargeable event: goods are delivered, services are performed or goods are imported. |
|---|---|---|

| Article 11 | Taxable amount | The principles of valuation are outlined. In circumstances where a supplier supplied goods to a retailer for less than the normal retail price, and where the retailer undertook to arrange gatherings at which the wholesaler's goods could be sold, the CJEC held that, for the purposes of Article 11A1(a) of the Directive, the taxable amount included not only the monetary consideration actually paid by the retailer for the product but also the value of the services provided by the retailer in obtaining and rewarding hostesses (being the difference between the normal wholesale price and the amount actually paid by the agents), so that VAT was chargeable on the whole of the normal wholesale price. *Naturally Yours Cosmetics Ltd v C & E Comrs (No 2)*, CJEC Case 230/87; [1988] |
|---|---|---|
| Article 12 | Rates | A minimum standard rate 15% is specified, with certain optional reduced rates of at least 5% on a restricted list of products, and protection for existing zero rates. |
| Articles 13–16 | Exemptions | Details the supplies which are to be exempted from VAT: activities in the public interest, eg public postal services, hospital and medical care, together with the other exemptions, eg insurance transactions, leasing and letting of immovable property. There are also provisions permitting Member States to allow taxpayers a right of option for taxation in cases of letting and leasing of immovable property and certain other land transactions and financial transactions. There are also provisions dealing with reliefs for certain imports, exports and international transport. |

| Articles 17–20 | Deductions | When deductible tax becomes chargeable, a corresponding right to deduct arises (*Lennartz*) . Conditions for exercising the right to deduct, such as the requirement to hold an invoice relating to the deduction and rules for calculating the deductible proportion, together with adjustments for initial deductions (as in the Capital Goods Scheme—**[38.89]–[38.94]**), are outlined. The ECJ held that input tax was only deductible under Art 17 of the EC Sixth Directive if the goods or services in question had a direct and immediate link with taxable transactions *BLP Group plc v C & E Comrs, CJEC Case C-4/94*; [1995] |
|---|---|---|
| Articles 21–23 | Liability | The persons who are liable to pay tax to the authorities and matters such as registration requirements, duty to keep records and tax invoices are outlined. The detailed rules for declarations and payments in respect of imports are left to the Member States to determine. |
| Articles 24–26C | Special schemes | Permits certain simplifications in applying the VAT system to small undertakings, a special flat-rate scheme for farmers (and, following FA 2002, many small businesses), a special scheme for travel agents and special arrangements for secondhand goods, works of art, collectors' items and antiques, investment gold and electronically supplied services. |
| Article 27 | Derogation | Member States may apply to the European Commission for permission to introduce special measures derogating from the provisions of the directive in order to achieve procedural simplifications or prevent tax avoidance. The CJEC ruled that Article 27(1) of the Sixth Directive was not confined to situations where there was a deliberate intention to avoid tax, but included business arrangements undertaken for genuine commercial reasons, if the effect of such arrangements was that tax was avoided.' *Direct Cosmetics Ltd v C & E Comrs (No 2); Laughtons Photographs Ltd v C & E Comrs*, CJEC Case 138/86; [1988] |

| Articles 28, 28A–28P | Transitional arrangements in the Single Market | As noted above, these are inserted by Directive (EEC) 91/680 and introduce the transitional system for intra-EU trade in the Single Market from 1 January 1993. The destination-based transitional rules continue in effect beyond the end of the four-year period until the date of entry into force of the definitive system, pending agreement on such a system. |
| Articles 29–38 | Miscellaneous provisions | **[37.6]–[37.20]** |

## II   RATES

### 1   In the EU

When the EU made its initial proposals for an origin basis of taxation it suggested, in order to avoid distortion of competition, that all Member States should have only two rates of VAT. As part of the arrangements for the introduction of the Single Market, the Member States reached a measure of agreement on the harmonisation of rates of VAT. From 1 January 1993 until 31 December 1996 (Member States are in the process of agreeing an extension of this), the standard rate of VAT applied by each Member State should not be less than 15%. Member States may apply one or two reduced rates to specified categories of goods and services that may not be less than 5%. On 16 July 2003 the Commission presented a proposal to amend the lower rates of VAT (COM (2003) 397 final).                          **[37.21]**

### 2   In the UK

During the transitional stage of the Single Market, Member States that applied lower rates than 5% that were in force on 1 January 1991, could retain them. These lower rates included the UK's zero rate. The zero rate is referred to in EC legislation as exemption with refund of the tax paid. This better describes the charging structure and differentiates the zero rate from a VAT exemption, in relation to which any directly attributable VAT is not recoverable. The UK now has seven groups of transactions that are liable at the reduced rate (VATA 1994 Sch 7A) (see **[38.6]**).                **[37.22]–[37.40]**

# 38   VAT—UK provisions

*Updated by Sinead Reid, BCL, LLM European Law, Barrister-at-Law, Senior Regulatory Advisor, DLA Piper Rudnick Gray Cary LLP*

## I   BACKGROUND

On becoming a member of the European Community (EC), the UK replaced two taxes (purchase tax and selective employment tax) with value added tax (VAT). Many of the provisions in FA 1972 (effective from 1 April 1973) and the subsequent Finance Acts and statutory instruments were consolidated in VATA 1983 and then again into VATA 1994.                                    [**38.1**]

### 1   UK legislation and administration

The basic legislation is in the consolidating VATA 1994. Many of the detailed rules are in orders, rules and regulations made by Statutory Instruments (VATA 1994 s 97). Notices and leaflets issued by the Commissioners of HM Revenue & Customs ('HMRC') set out their views on the operation of the legislation and do not generally have the force of law. Certain parts of these, however, are issued under statutory authority. They include parts of Notice 700 (The VAT Guide), Notice 727 and associated leaflets dealing with retail schemes and Notice 703 in regard to evidence of export. Extra-statutory concessions are contained in notices and leaflets (listed and catalogued in Notice 48).

HMRC are responsible for the collection and management of VAT (VATA 1994 Sch 11 para 1). Appeals against decisions of HMRC on specified matters lie to VAT tribunals (VATA 1994 s 83). Thereafter an appeal lies to the High Court (a single judge in the Queen's Bench Division), to the Court of Appeal and, finally, to the House of Lords.

Under what is now art 234 of the EC Treaty (formerly art 177), the European Court of Justice ('ECJ') has jurisdiction to give preliminary rulings on matters of the interpretation of EC law referred to it by national courts (which include VAT tribunals) but as noted in Chapter 31, the ECJ cannot decide the case. The decision to make a reference is one for the particular national court: an individual has no right of access to the ECJ (on this matter see *Naturally Yours Cosmetics Ltd v C & E Comrs* (1988) where a VAT tribunal obtained a ruling from the ECJ on the meaning of 'taxable amount'). Any court can make a reference to the ECJ, but the House of Lords is bound to make a reference if there is any question of doubt about the interpretation of European law (see **[30.72]**). An illustration of this is the case of *C & E Comrs v Sinclair Collis Ltd* (1999). The Court of Appeal had held that the agreement under which a pub owner allowed a company operating cigarette vending machines to site a machine in the pub was an exempt supply of a licence to occupy land. Three of the five Law Lords disagreed with the Court of Appeal but two agreed. Hence all five decided that a reference to the ECJ was appropriate. The ECJ emphatically rejected HMRCs' claims that the installation of a vending machine in a public house constituted the 'letting or leasing of immovable property'. Accordingly, the company was entitled to recover the related input tax. To the relief of most observers and the surprise of very few people outside HMRC, the ECJ has restored the decision that the VAT tribunal had reached in 1997.

In parallel with equivalent rules for direct tax, a requirement has been put into place by FA 2004 whereby taxpayers undertaking certain tax planning arrangements will need to provide details to HMRC.

The measure introduces a requirement for businesses with supplies of £600,000 or more to disclose the use of specific avoidance schemes that are listed in the Value Added Tax (Disclosure of Avoidance Schemes) (Designations) Order 2004 as amended. A business using a listed designated scheme must disclose its use to HMRC. This must be done within 30 days of the date when the first return affected by the scheme becomes due after 'listing'.

Failure to disclose will incur a penalty of 15% of the tax avoided. The measure also introduces a requirement for businesses with supplies exceeding £10 million a year to disclose the use of schemes that have certain of the hallmarks of avoidance. This must be done within 30 days of the date when the first return affected by the scheme becomes due.

The measure also includes provisions that provide a voluntary facility for those who devise and market VAT avoidance schemes (promoters) to register schemes that have the hallmarks of avoidance with HMRC. A business using a scheme registered by a promoter will not have to make a separate disclosure of its use. Failure to disclose will incur a flat rate penalty of £5,000.    **[38.2]**

## 2  Mechanics of VAT

VAT is an indirect tax (ie it is levied on consumption rather than on income) which is collected at each stage of a commercial chain.

In *Example 38.1* below a VAT rate of 17½% is assumed throughout and, for the sake of illustration, it deals with a single transaction. In reality, VAT is calculated on outputs during a given period and on 'inputs' (see note (1) to the example below) during that period, not on particular transactions (see further note (3) to the example).

**EXAMPLE 38.1**

| | Costs (£) (excluding VAT) | Sale (£) (excluding VAT) | VAT (£) on costs (input) | VAT (£) on sale (output) | Paid to HMRC (£) |
|---|---|---|---|---|---|
| Producer | — | 20,000 | — | 3,500 | 3,500 |
| Manufacturer | 20,000 | 30,000 | 3,500 | 5,250 | 1,750 |
| Wholesaler | 30,000 | 45,000 | 5,250 | 7,875 | 2,625 |
| Retailer | 45,000 | 60,000 | 7,875 | 10,500 | 2,625 |
| Customer | 60,000 | — | 10,500 | — | — |
| | | | | | £10,500 |

*Notes:*
(1)    Each taxable person in the chain must charge VAT on supplies made to customers (outputs) (this is subject to certain exceptions). This VAT is termed output VAT and must be accounted for to HMRC. So far as VAT on supplies which he has received (inputs) is concerned, this is input tax and can be recovered from HMRC provided that it is attributable to a taxable supply made or to be made (VATA 1994 s 26) and appropriate evidence is held. If input tax exceeds output tax the excess can be recovered in full provided, as stated above, that it is attributable to a taxable supply (VATA 1994 s 25(3)). Output tax is only charged on supplies made in the course or furtherance of a business: input tax is only generally refunded if inputs are used or are to be used for business purposes.
(2)    The final tax (£10,500) is wholly borne by the consumer (for VAT purposes this means someone who cannot recover VAT because he is not registered) or who does not make any taxable outputs, eg entirely exempt outputs (what is meant by exempt supplies is set out below).
(3)    The VAT mechanism is intended to ensure that ultimately the net VAT paid (£10,500) is exactly 17½% of the taxable value (£60,000). However, since supplies of goods or services which are exempt or outside the scope of VAT may have borne VAT which is not identified and not recoverable, this objective is not always achieved.

In order to ensure that all consumption is taxed, provision exists for the taxation of goods and services imported into the UK in certain circumstances (see [**38.103**]).                                                                    [**38.3**]

### 3   Characterisation of supplies and applicable rate

The general rule is that all supplies are subject to VAT at the standard rate. However, there are three specific reliefs from the obligation to charge VAT at this rate. Goods or services may be subject to a lower, but positive, rate of VAT such as fuel and power (effective rate of 5%), certain sanitary products and the importation of certain antiques and collectors' items (at an effective rate of 5% achieved by reducing the taxable value (VATA 1994 s 21)). VAT may also be charged at the zero rate, eg on most food and on books, magazines etc. The effect of a supply being 'zero–rated' is that a taxable person is not required to charge VAT on the supply; however, she/he retains the right to recover input tax incurred on costs attributable to making that supply. Lastly, a supply may be exempt from VAT. Where a supply is potentially both zero-rated and exempt, zero-rating takes precedence. In addition, supplies of goods and services made outside the UK are outside the scope of UK VAT.

[38.4]

a)    *The standard rate*

This rate applies to most transactions. Currently it is 17½% but, in the past, it has been 8%, 10% and 15%. The rate may be changed by SI upwards or downwards, by up to 25% of the rate then applicable (VATA 1994 s 2(2)). The Member States of what is now the EU have currently agreed a *minimum standard rate* of 15% subject to review. In practice, changes in the VAT rate have always been made in a Finance Act.                                    [38.5]

b)    *The reduced rate*

The range of reduced rate supplies is gradually being extended, albeit subject to extensive conditions, to include items such as child car seats, women's sanitary products, fuel for qualifying use, residential conversions, renovation and alteration of dwellings and installation of energy-saving materials (VATA 1994 Sch 7A).                                    [38.6]

c)    *Zero-rated supplies*

A supply that is zero-rated is a taxable supply that is taxed at a 0% VAT rate. As noted above, a person who makes zero-rated supplies is able to recover any input tax incurred in making those supplies provided s/he is registered for VAT.

The zero rate was introduced for social and political reasons and covers, eg supplies of most food, books and newspapers and children's clothing. Formerly, zero-rating covered a wider area (in particular, all new construction work) but the ECJ held that some cases were in breach of the Sixth Directive (Directive (EEC) 77/388) (see **[30.95]**) with the result that UK law was amended.

The following heads of supply (which are subject to restrictions and exemptions) are zero-rated (see VATA 1994 Sch 8):

Group 1     food

Group 2     sewerage services and water

Group 3     books, newspapers etc

Group 4     talking books for the blind and handicapped and wireless sets for the blind

Group 5     construction of dwellings etc

Group 6     protected buildings

Group 7     international services

Group 8     transport

Group 9     caravans and houseboats

Group 10    gold

Group 11    banknotes

Group 12    drugs, medicine, aids for the handicapped etc

Group 13    imports/exports etc

Group 14    tax-free shops (repealed with effect from 1 July 1999)

Group 15    charities etc

Group 16    clothing and footwear

**[38.7]**

d)   *Exempt supplies*

By contrast with zero-rating, a business which makes exempt supplies does not charge output VAT on its supplies because they are not taxable, but it cannot recover any input VAT incurred for the purpose of making those supplies. The following (listed in VATA 1994 Sch 9) are the heads of exempt supply:

Group 1     land

Group 2     insurance

Group 3     postal services

Group 4     betting, gaming and lottery

Group 5     finance

Group 6     education

Group 7     health and welfare

Group 8     burial and cremation

Group 9     trade unions and professional bodies and other public interest bodies

Group 10    sports, sports competitions and physical education

Group 11    works of art etc

Group 12    fundraising events by charities and other qualifying bodies

Group 13    cultural services etc

Group 14    supplies of goods where input tax cannot be recovered

Group 15    investment gold

The above paragraphs apply for determining the rate of VAT applicable to a supply of goods or services. However, in order to ascertain if a supply is within the charge to UK VAT, it is necessary to ascertain first where the place of supply is. This is because supplies which are made outside the UK are generally outside the scope of VAT and thus not liable to UK VAT. There are complex rules for determining the place of supply. Section 6 of Chapter 37 includes a summary of the place of supply rules within the EU Sixth VAT Directive. Section 7 of the UK VAT Act 1994 implements the place of supply rules.

Goods imported into the UK are liable to VAT and it is the Customs Office who is responsible for the imposition of VAT in such circumstances. Supplies that are outside the scope of UK VAT but would, if made in the UK, give rise to an entitlement to recover input tax, are treated as being equivalent to zero-rated supplies, ie no VAT is charged on the supply but input VAT is recoverable. Conversely, supplies that would not give rise to an entitlement to recover input tax are treated as exempt. This is subject to an exception, namely input tax incurred on certain exempt services will give rise to input VAT recovery where the supplies are made to a person who 'belongs outside the member states'. These supplies are referred to as out of scope with recovery supplies.

Businesses that make a mixture of taxable (including zero-rated) and exempt supplies are referred to as *partly exempt;* input VAT directly attributable to taxable supplies is recoverable; that directly attributable to exempt supplies is irrecoverable and that which cannot be directly attributed (eg. VAT on overheads) may be recovered in part: see further [**38.82**].

Certain business expenses (such as wages and salaries and local authority rates) are wholly outside the scope of VAT. Not all input tax is recoverable even if attributable to taxable supplies: examples include VAT on the cost of entertaining customers; on expenses incurred by a company in providing domestic accommodation to directors and their families; and on expenditure other than for business purposes. There are anti-avoidance provisions preventing VAT being avoided by overcharging on insurance premiums where exempt insurance is supplied in a package with other goods or services liable to VAT.                                                      [**38.8**]

e)   *The VAT fraction*

In *Example 38.1* above, note that the purchaser pays a total price of £60,000 + £10,500 = £70,500 for the goods. VAT as a percentage of that gross price is therefore £10,500/£70,500 = 7/47. This *'VAT fraction'* is used to calculate tax in cases where the price is 'tax inclusive'. It is particularly important at the retail level, where it is common for the price of goods to include VAT. If no mention is made of VAT and the contract does not provide otherwise, the consideration paid for the supply is VAT inclusive and the supplier must account for the tax. (See, however, VATA 1994 s 89, which provides that if, after the entering into of a contract, there is a change in the VAT rate (or a change in the VAT liability of a supply) then, unless the contract otherwise provides, the contractual price will be altered to take account of the change.)
                                                                        [**38.9**]

**EXAMPLE 38.2 – MIXED SUPPLIES – CREDIT**

Stefano, a computer supplier, also provides hire-purchase facilities directly to his customers. A customer buys a PC and accessories for £2,400 + VAT under an HP agreement over three years. The interest over the three years will be £200. So long as the documentation given to the customer shows the £200 as a separate charge, the total payments made will be £2,400 + £420 VAT for the goods and £200 exempt credit.

## 4   Relationship between VAT and other taxes

a)   *Capital gains tax*

SP D7 provides, in the context of CGT, that in cases where VAT paid on the purchase of an asset is recoverable, the CGT acquisition cost of the asset will exclude VAT. If no recovery is available the price will be VAT inclusive. On the disposal of an asset, VAT chargeable is ignored in computing the capital gain. Subsequent adjustments to VAT recovery, eg under the Capital Goods Scheme [**38.89**] ff, are treated as additional capital expenditure or disposal provisions in the period of adjustment **[38.10]**

b)   *Income tax*

For income tax purposes, irrecoverable VAT may be deducted as a business expense (see SP B1) except to the extent that it forms part of the cost of a capital item, in which case, it will be subject to capital allowances, if eligible.
**[38.11]**

c)   *Stamp duty/Stamp duty land tax*

The relationship between VAT and stamp duty is set out in SP 11/91. So far as stamp duty is concerned, the consideration on a sale is the price *inclusive* of VAT chargeable or potentially chargeable if the option to tax is exercisable. By contrast, VAT is *not charged* on stamp duty.

The former Inland Revenue has issued guidance in the *Law Society's Gazette* on several occasions (most recently 13 January 1999) regarding the stamp duty liability on transfers of a business (eg a property being let, where the landlord has exercised the option to waive exemption) as a going concern. In effect, early stamping is permissible providing certain undertakings are given. The adviser needs to confirm that the purchaser has been advised of his obligation and the purchaser needs to confirm that any additional stamp duty due will be paid. The interaction becomes considerably simpler under stamp duty land tax (SDLT) effective from December 2003. As regards SDLT, the charge is on the amount of VAT due on the consideration at the time of the transaction—the 'effective date' for SDLT purposes. There may be complications, however, where any additional VAT is not reserved as rent.
**[38.12]–[38.20]**

**EXAMPLE 38.3**

Ben, a retailer, acquired a Steinway concert grand piano for £23,500 (including VAT). He has just sold it to a customer, Charlie, for £50,000 (excluding VAT).
(1)    *VAT:* Ben must charge the customer output tax of £8,750. Input tax of £3,500 is fully recoverable.
(2)    *Income tax:* The purchase price, £20,000 net of VAT, is a deductible business expense (TA 1988 s 74). The sale consideration of £50,000 is an income receipt.
(3)    *CGT:* Charlie's acquisition cost for CGT purposes is £50,000 + £8,750 (VAT) = £58,750, assuming that Charlie cannot recover the VAT.

## II   TAXABLE PERSONS AND TRANSACTIONS

VAT is charged on *taxable supplies of goods* and *services* made in the UK by a *taxable person* in the course or furtherance of a *business* carried on by him (VATA 1994 s 4(1)). It is possible for a taxable person to make supplies otherwise than in the course or furtherance of his business, eg an individual who sells a private asset or a charity which makes a charitable disposal. Such supplies fall outside the scope of VAT. Goods imported into the UK from outside the EU are also chargeable (subject to a *de minimis* limit for small value items imported by post) irrespective of whether they are imported for business purposes and whether the importer is a taxable person. With regard to goods acquired from another Member State of the EU: see **[38.104]**. Certain services received from abroad are also chargeable to VAT on acquisition but, this only applies, if the services are received by a taxable person for the purpose of his business, and on a self-supply basis (see **[38.30]**). By contrast, exports of goods are generally zero-rated and some (although not all) exported services are zero-rated (see **[38.102]**).   **[38.21]**

## 1   A taxable supply

The supply must be made in the UK, which for these purposes means England, Scotland, Wales and Northern Ireland and the territorial sea but not the Isle of Man or the Channel Islands although the Manx VAT system is, in effect, identical with that of the UK. Good title does not have to pass for a transfer of goods to be a 'supply' for VAT purposes. The transfer of possession of goods in circumstances where it is contemplated that title will pass in the future may be a supply of goods.   **[38.22]**

## 2   A supply of goods

Schedule 4 of the VAT Act 1994 sets out those matters that are to be treated as supplies of goods and those that are supplies of services for VAT purposes. Because Sch 4 implements EC VAT law, in some cases the definitions are not consistent with established legal practice in other areas. The sale of a freehold interest in land or the grant, assignment or surrender of a lease exceeding 21 years is treated as a supply of goods (VATA 1994 Sch 4 para 4) whereas in common legal parlance, goods would not normally include land.

Where goods forming part of the assets of a business are disposed of so as no longer to form part of those assets, whether or not for a consideration, there is generally a supply of goods (VATA 1994 Sch 4 para 5(1)).

Where a person ceases to be a taxable person, goods then forming part of the assets of the business carried on by him are deemed to be supplied by him and VAT must be accounted for subject to a *de minimis* sum of £1,000 from 1 April 2000 (VATA 1994 Sch 4 para 8), ie the VAT on the deemed supply would not be more than £1,000. The rule does not apply to items in respect of which input tax was not claimed nor does it apply if on the occasion on which the person ceases to be a taxable trader, the business is transferred as a going concern to another taxable trader (VATA 1994 Sch 4 para 8(1)(a)—see **[38.26]**).

The gift of goods is not regarded as resulting in a supply provided it is made in the course or furtherance of the business and, subject to conditions, the cost to the donor, together with the cost of any other business gifts made to the same person in the same year, does not exceed £50 or is a sample of any goods (see *Example 38.3(6)*).   **[38.23]**

## 3  A supply of services

Section 5(2)(b) states that 'anything which is not a supply of goods but is done for a consideration is a supply of services'. The issue of shares or the coming into existence of a partnership interest following the subscription of funds by the investor/partner is not 'anything ... done for a consideration' (see *KapHag Renditefonds v Finanzamt Charlottenburg* (Case C-442/01) and *Kretztechnik A.G. v Finanzamt Linz* (Case C-465/03) ECJ cases).        **[38.24]**

### EXAMPLE 38.4

(1)  Monopoly supplies heating and lighting to X & Co. A supply of *goods* (Sch 4 para 3).

(2)  X & Co assign the remaining 30-year term on their lease to Fred. A supply of *goods* (Sch 4 para 4).

(3)  Big and Bob jointly own a stallion. Big sells his undivided share to Breeder & Co. A supply of *services.* Contrast the position if Big and Bob sold the horse to Breeder & Co (ie both shares were sold at the same time) when this would be a supply of *goods* (Sch 4 para 1).

(4)  Shine cleans Big's windows and Taylor makes up a suit with Big's cloth. Both are supplying *services* (Sch 4 para 2).

(5)  Concrete hires tools and machinery (a supply of *services*); it also sells goods on hire purchase (a supply of *goods*) (Sch 4 para 1(2)).

(6)  A, a publisher, gives a glossy calendar to a valued customer as a goodwill gesture. As an exception to the general rule in Sch 4 para 5(1) that the transfer of goods out of a business is a supply, even if no consideration is furnished, a gift of goods made in the course or furtherance of the business is not regarded as a supply provided that the cost of the goods—the calendar—to A does not exceed 50 (VATA 1994 Sch 4 para 5(2)(a)).

(7)  Sel sells power tools. One Saturday he borrows an item of trading stock for his own use. This is a supply of services and VAT will be charged on the cost (taken as being the depreciation for the period of use) of supplying the power tool (VATA 1994 Sch 4 para 5(4) and Sch 6 para 7).

## 4  Composite and multiple supplies

A taxable person may supply a combination of goods or services as part of what is nominally a single transaction. Where the liability of the individual supplies of goods and services would be the same as the liability of the goods or services regarded as a single package, no problems arise. However, disputes frequently arise as to whether there is a single (composite) supply or several different individual supplies, even though there is apparently a single consideration. Examination of this complex area of VAT is beyond the scope of this chapter. In essence the test of whether or not two identifiable supplies within a single transaction should be regarded as a single supply or not depends on whether they can be regarded as economically 'dissociable' from each other (see *EC Commission v UK* (1988) and *Card Protection Plan Ltd v C & E Comrs*, CJEC [1999] STC 270).        **[38.25]**

## 5  Transfer of a business as a going concern (VATA 1994 s 49)

When the provisions of the VAT (Special Provisions) Order 1995, SI 1995/1268 are satisfied, certain supplies of assets of a business as a going concern are treated as neither supplies of goods nor services and no VAT is chargeable on the consideration. This is not a matter of choice: if the conditions are satisfied and the vendor charges VAT in error, the purchaser is not entitled to recover the amount as input tax.

The conditions are that the assets must be used by the transferee in carrying on the same line of business as the transferor with no significant break (refurbishment or redecoration is acceptable); if the transferor is registered for VAT the transferee must likewise either be registered or become registered and where the assets form part only of the business, that part must be capable of separate operation. Where land is included in the transfer, certain other conditions may have to be satisfied.

Where the rules apply the transferee will become responsible in relation to the assets transferred for any future input tax adjustments under the Capital Goods Scheme (as to which see **[38.89]** and *Example 38.9*).

When assets are acquired as a transfer of a going concern and the assets are used exclusively to make taxable supplies, the VAT incurred on the costs of acquiring those assets will be attributed to those taxable supplies and is recoverable in full. Correspondingly, input tax relating to the disposal of such assets will also be recoverable in full (see *Abbey National plc v C & E Comrs* (2001) and *Higher Education Statistics Agency Ltd*) QB [2000] STC 332).

**[38.26]**

## 6   A taxable person

A taxable person is one who is either registered or required to be registered (VATA 1994 s 3). If the taxable supplies are, or will be, in excess of a ceiling (usually adjusted annually) the taxpayer is required to register with HMRC by submitting Form VAT 1 to, usually, his local VAT office (VATA 1994 Sch 3). The registration requirement is laid on the *person* rather than the business. An individual may therefore operate several businesses but will have only one VAT registration: by contrast a company is a distinct entity from its proprietors (for group registration, see **[38.52]**). For VAT purposes a partnership is treated as a separate taxable entity (VATA 1994 s 45).          **[38.27]**

## 7   A business

Supplies must be made in the course or furtherance of a business (VATA 1994 s 4(1)). Section 47 (predictably) states that a business 'includes any trade, profession or vocation'. 'Business', however, has a wider meaning than either trade or profession (see also the IHT provisions on 'business' property relief): and there is no requirement of profit motive. The Sixth Directive (see **[30.6]**) uses the term 'economic activity' (art 4) which is probably a wider term than 'business'. In *C & E Comrs v Lord Fisher* (1981), Gibson J identified the following indicia that should be considered in determining whether the activities carried on amounted to a business:

(1)   whether the activity is a 'serious undertaking earnestly pursued' or 'a serious occupation not necessarily confined to a commercial or profit making undertaking';

(2)   whether the activity is an occupation or function actively pursued with reasonable or recognisable continuity;

(3) whether the activity has a certain measure of substance as measured by the quarterly or annual value of taxable supplies made;

(4) whether the activity was conducted in a regular manner and on sound and recognised business principles;

(5) whether the activity is predominantly concerned with the making of taxable supplies to consumers for a consideration;

(6) whether the taxable supplies are of a kind which, subject to differences of detail, are commonly made by those who seek to profit by them.

The letting of property on a continuing or regular basis is a business activity.

In *C & E Comrs v Morrison's Academy Boarding Houses Association* (1978) the company ran boarding houses for students of Morrison's Academy. It was in all respects, carrying on an activity within the ordinary meaning of the word 'business' save that it charged rents which would produce neither profit nor loss and reserved its accommodation for students of the Academy. It was decided that it supplied services in the course of a business. By contrast, in *Three H Aircraft Hire v C & E Comrs* (1982) the court decided that although a single adventure could constitute a business or trade under other areas of the law it did not amount to a business activity for VAT purposes.

The taxable supply must be made in the course '*or furtherance*' of a business and activities that would not normally be thought of as falling in the normal course of a business may be taxable (such as the sale of assets to assist in the financing of the business). **[38.28]**

## 8 The value of a supply

VATA 1994 s 2 provides that VAT is charged on the value of the supply, determined in accordance with the Act.

Section 19(2) states that if the consideration for a supply is money 'its value shall be taken to be such amount as, with the addition of the tax chargeable, is equal to the consideration'. Accordingly, if £117.50 is paid for a supply taxable at the standard rate, the value of that supply is £100. If there is a supply made for no consideration (eg a gift) or for a consideration not wholly in money (eg an exchange), the value of the supply is 'such amount in money as, with the addition of the tax chargeable, is equivalent to the consideration' (VATA 1994 s 19(3)). Remember, however, that first there must be a supply and if services are performed for no consideration there is generally no supply for VAT purposes. **[38.29]**

### EXAMPLE 38.5

(1) A supplies goods to B for £1,762.50 inclusive of VAT. The value of A's supply is £1,500 being £1,762.50 minus the relevant VAT determined in accordance with the VAT fraction (see **[38.9]**): ie £262.50. A is responsible for the payment of this VAT to HMRC.

(2) A supplies goods to B who as a *quid pro quo* replaces A's existing windows. So far as A is concerned, the value in money of the work done by B (less VAT: see s 19(3)) is the consideration for his supply. For B, it is the value of A's goods.

(3) Silas, a solicitor, gives free tax advice to Mr Big, a local businessman, in the hope of obtaining Big's commercial business. No consideration is furnished

and there is no supply of services for VAT. Contrast the position if Mr Big had, in return, agreed to drop a negligence claim against Silas (this would constitute consideration so that there would be a taxable supply).

## 9   The reverse charge and self-supply

A number of occasions arise where a UK taxable person is required to account for VAT as if he had made a supply of goods or services to himself. Output tax is accounted for to HMRC and the taxable person may recover such tax in the usual way if he can attribute it in whole or in part to a taxable supply. One such charge arises under VATA 1994 s 8 where a UK taxable person receives certain services from abroad (see **[38.106]**). This method of accounting for VAT is termed '*a reverse charge*'.

### EXAMPLE 38.6

Paul receives legal advice from the lawyers Antonio and Carreras (Madrid) on the requirements of Spanish company law. He is charged £10,000. Under s 8 and Sch 5(3) of the VAT Act 1994, Paul is deemed to supply himself with these services and must account for output VAT on the value of the supply. Accordingly, VAT in the sum of £1,750 is payable. That same sum is also treated as input tax for Paul and, subject to the normal rules, can be recovered by Paul.

The 'reverse charge' is also applied to goods which are acquired by a business from another EU Member State (see **[38.104]**).

Goods produced for internal use in a business, or trading stock appropriated for such use, may also lead to a VAT charge. Such cases are referred to as '*self-supplies*' and the Treasury have powers to make orders that VAT should apply as if the relevant goods or services had been both supplied to a person for the purpose of his business and supplied by him in the course or furtherance of that business (VATA 1994 s 5(5)).

Orders have been made in the case of stationery produced by a firm's own printing department (this charge applied to exempt or partially exempt traders (SI 1995/1268) and was cancelled from 1 June 2002) and to motor dealers who acquire new cars for resale and then appropriate a car for use in the business. In such cases the dealer is put in the same position as any other trader buying a new car for use in his business (ie he suffers output tax on the conversion to own use and input tax is not generally recoverable) (VAT (Cars) Order 1992, SI 1992/3122). An order has also been made in the case of businesses which carry out their own in-house construction works other than for a consideration (Self-Supply of Construction Services Order 1989, SI 1989/472) and in respect of an exit from the flat rate scheme (SI 1995/2518 Regulations 55B(4), 55L(c), 55M, 55N(3)(4), 55P–55S; SI 2002/1142; SI 2003/1069, reg 7).                                    **[38.30]**

### EXAMPLE 38.7

Bonzo Motors acquired three cars for resale and has appropriated them for the purpose of its business. It is treated as making a supply of the cars itself and must account for output VAT.

## 10   Place and time of supply

a)   *Place of supply*

VAT only applies to supplies made in the UK (VATA 1994 s 1).

In the case of a supply of *goods* which are located in the UK, the supply is deemed to be in the UK so that UK VAT is chargeable (VATA 1994 s 7(2)). If those goods are exported the supply is then generally (see **[38.101]**) zero-rated. Goods supplied outside the UK and which do not enter the UK fall outside the UK VAT net.                                              **[38.31]**

b)   *Services*

The basic rule is that services are treated as being supplied in the place where the supplier belongs, which need not be the same place as where the services themselves are performed (on the concept of 'belonging', see VATA 1994 s 9). See, however, **[38.105]** for the many exceptions to this rule. **[38.32]**

c)   *Time of supply*

The time of supply (the *tax point*) usually determines both the rate of tax and the accounting period into which the supply falls. The general rule in the case of *goods* is that this is the time when they are removed by the customer or, if not removed, when they are made available to him (VATA 1994 s 6(2)). In the case of *services* it is the time when they are performed (VATA 1994 s 6(3)). If, before goods are supplied or services are performed, a tax invoice is issued or payment made, however, this will bring forward the time of supply (VATA 1994 s 6(4)) to the date of the invoice or the date on which payment was made. Furthermore, the general rules for time of supply may be overridden by statutory instrument (see especially VAT Regulations 1995, SI 1995/2518 Part XI).                                    **[38.33]**

d)   *E-commerce*

Much has been made of the potential consequences of e-commerce. As regards the supply of goods, the issues arising are the same as those encountered when using more conventional methods of trading. The place and timing of the supply of goods is unaffected by the method of procurement/delivery. As regards services, the use of new technology poses a range of problems. The basic rule that the place of supply is where the supplier belongs is overridden in the case of specified services (see **[38.105]**). A major issue arises as to the nature of the service being provided. By way of illustration, where music or text is downloaded is the supply one of data or a limited copyright? A further issue is the need to consider whether a server may comprise a fixed place of business. The nature of digitised goods and the need to prevent wholesale tax avoidance through the location of servers, etc in a low tax jurisdiction (or even outside the EU) are issues that are being addressed by the Member States and the EU Commission. The E-commerce Directive (Directive (EC) 2000/31) has been formally agreed and came into effect on 1 July 2003. Businesses based outside the EU, if supplying digitised services to consumers in the EU, need to register and account for the VAT due. Registration only needs to be in one Member State. Detailed provisions have been enacted in FA 2003 s 23 and Sch 2 (inserting new Sch 3B to VATA 1994). **[38.34]–[38.50]**

## III   REGISTRATION, ACCOUNTING FOR TAX AND PENALTIES

### 1   Registration requirements (VATA 1994 Sch 1)

A person must be registered if:
(1) at the end of any month the value of his taxable supplies over the *previous 12 months* exceeds £61,000 (from 1 April 2006) exclusive of VAT; or
(2) at any time there are reasonable grounds for believing that the value of the taxable supplies that *he will* make in the next 30 days will exceed £61,000 (from 1 April 2005) exclusive of VAT.

HMRC must be notified within 30 days of the end of the relevant month or within 30 days after the date on which reasonable grounds first existed. Registration can be avoided if HMRC are satisfied that, although taxable turnover in the previous 12 months exceeded £61,000, it will not exceed £59,000 in the next 12 months.

A business, which is required to be registered because it exceeds the registration limits, can be exempted from the requirement to be registered if it makes zero-rated supplies and its input tax would exceed its output tax (VATA 1994 Sch 1 para 14).

A business which is not required to register under the above rules may still do so on a voluntary basis if it can satisfy HMRC that it is making taxable supplies by way of business (VATA 1994 Sch 1 para 9(a)). This may be helpful for small businesses (whose customers can recover their input tax) desiring to recover input VAT.

A person, who is able to satisfy HMRC that he is carrying on activities preparatory to the making of taxable supplies (eg a feasibility study) is entitled to be registered for VAT (see *Merseyside Cablevision Ltd v C & E Comrs* (1987) (VATA 1994 Sch 1 para 9(b))).

For the purposes of the registration rules bear in mind that taxable supplies include zero-rated as well as standard-rated supplies but not exempt supplies.

Failure to register does not enable a person to escape his obligations. Registration will be backdated when notification is made outside the pre-scribed time periods and the person will be required to account for output tax from the earlier date whether he has in fact charged it to his customers or not. Penalties may be payable (see **[38.64]**).

A business, which is not required to be registered under the provisions because, for example, it only makes exempt supplies, may nevertheless have to register for VAT if it receives supplies of goods from other EU Member States where value exceeds £61,000 (from 1 April 2005) (VATA 1994 Sch 3 para 1).                                                                    **[38.51]**

## 2  Group registration

Corporate bodies within common control may obtain a single or 'group' VAT registration with the result that supplies of goods or services within the group are not subject to VAT (VATA 1994 s 43). This was particularly attractive when one or more companies in the group made exempt supplies and suffered restrictions on the recovery of input tax. The decision of the High Court in *C & E Comrs v Kingfisher plc* (1994) determined that the effect of the grouping provisions went further than merely allowing a number of VAT entities to account for VAT under a single registration (as HMRC had contended) and created a single taxable entity. In *Canary Wharf Ltd v C & E Comrs* (1996), it was held that group registration did not affect the characterisation of supplies by a group member to persons outside the group. Following the *Kingfisher* decision FA 1997 amended s 43.

Registration is in the name of a 'representative member' who becomes liable for VAT in respect of all group companies. Each individual company in a group remains jointly and severally liable for the tax payable by the representative. Companies may join and leave a group, previously on 90 days' notice. To qualify, companies must be resident or have an established place of business in the UK; 'control' depends on majority voting rights.

The rules were substantially tightened in FA 1999. HMRC are now able to exclude companies from a group that are no longer eligible or which pose a threat to the revenue. The rules regarding eligibility, in particular as to whether the company has sufficient presence in the UK, have also been tightened by adopting the terminology used in the directives. Existing groups had until 1 January 2000 to comply with the new criteria. Businesses' right of appeal was, however, extended to allow them to challenge a decision by HMRC, but only if their decision would be unreasonable.

A further tightening took place through FA 2004, section 20, from 1 August 2004 in order to ensure that artificial grouping could not be put in place. In particular, the Treasury will make an order modifying the rules on who can join a VAT group in particular cases. This power is to be used to impose additional conditions for VAT grouping in limited circumstances, in order to prevent abuse. So, if the economic benefits from the entity accrue to a third party and if the entity's accounts are not, or would not be, consolidated in the group accounts of the person controlling the VAT group then a VAT group will not be permitted. However, these additional rules will only apply where the entity managed for the benefit of the third party makes, or intends to make, positive-rated supplies to a member of the VAT group and the VAT group would be unable to recover VAT on such supplies in full. Any entity that is already a member of a VAT group, but fails either of these additional tests will automatically cease to be eligible to be a member of the VAT group.

The FA 2004 introduced new section 43D, VATA 1994, which ensures that a company cannot be in two VAT groups at the same time.

ANNEX A – Flowchart for new group eligibility rules from VAT Information Sheet 07/04

The chart assumes that the body corporate meets the normal VAT group eligibility requirements in VAT Act 1994 s 43A. It should be read in conjunction with the Information Sheet.                    **[38.52]**

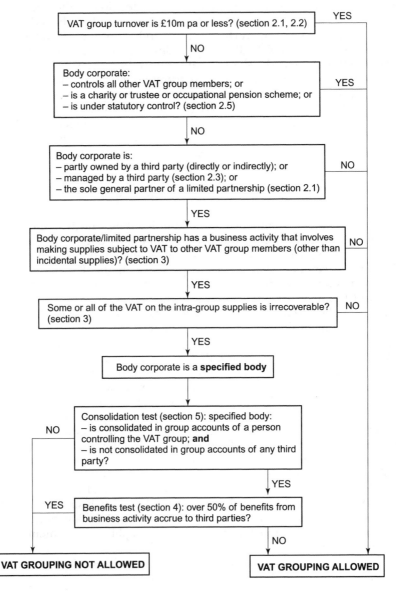

3   **De-registration**

HMRC may cancel a registration if satisfied that the business was not registrable at the time when it did in fact register (VATA 1994 Sch 1 para 13(2)). A registered 'intending trader' must notify HMRC within 30 days if he will not now make taxable supplies, otherwise penalties may be imposed (VATA 1994 Sch 1 para 11).

If a business permanently ceases to make taxable supplies it *must* notify HMRC within 30 days. A business may voluntarily de-register if it is expected that its taxable turnover will fall below £59,000 in the coming year. Unless there are very unusual circumstances, deregistration cannot be effected retrospectively.                                                                    **[38.53]**

## 4   Accounting for VAT

a)   *General rule*

VAT on supplies of goods and services must generally be accounted for on a quarterly basis with quarterly accounting periods being allocated to the trader at the time of his registration. The tax operates on the basis of self-assessment. Return Form VAT 100 is sent to the taxpayer towards the end of a quarterly period and must be returned completed, together with the tax payable so that it is *received* by HMRC by the end of the month following the end of the relevant quarter period. A seven-day extension is allowed if payment is by credit transfer but this has been withdrawn for businesses within the 'payments on account' provisions.

The taxpayer must pay the difference between output and input tax applicable to supplies during the quarter period. HMRC will repay excess input tax, normally within ten days of receiving the return (VATA 1994 s 25(3)). If a taxpayer has, by mistake, overpaid tax in an earlier period HMRC must refund that amount unless they can successfully argue unjust enrichment (see *Marks & Spencer plc v C & E Comrs* (1999)). All claims for refunds of VAT are subject to a three-year retrospective limit. The ECJ has ruled that the retrospective shortening of the limitation period was incompatible with the principles of effectiveness and protection of legitimate expectation (*Marks & Spencer plc* (Case C-62/00)).

A taxable person must keep detailed records and accounts for six years, together with full supporting documentation, and these are open to inspection by HMRC. Except in cases of fraud (when the limit is 20 years) there is a three-year limit on HMRCs' power to assess retrospectively for undeclared VAT.

Changes were made to VAT invoicing requirements with effect from 1 January 2004 to implement the EC VAT Invoicing Directive (2001/115/EC). C & E said they would adopt a light touch during 2004 to give businesses time to switch over to the new procedures and help minimise the cost of change. (VAT Information Sheet 16/03, para 2.4).

Unless C & E allow otherwise, a VAT invoice must show the following particulars:
(a)   An identifying number.
(b)   The time of the supply, ie tax point.
(c)   The date of issue of the document.
(d)   The name, address and registration number of the supplier.
(e)   The name and address of the person to whom the goods or services are supplied.

(f)    A description sufficient to identify the goods or services supplied.

(e)    Where services are supplied, a description of the services may be taken as sufficient to describe also the type of supply under (f) above and their extent under (h) below. For professional services, a description such as 'professional services rendered' is acceptable.

(g)    See 40.8 below for use of coded descriptions by cash and carry wholesalers. Coded descriptions may also be accepted in other circumstances (eg builders' merchants) where businesses whose trade is restricted to a large number of specialised parts or fittings issue illustrated catalogues to customers.

(h)    For each description, the quantity of the goods or extent of the services, the rate of VAT and amount payable, excluding VAT, expressed in any currency (before 1 January 2004, in sterling).

(i)    With effect from 1 January 2004, the unit price.

(j)    This applies to 'countable' goods and services. For services, the countable element might be, for example, an hourly rate or a price paid for standard services. If the supply cannot be broken down into countable elements, the total VAT-exclusive price is the unit price. Additionally, the unit price may not need to be shown at all if it is not normally provided in a particular business sector and is not required by the customer. (VAT Information Sheet 16/03, para 3.2.)

(k)    The gross amount payable, excluding VAT, expressed in any currency (before 1 January 2004, in sterling).

(l)    The rate of any cash discount offered.

(m)    Before 1 January 2004, each rate of VAT chargeable and the amount of VAT chargeable, expressed in sterling, at each rate. With effect from 1 January 2004, this information is optional.

(n)    The total amount of VAT chargeable expressed in sterling.    **[38.54]**

### b)    *Monthly returns*

Businesses likely to enjoy a refund of input tax (typically an export business) may submit monthly returns (SI 1995/2518 reg 25).    **[38.55]**

### c)    *Monthly payments on account*

'Very large' VAT payers (defined as those whose liability in the relevant reference period exceeds £2m in a year) are required to make monthly VAT payments on account in respect of each of the first two months of every quarter. The reference period is the year ending on the previous 31 March, 30 April or 31 May. A business that is within the payments on account scheme may only leave it if its liability falls below £1.6m.    **[38.56]**

### d)    *Annual returns*

Completing four VAT returns per year may present a burden to smaller businesses. As an alternative, such businesses with an annual value of taxable supplies *not exceeding £660,000* may make an annual VAT return. On the basis of the previous year's results, nine monthly payments must be made by direct debit; the final payment (adjusted as appropriate) together with the VAT return must then be made in the two-month period following the end of the year. From 1 April 1996, a business whose turnover does not exceed £100,000 and whose previous year's net VAT liability is less than £2,000 may elect to make three quarterly interim payments (instead of the nine monthly payments). **[38.57]**

### e) *Cash accounting*

Businesses whose annual value of taxable supplies does not exceed £660,000 may also be assisted by electing to make VAT returns on a cash basis: ie by reference to output tax collected in the quarter less input tax paid in that same period. In other cases returns are on the basis of invoices issued and received rather than cash received or paid. **[38.58]**

### f) *Bad debt relief*

In general, VAT is charged on the basis of invoices issued to customers irrespective of whether payment has been received. VAT relief in respect of bad debts was recast in FA 1990 s 11 (now VATA 1994 s 36) as further amended by SI 1997/1086.

The requirements for relief are that the taxpayer must have:
(1)   supplied goods or services on or after 1 April 1989; and
(2)   accounted for and paid VAT on that supply; and
(3)   written off the whole or part of the consideration in his accounts; and
(4)   notified the debtor, providing specified detail, that a claim for bad debt relief was being made.

For supplies made after 1 January 2003 (4) no longer applies. If an invoice is outstanding for six months, then the debtor will be obliged to repay the VAT to HMRC. In addition:
(a)   six months must have elapsed from the date on which payment became due and payable or, if later, the date of supply; and
(b)   claims must be made within three years and six months of the date on which payment became due or the date of supply, whichever is the later.

The result of a successful claim will be either a reduction in output VAT payable in the relevant quarter or, in appropriate circumstances, a refund of VAT. **[38.59]**

#### EXAMPLE 38.8—BAD DEBT RELIEF—GENERAL

HMS submits returns for the VAT period ending 31.1, 30.4, 31.7 and 31.10 and issued an invoice to a customer on 30 April 2003 for £20,000 + £3,500 VAT. Payment terms are 30 days from the tax point so settlement should have been received by 30 May. However, payment had still not been received by the end of October 2003. Bad debt relief is available six months from 30 May. The claim would be made in the January 2004 return.

#### EXAMPLE 38.9—BAD DEBT RELIEF DETAIL

Patrick is a trader who makes both standard-rated and zero-rated sales. He has made the following sales:

| Date of Supply 2003 | Due Date for Payment 2003 | Rate | Price excluding VAT | VAT | Total |
|---|---|---|---|---|---|
| | | | £ | £ | £ |
| 4 April | 31 May | Standard | 2,100 | 367 | 2,467 |
| 10 May | 30 June | Zero | 1,430 | – | 1,430 |
| 10 June | 31 July | Standard | 1,212 | 212 | 1,424 |
| 15 August | 30 September | Standard | 1,520 | 266 | 1,786 |
| 31 August | 30 September | Zero | 800 | – | 800 |
| | | | 7,062 | 845 | 7,907 |

Patrick received the following payments on account:

| 2003 | £ |
|---|---|
| 18 July | 1,800 |
| 7 September | 850 |

At a meeting of the creditors on 1 November 2003 the debt due to Patrick was proved and a resolution to wind up the company was passed.

Patrick submits his VAT returns quarterly for the periods ending 31 January, 30 April, 31 July and 31 October.

The bad debt relief that Patrick may claim for VAT purposes is as follows:

*Bad debt relief claimable under VATA 1994 s 36*

| Tax point | Payment Date | Gross Debt | Payment Received (FIFO*) | Unpaid | VAT Fraction | VAT |
|---|---|---|---|---|---|---|
| | | £ | £ | £ | £ | £ |
| 4.4.03 | 31.5.03 | 2,467 | 2,467 | – | – | – |
| 10.5.03 | 30.6.03 | 1,430 | 183 | 1,247 | – | – |
| 10.6.03 | 31.7.03 | 1,424 | – | 1,424 | 7/47 | 212 |
| 15.8.03 | 30.9.03 | 1,786 | – | 1,786 | 7/47 | 266 |
| 31.8.03 | 30.9.03 | 800 | – | 800 | – | – |
| | | | 2,650 | 5,257 | | 478 |

*Bad debt relief claimable:*

| Input Tax | Payment Due Date | Relief Claimable From | In Quarter Ended |
|---|---|---|---|
| £ | | | |
| 212 | 31.7.03 | 31.1.04 | 31.1.04 |
| 266 | 30.9.03 | 31.3.04 | 30.4.04 |
| Debt to be claimed from liquidator | | | £5,257 |

## 5  Penalties

The powers of HMRC to charge penalties and interest were drastically increased as a result of the Keith Report. In brief the rules are as follows:

*Default surcharge (VATA 1994 s 59)* Repeated default (lateness) in submitting returns (or making the appropriate payment) can lead to a default surcharge. One default can lead to the issue of a surcharge liability notice and further defaults during the operative period of that notice (12 months) will both extend the period for a further 12 months and lead to a surcharge of (at worst) 15% of the tax due for the period of default. The default surcharge may also be applied to the default of a business to make a monthly payment on account (see **[38.56]**).                    **[38.60]**

*Tax evasion (VATA 1994 s 60)* Where tax is evaded dishonestly a maximum penalty of 100% of the tax sought to be evaded is payable.            **[38.61]**

*Misdeclaration penalty (VATA 1994 ss 63 and 64)* This penalty was reformed by FA 1993 Sch 2 para 1 and the name of 'misdeclaration penalty' is now used in place of the old terms 'serious misdeclaration' and 'persistent misdeclaration' penalty. A penalty is charged when a return is made which understates tax due or overstates tax repayable (and also when a VAT assessment understates the tax due and the taxpayer does not draw this error to HMRCs' attention). The penalty is equal to 15% of the tax loss but will only apply if the lost tax equals or exceeds (in the case of an incorrect return) whichever is the lesser of £1m and 30% of the gross amount of tax (GAT) for the period (or, in the case of a failure to draw to HMRCs' attention an understatement of liability in an assessment, the lesser of £1m and 30% of the true amount of VAT for the period). The GAT is the aggregate of the correct amount of output tax and the correct amount of recoverable input tax for the period.

A penalty is also charged in the case of repeated errors. This penalty will only arise if returns for three out of 12 VAT periods contain errors and HMRC has issued a penalty liability notice. For a penalty to be chargeable, tax lost because of the inaccuracy must be at least £500,000 or 10% of the GAT for the period (whichever is the lesser). The penalty is 15% of the tax lost.                                                           **[38.62]**

*Failure to notify registration (VATA 1994 s 67(1)(a))* A penalty based on a percentage of the tax that would have been charged had correct registration occurred can be charged; for instance, at 5% for delays of up to nine months rising to 15% for delays in excess of 18 months.            **[38.63]**

*Penalties for breach of the VAT regulations (VATA 1994 s 9)* There are innumerable possible breaches—such as failure to keep appropriate records—and penalties are calculated on a daily basis.                    **[38.64]**

*Mitigation (VATA 1994 s 70)* In the case of penalties payable under ss 60, 63, 64 or 67 of VATA 1994 and assessed after 27 July 1993, there is a discretion available to HMRC (or, on appeal, to the tribunal) to reduce penalties if they see fit. In exercising their discretion, neither HMRC nor a tribunal may take account of the insufficiency of funds available to the taxpayer to pay the VAT or any penalty, the fact that there has been no VAT lost as a result of the default, or the fact that the taxpayer acted in good faith.                    **[38.65]**

*Interest (VATA 1994 s 12)* Interest, at a commercial rate, is payable on a VAT assessment and where there has been over-declaration of input tax or under-declaration of output tax. By a news release of 7 September 1994 HMRC announced their intention not to assess interest where there has been no loss to the exchequer, eg where a company has failed to charge VAT but, had it done so, another would have reclaimed it as input tax.          **[38.66]**

*The 'reasonable excuse' defence* This is a general defence to a claim for penalties. Lack of funds and reliance on another do not count (VATA 1994 s 21(1)). The question for the tribunal is one of fact and decisions show little consistency with the apparent honesty of the taxpayer often being decisive. Evidence that HMRC had been informed and their advice followed is highly material in establishing the defence. Taking proper professional advice and following that also helps.                                            **[38.67]**

*Repayment supplements and interest on overpayments* In cases where a refund of tax due to the taxpayer has been delayed, he may be eligible for a repayment supplement and there is a statutory right to interest in certain cases of official error.                                                  **[38.68]–[38.80]**

## IV   THE RECOVERY OF VAT, PARTIAL EXEMPTION AND THE CAPITAL GOODS SCHEME

### 1   The deduction principle

A taxable person is only entitled to deduct the VAT he has incurred from the output tax for which he must account if it was incurred in the course or furtherance of a business and then only if it was incurred in the making of taxable supplies, or supplies which are outside the scope of VAT because they were made outside the UK but which would have been taxable if made in the UK or supplies of 'out of scope' services to a person that does not belong in a Member State. Input tax on post cessation expenditure may continue to be regarded as deductible provided that there is a direct and immediate link between the payments made and the commercial activity and that the absence of any fraudulent or abusive intent has been established (*I/S Fini H v Skatteministeriet*, CJEC Case C-32/03).                            **[38.81]**

### 2   The need for apportionment

Technically, following the *Lennartz* decision (see **[30.1]**) in the ECJ, a taxable person is entitled to full recovery of the input tax on goods or services acquired but would need to treat any non-business use as a deemed supply. In practice (and, in relation to non-business use of business property, in law following the amendment made by FA 2003) a taxable person, who makes a combination of supplies on which recovery is allowed and those where it is not, must carry out an apportionment of any VAT incurred to determine how much is recoverable. Where a taxable person has made any supplies other-wise than in the course or furtherance of his business, he must first carry out an apportionment in order to identify and exclude that VAT from deduction. The remaining VAT is recoverable to the extent that it can be attributed to taxable supplies and does not fall within a category of expense for which there is no right to recover (see examples below).                    **[38.82]**

### EXAMPLE 38.10—BUSINESS GIFTS

(i)  Sophie buys 200 bottles of whisky and gives two each to 100 customers as Christmas gifts. Each bottle costs £10. Sophie may recover input tax in full on the purchase and no output tax is due because the value to each recipient is less than £50.

(ii) Michael buys 200 bottles of whisky and gives four each to 50 customers as Christmas gifts. Each bottle costs £20. Michael may recover input tax in full on the purchase but as the value to each recipient is more than £50 (ie £80), output tax is due on the cost. Michael must pay as output tax the same amount as has been claimed as input tax.

### EXAMPLE 38.11—INPUT TAX

(1)  Jack has a chain of bicycle shops and wishes to expand into Germany. He has identified suitable properties and engages the services of a local solicitor who charges €5,000. The invoice does not show VAT. Davies converts the value to sterling, say £3,000, adds 525 VAT at 17.5%, then on his next return pays £525 output tax and claims £525 input tax.

(2)  Anne Ltd imports parts from Germany. The latest assignment was for €10,000 without VAT. The company converts this to sterling, say £6,000, adds £1,050 VAT, and includes this as payable in its next return (ie the £1,050 is added to other output tax). It then claims back the same amount as input tax.

### EXAMPLE 38.12—PRE-TRADING

Adam sets up in business as a house builder. His plan is to buy land, build houses and sell them. He cannot start the business until he has worked his notice at his current employment. Before he leaves, he incurs the following set-up costs:

- Tools                              £6,000 + £1050 VAT
- Solicitors fees                    £1000 + £175 VAT
- Accountants fees                   £1,200 + £210 VAT

He may register immediately and reclaim the £1,435 input tax on his first return. He would probably complete returns monthly because all of his outputs (sales of houses) would be zero-rated and he would always be claiming a refund from HMRC.

### EXAMPLE 38.13—LATE CLAIM

Angela runs a clothing shop and is VAT registered, completing returns to the end of March, June, September and December. She bought a computer for £2,400 + £420 VAT on 30 June 1999. She also had some shop repairs carried out. The invoice was for £4,000 + £700 VAT and dated 30 December 2000. She failed to claim the input tax on either at the time.

When completing her September 2003 return, she realises the error. She can still reclaim the £700 on this return but the £420 cannot be claimed because the supply took place more than three years ago.

### EXAMPLE 38.14—ABORTIVE EXPENDITURE

Both Andy Ltd and Nash Ltd start research into a vaccine on 30 September 2001 and register for VAT as intending traders. On 31 December 2002, Andy Ltd launches its new successful product and starts making taxable supplies. However, Nash Ltd is unsuccessful and the research stops on 30 September 2003. Neither has made exempt supplies so all input tax reclaimed prior to making taxable supplies/ceasing research will not be disturbed and will not be clawed back by HMRC.

### EXAMPLE 38.15—CAR LEASING

Tracy leases a small fleet of cars from a leasing company that chooses to treat payments or rebates for early terminations as taxable supplies. All cars are subject to the 50% input tax restriction. Tracy terminates two agreements early. One requires an additional payment of £6,000 + £1,050 VAT which Tracy can recover in full as input tax, ie there is no 50% restriction. The other is a net rebate (after allowing for the termination payment) of £200 but Tracy only pays £17.50 VAT (rather than £35) on the amount received because the 50% restriction applied to the original rentals.

## 3   The partial exemption problem

A business that makes a combination of taxable and exempt supplies must attempt to attribute VAT to either its taxable business or its exempt business. Businesses such as insurance companies, banks and property developers usually make exempt supplies (see **[38.8]** and are obviously affected but other businesses, not at first sight affected by the partial exemption problem, may also be caught. Typically, rent received from property may give rise to an exempt output and so 'taint' the business. When a business makes exempt supplies the question is how much input tax should be attributed to those exempt supplies and so be irrecoverable (this is referred to as 'exempt input tax'). For the purposes of this apportionment, supplies that are outside the scope of VAT because they were made to a person who belongs outside the UK should be regarded as giving rise to a right of recovery (see *C & E Comrs v Liverpool Institute of Performing Arts* (1999)).                          **[38.83]**

## 4   The solution (VATA 1994 ss 25 and 26; SI 1995/2518)

The following rules apply:

*First,* input tax directly attributable to goods and services exclusively used or to be used in making taxable or other supplies carrying a right to recovery is fully recoverable.

*Secondly,* input tax directly attributable to goods and services exclusively used or to be used in making exempt supplies or in any other non-taxable activity is irrecoverable.

*Thirdly,* the residual input tax must then relate to both taxable and exempt (or non-taxable) activities (a common example is the cost of VAT incurred on overheads). This remaining tax must be apportioned in accordance with the standard method (a turnover based method) (see **[38.86]**) or in accordance with a reasonable method agreed with HMRC (referred to as the special method). **[38.84]**

## 5 Apportionment methods

A variety of methods are possible. Regardless of whether the standard (ie turnover-based) method or a special method is used, however, if input tax is incurred partly in relation to certain exempt financial supplies (such as the issue of shares) which are incidental to the taxpayer's business and partly in relation to other supplies, then the taxpayer can recover only that amount of such input tax used in making taxable supplies (VAT Regulations 1995, SI 1995/2518 reg 102(2)). This is an aspect that has attracted considerable attention by taxpayers and by HMRC. Further refinements were announced following the Budget 2005. In particular:

- A change in HMRC's policy on the use of the Special Method Override Notice (Notice).
- A new requirement that in future all special methods must be approved or directed in writing.
- New rules to deal with 'gaps' in special methods.
- New restrictions on rounding-up the results of partial exemption calculations in the standard method for very large businesses, and for new special methods. **[38.85]**

### a) *'Standard method'*

This method attributes residual input tax in accordance with the ratio of taxable outputs to all outputs. The fraction is reduced to a percentage. The fraction must be calculated for each VAT accounting period (monthly or quarterly) using the percentage rounded down to the nearest whole number. At the end of the VAT accounting year (called a 'longer period'), the values must be aggregated and an annual adjustment performed. The percentage is rounded up for the annual adjustment. Certain supplies made by the taxpayer, such as supplies of capital goods, incidental real estate transactions, incidental financial services and self-supplies are ignored for the purpose of this calculation (VAT Regulations 1995, SI 1995/2518 reg 101), ie the income derived from such transactions is not included as turnover. The standard method must be used unless and until an alternative method is approved by or imposed by HMRC. **[38.86]**

#### EXAMPLE—38.16

A taxpayer suffers the following input tax:

|       |                                       | £          |
|-------|---------------------------------------|------------|
| (i)   | That attributed to taxable supplies   | 500,000    |
| (ii)  | That attributed to exempt supplies    | 150,000    |
| (iii) | Residual input tax                    | 350,000    |
|       |                                       | £1,000,000 |

His taxable supplies total £10m and exempt supplies £2m.

To calculate the amount of residual input tax recoverable under the standard method:

(i)    calculate (as a percentage) the ratio of taxable supplies to all supplies:

$$\text{ie}\frac{10,000,000}{12,000,000} \times 100 = 83.33\% \text{ (rounded up to 84\%)}$$

(ii)   multiply residual (or 'non-attributable') input tax by this percentage to obtain input tax recoverable:

£350,000 × 84% = £294,000

Where the standard method is used it will be necessary to ensure that it does not work unreasonably by applying a 'use' method. This is referred to as the standard method override and was enacted in FA 2002 and is set out in VAT Information Sheet 04/02.

b)    *Special methods*

By virtue of SI 1995/2518 reg 102, HMRC may approve or direct the use of any other method of apportioning residual input tax, but any supplies of capital goods, incidental real estate transactions, incidental financial services and self-supplies must be ignored in making the calculation (SI 1995/2518 reg 101(3)). One alternative way of apportioning residual input tax (the 'input tax' based method which was formerly the standard method) is by employing the fraction:

$$\frac{\text{input tax directly attributable to taxable outputs}}{\text{input tax directly attributable to taxable and exempt outputs}}$$

Since the passing of the Finance Act (No 2) 2005, a special method must be in writing in order to be valid.    **[38.87]**

**EXAMPLE—38.17**

Taking the facts of *Example 38.7* the input tax based method would produce the following:

(i)    multiply residual input tax by the formula. Using the numbering in *Example 38.7* this becomes:

$$\frac{\text{(i)}}{\text{(i)} + \text{(ii)}}$$

(ii)   tax recoverable is:

$$£350,000 \times \frac{500,000}{650,000} = £269,230$$

**EXAMPLE 38.18—ALTERNATIVE SPECIAL METHOD**

A partly exempt business receives £4,000,000 taxable income excluding VAT and £2,000,000 exempt income. Total input VAT for the quarter is £300,000 of which

£120,000 is directly attributable to taxable supplies, £100,000 is directly attributable to exempt supplies and £80,000 is non-attributable.

The non-attributable input VAT is apportioned as follows:

$$£80,000 \times \frac{4,000,000\,(\text{value of taxable supplies})}{4,000,000 + 2,000,000\,(\text{value of total supplies})}$$

The ratio must be expressed as a percentage rounded up to the next whole number (in this case 66.66% rounded up to 67%) so here the recoverable amount is:
£80,000 × 67% = £53,600.

Total VAT recoverable for the period is therefore £120,000 (direct attribution) + £53,600 (partial exemption calculation) = £173,600.

## 6   De minimis

The *de minimis* rules provide that when the exempt input tax of a trader is not more than £625 per month on average or £7,500 pa, and provided this exempt input tax is no more than 50% of all input tax, all input tax shall be treated as attributable to taxable supplies so that the taxpayer is fully taxable and able to recover *all* input tax (SI 1995/2518 reg 106). This test must be applied for each VAT return and again when the annual adjustment is calculated at the end of the year.

In calculating whether the *de minimis* rules apply, input tax attributable to certain exempt supplies (such as a deposit of money) may be ignored provided the taxpayer's business is not that of a bank or certain other financial institutions. Such input tax may be treated as attributable to taxable supplies and therefore ignored in applying the *de minimis* rules. This provision is intended to permit small businesses to avoid partial exemption. There are special rules applicable to input tax relating to share issues.     [38.88]

### EXAMPLE 38.19—DETAILED ILLUSTRATION OF PARTIAL EXEMPTION

For the VAT year ended 31 March 2003 Sophie had the following transactions:

|  | £ |
|---|---:|
| General sales (standard rate VAT) | 240,000 |
| General sales (zero rate VAT) | 20,000 |
| Plant sold to UK trader | 10,000 |
| Plant sold to a trader in Australia and exported to him | 10,000 |
| Exempt supplies made | 200,000 |
| Wages to employees | 150,000 |
| New motor car purchased March 2003 for use by salesman (petrol only provided for business use) | 24,000 |
| (None of the above amounts include VAT) | |
| Input tax: | |
| Attributable to taxable supplies | 20,000 |
| exempt supplies | 12,000 |
| overheads | 8,000 |
| purchase of car | 4,200 |

The total amount of output tax for which Sophie is required to account and her deductible input tax for the year ended 31 March 2003 is as follows:

*Output tax and input tax for year ended 31 March 2003*

|  | £ | £ | £ |
|---|---|---|---|
| Outputs chargeable at standard rate: |  |  |  |
| Sales | 240,000 |  |  |
| Plant sold to UK trader | 10,000 | 250,000 |  |
| Outputs chargeable at zero rate: |  |  |  |
| Sales | 20,000 |  |  |
| Plant sold to Australian trader | 10,000 | 30,000 |  |
| Total taxable outputs |  | 280,000 |  |
| Exempt outputs |  | 200,000 |  |
| Total outputs |  | 480,000 |  |
| Output tax on taxable outputs of 250,000 at 17.5% |  |  | 43,750 |
| Input tax attributable to taxable supplies |  | 20,000 |  |
| Input tax attributable to overheads | 8,000 |  |  |
| Allowable proportion: |  |  |  |
| $\dfrac{260,000}{460,000} = 57\% \times £8,000$ |  | 4,560 | 24,560 |
| Net payment to HMRC for year |  |  | £19,190 |

*Note*

The sales of capital items, ie the plant sold to UK and Australia, traders, are distortive and left out of the fraction.

The irrecoverable input tax of £15,440 (£12,000 + (£8,000 − £4,560) = £3,440) will be treated as an allowable expense in computing Sophie's profit for income tax purposes.

The input tax on the purchase of the car is also irrecoverable and will count as part of the cost of the car for capital allowances purposes.

## 7  The Capital Goods Scheme

Rules were introduced from 1 April 1990 to deal with certain capital expenditure incurred by a business. The rules reflect the fact that capital expenditure will normally benefit a business over a period of time, in contrast to income expenditure that is primarily for the benefit of the current period of account.                                                                 **[38.89]**

Assets within the scheme

Expenditure on the following assets, incurred on or after 1 April 1990, is within the scheme:

(1) a computer or item of computer equipment to a value of at least £50,000;

(2) land or buildings and certain refurbishments to a value of at least £250,000. **[38.90]**

Initial deduction

In the year that an asset within the scheme is first acquired, a business calculates the proportion of VAT on the asset that it is entitled to deduct, in accordance with the usual rules (see **[38.81]–[38.88]**). **[38.91]**

Subsequent adjustments

In the second and subsequent 'adjustment intervals', the business must adjust the VAT initially claimed if the extent to which the asset is used for the purposes of the business's taxable supplies is greater or less than the extent to which it was used in the initial period. **[38.92]**

Period of adjustment

The number of 'adjustment intervals' depends on the nature of the asset. In the case of an interest in land having more than ten years to run, the VAT deducted is adjusted over ten intervals. There are only five adjustment intervals for computers and interests in land having less than ten years to run. The adjustment interval is the 'longer period' **[38.86]**, normally a year, ending on 31 March, 30 April or 31 May.

Where the asset is sold as part of the transfer of a going concern, an adjustment period will end on the day the asset is transferred. The transferor must then make an adjustment based on the use for that period. The transferee inherits the obligation to make any adjustments over the remaining number of intervals. An adjustment interval will also end where a company leaves or joins a VAT group. Therefore, although the adjustment interval is normally a year, it does not have to be and the adjustment period may therefore be less than ten years or five years. **[38.93]**

Making the adjustment

At the end of each tax year following the year of acquisition it is necessary to compare the input tax recovery percentage of the business with the recovery percentage in the year of acquisition. If that subsequent recovery percentage is *less* than the initial percentage, input tax has been over-recovered and an amount is payable to HMRC; if the then recovery percentage is *greater* than the first year's, a repayment is due from HMRC. Special rules apply where the capital item is disposed of during the period of adjustment and F(No 2)A 1997 included anti-avoidance provisions to prevent the artificial manipulation of the disposal price. **[38.94]–[38.100]**

**EXAMPLE—38.20**

Whatto plc purchases a computer for £200,000 exclusive of VAT that is £35,000. The company is partly exempt throughout the following four years but then leases the computer to another business for the fifth year.

| Year | % of use taxable | Input tax claims (£) | Adjustment % | Amount of adjustment (£) |
|------|------|------|------|------|
| 1 | 51 | 17,850 | | |
| 2 | 46 | | −5 | −350 |
| 3 | 49 | | −2 | −140 |
| 4 | 52 | | +1 | +70 |
| 5 | 100 | | +49 | +3,430 |

*Notes:*
(1)    The adjustment each year is:

$$\frac{\text{total input tax}}{\text{total years (5)}} \times \text{the adjustment percentage}$$

For instance, in *year 2*:

$$\frac{35,000}{5} \times 5\% = £350$$

(2)    The total input tax recovered (net of payments made to HMRC ) is *£3,010.*
(3)    Leasing the computer to another person results in 100% taxable use in *year 5.*

**EXAMPLE—38.21**

X Ltd purchases a new commercial property in June 1990 for £1m plus VAT. It exercises the option to tax and lets out the building. All VAT is therefore recovered. In June 1991 it sells the building to Y Ltd for £900,000 and Y Ltd exercises the option to tax (see **[39.27]**). Because Y buys subject to the existing letting, the sale is treated as the transfer of a business as a going concern so that no VAT is charged. Y Ltd now steps into X Ltd's shoes for the purposes of the scheme. In June 1993, Y Ltd obtains vacant possession of the premises and goes into occupation for the purposes of its own partially exempt business (property investment).

The consequence is that for the last seven years of the ten-year period, the building will not be used for fully taxable purposes and Y Ltd must repay part of the input tax recovered by X Ltd.

# V   INTERNATIONAL SUPPLIES OF GOODS AND SERVICES

## 1   General principle

The VAT treatment of the import and export of goods depends on whether or not the movement is between EU countries. Movements to and from non-EU countries are taxed on a destination basis, ie no tax is charged on exports, while VAT is chargeable on import. The treatment of goods movements between EU Member States depends on whether or not the person receiving the goods is a taxable person and registered for VAT purposes.

The treatment of international services is more complex. *First*, it depends on the categorisation of the service for VAT purposes. It is important to note that certain services fall outside the scope of UK VAT because they are regarded as being supplied where the customer is established or where the use and enjoyment of the service takes place. These exceptions apply notwithstanding the fact that the supplier is based within the UK. Similarly, services received from abroad may be regarded as supplied within the UK and, in principle, subject to UK VAT.

*Secondly*, it should be borne in mind that there is no blanket zero-rating of services to persons outside the UK.

It is also important to note that in the case of both goods imported from within the EU and certain services the liability to account for VAT is shifted to the person importing the goods and services (VATA 1994 s 8) (the customer). **[38.101]**

### 2 Export of goods to countries outside the EU

Under VATA 1994 s 30(6), a supply of goods is zero-rated if HMRC are satisfied that the person supplying the goods has (a) exported them to a place outside the EU, or (b) has shipped them for use as stores on a voyage or flight to an eventual destination outside the UK (other than for a private purpose). See VAT Regulations 1995, SI 1995/2518.

It is generally necessary for exports to be made directly to a customer for zero-rating to apply although there is an exception in the case of supplies to export houses in the UK who arrange for the export.

In order to justify zero-rating it is essential to be able to produce evidence of export to HMRC such as the airway bill or shipped bill of lading.

Two different types of retail export scheme are dealt with in the VAT Regulations: one applies to visitors to the UK, the other to UK residents and the crews of ships and aircraft. The taxable person is at risk if the goods are not exported and the safest course for the taxable person is to take a deposit of the VAT and return this to the customer when evidence of export has been provided. **[38.102]**

### 3 Import of goods from outside the EU

VAT is currently charged on the import of goods into the UK from outside the EU as if it were customs duty, and this is so whether or not the importer is a taxable person. The UK includes England, Scotland, Wales, Northern Ireland, territorial waters and, for this purpose, the Isle of Man.

Evidence of VAT paid on import (now in the form of a certificate C79) must be obtained by a taxable person and retained as evidence for input tax recovery. VAT paid on import can be recovered as input tax in accordance with normal rules.

VATA 1994 s 21 deals with the value of imported goods.

Payment of VAT on imported goods is due at the time of importation unless the importer or his agent has been approved under a scheme for deferral of tax which enables payment to be deferred until the fifteenth day of the month following import.

Currently, a number of exemptions from the VAT charge on importation apply. Some deal with temporary imports only and are dealt with in SI 1984/746. Limited categories of goods are exempted from VAT on import even if permanently imported: see SI 1992/3193.

It is also possible to defer payment of VAT on import by placing the imported goods in certain types of warehouse. Payment of VAT can by this method be deferred until the goods leave the warehouse and enter into free circulation in the EU.   **[38.103]**

### 4   Transfers of goods between EU countries after 1 January 1993

Where a registered taxable person in the UK despatches goods to a registered taxable person in another EU Member State, the supply will normally be zero-rated under regulations made under VATA 1994 s 30(8). No VAT will be paid as the goods cross the frontier. The customer will acquire the goods and will account for VAT on his own VAT return at the rate in force in the country of receipt. Where a UK registered business acquires goods from another EU country, he must now, instead of paying VAT on importation, account for VAT on the goods through his own VAT return.

Where a taxable person in one EU country despatches goods to a person who is not a VAT registered taxable person in another EU country, the supplier will generally charge VAT at the rate in force in the country of despatch. Thus, UK taxable persons who supply goods to customers in the EU who are not registered for VAT may not zero-rate those supplies. In addition, if the goods the supplier dispatches to unregistered persons exceeds certain limits, the supplier must register for, and charge, local VAT instead of UK VAT.

From 1 January 2005, VAT on the wholesale supply of natural gas and electricity is accounted for in the place where the customer is established. For other supplies, it is where the natural gas and electricity is consumed.   **[38.104]**

### 5   International services

Services are generally treated as made in the UK (and are hence liable to UK VAT) if the supplier 'belongs' in the UK (VATA 1994 s 7(10)). For the place where a supplier belongs, see VATA 1994 s 9. This basic rule is, however, modified by the VAT (Place of Supply of Services) Order 1992, SI 1992/3121, and further modified with effect from 1 January 1993 for, *inter alia*, certain supplies of transport services and supplies of certain interests in land. This may result in supplies of services made by taxable persons who belong in the UK being treated as made outside the UK and hence being treated as outside the scope of UK VAT. Notwithstanding that such supplies are treated as outside the scope of VAT, a UK taxable person may recover input tax attributable to such supplies if they would be taxable if made in the UK. Equally, it may result in non-UK taxable persons being treated as making supplies of services in the UK and hence being liable to register for UK VAT. Under the Order, services consisting of the transportation of passengers or goods are generally treated as supplied in the country in which the transportation takes place, and the letting or hire of any means of transport for use outside the EU is treated as made outside the UK. In relation to land, any supply of services which consists of the grant, assignment or surrender of an interest in land or a licence to occupy land or any lesser contractual right over land (as well as construction services and services of surveyors etc) is treated as made where the land is situate.

Also, under the Order, supplies of services of a kind listed in VATA 1994 Sch 5, paras 1–8 (including services of consultants, lawyers, accountants etc) and rendered to a person who either belongs outside the EU (but not in the Isle of Man) or who belongs in an EU country other than that in which the supplier belongs and receives the supply for business purposes, are treated as made where the recipient belongs and so are outside the scope of UK VAT unless for use in the UK. Again, a UK taxable person may recover input tax attributable to such supplies if they would be taxable if made in the UK.

The E-commerce Directive (Directive (EC) 2000/31) has been formally agreed and came into effect on 1 July 2003. It requires suppliers of digitised services into the EU from outside to register in a Member State and to account for VAT in that member state based on the VAT rate in the member state of the consumer. Provisions were introduced in the UK in new Schedule 3B to VATA 1994.

### EXAMPLE—38.22

(1) Cayco, a Cayman investment company, purchases a building in the UK and grants a five-year lease, having exercised the option to tax the building (see [**39.27**]). The grant is a supply of services made in the UK and Cayco must charge UK VAT.

(2) Lex and Lax (solicitors) provide for Hiram, in the USA, estate planning advice in connection with becoming UK resident and ultimately domiciled. This service is outside the scope of UK VAT; by contrast services in connection with the acquisition of a flat for him in London are standard-rated.

(3) Alternatively, they provide for François, a French resident who is not registered for VAT in France, advice in connection with his personal affairs. This service is standard-rated.

A further exception to the general rule relates to the supply of telecommunications services and access to the Internet. In relation to such services provided to UK business customers the place of supply is the UK and the customer is required to declare the VAT due under the reverse charge procedure (see [**38.106**]). Conversely such services provided by suppliers in the UK to persons outside the EU or to businesses outside the UK are outside the scope of UK VAT.

Services rendered by UK taxable persons to persons belonging outside the UK therefore, subject to the above provisions, are standard-rated unless they fall within the categories specified in VATA 1994 Sch 8 Group 7 or would be zero-rated if supplied in the UK, eg air travel, in which case zero-rating will apply. The services under this heading were substantially amended from 1 January 1993 and now comprise only:

(1) the supply of services of work carried out on goods intended for export outside the EU; and

(2)    the supply of services comprising the making of arrangements for the export of goods or supply of services outside the EU or for a supply of services detailed in (1) above.                                    **[38.105]**

## 6    The reverse charge

The 'reverse charge' applies, by virtue of VATA 1994 s 8, where services described as 'relevant services' are supplied by a person who belongs outside the UK to a person who belongs in the UK for the purpose of a business carried on by him. The recipient of the services will be treated as if the services had been supplied by himself to himself and must account for output tax (unless the services fall within an exempt or zero-rated category) and may recover the input tax charged to himself in accordance with normal procedures if it is attributable to taxable supplies he intends to make.

The services within the reverse charge are those set out in VATA 1994 Sch 5 provided that they do not also fall within Sch 9 (exempt services) and comprise:

(1)    transfers and assignments of copyright, patents, licences, trade marks and similar rights;

(2)    advertising services;

(3)    services of consultants, engineers, consultancy bureaux, lawyers, accountants and other similar services; data processing and provision of information (but excluding from this services relating to land);

(4)    acceptance of any obligation to refrain from pursuing or exercising any business activity or any such rights as are referred to in (1) above;

(5)    banking, financial and insurance services;

(6)    the supply of staff;

(7)    the letting on hire of goods other than means of transport;

(8)    telecommunication services, that is to say services relating to the transmission, emission or reception of signals, writing, images and sounds or information of any nature by wire, radio, optical or other electromagnetic systems, including the transfer or assignment of the right to use capacity for such transmission, emission or reception;

(9)    the services rendered by one person to another in procuring for the other any of the services mentioned in (1)–(8) above;

(10)   any services, where the place of supply is deemed to be the UK, not of a description specified in (1)–(7) and (9) when supplied to a recipient who is registered for UK VAT.

Anti-avoidance provisions prevent the routing of services tax free via an overseas branch of one of the companies forming a VAT group (see **[38.52]**).

                                                                    **[38.106]**

# 39 VAT on property

*Updated by Sinead Reid, BCL, LLM European Law, Barrister-at-Law, Senior Regulatory Advisor, DLA Piper Rudnick Gray Cary LLP*

I     Introduction [**39.1**]
II    Land, buildings and construction [**39.21**]

## I INTRODUCTION

The VAT treatment of supplies of land and buildings and construction services changed significantly in 1989. Prior to FA 1989, most transactions in land were exempt from VAT, although there was a significant category of zero-rated supplies. Only a limited number of supplies were standard-rated.

After FA 1989 the basic rule remains that the grant of any interest in or right over land or any licence to occupy land is *exempt* (VATA 1994 Sch 9 Group 1). The exceptions to this basic rule (which are standard-rated) were, however, extended, and the number of standard-rated transactions has been further increased by the introduction of the 'election to waive exemption' or 'option to tax' by which the person granting an interest in land can convert what would otherwise be an exempt supply of land into a standard-rated supply. The categories of zero-rated supply were reduced. Reduced rates (5%) apply to a range of construction services (see below).

Notice 742 (dealing with land and property) provides helpful guidance as to HMRC's practice in relation to property transactions.

*Construction services* are generally taxable at the standard rate save for certain supplies relating to the construction of new dwellings and other limited categories of residential/charitable buildings and works of alteration to some listed buildings, all of which are zero-rated (see [**39.23**]). Following proposals in the 2001 Budget, VAT at the reduced rate of 5% is chargeable on:

(1)   renovating and converting houses that have been empty for more than three years;
(2)   converting a house into flats;
(3)   converting commercial property; and
(4)   converting housing into a care home or bed-sit accommodation.

Further changes are made in the FA 2002 that took effect from 1 June 2002 (see [**39.26**]). **[39.1]–[39.20]**

## II   LAND, BUILDINGS AND CONSTRUCTION

### 1   **A grant of an interest in, or right over, land** (exempt supply)

You make a supply of land by making a grant of interest in, right over or licence to occupy land in return for consideration.

A grant of an *interest* in land includes a freehold sale as well as the grant, assignment or surrender of a lease.

A grant of a *right over* land includes a grant of mineral rights or easements. Grants of licences to occupy land fall into the exempt category, but must be contrasted with mere licences to use land that are standard-rated. Customs, in Notice 742, give as examples of the latter: allowing the general public to tip rubbish on your land; shared business premises; and the grant to the general public of admission to premises or events. The House of Lords referred the case of *C & E Comrs v Sinclair Collis Ltd* (1999) to the European Court of Justice ('ECJ'). The case related to an agreement under which a pub owner allowed a company operating cigarette vending machines to site a machine on the premises . The Court of Appeal had held that this was an exempt supply of a licence to occupy land. The ECJ emphatically rejected HMRC's claim that the installation of a vending machine in a public house constituted the 'letting or leasing or immovable property'. Accordingly the company was entitled to recover the related input tax. To the relief of most observers and the surprise of very few people outside HMRC , the ECJ has restored the decision that the VAT tribunal had reached in 1997 to the effect that the terms of arrangement between the owner and the installer of the cigarette vending machine did not amount, in the absence of exclusive occupation of a defined area or space, to the letting of immovable property.

**EXAMPLE 39.1**

(1)   On Saturday, Sid pays 35.25 to watch Arsenal FC. This is not a licence to occupy land: rather it is a licence to go on land and the supply is standard-rated.

On Sunday, he goes fishing on the Thames, paying £15 for a day licence. This is also a standard-rated supply.

(2)   Jack sells his freehold interest in two acres of freehold land to Jill and before completion she resells to Eric. Both have disposed of (exempt) interests in land.

In relation to the grant of a lease, the premium or rent payable is generally consideration for an exempt supply. Unless the landlord has exercised the option to tax, he will not charge VAT on any of these items.

The consideration paid by a landlord to his tenant for the surrender of an interest in land is exempt unless the tenant has exercised the option to tax.

Similarly, in the case of a 'reverse surrender' (being one where the tenant pays the landlord) the supply will be exempt unless the landlord has exercised the option to tax. The appropriate treatment of payments by landlords/original tenants to persuade a new tenant to take up residence was considered by the ECJ in the cases of *Cantor Fitzgerald* (Case C-108/99) and *Mirror Group plc* (Case C-409/99). The decision still leaves the VAT liability of any particular supply as uncertain. A payment made to be released from a lease is not for an interest in land and will generally be liable at the standard rate. **[39.21]**

## 2   Standard-rated supplies of land and buildings

The basic rule, already noted, is that grants of interests in or rights over land are exempt. The following are exceptions to this rule, listed in VATA 1994 Sch 9 Group 1:

(1) Freehold sales of new, or uncompleted, commercial buildings or civil engineering works. The legislation does not, in fact, use the term 'commercial building' but refers to a building that is neither designed as a dwelling nor intended solely for a relevant residential or charitable purpose (see **[39.23]**). Civil engineering works are likewise not defined, but include bridges, tunnels etc. A building or civil engineering work is *new* if it was completed within the last three years. It is treated as completed when the certificate of practical completion is issued or when it is fully occupied, whichever happens first.

**EXAMPLE 39.2**

(1) Dan Developer completes the construction of an office block on 1 August 1992 and on the same day sells the freehold interest to X-Ray for £5m. VAT at the standard rate is charged.

(2) If on 31 July 1995 X-Ray sells the freehold interest to Mad Mac Burgers for £7.5m, VAT at the standard rate is charged. Had the sale been delayed until 1 August 1995 the supply would have been exempt (unless X-Ray had exercised the option to tax: see **[39.27]**).

(3) A similar result would follow if X-Ray had effected an immediate sub-sale in favour of Mad Mac and the freehold had been conveyed directly from Dan Developer to Mad Mac.

(4) Instead of selling the freehold Dan Developer grants a long leasehold interest at a premium. The grant is an exempt supply (but note that prior to 31 March 1995 Dan Developer would have incurred a self-supply charge: see **[39.35]**).

(2) A supply made under a development tenancy, lease or licence. This is defined as a tenancy lease or licence of any building constructed, enlarged or extended after 1 January 1992 in respect of which the tenant, lessee or licensee, as the case may be, has incurred a developer's self-supply charge (see **[39.35]**).

(3) The grant of any interest in, right or licence consisting of a right to take game or fish except where, at the same time, the grantor also supplies the freehold to the grantee. Where land including the right to take game or fish is leased rather than sold freehold, VAT is chargeable on the proportion of the premium or rent attributable to the sporting rights.

**EXAMPLE 39.3**

Sid sells his freehold interest in a strip of the River Foul for £75,000. The freehold carries with it mooring and fishing rights. The sale of the freehold is an exempt supply and there is no question of apportioning the price to arrive at a value for the mooring rights or fishing rights.

(4)    The provision of accommodation in an hotel, boarding house or similar establishment.

(5)    The grant of an interest in, right over or licence to occupy holiday accommodation.

(6)    The provision of seasonal pitches for caravans.

(7)    The provision of facilities for camping.

(8)    The grant of facilities for parking a vehicle (see *Venuebest Ltd* [2002] AER (D) 66 (Dec) where the assignment of a lease of land was held to be the granting of facilities for parking) except where the facilities are provided in conjunction with domestic accommodation. The position as regards off street parking provided by local authorities was considered in the case of the *Isle of Wight Council* (LON/00/653) where the VAT and Duties Tribunal ruled that the Council provided off-street parking on the Isle of Wight under a public law regime and that, in its opinion, the relevant provision in the Sixth Directive (Article 4(5)) was not implemented in national law, concluding that the Commissioners are not in a position to raise any arguments concerning distortions of competition. The High Court has referred the case back to the Tribunal to consider the issues of distortion of competition.

(9)    The grant of a right to sell and remove standing timber.

(10)    The grant of facilities for housing or storage of an aircraft or mooring or storage of a ship, boat or other vessel.

(11)    The grant of a right to occupy a box, seat or other accommodation at a sports ground, theatre, concert hall or other place of entertainment.

(12)    The grant of facilities for playing sport or participating in physical recreation.

(13)    The grant of any right (such as an option) to call for or be granted an interest or right falling within (1) or (3)–(12) above.

Certain of the grants falling within (11) and (12) are nevertheless exempt if made by 'not for profit' bodies.

In addition to these taxable transactions, grants of interests in or rights over land or licences to occupy land which would otherwise be exempt may be converted to taxable supplies if the landowner concerned has exercised the election to waive exemption (the 'option to tax'): (see **[39.27]**).    **[39.22]**

### 3    Dwellings, qualifying residential and charitable buildings (zero-rated supplies)

The first grant or assignment of a major interest (defined to mean the freehold or a tenancy for a term certain exceeding 21 years—a lease for a term exceeding 21 years but with an earlier break clause will qualify) in certain qualifying buildings is zero-rated (VATA 1994 Sch 8 Group 5 Item 1).

To qualify, the building subject to the grant or assignment must have been:

(a)    a building, constructed by the grantor as a dwelling, number of dwellings or for a relevant residential or charitable purpose; or

(b)    a non-residential building or part thereof, which has been converted by the grantor into a dwelling, number of dwellings or for a relevant residential or charitable purpose. As from 1 August 2001 the VAT (Conversion of Buildings) Order, SI 2001/2305 introduced a relaxation in the rules to include buildings not used for residential purposes for only ten years, rather than the existing rule of buildings not used for residential purposes since 1 April 1973.

The conversion of a garage, which was previously occupied with a dwelling, is not zero-rated (VATA 1994 Sch 8 Group 5 Note (8)). Similarly, the conversion of a non-residential building that already contains a residential part, is not zero-rated unless the effect of the conversion is to create an additional dwelling or dwellings or is a conversion for relevant residential use (VATA 1994 Sch 8 Group 6 Note (9)). A useful summary of the zero-rating of renovated properties is contained in VAT Information Sheet 5/01.

**EXAMPLE 39.4**

(1)   Dick, the developer, builds a new house and grants a 99-year lease of it. The premium or first payment of rent is treated as consideration for a zero-rated supply. Further payments of rent are treated as consideration for an exempt supply.

(2)   By contrast if he granted a lease for less than 21 years then he would make an *exempt* supply (so that input tax would be restricted).

(3)   Fred Archer converts a barn into a dwelling that he then sells. The supply is zero-rated.

A *'dwelling'* includes a garage constructed (or converted) at the same time as the dwelling for occupation with it (VATA 1994 Sch 8 Group 5 Note (3)).

Use for a *'relevant residential purpose'* includes use as a residential children's home or old people's home, residential accommodation for school children or students and certain other similar purposes (see **[39.38]**) (VATA 1994 Sch 8 Group 5 Note (4)).

Use for a *'relevant charitable purpose'* means use *either* for something other than a business purpose *or* as a village hall or providing similar social or recreational facilities for a local community (VATA 1994 Sch 8 Group 5 Note (6)). Customs have issued guidance on a concession that allows zero-rating for charitable buildings which will have an insignificant business use. The concession allows zero-rating where the building intended for charitable non-business use would have less than 10% business use, measured by reference to time, persons, or floor area.

*'Construction'* does not include the conversion, reconstruction or alteration of an existing building and a building only ceases to be an existing building when either demolished completely to ground level or when the part remaining above ground level consists of no more than a single facade (or in the case of a corner site a double facade) the retention of which is a condition of a planning or similar permission (VATA 1994 Sch 8 Group 5 Notes (16) and (18)).                                                              **[39.23]**

**EXAMPLE 39.5**

Fred Flintstone constructs a building. The third floor is designed as a dwelling; the two lower floors as offices. He sells the property to Fred Archer. An apportionment of the consideration must be made: that portion attributable to the supply of the top floor is zero-rated whereas the remainder is standard-rated.

*Protected buildings* The first grant of a major interest in a 'protected building' by the person who has substantially reconstructed it is zero-rated provided that the building is intended solely for use as a dwelling, a number of dwellings or for relevant residential or charitable use (VATA 1994 Sch 8 Group 6 Item 1).

There have been a number of cases on the meaning of substantial reconstruction; HMRC's views are set out in Notice 708/02. The term 'protected buildings' covers listed buildings and certain other scheduled monuments.

Where there has been a zero-rated supply of a building intended for a relevant residential or charitable purpose and within a period of 10 years there is a change of use, the person to whom the zero-rated supply was made is treated as making a taxable supply on which VAT must be accounted for (VATA 1994 Sch 10 para 1).                                                    **[39.24]**

*Construction services* Supplies of construction services are generally standard-rated. However, where a builder provides supplies in the course of the construction of a new dwelling or qualifying residential or charitable build-ing, those works are zero-rated (VATA 1994 Sch 8 Group 5 Item 2 and see *Example 39.6*). In relation to listed buildings falling into one of these categories, building works are zero-rated if what is being carried out is an approved alteration (being, generally, an alteration requiring listed building consent) but not if it is a mere repair: VATA 1994 Sch 8 Group 6 Item 2.

Zero-rating is extended to building materials incorporated in a building (VATA 1994 Sch 8 Group 5 Item 4 and Group 6 Item 3). Input tax on materials incorporated in a building that are not building materials is not recoverable (VAT (Input Tax) Order 1992, SI 1992/3222 art 6).

DIY builders are able to obtain a refund of VAT incurred on goods used in the construction of buildings that would qualify for zero-rating (VATA 1994 s 35).                                                                    **[39.25]**

**EXAMPLE 39.6**

Lucky, a developer, owns Fairacre. He engages Brad, a builder to construct a residence on the land. Brad supplies carpets and fitted bedroom furniture. Subsequently Lucky sells the completed house to Sad.

(1)   Brad will zero rate the construction works (a supply in the course of the construction of the dwelling: Group 5 Item 2). Brad can also zero rate building materials. Lucky cannot reclaim the input tax attributable to the carpets and fitted furniture.

(2)   Lucky makes a zero-rated supply and can reclaim VAT paid in connection with the project (eg professional fees).

4   **Reduced rate: conversions and alterations**

The scope of the reduced rate is dealt with in VAT Information Sheet 03/02. The table below is included as an Annex to that document.

| | Single household dwelling(s) *after* conversion | Multiple occupancy dwellings *after* conversion | Relevant residential purpose building *after* conversion |
|---|---|---|---|
| **Single household dwelling(s)** *before* **conversion** | Normally **standard-rated** unless the number of dwellings changes when **reduced-rated** since 12 May 2001 | **Reduced-rated** since 12 May 2001 | **Reduced-rated** since 12 May 2001 |
| **Multiple occupancy dwelling(s)** *before* **conversion** | **Reduced-rated** since 12 May 2001 | **Standard-rated** | **Reduced-rated** since 12 May 2001 |
| **Relevant residential purpose building** *before* **conversion** | **Reduced-rated** since 12 May 2001 | **Reduced-rated** from 1 June 2002 | **Standard-rated** |
| **Any building not listed above** *before* **conversion, such as a building that has never been lived in** | **Reduced-rated** since 12 May 2001 | **Reduced-rated** from 1 June 2002 | **Reduced-rated** from 1 June 2002 |

[39.26]

## 5   Commercial buildings: the election to waive exemption (or option to tax)

A landowner may, in certain circumstances, convert what would otherwise be an exempt supply into a taxable supply by exercising the option to tax (VATA 1994 Sch 10 paras 2–3).

The consequence of the exercising of the option is that all supplies of the land or building made thereafter by that person (subject to any exercise by the taxpayer of the limited right to revoke) are taxable supplies, save to the extent that they relate to a dwelling or a building intended solely for a relevant residential purpose or relevant charitable purpose, other than an office.

Where one company in a VAT group has exercised the option over a building or land, it affects all other companies in the same group.

The main purpose of electing is to enable a landlord who has incurred input tax on the purchase or refurbishment or reconstruction of a non-residential building to recover that tax against a taxable supply (the grant of a lease or other interest in the land or sale of the freehold) that he makes.
                                                                        **[39.27]**

*What is affected by the option?* The option may be exercised over specified land or buildings, or generally over all land and buildings in the taxpayer's ownership.

Where the option is exercised in relation to part of a building, it will affect the whole. For this purpose, buildings linked internally or by a covered walkway and complexes consisting of a number of units grouped around a fully enclosed concourse are taken to be a single building.          **[39.28]**

### EXAMPLE 39.7

Lex, a property investor, owns a building which has shop premises on the ground floor, offices on the two floors above and a residential suite on the top floor. He exercises the option to tax. The consequence will be that all rents received thereafter in relation to the ground, first and second floors will be taxable, but the rent attributable to the residential suite will continue to be exempt. The rents will have to be apportioned to calculate the VAT liability.

*Mechanics of exercise* In a case where the taxpayer has not previously made any exempt supplies of the land or building concerned, consent of Customs is not required to its exercise and the taxpayer must merely notify Customs in writing of the exercise within 30 days thereafter. Notification can be done by way of a form VAT 1641 (new form introduced in March 2006). Where, however, the taxpayer has previously made exempt supplies of the land or buildings concerned then, from 1 January 1992, he will need prior consent from Customs to exercise the option (before that date no consent was required). Customs will only consent to the exercise the option to tax if they are satisfied that there will be a fair and reasonable attribution of input tax. Notification must be given to Customs of the exercise of the option within 30 days of exercise. It is important to note that the option to tax must be exercised after the consent is received.                          **[39.29]**

*Revocation* Prior to 1 March 1995, the option to tax was irrevocable. Since that date the taxpayer may (with the written consent of Customs) cancel the exercise of the option within three months of exercise provided that no VAT has in the meantime become payable or input tax been reclaimed as a result of its exercise and provided also that in the intervening period the land concerned has not been included in a transfer of a business as a going concern. Further, the option may be revoked (again with the written consent of Customs) once at least 20 years have elapsed since its exercise.     **[39.30]**

*Output tax* Following exercise of the option, the landlord must account for output tax on all supplies, including rent. Even though a tenant need not have been consulted before the landlord opted, nonetheless he will be liable to pay VAT in addition to the contractually agreed rent following exercise of the option *unless* the lease expressly provides that the agreed rent is to be inclusive of any VAT. This is because VATA 1994 s 89(3) provides that the exercise of the option to tax is equivalent to a change in the tax charged on a supply: see **[38.9]**. **[39.31]**

*Can the option be exercised?* FA 1997 s 37 restricts the option to tax in situations where an interest in, or works carried out on land or buildings, are a capital item within the Capital Goods Scheme. It applies where the owner makes a grant and he or the person funding his purchase of the property or any person connected to either intends or expects to occupy the property other than mainly for taxable business purposes. There is a transitional period of three years for grants on terms agreed in writing before 26 November 1996. **[39.32]**

*Should the option be exercised?* Given that the main purpose is to enable input tax to be recovered, if little or no such tax has been or is to be incurred there may be no need to exercise the option. Even if substantial input tax is to be incurred the impact of the exercise of the option on lettings and sales of the property must be considered. Exempt or partially exempt tenants (typically banks; insurance companies; building societies; trade unions; charities; schools; and private health care associations) may be unable to recover the whole of the VAT charged to them and may only be willing to pay a lower rent if VAT is imposed. Alternatively, existing leases may be VAT inclusive so that any VAT may be effectively borne by the grantor of the lease. This will in turn deplete the capital value of the property.

The rules in relation to the option to tax and the disapplication of the option have been the subject of a consultation exercise between HMRC and industry. In the pre-budget report and the December 2005 consultation document, it was stated that the complex option to tax provisions in Sch 10 VATA 1994 will be rewritten 'into language that is clearer and easier to use'. A Treasury Order will be made replacing Sch 10 of VATA 1994 and these changes are expected during the course of 2006. **[39.33]**

**EXAMPLE 39.8**

(1) Lenny purchases the fee simple in a newly constructed office block and intends to grant the Bond St Bank a 99-year lease of the premises in return for a substantial premium.
   (i) Lenny will suffer input VAT on the price paid for the freehold.
   (ii) If Lenny registers for VAT and exercises the option to tax, the Bond St Bank will suffer input VAT on the premium paid and on rent and service charges payable under the lease. As a partly exempt business full VAT recovery will be denied (although non-recoverable VAT will be added to the expenditure for direct tax purposes—potentially getting relief at the applicable corporation tax rate). From Lenny's point of view he is able to reclaim his input tax as he is charging output tax on the taxable grant.
(2) Jake lets a commercial building to the Dead End School. He has not exercised the option since to date he has not incurred substantial input tax. A major refurbishment will soon be necessary, however, and he may then wish to make the election.

The capital goods scheme allows for adjustments to be made to the initial amount of input tax claimed by a taxable person on capital items. The purpose is to reflect the use of capital goods in a business over a period of time ('the adjustment period'). If there is a change in the proportion of taxable use of a capital item during an adjustment period, then an adjustment must be made to the input tax claimed in respect of that item. The scheme applies to capital items with a value of £250,000 (net of VAT) or more; however, the value in respect of computers is £50,000 or more.

The relevant adjustment periods are:

- five intervals for computers;
- five intervals for an interest in land, buildings or civil engineering works that have less than 10 years to run when acquired; and
- 10 intervals for all other capital items.

The first interval is the period from the date of purchase of the capital item (or the date of first use if this is more relevant) to the day before the start of the next partial exemption tax year (eg the partial exemption year starts on 1 April 2006, a capital item is purchased on 5 August 2005, the first interval is the period from 5 August 2005 to 31 March 2006). If there is no change in use between the first and second interval, and the length of the two intervals together is less than 12 months, then the two intervals are rolled together and treated as the first interval. All subsequent intervals are normally in line with the partial exemption year.

### EXAMPLE 39.9—INPUT TAX ON CAPITAL GOODS

R & L Finance are a firm specialising in the provision of financial advice and investment products. They are VAT registered and their VAT year ends on 30 April.

(a)   On 10 July 1998 R & L took possession of a new office block. The purchase price was £1,000,000 plus VAT of £175,000. On the same day a mainframe computer was installed in the offices at a cost of £200,000 plus VAT of £35,000.

The offices and computer are both used by all aspects of the business and the agreed exempt proportion as at 10 July 1998 is 60%. Subsequently the 1999 annual partial exemption adjustment revised the exempt proportion to 65%.

(b)   The 2000 annual partial exemption adjustment revises the exempt proportion to 75%.

(c)   Due to expansion, on 1 January 2001 the business divides its activities into two parts. The taxation advice remains in the office block acquired in July 1998, and the sales of insurance etc are administered wholly from premises owned prior to July 1998. The computer remains in the new building and from that date is only used for taxation matters. The 2001 annual partial exemption adjustment gives an exempt proportion of 67%.

(d)   In January 2001 the firm received an offer from a Building Society to purchase its new office building, including the computer, for £2,000,000 for the building plus £1,000 for the computer, both figures exclusive of any VAT.

### R & L — purchase and sale of office building and computer

(a)   *10 July 1998 — VAT input tax recoverable*

| | £ | £ |
|---|---|---|
| Building — input tax Adjustment period — 10 intervals ie to 30.4.08 | 175,000 | |
| Computer — input tax Adjustment period — 5 intervals ie to 30.4.03 | 35,000 | |
| Recovery percentage (100 − 60) × 40% | 210,000 | £84,000 |

This claim should be included in the quarterly VAT return to 31.7.98.

1998 annual partial exemption adjustment

|  | £ |
|---|---|
| Revised recovery percentage (100 − 65) 35% × 210,000 | 73,500 |
| Original recovery | 84,000 |
| Payable on quarterly VAT return to 31.7.99 | £(10,500) |

(b)  *2000 annual capital goods scheme adjustment*

| | |
|---|---|
| First year recovery percentage (as adjusted) | 35% |
| 2000 recovery percentage (100 − 75) | 25% |
| Adjustment percentage | − 10% |

|  | £ |
|---|---|
|  | (1,750) |

$$\text{Buildings}\frac{175,000}{10\text{years}} \times (10\%)$$

|  | (700) |
|---|---|

$$\text{Computer}\frac{35,000}{5}\text{years} \times (10\%)$$

| Payable on quarterly VAT return to 31.10.2000 | £(2,450) |
|---|---|

(c)  *2001 annual capital goods scheme adjustment*
    Building and computer are in 33% taxable use from 1.5.2000 to 31.12.2000 = 245 days, and in 100% taxable use from 1.1.00 to 30.4.00 = 120 days. The percentage of taxable use for the year as a whole is therefore:

$$\frac{(33\% \times 245) + (100\% \times 120)}{365} = \quad 55.03\%$$

| First year recovery percentage | 35% |
|---|---|
| Adjustment percentage | +20.03% |
|  | 3,505 |

$$\text{Buildings}\frac{175,000}{10\text{years}} \times 20.03\%$$

$$\text{Computer} \frac{35,000}{5 \text{ years}} \times 20.03\%$$

1,402

Amount to be recovered on quarterly VAT return to 31.10.01 £4,907

(d)   *Offer from Building Society*

*Building* —   100% taxable use in 2002 to date of sale
— sale more than three years after completion therefore exempt
— remaining complete years of adjustment period 1.5.02 to 30.4.08 = 6 years

| | |
|---|---:|
| Adjustment percentage up to sale $(100 - 35)\%$ | + 65% |
| Adjustment percentage for remainder of adjustment period $(\text{Nil} - 35)\%$ | − 35% |

£

11,375

$$\text{For 2002:} \frac{175,000}{10} \times 65\%$$

(36,750)

$$\text{On sale:} \frac{175,000}{10} \times (35\%) \times 6 \text{ years}$$

*Computer* —   100% taxable use in 2001 to date of sale
— sale taxable
— remaining complete years of adjustment period 1.5.02 to 30.4.03 = 1 year

Adjustment percentage is $(100 - 35)\% = 65\%$ both for 2002 and for the remaining year of the adjustment period.

4,550

$$\text{For 2002} \frac{35,000}{5} \times 65\%$$

On sale, as above but restricted to output tax payable of $1,000 \times 17.5\%$    175

Amount *payable* on quarterly VAT return to 31.10.02 £(20,650)

| | |
|---|---:|
| Output VAT on sale: | |
| Building (exempt) | – |
| Computer £1,000 at 17.5% | 175 |
| Payable on quarterly VAT return to 31.1.02 | £175 |

**Anti-avoidance**

There have been numerous avoidance strategies that have resulted in countermeasures reflected in the considerable complexity in these rules.

The FA 2004 attempts to counter certain attempts to avoid VAT by use of artificial structures designed either to increase the amount of input tax they can claim or to spread the VAT cost of the purchase or construction over a number of years. The measures came into effect from 18 March 2004. One requires anyone making supplies under a lease (but who did not make the initial grant), to apply the option to tax disapplication test as though they had made a new grant and the other requires the transferor to be satisfied that the transferee has opted to tax. There will now be an additional requirement to tell the transferor whether or not the option they have made will be disapplied as a result of the new changes to paragraph 2 of Schedule 10.

In the recent ECJ cases of *University of Huddersfield* (Case C-223/03), *BUPA Hospitals Limited* (Case C-419/02) and *Halifax plc* (Case C-255/02), the ECJ decided that, while artificial avoidance transactions can be made in the course of an economic activity, they do not give rise to a VAT advantage, because the European law principle of abuse of rights prevents this. The principle of abuse of rights can be summarised as applying where:
  (i)  the transactions concerned result in the accrual of a tax advantage, notwithstanding the formal application of VAT law, that would be contrary to the purpose of the Sixth VAT Directive and the domestic legislation implementing it; and
  (ii) it is apparent, after taking into account a number of objective factors, that the essential aim of the transaction is to obtain a tax advantage. The 'essential aim' in this context actually means that the primary aim of the transaction must have been to obtain a tax advantage. Such an aim will not exist when there is some other explanation than the mere attainment of a tax advantage. This is to be determined objectively.
                                                                    **[39.34]**

## 6  The developer's self-supply charge

*Developmental leases* Since 1 January 1992, where the developer who incurs the self-supply charge merely has a lease or licence over the building concerned, he is obliged at the moment when the self-supply charge is incurred to notify his landlord or licensor in writing. From that date, the lease or licence is converted into what is known as a developmental lease or licence (VATA 1994 Sch 9 Group 1 Note (7)). The consequence of this is that the landlord must thereafter charge VAT on part of the rents payable. This is a most unusual provision which means that a supply made by the landlord which would otherwise be exempt becomes taxable as a result of an act, not of the landlord, but of the tenant. The tenancy will continue to be a developmental lease until it expires or is otherwise terminated.          **[39.35]–[39.36]**

## 7  Application of the transfer of a business rules (TOGC)

At first sight, one would not expect that the simple sale of a building would be treated as a transfer of a business, or part of a business, as a going concern.

However, the exploitation of property by the receiving of rental income amounts to a business for VAT, and so the sale of a let or partially let building could be treated as a transfer of part of that business as a going concern.

HMRC's view is that a sale of a let building subject to existing leases can be a transfer of part of a business as a going concern. Under the provisions of the VAT (Special Provisions) Order 1995, SI 1995/1268, it is necessary, where the sale of the building would otherwise be a taxable supply (because it is the freehold sale of a new commercial building or it is the sale of a commercial building in relation to which the vendor has exercised the option to tax), that not merely is the transferee registered for VAT (assuming that the vendor was a taxable person) but that he has, prior to the date of transfer, exercised the option to tax the building and notified Customs of this. Note the impact of the Capital Goods Scheme when a building is purchased under the transfer of business rules: *Example 38.10.*

Particular care needs to be taken when a property is sold via a nominee or by way of a sub-sale. As regards nominee purchases Customs will accept the sale is a TOGC provided the nominee is acting as a disclosed agent and the nominee, beneficial purchaser and vendor sign a declaration.

Following a referral to the European Court of Justice, it has been held that the input tax attributable to the transfer of a business as a going concern is entirely deductible where the assets are those of a business making only taxable supplies (such as when the option to tax has been exercised) (see *Abbey National plc v C & E Comrs* (Case C-408/98)).

Perceived abuse of the TOGC rules to enable input tax recovery to be indirectly provided to a non-taxable business has led to a further layer of complexity. There is now, with effect from 18 March 2004, an additional requirement to tell the transferor whether or not the option they have made will be disapplied as a result of the new changes to paragraph 2 of Schedule 10.                                                                                     [39.37]

## 8   Builders and contractors

The activities of builders and contractors, however, may be conveniently split into—
(1)   Work related to the construction of buildings for:
    (a)   use as dwellings;
    (b)   relevant residential use; or
    (c)   relevant charitable use.
(2)   Civil engineering work for the development of a permanent park for residential caravans.
(3)   Services in the course of an approved alteration to a protected building.
(4)   Construction of other buildings and civil engineering works (generally commercial construction).
(5)   The supply of materials and fittings in connection with the work in (1)–(4) above.

The activities under (1)–(3) are zero-rated, those under (4) are standard-rated whilst the liability of items under (5) generally follows the liability of the works.

'Relevant residential purpose' is use as one of the following:
(1)   a children's home;

(2)   a home providing residential accommodation with personal care for persons in need of personal care by reason of old age, disablement, past or present dependence on alcohol or drugs, or past or present mental disorder;

(3)   a hospice;

(4)   residential accommodation for students or schoolchildren;

(5)   residential accommodation for members of the armed forces;

(6)   a monastery, nunnery or similar establishment; or

(7)   an institution which is the sole or main residence of at least 90% of its residents.

Hospitals, prisons or similar institutions and hotels, inns or similar establishments are not regarded as being used for relevant residential purposes.

'Relevant charitable purpose' means use by a charity other than in the course or furtherance of a business. A building to be used by a charity as, eg, a church would qualify under this relief.

Where the supply of only part of a building qualifies for zero-rating, eg a shop with a flat over it, it is necessary to apportion the value of the supply between the zero-rated and other parts.                                **[39.38]**

### a)   *Soft landscaping*

As regards new buildings for charitable or domestic use, Customs accept that planting as well as just turfing can be eligible for zero-rating. Zero-rating can apply to both the labour element and the plants themselves. The soft landscaping must be:

(1)   done at the same time or immediately after the construction;

(2)   part of the planned construction;

(3)   shown on the landscaping scheme approved by the local authority.

**[39.39]**

### b)   *Supply of materials and fittings*

Information Sheet (December 2000) contains HMRC's policy on the VAT recovery for businesses developing or constructing a building, and describes when VAT incurred on materials used in the construction of new buildings is non-deductible. The rules for 'blocking' VAT incurred will apply to goods used in showhouses in the same way as for other houses on the development.

The supply of materials and builders' hardware ordinarily installed in conjunction with zero-rated construction services is zero-rated provided that it is supplied to the recipient of the building services. There has been considerable amount of litigation regarding wardrobes, cupboards etc and HMRC's guidance on these is now reasonably comprehensive. HMRC accept as qualifying, the following:

(a)   airing cupboards, under stair storage cupboards, cloaks/vestibule cupboards, larders, closets and other similar basic storage facilities which are formed by becoming part of the fabric of the building;

(b)   items which provide storage capacity as an incidental result of their primary function. Such items include shelves formed as a result of constructing simple box work over pipes, and basin supports which contain a simple cupboard beneath the basin; and simple bedroom wardrobes installed on their own with the characteristics outlined below.

The guidance provided by HMRC states: 'Other bedroom wardrobes, however fitted, are standard-rated as furniture; as are simple bedroom wardrobes which are installed as part of a larger installation of furniture in the room—typically as part of a matching range. The wardrobe encloses a space bordered by the walls, ceiling and floor. Units whose design includes, for example, an element to bridge over a bed or create a dressing table are standard-rated. The sides and back would be formed by using three walls of the room or two walls and a stub wall. For these purposes, the wardrobe could be fitted across the whole of the end of a room. The installation of a cupboard in the corner of a room where one side is a closing end panel is standard-rated. On opening the wardrobe you should see the walls of the building. These would normally be either bare or painted plaster. Wardrobes which contain internal panelling, typically as part of a modular or carcass system, are standard-rated. The wardrobe should feature no more than a single shelf running the full length of the wardrobe, a rail for hanging clothes and a closing door or doors. Wardrobes with internal divisions, drawers, shoe racks or other features are standard-rated'.

The following are generally recognised by HMRC as builders' hardware ordinarily installed in dwellings or other relevant buildings so as to qualify for zero-rating:

(1) window frames and glazing;
(2) doors;
(3) 'built in' wardrobes, where these are constructed on site and use at least two walls from the building as an integral part of their structure;
(4) letter boxes;
(5) fireplaces and surrounds;
(6) guttering;
(7) power points (including combination shaver points/lights but not light bulbs or tubes);
(8) outside lights (provided they are standard fittings but not light bulbs or tubes);
(9) immersion heaters, boilers, hot and cold water tanks;
(10) radiators;
(11) built-in heating appliances;
(12) burglar alarms;
(13) fire alarms;
(14) smoke detectors;
(15) air conditioning equipment;
(16) equipment to provide ventilation;
(17) dust extractors;
(18) lifts and hoists;
(19) work surfaces or fitted cupboards in kitchens (including those fitted in utility rooms);
(20) kitchen sinks;
(21) baths;
(22) basins;
(23) vanity units;

(24) lavatory bowls and cisterns;

(25) bidets;

(26) shower units;

(27) fixed towel rails; toilet roller holders; soap dishes etc; 'communal' TV aerials in blocks of flats etc; and

(28) warden call systems.

The following are examples of fixtures in particular buildings used for relevant charitable purposes (but not as dwellings or for relevant residential purposes) which would qualify for zero-rating:

*Schools*

(1) blackboards fixed to or forming part of the walls;

(2) gymnasium wall bars;

(3) name boards;

(4) notice and display boards;

(5) mirrors and barres (in ballet schools).

*Churches*

(1) altars;

(2) church bells;

(3) organs;

(4) fonts;

(5) lecterns;

(6) pulpits;

(7) amplification equipment;

(8) humidifying plant.

*General*

(1) air conditioning;

(2) central heating systems;

(3) lighting systems (excluding non-fixed bulbs and tubes);

(4) fire and burglar alarm systems;

(5) smoke detectors;

(6) blinds and shutters;

(7) mirrors.

Notice 708 details the above items and also sets out those items of fitted furniture which do not rank as builders' hardware ordinarily installed as fixtures. **[39.40]**


c) *Other commercial construction and civil engineering work*

All construction work, unless expressly zero-rated or outside the scope as relating to land situated outside the UK, is standard-rated. The consequence has been an increase in the amount of VAT suffered by businesses unable to recover all input tax, combined with the need to consider the possible use of the election to waive exemption and the effect of the Capital Goods Scheme.

The supply of *demolition services* is normally standard-rated. Where the demolition work is carried out as part of a contract for the construction of a zero-rated building and *carried out prior to first occupation*, the demolition services are zero-rated. Where building services are supplied in the course of construction of a building only part of which will qualify for zero-rating, eg a shop with a flat above, the supply has to be apportioned between the standard- rated and zero-rated elements. This provision applies only where an identifiable part of a building is to be used for a qualifying residential or qualifying charitable purpose.

Non-business charity buildings are often used indiscriminately by charities, sometimes for their non-business activities and sometimes not. Customs have stated that they will ignore indiscriminate business use for non-business charity buildings (or non-qualifying use of a relevant residential building) where it is not expected to exceed 10% of the time the building is normally available for use.                                          **[39.41]**

d)   *Refund of VAT to 'do-it-yourself' house builders*

Normally credit for VAT suffered as input tax is only available to a registered person where it is incurred for the purpose of any business carried on by him. Exceptionally, however, VAT may be reclaimed on goods supplied (or imported) by an individual lawfully building a dwelling house otherwise than for the purpose of a business carried on by him. The goods must be:
(1)   incorporated in the dwelling or its site; and
(2)   such that they would rank for input tax deduction as materials, builders' hardware, sanitary ware or other articles of a kind ordinarily installed by builders as fixtures.

The relief only applied to a house built as new and did not cover the conversion, reconstruction, alteration or enlargement of an existing building prior to 22 April 1994. From that date claims may also be made in relation to the conversion of a non-residential building and residential buildings not used as such since 1 April 1973. Recovery of VAT under these provisions is subject to a number of conditions, eg:
(1)   there must be documentary evidence of completion from the local authority;
(2)   all tax invoices in support of the claim must be attached to the completed VAT forms;
(3)   claims must be made within three months of completion.
For further details see Notice 719.                                          **[39.42]**

e)   *Speculative property developers*

Input tax in relation to speculative property transactions is dealt with by Business Brief 14/2004 (formerly Information Sheet 08/01 withdrawn by Business Brief 14/2004). This broadly requires the expenditure to be allocated to exempt, taxable or residual, with an adjustment being made if necessary.                                          **[39.43]**

## 9   Estate agents

The supply of services provided by an estate agent in arranging the purchase, sale or lease of a client's property is standard rated if the property is situated in the UK or the Isle of Man. Where the property is situated outside the UK or the Isle of Man then the supply will be 'zero-rated': technically outside the scope with input tax credit. The place of supply of services relating to land, and this specifically includes 'services such as are provided by estate agents', is where the land is situated.

The supply by the agent constitutes a single supply of services and it is not possible to break the service down into its constituent parts. Any payment received for expenses incurred when a sale is not made is also a single supply of services and standard-rated.                                      **[39.44]**

Property management

It is common practice for a landlord to appoint a managing agent to manage a property on his behalf, ie collect rents, deal with expenses such as insurance, repairs, porters' wages and so on. Thus tenants, suppliers, etc find themselves dealing with the managing agent rather than the landlord and rent demands and invoices may well be in the agent's name. The services rendered are by the agent and do not follow the liability of the property (*Nell Gwynn House Maintenance Fund Trustees v C & E Comrs* (1999)). However, Customs operate a concession in relation to services that the resident is obliged to accept because the service is supplied to the estate of buildings or blocks of flats as a whole.

This may lead to problems where the landlord has exercised the option to tax a particular property as it is vital that rent demands from the landlord meet the tests for VAT invoices. Customs and Excise have indicated that one of the following invoicing procedures is acceptable to them:

(1)    the landlord invoices the tenant direct; or

(2)    the agent invoices the tenant in his own name and applies the agency procedure in accounting to the landlord. This leaves the agent with the primary liability to account for the output tax on the rent invoices, pending recovery from the landlord; or

(3)    the agent invoices the tenant using the landlord's invoice with only the landlord's name, address and VAT registration number shown on the invoice. The agent's name may also appear on the invoice but only as the person through whom payment should be made. Customs have confirmed that the agent does not have to use the landlord's own blank invoice document but may generate his own invoice provided that it is not on the agent's own letter heading.

Expenses incurred by the agent in looking after the property should be treated as disbursements incurred on behalf of the landlord. The agent's own charges for managing the property will bear tax at the standard rate. **[39.45]**

# 40 Practical application of VAT

*Updated by Sinead Reid, BCL, LLM European Law, Barrister-at-Law, Senior Regulatory Advisor, DLA Piper Rudnick Gray Cary LLP*

## I  INTRODUCTION

The VAT legislation is drawn in general terms so that it can be applied to all types of business, person and supply. The legislation also contains special provisions that either supplement these general rules or derogate from them to meet specific circumstances. Transactions vary too widely in character for a uniform set of rules to apply to them all. A mixture of social, economic, administrative and political pressures have led to many exemptions, reliefs and anti-avoidance provisions which sometimes make it difficult to isolate which rules apply to a particular business activity and how they operate. Some of these special arrangements or Extra Statutory Concessions (ESC) are detailed in leaflets/notices (see Notice 48 for ESC)) and Notice 700/57/02 for certain special administrative arrangements) published by the Commissioners of HM Revenue and Customs ('HMRC'). It is recommended that, in cases of doubt, a written ruling is obtained from HMRC          [**40.1**]

### Analysis of transactions

A particularly important factor to consider is whether the person is accountable. The VAT legislation draws distinctions between different classes of person for a number of purposes, principally registration, business, exemption, zero-rating, special schemes and refund of tax. Separation is carried out according to a number of criteria that differ from one provision to another.

(1) *Legal personality:* largely, but by no means exclusively, concerned with registration.

(2) *Duties:* these are imposed under the legislation and differ according to whether a person is, or is not treated as, a taxable person. A distinction is also drawn between taxable persons according to whether they make taxable supplies, they intend to make taxable supplies or they neither make nor intend to make taxable supplies. This distinction is important in determining whether a trader is liable to register or merely eligible for registration.

(3)   *Capacity:* the legislation draws a distinction between traders who act on their own behalf (as principal) and those who act on someone else's behalf (as agent).

(4)   *Residence:* a number of reliefs depend, in broad terms, on the country where a person is resident (more specifically, by reference to a concept of belonging).

(5)   *Quality:* some reliefs are dependent upon some personal quality, eg as a charity, handicapped person or diplomatic mission.

(6)   *Activity:* some reliefs are dependent upon the supplier carrying out a specific activity.

(7)   *Identity:* some reliefs are given to named persons, eg zero-rating, refund of tax. In other cases, supplies made by a named person may be treated in a specified manner, eg the Post Office.

(8)   *Supplies:* some transactions call for considerable intellectual agility in determining their tax consequences-the classification of supplies between goods and services .                                      **[40.2]–[40.20]**

## II   BUSINESS ACTIVITIES

Specific aspects of a selection of commercial activities are considered below in order to draw attention to the application of some of the principles of VAT. The range and variation in activities are such that this approach can clearly not be comprehensive. The focus is on food and drink, social and welfare, leisure, business services, professional services, government, professional bodies and trade unions and special arrangements. Property transactions are dealt with in the preceding chapter.                                      **[40.21]**

## 1   Food and drink

### a)   *Farmers*

Until the flat rate farmer's scheme (see Notice 700/46/02) was introduced on 1 January 1993, farmers in the UK were not subject to any special regulations for VAT purposes. Thus they were subject to the same provisions regarding registration and accounting for VAT as any other trader; that said, however, farmers having a tax-exclusive turnover of not more than £660,000 a year may wish to take advantage of the simplification offered by the cash accounting option.

The restrictions on the application of the flat rate scheme, which is only available in relation to designated activities and where the farmer would be unable to charge a supplement materially in excess of the amount of the VAT on expenditure that would have been recoverable, makes it relatively unattractive.

Generally, because the larger part, if not the whole, of farmers' outputs are zero-rated, they are entitled to regular repayments of VAT and so may apply to make monthly VAT returns. Some farmers may find this discipline onerous and, notwithstanding the cashflow disadvantage, on application to their local VAT office may opt for quarterly tax returns if they prefer. Once this option has been made, the farmer will be expected to stay with it for at least a year.
                                      **[40.22]**

b)   *Catering*

The supply of food and drink in the course of *catering is* standard-rated. This is further defined to include:
(1)   any supply for consumption on the *premises*; and
(2)   any supply of *hot food* for consumption off the *premises*.
   It is therefore necessary to look closely at the definitions of the words in italics.                                                                         **[40.23]**

*Catering* is not clearly defined in the law. It is intended to cover the supply of food and drink at functions such as sporting events, conferences, exhibitions, wedding receptions, parties and dinner dances. It also includes meals, snacks, cold buffets, etc delivered to a customer, at home, at work or at a social event and preparing and cooking food for parties. It applies not only to complete meals but also to snacks, hot dogs, tea, coffee, etc.                          **[40.24]**

*Premises* includes:
(1)   the whole of any building and the surrounding grounds of eg, an office, factory, etc in which the catering is supplied. Where there is an independently run snack bar within an office block, which is split into a number of separate businesses, or within an institution such as a hospital which has its own premises, it should be possible to regard the snack bar premises as isolated from the remainder of the block, in which case some of the food sold could be zero-rated;
(2)   a totally enclosed ground, eg football ground, sports field, show ground, amusement park, pier or even garden;
(3)   for restaurants, cafes and public houses, the garden area is also regarded as 'premises';
(4)   if the premises are mobile vans, kiosks, etc which are located in public spaces (eg parks and picnic areas), unless suitable amenities are provided in the form of tables, chairs, etc the supply of food is not in the course of catering. It is therefore zero-rated provided the other zero-rating provisions can be satisfied;
(5)   if as a concession, a store or mobile van is operated from another person's premises, eg on a sports ground, the premises are still considered to be the whole area, the supplies are in the course of catering and, therefore, standard-rated.                                              **[40.25]**

*Hot food* means food which, or any part of which, has been heated to enable it to be consumed at a temperature above the ambient air temperature and which is, at the time of supply, above that temperature. If the food has been heated in order to comply with food hygiene regulations then the supply may be zero-rated.
   If there is an ingredient that is cold, eg the roll in the hamburger or hot dog, the whole supply is still standard-rated. Minor items for which there is no charge (eg salt, pepper, mustard, vinegar or sauces) are ignored.
   Where mixed supplies of both standard-rated and zero-rated items are sold, the price may be apportioned to calculate the tax value of each supply. Examples under this heading are baked potatoes with separately packaged coleslaw or salads, or meals consisting of hot and cold dishes supplied in separate containers. For further details see Notice 709/1/02.              **[40.26]**

c)   *Licensed trade*

*Public houses* There are three main categories of public houses (managed, free or tied) and these have different implications for VAT registration and accounting purposes. Tied houses are similar to free houses.          **[40.27]**

*Managed houses* As the name implies these are run by a manager who is an employee of the brewery that actually owns the public house. The retail sales are those of the brewery.

For the sale of beers, wines, spirits and intoxicating liquors the managed house will be VAT registered under the name of the brewery which will account for VAT on the sales.

It is often the case that the managed house also provides a catering service and this is often the private business of the manager and/or his wife. In this situation such catering activities fall to be considered separately for VAT registration purposes and the normal liability rules will apply if the registration limits are exceeded.

A similar position applies if the owner is not a brewery but runs the 'business' through a manager. The owner is then the person liable to be registered for VAT and to account for output tax on the sales.          **[40.28]**

*Free houses* These are public houses which are independently owned by a publican and/or his wife (or let by someone other than a brewery) and consequently have no restriction on where they buy their beers, wines, spirits and soft drinks.

The VAT position is similar to that for a tenanted house in that the licensee and/or his wife are self-employed persons and responsible for the corresponding VAT.          **[40.29]**

*Business splitting* Within the licensed trade a common feature is the separation of the business into retail sales of beers, wines and spirits (wet goods) on the one hand and catering supplies (dry goods) on the other. If it is sought to maintain that separate entities are operating these different aspects, great care must be taken to ensure that it cannot be alleged that they are in fact one business. This could result in the catering activities purported to be carried on by, eg, the wife, which might be below the registration limit, being brought into the husband's wet trade business, so giving rise to an assessment on him for undeclared sales.

If it were maintained that separate entities are operating separate businesses from the same premises, it would be wise to ensure that the following criteria are met in order to refute any suggestion that the activities are one:
(1)   separate bank accounts should be operated for each business and should be in the name of the person carrying on the business;
(2)   any wages and national insurance contributions paid in respect of staff that may be employed in the particular business should be borne by the person carrying on that business;
(3)   for income tax purposes each business should be assessed separately;
(4)   the person carrying on the business should be responsible for all the trading activities;
(5)   the normal day-to-day records should be separately maintained and annual accounts drawn up in the name of each business;

(6) purchase and any sales invoices should be made out in the name of the person who is operating the business;

(7) premises and equipment used by the business should be owned or rented by the person carrying on that business. In the case of a public house, if the registered person (the landlord) supplies any services or goods to the non-registered connected person (the caterer), such as catering equipment or if he rents out any part of the public house, then this consideration must be at market value and, if appropriate, VAT charged thereon.

HMRC has power, in certain circumstances, to make a direction (which cannot be retrospective) that the persons named in the direction shall be treated as a single taxable person carrying on the activities of the business described in the direction. One of the conditions that HMRC must fulfil before they may make a direction is that they must be satisfied that the main reason or one of the main reasons for the persons concerned carrying on the relevant activities in the way they do is the avoidance of a liability to be registered for VAT purposes. If, therefore, a wife or husband and wife in partnership run, say, the catering facilities provided in a public house separately from time husband's VAT-registered business, they should be clear as to the reasons for the separation of the activities and be in a position to demonstrate that the split was not made for VAT avoidance reasons.

**[40.30]**

*HMRC approach* The experience of HMRC over the years has indicated that the licensed trade is an area that requires close attention. This is borne out by the number of tribunal cases that have taken place. Sales are for cash and often difficult to substantiate because of the lack of supporting records (eg till rolls).

However, as there are generally few suppliers, prices are often fixed for long periods and with only one rate of output tax it is not too difficult to attempt to verify the declared takings by marking up the value of the goods purchased to arrive at an expected sales figure.

Before this can be accomplished there are a number of factors that have to be taken into account, and it is extremely worthwhile for landlords to give these careful and continued consideration, as they could have a distinct bearing on the credibility of the figures produced by the commissioners. The factors include the method of storing the beer (barrels, casks, etc), method of cleaning pipes, effect of drawing off loss due to spillage and effect of price reductions (eg happy hours). **[40.31]**

## 2 Social and welfare

### a) *Charities and the voluntary sector*

There is a general presumption that charities and similar non-profit making ventures intended for the benefit of the community, whether broadly or narrowly defined, should be exonerated from all forms of taxation. It is true that for many years charitable bodies have enjoyed a broad (though not total) exemption from income tax, corporation tax and capital gains tax.

It therefore comes as an uncomfortable, and possibly costly, shock to many worthy causes to find that this expected blanket exemption does not include VAT. Customs have issued guidance in Notice 701/1. However, it is not unusual to find that not only may there have been a failure to account for output tax on supplies made by the body concerned but penalties may arise for failure to register and, under the default surcharge, default interest, misdeclaration provisions-the list seems endless. However, this position has been progressively softened over the years since VAT was introduced by providing various reliefs from the tax for charities, either by the exemption or zero-rating of certain supplies made both by and to such bodies. It is important to understand, however, that such reliefs are drawn quite specifically and it is essential that those concerned with running charities clearly understand the scope of the reliefs as they apply (if at all) to their particular operation.

As a matter of practice, a body based in England or Wales will be recognised as a charity if it has been accepted by the Charity Commissioners and entered on their register; this will lead to its acceptance by HMRC as qualifying for the relevant direct tax benefits and as regards VAT. The writ of the Charity Commissioners does not run in Scotland; instead HMRC maintain a register which is intended to achieve the same ends. In theory, a body could exist for charitable purposes without being registered; in practice, such a body is unlikely to be allowed any tax exemptions, and its trustees would be in breach of their statutory duty to register and to file accounts etc, with HMRC. VATA 1994 does not provide a comprehensive definition of the term 'business'; it may be thought inappropriate that the terms 'charity' and 'business' are linked at all. However, a charity's work may constitute *economic activities* that come within the scope of 'business' so as to give rise to a possible liability to VAT. However, there are a number of activities that do not constitute 'business' activities and are therefore outside the scope of VAT, including the following:

(1)   Charges for advertisements in charity brochures, programmes, reports and the like, where these are clearly of a non-commercial nature and where the publication contains a significant proportion of non-commercial advertising from private individuals.

(2)   Flags and badges given in return for donations, but not where they are sold for a specified amount, as this would comprise a supply. By concession, the following are zero-rated when used in connection with collecting monetary donations:
    (a)   certain printed stationery;
    (b)   collection boxes;
    (c)   lapel stickers and similar tokens.

(3)   Religious activities, where fees are collected for the administration of various rites or where offertories are received from the congregation.

(4)   Goods and services supplied for the relief of distress to, eg the elderly, the handicapped, the chronically ill or the poor, gratuitously or consistently below cost.

(5)   Voluntary services provided free of charge where these are in accordance with the objects of the charity.

If the event held by a charity meets the criteria for VAT exemption, then it will automatically qualify for the purposes of exemption from income tax and corporation tax.                                                                    **[40.32]**

*Sponsored walks* The proceeds from most sponsored events are voluntary donations from individuals to the organisers for onward transmission to the charitable or other worthy cause and as such will be outside the scope of VAT. Commercially run events which benefit the organisers may be taxable supplies of services at the standard rate.                                **[40.33]**

### EXAMPLE 40.1 – CHARITY

A charity organises three concerts each year to raise funds. The event falls within the definition of a qualifying event for exemption from VAT. Therefore, all income generated from the events is exempt although much of it, eg admission charges and sponsorship, would normally be standard-rated.

The disadvantage is that VAT on any standard-rated costs of running the event (eg practitioners fees, catering charges) would normally be irrecoverable under the partial exemption rules.

b)   *Education*

The Sixth Directive (art 13A) specifically provides for exemption of a range of services related to education, together with the incidental supply of goods. The exemptions are specifically targeted and other services and the supply of goods may result in an obligation to register and account for VAT. The effect of making exempt supplies is that input tax on expenses may not be recovered. For organisations under local authority control the recovery of VAT will be facilitated through the special arrangements for local authorities. Where a school has opted out of local authority control, recovery of VAT will be restricted and compensation will be provided through the setting of the level of financial assistance.

In summary:
(1)   all fee-paying education supplied by schools, universities and further education colleges is exempt;
(2)   organisations covered by the order are able to exempt sporting and recreational courses and all courses in English as a foreign language;
(3)   exemption for private education is not restricted to one-to-one tuition;
(4)   free education and subsidised courses provided by local authorities are viewed as non-business activities;
(5)   there is an exemption for examination, assessment and similar services closely related to the measurement or maintenance of standards. This is broadly drawn to ensure relief is available for assessment and similar services made under the National Vocational Qualification system.
                                                                          **[40.34]**

*Correspondence courses* Correspondence courses or distance learning courses involve a combination of reading material, oral tuition and performance assessment. The overall supply maybe regarded as a single supply of education or a mixed supply. If the supplier is an eligible body then exemption extends to the supply of goods or services closely related to the provision of education; the supply may be regarded as exempt with the result that recovery of input tax would be restricted. If the supply was accepted as being a mixed supply then it would be partly exempt-education-and partly zero-rated-for the supply of books etc (when provided by an eligible body) or partly standard-rated and partly zero-rated (if supplied by other education providers). Examinations not provided in the course of a business are outside the scope of VAT. See Notice 701/30/02. In the case of *College Estate Management,* the House of Lords restored the Tribunal's decision that the printed materials were not an end in themselves for students and the college was providing, overall, a supply of education.                          **[40.35]**

### EXAMPLE 40.2 – EDUCATION AND BOOKS

(i)   A University sells books to a fee-paying school for use by its pupils. These supplies are exempt as both bodies are eligible and provide exempt education.

(ii)  The same University supplies books to a state comprehensive school. The latter provides free education to its pupils, therefore the books carry their normal zero-rated VAT liability.

c)   *Health*

In the main the provision of health care services is exempt from VAT. This is not exclusively so, however, and care must be taken to ensure that particular services fall within the scope of the exemption. Some services that might be thought to come within the definition of health care are excluded from exemption and are therefore standard-rated. This is largely because exemption is granted by reference to the supplier rather than solely by reference to the service. In Business Brief 05/05, a change in HMRCs' policy is announced concerning the date from which commercial providers of welfare services (such as domiciliary care agencies and independent fostering agencies) are 'state-regulated' and thereby required to exempt their services.

Where taxable (at the standard or zero rate) supplies are made, it is necessary to consider the obligations and opportunities of registering for VAT. The changes to the partial exemption *de minimis* limits from 1 April 1997 would enable full recovery of input tax where it amounts to no more than £625 per month on average. However, the addition of a further condition that exempt input tax must be less than 50% of all input tax has removed the opportunity for unacceptable tax planning.           **[40.36]**

*Supplies by qualified persons* The exemption extends primarily to the services performed by qualified medical personnel whose names appear in certain specified registers (see below) and to the supply of drugs, dressings and similar goods by such persons in connection with their supply of medical services. The exemption is not limited to supplies purely within the National Health Service (NHS) but extends to the private health sector.

The registers concerned are as follows:

(1)   the register of medical practitioners;

(2)   the dentists' register;

(3)   the register of ophthalmic opticians and the register of dispensing opticians;

(4)     any register kept under the Professions Supplementary to Medicine Act 1960 (eg chiropodists, dieticians, etc);

(5)     the register of osteopaths;

(6)     the register of chiropractors;

(7)     the register of qualified nurses, midwives and health visitors;

(8)     any roll of dental auxiliaries; and

(9)     the register of dispensers of hearing aids.

Any supply of professional medical services by a person or by a company which is not registered or enrolled in any of the statutory registers (or roll) mentioned above nevertheless qualifies for exemption when the services are performed or directly supervised by a person who is so registered or enrolled. The services concerned must clearly be within the ambit of the qualification of the person concerned in order to qualify for the exemption, eg acupuncture services provided by a state registered nurse would not be eligible for exemption.

The House of Lords, in the case of *Dr Beynon and Partners*, has held that the personal administration of drugs and appliances by GPs is not a taxable supply of goods, but is part of their VAT-exempt provision of medical treatment.

The exemption does not extend to any registers involving acupuncturists, psychoanalysts, herbalists or masseurs and such services are therefore always standard-rated. The ECJ has held that the exclusion of a particular profession or activity must be capable of objective justification on the grounds of professional qualifications and, thus, on the presumed quality of the services provided (*JE van den Hout – van Eijinsbergen* (C–444–04)).

Further, the exemption does not now apply to goods supplied in connection with medical care. This affects mainly spectacles, contact lenses and hearing aids bought from private hearing aid dispensers, the supply of which is standard-rated (see, however, *C & E Comrs v Leightons Ltd* (1995) although this decision pre-dated the criteria for single/multiple supplies set out by the ECJ in *Card Protection Plan Ltd v C & E Comrs* [1999] STC 270) which held that it was appropriate to apportion the consideration between exempt services and a standard-rated supply of goods). The supply of drugs and medicines on prescription and of appliances designed solely for the chronically sick and disabled is zero-rated. **[40.37]**

*Provision* of *care in hospitals etc* Exemption also applies to the provision of care or medical or surgical treatment and, in connection with it, the supply of any goods, in any hospital or other institution approved, licensed, registered or exempted from registration by any minister or other authority pursuant to a provision of a public general Act of Parliament.

The provision of care or medical or surgical treatment extends to cover such items as accommodation (including accommodation for parents sharing a room in a hospital with their sick children), catering, medical and nursing services and drugs, appliances, etc. HMRC interpret the term 'care' to mean the medical treatment, protection, control and guidance of the individual, provided it involves some personal and continuing contact between the person supplying the service and the patient. It includes the provision of light refreshments 'other than intoxicating liquor' provided to patients in the in-patients wards, the out-patients department or the casualty department of a hospital. It is not essential that the person providing care should be medically qualified. It does not, however, extend to the provision of a trolley telephone service.                                          **[40.38]**

*Pharmacists* The supply of any services by a person registered on the register of pharmaceutical chemists is exempt, but must be distinguished from the goods that might be sold through a chemist's shop. An example of an exempt supply would be a pregnancy test, carried out by the pharmacist, whereas the supply of a pregnancy testing kit would be standard-rated. When supplied by a registered pharmacist the following items are zero-rated:

(1)    drugs and medicines that have been prescribed for the patient by a doctor or dentist; and

(2)    dressings, appliances and chemical reagents, of a type which may be prescribed under the NHS drug tariffs, that have been prescribed for the patient by a doctor.

This applies where the goods are dispensed on the NHS. HMRC are of the view that drugs dispensed against private prescriptions are standard rated (refer VAT Information Sheet 03/2006 *Dispensing Doctors and VAT Registration*). Any supplies that are not supplied under a prescription are not within the zero-rating provision and therefore fall to be standard-rated.

Any supplies of human blood, products derived from human blood that are for therapeutic purposes, and human (including foetal) organs or tissue for diagnostic or therapeutic purposes or medical research are also exempt.

                                                                             **[40.39]**

*Opticians* Registered ophthalmic or dispensing opticians can exempt the supply of their professional services to a patient and also the supply in a hospital of spectacles, contact lenses and other appliances designed to correct or relieve a defect of sight if they are supplied in connection with ophthalmic services. It is important to determine the nature of the supply as HMRC may argue that the supply is a mixed supply, comprising an exempt supply of services and a standard-rated supply of goods, or a single supply of goods (standard-rated) rather than a single exempt supply of services.

                                                                             **[40.40]**

*Nursing agencies* There is an increasing tendency these days to provide nursing care through the auspices of a nursing agency, both within the NHS and in the private sector. The liability of supplies within this area depends upon an overall view of the facts, including the contractual arrangements between the parties concerned and the qualifications of the nursing personnel. Under the Nurses Agencies Act 1957, a nurses agency may only supply registered or enrolled nurses and midwives. The agency may be the agent of either the nurse or the client or, indeed, of both, or it may be acting as the principal. If the agency in fact employs the nursing personnel and is acting as a principal then any services provided are exempt. If acting on an agency basis, then any commissions, fees, etc in respect of arranging and administering the nursing care are standard-rated, while the nurses' services in carrying out the nursing care are exempt.

There is a similar situation in respect of employment agencies providing the services of nursing auxiliaries, except that the scope of the exemption is more limited. Because nursing auxiliaries are not entered on any register within the exemption schedule, their services may only be exempt if provided within the confines of a hospital or other approved institution. Where acting in an agency capacity, the fee or commission received by the agent will always be standard-rated. The nursing auxiliaries' services will be exempt if provided within a hospital, etc and standard-rated if supplied elsewhere (subject to the normal registration limits). If the agency acts as principal then there is a single supply that will be exempt if supplied to a hospital, etc but standard-rated if supplied elsewhere.

It is very important that agencies have a clear understanding of the nature of the various supplies they make and of those made by the nurses or auxiliaries concerned. Contracts or terms of engagement should clearly show if the agent is acting as principal or as agent in order to avoid any disputes with HMRC regarding the liability of the supplies being made. **[40.41]**

*Supplies to handicapped persons* As a further relief from the inherent VAT cost of exemption, certain goods and services supplied for the use of handicapped persons may be zero-rated. For this purpose 'handicapped' means chronically sick or disabled and includes anyone who is:
(1) blind, deaf or dumb or otherwise covered by the definition included in the Chronically Sick and Disabled Persons Act 1970; or
(2) substantially and permanently handicapped by illness, injury or congenital deformity.

It should be noted that the elderly do not fall within this category simply by virtue of age but must fall within one of the definitions above in order to be included. In *C & E Comrs v Help the Aged* (1997) it was held that the term handicapped included those whose health was so impaired on account of old age that they required the use of a wheelchair or walking aid. VATA 1994 Sch 8 Group 15, Notes 4A, 4B, introduced by FA 1997 s 34 with effect from 26 November 1996, were intended to restrict the scope of the zero-rating provisions to 'charities providing personal care or treatment predominantly for the handicapped ... in an institutional or a domiciliary setting'. Transitional relief was available and this was extended by HMRC—detailed in Business Brief 3/05.

The zero-rating provision for both goods and services is in respect of the supply to a handicapped person for domestic or personal use, or to a charity for making available to handicapped persons, by sale or otherwise, for domestic or personal use, of:
(1) medical or surgical appliances designed solely for the relief of a severe abnormality or severe injury;
(2) electrically or mechanically adjustable beds designed for invalids;
(3) commode chairs, commode stools, devices incorporating a bidet jet and warm-air drier and frames or other devices for sitting over or rising from a sanitary appliance;
(4) chairlifts or stairlifts designed for use in connection with invalid wheelchairs;
(5) hoists and lifters designed for use by invalids;
(6) motor vehicles designed or substantially and permanently adapted for the carriage of a person in a wheelchair or on a stretcher and of no more than five other persons;

(7)    equipment and appliances not included in (1)–(6) above designed solely for use by a handicapped person (including installation costs); and

(8)    TENS equipment (transcutaneous electrical nerve stimulators); and

(9)    parts and accessories designed solely for use in or with goods described in (1)–(8) above.

Installation and repair and maintenance costs in relation to any of the above are also zero-rated.

Costs of goods or services used in adapting any goods to suit the condition of a handicapped person can be zero-rated, whether they are supplied direct to that person or to a charity which will subsequently make them available to him. Any service or repair costs incurred later and the supply of goods in connection with such supplies also fall within the zero-rating provisions.

Whilst under normal circumstances any alterations to buildings fall to be standard-rated, exception is made in the case of some specific structural modifications made to facilitate movement by a handicapped person. In the case of a private residence, zero-rating can be applied in providing ramps or the widening of doorways or passages to ease entry and movement generally, and in providing, extending or adapting a bathroom, washroom or lavatory where the alterations are necessary by reason of the person's condition; the provision of specially designed hot water systems in individuals' bedrooms does not qualify as the provision of a 'washroom' for these purposes. It has been held that architect's fees incurred in drawing up plans for eligible alterations do not themselves fall within the zero-rating provision, and it must therefore be concluded that only direct costs involved in the service of constructing ramps, widening doorways, providing bathrooms, etc will be eligible for zero-rating. In another case zero-rating was disallowed with regard to a garage extension which allowed a handicapped person easier access to his car from a wheelchair and also in respect of modifications of kitchen fittings and the installation of remote control gear to open windows. It was held that a detached garage did not constitute part of a person's 'private dwelling', that the adaptation of kitchen fittings did not qualify as the adaptation of 'goods', and that remote control gear to open windows was not equipment designed solely for the use of handicapped persons. The lesson to be learned must be that great care should be taken in considering the detailed provisions before presuming zero-rate entitlement.

A charity can obtain a similar zero-rating provision on services of installing ramps or widening doorways or passages in any building, providing it is for the purpose of facilitating a handicapped person's entry to or movement within the building. Also zero-rated to a charity are supplies in respect of providing, extending or adapting a bathroom, washroom or lavatory for use by handicapped persons in a residential home and the provision of toilet facilities in any charity-run building such as day centres and church or village halls where it is necessary by reason of the condition of the handicapped persons.

Zero-rating is also applicable to both the cost and installation of lifts when installed in a handicapped person's home, or in a permanent or temporary residence or day centre for handicapped persons, where the lift was necessary for moving the handicapped persons between floors.

Alarm systems designed to be capable of operation by handicapped people and which are linked directly to specified persons or to a control centre are also eligible for zero-rating, whether supplied direct or to a charity which makes the system available to the handicapped. Ancillary costs such as fitting and subsequent control centre fees are also entitled to the relief. Alarm systems that do not make direct contact with specified persons or control centres, ie those which just sound a general warning, are excluded from the zero-rating provision.

In certain circumstances, motor vehicles that are leased to handicapped people in receipt of a mobility allowance can be zero-rated. The vehicle must be new, it must be hired for a minimum of three years and it must be provided by a lessor whose business consists 'predominantly of the provision of motor vehicles to such persons'. A further requirement is that the mobility allowance must be used for payment of the hire charge.

In order for a supplier to have authority to zero rate goods or services to handicapped people or charities, certificates must be provided giving declarations as to entitlement. HMRC do not provide set forms for this purpose and the certificates can be provided in whatever form is most convenient. However, there are suggested formats for particular circumstances. **[40.42]**

## 3 Leisure

### a) *Entertainers/performers*

An individual who normally lives abroad but who performs in the UK may come within the scope of VAT in the UK as cultural, artistic, sporting, educational or entertainment services are, since 1 January 1993, considered to be supplied where performed. Accordingly the performer may need to register for VAT in the UK and account for VAT. The extension of the scope of the reverse charge from 1 November 1993 to services regarded as supplied in the UK obliges UK VAT-registered customers to account for the VAT due on services supplied by an overseas supplier (unless the overseas supplier is registered for VAT in the UK). Registering for VAT does not in itself bring the individual within the scope of UK income tax (or corporation tax in the case of a company) as this is determined by different criteria.

It should be noted that performances outside the UK, particularly in other EU countries, may give rise to a liability to register for VAT in that country. In such circumstances it would be necessary to account for VAT (as output tax) on all receipts whilst claiming a refund for VAT suffered on costs, subject to the normal rules of the country concerned. **[40.43]**

*'Nett' acts* It is common practice for some entertainers to contract their services to a single theatrical agent for an agreed period and fee. In such circumstances it is the agent who is acting as principal in making supplies to the venue. On this basis the agent must account, as output tax, for VAT on the full value of the receipt from the venue. From this amount the agent will deduct his commission and any expenses according to the terms of the contract and pass the balance to the artist. This amount represents the output of the entertainer with the consequence that VAT must be accounted for by him accordingly. In such circumstances it is not unusual for the agent

to generate the individual's invoice under a self-billing arrangement. The amount paid over to the entertainer will represent an input to the agent. Further details of Customs' approach are set out in Notice 710/1/91.

Compare this with the situation where an agent introduces an entertainer to a venue for a fee or commission. In this instance the entertainer is the principal in the transaction and will invoice the venue directly. Similarly the agent will invoice the entertainer for his commission.    **[40.44]**

*Testimonials and benefits* In circumstances where a separate committee is set up to organise a benefit function or similar event, the proceeds of which are donated to an individual, the committee may need to consider whether it should be registered for VAT. Whilst the income in the hands of the individual may well not be subject to income tax this will not alter the fact that a supply is being made by the committee for a consideration. Should the taxable turnover in organising such a benefit exceed the registration limits, VAT registration will be mandatory. The turnover is likely to be in the form of admission charges, concession payments, etc. One way in which it might be reduced, so reducing the impact of VAT, would be to make a relatively low charge for admission or for other facilities, with the balance coming from the payer by way of a voluntary donation; however, it is essential that the donation element is genuinely free.    **[40.45]**

b)   *Bloodstock*

The main VAT problem faced by most bloodstock breeders is satisfying HMRC that the activities are not merely a hobby but a business that ought to be registered. If the breeder is already registered on account of other business activities, then the problem becomes one of establishing the right to recover input tax on bloodstock related expenditure within the existing registered business. With effect from 16 March 1993, significant relaxations were introduced to allow such activities to be treated as business (see revised Notice 700/67 (January 2002)). The main changes introduced in 1993 were that VAT registrations should be restricted to owners who have actually obtained sponsorship. Further, sole proprietors can apply 'the scheme' arrangements only to those racehorses in which they own at least a 50% share. Owners holding less than a 50% share in a racehorse must register for VAT as a partnership or club, etc.    **[40.46]**

*Stallion syndicates* A stallion that is to stand at stud may be 'syndicated' so that its ownership is split into (normally) 40 shares. Each share carries the right to 'nominate' a mare each season to be covered by the stallion and this share or the nomination may be sold at anytime. The sale of separate shares constitutes a supply of services and where the individual is a UK-taxable person who is selling in the course of his business, eg a breeder, VAT must be charged at the standard rate. In many cases the owning of a share will be recreational and its disposal will thus not attract VAT. When all the shares are sold as one lot, this is a supply of goods by each shareholder but again the VAT liability depends on the status of the individual. An export of a horse in these circumstances may be zero-rated.

It was agreed with the British Horseracing Board that, from 1 November 2000, sales of additional nominations by stallion syndicates should be treated

as supplies in the course of business. This means that syndicates will be liable to register and account for VAT if they exceed the VAT registration threshold.
**[40.47]**

*Racehorse syndicates* The rules about ownership of shares in a racehorse differ from those relating to stallion syndicates but the VAT principles are similar. Again the syndicate is not a 'person' for VAT and the liability of the sale of shares will depend on the status of the shareholder. A person will not be registrable on account of his share sales unless, exceptionally, he deals in them by way of business. **[40.48]**

*Nominations* Where a stallion nomination is sold this will constitute a supply of services and where the supplier is a taxable person making the supply in the course or furtherance of that business, VAT must be charged. Normally the rate applicable will be standard-rated but the zero rate will apply where:
(1)  the stallion stands outside the UK but the supplier belongs in the UK; or
(2)  the stallion stands in the UK and the mare nominated is owned by a person belonging abroad. The mare must have been acquired or imported for the sole purpose of being covered by the stallion and must be subsequently exported at the end of the breeding season following its importation or purchase. **[40.49]**

c)  *Clubs, associations and societies*

Clubs and similar associations generally fall into two main categories: those run by proprietors for the purpose of making commercial profits and those which are non-profit making, where any surplus is ploughed back for the benefit of club members. Though some clubs will have unique features, there are many facilities which are common to the majority, eg bars, catering, gaming machines, etc. Except where indicated, the VAT treatment is the same whatever the type of club.

Profit or gain is not an essential element of the concept of business. Furthermore the following are specifically treated as the carrying on of a business:
(1)  the provision by a club, association or organisation (for a subscription or other consideration) of the facilities or advantages available to its members; and
(2)  the admission for a consideration of persons to any premises.

What constitutes a club, association or organisation should be a matter of fact as determined by its constitution.

Because the provision of membership benefits is always treated as business activities for VAT, club-type organisations are subject to the normal rules about registration. Those with corporate status will be registered in the name of the company, whilst unincorporated bodies will be registered in the name of the club.

*Guidance and Memorandum of Understanding (MoU) with CIPFA*

A long-standing Memorandum of Understanding (MoU) between HMRC and the Chartered Institute of Public Finance and Accountancy (CIPFA) sets out the various scenarios relating to the provision of leisure services and their VAT consequences. It explains that VAT treatment generally depends on the circumstances in which the payments are made: in some cases they are simply grants and therefore outside the scope, whilst in others they are considera- tion for a supply. In the joined appeals of *Edinburgh Leisure, South Lanarkshire Leisure and Renfrewshire Leisure—EDN* 03/22, 03/29 and 03/30, the appellants were non-profit-making leisure trusts established by local authorities to take over the provision of leisure. It was agreed that the local authority would pay an amount to the leisure trust to cover any shortfall between operating costs and actual income. The issue related to the determination of the VAT status of that payment. The Tribunal decided that the payment was consideration for a supply as it was the local authority's statutory obligation to ensure that there was adequate provision of leisure facilities for inhabitants of their area; but also, it was the local authority's duty to ensure adequate facilities were available for people who cannot, for social and economic reasons, make use of facilities supplied for profit which as a result are costly.

HMRC are not appealing this decision but, in Business Brief 01/05, they have stated that in all cases the terms of the payment and the direct benefit received by the funding body must be considered.                [40.50]

*Bodies outside the scope of VAT* A body with objects in the public domain and of a political, religious, philanthropic, philosophical or patriotic nature is not treated as carrying on a 'business' for VAT purposes, so that its subscriptions are not subject to tax. A necessary condition is that subscriptions should not carry any benefit other than the right to receive accounts and to vote at meetings.

Subscriptions to charitable associations may be outside the scope of VAT to the extent that they provide benefits to the general public. Benefits for members other than the rights to receive annual accounts, to receive reports on activities and to vote at meetings are taxable.

Genuine donations, which are entirely voluntary and at the donor's discretion as to amount and timing and which secure no benefit for the donor, are also outside the scope of VAT.

Occasionally, a subscription obtains benefits that are also available to non-members but at a lower price, in which case only that part which represents an exclusive benefit to the member is taxable; the rest is outside the scope. In these circumstances it is wise to agree an apportionment with the local VAT office to avoid future difficulties. This is particularly important where input tax is restricted on account of 'non-business' activities, as input tax recovery may also be increased.                [40.51]

*Loans and levies* Any reduction or waiver of subscription as a result of the making of a voluntary loan is taxable at the standard rate, ie VAT must still be accounted for on the full subscription rate. Compulsory interest-free loans amount to additional fees for the supply of benefits by the club and VAT must be accounted for (usually at the time when subscriptions are due) on the value of these loans to the club (*Exeter Golf and Country Club Ltd v C & E Comrs* (1981)). This value is taken to be the notional interest the club would have incurred had it borrowed in the open market, ie normally base lending rate. If the loan is to a third party, but is still a condition of membership, the club is again liable to VAT as above. This ensures that the club does not avoid tax by arranging an indirect benefit, eg with a supplier or an associate. Levies are non-returnable payments and are regarded as additional subscriptions for the facilities provided by the club. As such, they will follow the liability of the subscription-normally standard-rated. 'Shares' or 'debentures' in clubs, where their purchase is compulsory or where reduced subscriptions are available if they are taken up, are not true securities, but are regarded as levies or interest-free loans depending on whether or not the amounts paid are refundable, as described above. The precise arrangements will need to be examined as, if there is a genuine share issue, the consideration for those shares may need to be closely scrutinised to determine whether any part of it relates to any membership facility that may be available to shareholders.

**[40.52]**

*Non-profit making activities* Reference has been made to making supplies 'otherwise than for profit'. This phrase has been tested in the courts where it has been made clear that a body which was not permitted by its constitution to distribute any part of its income or property to its members, but nevertheless budgeted for a surplus from an educational establishment operated by it with the intention of using that surplus to maintain and improve the quality of the establishment's facilities, was *not* profit making so far as those particular activities were concerned. Its supply was therefore held to be exempt from VAT *(C & E Comrs v Bell Concord Educational Trust Ltd* (1989)). HMRC clarified its position in relation to supplies of education and welfare following that decision. HMRC accept that supplies are made 'otherwise than for profit' if they are made by non-profit making organisations in circumstances where any surpluses are applied solely to the furtherance of the educational or welfare activity which generated the surplus. Where, however, such an organisation carries on more than one activity, eg the provision of education and the promotion of some other cause, and some surpluses arising from the educational activity are applied towards the benefit of the other activity, the education would not be regarded as being supplied otherwise than for profit. A similar view is taken where surpluses arising from the supply of a welfare activity are not applied to the general area of welfare (even though the other activities maybe charitable), so that the original supply would not be accepted as being otherwise than for profit.     **[40.53]**

*Sports* Sporting services supplied by non-profit making sports bodies and local authorities have been exempt under the Sixth Directive, Art 13.1(m) since 1 January 1990. A tightening of these provisions (with effect from 1 January 2000) was felt necessary due to provocative tax planning arrangements under which profit was extracted by way of remuneration and other tax efficient payments. Exemption applies to services closely linked and essential to sport or physical education where it is supplied by a non-profit making body to an individual, except where the body operates a membership scheme and the supply is to a non-member. The club will qualify for exemption *only* if:
(1)   it is non-profit making;

(2)   its constitution does not allow it to distribute any profits or surpluses it makes *other than* to:
   (a)   another non-profit making club, or
   (b)   the members on its winding up or dissolution;
(3)   it actually uses all profits or surpluses from its playing activities to maintain or improve the related facilities or for the purposes of a non-profit making body; *and*
(4)   it is not subject to 'commercial influence'.

A club is subject to commercial influence, if, at the time of the sports supply (eg the due date for playing subscriptions or other charges to members), over the 'relevant period' (the 'relevant period' is the three years, or the period from 14 January 1999 if shorter, leading up to the time of the sports supply), the club has:
(1)   paid a salary calculated by reference to its profits or gross income to anyone who was an officer or a shadow officer of the club (or was connected with such an officer); or
(2)   purchased certain goods or services (called 'relevant supplies') from anyone who was—
   (a)   an officer or a shadow officer of the club;
   (b)   acting as an intermediary between the club and the officer; or
   (c)   connected with any such person.

Included in the exemption are:
(1)   membership subscription of playing members;
(2)   subscriptions to sports governing bodies for sporting services;
(3)   hiring of equipment and facilities to members.

The sports that qualify are those that are on the Sports Council's list of recognised sports.

Affiliation fees charged by the golfing unions and County Associations and those charged by the governing bodies qualify for exemption. HMRC have agreed that commercial clubs are able to treat the fees as a disbursement for VAT purposes provided prescribed conditions are met.

Excluded from exemption are:
(1)   membership subscriptions of social and non-playing members;
(2)   subscriptions to sports governing bodies other than by individuals and where the service provided does not require active participation by an individual, eg priority right to purchase tickets;
(3)   temporary membership fees and charges to non-members;
(4)   transport, catering or accommodation.

Exemption is available for fund-raising events organised by non-profit making sports bodies exclusively for their own benefit.                    **[40.54]**

*Subscriptions, donations and fund raising* Members' subscriptions to a charity are outside the scope of VAT, provided that the members do not thereby receive any personal benefit or facility apart from the right to attend meetings and to receive periodic reports and accounts. Any additional benefit provided to members could result in the whole subscription being treated as a taxable supply. However, where members receive zero-rated materials, such as a journal or handbook, or exempt services, eg the making of arrangements for the provision of insurance, it should be possible to agree an apportionment of the subscription between standard-rated, zero-rated and exempt elements (*C & E Comrs v Automobile Association* (1974)). This case was distinguished in *British Sky Broadcasting plc* [1999] VATDR 283, As a general proposition, voluntary donations to charity, provided that no specific benefit is provided (other than, say, a flag or a badge), are outside the scope of VAT. This includes contributions made under a deed of covenant which provides income or corporation tax benefits to both donor and recipient. Where a fund-raising event is not covered by the exemption described above, admission charges will be standard-rated. However, where there is a set admission charge but those attending are invited to add a donation at their discretion, this will be recognised as a donation and so is not subject to VAT. However it is essential that any such additional contribution is not in any way a compulsory charge and the use of the correct wording on the tickets and any promotional material is absolutely vital (*C & E Comrs v Tron Theatre Ltd* (1994)). A relaxation has been announced in relation to affinity cards that are operated by some of the credit card companies for the benefit of various charities.                                                   **[40.55]**

*Participation and match fees* Charges for playing games and sports, such as court and green fees, are standard-rated. This includes match fees levied to offset overheads incurred, eg travelling expenses. The value for VAT is the gross receipts before payments of any kind (including commission to club professionals). Payments for snooker tables, squash courts, tennis courts, etc, which are illuminated by coin operated switches, or where extra charges are made for floodlighting, are also standard-rated as charges for the provision of sports facilities, and not regarded as the supply of electricity.

Payments for the right to enter a sporting competition are generally standard-rated unless:

(1)   the whole of the money is returned as prizes (money, goods, trophies); or

(2)   the sporting competition is organised by a non-profit making body established for the purpose of sport or physical recreation;

in which case the supply is exempt. However, if the fee entitles a competitor to gain admission or use facilities for which a charge is normally made on non-competition days the whole amount is standard-rated. This restriction does not apply if the competition is run on some other organisation's ground and it is that body which normally makes charges for admission or the use of facilities when there is no competition. Cash prizes and the award of cups and other trophies that remain the property of the club are outside the scope of VAT. Goods given as prizes or as presentations to officials or visitors will not give rise to any output tax if the cost to the donor is not more than £15; if it is more than that amount there may be liability to account for output tax on that cost unless it can be argued that the supply of the trophies is an incidental element in the overall supply-that of participating in the ceremony (*C & E Comrs v Professional Footballers Association (Enterprises) Ltd* (1993)). In either case input tax on the goods or trophies given may be reclaimed.
                                                         **[40.56]**

*Amusement and gaming machines* Amusement and gaming machines give rise to a number of VAT issues. The major ones are identifying the VAT supplies involved and how the consideration is calculated as regards supplies arising from the use of the machines. Although most betting and gaming is exempt from VAT, the net takings of gaming machines are liable to VAT at the standard rate. The definition of gaming machines for VAT covers those machines where the element of chance in the game is provided by means of the machine. This has meant that some machines have fallen outside of the scope of VAT by virtue of a remote random number generator where the element of chance was outside the machine and accordingly the income from such machines was treated as exempt.

In order to address the above, pre-budget 2006 it was announced that the VAT definition of 'gaming machine' would be amended to bring it into line with the definition contained in s 235 of the Gambling Act 2005 (although that has yet to be brought into force). The purpose is to ensure that all gaming machines are within the scope of VAT.

The VAT supplies involved in gaming machines are normally:

(1)    a supply of the use of the machine, when it is made available to a player;

(2)    a supply of the hire of the machine, when an owner rents a machine out, either for a fixed rental charge or perhaps, in the case of an amusement machine, for a share of the profit. This charge, however it is calculated, is always standard-rated. Where a guarantee is given that a certain revenue will be received from a machine, any payments made to honour this guarantee are not a consideration for a supply for VAT purposes so that no VAT charge arises;

(3)    when the owner of premises allows a machine to be sited on those premises HMRC used to consider this to be a supply of the right to occupy land so that it was exempt, unless the option to tax had been exercised by the owner.                                                           **[40.57]**

*Bingo* Apart from the exceptions mentioned below, charges for the playing of bingo are exempt. There is, however, a distinction between prize and cash bingo and their treatment for VAT purposes. The value of the exempt outputs is the total amount charged to play bingo less the tax inclusive cost of the goods given as prizes. Any cash prizes should also be deducted. No other deductions are allowed. VAT is not charged on goods given as prizes whatever the value: there is no separate supply for VAT purposes. Input tax on prizes is not recoverable as it is attributable to an exempt supply. Vouchers redeemed for goods should be ignored but the tax inclusive cost of the goods should be deducted. This applies also where someone else redeems the voucher and the club pays that person for supplying those goods. Any voucher used to play another game should be included in the value of exempt supplies. Any cash returned to players as prizes is outside the scope of VAT. Under the Gaming Act 1968 s 41 bingo may be played at functions for fund-raising purposes subject to a maximum payment to play and maximum prize values are laid down by law. As such charges are not admission charges, they are exempt.
                                                                          **[40.58]**

*Lotteries* A lottery is a game where prizes are awarded by lot or chance. Examples are raffles and instant bingo games. Competitions involving skill, eg spot-the-ball, are not lotteries. Charges to take part in a lottery are exempt from VAT. The value of this exempt supply is the amount collected on ticket sales less the value of cash prizes or the cost of goods given as prizes. The VAT position is not affected by the rules relating to societies formed for charitable purposes, for sporting or cultural activities or for other non-commercial purposes. It is the society, not the named lottery promoter, which makes the exempt supply. Clubs and societies may operate lotteries through development associations that promote lotteries. In such cases the development association is making exempt supplies and the net proceeds paid over to the society are outside the scope of VAT. This is an important point to note because the society cannot reclaim input tax on expenditure incurred on the lottery: such expenditure can only be an input of the development association. **[40.59]**

*Sponsorship* Moneys received from sponsors, and payments by them to third parties for staging events, as well as the value of any prizes given to competitors who take part under the sponsorship agreement, are all standard-rated. This is because the sponsor or his products, in return for moneys given, will get a degree of exposure. Where, exceptionally, the sponsor receives no benefit for his support, the payment may be treated as a donation, providing the only acknowledgement is a mention in the list of contributors in a programme or annual report. The acknowledgement must not be highlighted in any way so as to constitute an advertisement. **[40.60]**

*Jumble sales* Charges for admission to jumble sales are standard-rated. Sales of goods on the stalls will be subject to the VAT at the appropriate rates, eg standard rate for crockery, zero-rate for books. When the sale is organised by another body and the club merely makes a charge for the site, that is an exempt grant of a licence to occupy land (unless the option to tax has been exercised by the club). **[40.61]**

*Sales of assets* The disposal of surplus club assets is generally a taxable supply and output tax must be accounted for on all sales except motor cars which are sold below their original cost to the organisation. Such sales are frequently overlooked because they are unusual transactions outside the normal system and its records. Often the only evidence is a record of the cash received which may well be analysed in the cash book as 'miscellaneous' income. Failure to charge VAT will result in extra cost to the club unless the purchaser is registered for VAT and is prepared to accept a supplementary invoice for any VAT assessed (there is no reason why he should not if he is fully taxable and it is a business purchase on which VAT is reclaimable). The club may also incur penalties. **[40.62]**

d) *Museums and galleries*

Museums that do not charge for entrance are not 'in business' for VAT purposes, and cannot recover VAT on their costs. For publicly funded bodies this increases the funding requirement. Certain national museums and galleries are to be allowed to recover VAT on their costs when they provide free entry to the public (VAT (Refund of Tax to Museums and Galleries) Order 2001, SI 2001/2879). **[40.63]**

## 4    **Business services**

### a)    *Financial services*

A feature of the growth in financial services over the last few years has been the increasing complexity of the services being provided. Arranging a loan may now, eg, involve one swap arrangement as a safeguard against interest changes and another to minimise the effect of the volatility of foreign exchange rates. Quite apart from deciding whether such transactions are exempt or zero-rated, there are often problems of identifying the supply and consideration and the partial exemption implications. Thus it is necessary to be familiar with many aspects of VAT law if such transactions are to be given the correct VAT treatment; this is particularly so in relation to the outsourcing of services.    **[40.64]**

*Dealings in money* Dealings in money are exempt from VAT. 'Money' in this context includes coins and bank notes denominated in sterling or in any other currency, when supplied as legal tender in financial transactions. The sort of transactions which are regarded as falling within this area include the exchange of one currency for another. Other activities in this context are foreign currency options, forward rate agreements and interest rate swaps involving mutual supplies of services.

The value for VAT purposes of transactions of this type varies. For dealings in currency, following the decision in *First National Bank of Chicago v C & E Comrs* (1998), HMRC accept that where there is no specific consideration for the transaction, the value of the supply is the net result of the transactions over a period of time (ie the net profit), and not the values of the currencies exchanged (*Republic National Bank a/New York v C & E Comrs* (1998)).

The value of a supply of foreign currency options is the premium paid and the value of a supply of forward rate agreements is the full payment made. For interest swaps and currency swaps that are, in effect, mutual supplies of services, the value is whatever money changes hands under the agreement other than the principal sum of the loans.

Dealings in money that are not exempt include:

(1)    Dealings with bank notes or coins supplied as collectors' pieces or investment articles (eg proof coins, Maundy money). Such supplies are taxable at the standard rate of VAT on their full selling price. It should be noted, however, that there is a secondhand scheme for supplies of collectors' pieces.

(2)    Dealings in gold coin whether legal tender or not.

(3)    Issue and reissue of notes by the Bank of England and Scottish and Northern Irish banks payable to the bearer on demand. Such supplies are zero-rated.

(4)    Certain money flows which are not consideration for a VAT supply. Examples are the payment and receipt of dividends, and receipt of pension contributions and the payment of pensions out of a pension fund. This money flow does not create VAT supplies but any VAT incurred in connection with it may not be recoverable.

(5)    The safe carriage and custody of money. These services are chargeable to VAT at the standard rate.    **[40.65]**

*Securities for money* The supply of securities such as the following is exempt from VAT:
(1)   bills of exchange;
(2)   instruments and paper negotiable for cash;
(3)   commercial paper;
(4)   trading paper coupons; and
(5)   local authority and commercial bills.

This exemption also applies to issues of certain bonds, guarantees and other forms of indemnity provided by financial institutions for money which include only a guarantee or indemnity which:
(a)   is secondary to the primary contract; and
(b)   is a contract of security issued by a guarantor or surety obliging him to indemnify a party to the primary contract for any loss arising from the failure or default of the other party to fulfil his obligations under the primary contract.                                                      **[40.66]**

*Making arrangements for and underwriting of shares* To reduce the additional cost of raising capital caused by the partial exemption changes that took effect on 1 April 1987, the making of arrangements for and underwriting of new issues became exempt with effect from that date. With effect from 1 January 1990, following the Eighteenth Directive (Directive (EEC) 89/465), the exemption was extended to cover many stockbroking and underwriting services in the UK. Previously stockbroking services and making arrangements for any sales of securities other than of a new issue was standard-rated.

Advisory services of accountants or lawyers in connection with an issue are standard-rated, but if an accountant, for instance, is wholly responsible for arranging a management buy-out, the supply would be exempt provided that a preponderance of new shares was involved. Equally, if a merchant bank or similar organisation provides a service which is purely advisory, or falls short of making arrangements for an exempt supply, the supply is liable to VAT at the standard rate. Input tax recovery may be available if it can be argued that the buy-out etc is merely an intermediate economic step with no intervening exempt supply.                                                      **[40.67]**

*Loans; deposits and granting credit* The making of loans and the granting of credit are exempt supplies. The value for VAT purposes is the gross interest and/or any other sum received by whoever makes the loan or grants the credit. In common parlance, the exempt supply of a loan or of granting credit is often referred to as the exemption of interest. At the risk of stating the obvious it should always be remembered that it is the interest a business receives which is the consideration for its supply of a loan or credit and not the interest it pays.

Interest received on money deposited with a bank or building society is exempt as the consideration for the supply of an advance. Other examples of transactions that might give rise to exempt interest are budget accounts, customer accounts and credit club schemes.                                   **[40.68]**

*Instalment credit finance* Instalment credit finance covers supplies of credit by way of a hire-purchase agreement, conditional sale agreement or credit sale agreement. Each such agreement involves a supply of goods or services and a supply of credit if a separate charge is made for the credit that is disclosed to the customer. The supply of goods or services is subject to the appropriate rate of VAT, but any supply of credit is exempt. The measure of the value of the supply of credit is the amount of interest received with each payment. If the amount of the charge is not disclosed to the customer then the whole amount is subject to VAT at the rate applicable to the goods or services supplied.

If for administrative reasons, a business would prefer to account for the supply of credit at the same time, as the supply of goods or services, HMRC may be prepared to agree to an arrangement called an accommodation tax point under which this can be done. By this means the credit is treated as supplied as one item at the time of the underlying transaction rather than being spread over the period of credit.                                    **[40.69]**

b)    *Hire purchase and conditional sales*

*Repossession of goods* If goods are supplied to a customer under a hire-purchase or conditional sale agreement, including a reservation of title (Romalpa) agreement, the supplier must account for VAT at the outset. If the goods are subsequently repossessed or they are returned to the supplier, there is not a supply by the customer to the supplier for VAT purposes. For supplies made after 19 March 1997 bad debt relief can be claimed on the unpaid amount.
**[40.70]**

*Transfer of agreements* If a business owning goods which are the subject of a hire-purchase or conditional sale agreement assigns its rights, interest and ownership, the VAT position is as follows:
(1)    where made to a bank or finance company (eg under a block discount arrangement) the transfer is not taxable;
(2)    where made to a dealer (eg under a recourse agreement) the transfer is a single supply of goods and is chargeable with VAT in the normal way.

If a customer transfers his rights and obligations under a hire-purchase or conditional sale agreement, he is making (if he is registered for VAT) a standard-rated supply of services to the recipient. There is no supply for VAT purposes by the owner to the new customer. The original customer must account for VAT on the open market value of his supply, which is:
(1)    the total amount payable by the new customer to the owner to complete the agreement; plus
(2)    any amount received to secure the transfer (if the customer is not registered for VAT and the value of the supply does not require him to be registered, the transfer is not a supply for VAT purposes).    **[40.71]**

c)    *Dealings in securities*

The issue, transfer or receipt of, or any dealing with, any security or secondary security is exempt (please note recent ECJ decision in *Kretztechnik* which is discussed below). These terms are defined as:
(1)    shares, stock, bonds, notes (other than promissory notes), debentures, debenture stock or shares in an oil royalty;
(2)    any document relating to money, in any currency, which has been deposited with the issuer or some other person, being a document

which recognises an obligation to pay a stated amount to bearer or to order, with or without interest, and being a document by the delivery of which, with or without endorsement, the right to receive that stated amount, with or without interest, is transferable;

(3) any bill, note or other obligation of the Treasury or of a Government in any part of the world, being a document by the delivery of which, with or without endorsement, title is transferable, and not being an obligation which is or has been legal tender in any part of the world;

(4) any letter of allotment or rights, any warrant conferring an option to acquire a security included in this item, any renounceable or scrip certificates, rights coupons, coupons representing dividends, or interest on such a security, bond mandates or other documents conferring or containing evidence of title to or rights in respect of such a security; or

(5) units or other documents conferring rights under any trust established for the purpose, or having the effect of providing, for persons having funds available for investment, facilities for the participation by them as beneficiaries under the trust, in any profits or income arising from the acquisition, holding, management or disposal of any property whatsoever.

In contrast with the value of a supply of security for money the value for VAT purposes of a supply of any of these securities is the total consideration for any such supply together with any gross interest derived from the holding of these securities. The receipt of any dividend in respect of any of these securities is outside the scope of VAT.

The European Court of Justice (ECJ) handed down its judgment in the case of *Kretztechnik AG v Finanzamt Linz* (Case C–465/03) on 26 May 2005. Therein, the ECJ ruled that the first issue of shares by a public limited company is not a supply and the VAT incurred on the costs of such an issue is deductible input tax to the extent that the company's outputs are taxable transactions. In Business Brief 21/05, HMRC set out its position on share issues following the above decision. HMRC accept that the issue of shares is not a supply and that the Kretztechnik principles are not affected by the type of company issuing the shares or other types of security, such as bonds, debentures or loan notes, when the purpose of the issue is to raise capital for the issuer's business. Transfers of existing shares remain exempt for VAT purposes. **[40.72]**

d) *Brokerage services*

The intermediary services of mortgage brokers and money brokers in making arrangements for any advance of money or the granting of any credit are exempt unless, after 9 March 1999 and before 1 August 2003, they are performed as part of a supply of the management of credit.

Commission paid by building societies to agents for the introduction of investment business or mortgage transactions and commission paid by finance houses and other institutions to retailers and dealers for the introduction of hire purchase and other credit business is also usually exempt, although if the person receiving the commission does no more than make the introduction, the supply is standard-rated.

Brokerage charges in respect of securities for money are exempt, as (with effect from 1 January 1990) are those in respect of other securities and secondary securities. Any charge made by a broker for advice, investment guidance or similar services is chargeable with VAT at the standard rate unless these services fall within the description of the intermediary services in relation to the making of arrangements for the issue or transfer of shares in which case they are exempt.

Brokerage charges in respect of securities, other than those for money, are out of scope with recovery if they relate to a supply of securities that is itself out of scope under the rules relating to certain types of services exported to persons belonging in countries outside the EU. The effect is that VAT is not chargeable but input tax is recoverable.                                    **[40.73]**

e)   *Treatment of holding companies*

At one stage HMRC argued that VAT incurred by holding companies could not be recovered as the goods and services on which the tax had been charged were not used to make taxable supplies; this was particularly significant in relation to share acquisition costs.

A further attempt was made to adopt a restrictive approach to recovery of input tax by holding companies following the decision of the ECJ, in the case of *Polysar Investments Netherlands BV* (Case C-60/90) that a holding company was not carrying on a business. Only minor changes were made to take effect from 1 October 1993 and the approach therefore continues to be to compute the deduction of input tax on the following basis:

(1)   input tax on supplies to holding companies must be attributed to taxable, exempt or other non-taxable outputs to the greatest possible extent and the normal rules applied;

(2)   any residual input tax which cannot be directly attributed will be accepted as a general overhead of the taxable person (which may be the VAT group of which the holding company is a member);

(3)   the amount of residual input tax which can be recovered will be determined in accordance with the use of the related goods or services.
                                                                        **[40.74]**

f)   *Gold*

Over the years transactions in gold and gold coins have developed a VAT regime of their own. An investment gold scheme has now been introduced. Previously the rule was that supplies and importations were generally liable to VAT at the standard rate. However, some transactions were specifically zero-rated and others were outside the scope. The situation had, in fact, become so complex that it was first necessary to establish the meaning of the more common terms used in relation to trading in gold and gold coins:

(1)   *gold:* this covers all forms of gold bullion and gold coin;

(2)   *allocated:* gold or gold coins are allocated if they are set apart and designated as belonging to or reserved for specific persons or purposes. The supply of allocated gold or gold coins is the supply of goods for VAT purposes. If gold or gold coins are delivered they are, of necessity, allocated;

(3)   *unallocated:* gold and gold coins are unallocated if they remain as an unidentifiable part of a larger stock held by a supplier. The supply of

unallocated gold or gold coins is the supply of a service for VAT purposes. This service is a financial service for the purpose of VATA 1994 Sch 9; and

(4) *central banks:* these include the Bank of England and its counterparts in other countries.

Council Directive (EC) 98/80, 'Special Scheme for Investment Gold', is widely known as the Gold Directive. The scheme relieves supplies of investment gold from VAT and was implemented in all EU Member States on 1 January 2000.

As with shares, the price of gold is published daily. However, currently there is no significant UK market for private investment in gold. One reason for this is that gold is taxable, whereas shares (and most other financial investments) are exempt from VAT. Therefore investors have to pay 17.5% more than the published value of their investments. The special scheme exempts investment gold from VAT with effect from 1 January 2000. It gives traders in investment gold a limited right to input tax deduction in relation to certain costs and gives suppliers the option to charge VAT on their supplies of investment gold in certain circumstances. The scheme also protects the special treatment currently enjoyed by the London Gold Market. An option to tax is allowed when dealing with other taxable traders. Opting to tax means that traders will be able to reclaim all the VAT they incur (subject to the normal rules). In addition, traders in investment gold are able to reclaim the VAT they incur when they purchase or process gold, even if their subsequent supply of investment gold is exempt. As with financial services VAT on other costs and overheads will not be deductible.

The Gold Directive requires all Member States to exempt all supplies, acquisitions and imports of investment gold, allocated and unallocated, which are capable of physical delivery. It also requires Member States to exempt the services of agents where they are acting in the name of their principal.

Investment gold, is gold bars or wafers which are not less than 995 thousandths pure and gold coins which are sold for their bullion value as opposed to their rarity value. The European Commission will produce a list of qualifying gold coins, to be amended annually. Any gold coin included on this list will be regarded as investment gold for the whole period the list is extant.

The Gold Directive also deems that (for VAT purposes) investment gold coins are not coins of numismatic interest. This means that investment gold coins may not be included within the margin scheme.                **[40.75]**

g) *Terminal markets*

Many commodities are dealt with in the UK in commodity or terminal markets. Dealings in these markets are subject to special VAT provisions under which certain supplies of goods and services may be zero-rated.

The transactions in these markets that may be zero-rated are:

(1) Futures transactions in commodities ordinarily dealt with on the relevant market between:
    (a) two members; or
    (b) a market member and a non-member provided the transactions do not lead to a physical delivery of the goods (for this purpose

'delivery' takes place when instructions are given for the goods to be physically removed from the warehouse, vault, etc. If a futures contract leads to delivery, VAT must be accounted for on the basis of the original contract price unless the commodity is outside the UK and Isle of Man).

Since 1 January 1993 problems have arisen as some Member States have stated that transactions by London Metal Exchange members involving goods in warehouses outside the UK give rise to an obligation to register for VAT in the country of the warehouse. This can also apply to other commodities. Most Member States have now confirmed that no VAT should arise, though some are still insisting on registration in order to be able to quote a VAT number and benefit from the relief.

(2)   Actual transactions between two market members which result in the goods being delivered provided that:

   (a)   if the market is the London Metal Exchange, the transaction is between members entitled to deal in the 'ring';

   (b)   if the market is the London Rubber Market, the London Gold Market, the London Silver Market or the London Platinum and Palladium Market, the transaction is between members of the respective market;

   (c)   if the market is the Liverpool Barley Futures Market, the transaction is a sale registered at the Clearing House of the Liverpool Corn Trade Association Ltd;

   (d)   if the market is the London Grain Futures Market, the transaction is a sale registered at the Clearing House of the Grain and Feed Trade Association; or

   (e)   if the market is not any of those listed above, the transaction is a sale registered with the International Commodities Clearing House Ltd.

(3)   The grant of an option exercisable on a future date whether between two market members or a market member and a non-member is zero-rated. When an option is exercised the resulting transaction needs to be considered under (2)(a) or (b) above.

(4)   Brokers' or agents' services. If a person makes arrangements for a commodity transaction as a broker or agent, the supply of his services may be zero-rated if both:

   (a)   he is a member of the relevant market, and

   (b)   the transaction itself is zero-rated under (2)(a), (b) or (c) above.

If the transaction ceases to be zero-rated, eg because of an instruction for 'delivery' between a member and a non-member, then the market member's services as agent or broker become standard-rated.

Where a transaction in commodities does not fall within the scope of the terminal market provisions, the normal VAT rules apply. Examples of transactions not covered by these special provisions are:

(1)   any supply of goods between a market member and a non-member under a futures contract which leads to a physical delivery of goods;

(2)   any supply of goods between two non-members under a futures contract even if it does not lead to a physical delivery of goods;

(3)   any supply of brokers' or agents' services by a non-member; and

(4) any supply of precious metal other than gold, silver, platinum or palladium.

Where business is introduced to a broker for a fee or a share of his commission or brokerage, whatever is received is a consideration for a standard-rated supply of services, even if the broker is a market member who can zero rate his own service. **[40.76]**

h) *Supplies connected with Financial services*

The following supplies connected with financial services are not exempt and attract VAT at the standard rate:
(1) debt collection, credit control and sales ledger accounting services;
(2) equipment leasing;
(3) executor and trustee services and the administration of estates;
(4) investment advisory services by broker managers;
(5) investment, finance and taxation advice;
(6) management consultancy;
(7) merger and takeover advice;
(8) nominee services (unless for acting as a nominal holder of securities);
(9) paying agents' services;
(10) portfolio management;
(11) registrar services;
(12) safe custody services; and
(13) service companies' activities, eg administration, payment of salaries and wages. **[40.77]**

i) *Insurance*

The basic insurance transaction involves a person guaranteeing to make a payment to or otherwise compensate some other person in certain circumstances. It is seen for VAT purposes as a supply by the insurer to the insured, the consideration for which is normally the gross premium. Where the insurer is permitted to carry on insurance business in the UK such supplies are normally exempt from VAT. Certain supplies of insurance may take other liabilities though the only point of importance is whether or not recovery of related input tax is possible.

Insurance supplied by the Export Credits Guarantee Department is generally exempt.

The introduction of an insurance premium tax (IPT) was announced in the 1993 Autumn Budget. The tax is under the care and management of the now HMRC (see Notice IPT 1, March 2002). The tax is based upon the premium written and is due at a standard rate of 5% on contracts of insurance for specified risks and a higher rate of 17.5% for insurance supplied with selected goods and services. The detailed operation of the tax is beyond the scope of this book although many of the concepts and procedures appropriate to VAT have been adapted for the purposes of IPT.

Changes were announced as a result of an appeal case (*Card Protection Plan* (CPP)), which was referred to the ECJ by the House of Lords. CPP, who were not insurers, were able to procure insurance for their customers under a block insurance policy. The ECJ ruled that businesses in such a position should qualify for the exemption. The ECJ also said that the VAT exemption could not be restricted to authorised insurers. Following the ECJ decision, the case was referred back to the House of Lords. As it was directly applicable in the UK, HMRC implemented the ECJ decision and legislative changes were made which came into effect from 1 January 2005. In summary, the VAT exemption is extended to businesses that procure insurance cover under a block policy, under similar circumstances to CPP, or to businesses who provide insurance that have not previously been authorised to do so by the FSA, in addition to authorised insurers.                                    **[40.78]**

*Marine, aviation and transport (MAT)* The VAT liability of MAT insurance is to be generally determined by the country in which the recipient belongs. The place of belonging is to be determined using a set of rules agreed between Customs and the Association of British Insurers, Lloyd's of London, the Institute of London Underwriters and the British Insurance and Investment Association (see details in Notice 701/36/02). Input tax recovery is still available if the insurance covers the export of goods to a non-EU country. The previous concession allowing apportionment on a 50:50 basis for risks partly in and partly out of the EU is available in a modified form. It is now necessary to identify specific exports of goods in order to be able to recover attributable input tax.                                    **[40.79]**

*Reinsurance* Generally the VAT liability of reinsurance is similar to insurance. All classes of reinsurance (including facultative and treaty reinsurance) are exempt if supplied to a ceding company belonging in the EU.        **[40.80]**

*Brokers and other intermediary services* The making of arrangements by insurance brokers and other intermediaries for the provision or renewal of insurance or reinsurance by persons permitted to carry on an insurance business in the UK or by the Export Credits Guarantee Department, may be either exempt or 'zero-rated' (technically outside the scope with credit for related input tax). The identification of the appropriate item may be troublesome, but as 'zero-rating' increases the broker's recovery of input tax the effort can be worthwhile. Services such as market research, product design, valuation or inspection services etc are excluded from exemption.
   The normal VAT liability of the services of making arrangements for the provision of insurance is as follows:
(1)    exempt if the insured belongs in the UK or Isle of Man or elsewhere in the EU;
(2)    'zero-rated' if the insured belongs outside the EU.
   Making arrangements for the supply of insurance that can be clearly identified with journeys involving the carriage of goods liable to VAT as follows:
(1)    exempt if the journey is wholly within the EU and the Isle of Man;
(2)    outside the scope of VAT if the journey is to or from a place outside the EU and the Isle of Man. For fleet, hull and cargo covers, all journeys within the cover must meet this criterion.                                    **[40.81]**

*Claims handling* Claims handling is normally exempt when supplied to an insurer belonging in the UK, outside the scope without recovery if in another EU Member State and with recovery if outside the EU. Input tax recovery is available if the customer belongs outside the EU. However, the term 'handling' is interpreted narrowly by HMRC. It covers claims checking which is necessary to enable final settlement of a claim to be made but does not extend to specialist and professional services such as those of loss adjusters, average adjusters, motor assessors, surveyors and lawyers. However, if such a specialist does act as an agent for an insurer, providing a service of investigation and claims settlement, his services would be exempt or zero-rated', following the underlying insurance.

A 'trade agreement' has been reached in relation to the services provided by loss adjusters, motor assessors and similar experts.

By concession the VAT treatment may follow that of the underlying insurance if the claims handling service is performed by the broker who arranged the original policy.

Expenses incurred in respect of claims are considered by HMRC to relate to the general overheads and thus VAT on these expenses is subject to the partial exemption restriction. The High Court has, however, held that they relate to the insurance supplied and the VAT on the expenses should be directly attributable and thus fully deductible or fully disallowed (*C & E Comrs v Deutsche Ruck UK Reinsurance Co Ltd* (1995)).          **[40.82]**

*Other intermediaries* Where professional advisers such as accountants, solicitors or estate agents provide insurance brokerage, their services are exempt or out of scope with recovery under the same conditions as apply to the services of insurance brokers. It should, however, be borne in mind that this VAT treatment only applies if these businesses provide a comparable service to insurance brokers. Where the services of these businesses amount to no more than an introduction to an insurer or broker, any charge for this service is subject to the standard rate of VAT even if the recipient of the service belongs outside the EU.          **[40.83]**

*Underwriting agencies* The services of a non-Lloyd's underwriting agent are normally regarded as the 'making of arrangements for the provision of insurance', and are exempt or 'zero-rated' subject to the same conditions as apply to the usual services of an insurance broker. As the arrangements for providing insurance through Lloyd's underwriters are unique, and follow a pattern peculiar to Lloyd's, the Commissioners have entered into a special arrangement for determining VAT on this business.          **[40.84]**

*Agreements with trade bodies* A feature of the treatment of insurance and associated activities is the extent to which it is determined by agreement with trade bodies. Some of these agreements are not published and it is therefore important that insurance businesses keep abreast of information on VAT issued by their trade bodies. Other agreements are published in Notice 700/57/02.          **[40.85]**

5  **Professional services**

*Barristers* The normal VAT rules for registration and accounting for VAT apply for barristers. However, there are special rules for determining the tax point of services provided whilst practising and consequent upon ceasing to practise.

A barrister is registered as a sole trader at the chambers where he practises. Registration will need to cover any other business making taxable supplies, eg farming and lecturing.

A barrister is regarded as making supplies of legal services to the instructing solicitor that are generally subject to VAT at the standard rate. The value for VAT on the supply of those services will be determined by reference to the consideration. The consideration will normally be the value of the fee charged by the barrister to the instructing solicitor. If a barrister is instructed by a solicitor who 'belongs' outside the UK, his fees may be zero-rated.

Special rules apply in identifying the time of supply of the services supplied by a barrister (acting in that capacity) so that these are treated as taking place at whichever is the earliest of the following:
(1)    when the fee in respect of those services is received; or
(2)    when the barrister issues a tax invoice in respect of them; or
(3)    when the barrister ceases to practise.

Barristers will not normally issue a tax invoice until receipt of payment of their fee; instead they may be expected to issue a request for payment endorsed 'This is not a tax invoice'. This must *not* contain all the necessary ingredients that would constitute a tax invoice. In particular it must avoid showing the VAT number.

On ceasing to practise the barrister must notify his local VAT office within 30 days of cessation. It is understood that HMRC will allow the payment of VAT on outstanding fees at the time of ceasing to practise to be deferred until such a time as the fees are actually received or a tax invoice is issued, whichever is the earlier, provided that the barrister asks to adopt the special procedures permitted.

Where a barrister dies, the deceased barrister's clerk should notify the local VAT office of the death as soon as possible. The personal representatives should state whether they wish to pay VAT on the barrister's outstanding professional fees forthwith or to defer payment. This should be done within ten days of the grant of probate or letters of administration.    **[40.86]**

*Solicitors* Supplies of legal services are generally chargeable to VAT at the standard rate. Where services are supplied to a person who belongs outside the EU, or to a person in business in another Member State then, subject to exceptions, the place of supply of the service is outside the UK. The supply is thus outside the scope of VAT. The Law Society has issued guidance on the steps to be taken before treating a supply as outside the scope of VAT. Input tax on related expenses is recoverable and the value of the services should still be included in the turnover figures for VAT purposes. Indeed for partial exemption purposes VAT-exclusive values should be recorded if a value based method is used. The only real difference from 1 January 1993 is in relation to the obtaining of EU clients' VAT registration numbers which are regarded as best evidence that the client is in business in another Member State and this should be shown on the solicitor's invoice.    **[40.87]**

*Time of supply of legal services* The rules regarding the tax point for legal services are dependent on whether the supply is a single supply, eg preparation of a will, or a continuous supply, eg trustee work.

Work done over a period to enable a single supply to be made or a series of separate jobs for the same client over a period does not amount to a continuous supply. **[40.88]**

*Single supply* The basic tax point occurs when the supply of services is known to be completed and tax must normally be accounted for at this time.

This will usually be easy enough to determine and it is essentially a question of fact to be decided case by case.

This basic point can only be overridden if either:

(1) a VAT invoice is issued or payment is received before the basic tax point (if the amount invoiced or received constitutes only part of the consideration for the supply, the basic tax point is overridden only to the extent of that part); or

(2) a VAT invoice is issued within 14 days following completion of the service. In such circumstances the actual tax point becomes the date of issue of the VAT invoice or the date payment is received, whichever is the earlier.

The 14-day rule is extended to three months (under an agreement between the Law Society and HMRC) where a fee is not ascertained or ascertainable at or before the time when the services are completed, eg because the solicitor uses the services of an outside cost draftsman. **[40.89]**

*Continuous supply* There is no basic tax point for a continuous supply of services. A tax point occurs when a VAT invoice is issued or payment is received, whichever is the earlier. A typical case is where a regular payment is made on a retainer basis.

It should be noted that once a VAT invoice has been issued the tax shown on the invoice must be accounted for in the VAT return relevant to the VAT period in which the VAT invoice was issued. **[40.90]**

*Payments to solicitors by the Legal Services Commission-time of supply* On 1 January 2000, the Legal Aid Board (now replaced by the Legal Services Commission) introduced new arrangements for certain types of legally funded work, under which solicitors will receive regular monthly payments based on their anticipated level of that work over the coming year. HMRC anticipate that these payments will generally be received in advance of a supply being made to the client. On this basis, the date of receipt is to be regarded as the tax point. VAT will, therefore, be due at that time on the full amount received, unless the solicitor can demonstrate that an element of the payment will not be subject to VAT, eg because it includes non-taxable disbursements. Solicitors who account for VAT on the full amount at the time of receipt, but who subsequently find that an element was not liable to VAT, may adjust the amount of VAT previously accounted for accordingly. **[40.91]**

*Non-contentious business (non-legal aid funding)* If a fee is required to be reviewed by the Law Society under the Solicitors Remuneration Order 1972 the position is that tax remains due under the rules stated above, but if the fee is reduced the solicitor can issue a credit note for the difference and set off the VAT element in that credit note against his output tax for the quarter.

The same procedure applies if instead of, or in addition to, applying for a remuneration certificate a client (or third party entitled to apply) seeks taxation of the bill and it is varied.                                                    **[40.92]**

*Contentious business (non-legal aid funding)* A solicitor's services to his client include the settling of costs by the appointed procedure. Thus the basic tax point does not arise until the bill is agreed with the opposing solicitor or, in cases referred to the court for taxation, the taxation is complete. The normal 14-day, or longer, period follows from these dates for the issue of a VAT invoice by the solicitor preparing the bills. Note that a bill of costs prepared for taxation or for payment out of a fund cannot itself be a VAT invoice.

A *Practice Direction* detailing the VAT consequences of a bill of costs lodged for taxation after 8 February 1994 has been issued.                            **[40.93]**

*Credit notes* Where a VAT credit note is issued in accordance with the procedure recognised by HMRC, the solicitor issuing the credit note should adjust his VAT account to reflect the reduction in tax due. The issue of VAT credit notes can, however, only take place consistently with normal commercial practice. In the context of a solicitor's practice this will include the issue of a VAT credit note following a compulsory reduction in fees and it would also include cases in which fees are reduced voluntarily by agreement with the client in lieu of the latter seeking a remuneration certificate or taxation.
**[40.94]**

*Barristers' services* The services of barristers may be rendered to the instructing solicitor, who then makes an onward supply to the client, or the client directly. A taxpayer is only entitled to recover VAT on expenditure on goods or services supplied to the taxpayer. HMRC accept the practice of redirecting invoices, addressed to the solicitor, to the client where the client pays the bill directly. The invoice addressed to the solicitor, suitably endorsed by the solicitor, is acceptable as adequate documentation to support a claim for input tax credit.                                                              **[40.95]**

*Commission* Where a taxable person receives a commission (usually for arranging insurance or for introducing an investor to a stockbroker) from a third party in connection with making a supply to a client, and the commission must be accounted for to the client, then VAT is chargeable on the net fee. A commission for providing intermediary services (ie acting as an intermediary in arranging finance or for arranging insurance) is exempt.
**[40.96]**

*Disbursements* A solicitor often makes payments on behalf of his client that are the contractual responsibility of that client, eg stamp duty; these may not be subject to VAT. The solicitor should indicate clearly on the VAT invoice that such payments are disbursements in order to avoid having to include the value of such payments in the value of the invoice on which VAT is to be added.

Expenses which a solicitor incurs in order to provide his services to his client, eg air fares, train fares, stationery, postage, etc cannot be treated as disbursements and must be included in the value of the invoice on which VAT is to be added (*Rowe & Maw v C & E Comrs* (1975)).

The Law Society has, following discussions with the Commissioners, issued guidance on the payment of third party costs (and the extent to which the indemnity principle applies and the extent to which the payment constitutes part of the consideration for the supply) and confirmation that the telegraphic transfer fees are not disbursements and must therefore be subject to VAT when passed on to the client. **[40.97]**

## 6  Government

The increase in privatisation and competitive tendering for services that are being contracted out increased the need for central and local Government to be aware of the VAT consequences of transactions. The legislation provides for two types of 'relief'. The first, which applies to local authorities etc, enables the authority to recover input tax related to non-business activities. The second relief operates in a similar fashion by enabling a recovery of input VAT in respect of goods and services acquired otherwise than for the purpose of a business or deemed business if the Treasury so directs. A number of directions have been made and these are published in the *London Gazette*.

As noted, specific provision is made for the Crown and for local authorities and other statutory bodies. Where the goods and services supplied by these bodies would lead to significant distortion of competition then such supplies will result in their being treated as taxable persons. A number of activities are specifically stated to give rise to a need to consider the body as a taxable person unless the scale of activities is negligible:
(1)  telecommunications;
(2)  supply of water, gas, electricity and steam;
(3)  transport of goods;
(4)  port and airport services;
(5)  passenger transport;
(6)  supply of new goods manufactured for sale;
(7)  transactions of agricultural intervention agencies; and
(8)  running of trade fairs and exhibitions.
The classification of activities undertaken is of importance in determining the basis for recovering VAT on expenditure and guidance and has been provided by the Commissioners of Customs and Excise in Notice 749 (April 2002). **[40.98]**

### a)  *Local authorities*

Where a local authority makes any taxable supplies it is required to register for VAT. The special refund scheme is available in respect of VAT on expenditure and care needs to be exercised in order to ensure that it is operated correctly. Failure to do so may lead to penalties. A 'local authority' is defined to mean the council of a county, district, London borough, parish or group of parishes (or in Wales, community or group of communities), the Common Council of the City of London, the Council of the Isles of Scilly, and any joint committee or joint board established by two or more of the foregoing and in relation to Scotland, a regional, islands or district council within the meaning of the Local Government (Scotland) Act 1973, any combination and any joint committee or joint board established by two or more of the foregoing, and any joint board to which s 226 of that Act applies.

A number of detailed changes were announced by HMRC in 2002 dealing with:

(1)   partial exemption limits;
(2)   school trips;
(3)   transport of passengers;
(4)   repairs to private sewers in default;
(5)   sale of goods incidental to education; and
(6)   issue of decorating vouchers to local authority tenants.

Local authority purchasing consortia are not considered to be acting as public bodies. For HMRC's view on supplies of services by local authorities see C&E Manual VI–14.                                      **[40.99]**


b)   *Statutory bodies*

Specified bodies may make a claim to obtain a refund of VAT charged on supplies to them of goods purchased, imported or acquired for non-business purposes. Where the supply is partly for business and partly for non-business, then HMRC may apportion the VAT. There are restrictions on the right of refund in relation to lighthouse authorities and a nominated news provider. The apportionment will only be important where some of the business supplies are exempt and a restriction will be made under the partial exemption rules.

The bodies specified are:

(1)   a local authority;
(2)   a river purification board or a water development board;
(3)   an internal drainage board;
(4)   a passenger transport authority or executive;
(5)   a port health authority, a port local authority or a joint port local authority;
(6)   a police authority and the Receiver for the Metropolitan Police District;
(7)   a development corporation, a new towns commission and the Commission for the New Towns;
(8)   a general lighthouse authority;
(9)   the BBC;
(10)  a nominated news provider (previously ITN); and
(11)  any body specified by Treasury order.

The normal rules apply to statutory bodies so that they may register voluntarily and where supplies made exceed the statutory threshold they will be required to register.

Separate registration is normally required for every 'person' and this may give rise to an obligation on a committee or other body that is separate from but has close links to the body, eg a police authority or a joint committee of two or more bodies. An application may be made for this obligation to be waived if it is wished to account for VAT through the registration of the main body.

The acquisition of goods from a supplier in another Member State may also give rise to an obligation to register.                        **[40.100]**

c) *Refund scheme*

The main objective of the refund scheme is to avoid the movement of funds from one public pocket to another. Only where it is necessary to avoid distortion of competition in the single market is it necessary for VAT to be a commercial consideration. The scheme applies to goods and services supplied direct to the qualifying body. It is therefore necessary for the order to be placed by the body, for VAT invoices to be addressed to it and for payment to be made from its own funds.

Purchases made with trust funds where the local authority acts as sole trustee of funds and the objects of the trust relate closely to the activities of the authority, eg operating a village ball, also qualify for a refund. Relief may also be available for purchases made by the authority for its own purposes with funds given for specific purposes. No refund is generally available for the VAT on the acquisition of motor cars but VAT on entertainment relating to non-business activities is refundable.

Where a claim is made by a registered body, the claim will be made by including the refundable amount in the VAT return. Unregistered bodies may make claims for periods of at least one month and if the amount is less than £100 then the period must be of at least one year. **[40.101]**

d) *Government departments*

The Crown is not excluded from VAT and the normal provisions apply. The Treasury is enabled to make an order that directs that certain supplies made by a Government department, which are similar to supplies made by taxable persons should be treated as supplies in the course or furtherance of a business. Repayment of VAT may be made on expenditure subject to meeting conditions imposed by the Commissioners on record-keeping etc.

A Government department includes a National Health Service trust, a Northern Ireland health and social services body, any body of persons exercising functions on behalf of a Minister of the Crown and any part of such a department designated for this purpose by the Treasury. **[40.102]**

## 7 Professional bodies and trade unions

The dividing line between an 'association' falling within this section and an 'association' falling within the section on clubs and associations above may be narrow.

Often professional organisations operate through branches, chapters or sub-committees and these sub-units may themselves be considered to be separate persons. Where the branches, etc are regarded as part of a single entity there is a need to organise the collection of invoices, etc to ensure that accurate returns may be made so as to avoid potential penalties.

The need to pursue the objectives of the principal body and a need to raise funds often leads to activities which verge on the edge between business and non-business. Fund-raising activities may involve an element of gift which is outside the scope of VAT. The nature of the supply and the detailed documentation needs to be carefully scrutinised to ensure that the correct VAT status is attributed to the transaction.

The provision of facilities and advantages to members of clubs, associations and other such organisations are normally standard-rated but their provision by certain associations are exempt.

Exemption is available to:

(1)   a trade union or other organisation having as its main object the negotiation on behalf of its members of the terms and conditions of their employment;

(2)   professional associations: where membership is broadly restricted to individuals seeking a qualification appropriate to the profession (*Bookmakers Protection Association (Southern Area) Ltd v C & E Comrs* (1979): *City Cabs (Edinburgh) Ltd v C & E Comrs* EDN 79 30);

(3)   an association whose primary purpose is the advancement of a particular branch of knowledge or the fostering of professional expertise. It is essential that membership is restricted to individuals whose present or previous professions or employments are directly connected with the purposes of the association; and

(4)   an association whose primary purpose is to make representations to the Government on legislation and other public matters affecting the business or professional interests of its members. Membership must be restricted to persons whose business or professional interests are directly connected with the purpose of the association.

Exemption under (1)–(4) above is only available to non-profit making organisations and is not available in respect of the consideration for any right to admission to an event to which non-members are admitted for a consideration.

Registration fees, where registration is prescribed by law in order for the person to be able to practise, is outside the scope of VAT. In other cases it is necessary to examine the nature of the fee in order to assess whether it is akin to a membership subscription (exempt) or in return for particular services (generally taxable unless specifically exempted (insurance, finance) or zero rated (books)).

Hospitality provided without charge is standard-rated unless it is part of a function necessary to attain the association's aims, eg a conference. The business entertainment rules would debar a credit for input tax where the expenditure is for entertaining non-members.

Fund-raising events organised exclusively for their own benefit are exempt. A fund-raising event is defined to include fetes, balls, bazaars, gala shows, performances or similar events which are separate from and not forming any part of a series or regular run of like or similar events.

*Organisations of a political, religious, etc nature* Where a body has objects which are in the public domain and are of a political, religious, philanthropic, philosophical or patriotic nature, it is not treated as a carrying on of a business only because its members subscribe to it; providing the subscription provides no facility or advantage other than the right to participate in its management or to receive reports on its activities.   **[40.103]–[40.104]**

## 8  Special arrangements

a)  *Retailers*

The great majority of businesses which deal direct with the public are not required to issue detailed invoices for their sales nor, because they deal very largely for cash, do they need to keep their sales records in the same detail or format as manufacturing or wholesaling businesses would expect to do. They therefore do not have the same discipline of issuing VAT invoices that other businesses have and consequently would find difficulty in determining sales and output tax by conventional means.

HMRC have authority to allow retailers to operate special arrangements for determining the amount of output tax which they have to account for on their retail sales. It should be noted that 'exceptionally' under the relevant regulations, Notice 727 and the accompanying notices dealing with individual schemes do also have legal force.

For this purpose a 'retailer' is anyone, not simply a shopkeeper, who deals primarily with the final consumer. A retailer is regarded as a business that cannot be expected to account for VAT in the normal way on its sales. Such sales are generally of a low value, and are made to a large number of customers; for such businesses it is impractical to issue VAT invoices for all sales. A business making both retail and non-retail sales can use a retail scheme for the retail part of its business. An adjustment may be required where stocks of goods are transferred between the retail part and the non-retail part.                                                            [**40.105**]

*Gross takings* With effect from 1 March 1997, retailers must include in their daily gross takings:
(1)  all payments as they are received for cash sales;
(2)  the value of all sales made for which cash is not received, or where payment is made by other means, eg credit card; and
(3)  any adjustments to the daily gross takings record.            [**40.106**]

*Choosing a retail scheme* It is imperative from a tax planning point of view to choose the correct retail scheme from the outset. The choice of scheme can affect a retailer's cashflow and they have differing record-keeping requirements; the wrong choice can prove expensive.

HMRC have the power to refuse permission to use a scheme (eg if they consider it will not reflect the proper liability) but the retailer does have the right to appeal to a VAT tribunal against such refusal.

HMRC only allow a retrospective change of scheme in exceptional circumstances. In particular, a retailer who uses a scheme for which he is eligible will not be entitled to change his scheme retrospectively on the basis that a lower overall liability would have been achieved. For this reason it is important that great care be taken prior to using a scheme.

With effect from 1 April 1998, all retailers are obliged to use one of the published schemes, or have agreed a bespoke scheme. The turnover limit for compulsory negotiation of a bespoke scheme is £100m pa. The option of agreeing a bespoke scheme will continue to be open to any retailer if the published retail schemes are impracticable or do not produce a fair and reasonable result. Thought must be given to the administrative costs involved in operating a particular scheme, as well as the resulting VAT liability. Notice *727* provides a table of the five standard schemes. Note also that some schemes have certain restrictions, eg whether supplies of services can be included within the scheme.                                              **[40.107]**

*Secondhand goods* VATA 1994 s 50A provides for a margin scheme to operate for the sale of secondhand goods. This means that the calculation of output tax is based on the margin achieved on the goods, rather than on the total price of the goods. The scheme is voluntary, but it does provide for a reduced VAT liability. Certain conditions must be fulfilled.

Where secondhand goods meet certain conditions, in particular those with a purchase price below £500, the retailer may use the global accounting scheme. This enables him to cumulate his sales of secondhand goods, rather than issuing an invoice for each transaction.

Where a retailer makes sales of new and secondhand goods, his records must be sufficient to allow him to analyse sales and purchases accurately.

Detailed amendments were made to Notice 718, Margin schemes for secondhand goods, works of art, antiques and collectors' items, in May 2003.
                                                                      **[40.108]**

### EXAMPLE 40.3 – MARGIN SCHEME

Cost price of relevant item — £2,000 including VAT
  Selling price of relevant item — £2,800 including VAT
  Profit margin = £800 including VAT
  No input tax is claimed. Output tax is £800 × 7/47 = £119.14

### EXAMPLE 40.4 – SECONDHAND CARS

Tracey uses the margin scheme for second-hand car sales and meets all the required conditions for the scheme. In the quarter ended 31 January 2003 (all the amounts being stated inclusive of VAT where appropriate) the transactions are:

|  |  | Purchase Price | Repair Costs | Selling Price |
|---|---|---|---|---|
|  |  | £ | £ | £ |
| Second-hand car | (i) | 900 | 112 | 805 |
| Second-hand car | (ii) | 4,250 | 140 | 5,895 |
| Second-hand car | (iii) | 6,900 | 853 | 7,370 |
| Second-hand van | (iv) | 2,961 | 1,000 | 3,760 |
| Second-hand van | (v) | 4,230 | 480 | 5,875 |
| New car | (vi) | 17,860 | – | 19,975 |
| New car | (vii) | 11,750 | – | –* |
|  |  |  | 2,585 |  |

The second-hand vans were purchased on tax invoices from registered traders. The cars were taken in part exchange from private customers.
    * Used by Tracey personally — list selling price £14,995.
    The VAT consequences:

| *Second-hand car margin scheme* | *Cost* | *Selling Price* | *Margin* |
|---|---|---|---|

|  | £ | £ | £ | £ |
|---|---|---|---|---|
| (i) | 900 | 805 | (Loss) | |
| (ii) | 4,250 | 5,895 | 1,645 | |
| (iii) | 6,900 | 7,370 | 470 | |
| | | 14,070 | 2,115 | × 7/47 = 315 |

*Other outputs:*

| | | £ | |
|---|---|---|---|
| (iv) | Van | 3,760 | |
| (v) | Van | 5,875 | |
| (vi) | New car | 19,975 | |
| (vii) | Self-supply new car | 11,750 | |
| | | 41,360 | × 7/47 = 6,160 |
| | | | 6,475 |

*Inputs*

| | | £ | |
|---|---|---|---|
| Repair costs | | 2,585 | |
| Second-hand cars (i) (ii) and (iii) | | – | |
| Vans | (iv) | 2,961 | |
| | (v) | 4,230 | |
| New | (vi) | 17,860 | |
| cars | (vii) | 11,750 | |
| | | 39,386 | × 7/47 = (5,866) |

VAT payable                                                    £609

*Children's clothes* From 1 April 2001, the rules for determining whether young children's clothing and footwear qualify for relief from VAT were updated and simplified, allowing more children to benefit from zero-rating. Broadly, the articles must therefore be:
(1)   designed for young children (the design test); and
(2)   not suitable for older persons (the suitability test).
    The eve of the fourteenth birthday remains the age limit for a young child for VAT purposes. Details of the changes are contained in VAT Information Sheet 1/01 (March 2001).                                    **[40.109]**

b)   *Tour operators*

The scheme (referred to as the tour operators' margin scheme, or TOMS) came into effect in the UK on 1 April 1988 and has been subject to substantial amendments on a number of occasions. Detailed guidance is provided in Notice 709/6/02.
    At first sight the scheme resembles the secondhand goods schemes. However, one fundamental difference is that whereas the secondhand goods schemes are optional to the dealer, the tour operators' scheme is compulsory for those who are defined as within its scope (except for a *de minimis* exception for incidental supplies).

The essence of the scheme is that a tour operator will not charge output tax on the full value of supplies made by him and will not be able to recover input tax on supplies bought in by him for resale. Instead he will be required to account for output tax on the 'margin', ie the difference between the selling price and the bought-in cost.

However, unlike the secondhand goods schemes, the margin will be calculated on the basis of the eligible supplies made during a full financial year. The trader will be required to make a provisional calculation each quarter, based on the previous year's results. After the end of the year the trader will make a final calculation for the year and account for any adjustment with his next VAT return. It should be noted that the calculations are to be made by reference to the trader's financial year; the concept of the 'tax year' that is used for partial exemption purposes does not apply here.

Because of the specialised nature of the business area and of this scheme, a number of technical terms appear in the legislation and in the supporting documentation. An understanding of these is essential to understanding the detailed operation of the scheme.

The term, 'tour operator', includes a travel agent acting as principal and any other person providing for the benefit of travellers services of any kind commonly provided by tour operators or travel agents.

It will be appreciated that this definition goes much wider than the term 'tour operator' as it is commonly understood and includes any person who provides inclusive travel arrangements. Thus it could apply to a coach operator or a 'freebie' newspaper that offers a package holiday to members of the public as a promotional effort. Fortunately HMRC have issued guidance on when they consider that it does not apply.                    **[40.110]**

*Travellers* This term includes travellers of all kinds whatever the purpose of their journey, eg people who make their own travel arrangements but who buy accommodation or other services from a tour operator.            **[40.111]**

*Territorial scope* The scheme applies to supplies enjoyed by travellers to any part of the world, including journeys solely within the UK. Tax is only accounted for on the margin on supplies enjoyed within the EU, including the UK and the Isle of Man. Prior to 1 April 1988 the margin was apportioned on a reasonable basis between the EC and non-EC part of the journey. Since 1 April 1988 this is done automatically via the annual adjustment that apportions it on the basis of costs.
**[40.112]**

*Margin scheme* The goods and services covered by the scheme are those bought in from third parties and are referred to as 'margin scheme supplies'. These are at present split into two categories: margin standard-rated and margin zero-rated. However, with effect from 1 January 1996, the whole of the tour operators' margin became standard-rated, except to the extent that designated travel services are enjoyed outside the EU. These supplies must be brought into the calculations before deducting any agents' commission. In-house supplies are not included in the scheme.                                **[40.113]**

*Margin standard-rated supplies* Included under this head are:
(1)    hotel and other accommodation (including hire of tents and spaces on campsites);
(2)    catering;
(3)    entrance fees (theatres, places of entertainment, museums, sporting events, etc);
(4)    course fees, tuition charges, etc;

(5)    hire of sports equipment (eg ski packs) and facilities to play (eg green fees);
(6)    airport parking;
(7)    hire of cars, taxis, bicycles, boats.                                      **[40.114]**

*Margin zero-rated supplies* Included under this head are:
(1)    until 1 January 1996, air travel, including airport and baggage handling charges;
(2)    until 1 January 1996, ferry travel, including transportation of accompanied motor vehicles;
(3)    until 1 January 1996, rail, coach and bus travel, including transfers from airport to hotel;
(4)    margin standard-rated supplies when enjoyed in a non-EU country.
      In the case of cruises, the margin will have to be calculated by separating any zero-rated transport element from the standard-rated accommodation/catering elements.                                      **[40.115]**

*In-house supplies* These are supplies provided by the tour operators from their own resources rather than bought in from a third party. For example, if a tour operator owns an aircraft, or charters one without a crew, he is supplying travel in-house. On the other hand if a supply of passenger transport is made to a tour operator by a third party, that is a bought-in supply even if the transport is supplied under a charter-party contract. If an hotel is taken on a long lease so that day-to-day management of the hotel passes to the operator, the supply by the operator will be treated as an in-house supply. Accommodation that has been block booked is not treated as an in-house supply when sold by a tour operator.
      In-house supplies are not within the scheme and are dealt with in accordance with the normal rules. The VAT liability of such supplies is therefore different to the liabilities applicable to the margin scheme supplies. If a package is supplied which contains both in-house and bought-in supplies, then the figures for the two types of supply have to be separated so that the proper liability under the scheme can be calculated.                                      **[40.116]**

*Input tax* Tax incurred from third parties on margin scheme supplies as above cannot be treated as input tax. VAT incurred in non-margin supplies are regarded as overheads and tax on these may be reclaimed in the usual way. With effect from 1 May 1990, where passenger transport is supplied 'in-house' outside the UK, the supply is regarded as outside the scope of UK VAT; it can therefore be ignored for all purposes of the margin calculation in the UK.                                      **[40.117]**

*Foreign currency* Where margin scheme supplies are purchased from a third party, and billed in a foreign currency, the currency must be converted into sterling at the appropriate rate of exchange detailed in Notice 5.
      One of the following methods must be chosen to determine the rate of exchange to apply:
(1)    the rate of exchange published in the *Financial Times* using the Federation of Tour Operators' base rate current at the time of costing by the supplier;
(2)    the commercial rate of exchange current at the time that the supplies in the holiday brochure were costed;
(3)    the rate published in the *Financial Times* for the date that payment is made;
(4)    the rate of exchange which was applicable to the purchase of the foreign currency which was used to pay for the relevant supplies; and
(5)    the period rate of exchange published by Customs for customs purposes at the time the relevant supplies were paid for. (The VAT business advice centre in the relevant area will provide details of particular period rates.) **[40.118]**

*Time of supply* The normal rules for determining this do not apply. Instead the tour operator has the choice of either of the following as his tax point:

(1)   the date of the customer's departure or, if no travel is involved, the date on which the hotel accommodation is made available; or

(2)   the date of receipt of the main payment for the 'package'. The receipt of a deposit will not establish a tax point under this option provided that it is less than 20% of the total price.   **[40.119]**

*Supplies for use other businesses* Some operators or travel agents acting as principals buy in supplies of the kind that fall within the margin scheme for resale to other traders. Where the business customer is to be resold the supply then these supplies are outside the scope of the tour operators' margin scheme (TOMS) but may be included as part of a trade facilitation scheme.

Where the business customer is to use the services for their own consumption then the supplies fall, subject to a trade facilitation scheme, within TOMS. The trade facilitation scheme permits the supply to be excluded from TOMS and for VAT invoices to be issued. If the supply is enjoyed in another EU Member State, there must be evidence that VAT has been accounted for in that member state.   **[40.120]**

*Exception for incidental supplies* Some businesses whose main activity does not consist of making supplies of accommodation or travel that have been purchased from a third party may nevertheless make some purchases for resale to other margin scheme suppliers. One example is a hotelier who buys in car hire for resupply to some of his hotel guests; another is a coach operator who buys in tickets for admission to a stately home for resupply to his passengers. Provided that the value of the margin scheme supplies not consisting of accommodation or travel does not exceed 1% of the value of his total supplies the trader may apply to his local VAT office for approval (which should be obtained in writing) not to operate the margin scheme and so to account for VAT under the normal rules.   **[40.121]**

*Teaching of English as a Foreign Language (TEFL)* Following the decision of the Appeal Court in the case *of Pilgrim's Language Courses Ltd* (1999), it is accepted that services such as transport and accommodation which fall within the exemption for EFL tuition, either as integral parts of a single exempt supply of education, or as exempt closely related supplies, are not within the TOMS.   **[40.122]**

*Agents* Travel agents acting as true agents – arranging a supply between two other parties – are not affected by these provisions. Travel agents must, however, charge VAT on any commission they receive from a UK operator for arranging a margin scheme supply to any destination. In practice, such commission will almost certainly be self-billed to the travel agent by the operator and it is important therefore that the agent appreciates that the payment he receives contains a VAT element which he must account for to the Commissioners of Customs and Excise.   **[40.123]**

### EXAMPLE 40.5 – TOUR OPERATORS MARGIN SCHEME REGISTRATION

Hillingdon Manor Tours (HMT) starts trading on 1 January 2003 and sells 60 package holidays between 1 January and 30 June 2003 for £1,000 each. Therefore, total turnover to 30 June is £60,000. HMT only sells this type of holiday that consists entirely of designated travel services. HMT buys in each package for £500. Therefore, the total cost to 30 June is £30,000. HMT need not register yet because the margin between the aggregate selling and buying prices is only £30,000.

By the end of November 2003, HMT has sold £115,000 worth of package holidays and its total costs are £55,000. The margin is now £60,000. This is above the registration threshold of £58,000 so HMT must now register.

c)   *Auctioneers*

An auctioneer's services to his principal are taxable in the normal way unless he offers goods for sale as an agent of the seller, and he must account for tax in the same way as any other taxable person.

The normal rules for agents also apply to auctioneers. The charge for these services must for VAT purposes be treated separately from charges to the principal for other supplies. Similar considerations apply where agricultural goods are sold on behalf of a flat rate farmer. Where certain second-hand goods, works of art or collectors' items are sold, either the general margin scheme, the special margin scheme or the normal agents' rules are applied.                                                                 **[40.124]**

*Auctioneers' margin scheme* An auctioneer is defined as a person who offers for sale goods at any public sale where persons become purchasers by competition. The scheme was developed to allow auctioneers to take advantage of the facility to account for VAT on the margin. The scheme is optional and may be applied to some transactions whilst others are excluded. The requirements for the scheme are that the seller must not be registered for VAT, or a VAT registered person selling under a margin scheme or global accounting or an insurance company selling goods it has acquired under an insurance claim or a finance house selling goods it has repossessed.

The margin scheme calculations are detailed in Notice 718 (revised May 2003) which sets out the charges to be included/excluded under the scheme, together with the record-keeping requirements. The main changes in the revised version relate to the invoice and record-keeping requirements of the secondhand goods scheme and of global accounting.                      **[40.125]**

**EXAMPLE 40.6 – AUCTIONEERS**

Alison handles the following transaction:
1     Hammer price — £10,000
2     Commission charged to vendor — £1,000
3     Miscellaneous costs charged to vendor — £200
4     Net amount paid to vendor (1 – 2 – 3) = £8,800
5     Buyer's premium — £600
6     Costs recharged to buyer — £300
  The scheme purchase price is 1 – 2 – 3 = £8,800
  The scheme selling price is 1 + 5 + 6 = £10,900
  Therefore, the margin is £10,900 – £8,800 = £2,100
  Alison's output tax due on this transaction is £2,100 × 7/47 = £312.76

# Section 6    Business enterprise

**Chapters**

# 41 Corporation tax

*Updated by Michael Haig, Corporate Tax Manager, KPMG LLP (UK), Gatwick Office*

'With both the lowest corporate tax rates for businesses ever and the lowest ever capital gains tax rates for long term investors, Britain is now the place for companies to start, to invest, to grow and to expand.'
(Chancellor of the Exchequer, the Rt Hon Gordon Brown MP, Budget Statement,
21 March 2000.)
[41.1]

## I INTRODUCTION

Corporation tax was introduced by FA 1965 and applies to all resident bodies corporate including authorised unit trusts and unincorporated associations (see *Blackpool Marton Rotary Club v Martin* (1990)) but not to partnerships (although certain limited liability partnerships are treated as companies) or local authorities. It is levied on the profits of a company that are made up of income profits, computed according to income tax principles, and capital profits which will be assessed in accordance with CGT rules. The UK system of corporation tax was, until April 1999, generally referred to as the *imputation* system as part of the tax paid by the company was imputed to the shareholder by means of a tax credit attached to dividends paid to shareholders. This is still the case to a limited extent. The credit is not, however, repayable.

The process of reforming corporation tax is gaining momentum. Proposals have been made to further limit the application of the 'Schedular' system for identifying taxable income and to tax gains on property assets as income. These changes will, if enacted, follow the trend of recent years where the rules for computing income from rental businesses and trades have been more closely aligned and where gains on 'new' intangible assets are now treated as being of an income nature and, broadly, taxed according to the accounting treatment. [41.2]–[41.20]

II   GENERAL PRINCIPLES—RATES OF TAX

Corporation tax is charged by reference to financial years (FY) that run from
1 April to 31 March and are referred to by the calendar year in which they
commence. Hence, FY 2002 means the financial year from 1 April 2002 to
31 March 2003. Where companies are wound up, the rate charged during
their final financial year is generally that fixed for the preceding financial
year (TA 1988 s 342(2)). There are now two rates of corporation tax:
(1)    the small companies' rate of 19% (see **[41.24]**);
(2)    the full rate of 30%.
    The standard rate of corporation tax is, at present being set a year in
advance. The other rates are set in the Budget prior to, or early in, the FY.
Over the years the full rate has altered as follows:

| FY | Rate (%) |
|---|---|
| 1983 | 50 |
| 1984 | 45 |
| 1985 | 40 |
| 1986–89 | 35 |
| 1990 | 34 |
| 1991–96 | 33 |
| 1997 | 31 |
| 1998 | 31 |
| 1999–2007 | 30 |

Corporation tax is charged on a current year basis on the company's profits
for the financial year. Therefore, where a company's accounting period
straddles two financial years the profits must be apportioned on a time basis
(TA 1988 s 8(3)). The following example illustrates the computation problem with a change in the full rate. In recent years it has, in the main, been a
problem where small companies' relief is due.

**EXAMPLE 41.1**

Grr Ltd makes up its accounts to 31 December 1999 and its trading profits were
£2,000,000. The rate of corporation tax for FY 1998 was 31% and for FY 1999 was
30%.
    The tax will be calculated as follows:
*Profits of £2,000,000 apportioned:*
    1 January 1999–31 March 1999:
    3/12 of £2,000,000 = £500,000 taxed at 31% (FY 1998)
    1 April 1999–31 December 1999:
    9/12 of £2,000,000 = £1,500,000 taxed at 30% (FY 1999)

From FY 2000 to FY 2005 there were three rates of corporation tax. A
starting rate of 0% applied for FY 2004 and FY 2005. The operation of the
starting rate and the associated non-corporate distributions rate are
described below.

For all except large companies the tax is payable within nine months and one day after the end of the company's accounting period. Hence, in *Example 41.1* the tax will normally be due by 1 October in each year. The position of large companies is considered at [**41.185**]. [**41.21**]

## 1 Capital gains

Capital gains realised by a company are included in its profits and charged to corporation tax at the rate in force for the relevant financial year.

The corporation tax rate on a gain realised in FY 2006 is 30% (unless the starting rate or the small companies' rate applies). Unlike individuals, companies are not entitled to an annual exemption nor do they qualify for taper relief; the indexation allowance continues to apply to capital gains made by companies. [**41.22**]

## 2 The starting rate (TA 1988 s 13AA)

For FY 2004 and FY 2005 a starting rate of 0% applied to companies with profits of up to £10,000 (divided by the number of associated companies). Marginal relief is given on profits between £10,000 and £50,000 with the effect that the marginal rate of tax on profits in this band is 23.75%. The application of the associated companies test and the operation of marginal relief is the same as for the small companies' rate that is considered in the following paragraphs. From 1 April 2004 to 31 March 2006, the rate of tax was affected by any 'non-corporate distributions' paid in an accounting period when the 'underlying rate of tax' was not at least 19%. This is dealt with further in 4 below. [**41.23**]

## 3 The small companies' rate (TA 1988 s 13)

The small companies' rate is 19% for FY 2002 to FY 2006. This rate applies to any company (other than a close investment holding company: see [**41.129**]) whose profits, both income and capital, do not exceed £300,000 in the accounting period.

Where a company's profits exceed £300,000 but not £1,500,000 a marginal relief is available, the effect of which is (for FY 2006) to impose corporation tax at the rate of 32.75% on profits above £300,000 but below £1,500,000. The corporation tax definition of a small company is related to its profits for a financial year and for this purpose profits include franked investment income (FII) (see [**41.91**]). The £300,000 and £1,500,000 thresholds are reduced if the company has associated companies (below). The limits are divided by the total number of associated companies including the taxpayer company.

If a company wishes to take advantage of TA 1988 s 13 (or of s 13AA—the starting rate) it must submit a claim in the company's return that the profit should be charged at the small companies' rate or that marginal relief is appropriate. Any such statement should also indicate whether or not there are associated companies (see SP 1/91, ESC C9; for the position of holding companies, SP 5/94 and for companies which may not be carrying on any trade or business at any time during the accounting period, see *Jowett v O'Neill and Brennan Construction Ltd* (1998), *Land Management Ltd v Fox* (2002) and *HMRC Comrs v Salaried Persons Postal Loans Ltd* (2006)). Non-resident companies may be associated companies as can companies controlled by spouses, certain relatives and business partners and so are companies owned by trusts in relation to which a connected person is a settlor (see *R v CIR, ex p Newfields Developments Ltd* (2001), HL).

Changes in the small companies' rate and in the definition of the small company may be tabulated as follows:

| *FY* | *Small companies rate ( %)* | *Profit limit (£)* | *Higher limit (£)* | *Marginal rate ( %)* |
|---|---|---|---|---|
| 1993 | 25 | 250,000 | 1,250,000 | 35 |
| 1994–95 | 25 | 300,000 | 1,500,000 | 35 |
| 1996 | 24 | 300,000 | 1,500,000 | 35.25 |
| 1997 | 21 | 300,000 | 1,500,000 | 33.5 |
| 1998 | 21 | 300,000 | 1,500,000 | 33.5 |
| 1999–01 | 20 | 300,000 | 1,500,000 | 32.5 |
| 2002 | 19 | 300,000 | 1,500,000 | 32.75 |
| 2003 | 19 | 300,000 | 1,500,000 | 32.75 |
| 2004 | 19 | 300,000 | 1,500,000 | 32.75 |
| 2005 | 19 | 300,000 | 1,500,000 | 32.75 |
| 2006 | 19 | 300,000 | 1,500,000 | 32.75 |

**EXAMPLE 41.2**

(1)  Zee Ltd makes up its accounts to 31 March each year. For the year ending 31 March 2007 the company had trading profits of £80,000 and had made chargeable gains of £42,000.

The profits of Zee Ltd for corporation tax purposes are:

|  | £ |
|---|---|
| Trading (ie income) profits | 80,000 |
| Chargeable gains | 42,000 |
| Chargeable profits | £122,000 |

Zee Ltd will, therefore, qualify for the small companies' rate so that corporation tax will be charged as follows:
Chargeable profits (£122,000) at 19% = £23,180

(2)  Were the income profits of Zee Ltd to be £280,000 then, with the addition of chargeable gains (£42,000), the small company threshold of £300,000 would be exceeded by £22,000 so that the small companies' relief would apply as follows:

(i)  Corporation tax payable:    £
£322,000 (ie £280,000 + £42,000) × 30%    96,600

(ii)  *Less:* marginal relief (TA 1988 s 13(2)):

|  | (upper relevant amount – profits) × statutory fraction |  |
|---|---|---|
|  | ie (£1,500,000 – £322,000) × $^{11}/_{400}$ | 32,395 |
| (iii) | Total tax ((i) – (ii)) | £64,205 |

Two points should be stressed in connection with the small companies' rate (which apply also to the starting rate: see ([**41.23**])).

*First*, as noted above, provisions exist to prevent the fragmentation of a business among associated companies in an attempt to create a series of small companies (TA 1988 s 13(3)). This restriction only applies if the associated company was carrying on a trade or business at any time in the relevant accounting period: see s 13(4) and *Jowett v O'Neill and Brennan Construction Ltd* (1999) in which retaining a large sum of money in a bank account was not considered to involve a trade or business; for further discussion, see also *Land Management Ltd v Fox* (2002) and *HMRC Comrs v Salaried Persons Postal Loans Ltd* (2006).

### EXAMPLE 41.3

X Ltd has three wholly owned operating subsidiaries. The companies are associated and hence the lower and upper limits for each company are divided by one plus the number of associated companies. The lower and upper limits for each company in the X Group are, therefore, £75,000 and £375,000.

A company is treated as an associated company of another company if the same person controls both companies (see *Steele v EVC International NV* (1996) and TA 1988 s 13(4): control for these purposes is to be construed in accordance with TA 1988 s 416 on which see *R v IRC, ex p Newfields Developments Ltd* (2001)). There have been a number of further cases at the Special Commissioners that have confirmed that it is the wide-ranging s 416 test of control that is relevant. There is a concession (extra-statutory concession C9) that relieves certain companies where there is no commercial interdependence.

*Secondly*, the marginal rate applies where profits fall into the range £300,000 to £1,500,000, and the tax on profits in excess of £300,000 will be charged at an effective rate in excess of 30%. This is because the purpose of the small companies' relief is to increase gradually the average rate of corporation tax from the 19% payable by a company with profits of £300,000 to the 30% payable by a company with profits of £1,500,000. To achieve this result the rate applicable to the slice of profits between £300,000 and £1,500,000 has to *exceed* 30%. For FY 2006 this marginal rate is 32.75% calculated as follows:

| | |
|---|---|
| Tax on £300,000 at 19% | = £57,000 |
| Tax on £1,500,000 at 30% | = £450,000 |
| Difference (£450,000 – £57,000) | = £393,000 |

Therefore, £393,000 corporation tax has to be raised on profits falling between £300,000 and £1,500,000 (ie on £1,200,000).

Hence, as a percentage, tax on £1,200,000 will be:

$$\frac{393,000}{1,200,000} \times 100 = 32.75\%$$

Thus, continuing *Example 41.2(2)* above:
Corporation tax of £64,205 on profits of £322,000 can be analysed as:

|  | £ |
|---|---|
| First £300,000 of profits at 19% | = 57,000 |
| Final £22,000 of profits at 32.75% | = 7,205 |
|  | £64,205 |

In determining whether small companies relief is available, dividends received from other UK companies (franked investment income) are taken into account, but not dividends from the company's own subsidiaries (see **[42.91]** ff for the meaning of franked investment income and for an illustration of how this affects tapering relief).

The fact that a company's profits may just exceed £300,000 thereby attracting this relatively high marginal rate on the excess over £300,000 is of practical significance when considering how much money the directors of family companies should take by way of remuneration (or how much should be paid into the company's pension scheme). The marginal corporation tax rate exceeds the basic rate of income tax so that it may be advantageous to pay out such moneys in the form of salaries or by making increased contributions to the company pension scheme. Thus, in *Example 41.2(2)* above, the directors of Zee Ltd should consider paying increased salaries or bonuses of £22,000 for the year. In this way, the company's taxable profits for that accounting period will be reduced by £22,000 which would otherwise have been taxed at 32.75%, a saving of £7,205; this would be advantageous if the tax and NICs liability on the salaries paid do not exceed this amount: see further **Chapter 46**.

If the company is a member of a group and losses are available for group relief from other group members, the marginal tax rate in each group company should be considered when deciding how to surrender losses. Losses should be surrendered to companies with high marginal rates (eg 32.75%) of tax before other members of the group.                **[41.24]**

### 4    The non-corporate distribution rate

The starting rate proved to be so attractive that it had the 'unintended' effect of enormously increasing the number of businesses incorporating all or part of their business and extracting a substantial part of the profits by way of a dividend.

In order to prevent this FA 2004 introduced rules such that, where a distribution is made to a non-corporate shareholder and the underlying rate of tax is less than 19% (the lower rate), a further tax liability arises on the difference. These rules, along with the starting rate, are to be abolished with effect from 1 April 2006.

The size of the company is not a determining factor. Rather, the amount of profits chargeable to CT is the primary determining factor (along with the number of any associated companies) as to whether the company will be affected.

The measure will affect groups where a company within a group makes a distribution to a non-company shareholder and that company has profits chargeable to CT at the starting rate, or receives marginal relief from the small companies' rate.

The new rate applies when distributions are made to non-company shareholders on or after 1 April 2004 and before 1 April 2006. Where an accounting period straddles either of these dates the profits are apportioned.

If the distributions in an accounting period are more than the profits the excess is taken forward to the next or subsequent accounting periods to be 'franked' against future profits chargeable to corporation tax (PCTCT).

If the company is part of a group of companies, each company in the group needs to consider if it has made a distribution to a non-company shareholder and what rate of tax applies to its profits for that accounting period. Where there are insufficient PCTCT in the company to cover non-company distributions (NCDs), there are rules for allocating the excess to other companies within the group that can absorb the excess. Where there are insufficient PCTCT within the group to cover the distribution the remaining excess is carried forward to subsequent accounting periods.

*Example 1*

Assume that PCTCT for an accounting period are £9,000. These profits are distributed by way of a dividend to individuals.

| | | |
|---|---|---|
| PCTCT | £9,000 @ 0% = | £0.00 |
| Corporation Tax due | = | £0.00 |
| the underlying rate: (tax/PCTCT x 100) | 0.00/9,000 × 100 = | 0% |
| Non corporate distribution | £9,000 @ 19% = | £1,710.00 |
| Remaining PCTCT | | NIL |
| Total CT due | | £1,710.00 |

*Example 2*

Assume that PCTCT are £40,000. The distributions made in the accounting period totalled £36,000 of which £11,000 were made to a company.

| | | |
|---|---|---|
| PCTCT £40,000 @ 19% | = | £7,600.00 |
| Less: Marginal Relief (£50,000 − 40,000 × 19/400) | = | £ 475.00 |
| Corporation Tax due on basic profits | = | £7,125.00 |
| the **underlying rate** is 7125.00/40000 × 100 | = | 17.81% |

| | | |
|---|---|---|
| Non corporate distribution £25,000 @ 19% | = | £4,750.00 |
| Remaining PCTCT £15,000 @ 17.81% | = | £2,671.50 |
| Total CT due | | £7,421.50 |

## 5   The rate of corporation tax: a summary

The current position may be summarised in tabular form as follows:

| *Financial year* | *2006* |
|---|---|
| *Taxable profits* | |
| First £300,000 | 19% |
| Next £1,200,000 | 32.75% |
| Over £1,500,000 | 30% |

**[41.25]–[41.40]**

## III   HOW TO CALCULATE THE PROFITS OF A COMPANY

Profits of a company are defined as including both income profits and capital gains (TA 1988 s 6(4)(a)).                                                                     **[41.41]**

## 1   Income profits

a)   *General principles*

Generally, income profits have to be computed in accordance with the income tax rules that apply in the year of assessment in which the company's accounting period ends (TA 1988 s 9). Profits are calculated under Schedule A (property income), Schedule D Case I (trading income), Schedule D Case III (interest and other annual payments), Schedule D Case IV and V (overseas income) and Schedule D Case VI (other annual income not caught by the other schedules and cases). Until recently, these schedules and cases also applied for income tax purposes. However, since the enactment of ITEPA 2003 and ITTOIA 2005 references to schedules and cases have been removed from income tax law. Thus, a trading company having no other income will compute its profits in accordance with the rules of Schedule D Case I (ie trading income). In general the rules for what expenditure is deductible by individuals and partnerships (discussed at **[10.131]**) will apply equally to companies. Accordingly, the salaries and fees paid to its directors and employees will be allowable expenses under TA 1988 s 74, but note that TA 1988 s 337A(1)(b) prohibits the deduction as an expense (except in the case of insurance companies), of annual payments and annuities. Such payments must be relieved, if at all, as charges on income (see **[41.57]**).

So far as income from land is concerned, FA 1998 extended treatment of property rental income as a deemed business to companies (for the provisions of Schedule A (ie property income), see **Chapter 12**). As noted in the introduction, there are proposals that the distinction between property rental income and trading income should be further blurred. In particular, so far as companies are concerned:

(1) rental income from non-UK property is treated as the receipts of a separate business;

(2) in the context of group relief a distinction is drawn between 'true' trading losses and losses from a Schedule A business;

(3) TA 1988 s 768D deals with changes in ownership of a property business (see **[41.70]**);

(4) in computing Schedule A profits, related interest costs, exchange gains and losses etc are dealt with under the separate loan relationship rules which apply to companies (see **[41.50]** ff).

A problem in the case of a corporate group may arise from the common assumption that it represents a single commercial entity. This is not the case for tax purposes and so an expense may be non-deductible in the hands of the paying company if that expense was incurred for 'dual purposes': eg to benefit other group members (*Commercial Union Assurance Co Ltd v Shaw* (1998); however, see also *Vodafone Cellular Ltd v Shaw* (1997) where the Revenue was unsuccessful with a similar argument and **[43.21]**).

FA 2000 s 69, Sch 20 introduced an enhanced relief system of tax credits for small and medium-sized companies (SMEs) in respect of research and development ('R&D'). The definition of an SME is based on EU guidelines and is not the same as for UK Company law. The relief was extended to all companies from 1 April 2002. The relief operates so as to enhance the deduction by 50% for an SME and 25% for other companies. For an SME, if the result is that a loss is created or enhanced then the loss may be surrendered in return for a payment (although it is limited to the amount of PAYE Tax and NIC accounted for by the company).

An enhanced deduction is also available for costs in relation to removing harmful substances from contaminated land. Essentially, a company may claim an enhanced deduction of 150% of costs relating to land remediation. If this deduction creates or increases a loss then a tax credit of 16% of the qualifying loss can be claimed from HMRC (this is not limited to PAYE payments as under the R&D scheme) (FA 2001 s 70, Sch 22).　　　　**[41.42]**

b) *Foreign exchange gains and losses and financial instruments for managing interest rate and currency risk*

For accounting periods beginning on or after 1/10/02 the rules for the taxation of exchange gains and losses and on interest rate and derivative contracts are included in the rules which apply to loan relationships in FA 1996 (see FA 2002 s 82 and Sch 25 for exchange gains and losses and FA 2002 s 82 and Sch 26–28 for derivative contracts).　　　　**[41.43]**

c) *Transfer pricing (TA 1988 s 770A and Sch 28AA)*

The transfer pricing legislation was aimed at transfer pricing arrangements entered into by multi-national corporations. Such corporations can exploit the tax rules in the various jurisdictions to obtain a tax advantage. The rules on transfer pricing aim to eliminate such activity by requiring companies to calculate their taxable profits as if the arrangements had been effected on normal commercial terms. The rules provide that where any two persons have entered into a transaction which confers on one of them a UK tax advantage, the profits and losses of the advantaged party must be computed as if the transaction had been undertaken on arm's length terms. The company has to be satisfied that its transfer pricing policy meets HMRC's requirements and that arm's length prices are adopted in order to be sure that the profits and the tax in its CTSA return are calculated correctly. If the company fails to consider whether its arrangements are in accordance with the arm's length principle, penalties apply. The other party to the transaction may obtain relief through the competent authority procedure and, in the case of UK to UK transfer pricing rules, through corresponding adjustments.

Non-UK resident companies can also be subject to the transfer pricing regime. For example, a property investment company resident in Jersey may seek to eliminate any UK tax liability on rents received from a property situated in this country by borrowing the purchase price from an associated company and claiming the interest on that loan as a deduction from the rents. If the loan is not one that would have been made between non-associated companies dealing at arm's length and a UK tax advantage has resulted, the transfer pricing rules can operate to disallow the interest deduction and therefore to increase the UK taxable Schedule A profit of the Jersey company.

The Inland Revenue (now HMRC) sought to extend this principle to third party loans which are supported or guaranteed by a connected person (eg a group member) and to disallow part or all of the interest paid on such a loan (see *Tax Bulletin* 46, April 2000). Arguably, the extension of transfer pricing to all 'provisions' made between connected persons, from 1 April 2004, now deals with this issue. HMRC may also use TA 1988 s 787 to deny interest relief where arrangements have been entered into with the sole or main benefit being the obtaining of a deduction for the interest paid.

The transfer pricing rules apply in a wide variety of circumstances where transactions are undertaken between connected persons. A company will be connected with another if it is directly or indirectly 'controlled' by that other or both are controlled by a third company. There is a wide definition of 'control'. A person can also be connected with another by virtue of indirectly participating in the management, control or capital of the other person and this will include circumstances where the person has the right to acquire control at a future date.

The rules also cover joint venture arrangements by providing that a person can be deemed to control a company where that person has a 40% interest and another person also has 40% of the company.

From 1 April 2004, FA 2004 ss 30–37 and Sch 5 extended transfer pricing to UK to UK transactions. There is, however, an exclusion for small enterprises and a more limited relief for medium-sized enterprises and for dormant companies.

The definition of small and medium is derived from EU rules:
- Medium-sized
  - less than 250 employees; and
  - either turnover less than 50m Euros (c £35m); or
  - assets less than 43m Euros (c £30m)

- Small
  - less than 50 employees; and
  - turnover or assets less than 10m Euros (c £7m).

Detailed guidance has been provided by HMRC to assist businesses to comply.

The measures abolish separate thin capitalisation requirements and subsume them within general transfer pricing requirements and allow the connected UK business to make a corresponding adjustment in the calculation of its taxable income. In recognition of the practical issues for businesses in introducing or adapting systems to enable them to comply with transfer pricing requirements, there is a temporary relaxation of penalties for failing to keep evidence to demonstrate that a result is an arm's length result. This relaxation lasted until 31 March 2006.

FA 1999 ss 85–87 sets out the procedure to be followed by companies wishing to come to an advance agreement with HMRC on their transfer pricing policy (an 'advance pricing agreement'). **[41.44]**

### d) *Employee trusts*

Payments into employee trusts may constitute deductible expenditure if they are of an income nature (see *Heather v P-E Consulting Group* (1978), discussed at **[10.134]**). See also *Mawsley Machinery Ltd v Robinson* (1998) where the payments were disallowed as they were for the purpose of providing a fund to purchase the company's shares and *McDonald v Dextra Accessories Ltd* (2005) where payments were not allowed as a result of the restriction imposed under FA 1989 s 43 where payments relate to amounts intended to be emoluments not paid within nine months of the end of the accounting period. A deduction will only be given when emoluments are actually paid to employees.

For accounting periods ending on or after 27 November 2002 a tax deduction for contributions to an employee trust (which includes a payment of money or the transfer of an asset) is only allowed to the extent that the money or the asset is used within nine months of the end of the accounting period in providing qualifying benefits. These are payments or transfers of assets that give rise to a charge to income tax and NIC (see FA 2003 Sch 24). These new rules do not apply to most retirement benefit schemes or to share-related benefits where a statutory tax deduction is allowed. **[41.45]**

### e) *Franked investment income and income taxed at source*

In calculating income profits no account is taken of dividends and other distributions received by one UK company from another (TA 1988 s 208). The utilisation of such income is considered at **[42.91]**. Notice, however, that FII is included in the profits of a company for the purpose of determining the availability of the small companies' relief, although this income is not itself taxed (TA 1988 s 13(7) and see *Example 42.12*).

When income is received by a company net of income tax deducted at source, the gross income is included in the profits of the company and a credit is given from the corporation tax payable for the tax deducted at source.

Interest and other annual payments made after 31 March 2001 do not need to have income tax deducted at source where the recipient company is UK resident or where it is a non-resident company carrying on a trade in the UK through a permanent establishment and the payment is brought into charge in the UK.

**EXAMPLE 41.4**

Lexo Ltd makes up its accounts to 31 March each year. The accounts for the period ending 31 March 2006 show the following:

|  |  | £ |
|---|---|---|
| Trading profit |  | 260,000 |
| Profit from lettings |  | 40,000 |
| Interest received: |  |  |
| net | £60,000 |  |
| plus tax deducted | £15,000 |  |
| Gross |  | 75,000 |
| Total profits |  | £375,000 |
|  |  | £ |
| Corporation tax payable: |  |  |
| £300,000 at 19% (FY 2005) + £75,000 at 32.75% |  | 81,562 |
| *Less*: tax deducted |  | 15,000 |
|  |  | £66,562 |

*Notes:*
(1)    The trading profit is calculated according to the rules of Schedule D Case I, for 2005–06, and the profit from lettings according to the Schedule A rules.
(2)    If the tax deducted exceeded the corporation tax payable, the excess would be repaid to the company.

Income tax principles are relevant only in determining the amount of the company's income profits—other enactments of that legislation are not relevant. Thus the opening and closing year income tax provisions of Schedule D have no application to companies and there is no question of any personal reliefs or allowances applying. The system of capital allowances applies to companies with suitable modifications (see **Chapter 48**). The specific difficulties that may arise when an existing business is transferred to a company are dealt with in **Chapter 47**.                                    [41.46]

## 2    Capital gains

a)    *Basics*

A company's chargeable gains are computed in the same way as those of an individual. The definition of chargeable assets and the occasions when a disposal occurs are common to both individuals and companies. The annual exemption (£8,800 for 2006–07) is not available for disposals by companies and nor is taper relief (although the company retains the indexation allowance which in the case of assets with a high base cost is an advantage). The rules for the exemption of tax on the disposals by a trading company of a substantial shareholding in another trading company under TCGA 1992 Sch 7AC are examined at **[41.75]**. **[41.47]**

b) *Intra-group disposals*

A disposal between companies in the same group is treated as giving rise to neither gain nor loss until the asset is disposed of outside the group or the recipient company leaves the group within six years (see **[43.122]**). **[41.48]**

c) *Dangers of a double charge*

A disadvantage suffered by a company and its shareholders is that on any capital gain realised by the company there may be an element of double taxation. Not only will the company suffer corporation tax on the gain, but the shareholder whose shares may have increased in value as a result of the capital profit (albeit after tax) will suffer CGT when he disposes of those shares.

**EXAMPLE 41.5**

Saloman Ltd (a small company wholly owned by John Saloman) makes a chargeable gain of £100,000. It will suffer corporation tax of £19,000 (19%) on that gain. Saloman's shares will have increased in value by, say, £81,000 so that were he to sell them he would suffer CGT of (say) £32,400 at 40% (ignoring exemptions and reliefs). Effectively, therefore, the corporate gain has been subject to tax at 51% (19% paid by the company and 32% by Saloman). If Saloman Ltd were not a small company this percentage would be 58% (30% paid by the company and 28% by Saloman). He may, in that case, consider extracting the profit by the payment of a dividend because the dividend would bear tax at an effective rate of only 25% rather than 40%. The effect of taper relief, available to individuals and trustees, will have a significant impact. If full taper relief for a business asset (75%—giving a maximum effective rate of tax of 10% instead of 40%) is available then the total tax would be 27% (19% plus 10% of 81%) or 37% (30% plus 10% of 70%).

Holding appreciating assets in private companies therefore can be tax-inefficient and in some circumstances it may be better for the shareholder to retain those assets and lease them to the company. However, this judgment needs to take into account other reliefs (such as taper relief), and the effect on other taxes such as inheritance tax and stamp duty. **[41.49]**

## 3 Taxation of a company's loan relationships

a) *Principles of the loan relationships regime (FA 1996 ss 80–105, Schs 8–15)*

The intention is to bring the profits and losses on all 'loan relationships' within the corporation tax code on income. This is achieved on the basis of the accounting treatment in the company's statutory accounts (see FA 1996 ss 85 ff for authorised accounting methods). Significant changes were made in FA 2002 and the impact of the move towards the use of International Accounting Standards is addressed in FA 2005.                               **[41.50]**

b)   *Meaning of 'loan relationship' (FA 1996 s 81)*

A loan relationship can arise in one of two ways:
(1)   Where a company is either a debtor or creditor in respect of a money debt that arose from a transaction for the lending of money. A money debt is defined as a debt that falls to be satisfied by the payment of money or the transfer of rights under a debt which itself is a money debt.
(2)   Where a company issues an instrument as security for a money debt.

The regime does not apply to shares nor to any debt arising from rights conferred by shares (eg rights to a dividend or share capital) nor to gains or losses arising by reference to fluctuations in the value of securities which are convertible/exchangeable into shares and where there is (at the date of issue) more than a negligible likelihood that the conversion, etc, right will be exercised and the securities are not issued at a deep discount. Also excluded are trade debts including debts arising on the purchase of property or other goods or on the supply of services (hence the straightforward bad debt for goods supplied will be relieved under the company's trading account as an expense of the business).

However, interest and foreign exchange movements on a money debt which is not within the new regime (typically on a late payment of a trade debt) are caught and a similar treatment applies where interest is imputed on a debt, for instance as a result of a court award.          **[41.51]–[41.52]**

c)   *Extent*

The regime covers all profits, gains and losses including those of a capital nature arising as a result of a company's loan relationships and related transactions. Certain charges and expenses incurred by the company for the purpose of its loan relationships are taken into account: such as those incurred in bringing a loan relationship into existence; in entering into or giving effect to a related transaction and in making any payments under a loan relationship. In addition, relief is available for abortive expenditure incurred in connection with loans.

Interest or a discount that is treated as a distribution for income tax purposes is excluded (for the definition of a 'distribution', see **[43.1]** ff).
                                                                            **[41.53]**

d)   *Trading profits, losses and expenses*

When a loan relationship is entered into for the purposes of a trade any profits and gains are taxable and interest charges, expenses etc are deductible in computing the company's trading profits (FA 1996 s 82(2)). This means that there is no significant change to the treatment of bank interest paid on a loan raised for trading purposes although commitment fees, commission and interest are all now relievable on an accruals basis. While many companies are likely to have borrowed money for trading purposes, and are therefore entitled to a trading deduction for interest paid, HMRC consider that there are very few instances, other than banks and other financial institutions, when a company will be a creditor to a loan relationship for trading purposes giving rise to interest income taxable under Schedule D Case I. [**41.54**]

e) *Non-trading profits, losses and expenses (FA 1996 s 83)*

If the loan relationship is entered into for non-trading purposes any profits, gains and interest receivable are taxed under Schedule D Case III and losses, interest payable, expenses and charges are tax deductible (FA 1996 s 82(5) (6)). For each accounting period it is necessary to calculate the aggregate of non-trading credits less non-trading debits. If in any period the debits exceed the credits, tax relief is available as follows:

(1) As a deduction against the total profits of the company (ie which arise from any source) for the same accounting period. This relief is given before setting off trading losses for the same period or non-trading deficits carried back from a later period.

(2) By way of group relief against the current profits of other group companies in the corresponding accounting period (for group relief see [**43.41**]).

(3) By carry-back against profits from non-trading loan relationships of the company for the previous year.

Finally, deficits that cannot be relieved as above are carried forward against non-trading profits (including capital gains) in subsequent accounting periods. [**41.55**]

f) *Connected parties*

Although there are no rules specifically applying to intra-group loans there are provisions dealing with connected parties that are relevant in this situation. Because of the accruals basis it is not possible to achieve any timing benefit by having group lender and borrower companies with different accounting periods.

The loan relationship rules stipulate that gains and losses on a loan relationship must be calculated in accordance with generally accepted accounting practice. Where a loan relationship exists between two parties that have a connection, those parties must account for gains and losses in respect of that loan relationship using an amortised cost basis of accounting (as opposed to any other valid method, for example mark to market). For this purpose, parties have a connection if, at any time in the accounting period, one controls the other or both are controlled by the same person. Control in this case means the ability to secure that the affairs of the company are conducted according to one's wishes as a result of holding shares, having sufficient voting power or other power conferred by the company's constitutional documents.

*Impaired debt*

If a company is party to a loan relationship then, in the first instance, all profits and losses arising from that relationship are taxable or allowable.

Hence, a company that is a creditor in a relationship may recognise an impairment loss on a debt which is bad and obtain a tax deduction for that impairment. Conversely, if a debtor company has its debt released then that will result in a taxable credit arising.

This general principle is subject to a number of important exceptions. Where a debt is released, generally no taxable credit will arise if the parties to the relationship are connected. Likewise, if the parties to the relationship are connected, impairment losses cannot generally give rise to allowable debits. Similar rules apply in certain circumstances involving liquidations and capitalisation of debt.

*Late interest*

Where parties to a loan relationship are connected, interest is deductible on an accruals basis (based on generally accepted accounting principles). If, however, the creditor to a loan relationship is taxable on a receipts basis (eg an individual) or is not chargeable to UK tax (eg an overseas company) there could be an opportunity to accrue tax deductions with no corresponding taxable credit.

Rules exist to prevent a deduction being claimed if interest is not paid in respect of a debtor loan relationship within 12 months of the end of the period in which it is accrued, if that interest would not give rise to a credit under the loan relationship rules in respect of the creditor. These rules apply where:

(1)   debtor and creditor are connected;
(2)   the debtor is a close company and the creditor is:
    (a)   a participator in the debtor company (or a person who controls a company which is such a participator);
    (b)   the associate of a person who is or who controls a company which is such a participator or associate of a participator;
    (c)   a company controlled by a participator or a person who controls a company which is such a participator; or
    (d)   a company in which such a participator has a major interest
(3)   the debtor has a major interest in the creditor company, or vice versa; or
(4)   the creditor is a retirement benefit scheme.                     **[41.56]**

## 4   Deducting charges on income and capital

a)   *What are charges?*

The rules on charges on income for companies were changed by the second Finance Act of 2005. The only payments that now come under the legislation relating to charges on income are qualifying donations to charity and amounts allowed as charges in respect of donations to charity of shares or real property.

TA 1988 s 337A makes it clear that interest payments cannot be deducted as charges on income, these must be dealt with according to the rules in FA 1996 (as to which see **[41.53]**–**[41.54]**). Nor can losses from intangible fixed assets within FA 2002 Sch 29 be deducted except in accordance with that Schedule.                     **[41.57]**–**[41.58]**

b)   *Deduction against profits*

1)'Charges on income are allowed as deductions from a company's total profits ...

2)... as reduced by any other relief from tax other than group relief.' (section 338(1) and (2))

It follows that such charges may be set against all the company's profits, including chargeable gains. As the charges reduce profits any deductions made in calculating those profits cannot be deducted a second time as a charge (TA 1988 s 338A(3)). As s 338(4) only allows a deduction for payments made, it is important for a company to organise, so far as possible, its payments which constitute charges on income to be made at the end of one accounting period rather than at the beginning of the next in order to obtain the earliest possible tax relief. Where charges exceed the total profits for the year, the excess will still qualify for a measure of tax relief (see [**41.61**]; contrast the position of individual taxpayers who obtain no relief).     [**41.59**]

**EXAMPLE 41.6**

Zeus Ltd makes the following payments in the year ended 30 April 2006:
(1)   £5,000 pa to the Society to Promote Antiquarian Studies (a registered charity); and
(2)   £8,000 pa to the trustees of a trust fund set up by the company to educate the children of its employees and to provide evening classes in arts and crafts for its employees.
    *The payment of £5,000 pa:* will be a charge on income so long as it is a qualifying donation within the Gift Aid rules (TA 1988 s 339). The fact that the payment is recurring (and is for instance provided for in a deed of covenant) will not by itself enable the payment to be deducted as a charge: it must satisfy the Gift Aid requirements.
    *The payment of £8,000 pa:* is not a charitable payment (see *Oppenheim v Tobacco Securities Trust Co Ltd* (1951)) and will only be an allowable deduction if it can be shown to be allowable as a trading expense or under another schedule or case.

5   **Loss relief**

Different relieving provisions apply depending upon the type of loss that the company has made. In all cases, however, it is only the company (or another company in the same group: see [**43.41**]) that is entitled to the relief and never the shareholders of the company. The loss is thus 'locked into' the company and this is a matter of some significance in deciding whether to commence business as a company or partnership.
    Losses are deducted from the appropriate profits of the company in priority to charges on income.                                            [**41.60**]

a)   *Relief for trading losses: 'carry-forward' (TA 1988 s 393)*

A trading loss can be carried forward and set against trading profits (not capital gains) from the *same* trade in the future.
    Relief is given automatically by reducing the trading income of the succeeding accounting period or periods. In cases where such trading

income is insufficient to absorb the full loss, interest and dividends received by the company may be treated as trading income for the purpose of loss relief (TA 1988 s 393(8)) provided that such income would have been taxed as trading income if tax had not been assessed under other provisions. Dividends received by a company whose trade involves dealing in shares fall into this category but in *Nuclear Electric plc v Bradley* (1996) it was held that income produced by moneys set aside (although not placed in a segregated fund) for meeting future liabilities could not be treated as trading income:

> 'Whether income from investments held by a business is trading income must ultimately depend upon the nature of the business and the purpose for which the fund is held. At one end of the scale are insurance companies and banks part of whose business is the making and holding of investments to meet current liabilities. It has been suggested that tour operators might fall into this category but without a good deal more information I do not feel able to express an opinion on this matter. At the other end of the scale are businesses of which the making and holding of investments form no part. In between these two ends there will no doubt fall other types of businesses whose position is not so clear. However in this case it is absolutely clear that the business of NE was to produce and supply electricity. The making of investments was neither an integral nor any part of its business. Furthermore the investments which it did make were in no sense employed in the business of producing electricity during the year of assessment.'
> (Lord Jauncey)

Unrelieved charges on income may be carried forward as a trading expense but only to the extent that the payment was made 'wholly and exclusively for the purposes of the trade' (TA 1988 s 393(9) and see *Commercial Union Assurance Co plc v Shaw* (1998)). Thus, any charges not so made should be relieved against current year profits first, leaving only those payments to be carried forward which satisfy the 'wholly and exclusively' test.

**[41.61]**

**EXAMPLE 41.7**

Hee Ltd had the following corporation tax computation:

|  | £ |
|---|---|
| Schedule D Case I profit | 6,000 |
| Chargeable gains | 1,500 |
|  | 7,500 |
| *Less:* charges on income (total £8,500) limited to | 7,500 |
| Taxable profits | £Nil |
| Unrelieved charges | £1,000 |

If all the charges had been laid out wholly and exclusively for Hee Ltd's trade then £1,000 can be carried forward as a loss under s 393(1). But if only £500 had been so expended, the remaining £500 is unrelieved.

b)   *Relief for trading losses against current and previous profits (TA 1988 s 393A)*

A company may set its trading loss against profits of the same accounting period. As the relief sets the loss against other profits it follows that *all* current profits can be used, including capital gains.

**EXAMPLE 41.8**

Haw Ltd's accounts for the financial year show the following: a trading loss of £6,000; rental income of £5,000; chargeable gains of £3,000; and charges on income of £1,000. The corporation tax computation would be:

|  | £ |
|---|---|
| Schedule A | 5,000 |
| Chargeable gains | 3,000 |
|  | 8,000 |
| *Less:* trading loss | 6,000 |
|  | 2,000 |
| *Less:* charges on income | 1,000 |
| Profits for corporation tax | £1,000 |

Where a loss cannot be relieved, or cannot be fully relieved, against profits of the same accounting period a claim may be made to carry that loss back against profits of the accounting periods falling within the previous 12 months. The company must have been carrying on the same trade in the earlier period and the claim has to be made within two years of the end of the accounting period in which the loss was incurred (TA 1988 s 393A(10) subject to the Board's discretion to extend that period). Any claim for loss relief will take effect before charges on income are deducted but *after* any loss made in that earlier year.

**EXAMPLE 41.9**

How Ltd prepares its accounts to the year ended 31 May. Its accounts show the following:

|  | Trading profits (losses) | Schedule A income | Charges on income |
|---|---|---|---|
|  | £ | £ | £ |
| Year to 31 May 2006 | (5,000) | 4,000 | Nil |
| Year to 31 May 2005 | (7,000) | 4,000 | 1,000 |
| Year to 31 May 2004 | 2,000 | 4,000 | 1,000 |

In respect of the year ended 31 May 2005 a claim for s 393A relief would result in the following corporation tax computation:

| 31 May 2005 | £ | | | Loss memorandum £ |
|---|---|---|---|---|
| Schedule A | 4,000 | Schedule DI loss | | 7,000 |
| Less trading loss | (4,000) | Used in year | | (4,000) |
| Taxable profits | Nil | Losses remaining | | 3,000 |
| 31 May 2004 | £ | | | £ |
| Schedule A | 4,000 | | | |
| Schedule D I | 2,000 | | | |
| Total | 6,000 | | | |
| Loss carried back | (3,000) | Carried back | | (3,000) |
| | 3,000 | | | |
| Less charges | (1,000) | | | |
| Taxable profit | 2,000 | | | Nil |

As a result of the claim any tax paid on the 2004 profit will be recovered to the extent that losses cover profits of that year.

In respect of the year ended 31 May 2006, a claim under s 393A would result in all of the company's £4,000 Schedule A profit being covered by losses arising in the year with £1,000 remaining unused. This excess £1,000 cannot be carried back as there are no available profits in the year ended 31 May 2005. The losses must be carried forward under s 393.

A number of technical points should be made in connection with the relief under s 393A.

*First*, s 393A was amended in 1997. Formerly it had enabled the carry-back of losses for a three-year period and this is still the case with a terminal loss (see s 393A(2A)).

*Secondly*, on a claim being made a terminal loss will be set against profits of earlier accounting periods falling in the previous three years. It is not possible to claim to set the loss against a particular year in that three-year period: rather it must be offset against *later* periods first. A 2005 loss, for instance, will be offset against 2004; then 2003; and, finally, against the 2002 accounting period.

*Thirdly*, capital allowances may increase the loss to be relieved under s 393A although it should be noted that capital allowances carried forward from an earlier period cannot be included as part of the loss.          **[41.62]**

c)   *General restrictions on the availability of trading loss relief*

There are restrictions on the availability of trading loss relief under TA 1988 s 393 and s 393A.          **[41.63]**

*A commercial purpose* The trade must be carried on commercially with a view to the realisation of a gain if s 393A relief is to be available. Carry-forward (s 393) relief will, however, always apply. **[41.64]**

*Acquiring a tax loss company* TA 1988 ss 768 and 768A can operate to prevent the use of losses where, after the loss has been incurred, there has been a change in the ownership of the company's shares. The purpose of these provisions is to stop the practice of purchasing companies in order to utilise their accumulated tax losses or their past profits (and note that these provisions are extended to cover the sale of investment companies with surplus management expenses and companies carrying on a property business which have Schedule A losses: see **[41.70]**).

There are two relevant factors to be considered in deciding whether loss relief is available:
(1)   whether there has been a change of ownership; and
(2)   what has happened to the business of the company.

TA 1988 s 769 contains detailed rules setting out what constitutes a change in ownership; basically it amounts to a change in the beneficial ownership of more than 50% of the ordinary share capital.

So far as the business of the company is concerned the rules in s 768 apply if either:
(1)   there is a change in the ownership accompanied by a major change in the nature or conduct of the trade and both changes occur within a three-year period (for the interpretation of 'major' see *Willis v Peeters Picture Frames Ltd* (1982); *Purchase v Tesco Stores Ltd* (1984) and SP 10/91); or
(2)   a change in ownership follows a period when the trade carried on by the company has become small or negligible and only after that change of ownership has there been a revival, not necessarily within a three-year period.

HMRC accepts that a major change does not occur if changes are introduced to increase its efficiency; to keep pace with developing technology; or to rationalise the business by withdrawing unprofitable items. SP 10/91 provides the following illustrations of what does and does not amount to a 'major' change:

'*Examples where a change would not of itself be regarded as a major change*

(a)   A company manufacturing kitchen fitments in three obsolescent factories moves production to one new factory (increasing efficiency).
(b)   A company manufacturing kitchen utensils replaces enamel by plastic, or a company manufacturing time pieces replaces mechanical by electronic components (keeping pace with developing technology).
(c)   A company operating a dealership in one make of car switches to operating a dealership in another make of car satisfying the same market (not a major change in the type of property dealt in).
(d)   A company manufacturing both filament and fluorescent lamps (of which filament lamps form the greater part of the output) concentrates solely on filament lamps (a rationalisation of product range without a major change in the type of property dealt in).

(e)    A company whose business consists of making and holding investments in UK quoted shares and securities makes changes to its portfolio of quoted shares and securities (not a change in the nature of investments held).

*Examples where a major change would be regarded as occurring*

(f)    A company operating a dealership in saloon cars switches to operating a dealership in tractors (a major change in the type of property dealt in).

(g)    A company owning a public house switches to operating a discotheque in the same, but converted, premises (a major change in the services or facilities provided).

(h)    A company fattening pigs for their owners switches to buying pigs for fattening and resale (a major change in the nature of the trade, being a change from providing a service to being a primary producer).

(i)    A company switches from investing in quoted shares to investing in real property for rent (a change in the nature of investments held).'    **[41.65]**

*Corporate reconstructions* A company ceases to carry on a trade (eg when the trade is sold) even though the trade may be carried on by another company (TA 1988 s 337(1)). This means that losses cannot be carried forward although carry-back relief may be available.

Where a reconstruction has occurred as a result of which the trade passes from one company to another and both companies are under similar control, TA 1988 s 343 permits losses and capital allowances to be carried forward from the predecessor to the successor company.

There are restrictions on the amount of loss that can be carried forward, typically relevant when the transferor company is insolvent at the time of the transfer. Broadly, if the successor company fails to take over all the liabilities of the transferor (as when part only of the trade—the successful part—is being hived-down into a new 'clean' company) and the transferor has insufficient assets to cover them, the losses which can be transferred are reduced by the amount by which the predecessor's liabilities not transferred exceed the aggregate of the purchase consideration and the assets not transferred.

For s 343 to apply the same person or persons must, some time within the period of two years after the change, directly or indirectly, own the trade (or not less than a three-quarter share in it) and must have owned that trade or the same interest therein within the period of one year before the change. Ownership is normally determined by reference to the ordinary share capital, which is given by TA 1988 s 832 a wider definition than its normal meaning and includes all issued share capital except shares which carry a fixed rate dividend and no other interest in the profits of the company.

A normal hiving-down operation satisfies these requirements although restrictions on the amount of loss that can be carried forward have removed some of its attractions: when only a part of the transferor's trade is transferred (as in the typical hive-down) apportionments must be made to determine what fraction of the loss can be carried forward.

The successor company can amalgamate the predecessor's trade with another enterprise already carried on, although, in this situation, the carried-forward loss relief will only be available against future profits arising from the old trade (*Falmer Jeans v Rodin* (1990)).    **[41.66]**

**EXAMPLE 41.10**

The ordinary share capital of Zee Ltd and Pee Ltd is owned as follows:

|  | *Zee Ltd* | *Pee Ltd* |
|---|---|---|
| Alan | 10 | 8 |
| Ben | 6 | 12 |
| Claud | 30 | 40 |
| Dennis | 29 | 20 |
| Others | 25 | 20 |

A transfer of a trade from Zee Ltd to Pee Ltd would fall within s 343 since the 75% common ownership test is satisfied albeit that the relevant shares in Pee Ltd are owned by the same persons in different proportions.

d)   *Relief for income losses other than trading losses*

Losses of a Schedule A business are calculated in the same way as losses of a trade; however, they are relieved differently. Schedule A losses arising in any year must first be used to reduce total profits of that year. Any unrelieved loss cannot be carried back to the preceding period but must be carried forward to the next period (s 392A(1) and (2)). Schedule A losses brought forward to an accounting period are treated as losses arising in that period and so must be relieved against total profits of that period.

If a company with Schedule A losses ceases to carry on its Schedule A business, but continues to carry on an investment business, the Schedule A losses become excess management expenses. If the company does not have any investment business following the cessation of the Schedule A business, the losses will be extinguished.

Schedule D Case VI losses may be set against Schedule D Case VI income for either the current year or first available future accounting period (TA 1988 s 396).                                                                    **[41.67]**

e)   *Relief for capital losses*

Losses which would be deductible in computing liability to CGT can be set against the first available chargeable gains made by the company. Such losses cannot be offset against income profits.                                      **[41.68]**

## 6   Management expenses

a)   *The basic rule*

Companies with an investment business can deduct sums paid out in management expenses (such as salaries and general office expenditure) from their total profits (for a consideration of the meaning of 'management expenses', see *Camas plc v Atkinson* (2004)).

FA 2004 ss 38–44 and Sch 6, make a number of detailed changes. The main effect is that management expenditure that is capital in nature is not deductible and relief that is available is given only when any management expenses are charged to the profit and loss account. Hence capitalised expenditure will only be relieved if amortised.

A welcome change has been the removal of the restriction that allowed a deduction for management expenses only in companies defined as investment companies. A claim may now be made enabling expenses of management to be deducted to the extent that the expenses are in respect of so much of the company's business as consists in the making of investments provided the investments concerned are not held by the company for an unallowable purpose (ie not chargeable to UK tax) during the accounting period.

HMRC have issued guidance on their view as regards the dividing line between revenue and capital expenditure and on the new 'unallowable purpose' test.

If such expenditure is unrelieved, it can be carried forward and offset in future years, but cannot be carried back to a previous accounting period. Unrelieved charges can likewise be carried forward and treated as management expenses in future years so long as such charges were 'paid for the purpose of so much of the company's business as consists in the making of investments' (TA 1988 s 75(8)).

The term 'investment company' was defined as including:

> 'any company whose business consists wholly or mainly in the making of investments and the principal part of whose income is derived therefrom ...'
>
> (TA 1988 s 130)

For the purposes of the new rules, a company with investment business means any company whose business consists wholly or partly in the making of investments. This extends to non-resident companies undertaking an investment activity through a permanent establishment and eliminates the problem that arose with hybrid companies.

Whilst it is no longer necessary for the company's main activity to be to hold investments from which income in the form of rents, interest and dividends are received, there must be a 'business' with a financial return (see further *Cook v Medway Housing Society Ltd* (1996)).

Hence, authorised unit trusts and savings banks (with the specific exclusion of a trustee savings bank as defined under the Trustee Savings Bank Act 1981) are included. For companies whose business consists of managing land, expenses involved in administering that land will be deductible from the Schedule A profits, whereas the general running costs of the company will be management expenses. Difficulties may arise in obtaining a deduction for expenses such as brokerage and stamp duty relating to the sale of investments which may be classified as part of costs of purchasing and selling (ie as being of a capital nature).                    **[41.69]**

b)    *Sales of surplus management expenses companies*

TA 1988 s 768 (see **[41.65]**) is extended by s 768B so as to apply equally to sales of companies with surplus management expenses. As with the rules dealing with trading losses there has to be a change in the ownership of the company and the management expenses cannot be carried forward to periods beginning after that change in a number of situations. In addition to

those that apply for trading losses there is a further provision designed to prevent the purchaser pumping cash into the acquired company which would be invested to produce income to absorb the management expenses.
[**41.70**]

c)   *The division between investment and trading companies*

The division between trading companies and investment companies is important in that:
(1)   there is a different computation of taxable profits;
(2)   reliefs from capital taxes (CGT and IHT) may be available only to shareholders in trading companies: see, for instance, business assets taper relief for CGT and business property relief for IHT;
(3)   favourable tax treatment for certain corporate transactions, for example repurchase of shares or demergers, is only available to trading companies.
    A *trading company* exists 'wholly or mainly' for the purpose of carrying on a trade. In practice HMRC considers, in doubtful cases, that this phrase means more than 50% and will look at turnover, net profits, net assets and management time to see if this requirement is met. When a holding/subsidiary structure is used the holding company will often be an investment company albeit that its main function is to hold shares in trading subsidiaries. A company may fit in neither the trading nor investment category: in *Tintern Close Residents Society Ltd v Winter* (1995), a residents' company which owned and managed common property such as gardens, roads, footpaths etc and whose main source of income was membership subscriptions, was considered to be neither an investment company nor a trading company. As a result the claim to deduct management expenses was disallowed (see also *White House Drive Residents' Association Ltd v Worsley* (1996) and contrast *Cook v Medway Housing Society Ltd* (1996)).
    As noted above, a welcome change in FA 2004 has been the removal of the restriction determining what qualified for the reliefs available to investment companies. A company may now deduct expenses of management to the extent that the expenses are in respect of so much of the company's business as consists in the making of investments provided the investments concerned are not held by the company for an unallowable purpose (ie for the purpose of activities which are not commercial or not chargeable to UK tax) during the accounting period.                                                        [**41.71**]

## 7   Corporate Venturing Scheme (FA 2000 s 63, Sch 15)

This is a tax incentive scheme (closely mirrored on the EIS and VCT provisions that apply to individuals) designed to encourage companies to invest in small trading companies.                                                        [**41.72**]

a)   *The reliefs*

The investor company obtains tax relief at 20% on sums invested in new ordinary shares that are held for at least three years. For instance, if Xerxes Ltd makes a qualifying investment of £100,000, its corporation tax liability will be reduced by £20,000). When the shares are sold, tax that would otherwise arise may be deferred if the gain is reinvested (up to a year before and three years after the time when the gain is realised) in another qualifying shareholding. If the shares produce a loss on disposal the investor obtains relief for that loss (net of investment relief) against income if the losses are not deducted against gains.                                                    **[41.73]**

b)    *The requirements*

These largely follow the EIS/VCT requirements but the following may be noted:

(1)    the corporate investor cannot obtain relief if it controls the small company in which it invests (control, subject to two modifications, is defined in TA 1988 s 416(2)–(6): see Sch 15 para 8);

(2)    the corporate venturer's stake in the company must not exceed 30% taking into account ordinary share capital and share and loan capital which can be converted into ordinary share capital; and

(3)    the issuing company must not be quoted (although it may subsequently become quoted without relief being forfeited) and at least 20% of its ordinary shares must be owned by one or more independent individuals (Sch 15 para 18).

The gross assets test is the same as for EIS relief as is the trading activities requirement.                                                              **[41.74]**

## 8    Relief for disposals of substantial shareholdings (FA 2002 s 44, Sch 8)

A new relief that had been the subject of extensive consultation was introduced on 1 April 2002 to provide an exemption from tax in respect of gains on the disposal by a company of a substantial shareholding in another company.

The relief applies to capital gains realised by a trading company (or member of a trading group) on the disposal of shares in a trading company (or a member of a trading group). Such gains will be exempt from tax providing the shareholding was 'substantial' that is to say 10% or more of the ordinary share capital and has been held for a continuous period of 12 months during the two years before the disposal. Some key points are as follows:

(1)    The relief applies only to companies.

(2)    It applies to disposals of shares in overseas companies as well as UK companies.

(3)    The company making the disposal must have been a trading company or member of a trading group not only before the disposal but immediately afterwards. This may have the effect of denying the relief to a holding company with a single trading subsidiary.

(4)    A company qualifies as a trading company if its activities do not include to a substantial extent non-trading activities.

(5)    A company qualifies as a member of a trading group if, broadly, the activities of the members of the group taken together do not include to a substantial extent non-trading activities. The meaning of substantial in this context is more than 20% of the activities based on earnings, assets and employee time/expenses (see *Tax Bulletin* 62, December 2002).

(6) Where different companies in a group hold shares in a subsidiary, these may be aggregated for the purposes of establishing whether a 10% shareholding exists.

(7) Provided at least 10% of the ordinary shares have been held for the requisite period, the relief applies to disposals of all types of shares and also of 'assets related to shares' that includes options over shares and securities convertible into shares.

(8) In addition to holding at least 10% of the ordinary shares the company making the disposal must have been beneficially entitled to at least 10% of its distributable profits and at least 10% of its assets on a winding up.

(9) A capital loss made on the disposal of a shareholding that would qualify for the exemption will not be eligible for relief. This rule can not be circumvented by making a negligible value claim under TCGA 1992 s 24(2) and relating it back to a period before 1 April 2002.

**[41.75]–[41.90]**

## IV RAISING FINANCE

### 1 The sources of company finance

There are two major sources of corporate finance. Money can be raised by an allotment of *shares* so that the contributors become members of the company and will generally expect to receive dividends on those shares. Alternatively, money can be borrowed with the company creating *debentures* and paying interest to the debenture holders.

Interest may attract tax relief but dividends are not deductible in arriving at the company's profits. As a result of the limited imputation system a full double charge to tax is avoided but all the corporation tax paid by the company is not credited to the shareholders and so there remains a discrimination in favour of debentures and against raising funds by a share issue. **[41.91]**

### 2 Qualifying corporate bonds

a) *Basic rules for companies*

Certain loans to traders that prove to be irrecoverable qualify for capital gains loss relief (TCGA 1992 s 253). The majority of company loans, however, do not fall within this provision since they are 'debts on security' which are excluded from that section. Until 14 March 1989 this did not matter since relief was separately available for losses incurred by such investors under TCGA 1992 s 251 (relief for debts on security). From that date the law in this area has undergone a series of changes. It is important to appreciate at the outset that the rules for companies and the rules for individuals and trusts are different. For companies, profits and losses on loans are generally included in the company's income computation in accordance with the loan relationship rules so that the CGT rules do not apply. The following discussion is therefore concerned with the position of individuals and trusts. **[41.92]**

## b)    *Definition of a QCB (TCGA 1992 s 117)*

Qualifying corporate bonds (QCBs) are wholly exempt from CGT. Gains are therefore tax-free and no relief is available for losses. The original definition of a QCB involved a sterling denominated bond, debenture or loan stock whether secured or unsecured but restricted to securities which were *either* themselves quoted on the UK Stock Exchange *or* which were issued by a body with other securities so quoted.

FA 1989 widened the definition of a QCB to embrace such securities *whether or not issued by a quoted body*. The consequence was to extend the definition to include virtually all company securities. As a result, the disposal of such securities was wholly exempt from CGT with the result that losses incurred on that disposal were not tax allowable. Not surprisingly, attention was focused on the definition of a QCB in order to draw up an agreement which fell *outside* that definition but which still amounted to a debt on a security thereby enabling loss relief to be available under TCGA 1992 s 251.

**[41.93]**

## c)    *Preserving loss relief for debts on security*

Two devices were commonly employed. *First*, a QCB must be 'expressed in sterling and in respect of which no provision is made for conversion into or redemption in a currency other than sterling' (TCGA 1992 s 117(1)(b)). Accordingly, provisions for redemption in another currency or by reference to another currency could be included to take the bond outside the QCB definition. An *alternative* lay in the requirement that to be a QCB the debt in question must represent and have at all times represented a normal commercial loan (TCGA 1992 s 117(1)(a) and, for the definition of a normal commercial loan, TA 1988 Sch 18 para 1). Providing a right of conversion into shares would ensure that the test was *not* met so that the security was not a QCB.

**[41.94]–[41.95]**

## d)    *'Rolling into' a QCB*

Special rules exist to deal with the situation where a gain is 'rolled into' a QCB. Assume, for instance, that Toby sells his company to Vulture Ltd in consideration for an issue of securities in Vulture that fall within the definition of a QCB. Toby's gains on the disposal of his shares can be rolled into the replacement securities by virtue of TCGA 1992 ss 135–137. If the replacement securities are QCBs, special rules in TCGA 1992 s 116 apply and the gain is not 'rolled over' but merely postponed; to be triggered on a subsequent disposal of the QCB. In effect the gain is held in suspense and will arise *even if* the QCB is sold at a loss or is written off. Toby may therefore realise nothing on his QCB and yet be left with a tax liability. To add insult to injury, relief under TCGA 1992 s 254 will not be available even if the security has become of negligible value because the loan in question will not have been used wholly for trading purposes; it was created to enable Vulture Ltd to acquire Toby's company. If Toby dies still owning the QCB the suspended gain will pass to his personal representatives and fall into charge when they dispose of the bond. HMRC has, however, confirmed that the deferred charge can be avoided if a disposal is made to a charity within TCGA 1992 s 257. There will be no charge on the gift by the donor nor on the subsequent disposal of the bonds by the charity. **[41.96]**

e) *Paper for paper exchanges*

With the introduction of taper relief: **Chapter 20**, it can sometimes be more attractive to sell a company's shares in exchange for loan notes which are not QCBs so as to preserve entitlement to taper relief. **[41.97]**

## 3 Financing a UK subsidiary ('thin capitalisation')

There were no express provisions in the UK tax legislation that denied relief for interest paid by companies that are thinly capitalised (essentially, companies which had debt levels disproportionate to their share capital). The nearest equivalent was TA 1988 s 209(2)(e)(iv) which treated interest paid by companies in certain cases as being a distribution. This provision applied where the borrower was a 75% subsidiary of a non-resident lender *or* where the lender was non-resident and both it and the borrower were 75% subsidiaries of a third non-resident company *or* the borrower and a non-resident lender were 75% subsidiaries of a UK resident third company where less than 90% of the borrower's shares were directly held by a UK resident company. Under these provisions all interest payments were treated as distributions, ie they did not simply strike out 'excessive' payments. In practice the position was usually governed by double tax treaties, but this was not satisfactory since some treaties did not contain any override; in other cases the override did not apply where 'a special relationship' existed between borrower and lender (and it was on the basis of this that thin capitalisation claims were usually submitted by the Revenue). TA 1988 s 808A clarified the interpretation of the 'special relationship' provisions specifying that certain factors had to be taken into account regardless of the wording in the particular treaty.

FA 1995 s 87 repealed s 209(2)(e)(iv) and in its place were rules which apply where both of two conditions are satisfied: either the borrower is a 75% subsidiary of the lender or both are 75% subsidiaries of a third company *and* the whole or any part of the interest paid is greater in amount than would have been paid between unconnected companies. When these rules applied only the *excessive amount* of the interest is treated as a distribution (s 209(2)(da)) and see *Tax Bulletin 17*, June 1995, p 218. Whilst much depends on the business sector of the company concerned, the assets which might provide security, cashflow and the general state of the economy, HMRC is known to favour a debt:equity ratio of 1:1 and income cover of 3:1.

In addition, the recent Advocate-General opinion in the Thin Capitalisation Group Litigation test case (C-524/04) has stated that, even where the debt is not arm's length, so long as the arrangements between companies are put in place for genuine commercial reasons, there should be no need for an adjustment under the thin capitalisation rules (although it also admits that this may be quite rare). Furthermore, adjustments under the thin capitalisation rules should not be made between the UK and the EU unless a corresponding adjustment in the EU country can also be made. The ECJ has yet to deliver its final opinion on this case so this may not precisely follow the A-G's opinion.

From 1 April 2004, these rules have been repealed and the issue has been subsumed into the transfer pricing rules. Hence, arm's length rates and gearing levels must be applied to loans made between companies where one controls the other, or the same person can control both. As explained in **[41.43]** above, the definition of control used here is very wide.

**[41.98]–[41.120]**

## V    CLOSE COMPANIES

Companies controlled by one person or by a small group of individuals could be operated so as to secure tax advantages unavailable to the individual taxpayer or to the larger corporate taxpayer. As a result there have been special rules since 1922 aimed at preventing such arrangements.    **[41.121]**

### 1    What is a close company?

The definition of a close company is:

> 'one which is under the control of five or fewer participators, or of participators who are directors'

> (TA 1988 s 414(1))

Hence, it may be either director-controlled (irrespective of the number of directors involved) or controlled by five or fewer participators. In addition it may be close if it satisfies the winding up test in s 414(2).    **[41.122]**

### a)    *The meaning of 'control'*

A person (or two or more persons taken together) is deemed to have control of a company if:
(1)    he can exercise control over the company's affairs, in particular by possessing or acquiring the greater part of the share capital or voting power; or
(2)    he possesses or is entitled to acquire:
  (a)    such part of the issued share capital as would give him a right to the greater part of the income of the company if it were all to be distributed; or
  (b)    the right to the greater part of the assets available for distribution among the participators on a winding up or in any other circumstances.

In deciding whether a person has control there may be attributed to him any rights vested in his nominees, his associates and companies controlled by him or his associates. A 'nominee' is a person holding assets for another. **[41.123]**

### b)    *The meaning of 'participator', 'associate' and 'director' (TA 1988 s 417)*

'*Participator*' is defined as a person having a share or interest in the capital or income of the company and includes a person who is entitled to acquire share capital or voting rights and loan creditors (but not a bank lending in the ordinary course of its business; TA 1988 s 417(1) (9)).

'*Associate*' of a participator includes: (1) any person related to him as spouse, parent, remoter forebear, sibling, child or remoter issue, or as partner; (2) the trustees of any settlement set up by him or by any person related to him (see, for instance, *R v IRC, ex p Newfields Developments Ltd* (2001)); and (3) fellow beneficiaries under a trust of the company's shares or entitled to shares in the company under the will of a deceased shareholder (TA 1988 s 417(3)).

'*Director*' is defined as a person who occupies that post; any person in accordance with whose instructions the directors act; and a manager of the company who, with his associates, owns or controls 20% of the company's ordinary share capital (TA 1988 s 417(5)).                    **[41.124]**

c)   *Companies that are not close*

The following companies that would otherwise fall within the above definition are treated as not being close companies:
(1)   any non-resident company;
(2)   companies which are registered industrial and provident societies;
(3)   companies controlled by or on behalf of the Crown;
(4)   companies which are controlled by one or more companies which are not close companies and cannot be treated as close except by taking a non-close company as one of the five or fewer participators (therefore, the subsidiary of a non-close company is normally not a close company): note, however, s 414(6) which has the effect that the UK subsidiary of a foreign parent will be close if the parent would be close were it UK resident; and
(5)   companies whose shares have been listed and dealt in on a recognised stock exchange during the preceding 12 months, provided shares carrying at least 35% of the voting power are beneficially held by the public. Shares are not held by the public if (*inter alia*) they are held by a director of the company or his associates and the exception does not apply when the principal members (ie the five members who hold the greatest voting power in the company, but excluding any who hold less than 5% of the voting power) possess more than 85% of the total voting power.                    **[41.125]**

d)   *Illustrations of the definition*

Most small private companies will be close. Where there are fewer than ten shareholders the company must be close since five or fewer shareholders must control it.                    **[41.126]**

**EXAMPLE 41.11**

Aviary Ltd has an authorised and issued share capital of 60,000 ordinary shares of £1 each. Each share carries one vote. The shares are held as follows:

|                                       | *Ordinary shares* |
|---------------------------------------|------------------:|
| Mr A Robin, Chairman                  | 5,000             |
| Mr B Raven, Managing Director         | 2,800             |
| Mr C Crow, Director                   | 2,400             |
| Mr D Hawk, Director                   | 4,400             |
| Mr E Thrush, Director                 | 2,200             |
| Mr F Robin, son of A Robin            | 1,800             |
| Mr G Magpie, Sales Manager            | 3,600             |
| Mr H Magpie, father of G Magpie       | 3,000             |
| Mrs J Eagle, sister of G Magpie       | 3,000             |
| Mrs K Wren, sister of G Magpie        | 2,400             |
| Sundry small shareholders             | 29,400            |
|                                       | 60,000            |

Is Aviary Ltd a close company? It will be necessary to consider voting control and to discover whether it is either a company controlled by five or fewer participators or a company controlled by directors who are participators.

| *Participator/holding*                |        | *Five largest shareholdings* | *Shareholdings of all 'directors'* |
|---------------------------------------|-------:|-----------------------------:|-----------------------------------:|
| G Magpie—Sales Manager                | 3,600  |                              |                                    |
| *Add*: associate holdings:            |        |                              |                                    |
|     H Magpie—father | 3,000 |                             |                                    |
|     Mrs J Eagle—sister | 3,000 |                          |                                    |
|     Mrs K Wren—sister | 2,400 |                           |                                    |
|                                       | 12,000 | 12,000                       | 12,000                             |
| A Robin—Chairman                      | 5,000  |                              |                                    |
| *Add*: associate holding:             |        |                              |                                    |
|     F Robin—son   | 1,800  |                              |                                    |
|                                       | 6,800  | 6,800                        | 6,800                              |
| D Hawk—Director                       |        | 4,400                        | 4,400                              |
| B Raven—Managing Director             | 2,800  | 2,800                        |                                    |
| C Crow—Director                       |        | 2,400                        | 2,400                              |
| E Thrush—Director                     |        | —                            | 2,200                              |
| Total shares                          |        | 28,400                       | 30,600                             |

Although not controlled by five or fewer participators, Aviary Ltd is a close company because it is controlled by its directors. Notice that for this purpose, Mr G Magpie, the sales manager, is treated as a director because with his associates he holds 20% of the company's shares (TA 1988 s 417(5)).

## 2   Special rules that apply to close companies

a)   *Extended meaning of 'distribution' (TA 1988 s 418)*

Close companies are treated as making distributions when they incur expenses in providing living accommodation or other benefits in kind for a participator or his associates. This rule does not apply in cases where the benefit is subject to taxation under the provisions of ITEPA 2003 Part 3, and is designed to catch benefits conferred upon shareholders and debenture holders who are neither directors nor higher-paid employees of that company. The normal rules that govern the taxation of distributions apply (see **Chapter 42**).                                                                  [41.127]

> **EXAMPLE 41.12**
>
> DB Ltd, a close company, provides free holidays costing £1,500 each for Barry, a director, Barney, a shareholder and Betty, a debenture holder.
> (1)   *Barry's holiday* The cost will be a deductible business expense of DB Ltd. Barry will be assessed under the ITEPA 2003 rules on the benefit of £1,500 which he has received.
> (2)   *Barney's and Betty's holiday* In neither case will the expense be charged under ITEPA 2003 but, as both are participators, the expense will be treated as a distribution.

b)   *Loans to participators and their associates (TA 1988 s 419)*

A close company which makes a loan to a participator or his associate is obliged to pay to HMRC an amount equal to 25% of the loan. The loan itself is not a distribution and the borrower is not entitled to any tax credit. The payment to HMRC may best be described as a 'forced' loan so that when the participator repays the loan, HMRC will repay the amount paid. The amount will also be repaid if the loan is either released or written off but in those cases the participator will be assessed to income tax at the Schedule F higher rate (if applicable) on the amount of the loan grossed up at the Schedule F ordinary rate for the year of release (for the meaning of a release in this context see *Collins v Addies; Greenfield v Bains* (1992)). He will not be liable to the Schedule F ordinary rate and cannot reclaim any tax. The company must notify HMRC of the making of such a loan (for a consideration of when a debt was incurred, see *Gold v Inspector of Taxes; HCB Ltd v Inspector of Taxes* (1998)). The tax is due along with the corporation tax for the accounting period (nine months after the end of the accounting period). No payment is necessary if the loan has been repaid at the time the amount becomes payable.

These provisions also catch debts owed to the company, save for the situation where goods or services have been supplied in the ordinary course of the business of the company and the period of credit is either normal or does not exceed six months. Debts assigned to the company are likewise treated as loans but the misappropriation of a company's funds does not create a debt since the necessary consensus is lacking (*Stephens v Pittas* (1983)).

The rules do not apply to loans made in the ordinary course of a company's business of money lending nor to loans not exceeding £15,000 to someone who works full-time for the company and who does not have a material interest in it (a material interest is normally 5% of the ordinary shares).

Two other points must be mentioned. *First,* if the loan is to a director or higher-paid employee, income tax may also be charged under ITEPA 2003, on the beneficial loan based on the interest forgone; and, *secondly,* loans to directors are, in general, prohibited under the CA 1985 s 330.        **[41.128]**

c)    *Close investment-holding companies*

Special rules apply to close companies which are not trading companies or members of a trading group. For these purposes a company will be trading if it exists wholly or mainly for the purposes of trading so that it will not necessarily have to trade in every accounting period in order to satisfy the test. Companies that deal in land, shares or securities are trading companies for these purposes and a company carrying on property investment on a commercial basis will likewise be treated as a trading company and therefore will not be a CIC.

The consequence of being a CIC is that neither the small companies' rate of corporation tax (currently 19%) nor the starting rate (0% for FY 2005) is available: instead the company will suffer corporation tax at the main rate of 30%.                                                    **[41.129]–[41.150]**

## VI    THE OVERSEAS DIMENSION

### 1    Liability to tax

A company that is resident in the UK is liable to corporation tax on all its profits wherever arising (TA 1988 s 8(1)). A non-resident company is liable to corporation tax only if it trades in the UK through a permanent establishment and liability will then be restricted to the chargeable profits from that permanent establishment (TA 1988 s 11). A non-resident company having income arising in the UK but not trading through a permanent establishment cannot be assessed to corporation tax but may be subject to UK income tax. This will frequently be the position where a non-resident company owns investment property in the UK giving rise to rental income. In such cases, as the company will probably not have any UK presence, the UK Revenue may have problems of tax collection. In the case of rental income the problem is resolved by the obligation on the tenant to deduct tax from the rents. A charge (to corporation tax) under the CGT rules will only arise on the trade assets of non-resident companies trading through a permanent establishment in the UK (TCGA 1992 s 10B).                                    **[41.151]**

### 2    Computation of profits

The basic rule is that companies must compute and express their profits and losses and their corporation tax liability in sterling. However, companies that satisfy the relevant conditions must compute the profit or losses of a trade in either the company's accounting currency or its functional currency. That basic profit or loss is then translated into sterling at an appropriate exchange rate. FA 1993 ss 92–92E sets out the conditions that have to be met if a currency other than sterling is to be used: in simple terms the question depends on the currency the accounts are drawn up in and its functional currency. Functional currency is defined in FA 1993 s 92E(3) as the '... currency of the primary economic environment in which the company operates.'    **[41.152]**

## 3  The meaning of 'residence'

Formerly, companies were treated as UK resident and taxed accordingly if their central management and control was situated in the UK. The law developed in a series of cases and where precisely management and control is exercised is a factual question of some difficulty. Generally, of course, such powers will be vested in the board of directors, so that the problem becomes one of identifying where the board exercises its powers (see, for instance, *Untelrab Ltd v McGregor, Unigate Guernsey Ltd v McGregor* (1995)). Two general points should be stressed. *First,* that the overseas country where the company was incorporated is usually of small significance when it is a question of establishing UK residence. *Secondly,* it is possible under English law for a company to be 'dual resident', ie resident in more than one country.

This residence test is supplemented by an additional test based upon the place of company incorporation. UK incorporated companies will *always* be taxed as UK resident irrespective of where central management and control is exercised. This is subject to the qualification that 'dual resident' companies that would not be regarded as UK resident under the 'tie-breaker' provisions of a double tax treaty are not treated as UK resident. Subject to this qualification, there is now a dual test in operation as a result of which a company will be UK resident if *either* it was incorporated here *or,* in the case of companies incorporated abroad, its central management and control is located here (SP 1/90 sets out HMRC's views on these rules). There are exceptions and transitional provisions for certain companies which were carrying on business before the incorporation test came into effect.

The case of *Wood v Holden* (2006) emphasised that, if an overseas company holds its board meetings outside the UK then, *prima facie,* the central management and control of the company is outside the UK unless it can be shown that a UK resident 'outsider' had dictated or usurped the powers of the board. A board acting on the proposals and advice of another (rather than that other dictating the decisions to be taken) is still effectively managing and controlling the company.    **[41.153]**

### EXAMPLE 41.13

(1)  Styx Ltd, a UK incorporated company, was trading on 15 March 1988 (when the supplementary test based on UK incorporation was introduced) and, because its management was located in Liechtenstein, was then treated as non-UK resident. As the transitional period has expired it is now treated as UK resident unless it qualifies for one of the exceptions to the incorporation rule.

(2)  Aster Ltd was incorporated in the UK on 31 March 1995 and is managed and controlled from Liechtenstein. It is resident in the UK.

(3)  Rambo Ltd is incorporated in Panama and controlled by directors resident in the UK. It is resident in the UK.

## 4   Tax consequences of ceasing to be UK-resident

Subject to the 'tie-breaker' provisions, a UK incorporated company cannot lose its UK residence. In the case of overseas companies, however, if central management and control becomes located elsewhere, UK residence will cease and in that event a tax charge will arise on the unrealised gains of the company immediately prior to its change of residence. TCGA 1992 s 185 deems the company to have disposed of all its assets at market value immediately before it becomes non-resident and to have immediately reacquired them (note that if the tax is not paid within six months from becoming payable it may be collected from other persons: TCGA 1992 s 190). If at any later time the company carries on a trade in the UK through a permanent establishment the deemed disposal does not apply to any assets that are situated in the UK and are used in or for the trade, or are used or held for the permanent establishment.

**EXAMPLE 41.14**

On 1 August 2002 Rambo Ltd (see *Example 41.13*, above) ceases to be UK resident. At the relevant time it owns chargeable assets worth £200,000 on which its allowable expenditure is £50,000. Immediately before its change in residence it is deemed to sell the assets for £200,000, immediately reacquiring them, and thereby realising a chargeable gain of £150,000 (subject to the indexation allowance) in FY 2002.

The company must inform HMRC in advance of its intention to cease UK residence (see SP 2/90 for the procedure to be followed) and this should be done by notice in writing specifying the time when this change will occur and should include a statement of UK tax payable together with particulars of how that tax is to be paid. The tax in question will include any PAYE for which the company is liable. If such tax remains unpaid for more than six months, it may then be recovered from, *inter alia*, a controlling director or another company in the same group. Failure by the company to comply with the notification procedures before ceasing to be UK resident may lead to a penalty on both the company and certain other persons: the maximum amount payable being equal to the tax unpaid at the time when the company ceased to be resident.                                    **[41.154]**

## 5   Taxing resident companies

All profits wherever made by a UK resident company will be charged to corporation tax subject to any available double taxation reliefs.

When a trade is to be carried out by a UK company in a foreign country there are three possible methods of operation available.

*First*, the trade may be with that country so that there is no trading presence within the country and foreign tax is avoided (typically a representative office is established in the foreign country).

*Secondly*, a branch may be opened overseas which, from a UK tax point of view, results in any profits being subject to corporation tax. It also means that loss relief will be available. If a foreign branch is incorporated by the formation of a subsidiary company in the foreign jurisdiction it is possible to postpone the payment of UK tax on capital gains that would otherwise result: see TCGA 1992 s 140.

*Thirdly,* a subsidiary non-resident company may be formed with the result that corporation tax is generally avoided on profits until they are distributed to the UK by way of dividend. The attractions are obviously considerable when the tax rates in the overseas country are low in comparison with those in the UK and TA 1988 ss 747–756 contain provisions to prevent tax avoidance by the use of controlled foreign companies (see **[41.161]**).

Until recently, the UK group relief rules did not permit losses arising in overseas companies to be surrendered to cover profits in UK resident companies. Following the decision in *Marks & Spencer plc v Halsey* at the European Court of Justice, group relief has been extended to allow losses arising in subsidiaries based in the European Economic Area ('EEA') to be surrendered against profits of that company's UK parent and the parent's UK subsidiaries in certain circumstances. In particular, it is required that the loss has not been and cannot be relieved in any period in the EEA territory. This change has a very limited scope and does not address a number of other situations (for example group relief between an EEA company and a UK company that have a common parent company which is not resident in the UK): further developments are expected in this area in the coming years.

**[41.155]**

## 6   Double tax relief

### (a)   *General principles*

Double tax relief permits the set-off of foreign tax against UK corporation tax on the profits of the branch or distributions from a subsidiary company either by virtue of a double tax treaty with the relevant country (TA 1988 s 788) or by unilateral relief (TA 1988 s 790).          **[41.156]**

**EXAMPLE 41.15**

|  | £ |
|---|---|
| UK profits | 2,000,000 |
| Overseas branch profit (income and gains) | 80,000 |
| (overseas tax paid £25,000) | |
|  | £2,080,000 |
| Corporation tax (30%) | 624,000 |
| *less* relief (restricted) | 24,000 |
| UK tax payable | £600,000 |

*Notes*:
(1)   At its simplest double tax relief cannot exceed the amount of corporation tax attributable to the foreign income or gains; hence the maximum relief in this example is 30% of £80,000 = £24,000.

(2)    Double tax relief has become substantially more complex following changes made in FA 2000 and FA 2001 to deal with perceived abuse of mixer companies (see **[41.159]**).

### (b)    *Double tax agreements*

A large number of bilateral agreements are currently in place. Under these arrangements, certain classes of income derived from the participating countries are given complete exemption from income and capital gains taxes in the country from which they arise. In other cases relief from UK taxation is generally given in the form of a credit, calculated by reference to the foreign tax suffered. The credit is set against the UK tax chargeable on the doubly taxed income or gain.

Where double tax relief applies no deduction for foreign tax is generally allowed in assessing the foreign income or gain. If, however, a taxpayer does not take the credit allowable by an agreement, any foreign tax paid on that income, in the place where it arises, is deductible from the income for purposes of the UK tax assessment. Double tax agreements normally contain a 'mutual agreement procedure' that enables a taxpayer to present his case to the competent authority in his state of residence if he considers that the action of a tax authority has resulted, or will result, in taxation not in accordance with the agreement. The UK competent authority is HMRC.

**[41.157]**

### (c)    *Unilateral relief*

Where tax on overseas income is not relieved, or is only partly relieved, under an agreement, unilateral relief will normally apply.

The mechanics and limits are substantially the same as those under which the bilateral agreements operate.                                          **[41.158]**

### (d)    *Double tax relief and mixer companies (FA 2000 s 103, Sch 30)*

*Example 41.15* illustrates the use of the credit method of giving double tax relief. Much of the foreign tax relieved in the UK is underlying tax, ie tax paid on the profits out of which a foreign company pays a dividend. The purpose of a mixer company is to mix (or average out) foreign taxes paid in different countries to set against the UK tax charged at 30% on the single dividend that is paid out of the mixer company.

**EXAMPLE 41.16**

*Notes:*

|  |  | £ |
|---|---|---|
| (1) | Dividend paid to UK parent | 4,200 |
|  | Underlying tax | 1,800 |
|  |  | 6,000 |
|  | UK corporation tax (30%) | 1,800 |

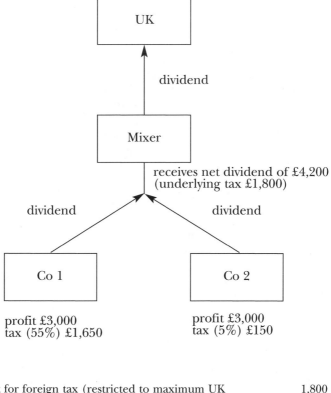

Credit for foreign tax (restricted to maximum UK           1,800
corporation tax payable)

Tax payable                                                Nil

(2)    If Co 1 had been directly owned by the UK company only 900 of the foreign tax suffered would have been relieved (*viz* 30% × £3,000).

In FA 2000 the Government restricted the use of mixer companies by introducing provisions to eliminate the tax advantage of routing overseas dividends through mixer companies in favourable foreign jurisdictions (such as the Netherlands). This applies to claims for credit relief made on or after 31 March 2001. The restriction applies to the relievable underlying tax in respect of any dividend paid up through an overseas subsidiary. Relief for underlying tax is generally restricted to the full corporation tax rate in force when the dividend is paid. However, a partial relief from this capping restriction is provided by the concurrent introduction of a system of 'onshore pooling' of certain foreign dividends. In such cases, relief is available up to a maximum of 45% in total. Relief may similarly be obtained up to the same overall 45% limit for unrelieved withholding and underlying tax on dividends received directly from overseas subsidiaries. The two main exclusions from the onshore pool are dividends paid by controlled foreign companies to satisfy the acceptable distribution policy test (see [**41.161**]), or dividends representing such dividends, and dividends for which relief is itself restricted.

**[41.159]–[41.160]**

## 7    Controlled foreign companies (CFCs): TA 1988 ss 747–756, Schs 24–26

This legislation enables the Board to tax UK companies on profits made by certain overseas corporations. Chargeable profits of the overseas entity are apportioned to those with an interest in the CFC and a UK resident company holding, with connected persons and associates, at least a 25% interest in the CFC will be assessed on its apportioned share of the profits. The provisions only apply if the CFC is under UK control and is resident in a 'low tax' area, defined as one where the tax is less than three-quarters of what would have been charged in the UK. 'Under UK control' for these purposes includes cases where a company is controlled jointly by a UK resident person and a foreign resident person and each of them has at least 40%, but not more than 55%, of their joint controlling interest (the test is aimed at joint ventures). Even then the CFC's chargeable profit (as to which see *Bricom Holdings Ltd v IRC* (1997)) must exceed £50,000 (reduced if the period is less than a full year). There are provisions to ensure that the charge will only arise where a CFC is used with the object of avoiding tax and to exclude CFCs which are pursuing an 'acceptable distribution policy', or which carry on 'exempt activities'. So far as the former is concerned, trading companies have to distribute 90% of their taxable profits less capital gains and foreign tax in order for the company to be pursuing an acceptable distribution policy. The provisions do not cover chargeable gains which may, however, be apportioned amongst UK shareholders under TCGA 1992 s 13 when the overseas company is one which would be close under UK rules. SI 1998/3081 sets out the regulations governing the countries in which residence and the carrying on of a business will not trigger a charge under the CFC legislation. So far as the exempt activities test (or EAT) is concerned the rules restrict the use of intra-group service companies and limit the cases where an overseas holding company qualifies for exemption.

A recent decision by the European Advocate-General (*Cadbury Schweppes* (Case C-196/04)) has indicated that the UK CFC rules are, to an extent, incompatible with EU law. Essentially, an EU subsidiary of a UK company should not be subject to the UK CFC rules even if the establishment of that company was done explicitly to benefit from more favourable tax rates. This basic position, however, can be overridden if the overseas company has no real substance in the overseas territory, ie it has no proper establishment there, its services are not actually performed there or the services performed by the company have no real value such that the profits arising in that company do not reflect the commercial reality. The ECJ has yet to deliver its final opinion on this case so the decision may not incorporate all of the A-G's opinions.

With the arrival of corporate self-assessment, companies need to have in place systems which will allow them to collect all information necessary to decide whether the CFC legislation will apply because if so, the company must account for any tax due.                                        **[41.161]**

## 8    Taxing non-UK resident companies

Companies not resident in the UK are subject to corporation tax on income arising from a trade carried on in the UK through a permanent establishment. The crucial factor in establishing a liability to UK tax is, therefore, whether a trade is carried on within the UK or not (see further **Chapter 18**). Other income arising from a UK source may be charged to income tax in the non-resident company's hands (TA 1988 s 6(2)). Hence, a property investment company with no permanent establishment in the UK, but owning land in the UK, would be subject to income tax on the profits arising from that land.

Capital gains are chargeable only if they arise from property associated with the trade carried on by the permanent establishment (TA 1988 s 11(2); TCGA 1992 s 10B). In the case, therefore, of a non-resident property company owning land in the UK, no chargeable gain will arise on a disposal of its capital assets. A UK resident subsidiary of an overseas company is a separate legal entity from the overseas company and will be subject to UK tax on its worldwide income. If a UK permanent establishment is transferred to a UK resident company in the same worldwide group as the transferor company the transfer falls within the capital gains group rules (TCGA 1992 s 171). **[41.162]**

## 9   Taxing non-resident shareholders of resident companies

The tax credit and FII provisions only apply to a resident shareholder. Therefore, a non-resident is not (subject to the provisions of a double tax treaty) entitled to any tax credit (TA 1988 s 231). The non-resident is not liable to income tax on the dividend (FA 1995 s 128).     **[41.163]–[41.180]**

## VII   CORPORATE SELF-ASSESSMENT

### 1   Introduction

Self-assessment for companies was introduced for accounting periods ending on or after 1 July 1999 (see FA 1998 s 117 and Schs 18 and 19).     **[41.181]**

### 2   The operation of pay and file and corporate self-assessment

a)   *Payment of tax and filing returns*

Since the introduction of Corporation Tax Self Assessment in 1999, HMRC no longer issue assessments of the company's tax liability. The tax return itself must include a self-assessment of the tax payable for that accounting period based upon the information contained in the return and taking into account any claims for relief or allowances. The self-assessment must include any sums due under eg TA 1988 s 419(1), the transfer pricing and the CFC legislation. In addition, it is necessary for the return to contain details of any tax 'schemes' that need to be disclosed under the Tax Avoidance Schemes (Information) Regulations introduced in the FA 2004.

In general, the company's taxable profits will automatically be determined on the basis of the self-assessment. HMRC may, by notice to the company, correct a return or make an amendment to a return for obvious errors or omissions within certain time periods. HMRC is also entitled to 'enquire' into the return and if it does so the taxable profits will be determined at the end of the enquiry.

The filing deadline for the corporation tax return is normally 12 months after the end of the period to which the return relates. When filing the return the company must deliver computations showing how the figures in the return were calculated and a copy of its audited accounts for the period.

Claims for group relief, capital allowances and certain tax credits must be made through the completed tax return. Under corporate self-assessment, the rules provide that claims and consents to the surrender of group relief can no longer be amended but must formally be withdrawn and replaced, if appropriate, by a new claim.

The requirement to make a return is not automatic. A company is only required to make a return if a form is sent to it. However, a company that is liable to pay corporation tax in respect of an accounting period must notify HMRC of this fact within 12 months of the end of that accounting period. Furthermore, the company must pay its estimated corporation tax liability by the normal due date.

FA 2004 s 55 has introduced a requirement for companies to notify HMRC (within three months) of the beginning of its first accounting period, and of the beginning of any subsequent accounting period that does not immediately follow the end of a previous accounting period.                    **[41.182]**

b)   *Interest*

Although tax returns need not be filed until 12 months after the end of the relevant accounting period, the normal due date for payment of corporation tax remains. For most companies this will be nine months after the end of the accounting period. Large companies (as defined by SI 1998/3175) may have obligations under the quarterly payments system (see **[41.185]**). Interest will run as from the date for payment if the tax has not been paid. Interest on any overpayment or underpayment will also be calculated from the due date. Not surprisingly, the interest on overpayments will not be as high as the interest on underpayments, and the rates of interest are closely linked to market rates.                                                            **[41.183]**

c)   *Late and incorrect returns* (*TMA 1970 s 94*)

If a completed return is not delivered to HMRC within the 12-month period, the following rapidly escalating penalties are automatically imposed:

| | |
|---|---|
| Return filed within 12 months: | no penalty |
| Return filed within 15 months: | £100 |
| Return filed within 18 months: | £200 |
| Return filed within 24 months: | £200 + 10% of unpaid tax |
| Return filed outside 24 months: | £200 + 20% of unpaid tax |

Companies which are guilty of persistent failure to make returns are subject to more severe penalties since if a penalty has been levied in respect of both of the two previous accounting periods, and the return for the third period is also late, the flat rate penalties become £500 (instead of £100) and £1,000 (instead of £200). The penalty for incorrect returns can be as much as the amount of the tax for the period for which the return is made.    **[41.184]**

**EXAMPLE 41.17**

A Ltd makes up its accounts to 31 October each year. Its corporation tax return for the year ended 31 October 2003 is submitted on:
(1)    15 November 2004; or
(2)    15 March 2005; or
(3)    15 January 2006: no tax was unpaid on 1 May 2005; or
(4)    15 January 2006: £1,000 tax was unpaid on 1 May 2005, but was paid by 10 June 2005.
   The penalties levied under each of these alternatives are:
(1)    £100 (£500 if the returns for the previous two accounting periods were also late);
(2)    £200 (£1,000 if the returns for the previous two accounting periods were also late);
(3)    £200 (or £1,000—no tax-related penalty is due);
(4)    £400 (or £1,200—a tax-related penalty (20% × £1,000) is added to the flat rate penalty).
   For the purposes of calculating penalties, 'unpaid tax' means the amount owing after 18 months, account being taken of credit for income tax withheld.

### d)   Quarterly payments

For accounting periods ending on or after 1 July 1999 large companies have to pay their corporation tax in instalments calculated according to their anticipated final tax bill for the current period. A large company is a company whose taxable profits in any accounting period exceed £1,500,000. The regulations provide, however, that a company is not a large company for the purposes of the quarterly payment regulations if its total tax liability for the accounting period does not exceed £10,000. There is a further exclusion in circumstances where the profits for the period do not exceed £10m and the company was not a large company in the 12 months preceding the accounting period. The idea is that companies within the new payment system are those which have sophisticated accounting and administrative systems in place already that can handle the quarterly payment charge quite easily. In determining whether a company is large or not any associated companies must be taken into account. The £1,500,000 limit and the £10m profit limit are reduced by dividing them between the number of companies in the group. The *de minimis* exclusions referred to above will still apply. All the above limits are reduced proportionately for periods of less than one year.
   In the case of a large company with a 12-month accounting period the payment dates for corporation tax will now be as follows:
(1)   six months and 14 days from the start of the accounting period;
(2)   nine months and 14 days from the start of the accounting period;
(3)   14 days after the end of the accounting period;
(4)   three months and 14 days from the end of the accounting period.

There are provisions for HMRC to repay tax to a company which believes that it has over-estimated the instalments which become due. Interest will be payable on late paid instalments and HMRC will pay interest on overpaid tax.

[**41.185**]

### 3   Anti-avoidance: company purchase schemes

When the ownership of a company changes hands and that company fails to pay corporation tax for any period before the date of the change, the tax may be assessed on any person who had control of the company before the change (or any company which that person controlled: see TA 1988 s 767A and s 767B). The relevant circumstances are similar to those which apply in relation to carry forward losses under TA 1988 s 768 (see [**41.65**]) and typically involve the vendor first stripping out trading assets to another group company then selling the company to a purchaser who leaves the company unable to pay its tax liabilities. Accordingly, great care needs to be exercised in structuring sales of companies and in drafting suitable tax indemnities.

[**41.186**]

# 42 Company distributions and shareholders

*Updated by Michael Haig, Corporate Tax Manager, KPMG LLP (UK), Gatwick Office*

---

---

## I   MEANING OF A DISTRIBUTION (TA 1988 PART VI CHAPTERS II AND III)

The term 'distribution' is widely defined to cover not only the payment of dividends but any method of transferring the company's profits to its members.

For the company, a distribution is not deductible in arriving at its profits for corporation tax: distributions are made out of profits after tax.

For individual shareholders the gross amount of the distribution is treated as income falling under Schedule F until 5 April 2005 and as savings and investment income under ITTOIA 2005 Part 4 thereafter.

Distributions received as corporate shareholders are called 'franked investment income' (FII).            **[42.1]**

The intention is to catch not merely the payment of profits to shareholders in the form of a dividend, but all payments and transfers by a company to its members other than repayment of capital subscribed, including the purchase by the company of its own shares (see **[42.21]**); other examples are discussed below.            **[42.2]**

### 1   Any distribution out of the assets of the company which is made in respect of shares except insofar as it is a repayment of capital or equal to any new consideration received (TA 1988 s 209(2)(b))

When sums are returned to shareholders on a reduction of capital, they will not be treated as distributions provided that they do not exceed the original amount subscribed (including any premium paid on the allotment of the shares). Payments to members on a winding up are expressly excluded from the definition of a distribution (such sums will usually be liable to CGT in the hands of the shareholders). The issue of bonus shares is not itself a distribution, but a repayment of share capital in the following ten years will be a distribution up to the amount paid up on the bonus issue: see TA 1988 s 211 (see also [42.4]). [42.3]

### EXAMPLE 42.1

U Ltd has a share capital of 100 ordinary £1 shares. It makes a 1:1 bonus issue by capitalising £100 of reserves. Later it repays the shareholders 50p per share on a reduction of capital. Each shareholder is treated as receiving a distribution on the reduction in capital.

*Position of a shareholder:* Originally, he owned one £1 share. After the bonus issue, he owns two £1 shares. After the reduction in capital, he owns two 50p shares and has £1 in cash. The shareholder is in the same position as if he had received a £1 dividend and is taxed as such.

## 2  A reduction of share capital followed by a bonus issue (TA 1988 s 210)

Essentially, this is the same operation as described at [42.3] but in a different order and it has similar taxation consequences. These consequences will not follow if the gap between repayment and the bonus issue exceeds ten years providing the bonus issue is not of redeemable shares and the company is not a closely controlled company within TA 1988 s 704. In addition, the bonus issue cannot be regarded as a distribution if the repaid share capital consisted of fully paid preference shares. [42.4]

### EXAMPLE 42.2

U Ltd has a share capital of 100 £1 shares. It makes a reduction of share capital by repaying 50p per share. It then issues 100 50p bonus shares (ie a 1:1 issue).

*Position of a shareholder:* originally, he held one £1 share. After the repayment of capital, he owns one 50p share and has 50p in cash. After the bonus issue, he owns two 50p shares and has received 50p in cash. Hence, he has shares of identical aggregate par value to the one share held at the start and has received a 50p payment from the company which will be treated as a distribution.

## 3  The issue of bonus redeemable shares and securities (TA 1988 s 209(2)(c))

A bonus issue of redeemable shares (ie shares which the company has express authority or an obligation to redeem in the future) and of securities is a distribution. Unlike the other types of distribution, this is a '*non-qualifying*' distribution, the taxation consequences of which are considered at [42.121]. It should be noted that the company is not, at the time of the distribution, paying out money to shareholders, but is entering into a commitment to do so in the future. The value of the distribution will, in the case of shares, be the nominal value together with any premium payable on redemption. In the case of other securities, it will be the amount secured together with any premium payable on redemption. When redeemable shares and securities are redeemed, the redemption will normally be a qualifying distribution. **[42.5]**

## 4 A transfer by a company to its members of assets or liabilities which are worth more than any new consideration furnished by the member (TA 1988 s 209(4))

The excess of the value of any assets or liabilities transferred by a company to its members over any new consideration furnished by the members is a distribution. **[42.6]**

### EXAMPLE 42.3

John is a member of J Ltd. He sells his house to J Ltd for £200,000 when the market value of the house is only £150,000. The excess £50,000 value will be taxed as a distribution in his hands.

## 5 Certain interest payments (see generally CTM 15515)

Interest payments geared to the profits of the company (irrespective of the reasonableness of the rate) or excessive interest (that which exceeds a reasonable commercial return) may be treated as distributions by TA 1988 s 209(2)(d), (e)(iii). Interest payments on bonus securities and on securities that are convertible whether directly or indirectly into shares in the company (unless listed on The Stock Exchange) are distributions. These rules do not apply if the payment is to another company within the charge to corporation tax, except to the extent that the interest exceeds a reasonable commercial return (and subject to certain other exceptions).

For the position of interest payments made to an overseas parent by a connected company see TA 1988 s 209(2)(da) discussed at **[42.98]** (repealed with effect from 1 April 2004; see also *Tax Bulletin*, 17, at p 218 and generally CTM 15515). **[42.7]**

### EXAMPLE 42.4

Zee Ltd borrows £50,000 from Con at a rate of interest of 10% pa. A reasonable commercial rate would be 6%. The company pays £5,000 pa to Con of which £3,000 is deductible from profits for corporation tax purposes. The excess (£2,000 pa) is a distribution on which Con will be taxed as savings and investment income under ITTOIA 2005 Part 4.

The intention of this provision is to prevent equity investment being artificially characterised as a loan in order to obtain corporation tax relief on the payment of the interest. From 21 March 2000 it has not caught 'ratchet loans': *viz* commercial loans with interest rates linked to profit so that the rate of interest reduces as business profits improve (or conversely the rate increases as business results deteriorate): see TA 1988 s 209(3B) inserted by FA 2000.

## 6 'Equity loans'

Equity loans are perpetual debt instruments issued by UK resident companies. The term itself is defined in TA 1988 s 209(2)(e)(vii) and (9). A typical illustration is a security with no fixed date for redemption. The UK formerly taxed payments under the instrument as 'interest' but the above provisions now reclassify such payments as distributions. Holding companies chargeable to UK corporation tax are generally unaffected (TA 1988 s 212).

[**42.8**]

### 7  The stock dividend option (see CTM 17005)

ITTOIA 2005 s 410(2) provides that where shares are offered to shareholders instead of a cash dividend, those shares will be treated as income in the shareholders' hands (see further [**42.150**] for a consideration of the enhanced stock dividend).    [**42.9**]

### 8  Special rules for close companies

Where a close company provides a benefit for a participator the cost of providing the benefit is treated as a distribution: see TA 1988 s.418 and [**42.127**].    [**42.10**]–[**42.20**]

## II  DISTRIBUTIONS AND COMPANY BUY-BACKS

The Companies Act 1985 ss 159–181 allows companies to purchase their own shares. Generally, such purchases must be paid for out of distributable profits, but private companies may use the proceeds of a fresh issue of capital. Any payment to a shareholder in excess of the sum originally subscribed on the allotment of the shares is treated as a distribution, unless the repayment occurs on a winding up of the company. TA 1988 s 219 provides that where certain conditions are satisfied, a purchase by a company of its own shares will *not* be treated as a distribution so that any profit made will be within the scope of capital gains tax. If the conditions of s 219 are not satisfied the buy-back will be treated as a distribution. The conditions are as follows.

[**42.21**]

### 1  The company

The company must be unquoted: that is to say, its shares must not be listed on the official list of a stock exchange but its shares may be dealt in on AIM. It must be either a trading company or the holding company of a trading group. A trading group is a group, the business of whose members taken together consists wholly or mainly of the carrying on of a trade.    [**42.22**]

### 2  The vendor of the shares

#### a)  *Qualifying vendors*

The vendor may be an individual, a trustee, the PR of a deceased share-holder, or a company. He must be resident and, if an individual, ordinarily resident in the UK throughout the tax year. Normally, the shares must have been owned for the whole of the five years ending with the transfer and it is not possible to aggregate different ownership periods. Accordingly, where assets are transferred to a trust or distributed by trustees to a beneficiary, the transferor must satisfy the five-year period. In the exceptional cases of husband/wife and of the deceased/his PRs and legatees, aggregation is permissible and in the latter case the aggregated ownership period need only be three years. [42.23]

b) *The 'substantial reduction' test*

The vendor must 'substantially reduce' his shareholding which means that his interest in the company must go down by at least 25%. In determining whether a substantial reduction has been achieved it should be remembered that shares bought back by the company are cancelled (see Companies Act 1985 s 160(4)). [42.24]

**EXAMPLE 42.5**

A Ltd has 100 shares in issue held by:

| | |
|---|---:|
| A | 40 |
| B | 30 |
| C | 20 |
| D | 10 |
| | 100 |

A Ltd buys back 10 of A's shares. A will then have 30 shares compared with the 40 shares he previously owned, which looks like a 25% reduction in his shareholding. However, when his 10 shares are purchased by A Ltd they are cancelled and the issued share capital is reduced to 90; A's shares therefore represent a 33.33% holding which is more than 75% of his previous holding. This will not satisfy the substantial reduction test.

For A to satisfy the substantial reduction test he would need to sell at least 15 shares so that his holding is reduced to 25 shares out of a total of 85: a 29.4% holding which is less than 75% of his previous holding of 40%.

c) *The 'connected' test*

After the purchase the vendor must not be 'connected' with the acquiring company (TA 1988 s 223). For this purpose 'connected' means holding more than 30% of the company's:
(1) issued ordinary share capital;
(2) share and loan capital (loan capital is widely defined in TA 1988 s 228(6) to include, eg a director's loan account); or
(3) voting power. [42.25]

d) *Other matters*

In calculating these fractions, spouses and associates are treated as one person. As any transactions in the same shares within 12 months of the sale will form part of the same transaction, it follows that replacement shares must not be acquired within a period of one year. [42.26]

## 3  The reason for the sale

There are two permissible reasons. First, the purchase by the company must benefit its trade (or that of a 75% subsidiary) and not be part of a scheme designed to enable the shareholders to participate in the company's profits without receiving a dividend or otherwise to avoid tax. The requirement that the purchase must be a 'benefit to the trade' is not an easy test to satisfy. For instance, the buying out of dissident shareholders is certainly for the benefit of the company but that is not necessarily the same as being for the benefit of the trade—unless it can be shown that the continued dissension was harming the management and therefore the trade of the company (contrast the position if money was needed urgently by the vendor, eg to fund a divorce settlement). In practice, HMRC has stated (see SP 2/82) that it will expect the requirement to be satisfied in such cases and where the vendor shareholder is genuinely giving up his entire interest in the company.

### EXAMPLE 42.6

(1)  It is proposed that WW Ltd (an unquoted trading company) purchases the shares of Mr Wam, one of the original founders of the company. He is willing to sell a 60% holding but wishes to keep a small (5%) holding for sentimental reasons. Mr Wam is retiring in favour of a new management team. On HMRC practice the transaction would be regarded as for the benefit of the trade of WW Ltd and, the other conditions being satisfied, the payment for the shares will not be a distribution.

(2)  Sal is the sole shareholder in Sal Ltd, an unquoted trading company. Profits amount to £100,000 for the present accounting period and Sal Ltd plans to use them to purchase 50% of Sal's shares. This proposal will not be within the provisions of TA 1988 s 219 because:

    (i)  it would appear to be a scheme designed to pass the profits to Sal without declaring a dividend;

    (ii)  Sal is not substantially reducing her holding since she will still own all the shares in Sal Ltd;

    (iii)  the purchase is not for the benefit of Sal Ltd's trade.

The second permitted reason for the sale of the shares is where the whole, or substantially the whole, of the proceeds of sale are to be used by the recipient in discharging his IHT liability charged on a death. The money must be so used within two years of death and it has to be shown that the IHT cannot be paid without undue hardship unless the shares are sold back to the company. In this case the above requirements as to the vendor of the shares do not apply. The IHT need not be due in respect of the shares.    **[42.27]**

### EXAMPLE 42.7

(1)  Sam inherits the family residence on his father's death. Under the terms of the will it is to bear its own IHT which can be raised by the sale of Sam's shareholding in Sham Ltd (a trading company which is not listed). The only alternative would involve the sale of the family house. If the shares are sold to Sham Ltd, the purchase money will not be treated as a distribution.

(2)  Sue inherits 30% of the share capital of Carruthers Ltd. She does not want the shares and arranges for the company to buy them back. Although this arrangement falls outside the relief for hardship on a death, there will be no distribution since such a payment will be for the benefit of the trade (see SP 2/82).

## 4 Position if the vendor is a UK company

If the vendor of the shares is a UK company and the payment is not treated as a distribution, it will be taxed as a chargeable gain in the ordinary way.

If the payment does not satisfy the s 219 requirements it will be treated as a distribution in the hands of the vendor company. Distributions are generally not liable to corporation tax by reason of TA 1988 s 208 which reads:

> 'Except as otherwise provided by the Corporation Tax Acts, corporation tax shall not be chargeable on dividends and other distributions of a company resident in the UK nor shall any such dividends or distributions be taken into account in computing income for corporation tax.'

Accordingly it would seem to be attractive for a company to arrange for a disposal of shares by means of a buy-back falling outside s 219 so that the proceeds would escape all taxation.

The Inland Revenue took the view (see SP 4/89) that the proceeds could still be brought into charge to capital gains tax. It said that s 208 has nothing to do with capital gains and merely excludes the distribution from a charge to tax as income. It does not exempt the distribution from tax as a chargeable gain. Although TCGA 1992 s 37 excludes from the computation of a capital gain amounts actually taxed as income, the receipt was not taxed as income and there was nothing to prevent it being charged as a capital gain.

This Statement of Practice attracted immediate criticism (see *Taxation*, 21 September 1989) and remained controversial until the decision of the Court of Appeal in *Strand Options and Futures Ltd v Vojak* (2003) which upheld the Inland Revenue arguments. **[42.28]**

### EXAMPLE 42.8

KP Ltd owns 500 shares in SJ Ltd for which it subscribed £1 each in March 1988. SJ Ltd buys the shares back for £10 each in June 2003.

(1) If the purchase is within s 219 KP Ltd's tax position would be as follows:

|  | £ |
|---|---|
| Sale proceeds for CGT purposes | 5,000 |
| *Less:* price paid by SJ Ltd | 500 |
| Capital gain (ignoring indexation) | £4,500 |

(2) If the purchase is outside s 219, and treated as a distribution, the distribution would not be taxed as income but it would be brought into charge to capital gains tax in the same way:

## 5 Advantages if the distribution rules apply

When the distribution rules apply, it is only the excess of the purchase proceeds over the amount originally subscribed for the shares that is treated as a distribution. As the sum treated as a distribution must then be ignored in calculating the individual vendor's CGT position (see TCGA 1992 s 37(1)), it is possible for him to make a CGT loss whilst selling the shares at a profit.

**EXAMPLE 42.9**

Risker subscribed for 50 shares in BB Ltd at par value of £1 per share. He sold the shares two years ago to Tusker for £500 and BB Ltd has now bought back the shares for £950. Assuming that the sale is taxed as a distribution Tusker's tax position is as follows:

| | £ |
|---|---|
| a) *Income tax* | |
| Total consideration received | 950 |
| | |
| Net distribution (950 – 50) | 900 |
| *Plus*: tax credit | 100 |
| | |
| Gross dividend | £1,000 |
| b) *CGT* | £ |
| Sale proceeds | 950 |
| *Less*: charged to income tax | 900 |
| | |
| | 50 |
| *Less*: price paid by Tusker | 500 |
| | |
| CGT loss | (£450) |

*Note:*
   There is a distribution to the extent that the sale proceeds exceed the sum originally subscribed for the shares (ie the sum paid by Risker).

Taper relief should also be taken into account as it can make a substantial difference to the tax payable:.                                              **[42.29]**

**EXAMPLE 42.10**

Alfie Ltd has an issued share capital of £20,000 comprising £20,000 £1 ordinary shares allotted at par. Harry, a higher rate taxpayer, acquired 10,000 shares by subscription at par on 6 April 1999. The company wishes to buy Harry's shares for £5 each in the accounting year ended 31 July 2005 during which it made profits of £200,000.
   *Harry's tax position*

| | | £ |
|---|---|---|
| (1) | If purchase is within s 219: | |
| | Sale proceeds for CGT | 50,000 |
| | *Less:* original subscription | 10,000 |
| | | |
| | Gain | 40,000 |
| | *Less:* taper relief (75%) | 30,000 |
| | | |
| | | 10,000 |
| | *Less:* annual exemption | 8,500 |
| | | |
| | | 1,500 |
| | | |
| | CGT at 40% | £600 |

| (2) | If purchase is a distribution: | £ |
|---|---|---|
| | Net distribution (£50,000 – £10,000) | 40,000 |
| | Plus tax credit | 4,444 |
| | Gross distribution | 44,444 |
| | Tax @ 32.5% | 14,444 |
| | *Less:* tax credit | 4,444 |
| | Tax payable | £10,000 |

## 6  Buy-backs from trustees

When a company buys back its shares from trustees and s 219 does not apply so that the distribution rules are in point, it was formerly the case that the trustees' income tax liability was limited to the basic rate (and this liability was satisfied by the tax credit). The reason for this somewhat anomalous position was that, although the income tax code with its extended definition of what amounts to a distribution includes the purchase of a company's own shares, as a matter of trust law the sum received by the trustees was capital. It was therefore not subject to the additional rate charge under s 686 (see **[17.28]**), and nor did it attract a higher rate charge in the hands of any life tenant (which was scarcely surprising given that the sum would be added to trust capital). This position was altered by FA 1997 to bring such sums into charge to income tax at 34% and from 6 April 2004 the rate has been increased to 40%. **[42.30]**

## 7  Clearances and stamp duty

Whenever a buy-back of shares is proposed, advance clearance can be obtained for the scheme and the same application can be used for a clearance under TA 1988 s 707 (see **[42.101]**). Similarly, if the arrangement is designed to fall outside TA 1988 s 219, negative clearance can be obtained. An article in *Tax Bulletin 21*, February 1996, at p 281 comments on various matters that are commonly overlooked or misunderstood when applying for a clearance.

No instrument of share transfer is necessary on a buy-back but the return that must be made by the company to Companies House (Form 169) is subject to stamp duty 'as if it were an instrument transferring shares on sale' (FA 1986 s 66). Accordingly, *ad valorem* duty at 1/2% is charged. (Note that the redemption of redeemable preference shares is outside the section and free from duty.) **[42.31]–[42.40]**

## III  TAXATION OF 'QUALIFYING DISTRIBUTIONS'

Prior to 6 April 1999 the payment of a dividend involved the payment of advance corporation tax that represented a partial discharge of the company's corporation tax liability. The shareholder was given a credit for this ACT so that he received his dividend together with a credit for income tax purposes. The rules applied to all qualifying distributions. This liability to ACT was abolished on 6 April 1999.                                        **[42.41]**

A tax credit of 10% now applies to dividends received (this is discussed further at **[42.76]**). The retention of the tax credit may have been determined because of the possible effect on dividends paid to or received from countries with which the UK has a double tax treaty.          **[42.42]–[42.45]**

## Utilisation of existing surplus ACT and the shadow ACT regime

a)  *Corporation Tax (Treatment of Unrelieved Surplus ACT) Regulations, SI 1999/358*

The regulations permit the carry-forward of surplus ACT at 6 April 1999 when it would have been available for use had ACT continued. Note that:
(1)  companies may therefore be divided into two: those with surplus ACT who may be concerned to ensure recovery of that tax and those without;
(2)  only companies with surplus ACT at 6 April 1999 are affected by the rules and they can 'opt out' if they decide not to seek to recover the ACT;
(3)  in the case of dividends paid during an accounting period which straddles 6 April 1999, the period is split at 6 April into two notional periods and any ACT which cannot be set against the profits apportioned to the period before 6 April is carried forward and dealt with under the new rules (FA 1998 Sch 3 para 12 (4), SI 1999/358 reg 4(4)).
                                                                        **[42.46]**

b)  *How do the rules work?*

They are based on the old rules governing relief for surplus ACT. Notional amounts of ACT ('shadow ACT') calculated in the same way and at the same rate as in FY 1998 arise when a company makes a distribution on or after 6 April 1999. The old limits on the set-off of ACT are retained so that a company can use ACT to meet its corporation tax liability up to a limit of 20% of its profits. However, the amount of surplus ACT that can be used will be determined by first deducting from that maximum amount the shadow ACT notionally treated as payable on the distributions made by the company. Insofar as distributions exceed profit an amount of surplus shadow ACT will be carried forward to be used first in a later period. In particular it should be understood that:
(1)  shadow ACT is a tool used in the computation of how much surplus ACT the company can use in a year. It does not involve the payment of any sum to the Revenue; and
(2)  shadow ACT does not reduce the amount of corporation tax that the company will actually pay (only surplus ACT can do that!).          **[42.47]**

### EXAMPLE 42.11

A company has surplus ACT of £100,000 at 6 April 1999. It has a 12-month accounting period ending on 5 April 2000, during which it pays dividends of £40,000 and has taxable profits of £120,000. In this case—

(1)   the limit on the set-off of ACT is £24,000 (that is 20% of £120,000);
(2)   there is shadow ACT of £10,000 (25% of £40,000) on account of its dividend payments;
(3)   the effect is to restrict the set-off of past surplus advance corporation tax to £14,000 (£24,000 less £10,000); and
(4)   its corporation tax liability is therefore reduced by £14,000, as is the figure for past surplus ACT carried forward to the next accounting period.

A group cannot use surplus ACT in any company in the group until a home has been found within the group for the notional offset of all shadow ACT generated by that group.                                             **[42.48]**

Notes:

(1)   Companies used to suffer corporation tax to the extent that dividends had been paid. With the abolition of ACT there is no minimum tax bill.
(2)   A company paying no corporation tax can still pass tax credits to its shareholders if it pays a dividend.
(3)   A company with no taxable income can fund itself equally as efficiently by shares (probably preference shares) as by debt.     **[42.49]–[42.75]**

## IV   TAXATION OF INDIVIDUALS (AND CHARITIES) WHO RECEIVE DISTRIBUTIONS

Dividends and other distributions received by UK shareholders are assessed to income tax under ITTOIA 2005 s 385 on the gross sum: ie on the dividend actually paid together with the appropriate tax credit (ITTOIA 2005 ss 397(1), 398(1)).
(1)   The tax credit is 10% (and the 'tax credit fraction' is one-ninth).
(2)   Individuals are not entitled to a repayment of any tax credit.
(3)   Charities are not entitled to recover tax credits but they received compensation from the government as a percentage payment of their dividend income over a transitional period as follows:

| *Tax year* | *Percentage of dividend income (%)* |
| --- | --- |
| 1999–00 | 21 |
| 2000–01 | 17 |
| 2001–02 | 13 |
| 2002–03 | 8 |
| 2003–04 | 4 |

(4)   Although these provisions concerning repayment of tax credits do not apply to non resident shareholders, the size of the tax credit coupled with the imposition of a withholding tax will produce little or no refund of the credit (see **[18.78]**).
(5)   Individuals subject to tax at either lower or basic rate have no further liability since the 'dividend ordinary rate' applicable in such cases is 10% (TA 1988 s 1B). Higher rate taxpayers are liable to 'the dividend upper rate' of 32.5%. From 6 April 2005 there is a special relief for

trusts to exclude the first £500 (£1,000 from 6 April 2006, but now subject to anti-splintering rules) of income which would otherwise be chargeable (in the case of dividend income) at the 'dividend trust rate' of 32.5% (see **[41.96]**).                            **[42.76]–[42.90]**

## V  TAXATION OF OTHER PERSONS WHO RECEIVE DISTRIBUTIONS

### 1  UK companies

a)  *No tax liability on distributions*

Dividends and other distributions received by one UK company from another are not generally subject to corporation tax in the recipient's hands. The sum paid, together with the tax credit thereon, is known as 'franked investment income' (FII) (TA 1988 s 208).                            **[42.91]**

b)  *Refund of tax credit*

Companies and pension funds are not entitled to any refund of tax credits.
                                                    **[42.92]–[42.93]**

c)  *Small companies relief and FII*

As noted at **[42.24]**, in determining whether the small companies' relief is available to a company its FII is taken into account. Broadly, the relief is not available on the profits of a company insofar as those profits include FII, other than FII received from a member of the same group of companies. Accordingly, if the profits of a company include FII the small companies' relief calculation is affected:                            **[42.94]**

**EXAMPLE 42.12**

HN Ltd makes up accounts to 31 March each year. For the year ended 31 March 2005 the company has trading profits of £300,000 and receives FII of £200,000 from another (non-group) UK company (ie £180,000 + £20,000 tax credit).
    The corporation tax calculation is as follows:

(i)     Tax at 30% on £300,000                                      £90,000

    (the dividend income is ignored at this stage)

(ii)    *Less:* small companies relief calculated as follows:

    (upper relevant amount – profits) × statutory fraction × *basic profits/profits*

    '*basic profits*' means profits subject to corporation tax;

    '*profits*' means basic profits plus FII, ie:

$$(1,500,000 - 500,000) \times \frac{11}{400} \times \frac{300,000}{500,000} = £16,500$$

(iii)   Total tax ((i)–(ii)) = £73,500

## 2  Trusts and estates

a)  *Interest in possession trusts*

The beneficiary receives the tax credit on dividend income and the income is taxed in his hands in the same way as with an individual directly entitled. Accordingly, any additional liability depends upon the level of that beneficiary's taxable income. **[42.95]**

b)  *Distributions received by discretionary trusts*

The tax credit on dividends paid is 10% of the gross dividend but a special tax rate applies to trusts, the dividend trust rate. This rate was 25% up to 5 April 2004 and 32.5% thereafter.

**EXAMPLE 42.13**

|  |  | £ |  | £ |
|---|---|---|---|---|
| Net dividend |  |  |  | 80.00 |
| Tax credit @ 1/9 of net | (10%) |  |  | 8.89 |
| Gross dividend |  |  |  | 88.89 |
| Tax at Trust rate | 32.5% | 28.89 |  |  |
|  |  |  |  | 28.89 |
|  |  |  |  | £60.00 |

For 2005–06 onwards the first £500 of income arising to a trust chargeable at the rate applicable to trusts or the dividend trust rate is, instead, chargeable at the basic, lower or dividend ordinary rate depending on the type of income: TA 1988 s 686D; FA 2005 s 14.

It is proposed in the 2006 Finance Bill to increase the basic rate band to £1,000 for 2006–07 and at the same time to introduce measures to group trusts made by the same settlor for the purposes of sharing one basic rate band between them.

The position of beneficiaries who receive distributions from the trust and the tax charge under TA 1988 s 687 is considered at **[16.33]**. **[42.96]–[42.120]**

## VI  TAXATION OF 'NON-QUALIFYING' DISTRIBUTIONS

An issue of bonus redeemable shares or securities is a non-qualifying distribution (TA 1988 ss 209(2)(c) and 14(2)). It is taxed in two stages: *first*, on the issue of the securities the recipient may be assessed at the dividend upper rate less the tax credit. *Secondly*, when the shares are redeemed, the redemption will be a qualifying distribution with the normal taxation consequences, save that, if the shareholder is then liable for income tax at the dividend upper rate, a deduction is made for any tax which he originally paid on the non-qualifying distribution: ITTOIA 2005 ss 400–401.

**[42.121]–[42.140]**

## VII   EXEMPT DISTRIBUTIONS AND SCRIP DIVIDENDS

### 1   **Demergers and the ICI test case**

The general topic of demergers is considered in **Chapter 47** where a distinction is drawn between 'direct' and 'indirect' demergers. From a tax point of view, provided that the requirements of TA 1988 ss 213–218 are satisfied (see [**47.51**]), the transfer of shares in the demerged company to the shareholders is not treated as a distribution and, for CGT purposes, the distributed shares are treated as a company reorganisation (TCGA 1992 ss127, 192(2)). If the shareholder sells the shares in either the original or the demerged company, the original cost of the shares is apportioned between the shares in the distributing company and the demerged company. For individuals, therefore, demergers can be effected without the necessity for a liquidation and without attracting fiscal penalties. Unfortunately this is not the case in certain situations where the shares are owned by trustees (see generally *CG33921* et seq). To understand why problems arise it is first necessary to consider the background trust and company law.        [**42.141**]

### a)   *Company and trust law*

*Hill v Permanent Trustee Co of New South Wales Ltd* (1930), a Privy Council case, confirmed that a company can only part with its assets to its shareholders by way of a distribution of profits unless it is in liquidation or making an authorised reduction in share capital.

> 'A limited company not in liquidation can make no payment by way of return of capital to its shareholders except as a step in an authorised reduction of capital. Any other payment made by it by means of which it parts with moneys to its shareholders must and can only be made by way of dividing profits. Whether the payment is called "dividend" or "bonus" or any other name, it still must remain a payment on division of profits ... Moneys so paid to a shareholder will (if he be a trustee) *prima facie* belong to the person beneficially entitled to the income of the trust estate. If such moneys or any part thereof are to be treated as part of the corpus of the trust estate there must be some provision in the trust deed which brings about that result. No statement by the company or its officers that moneys which are being paid away to shareholders out of profits are capital, or are to be treated as capital, can have any effect upon the rights of the beneficiaries under a trust instrument which comprises shares in the company.' (Lord Russell)

In the simple *direct* demerger, a company first declares a dividend out of distributable profits and then satisfies that dividend by an allocation of shares which it owns (accordingly the demerger will typically be of a subsidiary). By contrast in an *indirect* demerger the company will transfer part of its business into a newly formed company which will issue shares directly to the shareholders. Following on from the above statement the demerged shares will be income in the hands of the recipient so that if they are owned by trustees of an interest in possession trust those shares will belong to the life tenant. The consequences for the trust fund may be startling: for instance when Thomas Tilling Ltd made a distribution (which was considered by the courts in the case of *Re Sechiari* (1950)) the effect was to reduce the price of the company's shares by 77%. A windfall for income beneficiaries and a glaring injustice for those interested in the capital of the fund!        [**42.142**]

b) *The position of trustees on the assumption that the demerged shares are income*

On commonsense grounds and in the interests of fairness between the beneficiaries, trustees may wish to ensure that the trust capital is not depleted as the result of a proposed demerger.

The trustees could dispose of their shareholdings *before* the dividend is declared and demerger occurs and the trustees could subsequently buy back shares in either or both of the demerged companies. The acquired shares would then form part of the capital of the settlement. However, the sale of original shares may be commercially undesirable as it would represent a disposal (and possibly trigger a charge to capital gains tax).

The decision to sell may itself raise difficulties for the trustees: the deprived life tenant may argue that the decision was motivated solely to prevent him receiving income from the trust.

Alternatively, it is possible that the life tenant will agree that the shares should be added to the capital of the settlement. Were he to do so, not only might he suffer a CGT charge (disposing of shares which have become his property) but he would add property to the settlement and to that extent become a settlor himself.                                               **[42.143]**

c) *Tax position if the shares are trust income*

An individual who receives demerged shares, provided that the necessary conditions are met, will obtain an exempt distribution so that there will be no question of any income tax liability. Any CGT charge will be postponed until a disposal occurs.                                               **[42.144]**

*Trustees of life interest trusts* The income of a life interest trust (including the demerged shares if treated as income) belongs to the life tenant (subject only to the trustees' lien for costs) and, assuming that the relevant conditions are satisfied, that will be an exempt distribution for income tax purposes. For CGT purposes the position is not so straightforward and two approaches are possible. The shares could be treated as part of the trust fund to which the life tenant then became absolutely entitled. This raises the prospect of a charge under TCGA 1992 s 71. Alternatively, because the life tenant is treated as owning income as it arises, it could be argued that the distributed shares never became trust property so that s 71 is not in point. After initial doubts HMRC accepted that the income belongs to the life tenant as a result of the *Archer-Shee* decision so that TCGA 1992 s 71 is not in point (see *Tax Bulletin 13*, October 1994, p 164 and CG 33931).

One effect of the above is that the base costs of the trust cannot be apportioned to the life tenant and must be attributed only to the original shares (despite the diminution in their value flowing from the demerger). Accordingly, the trustees may realise a loss when those shares are sold (the oddness of this result in the case of direct demergers is well illustrated in *Private Client Business*, 1995, p 128). Turning to the life tenant, what is the base cost of the shares that he has received? HMRC has concluded that in the case of a *direct demerger* the allowable cost to the life tenant is the market value of the demerged shares as a result of TCGA 1992 s 17(1): see **[19.22]**. The disposal by the company would be the corresponding disposal for the purpose of s 17(2) (see *Tax Bulletin 13*, October 1994, p 162 and CG 33931).

In the case of an *indirect demerger*, however, there is no corresponding disposal (because the company does not dispose of the shares); accordingly the life tenant has no allowable cost.

As compared with individual shareholders, therefore, the life tenant may be placed at a CGT disadvantage in the case of indirect demergers (following the ICI test case (see **[42.148]**) it is, however, likely that such shares will be capital and so not belonging to the life tenant).

If the terms of a settlement provide for the payment of an annuity and for the balance of the income to be paid elsewhere the above analysis does not hold good. The reasoning in *Archer-Shee* cannot apply: the shares become part of the trust funds and a CGT charge under s 71 may arise when they are paid out to a beneficiary. **[42.145]**

*Discretionary and accumulation trusts where the demerged shares are accumulated*
The trustees receive the shares as an exempt distribution so that there is no liability to income tax under ITTOIA 2005 s 399. Although the shares are 'income' in the trustees' hands, provided that they exercise their powers to accumulate there are no further fiscal consequences. **[42.146]**

*Discretionary and accumulation trusts where the shares are paid out to a beneficiary*
Because the shares have been received as income by the trustees, if those shares (or their cash equivalent) are paid to a beneficiary the rules of TA 1988 s 687 will be in point. Given that the trustees received an exempt distribution, no s 686 credit will be available so that (subject to any unused credit in the tax pool) the payment is likely to attract an income tax charge at 40%. If the shares (rather than any cash equivalent) are paid out to a beneficiary, for CGT purposes a charge under TCGA 1992 s 71 may arise in addition to any income tax liability. A hold-over election is, however, generally available when property ceases to be held on discretionary trusts (see **[24.61]**). **[42.147]**

#### d)    *The ICI test case: are demerged shares income after all?*

The ICI demerger was 'indirect': the bio-chemical part of ICI's business was transferred to a new company (Zeneca plc) and the shares in that company were transferred directly to the ICI shareholders. *Sinclair v Lee* (1993) considered the position of trustees of an interest in possession will trust in receipt of Zeneca shares. The Vice-Chancellor concluded that the Zeneca shares formed part of the capital of the fund and that the *Hill* line of cases could be distinguished.

The judgment was deeply disappointing. Whilst it is true that ICI, for its own tax reasons, chose to effect its demerger by the 'indirect' method, to concentrate on that as a way of escaping from the manacles of precedent is hardly satisfactory. There should be no difference between the case where a shareholder receives as a distribution shares which had been owned by his company (the so-called direct demerger) and that where the company instead procures the issue of shares by a third party (as occurred in the *ICI* case). Having said that, there are *dicta* towards the end of the judgment that could, in the future, be used as ammunition against a mechanical application of the *Hill* decision:

'In the last analysis, the rationale underlying the general principles enunciated in *Hill's* case is an endeavour by the law to give effect to the assumed intention of the testator or settlor in respect of a particular distribution to shareholders. When the inflexible application of these principles would produce a result manifestly inconsistent with the presumed intention of the testator or settlor, the court should not be required to apply them slavishly. In origin they were guidelines. They should not be applied in circumstances, or in a manner, which would defeat the very purpose they are designed to achieve.'  **[42.148]**

e)  *Where are we now?*

Some other demergers have been carried out by the direct route, others by the indirect. In 1991, Racal Electronics plc distributed its shareholding in Racal Telecom plc to its shareholders (a direct demerger) whereas in the following year it demerged the Chubb Group by the indirect route. It is interesting to consider the position of an interest in possession trust owning Racal shares. In the first case the Racal Telecom shares should have been handed over to the life tenant whereas in the second we now know that the shares form part of the trust capital. How many trustees got it right? How many simply assumed—without even addressing the problem—that the shares must be added to the trust capital? And how many have retained the shares waiting for the matter to be cleared up? The best that can be said of *Sinclair v Lee* is that it solves half the problem.

Finally, the generally favourable tax treatment for interest in possession trusts in the case of direct demergers does not necessarily apply where the settlement is governed by foreign law. This will only be the case where the relevant law treats a life tenant as deriving his income directly from the trust investments in accordance with *Baker v Archer-Shee* principles.  **[42.149]**

## 2  Scrip dividends

a)  *The enhanced scrip (or stock) dividend*

The stock dividend option has been considered at **[42.9]**. In the absence of any element of 'enhancement', the shares are income in the hands of trustees. However, where the alternative to the cash dividend is shares which are worth significantly more, there is a degree of value enhancement which is particularly acute where the shareholders are offered the possibility of converting the scrip into cash by an immediate sale. A recent scrip offer illustrates all these points: the net cash dividend of 16.75p per existing share was well exceeded by the scrip offer of 25.125p per share and, if the shareholder wished to sell this scrip, the company had arranged a sale price of 23.87p per share.  **[42.150]**

b)  *Tax treatment*

For the shareholder there is no liability to income tax at the basic rate; the higher rate taxpayer, however, must gross up the cash equivalent of the scrip option, ie the cash dividend alternative which is then subject to an additional tax charge (ITTOIA ss 409–414). If the market value of the scrip exceeds the cash dividend by 15% or more of the market value, the cash equivalent is equal to the market value.

These rules apply to:

(1)   individual shareholders;
(2)   trustees of discretionary or A&M trusts; and
(3)   life tenants who are entitled to receive the scrip dividend (see further on the position of interest in possession trusts [42.152]).          [42.151]

### EXAMPLE 42.14

Jenni, a higher rate taxpayer, and an ordinary shareholder in Wizzo Ltd, opts to take an enhanced scrip dividend. Instead of receiving a cash dividend for £50 she accepts paid up shares having a value of £90. Her 2005–06 tax position is:

(1)   *Income tax:* The cash alternative (£90) must be grossed up at 10% (to £100) and Jenni will then be subject to an income tax charge at the dividend upper rate on this amount (ie to a tax charge of 32.5% less the tax credit, resulting in a liability of 22.5). See ITTOIA 2005 ss 409–414.

(2)   *CGT:* The shares are treated as a newly acquired asset and the cash equivalent of the share capital (£90) is her base cost: see TCGA 1992 s 142.

*Notes:*

(i)   The same rules will apply if the shares had been received by trustees of an A&M trust and for the purpose of the income tax charge the dividend trust rate (32.5%) would give an income tax liability of £22.50.

(ii)  Similarly, if the shares had been treated under an interest in possession trust as belonging to the life tenant, the above rules apply and, for CGT purposes under TCGA 1992 s 142, the shares are treated as acquired for a base cost equal to the cash equivalent of the share capital. Where, under the terms of an interest in possession trust, the shares are either treated as capital or, alternatively, the value is split between the life tenant and capital, the position is set out in the following paragraph.

c)   *Interest in possession trusts (and see SP 4/94)*

As with demergers it is interest in possession trusts which pose problems for scrip dividends. Traditionally, trustees have opted for cash rather than scrip: however, if there is a substantial element of enhancement, trustees should at least consider whether to take the scrip. If they do so, a familiar problem arises: are the shares income (and so the property of the life tenant) or must they be added to the capital of the trust? The normal non-enhanced scrip dividend will be treated in the same way as a cash dividend and so belong to the life tenant. In cases of enhanced value, however, there is some authority that the value of the scrip must be apportioned with the life tenant being entitled to the value of the cash dividend. Hence, although the shares themselves are added to the trust capital, the trustees must raise this sum and pay it to the life tenant (and so they may find it necessary to sell the shares). This was the result in *Re Malam, Malam v Hitchens* (1894). (Contrast, however, *Bouch v Sproule* (1887) in which the shares were allocated to capital and the *Hill* line of cases where they were treated as income.) Presumably the theory underlying apportionment is that the element of enhancement must be attributed to the value of the existing shares (and so treated as a form of capital reorganisation: see further *Law Society Gazette,* July 1993, p 17).

The tax treatment depends on how the shares are treated as a matter of trust law (this is expressly recognised by HMRC in SP 4/94 and a similar rule applies in the case of non-UK trusts). There are therefore three possibilities:

(1)   *Shares treated as trust capital:* No income tax liability arises and, for CGT purposes, the trustees acquire a new asset but apparently at a nil base

cost (since ITTOIA 2005 ss 409–414 do not apply to fixed interest trustees, proceeding on the assumption that the shares belong to the life tenant).

(2) *Shares treated as income:* The beneficiary with the interest in possession is treated as entitled to the income and taxed in the same way as an individual shareholder: see **[42.151]**.

(3) *A Malam apportionment:* The income tax position of the life tenant in a *Malam* type case is (according to SP 4/94) that he will be taxed on the income when it is paid out to him by the trustees under TA 1988 s 687 and, as the trustees have no tax credit on the scrip dividend, basic rate income tax must be accounted for by those trustees and the usual credit passed to the life tenant. The life tenant will be treated as receiving income equivalent to the cash dividend plus a tax credit (at the basic rate) and this will be income taxable as savings and investment income. The treatment applies whether the payment is made out of the proceeds of sale of the shares, out of other capital of the trust or by a distribution of some of the shares comprised in the scrip issue.

So far as the trustees' tax position on receipt of the shares is concerned, there is no question of any further income tax liability arising, since ITTOIA 2005 ss 409–414 have no application to interest in possession trusts. For CGT purposes, the scrip falls outside the provisions that enable the base cost of the shares to be equal to the 'cash equivalent of the share capital'. Accordingly, shares retained by the trustees will be treated as a new asset with a nil acquisition cost. These startling results arise because the relevant legislation proceeds on the assumption that the shares must belong to the life tenant in such cases who would be liable for higher rate income tax but would also be credited with an uplifted CGT base. If some of the shares are transferred to the life tenant there is a part disposal for CGT purposes.

**EXAMPLE 42.15**

In 2005–06 the trustees of the Dari Will Trust accept an enhanced scrip dividend from ABC plc under which, instead of receiving a cash dividend worth £80, they receive shares to a value of £120. The trustees decide under the terms of the trust that they are obliged to distribute the value of the cash dividend to the life tenant.

(1) The life tenant will receive £80 together with a credit for the basic rate income tax deducted at source (ie £102.56 in all). The trustees must, according to SP 4/94, pay income tax to HMRC under TA 1988 s 687 of £22.56.

(2) So far as the scrip dividend is concerned the trustees will not suffer any income tax liability thereon but the shares will be acquired at a nil base cost. Were the shares to be sold by the trustees a gain of £120 would result and accordingly they would face a CGT liability of £48 (subject to taper relief). On these particular facts therefore the trustees would be out of pocket as a result of accepting the scrip dividend since their costs total £80+£22.56 + £48 = £150.56, whereas the value received was only £120.

In the *Malam* case, Stirling J decided that 'the proceeds of the realisation of the shares should be applied in payment first of the dividend (to which the tenant for life is entitled …) and the balance ought to be applied as capital'. Pending sale of the shares, the life tenant would have a charge upon those shares equal to the value of the dividend. The view of HMRC—that the life tenant is to be treated as receiving savings and investment income falling under ITTOIA 2005 Part 4—is not free from doubt. It is arguable that any 'compensation' payment by the trustees does not constitute income and so escapes the income tax net altogether.                                      **[42.152]**

# 43 Corporate groups

*Updated by Richard Hayes and Stephen Whitehead, KPMG LLP (UK)*

## I  OPERATING STRUCTURES

Assume that Ron and Ed plan to set up in business together: Ron is a chef of renown and Ed has run (with some success) a hamburger chain. A corporate structure, rather than a partnership, is considered appropriate. A single company with two divisions—the catering/food production portion and the restaurant outlet—is one possibility. From a tax and risk perspective the company will be a single accountable entity (the fact that it is run as two separate divisions is purely for internal management purposes). Forming two separate companies—Ron Ltd and Ed Ltd—with different shareholdings may not meet their wishes and a group structure may be advantageous. A holding company—with shares owned 50:50 by Ron and Ed—may own two subsidiaries, Ron Ltd and Ed Ltd. From a risk and tax perspective there are then three separate legal entities: accordingly the insolvency of the restaurant business of Ed Ltd would not necessarily bring down Ron Ltd nor the holding company.

Commercially, groups of companies have obvious attractions: different enterprises can be segregated into different corporate units each with its limited liability and separate identity. Each trade will, to a greater or lesser extent, have a separate management and, in the event of a decision to sell any part of the enterprise, the appropriate company can be sold to the purchaser. From a taxation point of view, however, and despite the various reliefs considered below, forming a group may be disadvantageous because the various grouping provisions do not cause all the companies to be treated as one for tax purposes and, accordingly, certain reliefs are restricted. One significant problem with using groups which is sometimes overlooked is the application of the small companies' rate of tax to the members of the group. Where the companies are 'associated', the upper and lower limits for each associated company for calculating whether the small companies' rate of corporation tax is available are divided by the number of associated companies. This can lead to the loss of relief and hence a failure by the group as a whole to take full advantage of the small companies rate. With the introduction of the quarterly payments system, a large group could result in a number of relatively small companies becoming subject to instalment payments. Two companies are associated if they are under common control or if one has control of the other (TA 1988 s 13). If the two companies form a group, it may be possible to arrange for profits within the group to be configured in a way which minimises the tax payable. If the group overall has profits below the lower limit for small companies, it is usually best that they are distributed evenly around the group in order to avoid them falling within the marginal relief band. The requirement that transactions between associated companies must now be conducted at arm's length may make this more difficult to achieve, although this requirement does not, in general, apply to small- and medium-sized enterprises.                    **[43.1]–[43.20]**

### EXAMPLE 43.1

Fred Ltd has one wholly owned subsidiary, Barney Ltd. Both companies make up their accounts to 31 March and for the year ending 31 March 2006 both have taxable profits of £150,000. The lower limit for each company is £150,000 (£300,000 ÷ 2) and therefore both are taxed at 19%, making £57,000 tax payable in total.

If Fred Ltd had profits of £250,000 and Barney Ltd profits of £50,000, the position would be different. Fred Ltd has profits falling within the marginal band and therefore pays tax of £61,250 and Barney Ltd pays £9,500—making a total of £70,750 an increase of £13,750.

### EXAMPLE 43.2

Wilma Ltd makes profits of £400,000 and has three subsidiaries whose results are as below for the year ended 31 March 2006:

| Rock Ltd | profit | £25,000 |
| Stone Ltd | loss | £10,000 |
| Granite Ltd | loss | £5,000 |

There are four associated companies so not only does Wilma Ltd pay tax at the full rate of 30% (because the upper limit of £1.5 million is divided by 4 so that the company pays the full rate when profits exceed £375,000) but the quarterly payments system also applies to Wilma.

## II   WHAT IS A GROUP?

A group of companies will comprise at least a parent company (a holding company) which controls another company known as a subsidiary. Groups may consist of any number of interlocking companies; and reference to a company may include an industrial and provident society; a trustee savings bank; and a building society. Commercially, a group may be regarded as a single entity; however, as far as the law is concerned the companies are generally treated as separate legal entities. The tax legislation confers a number of useful reliefs upon companies in a group. These reliefs depend upon the structure of the group: some are available to '51% groups'; some to '75% groups' and 'consortia', whilst provision is made for the case where a company is both a member of a group and either one of the joint owners of a consortium company or a company owned by a consortium.

A '51% group' exists where more than 50% of the ordinary share capital of one company is beneficially owned, directly or indirectly, by another company; and a '75% group' where at least 75% of the ordinary share capital of one company is so owned (TA 1988 s 838). Certain privileges may be available even if the 75% or 51% group requirement is not satisfied, in cases where a company is owned by a consortium of corporate members. A company is owned by a consortium if 75% or more of the ordinary share capital is beneficially owned by companies of which none owns less than a 5% share and none owns 75% or more.

How does the existence of a group affect the tax position of an individual shareholder? For CGT taper relief purposes, the relief is given on a disposal of shares in the holding company of a trading group and the requirements to be met are discussed in *Tax Bulletins* 53, June 2001, and 62, December 2002. Relief may also be available under the IHT business property relief provisions provided that the conditions in IHTA 1984 s 105(4)(b) and s 111 are met.

**[43.21]–[43.40]**

## III   GROUP AND CONSORTIUM RELIEF (TA 1988 s 402)

### 1   **When is relief available?**

Group relief applies to 75% groups and to consortia. In addition to the requirements as to the ownership of share capital, certain economic ownership tests must also be met. TA 1988 s 413(7)–(10) provides that for group relief to be available the parent company must also be entitled to not less than 75% of the profits available for distribution and not less than 75% of the assets on a winding up. For consortium relief a consortium member's interest in the consortium company is taken as the lowest of the percentage share capital, entitlement to profits available for distribution and entitlement to assets on a winding up.                                  **[43.41]**

### 2   **The international dimension**

Until 1 April 2000, the group relief legislation required both the surrendering company and the claimant company in a group relief claim to be UK residents. This restriction in the UK legislation was tested in the courts in the EU context on the basis that EU companies should benefit from arts 52 and 58 of the EC Treaty (now arts 43 and 48 EC) providing for freedom of establishment. The argument was that the UK group relief legislation restricted freedom of establishment by providing that tax benefits were not available to non-UK companies. So far as consortium relief was concerned, the case of *ICI v Colmer* (1996) was particularly significant and involved two UK-resident companies each owning half the shares in a holding company with a number of wholly owned trading subsidiaries, the majority of which were non-UK resident (although a minority were resident in the EU). The Revenue contended that the holding company did not fall within the definition in TA 1988 s 413(3)(b) because the subsidiary trading companies had to be UK resident. The matter was referred to the European Court of Justice (ECJ) which decided that the UK restriction was not contrary to EC law but that it should be possible to establish a group or consortium relationship through companies resident in the EU. After the matter had been referred back to the House of Lords by the ECJ, ICI contended that since the effect of the decision of the ECJ was that, if a majority of the subsidiaries concerned had been resident in countries within the EU, consortium relief could not have been denied, it was no longer permissible for the UK to limit the relief to companies resident in the UK. The House of Lords said that although it might seem anomalous, if a majority of a company's subsidiaries were non-UK and non-EU companies, the business of that company was not a 'holding company' within the terms of group relief legislation and so no relief was available. Had the company had a majority of EU subsidiaries things would have been different.

The matter has been resolved by FA 2000 which provides that the group relief rules now permit groups and consortia to be established through companies resident anywhere in the world. This means that fellow UK resident subsidiaries of a non-UK company can surrender losses etc between themselves (it is still an open question whether the foreign parent will be able to surrender down losses for use by the subsidiaries against their UK tax liability—see the discussion concerning the *Marks & Spencer* case below). Group relief has also been extended to UK permanent establishments (PEs) of non-resident companies so that, for example, the UK PE of a US company could surrender the losses of the UK trade to a UK subsidiary of the same US company. Such losses would need to be attributable to activities of the UK PE within the charge to UK corporation tax, which would not be exempt from such tax by virtue of any double taxation arrangement and which are not relievable against non-UK profits of any person for the purposes of any foreign tax (TA 1988 s 403D).

The position is therefore as follows:

**EXAMPLE 43.3**

In *Example 43.3* the two UK subsidiaries are now members of the same group, whatever the country of residence of the parent. The two UK subsidiaries will therefore be able to claim and surrender group relief between each other.

In addition, if the non-UK resident parent trades in the UK through a PE, the PE will be able to claim group relief from the UK resident subsidiaries. It will also be able to surrender losses and other amounts to the UK resident subsidiaries providing those amounts are not relievable against non-UK profits in the overseas country.

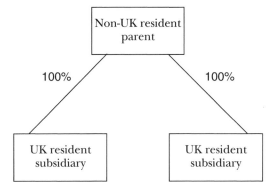

**EXAMPLE 43.4**

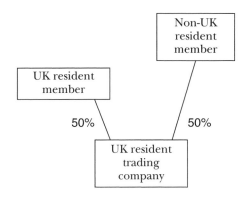

In *Example 43.4* the three companies form a consortium, whatever the country of residence of the non-UK resident member. The UK resident member of the consortium and the UK resident trading company are able to claim and surrender group relief between each other. **[43.42]**

## 3 Operation of the relief

**EXAMPLE 43.5**

A, B, C and E form a 75% group. A only owns 72% of F and 60% of G. The latter two companies cannot, therefore, form part of a 75% group with A. However, C, E, F and G form a further group.

The relief enables trading losses or excess charges on income, or management expenses and certain other items (see TA 1988 s 403) to be surrendered to another company in the group or consortium except that such items may not be surrendered by a dual resident investing company to another member of a UK group (TA 1988 s 404). Generally, however, these amounts can be used to reduce the taxable profits of the 'claimant' company on being given up by the 'surrendering' company. It is not necessary to make a payment for group relief but if one is made it is ignored in computing

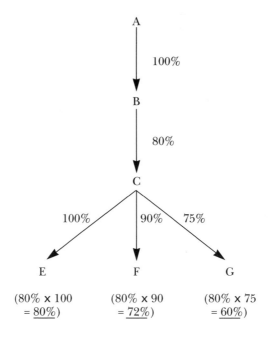

profits and losses of both companies for tax purposes provided the payment does not exceed the amount surrendered.

The amount of available loss or expense which it is possible to surrender is the amount generated in the part of the accounting period of the surrendering company which overlaps with the accounting period of the claimant company. The maximum loss which may actually be surrendered is restricted to the profit of the claimant company attributable to the overlapping period. There are certain further restrictions where the surrendering company has profits against which the loss etc can be offset (TA 1988 s 403 and s 403ZE) The relief is more restrictive in the case of consortia since losses may be surrendered to the consortium members only in proportion to their percentage interest in the consortium company. Similarly, losses may be surrendered by the consortium members only up to the amount of the consortium company's profits corresponding to their percentage interest in the consortium company.

**EXAMPLE 43.6**

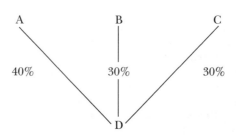

D makes a loss of £60,000. It can be surrendered to A, B and C as follows:
  A = £24,000 (40% of £60,000)
  B = £18,000 (30% of £60,000)
  C = £18,000 (30% of £60,000).
  If D had made profits of £100,000 and A and B had made losses of £50,000 and £40,000 respectively then they could have surrendered losses to D as follows:
  From A = £40,000 (40% of £100,000)
  From B = £30,000 (30% of £100,000).

The claimant company must use the relief in the year of surrender; it cannot be carried back or forward and is deducted from total profits after any charges on the income of the claimant company. It need not be surrendered in full (contrast loss relief under TA 1988 s 393A where the full loss must be relieved if there are sufficient profits). **[43.43]**

**EXAMPLE 43.7**

Little Ltd is the wholly owned subsidiary of Large Ltd. Both companies make up accounts to 31 March and for the year ended 31 March 2006, Little Ltd has trading losses of £20,000 and Large Ltd profits of £400,000. All the loss could be surrendered to Large Ltd resulting in the profits being reduced to £380,000. Alternatively, Little Ltd might carry back all or a part of the loss under TA 1988 s 393A and merely surrender the balance. If Large Ltd were to pay £5,000 for the surrender, that sum would be ignored for tax purposes.

## 4 The *Marks & Spencer* Case

The effect of European law on group relief has been further accentuated by the case of *Marks & Spencer plc v Halsey* (2005) C-446/03. Marks & Spencer established subsidiaries in Belgium, France and Germany but the retail operations were not a success and substantial losses were incurred. Group relief was claimed under TA 1988 s 402 but the claim was denied by HMRC. One of the conditions for group relief in the UK is that the subsidiaries are resident in the UK or at least carrying on business in the UK through a branch or agency so under domestic legislation Marks & Spencer were clearly not entitled to the relief.

However, they claimed that the domestic group relief provisions were discriminatory and contrary to article 43 (freedom of establishment) of the Treaty.

The ECJ has now given its judgment. Broadly, the court concluded that the freedom of establishment provisions did not preclude provisions of a member state which generally prevented a resident parent company from deducting from its taxable profits losses incurred in another member state. However, it was contrary to the freedom of establishment provisions to prevent a resident parent company from doing so where the non-resident subsidiary had exhausted the possibilities in its state of residence of having the losses taken into account for the current or any previous accounting period and where there were no possibilities for those losses to be taken into account in its state of residence for future periods either by the subsidiary itself or a third party.

In the FA 2006 the Government has changed the law to accommodate the decision in the *Marks & Spencer* case. The principal features of these changes, which have effect from 1 April 2006, are as follows:

- The surrendering (ie loss-making) company must be within the charge to tax under the law of any EEA territory either because it is resident there or because it trades through a PE in that EEA territory.
- The surrendering company must be a subsidiary of a claimant company which is resident in the UK or the surrendering company and the claimant company must be 75% subsidiaries of a third party which is resident in the UK (note consortium group relief is not available under these proposals).
- The surrendering company must have sustained an overseas loss equivalent to the items which can be surrendered as group relief. The overseas loss must be determined under the law of the relevant EEA territory.
- The overseas loss must not have been relieved in any territory outside the UK or be capable of being relieved in the relevant EEA territory or other specified territories for any period, including future periods.
- The actual loss surrendered by the company is limited to the amount determined applying UK tax rules.

As mentioned these proposals come into effect on 1 April 2006. Before that date taxpayers will have to rely on the judgment in *Marks & Spencer* to obtain relief for overseas losses. It seems that the Government has taken a narrow view of the judgment in *Marks & Spencer* and there may still be features of the UK group relief system which run counter to the provisions of the EC Treaty.    **[43.44]**


## 5  The *European Vinyls* Case

In *Steele v EVC International* (1996) ('the *European Vinyls* case') the court held that a shareholders' agreement providing for the constitution and control of a jointly owned company caused the shareholders to be connected to each other for the purposes of TA 1988 s 839(7).

It was feared that this case, although not directly concerned with consortium relief, could have had a serious impact on its availability in the case of consortia where the owners had agreed to implement a policy for the company and especially in joint ventures. This is because if all the owners of the company are deemed to be connected, they are each deemed to control not less than 75% of the votes so there will be no consortium relief by virtue of TA s 410(2). HMRC confirmed in *Tax Bulletin 26*, December 1996 that where members of a consortium had entered into an ongoing agreement to operate the consortium company in accordance with their collective will the case would be applied to consortia and could deny relief. As a result FA 1997 s 68 (arguably retrospectively) was enacted to disapply the connected persons test of s 839(7) in the context of claims for group or consortium relief.    **[43.45]**


## 6  Claims

A claim for relief must be made by the first anniversary of the filing date, which normally means within a two-year period from the end of the accounting period. However, if there is an enquiry into the tax return the time limit is extended to 30 days after the enquiry is concluded, the return amended by HMRC or any appeal determined.

A claim for group relief must be made in the claimant company's tax return for the accounting period for which the claim is made. The claim can be made in the original or amended return. The claim must specify the amount of relief claimed and the name of the surrendering company. A claim for group relief requires the written consent of the surrendering company and, in the case of a consortium, all the members of the consortium must consent in writing. It is possible for a group to enter into arrangements with HMRC under which claims and consents can be made in a single document (often referred to as a joint amended return). **[43.46]**

## 6 Tax avoidance

TA 1988 s 410 is designed to prevent artificial manipulation of the group relief provisions: in particular, the forming of groups on a temporary basis and in order to obtain the relief. Under the terms of this section a company will not be regarded as a member of a group if '*arrangements*' are in existence for the transfer of that company to another group or for any person to take control of the company but not the other companies within the group (for the meaning of 'arrangements', see SP 3/93, ESC C10 and on the general interpretation of this section *Pilkington Bros Ltd v IRC* (1982)). Relief is not available during any period when such arrangements are in force. In *Shepherd v Law Land plc* (1990), for instance, arrangements (an option to purchase the shares of the subsidiary company) came into existence on 6 January 1983 and ceased five weeks later on 11 February 1983 (the option was never taken up). In the accounting period ending 31 March 1983 group relief was therefore not available for that five-week period.

In *J Sainsbury plc v O'Connor* (1991) a joint venture company (Homebase) was formed by Sainsbury's and a Belgian company in which Sainsbury's held 75% of the issued share capital and the Belgians the remaining 25%. There was, in addition, a cross-option agreement whereby 5% of that share capital could be acquired by the Belgians. The options were not exercisable for a five-year period and, in the event, were never exercised. Did their existence prevent Sainsbury's being entitled to group relief? The Court of Appeal decided that they were so entitled: *first,* because mere existence of the options did not deprive Sainsbury's of their beneficial ownership in the relevant shares: accordingly they satisfied the 75% test. *Secondly,* because the existence of the options did not amount to arrangements which affected the rights of the relevant shares within the test for such arrangements laid down in TA 1988 Sch 18. Legislation was introduced whereby 'arrangements' was extended to include such changes in the ownership of shares that could arise under options to buy and sell. **[43.47]–[43.100]**

## IV GROUP ARRANGEMENTS FOR PAYMENTS OF INSTALMENTS OF CORPORATION TAX

Groups of companies can arrange to account for corporation tax on a group basis. The idea is that the group, via a nominated member company, can enter into a binding arrangement with HMRC under which the nominated company undertakes to pay the corporation tax liability of all the companies in the specified group. To be eligible to enter into the group payment arrangements, the participating members of a group constitute parent companies and their subsidiaries and also their subsidiaries, all the way down a chain of holding. Although an indirect holding by the ultimate parent in a company at a lower tier might be considerably less than 50%, the whole tier can benefit from these arrangements as long as each company in the tier owns more than 50% of the equity capital in the company at the tier below it. Not all group companies eligible to participate in such an arrangement need to do so. It is also possible to have several group payment arrangements in place for a wider group each comprised of different specified members. Group members still need to file individual self-assessment returns separately and each needs to compute its own corporation tax liability for the account-ing period. However, each company's liability is met out of an allocation of the group payments made under these arrangements. Interest on underpaid tax will remain the liability of the individual group company as will any late fine or penalty that may be incurred.

If companies in a group do not participate in the group payment arrange-ments, amounts of instalments overpaid by one group member (and presum-ably amounts overpaid under the group payment arrangement) can be surrendered between companies.                    **[43.101]–[43.120]**

## V   CAPITAL GAINS

### 1   What is a group for these purposes?

For chargeable gains purposes, a group consists of a principal company and all its 75% subsidiaries. If any of those subsidiaries also have 75% subsidiaries they are included within the group provided they are effective 51% subsidi-aries of the principal company (TCGA 1992 s 170).                    **[43.121]**

#### EXAMPLE 43.8

A, B, C and D form a s 170 group. E is not in the group as it is not a 51% subsidiary of A the principal company.

### 2   Intra-group transfers

The transfer of an asset within a group is treated as being for a consideration that gives rise to neither gain nor loss (TCGA 1992 s 171: for the IHT position if the disposal involves a transfer of value, see IHTA 1984 s 97). The result is to defer any gain until the asset is disposed of outside the group or if the company owning the asset leaves the group within six years (TCGA 1992 s 179). A potential purchaser of a company should, therefore, check whether the company will be subject to such 'exit' charges in the event of its leaving its existing group, or whether any company in a group he acquires has any member company with such a potential 'exit' charge.

TheFA 2000 updated the rules for chargeable gains and companies. The changes were intended to allow the tax neutral transfer of assets between

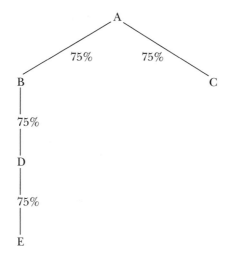

companies in a wider variety of circumstances. In particular it changed the definition of a 'group' for these purposes and enabled transfers of assets within a group even if the relevant members of the group were not resident in the UK. The rules allow any company, whatever its country of residence, to be a member of a group but transfers within the group will only be on a tax neutral basis if the asset remains within the UK tax net.

Prior to FA 2000, if company B (in the structure set out in *Example 43.9* below) transferred an asset to company C, company B was treated as making a disposal of the asset at its market value, and charged to corporation tax on any gain arising.

**EXAMPLE 43.9**

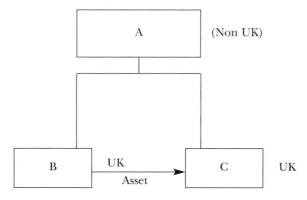

The FA 2000 changes mean that even though company A is not resident in the UK, company B and company C can transfer assets between themselves on a no gain/no loss basis, as if company A were UK resident.

The changes to the rules also mean that a UK subsidiary can transfer assets to a non-UK subsidiary of the same parent provided that the asset will be used by that non-UK subsidiary for its trade in the UK. Since the assets will remain within the corporation tax charge after the transfer, the no gain/no loss treatment applies. The de-grouping rule was amended so that TCGA 1992 s 179 focuses on a company leaving the worldwide group.    **[43.122]**

## 3   Sub-groups

Where two or more companies which between themselves would form a group leave the group at the same time no exit charge arises on assets which they acquired from each other (see further *Dunlop International AG v Pardoe* (1999)). TCGA 1992 s 179(2A) may apply to create an exit charge in situations where, after the sub-group has left the original group, the recipient company of the earlier intra-group transfer leaves the subsequent group (note that FA 1998 strengthened this provision by widening the 'common control' test in s 179(2B)).    **[43.123]**

## 4   Triggering a loss

Before 5 December 2005 it was possible to use TCGA 1992 s 179 to crystallise a capital loss as the following example illustrates.    **[43.124]**

**EXAMPLE 43.10**

Alpha Ltd transfers a chargeable asset showing a capital loss to subsidiary company Beta Ltd which has realised capital profits. TCGA 1992 s 171 ensures that the transfer is at no gain/no loss. Beta Ltd then issues shares to a non-group company (Omega Ltd) so that there is a deemed disposal of the asset under TCGA 1992 s 179 and the loss is thereby realised which can be used to offset Beta's capital gains. Omega then sells the shares to Alpha Ltd. Notice that the transaction has resulted in a permanent change in the capital structure of Beta Ltd.

FA 2006 contains proposals which have effect for disposals on or after 5 December 2005 and are likely to deny the offset of any loss crystallised in this way. The proposals are far-reaching and apply to any arrangements of which the main purpose or one of the main purposes is to secure a tax advantage. HMRC has issued guidance notes to explain when they consider these proposals apply. Broadly, they state that a loss is likely to be caught if there is no commercial loss or no commercial disposal.

## 5   Trading stock

If the asset transferred had not formed part of the trading stock of the transferor but is appropriated to the trading stock of the transferee, the transfer itself is covered by the no gain/no loss rule of s 171; but the transferee is then given an election when the asset is appropriated to his stock (see TCGA 1992 s 173). *Either* that appropriation is taxed as a disposal at market value thereby triggering any capital gain (or loss) *or*, alternatively, the transferee may elect to convert that gain into a trading profit (or loss) by postponing any tax until the asset is sold.

In *Coates v Arndale Properties Ltd* (1984) an attempt to take advantage of the election to obtain group relief for a loss on a capital asset was unsuccessful.

The House of Lords concluded that the transferee never acquired the asset as trading stock because it was immediately resold to another member of the same group. Hence, the transaction was not covered by the election. This 'constructional' approach to a tax relieving provision may be contrasted with the House of Lords decision in *Furniss v Dawson*. In *Reed v Nova Securities Ltd* (1985) the House of Lords were again concerned with the question of when assets are acquired as trading stock and concluded that, not only must those assets be of a kind which were sold in the ordinary course of the company's trade, but also that they must have been acquired with a view to resale at a profit.                                                     [43.125]

## 6   Capital losses

The group relief provisions do not provide for the surrender of capital losses. In the past it was common for chargeable assets to be transferred within the group (taking advantage of TCGA 1992 s 171 which prevents any chargeable gain arising: see above) to enable losses to be utilised.

### EXAMPLE 43.11

Subsidiary company Alpha intends to sell land to P, but will realise a capital gain of £80,000 on that sale. Assume that another subsidiary company (Beta) has unused capital losses of £100,000. The land could be sold to Beta for full value and then resold by Beta to P.
(1)   *On the sale to Beta:* the disposal is on a no gain/no loss basis irrespective of the actual consideration paid (TCGA 1992 s 171: above). No gain is, therefore, realised by Alpha.
(2)   *On the sale to P:* the gain of £80,000 is realised by Beta, which can use its losses to avoid any corporation tax charge.

FA 2000 changed the position by enabling two companies within a group to elect that an asset can be treated as though it had been transferred between themselves immediately before being sold to a person outside the group. The idea is to enable groups to bring together (in effect) chargeable gains and allowable losses in a single company without the need to make an actual transfer of ownership of the asset within the group. The election must be made within two years of the end of the accounting period of the company that made the actual disposal (TCGA 1992 s 171A). When such an election is made the incidental costs of disposal incurred by the actual disponor will be treated as made by the notional disponor. Note that this election can only be made where an asset is disposed of outside the group; the election may not be made in respect of other events which can give rise to capital gains disposals.                                        [43.126]

## 7   Anti-avoidance

In *News International v Shepherd* (1989) Vinelott J held that the acquisition of a loss-making company to which the parent then transferred shares for sale on the Stock Market did not involve a composite transaction so that the *Ramsay* principle was inapplicable. Crucially, in that case the terms of the actual sale had not been arranged before the intra-group transfer. It did not matter that the subsidiary was acquired for the express purpose of utilising its unrelieved losses. The *News International* case reawakened interest in the acquisition of a company by a group in order to take advantage of its capital losses. FA 1993 inserted section 177A into TCGA 1992 and a new Sch 7A providing for capital losses brought into a group to be 'ring fenced'. Broadly, these rules mirror the legislation that deals with income losses in similar cases. The rules are widely drafted to catch unrealised as well as realised losses and apply to a loss-making company joining a group if gains are realised that would otherwise be set against those losses. These anti-avoidance issues were complex and still allowed some capital losses to be transferred to a third party; furthermore it was possible for companies with potential gains to be sold to groups with actual or potential losses which could be used to shelter these gains. FA 2006 contains further anti-avoidance proposals, which are now enacted as s 184A to s 184I TCGA 1992, designed to reinforce the ring-fencing of capital losses and ensure they can only be offset against gains which are realised on assets owned by the same group which has sustained the loss.                                                                    **[43.127]**

## 8   Roll-over relief

For roll-over relief, trades carried on by companies in a 75% group are treated as a single trade (TCGA 1992 s 175). HMRC considers that this section means that a chargeable gain made by one group member on a disposal of an asset outside the group can be rolled over into an asset acquired from outside the group by another group member (SP D19).

### EXAMPLE 43.12

R Ltd, S Ltd and Q Ltd are members of a 75% group. The following transactions occur:
(1)   R Ltd disposes of an office block with a base cost of £100,000 to Q Ltd when its value is £150,000;
(2)   Q Ltd sells that asset to T Ltd for £150,000; and
(3)   S Ltd acquires a new office block for use in its business for £200,000.
   The taxation consequences of these transactions are:
(1)   *The intra-group transfer from R Ltd to Q Ltd* This is treated as being for no gain/no loss so that tax on the gain (£50,000) is postponed. Q's base cost is, therefore, £100,000.
(2)   *The sale by Q Ltd to T Ltd* The asset leaves the group so that a chargeable gain of £50,000 arises to Q Ltd.
(3)   *The replacement asset purchased by S Ltd* On a claim being made by both companies (Q Ltd and S Ltd) the gain of Q Ltd can be rolled over into the purchase by S Ltd. Hence, S Ltd's base cost of the new asset will be £150,000 (£200,000 – £50,000) and Q Ltd will not be assessed on a gain as a result of the disposal to T Ltd.

In *Campbell Connelly & Co Ltd v Barnett* (1992) doubt was cast on this view:

'It was submitted to me that the inference should be drawn in relation to [s 175(1)] that not only should the trades carried on by members of a single group of companies be treated as a single trade and thereby the same trade but that members of a group of companies should be treated as a single person and thereby the same person. That does not seem possible to me as a matter of construction, given the very startling difference Parliament provided in the clearest possible way in [s 175(3)].'

(Knox J whose judgment was affirmed by the Court of Appeal (1993).)

The result was to leave the interpretation of s 175(1) in a state of confusion and the Financial Secretary indicated that irrespective of the *Campbell Connelly* case:

'The Revenue's practice seems to me to be sensible and to reflect how commercial transactions are commonly organised. We will ensure that it continues to apply. What needs to be done will depend on the outcome of the appeal.'

(See [1992] STI 834.)

As from 29 November 1994 this view was given statutory effect: relief is available provided that the disposing and acquiring companies are members of the group at the time of *their own* transaction. They do not have to be members of the group at the time of both events. **[43.128]**


## 9 'Roll around' relief

FA 1995 contained provisions preventing roll-over relief from being available where a company which had realised a gain on disposal of an asset acquired a replacement asset from another group member (this commonly being referred to as 'roll around' relief). The replacement asset was acquired on a no gain/no loss basis so that the amount deemed to be invested was linked to the original cost to the group of the asset (together with any indexation allowance). Nonetheless this device could be used to shelter a gain and had the merit of avoiding the payment of cash outside the group. (See TCGA 1992 s 175(2C).) **[43.129]**


## 10 Group property companies

Roll-over relief is limited to trading companies and so, as a matter of strict law, was not applied to non-trading companies within a group which held assets for use by the trading companies. In fact, relief was extended by means of ESC D30: this concession was given statutory force by FA 1995 and that company is now treated as if it were carrying on the 'group trade' in relation to disposals or acquisitions used wholly for the purposes of the group trade (TCGA 1992 s 175(2B)). It is thought that the non-trading company may hold assets used by non-group members and that this will not jeopardise the above relief although such assets will not themselves be eligible for roll-over relief. **[43.130]**


## 11 Compulsory acquisition of land

TCGA 1992 s 247 applies when land is compulsorily acquired to enable the vendor to roll over his gains into the acquisition of other land. FA 1995 extended this relief to the situation where the replacement land is acquired by a company in the same capital gains group as the company which made the compulsory disposal.                                                    **[43.131]**

## 12   Linked transactions

The CGT rules in TCGA 1992 ss 19–20 (dealing with assets disposed of in a series of linked transactions) do not apply to transactions between companies in the same (75%) group which, under TCGA 1992 s 171, give rise to neither gain nor loss. Thus such transactions do not count as part of any linked series (contrast the situation where there is a transfer between spouses). Special provision is, however, made for the following case.                         **[43.132]**

### EXAMPLE 43.13

Asset 1 is transferred by a series of intra-group transfers from Slim Ltd to Short Ltd; then to Tall Ltd and finally from Tall Ltd to a connected outsider Wilbur. Asset 2 is transferred directly by Slim Ltd to Wilbur. So long as Wilbur is connected with both Tall Ltd and Slim Ltd the disposal of Asset 1 is treated as having been made by Slim Ltd to him and hence can be linked to the disposal of Asset 2. Any increase in the tax chargeable on the disposal of Asset 1 remains the liability of Tall Ltd (TCGA 1992 s 19(6)).

## 13   Roll-over claims

In exercise of its powers under TMA 1970 s 42(5) the Revenue has determined the form of a roll-over claim: claims under s 175(2A) must be made jointly by the two companies involved (IR Press Release, 29 November 1994).
**[43.133]–[43.150]**

## VI   DEPRECIATORY TRANSACTIONS AND VALUE SHIFTING (TCGA 1992 s 176 AND ss 30–34)

Anti-avoidance provisions within the legislation may apply to prevent the exploitation of the rules for transfer of assets around groups to secure a tax advantage. TCGA 1992 s 176 operates to restrict allowable capital losses made on a disposal of shares by a group member following an earlier depreciatory transaction which resulted in the value of the share being reduced.

TCGA 1992 ss 30–34 deal with value shifting and operate to both restrict allowable losses and increase capital gains in certain circumstances. The rules can apply where dividends are paid out of profits artificially created by intra-group asset transfers, or where an intra-group asset transfer takes place for less than both cost and market value and is followed by the sale of shares in the transferor company. For the rules to apply a scheme has to be carried out to reduce the value of an asset materially and some person must secure a tax-free benefit.                                          **[43.151]–[43.170]**

### EXAMPLE 43.14

Bigco Ltd intends to sell its subsidiary Smallco Ltd for £5,000. The base cost of the Smallco shares is £1,000 which would give Bigco a gain of £4,000 (ignoring indexation). Before the sale Smallco transfers one of its assets which has a market value of £2,000 to Bigco for £500. Smallco originally paid £1000 for the asset. As a result of the transfer Smallco is only worth £3,500 and on the sale Bigco makes a gain of £2,500. At the same time Bigco sells the asset for £2,000 making a gain of £1,000 (as Bigco took over Smallco's base cost). The total gain made by Bigco has been reduced from £4,000 to £3,500, so the value shifting rules would be applied to increase the gain.

(If it could be shown that the asset was transferred for *bona fide* commercial reasons and not as part of a scheme to avoid tax, the value shifting provisions would not apply.)

## VII   SCHEMES OF RECONSTRUCTION

Assume that Alpha Ltd, with a wholly owned subsidiary Beta Ltd, now acquires all the issued share capital in a further UK company, Gamma Ltd. It then desires to merge the businesses of Beta Ltd and Gamma Ltd by liquidating Gamma once its assets have been transferred to Beta. A tax-efficient way of achieving this result would be a scheme of reconstruction falling within the Insolvency Act 1986 s110. This would involve the transfer of Gamma Ltd's business to Beta in return for an issue of shares by Beta (at the instruction of the liquidator) to the shareholders in Gamma . The transfer of the undertaking will be governed by TCGA 1992 s 139 since it falls within a scheme of amalgamation or reconstruction. Under this provision no corporation tax will arise on the transfer of chargeable assets that are rolled over into the new company. Equally, the transfer should not attract stamp duty land tax by reason of stamp duty land tax group relief or reconstruction relief under FA 2003 Sch 7. The issue of the further shares by Beta to Alpha will be governed by TCGA 1992 s 136 that ensures that so far as Alpha is concerned the old shares are treated as merged with the new. Accordingly, no charge will arise but the whole operation should be submitted to the Revenue in advance for clearance.                                   **[43.171]–[43.190]**

## VIII   VAT

Corporate bodies within common control may obtain group VAT registration with the result that supplies of goods or services within the group are not subject to VAT (VATA 1994 s 43). This may be particularly attractive when one or more companies in the group make supplies to another group company that in other circumstances would be exempt from VAT, as it may reduce the overall VAT burden of irrecoverable VAT. The decision of the High Court in *C & E Comrs v Kingfisher plc* (1994) determined that the effect of the grouping provisions went further than merely allowing a number of VAT entities to account for VAT under a single registration (as HMRC had contended) and created a single taxable entity.

Registration is in the name of a 'representative member' who becomes liable to report VAT in respect of all group companies. Each individual company, however, remains jointly and severally liable for the VAT position of the group. Companies may join and leave a group, generally on 90 days' notice. To qualify, companies must be resident or have an established place of business in the UK; 'control' depends on majority voting rights.

HMRC may refuse an application to form a group or an application by any company to join or leave a group if they perceive a VAT avoidance motive. FA 1996 contains further provisions giving HMRC extensive powers to counter VAT avoidance using the group registration rules.

These anti-avoidance provisions arose out of a VAT avoidance scheme involving the exploitation of the grouping provisions. The scheme involved mitigating irrecoverable input tax by making substantial prepayments for goods whilst supplier and customer were within a group and then actually supplying the goods once the supplier had left the group. Following the decision of the House of Lords it appears the scheme did not in fact work and therefore the anti-avoidance provisions may now be a matter of overkill (see *C & E Comrs v Thorn Materials Supply Ltd* (1998)).

Applications for group treatment take effect from the dates they are received by HMRC or such other time as HMRC may allow. HMRC have powers to remove companies from groups on ineligibility or Revenue protection grounds.                                **[43.191]–[43.210]**

## IX   STAMP DUTY LAND TAX

Stamp duty land tax is not charged on an instrument by which one company transfers property to an associated company. The detailed requirements are in FA 2003 Sch 7 which requires that one of the companies in question beneficially own, directly or indirectly, at least 75% (by nominal value) of the ordinary share capital of the other, or a third company beneficially owns, directly or indirectly at least 75% of the ordinary share capital of each. The grant of a new lease from one group company to another qualifies for relief in the same way as an assignment.

FA 2003 Sch 7 contains provisions to prevent abuse of the group relief. In particular the consideration for the transfer must not be provided directly or indirectly by a person outside the group. It is also important that the relief is not part of an arrangement whereby the transferor's interest in the transferee's share capital will be reduced below 75%. Relief must be claimed in a land transaction return or an amendment of such a return.          **[43.211]**

# 44 The taxation of partnerships

*Updated by Colin Ives, Professional Practices Tax Director, Smith &* *Williamson*

---

---

Unlike companies and unincorporated associations, a partnership, whether trading or professional, is not subject to special rules of taxation. A partnership is fiscally transparent and the normal principles of income tax and CGT apply to each partner individually. For IHT the partners are taxed individually on their interest in the partnership, but the assets of the partnership are not treated as the assets of the individual partners. The position is different for VAT where a partnership is treated as a separate taxable entity (VATA 1994 s 45 and see *Hawthorn v Smallcorn* (1998)). [**44.1**]

## I INCOME TAX

Historically, a trading partnership was taxed under Schedule D Case I and a professional partnership under Schedule D Case II, although for all practical purposes the rules were the same. For partnerships of individuals, the distinction has now been abandoned and trades, professions and vocations are all charged under ITTOIA Part 9. Under self-assessment there are no longer partnership assessments (and individual partners are required to include their share of partnership profits in their own tax return) but a partnership return is still required to enable the calculation of the partnership profits to be dealt with centrally (TMA 1970 ss 12AA). [**44.2**]

### 1 How to calculate the profits of the partnership

a) *Contrast the sole trader/practitioner*

The procedure for calculating the profits of a partnership is the same as for the sole trader or practitioner (see **Chapter 10**).

In *MacKinlay v Arthur Young McClelland Moores & Co* (1989) the Court of Appeal allowed a partnership to deduct removal costs paid to encourage two partners to move house: in one case from London to Southampton, in the other from Newcastle to Bristol. In both cases the move was desirable from the point of view of the firm's business and neither partner would have agreed to move had his relocation expenses not been borne by the firm. Slade LJ explained the Court of Appeal decision and distinguished the *Mallalieu* case (see [10.137]) as follows:

> 'The analogy between the case of expenses incurred by a sole trader of which he is the beneficiary and the case of expenses incurred by a partnership, of which one partner is the beneficiary, is a misleading one. Section 74(a) ... directs attention to the object of the *spender*, not the recipient. In the first of those two cases it is impossible to differentiate between the objects of the taxpayer *qua* spender and *qua* beneficiary; ... in the second case, where the payer and the beneficiary are not the same, it is clearly possible to evaluate the objects of the payer in incurring the expenditure separately and distinctly from those of the beneficiary ... The Revenue [must] ascertain the purpose of the expenditure at least primarily by what was referred to in argument as the "collective purpose" of the partnership in incurring it.'

The House of Lords reversed the Court of Appeal decision and, in so doing, restated the principles underlying the rules governing the deduction of business expenditure. Their Lordships held, first, that there was no difference for these purposes between a partnership—even a large professional body run by a management committee on corporate lines—and a sole practitioner. In both cases, to be deductible, expenditure must be 'wholly and exclusively laid out or expended for the purposes of the trade, profession or vocation'. Only in very limited situations is an English partnership a separate entity for tax purposes and the speeches of the Law Lords emphasised again that tax rules applicable to individuals must apply to unincorporated bodies. In some cases this is easier said than done: for instance, the application of CGT principles to partnerships is far from straightforward, as will be discussed later.

A second principle to emerge from the speeches was that (in the words of Lord Oliver) 'a partner working in the business or undertaking of the partnership is in a very different position from an employee'. Crucially, he is also a proprietor and accordingly any money which he withdraws from the business whether in the form of a share of profits, 'salary', or interest on partnership capital, must be treated as a share of profits. It remains, however, an over-simplification to assume that *no sums* paid out by the firm to a partner can amount to a deductible business expense for the firm. Rent, for instance, paid to a partner who leases premises to his firm (provided, of course, that the sum involved is not excessive) will be deductible by the firm and attract an income tax charge in the hands of the recipient partner.          [44.3]

b)   *The basis of assessment*

Since 6 April 1999, the taxable profits of a partnership are based on the accounting profits including work-in-progress for the accounting year ended in the tax year (see **Chapter 10**). Barristers are able to use the cash basis for the first seven years of their career. Transitional relief is available for professional practices in general and barristers in particular. The transitional relief takes the form of spreading the adjustment arising on the change of accounting basis (and in particular the inclusion of professional work-in-progress) over a period of up to ten years (ITTOIA 2005 Part 2 Chapter 17 and s 860).                                                                       **[44.4]**

c)   *Arriving at a firm's taxable profit*

ITTOIA 2005 s 25 requires generally accepted accounting practice to be used in arriving at the taxable profit (*subject to any adjustment required by law in calculating profits*), a number of specific matters merit comment:          **[44.5]**

*Salary paid to partners* How a partner's salary is taxed depends on whether he is a partner or merely an employee of the firm. The terms employed by the parties themselves are not decisive of the matter; it is the substance of the relationship between them, as determined from the partnership agreement, that needs to be considered. In view of the high level of national insurance contributions payable by an employer in respect of his higher-paid employees, the firm should consider carefully how it wishes new 'partners' to be taxed and draft the partnership agreement accordingly.

If the individual is an employee the salary paid is a deductible partnership expense on which he should be assessed as earnings from an employment, with tax deducted at source under PAYE. If the individual is a partner, the salary is not an allowable expense of the firm but merely part of his share of profits. The firm's accounts must show the profits as including salaries paid to partners that are then taken into account when apportioning those profits amongst the partners.                                                                       **[44.6]**

**EXAMPLE 44.1**

Balthazar, Mountolive and Justine are in partnership sharing profits in the ratio 3:2:1 after deducting salaries agreed at £1,000, £2,000 and £3,000 respectively. In the year ended 31 December 2006 the business profits (after deducting salaries) were £12,000.

This profit will be divided between the partners in accordance with their profit sharing arrangements in the year ended 31 December 2006.

For 2006–07 the current year basis applies and the assessment will be on £18,000 (HMRC treating the salaries as part of the profit shares) attributed to the partners as follows:

| | | | | | | |
|---|---|---|---|---|---|---|
| *Balthazar:* | £1,000 | (salary) plus | £6,000 | (3/6 × £12,000) | = | £7,000 |
| *Mountolive* | £2,000 | (salary) plus | £4,000 | (2/6 × £12,000) | = | £6,000 |
| *Justine:* | £3,000 | (salary) plus | £2,000 | (1/6 × £12,000) | = | £5,000 |
| | £6,000 | (salaries) + | £12,000 | (balance of profits) | = | £18,000 |

*Interest paid to partners* Partners may be paid interest on capital they contribute to the firm. As with salaries, the interest is not a deductible expense, but is treated as an appropriation of profit. The profits must be adjusted by adding back the interest and the share of each of the partners in the profits then calculated.                                                                    **[44.7]**

*Rent paid to a partner* Where premises are owned by one partner and leased to the firm, any rent paid will be an allowable deduction from the firm's profits, unless the amount exceeds the market value; the partner concerned will be taxed on that rent as property income. It may be more attractive for the premises to be let to the partnership at a nominal rent and for the partner to receive an increased share of the profits. This will not of course be tax deductible by the firm, but the partner concerned will be taxed on the income as trading profits (rather than as property income) and, thus could improve his pension position and give greater scope in the event of loss relief. However, the increase in Class 4 NIC liability since 6 April 2003 can tip the balance of advantage back to property income treatment.

When the partner has taken out a loan for the purchase or improvement of the premises which are used by the firm, he needs to ensure that the interest paid on the loan qualifies for income tax relief. If he receives rent from the firm or if the firm discharges the interest payments (which will be treated as 'deemed rent') income tax relief will be obtained by setting the interest due against the rent (or the deemed rent arising from the interest paid by the firm). If the premises belong to all the partners they cannot let those premises to the firm since a person cannot let property to himself (see *Rye v Rye* (1962)).                                                                    **[44.8]**

*Losses* Losses incurred by the partnership will be apportioned between the partners in the same way as any profits (ITTOIA 2005 s 849), each partner dealing with his share of the loss under the normal relieving provisions (see **Chapter 11**). In the case of a limited partner (whether an individual or a company), loss relief is restricted to the amount that that partner has at risk in the partnership (see TA 1988 s 117 reversing *Reed v Young* (1986)). The FA 2004 and FA 2005 introduced anti-avoidance rules to prevent the use of partnership losses in avoidance schemes (see **[11.122]**).                                     **[44.9]**

## 2   Interest relief on loans to acquire a share in a partnership

Tax relief is available for interest on money which is borrowed to acquire a share in a partnership, or to be used by the firm, or to acquire machinery or plant to be used by the firm. It is important to be able to demonstrate the purpose of the borrowing. In *Lancaster v IRC* [2000] STC (SCD) 138 the taxpayer failed to convince the Special Commissioner that the purpose of borrowing money was to use it within the business rather than funding a transfer of value to his spouse. The relief operates by enabling the borrower to deduct the interest from his income (TA 1988 ss 362, 359(1), (2); see **[7.45]**). In contrast, where the firm borrows money, any interest paid is normally a deductible business expense (ITTOIA 2005 s 29; see **[10.131]**).
**[44.10]**

## 3   Changes in the partnership

Partnership changes are considered in detail in **Chapter 10**.                    **[44.11]**

## 4  **Leaving the partnership**

a)  *Consultancies*

An outgoing partner may be retained as a consultant whereupon he will often be paid a fee in return for some continuing duties. For income tax purposes, the consultant is not a partner so that any sum paid to him by the firm will be a deductible business expense assuming that it can be justified according to the 'wholly and exclusively' test (see **[10.131]**, *Copeman v Flood* (1941); and *Earlspring Properties Ltd v Guest* (1995)). The consultant may be an employee so that PAYE must be operated and he may benefit from joining the firm's pension scheme for a few years. Even if a PAYE obligation does not arise directly, the individual may be within the personal service company rules in ITEPA 2003 Part 2 Chapter 8. He may be able to establish that he is exercising a profession or vocation and should be assessed under ITTOIA 2005 s 847. This treatment is more likely to apply where the individual holds consultancies with several different bodies. In view of the increased national insurance contributions payable in respect of employees, the firm should consider whether it will be preferable to retain the individual as a partner with a reduced profit share rather than as a consultant. **[44.12]**

b)  *Payment of annuities by continuing partners*

Professional partnership agreements may make provision for the payment of annuities to retiring partners in consideration for the outgoing partner surrendering his share of the firm's goodwill and of its capital assets (see **[44.34]** ff). It is largely a matter of commercial expediency whether such annuities are to be payable and if so for how long and for what amount. The recipient would probably prefer an annuity linked to the profits of the business (eg 10% of the net profits) rather than a fixed sum, as this should offer 'inflation proofing'. The following income tax provisions should be noted: **[44.13]**

*Position of paying partners* It is usual for the cost of an annuity to be borne by the partners in the same proportion as they share the profits. They are treated as annual payments which means that the payments are deductible from their personal income and should be paid net of basic rate income tax. The annuity will be a tax-effective settlement of income provided that it is payable under a partnership agreement to a former member of that partnership, or his widow or other dependants (where the partner is dead the annuity must not be payable for more than ten years) and is payable under a liability incurred for full consideration (ITTOIA 2005 s 727 and s 627(2)). The annuity will also be an effective annual payment if it is paid in connection with the acquisition of a share in the business of the outgoing partner.

The partnership agreement will often provide for any incoming partner to take over the cost of an appropriate share of the annuity and that, should the firm cease to exist, the outstanding years of the annuity are to be valued and treated as a debt owed by the partners in the partnership at the date of its cessation. **[44.14]**

*Position of the recipient* The recipient will be taxed on the annuity with a credit for basic rate tax deducted at source. The annuity will be taxed in his hands as earned income to the extent that the amount payable does not exceed one half of the average of his best three years' profits out of the last seven; any excess is unearned income (TA 1988 s 628). Those profit figures are index-linked. Hence, where he is paid a fixed annuity the proportion treated as earned income may vary from year to year.

If the annuity is payable after the recipient's death to a widow(er) or dependants, they may have problems enforcing the payments should the continuing partners default (see *Beswick v Beswick* (1967)). **[44.15]**

**EXAMPLE 44.2**

The partnership agreement of Falstaff & Co provides for retiring partners to be paid an annuity for ten years after retirement amounting to 10% of the annual net profits of the firm earned in the preceding accounting year.

Hal retires as a partner on 5 April 2006. His share of the profit (index-linked) in the last seven years before his retirement is as follows:

| | | | |
|---|---|---|---|
| 2005–2006 | £20,000 | 2001–2002 | £11,000 |
| 2004–2005 | £14,000 | 2000–2001 | £8,000 |
| 2003–2004 | £8,000 | 1999–2000 | £9,000 |
| 2002–2003 | £7,000 | | |

In the tax year 2006–07 Falstaff & Co's net profits amount to £90,000. The continuing partners will pay Hal £7,020, ie 10% × £90,000 = £9,000 less basic rate income tax deducted at source. Hal must enter the gross amount of the payment (£9,000) in his income tax calculation for 2006–07 with a tax credit for £1,980 (basic rate tax of 22%).

The £9,000 is treated as earned income in Hal's hands up to a limit of £7,500 (being half the average share of his taxable profits in the best three of the last seven years before retirement (ie 2005–06; 2004–05; 2001–02). The balance of £1,500 is treated as unearned income.

c) *Retirement annuities and personal pension schemes*

In addition to or instead of (b) above, partners as self-employed individuals could provide for their retirement by making pension contributions personally. Prior to 1 July 1988, such insurance had to take the form of a retirement annuity contract approved by the Inland Revenue under TA 1988 s 619. However, in order to bring retirement provision for the self-employed into line with that available to employees, TA 1988 ss 630–655 required both employees who contract out of occupational pension schemes and partners who provide for their retirement after the same date to enter new personal pension scheme arrangements. On 6 April 2006, the UK pension regime was further simplified with an annual contributions limit subject to an overriding fund value cap. Pensions are considered further in **Chapter 50**.

**[44.16]–[44.30]**

## II   CAPITAL GAINS TAX

### 1   **General**

The application of CGT principles causes difficulties which are exacerbated by the failure of the legislation to make express provision for the treatment of partnerships. It is necessary to apply rules designed for individuals to firms and rely on SP D12, SP 1/79 and SP 1/89 as a substitute for proper legislation in this field. Further, the position as regards taper relief is complex, with partnership property interests being treated differently from other assets—broadly, partnership interests are considered to be a single asset that grows or diminishes as the parties' interest increases or falls.

Where the partnership is carrying on a trade, any dealings with the assets of the partnership are treated as dealings by the partners individually (TCGA 1992 s 59). In the absence of any specific agreement, the treatment of capital gains and losses follows the profit sharing arrangements. Sometimes the asset surplus entitlement will be different from the profit sharing ratio to reflect the partners' contributions to the capital of the business. It may be uncertain whether a particular asset is partnership property or owned by one of the partners and merely used, often without any formal arrangement being entered into, by the firm (see, in relation to milk quota, *Faulks v Faulks* (1992)).                                                               **[44.31]**

#### EXAMPLE 44.3

(1)   Flip & Co, a partnership trading in goods from the East, has three partners, Flip, Flap and Flop, who share asset surpluses in the ratio 3:2:1. In 1998 the firm acquired a valuable Ming vase which was put on display in the firm's reception area at a cost of £60,000; they sell it subsequently for £180,000. The gain of the firm (ignoring any incidental costs of disposal, the indexation allowance and taper relief) is £120,000. CGT must be calculated separately for each partner:

Flip owns 3/6 of the asset and, therefore, has a base cost of £30,000 and is entitled to 3/6 of the sale proceeds (£90,000); his gain is £60,000 (ie he is entitled to 3/6 of the partnership gain).

Flap's base cost is 2/6 of £60,000 (£20,000) and his share of the proceeds is 2/6 of £180,000 (£60,000) so that his gain is £40,000.

Flop's base cost is 1/6 of £60,000 (£10,000) and his share of the proceeds is 1/6 of £180,000 (£30,000) so that his gain is £20,000.

(2)   Assume that the Ming vase is given to Flip in recognition of his 25 years' service with the firm. It is worth £180,000 at the date of the gift. The position of Flap and Flop is basically unchanged and they have made gains of £40,000 and £20,000 respectively. Tax may be postponed by an election under TCGA 1992 s 165 if the donors and Flip agree. In that event Flap will dispose of his 2/6 share for £20,000 and Flop his 1/6 share for £10,000.

The position of Flip is that since he is given the asset he is not treated as making a disposal of his original 3/6 share in the asset (see SP D12, para 3). Hence, the only difficulty is to discover Flip's base cost. Under general principles it will be:

|  | £ |  |
|---|---|---|
|  | 30,000 | (cost of original 3/6 share) |
| *Plus* | 60,000 | (market value of Flap's 2/6 share at date of gift) |

| | | |
|---|---|---|
| *Plus* | 30,000 | (market value of Flop's 1/6 share at date of gift) |
| | £120,000 | |

The result is that Flip's own gain (£60,000) is held over until such time as he disposes of the vase.
If claims are made under TCGA 1992 s 165 Flip's base cost becomes:

| | £ | |
|---|---|---|
| | 30,000 | (as above) |
| *plus* | 20,000 | (balance after deducting held-over gain on Flap's share) |
| *plus* | 10,000 | (balance after deducting held-over gain on Flop's share) |
| | £60,000 | |

## 2   Changing the asset surplus sharing ratio

CGT may be triggered when the asset surplus sharing ratio is altered.

| *Old partners* | *New partners* | *Old asset surplus sharing ratio* | *New asset surplus sharing ratio* |
|---|---|---|---|
| (1) AB | ABC | 1:1 | 1:1:1 |
| (2) AB | AB | 1:1 | 2:1 |
| (3) ABC | ABD | 1:1:1 | 2:2:1 |

In all the above cases there has been a change in the entitlement to asset surpluses (and, therefore, to the beneficial ownership of the capital assets). No asset has been disposed of outside the firm, but there has been a disposal of a share of the assets between the partners.

In (1), above, A and B formerly owned the assets equally; C now joins the firm and is entitled to 1/3 of the asset surpluses. A and B have each made a disposal of 1/3 of their original share in the assets. A, for instance, is now entitled to 1/3 instead of 1/2 or, to put the matter another way, they have together made a disposal of 1/3 of the total assets to C. In (2), although the partners remain the same, the sharing ratio is altered so that B is making a disposal to A of 1/3 of his share of the assets. In (3), C is disposing of a 1/3 share in the assets amongst the continuing partners, A, B and D (A and B each acquire an extra 1/15 of the assets and D 3/15).

Such changes in the sharing ratio are likely to occur principally in three cases: (i) on the retirement of a partner; (ii) on the introduction of a new partner; and (iii) on the amendment of the partnership agreement. It should be noted that the mere revaluation of an asset in the accounts of the firm has no CGT consequences since the revaluation is neither a disposal of an asset nor of a share in assets. However, a charge will arise if an adjustment to the profit sharing ratio is made as a result of the revaluation. Where the revaluation is credited to the partners' accounts and there is a change in profit sharing ratio, a capital gain arises, despite the fact that no actual disposal of the asset takes place. SP D12 paragraph 4 only applies where no revaluation of the asset concerned has occurred.

**EXAMPLE 44.4**

(1) Fleur and Camilla have been in partnership sharing profits and asset surpluses equally. The only substantial chargeable asset of the business is the freehold shop that cost £40,000 in 1998. Fleur now sells her share to Charlotte for £75,000.

Fleur has made a disposal of her half share in the asset and her gain (ignoring any incidental costs of disposal, indexation and taper relief) will be:

|  | £ |
|---|---|
| Consideration received | 75,000 |
| *Less:* base cost (50% of £40,000) | 20,000 |
| Gain | £55,000 |

(2) Slick and Slack are in partnership owning asset surpluses in the ratio 2:1. The main capital asset is the firm's premises which cost £30,000 in 1988 and have recently been revalued at £75,000. The two partners have the following interests in this capital asset:

|  | *Slick* | *Slack* |
|---|---|---|
|  | £ | £ |
| Original expenditure | 20,000 | 10,000 |
| Share of increased value | 30,000 | 15,000 |
|  | £50,000 | £25,000 |

Sloth joins the firm and Slick disposes of 1/2 of his share to Sloth with the result that the sharing ratio becomes 1:1:1. The capital account of Slick will be credited with the value of the share transferred and ultimately he will be paid that sum of money. Slick has thus disposed of 1/3 of the asset (or 1/2 of his share) which has a value of £25,000. That sum will be credited to his capital account with the result that he will have made a gain of £25,000 (consideration for the share disposed of) less £10,000 (base cost of the share disposed of) = £15,000.

Slick will be assessed to CGT on this gain despite the fact that he may not be entitled to receive the £25,000 until the firm is dissolved or until he leaves it. So far as the incoming partner Sloth is concerned, he will acquire a 1/3 share of the capital asset, of a value of £25,000, and that figure will be his base cost (it will often be the capital sum that he will pay into the firm on becoming a partner).

(3) If in (2) above Slick and Slack had never revalued the premises (which appear in the accounts at their original cost price of £30,000), on the change in profit sharing ratio Slick will be treated as transferring half of his share for its book value (£10,000) with the result that he will have made no gain. Correspondingly, Sloth's base cost will be £10,000.

A failure to revalue an asset, with a subsequent transfer of it at cost, might be viewed as a gift to the incoming partner so that market value should be substituted for the share transferred. In *Example 44.4* this would produce a gain for Slick of £15,000 (£25,000 – £10,000). However, although partners are generally connected persons, they are not so treated in respect of transfers of partnership assets (TCGA 1992 s 286(4)). Hence, the market value rule will not apply unless the partners are connected in some other capacity, eg parent and child, and even in those circumstances HMRC states that 'market value will not be substituted ... if nothing would have been paid had the parties been at arm's length' (SP D12, para 7). In all cases, therefore, there will be no question of market value being substituted *so long as the transaction can be shown to be one entered into at arm's length.* Normally, the commercial nature of the arrangement will be assumed. Where there are connected persons, however, the onus is on the taxpayer to show that identical transactions would have been made with a stranger. This onus will usually be discharged by showing that the incoming partner was assuming a large share of responsibility for the running of the business and, thus, furnishing consideration for his share of the assets.

If the bounty element is so great that the transfer must be treated as a gift, HMRC has stated that 'the deemed disposal proceeds will fall to be treated in the same way as a payment outside the accounts'. In such a case any CGT can be postponed by the parties electing to hold over the gain under TCGA 1992 s 165.                                                                                          **[44.32]**

**EXAMPLE 44.5**

Jake and Jules are brothers and are in business together sharing profits equally. The chargeable assets of the firm cost a total of £20,000 and are now worth £200,000 although they have not been revalued in the firm's books. Jake now transfers his 50% share to his two sons, Jason and Jasper. This would clearly not be a bargain at arm's length and a disposal for CGT at market value would arise giving rise to a charge to CGT. However, Jake, Jason and Jasper could make a claim under TCGA 1992 s 165 to hold over Jake's gain.

## 3   Goodwill

Goodwill is a chargeable asset for CGT purposes. Thus, the disposal of the whole or part of a firm's goodwill may be an occasion of charge to CGT. Problems have arisen in recent years (especially with regard to professional partnerships) when the existing partners decided not to charge future incoming partners for any share of the firm's goodwill and, therefore, to write off the goodwill in the partnership's balance sheet. On the question as to whether those partners who originally paid for a share of that goodwill (usually on becoming partners in the firm) can then claim immediate CGT loss relief, the following principles may be suggested.

*First,* on an actual disposal of the goodwill, whether on retirement or to an incoming partner, provided that its value has been written off in the partnership's balance sheet, an allowable loss for CGT purposes may be claimed by the disposing partner.

**EXAMPLE 44.6**

Alfie is a partner in Cockney Films & Co. When he joined the firm in 1995 he paid £10,000 for a share in the goodwill. The firm has decided to write off goodwill since incoming partners will no longer be expected to pay for a share of it. When he retires and a new partner, Slicker, joins there will be no payment for Alfie's share of goodwill and Alfie will have made a loss for CGT purposes of £10,000 (being the difference between what he originally paid for the asset and the consideration received on its disposal).

*Secondly*, at the time when the goodwill is written off in the balance sheet, the partners may wish to claim immediate loss relief under TCGA 1992 s 24(2) which allows a claim for loss relief when 'the Inspector is satisfied that the value of an asset has become negligible'. HMRC does not agree that the mere writing off of goodwill has this result but takes the view that goodwill retains its value even though no longer paid for by incoming partners or shown in the firm's balance sheet, on the grounds that if the business were sold, the consideration would include a sum for goodwill (see CGT Manual, paragraph 68760). [**44.33**]

## 4 Payment of annuities

When a partner leaves the firm any annuity payments that he receives from the continuing partners will be subject to income tax ([**44.13**]) and, in addition, their capitalised value may be treated as consideration for the disposal of a share of the partnership assets (TCGA 1992 s 37(3)) and CGT levied on any resultant gain. In SP D12 Paragraph 8 HMRC has indicated when this will be the case:

'The capitalised value of the annuity will only be treated as consideration for the disposal of his share in the partnership assets, if it is more than can be regarded as a reasonable recognition of the past contribution of work and effort by the partner to the partnership. Provided that the former partner had been in the partnership for at least ten years an annuity will be regarded as reasonable for this purpose if it is no more than two-thirds of his average share of the profits in the best three of the last seven years in which he was required to devote substantially the whole of his time to acting as a partner.

For lesser periods the following fractions will be used instead of the two-thirds

| Complete years in partnership | Fraction |
|:---:|:---:|
| 1–5 | 1/60 for each year |
| 6 | 8/60 |
| 7 | 16/60 |
| 8 | 24/60 |
| 9 | 32/60' |

Where the partner receives both an annuity and a lump sum, the view of HMRC is that:

'If the outgoing partner is paid a lump sum and an annuity, the Revenue will not charge CGT on the capitalised value of the annuity provided that the annuity and one-ninth of the lump sum together do not exceed the relevant fraction of the retired partner's average share of the profits.' (SP 1/79)

The lump sum will, therefore, always be charged to CGT and it may cause the capitalised value of the annuity to be taxed. [**44.34**]

**EXAMPLE 44.7**

(1)   Charles and Claude agree to pay their partner, Clarence, who retires on 5 April 2007 after 18 years as a partner, an annuity of £3,000 pa for the next ten years. His share of the profits in the last seven years of the partnership was as follows:

| Tax year | Profits | Tax year | Profits |
|----------|---------|----------|---------|
|          | £       |          | £       |
| 2006–07  | 10,000  | 2003–04  | 2,000   |
| 2005–06  | 14,000  | 2002–03  | 4,000   |
| 2004–05  | 12,000  | 2001–02  | 5,000   |

The annuity does not exceed two-thirds of Clarence's average share of profits in the best three years of the last seven years before retirement, ie 2/3 × £36,000 divided by 3 = £8,000. Therefore, no CGT is paid on the capitalised value.

Contrast the position if Clarence had been paid an annuity of £9,000 pa. As the permitted £8,000 figure is exceeded the entire capitalised value of that annuity would be subject to CGT.

(2)   Assume that, in addition to the annuity (in (1)), it is agreed that Clarence is to receive a lump sum of £54,000. His CGT position is as follows:

   (i)   the annuity will be subject to income tax;

   (ii)  the lump sum (£54,000) will be subject to CGT insofar as it represents consideration for a disposal of chargeable assets; and

   (iii) the capitalised value of the annuity will also be included for CGT purposes since the annuity (£3,000) plus 1/9 of the lump sum (£6,000) exceeds the 2/3 limit of £8,000.

## 5   Reliefs

CGT reliefs have been considered in detail earlier. Those of particular relevance to partnerships are:                                                    **[44.35]**

*Hold-over relief* Under TCGA 1992 s 165 for gifts of business assets.   **[44.36]**

*Roll-over (business asset replacement) relief (TCGA 1992 s 152)*. The extension of the relief in two circumstances should be noted. *First*, it applies to assets which are owned by an individual partner and used by the firm, so long as the entire proceeds of disposal are reinvested in another business asset used by the firm or used in a new trade carried on by the partner. *Secondly*, where land (or another qualifying asset) is partitioned between the partners it is treated as a new asset for the purpose of this relief provided that the firm is dissolved immediately afterwards (see ESC D23).                        **[44.37]**

*Roll-over (incorporation) relief (TCGA 1992 s 162)* This relief is available on the incorporation of a partnership. Care is needed over the impact on business taper relief.                                                                        **[44.38]**

*Taper relief (TCGA 1992 s 2A, Sch A1, para 5)* A business asset qualifies for an enhanced rate of taper. A business asset includes an asset used wholly or partly for the purpose of a trade carried on by a partnership. It should be noted that the use of roll-over relief (both of the above forms) and hold-over relief may result in the loss of taper relief as the period of ownership relevant, on the eventual disposal, is that of the transferee/replacement asset. With business taper relief having been enhanced from 6 April 2002 so as to provide full relief after only two years, it is a relief that needs to be carefully considered as failure to meet the conditions may result in a substantial loss of relief. From 6 April 2002 in the case of incorporation of a business in exchange for shares under s 162 it is possible for each individual partner to elect for the incorporation relief not to apply so as to preserve entitlement to taper relief. (See TCGA 1992 s 162A.)                    **[44.39]–[44.50]**

## III   INHERITANCE TAX

A partnership is not a separate legal entity but a collection of individuals and inheritance tax applies to each partner as an individual in respect of his interest in the partnership. The partnership is not transparent and the partnership assets are not treated as the assets of the partners.

Normally, the share of a retiring partner in the firm will pass to the continuing partners. There will be no IHT charge where full consideration is paid, or if the transfer is a commercial transaction within IHTA 1984 s 10(1).

**EXAMPLE 44.8**

Big & Co has 20 partners all equally entitled to profits. The following changes occur:
(1)   Partner Zack is retiring and is to receive an annuity. His share of goodwill is to pass automatically under the partnership deed to the continuing partners.
(2)   Partner Uriah is to devote less time to the business and will receive a reduced share of the profits (including capital profits). At the same time, partner Victor is to be paid an increased profit share to reflect his central position within the firm.
(3)   Partner Yvonne is retiring and her place is to be taken by her daughter Brenda. No payment is to be made by Brenda.
   The IHT consequences of these transactions are as follows:
(1)   *Zack* There is no risk of an IHT charge since consideration is given for his assets (there may not even be a fall in value in his estate). Regarding the automatic accrual of goodwill, it is generally thought that the estate duty case of *A-G v Boden* (1912) is still good law for IHT. Mutual covenants by the partners that goodwill shall pass to the surviving partners on death or retirement without any cash payment will make the transfer of goodwill non-gratuitous within IHTA 1984 s 10(1). This principle should apply even where the other parties are, or include, connected persons since it should be possible to show that identical arrangements would have been made with partners who were not so connected.
(2)   *Uriah* The loss to Uriah's estate is the result of a commercial bargain since he is being allowed to devote less time to the business; no transfer of value arises. Likewise, increasing the profit sharing ratio of Victor is merely a commercial judgement by the other partners of his importance to the firm.
(3)   *Yvonne* The new partner is a connected person and Brenda's acquisition of an interest in the partnership will be treated as a transfer of value by Yvonne unless the same arrangement would have been made with a new partner who

was not connected to Yvonne.

The major IHT reliefs applicable to trading and professional partnerships will be business property relief, agricultural relief, and the instalment option. There are three points of particular relevance to partnerships:

*First*, on a transfer of assets held outside the firm and consisting of land, buildings and machinery or plant, business property relief at 50% may be available. If the asset is owned by the partnership, the full 100% relief may apply on the partners' interest in the partnership.

*Secondly*, the IHT business reliefs are not available where a partner's share is subject to a binding contract of sale at the time of transfer (see IHTA 1984 s 113). If it is desired to ensure that on the death or retirement of a partner his share shall pass to the survivors whilst at the same time preserving IHT business property relief, the partnership deed should avoid either imposing an obligation on the remaining partners to purchase his share or even providing for his share to accrue automatically to them. Instead the deed should give the surviving partners *an option* to purchase that share (see *Law Society Gazette*, 4 September 1996, at p 35).

*Finally*, in *Gray v IRC* (1994), HMRC succeeded before the Court of Appeal in lotting the deceased's freehold interest in a landed estate with her share in a farming partnership which owned a lease over the land thereby causing a much higher value to be attributed to the property. The case represents a considerable extension of the old authorities, especially with regard to the rejection of any requirement that to be lotted for valuation purposes property must form a 'natural unit'. It may turn out, however, that the actual decision turned on particular facts since the other partners were not members of the family and had no wish to continue in the business, being only too willing to sell their partnership shares to the hypothetical purchaser of the entire estate: *Private Client Business* (1994) Issue 4).    **[44.51]–[44.70]**

## IV  VALUE ADDED TAX

A partnership is regarded as a separate person for VAT registration purposes. The registration of persons carrying on business in partnership may be in the name of the firm. A notification of liability to register by a partnership is to be accompanied by Form VAT 2, which shows the name, address and signature of each partner.

The admission of a new partner or retirement of an existing partner creates a new partnership. However for VAT, in determining whether goods or services are supplied to or by persons carrying on a business in partnership, no account is taken of any change in the partnership. This does not apply to a change if there is an outright sale of the business by one group of individuals to another and value of taxable supplies exceeds the registration threshold.

Where the same individuals carry on two separate and distinct businesses in partnership there need not be separate registrations in respect of each partnership (*C & E Comrs v Glassborow* (1974)). This decision was distinguished where two limited partnerships existed, see *Saunders v C & E Comrs* (1980).

Changes in the composition of a continuing partnership must be notified to the commissioners in the same way as other changes affecting the registered particulars of a taxable person. Until such time as a retirement is notified, a former partner is regarded as a continuing partner for the purposes of VAT and, therefore, remains liable for any ongoing VAT liability.

**[44.71]**

# 45 Limited liability partnerships

*Updated by Colin Ives, Professional Practices Tax Director, Smith &
Williamson*

## I  BACKGROUND

a)  *The options*

The main choice of business vehicle for many new businesses was between a
company and a partnership (or sole-trader) ie corporate or unincorporate.
Recent tax changes, with the exception of the new rules for personal service
companies and those in respect of non-corporate distributions, made incorporated entities very attractive. The tax advantages of operating a company
are, primarily, the lower rates of tax on retained profits and the absence of
National Insurance on profits extracted by way of dividends but, in some
circumstances where profits are not retained in the business, a partnership or
LLP can be more tax-efficient than a limited company. In reality the tax
issues are complex and need to be considered very carefully (see further
**Chapter 46**).

   The main commercial advantage was the ability to limit liability, although
this benefit may frequently be eroded by the demand for personal guarantees
by lenders. A further, not inconsiderable, advantage was the increased
credibility of the corporate business. This included the enhanced ability to
raise funds with floating charges, the ability to enter into asset finance leases
etc. These issues have, to a degree, been obviated with the LLP structure.

[**45.1**]

b)  *Limited partnerships*

The Partnership Act 1890 was followed by the Limited Partnerships Act 1907,
which permitted some limited liability. Probably the most significant require-

ment of these provisions is that a partner with limited liability may not take any part in the management of the firm. Since active partners will often exercise management and control they will be disqualified from the limited liability protection otherwise available. Accordingly, as a general business vehicle, the limited partnership has not enjoyed the popularity of the limited liability company for this and a number of further reasons. It has, however, gained acceptance as a vehicle for investment 'funds'. This latter advantage may be eroded by the proposed new UK REIT (real estate investment trust) that appears to be aimed at emulating the American REITS and to bring collective investment schemes back onshore.                **[45.2]**

### c)  *LLPs—general*

Since 6 April 2001 a variant of the limited partnership, the 'limited liability partnership' (LLP) has been introduced which provides a vehicle whereby the partners enjoy a measure of limited liability whilst continuing to benefit from the transparent tax nature of a partnership. The tax treatment of partnerships is considered in **Chapter 44**. In this Chapter the tax and other related issues specific to an LLP are considered. Formally, in legal terms, an LLP is a 'body corporate' (ie a company) with a separate legal personality. Its management acts on behalf of the LLP and not on behalf of the members. An LLP will enter into contracts in its own right. However, a major attraction is that the LLP, generally, has the tax status of a partnership (ie is transparent) whilst the members are provided with some limited liability. Individual members of the LLP will thus be protected from debts or liabilities arising from negligence, wrongful acts or misconduct of *another* member, employee or agent of the LLP.                **[45.3]**

## II  NON-TAX ASPECTS OF AN LLP

### a)  *LLPs and companies*

At a practical level, it is essential to remember that an LLP is a body corporate and not an unincorporated entity. As regards taxation, however, in most ways, the members of the LLP are taxed in the UK as if the LLP were a partnership. The price of limited liability is that an LLP must follow the Companies Act requirements for reporting, filing accounts etc which are almost identical to those that apply to limited companies. The major difference between the company and LLP financial regimes is that no maintenance of capital principle applies to LLPs.

The key non-tax features of an LLP are:

- need to register with the Registrar of Companies;
- need to comply with disclosure requirements – eg to file annual accounts on a 'true and fair' basis;
- the LLP has full legal capacity;
- the members of the LLP are in a similar position to company directors regarding wrongful trading etc;
- the Insolvency Act 1986 applies with necessary amendments.

Specifically, from a tax perspective, an LLP is not a company for group relief purposes (TCGA 1992 s 170(a)(b)). It would, however, be eligible to be a member of a VAT group as it is a body corporate.                               **[45.4]**

b)   *Limited liability*

The liability of a member of an LLP is limited to:
- the capital contributed; and
- the amount that the member agrees to contribute in the event of the LLP being wound up.

There are some notable exceptions. In particular there will not be a limitation where a member has accepted a personal duty of care to a third party or a personal contractual commitment.

There may also be additional liabilities in the event of an LLP becoming insolvent when 'clawback' rules are in point. The 'clawback' rules relate to any amounts withdrawn by members in the two years leading up to a winding up where the member knew or ought to have known that after the withdrawal there was no reasonable prospect that the LLP would pay its debts or avoid insolvent liquidation.

Members must ensure that they make it clear that the firm is a LLP (eg note paper, trading name, promotional material, etc) otherwise it may be argued that there was, in fact, an ordinary partnership.                               **[45.5]**

c)   *Capacity*

Every member is deemed to be an agent of the LLP. The extent of the agency can be limited by the constitutional documents. With the exception of a basic default structure, members must create the necessary legal relations between themselves and between members and the LLP. The general law of partnerships or companies will not determine those relationships.

It is therefore advisable for a comprehensive agreement to be made to govern these relations. This is often known as the Members Agreement and will deal with profit sharing and ownership issues.                               **[45.6]**

d)   *Accounts*

As noted, the accounting and audit provisions of the Companies Act 1985 apply to an LLP. All relevant FRSs, SSAPs and SORPs apply (as, in due course, will the International Financial Reporting Standards – IFRSs or IASs).

Accounting practice is important in determining both the quantum of profit and the timing aspect of recognising income and expenditure. In view of the specific issues arising as regards LLPs, a SORP has been prepared and recently updated specifically for LLPs. It is not appropriate, in this text, to consider the detailed provisions of the SORP further. However it should be noted that SORPs are recommendations on accounting practices for specialised industries or sectors. They supplement accounting standards and other legal and regulatory requirements in the light of the special factors prevailing or transactions undertaken in a particular industry or sector. SORPs are issued not by the Accounting Standards Board (ASB) but by industry or sector bodies recognised for the purpose by the ASB.                               **[45.7]**

e)   *International*

It will only become apparent on a country-by-country basis, over time, whether the tax transparency of an LLP will be respected in tax jurisdictions other than the UK. For those countries where the separate legal personality of an entity under general law determines its tax treatment as a body corporate, the likelihood is that the UK LLP will be taxed as a company and will not be tax transparent. If, however, specific criteria contained in the constitution is critical then it may be treated as an unincorporated body. A number of countries accept or have indicated they will accept a UK LLP as tax transparent and consideration of Double Tax Treaties will be relevant.

[**45.8**]

## III   TAXING PROFITS AND GAINS

### 1   General

As noted, LLPs are treated as partnerships for tax purposes in most circumstances. The main exceptions to this general rule relate to LLPs in liquidation and LLPs which are not carrying out a business with a view to profit.

In general therefore, the LLP will not itself be chargeable to tax on its profits or gains, instead each member will be taxed on his share of those profits and gains. This contrasts with the tax treatment of companies. [**45.9**]

### 2   Trading LLPs (TA 1988 s 118ZA–O)

Where an LLP carries on a trade, profession or business with a view to profit, the members will be treated for the purposes of income tax, corporation tax and capital gains tax as if they were partners carrying on that business in partnership. Hence a trading, professional or business LLP will be treated as tax transparent and the detailed provisions discussed in **Chapter 44** will be relevant as regards each member (ITTOIA s 863 and TCGA 1992 s 59A). The partnership rules relating to income and gains for both individual and company members applies to LLPs.

Concern that this vehicle could be 'abused' has resulted in special rules being introduced that apply to 'investment' and 'property investment' LLPs (see [**45.13**]).                                                                [**45.10**]

### 3   Losses

As regards loss relief, members of trading (but not professional) LLPs are subject to the restrictions imposed on limited partners in trading limited partnerships (see [**44.9**]). Consequently, the ability to set losses, etc against income or profits from other activities will be limited by reference to the amount of the capital contribution made plus the amount of agreed liability on a winding up.

Further anti-avoidance rules have been introduced in the FA 2004 and FA 2005 to deal with Film Partnerships and LLPs, partnerships involving non-active partners, partnerships involving companies and individual partners where losses have been derived from exploiting any licence and an individual receives consideration not otherwise taxable.

Unrelieved losses can be carried forward to the next period for set-off, subject to the limit on loss relief, against other income for that period.

[**45.11**]

## 4 Specific matters

The following tax considerations are worthy of particular note:

(a) A change from an ordinary partnership to an LLP will generally be tax neutral as it will not, of itself:
  – give rise to a cessation of the business; or
  – give rise to a balancing event for the purposes of the capital allowance provisions; or
  – constitute a disposal by the partners of their interests in the old partnership's assets; or
  – affect the availability of indexation allowance; or
  – affect the holding period for taper relief.

(b) Members of an LLP, who are individuals, will be entitled to claim interest relief on the loans they take out for the purposes of the LLP provided that they otherwise meet the conditions of the relief (see [**7.45**]. Relief will not, however, be available for funds provided to an investment or property investment LLP (see [**45.13**]). In these circumstances, consideration should be given to raising required finance via the LLP itself.

(c) Undrawn profits of a member of an LLP cannot normally be added to their subscribed capital in order to calculate the limit of relief for any trading losses (see [**45.11**]. [**45.12**]

## 5 Investment LLPs and property investment LLPs

a) *An 'investment LLP' (TA 1988 s 842B(1))*

The definition of an investment LLP closely follows the definition of an investment company so that the case law and guidance relating to the definition of an investment company may be applied to LLPs (TA 1988 s 842B(1)). A representative period will be taken to form a view as to whether the principal part of income is derived from the business so that an LLP is an investment or property investment LLP, but that view will then be taken to apply for the whole period of account.

b) *A 'property investment LLP' (TA 1988 s 842(B)(1))*

The definition of a property investment LLP builds on that of an investment LLP. Two particular rules should be noted:

(1) As regards property activities, individuals will not be able to obtain interest relief on loans to buy into a property investment LLP (TA 1988 s 362(2)). On one level this is not surprising, since interest relief is currently restricted for limited partners in a limited partnership registered under the Limited Partnership Act 1907. The restriction for LLPs matches this restriction.

(2)   Exemptions for income and gains will not apply for pension funds, the pension business of life insurance companies and the tax-exempt business of friendly societies where the income and gains are received in their capacity as a member of a property investment LLP (TA 1988 s 659E).                                                                      **[45.13]**

## 6   Capital gains

A member's interest in a trading or professional LLP will not be regarded as a separate chargeable asset, and the members will be taxable on their share of chargeable gains arising on the disposal of the LLP's assets (TCGA 1992 s 59A). SP D12 applies (see **[44.31]**) to members of an LLP. An LLP cannot be the member of a group of companies. Any tax reliefs that would be available if it had corporate status for tax purposes are not available (TCGA 1992 s 59A).                                                                      **[45.14]**

## IV   TAX ON CESSATION OF ACTIVITIES

### 1   General

The LLP is treated as being transparent for tax purposes until it ceases to carry on a trade or business either at the end of a winding-up process or by going into liquidation. In these circumstances the LLP reverts to corporate status.

In order to prevent avoidance of tax when an LLP ceases to be transparent, there is a charge to tax based on an amount equal to the postponed gain or gains which have not otherwise, by then, come back into charge (TCGA 1992 s 169A). The temporary cessation of trading will not, however, change the normal tax treatment.                                                                      **[45.15]**

### 2   Winding up and liquidation

#### a)   *Winding up*

Where the members of an LLP proceed to wind up its affairs the transparency of the LLP will be preserved during the period in which the assets are being disposed of provided that:
(1)   the LLP is not being wound up for reasons connected in whole or in part with the avoidance of tax; and
(2)   the period of winding up is not unreasonably protracted.
    HMRC will treat an informal winding up in the same way (see IR Tax Bulletin 50 (December 2000)).
    If these conditions are not met, then the transparency of the LLP may be regarded as coming to an end before the informal winding-up process has been completed.                                                                      **[45.16]**

#### b)   *Liquidation*

In the liquidation period, the LLP's capital gains will be treated in exactly the same way as for any other body corporate. Chargeable gains will be computed by reference to the date on which assets were first acquired by the LLP and their cost at that date. As with shareholders, LLP members will be taxed on any gain (or granted relief for losses) that arises on the disposal of their capital interests in the LLP. The allowable acquisition cost of each partner's interest is determined according to the historical capital contributions made as if the LLP had never been transparent. To state the obvious, this treatment does not extend to the pre-liquidation asset disposals: their tax treatment remains undisturbed. It should be noted that the base cost of a partner's capital interest is not equal to the market value of that interest at the time when transparency is lost – there is no rebasing. Accordingly, the impact of going into liquidation should be carefully considered.

Each member who has postponed a gain is deemed to have a chargeable gain accruing to him or her immediately before the LLP ceases to be transparent. The gain is equal to the amount of the postponed gain or gains, which has not then come back into charge (TCGA 1992 s 156A).    **[45.17]**

## V  TRANSFER OF AN UNINCORPORATED BUSINESS TO AN LLP

The effect of a transfer of a business to an LLP is in line with any change in tax transparent form (sole trader to partnership, partnership to sole trader or partnership to another partnership or partnerships). The key points to note are:

- *Capital allowances* – No balancing charges or allowances will arise.
- *Interest relief* – Members continue to enjoy tax relief for interest on qualifying borrowings. ESC A43 reflects this.
- *Spreading rules* – The spreading rules for the 'catching up charge' set out in FA 2002 Sch 22 continue to apply as if the conversion had not occurred. Similarly, the spreading rules included in the Finance Act 2006 in respect of the change in rules for income recognition (UITF 40) will continue to apply.
- *Cessation* – Incorporation as an LLP will not, of itself, involve the cessation of the trade or profession.
- *Overlap relief* – no overlap relief will be utilised or created unless there is a change of accounting date.
- *Tax returns* – If a conventional partnership incorporates as an LLP *during* an accounting period, then if the partners so wish, a single partnership return may be made for the accounting/tax year in question.
- *PAYE returns* – a single return may be made for the tax year in which a conventional partnership incorporates as an LLP.
- *Non-UK resident members* – As noted above the country in which the member is resident may treat the LLP as liable to corporate taxes rather than income tax.
- *Capital Gains tax* – the incorporation will not, of itself, constitute a disposal by the partners in their interests in the old partnership's assets. The transfer will not affect:
  - The availability of indexation allowance.
  - The holding period for taper relief.
- *Annuities* – assuming that the rights remain substantially the same:
  - the transfer of a partner's annuity rights and/or

>       –   the transfer of annuity obligations to former members will not be
>           regarded as a chargeable disposal.

The same treatment is accorded where an annuitant agrees to the substitution of the LLP for the predecessor partnership as the payer of the annuity.

**[45.18]**

It will be a matter of fact as to whether an LLP has succeeded to the business of a partnership. The basic test is whether or not the business carried on by the LLP is recognisably 'the business' previously carried on by the old partnership. The issues to be considered in determining whether or not a succession has occurred are set out in SP 9/86. Where only part of an existing trade or profession is transferred, the cessation of business provisions may apply to the old partnership. The previous overlap relief will be crystallised and commencement provisions will apply to all members of the LLP giving rise to fresh overlap profits.               **[45.19]**

## VI   ANTI AVOIDANCE: INVESTMENT AND PROPERTY INVESTMENT LLPS

Provisions introduced by FA 2001 Sch 25 are intended to discourage the use of LLPs for purposes other than trading and professional activities. The property investment partnership is particularly identified and dealt harsh treatment to prevent pension funds investing in property through LLPs. For exempt pension funds and the pension side of life offices' business, the normal exemption from income and capital gains tax afforded to the profits of such funds is not available (ICTA 1988 s 659E and ICTA 1988 s 438B).

Ordinary investment LLPs (those 'whose business consists wholly or mainly in the making of investments and the principal part of whose income is derived therefrom') are penalised by prohibiting interest relief under ICTA 1988 s 362(2) on borrowings to subscribe capital, lend to the LLP, etc for individual members (FA 2001 Sch 25 para 9).

Interest relief will, however, be available if an individual investor can satisfy the conditions of other interest relieving provisions, eg property income.

**[45.20]**

## VII   OTHER TAXES

### 1   Stamp duty/Stamp Duty Land Tax (SDLT)

The Limited Liability Partnership Act 2000 s 12 provides for relief from stamp duty on the transfer of assets from a partnership to an LLP. This relief is replicated for SDLT in FA 2003 s 65. The relief is available for transfers on conversion or within 12 months of the date of incorporation of the LLP. Technically, the legislation does not fit in with the proper analysis of a member's interest in an LLP. However, HMRC (in *Tax Bulletin 50* December 2000) say that they will not take the point. The key practical considerations are

● the partners' proportional interests in the assets transferred to the LLP must correspond to those held by them through the LLP immediately after incorporation; or

- if there are any changes, the proportions have not been changed for tax avoidance reasons; and
- the people making the transfers (ie the partners in the old firm) must be exactly the same as the members of the LLP immediately after incorporation.

Interests in LLPs are not 'marketable securities' and, as a result, the rate of duty on the conveyance or transfer on sale of interests in an LLP will be at the *ad valorem* rates (0% to 4%).

SDLT applies to partnerships and LLPs with effect from Royal Assent to the Finance Act 2004. However, the Finance Act 2006 has brought in changes to remove most transactions between partners from the charge to SDLT. A charge may arise on the contribution of a property to a partnership or LLP. The detailed rules are beyond the scope of this chapter – see **Chapter 40** for further detail. **[45.21]**

## 2   National insurance and salaried members

The taxation and NIC position of members of an LLP is complex and uncertain at this time. Where a partner satisfies all of the normal badges of self-employment then they will be treated as self-employed. However, in addition, HMRC currently view all salaried members as self-employed based on an interpretation of ICTA 1988 s 118ZA(1)(a). However, LLPA 2000 s 4(4) clearly allows for employee members, which would imply that such salaried members will be treated as an employee of the LLP. It is understood that HMRC have issued some rulings under Code of Practice 10 to the effect that certain salaried members are to be taxed as self-employed for taxation purposes. Such rulings are dependent upon the particular circumstances of each set of facts, and are also capable of being withdrawn at any time. It is the view of the author of this chapter that if it is intended that salaried members are to be taxed as self-employed their arrangements should be capable of meeting the normal criteria of self-employment. Typically this would include the requirement for the members in question to provide capital to the LLP and participate in the variable profits of the business (and possibly losses to some degree (see the discussion at **[12.13]**).

Where members of an LLP are treated as partners, not employees, the self-employed (Class 2 and Class 4—and Class 3) rates of National Insurance will apply and employers National Insurance will not be due. **[45.22]**

## 3   VAT

Business Brief 3/2001 sets out the VAT position of LLPs. The basic rules of VAT apply to any form of business. As regards the incorporation of a partnership, broadly, the LLP will need to apply for a separate registration unless the partnership ceases to trade at the same time. Where the partnership ceases at the same time the existing registration can be transferred to the LLP. This will, generally, not give rise to a VAT charge as it will be a transfer of a going concern (TOGC) subject to the normal rules, so no VAT will be payable. Although an LLP cannot be a member of a direct tax group, it can be a member of a VAT group. This facility may make the LLP attractive when compared to an ordinary partnership or limited partnership when it is desired to limit the VAT leakage on management fees whilst retaining favourable NIC treatment.                                                              **[45.23]**

## 4  Inheritance tax

IHTA 1984 s 267A treats an LLP as tax transparent for IHT purposes. Therefore, the inheritance tax position is not affected by a conversion of a partnership to a LLP.                                                                      **[45.24]**

# 46 Choice of business medium

*Updated by Peter Vaines, Squire, Sanders & Dempsey*

---

I     Introduction—the available options **[46.1]**
II    Non-tax factors **[46.21]**
III   The taxation factors **[46.41]**
IV   General conclusions **[46.81]**

---

## I   INTRODUCTION—THE AVAILABLE OPTIONS

When commencing a business the participators will normally have an unrestricted choice between operating through the medium of a company or partnership. Professions which operate through the medium of a partnership may set up a company to service the running of their premises and to provide staff, furniture and equipment. The Limited Liability Partnership has been introduced as a hybrid between the limited liability company and the unlimited liability of the traditional partnership.

The typical company will be the private limited company and the typical partnership will consist of a number of partners with unlimited personal liability. **[46.1]**

There are, however, other possibilities such as:

*The public company:* Its attraction is the ability to raise funds from the public (contrast the restriction on private companies: Companies Act 1985 s 81). In practice, of course, it is unlikely that a new business would commence as a public company since the costs involved are considerable and only in very limited cases would a Stock Exchange listing or permission to deal in the company's shares on the Alternative Investment Market be granted for a completely new enterprise. **[46.2]**

*The unlimited company:* This suffers from the disadvantage that the liability of the shareholders is unlimited—hence, they are in the same position as partners (albeit with the convenience of corporate personality). However, the unlimited company need not file the statutory company accounts, enabling it to preserve a greater degree of confidentiality. Many of the restrictions which apply to limited companies for the protection of creditors do not apply, such as the ability to reduce or repay its share capital without the sanction of the court. **[46.3]**

*The old style limited partnership under the Limited Partnerships Act 1907:* The creation of an old style limited partnership is regulated by formalities similar to those which have to be satisfied if a company is to be formed and although there can be partners whose liability for the debts of the firm is limited, there must also be at least one general (or unlimited) partner. Furthermore, if a limited partner takes any part in the management of the firm, he loses the protection of his limited liability and becomes a general partner. Thus, a limited partner who has put capital into the firm might be obliged to allow his money to be lost by inept management since any attempt to interfere would put at risk the whole of his personal fortune. In recent years the investment and tax planning opportunities afforded to limited partnerships have proved attractive both for income tax and IHT as the partnership interest can qualify for business property relief at 100%.                                        **[46.4]**

*The limited liability partnership (LLP):* This new form of legal entity was introduced by the Limited Liability Partnership Act 2000 (see **Chapter 45**). An LLP is a body corporate which exists as a legal person separate from its members. The introduction of this legislation stemmed from the concerns felt by professional partnerships over the unlimited liability of the partners and the unsatisfactory operation of the Limited Partnerships Act. An increasing number of professional partnerships are converting to LLPs although some will be deterred by the company law disclosure requirements that apply. The existing tax rules for partnerships and partners generally apply to LLPs and members of LLPs which are carrying on businesses as if they were partnerships and partners respectively. Accordingly whether to operate through a general partnership or an LLP is tax neutral and converting an existing partnership into an LLP will not normally lead to any tax charge.
**[46.5]**

*Partnerships with companies:* This hybrid arrangement involves an individual joining in partnership with a limited company. If the individual is also a director of the company concerned, making him a limited partner offers attractions since he can participate in the management of the business in his capacity as director of the company. The particular advantages afforded by the arrangement lie in the regulation of profit sharing ratios to take account of different income and corporation tax rates and to maximise the use of business losses.                                        **[46.6]**

*The IR 35 rules:* It will not be attractive for a taxpayer to form a company in circumstances where these rules apply, although there might be strong commercial pressures to do so despite the tax disadvantages. **[46.7]–[46.20]**

## II  NON-TAX FACTORS

### 1  Limited liability

A limited company is a separate legal entity and is solely liable for its debts and obligations. The shareholders' liability is restricted to the sum invested by way of share capital and this liability cannot be increased without their consent (Companies Act 1985 s 16). The limited company offers the ideal vehicle for the individual who wishes to set up in business, but who is not prepared to risk his entire personal fortune in the venture.

**EXAMPLE 46.1**

Brian is the sole shareholder in Wretched Ltd. The company is in liquidation with total debts of £50,000 and assets of only £20,000. Brian has a personal wealth of £100,000, but because of the limited liability of the company, the creditors of Wretched Ltd cannot generally look to Brian for payment of the shortfall.

There are exceptions to the principle of limited liability and in certain circumstances the 'veil of incorporation' has been lifted to make shareholders liable for the company's debts. Although these instances are rare, the director of a private company should be aware that there are circumstances in which he might be liable for the debts of the company. Most notably, a director of a company which has entered insolvent liquidation who is found guilty of wrongful trading under the Insolvency Act 1986 s 214 can be ordered by a court to contribute to the assets of that company.

On a practical level, in order to obtain finance for his company a shareholder/director will often be required to give security for the liabilities of the company by way of a personal guarantee. To the extent that personal guarantees are given, limited liability will be illusory. However, it is only major lenders, lease finance companies and landlords who are likely to require guarantees—not trade creditors and certainly not customers. **[46.21]**

## 2 Corporate personality

A company will never die: it can only be liquidated or dissolved. The death of a shareholder does not affect the company; the only result will be a transmission of some of the shares of the company. Sole traders enjoy no such advantages, because the assets of the business will be vested in them so that death will bring the business to an end. Further, from the point of view of simple estate planning, the company's shares are easy to transfer and easy to divide into separate parcels. A large shareholding can be fragmented between different members of the shareholder's family whereas the ownership of an unincorporated business is not easily divisible.

The existence of a separate legal entity (the company) means that the shareholder/proprietor can enter into legally binding contracts with it (see *Lee v Lee's Air Farming Ltd* (1961)). Normally the shareholder in the small private company will be concerned in the management of the business as a director and will ensure that he enters into a lucrative long-term service contract with the company. Amongst a number of advantages that such contracts offer will be the protection in the event of the employment being prematurely terminated and preferential treatment for arrears of wages in the event of the company's insolvency.

Incorporation will have an effect on the valuation of the interest in the business. A 10% partner, for instance, is treated as owning 10% of the firm's assets but a 10% minority shareholding would be valued at a substantial discount (because of the very limited rights possessed by a 10% shareholder). This can give rise to an advantage for tax purposes and incorporating a business may be a useful first step as a prelude to a gift of part of the business.
**[46.22]**

### 3  Obtaining finance

Companies have advantages when it comes to raising finance. Apart from issuing risk capital in the form of shares, money can also be raised by loans secured by fixed and floating charges. The fixed charge is common to both incorporated and unincorporated businesses (eg the land mortgage), but a floating charge is only applicable to companies. It operates as a charge over (usually) the entire undertaking and has the advantage of leaving the company free to deal with the assets of the business as it sees fit save to the extent that the terms of the charge provide otherwise. The floating charge will only crystallise on liquidation or when a default, as specified in the deed of charge, occurs.

How advantageous is the floating charge? This question can only be answered by considering whether creditors will be satisfied with the protection afforded by it and in many cases they will not be. Quite apart from the inherent defects of a non-crystallised charge, the existence of preferential creditors on an insolvency has weakened the attractions of such charges. Accordingly, the characteristic feature of company charging in recent years has been the practice of creditors to demand fixed security (see, eg *Siebe Gorman & Co Ltd v Barclays Bank Ltd* (1979) and the growth of *Romalpa* clauses).                                                                        **[46.23]**

### 4  Formality, rigidity and costs

By comparison with the unincorporated business, a company suffers from formality and rigidity and has greater operating costs. A partnership or sole trader can establish a business with negligible documentation and formality. A company can be bought 'off the shelf' quite cheaply but the costs of a tailor-made company are usually higher. The obligation to file forms is a regular feature of a company's life, especially the annual return and it is necessary to submit annual accounts to the Registrar of Companies. Such requirements, however, are probably a small price for the benefits of limited liability and, in practice, the costs of a well-drafted partnership deed may be equal to the expense involved in company formation.

As an artificial entity, a company must be formed for specific purposes set out in the objects clause of its memorandum of association. Actions outside the scope of these prescribed objects are *ultra vires* and are void. This difficulty should not be exaggerated since, objects clauses are generally drafted in such wide terms that they will embrace all conceivable activities. Furthermore, as a result of the Companies Act 1989, a company's memorandum may state that the object of the company is to carry on business as a general commercial company (ie any trade or business whatsoever).

**[46.24]–[46.40]**

## III   THE TAXATION FACTORS

The formation of a company generally means that the company will be taxed as an entity distinct from its members and distributions from the company will be taxed in the hands of the shareholders, resulting in double taxation. Specific provisions dilute this problem, but it remains a major argument against incorporation. Any comparison, however, cannot be just between the taxation of individuals and the taxation of companies, since there is also the need to consider the individual as a director or employee of the company. The topic must, therefore, include some discussion of the pros and cons of being employed as opposed to self-employed. **[46.41]**

## 1 Taxation of income profits

a) *Rates of tax*

Income tax on the profits of a partnership or sole trader will be taxed at 40% when the individual's taxable income for 2006–07 exceeds £33,300. Corporation tax will be charged on the profits of the company at either 30% or 19% depending upon the profits of the company (see **[41.21]**).

For an individual whose taxable income exceeds £33,400, the marginal rate will be 40%, but this will, of course, only apply to the slice of income above that level. For small companies whose profits exceed £300,000 but fall below £1,500,000 there is a system of tapering relief and tax on profits which fall within that zone is charged at the marginal rate of 32.75%.

It may be advantageous to ensure that the company avoids making profits taxed at this marginal rate: keeping a company's profits below £300,000 can be achieved by a number of methods: eg paying out additional tax deductible sums to its directors in the form of salaries or bonuses or by making extra contributions to a pension scheme (see *Example 46.3*). **[46.42]**

b) *National Insurance contributions*

The rates for 2006–07 are set out as **Appendix A** at the end of this chapter. National insurance contributions (NIC) costs must be borne in mind when extra salary/bonuses are paid out to directors and employees. **[46.43]**

c) *The effect of paying all the profits out as remuneration*

Employees' remuneration is deductible as a business expense of the company and will be subject to income tax as earnings in the hands of the employee. The amount paid to a full-time working director is unlikely to be challenged as excessive so that, if all the profits are paid out as remuneration, the company will pay no corporation tax (contrast *Copeman v William J Flood & Sons Ltd* (1941) and *Earlspring Properties Ltd v Guest* (1993) which illustrate that excessive payments to a director's family may be challenged). The only differences between a shareholder/director who extracts all the profits as salary and the self-employed sole trader are as follows:
(1) Dates for paying the tax: this is discussed in more detail at **[46.45]** below.
(2) Pension entitlements: the pensions available for employees and for the self-employed are discussed in **Chapter 50**. It should be remembered that, although the pension choices are now similar in both cases, one advantage for employees is that tax deductible contributions to their pension schemes can also be made by their employer (ie by the

company), thus boosting their eventual entitlement under the scheme (see also *Taxation*, 24 May 2001, p 191).

(3)  Social security aspects: the salary paid to employees, including directors, attracts Class 1 NICs payable by both employer (the company) and the employee.                                                            **[46.44]**

### d)  *Dates for paying tax*

Companies have a maximum delay of nine months from the end of the accounting period to the payment of corporation tax. The system of quarterly payments for corporation tax means that large companies have to pay tax during the accounting period and, therefore, the advantage in payment timing may be less. Where company profits are all paid out in directors' fees, tax and NIC will be deducted and paid under the PAYE system.

For individuals the self-assessment regime involves profits charged for a tax year being those shown in the accounting period ending in the year of assessment (this tax is paid in two instalments, on 31 January in the year of assessment and on the following 31 July). A final, balancing, payment is then made the following 31 January. Drawing up accounts to end early in the tax year (eg on 6 April) therefore produces the longest delay before the tax liability is finally settled.                                              **[46.45]**

### e)  *Trading losses*

The relief for trading losses is generally more advantageous with an unincorporated business. Company losses are 'locked in' so that they cannot be used by the owners to set against their other income, and instead relief will only be given when the company makes profits (see **[41.60]**). Formerly, the ability to set a trading loss against capital gains in the year in which the loss was incurred was the one real advantage that the company had over the unincorporated trader. However, an unincorporated trader can set trading losses against capital gains for the year of the loss and one following year (see **[11.61]**). The unincorporated trader is also able to set his trading losses against his other income under the provisions of TA 1988 s 380 and, so far as early losses are concerned, against previous income as a result of TA 1988 s 381. It is often argued that when a new business is likely to show early losses, it is best to start the business as an unincorporated trade and to incorporate the business when it becomes profitable. However, if early losses exceed the wildest expectations of the trader, the advantage of income tax loss relief will not compensate for the disaster of bankruptcy. Had the loss been realised by a company, the limited liability may have protected the proprietors from bankruptcy.                                                          **[46.46]**

**EXAMPLE 46.2**

Having worked in the Civil Service for many years, Samantha has resigned to open a boutique. She anticipates trading losses in the early years. She has a substantial private income.

(1)    If she forms a company to run the business, trading losses can be relieved only against future corporate profits.

(2)  If she operates as a sole trader the losses can be set against her private income (and capital gains) for the year of the loss (TA 1988 s 380) or against her income, including that from the Civil Service, in previous years (TA 1988 s 381) or against both (*Butt v Haxby* (1983)).

### f)  *Interest relief*

Income tax relief is generally available on the interest paid on loans to acquire a share in either a partnership or a close company. To qualify, the taxpayer no longer has to work for the greater part of his time in the business (see generally **Chapter 7**). Relief is also available on loans raised for the benefit of the close company or partnership. Interest paid on loans to finance the business will usually be a deductible business expense; companies are subject to special rules whereby all profits and losses (whether as borrowers or lenders) are treated as income with interest payments taxed or relieved as they accrue rather than as they are paid.            **[46.47]**

### g)  *Corporate investment reliefs*

Various reliefs have been introduced in an attempt to stimulate investment in qualifying trading companies.            **[46.48]**

*Loss relief* (*TA 1988 s 574*) Section 574 is intended to encourage the subscription of shares in certain unquoted trading companies by allowing a loss on disposal of the shares (including failure of the venture) to be relieved against income (see further **[11.121]**). It is not available for moneys lost in an unincorporated enterprise, but the partner who lends money to the partnership may be able to claim a capital loss under TCGA 1992 s 24 if the partnership defaults and the debt is a debt on a security, or otherwise under TCGA 1992 s 253.            **[46.49]**

*Enterprise Investment Scheme* (*TA 1988 s 289*) Subject to detailed provisions being satisfied, tax relief at 20% on the sum invested in a qualifying company is available and the investment may also enable capital gains to be sheltered (see **Chapter 15**).            **[46.50]**

### h)  *Illustrations*

#### EXAMPLE 46.3

AJ Ltd has taxable profits for the year ended 31 March 2006 of £310,000 after paying its two directors salaries of £23,000 each. To avoid paying corporation tax at 32.75% on profits above £300,000, AJ Ltd pays each of the two directors a further cash bonus of £5,000.

This has the following results (assuming that the directors have no other income and are entitled to the personal allowance).

| | | £ | £ |
|---|---|---|---|
| (1) | *Taxation of AJ Ltd* | | |
| | Taxable profit to date | | 310,000 |
| | *Less*: bonuses to directors (£10,000) | | |
| | and NIC (at 12.8% = £1,280) | | 11,280 |

|  |  |  |  |
|---|---|---:|---:|
|  | Revised profit for year |  | £298,720 |
|  | Corporation tax at 19% |  | 56,756.80 |
| (2) | *Taxation of the directors* |  |  |
|  | Total income (£23,000 + £5,000) | 28,000 |  |
|  | *Less*: personal relief | 4,895 |  |
|  | Taxable income | £23,105 |  |
|  | Income tax payable by each: |  |  |
|  | £2090 at 10% | 209.00 |  |
|  | £21015 at 22% | 4,832.30 |  |
|  | Total income tax paid (2 × £4832.30) |  | 9,664.60 |
| (3) | Total tax paid |  | £66,421.40 |

*Notes*:
(a)   Dividends cannot be used to reduce profits.
(b)   Had the bonus payments not been paid, the total tax bill would have been:

| (1) | *Taxation of AJ Ltd* | £ | £ |
|---|---|---:|---:|
|  | Taxable profits |  | 310,000 |
|  | Corporation tax payable: |  |  |
|  | £300,000 at 19% |  | 58,000 |
|  | £10,000 at 32.75% |  | 3,275 |
|  |  |  | 61,275 |
| (2) | *Taxation of directors* |  |  |
|  | Total income | 23,000 |  |
|  | *Less*: personal relief | 4,895 |  |
|  | Taxable income | £18,105 |  |
|  | Income tax payable by each: |  |  |
|  | £2090 at 10% | 209.00 |  |
|  | £16,015 at 22% | 3,523.30 |  |
|  | Total income tax paid (£3,773.90 × 2) |  | 7,464.60 |
| (3) | Total tax paid |  | £68,739.60 |

Hence, the tax saving arising from making the bonus payments is £68,739.60 − £66,421.40 = £2,318.20

(c)   The bonus payments also result in an NIC liability of 1% on the employee (ie 100) .

(On ways to avoid NIC on bonus payments, see [46.60].)

The decision to extract funds from the company by way of bonus or dividend will depend upon the rate of tax paid by the company:

*Bonus* (assuming all basic rate band fully utilised)

| | | |
|---|---:|---:|
| Profits | | 100,000 |
| Bonus | 88,652 | |
| NIC at 12.8% | 11,348 | 100,000 |
| Corporation tax | | NIL |
| Bonus received | | 88,652 |
| Income tax on bonus at 40% | 35,461 | |
| NIC at 1% | 886 | 36,347 |
| Net received by individual | | £52,305 |

*Dividend*

| | |
|---|---:|
| Profits | 100,000 |
| Corporation tax at 19% | 19,000 |
| | 81,000 |
| Dividend | 81,000 |
| Effective income tax rate at 25% | 20,500 |
| Net received by individual | £60,500 |

If the company pays tax at 30% the position is:

| | |
|---|---:|
| Profits | 100,000 |
| Corporation tax at 30% | 30,000 |
| | 70,000 |
| Dividend | 70,000 |
| Income tax at 25% | 17,500 |
| Net received by individual | £52,500 |

If the company pays tax at the marginal rate of 32.75% the position changes:

| | |
|---|---:|
| Profits | 100,000 |
| Corporation tax at 32.75% | 32,750 |
| | 67,250 |
| Dividend | 67,250 |
| Income tax at 25% | £16,813 |
| Net received by individual | £50,437 |

The clear conclusion is that despite the NIC liability a dividend is much better if the company is paying tax at the small companies rate—and still marginally better where the company is paying tax at the full rate of corporation tax. Where the company is in the marginal rate band of 32.75% a dividend is the worst option.

Where the individual is not paying tax at the higher rate a dividend will be effectively tax-free and that would obviously be most advantageous.

*Example 46.4* shows the advantages of a small company when it is desired to retain profits for use in the business.

**EXAMPLE 46.4**

Business profits are estimated to be £40,000 in the year ended 31 March 2007 and the proprietor will take £15,000, leaving the remainder in the business to finance expansion.

(1)    If an unincorporated business:

|  | £ | £ |
|---|---|---|
| Taxable income (ignoring reliefs) | | £40,000 |
| Income tax on £40,000: | | |
| 2,150 at 10% | 209.00 | |
| 31,150 at 22% | 6,853.60 | |
| 6,700 at 40% | 2,680.00 | |
| | £9,742.60 | |
| NIC | | |
| Class 2 | 109.20 | |
| Class 4 | 2,345.00 | |
| | £2,454.20 | |

|  | | £ |
|---|---|---|
| Profit: | | 40,000.00 |
| *Less*    Income tax | 9,742.00 | |
| NIC | 2,454.20 | 12,196.20 |
| | | £27,803.80 |

(2)    If the company paid out £15,000 as emoluments and the balance retained:

|  | £ | £ |
|---|---|---|
| *Employee:* | | |
| Taxable income (ignoring reliefs) | | 15,000.00 |
| Tax on £15,000 @ 10% and 22% | 3,036.00 | |
| NIC on £15,000 | 1,650.00 | 4,686.00 |
| Total amount received after tax and NIC | | £10,314.00 |

|  | £ |
|---|---|
| *Company:* | |
| Total profits | 40,000.00 |

| | | |
|---|---:|---:|
| *Less:* remuneration | 15,000.00 | |
| NIC on remuneration | 1,920.00 | 16,920.00 |
| Taxable profits | | 23,080.00 |
| Corporation tax at 19% | | 4,385.20 |
| Retained profit | | £18,694.80 |

(3)  In summary, the amount of tax and NIC payable as a sole trader amounts to £12,196.20 whereas the amount paid by the company amounts to £10,991.20, a saving of £1205.00; the saving will vary depending upon the amount of profit retained or paid out by the company.

If the business is generating profits in excess of the needs of the proprietor(s), the ability to use the lower corporation tax rates to retain profits represents one of the attractions of incorporation. Hence, the retention of profits is a factor of importance in most businesses.            **[46.51]**

## 2  Extracting cash from the business

One of the drawbacks of a company is exposed when the individual wishes to extract surplus profits for his own benefit. The company is a separate taxable entity and the funds extracted will be charged to tax on the individual. As the company's profits have already been charged, there is a risk of double taxation. The major methods of 'extracting' profits are:            **[46.52]**

*Paying dividends:* A shareholder may waive his entitlement to a dividend before it is declared and it will not then be treated as paid to him since he never becomes entitled to it. Accordingly, it does not form part of the income of the shareholder for income tax purposes. Further by IHTA 1984 s 15, a dividend waiver will not be a transfer of value if it is made within one year before the dividend is declared. Two common uses of the waiver may be noted: *first*, to enable the company to pay a larger dividend on the other shares; *secondly*, to enable profits to be extracted by shareholders who are not directors by the latter waiving their dividend and taking additional remuneration. However it is necessary to consider the NIC implications and the settlement provisions in Taxes Act 1988 Part XV in respect of any proposed dividend waiver.            **[46.53]**

A dividend waiver is certainly capable of being a settlement where there exists an element of bounty. Accordingly a dividend enabling another shareholder to receive an increased dividend would be a settlement within the meaning of ITTOIA 2005 s 624. The person waiving the dividend would be the settlor and would remain taxable on the whole of the amount waived. (See *Tax Bulletin* 64, April 2003 for further examples of settlements.)

However, this does not have to be the case. A dividend waiver is the temporary abandonment of a contingent right to future income. It does not necessarily increase the amount payable to any other shareholder unless the dividend is declared for a fixed monetary amount.

**EXAMPLE 46.5**

Magna is a higher rate taxpayer with 7,500 shares, a 75% shareholding in Magna Ltd. His daughter Minima has 2,500 shares, a 25% shareholding.

(a) Magna waives his rights to dividend and the company declares a dividend of £50,000. The whole of the dividend is therefore paid to Minima. She would have received only £12,500 if Magna had not waived his dividend and the extra £37,500 is therefore a settlement and will be taxed on Magna.

(b) If the company had instead declared a dividend of £20 per share Minima would receive £50,000 but Magna would receive nothing. His waiver would not have affected her dividend; it would merely have eliminated his dividend. The waiver would not be a settlement—subject to (c) below.

(c) If the company had insufficient distributable profits to pay a dividend on all the shares, there would be a settlement. If the company only had £160,000 distributable profits, Minima would only have been entitled to a maximum of £40,000 and it is only because of the waiver by Magna that she was able to receive more. This excess £10,000 will be taxed on Magna as a settlement.

(d) Although the dividend waiver might not itself be a settlement, the payment of the dividend or the generation of profits could be a settlement. Magna might take a very low salary from the company with the intention of boosting the profits that are paid out by dividend to Minima. This could be a settlement because the provision of services would be bounteous, enabling income to be transferred to Minima (see *Jones v Garnett* (2005)).

*Interest payments:* Excessive interest payments, and any attempt to link the interest to the profits of the company, may result in the interest being treated as a distribution and not tax deductible from the company's profits (see **[42.7]**). Interest payments have to be in respect of *bona fide* loans.    **[46.54]**

*Lending the profits:* Apart from restrictions on the making of loans to directors in the Companies Act 1985, the company will usually be a close company so that the provisions of TA 1988 s 419 will apply (see **[41.128]**). This means that any loan to a shareholder will give rise to a payment of notional tax of 25% of the loan. This notional tax is repayable only when the loan is repaid. In addition, the recipient may be liable to income tax on a benefit in kind from the receipt of a beneficial loan.    **[46.55]**

*Extracting the profits by selling the shares:* Profits made by the company will be reflected in the value of the shares. Hence, a sale of the shares will ensure that the profit is obtained by the shareholder as a capital gain. This will inevitably give rise to double taxation since not only will the company's profit be subject to corporation tax, but also the proceeds of sale of the shares will be taxable on the shareholder.    **[46.56]**

**EXAMPLE 46.6**

Hoco Ltd makes profits of £100. Corporation tax at 19% is £19 so that £81 is retained by Hoco Ltd. If all the shares are owned by Mr Hoco they would be worth £81 more. Therefore, were he to sell his shares for the asset value, he would make a gain of £81 subject to (say) 40% CGT = £32.40. The total tax attributable to the company's £100 profit is therefore £51.40 (£19 paid by Hoco Ltd and £32.40 paid by Hoco.) The tax would be much less if the shares qualified for business assets taper relief as this could reduce the capital gains tax on the shares to a rate of only 10%.

Advantages clearly exist in taking a profit as capital gain (rather than as income) particularly having regard to business assets taper relief (see **[19.141]**).

*Buy-backs* This topic is considered at [**42.21**]: reference should be made to TA 1988 s 219 and SP 2/82. [**46.57**]

**EXAMPLE 46.7**

Doug gives his adult children some shares but then causes a dividend to be paid of £90,000 to each child. The income tax would be:

| | |
|---|---:|
| 32.5% on the gross equivalent of £100,000 | 32,500 |
| less tax credit | 10,000 |
| | £22,500 |

This is an effective rate of only 25% on a dividend received of £90,000.

*Extraction in the form of remuneration:* As already discussed, this method avoids any double charge to tax since the sum paid will be deductible for corporation tax and subject only to income tax and NIC in the hands of the individual. In the typical private company, where the shareholders are also full-time working directors, profits may easily be extracted in this fashion. (See *Ebrahimi v Westbourne Galleries Ltd* (1973) for a practical illustration of such a private company and for a salutary lesson in what can happen if things go wrong!) The amount of NIC borne by the company (discussed above) should also be borne in mind when fixing levels of remuneration. [**46.58**]

*Tax-efficient benefits* Modest savings can be obtained by the provision of certain benefits in kind (see generally *Taxation*, 28 September 2000, p 664): for instance:
(1) holiday accommodation or a second home subject to a possible benefit in kind charge;
(2) assets which directors can use for a limited time so as to keep the benefit at a low level (for instance, use of a yacht/aircraft etc);
(3) are there still attractions in the company car and company fuel? It is necessary to compare the cost savings to the individual by having the car purchased and paid for by the company, with the tax and NIC payable on the benefits in kind. The use made of the car will be crucial in this calculation and the alternative of a mileage allowance (tax-free under the Fixed Profit Car Scheme—now known as the Approved Mileage Allowance Payments Scheme). In extreme cases the provision of a van as a second car may be attractive since this will result in a significantly lower taxable benefit. Indeed from 6 April 2005 the taxable benefit on a van was removed entirely if the employee is prohibited from any private use other than ordinary commuting. Where this restricted private use condition cannot be satisfied the benefit in kind will remain at £500 (£350 for vans more than four years old at the end of the tax year). However, on 6 April 2007 the benefit in kind increases to £3000 irrespective of the age of the van, unless the restricted private use condition is satisfied;
(4) as far as NIC mitigation is concerned the loopholes in this area have been steadily reduced over the years and NIC now also applies to most benefits in kind. [**46.59**]

*Dividends or remuneration?* The main choice facing proprietors of the private company is between dividends and salary. The payment of salary has obvious attractions being fully deductible by the company. The increasing level of NIC has improved the position of the dividend, and reverses the advantages of paying emoluments except where the company pays tax at the marginal rate in excess of 30%: see **[46.51]**. In cases where husbands and wives are both engaged in the business of a private company it is necessary to give detailed consideration to the possible application of ITTOIA 2005 s 624. In *Jones v Garnett* (2005) (more popularly known as *Arctic Systems Limited*) the company provided computer consultancy services that were supplied by Mr Jones. Mrs Jones dealt with all the financial administrative requirements. Mrs Jones took a small salary and the profits were mainly extracted by way of dividend. HMRC argued that the arrangements represented a settlement for the purposes of ITTOIA s 624 so that the dividend paid to Mrs Jones could be treated as the income of Mr Jones. There were two important issues—first whether these arrangements represented a settlement by Mr Jones and secondly whether such a settlement could be excluded from these provisions by the exemption provided by s 626 for outright gifts from one spouse to another of property which is not wholly or substantially a right to income.

The High Court decided that a settlement did exist and the settlement was not simply the one share acquired by Mrs Jones but the whole of the arrangements whereby she received income from the share. The exemption did not apply because the arrangements covered more than merely an outright gift but a composite arrangement involving many different elements to cause income to become payable to Mrs Jones. (This decision was reversed by the Court of Appeal who held that there was no bounty and this was all a commercial arrangement. Accordingly there was no settlement and Mr Jones could not be taxed on the income or Mrs Jones:

> 'No doubt the acquisition by Mrs Jones of her share would enable her to receive dividends in the future, but it did not follow that Mrs Jones would receive any dividends; nor if she did, that each and every dividend then received by her constituted an element of bounty. That would all depend on the future trading of the company and the contribution made by Mrs Jones. The structure did not guarantee any profits. The fact that a profit and a dividend may result is not in my view enough, nor do I think it is contemplated by the decided cases.' (Chancellor of the High Court)

And further:

> 'The settlement must be identifiable by a particular point in time, as opposed to there being something which may or may not turn out to be a settlement if certain future events happen.' ((Keene LJ))

The Court of Appeal also held that, although there was no outright gift from the taxpayer to his wife and the exemption in s 626 could not apply, had there been an outright gift of the share to Mrs Jones, the share would not have been wholly or substantially a right to income and the exemption would have applied.

This case may not have reached a final conclusion yet as leave to appeal to the House of Lords has been granted.                                    **[46.60]**

3 **Capital taxes**

a) *General*

Recent changes in the capital taxation of companies have placed the small company in an improved position compared with the unincorporated business.

Sole traders and partners are subject to CGT at a rate of 22% or 40% with an annual exemption (for 2006–07) of £8,800. For partnerships, the rules for calculating the CGT liability of the individual partners are applied in accordance with SP D/12 (see **Chapter 44**). So far as companies are concerned, capital gains are taxed at the normal corporation tax rate, ie at either, 19% or 30%. Such gains are included in determining whether the small company rate is applicable. In terms of tax rates, therefore, companies may be at an advantage since the individual will usually find that a 40% rate of tax will apply to his gain whereas the company will, at worst, be subject to a 30% rate.

In many cases both individuals and companies will be able to defer a charge by claiming roll-over relief under TCGA 1992 s 152 (see **[22.72]**) or by EIS deferral relief. In other cases, the company should consider disposing of the asset in a year when its trading profits are low so that it may come within the small company's 19% rate of charge. Capital profits can be taken out of the company by means of a dividend. In this way, a shareholder who is liable to tax only at the basic rate and who wishes to realise the capital profit on his shares can avoid the double charge to tax that would otherwise result when he sells those shares (see *Example 46.9*). **[46.61]**

**EXAMPLE 46.8**

In its accounting period ending 31 March 2006, Kafka Ltd, a small company, makes capital profits of £30,000. K, a basic rate taxpayer, is the sole shareholder/director and wishes to obtain the benefit of this profit.
(1) *Sale of shares:* Kafka Ltd incurs a corporation tax charge of £5,700 on the capital profit. Accordingly the net profit of £24,300 is retained in the company. If K were to sell his shares for a price reflecting this retained profit he would be subject to CGT of 17.82% on the retained profit (ie 22% × £24,300). Hence, assuming K has already utilised his CGT annual exemption, the total tax attributable to the company's capital profit will be 36.82%). (19% corporation tax + 17.82% CGT).
(2) *Payment of dividend:* If, instead of selling his shares, K arranges for Kafka Ltd to distribute the profit by way of dividend the tax position is as follows:

|  | £ |
| --- | --- |
| Dividend | 24,300 |
| Tax credit thereon | 2,700 |
|  | £27,000 |

K's income

No further charge for the basic rate taxpayer

| Total tax paid | £5,700 |
| --- | --- |
|  | (19%) |

Hence, K saves the 17.82% CGT. Note, however, that no account has been taken of the availability of taper relief on a sale of the shares by K—the maximum amount of business assets taper is 75% which would reduce K's CGT bill from 17.82% to 4.45%.

b)    *Retention of assets outside the business*

It is a common practice to keep appreciating capital assets out of a company. In part, this is to avoid any risk of a double charge to CGT: but undoubtedly the most compelling reason is very often the desire of the owner of the asset to retain all of any future profits made from the sale of that asset! In such a case, therefore, the relevant shareholder will allow the asset to be used by the company, but will retain its ownership.

On its disposal, any gain will be subject to CGT only in the hands of the shareholder. The difficulty is that although a double charge may be avoided, other problems can be created, for instance:

(1)    *IHT business property relief:* Relief may be available on such an asset, but only at 50% and, in the case of an asset used by an unquoted company, only if the owner is a controlling shareholder (which limits the relief to those cases where the individual has more than 50% of the company's voting shares). For a partner the relief at 50% is available whatever the size of his share in the partnership (see **[31.43]**). The possibility of 100% relief is a crucial factor which may encourage assets to be held within partnerships and companies.

(2)    *Payment for use of the asset:* Apart from such payments being subject to income tax as property income they will restrict the amount of gain which can be wiped out by the relief. Hence, it may be better for the taxpayer to take, instead, an increased share of the profits or, in the case of a company, a greater salary. If rent is paid the company should obtain a corporation tax deduction (provided that it is not excessive): rent in excess of a market rent paid to a shareholder is treated as a distribution. Interest paid on a loan to acquire property can only be set against rental income whereas interest on a loan to purchase shares in, or make a loan to, the company can be deducted from the taxpayer's total income.

(3)    *Section 162 relief:* The relief for CGT on the incorporation of a business will not be available if assets (except cash) are retained outside the company.

(4)    *Paying IHT by instalments* is generally not available in the case of assets held outside a company except for land (when interest will be charged on the unpaid IHT).                                                    **[46.62]**

c)    *VAT aspects*

If a new commercial building is acquired, the purchaser may have to pay VAT on the purchase price. If this VAT is to be recovered, the purchaser will need to register for VAT and to charge VAT on the rent which he receives. **[46.63]**

4    **Stamp duty land tax**

Sales of a business involving land will give rise to a charge to stamp duty land tax. On a share transfer stamp duty or stamp duty reserve tax is charged at an *ad valorem* rate of only ½%. If the business to be sold consists of valuable dutiable assets, the purchaser may (obviously depending on other commercial considerations) prefer to reduce his stamp duty cost by acquiring the shares.                                                        **[46.64]–[46.80]**

## IV   GENERAL CONCLUSIONS

Although non-taxation factors tend to favour incorporation (notably the benefit of limited liability), tax considerations will favour the unincorporated trader at lower levels of profit. Note, however, in particular:

(1)   The small companies rate of 19%, encourages the retention of profits (up to £300,000 pa) in the company (see *Example 46.3*).

(2)   The top rate of corporation tax (30%) is less than the higher rate of income tax (40%) and applies to both income and capital profits.

(3)   Dividends still carry a tax credit which offsets (at least in part) tax suffered by the company.

(4)   The danger of an investor being 'locked-into' the private company has been reduced by the 'buy-back' provisions (see **[42.21]**).

(5)   Taxpayers are given incentives to invest in corporate trades through the Enterprise Investment Scheme and CGT deferral relief.

Two final points may be mentioned. *First,* questions of commercial 'prestige' favour incorporation: the label 'company director' is more impressive than 'sole trader'. *Secondly,* and by way of a cautionary note, considerable tax reliefs are given to encourage firms to incorporate and new corporate businesses to commence, but the same is not true on disincorporation. A company is easier to get into than to escape from and this is a factor to be remembered when the decision to incorporate is taken.            **[46.81]**

APPENDIX A: TABLE OF RATES OF NATIONAL INSURANCE
CONTRIBUTIONS FOR 2006–07

The table below shows the rates of national insurance contributions for the
year 2005–06.

| CLASS 1 (EMPLOYMENT)—NOT CONTRACTED OUT | | | |
|---|---|---|---|
| | | *Employer* | |
| | | *% of all earnings* | *Employee* |
| *Weekly earnings bands* | | | |
| £0–£97 | | 0.0 | 0% |
| £97–£645 | | 12.8 | 11% |
| Over £645 | | 12.8 | 1% |
| Men 65 and over and women 60 and over | | 12.8 | Nil |
| Class 1A—on benefits | | 12.8 | Nil |
| Class 1B—on PAYE settlement agreements | | 12.8 | |
| **Class 2** | Self-employed | | £2.10 per week |
| | Limit of net earnings for exception | | £4,465 pa |
| **Class 3** | Voluntary | | £7.55 per week |
| **Class 4*** | Self-employed on profits | | |
| | £5,035 – £33,540 | | 8% |
| | over £33,540 | | 1% |
| * Exemption applies if state retirement age is reached by 6 April 2006 | | | |

# 47 Incorporations, acquisitions and demergers

*Updated by Peter Vaines, Squire, Sanders & Dempsey*

| | | |
|---|---|---|
| I | Transfer of an unincorporated business to a company | **[47.2]** |
| II | Company acquisitions | **[47.31]** |
| III | Demergers and reconstructions | **[47.51]** |
| IV | Management buy-outs | **[47.71]** |

Some aspects of business takeovers will be considered in this chapter, although in view of the complexities and technicality of the subject all that is attempted is a general introduction to the problems involved. **[47.1]**

## I TRANSFER OF AN UNINCORPORATED BUSINESS TO A COMPANY

This section is concerned with the issues that arise when an existing unincorporated business is transferred to a company. There are a variety of ways in which this might happen, for instance:

(1) The business could be transferred to an existing company or to a company formed or purchased 'off the shelf' by the proprietor to take over the business.

(2) The business might be acquired by the company in return for shares in the company, loan notes, cash, deferred or contingent consideration or a combination of all four. **[47.2]**

### 1 Income tax

Until 6 April 2005 unincorporated businesses were subject to income tax under Schedule D Case I but now the code is contained in ITTOIA 2005 Chapter 2. The principles on which income tax is charged are unchanged and where the business is transferred to a company the closing year rules will apply. Where assets only are sold and the proprietor continues the same trade, there will not be a cessation of the business and he will continue to be taxed according to the current year rules.

Termination of a business may lead to a claim for terminal loss relief (TA 1988 s 388(1)). As an alternative, where the business is transferred to a company wholly or mainly for shares, the taxpayer can elect for any year throughout which he retains beneficial ownership of the shares to set off unrelieved trading losses against income that he receives from the company.

The set-off must first be used against salary if the proprietor is employed by the company but any balance can be relieved against dividends paid by the company (TA 1988 s 386). The loss cannot be transferred to the company.

A discontinuance may result in a clawback of capital allowances by a balancing charge. Where the transfer is to a company controlled by the transferor, an election can be made by both parties, in the case of machinery and plant, that the company takes over the assets at written down value for capital allowances. That election must be made within two years of the date of succession.                                                                    **[47.3]**

## 2   Capital gains tax

### a)   *The available reliefs*

The incorporation of the business will involve the transfer of chargeable assets to the company with a consequent risk of a CGT charge. A number of reliefs may be available:                                                           **[47.4]**

*Where the transfer is in exchange for shares:* relief is provided by TCGA 1992 s 162 which operates to roll any gain on the business assets into the shares acquired in exchange. The capital gain will, therefore, be postponed until the shares are sold. (Note, however, that the company acquires the business assets at market value, ie there is a tax-free step up which will reduce the capital gain on a disposal of the assets by the company.) For the relief to apply, all the business assets (except cash) must be transferred to the company in exchange for shares. It follows that retention of appreciating business assets prevents s 162 from applying. Any attempt to remove those assets from the business prior to incorporation (eg by transferring them to a spouse) may result in HMRC denying the relief on the grounds that not all the assets of the business had been transferred. If the consideration is partly shares and partly cash an appropriate portion of the gain will be subject to charge and only the balance will be rolled into the shares (see ESC D32 on liabilities of the business.) Special rules operate if part of the consideration is a qualifying corporate bond. Accrued taper relief of the transferor may be lost subject to a claim under s 162A.                                                           **[47.5]**

*A transfer for cash:* Roll-over relief under TCGA 1992 s 152 may be available if the transferor reinvests the proceeds of sale of permitted assets in the same or a new trade within the prescribed period. This is most unlikely to arise if the trade has been transferred.                                                           **[47.6]**

*A gift to the company:* Where business assets are transferred to the company for no consideration or at an undervalue the disposal will be treated as taking place at market value. The gain arising can be held over under TCGA 1992 s 165 (see **[24.21]**). The use of this hold-over election under s 165 should, however, be carefully considered since the effect is to transfer any capital gain in the assets to the company. Accordingly it can lead to a double charge when that gain is ultimately realised by the company (see further **Chapter 46** and *Example 47.1*, below).                                                           **[47.7]**

*The retention of appreciating assets outside the company:* The double charge which may arise when capital gains are realised by a company means that where a business is incorporated there may be attractions in retaining outside the company assets which are likely to appreciate substantially in value and to allow the company to use or lease those assets. TCGA 1992 s 162 will not apply to the incorporation in these circumstances so that, unless hold-over relief is available, gains on the incorporation will be subject to charge. The owner of the asset may, however, sell the asset and reinvest the proceeds claiming roll-over relief under TCGA 1992 s 152. Deferral relief under EIS may also be available. A gift of the retained asset should attract hold-over relief under TCGA 1992 s 165 and business property relief for IHT at a rate of 50% so long as he controls (within the IHTA 1984 s 269 definition) the company (but note that 100% business property relief will *not* be available).

**[47.8]**

### EXAMPLE 47.1

Slick intends to incorporate his existing business. Accordingly, Slick Ltd is formed with £100 share capital. Slick then sells to Slick Ltd goodwill for a nominal sum and other assets at their CGT base cost. The consideration may either be paid in cash or left outstanding as a loan to Slick Ltd. An election under TCGA 1992 s 165 is then made. The following matters should be noted:

(1)   Slick is free to retain the ownership of whichever assets he desires (hence avoiding the problems of s 162).

(2)   Under s 165 the gain is rolled over to reduce Slick Ltd's base cost of the assets whereas under s 162 it is the base cost of the shares held by the shareholder that is reduced, the company acquiring the assets at market value. Note, however, that Slick Ltd will obtain the benefit of the CGT indexation allowance only on the base value of the assets transferred. A major problem which may arise if s 165 is used is that the postponed gain may be taxed twice—once on disposal by the company of chargeable assets and the second time when the shares showing an increased value are sold.

b)   *Valuation*

In *Tax Bulletin* 76 (April 2005) HMRC explained their practice on the treatment of goodwill when a sole trader transfers their business to a company in which they have a controlling interest. The transfer of the goodwill represents a transaction between connected parties and market value needs to be substituted for the actual consideration: TCGA s 17. Where the goodwill is over valued HMRC will treat the excess not as a capital gain but as earnings or as a benefit in kind, chargeable to income tax and class 1 NIC. Where there is no evidence that any excess value constitutes earnings (for example, it may have been received in his capacity as a shareholder rather than employee) they consider the excess would be regarded as a distribution, providing there are sufficient distributable profits for such a distribution to be lawful.

Where the excess value arises inadvertently (because neither side intended to transfer the goodwill as an excess value) HMRC will allow the transaction to be unwound by the company repaying the excess value to the sole trader or rewriting the loan account to remove the excess amount.       **[47.9]**

c)   *Taper relief*

A taxpayer who has built up taper relief on business assets will lose that accrued relief if he incorporates the business under s 162 and likewise if he gives the assets to a company claiming hold-over relief under s 165. Section 162A introduced by FA 2002 allows the taxpayer to disapply s 162 so that the transfer gives rise to a disposal enabling taper relief to be obtained at that time. This would be a substantial advantage if a sale of the shares were to take place within two years before full business asset taper had been built up on the shares.                                                                    **[47.10]**

## 3   Stamp duty land tax

The sale of a business to a company may involve a charge to stamp duty land tax unless the contract contains a certificate of value (so that the nil rate applies). Duty will only be charged on the land, as the charge to stamp duty on intellectual property was abolished by FA 2000 and on goodwill in 2002. It need not be charged on goods that can be transferred by delivery. An apportionment of consideration between the chargeable and non-chargeable assets must be made and duty will be charged on liabilities taken over by a purchaser.                                                                    **[47.11]**

**EXAMPLE 47.2**

Yol agrees to sell his business to M Ltd for £157,000 on 1 April 2006. M Ltd further agrees to take over Yol's outstanding liabilities to secured and trade creditors. The state of Yol's business is:

| *Liabilities* | £ | *Assets* | £ |
|---|---|---|---|
| Secured creditors | 6,000 | Freehold | 112,000 |
| Trade creditors | 14,000 | Goodwill | 16,000 |
| | | Stock | 14,000 |
| Excess of assets | | Book debts | 22,000 |
| over liabilities | 157,000 | Deposit a/c | 13,000 |
| | £177,000 | | £177,000 |

M Ltd will purchase the business for a consideration for stamp duty land tax purposes of £132,000 being the value of the freehold and the creditors taken over. The other assets acquired are not subject to duty.

Stamp duty land tax would be reduced if the cash were used to discharge some of the creditors thereby reducing the consideration for stamp duty land tax to £119,000, ie below the £120,000 threshold.

## 4   Problems for a purchasing company

Where the business is not being incorporated but is being sold to an existing company other difficulties for that purchaser should be noted. For instance, if the business is acquired as a going concern it must be treated separately for corporation tax purposes from any existing trade already carried on by the company. The price paid for items such as land, plant and machinery, and goodwill constitute the purchaser's base cost for the purpose of computing any future capital gains. So far as capital allowances are concerned, a conflict of interest is likely with the vendor being concerned to attribute as small a sum as possible to such assets in order to avoid a balancing charge whilst for the purchaser a high figure will give him a greater capital allowance. The agreed apportionment will normally be accepted by HMRC, but will probably only be reached after hard bargaining between the parties.          **[47.12]**

## 5  Other matters

A number of ancillary matters should also be considered on incorporation or sale of a business. The following summarises the more important:

(1)   If an existing trade is incorporated, contracts of employment automatically transfer with the business. Where assets alone are sold, however, claims for redundancy will occur if staff are reduced. (See especially the Employment Rights Act 1996 and the Transfer of Undertakings (Protection of Employment) Regulations 1981.)

(2)   If the vendor of the business is a director of the purchasing company (this will normally be the case when a business is being incorporated), a general meeting of the company will usually have to approve the agreement under Companies Act 1985 s 320 (CA 1985). If new shares are to be issued it will be necessary to ensure that the company has available authorised share capital (if necessary, the authorised share capital should be increased: see CA 1985 s 121); that the directors have the power to allot such shares (see CA 1985 s 80); and that any pre-emption provisions in the articles of association have either been satisfied or do not apply to shares issued in return for a non-cash consideration.

(3)   Providing the company is registered for VAT before the transfer of the business as a going concern, there will be no charge on the transfer of items which are subject to VAT on the sale of the business (VATA 1994 s 49). VAT may be charged on a mere transfer of assets.

(4)   Ensure that all necessary consents are obtained and/or documents amended, eg a landlord's consent to the assignment of a lease.

(5)   If the business is sold for cash, the vendor should remember that for IHT purposes, business property relief and the instalment option will be lost because an asset which qualifies for relief for IHT is being exchanged for cash that enjoys no such relief.          **[47.13]–[47.30]**

## II  COMPANY ACQUISITIONS

A sale of a company may take different forms. The assets of the target company may be purchased; or the shares of that company may be acquired. In the former, the shareholders of the target will be left with a company whose sole asset is cash; in the latter, the shareholders themselves will be left with cash. Alternatively, the takeover may be by a share exchange in which case the vendors will be left with shares in the purchaser. On a share acquisition, the purchaser will have acquired the entire enterprise as a going concern and, if a corporate purchaser, will have acquired a subsidiary company. In an assets takeover, the purchaser may simply amalgamate those assets with his existing business so that instead of acquiring a new enterprise he may simply be expanding the existing business.            **[47.31]**

## 1   Considerations on an assets sale

a)   *The vendor*

If the vendor company intends to continue in business, an asset sale has the advantage that the vendor company may be able to roll over any gains (under TCGA 1992 s 152) into the purchase of new assets within the permitted time. It is possible to reinvest in a completely different trade (see SP 8/81). A disposal of stock results in a corporation tax charge and a disposal of machinery and plant may lead to balancing charges.

   If the company plans to discontinue trading permanently, the consequences are far from satisfactory. The company will be liable to tax on any capital profits made on the sale. The normal carry-back of losses to the previous year will be available, but carry-forward relief will be lost. Problems will arise if the shareholders wish to extract the cash from the company. The result will be either an income tax charge on a distribution, or a charge to CGT on a liquidation in addition to the tax charge already borne by the company. Generally, if the vendors plan to discontinue the business, and to obtain all the sale proceeds personally, the company should not sell its assets; it is better for the shareholders to sell the shares. However, where the shareholders have no real need for the money other than to invest, they may prefer to arrange for the company to sell its assets and for the proceeds to be invested by the company. In this way the rate of tax on the disposal might be lower (depending on how much taper relief is available to the shareholders) and the investment return will be taxed at a lower rate inside the company than if they invested the proceeds themselves.            **[47.32]**

b)   *The purchaser*

The *first* and most obvious attraction is that the purchaser can select which assets he wants to acquire since he will not be acquiring the entire entity. *Secondly*, save in respect of employees (which the purchaser will take over if there is a transfer of a business as a going concern), the purchaser will not run the risk of acquiring liabilities which he does not want and/or of which he is not aware. *Thirdly*, the purchaser will be entitled to capital allowances (eg on the purchase of plant and machinery) and to roll over relief on the purchase of prescribed assets.            **[47.33]**

## 2   Considerations on a share sale

a)   *The vendor*

. The sale of shares will be a disposal for CGT purposes and, if the requirements are satisfied, taper relief will be available. Because the company is sold, there is no change of owner of the business so that continuity of employment is automatically preserved and all debts and liabilities effectively pass to the purchaser. The vendors will normally be required to give certain undertakings and warranties to the purchaser so that there will be some continuing personal liability.

If the purchase money is to be paid in instalments, CGT will still be charged on the total sum at the outset unless HMRC allows the tax to be paid by instalments (see TCGA 1992 s 280). Where the consideration is partly deferred, the deferred consideration may need to be brought into charge immediately if it is able to be quantified, or at its present value at the date of the contract if it is unable to be ascertained or quantified (*Marren v Ingles* (1980), see [**19.7**]).

If the vendors intend to stay in business, a share sale may not be ideal since, for CGT, gains on the sale of the shares can only be rolled over into the purchase of replacement shares in a qualifying EIS company, although if full business taper relief applies and the vendors can realise the gain at a rate of only 10%, they might regard that as an acceptable result. The position of the vendor if consideration for the sale is in the form of shares or loan notes is considered below. [**47.34**]

b)   *The purchaser*

The acquisition of the company's shares will usually ensure continuity of the business. However, there will be no tax relief for the purchase of the shares themselves. It is possible to carry forward trading losses suffered by the company prior to the sale of the shares but by TA 1988 s 403(1) these losses may only be set against profits *in the same trade*. If the trade has ceased, carry-forward is not possible even if an identical trade is later restarted. Further, TA 1988 s 768 prevents relief in the event of a 'major change in the nature or conduct of the trade' within a period of three years of the sale (see *Willis v Peeters Picture Frames Ltd* (1983) and SP 10/91; [**41.65**]). The prudent purchaser should tread warily for three years before attempting any major revitalisation of the target company if he wants to preserve any losses which may be available in the company.

It is essential for the purchaser to ascertain what skeletons are hidden in the target company's cupboards. To protect himself, warranties and indemnities will normally be sought. In a typical share acquisition agreement the vendor will be asked to warrant at the time of sale that the company has no undisclosed tax liabilities. Since the function of tax warranties is not only to protect the purchaser against future liabilities but also to extract for the purchaser information about the company, tax warranties normally involve detailed points. For example, the vendor will be asked to warrant that the company has duly and punctually paid all taxes, has operated the PAYE system correctly and has not been involved in any anti-avoidance scheme. It is usual to back up these warranties with a deed of tax indemnity whereby the vendor indemnifies the purchaser against any tax liability of the company which comes to light after the sale but by reference to a pre-completion event and which was not disclosed to the purchaser. As a result of *Zim Properties Ltd v Proctor* (1985) (see [**19.114**]) payments made under such indemnities were thought to be taxable in the hands of the recipient as the proceeds of the disposal of a *chose in action* (ie the right to sue was considered a separate asset). This led to the practice of inserting a 'grossing-up' clause in the deed of indemnity to ensure that the amount payable in the event of a claim would equal the liability under the deed plus the tax payable by the purchaser thereon. However, ESC D33 makes it clear that, *provided that payments under indemnities are made to the purchaser*, they will be regarded as a reduction in the purchase price and therefore not subject to tax (contrast the position if payments are made to the company). Notwithstanding this, grossing-up clauses are often still found in deeds of tax indemnity.

When purchasing a company out of a group, special considerations arise. In particular, there may be a clawback charge under TCGA 1992 s 179 in respect of assets transferred to the subsidiary by another group company on a no loss/no gain basis under s 171.                                    **[47.35]**

c)   *Pre-sale dividend strip*

The use of a pre-sale dividend to extract value from a subsidiary before its sale is a well-used tax saving device subject to the availability of distributable profits and the value shifting rules (see **[26.61]**). With the equalisation of rates of income tax and CGT, the pre-sale dividend strip also became popular with individual vendors of private companies as a means of reducing the CGT liability on sale. However, the availability of business assets taper relief necessitates a careful review of the situation because taper relief might well give rise to a much lower tax liability than that arising from a pre sale dividend.                                                           **[47.36]**

> **EXAMPLE 47.3**
>
> (1)   SJ Ltd has substantial undistributed profits. The owner, Mr Wise, has been offered £2m for his shares, producing a capital gain of £1.2m which, taxed at 40%, would lead to a CGT liability of £480,000.
>
> If, shortly before the sale, a dividend of £1 m is paid to Mr Wise and the sale price is reduced accordingly, he will suffer a CGT liability of £80,000 on his reduced gain of £200,000 plus Schedule F higher rate income tax of £250,000 on his dividend. Thus, Mr Wise will pay tax totalling £330,000, a saving of £150,000.
>
> There is no longer an obligation on the company to pay any ACT on dividends and so the purchaser will not be concerned about the potential extra cost within the company.
>
> (2)   As illustrated in the first part of this example a pre-sale dividend is taxed in Mr Wise's hands at 25% instead of at his capital gains tax rate of 40%. However, if business assets taper is available the CGT rate may be reduced to 10% and it would be preferable for Mr Wise to take all the consideration on the share sale because the tax may only amount to £120,000. Business asset taper rates are set out at **[19.37]**.

d)   *Pre-sale stock dividends*

Instead of a pre-sale cash dividend the vendors may receive a stock dividend from the company prior to sale (the tax treatment of stock dividends is considered at **[43.210]**). Such arrangements have been commonly used where the company has insufficient reserves to pay a pre-sale cash dividend. Typically, the company declares a stock dividend alternative that should be as early as possible in the company sale process. Each shareholder is offered a choice between a cash dividend and an issue of new shares at par. Shortly before the sale, the shareholders take up their stock dividend entitlements. This reduces the risk of the sale falling through after the dividend has been taken up, which could leave the shareholders with an income tax charge but no cash with which to pay it. For company law purposes, the amount charged to reserves is the *nominal* value of the new shares not their market value. The tax saving (as with a pre-sale cash dividend) is 15% (ie the stock dividend rate of 25% as against the CGT rate of 40%). Where business assets taper is available it will not be advantageous to have a pre-sale stock dividend because the rate of capital gains tax would be lower (see *Example 47.3*).          **[47.37]**

## 3  Acquisition by means of a share issue

Shares or assets in the target may be acquired in exchange for an issue of shares in the acquiring company. In such an event:

(1)    On a share exchange CGT will not usually be payable by the vendors since a roll-over deferral is available provided that the arrangement is a *bona fide* commercial one and, generally, that more than 25% of the target's shares are owned or acquired by the purchaser (TCGA 1992 s 135 and s 137). Deferral is also available if the exchange is as a result of a general offer made to the shareholders of the target that is conditional upon the purchaser acquiring control of the target and is for *bona fide* commercial purposes. A clearance can be obtained from the Revenue that this requirement is satisfied. It is also possible to exclude s 135 (in whole or in part) when the vendor wishes to take advantage of EIS deferral relief.

(2)    *Marren v Ingles* (see **[19.7]**) can present problems in share-for-share transactions where shares in the vendor are transferred to a purchaser in return for an immediate issue of shares in the purchaser together with a future right to further consideration, possibly in the form of shares (an arrangement sometimes referred to as an 'earn-out' since the further consideration is often made dependent on a future profit target being met). These future shares (ie the deferred consideration) do not fall within TCGA 1992 s 135 and accordingly cannot benefit from the deferral. A number of arrangements were employed to avoid this difficulty usually involving an issue of loan stock by the purchaser that was ultimately converted into shares (ie the deferred shares) in the purchaser. The immediate exchange of shares for convertible loan stock fell within TCGA 1992 s 135 whilst the subsequent conversion of the loan stock was free from CGT under TCGA 1992 s 132.

The problems of earn-outs were eased by ESC D27 that provided that:

'where an agreement for the sale of shares or debentures in a company creates a right to an unascertainable element (whether or not subject to a maximum) against the purchaser which is acquired by the vendor at the time of disposal and that right falls to be satisfied wholly by the issue of shares or debentures, then, notwithstanding a concurrent right to consideration other than in the form of shares or debentures, the Board are prepared to treat the right to shares or debentures in the hands of the vendor as a security within the meaning of [TCGA 1992 s 132].'

Relief under s 135 was therefore available if the other conditions are satisfied. The concession was not happily worded but the Revenue applied it to the extent that the future consideration could only be satisfied by an issue of shares or debentures and therefore ignored the existence of a concurrent or separate right to a cash payment. The concession was revised by the insertion of a final paragraph in two situations that extended its ambit. *First*, if the original purchaser was itself subsequently purchased on a share-for-share basis by another company (not in the same group) and the initial vendor's earn-out rights were exchanged for similar rights in the new purchaser and, *secondly*, if there was a subsequent variation in the terms of the original sale agreement (eg by extension of the earn-out period or to record an agreed settlement). In both cases the original s 135 roll-over was not prejudiced.

TCGA 1992 s 138A put the extra-statutory concession onto a legislative basis: the legislation is, however, more detailed; for instance, it defines 'unascertainable' and it is clear that although the relief is only available if the earn-out is satisfied by paper, there can be two separate earn-outs, one for cash and one for paper.

**EXAMPLE 47.4**

Jon owns shares in J Ltd that is taken over by P Ltd. For his shares J receives an initial cash sum together with a right to further (deferred) consideration depending on the profits of J Ltd and to be satisfied by an issue of shares in P Ltd (at the time of the takeover the value of the deferred consideration is unascertainable). Jon's CGT position is as follows:

  (i)  under general principles the consideration for the disposal of his shares will include the value of the earn-out right (which is a separate asset: see *Marren v Ingles* (1980));

  (ii)  under s 138A any gain that would have resulted from the value attributed to this right is deferred;

  (iii)  when the right is satisfied by an issue of shares this can be treated as a conversion of securities so that the charge is further deferred until such time as Jon sells the P Ltd shares;

  (iv)  if the earn-out is satisfied by an issue of securities in the form of qualifying corporate bonds the new legislation makes it clear that the postponed tax will be charged on the disposal of the qualifying corporate bond.

(3)   If assets of the target are transferred in return for shares by way of a *bona fide* commercial arrangement with the target going into liquidation, there will be no corporation tax on the transfer of assets by the target. Instead, the assets will be transferred at no gain/no loss, so that tax will be deferred until the purchaser sells (TCGA 1992 s 140). The shares in the purchaser company received by the vendor's shareholders are not subject to CGT until sold (TCGA 1992 s 136): but see the case of *Snell v HMRC* SpC 532. Clearance is available under both these provisions.     **[47.38]**

## 4  Acquisition by means of loan notes

The vendor should ensure that the loan arrangements are structured as a debt on security (see **[22.44]**). The paper-for-paper exchange will fall under the roll-over provisions of TCGA 1992 s 135 and the vendor may be able to spread his gain by encashing the notes in different tax years. Sometimes an individual vendor will prefer to arrange that the security is not a qualifying corporate bond so that he would be entitled to loss relief in the event of the purchasing company defaulting (see [41.94]). [47.39]

## 5 The impact of taper relief

Taper relief should always be considered when structuring a sale. For instance, if loan notes are to provide the consideration then (subject to the satisfaction of the bona fide commercial test) the position is:

(1) there will be no CGT on the sale (see TCGA 1992 s 135 ff);

(2) if the notes are *not* QCBs, then the gain and taper relief will not be frozen at the time of sale (for the meaning of a QCB, see [41.93]). The notes themselves may continue to attract business assets taper provided that they are securities for these purposes, (see *Tax Bulletin*, June 2001, p 858) and enable a taxpayer who has, say, only one year's accrued taper when he sells the business to obtain further relief on the loan notes so that by the time that they are encashed full business taper will be available.

(3) an earn-out satisfied by loan notes which are not QCBs, may allow a gain to be tapered to 10% over the period of the earn out (see further (2001) PTPR 79).

(4) if maximum taper has already been built up an earn out satisfied by QCB's will freeze the taper and avoid any loss of taper relief if the company should change its activities and cease to qualify for taper relief.

The case of *Snell v HMRC* SpC 532 should be considered where loan notes are taken by the vendor prior to becoming not resident. [47.40]–[47.50]

## III DEMERGERS AND RECONSTRUCTIONS

Splitting up groups of companies or splitting a company into separate parts under separate ownership is the subject of relieving provisions. TA 1988 ss 213–217 takes distributions which are made to achieve a demerger outside the normal income tax treatment of distributions (under TA 1988 s 209) whilst TCGA 1992 s 192(2) prevents the shareholders from suffering a CGT charge by treating the demerged shares as if they had been received on a reorganisation of share capital. It should, however, be noted that the demerger code in TA 1988 does not deal either with the company's CGT position or with stamp duty land tax.

The conditions to be satisfied are technical and cannot be used to separate trades from investments (see generally SP 13/80). In general, three types of transaction constitute a demerger and qualify for advantageous tax treatment:

(1) A transfer to ordinary shareholders of shares in another company of which the transferor owns at least 75% of the ordinary share capital. This is the so-called '*direct demerger*' in the sense that the shares pass directly to the shareholders of the demerged company and the distributing company may suffer a CGT charge on the distribution.

(2)    Pursuant to an agreement between the transferor company, its shareholders and the transferee company, the transferor declares a dividend
*in specie* of part of its undertaking which it transfers to the transferee in
return for an issue of shares to the shareholders of the transferor. This
and (3) below are '*indirect demergers*' since the trades or subsidiaries pass
first to a company which then issues shares to the original shareholders
in the demerged company (this was the type of demerger carried out by
ICI and considered by the court in *Sinclair v Lee* (1993)). In both cases a
CGT charge on the company is prevented by TCGA 1992 s 140.

(3)    An amalgamation of (1) and (2): namely, shares in company 1's 75%
subsidiary are transferred to company 2 in return for an issue of shares
in that company.

Even where a transaction would appear to fall within one of these
categories, further conditions have to be satisfied if relief is to be available.
Only trading companies and groups are covered, and each entity resulting
from any split must be a trading entity. Further, the reason for the split must
be to benefit some or all of the trading activities that before the distribution
were carried on by a single company and after the distribution by two or
more companies. The purpose of the demerger must not be to save tax nor
must it be intended as a means of transferring control of the company to a
third party. A clearance procedure is available and the form of application is
set out in SP 13/80.

The transfer of an 'undertaking' is exempt from stamp duty land tax under
FA 1986 s 75 and a direct demerger, because it involves no sale, is not
potentially subject to duty.

The demerger procedure may be employed to effect a partition as
illustrated in the following example:                                   **[47.51]–[47.70]**

**EXAMPLE 47.5**

Audivis Ltd carries on two separate trades as a result of a merger of two existing
businesses (Audi and Vis). Its shareholders are family A and family V who are
concerned in the running of the different trades. The merger has failed and so
two classes of share are created (A and V shares); a dividend is declared in respect
of the A shares which is satisfied by the transfer of the 'Audi' trade to a transferee
company which issues shares to the A shareholders.

## IV    MANAGEMENT BUY-OUTS

The distinction between an MBO and an employee buy-out is that in the
latter the business is purchased by all or a part of the workforce not just by
the managers. There are three typical situations when a buy-out may occur;
*first*, when a subsidiary (or division) is purchased from a group of companies;
*secondly*, when the owners sell the family company or its business; and *thirdly*,
when a receiver or liquidator sells all or a part of the failed undertaking often
by means of a hive-down. As with any takeover the management may
purchase either shares of the target company or the assets of the business and
similar considerations to those discussed at **[47.32]** apply in deciding which is
the most advantageous method for vendor and purchaser.

When the company is purchased (ie a share purchase) the normal
indemnities and warranties should be sought by the management team

although the vendors will often take the view that if there are 'skeletons in the cupboard' this is a matter of which the managers will have knowledge.

The major difficulties involved in buy-outs relate to the financing of the purchase since the management team will lack sufficient funds to purchase the business out of their own resources. Accordingly the bulk of the finance must be supplied by institutional investors and the target company or business is generally purchased by a newly formed company ('Newco') in which the managers have voting control but in which the majority of the finance has been provided by the institutions (this will normally be in the form of unsecured loan stock and convertible preference shares).

It may be possible to use the assets of the target company to assist in the purchase of its own shares (see the CA 1985 Part V Chapter VI). Dividends or loans may be paid to Newco to enable it to discharge interest payments to the institutions (care should be taken to ensure that when Newco is a holding company it has sufficient profits against which to obtain tax relief for the interest payments). Finally, the target could be liquidated after its purchase and its assets transferred up to Newco. This would have the attraction of ending the holding company/trading subsidiary structure but care should be taken to ensure that the transfer of assets does not trigger a CGT charge (see TCGA 1992 s 122). Accordingly, it might be more satisfactory to transfer the business of the target as a going concern at book value and to leave the consideration outstanding on an inter-company loan account. The target would then be left as a 'shell' company.

So far as the managers are concerned, apart from using their own personal wealth to purchase shares in Newco, it will often be necessary for them to raise additional funds by way of loans. Income tax relief may be available on the interest paid on such loans (see generally *Lord v Tustain* (1993) and **Chapter 7**). Under TA 1988 s 360 relief is given if the taxpayer works for the greater part of his time in the actual management or conduct of the company. When the buy-out is arranged through Newco, it is essential to ensure that it satisfies the test for a close trading company if s 360 relief is to be available (see *Lord v Tustain* (1993): a company formed to acquire a business existed for the purpose of carrying on that business). In practice, this means ensuring that 75% or more of its income is derived from trading subsidiaries and HMRC accepts, that, so long as it is in receipt of the appropriate amount of dividends or income from the target during its first accounting period, this requirement will be treated as satisfied at the time when the managers make their investment. Thus, if at some later date Newco ceases to satisfy the conditions of s 360, relief will not be withdrawn. Relief may alternatively be available under TA 1988 s 361. Newco must be employee-controlled (ie full-time employees should control more than 50% of the ordinary share capital and votes) and it must be an unquoted trading company or the holding company of a trading group. For the purpose of this requirement Newco may qualify even though it has only the one trading subsidiary. If the company ceases to be employee-controlled, however, tax relief is withdrawn. Reference has already been made to the potential income tax liability of managers under ITEPA 2003 Part 7 chapter 2 resulting from an acquisition of shares in their capacity as employees (see further **Chapter 9**). Further, if shares are offered at below market price an income tax liability under the general provisions taxing benefits in kind could arise. **[47.71]**

# 48 Capital allowances

*Written by Andrew Farley, Partner, Wilsons and updated by Martin Wilson, Partner, The Capital Allowances Partnership*

## I  THE GENERAL SCHEME OF CAPITAL ALLOWANCES

In general, taxpayers cannot deduct capital expenditure in arriving at their taxable income or profits (an exception is the Private Landlord's Energy Saving Allowance introduced by FA 2004). Nor is depreciation in commercial accounts allowed as a deduction for tax purposes. Capital allowances, broadly speaking, take the place of depreciation charged in commercial accounts and allow the cost of certain capital assets to be written off over a period against a business's taxable profits.

### 1  The legislation

The governing legislation for capital allowances is the Capital Allowances Act 2001 (CAA 2001), the first Act of Parliament to result from the Tax Law Re-Write project. CAA 2001 became law on 22 March 2001. Basically, it was consolidating legislation: the substantive rules on capital allowances hardly changed and the substantial body of case law (eg on what constitutes 'plant and machinery') continues to be relevant. Yet CAA 2001 was more than simple consolidation because there was a substantial tidying up of obsolete and anomalous provisions. The primary emphasis of the Tax Law Re-Write has been to make the language of tax legislation simpler and clearer.

References to sections, without more, are references to sections of CAA 2001.                                                                    [**48.1**]

### 2  The different forms of allowances

Capital allowances give taxpayers relief for certain kinds of capital expenditure. CAA 2001 deals with who gets relief for what expenditure, when and how. Part 1 of CAA 2001 sets out the basic rules on how allowances affect the calculation of tax, defines some of the key terms used throughout the Act and stops double relief. Leaving aside Part 3A (see below) each of the next ten Parts deals with a specific allowance, providing allowances for expenditure on:

(1)  *plant and machinery* (Part 2);
(2)  *industrial buildings* (Part 3);
(3)  *agricultural buildings* (Part 4);
(4)  the renovation and conversion of vacant space above shops and commercial properties to provide flats for rent ('*flat conversion* allowances', introduced by FA 2001) (Part 4A);
(5)  *mineral extraction* (Part 5);
(6)  *research and development* (Part 6);
(7)  the acquisition of certain industrial information or techniques ('*know-how*') (Part 7);
(8)  the purchase of *patent rights* (Part 8);
(9)  *dredging* (Part 9);
(10) the construction of *dwelling houses let on assured or certain other tenancies*— but only where the expenditure was incurred between 9 March 1982 and 1 April 1992 (Part 10).

Part 3A was inserted by FA 2005 but, one year on, the date on which it comes into effect has still not been determined. If implemented, it will provide allowances on the costs of renovating business premises in disadvantaged areas.

Part 11 deals with contributions one person makes to another's expenditure, and Part 12 deals with miscellaneous issues such as capital allowances for life assurance businesses, the interaction between capital allowances and the VAT capital items legislation, partnerships, and the succession and transfer of businesses.

Broadly speaking, where an allowance is made under one of the above codes the taxpayer cannot obtain an allowance under another in respect of the same expenditure.                                                    [48.2]

## 3  Capital expenditure

### a)  *Problems in identifying expenditure of a capital nature*

Capital allowances are generally due only in respect of *capital* expenditure—provided that it is also qualifying expenditure for the particular form of allowance being claimed. Usually taxpayers will prefer the expenditure to be classed as *revenue* expenditure so as to obtain a deduction for it in arriving at their profits and thus receive 100% tax relief immediately: ie for the chargeable period related to the accounting period in which the expenditure was incurred. By contrast, much capital expenditure is not deductible at all; and even capital expenditure which qualifies for capital allowances does not usually entitle the taxpayer to a 100% deduction in the first year. (There are some exceptions: see the 100% allowances for certain plant and machinery expenditure ([48.49]–[48.54]), the 100% allowances for flat conversions ([48.122]) and for R&D expenditure ([48.123]) and the 100% allowances for certain expenditure on the construction of certain industrial buildings, hotels and commercial buildings in enterprise zones and on plant and machinery within those buildings.) Accordingly, the distinction between capital and revenue expenditure is very significant.

What is capital expenditure and what is a capital sum? The legislation is unhelpful, only stating what capital expenditure is *not*, ie it cannot include:

(1)   in relation to the payer, expenditure which is deductible in computing the taxable profits or gains of a trade, profession, office, employment or vocation, or

(2)   in relation to the recipient, a sum which in his hands counts as a receipt in computing his trading profits, or

(3)   annual payments within TA 1988, s 348 or s 349, eg rent and royalties which are made after deduction of tax at source: s 4.

Viscount Cave's test in *Atherton v British Insulated and Helsby Cables Ltd* (1925) has stood the test of time:

> '... when an expenditure is made, not only once and for all, but with a view to bringing into existence an asset or an advantage for the enduring benefit of a trade ... there is very good reason (in the absence of special circumstances leading to an opposite conclusion) for treating such an expenditure as properly attributable not to revenue but to capital'.

The distinction between capital and revenue expenditure is often difficult to draw when considering expenditure on an existing asset, namely, whether the expenditure is a repair (revenue) or an improvement (capital). Is the expenditure for the purpose of maintaining the asset in its present condition or at its present value (revenue), or is the effect to alter the very nature of the asset so as virtually to bring into existence a new asset (capital)? Also, where *part* of an asset is replaced there can be circumstances in which the replacement is regarded as a separate asset in itself so that the expenditure will be capital expenditure: see, for instance, *O'Grady v Bullcroft Main Collieries Ltd* (1932).

Certain expenditure that would otherwise be classed as capital may be treated as revenue expenditure by virtue of specific provisions in the tax legislation. One example is a premium paid by a trader on a short lease, part of which can be deducted from his trading income over the duration of the lease: ITTOIA 2005 ss 60–65 (see **[12.85]**).

CAA 2001 sometimes makes specific provision for the demolition costs of an asset to be treated as qualifying expenditure for capital allowances purposes, eg s 26, in respect of the demolition costs of plant and machinery.

**[48.3]**

b)   *Contributions*

Part 11 of CAA 2001 (ss 532–543) contains special provisions relating to subsidies and other contributions paid by one person to another person's capital expenditure. Broadly, ss 532 and 535 provide that a recipient cannot obtain capital allowances on expenditure to the extent that it is funded by a contribution (not counting insurance moneys), but ss 537 ff enable the contributor to do so if the contribution is made for the purposes of a trade or 'relevant activity' carried on by him and the recipient is an unconnected person whose expenditure would (but for s 532) have entitled the recipient to claim allowances.

It should be noted in particular that expenditure is not treated as incurred by a person if it has been met, directly or indirectly, by a central or local Government grant (there are exceptions to this, for instance, Northern Ireland regional development grants): ss 532 and 534.

'Relevant activity' is defined by s 536(5) to include not only a profession or vocation but also a property business including that of furnished holiday lettings and an overseas property business, and also the management of an investment company; and in this respect CAA 2001 represents a change in the legislation that is favourable to contributors.

All expenditure qualifying for a contributions allowance has to be allocated to a single asset pool: s 538(3) and see [48.57].                    [48.4]

c)    *The VAT element*

The treatment of the VAT element of capital expenditure qualifying for allowances will depend on a person's VAT status. The treatment is prescribed by SP B1 as follows:

(1)    For a person who is not a taxable person for VAT the cost of an asset for capital allowance purposes will include the VAT. His input VAT forms part of his expenditure for tax purposes generally.

(2)    A person whose output is wholly taxable for VAT (whether at the standard rate or zero rate) will be able to reclaim input VAT suffered. Therefore, for him the cost of an asset for capital allowance purposes is exclusive of VAT (with the exception of motor cars where reclaiming VAT is expressly prohibited).

(3)    For a taxable person whose supplies are partly exempt, the VAT inputs which cannot be reclaimed must be attributed, however approximately, to the individual items of expenditure to which they relate. If such an item is an asset qualifying for capital allowances, its cost for that purpose will be its net cost plus the proportion of the VAT suffered thereon which cannot be reclaimed.

Where the capital expenditure is incurred on a 'capital item' within the VAT Capital Goods Scheme (see [38.89]) detailed provision is made in the various allowances for account to be taken of any VAT adjustments caused by the operation of the Scheme. Broadly speaking, any additional VAT which a person becomes liable to pay during the VAT adjustment period (because the proportion of exempt use has risen) is to be treated as capital expenditure incurred by that person; and any additional VAT which a person becomes entitled to deduct during the VAT adjustment period (because the proportion of exempt use has fallen) is regarded as a (or as additional) 'disposal value' reducing his qualifying expenditure for future writing-down allowances. See, for example, CAA 2001 Part 2 Chapter 18 in respect of plant and machinery allowances.                    [48.5]

4    **Claiming capital allowances**

For both individuals and companies the granting of capital allowances is not mandatory: allowances have to be claimed—s 3(1). Similarly, it is not compulsory to claim full writing-down allowances (WDAs): a taxpayer claiming WDAs for any chargeable period may claim a reduced allowance of whatever amount he chooses: see s 56(5). Occasionally a taxpayer may have good reason not to claim allowances, or to claim only a reduced WDA, for a particular chargeable period, for example, to maximise the amount of taxable income or profits available in the period for other tax reliefs or for the offsetting of trading losses brought forward. With WDAs calculated on a reducing balance basis (eg for plant and machinery: see **[48.55]**) the effect of not claiming the allowance, or of making a reduced claim, for a particular period is to increase the balance of qualifying expenditure carried forward to the succeeding period. Thus the allowances for the succeeding period will be greater (and any balancing charge will be less) than would otherwise have been the case. The taxpayer does not lose the benefit of allowances not claimed. Where WDAs are calculated on a straight-line basis, ie where the allowance is based on a fixed percentage of the original expenditure over a specific writing-down period (eg industrial buildings allowances), a failure to claim all or part of the DDA for a year will result in the extension of the writing-down period. For example, if the first year's IBA is not claimed, the cost will be written down in equal amounts from years 2 to 26.

It is important to remember that capital allowances are given for periods of account (or 'chargeable periods'), not for tax years.                               **[48.6]**

## 5   When is capital expenditure incurred?

It is often important to determine the time when capital expenditure is incurred, because an allowance will be available for a chargeable period only if the expenditure has been incurred in that (or a previous) period. If the expenditure is incurred in a chargeable period, the allowance generally becomes available even if the asset has not been brought into use in the business in that period (IBAs are an exception: see **[48.55]**).

Subject to certain exceptions, an amount of capital expenditure is treated as incurred as soon as there is an unconditional obligation to pay it (when title will normally pass) even though the agreement may provide a credit period for payment: s 5(1) and (2).

One of the exceptions to the above is where there is a credit period exceeding four months from the date when the obligation to pay becomes unconditional. In this event the expenditure is treated as incurred on the date by or on which, under the credit agreement, it is required to be paid: s 5(5).

Furthermore, as an anti-avoidance measure, if the obligation to pay arises earlier than normal commercial usage for that trade would dictate, and the only or main benefit that results is the bringing forward of capital allowances to an earlier chargeable period, the expenditure will be deemed to be incurred on the later date by or on which payment must actually be made: s 5(6).

A 'chargeable period' means, broadly, for a company, partnership or self-employed individual its or his accounting period; and for an employee the tax year: s 6.                               **[48.7]**

## 6   How is a capital allowance given?

With the introduction of the current year basis of assessment for individuals and partnerships ushered in by FA 1994, the method of making allowances for income tax has been assimilated to the method used for corporation tax. Thus, for both income tax and corporation tax first year allowances, writing-down allowances and balancing charges are now generally treated as expenses and receipts of the trade for the accounting period in which they arise (see, eg ss 247–252 in relation to plant and machinery allowances). Therefore, in contrast to the situation for income tax up to 1996–97 (for trades which commenced before 6 April 1994) capital allowances and balancing charges are taken into account in the calculation of the trading result, rather than being deductions from, or additions to, the assessable trading profits; and if this results in a loss, no part is now ascribed specifically to capital allowances and treated separately. For individuals and partnerships, the loss can simply be carried forward and set against future profits (under TA 1988 s 385); alternatively, the taxpayer may elect to carry across the loss against his general income of the year when the loss arises, or of the preceding year (TA 1988 s 380)); or, if appropriate, he can elect to carry it back under TA 1988 s 381) (see **Chapter 11** for a consideration of loss relief).

For companies carrying on trades the provisions of TA 1988 s 393 and s 393A have a broadly similar effect in that trading losses can be carried forward indefinitely or (by election) carried back for a period of one year.

Capital allowances and balancing charges are treated similarly as regards the property business of an individual, partnership or company (including a business of furnished holiday lettings), ie as expenses or receipts of that business: see, for example, ss 248 and 249. If capital allowances result in a property business loss, then—contrary to the general principle that applies to property business losses—that loss may be relieved against other income of the taxpayer in question (but only to the extent that the loss is attributable to capital allowances). Capital allowances are also given for plant and machinery used in the management of an investment company: s 253. **[48.8]–[47.30]**

## II  PLANT AND MACHINERY

### 1  **The conditions**

Section 11 is the general provision by which plant and machinery allowances are granted. The effect of this section is that allowances are granted under CAA 2001 Part 2:
(1)  to a person carrying on a *qualifying activity*
(2)  who *incurs*
(3)  *capital expenditure*
(4)  on the provision of *plant* or *machinery*
(5)  *wholly or partly* for the purposes of that qualifying activity
(6)  provided the plant or machinery is then *owned* by that person as a result of incurring the expenditure.

Each of these constituent elements will be examined in turn. If elements (3)–(6) are met the capital expenditure is called *qualifying expenditure.* **[48.31]**

### a)  *'A person carrying on a qualifying activity'*

Under CAA 2001 entitlement to plant and machinery allowances is by virtue of carrying on a 'qualifying activity'. This includes both a trade and certain non-trading activities, such as:

(1)   a UK property business, including a furnished holiday lettings business;
(2)   an overseas property business;
(3)   a profession or vocation;
(4)   the management of an investment company;
(5)   an employment or office.
   (1) and (2) above highlight the availability of capital allowances for fixtures in investment properties, held either by UK investors or by non-resident investors (non-resident investors benefit from capital allowances because they are liable to UK income tax on the net profits of their UK property business).
   Note, however:
(a)   Plant and machinery for use in a *dwelling house* does not qualify for capital allowances if the expenditure is incurred by a landlord carrying on a property business (UK or overseas property): s 35. An exception is where the landlord is carrying on a business of furnished holiday lettings. For non-holiday furnished lettings the taxpayer usually takes advantage of ESC B47 and deducts 10% of the rent (net of council tax and water rates) as an allowance for the cost of renewing furniture, furnishings and fixtures (see **[12.45]**).
(b)   Plant and machinery such as boilers and lifts in the common parts of blocks of flats will be allowable as they are not being used in a dwelling house.
   Finally, although a person may be carrying on a qualifying activity, a particular allowance may be restricted by the legislation to a specified category of taxpayer: for example, the current 40% first-year allowances available to small- or medium-sized enterprises (see **[48.48]**).        **[48.32]**

b)   *'Who incurs'*

This has already been considered in relation to capital allowances generally, see **[48.4]** and **[48.7]**.                                             **[48.33]**

c)   *'Capital expenditure'*

This has also been considered in relation to capital allowances generally, see **[48.3]**.
   It should be noted that expenditure on plant or machinery held as *stock in trade* will be revenue not capital expenditure and will not qualify for allowances. Therefore, in the case of a property company it is important to ascertain whether the property is held in a trading or investment portfolio because capital allowances will not be available on plant and machinery in properties held in a trading portfolio for such items, like the properties themselves, will be stock in trade: for instance, plant in properties held by a property dealer or in properties being constructed by a development company for sale, as opposed to letting.
   There are special rules relating to the ascertainment of the capital expenditure incurred on plant and machinery in the common situation where a building, with plant and machinery already installed as fixtures, is purchased for a single price. These are considered in detail at **[48.64]** ff.
   If a taxpayer is given an asset which he then uses for a qualifying activity, he will be entitled to writing-down allowances as if he had incurred capital

expenditure equal to the open market value of the asset at the time it was brought into use: s 14. If however, the donor and the taxpayer are 'connected' the taxpayer's expenditure will generally be taken to be the cost of the asset to the donor if this is less than its open market value when brought into use: ss 213(3) and 218.

First year allowances are not generally available where an asset is received as a gift.                                                                                    **[48.34]**

d)    *'On the provision of plant or machinery'*

*Definition* The terms 'plant' and 'machinery' have never been defined in legislation. Having said that, FA 1994 provided that buildings, structures, land and alterations to land *cannot* now qualify as plant and, furthermore, set out columns of assets (now List A in s 21(3) and List B in s 22(1)) which would be deemed to be included in the expressions 'building' and 'structure' and so fall outside the definition of plant and machinery (such as walls, ceilings, mains services, lift shafts, stairs). But these provisions only seek to identify what is *not* plant and machinery. They do not define what is included in those expressions (for the application of these principles to the construction of a football pitch, see *IRC v Anchor International* (2005)).

These changes, as well as setting out columns of assets included in the expressions 'building' and 'structure', also set out a list of assets which—although comprised within buildings and structures—were *not* automatically excluded from plant and machinery. This is now List C in s 23(4). These assets can still be considered on their own merits and on the basis of the relevant case law (see **[48.36]** and **[48.37]**). Examples include lighting systems provided mainly to meet the particular requirements of the qualifying activity, air conditioning plant (including ceilings and floors comprised in the system), lifts, sprinkler systems, burglar alarm systems, de-mountable partitions, swimming pools, dry docks, and grain silos. Interestingly, this list also includes 'decorative assets provided for the enjoyment of the public in the hotel, restaurant or similar trades', reflecting increasing recognition by the courts prior to FA 1994 that in such trades the ambience or setting is part of what the trader is selling. For all such items, as well as the innumerable capital assets which do not form part of a building or structure, it is case law alone which determines whether they qualify as plant or machinery.

Moreover, the FA 1994 changes do not apply to any expenditure on buildings or structures, or assets comprised within buildings and structures, which was incurred on or before 29 November 1993. In relation to all such expenditure the position is still governed entirely by case law.

Case law is still therefore extremely important.                                     **[48.35]**

*Case law: Machinery* 'Machinery' is easier to identify than 'plant'. Assets with moving parts such as lifts, escalators, pumps and air conditioning plant are invariably accepted as machinery.                                                           **[48.36]**

*Case law: Plant* 'Plant', on the other hand, is more difficult to identify. The meaning has been the subject of litigation for over 100 years. From the earliest case of *Yarmouth v France* (1887) the broad distinction developed between (a) assets which are used in the course of a trade (plant) and (b) assets which form part of the premises or the setting in which the trade is carried on (non-plant). Over the years the usefulness of this broad distinction was seen to have its limitations. As Pennycuick J commented in *Jarrold v John Good & Son* (1963) 'the setting in which a business is carried on, and the apparatus used for carrying on a business, are not necessary mutually exclusive'. With some items the application of the 'premises test' by itself would lead to one conclusion, whilst the 'business use' test would lead to the opposite result: for instance, in the case of fittings designed to attract custom. For a time the judicial emphasis was on the application of a test of function: if the asset in question performed a function in the business then it was considered to be plant; otherwise it was considered merely part of the setting and disallowed. Although there was some judicial recognition of the need to place some limit on this approach—in the House of Lords case of *IRC v Barclay Curle & Co Ltd* (1969) (a case which the Revenue lost) Lord Hodson in a dissenting judgment observed that although 'function is a useful test and relevant in considering whether or not a thing is properly described as "plant", [it] is not decisive'—the position became increasingly unworkable in that it became difficult to state which structures, and assets forming part of structures, would, and which would not, qualify as plant. The case law often appeared contradictory. Hence the same type of item (light fittings) was allowed as plant for a fast food chain company, on the ground that the volume of light was important for that trade rather than just being for general illumination (*Wimpy International Ltd v Warland* (1988)), but not for a departmental store, where the indoor lighting was regarded as merely a part of the setting in which the trade was carried on (*Cole Bros Ltd v Phillips* (1982) but contrast the specialist window lighting of the store which was accepted as plant became it was designed to attract custom).

It was against this unsatisfactory case law background that FA 1994 introduced the columns of assets included in the expressions 'building' and 'structure' referred to above. The Revenue explained to the Chartered Institute of Taxation at the time:

> 'Court cases have, over the years, increasingly reclassified expenditure on buildings and structures as being expenditure on plant. This erosion has affected Exchequer receipts and has itself created continuing uncertainty. The intention behind the legislation is therefore to strengthen the current boundary [between plant and premises] and to ensure that no further erosion takes place.'

This legislative intent with regard to post-29 November 1993 expenditure on buildings and structures has been supplemented, in relation to expenditure on buildings and structures incurred on or before that date, by a change in the judicial approach to the boundary between premises and plant, illustrated by three cases in which exalted status has been given to the premises test. The Court of Appeal (upholding the decision of the High Court) in *Gray v Seymours Garden Centre* (1995) in relation to a structure in a garden centre designed to maintain plants in a favourable condition; the Court of Appeal (again upholding the decision of the High Court) in *Attwood v Anduff Car Wash Ltd* (1997) in relation to a car wash hall; and the High Court in *Bradley v London Electricity* (1996) in relation to an underground substation, all overruled decisions of the General or Special Commissioners in favour of the taxpayer and applied the 'premises' test *in addition to* the 'business use' test. The fact that the structure in question performed some business purpose did not save it from disqualification since its *function* (or primary function) was not as apparatus with which the business was carried on but rather as the premises upon which the business was carried on. In the words of Fox LJ in *Wimpy* (quoted with approval by the Court of Appeal in both *Seymours Garden Centre* and *Anduff*): 'The fact that the building in which a business is carried on is, by its construction, particularly well-suited to the business, or indeed was specially built for that business, does not make it plant ... it remains the place in which the business is carried on and is not something with which the business is carried on'.

*Seymours Garden Centre, Anduff* and *London Electricity* all concerned expenditure incurred before 29 November 1993 on particular buildings or structures. It remains to be seen whether this hardening of the judicial attitude to the boundary between premises and plant will be extended to the other area of uncertainty where the issue is still governed by case law alone, ie those assets which, although forming part of a building or structure, are declared by what is now List C in s 23(4) not to be automatically excluded from being plant and machinery. Examples have been given above (see **[48.35]**). It has been incorrectly assumed by some that exclusion from disqualification is tantamount to qualification as plant, mainly because many of the items listed have been held, on the facts of particular cases, to be plant. Each case turns on its own facts, however, and a previous case in which a particular asset was held to be plant cannot necessarily be relied upon when considering an asset of the same type, especially in light of the judicial approach adopted in these recent cases, and particularly so where the context or design of the two assets is significantly different.                                            **[48.37]**

*Building alterations* Where a person carrying on a qualifying activity incurs capital expenditure on alterations to an existing building *incidental* to the installation of plant or machinery for the purposes of his qualifying activity then that expenditure will be treated as if it were incurred on the provision of the plant and machinery and therefore as eligible for capital allowances, see s 25. Note that 'incidental' has a wider meaning than 'necessary': see *IRC v Barclay Curle & Co Ltd* (1969).

This provision can enable an item to qualify for capital allowances which would not otherwise do so. For example, expenditure on a lift shaft does not normally qualify since it counts as part of the 'building' in List A in s 21(3)). However, the installation of a new lift in an existing building may require the construction of a new lift shaft and this could count as building alterations connected with the installation of the lift and thus fall within s 25.    **[48.38]**

*Demolition costs* Where any plant or machinery is demolished and replaced the demolition costs (net of any moneys received for the remains of the items) are treated as part of the expenditure incurred on the replacement items: s 26(2).

If the demolished items are not replaced the net demolition costs are added to the taxpayer's pool of 'qualifying expenditure' for the purpose of future WDAs (see **[48.57]**: s 26(3))).                                       **[48.39]**

*Other expenditure treated as being on plant and machinery* Certain expenditure which would not normally be described as being on the provision of plant or machinery is nevertheless treated as such by statute for the purposes of capital allowances. The theme of such expenditure is one of safety, for instance:

(1)  Expenditure incurred by a trader in taking steps specified in a notice issued by the fire authority under s 5(4) of the Fire Precautions Act 1971 or specified in a prohibition notice issued under s 10 of the same Act: s 29. It should be noted that notices under s 5(4) of the 1971 Act are issued only in relation to premises which are designated, by regulation, as subject to the requirement for a fire certificate; and it is understood that whereas most hotels, factories, shops and offices fall within the categories of buildings which have been so designated, many nursing homes, schools and colleges do not.

(2)  Expenditure on thermal insulation of an existing industrial building, where the expenditure was incurred either by the occupying trader or by the landlord: s 28.

(3)  Expenditure in taking steps specified in a safety certificate issued for a regulated stand at a sports ground (s 31) or for a ground designated under the Safety of Sports Grounds Act 1975 (s 30).                    **[48.40]**

e)  *'Wholly or partly for the purposes of the qualifying activity'*

This expression cannot be taken at face value because CAA 2001 Chapter 15 (ss 205–208) restricts allowances (and balancing charges) for plant and machinery which is used only partly for the purposes of a qualifying activity: see **[48.63]**.

If a taxpayer purchases an asset for private use, or for some other purpose which does not qualify for capital allowances, and subsequently uses that asset for a qualifying activity, he is treated as if he had incurred capital expenditure on the provision of the asset for the purposes of the qualifying activity; but the qualifying expenditure is the open market value of the asset at the time it is brought into use for the qualifying activity or, if lower, the original cost to the taxpayer: s 13.                    **[48.41]**

f)  *'Provided the plant or machinery is then owned by that person as a result of incurring the expenditure'*

The general rule is that to qualify for capital allowances the plant and machinery must be 'owned' by the person incurring the capital expenditure. An exception is where plant is leased under a long funding lease (generally one of more than five years), in which case, provided various conditions are met, allowances are available to the lessee, rather than to the lessor, who is the actual owner of the plant (FA 2006 Sch 9). This provision does not apply to fixtures and plant leased with a building.

Special rules are needed to deal with fixtures, since land law usually treats them as belonging to the owner of the freehold. In many cases this will mean that the person incurring expenditure on them for use in a qualifying activity (eg the tenant) will not become the legal owner of the fixture. In the absence of special rules, many taxpayers incurring capital expenditure on fixtures would thus fail to qualify for allowances.                    **[48.42]**

*Installation of fixtures by tenant* Until July 1984 expenditure by a tenant on true fixtures—as opposed to tenant's or trade fixtures—qualified for capital allowances only if the tenant was obliged *by the terms of his lease* to incur the expenditure. Thus in *Stokes v Costain Property Investments* (1984) a tenant who incurred expenditure on the installation of lifts and central heating *under a development agreement* before the commencement of his lease could not claim allowances as a consequence of the above position. Nor could the landlord claim, as he had not incurred the expenditure in question. This led to a change in the law, introduced by FA 1985.

As regards the installation of fixtures, the general position is now contained in s 176(1). This provides that if a person who has an 'interest in land' incurs capital expenditure in providing a fixture (eg on the construction or refurbishment of a building) for the purpose of a qualifying activity carried on by him, he will be treated as the owner of the fixture. An 'interest in land' for this purpose is broadly defined to include a freehold or leasehold estate, an agreement to 'acquire' the same, an easement and a licence to occupy: ss 175(1) and 174(4). Thus a tenant can be entitled to capital allowances for fixtures he installs even though as a matter of property law he may not own the fixtures in question.

The pre-July 1984 provision is now much more restricted in its scope and simply provides that if a tenant, pursuant to an obligation in his lease, incurs capital expenditure in providing plant or machinery which does not become a fixture, and the tenant would not otherwise own the item under general law, then he is to be treated as the owner of the item for capital allowances purposes for so long as it is used for the tenant's qualifying activity: s 70.

**[48.43]**

*Acquisition of property with fixtures already installed* The provisions of s 176(1) are supplemented by those of s 181 the effect of which is that where, after an item has become a fixture, a person acquires an existing interest in the land (freehold or leasehold) and the consideration given by him includes an element for the fixture, the fixture is treated as belonging to him, whatever the position under property law.

The provisions of s 176(1) are further supplemented by those of ss 183 and 184 which apply where a lease (ie a new interest) is granted to a tenant for a premium which includes an element for fixtures already installed. If the landlord is (or would be) entitled to allowances in respect of the fixtures, the landlord and tenant may jointly elect within two years after the grant of the lease for the tenant to be treated as the owner of the fixtures: ie for the allowances to be transferred to the tenant: s 183. If no joint election is entered into, then the allowances vest (or continue to vest) in the landlord. For this reason if a prospective vendor suggests that, instead of selling the freehold, he grants a long leasehold interest to the prospective purchaser for a premium, the purchaser may wish to seek an undertaking from the vendor-landlord that he will enter into a joint declaration under s 183.

Where the landlord is not entitled to claim allowances (as where he is a non-taxpayer or property dealer) the tenant is automatically treated as the owner of the fixtures: s 184.

**[48.44]**

*Joint expenditure on fixtures* The 'deeming' provision of s 176(1) could result in two or more persons with different interests in the land 'owning' the same fixture at one and the same time: for instance, if a landlord and tenant share the cost of installing a fixture. In these circumstances s 176(2) and (3) lays down an order for priority of entitlement whereby only one person can own the fixture at a time—generally the person with the most subordinate interest. **[48.45]**

**EXAMPLE 48.1**

Two property investment companies, L and T, plan to purchase and redevelop a property jointly for letting, sharing the eventual occupational rents. To make their eventual interests more marketable L and T adopt a vertical structure whereby L buys the property and grants a 150-year lease to T on a rent formula which effectively secures 50% of the eventual occupational rents for L. L and T enter into a separate development agreement providing for equal sharing of the redevelopment costs including the substantial expenditure on plant and machinery which are to become fixtures in the building.

T's expenditure on the plant and machinery will qualify for capital allowances under normal principles. The Revenue has declined in one case to accept an argument (based on what are now ss 270 and 571(1) – shares in, or parts of, plant and machinery), to the effect that s 176(2) and (3) can be ignored on the ground that L and T have each purchased separate items, ie their respective 'shares' of each of the fixtures. However, allowances would be available to L under the 'contributions' rules (Part 11 – see **[48.4]**).

*Disposal of property with fixtures* The 'deemed ownership' provisions of ss 176, 181, 183 and 184 are mirrored by s 188 which provides that where a person who is treated as the owner of a fixture by any of those sections ceases to hold the 'qualifying interest' (eg the lease) he is generally treated as ceasing to be the owner of the fixture at the same time, with the consequence that a disposal value then has to be brought into account (see **[48.56]**).

Exceptions to the above apply:
(1)   where a lease merges into a superior interest acquired by the tenant;
(2)   where a lease terminates and a new lease of the same property is granted to the same tenant;
(3)   where a lease terminates but the tenant remains in possession with the consent of the landlord: s 189. **[48.46]**

*Equipment lessors* Besides tenants, equipment lessors are the beneficiaries of other 'deemed ownership' provisions resulting from the problems of fixtures. Basically an 'equipment lessor' is a person who installs a fixture on another's property and lets out that item (a 'fixtures lease') to the occupier: s 174. Under the general rule in s 176(1), the equipment lessor would be denied capital allowances because he would have no interest in the land itself, one of the conditions under that section for him to be treated as the owner of the fixture. Section 177(1) deals with this by making provision for the equipment lessor and the equipment lessee to elect that the equipment lessor shall be treated as the owner of the fixtures.

Note, however, that this election cannot generally be made if the fixture is not provided for the purpose of a qualifying activity carried on (or to be carried on) by the equipment lessee or if the equipment lessee is a non-taxpayer, such as a pension fund, local authority or charity: ss 178(a) and (b). The latter measure was introduced by FA 1997 and was aimed at arrangements whereby non-taxpayers would indirectly benefit from capital allowances to which they were not entitled, for instance, by the equipment lessor passing back the value of the capital allowances via reduced leasing charges. (There are exceptions to s 178 and the denial of allowances to an equipment lessor where the fixture is not provided for the purpose of a qualifying activity of the equipment lessee or where the equipment lessee is a non-taxpayer. The election can be made, notwithstanding that one or both of these provisions may be offended, in the case of certain leases of fixtures attached to land rather than to buildings, eg street furniture such as bus shelters (s 179); and also in the case of leases of domestic heating equipment installed as part of the Affordable Warmth Programme introduced by FA 2000 (s 180). Both s 179 and s 180 contain additional conditions to be met in those cases.)

The effect of an election under s 177 is that the equipment lessor is treated as the owner of the fixture (and thus entitled to capital allowances) from the time he incurred the expenditure or, if later, from the time the equipment lessee begins to carry on the qualifying activity.                    **[48.47]**

## 2   First-year allowances (FYAs)

a)   *40% FYAs for small- or medium-sized enterprises: ss 44 and 46–52*

Limited FYAs for plant and machinery expenditure by small and medium-sized enterprises have been continuously available since 1 July 1997. 'Small or medium-sized enterprises' are defined by reference to the definition of a 'small- or medium-sized' company under CA 1985 s 247. This means, broadly, that the company or business must satisfy at least two of the following three conditions in the financial year in which the expenditure was incurred or in the previous financial year:
(1)   turnover of not more than £22.8m;
(2)   assets of not more than £11.4m; and
(3)   not more than 250 employees.
If a company is a member of a group, the whole group must comply with the above limits if the company is to qualify.

The financial limits in (1) and (2) above were increased from the previous thresholds on 30 January 2004 and they apply to financial years ending on or after that date.

FYAs for small- and medium-sized enterprises were initially introduced at 50% but they have been generally set at 40% since 1 July 1998, ie in relation to expenditure incurred since that date. In the case of small enterprises (see **[48.49]**) the rate of FYAs temporarily reverted to 50% for expenditure incurred in the 12 months from 1 April 2004 (corporation tax) or 6 April 2004 (income tax): FA 2004. Finance Act 2006 s 30 has re-introduced this rate for expenditure incurred from 1 (or 6) April 2006, after a gap of one year.

Section 46 contains overriding provisions disqualifying certain expenditure from FYAs generally. Assets which are 'long life-assets' (see **[48.62]**) do not qualify for FYAs. Furthermore s 46 disqualifies from most FYAs expenditure on plant and machinery for leasing, cars and certain other assets (though see **[48.50]**–**[48.52]**) and it also excludes any qualifying expenditure a person is treated as incurring if he brings into use for a qualifying activity:
(1)   plant or machinery previously used for other purposes; and
(2)   plant or machinery received as a gift, because FYAs may already have been given for this plant or machinery when it was originally bought.

Section 46 also precludes FYAs for expenditure incurred in the chargeable period in which the qualifying activity permanently ceases.

It is particularly important to note the exclusion of expenditure on plant and machinery acquired for leasing: subject to the exceptions referred to in **[48.50]** and **[48.52]**, this denies FYAs on all items fixed to a building held for investment purposes. Fixtures accordingly qualify for FYAs only if acquired by an owner-occupier that is also a small or medium-sized enterprise (on plant hire, see further (2003) SWTI 1041).

After the 40% (or 50%) FYA, writing-down allowances are given in subsequent chargeable periods at 25% pa on the reducing balance basis (see **[48.55]**). **[48.48]**

b)  *100% FYAs for ICT expenditure by small enterprises: ss 45 and 46–52*

100% FYAs were available for expenditure incurred on information and communications technology (ICT) by 'small enterprises' between 1 April 2000 and 31 March 2004.

ICT included computers, computer peripherals and cabling and data connection equipment; wireless application protocol telephones, third generation mobile telephones and TV set data connection devices; and related software (though not software acquired for sub-licensing on or after 26 March 2003: s 166 FA 2003).

A 'small enterprise', broadly speaking, means a company or business which satisfies at least two of the following three conditions in the financial year in which the expenditure was incurred or in the previous financial year:

(1)  turnover of not more than £5.6m;
(2)  assets of not more than £2.8m; and
(3)  not more than 50 employees.

If a company is a member of a group, the whole group must comply with the above limits if the company is to qualify.

The financial limits in (1) and (2) above were increased from the previous thresholds on 30 January 2004 and they apply to financial years ending on or after that date (though this has limited relevance to these particular FYAs since they do not apply to expenditure incurred after 31 March 2004).

The disqualifying provisions of s 46 (see **[48.48]**) applied to 100% FYAs for ICT expenditure by small enterprises in the same way as they do still to 40% FYAs under s 44. **[48.49]**

c)  *100% FYAs for expenditure on designated energy-saving plant and machinery: ss 45A–C and 46*

Sections 45A–C were introduced by FA 2001 as part of a package of measures to encourage investment in a new generation of environmental technologies. To qualify for these 100% FYAs the expenditure must be incurred on or after 1 April 2001 on new plant or machinery of a description, and meeting energy-saving criteria, specified by the government.

For this purpose, the Department for Environment, Food and Rural Affairs has published Energy Technology Criteria and Product Lists. The Lists are given statutory force by the Capital Allowances (Energy-saving Plant and Machinery) Order 2001, SI 2001/2541 and the Capital Allowances (Energy-saving Plant and Machinery) (Amendment) Order 2002, SI 2002/1818.

The disqualifying provisions of s 46 (see **[48.48]**) apply to 100% FYAs for energy-saving plant and machinery in the same way as they do to 40% (or 50%) FYAs. With effect from 1 April 2006, the allowance for such assets which are leased is restricted to those cases where the assets concerned are 'background plant or machinery' (generally fixtures in a property).    **[48.50]**

d)    *100% FYAs for expenditure on new low-emission cars: ss 45D and 46*

In FA 2002 the Government continued its policy of encouraging the development of environmentally friendly technologies by introducing 100% FYAs for expenditure (by any business, large or small) on new cars which either emit no more than 120 grams of $CO_2$ per kilometre driven or are electrically propelled. These FYAs apply to expenditure incurred from 17 April 2002 to 31 March 2008.

Cars qualifying for the 100% FYAs are exempt from the single asset pool rules in s 74 for cars costing more than £12,000 (see **[48.74]**.

Expenditure incurred on new low-emission cars for leasing also qualifies for the new 100% FYA. The other disqualifying provisions of s 46 (see **[48.48]**) apply.    **[48.51]**

e)    *100% FYAs for expenditure on new natural gas and hydrogen refuelling equipment: ss 45E and 46*

FA 2002 also introduced 100% FYAs for expenditure on plant and machinery installed at gas refuelling stations for use solely in connection with refuelling vehicles with natural gas or hydrogen fuel. Again, the expenditure has to be incurred between 17 April 2002 and 31 March 2008.

Expenditure incurred on natural gas and hydrogen refuelling equipment for leasing also initially qualified for the new 100% FYA. With effect from 1 April 2006, the allowance for such assets which are leased is withdrawn (FA 2006 Sch 9 para 11). The other disqualifying provisions of s 46 (see **[48.48]**) apply.    **[48.52]**

f)    *24% or 100% FYAs for expenditure on plant and machinery used wholly for a 'ring-fence' trade: ss 45F–G and 46*

A 'ring-fence' trade is a trade for the extraction of oil or gas in the UK or on the UK Continental Shelf, and a company carrying on such a trade is subject to a supplementary charge to corporation tax on its profits from that trade (TA 1988 s 501A). By FA 2002, however, FYAs are given on expenditure incurred by a company on equipment used wholly for the purposes of a ring-fence trade, the amount of the FYA being 24% if the expenditure is on a long-life asset (see **[48.62]**), and 100% in other cases.

The new s 45G contains provisions for the withdrawal of the FYA if the equipment is not used, or not used exclusively, for a ring-fence trade throughout the first five years after the expenditure was incurred or, if shorter, throughout the company's ownership of the equipment.

These FYAs apply to expenditure incurred from 17 April 2002. There is as yet no closing date.    **[48.53]**

g) *100% FYAs for expenditure on environmentally beneficial plant or machinery: ss 45H–J and 46*

FA 2003 s 167 introduced 100% FYAs for expenditure incurred from 1 April 2003 on new environmentally beneficial plant or machinery of a description, or meeting environmental criteria, specified by Treasury Order. The idea is to promote the use of technologies and products designed to prevent or remedy damage to the physical environment or natural resources.

Assets which are 'long-life' assets (see [48.62]) do not qualify and the disqualification provisions of s 46 (see [48.48]) also apply. With effect from 1 April 2006, the allowance for such assets which are leased is restricted to those cases where the assets concerned are 'background plant or machinery' (generally fixtures in a property).

The new s 45J provides for the apportionment of expenditure where some, but not all, of the components of the plant or machinery meet the description specified by Treasury Order. **[48.54]**

## 3 Writing-down allowances (WDAs)

a) *WDAs: the basic idea*

The various FYAs for plant and machinery have been considered at [48.48]–[48.54]. The most usual form of plant and machinery allowance however is not a FYA (whether at 40%, 50%, 100% or 24%) but the annual writing-down allowance (WDA).

Taking the case of a single asset of plant or machinery, a WDA is available at (generally) the rate of 25% per annum of the unrelieved 'qualifying expenditure' attributable to the asset, on a reducing balance basis. The unrelieved qualifying expenditure means the original 'qualifying expenditure' (see [48.31]) less any FYAs or WDAs already given. **[48.55]**

### EXAMPLE 48.2

Wilson Property Company Ltd, a new property investment company, makes its first acquisition and incurs, as an apportionment of the purchase price of the property, capital expenditure of £800,000 on plant. Wilson will be entitled to claim WDAs during each year that the plant remains in its ownership as follows:

| | £ |
|---|---|
| *Year 1* | |
| Capital expenditure on plant | 800,000 |
| *Less:* 25% WDA | 200,000 |
| Unrelieved qualifying expenditure carried forward | 600,000 |
| *Year 2* | £ |
| *Less:* 25% WDA | 150,000 |
| Unrelieved qualifying expenditure carried forward | 450,000 |

etc, etc …

Thus in each of the first two years WDAs of £200,000 and £150,000 could be offset against Wilson's taxable profits from its property business. This would continue until the property was sold, when a disposal value would be brought into account (see [48.56]).

If a chargeable period is more or less than a year the rate of WDA for that period is proportionately increased or reduced (in contrast to FYAs). It is similarly reduced proportionately if the qualifying activity has been carried on for only part of the chargeable period.

A WDA is not however available in the chargeable period in which the qualifying activity ceases: s 55(4). Instead, there is either a balancing allowance or a balancing charge: see [**48.56**].

b) *Disposals and balancing allowances/charges: the basic idea*

When an item of plant or machinery is disposed of, the 'disposal value' of that item is brought into account to ensure that the allowances which have been given correspond to the actual depreciation cost of the item to the business: s 61(1). A disposal (or 'disposal event', to use the CAA 2001 expression) occurs for these purposes whenever:

(1)   the taxpayer ceases to own the asset, for instance by selling it;
(2)   the asset ceases to be in his possession, for instance by theft;
(3)   the asset ceases to exist, for instance by destruction or dismantling;
(4)   the asset ceases to be used wholly for the purposes of the qualifying activity;
(5)   the qualifying activity is permanently discontinued, for instance, on a sale or incorporation of the business.

The 'disposal value' will usually be the net sale proceeds or insurance moneys or in other cases the open market value of the item: see the table set out in s 61(2).

**EXAMPLE 48.3**

(continuing from *Example 48.2*)
   *Year 3*
   Wilson Property Company switches out of property investment and sells the building. £400,000 of the net sale proceeds is attributed to the plant. This is the disposal value and since it is less than the unrelieved qualifying expenditure of £450,000 Wilson will have a *balancing allowance* of £50,000, which is deductible in calculating the profits of its property business for the chargeable period in which the sale took place.
   If the proportion of the net sale proceeds attributable to the plant (the disposal value) had been £520,000 there would be a *balancing charge* of £70,000, taxed as a receipt of the property business in the chargeable period of sale.

Notwithstanding s 61(2), however, the disposal value of any plant or machinery cannot exceed the qualifying expenditure incurred by the taxpayer when he acquired it: s 62. In the unlikely event of an item of plant or machinery being sold at a gain, the excess of the net sale proceeds over the acquisition cost will be chargeable to CGT: see [**19.65**].

Moreover, despite the table of disposal values in s 61(2), the disposal value is nil if the taxpayer gives the item of plant or machinery to a charity or disposes of it in circumstances where a tax charge arises under ITEPA: s 63 (eg a gift to an employee).

A disposal value also has to be brought into account where a person who has been treated as the owner of a fixture subsequently ceases to hold the qualifying interest (usually the lease) and is thereby treated by s 188 as ceasing to own the fixture (see [48.46]). Section 196 contains the detailed rules. A tenant is not, however, treated as ceasing to hold the qualifying interest, and hence no disposal value has to be brought into account, where any of the exceptions referred to in [48.46] apply. Moreover, s 196(1) provides that where a tenant ceases to own a fixture by virtue of the expiry of his lease his disposal value will be nil unless he receives compensation for the fixture.

It should be emphasised at this point that a balancing allowance (ie an allowance equal to the amount by which the disposal value is less than the unrelieved qualifying expenditure) is available only if there is a permanent discontinuance of the qualifying activity, as in *Example 48.3*: ss 55(4) and 65. If Wilson had remained in property investment the disposal value would simply have been deducted from the WDA of £450,000 before calculating the 25% WDA for Year 3: see 'Pooling' below. [48.56]

## 4 Pooling

### a) *General*

For ease of explanation, *Examples 48.2 and 48.3* have shown the operation of WDAs and balancing allowances/charges by reference to a taxpayer, Wilson, which acquired a single building, containing a single item of plant. In practice, however, it is more usual for property investment companies to acquire a number of properties (and for them and traders to acquire a number of items of plant and machinery) over a period of time. In such circumstances the qualifying expenditure has to be pooled to calculate WDAs and balancing allowances or charges: s 53.

There are in fact three different kinds of pools:

(1) A *'single asset pool'* The principal single asset pools are those for expenditure on expensive cars (see [48.74]); short-life assets (see [48.61]); assets used only partly for a qualifying activity (see [48.63]); and assets to which the taxpayer has made a capital contribution (see [48.4]): s 54(3). Each single asset pool may not contain expenditure in respect of more than that one asset: s 55(2). WDAs will be available until the first chargeable period in which a disposal event occurs (see [48.56]). This is the 'final chargeable period' for a single asset pool and will trigger a balancing allowance or a balancing charge.

(2) *'Class pools'* There are two class pools, one for long-life assets (see [48.62]) and the other for overseas leasing: s 54(5). Each class pool may contain expenditure relating to more than one asset within that category. The reason for these class pools is that they have their own separate WDAs (see [48.58]).

(3) *The 'main pool'* Qualifying expenditure falls into the main pool if it does not have to be allocated to a single asset pool or a class pool: s 54(6).

For both a class pool and the main pool the 'final chargeable period' means the chargeable period in which there is a permanent discontinuance of the qualifying activity. Only in this period can a balancing allowance arise in these pools. Note there is no balancing allowance in a pool simply because all the assets in that pool have been disposed of, unless that coincides with the permanent discontinuance of the qualifying activity.

If a person carries on more than one qualifying activity, expenditure relating to the different activities must not be allocated to the same pool: s 53(2). Thus a property company which engages in both property investment (an ordinary Schedule A business) and property development (a trade) will need to maintain two main pools; and if it incurs expenditure on long-life assets in each of its activities it will similarly need to maintain two class pools for its long-life assets, one for each qualifying activity.

WDAs and balancing allowances and charges for each chargeable period are determined separately for each pool. The key concepts are:

(a)    AQE, which means the *available qualifying expenditure* in the pool for that period. This will consist of

   (i)    any qualifying expenditure allocated to the pool for that period *together with*

   (ii)   any unrelieved qualifying expenditure carried forward from the previous chargeable period: s 57(1).

   A person is generally free to allocate or not allocate qualifying expenditure to the appropriate pool in any chargeable period, ie he may add qualifying expenditure to the appropriate pool in a chargeable period after the one in which the expenditure was incurred.

(b)    TDR, which means the *total of disposal receipts* to be brought into account in that chargeable period. 'Disposal receipts' means the actual disposal values which have to be brought into account as the result of any disposals, taking account of the effect of sections such as s 62 and s 63 which, if applicable, will limit the disposal values specified in the table set out in s 61(2) (see **[48.56]**).                    **[48.57]**

b)    *Pooling: WDAs*

Except in relation to long-life assets and overseas leases, the amount of WDAs for a chargeable period is 25% of the excess of AQE over TDR, adjusted up or down if the chargeable period is more or less than a year or if the qualifying activity is carried on for less than the whole chargeable period: s 56(1), (3) and (4).

For the class pool of long-life assets the amount of WDAs is 6% of the excess of AQE over TDR: s 102. For the class pool for overseas leasing it is 10%: s 109. For leases finalised on or after 1 April 2006, the reduced rate of allowances is withdrawn (FA 2006 Sch 9, para 13). From that date, assets used for overseas leasing qualify for allowances at the 'usual' rate of 25% per annum.                    **[48.58]**

c)    *Pooling: balancing allowances and charges*

As stated, the 'pooling' provisions mean that, except in relation to single asset pools, so long as the business continues no balancing allowances will arise and it is unlikely that any balancing charges will become due. Whether the disposal value of any plant or machinery is more or less than the unrelieved qualifying expenditure (the written-down value) of that item considered in isolation, the disposal value will simply be used to reduce the AQE of all the remaining items in the pool on which future WDAs will be calculated. Therefore any negative tax effect on disposal will be spread over many years rather than hitting the taxpayer immediately.

**EXAMPLE 48.4**

Wilson Property Company buys three investment properties in successive years incurring, as an apportionment of the respective purchase prices, the following capital expenditure on the plant and machinery within those properties:

| | |
|---|---|
| *Year 1* | Property A—plant and machinery expenditure of £600,000 |
| *Year 2* | Property B—plant and machinery expenditure of £800,000 |
| *Year 3* | Property C—plant and machinery expenditure of £1,000,000 |

| | £ |
|---|---:|
| *Year 1* Capital expenditure—AQE (Property A) | 600,000 |
| *Less:* 25% WDA for year | 150,000 |
| Unrelieved qualifying expenditure carried forward | 450,000 |
| *Year 2 Add* capital expenditure (Property B) to pool | 800,000 |
| AQE in pool | 1,250,000 |
| *Less:* 25% WDA for year | 312,500 |
| Unrelieved qualifying expenditure in pool carried forward | 937,500 |
| *Year 3 Add* capital expenditure (Property C) to pool | 1,000,000 |
| AQE in pool | 1,937,500 |
| *Less:* 25% WDA for year | 484,375 |
| Unrelieved qualifying expenditure in pool carried forward | 1,453,125 |

Suppose that in *Year 4* Wilson sells property A with the disposal value of the plant and machinery being £453,125:

| | £ |
|---|---:|
| *Year 4* | |
| AQE in pool | 1,453,125 |
| Less: disposal value | 453,125 |
| | 1,000,000 |
| *Less:* 25% WDA for year | 250,000 |
| Unrelieved qualifying expenditure in pool carried forward | 750,000 |

A balancing charge will, however, arise in any chargeable period in which TDR exceeds AQE: s 56(6). In a class pool or the main pool this could occur before the permanent discontinuance of the qualifying activity if several assets in the pool were sold in the course of business at prices which compared favourably with the rate of depreciation assumed in the WDAs already claimed.

A balancing allowance will arise in a class pool or in the main pool only in the chargeable period in which the qualifying activity is permanently discontinued (the final chargeable period) and then only if the AQE for that period exceeds TDR: s 56(7).

AQE, basically, represents the value which the assets in the pool are assumed to have on the basis of the depreciation allowed for through the WDAs claimed. Hence if those assets are then disposed of (TDR) for *more* than the AQE, a balancing charge arises; if for less, a further (balancing) allowance becomes due.

Both a balancing allowance and a balancing charge have the effect, in colloquial terms, of 'emptying the pool'.                                    **[48.59]**

### d)    *Sale of business*

As stated, in a chargeable period in which a business terminates there is no WDA. Instead, there will either be a balancing allowance (if the TDR of the plant and machinery is less than the AQE) or a balancing charge (if it is greater): s 56.

Where the termination of the business is by reason of its sale the amount of the purchase price attributed to the plant and machinery is a matter for hard bargaining between the parties with the vendor wanting a low figure (to reduce the risk of a balancing charge or to increase the balancing allowance) and the purchaser wanting a high figure for the purpose of his future WDAs. In practice, HMRC will normally accept the figure the parties agree, since it cannot lose.

Balancing allowances and charges can be avoided on the occasion of a sale or transfer of a business between connected persons. The connected persons can jointly elect within two years after the sale or transfer that the disposal value shall be an amount which gives rise to neither a balancing allowance nor a balancing charge, ie the transferee takes over the allowances position of the transferor: ss 266 and 267. This election will normally be used when a business is incorporated.                                    **[48.60]**

### e)    *Single asset pools for short-life assets, by election: ss 83–89 (Part 2 Chapter 9)*

The taxpayer may irrevocably elect within two years after the end of the chargeable period in which the expenditure on the asset was incurred for that asset to be a short-life asset. The qualifying expenditure in respect of the asset will then be allocated to a single asset pool (a 'short-life asset pool') on which the WDAs will be calculated separately from the WDAs on the main pool of qualifying expenditure. If the short-life asset is then disposed of within four years after the end of the chargeable period in which the expenditure was incurred ('the four-year cut-off'), the disposal proceeds will trigger an immediate balancing allowance (or, less likely, balancing charge) for the taxpayer, instead of effecting only a reduction in the qualifying expenditure in the main pool.

A short-life election is not available for items such as ships, cars, and certain leased items. It is intended for, although not specifically limited to, assets with an anticipated working life of less than four years, typically computers. Note, however, that the important factor is the length of owner-ship by the person making the election, not the whole life of the asset. The election is not available for assets which are acquired only partly for the purpose of a qualifying activity and partly for some other purpose (see [**48.63**]).

Thus the cost of a short-life asset can effectively be written off for tax over the same period that it is likely to depreciate. The only occasion on which a short-life election might have an adverse effect is where the asset is sold before the four-year cut-off for more than its unrelieved qualifying expenditure (or 'written down value').

If the asset is not disposed of before the four-year cut-off then at that time the AQE (which will comprise just the unrelieved qualifying expenditure of the asset) must be transferred to the main pool.

To prevent the short-life election from being abused by a sale to a connected person before the four-year cut-off, s 89(4) and (5) provide that the purchaser in such a case will be deemed to have made a short-life election and the existing four-year cut-off will be preserved, ie the purchaser must transfer the asset into his main pool on the same date as the vendor would otherwise have done. The connected vendor and purchaser may, however, jointly elect within two years after the end of the chargeable period of the sale for the asset to have been transferred between them at its AQE rather than its market value, with the result that the vendor at least avoids a balancing charge (or allowance) on that occasion: s 89(2) and (6). [**48.61**]

f) *The class pool for long-life assets: ss 90–104 (Part 2 Chapter 10)*

The capital allowances system was considered to be too generous towards assets with a long 'useful life expectancy'. Accordingly FA 1997 introduced special provisions for capital expenditure incurred on or after 26 November 1996 on 'long-life assets'. The definition of a 'long-life asset' is plant or machinery which it is reasonable to expect will have a useful economic life of at least 25 years (or where such was the reasonable expectation when it was new).

Subject to certain exceptions, post-26 November 1996 expenditure on all long-life assets has to be pooled in a separate class pool. This class pool then qualifies for WDAs at the reduced annual rate of 6% instead of 25%.

These unfavourable rules do not, however, apply to expenditure incurred on fixtures in a dwelling house, retail shop, showroom, hotel or office (note that certain buildings are not included in this exempt category: for instance, industrial buildings and leisure centres). Nor do the rules apply to second-hand assets where the previous owner properly claimed allowances under the pre-FA 1997 rules: CAA 2001 Sch 3 para 20 (so the qualification of an asset for 25% WDAs is preserved for subsequent purchasers notwithstanding the introduction of these new rules). By the same token, however, once an asset has been treated as a 'long-life asset' it cannot be reclassified as non-long-life in the hands of a subsequent purchaser: s 103. This broadly means that second-hand assets are treated in the same way as they were when new.

There is also a *de minimis* limit below which these new provisions do not operate. Generally speaking, the new provisions do not apply to expenditure on 'long-life assets' which does not exceed £100,000 during any chargeable period (adjusted up or down if the chargeable period is more or less than a year). If the limit is exceeded, all the relevant expenditure is long-life asset expenditure. But expenditure of any amount on the provision of long-life assets *for leasing* is caught: s 98(4).    **[48.62]**

g)    *Single asset pools for assets used only partly for a qualifying activity: ss 205–208 (Part 2 Chapter 15)*

Section 11 grants plant and machinery allowances where the expenditure is incurred 'wholly or partly' for the purposes of a qualifying activity. CAA 2001 Part 2 Chapter 15 explains how the allowances are computed if the qualifying use is only 'partly for the purposes of a qualifying activity'. The idea is that the allowances are reduced proportionately for the non-qualifying use, eg for private use in the case of a sole trader. It would be impossible to achieve the correct adjustment if the expenditure was pooled with expenditure on other plant or machinery, so where expenditure is incurred on an item only partly for the purposes of a qualifying activity this expenditure is kept outside the main pool and allocated to a single asset pool.

Further, if an asset in the main pool ceases to be used wholly for the qualifying activity and becomes only partly so used, this is treated as a disposal of the asset (see **[48.56]**). The disposal value of the asset reduces the qualifying expenditure in the main pool but an amount equal to the disposal value is transferred to a single asset pool in the same chargeable period. The disposal value will be the market value, derived from the table in s 61(2).

In both the above cases, WDAs on the single asset pool for any chargeable period are reduced to such an extent as is just and reasonable having regard in particular to the extent to which the asset is used for the purposes of the qualifying activity in that period. If a taxpayer's inspector raises an enquiry into the taxpayer's own assessment of the proportion of qualifying use, the determination is usually negotiated between the taxpayer and his inspector. It is however the full amount of the WDA, before the reduction, that is deducted in determining the amount of unrelieved qualifying expenditure carried forward to the following chargeable period.

If the asset is disposed of (which includes ceasing to use it for the purposes of the qualifying activity at all) the disposal value of the asset will give rise to a balancing allowance or charge. That allowance or charge will be reduced in the same proportion that the total amount of allowances previously given bears to the amount which would have been available had there been no non-qualifying activity use.

Furthermore, if in any chargeable period there is a reduction in the amount of qualifying use of an asset, and at the end of that period the open market value of the asset is greater than the AQE by more than £1m, a disposal value has to be brought into account for that chargeable period (s 208). By the table set out in s 61(2) the disposal value will be the open market value, with the result that a balancing charge will arise. The taxpayer is then treated in the following chargeable period as incurring qualifying expenditure, equal to the disposal value, on the fresh provision of the asset. This measure, introduced by FA 2000, is aimed mainly at non-residents and other persons, the degree of whose taxable trading (or Schedule A) activities in the UK is liable to vary. Where the rule applies its effect is to adjust the allowances given so that they are brought into line with the depreciation actually suffered.    **[48.63]**

## 5 Allowances: ascertaining the 'qualifying expenditure' on fixtures in purchased buildings

### a) Basic principles

In order to claim capital allowances it is first necessary to identify the qualifying expenditure. In the case of a purchase of a 'stand alone' identifiable asset the qualifying capital expenditure is simply established by reference to the actual cost incurred in its acquisition by the taxpayer. Similarly, capital expenditure incurred on plant and machinery fixtures installed in the construction of a new building, or in the alteration or refurbishment of an existing building, may be readily established in most cases by separating out the assets in question and abstracting the cost of providing and installing them directly from invoices or priced documentation.

In the case of the purchase of an existing building containing fixtures, however, the only known cost will usually be the price paid by the purchaser for the entire building. Within that purchase price would be an element for the lifts, heating, sanitary ware etc which qualify for capital allowances. How is the price for those fixtures to be determined? **[48.64]**

### b) The 'just apportionment' under s 562

The position in such circumstances is governed by s 562. This provides for 'a just apportionment' of the sale price of a single bargain in order to arrive at the proportion properly attributable to the plant and machinery. This applies even if a separate price is, or purports to be, agreed for the plant and machinery and even if the plant and machinery is sold, or purportedly sold, under a separate contract. Since the largest of capital allowances claims are made on plant and machinery fixtures within the acquisition cost of existing buildings, the operation of s 562 is particularly important.

For the purposes of a s 562 valuation, a property purchaser is regarded as acquiring three main assets: the land, the building and the plant and machinery within the building. Under the valuation method approved by the Revenue, it is necessary, in broad terms, to ascertain three figures, ie the value of the land as a cleared site (with planning permission for a contemporary equivalent of the building *in situ*), the reinstatement cost of the building excluding plant, and the reinstatement cost of the plant and machinery itself. The actual purchase price must then be apportioned between these three elements. The proportion of the total purchase price attributable to the plant and machinery is the same proportion as the plant and machinery reinstatement cost bears to the total of the three elements described.

#### EXAMPLE 48.5

In 1990 a pension fund redeveloped a building for investment, incurring expenditure of £200,000 on the plant and machinery installations. (Being a non-taxpayer, the pension fund would not have claimed capital allowances on that plant and machinery.)

In 2004 Wilson Property Company purchased the building for £2.2m. Under the approved valuation method the three constituent elements are valued as follows:

|  | £ |
|---|---|
| Land as cleared site | 200,000 |
| Reinstatement cost of plant and machinery | 300,000 |
| Reinstatement cost of building | 1,900,000 |
|  | 2,400,000 |

A s 562 apportionment of the £2.2m sale price would produce a proportion for the plant and machinery of:

$$\frac{300,000}{2,400,000} \times 2,200,000 = £275,000$$

Wilson's opening qualifying expenditure for the plant and machinery is more than the sum spent on the initial plant and machinery installation, and obviously far more than the written-down value (unrelieved qualifying expenditure) of the plant and machinery at the time of the 2004 sale. The effect of a s 562 apportionment of the sale price is that the valuation of the plant and machinery actually reflects (benefits from) any increase in property prices generally.

The fundamental points to bear in mind with regard to a s 562 apportionment are:

(1) The exercise is aimed at arriving at the proportion of the total *purchase price* which is properly attributable to the plant and machinery. The written-down value, market value, and original cost of the machinery and plant are all irrelevant to the s 562 computation.

(2) It is not only the purchaser to whom s 562 applies. The vendor is also required to apportion the total sale price in order to ascertain the disposal value of his plant and machinery: see item 1 of the table in s 196(1).

(3) However, the ascertainment of the sale/purchase price of the fixtures by a s 562 apportionment does not necessarily determine the vendor's disposal value that he has to bring into account for the fixtures sold; or the purchaser's qualifying expenditure that he can add to his pool.

As far as the vendor is concerned, his disposal value cannot exceed the expenditure he incurred in acquiring the items (see s 62(1) and **[48.56]**). Thus, if in *Example 48.5* a taxpaying property investor, instead of a pension fund, had redeveloped the property and subsequently claimed capital allowances on the £200,000 incurred on plant and machinery, the disposal value for the plant and machinery on the sale in 2004 would have been £200,000, not £275,000.

As far as the purchaser is concerned, there are now a number of statutory provisions which limit, or determine, the amount of expenditure which qualifies for capital allowances in his hands. These provisions are now considered.                                                                **[48.65]**

c)   *Transactions between connected persons and sale and leasebacks: ss 214–218*

Where:

(1) the vendor and purchaser of plant and machinery (whether fixtures or not) are connected, *or*

(2) the plant and machinery continue to be used for the purposes of a qualifying activity carried on by the vendor, for instance on a sale and leaseback of a building

then no FYA is available (where one would otherwise be due) and the amount of qualifying expenditure which the purchaser can allocate to the relevant pool for his WDAs cannot exceed the disposal value brought into account by the vendor.

If no disposal value is brought into account by the vendor (as where the vendor is a non-taxpayer or the sale was on trading account) the amount of the purchaser's qualifying expenditure cannot exceed the lower of:
(a)  the open market value of the plant and machinery;
(b)  the capital expenditure (if any) incurred by the vendor, or any connected person, on the plant and machinery. It should be noted that this particular limitation will not apply where the vendor is a property trader since his expenditure on the plant and machinery will not have been *capital* expenditure (see s 4(2)).

By CAA 2001 ss 227, 228 the limitation in (a) above—the restriction to open market value—will not apply if an election is made to that effect by the vendor and the purchaser (usually a finance company), and
(1)  the vendor incurred capital expenditure on the provision of the asset, thus ruling out property traders and other vendors who acquired equipment as trading stock;
(2)  the asset was new when acquired by the vendor and the sale occurs within four months after it was brought into use;
(3)  the vendor did not himself acquire the asset through a sale and leaseback transaction or from a connected person; and
(4)  the vendor has made no claim for allowances in respect of the expenditure incurred on the asset.

By removing the restriction to open market value for the purchaser's (finance company's) qualifying expenditure, this rule facilitates businesses financing the purchase of new equipment through leasing.          **[48.66]**

d)  *The first general restriction applying to fixtures: FA 1985*

The first general restriction aimed at limiting a purchaser's qualifying expenditure on fixtures was introduced by FA 1985. This provided that a purchaser's qualifying expenditure in respect of any fixtures could not exceed the disposal value brought into account by the vendor on those items. However, this restriction applied only if the immediate vendor had made a claim for plant and machinery allowances in respect of the fixtures (for expenditure incurred after 11 July 1984). Thus if the vendor was a non-taxpayer or not entitled to claim capital allowances (or omitted to do so) then the purchaser would still have been entitled to an unrestricted claim for allowances based upon what is now a s 562 'just apportionment' of his total purchase price (the majority of cases in practice).

If this provision had remained unamended, most buildings would have become unrestricted at some point in time and so qualifying expenditure on the plant and machinery would then have been 'regenerated' reflecting the increase in property values. Partly as a consequence of this, the FA 1985 provision was replaced by more far-reaching provisions introduced by FA 1997 (now CAA 2001 s 185).          **[48.67]**

e)    *Fixtures acquired after 23 July 1996 and on which any former owner had claimed an allowance: s 185 and Sch 3 para 38*

Where fixtures are now acquired on the purchase, etc of property the amount of the purchaser's qualifying expenditure can be no greater than the disposal value brought into account by the vendor *or by any other previous owner on a disposal after 23 July 1996.* The effect is that the purchaser is restricted to the most recent post-23 July 1996 disposal value brought into account, whether by the vendor or any previous owner; and the purchaser will be restricted to the disposal value of *all* the fixtures on which the vendor (or previous owner) claimed allowances, including any on which the expenditure was incurred pre-July 1984.

It follows from these changes that it is no longer prudent for a purchaser who is concerned as to his capital allowances position to restrict his enquiries solely to the vendor. If the vendor himself did not claim allowances but acquired the property after July 1996, the purchaser will now need to establish whether the previous owner made claims because this also could restrict his entitlement.

This line of enquiry will have to go back through every prior vendor since July 1996 until the last post-July 1996 claimant is identified. These enquiries are likely to become more exhaustive as time progresses, and accurate record-keeping will become increasingly important in order that such enquiries can be satisfactorily answered on a sale. The Revenue Manual makes it clear that it is the responsibility of the taxpayer to obtain and provide details of previous claimants and their disposal values.

It should, however, be noted that notwithstanding s 185 there will still be no restrictions on a s 562 apportionment for a purchaser in respect of fixtures on which the vendor has not claimed capital allowances (as where the vendor is a non-taxpayer or a property developer holding the building on trading account, or a person who has omitted to claim allowances) as long as there has not been any post-23 July 1996 sale by an owner who *did* claim allowances on those fixtures. In respect of any such fixtures, the purchaser will be entitled to capital allowances based on a s 562 'just apportionment' of his purchase price of the property, unrestricted by past disposal values brought into account by any owners before the vendor.

As illustrated in *Example 48.5*, if a taxpaying property investor, instead of a pension fund, had redeveloped the property, and claimed capital allowances, his disposal value for the plant and machinery on the sale in 2004 would have been limited by s 62(1) to the original cost, £200,000. The effect of s 185 is that, because this sale took place after 23 July 1996, no subsequent purchaser of the property can have qualifying expenditure for these plant and machinery items of more than £200,000 (their original cost). Where there has been a post-23 July 1996 sale, s 185 ensures that no s 562 apportionment on a subsequent sale can have the effect, for instance in a rising property market, of 'regenerating' the qualifying expenditure for these items to a level higher than their original cost.

It is, of course, in the interest of a vendor to enter as low a disposal value as he can justify. It is not unknown for a vendor who is selling at a substantial profit to try to avoid doing a s 562 apportionment at all, to include a disposal value in his tax return well below original cost (or no disposal value at all) and to succeed in getting this accepted—incorrectly—by his inspector without enquiry. If this should happen, a purchaser might find that his inspector insists on applying s 185 in these circumstances, even though the low disposal value has been accepted incorrectly by the vendor's inspector. As a last resort, the purchaser could go to the General or Special Commissioners under s 563, with (if the vendor's approach has clearly been unreasonable) a high chance of success. **[48.68]**

f) *Conclusions for a purchaser*

It follows from the above that a purchaser who is concerned about his capital allowances position should seek to establish, before contracts are exchanged, the following:
(1) What plant and machinery items have been the subject of capital allowance claims by the vendor?
(2) What was the vendor's original expenditure on those items?
(3) Is the vendor prepared to warrant that he will return a proper disposal value for these items, ie a disposal value ascertained by a s 562 apportionment subject only to the 'cap' imposed by s 62(1)?
(4) Are there any other plant and machinery items in the building?
(5) If so, has any previous owner claimed allowances on these and brought a disposal value into account (eg on a sale of the property) *after* 23 July 1996?

In regard to (4), it should be noted that several property investors—mainly small or medium-sized companies—on purchasing a building with fixtures for refurbishment, claim allowances for the plant and machinery they install as part of the refurbishment, but omit to claim allowances for the items that were in the building at the time they purchased and which were incorporated within the refurbishment. Unless the company purchased the property post-23 July 1996 from an owner who had himself claimed allowances on these items, when the company sells the property its purchaser will be able to claim allowances on those items based on a s 562 apportionment unrestricted by s 185.

Solicitors acting for a purchaser should, however, note that if the vendor has not made a claim for allowances he will nevertheless be entitled (subject to satisfying certain conditions) to make a retrospective claim after his disposal of the property. If this should happen the purchaser could unwittingly find his s 562 claim limited by s 185. It may therefore be advisable for the purchaser's solicitor to insert in the sale contract a warranty from the vendor agreeing not to make any retrospective claims for capital allowances on any unclaimed items.

Even a purchaser who is not entitled to claim allowances (eg a gross fund or a property dealer) would be well advised to ascertain the full capital allowances history so that he can give this information to his eventual purchaser.

A word of warning: purchasers should be wary of alerting the vendor to the value of capital allowances which he has hitherto overlooked, lest the vendor seeks additional payment, or looks to retain the rights to allowances using s 198 (see **[48.70]**). **[48.69]**

g)    *Election between vendor and purchaser: s 198*

From 19 March 1997 a vendor of property who has claimed capital allowances on fixtures has been able to enter into a joint election with the purchaser to determine the amount of the total sale price that is to be apportioned to the fixtures. This determines both the disposal value to the vendor and the amount of qualifying expenditure for the purchaser. It also binds HMRC, unlike an apportionment specified in a contract for sale.

An election once made is irrevocable.

Note that a s 198 election can be made only in respect of fixtures on which the vendor has claimed allowances. Thus, a purchaser buying from a gross fund or a property dealer will not be able to bind HMRC to a figure for his qualifying expenditure through such an election.

The amount specified in the election may not exceed either the cost of the fixtures to the vendor or the total purchase price paid by the purchaser (so in *Example 48.5* an election could not have been made at a figure above £200,000). In most cases the 'cap' for the election will be the vendor's cost. Subject to these limits, the election can be of an amount in excess of what the apportioned cost under s 562 would be.

If the parties contemplate making an election at a figure less than the 'notional written-down value' there may be a risk of the anti-avoidance provisions of s 197 applying, by which the notional written-down value will be substituted. These provisions apply only if there is a tax avoidance objective to the whole transaction, not merely to the making of a s 198 election. 'Notional written-down value' is defined to mean, broadly, the value which the items would currently have for capital allowances if allowances had been claimed on them individually and separately from any pool, ie the value which, as a disposal value, would give rise to neither a balancing allowance nor a balancing charge.

Subject to these anti-avoidance provisions there can be particular advantages in having a s 198 election where one party to the transaction has a significantly higher overall tax rate than the other, ie an election favouring the former, with a suitable adjustment of other terms of the transaction.

There are also cases in which a purchaser is not greatly concerned about the capital allowance position or the disposal value which the vendor would like to bring into account: for instance, if the purchaser is a non-taxpayer or a property dealer and is not entitled to claim allowances, or if he has present and pending losses which are likely to mean that any allowances he has are unlikely to benefit him for a few years and his main concern is simply to purchase the investment property. In these cases the vendor is in a good position to get a low disposal value agreed by a joint election under s 198. The purchaser should however be aware that a low disposal value agreed by him may have an adverse impact on the price he can get when he sells the property since this disposal value will determine the maximum amount a purchaser from him can claim by way of qualifying expenditure.

A purchaser will usually seek to elicit at the pre-contract stage whether the vendor is proposing a s 198 election and, if so, the proposed sale price for the fixtures. He can then take specialist advice as to whether this is a reasonable figure for the fixtures in question or whether he is likely to fare better with a s 562 apportionment subject to any restriction under s 185.

Elections must be made within two years after the date of the purchaser's acquisition of his interest. For other rules about the content of elections and procedure, see ss 200 and 201. It is important from the purchaser's point of view that the election is very specific as to the particular plant it relates to, so that he clearly retains the right to a s 562 apportionment (subject to any s 185 'cap' applicable) in relation to plant not intended to be covered by the election.

Strictly, since the fixtures rules in CAA 2001 work on an asset-by-asset basis a s 198 election would need to be made in relation to each individual fixture. In practice, HMRC normally accept a single s 198 election covering a group of fixtures in a single building but not one covering fixtures in different properties eg where a portfolio of properties is being sold. **[48.70]**

h) *Agreed sale price of fixtures without election*

Sale contracts sometimes specify the proportion of the sale price which the parties agreed should be attributed to fixtures. This is rarely done with capital allowances in mind. An allocation such as this would not be binding on the Revenue: s 562(2).

Purchasers should be wary of vendors who suggest inserting plant and machinery values within a purchase contract. Such a figure is likely to be in the vendor's rather than the purchaser's interest, for the purchaser is likely to be entitled to a higher figure for his qualifying expenditure, whether through an unrestricted s 562 apportionment or through a s 562 apportionment subject to the s 185 maximum. Should a purchaser agree a value for plant and machinery in his purchase contract and subsequently attempt to establish a qualifying expenditure at a higher figure with his inspector, he could be in breach of contract (although it is arguable that a contract cannot be used to force a taxpayer to ignore the requirements of statute). **[48.71]**

### 6 Allowances on cars

a) *Introduction*

The 100% first year allowances (FYAs) introduced by FA 2002 for new low-emission cars are explained in **[48.51]**. However, very few cars satisfy the low-emission requirements and are thus capable of qualifying for 100% FYAs. For most cars the capital allowances treatment is different and depends on whether or not they cost in excess of £12,000.

'Car' is defined as 'any mechanically propelled road vehicle' but there are a number of exclusions, the first being vehicles which are of a construction primarily suited for conveyance of goods: s 81. Lorries and vans are therefore generally excluded from the special treatment accorded to cars. Some vehicles can be designed either for goods or for passengers, and their tax treatment will depend on the precise construction of the relevant vehicle. The Revenue has confirmed that Land Rovers are capable of falling within this exclusion, Range Rovers and estate cars are not.

If a vehicle is not a 'car' it is dealt with in the same manner as most other items of plant, ie as part of the main pool.

Cars are excluded from the operation of the provisions relating to short-life assets (s 84) and long-life assets (s 96). **[48.72]**

b)    *'Inexpensive cars'*

The term 'inexpensive car' is not an expression defined in the legislation but is used here to indicate a car (other than a low-emission car in respect of which a 100% FYA is available under the new s 45D) with a cost to the present taxpayer of £12,000 or less and which is used wholly in the taxpayer's qualifying activity.

An 'inexpensive car' is treated for capital allowances in the same way as most other items of plant, ie as part of the main pool. Until fairly recently expenditure on all 'inexpensive cars' was pooled separately from the main pool but this requirement was abolished with effect for all chargeable periods ending after 31 March 2000 (for corporation tax) or 5 April 2000 (for income tax) or, if the taxpayer elected, for all chargeable periods ending after the date one year later. Any balance of qualifying expenditure in the car pool at the relevant date was added to the taxpayer's main pool.

It should, however, be noted that a car costing £12,000 or less which is used partly for private purposes will still need to be kept outside the main pool and allocated to a single asset pool under CAA 2001 Part 2 Chapter 15 (see [48.63]). Separate records will thus still continue to be required for such cars.

[48.73]

c)    *'Expensive cars': ss 74–82 (Part 2 Chapter 8)*

The term 'expensive car' means a car (other than a low-emission car in respect of which a 100% FYA is available under the new s 45D) with a cost to the present taxpayer of more than £12,000. These are dealt with in CAA 2001 Part 2 Chapter 8. In the case of a new car 'cost' is accepted as including factory-fitted extras but not additions made after the car has been brought into use unless these were contracted for at the time of the acquisition of the car. Subsequent additions are added to the main pool.

There are two special features of the capital allowances treatment of 'expensive' cars:

(1)    The expenditure on such a car has to be allocated to a single asset pool: s 74. It follows from this that, unlike disposals from the main pool (or the old car pools), a balancing adjustment will arise whenever an individual 'expensive' car is disposed of.

(2)    The annual WDA for 'expensive' cars is restricted to £3,000, proportionately adjusted where the chargeable period is more or less than a full year: s 75.

In general terms it will often be advantageous for a taxpayer with a fleet of cars to buy an 'expensive' car rather than add another 'inexpensive' car to his main pool, especially where it is anticipated that the car will be sold after a relatively short time for a low value. With the expenditure being kept in its own single asset pool, the disposal proceeds will trigger an immediate balancing allowance for the taxpayer, instead of effecting only a reduction in the overall qualifying expenditure in the main pool.

The WDA for an 'expensive' car is proportionately reduced in the following circumstances:

(a)    Where the taxpayer receives a contribution, eg from an employee, towards the purchase price: s 76. The person making the contribution can also claim allowances, although his WDAs will be restricted to such proportion of £3,000 as his contribution bears to the total expenditure: s 76(4).

(b) If the car is used partly for purposes other than the purposes of the actual qualifying activity: s 77(2). In these circumstances the WDAs will be reduced according to what is 'just and reasonable' in the same way as under CAA 2001 Part 2 Chapter 15. This often ends up being negotiated between the taxpayer and the inspector after an enquiry into the taxpayer's own assessment of the appropriate reduction. The reduction is commonly based on the proportion which private mileage bears to total mileage. It is understood that in practice cars used by employees and directors are normally regarded by inspectors as used wholly for the business purposes of the employing company for capital allowances purposes, notwithstanding that they might be used privately by the employee or director. A tax charge would normally arise on the benefit in kind under the benefits code of ITEPA Part 3.

HMRC may also seek to restrict allowances where there is a 'blatant incongruity' between the type of car and the size and nature of the business (Revenue Manual CA2422).

If an expensive car bought wholly for a qualifying activity later begins to be used partly for other (eg private) purposes there is no disposal event (and hence no balancing adjustment) as there would normally be under s 61(1): s 77(1). The single asset pool under Chapter 8 takes the place of the single asset pool that would normally be required under Chapter 15 in this event and the 'just and reasonable' reduction rules in Chapter 8 take effect in the same way as the corresponding rules in Chapter 15.

To prevent traders circumventing the allowance restriction for 'expensive cars' by leasing rather than buying and then claiming the deduction of the whole rental as a business expense, the deduction under TA 1988 s 74 is limited to the proportion that £12,000 plus one half of the excess above £12,000 bears to the total cost of the car when new. **[48.74]**

**EXAMPLE 48.6**

Footsore hires a car, which cost £16,000, for business use at a rent of £1,020 for one year. The hire charge that he can treat as a business expense is limited to:

$$\frac{£12,000 + 1/2 \left(£16,000 - £12,000\right)}{£16,000} \times £1,020 = £892.50$$

## 7 Hire purchase: ss 67–69 (Part 2 Chapter 6)

In the absence of specific legislation, a person acquiring plant (eg a car) under a hire-purchase agreement would not be able to fulfil the 'ownership' requirement (see **[48.42]**) because title would not generally pass until all instalments have been paid. Special rules apply however where a taxpayer incurs capital expenditure on plant or machinery under a contract which provides that he 'shall or may become the owner of the machinery or plant on the performance of the contract': s 67(1). Thus these special rules apply to leases which contain an option under which it is possible for the hirer to acquire the asset at the end of the period of hire; and to contracts where title to the asset passes automatically to the purchaser on payment of the final instalment of the purchase price. HMRC's view is that expenditure is incurred 'under a contract' only if the contract is legally binding and commits the taxpayer to incur that expenditure.

In such cases s 67 has two effects:

(1)    the 'ownership' requirement is treated as satisfied at any time when the taxpayer is entitled to the benefit of the contract, and

(2)    all capital expenditure to be incurred under the contract after the time when the plant or machinery is brought into use for the purposes of the qualifying activity is treated as having been incurred at that time.

It is of course only the capital element of the hire-purchase instalments that is treated in the way described in (2) above. The interest element is generally a fully deductible business expense in the year it is paid.

There are two exceptions to the operation of s 67 on hire-purchase contracts:

(a)    Section 67 does not apply to hire-purchase contracts for fixtures. Fixtures have their own 'deemed ownership' provisions (see **[48.43]** and these apply even if the fixture is acquired under a hire-purchase contract.

(b)    For chargeable periods ending on or after 2 July 1997, the effect of (2) above does not apply where the plant or machinery is let under a finance lease: s 229(3). Where this is the case,capital expenditure on the asset will qualify for allowances only as and when it is incurred and not when the asset is first brought into use.

Where s 67 does apply, and the taxpayer subsequently ceases to be entitled to the benefit of the contract, he is treated as ceasing to own the asset at that time and has to bring a disposal value into account. The disposal value is the total of any sums he receives by way of compensation or insurance money plus the residue of the expenditure still to be paid under the contract.

**[48.75]–[47.90]**

## III   INDUSTRIAL BUILDINGS

Capital allowances in the form of Industrial Buildings Allowances (IBAs) are available under CAA 2001 Part 3 if expenditure has been incurred in the construction of an industrial building or certain other buildings.

There are significant differences between the provisions relating to IBAs and those in CAA 2001 Part 2 relating to plant and machinery allowances:

(1)    For IBAs, there is normally a single amount of qualifying expenditure which is quantified at the outset. Allowances on this sum of expenditure may then be granted to successive owners of the building.

(2)    For IBAs, expenditure is not 'pooled' for the purposes of working out allowances and charges.

(3)    WDAs for IBAs are made on what is generally known as a 'straight-line' basis rather than a reducing balance basis. In brief, a fixed proportion of the qualifying expenditure is allowed annually.

(4)    Balancing adjustments are not normally made more than 25 years after the first use of the building.    **[48.91]**

## 1 Industrial building

Unlike plant and machinery, an industrial building is defined in detail in CAA 2001 (in Part 3, Chapter 2). The main type of 'industrial building' is a building or structure which is *in use* for the purposes of a 'qualifying trade'. Thus the trade carried on by the tenant or other occupier is all important. Table A in s 274 sets out seven trades which are qualifying trades; and Table B in the same section sets out ten undertakings which are qualifying trades if they are carried on by way of trade. The Table A trades include all manufacturing and processing trades, certain storage trades, agriculture contracting, and fishing. The Table B undertakings include undertakings for the generation or distribution of electricity, the supply of water and hydraulic power, and transport, highway, tunnel, bridge and dock undertakings.

Other buildings which qualify as 'industrial buildings' for capital allowances are:
(1) certain hotels, ie hotels in which there are at least ten letting bedrooms, which offer breakfast and an evening meal, and are open for at least four months between April and October: s 279;
(2) sports pavilions provided for the workers of a trade: s 280;
(3) commercial buildings, eg offices, in relation to 'qualifying enterprise zone expenditure': s 281.

Buildings used as dwelling houses, retail shops, showrooms, hotels (other than those referred to above) and offices outside enterprise zones are not generally industrial buildings: s 277. In many instances part of a building will be used for non-industrial purposes but part for purposes which would qualify that part as an 'industrial building'. In such cases, if the qualifying expenditure on the non-industrial part is no more than 25% of the qualifying expenditure relating to the whole building, the whole building will be regarded as an 'industrial building': s 283.                               **[48.92]**

## 2 'Relevant interest'

IBAs are given to the person who holds a 'relevant interest' in the industrial building. The general rule is that the relevant interest is the interest in the building which was held, at the time, by the person who incurred the expenditure on the construction of the building: s 286. If a person acquires an interest in the building on *or as a result of* the completion of the construction (eg under a building lease) he is treated as having had that interest when he incurred the expenditure: s 287.

The relevant interest remains even if a lease or other interest is subsequently granted out of it: s 288. If the relevant interest is a lease and the lease is subsequently surrendered, the reversionary interest becomes the relevant interest: s 289. Note that there can be more than one relevant interest, for example if a lessee incurs qualifying expenditure, the lease will be his 'relevant interest', even if the freehold is already a 'relevant interest' for the landlord. Each can claim on his own expenditure.                               **[48.93]**

## 3 Qualifying expenditure

IBAs are given in relation to 'qualifying expenditure'. The basic point to note is that there are circumstances in which this will not be the construction cost.

CAA 2001 Part 3 Chapter 4 defines 'qualifying expenditure' differently according to whether or not a developer (ie a person who carries on a trade consisting of the construction of buildings with a view to sale) was involved in the construction, and whether or not the building has been used. There are five circumstances:

(1)    where capital expenditure is incurred in the construction of a building by a person who then uses the building (ie in practice a non-developer) whether or not he subsequently sells the relevant interest—the qualifying expenditure is the construction cost: s 294;

(2)    where a building is sold by a non-developer *before* being used—the qualifying expenditure is the lower of the construction cost and the purchase price: s 295;

(3)    where a building is sold by a developer *before* being used—the qualifying expenditure is the purchase price, except if there is a further sale (or sales) before the building is first used in which case the second (or last) purchase price will apply if that is lower than the first: s 296;

(4)    where a building is sold by a developer *after* it has been used—the qualifying expenditure is the developer's construction cost as adjusted by all WDAs and the balancing adjustment on the sale that would have been made to the developer if his expenditure had been capital expenditure and he had accordingly qualified for capital allowances: s 297;

(5)    where the expenditure is 'qualifying enterprise zone expenditure'. The main significance of such expenditure is that it can qualify for 100% initial allowances (see [48.95]).

The qualifying expenditure under (1) to (3) above (ss 294–296) will be qualifying enterprise zone expenditure if the construction costs were incurred within ten years of the site first being included in the enterprise zone (or within 20 years, if incurred under a building contract entered into within the first ten years). As regards the provisions of s 297, these need to be read with those of s 301, which allow qualifying enterprise zone expenditure—differently calculated according to whether or not a developer is involved—only in cases where a person buys an enterprise zone building within two years of it first being used. Special rules apply (ss 302–304) where only part of the construction costs of an enterprise zone building are incurred within the specified time limit.

Expenditure on the construction of a building does not include expenditure on the acquisition of the land itself, or of rights over the land; but the costs of tunnelling, levelling and preparing the land as a site for the construction of a building are included (s 273).                    **[48.94]**


4    **Allowances**

a)    *Initial allowances: ss 305–308 (Chapter 5)*

100% allowances are given for qualifying enterprise zone expenditure as long as the building is to be an industrial building (which for this purpose includes a commercial building: see [48.92]) occupied either by the person who incurred the expenditure or by a lessee under a lease granted by that person or by the successor to his interest in the building. The 100%

allowance is given for the chargeable period in which the qualifying expenditure was incurred. A person may claim less than the full amount.

Because the entitlement to the initial allowance is for a building which is 'to be' an industrial building there are provisions (in s 307) denying or withdrawing the initial allowance if the building is not in fact an 'industrial building' when first used or if the person to whom the allowance was given sells the relevant interest before the building is first used. Further provisions (s 308) deny or withdraw initial allowances if, and to the extent that, the expenditure is met by certain grants. **[48.95]**

b)  *Writing-down allowances: ss 309–313 (Chapter 6)*

WDAs are given on all qualifying expenditure, not just qualifying enterprise zone expenditure. A person is entitled to a WDA for a chargeable period if, at the end of the period, he is entitled to the relevant interest and the building is an industrial building. By definition, the building must be in use on the last day of the accounting period.

The basic rule is that WDAs are given for each chargeable period at 4% of the qualifying expenditure, or 25% of qualifying enterprise zone expenditure, adjusted up or down if the chargeable period is more or less than a year. Of course, if 100% initial allowances have been given for qualifying enterprise zone expenditure there will be no residue of qualifying expenditure left for WDAs: s 312. A person may claim less than the full amount of WDAs in any chargeable period.

It will thus be seen that in relation to IBAs, other than for qualifying enterprise zone expenditure, an industrial building will have a 'tax life' of 25 years. Once the relevant interest in the building has been sold, however, the WDA position is different: see **[48.98]**. **[48.96]**

c)  *Balancing allowances and charges: ss 314–340 (Chapters 7 and 8)*

A balancing adjustment (ie a balancing allowance or balancing charge) has to be made whenever a 'balancing event' occurs. The principal balancing events are:
(1)  the sale of the relevant interest;
(2)  if the relevant interest is a lease, the expiry or surrender of the lease;
(3)  the demolition or destruction of the building;
(4)  the building ceasing altogether to be used (other than for a period of temporary non-use): s 315.

There is an additional balancing event in the case of a building which is, or has been, an industrial building in an enterprise zone, where *capital value* is realised within seven years after the agreement under which the qualifying expenditure was incurred was entered into. This was introduced in FA 1994 to prevent the abuse of enterprise zone allowances. No balancing allowance can arise on such a balancing event, only a balancing charge, and special rules apply to its calculation: ss 328–331.

If the proceeds of a balancing event are less than 'the residue of qualifying expenditure immediately before the event', a balancing allowance equal to the difference will arise. If the proceeds are greater than the residue of qualifying expenditure immediately before the event, a balancing charge is made: s 318. The 'proceeds' from a balancing event are (on a sale of the relevant interest) the sale proceeds or (on other balancing events) the net amount, if any, received for the building or its remains, whether through insurance or otherwise: s 316. The proceeds may need to be apportioned on a 'just and reasonable' basis in order to arrive at the sum attributable to the building, as opposed to the land. This will clearly be required if the balancing event is a sale. Only the sum apportioned to the building is taken into account for the purposes of the balancing adjustment: s 356.

If the proceeds of a balancing event have been artificially depressed by a tax avoidance scheme, the taxpayer is denied *any* balancing allowance: s 570A introduced by FA 2003.

The 'residue of qualifying expenditure immediately before the event' means, broadly, the original qualifying expenditure less:
(a)    any initial allowances—these are written off when the building is first used: s 333; and
(b)    all WDAs previously given—these are written off at the end of the respective chargeable period for which they are made: s 334.

If there has been any period during which the building was not an industrial building notional WDAs, based on the WDAs that would otherwise have been given, are written off when the residue has to be ascertained: s 336. If the building has not been an industrial building throughout the taxpayer's period of ownership, the calculation of the balancing adjustment is modified: s 319.

There is an overall limit on a balancing charge: the charge cannot exceed the amount of the allowances given: s 320. Hence if the proceeds of a balancing event exceed the qualifying expenditure (eg the construction cost) the excess represents a chargeable gain for CGT purposes.          **[48.97]**

### d)    *WDAs to a purchaser of a secondhand industrial building: s 311*

Following the sale of an industrial building, the purchaser will be entitled to WDAs on the residue of qualifying expenditure. For this purpose the residue of qualifying expenditure immediately before the sale (see **[48.97]** is reduced by the amount of any balancing allowance given to the vendor; or increased by the amount of any balancing charge made against him: s 337. The residue of qualifying expenditure, as so calculated, represents the qualifying expenditure less the net allowances given to date (restricted to original cost). This is then written off for the purchaser on a straight-line basis over the remainder of the 25 year 'tax life' of the building, if he retains the relevant interest that long. If there is a further sale, the subsequent purchaser's WDAs are further adjusted in accordance with the same provisions.          **[48.98]–[47.119]**

**EXAMPLE 48.7**

Arkwright builds a jute spinning mill at a cost of £1m in 1992. In 2005 he sells the mill to Hargreaves for £900,000. Hargreaves continues to use the mill for the jute spinning business.
(1)    *Position of Arkwright:* He will qualify for allowances between 1992 and 2005 (13 years) at a rate of 4% pa on £1m. In 2005, at the time of the sale, he would have received WDAs totalling £520,000 and his residue of qualifying expenditure is £480,000.
(2)    On the sale to Hargreaves, Arkwright will suffer a balancing charge of £420,000 (£900,000 − £480,000).

(3)  *Position of Hargreaves:* He will qualify for WDAs for the next 12 years on the residue of expenditure of £480,000, plus the balancing charge of £420,000, namely on his acquisition cost of £900,000. This is spread evenly over the remaining 12-year period *and is not tied to a 4% figure.*

If the purchase price had been £1.2m, Arkwright would have suffered a balancing charge of £520,000 (ie a clawback of all the allowances he had previously claimed), and Hargreaves's claim would be limited to £1m (original cost).

If a vendor is denied any balancing allowance because of a scheme which artificially depressed the amount of the proceeds, (see [48.97]), the residue of qualifying expenditure is nevertheless calculated (ie reduced) as if the balancing allowance had been made: s 507(A)(4) introduced by FA 2003. Hence the purchaser's WDAs are calculated on the amount he actually paid just as they would have been had a balancing allowance been made to the vendor.                                                                  [48.120]

## IV  OTHER CATEGORIES OF EXPENDITURE ELIGIBLE FOR CAPITAL ALLOWANCES

### 1  Agricultural buildings (CAA 2001 Part 4)

Capital allowances in the form of Agricultural Buildings Allowances (ABAs) are given for capital expenditure on the construction of farmhouses, farm buildings, cottages, fences and other works for the purposes of husbandry on land in the UK. The meaning of 'husbandry' has been examined by the courts on several occasions over the years and its meaning is expressly widened by the legislation to include commercial fishing: s 362.

The following points should be noted:
(1)  The building, etc need not be standing on the relevant agricultural land. What is required is that it is used for the purposes of husbandry carried out on that land.
(2)  A landlord may claim ABAs in relation to buildings, etc let to a tenant carrying on husbandry on the related agricultural land.

There are many parallels with Industrial Buildings Allowances (IBAs) in the way ABAs are granted. Both give allowances:
(a)  for capital expenditure incurred on the construction of buildings;
(b)  to the person who for the time being has the 'relevant interest'; and
(c)  on a 'straight-line' basis over a 25-year period.

The concept of 'relevant interest', though similar to that for IBAs, is not however the same. In particular, for ABAs the relevant interest is not in the building constructed but in the related agricultural land. The freehold or leasehold interest in that land held, at the time, by the person who incurred the expenditure is the 'relevant interest': s 364. Also, if the relevant interest is a lease and on its expiry a new lease is granted to the same person, the new lease becomes the relevant interest. In this connection CAA 2001 has changed the law by providing that where the new lease is of part, rather than the whole, of the agricultural land that was the subject of the old lease, the tenant under the new lease is treated as having the relevant interest in the *whole* of the related agricultural land. This change favours the tenant farmer because it means that his allowances will not pass to the landlord.

The qualifying expenditure, broadly, is the capital expenditure incurred on the construction: s 369(1). However, as regards farmhouses only one-third of the expenditure qualifies—and if the accommodation and amenities of the farmhouse are disproportionate to the nature and extent of the farm a (lower) just and reasonable proportion of the expenditure is taken: s 369(3) and (4).

WDAs are broadly given on the same basis as for IBAs: 4% of qualifying expenditure per chargeable period over a 25-year period, adjusted up or down if the chargeable period is more or less than a year: s 373. However, following the transfer of the relevant interest, whether by sale or otherwise, a balancing adjustment is made only if both the former owner and the new owner so elect: ss 380 and 381. If such an election is made, the calculation of the balancing adjustment follows that for IBAs (see **[48.97]**), thus enabling the WDAs granted to the former owner to be brought into line with actual depreciation.

Subject to any such joint election the new owner simply takes over the entitlement to 4% WDAs from the former owner: s 375. If an election is made, however, the new owner's WDAs are calculated in a similar way to that set out in **[48.98]** in relation to IBAs: ss 383–390.

The FA 2003 legislation countering the effect of tax avoidance schemes which artificially depress the proceeds of a balancing event (see **[48.97]** and **[48.98]**–**[48.119]**) applies to ABAs as it does to IBAs.                    **[48.121]**

## 2    Flat conversions (CAA 2001 Part 4A)

This legislation was introduced by FA 2001 and gives 100% capital allowances (and in some cases WDAs) for qualifying expenditure incurred in connection with the conversion or renovation of part of a 'qualifying building' into a 'qualifying flat'.

Not all types of expenditure will qualify even if these are of a capital nature. Examples of non-qualifying expenditure include:

(a)    the cost of the acquisition of land, or of rights in or over land;

(b)    the cost of building an extension unless this is to provide access to the flat;

(c)    the provision of furnishings or chattels (s 393B(3)).

Expenditure on capital repairs related to the conversion will be allowable as long as it does not qualify as a deduction in calculating the profits of a UK property business.

Only the person who incurs the expenditure qualifies for flat conversion allowances. The interest in the flat to which that person was entitled when he incurred the expenditure is called the 'relevant interest' but there is no provision for any transfer of allowances to a new owner of that interest.

To be a 'qualifying building' a building must meet all of the following four conditions (s 393C):

(1)    all or most of the ground floor must be authorised for business use under planning law;

(2)    it must appear that when the building was constructed the floors above the ground floor were primarily for residential use;

(3)    the building must not have more than four storeys (not including an attic) above the ground floor;

(4)   the building must have been originally built and completed before 1 January 1980 with any subsequent extensions completed by the end of December 2000.

There are a number of conditions that the converted flat must meet for it to be a 'qualifying flat' (s 393D). It must, for instance:

(a)   be suitable for short-term (not more than five years) letting as a dwelling;

(b)   be possible to gain access independently of the ground floor business;

(c)   have not more than four rooms, excluding for this purpose any kitchen or bathroom, and any cloakroom or hallway not exceeding 5 sq metres;

(d)   not be a 'high value flat' (see below);

(e)   not be let to a person connected to the person who incurred the expenditure.

Under s 393E a flat will be a 'high value flat'—and thus exclude a claim for flat conversion allowances—if the rent that could reasonably be expected when the expenditure is first incurred (assuming the conversion was then completed and the flat let furnished) exceeds certain 'notional rent limits'. These limits are set at very low levels, particularly for Greater London, though there is provision for them to be amended by regulations:

Notional rent limits

| Number of rooms in flat | Flats in Greater London | Flats elsewhere |
| --- | --- | --- |
| 1 or 2 rooms | £350 per week | £150 per week |
| 3 rooms | £425 per week | £225 per week |
| 4 rooms | £480 per week | £300 per week |

The 100% initial allowance is given to the person who incurred the renovation and conversion expenditure but there is no compulsion to take the full amount. A reduced amount can be claimed: s 393H.

The initial allowance will be given only on a flat which, when first suitable for residential letting, is a qualifying flat and will not be made if the person incurring the expenditure sells his interest before the flat is suitable for residential letting. Provision is made for any initial allowance already given to be withdrawn in the event of a breach of either of these conditions: s 393I.

If no claim for the 100% initial allowance is made, or only a reduced claim is made, WDAs will be due to the person who incurred the renovation and conversion expenditure for each chargeable period at the end of which the flat is a qualifying flat, provided he retains the relevant interest in the flat and has not granted a long lease (one exceeding 50 years) of the flat out of his interest for a premium: s 393J. WDAs are given for each chargeable period at 25% of the qualifying expenditure, adjusted up or down if the chargeable period is more or less than a year, but the WDA for any chargeable period is limited to the amount of qualifying expenditure not yet written off: ss 393K and 393L

If a 'balancing event' takes place within seven years of the time when the flat was first suitable for residential letting, a balancing adjustment will be made in the normal way to ensure that the allowances given to the person who incurred the qualifying expenditure are brought into line with actual depreciation. Any material change in the ownership of the relevant interest in the flat will amount to a 'balancing event', eg:

(1)    if the relevant interest in the flat is sold or otherwise transferred into new ownership;

(2)    if a long lease is granted out of the relevant interest in return for a capital payment;

(3)    if the relevant interest is a lease and that lease expires;

(4)    the death of the person who incurred the expenditure;

(5)    the demolition or destruction of the flat; or

(6)    if the flat ceases to be a qualifying flat (s 393N).

For the purpose of calculating the balancing adjustment, s 393O gives the proceeds for each balancing event (sale proceeds, premium, market value of the relevant interest or insurance moneys, as appropriate) and these are compared with the qualifying expenditure not yet written-off to produce either a balancing allowance or a balancing charge as the case may be. There is provision (s 393U) for all necessary apportionments to be made, eg to arrive at the sale proceeds of the relevant interest in the flat if the whole building is sold.

No balancing adjustment is made if the balancing event occurs more than seven years after the time when the flat was first suitable for residential letting.

The FA 2003 legislation countering the effect of tax avoidance schemes which artificially depress the proceeds of a balancing event (see **[48.97]** and **[48.98]–[48.120]**) applies to flat conversion allowances as it does to IBAs.

**[48.122]**

## 3   Research and development (CAA 2001 Part 6)

FA 2000 introduced 100% allowances for qualifying expenditure on research and development. These extend the 100% allowances previously available for expenditure on scientific research and indeed the new definition of 'research and development' (R&D) covers much the same range of activities that previously qualified as 'scientific research'. There is however now greater clarity as to what is, and what is not, covered. The provisions are now found in CAA 2001 Part 6 (ss 437–451).

To qualify as R&D the activity:

(1)    must be one that is treated as R&D under normal accounting practice in the UK, as set out in Accounting Standard SSAP 13; and

(2)    must also fall within guidelines issued by the Secretary of State for Trade and Industry.

The key theme is that the activities must be creative or innovative work in the fields of science or technology, and undertaken with a view to the extension of knowledge. R&D is characterised by work that contains an appreciable element of innovation and breaks new ground or aims to resolve scientific or technological uncertainties. Such works can range from research in areas that are purely theoretical to applied research and experimental development directed towards a practical aim or product. But commercial development undertaken without such scientific or technological investigation, or undertaken only after the resolution of such uncertainty, is not R&D.

For capital allowances purposes R&D expressly includes oil and gas exploration and appraisal.

If, following an enquiry on the taxpayer's self-assessment return, a taxpayer and inspector are unable to agree whether an activity is R&D the taxpayer's appeal will now be heard by the General or Special Commissioners and not, as was the case prior to FA 2000, by the Secretary of State.

The new definition of R&D applies for all purposes for the tax year 2000–01 onwards for income tax, and for accounting periods ending on or after 1 April 2000 for corporation tax. The change in the appeal system also applies for these periods onwards.

Qualifying expenditure means capital expenditure incurred by a person on R&D:

(a)   undertaken either by him or on his behalf; and

(b)   that relates to a trade he is carrying on or has commenced since incurring the expenditure: s 439.

Expenditure on land does not qualify for R&D allowances, but expenditure on acquiring an existing building or structure, or plant and machinery in such a building or structure, is capable of qualifying. For this purpose a 'just and reasonable' apportionment will need to be made to identify the non-qualifying proportion attributable to the land: s 440.

An R&D allowance is generally given in the chargeable period in which expenditure is incurred, at the rate of 100%. If the trade is yet to commence, however, the allowance is given in the chargeable period of commencement: s 441. A claim for a reduced allowance may be made although, as there is no provision for the remainder to be claimed in later years through WDAs, such a claim is unlikely in practice.

Strict rules apply for the recovery of an R&D allowance where an asset representing allowable expenditure is transferred or sold by the person who incurred the expenditure. In this event, or if the asset is demolished or destroyed, a balancing event occurs and if the proceeds exceed the amount of any unclaimed allowance a balancing charge will arise equal to the excess. The 'proceeds' means, in the event of an arm's length sale, the net sale proceeds; in the event of any other sale or transfer, the market value; and in the event of the demolition or destruction of the asset any amount received for the remains plus any insurance moneys or other compensation. If the balancing event occurs after the permanent cessation of the relevant trade, the balancing charge is made in the chargeable period of the cessation: ss 441–444.

Finally, R&D allowances are not to be confused with the tax credit scheme for *non*-capital expenditure on R&D that was introduced by FA 2000 for small and medium-sized companies, and then extended to all companies and also enhanced in value (particularly in relation to R&D on vaccine research) by FA 2002, and improved further by FA 2003 and FA 2004.          **[48.123]**

# Section 7    Stamp taxes

**Chapters**

# 49 Stamp taxes

*Substantially rewritten and updated by Gordon Keenay, Deputy Head of KPMG's Stamp Taxes Group*

---

I     Introduction **[49.2]**
II    Stamp duty land tax (SDLT) **[49.22]**
III   Stamp duty reserve tax (SDRT) **[49.83]**
IV   Stamp duty on stock and marketable securities **[49.107]**

---

'The law upon the subject of stamps is altogether a matter *positivi juris*. It involves nothing of principle or reason but depends altogether upon the language of the legislature.'

(Taunton J in *Morley v Hall* (1834).)
**[49.1]**

## I   INTRODUCTION

The first stamp duties were introduced in 1694 during the reign of William and Mary and they have since remained a feature of the fiscal landscape. The cardinal feature of stamp duty and one that distinguishes it from the other direct taxes has been that it is strictly a charge on *instruments* and not on either transactions or on persons. Much of stamp duty is, therefore, concerned with purely legal concepts (eg 'a conveyance or transfer on sale') and there is less scope for the application of the *Ramsay* principle (see **[42.39]**) although it is clear that the *Ramsay* principle is capable of applying to stamp duty: see *Ingram v IRC* (1985) and *MacNiven v Westmoreland Investments Ltd* (2001).

In modern times the bulk of the revenues from stamp duty had become focused on two main areas: conveyances of UK land and transfers of shares in UK companies. Stamp duty was cheap for the Stamp Office to collect—since taxpayers and their advisers did most of the work. But the arrival of the electronic age, and the ingenuity of those who sought to carry out transactions without creating stampable documents, resulted in the introduction of numerous anti-avoidance provision and two additional transaction taxes.

The fact that stamp duty is charged on certain legal documents, and that stamping is a prerequisite for those documents to be usable for registration or evidence in court, has led to it being a very legalistic tax. This characteristic has largely been inherited by the successor transaction taxes and stamp taxes remain of particular relevance to legal practice. **[49.2]**

## 1   Reform of stamp duty on shares

FA 1986 introduced stamp duty reserve tax (SDRT) to protect the revenue from stamp duty on shares as the trading of shares entered the electronic age. SDRT is a mandatory tax with modern enforcement provisions charged to the transferee whenever there is an agreement to transfer shares within the scope of the tax. It is aimed at transactions rather than instruments. But stamp duty on shares remained (and remains) in place. A double charge to both taxes is prevented since the liability to SDRT is removed if an instrument transferring the relevant shares is duly stamped within six years of a transaction. This also provides continued access to certain reliefs against stamp duty that have not been replicated in the SDRT provisions. Other than for deals carried out on Stock Exchanges and settled electronically, it is generally necessary to submit stock transfer documents for stamping to enable the registration of changes in legal ownership of shares in private companies or in the subsidiaries of public companies.

A reform envisaged in FA 1990 would have removed both stamp duty and SDRT from all transactions in shares to coincide with the introduction of paperless dealing under The Stock Exchange's planned share transfer system ('Taurus'). In the event the collapse of Taurus meant that the charge on shares was left in place. By the time that the replacement system, Crest, went live in 1996 the political desire to abolish this source of revenue had waned and the Crest system automatically collects SDRT on share transactions that it settles electronically.                                                                          **[49.3]**

## 2   Reform of stamp duty on land

The modernisation of stamp duty on land was announced in the 2002 Budget and stamp duty land tax (SDLT) is contained in FA 2003 Part 4 (as extensively amended by a number of statutory instruments and subsequent Finance Acts). SDLT took effect from 1 December 2003 and, with some transitional provisions, abolished stamp duty except for transfers relating to stock and marketable securities.

The introduction of SDLT paves the way for electronic conveyancing. But, it was mainly prompted by the Government's determination to protect revenues from avoidance schemes that could exploit the non-mandatory nature of a tax on legal documents. Taxpayers' desire to avoid stamp duty on land had been accentuated by increases in the rates of stamp duty on land from 1997. Until the change of Government in 1997 the maximum rate of stamp duty had been 1% for more than a decade and had never exceeded 2% in its 300-year history. By 2000 the top rate was 4%. FA 1999 strengthened the penalty and interest regime for stamp duty and FA 2000 included anti-avoidance measures as well as a wide-ranging power to vary stamp duties with immediate effect (s 117 and Sch 33), a measure designed to frustrate avoidance schemes. The power cannot be used to effect general changes in tax rates or thresholds. SDLT retains this feature and shows its roots in stamp duty in a number of respects.                                          **[49.4]–[49.20]**

### 3 Current structure of stamp taxes

Key features of the current stamp taxes regime are:

(a) Stamp duty land tax (SDLT) applies to transactions in UK land, including acquisitions of existing land interests, creation of new interests and variations and surrenders. It also applies to transfers of partnership interests where the property of the partnership includes UK land. The tax is mandatory with modern enforcement powers and the taxpayer has to self-assess, and send in a return and the associated payment within 30 days of a transaction.

(b) Stamp duty reserve tax (SDRT) applies, with full enforcement powers, to agreements to transfer chargeable securities (essentially UK equities). However, except for electronic transfers related to deals on a stock exchange, the charge is generally by-passed by submitting a stock transfer document for stamping.

(c) Stamp duty applies to documents relating to transactions involving shares (including bearer shares) and is not in general mandatory – though absence of stamping impedes the use of documents for registration and as court evidence.

The words 'stamp' and 'duty' are confusingly included in the names of SDRT and SDLT, notwithstanding that neither directly involve stamps and they are taxes rather than duties. But the naming of taxes is a political matter and these names were no doubt chosen to emphasise continuity with the long-standing predecessor rather than their novelty as new taxes.     **[49.21]**

## II  STAMP DUTY LAND TAX (SDLT)

The legislative provisions are in FA 2003 Part 4, as extensively amended by subsequent Finance Acts and statutory instruments. References in this section are to FA 2003 unless otherwise specified.

SDLT replaced stamp duty on land from 1 December 2003. There is no interaction with stamp duty legislation—except insofar as the transitional provisions determine which tax applies to transactions that started while stamp duty applied and finish when SDLT applies. A knowledge of stamp duty is not required in order to understand SDLT—even though many features were carried forward in some form to the new tax. But the Government's anti-avoidance motive for introducing the tax led to key SDLT provisions being designed around the structure of specific stamp duty mitigation schemes. This starting point led to the extraordinary complexity of the charging provisions for ordinary conveyances and lease grants. Some references to the stamp duty schemes will therefore be made to help the reader to understand why the SDLT provisions are structured in the way that they are.     **[49.22]–[49.25]**

### 1  Scope of the tax

The scope of SDLT is limited to land in the UK (s 48(1)(a)) but it does not matter how or where the transaction was effected or whether any party to the transaction is present or resident in the UK (s 42(2)).

The charge applies to 'land transactions' (s 43) which are acquisitions of 'chargeable interests' (s 48) that are widely defined and include freeholds, leaseholds and options relating to land. But licences to occupy land and security interests over land such as mortgages are excluded as exempt interests and do not trigger a charge to SDLT.

Transfers of partnership interests are brought within the scope of SDLT when the partnership property includes chargeable interests in land. And there are special rules when partners transfer land into partnerships and vice versa.                                                                      **[49.26]**

## 2   **Basics**

The tax, and associated tax returns and administration, are triggered in relation to four concepts:

(a)   There must be a *land transaction* (s 43) which is defined as the acquisition of a *chargeable interest* (s 48). But 'acquisition' is given an extended meaning to include the creation, surrender, release or variation of a chargeable interest.

(b)   The *purchaser* (s 43) is potentially liable to the tax and is responsible for self-assessment, payment of any tax, and delivery of *land transaction returns* (s 76) if the transaction is *notifiable* (s 77).

(c)   There is no tax consequence until the *effective date* of the transaction (s 119)—notification and any payment are required within 30 days of that date.

(d)   The amount of tax payable is based on the *chargeable consideration* (Sch 4) and is charged at rates as follows (s 55):

Table A: Residential

| *Relevant consideration* | *Percentage* |
| --- | --- |
| Not more than £125,000 | 0% |
| More than £125,000 but not more than £250,000 | 1% |
| More than £250,000 but not more than £500,000 | 3% |
| More than £500,000 | 4% |

Table B: Non-residential or mixed

| *Relevant consideration* | *Percentage* |
| --- | --- |
| Not more than £150,000 | 0% |
| More than £150,000 but not more than £250,000 | 1% |
| More than £250,000 but not more than £500,000 | 3% |
| More than £500,000 | 4% |

The rate applies to the entirety of relevant consideration (known as the 'slab' system) rather than progressively to the 'slices' of consideration above each threshold (as in income tax). So a house bought for exactly £250,000 will trigger SDLT of £2,500, while the SDLT on a house bought for £250,001 will be £7,500 (the land transaction return allows you to ignore the 3p tax on the final £1).

There is also a charge on the rental element of new leases (and sometimes on the rental element of an existing lease which is assigned)—see below for details.

At this point we appear to have, in a completely re-written tax, the features that would be expected for a relatively straightforward tax on transactions—a definition of transactions covered, an identified taxpayer, a date for the taxable transaction, a quantum of consideration which will be subject to the tax, and a tax-rate schedule. Of course, we might expect a degree of complexity in relation to forms of consideration that are not money; and individual exemptions and reliefs may be intricate. But simplicity is about to fall apart when we look at the charging provisions for the bulk of actual transactions—that is to say contracts completed by conveyance and agreements for lease. However, first let us consider the general definitions relating to land transactions in more detail. **[49.27]–[49.30]**

## 3 Land transactions

A land transaction is defined by s 43(1) as an 'acquisition' of a 'chargeable interest' in land. So we need to consider s 48 to see the scope of these interests. **[49.31]**

### a) *Chargeable interests*

Only land in the UK is to be considered. The definition of the UK is not extended to include territorial waters and therefore stops at the low water mark. Section 121 tells us that land includes buildings and structures, and land covered by water.

Then things become more difficult since s 48 has a very wide definition of 'chargeable interest' from which certain categories of interest are exempted.

The wide definition comprises:
(1) an estate, interest, right or power in or over land in the UK; and
(2) the benefit of an obligation, restriction or condition affecting the value of any such estate, interest, right or power.

The first part of the definition includes freehold and leasehold interests. And it includes equitable as well as legal interests. The inclusion of rights over land brings in the granting of easements. Powers over land include powers of appointment by trustees where a beneficiary might pay consideration in order to vary a land interest. The second part brings payments to vary restrictive covenants into the charge, for example.

Section 48 excludes, as exempt interests:
(1) security interests;
(2) licences to use or occupy land;
(3) tenancies at will; and
(4) advowsons, franchises, or manors.

Security interests are defined as 'an interest or right (other than a rentcharge) held for the purpose of securing the payment of money or the performance of any other obligation'. This means that lenders or creditors taking a charge over property will not be acquiring a chargeable interest in land. In particular, normal mortgages or re-mortgages will not trigger payments of SDLT.

Licences are exempt interests and are not specially defined for SDLT purposes. The *Street v Mountford ([1985] 2 All ER 289, HL)* authorities on the distinction between leases and licences will therefore be of use in determining whether a particular contract is within the scope of SDLT.

Leases are defined for the purposes of SDLT in Sch 17A para 1 as

(1)    an interest or right in or over land for a term of years (whether fixed or periodic); or

(2)    a tenancy at will or other interest or right in or over land terminable by notice at any time.

The key determinants would seem to be that a licence is a personal rather than a proprietary right, and leases involve exclusive possession. But there are bound to be situations where it is difficult to distinguish between a contractual licence and a lease.

While licences are exempt interests and so their acquisition cannot be a land transaction, they may have significance for the effective date of an SDLT charge.                                                                          **[49.32]**


b)    *Acquisitions*

Where an existing land interest is transferred it is clear that the transferee acquires the interest. But the scope of chargeable land transactions is wider than transfers. To achieve this, the definition of 'acquisition' is extended (s 43), with corresponding extensions of the concepts of 'vendor' and 'purchaser'. These extensions are as follows, and in each case the person or persons deemed to 'acquire' the interest are specified:

| *Event* | *Deemed acquisition and purchaser* |
| --- | --- |
| the creation of an interest | an acquisition by the person becoming entitled to the new interest |
| the surrender or release of an interest | an acquisition by the person whose interest is benefited or enlarged by the transaction |
| the variation of an interest (other than a lease) | an acquisition by the person benefiting from the variation |
| the variation of a lease | an acquisition by the person benefiting from the variation, but only if it takes effect or is treated (for the purposes of SDLT) as a new lease; the amount of rent or the term of the lease is reduced; or other variations where the lessee provides consideration in money or money's worth (other than an increase in rent) for the variation. |

Here we have the first sign that leases are to be treated rather differently from other land transactions. Only a limited range of lease variations count as land transactions. The first category allows for variations that increase rent (other than rent reviews within the existing terms of the lease) and increases of the demise (which operate in property law as a surrender and re-grant of the lease). Variations of the rent are treated as significant for SDLT because they have implications for the SDLT charge on rents or on the value of the freehold or superior leasehold interest out of which the lease has been granted. **[49.33]**

c) *The purchaser*

The purchaser is the person who potentially has a liability to SDLT and who may be required to carry out the administrative responsibilities. So, once there is a chargeable land transaction, we must identify the purchaser or purchasers. Based on the extended definition of acquisition, the purchaser is the person who acquires the chargeable interest. Four cases identify the purchaser as follows:

| Trans-action | Purchaser | Example |
|---|---|---|
| Transfer | The transferee | Purchaser of an existing freehold or leasehold interest |
| Creation | The person becoming entitled to the new interest | The tenant to whom a lease is granted |
| Surrender | The person whose interest is benefited or enlarged | The landlord when a lease is surrendered |
| Variation | The person who benefits from the variation | The tenant who pays the landlord to agree to a rent reduction. The landlord who pays the tenant to modify the rent upwards (eg by inserting market rent reviews into a fixed rent lease) |

But s 43(5) restricts the definition by specifying that a person is only treated as a purchaser if he is a party to the transaction or has given consideration for it. This prevents the owners of land interests related to the subject matter of a land transaction from inadvertently becoming subject to an SDLT charge by virtue of an indirect benefit to their own land interest. But it does not widen the scope of the charge to include everyone who is a party to a land transaction or who provides consideration. A 'purchaser' must 'acquire' a chargeable interest *and* also be a party to the transaction or provide consideration. **[49.34]**

d) *The effective date*

For a land transaction the effective date is the trigger to notify and pay tax within 30 days, so it is crucial to identify it. The general rule in s 119 is that the effective date is the date that the transaction is completed. However, the general rule rarely applies in practice since most transactions are charged under the provisions for contract and conveyance (starting with s 44) that set the effective date or dates depending on actions of the purchaser. **[49.35]**

## 4   Contract and conveyance

Three factors lead to the complexity of the SDLT charging provisions:

(1)   The normal purchase of a freehold or leasehold interest is generally achieved in two steps—a contract completed by a conveyance. Similarly, the grant of a new lease is usually preceded by a contractual agreement for lease.

(2)   Stamp duty avoidance schemes had been used for the acquisition of commercial property that relied on the fact that conveyances were stampable but contracts had not been (until FA 2002 which included a temporary anti-avoidance measure charging some contracts). The use of nominee companies to hold the bare legal title of a property while the beneficial interest could be traded by means of uncompleted contracts led the designers of the new tax to include both contract and completion by conveyance as land transactions. This led to the need for provisions limiting the resulting multiple charges to one effective tax hit for each deal.

(3)   The decision was taken to impose a substantially higher charge on the rental element of new leases than had been the case under stamp duty. Given that assignments of leases would generally not be charged on the rental element, the charge on new leases required special features.

**[49.36]**

a)   *The simple case*

Section 44 gives the basic rule where a contract for a land transaction is entered into and is to be completed by a conveyance. The term 'contract' includes any agreement (including an agreement for lease) and 'conveyance' is defined to include any instrument (including a lease). So the rules here cover standard purchases of freehold and leasehold interests and grants of new leases unless they come within the special rules in Schedule 17A.

Taking firstly the case where completion follows contract without any intervening contract, assignment or variation, s 44 firstly lifts the general charging provision and then re-applies it. The style of the provision is driven more by the desire to impose a charge as early as reasonably possible rather than clarity. There are two cases:

(i)   completion occurs without an earlier *substantial performance* of the contract

In this case the contract and conveyance are treated as a single land transaction with the date of completion as the effective date.

(ii)   *substantial performance* occurs before completion.

Agreements for lease are subjected to Schedule 17A instead of s 44.

Otherwise, s 44(4) deems there to be a land transaction as if all of the transaction envisaged in the contract had occurred on the date of substantial performance. The effective date is the date of substantial performance.

The subsequent completion is a separate land transaction and is notifiable in its own right. But it is chargeable only to the extent (if any) that the amount of tax chargeable on it is greater than the amount of tax chargeable on the contract. It will therefore be rare for an additional charge to apply at completion.

If, after substantial performance, a contract is rescinded or annulled (wholly or partly) then the tax paid can be (proportionately) reclaimed (s 44(9)).

The statutory definition of substantial performance is contained in s 44(5)–(7). Any of the following are sufficient to trigger substantial performance:

(1) payment of 90% or more of the part of the consideration which is not rent (the statute merely says 'a substantial amount' but HMRC practice is to use 90% or more as their interpretation;

(2) the purchaser (or a connected person) taking possession of the property, even if this is under a licence

(3) (in the case of a lease) paying rent;

(4) receiving or becoming entitled to profits or rents derived from the land interest.

So the effective date, and therefore the timing of any tax payment, depends on whether or not substantial performance occurs before completion. **[49.37]**

The following example illustrates a simple case of a house sale.

**EXAMPLE 49.1**

Jasper agrees to buy Jennie's house for £300,000. The contract is entered into on 1 January 2004. Jasper pays a 5% deposit, but does not get the keys to the door until completion that occurs on 1 February.

Because this transaction is completed without previously being substantially performed:

(a) Entering into the contract is not regarded as being a land transaction.

(b) Contract and completion are regarded as a single transaction with the effective date of the transaction being 1 February (s 44(3)).

(c) Jasper must deliver a 'land transaction return' before the end of the period of 30 days after 1 February (s 76(1)) and must at the same time pay the tax (s 86(1)).

(d) The sale will not be registered at the Land Registry unless a certificate of compliance with the SDLT provisions is produced. A Revenue Certificate will be issued following acceptable filing of the return.

(e) The legislation contains a raft of provisions dealing with interest, penalties and compliance.

b) *Sub-sales*

A may contract to sell a property to B, and before completion B contracts to sell to C or assigns his rights under the original contract to C. Both contracts may then be completed by A conveying to C (at B's direction). Under a tightening of the rules under SDLT (compared with stamp duty where generally the conveyance was stamped by C on the basis of his purchase but B had nothing to pay) B is likely to have to pay SDLT on the basis of the purchase price under his original contract with A. C has to pay on the basis of his purchase price. B has a land transaction if he has substantially performed his contract with A before the conveyance from A to C.

The provision that produces this result (and provides for longer chains of contracts with the same result that intermediate purchasers are liable to SDLT if they substantially perform, but not otherwise) is s 45. This section again suspends the general rules and re-imposes them with modifications. An example is as follows: **[49.38]**

**EXAMPLE 49.2**

A enters into a contract to sell land to B for £100,000 paying a deposit of £10,000. B goes into occupation of the property (or otherwise substantially performs the contract). He then sells his rights under the contract to C for £20,000 and requires A to convey the land to C who pays the balance of £90,000 to A. SDLT is triggered by each agreement as follows:

*A and B:* as a result of substantial performance SDLT is payable by B on the consideration of £100,000.

*B and C:* s 45 treats s 44 as applying on the basis of a 'secondary contract' under which C is the purchaser and the consideration for the transaction is (a) the sum paid to B for the assignment (£20,000) plus (b) the sum paid to A to complete the A/B contract (£90,000). SDLT is therefore payable by C on £110,000.

c)   *Development agreements providing for sub-sale*

Sections 44A and 45A were introduced by FA 2004 to clarify the SDLT position on certain development contracts. For example, if a developer may contract with a landowner such that he will build houses on the land, arrange their sale, and then direct the landowner to convey the relevant parcel of land to the end purchaser. Section 44A ensures that where there is a contract between A and B under which B may subsequently direct A to convey to C, who is not a party to the initial contract, then B has a land transaction if he substantially performs the contract. If the development proceeds, B obviously will substantially perform since he will take possession of the site to build the houses. Section 45A covers the position when B assigns rights under such a contract to D.

What is in some doubt is whether these provisions are restricted to development situations. Section 44A states that a contract merely has to provide for B to have the right to direct A to convey to C, and this is allowed for in many standard contracts. So there is some doubt as to whether ss 44A and 45A apply in only the limited range of circumstances envisaged. However, it seems to be the view of HMRC that in situations where s 44 and s44A are both capable of applying then s 44 will take precedence. This will leave s 44A and s 45A to apply when B did not have a contract for a land transaction within the scope of s 44—or at least where it is unclear whether s 44 applies. **[49.39]**

5   **Options**

Options and rights of pre-emption appear to be provided for in s 46. In fact most options to purchase land are covered in the general definition of land transaction and s 46(4) expressly excludes the application of s 46 to options covered elsewhere. The purpose of the section is to bring 'put' options relating to land interests within the scope of SDLT and to remove doubt about options under Scots Law.

The acquisition of an option is a separate land transaction from the subsequent exercise of the option, and has an effective date when it is acquired (rather than when it becomes exercisable).

The acquisition of an option and its exercise (if it is exercised) may well be 'linked' transactions (see below).                                                    **[49.40]**

## 6   What is chargeable consideration?

a)   *The general rule*

The chargeable consideration for a land transaction is defined in Schedule 4. The general rule is that it includes any consideration in money or money's worth given for the subject-matter of the transaction, directly or indirectly, by the purchaser or a person connected with him. Then there are rules about debt, apportionment, exchanges, and extensions to the definition in relation to building services and other services. The special rules are summarised below.                                                                                         **[49.41]**

b)   *Special rules*

i)   *Value added tax*

Chargeable consideration includes value added tax chargeable in respect of the transaction, so SDLT is a tax that is charged on a tax. VAT is not included in chargeable consideration if it is charged under an election to tax (under VATA 1994 Sch 10 para 2) if that election was made *after* the effective date of the land transaction.                                                                    **[49.42]**

ii)   *Postponed consideration*

There is no discount where the payment of consideration is postponed. (However, see below for the rules on uncertain consideration.)        **[49.43]**

iii)   *Just and reasonable apportionment*

Where an overall bargain contains more than one land transaction or relates to other matters as well as land transactions, the consideration is to be apportioned on a just and reasonable basis in order to determine the amount of chargeable consideration for the land transaction or land transactions within the bargain.                                                               **[49.44]**

iv)   *Exchanges*

Exchanges of land interests are treated as two land transactions. The general rule for chargeable consideration on a land transaction that is part of an exchange is that it is the market value of the land interest that is acquired, so long as a major interest in land (a freehold or leasehold) is involved in the exchange. Detailed rules are in Sch 4 para 5.                              **[49.45]**

*v)   Partition or Divisions*

For land transaction giving effect to a partition or division of a chargeable interest to which persons are jointly entitled, the share of the interest held by a purchaser immediately before the partition or division is disregarded in calculating the chargeable consideration.                    **[49.46]**

*vi)   Non-monetary consideration*

Chargeable consideration that is not in the form of cash or debt is generally included at its market value at the effective date of the transaction.   **[49.47]**

*vii)   Debt as consideration*

The rules are in Sch 4 para 8.
   Where chargeable consideration includes:
(1)   the satisfaction or release of debt due to the purchaser or owed by the vendor; or
(2)   the assumption of existing debt by the purchaser;

   then the amounts of debt satisfied, released or assumed are included in the chargeable consideration for the transaction.
But, if the effect of this is that the amount of the chargeable consideration for the transaction exceeds the market value of the subject matter of the transaction, the amount of the chargeable consideration is treated as limited to that value.                    **[49.48]**

*viii)   Foreign currency*

Amounts in foreign currency are converted to sterling by reference to the London closing exchange rate on the effective date of the transaction (unless the parties have used a different rate for the purposes of the transaction).
                    **[49.49]**

*ix)   Carrying out of building works*

There special rules in Sch 4 para 10 concerning the situation where the whole or part of the consideration for a land transaction consists of the carrying out of works of construction, improvement or repair of a building or other works to enhance the value of land.
   Generally, the works score as chargeable consideration, calculated on the basis of their open market value.
   But they are not included as chargeable consideration if:
(1)   the works are carried out *after* the effective date of the transaction;
(2)   the works are carried out on land acquired or to be acquired by the purchaser, or on any other land held by the purchaser or a connected person; and
(3)   it is not a condition of the transaction that the vendor carries them out on the purchaser's behalf.
   Where there are two effective dates because the contract was substantially performed before completion, it is sufficient for the works to be carried out after the earlier effective date (Para 10(2A)).
   HMRC have given the following example (see SDTLM 4060a):

**EXAMPLE 49.3**

P Ltd, a construction company, enters into a contract to acquire a plot of land from V Ltd on 1 July 2004.
Under the terms of the contract, P Ltd is to pay £1m and to build a new workshop for V Ltd on a plot of land owned by V Ltd in a nearby town.
The cost of constructing the workshop is £750,000.
The chargeable consideration for Stamp Duty Land Tax is £1,750,000.     **[49.50]**

### *x)   Provision of services*

Where the provision of services (other than building works) is consideration for a land transaction, the value of that consideration is the amount that would have to be paid in the open market to obtain those services.   **[49.51]**

### *xi)   Employer-provided accommodation*

Schedule 4 paragraph 12 applies where a land transaction is entered into by reason of the purchaser's employment, or that of a person connected with him, if the transaction gives rise to a charge to tax under the ITEPA 2003 Part 3 Chapter 5 (taxable benefits: living accommodation). Cash equivalent chargeable to income tax is added to the consideration for the transaction.
**[49.52]**

### *xii)   Obligations under a lease*

On the grant of a lease, the usual undertakings and obligations of a tenant do not add to the chargeable consideration, under the provisions of Sch 17A para 10. Nor does an assignee's taking on of rent or other tenant obligations contribute to chargeable consideration (para 17). See the lease section below for more on leases.     **[49.53]**

### *xiii)   Reverse premium*

A reverse premium for a lease does not count as chargeable consideration.
**[49.54]**

### *xiv)   Indemnity given by purchaser*

Where the purchaser agrees to indemnify the vendor in respect of liability to a third party arising from breach of an obligation owed by the vendor in relation to the land that is the subject of the transaction, neither the agreement nor any payment made in pursuance of it counts as chargeable consideration.     **[49.55]**

### c)   *Contingent, uncertain or unascertained consideration*

All or part of the consideration for a transaction may be unclear at the effective date. Section 51 provides for this.     **[49.56]**

### i)    *Contingent consideration*

'Contingent' here means that an amount is to paid or is not to be paid if some uncertain future event occurs. An example is where a plot of land is acquired for consideration of £1 million and an additional contingent payment of £1.5 million should planning permission be obtained for an intended development.

In the first place, tax is chargeable on the basis that the contingent amount is paid (or does not cease to be paid). In other words SDLT is charged on the maximum amount for any contingency or set of contingencies. But see below for the rules on deferment.                                                              **[49.57]**

### ii)    *Uncertain consideration*

This is defined as an amount that depends on uncertain future events. An example is where a developer buys a plot of land and agrees that he will pay to the vendor an overage payment of a percentage of profits or turnover when the buildings are completed and sold on to third parties.

Again in the first place, SDLT is chargeable on the basis of a reasonable estimate of the total consideration that will be paid.                          **[49.58]**

### iii)    *Unascertained consideration*

This is an amount that can in principle be determined at the effective date—it does not depend on future events—but in practice is unknown. For example, the consideration may be based on a set of business accounts to be made up to the day before signing the agreement. Until the accounts have been settled, the amount of consideration is not determined.

As with uncertain consideration, SDLT is at first chargeable on the basis of a reasonable estimate of the amount that will be paid.                      **[49.59]**

### iv)    *Adjustments*

Section 80 provides for an adjustment where a contingency crystallises or initially unascertained consideration becomes ascertained. If the effect is to increase liability for SDLT or to make a transaction notifiable, the adjustment or notification must be made as if the effective date was the date of the event that removed the uncertainty. If the adjustment is downwards then the taxpayer is entitled to claim repayment of the overpaid tax.          **[49.60]**

### v)    *Deferred payment of SDLT*

Section 90 provides for a purchaser to apply to HMRC to defer payment of SDLT in respect of contingent or uncertain consideration (though not for unascertained consideration). An application can only be made in respect of consideration that falls to be paid or provided on one or more future dates of which at least one falls, or may fall, more than six months after the effective date of the transaction.

The rules that HMRC will apply when deciding whether to allow deferments are in The Stamp Duty Land Tax (Administration) Regulations, SI 2003/2837, Part 4 (regs 10–28).                                            **[49.61]**

*vi)  Contingent, uncertain or unascertained consideration in the form of rent*

The adjustment and deferral provisions do not apply to consideration in the form of rent. See the lease section below for the special rules.  **[49.62]**

d)  *Transfers of land to a connected company*

SDLT generally applies to actual consideration paid rather than market value of the land. Gifts do not usually even require a land transaction return to be filed.

Where the purchaser in a land transaction is a company connected to the vendor, s 53 deems the consideration for a land transaction to be no less than the market value of the land transferred. This is an anti-avoidance provision to prevent a gift into a wholly-owned company followed by a sale of the shares in the company to a third party from being liable only to the shares rate of stamp duty rather than SDLT.

Such a transfer might be subject to a relief (for example, the relief for transfers within corporate groups), in which case the amount of consideration would be irrelevant.  **[49.63]**

e)  *Linked transactions*

Linked transactions are defined in s 108 as those which form part of a single scheme, arrangement or series of transactions between the same vendor and purchaser or, in either case, persons connected with them. The purpose of this anti-avoidance rule is to prevent the fragmentation of land deals so as to gain the advantage of lower rates.

**EXAMPLE 49.4**

A vendor advertises a house with a garden for sale at an asking price of £650,000. Mr and Mrs X are interested in the property and, after negotiations, the purchase is structured so that Mr X buys the house for £500,000 and Mrs X buys the gardens for £100,000.

HMRC will regard these purchases as linked transactions. The rate of tax is determined by reference to the sum of the chargeable considerations (£600,000) and a rate of 4% applies to each land transaction, giving a total tax charge of £24,000. Had it not been for this rule, Mr X would have paid 3% of £500,000 (£15,000) and Mrs X would have paid nothing on her transaction below the £125,000 threshold for residential property.

A circumstance where transactions are linked is where a property portfolio is acquired under a single negotiated deal. This can be contrasted with the position where a number of properties are acquired as separate lots at a public auction. Stamp duty case law established that separately struck deals made in this manner are not regarded as a 'series' of transactions to be aggregated as one transaction.

**[49.64]**

### 7   Leges

*a)   The charge on a new lease*

When a new lease is granted, any premium is treated as consideration as for a transfer of an existing freehold or leasehold interest. There are, however, anti avoidance provisions where the annual rent for the lease exceeds £600: in such cases there is no zero band for the premium (ie the minimum charge is 1%). Reverse premiums paid by the landlord to the tenant are not charged (Sch 17A Para 18).

What distinguishes the lease regime is that there is an additional charge in relation to the rent that is payable under the lease. SDLT, like the other stamp taxes, makes a single charge when a transaction is carried out (subject to subsequent corrections if some or all of the consideration is uncertain). So, rather than charge the rent paid each year, SDLT charges in relation to the 'net present value' (NPV) of the rent calculated over the whole lease term when the lease is granted (but see below about agreements for lease).

Schedule 5 (as amended) contains the rules for calculating the amount of tax chargeable. Schedule 17A contains further provisions relating to leases.

**[49.65]**

*i)   Tax chargeable on rent*

In respect of the rent on a new lease, the charge is based on a 'slice' system. That is to say, the charge is a percentage of the extent to which the 'net present value' (NPV) exceeds the relevant threshold. The rates and thresholds are as follows (Sch 5 Para 2):

**Table A: Residential**

| Rate bands | Percentage |
|---|---|
| £0 to £125,000 | 0% |
| Over £125,000 | 1% |

**Table B: Non-residential or mixed**

| Rate bands | Percentage |
|---|---|
| £0 to £150,000 | 0% |
| Over £150,000 | 1% |

This means that the thresholds are as for the charge on transfers, the only rate (apart from zero) is 1%, and this is applied to the excess over £125,000 or £150,000, as appropriate.

**[49.66]**

*ii)   NPV of the rent*

The net present value (NPV) of the rent is based on totalling the rent over the whole lease term, but with a discount factor that counts a decreasing percentage of the rent for future years. Here is the formal definition from Sch 5 para 3.

**Definition of net present value of rent payable over the term of the lease**

The net present value of the rent payable over the term of a lease is calculated by applying the formula

$$NPV = \sum_{i=1}^{n} \frac{r_i}{(1+T)}$$

where:
**NPV** is the net present value.

**$r_i$** is the rent payable in year i. (However, this is modified by Sch 17A para 7 to substitute for years 6 onwards the maximum rent payable in any 12-month period in the first five years of the lease.)

**i** is the first, second, third, etc year of the term.

**n** is the term of the lease.

**T** is the temporal discount rate, initially set at 3.5% (it seems unlikely that this rate will change, even though Sch 5 para 8 provides a power to do so by regulation).

Thus, the net present value is the total of the net present values of the rents each year.

A tool is available on the Stamp Office website at www.hmrc.gov.uk/so to assist in the calculation of the net present value of rents.

**EXAMPLE 49.5—A SIMPLE COMMERCIAL LEASE**

A lease is granted for a term of four years at a rent of £100,000 a year. VAT is not chargeable. The calculation of NPV is as follows:

| Year | Rent | Rent discounted |
|---|---|---|
| 1 | £100,000 | £96,618 |
| 2 | £100,000 | £93,351 |
| 3 | £100,000 | £90,194 |
| 4 | £100,000 | £87,144 |
| Total | £400,000 | £367,308 |

Note the following:

The rent for the first year of the lease is discounted. The formula specifies that the rent for year 1 be divided by 1.035, giving the result £96,618.

For year 2, the rent is divided by 1.035 twice. That is to say:

£93,351 = £100,000/(1.035 × 1.035).

The NPV for rent in years 3 and 4 is calculated in a similar manner and the four figures totalled to obtain the NPV for the entire lease term as £367,308 (compared with the total undiscounted rent of £400,000).

Since the lease is non-residential, the threshold is £150,000 and only £217,308 of the NPV is chargeable to tax at 1%. This gives a tax charge of £2,173.

**EXAMPLE 49.6—NPV CALCULATION WHERE THE RENT VARIES**

A lease has a fixed term of five years and the rent payable in each year is as follows:

| | |
|---|---|
| Year 1 | £4,000 |
| Year 2 | £5,000 |

| | |
|---|---|
| Year 3 | £6,000 |
| Year 4 | £7,000 |
| Year 5 | £8,000 |
| Total | £30,000 |

The net present value of the rental over this period is calculated as follows:

| | | |
|---|---|---|
| Year 1 | $4,000/(1+0.035)$ | £3,864.73 |
| Year 2 | $5,000/[(1+0.035) \times (1+0.035)]$ | £4,667.55 |
| Year 3 | $6,000/[(1+0.035) \times (1+0.035) \times (1+0.035)]$ | £5,411.65 |
| Year 4 | $7,000/[(1+0.035) \times (1+0.035) \times (1+0.035) \times (1+0.035)]$ | £6,100.09 |
| Year 5 | $8,000/[(1+0.035) \times (1+0.035) \times (1+0.035) \times (1+0.035) \times (1+0.035)]$ | £6,735.78 |
| Total | | £26,779.82 |

The net present value is £26,779, which is below the threshold.

(d)    Any variation in the lease resulting in a rent increase causes SDLT to be payable on the variation in respect of the additional rent.    **[49.67]**

b)    *Variable or uncertain rents*

As already noted, the calculation of NPV on the grant of a lease is based on the pattern of rents over the first five years (rents for the later years in the formula being taken as the maximum rent for any 12-month period within the first five years. Sch 17A para 7 provides for uncertainty in the rent within the first five years. Except for adjustment in the rent in line with the retail prices index, which are ignored, the taxpayer must make a 'reasonable estimate' of future changes for the initial payment of tax. There will then be one adjustment (upwards or downwards) either at the five-year point or earlier if all the uncertainties crystallise earlier.    **[49.68]**

c)    *Anti-avoidance rules to defend the NPV charge*

i)    *Abnormal rent increases after five years*

The charge on the NPV of rents was controversial since it greatly exceeded the corresponding stamp duty charge for commercial occupational leases—often by more than a factor of five. The Government became particularly sensitive about avoidance of this aspect of the charge following publication of a proposed avoidance scheme in relation to an earlier proposal.

Accordingly, the rule for taking account only of variation in rent during the first five years of a lease has been backed up by a provision for charging 'abnormal' rent increases later in the life of the lease. Schedule 17A paragraph 14 provides for such an increase (whether it occurs under the provisions of the lease or as a variation) to be deemed to be treated as the grant of a new lease for the remaining term of the lease with a charge based on the part of the rent that is additional to the rent already taken into account for the earlier SDLT charge. Paragraph 15 contains three steps to determine whether a particular rent increase is 'abnormal'. The essential idea is that abnormality is when the increase is of more than 20% per complete year (without compounding) measured against the level of rent which was last taken into account for SDLT purposes ('the rent previously taxed') and the 'start date' for that rent.

### EXAMPLE 49.7—ABNORMAL INCREASES IN RENT

A lease was granted for a term of 15 years at a rent of £100,000 a year with market rent reviews five years and one quarter and 10 years and one quarter into the term of the lease. VAT is not chargeable. SDLT was paid on any premium and on the NPV of the rent assumed to be £100,000 a year for the whole term of the lease. A deemed grant of a lease for the excess rent will apply at the rent review points as follows:

- at the first rent review if the rent is greater than £200,000 – that is to say the increase above £100,000 exceeds five times 20%;
- at the second rent review if the rent is greater than £300,000 (an increase of 200% which is 10 times 20%).

If the rent as a result of the first review is greater than £200,000, the second rent review will only trigger a land transaction if rent is set at more than double the amount set at the first rent review.

This provision will only apply from December 2008, when the first SDLT leases reach their five-year point. **[49.69]**

### ii) *Assignment of lease treated as grant of lease*

The charge on the NPV of rent usually applies only to the grant of a lease. Mindful that a lease for rent might be eligible for a relief or exemption and that it might then be assigned for a small premium (leases at market rent have little capital value), Sch 17A para 11 was introduced to trigger the NPV charge in such a case on the first assignment of a lease which was not covered by a list of specified exemptions. The exemptions in the list include group relief and charities relief. **[49.70]**

### d) *Surrenders and re-grants*

When an existing lease is surrendered in return for a new lease, Sch 17A para 16 lifts the Sch 4 para 5 rules for exchanges and states that the grant is not treated as consideration for the surrender or vice versa.

Paragraph 9 provides that the NPV charge on the new lease is based only on rent insofar as it is additional to rent already taken into account for SDLT purposes on the surrendered lease. This means that a full NPV charge is made on the new lease when a stamp duty lease is surrendered. **[49.71]**

### e) *Agreements for lease and grants of leases—charging provision*

We have seen above that a contract that is to be completed by a conveyance is subject to special rules if the contract is substantially performed or the rights assigned prior to completion by conveyance. The corresponding rules for a new lease are separately specified in Sch 17A paras 12A and 12B (except that the rules for leases and missives of let under Scots law are in paragraph 19. The definition of substantial performance is carried forward from s 44.

If an agreement for lease is substantially performed before the lease is granted then paragraph 12A treats the agreement as the grant of a 'notional' lease in accordance with the agreement on the date of substantial performance. The subsequent grant is then treated under the surrender and re-grant rules in paragraph 9 so that rent taken into account for the notional lease is not charged again for the real lease.

As in the corresponding provisions in s 44, s 44A, and Sch 17A para 19 there is a provision for tax to be refunded if a substantially performed contract is subsequently rescinded or annulled (para 12A(4)).

If the rights under an agreement for lease are assigned, paragraph 12B distinguishes between situations where the agreement has not been substantially performed before the assignment and when it has. In the former case then the assignee stands in the assignor's shoes but with any consideration for the assignment added to the consideration for the lease. If there is a previous substantial performance—and therefore a notional lease has been deemed to have been granted—then the assignment is taken as a separate land transaction with the date of the assignment as the effective date. When the lease is granted it will presumably then be the assignee who is taken as being involved in a surrender and re-grant as envisaged in paragraph 12A.

**[49.72]**

## 8    Partnership transactions

In the Government's consultative document on *Modernising Stamp Duty* published in 2002, the proposal was made that transfers of interests in 'land-rich' entities should be subject to an SDLT charge on the proportion of the underlying land that was effectively transferred. This proposal was not implemented in respect of companies or unit trusts, so company shares or units in unit trusts can be traded without any indirect charge to SDLT – though transfers of shares may trigger clawbacks of reliefs on an earlier transfer of the land (see **[42.79]**) . But transfers of partnership interests, where the partnership owns chargeable interests, are subject to SDLT under a special regime in Part 3 of Sch 15.

The special regime applies to three types of transaction:
(1)    transfers of a chargeable interest from a partner to a partnership (para 10);
(2)    transfers of an interest in a partnership (paras 14, 17, 31, 32);
(3)    transfers of a chargeable interest from a partnership to a partner (para 18).

'Partnership' is defined for the purposes of SDLT as including general partnerships within the Partnership Act 1890, limited partnerships within the Limited Partnerships Act 1907, and limited liability partnerships under the Limited Liability Partnerships Act 2000. Entities of a similar character formed under a foreign jurisdiction are also included (para 1).

Further general provisions disregard the legal personality of a partnership (if it has one) and treat its holding of chargeable interests and entering into land transactions as being done by or on behalf of the partners. And partnerships are deemed not to be unit trusts or open-ended investment companies (paras 2–4).

Normal rules apply to land transactions to which the partnership is a party and which do not fall within the three special categories. So an acquisition from a vendor or a sale to a purchaser where the vendor or purchaser is independent of the partnership is subject to a charge under the normal rules.

The general aim of the special provisions (para 9 onwards) seems to be to charge these land transactions as if ownership of land through a partnership broadly equated to ownership of a tenancy in common in proportion to partnership shares (those shares being defined as the rights to a share of income profits of the partnership: para 34). This aspiration, if indeed it is the aim, is neither stated authoritatively nor precisely achieved. Nevertheless, the idea may help to make some sense of the special rules.

The three elements of the special regime apply broadly as follows:

(1)  When a partner transfers a chargeable interest to a partnership, the charge is based on a proportion of the market value of the interest. The proportion, expressed as a percentage, is 100 less that partner's percentage share of the partnership after the transaction. So, where the partner has a 15% share in the partnership after the land transfer he is taken as having disposed of 85% of the property to the other partners of the partnership and 85% of the market value is charged to SDLT.

(2)  When a partner transfers an interest in a partnership to someone else, the transferee is charged to SDLT on a proportion of the market value of any chargeable interests held by the partnership – that proportion being the acquired proportionate interest in the partnership that has been acquired. Leases for a market rent (with reviews to market rent) are excluded from the valuation of land in the partnership. This charge only applies to transfers of interests in partnerships whose sole or main activity is investing in, dealing in, or developing property (so professional partnerships are excluded).

(3)  When a partnership transfers a chargeable interest to a partner, the charge is based on a proportion of the market value of the interest. The proportion, expressed as a percentage, is 100% less that partner's percentage share of the partnership before the transaction. So, where the partner has a 15% share in the partnership before the land transfer he is taken as having acquired 85% of the property (since he already effectively held 15%) and 85% of the market value is charged to SDLT.

**EXAMPLE 49.8**

A and B establish a partnership, each making a capital contribution of £1 million. So each have a 50% interest. A owns a property with a market value of £0.5 million and this is to be transferred to the partnership in one of two possible ways.

(i)  A receives cash consideration of £0.5 million.

In this case A would not have a larger share of the partnership after the transaction since the cash he has received matches the capital item he has transferred.

SDLT is charged in respect of a total of £250,000, which is 50% of the market value on the basis that A in effect retains 50% of the property by virtue of his 50% partnership interest.

(ii)  A receives no cash consideration, but his partnership share is adjusted to allow for the fact that he has contributed a total of £1.5 million to the partnership whereas B contributed £1 million. After the transaction, therefore, A has a 60% interest.

        SDLT is charged on 40% of the £0.5 million market value (£200,000) on the basis that after the transaction, A in effect retains 60% of the property.

(iii)    After the position reached by (ii), C buys A's partnership interest for £1.5 million.

        This is deemed to be a land transaction. The chargeable consideration is taken to be 60% (the partnership interest acquired) of the market value of the land held by the partnership (£0.5 million), that is to say £300,000.

Formulae in the legislation define the amount of chargeable consideration which is charged to SDLT. These also take account of people who are connected to partners and are parties to the land transaction. The proportionate reduction in the charge compared with 100% of market value in (1) and (3) does not apply in circumstances where the partnership consists entirely of bodies corporate and SDLT group relief might be expected to apply (forcing taxpayers to claim group relief if they can and then to face the three-year clawback rules).

Exemptions and reliefs generally apply to partnership transactions – in some cases with amended wording to explain the detailed application of a relief (para 25).

Generally, cash contributions to and cash withdrawals from partnerships when new partners join or existing partners retire are not taken to trigger a charge. But there is an anti-avoidance provision to treat as transfers of interests 'arrangements' under which both circumstances are to happen (para 36). And withdrawal of money other than income profit by a partner within three years of his transferring land into a partnership is subject to a charge as a deemed land transaction (para 17A).

In a bizarre twist to the modernisation process, a stamp duty charge is not removed from documents transferring partnership interests (Sch 15 paras 31–33). It seems that the aim is to protect the 0.5% stamp duty charge where the property of the partnership consists largely of UK equities. The stamp duty charge does not exceed the charge to stamp duty that a transfer of the underlying stock and marketable securities would incur.     **[49.73]**

## 9  Exemptions and reliefs

Under stamp duty, many of the reliefs were subject to 'adjudication' that required the taxpayer to submit the relevant documents and claim the relief. Adjudication of a relief gave certainty, usually fairly quickly. In contrast, under SDLT the taxpayer has to self assess and enter a code in the relevant box in the land transaction return if he feels that he is entitled to a relief. If no immediate query is raised and an SDLT certificate is issued, then there is still a period of nine months during which HMRC can open an enquiry and challenge the availability of the relief.     **[49.74]**

### a)  *Disadvantaged areas relief*

Between 10 April 2003 and 16 March 2005 this was a very important relief for commercial property transactions since it removed any SDLT liability from non-residential land transactions within the designated areas. The relief had been intended to encourage urban regeneration. HMRC Statement of Practice SP1/2004 sets out HMRC's interpretation of the rules, including the definition of 'residential'. Bulk purchases of at least six residential properties count as non-residential for the purposes of the relief. The designated areas are specified as local authority wards or (in Scotland) postcode sectors that are listed in the Stamp Duty (Disadvantaged Areas) Regulations 2001, SI 2001/3747. The areas were defined in relation to 1991 Census data and that there have been ward reorganisations and postcode changes since then. The HMRC Stamp Taxes website contains a postcode lookup facility to assist in identifying whether the postcode is situated within a designated area.

The abolition of the relief for transactions with effective dates from 17 March 2005 was not explained though it seems likely that the relief was considered to be costing too much in lost revenues. Transitional provisions preserve the relief for land transactions pursuant to pre-17 March 2005 contracts and agreements. If such contracts were not substantially performed before that date then the relief applies only if there is no variation, subsale or exercise of options or pre-emption rights from that date. The relief will remain relevant for some major projects where there is a development agreement with a public authority and the transfer of the land or grant of a headlease will occur only at the end of the project—which may be several years in the future.

The relief is still in place for purchases of residential property but is of limited application since purchases above £150,000 do not qualify for the relief. The relief, therefore, applies only to residential purchases for more than £125,000 and up to £150,000. **[49.75]**

b) *Group relief*

This corresponds to the relief available from stamp duty under FA 1930 s 42 and provides for exemption from SDLT for transfers of properties between companies within a group. For this purpose *group* means a '75% group' as defined for corporation tax group relief purposes) (s 62, Sch 7 Part 1).

Group relief is not available if there are arrangements at the effective date for the transferee to be de-grouped from the transferor or for consideration to be provided from outside the group. HMRC have published administrative and technical guidance including a description of how they will interpret the arrangements test in *Tax Bulletin* 70 (which is largely derived from SP 3/98 which provides equivalent guidance in relation to stamp duty).

FA 2005 introduced a further test for group relief to apply. This is that there must be a *bona fide* commercial motive and that avoidance of tax (including stamp duty, income tax, corporation tax and capital gains tax) is not a main motive.

The relief is subject to a clawback if certain corporate events occur within three years of the effective date of the transaction or under arrangements entered into before the end of the three-year period. These include the transferee company leaving the group while it or a relevant associated company holds the chargeable interest and certain cases when control of the transferee follows successive transactions eligible for group relief. **[49.76]**

c) *Reconstruction and acquisition reliefs*

These reliefs (s 62, Sch 7 Part 2) match those available for stamp duty under FA 1986 s 75 or 76 as follows:

(1)  Reconstruction relief provides a full exemption from SDLT where a land transaction is in connection with a scheme of reconstruction of the 'target' company in exchange for non-redeemable shares and, possibly, the assumption or discharge of liabilities of the target company by the 'acquiring' company.

(2)  Acquisition relief reduces the rate of SDLT to 0.5% where the land transaction is entered into in connection with the acquisition of an undertaking of the target company in exchange for non-redeemable shares or for such shares and cash up to 10% of the nominal value of the shares and also, possibly, the assumption or discharge of liabilities of the target company by the 'acquiring' company.

Both reliefs are subject to the motive test as for group relief and may be withdrawn in the following circumstances:

(1)  The transferee company leaves the group within three years of the effective date of the transaction (or under arrangements entered into before the end of the three-year period) while still holding an interest in property (or an interest derived from it) which it held at the date of the transaction.

(2)  There is a change of control of the transferee company within three years of the effective date of the transaction (or under arrangements entered into before the end of the three-year period) while still holding an interest in property (or an interest derived from it) which it held at the date of the transaction.                                           **[49.77]**

d)  *Exemptions under Schedule 3*

The exemptions under Schedule 3 (which lift the notification requirement) are as follows:

| *Exempt land transactions (under Schedule 3)* | *Statutory reference* |
| --- | --- |
| Gifts (transactions where there is no chargeable consideration) | s 50, Sch 3, para 1 |
| Certain grants of leases by registered social landlord | Sch 3, para 2 |
| Transactions in contemplation of or in connection with divorce or separation | Sch 3, para 3 |
| Variation of testamentary dispositions, etc | Sch 3, para 4 |

**[49.78]**

e)  *Other reliefs*

A land transaction return is needed for these other reliefs (if the transaction would have been notifiable, absent the relief).

| Reliefs | *Statutory reference* |
| --- | --- |
| Disadvantaged areas | s 57, Sch 6 |
| Leaseback element of sale and leaseback | s 57A |
| Certain acquisitions of residential property | s 58A, Sch 6A |
| Part-exchange (house building company) | s 58A, Sch 6A |
| Acquisition by property trader | s 58A, Sch 6A |

| | |
|---|---|
| Re-location of employment | s 58A, Sch 6A |
| Compulsory purchase facilitating development | s 60 |
| Compliance with planning obligations | s 61 |
| Group relief | ss 62, 126, Sch 7, Part 1 |
| Reconstruction relief | s 62, Sch 7, Part 2, paras 7, 9–13 |
| Acquisition relief (tax limited to 0.5%) | ss 62, 127, Sch 7, Part 2, paras 8–13 |
| Demutualisation of insurance company | s 63 |
| Demutualisation of building society | s 64 |
| Incorporation of limited liability partnership | s 65, Sch 15 |
| Transfers involving public bodies | s 66 |
| Transfer in consequence of reorganisation of parliamentary constituencies | s 67 |
| Charities | s 68, Sch 8 |
| Acquisition by bodies established for national purposes | s 69 |
| Right to buy transactions | s 70, Sch 9 |
| Registered social landlords | s 71 |
| Alternative property finance | ss 72, 73 |
| Collective enfranchisement by leaseholders (does not apply in Scotland) | s 74 |
| Crofting community right to buy (applies in Scotland only) | s 75 |
| Private Finance Initiative (PFI) transactions | Sch 4, para 17 |

Some stamp duty reliefs were carried forward into SDLT by The Stamp Duty Land Tax (Consequential Amendment of Enactments) Regulations 2001, SI 2003/2867. Reliefs in the following Acts are of particular significance:
(1) Friendly Societies Act 1974 — Land transactions effected by or in consequence of an amalgamation of two or more registered societies or a transfer of engagements are exempt from charge:
(2) National Health Service (Scotland) Act 1978;
(3) National Health Service and Community Care Act 1990;
(4) Building Societies Act 1986 — A land transaction effected by or in consequence of an amalgamation of two or more building societies or a transfer of engagements between building societies is exempt from charge. **[49.79]**

f) *Clawbacks*

Four reliefs are subject to clawbacks if 'disqualifying events' occur within three years. For group relief, clawback is potentially triggered by corporate-level events that de-group the purchaser. For acquisition and reconstruction reliefs, change of control of the purchaser can cause a clawback. And for charities relief the clawback may result from loss of charitable status or a disqualifying change of use of the land by the purchaser. If a disqualifying event occurs a land transaction return is required within 30 days.    **[49.80]**

### 10   Administration

If a land transaction is notifiable (s 77), then it is necessary to file a return and pay any tax due (s 76). This requirement is also linked to the process of land registration since, for a notifiable transaction, a Revenue Certificate is needed for the purposes of registration of the land interest. For non-notifiable transactions, self-certificates need to be used.

Even when HMRC has issued a certificate, it has a period of nine months after the filing date to open an enquiry into the land transaction return—longer in the case of non-disclosure, negligence, etc (s 78, Sch 10).

Notifiability always applies when there is a charge to SDLT. But the following land transactions are also notifiable:
(1)   Transactions that would give rise to a charge were it not for a relief (except that transactions exempt under Schedule 3 are not notifiable).
(2)   Grant of a lease for seven years or more that is granted for chargeable consideration.
(3)   Other acquisitions of major interests (defined in s 117 as a freehold or leasehold interest) for chargeable consideration.

The following land transactions are not notifiable:
(1)   Acquisitions of major interests for no chargeable consideration.
(2)   Transactions in connection with divorce or separation.
(3)   Transactions arising from variation of testamentary dispositions.

The last two of these are exemptions within Sch 3, together with the exemption for gifts. The rationale for them not to be notifiable, while other reliefs require notification, is mysterious.

Schedule 10 Part 2 establishes a duty for purchasers to keep and preserve records relating to a land transaction return for at least six years. There is a corresponding requirement in Sch 11 Part 2 in relation to self-certificates.

**[49.81]**

### 11   Transitional provisions

Land transactions may or may not be 'SDLT transactions' to which SDLT rather than stamp duty applies) under the transitional provisions set out in Schedule 19. HMRC Stamp Taxes produced the following flowchart to indicate whether a transaction attracts SDLT. Royal Assent of FB 2003 was on 10 July 2003 and implementation of SDLT was on 1 December 2003.

The main categories of document which are executed on or after 1 December 2003 but which are still subject to stamp duty rather than SDLT are:
(1)   Conveyance executed to complete a contract for sale executed before 11 July 2003, without any variation of the contract or intervening assignment of rights or subsale or exercise of an option, etc.
(2)   Leases granted in conformity with agreements for lease executed before 11 July 2003 without any variation, etc.

These circumstances are by now unusual. However, there are still a reasonable number of agreements for lease in relation to new developments where the lease will only be granted on completion of the building works. Even for these, if material variations in the agreement are made the subsequent grant of the lease will fall within SDLT. The other circumstance where stamp duty applies in practice is where granting of the lease has been overlooked – landlord and tenant having had no legal difficulties in relying on the agreement for lease – and a formal grant becomes desirable. **[49.82]**

## III   STAMP DUTY RESERVE TAX (SDRT)

The statutory provisions for SDRT (mostly in FA 1986 Part 4) ensure that the substantial revenues from stamp taxes on UK shares (£2.6 billion in 2003–04) continue to be paid. SDRT can be regarded as the primary tax since it imposes a charge on the transferee whenever there is an agreement to transfer chargeable securities (FA 1986 s 87) with modern administrative, compliance, and enforcement procedures (SI 1986/1711). There is a separate SDRT regime for surrenders of units in UK unit trusts and shares in open-ended investment companies (OEICS) (FA 1999 Sch 19).

But, with the important exception of those who play a direct role in the financial markets, most taxpayers need take little notice of SDRT. This is because stamp duty is fully in place for documents that transfer shares and the vast bulk of off-market share transactions require a stamped stock transfer form to enable registration of the change in legal ownership. And a number of important reliefs can only be obtained by claiming stamp duty relief on a transfer document. A stamped transfer document removes the SDRT charge on the associated agreement (FA 1986 s 92) or allows the reclaim of SDRT already paid.

This Part describes SDRT as it applies to market transactions where no physical document is required and to the relevant minority of non-market transactions. The next Part describes stamp duty proper which applies to documents relating to stock and marketable securities.     **[49.83]–[49.100]**

## 1   **The Basics**

### a)   *Territorial scope*

SDRT applies wherever agreements are made or effected, ie whether or not the transaction is effected in the UK and any party is resident or situated in the UK (FA 1986 s 86(4)).     **[49.101]**

### b)   *The principal charge*

SDRT is a charge on agreements to transfer stocks and shares issued by UK incorporated companies. Securities issued by a Societas Europaea (SE) (a new European company created by Council Regulation (EC) 2157/2001, 8 October 2001) are within the scope of the charge if the SE has its registered office in the UK, irrespective of where the SE was incorporated.

The principal charge (FA 1986 s 87) applies when A agrees with B to transfer 'chargeable securities' (defined in detail in FA 1986 s 99(3) onwards), whether or not to B, for a consideration in money or money's

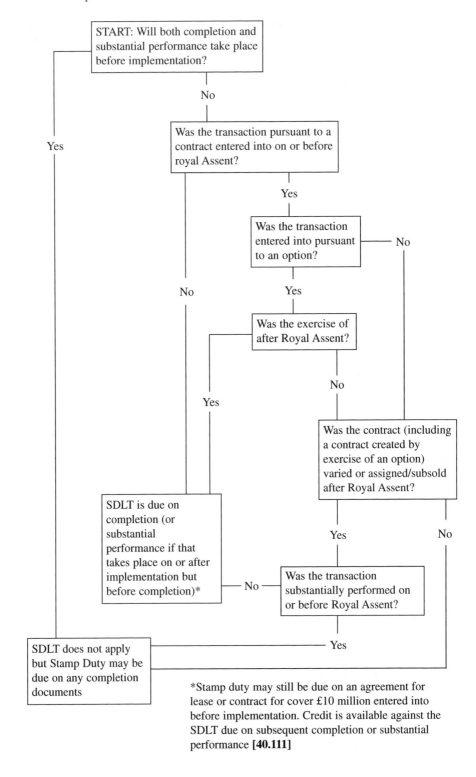

START: Will both completion and substantial performance take place before implementation?

Yes

No

Was the transaction pursuant to a contract entered into on or before royal Assent?

Yes

No

Was the transaction entered into pursuant to an option?

No

Yes

Was the exercise of after Royal Assent?

Yes

No

Was the contract (including a contract created by exercise of an option) varied or assigned/subsold after Royal Assent?

Yes

No

SDLT is due on completion (or substantial performance if that takes place on or after implementation but before completion)*

No

Was the transaction substantially performed on or before Royal Assent?

Yes

SDLT does not apply but Stamp Duty may be due on any completion documents

*Stamp duty may still be due on an agreement for lease or contract for cover £10 million entered into before implementation. Credit is available against the SDLT due on subsequent completion or substantial performance [40.111]

worth and is charged at 0.5% of consideration. The principal charge is cancelled if an instrument of transfer covering those securities is executed in pursuance to the agreement and duly stamped within a period of six years (FA 1986 s 92). B is liable to the tax though others, such as the broker who arranges the deal, may also be accountable under administrative regulations.

The definition of chargeable securities includes interests in or rights arising out of stocks, shares or loan capital. So transfers of derivative financial instruments are within the scope of the tax, though the issue of a derivative will not trigger the principal charge; nor will there be a charge if a derivative contract is settled by a cash payment.

The SDRT charge does not apply to securities that are exempt from all stamp duties (FA 1986 s 99(5)) this includes gilt-edged securities and other loan capital exempt under FA 1986 s 79, see [**49.124**]); nor to stock or securities subject to charge under the bearer head of stamp duty (FA 1999 Sch 15).

Since 1996 the electronic system CREST has settled deals made on the London Stock Exchange without the use of physical stock transfer forms. The tax is levied on the consideration paid except where an exemption can be claimed by the use of flags in CREST transactions, and share registers are automatically updated, CREST (and any other approved paperless system) has a statutory obligation to collect and account for SDRT on transactions carried out within its system or reported through it for regulatory purposes.

**[49.102]**

c)  *The higher charge*

SDRT applies at a higher rate to shares converted into depositary receipts (FA 1986 s 93) and to shares put into a clearance system (FA 1986 s 96). It supplements the charge to duty on depositary receipts (see [**49.121**]) and is charged at a rate of 1.5% subject to an option, in FA 1986 s 97A, enabling as an alternative clearance services to opt for the normal SDRT charges to apply to transactions within the service. The higher charge acts as a 'season ticket' up-front charge since subsequent effective changes in ownership of the underlying UK shares are not subject to any charge. For this reason, issues of new shares are subject to the higher charge as well as transfers of existing shares—unlike the principal charge that does not apply to new issues.

There are reliefs for transfers of shares between systems, where the higher charge applied on the original entry to such a system (FA 1986 ss 97AA and 97B). Though other transfers of shares out of such a system bring them back into the scope of the principal charge. **[49.103]**

2  **Exemptions for certain financial market transactions**

When shares are bought on the financial markets there are likely to be a series of transactions carried out by brokers, market makers, etc to effect the one trade. Some of these intermediate dealers may act as agents for others. But others act in a principal capacity and would be charged to SDRT. The intention of the SDRT provisions is just to charge the end purchaser. So there are reliefs for market intermediaries (FA 1986 s 88A) and for additional transactions in relation to public issues (FA 1986 s 89A) as well as for within-market stock lending (FA 1986 s 89AA). **[49.104]**

### 3   Off-market transactions subject to SDRT

The existence of SDRT protects the stamp duty charge on changes in ownership of UK shares, In particular, avoidance schemes which depend on restricting the need for stock transfer documents are ineffective since any agreement to transfer shares which does not require the execution of a stampable document triggers a free-standing SDRT charge.

Some examples where SDRT, but not stamp duty, applies are as follows:

**EXAMPLE 49.9**

(1)   Adam receives a renounceable letter of allotment of shares in Zeta Ltd.
   (i)   If he applies to be registered there will be no charge to duty since there has been no transfer of the rights comprised in the letter.
   (ii)   If he renounces the rights and transfers the letter of allotment to Bertha who in turn transfers to Charles, SDRT may apply to those transfers.
(2)   Bertram buys and sells securities within the same Stock Exchange account or there is a purchase of shares that are registered in the name of a nominee acting for both seller and purchaser. Given that in both cases there is an agreement to transfer chargeable securities for consideration, Bertram is subject to SDRT.                                                        **[49.105]**

### 4   The charge on units in unit trusts

Unlike the principal charge to SDRT, the special regime for units in UK unit trusts operates as a free-standing tax regime without any overlap or interaction with stamp duty. The provisions are in FA 1999 Sch 19 which removes stamp duty from instruments relating to units under a unit trust scheme (para 1) except that units are treated as stock where they are consideration in relation to an otherwise stampable document (para 19) or where they fall within the bearer instrument regime.

The SDRT charge applies to surrenders of units and is in the first place charged at 0.5% on the market value of the units. The taxpayers are the trustees of the unit trust who will undoubtedly ensure that the trust deed provides for any tax to be financed out of the fund or from charges to unit holders. FA 1986 s 99(5A) exempts from the charge unit trusts with no register in the UK and no UK-resident trustees.

The full 0.5% charge is proportionately reduced by two formulae. Firstly the tax amount is multiplied by $I/S$ if I, the number of units issued in the week of the surrender and the week after, is smaller than S, the total number of surrenders in the same two week period. This may seem odd. The tax policy rationale is that if all redeemed units are re-issued then the full charge should apply since, in effect, the ownership of the underlying property (eg shares) has changed hands and there would have been a charge to stamp duty or SDRT if that property had changed ownership directly. If, in contrast, there are no new issues within a reasonable time of the surrender then the unit trust is likely to have to sell the underlying assets corresponding to the surrendered units. In this case the stamp duty or SDRT charge on the sale of the assets (albeit charged on the purchaser) means that the charge on the surrender can be removed without net effect on total revenues. The formula reduces the SDRT charge to the extent that issues match surrenders.

The second proportionate reduction is also based on looking through the units to the underlying property. This reduction is to multiply by the formula N/(N+E) where N is the value of non-exempt investments and E is the value of exempt investments in the fund. Exempt investments are defined in FA 1986 s 99(5A)(b) and are in broad terms securities outside the scope of stamp duty (eg non-UK shares) and units in unit trusts that only invest in bonds.

The unit trust regime is applied to OEICS, with appropriate changes in terminology, by regulations in SI 1997/1156. Regulation 4A specifically relates to the FA 1999 Sch 19 regime. **[49.106]**

## IV STAMP DUTY ON STOCK AND MARKETABLE SECURITIES

### 1 General structure of stamp duty

Stamp duty depends primarily upon the Stamp Act 1891 and the Stamp Duties Management Act 1891 as amended by subsequent Finance Acts. From 1 December 2003, when SDLT commenced, FA 2003 s 125 restricts stamp duty to instruments relating to stock and marketable securities, except for some documents relating to land which stay within stamp duty under the transitional provisions for SDLT. Stamp duty on land transactions where partnerships acquire or dispose of land from or to partners and transfers of partnership interests where the partnership owns land ceased when these transactions were brought within SDLT from 23 July 2004 (FA 2003 Sch 15). **[49.107]**

#### a) *Written instruments*

Stamp duty applies to any 'instrument' (the term includes 'every written document') which falls within the description of what were termed 'Heads of Charge' in the Stamp Act 1891 and were restated in FA 99 Schs 13 and 15, and is not covered by an exemption. If a transaction transferring chargeable securities is effected without a written instrument then SDRT is likely to apply. **[49.108]**

#### b) *Rates, interest and penalties*

The amount of stamp duty to be paid will be either a fixed duty of £5 or an *ad valorem* duty calculated (usually) by reference to the amount or value of the consideration recorded in the instrument (rounded up, if necessary, to a multiple of £5). SA 1891 s 15 (amended by FA 1999) provides that an instrument may be stamped after execution 'on payment of the unpaid duty and any interest or penalty payable'. Note the following:
(1) *Interest (s 15A)*: after 30 days interest is payable at a rate fixed by regulations but not if the interest is less than £25. This charge applies to all documents that are chargeable, including those executed overseas. In all cases the 30-day period runs from the date of execution.
(2) *Penalties (s 15B)*: after the 30-day period a penalty arises. If the document is presented for stamping within one year of the end of the 30-day period the maximum penalty is £300 or, if less, the amount of

duty. After one year the maximum penalty is the amount of the duty or, if more, £300. Where an instrument is executed and retained offshore, the 30-day period for the penalty is delayed to the point where it is brought into the UK. However, this is of little practical importance where SDRT potentially applies.

(3)  There is a power for the Commissioners to mitigate any penalty (s 15B(4)) and 'no penalty is payable if there is a reasonable excuse for the delay in presenting the instrument for stamping' (s 15B(5)). An appeal against late stamping penalties may be made to the Special Commissioners and then to the High Court (FA 1999 Sch 12).

(4)  The '30-day rule' may create problems in cases where the amount of duty is uncertain (for instance when the sale price depends upon a set of accounts yet to be prepared) or where a statutory exemption from duty is claimed (see *Tax Journal*, 24 May 1999, p 8 and *Stamp Taxes Manual* para 4.308).                                      **[49.109]**

c)  *Who is accountable for duty?*

The legislation does not generally state who is accountable for the duty. Apart from the fact that SDRT is enforceable on the transferee in relation to transfers of chargeable securities, the main sanction for non-payment is that, unless properly stamped, no document executed in the UK or relating to any property that is situated in the UK, will be admissible in evidence in any civil proceedings (SA 1891 s 14(4) and company registrars are not permitted to register changes without having a stamped document (SA 1891 s 17). There is, however, a penalty for failure to submit bearer instruments for stamping in accordance with FA 1999 Sch 15 para 1.                          **[49.110]**

d)  *Administration*

The administration of stamp duty is under the Commissioners of Revenue & Customs but the day-to-day work of administration is carried out by the appropriate Stamp Offices. In the event of a dispute there will normally be an adjudication followed by the stating of a case by the commissioners with a hearing in the Chancery Division of the High Court. There is a right of appeal to the Court of Appeal and, ultimately, to the House of Lords. Unlike other taxes the taxpayer (or, rather, the person who wishes the document to be duly stamped) has to pay the assessed duty before the appeal is heard.                                                           **[49.111]**

e)  *Adjudication*

If required to do so the commissioners must state whether, in their opinion, any executed instrument is subject to a stamp duty charge and if so must state the amount of duty chargeable (the *adjudication* process: SA 1891 s 12). Adjudication may be voluntary, in which case the individual will be asking the commissioners to confirm that no duty is payable on the instrument, or, alternatively it may be necessary to ascertain the correct duty to be paid. In certain cases, however, legislation makes adjudication compulsory to ensure that the correct amount of duty is paid or to ensure that an instrument is covered by an exemption from duty (eg where there is a transfer between associated companies or a company reconstruction and exemption from duty is sought: see [**49.125**] and [**49.126**]). Such instruments are deemed not to have been properly stamped unless adjudicated bearing a stamp to that effect.

The process of adjudication is an essential step in the appeals procedure and it also provides a definitive means by which a third party can be satisfied as to the correctness of the stamp duty paid—since the Stamp Office cannot change its mind about the stamp duty payable on a document after formal adjudication. This ability to require HMRC to take a binding view as to the tax position is in contrast to the provisions for modern taxes. The norm in recent legislation is for the taxpayer to be required to self-assess and take the risk if, on enquiry, he turns out to have underpaid. Statutory clearance procedures are relatively rare (and new ones have not been included in recent years) and administrative procedures for rulings tend to be restricted to areas where the meaning of the law is in doubt in a particular circumstance. [**49.112**]

## 2 Instruments subject to stamp duty on sale

a) *Conveyance or transfer on sale (FA 1999 Sch 13(1))*

Stamp duty is chargeable on a document which transfers stock or marketable securities on sale and the duty charged is *ad valorem* at a rate of 0.5% of consideration (rounded up to a multiple of £5 if necessary). Generally these documents will be stock transfer forms though they may, for example, be declarations of trust or letters of direction to a nominee where these effect a transfer.

'Sale' is not defined but there must be a vendor, a purchaser, and consideration (although there is no requirement that the consideration must be adequate). Duty is charged on the amount or value of the consideration and where it is in sterling, there will be no problem. If the consideration is in foreign currency, duty is charged on the sterling equivalent at the rate of exchange applying on the date of execution of the instrument (FA 1985 s 88). [**49.113**]

*i) Meaning of 'consideration'*

Although the consideration for a sale will often be money, for stamp duty purposes stock or marketable securities and debts and other liabilities are also treated as chargeable sale consideration (SA 1891 ss 55, 57). A right to receive shares or securities in the future is dutiable consideration: for the purpose of valuing that consideration and the possibility that it may not be issued is ignored (s 55(1A)). Reorganisations of corporate groups often involve share for share exchanges. If shares are transferred and the consideration is an issue or transfer of other shares, then the consideration shares must be valued to calculate the amount of stamp duty payable.

An example where consideration is not in the form of cash, securities or debt is a merger of pension schemes where the only consideration for the transfer of assets from the transferring scheme to the receiving scheme is the assumption by the receiving scheme of the obligation to pay pension benefits. This is not chargeable consideration for stamp duty purposes so the transfer instruments that give effect to the transfer of stock or marketable securities from the transferring scheme to the receiving scheme are not stampable *ad valorem*. Instead they are liable to fixed duty of £5 (see **[49.118]**).                                                                                              **[49.114]**

ii)    *Unascertainable consideration and the contingency principle*

Consideration may be uncertain at the time of the sale due to elements that depend on future events. For example, the shares in a company which runs a business might be sold for an amount which depends on the amount of profits over, say, the three years following the sale. If there is a specified *maximum* consideration provided for under contingencies which are provided for, then *ad valorem* duty is charged on that amount even though there may be little practical likelihood of it being paid. If there is no maximum sum stated but a minimum figure, *ad valorem* duty is charged on the minimum figure. If, however, there was no maximum nor minimum figure the consideration is wholly unascertainable with nothing to stamp and only fixed duty payable (see *Coventry City Council v IRC* (1978); *LM Tenancies 1 plc v IRC* (1996), CA; affd (1998), HL.                                                                                 **[49.115]**

b)    *Partnership dissolutions*

Documents relating to partnerships may be within the scope of stamp duty if the partnership owns stock or marketable securities (FA 2003 Sch 15 para 33). On the dissolution of a partnership, the division (or partition) of the assets between the partners will not be treated as a sale (*MacLeod v IRC* (1885)) but, if an outgoing partner is 'bought out', the instrument effecting that arrangement will be a sale (*Garnett v IRC* (1899)). A partition document is subject to a fixed duty. The mere withdrawal of partnership capital does not attract any charge and neither does the introduction of cash by an incoming partner. However, when an incoming partner pays for an interest in the business, the relevant document may operate as a conveyance on sale. Given these permutations, considerable care should be exercised in structuring both the admission of new partners and the retirement of old partners. To the extent that partnership property consists of interests in land, SDLT special rules apply and require even more care (see **[49.73]**).

**EXAMPLE 49.10**

Dave joins the partnership of Bob, Mick and Tom that has no land assets. He contributes capital of £100,000. This by itself will not amount to a sale. If, however, he pays the money to the other partners or they make a simultaneous withdrawal of capital, the deed or instrument of partnership effecting the transaction will be charged as a conveyance or transfer on sale of partnership property to Dave. However, the amount of stamp duty to be charged will depend on the extent to which partnership property consists of chargeable securities.                                      **[49.116]**

c)    *Exchanges of shares*

An exchange of shares is a sale not an exchange (*Chesterfield Brewery Co v IRC* (1899)). FA 2000 s 122 ensures that both transfers are stampable *ad valorem* (unless exempt). This overrides a former practice under which a sale of shares for shares as consideration resulted in only one charge to *ad valorem* duty—the other transfer being stamped at £5. **[49.117]**

## 2 Conveyance or transfer not on sale

### a) *General*

In the case of conveyances or transfers other than on sale the duty is fixed at £5. This includes the dispositions considered below and decrees or orders of the court or commissioners whereby property is transferred or vested in any person (SA 1891 s 62). The 1987 Regulations (SI 1987/516, see **[49.121]**) provide an exemption from the fixed duty in a number of the more common situations where property is transferred otherwise than on sale. There will still be cases, however, where duty remains payable; for instance:
(1)  transfer from a beneficial owner to his nominee (including a declaration of trust: see below);
(2)  transfer from a nominee to the beneficial owner;
(3)  transfer from one nominee to another nominee of the same beneficial owner;
(4)  transfer by way of security for a loan or re-transfer to the original transferor on repayment of a loan;
(5)  transfer from the trustees of a profit sharing scheme to a participant in the scheme. **[49.118]**

### b) *Gifts and voluntary dispositions*

There is no *ad valorem* duty on gifts (though these were charged prior to FA 1985). Instead they are charged to fixed duty of £5. In some cases even fixed duty does not apply provided that the appropriate certificate is included in the transfer (see next paragraph).

Bad bargains and sales at undervalue are charged as 'conveyances on sale' with duty being levied on the actual consideration furnished.

*A declaration of trust* Trusts may be created by self-declaration or by transferring the property to trustees to hold for the intended beneficiaries. Instruments which declare trusts (except when the declaration is within a life insurance policy, are subject to a fixed charge of £5 but the transfer of assets by the settlor to the trustees will not attract duty, provided that the appropriate certificate is included, unless consideration is furnished (when it will be a sale). A trust created by will is not subject to duty. Deeds effecting changes of trustees are not subject to duty provided a certificate is included (Category A of the 1987 Regulations (see **[49.121]**) and in practice duty is not charged on automatic vestings under the Trustee Act 1925 s 40). **[49.119]**

*Orders under the Variation of Trusts Act 1958* When a variation order is made by the courts, there is no longer any requirement to submit a duplicate of the order for stamping (see Practice Direction (Chancery: Stamp Duty on Orders under the Variation of Trusts Act 1958) (No 3/89)). Arrangements will normally involve either a voluntary disposition (falling within Category L) or a declaration of trust attracting a £5 stamp. **[49.120]**

c)   *Stamp Duty* (*Exempt Instruments*) *Regulations 1987* (*SI 1987/516*)

Instruments falling within the categories listed in the Schedule to these Regulations, which are correctly certified, are exempted from the fixed duty of £5 that would otherwise be chargeable and should not be presented at stamp offices for adjudication. The appropriate certificate should be included in, endorsed or attached to, the instrument and should refer to the category in the Schedule under which exemption is claimed. The following is a suggested form of wording for such certificates:

> 'I hereby certify that this instrument falls within category in the Schedule to the Stamp Duty (Exempt Instruments) Regulations 1987.'

These are the exempt categories:

*Category A:* The vesting of property subject to a trust in the trustees on the appointment of a new trustee or in the continuing trustees on the retirement of a trustee.

*Category B:* The conveyance or transfer of property subject of a specific devise or legacy to a beneficiary named in the will (contrast Category D below).

*Category C:* The conveyance or transfer of property which forms part of an intestate estate to the person entitled on intestacy.

*Category D:* The appropriation of property in satisfaction of a general legacy of money or in satisfaction of any interest of a surviving spouse in an intestate's estate.

*Category E:* The conveyance or transfer of property forming part of the residuary estate of a testator to a beneficiary entitled under the will.

*Category F:* The conveyance or transfer of property out of a settlement in or towards the satisfaction of a beneficiary's interest in accordance with the provisions of the settlement (the relevant interest must not have been acquired for money or money's worth since the *ad valorem* charge is not exempted by these regulations).

*Category G:* The conveyance or transfer of property on and in consideration of marriage to a party or to trustees to be held on a marriage settlement.

*Category H:* The conveyance or transfer of property in connection with divorce etc (see [**49.124**]).

*Category I:* The conveyance or transfer by the liquidator of property that formed part of the assets of the company in a liquidation to a shareholder in satisfaction of his rights on the winding up.

*Category J:* The grant in fee simple of an easement in or over land for no consideration in money or money's worth.

*Category K:* The grant of a servitude for no consideration in money or money's worth.

*Category L:* The conveyance or transfer of property as a voluntary disposition *inter vivos.*

*Category M:* The conveyance or transfer of property under a post death variation.

*Category N:* The declaration of any use or trust of or concerning a life policy, or property representing, or benefits arising under, a life policy.   [**49.121**]

## 3 The higher charge for depositary receipt systems and clearance services (FA 1986 ss 67–72A)

A 1.5% charge is generally imposed when UK shares are converted into depositary receipts or transferred to a clearance service that enables UK shares to be bought and sold without payment of stamp duty or SDRT. The charge is levied on the consideration paid if the transfer is on sale: otherwise it is levied on the value of the shares at that time. This provision complements the higher charge of SDRT (see further [49.102] and see FA 1986 s 97A). [49.122]

## 4 Other documents subject to stamp duty

In addition to the occasions of charge already considered, *ad valorem* duty is chargeable on certain bearer instruments (see FA 1999 Sch 15) at varying rates from 1.5% of the market value to 0.2% of the market value and bonds, covenants or instruments increasing the rent reserved by another instrument are dutiable as a lease in consideration of the additional rent thereby made payable. Unlike the generality of stamp duty charges, the charges on bearer instruments are mandatory with penalties for default (see FA 1999 Sch 15 paras 21–23).

Fixed duty is chargeable in respect of the following documents:
(1) conveyance or transfer other than on sale (see [49.117]);
(2) duplicate or counterpart of any instrument chargeable with duty (see SA 1891 ss 72, 11);
(6) release or renunciation of any property or interest in property and which is not subject to sale duty (eg a partnership share) see [49.115];
(7) surrender of any kind which is not chargeable to sale duty;
(8) transfers from a beneficial owner to his nominee and *vice versa*;
(9) transfers by way of security for a loan or retransfer on repayment;
(10) transfers from trustees of a profit sharing scheme to a participant.
[49.123]

## 5 Exemptions and reliefs from stamp duty

a) *General*

Exemption from duty is conferred upon a number of documents, in particular:
(1) A deed of variation of a deceased person's property made in consideration of the making of a variation in respect of another of the dispositions.
(2) An assent whereby property is appropriated by a PR in or towards the satisfaction of a general pecuniary legacy or in satisfaction of the interest of a surviving spouse on an intestacy.
(3) Transfers in contemplation or connection with divorce or separation are subject to a fixed duty (FA 1985 s 83) and SI 1987/516 provides an exempt category (H) against the fixed duty.
(4) Transfers to a charitable body, charitable trust or to the trustees of the National Heritage Memorial Fund (FA 1982 s 129).

(5) Renounceable letters of allotment with a renunciation period not exceeding six months (although if transferred for value they will attract SDRT, see **[49.101]**).

(6) Transfers of gilts and loan stock (including ratchet loans) which are neither convertible into equities nor carry a right to interest at a rate which is determined by reference to the results of a business or which exceeds a reasonable commercial return on the nominal value of the stock (FA 1986 s 79).    **[49.124]**

b) *Exemptions for companies*

*i)   A demerger which is effected by a direct distribution of a subsidiary's shares since this is not a conveyance on sale*

*ii)   Transfers between associated companies 'group relief' (FA 1930 s 42)*

Conveyance or transfer duty is not charged on an instrument by which one company transfers property to an associated company. The detailed requirements are in FA 1930 s 42 which requires that one of the companies in question must beneficially own, directly or indirectly, at least 75% of the ordinary share capital of the other, or a third company beneficially owns, directly or indirectly at least 75% of the ordinary share capital of each. There is no residence restriction: foreign companies may benefit from the relief and their inclusion in a group will not prevent the group qualifying for the relief (*Canada Safeway v IRC* (1973)). The 'grouping' test was tightened up by FA 2000: to have regard to the tests in TA 1988 Sch 18. The test of association is also not satisfied if a person or persons together has or have or could obtain control of one (but not both) of the otherwise associated companies (see new s 42(2C) and for the interpretation of such clauses *Pilkington Bros Ltd v IRC* (1982)).

FA 1967 s 27(3) contains provisions to prevent abuse of the s 42 relief. In particular the consideration for the transfer must not be provided from outside the group. The relief will not be allowed if it forms part of an arrangement whereby the transferor's interest in the transferee's share capital will be reduced below 75%.

It is necessary to apply for adjudication of the instrument effecting the transfer in order to obtain the relief. Claims for group relief require a formal (but not statutory) declaration by a director or company secretary of the company establishing the group (see SP 3/98) and *Stamp Taxes Manual* 6.163 onwards). In contrast to the corresponding group relief in SDLT, there is no motive test or clawback rule for group relief on shares.    **[49.125]**

*iii)   Reconstructions where there is no real change of ownership (FA 1986 ss 75– 77)*

Exemption from *ad valorem* duty is given when, pursuant to a scheme of reconstruction of the target company, the whole or part of its undertaking (s 75), or the whole of its issued share capital (s 77), is acquired by the acquiring company for an issue of non-redeemable shares and perhaps the assumption or discharge of liabilities. Section 76 formerly provided a partial relief for transfers of land but has no utility for share transfers since it merely restricts the duty to 0.5%. For the meaning of a scheme of reconstruction, see SP 5/85 and see also *Fallon v Fellows* (2001) and the provisions in FA 2002 putting the practice on a statutory basis.

From the day after Royal Assent to FA 2006, the statutory provision no longer requires the registered office of the acquirer to be within the UK for these reliefs. On 22 July 2005, HMRC announced that: 'Following legal advice, the Government now accepts that this requirement is defective in law. HMRC will, therefore, from the date of this announcement, and provided that all other conditions for the relief are satisfied, accept claims to relief where the registered office of the acquiring company is in any EEA State.' The condition will not be applied in future and reclaims will be made for transfers within the two years preceding the announcement, provided that other conditions were satisfied. It is assumed that EU law is the law that makes this provision defective, but neither HMRC nor the Government chose to reveal their analysis.

Section 77 enables the interposition of a holding company and s 75 provides for demergers. Other conditions for these reliefs are that, apart from the assumption of liabilities consideration must be in the form only of shares which must be issued to all shareholders of the target company only (and not to that company itself). The acquisitions must be for *bona fide* commercial reasons and not have any tax avoidance as a main purpose. After the acquisition each shareholder in the target company must hold shares in the acquirer and *vice versa* and the proportion of the shares of one company held by any shareholder must be the same as the proportion of the shares in the other company held by that same shareholder. From FA 2006 the conditions in ss 75 and 77 reliefs that the proportions must be 'the same proportion' has been softened to read 'the same proportion, or as nearly as may be the same proportion' to allow for circumstances where precise matching cannot be achieved for practical reasons. Section 77 also requires that share classes of the target match the classes of the consideration shares in the acquiring company.

Any instrument employed to convey or transfer property under any of the reconstructions requires adjudication. These arrangements normally take place pursuant to TCGA 1992 s 139 in respect of which a clearance procedure is available under s 138 (this will usually be accepted by the Stamp Office). Given these requirements, which ensure that the undertaking is held by the same shareholders before and after the acquisition, this exemption is extremely limited. A reconstruction under the Insolvency Act 1986 ss 110–111 may fall within this relief as illustrated in *Illustration 1* below:

Company 1 is liquidated and its two component trades are split with the ownership being transferred to Newco (1) and Newco (2). Those companies then issue shares to the shareholders of Company 1. This reconstruction qualifies for relief: contrast, however, the following illustration (a demerger) that does not:

In *Illustration 2* there is a similar partition but, instead of the shares in the two new companies being divided amongst all the original shareholders, the shares in A Co now pass only to the original shareholders who comprised the A family and the B Co shares to the B family.

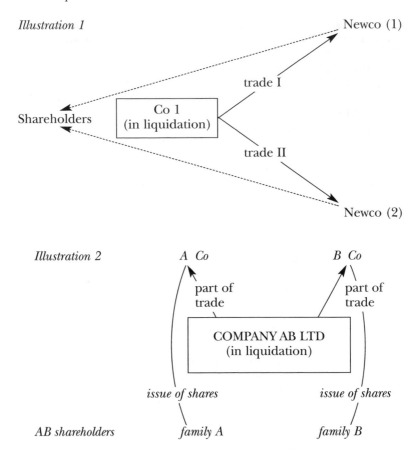

*Illustration 1*

*Illustration 2*

There are equivalents to FA 1986 ss 75 and 76 reliefs in SDLT (in FA 2003 Sch 7) relating to the transfer of land assets. There are some detailed differences, including clawback rules.   **[49.126]**

# Section 8    Pensions

**Chapters**

# 50 Pensions

*Updated by Alec Ure, Alec Ure & Associates, Pensions and Taxation Specialists*

## I INTRODUCTION

At present the taxation of pensions and pension schemes is subject to the following legislation:

| Legislation | Provision | Subject matter |
| --- | --- | --- |
| IHTA 1984 | s 5 | Lump sum death benefits |
| | s 151(2) | |
| Companies Act 1985 | s 311 | Prohibition on tax-free payments to directors |
| TA 1988 | s 189 | Lump sum benefits on retirement |
| | Part XIV ss 590–659E | Pension schemes, social security benefits, life annuities etc |
| | Sch 22 | Reduction of pension fund surpluses |
| | Sch 23 | Occupational pension schemes: schemes approved before 23 July 1987 |
| ITEPA 2003 | Part 9 ss 386–416 | Pension income (previously TA 1988 Sch E) Approved and unapproved schemes |
| FA 1989 | s 76 | Unapproved retirement benefits schemes |
| | Sch 6 | Retirement benefits schemes |
| | Sch 7 | Personal pension schemes |
| FA 1995 | s 61 | Cessation of approval of certain retirement benefits schemes |

| FA 2004 | ss 149–284 | Pension schemes |
| | ss 306–319 | Disclosure of tax avoidance schemes |
| | Schs 28–36 | Pension Schedules |
| FA 2005 | Sch 10 | Amendments to FA 2004 |
| FA 2006 | Sch 21 | Amendments to FA 2004 |
| | Sch 23 | Amendments to FA 2004 |

With effect from 6 April 2006 a new, simplified, tax regime was introduced for tax-advantaged schemes, replacing the eight regimes which had been in existence prior to that date. At the same time, the discretionary powers of Her Majesty's Revenue and Customs (HMRC, previously the Inland Revenue) were removed almost in their entirety. Nevertheless, HMRC has a continuing involvement in monitoring certain events. The changes are contained in the Finance Act 2004 as revised by the Finance Act 2005, and subsequent regulatory law. In the future all pensions rules will be contained in statutes and secondary legislation. The new rules are discussed in depth later in this chapter, together with the associated transitional protection rules which protect many accrued rights and entitlements which were in place as at A-Day.

HMRC has published a comprehensive pensions manual for the purpose of explaining the new tax regime on its website. The publication is entitled 'The Registered Pension Schemes Manual'. The tax changes have been accompanied by changes in pensions regulation under the Pensions Act 2004, in particular in connection with final salary schemes, with associated levies and transfer rules.                              **[50.1]–[50.20]**


## II   STATE PROVISION

The state pension scheme is funded by NI contributions and is split into two parts, the basic state pension and the additional pension. From April 1978 to April 2002 the additional pension was the State Earnings Related Pension Scheme (SERPS). From April 2002 SERPS was replaced by the State Second Pension (S2P).

The basic state pension is payable to all individuals who have:
(1)   reached state pension age;
(2)   made sufficient NI contributions; and
(3)   made a claim for the state retirement pension.

The state pension age for men is 65 and for women born before 6 April 1950 is 60. However, the state pension age for women will rise gradually from age 60 to age 65 over a ten-year period between 2010 and 2020. The overall effect of this change is that women who were born on or after 5 April 1955 will have a state pension age of 65. For women born between 6 April 1950 and 5 April 1955, state pension age is determined in accordance with a sliding scale as set out in PA 1995 Sch 4 which sets out the state pension age for women based on how long after 6 April 1950 they were born.

The full rate of the basic state pension for the year 2005–06 is £82.05 per week. The other main rates are:
(1)   based on a spouse's NI contributions: £49.15
(2)   non-contributory: Over-80 pension: £49.15
(3)   age addition: £0.25

The Government guaranteed in the March 2004 Budget that the basic state pension will continue to rise each April by 2.5% or the increase in the Retail Prices Index for the previous September, whichever is higher. In order to qualify for a full basic state pension a person must have been paid, or been credited with, full NI contributions for approximately 90% of his or her working life. This corresponds to 44 years for a man and between 39 and 44 years for a woman. The DWP publish a leaflet *GL23* showing pension rates from the state.

The additional pension provided by the S2P is based on an individual employee's earnings between 1978 and 2002. The S2P is discussed in more detail below. **[50.21]**

### 1 Pension Credit

From April 1999 to October 2003, individuals aged 60 or over could claim the Minimum Income Guarantee (MIG), which was paid as a means-tested income support to top up the basic state pension (see above). From October 2003, the MIG was replaced by a new two-tier pension credit system (Pension Credit) that provides a guaranteed minimum income for pensioners and a reward for those with modest savings or second pensions.

The Pensions Credit consists of:

(a) a *guaranteed credit*, which guarantees a minimum level of income to those aged 60 or over; and

(b) a *savings credit*, which provides income support to those aged 65 or over on low or modest incomes to top up the basic state pension.

Additional benefits include a winter fuel allowance for persons aged over 60 and a tax-free lump sum Christmas bonus to all state pensioners and other beneficiaries. **[50.22]**

### a) *Guaranteed credit*

This applies to people aged over 60 or whose income is below the minimum amount the Government claims is required to live on. An individual may be entitled to a guaranteed credit if his or her income is less than £109.45 if single or £167.05 for couples. (In some circumstances, for instance if the individual is severely disabled or has outstanding mortgage costs, the individual may be able to obtain more than these amounts.) When assessing guaranteed credit, the Department for Work and Pensions (DWP) looks at the individual's income, taking into account state, and any other, pensions. It will ignore income derived from various other social benefit allowance sources. **[50.23]**

### b) *Savings credit*

Income or savings (including a works or private pension, earnings and savings over £6,000) can count towards a savings credit. When working out the credit, the DWP looks at weekly income over a certain level. An individual can get 60p for each £1 of income they have over that level. The levels are £82.05 for single individuals or £131.20 for individuals with a partner. The maximum amount of savings credit is £16.44 per week or £21.51 if the individual has a partner.

Any entitlement to Pension Credit will be calculated at retirement (instead of through weekly and annual means tests) and may be adjusted if there is a significant change in circumstances.                                    **[50.24]**


## 2    State second pension (S2P) and contracting-out

The S2P, which has replaced SERPS since April 2002, raises the additional pension for low and moderate earners and provides a second pension for many carers and disabled people. SERPS ceased accruing from April 2002 but existing entitlements are protected and are payable when the claimant reaches state pension age. Contributions from 6 April 2002 are now used to build up rights to the additional pension provided by the S2P.

For the initial phase ('phase 1') the S2P operates as an earnings-related pension based on earnings between the Lower Earnings Limit (LEL) (£4,264 for 2005–06) and the Upper Earnings Limit (UEL) (£32,760 for 2005–06). There are three different rates of accrual:

(1)  *Band 1*: 40% of an employee's average revalued annual earnings between the LEL and the lower earnings threshold (LET—£12,100 for 2005–06). However, the earnings of anyone earning less than the LET will be deemed to be equal to the LET.

(2)  *Band 2*: 10% of an employee's average revalued earnings between the LET and the upper earnings threshold (UET — £27,801 for 2005–06).

(3)  *Band 3*: 20% of an employee's average revalued earnings between the UET and the UEL.

The full pension is scaled down for people without a lifetime's earnings. For individuals who reach pension age before April 2009, the Phase 1 pension will be topped up where needed to the level SERPS would have given. Rights for members of occupational pension schemes which wind up underfunded may be restored under the Occupational Pension Schemes (Contracting-out) (Amount Required for Restoring State Scheme Rights) Amendment Regulations 2005 (SI 2005/891).

People over a certain age (approximately 45) will stay in phase 1 for the rest of their working lives. For those under that age, no pension will accrue under Band 2 or 3. The S2P is now a second flat rate scheme aimed at those on lower earnings. Actual earnings govern contributions but all individuals are treated as if earnings are equal to the LET. However, actual earnings are still used for NI contribution purposes.

In general, lower paid individuals have benefited most from the change from SERPS to the S2P. Moderate earners also benefit. Individuals with earnings up to the LET accrue in the region of twice the benefits under the S2P than they would have under SERPS. As those with earnings of less than the LET are treated as if they had earnings of the LET, their benefits have increased even more. Those who gain the most are individuals who were previously excluded from SERPS but now qualify for the S2P, that is, carers and the long-term disabled.

When SERPS was originally introduced in 1978, the Government decided to allow employers to contract-out of it as long as contributions in respect of employees were paid to a suitable private arrangement. Contracting-out allows employers and employees to reduce the rate of NI contributions that they pay to make up for the additional state pension which has been given up.

If an individual is a member of a contracted-out final salary scheme, the pension they will get when they retire or otherwise leave pensionable service will be based on salary at the date they left pensionable service and the length of pensionable service they have accrued in the scheme. Before 6 April 1997, one of the conditions that final salary schemes had to satisfy to obtain a contracting-out certificate was to offer members a 'guaranteed minimum pension' (GMP) when they retired which equated to the same amount of SERPS which would have been accrued had the member not been in a contracted-out scheme. After 6 April 1997, schemes were not required to pay GMPs, but have to meet a new test of overall quality. The result of this is that contracted-out schemes must provide benefits that are broadly equivalent to, or better than, those set out in the new test.

Individuals who are members of a contracted-out money purchase scheme are given a minimum payment by their employer to their pension to satisfy the contracting-out conditions. This payment will equate to the total of both the employer and the employee's NI rebate. HMRC will also pay an annual extra age-related rebate to the individual's pension based on a percentage of the individual's earnings between the LEL and the UEL. The HMRC website is http://www.hmrc.gov.uk. **[50.25]–[50.40]**

## III   OCCUPATIONAL PENSION SCHEMES

An employer can provide pension benefits through a promise to pay a pension on retirement according to a formula or at a set rate. More commonly, the promised benefits are pre-funded (ie money is set aside and invested to meet employee claims on reaching retirement). These types of arrangements are known as occupational pension schemes.

Usually, occupational schemes are of two types—money purchase (otherwise known as defined contribution schemes) or final salary (otherwise known as defined benefit schemes). It is possible to have a hybrid arrangement providing both money purchase and final salary aspects.

An occupational pension scheme can be funded or unfunded, and it can relate to an entire workforce, a specified group of employees or an individual. It can be established and governed by a contractual promise or, more likely, by a trust deed (although a trust is not essential for any type of tax-advantaged scheme or arrangement from A-Day). Prior to A-Day only schemes established under irrevocable trusts could be granted 'exempt approved' status and benefit from various tax reliefs (TA 1988 s 592(1)). TA 1988 s 592(1) was repealed with effect from A-Day by FA 2004 s 326 and Sch 42 Part 3, with transitional provisions and savings.

Traditionally, pension benefits are pre-funded through a trust, where contributions are held for the benefit of employees and are protected from the employer's creditors. For tax purposes, prior to A-Day, schemes could be approved by HMRC or could be unapproved. Unapproved schemes have lost most, if not all, of their attraction from A-Day, and tax-advantaged schemes have been reclassified as 'registered'. As from A-Day all existing approved schemes were automatically registered unless they chose to opt out. **[50.41]**

## 1   Types of occupational pension scheme

### a)   *Final salary schemes*

In a final salary scheme (also known as a 'defined benefits scheme'), the amount of pension a member receives on retirement will depend on his remuneration at the date of his retirement. Although a minority of schemes are non-contributory, employees will usually be required to pay a proportion of their remuneration as contributions. The balance of the cost of providing the benefits is met by the employer. In a final salary scheme the financial risk lies with the employer as the exact cost of providing the benefits will not be known until the last beneficiary dies.

The maximum total benefits a member may receive on retirement are calculated by reference to the employee's length of service and his 'final remuneration'. 'Remuneration' includes pension income chargeable to tax under ITEPA 2003 Part 9 except:

(1)   sums arising from the acquisitional disposal of shares, or from a right to acquire shares; and

(2)   payments on the termination of office (eg redundancy payments and golden handshakes).

(Glossary to the Practice Notes and TA 1988 s 612.)

Prior to A-Day, an 'earnings cap', or 'permitted maximum', was imposed by TA 1988 s 590C on the level of remuneration which may be taken into account for the purposes of determining the maximum benefits payable. It increased annually in line with the retail prices index, and was rounded up to the nearest multiple of £600 (TA 1988 s 590C(5)). The earnings cap for the last year of operation 2005–06 was £105,600 (Retirement Benefits Scheme (Indexation of Earnings Cap) Order 2005 (SI 2005/720)). The earnings cap applied to all members of schemes established on or after 14 March 1989 and members of schemes established before that date who became members on or after 1 June 1989. However, it did not apply if a member moved from one pension scheme that he joined before 1989 to another scheme of the same employer, as his membership was treated as continuous (Retirement Benefits Schemes (Continuation of Rights of Members of Approved Schemes) Regulations 1990 (SI 1990/2101)). TA 1988 s 590C was repealed with effect from A-Day by FA 2004 s 326 and Sch 42 Part 3, with transitional provisions and savings.

The effect of A-Day is that those persons who previously escaped the earnings cap will find themselves restricted for the first time. This will only affect persons whose pension entitlements exceed the Lifetime Allowance, which is described later in this chapter.

Schemes which existed as at A-Day may decide to retain a cap on pensionable earnings on a voluntary basis/basis of cost. All schemes should either have already reviewed, or should consider reviewing, their existing documentation in the light of the new developments.          **[50.42]**

### b)   *Money purchase schemes*

Under a money-purchase scheme (also known as a 'defined contributions scheme') contributions are invested for the benefit of the individual. A member has a notional 'individual account' or 'pot' of money that is credited with contributions and the investment growth attributable to them. It is then used to provide retirement benefits. In contrast to a final salary scheme, no level of benefit is guaranteed, and the risk of the investment falls on the employee. When a member retires, assets equal to the value of his 'individual account' will be realised and used to purchase an annuity to provide him with income in retirement. As from A-Day schemes may formally earmark assets for their members for the first time.

The rules of a money purchase scheme will usually specify the contributions the member and the employer are required to make. The amount of pension received depends on the contributions made, the investment growth achieved and the prevailing annuity rates at retirement. It is not related to a member's earnings at or before retirement. A money purchase scheme is often more attractive to an employer as the cost of financing the scheme can be predicted with certainty and is generally lower than for final salary schemes. However, they are less attractive to employees because they carry the risk of poor investment return and poor annuity rates.

The earnings cap also applied to money purchase schemes, for the purposes of determining the maximum benefits payable. Often, the benefits provided under a money purchase scheme were insufficient to provide the maximum set by HMRC. If the funds available in a money purchase scheme were more than sufficient to provide the maximum benefits payable, then the excess, less tax, would normally have to be refunded. **[50.43]**

c)  *Small self-administered schemes*

A small self-administered scheme (SSAS) is an occupational scheme with fewer than 12 members. It provides a flexible means of providing pensions for controlling shareholders of private companies, while allowing the money in the fund to continue to work for the business by way of loans and leasebacks (this was in contrast to a more restrictive HMRC regime which applied prior to A-Day to the occupational schemes. A SSAS offers a facility for the directors of a private company to be the trustees of a pension scheme to which they belong as members. They have almost complete control over the scheme (apart from certain restrictions imposed by HMRC – prior to A-Day, these restrictions included the appointment of a professional 'pensioneer trustee'—see below).

The term 'SSAS' will, at some time in the future, become purely of historical interest. The post A-Day changes have brought all registered schemes into a single regime, subject to transitional provisions and savings. However, there are some exceptions, and these mainly concern the investment activity of small schemes. The existing investment exemptions for SSASs under the Pensions Act 1995, and certain other investment legislation, largely remain, but are mainly extended by EU investment rules which provide exemptions for schemes with fewer than 100 members. Many of the funding constraints and investment restrictions have been removed. SSASs are now regarded as 'self-directed' schemes (being schemes where the member has influence directly or indirectly over where the scheme monies are invested). This term also extends to schemes where 10% or more of the membership have such control. These matters are described in greater detail in **[50.160]** and **[50.160A]** below.

The following rules applied prior to A-Day:

(1) To obtain HMRC approval, a SSAS had to be established under an irrevocable trust, either by deed or by a company resolution. HMRC Savings, Pensions, Share Schemes Office (HMRC SPSS) announced, in Pensions Update No 103, that a definitive deed and rules must accompany all applications for approval from 6 April 2002. HMRC had the power to withdraw approval on a discretionary basis (TA 1988 s 591B(1)). Approval could be withdrawn for serious rule breaches and for failing to amend scheme documentation to incorporate regulatory changes within the set time limits. TA 1988 s 591B was repealed with effect from A-Day by FA 2004 s 326 and Sch 42 Part 3, with replacement procedures for loss of tax registration and transitional provisions and savings.

(2) Under TA 1988 s 591C(2) (repealed, as above, by FA 2004), there was a 40% charge (under Case VI of Schedule D) on the market value of the scheme's assets for CGT purposes if the scheme lost approval for any reason. If approval was withdrawn benefits became taxable, employees became liable to tax on subsequent contributions by the employers, all exemptions and reliefs ceased, and the CGT exemption was withdrawn from any capital gains realised on or after the withdrawal of approval (IR 12).

(3) A SSAS had to have a professional trustee called a pensioneer trustee (SSAS Regulations 1998 (SI 1998/728)), who exercised a general supervisory function and would oversee any winding up of the scheme. From 1 April 1998 legislation made it more difficult for pensioneer trustees to be removed or otherwise terminate their appointment. This could only be done where the pensioneer trustee died, was removed by a court or by Opra (now the Pensions Regulator) order, on withdrawal by HMRC of pensioneer trustee status, or where an immediate replacement was effected. With effect from A-Day the special status of a pensioneer trustee is no longer required by HMRC. However, the expertise of such a person in the form of an independent trustee is likely to be indispensable for some time to come. There are transitional rules that ensure that existing investments may be retained, generally if they are not varied and DWP legislation calls for independent trustees to be appointed in some circumstances.

(4) There were strict funding controls on SSASs. Checks had to be carried out on the funding status of a scheme or arrangement as at A-Day using the existing 1996 funding method. Under this method the assumptions were tied into the surplus regulations. Pensions Update No 137 introduced the latest published funding requirements for SSASs prior to A-Day and replaced Appendix IX to the Practice Notes.

(5) The trustees of SSASs normally had wide investment powers and, subject to the consent of HMRC they could employ the fund for the benefit of the company. They could purchase the business premises and lease them back to the company, provided that certain conditions were met. The rent was tax deductible for the company and tax free in the hands of the trustees. Any rent that was written off would have been treated as a refund to the employer and taxed at 35% (the trustees did not incur CGT on the property when they dispose of it). The 35% tax

charge was free-standing and remains for all schemes which make refunds to employers from A-Day. Investment in the shares of unlisted companies was restricted to shares which carried 30% or less of the voting power in the company or which entitled the holder to 30% or less of the dividends declared for that class of share.

(6) Trustees could also make loans to the company and invest in the company's shares. The facility to reinvest contributions could be very advantageous. The contributions would have received relief from corporation tax and the interest on the loan would also attract relief when the company paid it. The trustees were able to reclaim any tax deducted from interest payments where the interest was paid net of tax. Such 'self-investments' were, however, subject to conditions and to HMRC limits (SSAS Regulations 1991 and IR 12). SSAS Regulations reg 7 restricted trustees' investment in, loans to, and shares in an employer company. The term 'loan' included debentures and loan stock issued by the employer or an associated company. For the first two years of a SSAS's life, self-investment could not exceed 25% of the market value of the scheme assets derived from contributions since the date of establishment. After two years it could not exceed 50% of the market value of all the scheme assets as at the date the loan was taken out. When applying the 25% or 50% limit, there had to be excluded any portion of scheme funds which underpinned retired members', ex-spouses', widowers'/ widows' or dependants' benefits in payment where the purchase of an annuity had been deferred.

(7) A loan had to be evidenced by written agreement, repayable (if, for example, the borrower is in breach or is insolvent) and for a fixed term. From 10 October 2002 a company was no longer required to deduct tax from interest under TA 1988 s 349 where, at the time interest was paid, the company reasonably believed that the payment was to be made to the administrator of an approved pension scheme. There was therefore no requirement for the borrowing company to deduct tax from interest paid on or after 1 October 2002 in respect of a loan made by a SSAS, regardless of when the loan was made.

(8) Pensions Update No 143 required the administrator to notify HMRC SPSS of any loan defaults. This had to be done within 90 days of the date of the default and a further notification had to be sent within the following 90 days explaining the steps which were being taken by the trustees to recover the debt. Penalties and/or possible withdrawal of approval could follow a failure to pursue an outstanding loan debt.

**[50.44]**

d) *Funded unapproved schemes—FURBS*

FURBS did not fall under the new tax regime from A-Day, unless they registered to do so. From that date, non-registered funded schemes are designated employer-financed retirement benefits schemes ('EFRBS'). EFRBS are described in **[50.160H]** below. The status of existing unapproved schemes prior to A-Day remains important in relation to the benefit entitlements which accrued prior to that date. In general, these entitlements are protected, subject to post A-Day indexation. In addition to FA 2004 ss 245 to 249 and Sch 36, the Employer-Financed Retirement Benefits (Excluded

Benefits for Tax Purposes) Regulations 2006 (SI 2006/210) and the Employer-Financed Retirement Benefits Schemes (Provision of Information) Regulations 2005 (SI 2005/3453) make the relevant changes.

Prior to A-Day, the following rules applied:

(1) The FA 1989 provided that only benefits granted under approved schemes had to be aggregated in calculating whether the benefit limits including the earnings cap had been reached. To compensate employees who were subject to the earnings cap many employers chose to provide unapproved 'top-up' schemes for executives and high earners. As the earnings cap is increased annually in line with the retail price index (rather than salary increases which have tended to be higher) more individuals became subject to the earnings cap. Unapproved schemes could be funded or unfunded.

(2) In a funded unapproved retirements benefits scheme (FURBS), contributions were paid and accumulated, usually within a trust, until the benefits became payable. The scheme assets, therefore, accumulated separately from the control of the company or its creditors. If the arrangement was correctly structured the investment growth of a FURBS was taxed at the basic rate of income tax. However, income tax on the fund was increased from 22% to 40% from 6 April 2004. FURBS could, until that time, be attractive to a large employer paying corporation tax at the standard rate.

(3) For most investment gains, capital gains tax was chargeable at the rate applicable to trusts (RAT). The rate increased from 34% to 40% on 6 April 2004, although HMRC stated , for RATS generally, the basic rate of tax would apply on the first £500 from 6 April 2005. This was expected to remove one-third of trusts from the RAT. Tax returns were only likely to be issued every five years in such cases, although taxable income had to be declared if it arose.

(4) An employee was liable for income tax on the contributions paid by his employer in respect of him (ITEPA 2003 s 386(1)) so the employee was taxed when the employer made a payment to a scheme, even though the employee had not yet received any cash (separate contributions for the establishment and running costs of the scheme were not taxed). If a pension was paid it was also taxable in the hands of the employee even though the contributions had already been taxed (s 393(2)). Conversely, lump sums were tax-free, meaning that FURBS invariably paid out, and will continue to pay out, their benefits in lump sum form.

(5) Contributions made to a FURBS by a company were deductible for corporation tax purposes under TA 1988 s 74, if the expenditure could be classified as an income expense. It was inadvisable for an employee to make contributions to a FURBS. *First*, as there was no tax relief, it would be better for an employee to make voluntary contributions to an approved scheme. *Secondly*, an employee's contributions could be regarded as providing funds for the purpose of a settlement. The income of the FURBS could then be treated as the employee's income and taxed at his highest marginal rate (TA 1988 s 660A).

(6) An employer could decide to meet the employee's tax liability on contributions paid by the employer by 'grossing-up' the contributions. This would usually result in additional salary being paid, on which the

employer would have to pay NI contributions. The grossed-up equivalent of the chargeable contribution and the tax figure was included on the employee's pay record. Grossing-up was not possible for directors as it is unlawful for a company to pay a director remuneration that varies with the amount of his income tax (Companies Act 1985 s 311), but it could have been possible to gross-up indirectly by means of a discretionary bonus.

(7) For schemes entered into on or after 1 December 1993, lump sums paid from FURBS were liable to tax if any of the scheme's income or gains had not been brought into the tax charge (ITEPA 2003 s 395(3)–(4)). The 40% tax payable under s 511C where approval was withdrawn from certain approved schemes was not viewed as a charge on the scheme's income and gains, and so tax under ITEPA 2003 s 394 was also payable (*Tax Bulletin*, August 1995). The lump sum was taxed subject to a deduction for any sums on which the employer had been taxed under ITEPA 2003 s 386(1)–(4) and any employee contributions that were paid to provide the lump sum.

As stated above, unapproved schemes lost most of their attraction after A-Day under the new tax regime. Existing FURBS may enjoy the protection of a tax-free lump sum element, but only inclusive of indexation not fund yield, on values up to A-Day where such payments have qualified for relief either by virtue of the taxation of employer contributions on the member or the taxation of all income and gains under the fund. The normal inheritance tax exemptions for discretionary distributions apply to pre A-Day assets in FURBS, but not post A-Day accrual, and future accrual will attract full tax charges on the rate applicable to trusts.  **[50.45]**

### e) *Unfunded unapproved schemes—UURBS*

In an unfunded unapproved retirement benefit scheme (UURBS) no provision was made for benefits until they became payable. The benefits were usually paid directly from the employer on a 'pay as you go' basis. As there was no separation of assets an UURBS could be established by a bare contractual promise in the employment contract, although a greater degree of flexibility could be retained by using separate documentation.

The taxation position of an UURBS was more straightforward than that of a FURBS. The only tax consequences arose, under TA 1988 s 595, when benefits were paid out. Payment could simply be reduced to take account of the tax charge. For an employee, all benefits were chargeable in full to income tax. The employer qualified for a deduction in respect of the benefit payments as a business expense. The result was a tax regime similar to that of a FURBS; the only difference is that there was no tax-free lump sum.

The employee's pension was taxed as pension income at his highest marginal rate under ITEPA 2003 Part 9. ITEPA 2003 ss 393–394 also imposed a specific charge designed to catch lump sums and other benefits provided through UURBS that might otherwise escape income tax. If the lump sum was not paid to an individual, the administrator of the scheme would be liable to tax under Case VI of Schedule D at 40% (ITEPA 2003 s 394(2) and (4)). Authority for deducting this tax from the benefit payment had to be included in the governing documentation. The tax liability could not be mitigated by directly purchasing an annuity payable to the individual as TA 1988 s 657(2)(d) prevented such favourable treatment.

Payments made to an employee under an UURBS were deductible for corporation tax purposes under TA 1988 s 74, as long as the payment was not excessive in relation to the employee's service. FA 1989 s 76 did not prevent a deduction as the benefits were taxable in the hands of the employee (s 76(2)(b)). No deduction was allowed for book reserves, therefore, the corporation tax deduction could only be claimed when the benefits are paid.

If an UURBS was used to provide death benefits, which was likely to be calculated as a multiple of earnings, no inheritance tax would be payable if the recipient was determined at the discretion of a third party, such as the employer or the trustees. This was because the payment would not form part of the employee's estate (IHTA 1984 s 5). The employee's estate had to be excluded from the class of potential beneficiaries for the avoidance of doubt. There would, however, probably be liability for income tax. The exemption contained in ITEPA 2003 s 396(1) did not apply, unless the lump sum benefit was insured, as the employee would not have paid sums that were assessable to tax to provide the benefit. If the death benefits were insured, the UURBS was treated as if it were funded and income tax would have been payable on the insurance premiums. Income tax would not then be payable on receipt of the death benefit.

UURBS do not fall under the new tax regime from A-Day, unless they register to do so by 7 July 2006. There are transitional protections for promises made under UURBS prior to that date. In general, such arrangements are not tax-attractive from A-Day, although they are seen by some employers as an alternative to FURBS or cash.                                    **[50.46]**

f)   *Secured unfunded unapproved schemes—SUURBS*

SUURBS (secured unfunded unapproved retirement benefit schemes) were developed in an attempt to counter the problem of purely unfunded schemes not having assets to provide the benefits promised by the employer. In accordance with this promise, a reserve was accumulated in the balance sheet. Simultaneously, the company would buy assets that it secured by way of a charge with payment of the benefits. As long as the payment of the benefits was intended to come from company resources rather than the charged assets, purchase of the assets was not treated as funding. It is still possible to back a benefit (where appropriate) after A-Day by an asset or security but the member must pay a benefit-in-kind tax charge on the cost to the employer of providing security and or underwriting.                                    **[50.47]**

## 2   HMRC approval of occupational pension schemes pre A-Day

Most occupational pension schemes were approved by the HMRC SPSS. HMRC approved schemes benefited from certain tax reliefs for the employer, the members, the employees and the scheme under TA 1988. A scheme was approved if it complied with the conditions set out in TA 1988 s 590.

The alternative mandatory approval was rare in practice but it had to be given if the following conditions were met by the scheme:
(1)   normal pension age was between 60 and 75;

(2)   pensions accumulated at a rate of no more than 1/60th of final pensionable salary for each year up to a maximum of 40 years;
(3)   widow/er's pensions were limited to two-thirds of a member's pension; and
(4)   any commutation of pension was on the basic scale of 3/80ths of final remuneration for each year of service up to a maximum of 40 years.

No additional benefits could be provided under s 590 so many schemes sought discretionary approval under TA 1988 s 591. Discretionary approval was normally granted by the HMRC SPSS if the requirements set out in HMRC's Practice Notes IR 12 (2001) were satisfied. Many of these related to the maximum benefits that could be paid but there were also limits on the contributions that members could make. TA 1988 s 591(2) stated that HMRC could approve a scheme that provided 'relevant benefits', defined by s 612 as retirement and related benefits, within certain parameters.

To obtain all the available tax advantages, a scheme could also have been 'exempt approved' under TA 1988 s 592. Any schemes approved under s 590 or s 591 can be granted exempt approved status. The scheme had to be established under an irrevocable trust, to the satisfaction of HMRC, or be a scheme which HMRC directed should be treated as an exempt approved scheme (TA 1988 s 592(1)). Until formal approval was granted no relief could be given under s 592(4) on the employer's contributions.

HMRC required employer contributions to be made before it would grant approval, although it could waive this requirement if there was a statutory surplus in the scheme (ie if assets exceed liabilities by more than 5%) and an employer's contribution holiday had been authorised in order to reduce the level of the surplus, where the scheme was being operated as a closed scheme to which no contributions were being made, or where the scheme was being wound up. There was no fixed upper limit on an employer's contributions to an occupational scheme. Employer contributions were not taxed as emoluments of the employee and they were deductible in arriving at the profits of the employer. They, therefore, could prove more attractive than paying a higher rate or bonus, because they were not subject to Nl.

Pension schemes had to keep any surplus of assets over liabilities within a prescribed limit, to prevent funds that were not needed to provide benefits being rolled up tax free in an approved pension scheme and then returned to an employer when he had sufficient losses to avoid paying tax on the refund. If the limit was exceeded, the surplus had to be reduced by improving benefits, by giving contribution holidays to employers and/or employees, or by refund to the employer or tax advantages on the surplus funds would be lost (see **[50.103]** below). TA 1988, regulations and HMRC discretionary practice included provisions to prevent overfunding and for the elimination of surpluses. Any refunds were subject to a 35% tax charge deducted at source (TA 1988 s 601) whatever the tax position of the employer (even if the employer had trading losses).

If the benefits to be provided by a scheme already equalled the HMRC limits set out in IR 12, an employee had to cease making additional voluntary contributions (AVCs). Excess voluntary contributions would be refunded. Tax at 32% was deducted from the refund (Income Tax (Charge to Tax) (Payments Out of Surplus Funds) (Relevant Rates) Order 2000 (SI 2000/600)). This satisfied the employee's basic rate liability on the refund. The extra 10% reflected the benefit received from the contributions having grown tax-free when it was in the fund. Higher rate taxpayers had to pay tax at their marginal rate on the amount of the repayment after deduction of tax at 35% (TA 1988 s 599A). If an employee's contributions were refunded, s 598 imposed a 10% tax charge on the administrator of the scheme.

TA 1988 ss 590–591, 598 and 601 were repealed with effect from A-Day by FA 2004 s 326 and Sch 42 Part 3, with transitional provisions and savings. TA 1988 ss 599A was revised with effect from 2003–04 by ITEPA 2003 ss 722–724.

[**50.48**]

a)    *Consequences of withdrawal of approval and reporting transfer payments pre A-Day*

HMRC could withdraw either full or partial approval of a scheme if it considered that it was no longer warranted (TA 1988 s 591B(1)). This could have been due to overfunding or the use of the scheme for tax avoidance. Approval would also lapse automatically where the scheme made an unapprovable alteration (TA 1988 s 591B(2)) or failed to comply with the regulations made under that section within a period of three years. No scheme should have faced loss of approval as long as the trustees acted in accordance with the scheme's trust deed and rules and their statutory obligations.

The consequences of withdrawal of approval were as follows:
(1)    all benefits payable from the scheme on or after 27 July 1989 became chargeable to tax under s 591A except to the extent that they were chargeable under ITEPA 2003 Part 9 or TA 1988 s 58;
(2)    employees became liable to tax under ITEPA 2003 s 386 in respect of any subsequent contributions by employers;
(3)    all exemptions and relief flowing from the exempt approval were forfeited;
(4)    exemption from CGT under TCGA 1992 s 27(1)(g) was not available on any capital gains realised by the scheme on or after the date of withdrawal of approval;
(5)    taxation continued to be chargeable:
    (a)    under s 598 on repayment to employees of contributions paid before the scheme ceased to be exempt approved;
    (b)    under s 601 on repayments to an employer out of funds held at any time for the purposes of the scheme;
    (c)    under s 599A on repayments of surplus of funds arising from the payment of AVCs; and
    (d)    under s 600 on payments made between 26 July 1989 and the withdrawal of approval not expressly authorised by the rules of the scheme.

The Finance Act 2004 introduced many changes from A-Day on the matter of withdrawal of registration status and penalties, charges and sanctions.

HMRC worked closely with Opra, later the Pensions Regulator, to prevent similar arrangements to the *Roux* case, which is described below, from operating in future. With effect from A-Day, under FA 2004, unauthorised payments charges apply to such cases. Prior to that date, the main HMRC guidelines on 'trust-busting' were in Pensions Update 132 (May 2002), and the Pensions Regulator website contained (and still contains) updates and guidelines on unacceptable forms of 'pensions liberation'. In addition, the following were issued:

(1) Update 150—Pre-A-day avoidance: where HMRC came across a scheme that was trying to circumvent the boundaries of discretionary approval, it would consider whether this affected the approval of the pension scheme concerned.

(2) The Occupational and Personal Pension Schemes (Pension Liberation) Regulations 2005 (SI 2005/992)

The Retirement Benefits Schemes (Information Powers) Regulations 1995 (SI 1995/3103) were amended with effect from 6 April 2003 by the Retirement Benefits Schemes (Information Powers) (Amendment) Regulations 2003 (SI 2003/3006) so that there was no longer a requirement to receive the prior consent of HMRC to transfers-out, with the exception of schemes not yet approved and most overseas transfers. However, aggregate transfers in a year of £250,000 had to be reported to HMRC within 28 days of the transfer on form PS7050.

The post A-Day rules are described in **[50.160I]** and **[50.160K]** below.

**[50.49]**

b)  *R v IRC, ex p Roux Waterside Inn (1997)*

This is an important tax avoidance case which is often quoted, and a summary of the main issues is given below. Under the post A-Day regime the events which give rise to unauthorised payment charges, and other sanctions, are contained in statute and the charges on such unacceptable activities are automatically incurred.

The circumstances of the case were:

(1)  A trustee of an exempt approved pension scheme, of which he and his wife were the only members, made a transfer payment into a new scheme that the Inland Revenue, as it was then known, had indicated it would approve.

(2)  On the same day non-resident trustees were substituted for the trustees of the new scheme so that it could not obtain tax approval.

(3)  This resulted in a 40% tax charge on the new scheme's assets as at the day before approval was lost. This was also the day before the transfer payment, which meant that it was not caught.

(4)  The Inland Revenue subsequently withdrew approval from the transferring scheme with effect from the day before the transfer payment, so that there was a charge to tax of 40% on the transferring scheme's assets before the date of the transfer.

(5)  The High Court dismissed the trustee's application for judicial review. It held that the Inland Revenue was entitled to withdraw approval where the transfer was not permitted under the Practice Notes and was entitled to look at the purpose for which the scheme was being used. This was a pre-planned tax avoidance scheme and the withdrawal of tax approval was held to be justified whether or not the tax avoidance scheme in fact worked.

In connection with the withdrawal of approval it should be borne in mind that, apart from income tax and CGT, pension schemes may incur other tax liabilities. These may include stamp duty, stamp duty reserve tax or stamp duty land tax on some transactions and, as schemes incur professional fees, the proper treatment of VAT charges may be of considerable importance. The matter of withdrawal of registration under the post A-Day regime is described in **[50.160L]** below.                                                     **[50.50]**

### 3   Employee tax relief – pre A-Day rules

The pre A-Day rules are described below:

(1)   In occupational schemes that were exempt-approved any contribution paid under the scheme by an employee could be deducted as an expense from taxable income, subject to a limit of 15% of his remuneration up to the earnings cap for post-1989 joiners (TA 1988 s 592(7)–(8)). It should be noted that cerd anything which was chargeable to tax as employment income and which arose from the acquisition or disposal of shares (or from an interest in shares or a right to acquire shares), or anything in respect of which tax was chargeable on payments or benefits on termination of employment.

(2)   In an unapproved scheme employee contributions were not deductible from the employee's taxable income. In practice most unapproved schemes were non-contributory, particularly those established before 1 December 1993 and which had not been varied to fall within FA 1994 s 108(6). Where ITEPA 2003 s 394 applied, if the employer wished to act as agent in the collection of employee contributions, they had to be collected out of after-tax income.

(3)   At their normal retirement date, members were also allowed to commute some or all of their pension for a tax-free cash lump sum (IR12 (2001) Part 8). The lump sum could be no more than 3/80ths of final remuneration for each year of service up to a maximum of 40 years. This provided a lump sum of one and a half times final remuneration to be paid after 40 years of service.

(4)   Members' contributions to personal pension schemes were subject to HMRC limits as summarised in **[50.101]**. They were treated as if they are paid net of basic rate income tax (from 6 April 2001). The member deducted tax at the basic rate and retained this amount. The administrator reclaimed tax from HMRC (s 639). This applied to employees, the self-employed and minors whether they were non-taxpayers, basic rate taxpayers or higher rate taxpayers.

FA 2004 introduced far-reaching changes from A-Day on the matter of contributions and tax relief, giving scope for far higher contributions to be made by many. These matters are described in greater detail in **[50.142]** and **[50.144]** below.                                                     **[50.51]**

Venables v Hornby (2003)

With the introduction from A-Day of the ability for most schemes, rules permitting, to pay benefits while remaining in service, the decision of the House of Lords in *Venables v Hornby* (2003) is of diminishing importance. Nevertheless, the decision raised the importance of the meaning of the term 'retirement', and the facts of the case are summarised briefly below:

(1)   Historically, the Inland Revenue (HMRC) had allowed early retirement benefits to be taken, provided that the role of the individual has changed significantly.

(2)   In this case, Venables was a member of a final salary scheme which contained a provision enabling the trustees, with the consent of the founder, to award an immediate pension to a member who '*retires in normal health at or after age 50*'. 'Retirement' was not otherwise defined in the documentation.

(3)   Venables retired as a non-executive director of the sponsoring company, taking benefits, but continued to act as an unpaid non-executive director. The Inland Revenue considered that the lump sum payment to Mr Venables was taxable.

The matter eventually went to the Court of Appeal, on appeal from the Revenue Commissioners who had taken the view that the wording of the scheme had to be construed in conjunction with the relevant legislation (the Taxes Act 1970, the provisions of which were then contained in TA 1988) to understand the meaning of 'retire' in the legislation and thus by reference to the scheme.

The Court of Appeal held that in the context of the legislative provisions, 'retirement' means cessation of service as an employee of the employer in question and that 'retire' must be construed accordingly. It also concluded that there can be a situation whereby a scheme can define employment in a different manner, for example to confine service with the employer in question to service in a particular role. In such a case, service would cease on termination of a particular role, notwithstanding that the employee stayed on with the employer in a different role. However, it did not consider that to be the case in connection with this case, and concluded that the payments made to Venables were not authorised by the scheme rules, that Venables had not retired and accordingly that the tax-free lump sum would be taxable.

A subsequent House of Lords decision overturned the Court of Appeal decision. It was held (albeit by a 4 to 1 majority) that payments made to Venables out of funds held for the purposes of the scheme were not unauthorised and were not therefore assessable to income tax. The reasoning was that, strictly speaking, the question turned on the meaning of '*retire*' in the trust deed and not in the legislation (but that in Venables' case there was no material difference). The House held that:

(1)   The reasoning of the Court of Appeal was accepted up to the point that service as an employee of the company must include service as a director of the company. However, it did not follow from this that an employee who was also a director had to retire from **both** his employment and his office as director before he could be said to retire within the meaning of the trust deed. It was stated that the Court of Appeal had wrongly interpreted the effect of the definition of the word 'employee'.

(2)   The best way of dealing with the word 'employee' wherever it appeared in the trust documentation was to substitute it for the words 'whether as employee or director'. This allowed the member to retire from either and receive the benefits attributable to the position from which he had retired. It followed that to 'retire' meant to retire from the service of the company whether as an employee or director.

(3)    As the scheme was final salary, benefits under it were linked to final remuneration. As Venables was unpaid in his position as non-executive director this could not be counted as pensionable service. The House of Lords went further to say that even if he had been in receipt of director's fees, this would have made no difference, as he would have still retired from his pensionable occupation as an employee. In this situation, all that would happen would be that his benefit would be calculated without reference to his fees as a director.

(4)    At first instance, the Commissioner was entitled to find that Venables was both a paid employee and an unpaid director of the company. It was satisfied that, on a true construction of the trust deed, Venables retired from service as an employee on that date even though he had continued to be an unpaid non-executive director thereafter.

**[50.52]–[50.70]**

## IV   PERSONAL PENSIONS

### 1   Applicable tax regime

Personal pension schemes are a type of pension scheme that a person may join privately, to save for an income in retirement to supplement their state pension. Prior to A-Day, personal pension schemes were approved by HMRC and received tax advantages. From 6 April 2001 an individual did not have to be working to join or pay into a personal pension scheme. With effect from A-Day all personal pension schemes fall under the new tax regime.

The following types of personal pension scheme exist:

(1)    *individual personal pension schemes*: introduced to allow individuals who did not have access to company sponsored group schemes, or who wanted to opt out of such schemes, to build up their own pension entitlement.

(2)    *group personal pensions* (*GPPs*): an employer may arrange through a pension provider a personal pension scheme for each employee, collectively known as a group personal pension scheme. These are not classed as employers' occupational pension schemes for which there are different tax, benefits and contribution rules;

(3)    *stakeholder pension schemes*: stakeholder pension schemes became available from 6 April 2001. Such schemes must meet strict standards set by the government, eg on costs, flexibility, and the way the scheme is run. For tax purposes a stakeholder pension receives exactly the same treatment as a personal pension scheme. Most employers with five or more employees must offer access to a stakeholder pension scheme, unless they already offer a suitable alternative pension scheme. There is no requirement for an employer to contribute to a stakeholder scheme. From A-Day all schemes fall under the single tax regime. Prior to A-Day contributions could be made up to £3,600 irrespective of the member's earnings (ie even if he has no earnings). The limit referred to total contributions plus tax relief recovered by the pension provider on the contributions but it excluded any contracted-out rebate. Contributions to stakeholder schemes above the earnings threshold were earnings-related and, once evidence of one year's earnings had been submitted,

this level of contributions could be allowed for the following five years. Higher contributions were subject to the pre A-Day limits of personal pensions. To a certain extent the contributions were also divorced from earnings as they could continue for up to five years after earnings had ceased. All contributions were paid net of basic rate tax (with personal pensions, the self-employed paid gross). The pension provider reclaimed the tax from HMRC. Higher rate taxpayers received relief through their self-assessment return;

(4) *appropriate personal schemes and appropriate personal pensions stakeholder pension schemes*: as well as the basic state pension, employees can get an additional pension from the state through the S2P, which is earnings-related. Since April 1987 employees have been able to use a personal pension scheme (or, from April 2001, a stakeholder pension scheme) to contract out of SERPS or the S2P. This means that part of their NI contributions goes into their personal or stakeholder pension scheme that will then provide a replacement for SERPS or the S2P. Schemes that are authorised to do this are called appropriate personal pension schemes or appropriate personal pension stakeholder pension schemes.

(5) *other features of stakeholder schemes:* stakeholder pensions have a maximum Charges, Access, Terms (CAT) standard charge of 1% Annual Management Charge (AMC), which has increased for new schemes from 6 April 2005 to 1.5%. Savings are required to move to less volatile investments five years before retirement, subject to a voluntary opt-out, a form of investment known as 'lifestyling'. The Stakeholder Pension Schemes (Amendment) Regulations 2005 (SI 2005/577) came into force on 6 April 2005 and amended SI 2000/1403. Market Value Adjustments (MVAs) may be made from stakeholder pensions.

The procedures for applications for tax-registration and registration with the Pensions Regulator are laid down on the Pension Regulator's website.

**[50.71]**

## 2 Tax approval pre A-Day

The following tax incentives were available in relation to personal pensions (and remain under the new tax regime, which is described in **[50.141]**–**[50.160L]** below):

(1) individuals obtained tax relief on payments made to a personal pension scheme;

(2) individuals were not taxed on any contributions their employer made to the scheme;

(3) an employer received tax relief on contributions made to the scheme;

(4) the scheme itself paid no tax on the income and gains it made while investing the funds on the individuals' behalf;

(5) some of the individuals' benefits could be taken from the scheme free of income tax in the form of a lump sum.

The main legislation relating to the approval of personal pension schemes was contained in TA 1988 Part XIV Chapter IV. Schemes had to operate in accordance with the guidance laid down by HMRC in the Personal Pension Schemes Guidance Notes (IR 76 (2000). The tax treatment of a personal pension scheme was governed by TA 1988 Part XIV Chapter IV and IR 76.

Personal pension schemes are money purchase contracts, the accumulated savings from which are used to buy an annuity from a life insurance company. The eventual pension is not linked to the individual's earnings but depends on contributions, investment growth and prevailing annuity rates of retirement.

Maximum contributions were calculated by reference to a percentage of the individual's 'net relevant earnings' (defined in TA 1988 s 644) depending on the taxpayer's age. They were as follows:

| Age | Maximum contribution |
|---|---|
| 16–35 | 17.5% |
| 36–45 | 20% |
| 46–50 | 25% |
| 51–55 | 30% |
| 56–60 | 35% |
| 61 and over | 40% |

(TA 1988 ss 638(5) and 640(2)).

Approved personal pension schemes were exempt from tax on the income from investments, other than UK dividends, or deposits held for the purposes of the schemes (s 643(2)) and from CGT on the gains arising from the disposal of investments (TCGA 1992 s 271(1)(h)).

At the date on which the benefits are paid, the 'pension date', the member had to elect to:

(a) purchase an annuity;

(b) defer purchasing an annuity under s 634 until age 75 and take income withdrawals—the amount withdrawn had to be between 35% and 100% of the amount of the annuity which could have been purchased;

(c) purchase an annuity with part of the assets and continue to take income withdrawals from the residual fund;

(d) take benefits from part of the arrangement's assets and continue to take income withdrawals; or

(e) take part of the benefits as a tax-free lump sum—this could not exceed 25% of the difference between the value of the fund when the benefits were commuted and the value of the protected rights (s 635). If the personal pension scheme was established before 27 July 1989 the member could elect to commute 25% of the total value of the fund that had accumulated to provide benefits for the member.

An annuity paid under a personal pension scheme was chargeable to income tax as pension income under ITEPA 2003 Part 9 and collected through PAYE (TA 1988 s 648A). There was no general exemption from income tax where the annuitant was resident abroad, although an exemption could be available under a double taxation treaty or on application to HMRC under s 278. From 6 April 2001 an individual earning less than £30,000 pa could contribute to a stakeholder pension scheme even if they were already a member of an occupational scheme. This was known as concurrency. (Concurrent membership is available from A-Day in respect of all registered schemes, whatever their nature).

From 6 April 2001, all member contributions were treated as amounts paid net of basic rate tax, whether an individual was employed, self-employed or not employed at all. The pension scheme administrator then claimed tax relief at basic rate from HMRC on the individual's behalf and added it to the fund. Higher rate taxpayers could claim the balance of tax relief due from HMRC by completing the relevant section on their self-assessment income tax return.

On top of the tax relief that individuals were given on contributions, pension funds were exempt from tax on the profits and gains from the investments made with the contributions selected by the individual. Some benefits paid by the scheme may also be free of income tax. If an individual chose to take up to 25% of the fund as a lump sum, he also had to buy an annuity or take income withdrawals at the same time. The part of the fund built up from NI contributions whilst contracted out of SERPS, or the S2P, (known as protected rights) could not be taken into account, because protected rights could only be used to provide pension benefits, not lump sums. Further a lump sum entitlement could be restricted if any part of the fund was transferred in from an occupational pension scheme and the individual was in a category that needed a lump sum certificate (ie controlling directors and high earners). There have been certain relaxations on the payment of contracted-out rights. The latest developments are:

(1) The Social Security (Deferral of Retirement Pensions) Regulations 2005 (SI 2005/453) allow contracted-out benefits to be paid as part of a cash lump sum. They remove some of the restrictions on when and how contracted-out benefits can be paid.

(2) The Protected Rights (Transfer Payment) (Amendment) Regulations 2005 (SI 2005/2906) permit transfers out from money purchase schemes to apply to deferred members in certain circumstances, such as an untraceable member.

(3) The Contracting-out, Protected Rights and Safeguarded Rights (Transfer Payment) Amendment Regulations 2005 (SI 2005/555) remove the requirement that trustees must satisfy themselves that a member has permanently emigrated before making a transfer of contracted-out or safeguarded rights to an overseas scheme from 6 April 2005.

(4) The Occupational and Personal Pension Schemes (Miscellaneous Amendments) Regulations 2006 (SI 2006/778) bring in associated regulatory changes to other regulations and other relevant changes to practice.

(5) The Contracting-out, Protected Rights and Safeguarded Rights (Transfer Payment) Amendment Regulations 2005 (SI 2005/555) remove the permanent emigration requirement in relation to transfer payments to overseas schemes or arrangements in respect of guaranteed minimum pensions, protected rights and safeguarded rights. They also bring the detailed provisions applying to different types of contracted-out and safeguarded rights into line with one another.

FA 2004 contains provisions for great flexibility in the membership and benefit design of pension schemes and arrangements after A-Day. There is greater access to monies, including whilst remaining in service, and for levels of contributions and benefits that may be paid. **[50.72]**

### 3   Carry-back and carry-forward relief

If the amount of the individual's contribution is less than the allowable maximum, the unused relief could be carried back if the contribution was paid between 6 April and 31 January and the election to carry back was made at or before the time of payment (IR 76, Part 6B). Contributions paid on or after 6 April 2001 and carried back were to be paid net of basic rate tax, even if the member was self-employed. Employers' contributions could not be carried back. The carry-forward facility was discontinued from 6 April 2001. From 31 January 2002 carry-forward and carry-back relief could no longer be combined.

Under the old regime any unused relief could be carried forward for up to six years, set against earlier years before later years. Members could elect to have a contribution, or part of it, treated as if it was paid in the previous tax year, or the tax year before that, if there were no relevant earnings in the previous year. Employer contributions could not however be carried back. An election to carry back had to be made within the first three months of the tax year in which the contributions were in fact paid. Carry-back and carry-forward relief could be combined up to 31 January 2002. This meant that any amount carried back could exceed the percentage limit of net relevant earnings for the previous year. The tax relief due was calculated by reference to the basic rate in force in the tax year to which the payment was carried back rather than the tax year in which it was actually paid.

For the transitional period from 6 April 2001 to 31 January 2002 the two reliefs could be combined where the member paid a contribution before 31 January 2002 and elected to carry it back to the tax year 2000–01 and still had some unused relief available from the preceding six tax years. A worked example is provided by IR 76, Part 6B.

FA 2004 contains provisions for great flexibility in the level of tax relievable contributions after A-Day, making the carry-back facility unnecessary. Under FA 2004 Sch 36 Part 4 para 39, any elections for a carry-back of contributions by retirement annuities must be made by 31 January 2007. PAYE will apply to retirement annuities from 6 April 2007.                          **[50.73]**

### 4   Self-Invested Personal Pensions (SIPPs)

SIPPs are personal pension plans that offer the member the opportunity to select where his contributions are invested (subject to certain limitations). SIPPs are available to both the employed and the self-employed and offer a wide range of investment opportunities. SIPPs became increasingly popular following the introduction of 'income drawdown' in FA 1995. This meant that income can be paid from the SIPP on retirement rather than purchasing an annuity. Again, as with other personal pensions, the earnings cap applied.

All contributions paid to a SIPP were paid net of basic rate tax. The basic rate tax was then reclaimed from HMRC.

There was a wide range of available investments for a SIPP including:
(1)   stocks and shares in the UK and overseas;
(2)   unit trusts, investment trusts and OEICs;
(3)   insurance company funds;
(4)   deposit accounts; and
(5)   commercial property.

It was also possible for SIPP holders to pool together their assets and jointly purchase a property for commercial use. The tax regime that came into force on 6 April 2001 following the introduction of stakeholder pensions introduced changes relating to funding and created differences with other approved pension schemes and personal pensions prior to 6 April 2001. This included the ability to carry forward and carry back unused tax relief for up to six years.

Most of the existing investment restrictions, such as residential property, were removed by FA 2004, subject to the requirements of the DWP and any EU constraints. Reliance will mainly be placed on the prudence of, and compliance with, the statutory duties of trustees or administrators as the determining factor on new investments. All investments, including loans to third parties, must be on commercial terms and not remove value from the fund. However, like SSASs, SIPPS are now regarded as 'self-directed' schemes (being schemes where the member has influence directly or indirectly over where the scheme monies are invested). There are special restrictions on the activities of such schemes, which have been unexpected and unwelcomed. These matters are described in greater detail in **[50.160]** below. **[50.74]**

## 5 HMRC providers of personal pension scheme, and model rules, pre A-Day

A personal pension scheme would only be approved by HMRC if it was established by a permitted provider. Under TA 1988 s 632 they were:

(1) a person who had permission under the Financial Services and Markets Act 2000 (FSMA 2000) Part IV to effect or carry out a long-term insurance contract or to manage authorised unit trust schemes;

(2) an EEA firm which had permission under FSMA 2000 Sch 3 to effect or carry out a long-term insurance contract or permission under FSMA 2000 Sch 4 to manage authorised unit trust schemes;

(3) a person who was authorised to operate a collective investment scheme under FSMA 2000 Sch 5;

(4) a building society (as defined in the Building Societies Act 1986 (BSA));

(5) a bank (as defined by TA 1988 s 840A(1)(b)); or

(6) a corporate body which was a subsidiary or holding company of a bank as defined.

HMRC also had discretion to approve a personal pension scheme established by another provider if the scheme is established under a trust. The post A-Day permitted providers of registered schemes are described in **[50.160F]** below.

HMRC produced model rules for personal pension scheme approval (IMR 2003), which covered tax approval, contracting-out and stakeholder status. There were separate model rules for basic personal pension provision (IMR 2003PP), contracting-out (IMR 2003CO) and stakeholder status (IMR 2003SHP). While the models were not compulsory, they were designed to speed up approval and registration. **[50.75]–[50.100]**

## V   PRE A-DAY HMRC RESTRICTIONS

### 1   **HMRC pre A-Day limits**

The HMRC limits represented the maximum benefits that could be provided on retirement, leaving service or on death. There was no requirement for schemes to provide benefits at that level, and lower benefits were often targeted. An overriding limits rule facilitated the granting of exempt approval and ensured that limits were not exceeded. The limits prevailed over any conflicting provisions in a scheme's governing documentation. They disappeared from A-Day under the tax simplification legislation, subject to transitional arrangements and protection.

Pensions provided under a final salary scheme were dependent on the definition of pensionable remuneration under the scheme. A definition of 'final remuneration' was provided by the Glossary in Appendix I (IR 12 (2001)). It could not be greater than either the highest remuneration for any one of the five years before retirement, with additional remuneration averaged over a minimum of three years; or the average of total emoluments for any three or more consecutive years ending no later than the ten years before retirement. There were additional restrictions for 'controlling directors' and those who had final remuneration in excess of £100,000, for whom the three-year averaging method had to be used.

Benefits-in-kind could be included in pensionable pay. Pensionable benefits excluded share options and golden handshakes but could include childcare facilities, company cars, maternity benefits, medical treatment, season tickets and sickness benefits. For limits purposes these were 'fluctuating emoluments' and had to be averaged over a minimum of three years. Termination payments were excluded, together with any emolument that arose from the acquisition or disposal of shares or an interest in shares, or from a right to acquire shares.

In straightforward terms, the maximum aggregate benefits payable were:
(1)   a pension of 1/60th of final remuneration for each year of service, up to a total of 40 years;
(2)   benefits greater than 1/60th up to a maximum of 1/30th of final remuneration for each year of service up to a maximum of 20 years, provided that the aggregate of the benefits provided by current service and any retained benefits did not exceed two-thirds of final remuneration;
(3)   retained benefits normally had to be taken into account when calculating the maximum benefits under the limits for 'controlling directors', high earners, those with an accrual rate in excess of 1/60th and when calculating benefits on the early termination of employment.

'Retained benefits' meant, in general, those benefits pertaining to membership of other pension arrangements.

The pension benefits of controlling directors were closely regulated. A controlling director was, broadly, a director who alone or with associates controlled 20% or more of the ordinary share capital of the employer company. Where a scheme existed wholly or mainly for the benefit of controlling directors the additional restrictions relating to small self-administered schemes could applied.                          **[50.101]**

## 2  Company tax advantages/reliefs

In an exempt approved scheme employers could claim tax deductions for ordinary annual contributions (s 592(4)) in the accounting period in which the contributions are paid. 'Special contributions', which were contributions in excess of ordinary annual contributions, had to be spread over a number of years (s 592(6)) if the contributions exceeded £500,000. The number of years over which they were spread depended upon the amount paid (similar rules apply post A-Day). Special contributions had to be reported to HMRC within 180 days of the end of the scheme year (SI 1995/3103). The costs of establishing and running a scheme were not deductible under s 592 but were allowed as an expense for the chargeable period in which they are paid (IR 12, para 5.11).

In an unapproved scheme an employer could not claim a tax deduction for contributions unless the employee received a benefit on which he was taxed or the employee was taxable under ITEPA 2003 s 386 on the contributions. This means that there was a right to deduction if the payments led to a tax charge being imposed on the employee; the employer did not also need to show that the contributions were made 'wholly and exclusively' for the purposes of a trade. Payments for the establishment and running costs of a scheme were only deductible if they were deductible under normal principles.

FA 2004 replaced the above legislation from A-Day, with attaching transitional provisions and savings.                                    **[50.102]**

### a)  *Tax on surpluses*

The Finance Act 1986 removed the tax advantages available to schemes with excessive surpluses by imposing tax on the income and gains arising from scheme assets that were in excess of 105% of the value of the scheme's liabilities when calculated in accordance with the statutorily prescribed assumptions. The Surplus Funds section of HMRC SPSS required schemes to investigate their funding position regularly. This was governed by TA 1988 Sch 22 and the Surplus Regulations 1987 (SI 1987/412).

The legislation covered exempt approved schemes (except for SSASs), insured schemes where the level of contributions took account of the surplus or only provided a lump sum death-in-service benefit, and simplified defined contribution schemes (now defunct). Where a surplus was reduced by making a payment to an employer, this payment was subject to a 35% tax charge (40% for payments made prior to 11 May 2001) (s 601). The scheme administrator deducted the tax before payment and made a return to HMRC within 14 days of payment to the employer. The same flat rate tax charge was levied on any payment to an employer out of the scheme assets of exempt approved schemes, whether or not this was under Sch 22. Exceptions were provided by s 601(3) and regulations (SI 1987/352). There was no charge in the case of charities.

A sanction wais imposed on schemes that hold assets that amount to more than 105% of their liabilities and which failed to make acceptable proposals for the reduction of scheme assets. HMRC could specify what percentage of the surplus would continue to receive tax advantages, but the scheme would normally lose all tax relief in respect of income and gains from assets above the 105% threshold.

From A-Day, it is still possible for employers to receive surplus monies from pension schemes subject to a fixed tax charge of 35%. Otherwise, all the pre A-Day legislation and practice that related to the reduction of surpluses, the regular reviews for surpluses etc has ceased. Any earlier periods must be administered under the old rules.                                                    **[50.103]**

b)   *Tax advantage by way of dividend on share buy-back*

In *IRC v Trustees of the Sema Group Pension Scheme* (2002), the High Court, on appeal from the Special Commissioners, found that the trustees of the Sema Group Pension Scheme had received an abnormal amount by way of dividend on a share buy-back, and that they had obtained a tax advantage. The trustees denied this and argued the transaction had been carried out for *bona fide* commercial reasons.

The trustees purchased shares in Powergen in two batches, one at £5.39 a share and one at £5.35 a share. Later, they sold shares back to Powergen in two different batches for £5.25 and £4.83 a share, and claimed the tax credit attaching to the share buy-back. The (then) Inland Revenue issued a notice on the basis that the trustees had received an abnormal amount by way of dividend and a tax advantage. The Special Commissioners had allowed an appeal by the trustees on the basis that the amount of the dividend was not abnormal.

The criterion for normality was the normality of the return expected to be paid on securities of the type in question. The court found that the fact that the dividend was paid on a share buy-back should not be taken into account. A dividend paid on a buy-back could, therefore, not qualify as normal.

The Court agreed with the Inland Revenue in finding that the main object of the transactions had been to obtain a tax advantage, despite the trustees' argument that the transactions had been carried out for *bona fide* commercial reasons.

On appeal, the trustees contended that the High Court judge had been wrong to consider the distribution of the purchase price as a dividend, that they had not gained a tax advantage, and that obtaining a tax advantage was not one of the principal reasons for the buy-backs.

The Court of Appeal overturned the High Court decision and ruled that the buy-back scheme was not caught by the anti-tax legislation. What the trustees received was a normal return on the consideration that they had originally provided for the shares. However, the court did comment that the IRC were fully entitled to find that the main objective of the sale was to gain a tax advantage.                                                    **[50.104]–[50.120]**

## VI   INHERITANCE TAX AND LUMP SUM 'DEATH-IN-SERVICE' BENEFITS

IHTA 1984 s 151 deals with the treatment of lump sum death-in-service benefits and these provisions apply to exempt approved occupational schemes and approved personal pension arrangements. To mitigate against the prospect of a charge to inheritance tax on lump sum death-in-service benefits arising when a member dies, the benefit must be dispensed via a discretionary trust. This means that the trustees of the arrangement have discretion as to whom the recipient of the benefit will be. Generally members will be asked to complete a statement of wishes form, indicating the person (or body) that the member would like to benefit. The trustees are, however, not bound by this statement although they will usually be guided by it.

In the Budget 2006, the Chancellor stated that monies held in an alternatively secured pension (see **[50.151]** below) by an investor aged 75 or over will be subject to inheritance tax at 40% when the investor dies. This applies to assets over the nil rate band of £285,000 next year, and it will be deducted directly from the fund by the administrator. The charge is based on the value of the taxable property at the time the charge arises, calculated by reference to the assets over the nil rate band and the rate of tax at the time. There will be provision to cover two instances where the tax charge on alternatively secured pension funds overlap. Funds passed to charities will escape the tax. Funds paid to provide pension benefits for a spouse, civil partner or financial dependant will not be chargeable until the entitlement to the benefit ceases.

In addition to the above, the Finance Act 2006 legislates an existing 1992 concessionary practice in relation to an IHT charge which can arise when a person aged under 75 exercises a choice which reduces his chargeable estate and increases that of another (unless on an arm's length basis, and so excepted as a transfer of value). The exemption can apply in a pension scheme where the member exercised his right not to take pension. For example, where the member was in good health when the decision was made, but subsequently his life expectancy was seriously impaired and an enhanced death benefit is paid. The Act also extends the concession to dispositions to charities. Exemptions continue to apply to payments made to a spouse, civil partner or financial dependant. However, funds could be subject to IHT if HMRC considers that a person had deliberately avoided purchasing an annuity in an attempt to avoid the tax. This is a rather confusing statement and further details are required.

Children and grandparents are also likely to be disadvantaged by further IHT restrictions. Tax will be payable on trusts when they are set up if the value of the trust is higher than the nil IHT band (see above). A further tax charge will be levied on the tenth anniversary after they are set up. These measures apply to trusts set up in the future and to existing ones from 2008. The main impact will be on Accumulation and Maintenance Trusts and Interest in Possession Trusts. All transfers into new trusts are taxable at 20% above the nil rate band plus a further 6% charge every 10 years. Existing trusts will only be charged at 6% – the 10-yearly charge. The new rules also extend to certain divorce cases.                     **[50.121]–[50.140]**

## VII  FRS17 AND SCHEME ACCOUNTS

Financial Reporting Standard (FRS) 17 *Retirement Benefits* introduced in November 2001, applies to all financial statements that are intended to give a true and fair view of the reporting employer's financial position and profit and loss (or income and expenditure) for an accounting period. It addresses all retirement benefits provided by an employer, including those arising overseas.

In contrast to the previous accounting standard, SSAP24, FRS17 is designed to make the retirement benefits section of company accounts more transparent and easier to understand by ensuring that:

(1)    the scheme assets are measured using current market values;
(2)    the scheme liabilities are discounted at a high quality corporate bond rate; and
(3)    the scheme surplus or deficit is recognised in full on the balance sheet at the accounting date.

In order to allow companies to accumulate the data necessary to adopt the standard in full, FRS17 had a long implementation period. Disclosures in the notes to the closing balance sheet were required for accounting periods ending on or after 22 June 2001. For accounting periods ending on or after 22 June 2002, both opening and closing balance sheet information and performance statement information (both profit and loss and the statement of total recognised gains and losses) had to be given in the notes.

However, the UK Accounting Standards Board (ASB) agreed that companies could delay full implementation of FRS17 until 1 January 2005, meaning that until 2005 companies needed only disclose the surplus or deficit in the notes to the accounts, rather than show them in full on the balance sheet. The stated reason for the delay was that under new EC regulations, all companies listed and based in the EU must comply with international accounting standards (IAS19) from 1 January 2005 and the ASB did not want two quick changes in UK accounting laws in succession.

Under the new EC regulations, by 2005 FRS17 had to be consistent with IAS19 *Employee Benefits* (the International Financial Reporting Standard which covers post-employment benefits, including pensions costs). The main difference currently between the two accounting standards is that whilst under FRS17 actuarial gains and losses must be recognised immediately on the balance sheet, under IAS19 actuarial gains and losses can be spread over the lives of the employees. IAS19 has been undergoing a comprehensive review, which may ultimately bring it broadly into line with FRS17.

In addition, the ASB has issued an exposure draft on FRED 33, which concerns financial instrument disclosures. It is expected that this will eventually apply to all UK financial statements that fall under UK accounting standards. The information must be qualitative and quantitative.

Under the self-assessment rules, schemes have to submit scheme accounts with their tax returns. Where accounts are not yet available, a statement of assets and liabilities at the beginning and end of the tax year, ie as at 6 April 2005 and 5 April 2006 for the 2005–06 return, must be provided. HMRC must give at least 30 days' notice in order to ask for scheme accounts (s 252, Finance Act 2004), and it will normally give schemes the later of 30 days from the date of notice and seven months from the end of the previous scheme year. The seven months is designed to link in with the DWP's Disclosure Regulations which require scheme accounts to be completed within seven months of the scheme year end. Actuaries generally ask for scheme accounts at the time of any scheme valuation.

The relevant tax legislation is in the Registered Pension Schemes (Accounting and Assessment) Regulations 2005 (SI 2005/3454), and the Registered Pension Schemes (Audited Accounts) (Specified Persons) Regulations 2005 (SI 2005/3456)                                                    **[50.141]**

## VIII   THE NEW TAX REGIME, POST A-DAY

### 1   New simplified tax regime

Preceding the coming into force of ITEPA 2003, which began the task of clarifying the multitude of taxation legislation applicable to pensions in December 2002, the (then) Inland Revenue produced proposals for changes to the taxation of tax-approved pensions. The main aim of the proposals was to replace the current eight different sets of tax regimes applying to UK private pension provision with one universal scheme. Following consultation, a revised tax simplification report was published by the Inland Revenue Pensions Simplification Team/HM Treasury 'Simplifying the Taxation of Pensions: The Government's Proposals' (10 December 2003). The main purpose of that document was to introduce a single set of new tax rules after 'A-day' — which was announced as 6 April 2006 in the Budget 2004.

The concept of the new tax regime was subsequently brought into force by FA 2004 with effect from A-Day. Sections 149–284 cover pension simplification, ss 306–319 cover the disclosure of tax avoidance schemes and Schs 28–36 cover other pension rules, including transitional provisions and savings. Part 4, Chapter 8 ss 275–280, contain the main definitions and abbreviations that are used in the text of the Act.

From A-Day registered schemes fall into four defined categories, which are of importance in determining the level of the 'input amount' in each year for the purpose of measuring the Annual Allowance (see below). Schemes and arrangements are free to choose whatever style of benefit provision they wish. The description of a stakeholder scheme remains in place for registered schemes of that nature after A-Day. The main form of scheme design is becoming money purchase, which is consistent with developments elsewhere in the European Union.

Several developments took place in the year 2005. There were three Finance Bills:
(1)   the first Finance Bill 2005 (published 24 March 2005);
(2)   the Finance (No 2) Bill (published 6 April), which was enacted as FA 2005; and
(3)   a new Finance Bill 2005 which was enacted as F(No 2)A 2005.

The F(No 2)A 2005 brought back much of the provisions of the first Bill, which were omitted from the second Bill, together with some new provisions (in particular concerning capital gains tax avoidance by temporary non-residents and trustees and matters involving the disposal of assets overseas by residents and non-residents).

The most significant changes are the introduction of a tax-free pension fund Lifetime Allowance and an annual tax allowable Annual Allowance (input limit) into pension funds. The self-assessment procedure will be used to manage the allowances, together with new reporting procedures. The main details are summarised below. Many decisions may have been made prior to A-Day, and trustees and managers should review any that were made. These may include:

(1)    whether a member's fund was built up, within HMRC's permitted limits, in order to enjoy a higher personal Lifetime Allowance;

(2)    whether registration for enhanced protection or for primary protection from the standard Lifetime Allowance was to be made (members needed to decide whether or not to cease contributions/cease relevant benefit accrual at A-Day);

(3)    whether member contributions to any retirement annuities were maximised (carry-back reliefs will cease on 31 January 2007 and the carry-forward facility for unused reliefs was abolished from A-Day);

(4)    whether to retain AVC facilities;

(5)    whether death benefits should be restructured as lump sums;

(6)    whether to adopt the new limited price indexation cap of 2.5% for future benefit accrual;

(7)    how to track earnings in excess of, or close to, the earnings cap, identify the percentage of the Lifetime Allowance taken up, review employment terms (including flexible retirement, and early retirement) and retained benefits and review investments;

(8)    to compare the member's lump sum benefit entitlement pre and post A-Day (for example, did any member defer taking their lump sum until after A-Day?);

(9)    whether to use the new income withdrawal facilities;

(10)    what new investment decisions, if any, were made before A-Day (there is transitional protection for existing holdings, although the post A-Day rules are generally less onerous than the past ones);

(11)    whether to introduce a maximum benefit structure for post A-Day.

The main FA 2004 changes, describing firstly the allowance limits, are as follows.                                                                  **[50.142]**

### Annual Allowance

The aggregate Annual Allowance limit for tax relievable contributions is £215,000 per annum as at A-Day. There are different methods of calculation for defined benefits schemes and defined contributions schemes. The allowance will increase steadily to £255,000 by the year 2010, as shown below:

—    tax year 2006–07—£215,000;
—    tax year 2007–08—£225,000;
—    tax year 2008–09—£235,000;
—    tax year 2009–10—£245,000;
—    tax year 2010–11—£255,000.

There will, thereafter, be five-yearly reviews.

The allowance is regulated by the self-assessment return, and tax will be clawed back on any excess at 40%. The allowance will not apply in a year where the limit has been tested and the pension has vested in full. The test against the allowance requires the 'pension input amount' to be measured over the 'pension input period'.

The pension input amount is calculated according to the type of scheme or arrangement concerned:

*Cash balance arrangement:* The pension increase amount is the increase in the value of an individual's rights within the pension input period in the tax year concerned. The pension value at the beginning of that period is compared with the pension value at the end of that period. In order to determine the value at the two relevant dates, the opening value and the closing value must be determined. The opening value is the amount which would have been available to provide benefits on the assumption that an entitlement to their payment arose at the beginning of the pension input period. The amount is increased by RPI or 5%, whichever is higher, unless another amount is laid down in regulations. The closing value is the amount which would be available to provide benefits on the assumption that an entitlement to their payment arose at the end of the period.

Pension debits which occur in the period are added back, and pension credits which occur in the period are deducted. The amount of transfers to registered, or qualifying recognised overseas schemes, together with the market value of the assets is added back. The amount of transfers in from registered, or qualifying recognised overseas, schemes, together with the market value of the assets is discounted. Benefits which have crystallised are added back, unless the member has become entitled to the whole benefit, or died and any minimum payments under PA 1993 are subtracted.

*Other money purchase arrangement:* For money purchase arrangements which are not cash balance arrangements, the amount of the increase within the pension input period in the tax year concerned is the total tax-relievable contributions paid by or on behalf of the individual; and the contributions paid in respect of the individual under the arrangement by an employer of the individual. For cash benefit schemes, any minimum payments under PA 1993 are deducted.

*Defined benefits arrangement:* The pension increase amount is the increase in the value of an individual's rights within the pension input period in the tax year concerned. The pension value at the beginning of that period is compared with the pension value at the end of that period. Pension debits which occur in the period are added back and pension credits which occur in the period are deducted.

The amount of transfers to registered, or qualifying recognised overseas, schemes together with the market value of the assets is added back. The amount of transfers in from registered, or qualifying recognised overseas, schemes together with the market value of the assets is discounted.

Benefits which have crystallised are added back, unless the member has become entitled to the whole benefit or died. Any minimum payments under PA 1993 are deducted. There are special provisions for the valuation of deferred benefits. The Registered Pension Schemes (Defined Benefits Arrangements – Uprating of Opening Value) Regulations 2006 (SI 2006/130) prescribe an alternative percentage. This is the greatest of 5%, the RPI increase and any percentage prescribed by regulations.

*Hybrid arrangement:* The pension increase amount is the greater or greatest of such of input amounts A, B and C as are relevant input amounts:

A is what would be the pension input amount under ss 230–232, FA 2004, if the benefits provided to or in respect of the individual under the arrangement were cash balance benefits;

B is what would be the pension input amount under s 233, FA 2004, if the benefits provided to or in respect of the individual under the arrangement were other money purchase benefits;
C is what would be the pension input amount under ss 234 to 236, FA 2004, if the benefits provided to or in respect of the individual under the arrangement were defined benefits.

The pension input period can be the period which best suits the administrator. It is known as the 'nominated date'. The nomination can be made by the administrator or, in the case of a money purchase arrangement other than a cash balance arrangement, the individual member or the administrator. The only other criterion is that there must be a pension input period in every tax year. The first pension input period will commence on the day that the member's pension rights begin to accrue under the registered scheme. A preferred end date may be chosen (for example, the end of the scheme accounting period, or the end of the tax year). The total of all pension input amounts paid in that tax year will be the amount which is tested against the Annual Allowance. Any excess will be subject to the Annual Allowance charge. **[50.143]**

**Annual Allowance charge**
If the Annual Allowance is exceeded, a free-standing charge of 40% is applied to the excess. The member is liable to pay the charge, and must inform HMRC if he has not been issued with a personal tax return. The charge is incurred whatever the residence or domicility of the administrator or member. The net balance of the excess may remain in the scheme, subject to the ultimate application of the Lifetime Allowance. The excessive amount is not treated as pension income (or any other income) for the purposes of UK bilateral double taxation conventions.

The Annual Allowance test disregards:
(1)    transfers between registered funds, and recognised and regulated overseas schemes;
(2)    amounts in a year when the annual allowance has already been tested and the pension has vested in full;
(3)    member contributions which exceed the member's earnings and so do not qualify for tax relief;
(4)    additional voluntary contributions which are paid for the purpose of securing added years; and
(5)    where the individual has died before the end of the tax year concerned.
**[50.144]**

**Lifetime Allowance**
The aggregate Lifetime Allowance on the amount of tax-free pension saving is £1.5 million as at A-Day. It is tested at various crystallisation dates and events. The allowance will increase steadily to £255,000 by the year 2010. Defined contributions schemes will be measured at market value, and defined benefits schemes must use a factor of 20:1 (a different factor must be agreed if the increases to benefits exceed RPI, or a fixed 5% per annum, or for survivors' benefits which in aggregate exceed the member's pension).

The allowance will increase steadily to £1.8 million by the year 2010, as shown below:

— tax year 2006–07—£1,500,000;
— tax year 2007–08—£1,600,000;
— tax year 2008–09—£1,650,000;
— tax year 2009–10—£1,750,000;
— tax year 2010–11—£1,800,000.

There will thereafter be five-yearly reviews.

If the value of a member's aggregate pension benefits as at A-Day are more than the allowance, a higher certified allowance, increasing in line with the main allowance, may be provided—including a protected higher lump sum. For pension-splitting orders made after A-Day, pension credits will count against the recipient's Lifetime Allowance but pension debits will not count against the donor's Lifetime Allowance, nor towards the Annual Allowance. Pre-A-Day rights of benefits can be protected and an additional Lifetime Allowance is available. Where pension-splitting orders are in place as at A-Day, the value of the Lifetime Allowance may be ignored for the purpose of the Lifetime Allowance for both parties.                              **[50.145]**

## Lifetime Allowance charge

A charge (the 'Lifetime Allowance charge') will be imposed on benefits that exceed the member's Lifetime Allowance. The test will take place when benefits become payable. Any benefits that are already in payment must be taken into consideration. The charge is 25% on the excess over the allowance. The remainder may be paid as a pension and taxed accordingly. By way of an alternative, benefits may be taken in lump sum form. The lump sum charge is 55% on the excess. The administrator shall withhold the charge, and remit it to HMRC.

There are two forms of protection from the charge, which are described below:                                                                       **[50.146]**

## Primary protection

Under primary protection, the member's aggregate pension rights and benefits in excess of the standard Lifetime Allowance will be valued on the basis of the member having attained his expected retirement date on A-Day. The member may also take his lump sum from any of his arrangements that he chooses. The protected allowance is the lower of the value of the accrued lump sum, without early retirement factors, and the maximum lump sum allowed under HMRC's discretionary approval regime on A-Day (subject to certain assumptions). Under primary protection, the member's personal Lifetime Allowance increases in proportion to the increase in the standard Lifetime Allowance.                                                   **[50.147]**

## Enhanced protection

This form of protection applies to the member's aggregate pension rights and benefits as at A-Day, where the member ceases active membership at that date (that is, he and his employer, if any, cease to make contributions and he ceases to accrue benefits), provided that he does not join another registered scheme. Enhanced protection will also be lost on the crediting of additional benefits and the receipt of any transfer payment. The member's benefits can be recalculated at the first benefit crystallisation event, according to various assumptions. If the aggregate of the benefits do not exceed the higher of those two amounts, enhanced protection will be retained. His earnings for a three-year period to the earliest of his death, leaving employment with the sponsoring employer and the first relevant event are taken into account.

The key requirement for preserving enhanced protection is that there must be no further 'relevant benefit accrual' from A-Day.

Relevant benefit accrual means the following:

*For a money purchase arrangement (but not a cash balance arrangement)*: where a contribution is paid which is:

(1)   a tax relievable contribution paid by or on behalf of the individual;

(2)   a contribution in respect of the individual by his employer;

(3)   any other contribution which becomes held for the benefit of the individual.

*For a cash balance or defined benefits arrangement*: where, at the time when a benefit payment is made (or on making a permitted transfer to a money purchase arrangement), the crystallised value of the benefit exceeds the higher of:

(a)   the value of an individual's rights on 5 April 2006, increased to the date of payment by the highest of:

  •   5% compound;

  •   the increase in the Retail Prices Index;

  •   an increase specified in statutory order applicable to contracted-out rights.

(b)   the benefit derived by using pensionable service to 5 April 2006, the scheme's accrual rate, and the amount of pensionable earnings at the actual date of payment, which may be some time after A-Day (the elements included in earnings must be the same elements that were pensionable prior to A-Day).

The elements in (b) above are:

(a)   if the member was subject to the post-1989 tax regime on 5 April 2006, his earnings are limited to the highest earnings in any consecutive 12-month period in the three years before retirement, or 7.5% of the standard Lifetime Allowance if that is lower;

(b)   if the member was not subject to the post-1989 tax regime on 5 April 2006, his earnings are similarly calculated as the highest earnings in any consecutive 12-month period in the three years before retirement, but if they exceed 7.5% of the standard Lifetime Allowance they must be restricted to a three-year average or to 7.5% of the standard Lifetime Allowance, whichever is greater.

Defined benefits may continue to accrue post A-Day under enhanced protection as long as the eventual amount crystallised on retirement does not exceed the appropriate limit set out above. This allows for modest pay rises to the date of retirement, but, more importantly, it allows for normal accrual to continue and for early retirement to be taken where the early retirement reduction factor takes the value of the actual benefit paid under the appropriate limit.

There are exceptions whereby transfers are permitted without loss of protection:

(1) where all the sums and assets or all pension rights of the individual under the arrangement are transferred;

(2) where the sums and assets or pension rights are transferred to form all or part of the assets of one or more money purchase arrangements under a registered pension scheme or recognised overseas pension scheme (if the transfer is in connection with winding up of a scheme under which the individual has defined benefit or cash balance rights, his rights can be transferred to another cash balance or defined benefits arrangement for the individual – provided that the receiving arrangement is a registered pension scheme or recognised overseas pension scheme relating to the same employment as the wound-up arrangement);

(3) where defined benefit or cash balance pension rights are transferred to a money purchase arrangement, and the value of the sums and assets received by the money purchase arrangement are actuarially equivalent to the rights being transferred.

A transfer of rights which is made to a scheme for an ex-spouse following a pension sharing order is a permitted transfer. **[50.148]**

## Notice of intention to rely on primary or enhanced protection

A notice of intention to rely on primary or enhanced protection must be given no earlier than A-Day and no later than 5 April 2009. The notice should be given online. A new registration procedure will require various information to be provided, according to the type of protection that is being sought. HMRC will issue a certificate showing the extent of the protection given. **[50.149]**

## Benefit crystallisation events

There are eight events when a test must be made against the Lifetime Allowance (FA 2004, s 216). These are:

*Event 1:* By the designation of sums or assets held for the purposes of a money purchase arrangement under any of the relevant pension schemes as available for the payment of unsecured pension to the individual.

The amount crystallised is the aggregate of the amount of the sums and the market value of the assets designated.

*Event 2:* By the individual becoming entitled to a scheme pension under any of the relevant pension schemes.

The amount crystallised is RVF × P.

*Event 3:* By the individual, having become so entitled, becoming entitled to payment of the scheme pension, otherwise than in excepted circumstances, at an increased annual rate which exceeds by more than the permitted margin the rate at which it was payable on the day on which the individual became entitled to it.

The amount crystallised is RVF × XP.

*Event 4:* By the individual becoming entitled to a lifetime annuity purchased under a money purchase arrangement under any of the relevant pension schemes.

The amount crystallised is the aggregate of the amount of such of the sums, and the market value of such of the assets, representing the individual's rights under the arrangement as are applied to purchase the lifetime annuity (and any related dependants' annuity).

*Event 5*: By the individual reaching the age of 75 when prospectively entitled to a scheme pension or a lump sum (or both) under a defined benefit arrangement under any of the relevant pension schemes.

The amount crystallised is (RVF × DP) + DSLS.

*Event 6*: By the individual becoming entitled to a relevant lump sum under any of the relevant pension schemes.

The amount crystallised is the amount of the lump sum (paid to the individual).

*Event 7*: By a person being paid a relevant lump sum death benefit in respect of the individual under any of the relevant pension schemes.

The amount crystallised is the amount of the lump sum death benefit.

*Event 8*: By the transfer of sums or assets held for the purposes of, or representing accrued rights under, any of the relevant pension schemes so as to become held for the purposes of or to represent rights under a qualifying recognised overseas pension scheme in connection with the individual's membership of that pension scheme.

The amount crystallised is the aggregate of the amount of any sums transferred and the market value of any assets transferred.

The following terms have the following meanings:

**P** is the amount of the pension which will be payable to the individual in the period of 12 months beginning with the day on which the individual becomes entitled to it (assuming that it remains payable throughout that period at the rate at which it is payable on that day);

**RVF** is the relevant valuation factor;

**XP** is (subject to the above) the amount by which the increased annual rate of the pension exceeds the rate at which it was payable on the day on which the individual became entitled to it, as increased by the permitted margin;

**DP** is the annual rate of the scheme pension to which the individual would be entitled if, on the date on which the individual reaches 75, the individual acquired an actual (rather than a prospective) right to receive it;

**DSLS** is so much of any lump sum to which the individual would be entitled (otherwise than by way of commutation of pension) as would be paid to the individual if, on that date, the individual acquired an actual (rather than a prospective) right to receive it.                    **[50.150]**

### Administrator, and administration expenses

The administrator's duties are extensive, and the reporting procedures involve various parties (primarily administrators) to notify HMRC and certain other parties on the occasion of notifiable events.

Administration expenses must not exceed those that might be expected to be paid to a person at arm's length.                    **[50.151]**

### Annuity purchase, alternatively secured pensions, income withdrawal and unsecured pensions

Buy-out policies must be provided through a registered scheme. They may no longer be free-standing. There need be no monetary limits, and a tax-free lump sum of up to 25% of value may be paid. Defined contribution contracts must use a factor of 20:1 for determining limits. Pre-A-Day bought-out benefits remain subject to the limits that were written into those contracts.

The Act introduced alternatively secured pensions (ASP). Alternatively secured means an entitlement that is limited by income limits and annual reviews from being depleted too rapidly. ASP provides that an annual maximum income may be paid by the scheme of 70% of the amount that could be generated from applying an annuity rate for the member's age and sex up to age 75, and as at age 75 for a member who is aged 75 or more. ASI is applied firstly to secure dependants' pensions, and in the absence of dependants shall be returned to the scheme with the exception of lump sum benefits to charities.

Schemes may offer value protection for secured pensions. Secured pensions means a scheme entitlement that is backed by an employer or guaranteed by an annuity purchase. Value protection permits the return of the balance of initial capital value of the pension (less any instalments paid up to the death of the member, if aged less than 75)—subject to a tax charge of 35%. Alternatively, a guaranteed pension for a period not exceeding ten years may be offered (and existing ten-year guarantees may continue).

Unsecured pensions means returns on widely invested funds which deliver growth rather than security up to age 75. There is a maximum annual income withdrawal of 120% of the flat-rate single life annuity that could be bought out of the member's credit with five-yearly reviews. As an alternative, term-certain annuities may be purchased.

Income withdrawal, which means unsecured or alternatively secured pension, depending on age, is available for defined contribution schemes. Defined contribution occupational schemes must offer members an open market option when purchasing an annuity. **[50.152]**

### Audit and compliance

HMRC will operate audits and checks on a random selection basis and on a risk assessment basis. The Act provides for penalties and sanctions to be imposed in various circumstances, including false claims to transitional relief and for payments that are not made in accordance with the agreed transitional rules for the member concerned. **[50.153]**

### General benefits rules

There are general benefit rules that apply in all cases, with certain exceptions under the transitional arrangements. These are:
(1) tax-free lump sums are limited to 25% of the capital value of the pension;
(2) benefits must commence before age 75;
(3) benefits must not normally commence before age 55 as from 2010;
(4) pensions must generally be paid for life, but they may cease on remarriage;
(5) pensions must be paid in at least annual instalments;
(6) pensions must be non-assignable, except where otherwise permitted by HMRC;
(7) pensions must not normally be guaranteed for more than ten years;
(8) schemes must not offer a capital guarantee of more than value protection up to age 75;
(9) pensions must normally be taxed as income under ITEPA, formally PAYE.

For death benefits, the general benefit rules are:
(1) childrens' pensions must cease at age 23 unless dependency continues by reason of disability;

(2) adult's dependants pensions may be paid for life;

(3) a dependant may include a person financially dependant on the member; mutually dependent, or dependent because of physical or mental impairment;

(4) own right pensions do not need to be restricted to the member's pension level, but must not be value protected or guaranteed; and

(5) the non-assignment and non-surrender rules apply (except where a pensions sharing order is in point) and non-commutation rules apply except in cases of triviality. **[50.154]**

## Pensions

There is no monetary limit on the level of pensions that may be paid. **[50.155]**

## Lump sums

Lump sums must come into payment before the member's Lifetime Allowance has been fully used up and by age 75. They must also be paid within three months of entitlement arising. The calculation of lump sums is complex. Essentially, the calculations utilise the new concepts of 'permitted maximum' and an 'applicable amount'. The permitted maximum is calculated using a divider of 25% of the standard Lifetime Allowance after the deduction of any crystallised benefits, the applicable amount is one-third of the market value of the assets underlying the member's unsecured fund on income withdrawal, or one-third of the annuity purchase price if the lump sum is linked to the Lifetime Allowance. Excessive lump sums that are repaid will be taxed at 55%.

There are two main protections from the new limits for existing rights as at A-Day:

(1) lump sum entitlements which exceed £375,000;

(2) uncrystallised rights that are greater than 25% of uncrystallised rights for members who are not entitled to a valid claim for transitional protection (this is only available at the first crystallisation event after A-Day).

Existing lump sum certificates can be ignored once post A-Day valuations for transitional protection have taken place. However, for personal pension schemes that received a transfer from an occupational pension scheme the lump sum must not exceed that shown on the certificate.

Trivial commutation is a 'once only' option and not available before THE age of 60 or later than 75. Tax will be charged on 75% of the commuted value. There is an exception for low aggregate value pensions. **[50.156]**

## Death benefits

Despite the clear simplification of most of the pensions tax regime, it must be stated that the tax rules for death benefits are far from straightforward. The main features are:

(1) vested pensions not yet in payment may be paid to dependants either in pension form or, if a member has not yet reached age 75, as a lump sum;

(2) the lifetime allowance charge of 55% applies to any excess payments (but there will be no additional charge on pension payments;

(3) no capital payments may be made after age 75;
(4) existing five-year guarantees may continue;
(5) existing inheritance tax exemptions for approved schemes will continue.

The tax position is that a 35% charge on the administrator applies on:

(1) any pension protection lump sum death benefit (meaning value protection on the pension from a defined benefits scheme);
(2) any annuity protection lump sum death benefit (meaning value protection on the annuity from a defined contributions scheme ); and
(3) any unsecured pension fund lump sum death benefit (meaning return of fund under income drawdown).

There is no 35% charge on a defined benefits scheme lump sum death benefit if:

(1) the member had not reached age 75 at date of death;
(2) the benefit is paid in respect of a defined benefits scheme;
(3) the benefit is paid before the end of two years from date of death; and
(4) the benefit is not a pension protection lump sum death benefit; a trivial commutation lump sum death benefit; or a winding up lump sum death benefit. **[50.157]**

### Recipients of lump sum death benefits

Lump sum benefits may be paid to any person. A dependant may include a person who was married to the member when the pension commenced but divorced before the member's death. Exceptions to this are the cases of triviality commutation and winding up, in which events payment must be made to dependants (FA 2004, s 168 and Sch 29, Pt 2).

Payments may be made on a tax-free basis to charities where a member or dependant dies on or after age 75. This facility is only available where the member or dependant had an alternatively secured pension and no dependants. If the member dies after attaining age 75 the aggregate of all dependants' benefits must not exceed the amount of the member's pension at death. Future pension increases must be restricted in order to avoid evading this initial limit.

If the lump sum death payments are not paid directly to the legal personal representative, that person must be notified of the payment. It is also a requirement that the amount of the Lifetime Allowance used up is declared, and a charge of 55% on any excess will fall on the beneficiary. However, there will be no additional charge on any pension payments made.

If a scheme provided a capital payment on the death of a member in retirement for the purpose of assisting with the payment of funeral benefits as at A-Day, it may continue. This is only available in circumstances where the right would have been a member right if he had joined the scheme on 10 December 2003 and retired before A-Day. No such benefit must be provided for members who are age 75 or over at the date of death. **[50.158]**

### Early retirement

An abatement percentage of 2.5% per annum is applied to the Lifetime Allowance on taking benefits before normal 'minimum pension age'. The abatement applies to persons who have a protected right to take a pension before age 50. The member's protected pension age is the age from which he or she had an actual or prospective right to receive payment of benefits as at A-Day. The right may be protected on making a block transfer into a scheme.

Except in the case of some statutory schemes, any age lower than 55 must be in place throughout the period commencing on the publication date of the tax simplification paper (10 December 2003). However, FA 2004 does not have effect so as to give a member a protected pension age of more than 50 at any time before 6 April 2010. The draft Pension Schemes (Prescribed Schemes and Occupations) Regulations 2005 list the prescribed occupations under which benefits may be taken before normal minimum retirement age. The member must have had that right or prospective right on 5 April 2006 and the rules of the scheme must have included such provision on 10 December 2003.

Ill-health and incapacity pensions are still permitted. On serious ill-health, the administrator must obtain written medical evidence and must notify HMRC. There will be no tax liability on the payment if the lifetime allowance is not exceeded.

FA 2004 Sch 36 Part 2 para 19 describes the annual 2.5% abatement for early retirers before minimum pension age. Schedule 36 Part 3 covers the transitional provisions for rights to a low pension age and the transitional provisions for early retirement pension.                                    **[50.159]**

### Investment rules

FA 2004 removed many of the current investment restrictions (such as residential property) for registered schemes. Transactions must be conducted at commercial rates and any associated tax charges on acquisitions and disposals met by the appropriate party. Tax will be charged on income received by members or on the level of benefit-in-kind obtained where this is applicable. However, there are new restrictions for self-directed and investment-regulated pension schemes-directed schemes, which are described below. The changes have in the main taken into account the requirements of the European Union Pensions Directive (2003/41/EC) on IORPS. Investments must be made on a prudent basis, and consideration must be given to an appropriate level of scheme liquidity. Disposals and acquisitions by registered schemes must be transacted at commercial rates, and must be permitted by the scheme rules. The Occupational Pension Schemes (Investment) Regulations 2005 (SI 2005/3378) revoked the Occupational Pension Schemes (Investment) Regulations 1996 (SI 1996/3127). Regulation 12, states (subject to an exemption from the following requirement for schemes with fewer than 12 members):

(1)    not more than 5% of the current market value of the resources of a scheme may at any time be invested in employer-related investments; and

(2)    none of the resources of a scheme may at any time be invested in any employer-related loan.

Additionally, under the Act:

(1)    Borrowing is not to exceed 50% of fund value, and transactions must be on commercial terms.

(2)    Loans are permitted under the Act, other than member loans. Aggregate loans must not exceed 50% of total fund value; be secured and not exceed five years' duration. If a loan cannot be repaid within the period

under the agreement it may be rolled over once for a further period not exceeding five years. A loan reference rate of 1% more than the relevant interest rate, which is an average of the base rates of a specified group of banks on the sixth working day of the month which follows the start of the period, must be charged.

(3) Loans which are made to employers are 'employer-related investments', which means that they fall under the restrictions on such investments which are described above.

(4) There are restrictions for most schemes on shareholdings in the sponsoring company and associated/connected companies (5% of the fund value, 20% where there is more than one employer).

(5) Existing investments may be retained, preserving (in particular) the life of some small schemes investments that are no longer permitted under the new rules.

(6) All member transactions must be conducted on a commercial basis. A member's business may purchase assets from the scheme on an arm's length basis.

(7) Again, all member transactions must be conducted on a commercial basis. A member's business may sell assets to the scheme on an arm's length basis. The member should check whether capital gains tax is payable, and declare the sale on his self-assessment tax return.

(8) There are no restrictions on scheme trading. However, the scheme is liable to pay tax on any income derived from a trading activity, and the income must be returned on a self-assessment tax return.

(9) Transactions between an employer's or member's business and a registered scheme must be at commercial rates and on an arm's length basis; they are not to be treated as unauthorised payments. **[50.160]**

## Self-directed schemes

Special rules apply to self-directed schemes. These arose from a pre-Budget Report (Technical Note dated 5 December 2005), in which the Government published its latest thinking on tax simplification in respect of 'registered pension schemes which are self-directed'. The Government stated that it wished to avoid the potential misuse of schemes for buying second homes. The Report concerned tax avoidance in general, and stated that SIPPS 'will be prohibited from obtaining tax advantages when investing in residential property and certain other assets such as fine wines from A-Day'.

The Registered Pension Schemes Manual reflects the growing concern of the Government in the area of investment by SIPPS in residential property (RPSM07101060), and warns of the potential taxation consequences of investing in a buy-to-let residential property or holiday home or any other type of residential property. The latest legislation concerning investment-regulated pension schemes goes beyond the original intent, and is described in detail below. **[50.160A]**

## Investment-directed schemes

Schemes with fewer than 100 active and deferred members are exempted from many of the requirements of the legislation concerning investments, other than the need for diversity in investment choice, in accordance with the EU Directive. However, there has been a further tightening-up of the rules which apply to schemes in which the members can influence invest-ment choice. This affects not only to SSASs and SIPPS, but any scheme which falls within a newly-defined terms of 'investment-regulated pension scheme' and 'self-directed schemes'. The effect is that a tax charge may be incurred in respect of indirect investment activity in 'taxable property'.

Investment-regulated pension schemes are schemes where there are 50 or fewer members, and one or more meets the following condition, or at least 10% meet that condition. The condition is that either the member or a person related to the member is or has been able (directly or indirectly) to direct, influence or advise on the manner of investment of any of the sums and assets held for the purpose of the scheme. The new measures also impact on investment in unquoted shares in companies controlled directly or indirectly by a scheme member or someone connected with a scheme member. Major tax charges can be incurred where a company is used as a vehicle for an indirect holding and the scheme and/or its members and persons connected with them control the company in question. If the SSAS holds, say, 10% of the company shares, it will be taxed on 10% of the taxable property of the company. The Finance Act 2006 contains the relevant provisions under Sch 21 which also inserts a new Sch 29A to FA 2004. The provisions are summarised below:

(1) Tax charges will apply where an investment regulated pension scheme holds investments that are taxable property.

(2) Taxable property consists of residential property and most tangible moveable property. Residential property can be in the UK or elsewhere and is a building or structure, including associated land, that is used or suitable for use as a dwelling. Tangible moveable property is things that you can touch and move. It includes assets such as art, antiques, jewellery, fine wine, classic cars and yachts.

(3) The provisions apply to taxable property that is held directly and also to indirect holdings of property except through genuinely diverse com-mercial vehicles.

(4) If an investment regulated pension scheme directly or indirectly acquires taxable property (residential property or tangible moveable property) this will create an unauthorised payment tax charge on the member whose arrangement acquires the asset. In addition, the scheme administrator will be liable to a scheme sanction charge both on income from the taxable assets and capital gains on their disposal.

(5) The tax charges will remove the tax advantages on taxable property that may create an opportunity for personal use. So the benefit-in-kind charge on personal use of registered pension scheme assets will not apply to assets taxed under these measures.

(6) Income received from taxable property will be charged on the scheme administrator. This will be a charge under the scheme sanction charge and will be taxed at a rate of 40%. If the net income from the property is less than 10% of the value of the property then in place of the actual income the scheme administrator will be taxed on a deemed income. The amount of the deemed income will be 10% of the value of the property.

(7) Capital gains arising on disposal of taxable property will also be taxed on the scheme administrator as a scheme sanction charge and this will

be charged at 40%. The gain will be calculated as if it had been made by a UK resident and domiciled person.

Further regulations have also been issued, namely the Pension Schemes (Taxable Property Provisions) Regulations (SI 2006/1958) and the Investment-regulated Pension Schemes (Exception of Tangible Moveable Property) Order (SI 2006/1959)

The legislation on taxable assets will not affect the tax treatment of any income or lump sum paid out of the registered pension scheme. For example pension benefits, based on taxable property assets, will be taxed in exactly the same way as any other payment from a pension scheme. Some protection will exist for assets acquired before A-Day. Additionally, where alternatively secured pensions are in payment, any leftover funds, once used by the spouse, civil partner or person who is financially dependent (the beneficiary) has come to an end, will be chargeable to inheritance tax on the earlier of the cessation of those benefits and the death of the beneficiary. This is a further restriction, which mainly affects SSASs (and SIPPS), as the remaining funds will be treated as if they were an addition to the original scheme member's estate.

There are special rules to deal with UK tax relieved funds that are put into overseas schemes. **[50.160B]**

### Levies for the Pension Protection Fund

New levies were required in view of the provisions of PA 2004 ss 117, 174 and 209. They are for the provision of the new Pension Protection Fund ('PPF'), and the following apply:

(1) an administration levy;
(2) a PPF Ombudsman levy (no PPF Ombudsman levy was payable for the financial year which ended on 31 March 2006);
(3) an initial levy; and
(4) a pension protection levy.

The administration levy for the financial year ending with 31 March 2006 ranges from £24 to £10,600, dependent on the number of scheme members.

The PPF Ombudsman levy is not payable in respect of the financial year ending 31 March 2006.

The initial levy is payable on 6 April 2005 at a rate of £15 per member and pensioner, and £5 per deferred member and pension credit member who is not entitled to present payment of a pension as a result of his pension credit rights. Schemes with fewer than 100 members are exempted from the risk-based levy and will effectively pay a flat-rate levy.

The existing pensions compensation levy is being charged for the current year at the maximum rate of £23 per member and may increase.

The relevant legislation is:

(1) the Occupational Pension Schemes (Levies) Regulations 2005 (SI 2005/842), in force on 1 April 2005;
(2) the Pension Protection Fund (Pension Protection Levies Consultation) Regulations 2005 (SI 2005/1440), in force on 20 June 2005;
(3) the Pension Protection Fund (PPF Ombudsman) Order 2005 (SI 2005/824), which made provision in respect of the new PPF Ombudsman and the Deputy PPF Ombudsman with effect from 6 April 2005;

(4)    the Pension Protection Fund (Pension Compensation Cap) Order 2005 (SI 2005/825) (the amount of the compensation cap is £27,777.78).

Additionally, at least 80% of the PPFs occupational scheme levy must be risk-based and in place within a year. Valuations must be no earlier than 1 November 2004 and no later than 5 April 2008 for the purposes of s 179, Pensions Act 2004. The Pension Protection Fund (Pension Protection Levies Consultation) Regulations 2005 (2005/1440) came into force on 20 June 2005.

Schemes are exempt from paying the risk-based element of the levy if they are more than 125% funded on a s 179, Pensions Act 2004, basis. The s 179 basis is calculated by the actuary by multiplying a scheme's under-funding risk by its insolvency risk. The scheme's risk exposure is then multiplied by 0.8 and by a levy scaling factor of 0.53 to determine the amount of levy the scheme will have to pay. The levy applies to defined benefits schemes and defined contribution schemes with a defined benefit underpin (and vice versa).

If a scheme submitted a PPF valuation prior to 31 March 2006, it will be charged a levy based on risk using the information provided in that valuation.                                                              **[50.160C]**

**Membership**
In future, scheme membership will be open to all—whatever the employment or residence status of the individual concerned. Under the new tax rules and members may concurrently be a member of any type or any number of scheme (for example, occupational pension schemes and personal pension schemes).                                          **[50.160D]**

**Modification powers**
The documentation of all schemes and arrangements became out of date as at A-Day, unless it had been amended to meet the requirements of the new tax regime. Importantly, the Act provides transitional protection to schemes if administrators or trustees do not amend the documentation to comply with the new tax regime. The protection will end on 6 April 2011, or on any earlier date of amendment to the scheme. The Pension Schemes (Modification of Rules of Existing Schemes) Regulations 2005 (SI 2005/705) provide a rule of construction and give the trustees discretion over whether or not to make a payment which would fall to be treated as an unauthorised payment under the new regime.

It is important for trustees to seek legal guidance if they are to rely on the overriding legislation. The new discretionary power conferred on the trustees could lead to a complaint by an aggrieved party in the future. A particular area of concern must be what the trustees should do in the event of a surplus arising which, under the existing regime, should be returned to the employer but, under the new regime, may remain within the member's Lifetime Allowance.                                              **[50.160E]**

**Overseas considerations**
There are significant changes for overseas members and transfers. Migrants who come to the UK will be given tax relief on their contributions in place of corresponding relief provisions ('MIGRANT MEMBER RELIEF'), subject to

certain conditions. Additionally, UK-registered schemes will be able to transfer a member's fund to an overseas scheme if the overseas scheme is regulated as a pension fund in its country of establishment and undertakes to comply with information reporting requirements. **[50.160F]**

### Providers of registered schemes

The following persons may establish a registered pension scheme:

(1)  a representative body that is itself an employer may establish a pension scheme for people who are employees in a particular industry; and

(2)  one or more employers within a geographical area may set up a pension scheme for employees of theirs within that geographical area.

An employer (or employers) establishing a pension scheme may specify, for example, that the membership is for employees in a group of companies plus self-employed individuals who work with them.

An application to register a pension scheme may be made only if the scheme is an occupational pension scheme or has been established by:

(1)  an insurance company;

(2)  a unit trust scheme manager;

(3)  an operator, trustee or depositary of a recognised EEA collective investment scheme;

(4)  an authorised open-ended investment company;

(5)  a building society;

(6)  a bank; or

(7)  an EEA investment portfolio manager.

A scheme need not be established under trust, and there is no requirement that the employers in a multi-employer scheme should be connected. **[50.160G]**

### Registration

Existing approved schemes were automatically registered, unless they opted out of the new regime. New schemes need to register, and core information is required. The main forms are on the HMRC website. Schemes which were only interim approved before A-Day (this was only permitted where a scheme was set up as a result of the sale of an employer or part of an employer's trade) will need to have formal documentation in place in order to gain registration status.

The core information is:

*  the legal structure of the arrangement;

*  the size of the membership (bands of 0, 1–10, 11–50, 51–10,000 and over 10,000 apply);

*  the degree of control that a member has over the assets;

*  who established the scheme (a connected employer is to carry more risk than an 'off-the-shelf' product);

*  who the administrator is, together with a declaration of compliance and understanding from the administrator or authorised practitioner;

*  registration with the Pensions Regulator for schemes with more than one member;

*  an election to contract-out of S2P, where this is relevant;

*  a registration for contributions relief at source where this is applicable;

*  registration of a stakeholder plan, where this is relevant.

The main forms and reports are:

- Registration for tax relief and exemptions;
- Registration for relief at source;
- Contracting out (Industry wide schemes);
- Contracting out (other schemes);
- Event Report;
- Accounting for Tax Return;
- Registered Pension Scheme Return;
- Protection of Existing Rights;
- Enhanced Lifetime Allowance (Pension Credit Rights);
- Enhanced Lifetime Allowance (International);
- Declare as a Scheme Administrator of a Deferred Annuity Contract.

The following maintenance forms have been published:

- Pre-register as a Scheme Administrator;
- Notify Scheme Administrator details;
- Change of Scheme Administrator/Practitioner details;
- Authorising a Practitioner;
- Add Scheme Administrator;
- Amend Scheme details.

The administrator must make the registration application, and HMRC will have 12 months from registration to raise any queries. Standard forms should be completed online. There will be a choice of written application for contracting-out forms. The scheme return SA 970 will not be available online at present. If a scheme applies for non-registration, or loses registration, a 40% tax charge will be imposed on the assets.

It is no longer a requirement for a registered scheme to be set up under a trust, but the use of a trust can protect the members' interests and provide discretionary distribution powers in order to mitigate inheritance tax charges.                                                                                          **[50.160H]**

### Employer-financed retirement benefit schemes

FURBS are renamed employer-financed retirement benefit schemes ('EFRBS') and are covered by transitional arrangements. Their tax-free lump sum element, plus indexation, is protected on values up to A-Day if payments have qualified for relief either by virtue of the taxation of employer contributions on the member or the taxation of all income and gains under the fund. The inheritance tax exemptions continue to apply, but only to pre A-Day assets that are under a discretionary trust. If contributions are made after A-Day, the tax-free lump sum must be adjusted to take account of the earlier tax-free elements. NIC charges will be incurred on some payments and employers will not receive relief on contributions and expenses until benefits come into payment. Additionally, investment gains will be taxable at the rate applicable to trusts, which increased from 34% to 40% on 6 April 2004 and income charged at 40%. No additional tax charge will arise on the fund/lump sum for a FURBS that ceases contributions/input before A-Day.

It is still be possible to back an unfunded unapproved retirement benefits schemes (UURBS benefit) by an asset or security but the member must pay a benefit-in-kind tax charge on the cost to the employer of providing security and, or underwriting, and it will be possible to insure UURBS promises against employer default if the premiums are taxed on the member as a benefit-in-kind. UURBS could be consolidated and rolled into the new regime on application by 7 July 2006, if wished. **[50.160I]**

**Reporting requirements**

The main reporting requirements under the new regime are the self-assessment return, the pension scheme return and the events reports. The events reports will initially appear complex, until automatic procedures are put in place. The Registered Pension Schemes (Provision of Information) Regulations 2006 (SI 2006/567) apply, and have replaced the Retirement Benefits Schemes (Information Powers) Regulations 1995 (SI 1995/3103). The reporting service is being introduced in stages, on a 'needs' basis. Failure to provide information can lead to fines normally at a level of £300, plus £60 per day for continued non-compliance. In the case of fraudulent statements, or negligence in making returns, transfers and statements and providing information, fines may be increased up to £3,000. Most reports must be made after 5 April of the year following the relevant event, and before the following 31 January.

Among other things, the administrator has a general duty to report certain events in relation to the Lifetime Allowance for the year concerned. There are also requirements for the provision of information on certain events by insurance companies (etc) on annuity purchase and to personal representatives (PRs) on death; by PRs to HMRC; between the scheme administrator and member on the enhanced Lifetime Allowance and by schemes (quarterly) to HMRC on the lifetime allowance charge.

The main events which must be reported by the administrator to HMRC are:

- any change in the legal structure of a scheme, the number of members or the rules;
- any change to the rules of pre-commencement schemes treated as more than one scheme;
- benefit crystallisation events, enhanced lifetime allowance or enhanced protection;
- early payment of benefits;
- an overseas event check on the lifetime allowance;
- payment of a lump sum payment after the death of a member aged 75 or over;
- payment of an alternatively secured pension;
- payment of a pension commencement lump sum which, when added to the crystallised amount, exceeds 25% of the total; and is more than 7.5%, but less than 25%, of the current standard lifetime allowance;
- payment of a transfer lump sum death benefit;
- payment of a pension commencement lump sum – primary and enhanced protection, where lump sums exceed £375,000;
- payment of a serious ill-health lump sum;
- suspension of an ill-health pension;
- transfers to a qualified and recognised overseas pension scheme;
- unauthorised payments by members or employers;
- where a member is able to control scheme assets;
- on the termination of his appointment together with the date on which termination took effect, within 30 days of the event;

- on a scheme wind up and the date on which the winding up was concluded – the prescribed time for making the notice is any time on or before the last day of the period of three months beginning on the day on which the winding up is completed; or the last day otherwise prescribed by the regulations for the purpose of that information; whichever is the earlier.

The normal timescale for submission applies, being 31 January following the relevant tax year (or three months after any notice which is given after 31 October in the relevant tax year, or three months from the completion of the winding up of a scheme which wound up before that date).

An accounting for tax return must be completed by the administrator concerning any lifetime allowance charges, lump sum refunds, death benefits, surplus refunds and deregistration charges. Payment is due quarterly and must be made within 45 days of quarter end. Members must be notified of their fund value at vesting, the percentage of the lifetime allowance used (the P60 form) and any benefits-in-kind by 19 July following the relevant tax year end.

Schemes also have to submit scheme accounts with their tax returns. However, schemes will only need to send in the new registered scheme tax return if they have declarable income or if a notice is served on the trustees by HMRC for a return to be completed. HMRC must give at least 30 days' notice if it requires any accounts or investment details. The Registered Pension Schemes (Accounting and Assessment) Regulations 2005 (SI 2005/3454) and the Registered Pension Schemes (Audited Accounts) (Specified Persons) Regulations 2005 (SI 2005/3456) apply.

As a result of PA 2004, in respect of final salary schemes, actuarial valuations must be completed annually, or triennially where interim reports are received at least annually. They concern a scheme's technical provisions for meeting the statutory funding objective. The interim reports are not required for schemes with fewer than 100 members.                **[50.160J]**

### Tax reliefs and charges

The Act relaxes the current tax allowable contributions rules and charges for most from A-Day, and pension investment funds may continue to build up tax-free. The details are:

(1)   member tax relief on contributions up to 100% of earnings, or £3,600 if higher (at marginal tax rate);

(2)   employers' contributions allowed against corporation tax/profits, restricted by the aggregate Annual Allowance on tax relievable input;

(3)   tax-free lump sums may be paid up to 25% of the value of the fund benefits for the member.

The new tax spreading rules for large employer contributions remain much as before, with transitional arrangements. Contributions exceeding 210% of an amount paid in a preceding accounting year must be considered for spreading:

| *Excess amount* | *Period of spread* |
|---|---|
| Between £500,000 and £1m | Over two years |
| Between £1m and £2m | Over three years |
| More than £2m | Over four years |

Most additional voluntary contributions arrangements will begin to fall into disuse, due to the new (more generous) limits.

There is no limit on contributions, only on the tax reliefs available. The maximum tax-relievable input by way of contributions and/or benefit increases for the year 2006/07 is £215,000. **[50.160K]**

### Transfers

Registered schemes may:

(1) transfer to other registered schemes without restriction, and without having to test for the Lifetime Allowance;

(2) transfer to a scheme in another country which is recognised and regulated in that country as a pension scheme;

(3) receive a direct transfer from other registered schemes;

(4) disregard transfers from acceptable schemes described above from the Annual Allowance; and

(5) disregard transfers from overseas regulated schemes from the Lifetime Allowance if they do not include monies which have received UK tax relief.

Any breaches shall be treated as unauthorised payments, the scheme will be deregistered and a 40% scheme sanction tax charge imposed. Trust-busting will also be subject to a civil penalty of up to £3,000 for each member event. Any false request to obtain a transfer out of a registered scheme will fall within this.

The regulations which concern qualifying overseas pension schemes, to which transfers may be made without tax charge, are the Pension Schemes (Categories of Country and Requirements for Overseas Pension Schemes and Recognised Overseas Pension Schemes) Regulations 2006 (SI 2006/206). The following regulations also apply to overseas schemes and members:

(1) the Pension Schemes (Application for UK Provisions to Relevant Non-UK Schemes) Regulations 2006 (SI 2006/207);

(2) the Pension Schemes (Information Requirements – Qualifying Overseas Pension Schemes, Qualifying Recognised Overseas Pensions Schemes and Corresponding Relief) Regulations 2006 (SI 2006/208);

(3) the Pension Schemes (Relevant Migrant Members) Regulations 2006 (SI 2006/212).

A scheme is a 'relevant non-UK scheme' if:

● migrant member relief has been given;

● double taxation relief has been given post A-Day;

● members have been exempted under s 307, ITEPA 2003 from tax liability relating to pension or death benefit provision at any time after A-Day when the scheme was an overseas scheme; and

● there has been a relevant transfer from a UK scheme after A-Day when the scheme was a qualifying recognised overseas scheme. **[50.160L]**

### Unauthorised transactions

Any activity which involves an unauthorised transaction which falls within the meaning of 'payment' under ss 160–163, Finance Act 2004, is liable to a charge and/or penalties and sanctions. Transfers of assets or of monies or monies worth are deemed to be payments by the Act. Unacceptable investment activity includes:

(1)    taking value out of a pension scheme for unauthorised reasons;
(2)    pensions liberation;
(3)    value shifting of assets;
(4)    non-commercial transactions;
(5)    acquisition of wasting assets (that is, assets that have an anticipated life of less than 50 years, such as properties with less than 50 year leases, cars, racehorses, plant and machinery etc);
(6)    waivers of debt.

The main charges, surcharges, penalties and sanctions are:
- the Annual Allowance and Lifetime Allowance charge;
- the charge on unauthorised payments of 40%;
- the benefit-in-kind charge;
- the charge on deliberately winding up a scheme;
- the deregistration of a scheme charge;
- penalties on failures to provide documents or required particulars;
- failure to provide information penalties;
- fraudulent or negligent statements penalties;
- liberated pension savings charges and penalties;
- charges on Relevant Non-UK Schemes;
- charges on false or fraudulent information concerning the Lifetime Allowance;
- charges on surplus repayments (35%);
- charges on value shifting transactions;
- charges on withholding information;
- the unauthorised payments surcharge; and
- the scheme sanction charge.                              **[50.161]**

## 2   Pensions Act 2004

Although the Pensions Act 2004 is not directly concerned with taxation, it was brought about as a response to many of the Green Paper proposals for pension reform issued by the DWP in December 2002 and the White Paper that was published in June 2003. It is therefore integral to the combined tax and pensions simplification objectives of government. Many of the measures came into force in April 2005. A digest of the main subjects is given below.

**Pension Protection Fund:**
(1)    The introduction of provisions relating to the Pension Protection Fund (PPF) from April 2005, under ss 173–181, a form of insurance fund (funded by a set levy from pension schemes) which will provide compensation to members where the principal employer of a defined benefit scheme or hybrid pension scheme becomes insolvent and is unable to fund the scheme sufficiently.
(2)    The PPF impacts mainly on defined benefits schemes, but it will also apply to defined contributions schemes in the event of fraud and misappropriation of assets.
(3)    The levies for the PPF are described above.

**Moral hazard provisions:**
(4)    There are provisions in the Act that are intended to stop companies moving their deficits to the PPF. The Regulator can issue a contribution

notice, restoration order or deliberate failure to act order. It had been felt by many that these 'moral hazard' provisions would stifle UK business restructuring and transactions, and a 'green light' clearance system was called for on pensions liability issues, in advance of deals. As a result, ss 38–42 were inserted to provide a clearance procedure for legitimate corporate transactions and corporate restructuring, and a six-year time limit on an entity's continuing potential liability if it has endeavoured to avoid or reduce a buy-out debt.

**Financial assistance scheme:**

(5)    A financial assistance scheme (FAS) has been established to provide compensation to members of schemes who lost out when their schemes had wound-up. The FAS will receive £400 million from public funds over 20 years, and may also be supported by industry. It will be reviewed in three years.

(6)    Three main sets of Financial Assistance Scheme Regulations have been made, the FAS will include only those who will receive at least £10 a week, or equivalent, from the scheme and it is intended to have a maximum ceiling of £12,000 per year. Assistance levels will be geared with reference to the number of years an individual is from their retirement, and the Government is considering making payments for all individuals at age 65.

(7)    A White Paper was launched on 25 May 2006 on Pensions reform 'Security in retirement: towards a new pensions system'. The FAS was to have been limited to persons who are within three years of retirement, and this is extended to 15 years as at 14 May 2004. Pensions will be topped up to 80% of core pension for those within seven years of scheme pension age; 65% for those within eight to eleven years and 50% for the remainder.

(8)    Members of schemes that commenced winding up before 1 January 1997 will not be eligible. The possible options for delivery include a top-up pension, a cash lump sum, or purchase of an annuity at age 65. Payments are unlikely to commence before late summer or autumn 2005.

**Scheme specific funding objective:**

(9)    The Act provided for the replacement of the statutory minimum funding requirement with a scheme specific funding objective which, the Government hopes, will mean that schemes will have more flexibility to adopt a suitable funding strategy to meet their specific pension commitments.

(10)  The objective was intended to apply from September 2005, in line with EU Pensions Directive, and the provisions are set out in ss 222, 223. In practice, the objective was not brought into force until 30 December 2005 in respect of valuations as from 22 September 2005. Ongoing schemes must hold sufficient funds to meet their accrued pension commitments when they fall due to be paid.

(11)  The MFR transitional period was extended to 6 April 2006 by The Occupational Pension Schemes (Minimum Funding Requirement and Actuarial Valuations) Amendment Regulations 2004 (SI 2004/3031).

**Schemes in deficit:**

(12) Under s 226, a recovery plan must be put into place for schemes that are in deficit, in order to meet a new statutory funding objective. The Government considers that the IORP (European Investment Directive) requires schemes to be able to meet their accrued pension commitments on a full actuarial solvency basis. The new Regulator can issue a financial support direction under ss 42–51, and has power to issue a clearance statement.

(13) For schemes which enter wind-up on or after 11 June 2003, with solvent employers, the statutory debt under PA 1995 s 75 will be calculated on a full buy-out basis (the Occupational Pension Schemes (Winding Up and Deficiency on Winding Up etc) (Amendment) Regulations 2004 (SI 2004/403) came into force on 15 March 2004, and amend SI 1996/3126 and SI 1996/3128).

(14) For multi-employer schemes, the Pension Protection Fund (Multi-employer Schemes) (Modification) Regulations 2005 (SI 2005/441) describe the application of debts under section.

(15) Occupational Pension Schemes (Winding Up, Deficiency on Winding Up and Transfer Values) (Amendment) Regulations 2005 (SI 2005/72) came into force on 15 February 2005. They describe the changes in the calculation of liabilities where winding up commences, and date of calculation falls, on or after 15 February 2005 for the purposes of s 75. They require the trustees to inform members who request a transfer payment that their cash equivalent may be affected by the wind-up and that the member should consider taking independent financial advice.

(16) Occupational Pension Schemes (Winding up etc) Regulations 2005 (SI 2005/706) came into force on 6 April 2005 (except where otherwise stated), largely in respect of schemes which begin to wind up from that date. They prescribe when trustees or managers of schemes are required to adjust entitlements to discretionary awards and to survivors' benefits when schemes are winding up and make additional miscellaneous provisions.

(17) Occupational Pension Schemes (Winding Up) (Modification for Multi-employer Schemes and Miscellaneous Amendments) Regulations 2005 (SI 2005/2159) modify the Pensions Act 1995 for schemes with more than one employer, or with more than one employer at any time since 6 April 2005, whose rules do not provide for the partial winding up of the scheme if it is being wound up. They apply where an insolvency event has occurred in relation to one of the persons who is an employer in relation to an occupational pension scheme since 6 April 2005, and where the trustees or managers of the scheme have determined in the last three months that it is probable that the scheme will enter an assessment period in the next 12 months (that is, a period when the Board of the Pension Protection Fund determine whether to assume responsibility for the scheme for the purposes of pension protection).

The normal obligation of the trustees or managers to reduce the benefits that they pay out in respect of a member during the winding-up period, so that members do not receive more than they should according to the priority rules, is modified by the regulations. Trustees may, if they wish, pay in full the level of benefits that would be payable if the Board were to assume responsibility for the scheme.

**Pensions Regulator:**

(18) A new Pensions Regulator replaced OPRA from April 2005. The Regulator has a more targeted, proactive and proportionate approach to pension scheme regulation. The Regulator is described in ss 1–7, and will act on the major issue of member protection and use its power to counter pensions liberation.

(19) The Regulator may issue a restoration order in appropriate circumstances and may make a temporary freezing order, under s 23 of the Act, if there is an immediate risk to interests of the members. Schemes with an insolvent employer may be ordered to wind-up if it is in the interests of the members.

**Other:**

The Act is of considerable length. The further subjects that are covered include:

— Actuarial reporting.
— Administration procedures.
— Automatic vesting after three months' pensionable service.
— Combined Pension Forecasts.
— Consultation between employer and employees.
— Contracting-out changes.
— Internal dispute procedure.
— Indexation.
— Member-nominated trusteeship.
— Overseas matters.
— Registration requirements.
— Trustees' duties.
— TUPE review.

Most commentators believe that the Act fails to represent the move to a system of simplified pensions legislation that had been hoped for by the pensions industry. **[50.162]**

## 3 EU Pension Fund Directive

In September 2003, the EU issued EU Pension Fund Directive 2003/41/EC, a directive on the activities and supervision of institutions for occupational retirement provision. The intent was to remove many of the obstacles to cross-border pension provision, and to seek a unification of the tax treatment of pensions between member states. Accordingly, the Directive set out basic requirements for occupational pension funds across the EU, specifically relating to technical provisions, cross-border co-operation and investment principles based on the following broad principles:

(1) *Boundaries*: Schemes where the benefits are directly paid via company funds from employer to employee will be excluded along with 'pay as you go' schemes.

(2) *Technical provisions and prudential requirements*: The European Commission's approach to qualitative calculation of technical provisions is recognised. The Commission would now be required to present a bi-annual report on this matter to the Pensions Committee.

(3) *Cross-border co-operation*: A mechanism to enhance co-operation and notification between the regulators, especially between the country

where the pension fund is established and the country where the members are domiciled, is to be set up. Cross-border pension funds will be subject to few investment limits provided that they abide by the so-called 'prudent person' rule: this gives fund managers the freedom to invest, provided they hold a diversified portfolio and manage it prudently.

(4)   *Investment principles:* It is proposed that asset allocation must be on a qualitative basis and should be based on a consideration of the risks and liabilities of each fund rather than on an established set of rules which would apply to all schemes covered by the directive. On a national level, individual countries would be allowed to apply more stringent rules within certain limits. The directive also calls for parity of regulations between the country that is home to the pension fund and the country that is home to the members of the fund.

Member States were required to implement the Directive in full by 23 September 2005, with a limited opportunity for deferral of compliance with certain articles until 23 September 2010 for schemes which operate solely in a member state's own jurisdiction. However, since that date, the European Commission has sent reasoned opinions to Belgium, Cyprus, the Czech Republic, Finland, France, Italy, Lithuania, Slovakia, Slovenia, Spain and the United Kingdom for a failure to comply with the Directive or for having done so only partially. The Commission's opinion included the following statement:

'Whilst recognising that member states' systems for occupational pensions differ widely, the directive provides harmonised rules for prudential supervision and capital requirements for these institutions'.

**UK developments**
In the UK, the Occupational Pension Schemes (Investment) Regulations 2005 (SI 2005/3378) revoked the Occupational Pension Schemes (Investment) Regulations 1996 (SI 1996/3127), and supplement the changes to the PA 1995 which were made by the PA 2004. The regulations had been subject to consultation in draft form. in order to seek views on proposals to implement certain requirements of the Directive. The main topics were:

- a 'prudent person approach', as the underlying principle for capital investment, in accordance with Art 18 of the Directive;
- a written statement of investment policy principles, under Art 12 (s 35, Pensions Act 1995 refers);
- investment restrictions and requirements, including where there is more than one employer.

The regulations contain the relevant provisions, including:

(1)   Assets must be invested in the best interests of members and beneficiaries; and in the case of a potential conflict of interest, in the sole interest of members and beneficiaries.

(2)   The powers of investment, or the discretion, must be exercised in a manner calculated to ensure the security, quality, liquidity and profitability of the portfolio as a whole.

(3)   Assets must consist predominantly of investments admitted to trading on regulated markets, and other investments must be kept to a prudent

level. There must also be diversification of assets, and special rules apply to derivatives and collective investment schemes.

(4)   The requirements of the Directive are adopted in a proportionate and flexible manner, where appropriate using the 'small scheme exemption' which is contained in Art 5. Schemes with fewer than 100 active and deferred members are exempted from many of the requirements of the regulations, but are still required to have regard to the need for diversification on investment rule.

(5)   A triennial review of the statement of investment principles is required. The previous requirements on the statement's contents are largely restated.

(6)   Trustees must consider 'proper advice' on the suitability of a proposed investment, and there are specific requirements in relation to borrowing and a restriction on investment in the 'sponsors' undertaking' to no more than 5% of the portfolio (where a group is concerned, the percentage is no greater than 20%).

## Exemption regulations

The Occupational Pension Schemes (Trust and Retirement Benefits Exemption) Regulations 2005 (SI 2005/2360) prescribe the description of schemes which are exempt from:

- the requirement in s 252(2), PA 2004, that trustees or managers of an occupational pension scheme with its main administration in the UK must not accept funding payments unless the scheme is established under irrevocable trust;
- the requirement in s 255(1) of the Act that an occupational pension scheme with its main administration in the UK must be limited to retirement-benefit activities.

The effect is:

- s 252(2) transposes Art 8 of the Directive (Art 8 requires legal separation of the assets of an occupational pension scheme and those of a sponsoring employer);
- s 255(1) transposes Art 7 of the Directive (Art 7 requires that occupational pension schemes are limited to retirement-benefit activities).

[**50.163**]

# Section 9 The family

**Chapters**

# 51 Taxation of the family unit

*Written and updated by Natalie Lee, Barrister, Senior Lecturer in Law, University of Southampton*

'Family life is the foundation of society, and our first principle in society's support for the family is that the interests of children must be paramount.

For the last third of this century families with children have been losers in the tax system. Their tax burden has risen by nearly 20 per cent under successive governments—even though the time when children are growing up is the time when families need tax help most.

So it is time to reform the tax and benefit system to strengthen the family by putting children first.'

(The Chancellor of the Exchequer, the Rt Hon Gordon Brown MP, Budget Speech, 9 March 1999.)

'A tax and benefit system that puts families first in the modern world would not just recognise the family as the bedrock of society, and the rights and responsibilities of parents, but also the very real pressures parents face right up to the income scale. It would materially help them balance the needs of work and family and it would be generous enough to ensure for each child a good start in life.

To create a truly friendly tax system we must integrate tax and benefits.'

(The Chancellor of the Exchequer, the Rt Hon Gordon Brown MP, Budget Speech, 17 April 2002.)

'... tax credits are the modern route to eradicating poverty by making work pay.'

(The Chancellor of the Exchequer, the Rt. Hon. Gordon Brown MP, Budget Speech, 17 April 2003.)

'The Government's policies to modernise the tax and benefit system constitute the most fundamental programme of welfare reform since the 1940s.'

(Tax credits: reforming financial support for families, The Modernisation of Britain's Tax and Benefit System No 11, HM Treasury, March 2005)

[**51.1**]

## I   INTRODUCTION

Since 1997, there has been a sea change in the impact of taxation on the family unit. No longer are we concerned with tax allowances for married couples (apart from the age-related married couples allowance (see **[51.23]**–**[51.27]**) or mortgage interest relief (see **[51.44]**). Rather, we are learning the new language of tax credits, introduced to reduce poverty in families, particularly amongst children, and to provide an incentive to work by making work pay (see the Green Paper on *Welfare Reform* (1998)). Formerly, the interaction of the benefits and taxation systems frequently resulted in a disincentive to work, with the sharp withdrawal of means-tested benefits and the relatively low threshold for the payment of income tax. This problem was exacerbated for a family bearing the extra costs of childcare, and which was in receipt of higher out-of-work benefits as a result. In such a case, the gap between the benefits levels and pay levels was often very narrow, and the family could well have found itself worse off by being a working family. Thus it was that in November 1997, the Chancellor of the Exchequer promised the greatest reform of the tax and benefits systems for a generation. This reform has occurred in stages, beginning with the Working Families' Tax Credit (WFTC) and the Children's Tax Credit (both now abolished—for details of these credits, see earlier editions of this book), and culminating in the new tax credits, the Child Tax Credit and the Working Tax Credit. These newly extended tax credits, which have been in operation since 6 April 2003, and which are discussed in detail at **[51.29]**, build upon the framework provided by WFTC and the Children's Tax Credit, and are administered by HMRC. As with WFTC, the concepts of joint income and couples, whether married or not, are central to the new credits, both of which are alien to the current tax system. However, in so far as there are no longer any capital limits acting as a bar to eligibility, determination of income is tax based and income is calculated on the basis of tax years, the new tax credits differ fundamentally from WFTC and all other social security benefits.

Another major change is the parity of treatment (from 5 December 2005) between married couples and civil partners (see **[51.130]**) and, in each case, those treated as such. Whilst this chapter continues, in the main, to refer to 'spouses', the equal treatment of civil partners should be borne in mind.

**[51.2]–[51.20]**

## II   INCOME TAX

### 1   Independent taxation of husband and wife (see generally IR 93 and the Independent Taxation Manual)

From 6 April 1990, every taxpayer resident in the UK has been entitled to a personal allowance (£5,035 for 2006–07) that can be set against all types of income, both earned and unearned. This is in stark contrast to the position that existed prior to that date when a married woman's income chargeable to income tax was deemed to be that of her husband for income tax purposes (details of the previous position may be found in earlier editions of this book). It should be noted that, just like the WFTC, the new tax credits are to be determined on the basis of the income of the family, marking a return to the assessment of joint income, albeit only for the purposes of tax credits (see **[51.29]**). **[51.21]**

## 2 The married couple's allowance—the position from April 2000

The married couple's allowance (MCA) was withdrawn for the year 2000–01 and subsequent years of assessment where neither party to the marriage had reached the age of 65 on or before 5 April 2000. For the position where at least one spouse had attained the age of 65 on or before 5 April 2000, see **[51.24]**. **[51.22]**

## 3 The age-related married couple's allowance

Where at least one of the parties to the marriage attained the age of 65 on or before 5 April 2000, the married couple's allowance is retained. Whilst new claims cannot be made after that date when one of the spouses reaches the age of 65, where a person born on or before 5 April 1935 newly marries, they or their spouse will be eligible to claim the relief. **[51.23]**

a) *Basic requirements*

A man who is married and whose wife is living with him for any part of the tax year is entitled to a married couple's allowance for that year in addition to the personal allowance. TA 1988 s 282 defines the phrase 'living together' as follows:

'(1) A husband and wife shall be treated for income tax purposes as living together unless—
(a) they are separated under an Order of a Court of competent jurisdiction, or by Deed of Separation, or
(b) They are in fact separated in such circumstances that the separation is likely to be permanent.'

For income tax purposes, therefore, a marriage ends at the time of actual separation. Continuing to live in the same house will not normally amount to separation, although if the building is divided into two flats that are self-contained, it is likely that the couple will be living apart for income tax purposes (TA 1988 s 257A). In *Holmes v Mitchell* (1991) the husband and wife had ceased to be one household in 1972 and become two households even though they continued to live under the same roof and there was no physical division of the dwelling space. With the husband's subsequent declaration of intent to seek a divorce some ten years later the circumstances of the separation were then such that it was likely to be permanent.

The married couple's allowance for 2006–07 is £6,065 for those aged 65–74, and £6,135 for those aged 75 or over. These allowances are reduced if, for 2006–07, the taxpayer's income exceeds the income limit of £20,100, although they cannot fall below £2,350. The increased allowances available in such cases are discussed more fully in **Chapter 7**. **[51.24]**

b)    *Restriction of relief*

The claimant's entitlement is by way of a *reduction in respect of the income tax liability* arising on his total income, in other words, a tax credit. This tax credit is an amount equal to a percentage of the allowance, 10% for 2006—07 or, if less, an amount that would reduce the claimant's tax liability to nil.

### EXAMPLE 51.1

Porgy, who celebrated his 65th birthday in March 2000, and Bess are married and living together throughout the tax year 2006—07. Porgy's gross income (all earned) is £40,000; Bess has no income.
    Porgy's income tax liability for 2006–07 is computed as follows:

|  |  | £ |
|---|---|---|
| Income |  | 40,000 |
| *Deduct:* personal allowance (age allowance restricted because of total income) |  | 5,035 |
|  |  | £ 34,965 |
| Income tax liability: | £2,150 at 10% = £ 215 |  |
|  | £ 31,149 at 22% = £ 6,852.78 |  |
|  | £1,666 at 40% = £666.40 | 7,734.18 |
| *Deduct:* relief for age-related MCA (restricted due to income limit): |  |  |
| £ 2,350 × 10% |  | 235.00 |
| Net income tax liability |  | £ 7,499.18 |

If, instead, Porgy's gross income for 2006–07 was only £10,000, his tax liability would be computed in the following way:

|  |  | £ |
|---|---|---|
| Income |  | 10,000.00 |
| *Deduct:* personal allowance (age 65–74) |  | 7,280.00 |
|  |  | 2,720 |
| Income tax liability: | £2,150 at 10% = £215.00 |  |
|  | £570 at 22% = £125.40 | 340.40 |
| *Deduct:* | relief for age-related MCA: £6,065 × 10% = £606.50 |  |
|  | restricted to £340.40 | 340.40 |
| Net income tax liability |  | Nil |

A claimant's tax liability is determined *after* giving effect to any reduction in respect of relief for qualifying maintenance payments (see [51.6]), and by excluding tax at the basic rate which the claimant is entitled to deduct or retain out of charges on income (such as a payment to a charity). Further, any double taxation relief to which the claimant may be entitled either unilaterally or by virtue of a double taxation agreement is ignored. **[51.25]**

### c)   *Use of the allowance*

The allowance goes automatically to the husband, but there are provisions that allow a married couple to decide how to allocate part of the allowance (the specified amount) between them. The specified amount for 2006–07 is £2,350. Before the beginning of the appropriate tax year *either* the couple may elect jointly that the wife should be allocated the whole of the specified amount, *or* the wife can elect to receive one half of the specified amount. In either case, the wife will become entitled to a reduction from her income tax liability of an amount equal to 10% (for 2006–07) of the specified amount or of her allocated portion of the specified amount. Any election must be made on a prescribed form and, once made, will continue until revoked by a subsequent election made before the start of the later tax year (see *Taxation*, 21 September 1995, p 641 and *Independent Taxation Manual*, para 470).

Where the relief afforded in respect of the married couple's allowance cannot be fully utilised, whether by the husband or the wife, because his or her tax liability is insufficient to absorb the allowable percentage reduction, that spouse may give notice that the other spouse should be entitled to an income tax reduction calculated by reference to the unused part of the allowance.

### EXAMPLE 51.2

Susan and Nicholas, who was 65 in February 2000, are a married couple living together throughout the tax year 2006–07. Nicholas has a part-time job bringing in £8,000 pa. Susan earns £21,000 pa and has elected to receive one half of the specified amount of the age-related married couple's allowance. Relief in respect of this allowance will be split between them in the following way:

*Nicholas*

|  | £ |
|---|---:|
| Income | 8,000 |
| *Deduct:* personal age-related allowance | 7,280 |
|  | £720.00 |
| Income tax liability: £720 at 10% | 72.00 |
| *Deduct:*   relief for age-related MCA (full amount less Susan's portion): £6,065 × 1/2 × 10% = £303.25 |  |
|  restricted to £72.00 | 72.00 |
| Net income tax liability | Nil |

As Nicholas has used only £72 of the possible £303.25 in reducing his tax liability to nil, the remaining £231.25 should be transferred to Susan to further reduce her income tax liability.

*Susan*

|  |  | £ |
|---|---|---|
| Income | | 21,000.00 |
| *Deduct:* personal allowance | | 5,035 |
| | | 15,965.00 |
| Income tax liability: | £2,150 at 10% = £215 £13,815 at 22% = £3,039.30 | 3,254.30 |
| *Deduct:* | her portion of relief for age-related MCA: £6,065 ×1/2 × 10% = £303.25 plus unused part transferred from Nicholas of £231.25 | 534.50 |
| Net income tax liability | | £ 2,719.80 |

By contrast, a husband and wife cannot transfer any part of the personal allowance to each other. If the married couple's allowance has been reduced in the year of marriage (see **[51.27]**) it is that reduced allowance that forms the maximum amount which can be transferred to the other spouse. **[51.26]**

## 4   Tax in year of marriage

The personal allowance is available to both husband and wife in the year of marriage in the normal way. However, the age-related married couple's allowance for the year of marriage is reduced by one-twelfth for each complete tax month before the date of marriage. For example, in the case of a couple marrying on 4 August where there has been no election as to the allocation of the allowance, the man would lose three-twelfths of the married couple's allowance since there are three complete tax months in that tax year during which the couple are not married.

Where a man marries who is already entitled to the age-related married couple's allowance (because of a previous marriage in the same tax year) only one allowance is available.

If a married couple separate in one tax year but are reconciled in a later year, and were not divorced in the meantime, the husband will get the full age-related married couple's allowance in the year of reconciliation. There is no *pro rata* reduction, as there is for the year of marriage (TA 1988 s 257A(6)).    **[51.27]**

## 5   Death of either spouse

If the wife dies, the husband will get the full age-related married couple's allowance for that tax year, in addition to his personal allowance. For subsequent years he will receive only the personal allowance (assuming that he does not remarry). If the husband dies, in addition to her personal allowance the wife will receive any unused relief in respect of the age-related married couple's allowance. A discussion of the widow's bereavement allowance (abolished with effect from April 2000) can be found in earlier editions of this book. [**51.28**]

## 6 The child tax credit and the working tax credit

a) *Introduction*

The aim of the new tax credits, the Child Tax Credit (CTC) and the Working Tax Credit (WTC), is to separate the support for working adults in a household from support for children. This is to ensure both that children may be properly provided for within households out of work as well as in working households, and that those who are low -paid receive more financial help whether or not they have children. Accordingly, CTC may be claimed irrespective of whether an adult in the household is in work, and WTC may be claimed even though there may be no children in the household. This is in contrast to WFTC, eligibility for which had depended upon at least one of the adults in the family being in remunerative work, and there being one or more children in the household.

Tax credits must actually be claimed by use of the appropriate form (TC600), except by those who, immediately prior to 6 April 2003, were in receipt of Income Support or Income-related Job Seeker's Allowance and who are automatically entitled to the maximum amount of CTC without having to undergo the income test for the new tax credits and the means test for out-of-work benefits. An individual or family's award is based on two factors: *first*, their current circumstances (for example, for CTC, how many children they have, and for WTC, how many hours they work and the amount of eligible childcare costs), and *secondly*, their gross income (or the joint gross income of a couple). A 'couple' is defined as a man and a woman who are married, or two people of the same sex who are civil partners of each other (see [**51.130**]), and not separated (Tax Credits Act 2002 s 3(5) as amended (the tax definition)), or a man and a woman, or two people of the same sex, living together as if they were married or civil partners, a matter of fact that is likely to be determined by reference to the social security approach. The new tax credits run from 6 April in any year for a period of 12 months and, generally, awards will be made on the basis of the claimant's current circumstances and previous year's gross income, with changes in circumstances (for example, the birth of a new child) or in income during that period being reflected in the amount paid to the claimant (see [**51.39**]–[**51.40**]). This 'responsiveness' is achieved through a three-stage process. On a claim for a tax credit being made, HMRC make an initial decision as to whether an award should be made, and the rate at which to award it. Following notification of a change of circumstances during the year, HMRC may revise their initial decision and amend the award from the date of the change. At the end of the period of award, that is, at the end of the tax year in which the award was made, the person to whom a tax credit was awarded is required to confirm that the circumstances/income affecting their entitlement to tax credits were the same for the current year as for the previous year or, if they were not, to declare how they differ. HMRC will then make a final decision as to entitlement and, until April 2007, any underpayment will be made by way of a single payment of the outstanding credit owed. From that date, any underpayment will only be refunded after the award has been finalised at the end of the tax year. Overpayments are recovered either by a notice to repay a specified sum within 30 days of service of the notice (for overpayments arising in 2003–04 and 2004–05, claimants were permitted to pay in 12-monthly instalments: see *Inland Revenue Code of Practice 26*, August 2004), or by a reduction in tax credit payments. From November 2006, a reduction in tax credit payments will be limited to a maximum of 25%.

**[51.29]**

b)    *Child Tax Credit*

(*i*)    *Elements of the credit*

There are three basic elements:
(1)    a family element up to a maximum of £545 (for 2006–07) per year;
(2)    an additional family element up to a maximum of £545 (for 2006–07) per year for families who have one or more children under the age of one, continuing until the youngest child's first birthday;
(3)    an individual element for *each* child within the family up to a maximum of £1,765 (for 2006–07) per year. This element of CTC will rise at least in line with earnings up to and including 2007–08.
An extra credit is available for each child with a disability.

Unlike WTC (see **[51.33]**, there is no additional second adult element that distinguishes between couples and lone parents; CTC is independent of the status of the adults in the family or the number of parents in or out of work, and the calculation of the credit is based on the *children* in the household. Further, in contrast to the recently abolished Children's Tax Credit, a claim for CTC will be based on the *joint* income of a couple.

The actual award of CTC is based on the aggregate of these separate elements, which is then adjusted according to the claimant's income. For 2006–07, CTC is paid at the maximum rate until the income of the family reaches £14,155 per year (the first threshold for those entitled to CTC only). Thereafter, the award is gradually reduced at the rate of 37p for every pound of gross income over the threshold. The family element is retained until income exceeds £50,000 a year (the second threshold), and tapers away at that point at the rate of 6.67p for every pound of gross income above the second threshold.

**[51.30]**

(*ii*)    *Conditions of entitlement*

A claim may be made in respect of a child or children of a family irrespective of whether one or both of the adults are working. The support continues until 1 September following the child's 16th birthday or, for those who continue in full-time secondary education, until the young person's 19th birthday. It is also now available in respect of 16–19 year olds on unwaged work-based training programmes.

**[51.31]**

(*iii*) *Payment of the credit*

CTC (along with the childcare element of WTC (see [**51.38**])) is paid directly to the main carer. The persons or families with whom the child normally lives may decide which of them is mainly responsible but, if they do not decide, HMRC will decide on the basis of the available information.　　　　[**51.32**]

(c)　*Working Tax Credit*

(*i*)　*Elements of the credit*

There are broadly four elements:
(1)　a basic element in respect of all persons entitled to the credit, up to a maximum of £1,665 per year (for 2006–07);
(2)　an element in respect of persons being a couple (whether married or not) or a lone parent, up to a maximum of £1,640 per year (for 2006–07);
(3)　a 30 hour element giving extra credit to a person who, or persons who between them, works for more than 30 hours per week, up to a maximum of £680 per year (for 2006–07); and
(4)　a childcare element of 80% of eligible childcare costs, up to maximum costs of £175 per week for one child, and £300 per week for two or more children (for 2006–07).
There are additional elements to help those who may be particularly disadvantaged by their personal circumstances in the work market, for example disabled workers and those aged 50 and over who are returning to work after a period of unemployment.

As with CTC, a WTC award is the aggregate of these separate elements, adjusted according to the claimant's income. For 2006–07, individuals and couples with income below £5,220 per year receive the maximum amount of credit; for those whose income exceeds that threshold, the award is gradually reduced at the rate of 37p for every pound of gross income above the threshold. Claimants eligible for both WTC and CTC have their maximum awards reduced in the following order:
● 　WTC apart from the childcare element;
● 　the childcare element of WTC;
● 　CTC apart from the family element; and
● 　the family element of CTC.　　　　　　　　　　　　　　　　[**51.33**]

(*ii*)　*Conditions of entitlement*

1　**Couples with children and workers with a disability**
　Families/workers are eligible for WTC provided they are over the age of 16 and work at least 16 hours per week. Couples with children are eligible for an extra credit element if jointly they work at least 30 hours per week, provided that one of them works at least 16 hours. Where the claim for the credit is made jointly, the couple are entitled to a further second adult element.
　　　　　　　　　　　　　　　　　　　　　　　　　　　　[**51.34**]

## 2    Lone parents

Single persons are eligible provided they are over the age of 16 and work at least 16 hours per week. They are further entitled to additional elements in respect of working at least 30 hours per week and for claiming as a single parent.                                                                 **[51.35]**

## 3    Workers with no children and no disability

This category is entirely new, eligibility for the former WFTC being dependent upon having responsibility for children, whether as a lone parent or as a couple. The claimant must be aged 25 or over, and working for at least 30 hours per week. In the case of a joint claim, the couple will be entitled to the second adult element, provided that one of them works at least 30 hours per week. There has been criticism that those below the age of 25 and without children are not eligible for tax credits, since research has revealed in-work poverty in the 18–25 age-group.                          **[51.36]**

### (*iii*)    *Childcare element*

Families will be eligible for the childcare element of WTC where a lone parent or both partners in a couple work for at least 16 hours per week and incur relevant childcare charges. For these purposes, a person is a child until the last day of the week in which falls 1 September following the child's 15th birthday (or 16th if the child is disabled). The childcare element is available for approved childcare schemes, and in England these would include registered minders, nurseries, play schemes, nannies, au-pairs, and out of school clubs.                                                         **[51.37]**

### (*iv*)    *Payment of the credit*

WTC (apart from the childcare element) is paid directly by HMRC to the self-employed. Whilst WTC was previously paid to employees by their employers through the pay packet, since 7 November 2005, new employees have received the credit directly from HMRC; all other employees have been paid directly by HMRC since April, 2006. For couples, it is paid to the partner who is engaged in remunerative work, and if both work at least 16 hours per week, they can decide between them which of them is to receive the payments. In the event that they do not reach a decision, HMRC will decide to which partner the credit will be paid.                                      **[51.38]**

### (d)    *Changes in circumstances*

Although a change in circumstances will generally only affect the rate of entitlement, an award will come to an end prior to the end of the tax year if eligibility for the credit ceases, for example because there is no longer a 'child' or 'young person' in the family. Further, an award will only last until either a couple who have made a joint claim separate, or a single person who has made a claim becomes part of a couple (at which time, a new claim would have to be made). In these circumstances, there is a formal requirement to notify HMRC of such a change within three months of its occurrence. From November 2006, notification will also be required where there are changes in work status and the number of children for which the family can claim support. There is also a requirement to notify HMRC when the claimant or partner leaves the UK permanently or for more than eight weeks, or where the claimant goes abroad due to an illness, family illness or bereavement for more than twelve weeks. Where a change merely affects the rate of the award, formal notification of the change, again within three months, is only required where there is either a cessation of, or a significant reduction in, childcare costs. From April 2007, the time for reporting all of these changes will be reduced from three months to one. With respect to any other changes, there is no formal requirement to notify where the change might have the effect of reducing the rate of entitlement (the overpayment of a tax credit, with the need to pay it back at the end of the year, is a deterrent to not notifying), but where it would have the effect of increasing the rate of entitlement, for example the birth of a new baby, or an increase in the number of hours worked (giving rise to eligibility for the 30-hour element), then provided HMRC is notified, the tax credit award will be revised from the date of the change. Any other changes not notified to HMRC in the course of the year and not requiring notification, will come to light at the end of year (see **[51.29]**). **[51.39]**

(e)   *Changes in income*

In the case of the initial decision on an award of a tax credit, a determination is made on the basis of the income of the previous tax year. However, entitlement is only finally determined at the end of the tax year for which the claim is made, and consideration must then be given to both the previous tax year and the year in which the claim is made, the current tax year. Where there is an increase in the family income during the current year, it is the current year income that will form the basis of the final award, subject to a £25,000 disregard (for 2006–07 and subsequent years – TCA 2002 s 7(3)(b) and the Tax Credits (Income Thresholds and Determination of Rates) Regulations 2002 as amended). If, however, the current year income is no more than £25,000 (for 2006–07 and subsequent years) than that of the previous year, then it is the income of the previous year that is taken (TCA 2002 s 7(3)(a) and the Tax Credits (Income Thresholds and Determination of Rates) Regulations 2002 as amended). Perhaps surprisingly, where the current year income is less than that of the previous year, it is the current year income that will form the basis of the assessment regardless of the amount in question (TCA 2002 s 7(3)(e)). This is despite the fact that it was clearly the intention of Parliament to ignore any movement in income of less than £2,500, and to disregard the first £2,500 of any increase or decrease (£2,500 being the amount of the disregard under TCA 2002 s 7(3)(a), (b) until 6 April 2006). This is a default position that must be relied upon in the absence of any regulations having been made in respect of the applicable threshold in these circumstances. **[51.40]**

**EXAMPLE 51.3**

Edwina is a lone parent who has been awarded CTC and WTC for 2006–07. Her gross income for 2005–06 (the 'previous' year income) was £20,000. Her final award, determined at the end of 2006–07, will depend upon her gross income for the current year, 2006–07.

(1)   If Edwina's income for 2006–07 is £30,000, the final award will continue to be based on the income of the previous year (TCA 2002 s 7(3)(a)). This is because the current year income exceeds the previous year income by no more than £25,000.

(2)   If Edwina's income for 2006–07 is £48,000, the final award will be based on the income of the current year reduced by £25,000, ie £23,000 (TCA 2002 s 7(3)(b)). This is because the current year income exceeds that of the previous year by more than £25,000.

Had Edwina's gross income for 2005–06 been £40,000, then:

(a)   if Edwina's income for 2006–07 is £10,000, the current year income will form the basis of the final award (TCA 2002 s 7(s)(e) in the absence of any regulations having been made to cover this event).

(b)   if Edwina's income for 2006–07 is £25,000, it is once again the current year income that will form the basis of the final award, despite the fact that the drop in income is less than £25,000 (TCA 2002 s 7(3)(e)).

(f)   *Appeals*

Although it was the clear intention of Parliament that tax credits appeals should be heard by the Commissioners of Income Tax (TCA 2002 s 39), until the Treasury directs otherwise, all appeals will go to the Social Security Appeals Tribunal and Commissioners (TCA 2002 s 63), and the procedure is a compromise between the Social Security Act 1998 and the Social Security Decisions and Appeals Regulations on the one hand, and the Tax Credits Act 2002 and the Taxes Management Act 1970 on the other. If the case is a 'difficult' one, then membership of the tribunal must include a financially qualified person. Claimants may appeal against the initial decision, a decision to terminate an award, any other revision or refusal to revise, a decision as to entitlement after the final notice at the end of the period of award and any later revision. There is no right of appeal against a decision by HMRC to collect an overpayment.                                     **[51.41]**

(g)   *A Case Study*

**EXAMPLE 51.4**

Alan and his wife Charlene have three children, Alice aged nine, Ben aged six, and Claire who was born on the 6 April 2006. Their joint gross income for 2005–06 was £14,500 and £65,000 for 2006–07. They have always worked in excess of 40 hours each week.

Since both Alan and Charlene are away from home during the day, they incur childcare costs. Prior to the birth of Claire, these amounted to £120 per week, but thereafter rose to £320 per week.

**1.   Calculating the initial award**

(a)   *Entitlement to claim*

The family will be entitled to claim tax credits in respect of the tax year 2006–07 by completing form TC600. The initial claim will be based upon the income for 2005–06, the preceding tax year.

(b)   *Calculating initial entitlement to CTC*
The basic entitlement to CTC comprises:

|  | £ |
|---|---|
| Family element | 545.00 |
| Child element (£1,765) for 2 children | 3,530.00 |
| Maximum basic CTC entitlement | £4,075.00 |

However, the detailed rules of calculation convert each element to a daily sum, rounding certain (but not all) figures up or down, and then converting the result back into an annual sum. This exercise is done to allow for the extra day occurring in a leap year. The result of this is that the basic entitlement on the initial claim becomes:

|  | £ |
|---|---|
| Family element | 543.85 |
| Child element for two children | 3,533.20 |
| Maximum basic CTC entitlement | £4,077.05 |

(c)   *Calculating entitlement to WTC*
The basic entitlement to WTC comprises:

|  | £ |
|---|---|
| Basic element | 1,665.00 |
| Second adult element | 1,640.00 |
| 30-hour element | 680.00 |
| Maximum basic WTC entitlement | £3,985.00 |

Applying the conversion rules discussed above, the basic entitlement on the initial claim becomes:

|  | £ |
|---|---|
| Basic element | 1,664.40 |
| Second adult element | 1,638.85 |
| 30-hour element | 678.90 |
| Maximum basic WTC entitlement | £3,982.15 |

There is entitlement to the childcare element, which is limited to 80% of the childcare costs and, with more than one child, to a maximum of £300 per week. In this case, the amount paid at the time of the initial application was less than £300, and the entitlement (after applying the conversion rules) is:

|  | £ |
|---|---|
| Childcare cost of £120.00 per week | 6,240.00 |
| Childcare element: 80% of £6,240 | £4,992.00 |

(d)    *Calculating maximum initial tax credits award*

The initial award is the aggregate of CTC, WTC and the childcare element of WTC:

|  | £ |
|---|---|
| CTC | 4,077.05 |
| WTC | 3,982.15 |
| Childcare element of WTC | 4,992.00 |
| Maximum initial award | £13,051.20 |

(e)    *Calculating the reduction in the initial award*

(i)    WTC is reduced by 37% of the amount by which the claimant's income, calculated as above, exceeds the threshold (£5,220 for 2006–07). The reduction in the award is thus:

|  | £ |
|---|---|
| Income | 14,500.00 |
| *Less* threshold | 5,220.00 |
|  | 9,280.00 |
| Reduction in award: 37% × £9,280 | 3,433.60 |

(ii)    CTC is reduced by 37% of the amount by which the claimant's income exceeds the threshold (£14,155 for 2006–07). The reduction in the award is this:

|  | £ |
|---|---|
| Income | 14,500.00 |
| *Less* threshold | 14,155 |
|  | 345 |
| Reduction in award: 37% × £345 | 127.65 |

(iii)    Reductions are made in the following order:
WTC
Childcare element of WTC
Child element of CTC
Family element of CTC

(f)    *Calculating the actual award*

|  | £ | £ |
|---|---|---|
| WTC | 3,982.15 | |
| *Less:* reduction in award | 3,433.60 | |
| Actual WTC award | | 548.55 |
| Childcare element of WTC | 4992.00 | |
| *Less:* reduction in award | 127.65 | |
| Actual childcare element award | | 4,864.35 |
| CTC | | 4,077.05 |
| Total tax credits payable | | 9,489.95 |

## 2. Calculating the effect of the change in circumstances following the birth of Claire

Provided that HMRC were notified of this change in circumstances (which will have the effect of increasing the tax credits award) within three months of the date of the change, the revised award takes effect from the date of change. Otherwise, the award will only be effective as from the date of notification.

The birth of Claire and the increase in childcare costs will both cause the tax credits award to be revised:

|  | £ | £ |
|---|---|---|
| CTC (applying the conversion rules): |  |  |
| Family element (with a child under the age of one year) | 1,087.70 |  |
| Child element for 3 children | 5,299.80 |  |
| Revised CTC award |  | 6,387.50 |
| Childcare element of WTC (limited to £300 per week and after applying the conversion rules) |  | 12,515.12 |
| WTC remains the same |  | 548.55 |
| Total tax credits payable after the birth of Claire |  | 19,451.17 |

## 3. Calculating entitlement after the final notice at the end of the tax year 2006–07

The award is reassessed at the end of the year, and a comparison is made between the income of the previous year (2005–06 on the facts of this case study) and that of the current year (2006–07).

|  | £ |
|---|---|
| Gross joint income for 2005–06 | 14,500.00 |
| Gross joint income for 2006–07 | 65,000.00 |

At this level of income, the whole of the award would be withdrawn apart from the family element of CTC that is restricted by 6.67% of the amount by which the income for the relevant period exceeds £50,000 (£65,000–£50,000 × 6.67% = £1,000.50).

|  | £ | £ |
|---|---|---|
| WTC |  | 0 |
| Childcare element of WTC |  | 0 |
| CTC (apart from family element) |  | 0 |
| Family element of CTC | 1,087.70 |  |
| *Less:* restriction | 1,000.50 | 87.20 |
| Initial revised award | 19,451.17 |  |
| Final award | 87.20 |  |
| Overpayment | £19,363.97 |  |

If Alan and Charlene have no current entitlement to tax credits (which seems likely), they will be asked to repay £19,363.97 within 30 days of notice being given to them by HMRC). Wherever possible, a previous year's overpayment will be collected by reducing the claimant's payments for the current tax year (see *Tax Bulletin*, December 2004, p 1164 and **[50.29]**). A decision by HMRC to collect the overpayment is not subject to appeal.

## 7   Child Trust Fund

The child trust fund, provided for by the Child Trust Funds Act 2004, is intended as a new long-term savings and investment account for children. Its aim is to ensure that all children have a financial asset behind them when they reach the age of 18, and to encourage a savings culture for both families and children.                                                   **[51.42]**

### a)   *Operation of the scheme*

All children in the UK born after 31 August 2002 will have a child trust fund account, and will receive an initial government payment of £250, with children being looked after by local authorities receiving a higher rate. Children who are part of a family claiming child tax credit with a household income below the income threshold for child tax credit (£14,155 for 2006–07), or part of a family receiving income support or job seeker's allowance and who have not yet moved on to child tax credit, qualify for a further contribution from the Government of £250. The Government is consulting on making a further payment at age seven (primary school age) into all child trust fund accounts in a similar manner to the initial payment, and also on the issue of a further payment at secondary school age. Payment is by means of a voucher, which parents can use to open an account of their choice with a participating financial provider. Building societies, other financial institutions and high street retailers must seek the approval of HMRC to be an account provider and it is a condition of approval that they offer equity-based stakeholder accounts, although cash accounts may also be offered. Children, parents, family and friends, together with institutions or organisations such as businesses, community groups, charities and local authorities, are able to contribute up to £1,200 per annum to each account. There exists no provision for income tax relief on such a subscription and any payment by an individual is taken into account in determining the annual exempt amount for inheritance tax purposes (see: **[31.3]**), unless it is made on a regular basis and qualifies for exemption as normal expenditure out of income (see: **[31.4]**). Until the child reaches the age of 16, the account is managed by the person with parental responsibility. On reaching 16, a child may manage his own child trust fund account, but there will be no access to the money until he reaches the age of 18, at which time he may use it as he chooses.                                         **[51.42A]**

### b)   *Relief from income tax and capital gains*

Neither the child nor the account provider is liable for any income tax on the income from child trust fund savings and investments, including dividends, interest (which may be made gross to the account provider) and bonuses, on any annual profits or gains treated by TA 1988 s 714(2) as amended (the accrued income scheme: see **[42.100]**) as having been received by them in respect of account investments, or on an offshore income gain arising from a disposal of an account investment that would otherwise be treated as a profit or gain by virtue of TA 1988 s 761(1) (see: [**13.6**]). Importantly, income arising from account investments is not deemed to be that of the parent subscriber under ITTOIA 2005 s 629 (see: [**16.95**]). Further, the child pays no capital gains tax arising on the disposal of account investments. However, the child trust fund investments are effectively ring-fenced from any other investments held by the child concerned, since any capital losses arising on the disposal of child trust fund investments are not deductible from any capital gains made outside the child trust fund. [**51.43**]

## 8 Reliefs and exemptions

### a) *Mortgage interest relief*

Mortgage interest relief was abolished with effect from 6 April 2000. Details of how mortgage interest relief operated as between spouses prior to that date may be found in earlier editions of this book. [**51.44**]

### b) *Enterprise Investment Scheme (EIS)*

From 1 January 1994, the old Business Expansion Scheme (BES) was replaced by EIS. From 6 April 1998, a new EIS, a product of the rationalisation of the original EIS and CGT reinvestment relief came into being). As with the original EIS, husband and wife each have their own minimum (£500) and maximum (£400,000 from 2006–07 and for subsequent years) limits for EIS relief on qualifying share subscriptions. Inter-spouse transfers do not result in withdrawal of the relief: the transferee spouse is instead treated as the original subscriber for the shares. [**51.45**]

### c) *Close company loans*

Close companies are exempt from a tax charge on loans to full-time employees without a material interest in their company, and their husbands or wives, if the sum of outstanding loans to the employee and the employee's husband or wife does not exceed £15,000 (TA 1988 s 420). Under independent taxation there are separate £15,000 limits for husband and wife if both are employees of the company and if a loan is made for the first time on or after 6 April 1990. [**51.46**]

### d) *Capital allowances and charges*

Capital allowances due by way of discharge or repayment are given against income of a specified class or, on election, against other income for the year or the following year. Such allowances can be set only against the income of the person who incurred the expenditure. So far as charges on income are concerned, for example the payment of an annuity, if a married couple are jointly liable to make a payment, the amount each person *actually pays* is the amount of his or her charge for tax purposes. If it is unclear how much each person pays, the tax office will adopt a 50:50 split. [**51.47**]

## 9    Trading losses

The trading loss of one spouse cannot be offset against the income of the other spouse. Instead, any unused loss may be carried forward to set against the income in the following year of the spouse who incurred the loss.

**[51.48]**

## 10    Jointly held property

In order to give a clear and simple basis of taxation without the need for enquiries where assets, such as rental property, are jointly owned by both spouses, special rules exist whereby 'income from assets held in the names of a husband and wife who are living together' (TA 1988 s 282A(1)) is treated as income to which husband and wife are entitled equally (TA 1988 s 282A). Thus, if husband and wife have a joint building society account, even if they have contributed to it in unequal proportions, for income tax purposes each is treated as owning one-half of the interest arising, and taxed accordingly. Indeed, some spouses actively rely on the 50:50 rule when, in fact, the asset is owned between them in different proportions. Say, for example, the husband owns an income-producing asset worth £1,000. He might transfer it into the joint names of himself and his wife but only give his wife a 1% beneficial interest in the asset. Despite this, under the 50:50 rule the wife will be taxed on 50% of the income. Nevertheless, the husband will remain the owner of 99% of the asset. However, for the tax year 2004–05 and subsequent years, the general 50:50 rule does not apply where the property in question is shares in a close company, and one spouse is beneficially entitled to all of the shares and income, or the spouses are entitled to the shares and income in equal or unequal proportions (TA 1988 s 282(4A)). Close company shares are given the same meaning as in TA 1988 s 254. This new provision is aimed at preventing the general measure from being used as a device to circumvent the anti-avoidance settlements legislation.

**EXAMPLE 51.5**

Jimbo Ltd provides the services of Jim as a consultant to a number of clients working in the telecommunications industry. Jim is the sole director of the company. His wife, Tanya, takes no active part in the company and has no other income. The company's share capital is £100 consisting of 100 £1 shares, for which Jim and Tanya subscribed jointly. By virtue of a declaration of trust, Jim is entitled to 99% of the beneficial ownership of the shares, with Tanya being beneficially entitled to the remaining 1%. During the tax year 2003–04, on a turnover of £100,000, the company incurred expenses of £5,000, Jim received a salary of £10,000 and a dividend of £70,000 was declared. Although Jim controls the company, when the dividend was paid out TA 1988 s 282A deemed the income from the shares to arise 50:50, so that for tax purposes £35,000 was treated as Jim's and £35,000 as Tanya's. Until recently, it had been thought that the settlements legislation in ITTOIA 2005 Part 5 Chapter 5 (formerly TA 1988 ss 660A–660G), which was designed to prevent individuals from securing a tax advantage by transferring their own income to another individual who is taxed at a lower rate, would not have applied since Jim had not given anything away—apart from 1% of the shares and income, to which the settlements legislation could apply—thus saving Jim and Tanya significant amounts of tax. However, the case of *Jones v*

*Garnett* (2005) (see [**51.50**]) has questioned this assumption. Although the High Court held that the settlements legislation did apply to these types of circumstances, the Court of Appeal took the opposite view on the facts of the case. The question remains in the balance, with an appeal to the House of Lords pending.

In any event and in contrast, if the same facts occurred during the tax year 2006–07, TA 1988 s 282(4A) would require that Jim and Tanya be taxable on the actual income to which they are entitled. Accordingly, Jim would be taxed on 99% of the income, and Tanya would be taxed on 1%.

More generally, the 50:50 rule does not apply to income to which neither spouse is beneficially entitled; to partnership income from a trade or profession; to the income of a married couple who are separated; to the situation where property is held in the name of one party only; or where some other legislation (eg that governing settlements) directs that the income should be taxed in a different way.

It is, however, possible for the general 50:50 rule to be displaced (eg in respect of income to which one spouse only is beneficially entitled or in respect of income to which they are beneficially entitled in unequal shares). For the rule to be displaced, an appropriate declaration must be made specifying the shares in which the income is, in fact, beneficially enjoyed by one or both spouses. Any declaration must relate to both the income arising from the property and the property itself, and the income cannot be shared in different proportions from the capital. It has effect in relation to income arising on or after the date of the declaration.

Notice of any declaration must be given to the appropriate tax inspector within the period of 60 days beginning with the date of the declaration and must be made on the prescribed Form 17.

**EXAMPLE 51.6**

John and Susan jointly own £1,000 10% loan stock in XYZ plc producing annual interest of 100. Each will be taxed on one half of the income. They may enter into a declaration of trust giving John a 1% beneficial interest in the stock and Susan a 99% beneficial interest. If, following that trust, the appropriate declaration is made on Form 17 and submitted to the Revenue within 60 days, as from the date of that declaration Susan will be taxed on 99% of the income and John on 1%. [**51.49**]

## 11 Planning opportunities

The rules offer planning opportunities to many couples. In particular, if one spouse or civil partner is a higher rate taxpayer and the other is subject to the starting or basic rate only, it will be advantageous for income tax purposes for the former to transfer income-producing assets to the other spouse to ensure that the personal allowance and basic rate band is fully utilised. There may be other advantages (see [**51.59**]). However, care must be taken to ensure that any transfer is an outright gift of assets with 'no strings'. Certain gifts will *not* be treated as outright gifts, namely:

(1)  a gift not carrying the right to the whole of the income from the property given; or

(2)  a gift which is wholly or substantially a right to income (without being a gift of the underlying capital); or

(3)  a gift subject to conditions; or

(4)  a gift where the property given or any income or property derived from it is or might be paid to or for the benefit of the donor.

In such circumstances, the gift will be treated as a settlement and any income arising treated as the donor's for income tax purposes (ITTOIA 2005 s 624(1), formerly TA 1988 s 660A). To be certain that the inter-spouse gift is effective for income tax purposes it is vital to ensure that the gift is outright, incapable of being revoked, unconditional and of matching proportions of income and capital. For a gift that was considered to be wholly or substantially a right to income, see *Young v Pearce, Young v Scrutton* (1996). In fact, that case was one of the first cases to reveal just how widely HMRC is prepared to use the settlement legislation to combat what it views as a transfer of income between co-shareholders or partners where the effective reward by way of dividend or partnership share is not commensurate to the way in which the money is earned (see *Tax Bulletin*, April 2003, p 1011 and February 2004, p 1085. This important issue has recently been revisited by the Court of Appeal in the case of *Jones v Garnett* (2005), otherwise known as the *Arctic Systems* case). In that case, the only business of a company, which was owned equally by husband and wife, each paying £1 for the purchase of the shares, was the supply of consultancy services provided by the husband alone. The husband was the sole director and the wife provided some administrative services. Both received small salaries from the company; although substantial dividends were paid equally to husband and wife in certain years. Bearing in mind the modest services being provided by the wife, the Revenue was of the view that the dividends were being paid in lieu of a salary in order for the income to be taxed at the lower rate applicable to the wife rather than to the higher rate of the husband. Accordingly, the question to be decided was whether the dividend income paid to the wife during those years was income arising under a settlement made by the husband and thus to be treated as the income of the husband as settlor under s 660A(1) (now ITTOIA 2005 s 624(1)). There were two main questions to be decided before the High Court and subsequently the Court of Appeal: *first*, was there a settlement, which term includes an arrangement, within the meaning of the relevant statutory provisions; and *secondly*, did the outright gift exclusion in TA 1988 s 660A(6) (now ITTOIA 2005 s 626: see **[16.102]**) apply so as to prevent the anti-avoidance rules from having effect? In the High Court, Park J, relying on a number of authorities, in particular, *IRC v Plummer* (1980), concluded that the corporate structure created by the taxpayer had been done so with the intention that it should provide the means of bounty in future years and was thus an arrangement falling clearly within the meaning of the legislation. That being the case, it could be concluded that the taxpayer was the settlor and that the dividends paid to his wife had to be treated as his income for tax purposes. As far as the second issue was concerned, Park J held that far more was comprised in the arrangements in question than could be covered by the term 'outright gift' and that what constituted the 'settlement' was not an outright gift at all. Moreover, the taxpayer did not give to his wife her share—she had purchased it for £1. Accordingly, TA 1988 s 660A(6) (now ITTOIA 2005 s 626) did not take the case out of the scope of the charging provision. Like the presiding Special Commissioner, Park J set great store by previously decided cases where, in each case, the arrangements were entered into entirely for tax avoidance purposes. It is suggested that this coloured his view of the facts of the case, where it appears clear that the formation of the company and even the division of the share capital, were motivated by commercial considerations rather than tax planning. The Court of Appeal took a different view from the High Court. As to the first question, whether there was an arrangement and thus a settlement within the terms of the legislation, the Chancellor (with whom Keene and Carnwath LLJ agreed) was of the view that, at the time of the acquisition for value of her share by Mrs Jones, there could be no arrangement because there was no bounty; that, although there were subsequent bounteous elements, such as the declaration of dividends in the wife's favour, these could not be included in the original arrangement because they were not arranged in advance. In distinguishing previous cases such as *Crossland v Hawkins* (1960) and *Mills v CIR* (1974), the Chancellor was of the view that these cases 'had a "unity" and probability which in this case is lacking.' Nor did the fact that the acquisition by Mrs Jones of her share would enable her to receive dividends in the future mean that she would *actually* receive a dividend, or that every dividend received by her would constitute an element of bounty; there was no guarantee of any profits. Finally, the Chancellor was of the view that intention alone could not be an arrangement or part of an arrangement. As far as the interpretation and application of s 660A(6) (now ITTOIA 2005 s 626) was concerned, the issue of which could only arise if the taxpayer's first argument had failed, the Chancellor agreed with the reasoning of Park J and his conclusion that this was not an outright gift but, on the further issue that, in the circumstances, did not arise, he took the view that, had the property been given to Mrs Jones, it was not 'wholly or substantially a right to income'. As an item of property, Mrs Jones' share carried with it exactly the same rights as that of her husband's, those rights being more than just a right to income. Given that an appeal to the House of Lords is pending, people intending to set up a new company should err on the side of caution and ensure that both husband and wife are appointed as directors, and complete their tax returns on the basis of the dividends actually paid.

The above rules do not catch a gift where the donee, of his or her own accord, chooses to apply the income or capital in some way that might benefit the donor. The previous Inland Revenue practice whereby property which might return to the donor following the death of the donee under the donee's will or under the intestacy rules would not, for that reason, fail to be treated as an outright gift is now expressly enacted in ITTOIA 2005 s 625(4)(c), formerly TA 1988 s 660A(3)(c).

As noted above, the one way of making an outright gift of unequal amounts of income and capital is to arrange for the capital to be owned jointly, albeit in unequal shares, and then to rely upon the presumption of equality to ensure that half of the income is taxed as that of the spouse with the small capital entitlement. Such presumption will not apply where the assets concerned are shares in a close company.               **[51.50]**


## III   CAPITAL GAINS TAX

### 1   Separate taxation of gains

The gains of each spouse are calculated separately and each is entitled to an annual exemption (£8,800 for 2006–07).               **[51.51]**

## 2   Losses

The losses of a spouse can only be offset against his or her own chargeable gains and not set against the gains of the other spouse.         **[51.52]**

## 3   Inter-spouse transfers (TCGA 1992 s 58)

The disposal of an asset by one spouse to another, or from one civil partner to the other, is treated as being for such consideration as gives rise to neither gain nor loss. This rule operates whether or not any consideration is furnished for the transfer and in spite of the couple being connected persons. Effectively, therefore, gains are held over and the asset will be acquired at the base cost of the disponer spouse together with any incidental costs involved in the disposal. The indexation allowance (available only for periods up to April 1998) will be included in the deemed consideration.

### EXAMPLE 51.7

Jim gives his wife Judy two birthday presents on 1 June 2006, a Ming vase which he acquired from Christie's on 1 April 1988 and a painting by William Roberts acquired on 10 April 1986.

The disposal by Jim will be at no gain/no loss and Judy's base costs will include an indexation allowance on the vase from April 1988 to April 1998 and on the picture from April 1986 to April 1998. (The indexation allowance has been abolished for the months after April 1998 in the case of individuals.)

The rule in s 58 applies only so long as the spouses or civil partners are 'living together', and a couple will remain living together for these purposes, and therefore taxed as a married couple, where one is, but the other is not, resident in the UK during a year of assessment, and also when, although both are UK resident, one is absent from the UK throughout the relevant tax year.         **[51.53]**

## 4.   Retirement relief

Retirement relief has been completely phased out for the tax year 2003–04 and subsequent years. Earlier editions of this book explain how it operated.         **[51.54]**

## 5   Taper relief

The withdrawal of retirement relief and the removal of the indexation allowance have been accompanied by the introduction of taper relief, discussed in detail in **Chapter 20**. When an asset has been transferred between spouses, taper relief on the eventual disposal of that asset is based on the combined period of ownership of both spouses.         **[51.55]**

### EXAMPLE 51.8

Dan owns 5% of the shares in Computrade Ltd (a qualifying company), and has done so since May 2002. His wife Doris acquired 10% of the shares in the same company in April 2005.

*Present position:*

(a)    Dan is entitled to maximum business asset taper in 2006–07 of 75%.

(b)    Doris does not qualify for maximum business assets taper until April 2007.

    *But if:*

(i)    Doris gave her shares to Dan in May 2006; and

(ii)    He sells his entire 15% holding in June 2006,

    then he is entitled to 75% business assets taper relief on the entire shareholding.

    *Notes*:

(1)    Dan is treated as having acquired Doris's shares from the date when she acquired them for taper purposes.

(2)    It is Dan's qualification for maximum business taper that determines the availability of the relief (hence Dan should not give the shares to Doris).

(3)    For identification purposes, the date of the gift is relevant.

## 6  Cohabitees and children

General CGT principles operate for disposals between cohabitees and between parents and their children. In the case of disposals to children the connected persons rules operate with the result that any disposal will be deemed to be made at market value (TCGA 1992 ss 17, 18). **[51.56]**

## 7  Principal private residence

Only one principal private residence exemption is available where a married couple live together (TCGA 1992 s 222(6) and see **[23.42]**). **[51.57]**

## 8  Jointly held assets

Where assets are disposed of which were held in joint names of husband and wife, each spouse will be regarded as owning a half share of the asset and charged to CGT accordingly. This is subject to the couple having made a declaration that the asset is held in different shares: in such a case the gain is charged *pro rata* according to their respective shares in the property.

Any declaration that has been made for income tax purposes regarding jointly held property (see **[51.49]**) will have a corresponding effect for CGT purposes. **[51.58]**

## 9  Planning opportunities

If one spouse's annual CGT exemption will not be utilised whilst the other spouse's is fully utilised, it may be worth the couple transferring assets (at no gain/no loss under s 58 as discussed above) to the 'poorer' spouse so that both exemptions are used. Similar advice should be given where one spouse has a CGT rate (say 40%) which is in excess of that of the other.

**[51.59]–[51.70]**

## IV  INHERITANCE TAX

## 1  General principles

There is no aggregation of spouses' chargeable transfers for IHT purposes. They are treated as separate taxable entities, each entitled to the full exemptions and reliefs. It is immaterial whether they are living together and, unlike the position with respect to income tax and CGT, a couple remain married for IHT until the decree absolute that terminates the marriage. If care is taken with the associated operations and related property rules, transfers between spouses offer an opportunity to mitigate IHT since they are exempt without limit (except where the donee spouse is domiciled abroad, when only £55,000 may be transferred free of IHT). This inter-spouse exemption means that full use may be made of both spouses' exemptions and reliefs and benefits may be obtained by ensuring that the nil rate band (currently £285,000) of each spouse is fully used. In his Budget speech on 16 March 2005, the Chancellor of the Exchequer announced that the threshold would rise to £300,000 for 2007–08.                    **[51.71]**

## 2   PETs and the nil rate band

There are only two rates of tax (0% and 40%), and accordingly the *ideal* IHT planning for spouses should ensure that full use is made of PETs and of the nil rate band.                                                    **[51.72]**

### a)   *Making full use of PETs*

Whenever practicable, PETs should be employed to transfer wealth *inter vivos* to future generations. The spouse with the greater life expectancy should make the bulk of such transfers in order to minimise the risk of the PET failing. Since the making of any kind of inter-vivos trust, apart from a trust for a disabled person, on or after 22 March 2006, will now be subject to the same inheritance tax regime that formerly only applied to discretionary trusts, it is suggested that outright gifts should be made to avoid any charge that might arise in respect of property of a value in excess of the nil rate band (see **[28.41]**–**[28.42]**). If necessary, property can be transferred from the wealthy to the poorer spouse to enable the transfer to be made without the risk of the associated operations provisions applying.                                **[51.73]**

### b)   *Making full use of the nil rate band*

In drafting family wills it is desirable to ensure that both spouses fully exhaust their nil rate bands, ie that both make chargeable gifts to, for example, children of £285,000 and in addition give any property attracting 100% business or agricultural property relief. Above that level there is no IHT advantage in the first spouse to die making further chargeable transfers. Rather he should be advised to leave the balance to his surviving spouse who may then dispose of it to children either by means of PETs or by will. In such cases even if the transfer by the surviving spouse turns out to be chargeable no extra IHT will arise since all such transfers will fall within the 40% rate band.                                                        **[51.74]**

**EXAMPLE 51.9**

(1) Husband (H) has an estate of £500,000; wife (W) an estate of £84,000.
(i) *If H leaves all to W and dies first:*

| | |
|---|---|
| IHT on H's death | Nil (spouse exemption) |
| IHT on W's death | £119,600 (on £584,000) |

(ii) *Contrast if H leaves £285,000 to his children with remainder only to W:*

| | |
|---|---|
| IHT on H's death | Nil (on £285,000) |
| IHT on W's death | £5,600 (on £299,000) |

Accordingly, IHT saved is £114,000 (ie 40% × £285,000).
(iii) If W dies before H, full use could not be made of her nil rate band (because her estate only amounts to £84,000). It is therefore desirable on these facts for H to make an *inter vivos* transfer so that W has an estate large enough to cover the nil band.
(iv) When drafting a family will designed to utilise the nil rate band it is possible to leave a legacy equal to £285,000 (the current nil rate band) or, alternatively, if it is desired to take account of future increases in the threshold of that band, to employ a formula along the following lines:

'I GIVE such sum as at my death equals the maximum amount which could be given by this will without IHT becoming payable in respect of the gift.'

One risk thrown up by employing a formula is that should a future government dramatically increase the nil rate band (for example to £500,000) then the testator might find that his entire estate is going to the children so that inadequate provision is made for his spouse. When the combined estates for the husband and wife are relatively modest (below say £375,000), leaving £285,000 outright to the children on the death of the first spouse may be unacceptable since the couple will probably wish the bulk of the estate to pass to the survivor. The mini-discretionary trust (illustrated in (2), below) provides a halfway house that may be employed in such cases.

(2) Ma and Pa are relatively poor: joint assets below £375,000 including their dwelling house. It is likely that all or at least the bulk of the combined estate will be needed by the survivor and the scope for lifetime planning is non-existent. As discussed above it is desirable that part (at least) of the nil rate band of the first to die is utilised. In this case, however, leaving £285,000 away from the surviving spouse is probably unacceptable since it will be desirable to ensure that the surviving spouse can obtain all the property should the need arise. At the same time, there are advantages of using up the nil rate band in favour of (say) children. One way of achieving both objectives is to set up a discretionary trust, often called a 'mini discretionary trust', of £285,000 in the following terms:
   (a) *duration of trust:* the full perpetuity period—say, 80 years;
   (b) *beneficiaries:* surviving spouse, children and grandchildren;
   (c) *the discretion:* a wide discretion in the trustees to appoint both income and capital during the trust period;
   (d) *provision in default:* should there still be unappointed assets at the end of the trust period the amount should be divided in equal shares amongst the living beneficiaries; and
   (e) *protection of surviving spouse:* provision that the surviving spouse is to be the beneficiary with the greatest claim upon the trustees (if desired, the spouse could be appointed a trustee).
Such a trust has the attractions that there will be no IHT payable on creation through the use of the testator's nil rate band; assuming that the rates of

IHT remain linked to inflation, subsequent anniversary and exit charges are likely to be nil or very small; and the paramount wish of the testator for flexibility is achieved since, if the need arises, the entire fund can be distributed to the surviving spouse; otherwise full use has been made of the testator's nil rate band.

(3)   Bill owns a farm (qualifying for 100% agricultural property relief (APR)) worth £1m. On his death it will be run by his wife, Daisy. If he leaves it to her in his will, APR will be lost since the gift will be spouse exempt. Bill should therefore consider leaving the farm to his daughter, Tulip. Because of APR at 100% IHT will not be charged on that gift. Tulip could then sell the farm to her mother, Daisy, for its market value of (say) £1m with the result that:

   (i)   on Daisy's death APR may again be available at 100% provided that she occupies the farm for two years (the relief has been 'recycled');

   (ii)   if Daisy cannot afford £1m, consider leaving the price outstanding on an interest-free loan.

## 3   How to leave property to a spouse: outright and limited gifts

A separate problem is whether a spouse gift should be absolute or for a limited (for example, life) interest. So far as IHT is concerned, both types of gift fall within the spouse exemption so that the tax is neutral. Accordingly, the decision can be made on non-fiscal grounds.

The *outright gift* has the attraction of flexibility. The surviving spouse is free to use the property for any purpose and may therefore employ it to the best advantage of the family in the future. As a corollary, however, because the assets are given free from all conditions, an imprudent spouse may fritter away the inheritance and leave nothing for the children.

A *life interest* avoids the dangers inherent in the absolute gift by ensuring that the capital assets will eventually pass to persons entitled in remainder (usually children or grandchildren). Giving an interest in income may, however, be inadequate for the needs of the surviving spouse. A sudden emergency requiring a substantial capital outlay, for instance, may arise and if the absolute gift suffers from being too flexible the limited interest may well prove too inflexible! It had been the Government's intention to treat for inheritance tax purposes such a post-death interest in possession trust in the same way as a discretionary trust from 22 March 2006, but it subsequently changed its mind in the face of extreme criticism from a number of professional bodies.

An alternative to the two major types of gifts considered above is for a limited interest to be conferred on the spouse, but for the trustees of the will to be given a power to advance capital sums to the spouse. Such a power can then be exercised should the need arise, bearing in mind that capital sums advanced to the interest in possession beneficiary are free from IHT (IHTA 1984 s 52(2)). Giving only a life interest to a surviving spouse may give rise to a further disadvantage in restricting the ability of that person to pass on the property by means of potentially exempt lifetime transfers. It is true that by including a power to advance capital as set out above, the problem can be partly solved: however, the end result is somewhat cumbrous with the trustee advancing assets to the life tenant in order for that person to make PETs of the same property.

A life interest may, however, be employed *to ensure that the surviving spouse makes a PET*. Assume, for instance, that a husband wishes the bulk of his estate to pass on his death to his grandchildren on accumulation and maintenance trusts. His wife is much younger but he is concerned that, should he leave the property to her absolutely, it will never find its way to the grandchildren. On these facts the husband should be advised to settle property in his will with his spouse being given an immediate interest in possession. The trustees should then be given the power to terminate the interest (say six months after his death) whereupon the will should provide for the property to be held on the desired trusts for the grandchildren. There is no IHT charged on the husband's death because of the spouse exemption and the subsequent termination of the interest in possession will be a PET by the surviving spouse. However for deaths occurring on or after 22 March 2006, while the spouse exemption would still apply, the subsequent termination of the interest in possession would now be the occasion of a chargeable transfer (see **Chapter 30** for a discussion). **[51.75]**

### 4 Cohabitees and children

The general principles of IHT apply to transfers between cohabitees (so that *inter vivos* transfers will be PETs: death transfers chargeable) and between parents and children. In the latter case the connected person rules apply.

**[51.76]**

### 5 Post mortem adjustments

The rules governing *post mortem* rearrangements (see **Chapter 30**) are bolstered up by an anti-avoidance provision in IHTA 1984 s 29A which is relevant when there is an exempt transfer on death (for example, to the surviving spouse) and the recipient then, in satisfaction of a claim against the estate of the deceased, disposes of property 'not derived from the death transfer' (see **Chapter 30**). **[51.77]–[51.90]**

## V STAMP DUTY AND STAMP DUTY LAND TAX

A gift between spouses is (like other voluntary dispositions) exempt from *ad valorem* duty; a sale between spouses is subject to *ad valorem* duty only if it is made otherwise than in connection with the breakdown of the marriage (see FA 1985 s 83, and **Chapter 49**). The residual charge to duty and adjudication requirement was removed for instruments executed after 1 May 1987 if the appropriate certificate is completed (Stamp Duty (Exempt Instruments) Regulations 1987, SI 1987/516 as amended—and see in particular categories H and L of the Schedule). **[51.91]–[51.110]**

## VI ADMINISTRATION

From 1990–91 each spouse's tax affairs have been dealt with separately, not necessarily by the same tax office. It is each spouse's own responsibility to furnish, if required, a tax return in respect of his or her income and gains for the tax year in question.

HMRC are not permitted to disclose information regarding one spouse's tax affairs to the other without the spouse in question's written permission.

From 5 December 2005, these principles have applied with equal force to same-sex civil partners (see [51.130]).                    [51.111]–[51.129]

## VII   CIVIL PARTNERSHIPS

CPA 2004, which came into force on 5 December 2005, creates a new legal status of civil partner, giving same-sex couples in the UK the opportunity of acquiring a legal status for their relationship, and gaining rights and responsibilities that mirror those available to a married couple. Although taxation measures were not provided for in the Act itself, the FA 2005 enables the Treasury to make regulations providing similar treatment for civil partners and civil partnerships as is given to married persons and marriage. The effect of this means that, from 5 December 2005, tax charges and reliefs, together with the various anti-avoidance rules, have applied to married couples and civil partners alike. The most significant change is the exemption from inheritance tax of transfers between civil partners during their lifetime or on death. Same sex couples (like cohabitees: see [51.131]) had argued for some considerable time that the exemption in favour of married couples, but not in favour of those who were not legally married, was discriminatory and, taken together with Article 1 of Protocol No 1, was a breach of the European Convention on Human Rights (see [55.21], [55.42]–[55.60]). Whilst this argument was discounted in respect of heterosexual cohabitees, who had the choice of whether or not to marry (see [55.42]–[55.60]), it was believed that same sex couples might have been successful had such argument been brought before the domestic courts under the HRA 1998. Another area affected includes the capital gains tax legislation where: (i) only one property owned by a couple who are civil partners may be treated as the principal private residence of either of them at any time for the purpose of the principal private residence exemption; (ii) transfers of assets between persons who are civil partners who are living together are on a no gain no loss basis; (iii) civil partners are treated as 'connected persons' and are also connected with other persons such as close relatives of their civil partner in the same manner as husbands and wives; and (iv) a settlement of assets by one civil partner under which the other partner can benefit may result in the settlor being liabile to capital gains tax on capital gains realised by the trustees, provided other conditions are met (see [19.85]). As far as income tax is concerned: (i) where one of the partners was born before 6 April 1935, the partners are entitled to an allowance equivalent to the married couple's allowance (see [51.23]); and (ii) the income tax anti-avoidance provisions dealing with transfers of assets abroad where, as a result of the transfer, income becomes payable to a person resident or domiciled outside the UK, also apply to civil partners. Pension tax legislation amendments provide that references to husband, wife, ex-husband, ex-wife, spouse, ex-spouse, surviving spouse, widow and widower now include civil partner, former civil partner and surviving civil partner. Pension tax simplification legislation, which came into force on 6 April 2006, also reflects the terms of the CPA 2004. Finally, there is an exemption from stamp duty and stamp duty land tax for transactions effected in connection with the dissolution of a civil partnership so that transfers of shares or the transfer of an interest in the partners' home into the sole ownership of one of the ex-partners is exempt (see **[51.66]**).

**[51.130]**

## VIII COMPARISONS IN THE TREATMENT OF SPOUSES AND COHABITEES

The withdrawal of the married couple's allowance from 2000–01, together with the uniform personal allowance for all individuals irrespective of marital status, has meant that married and cohabiting couples are now on a par with each other for income tax purposes. In a similar fashion, for CGT purposes, the annual exempt amount (up to £8,800 for 2006–07) is available to *all* taxpayers (and hence as much to the advantage of both husband and wife as to each of a cohabiting couple), whilst for IHT, the general exemptions (£3,000 pa, gifts in consideration of marriage and normal expenditure out of income) are available to all. Moreover, with the introduction of the working tax credit and the child tax credit from April 2003, no distinction is made between married and cohabiting couples: both credits are available irrespective of whether a couple are married or living together as husband and wife. They are also available to lone parents. These credits, particularly CTC, are concerned mainly with children; it is the children who make up the family, and it is the children who should be supported irrespective of whether their parents or carers are married or not. It was believed by some that to treat cohabitation on a par with marriage for taxation purposes would be impractical in cases where that relationship was likely to be transitory; in other cases (notably situations falling within the old idea of 'common law marriage') a different argument could be thought persuasive, albeit that deciding when a temporary arrangement had become permanent could be far from easy. These concerns are no longer critical when it is the *child* of the relationship that is being supported rather than the relationship itself.

That having been said, the distinction in tax law between married couple and those living together as husband and wife (andthose living together as civil partners) persists in other important areas. Crucially, special reliefs are available to a married couple that enable assets to be transferred *inter se* without the risk of any tax charge. For IHT purposes this relief is unlimited in amount save for the situation where the donee spouse is a non-UK domiciliary (and therefore potentially outside the UK tax net). For CGT purposes, disposals between spouses are treated on a no gain/no loss basis (see TCGA 1992 s 58) and taper relief operates in relation to the combined holding period of the spouses. As some (limited!) compensation, it may be noted that various anti-avoidance rules based upon a 'connected persons' test will not normally apply to cohabitees. In such cases transactions between the cohabiting couple will be taxed in the same way as transactions between strangers. Take, for instance, IHTA 1984 s 10, which is intended to ensure that IHT does not catch the bad bargain. In the case of a transfer between cohabitees, in order to avoid any question of an IHT charge, it is only necessary to show an absence of gratuitous intent on the part of the transferor. It is not necessary to go further, as is the case when the transferee is a connected person, and to show the transfer in question is one that would have been entered into with a third party. Admittedly this is small beer in the majority of cases where the crucial point in any case where property is transferred between a couple (whether married or otherwise) will be the exemption from charge for inter-spouse transfers. Consider, however, as a second illustration the CGT rules which tax the settlor on the gains realised by his trustees in cases where he has retained an interest in his trust. For UK trusts, TCGA 1992 ss 77, 78 limit the charge to situations where the settlor or his spouse (no mention of other members of the family, nor of cohabitees) can benefit directly or indirectly from property in the settlement (see **Chapter 19**). The legislation on offshore trusts goes further: a settlor has an interest if a benefit may be enjoyed by a category of 'defined persons' which includes children (plus their spouses), stepchildren, grandchildren and companies controlled by such persons (including any company controlled by that company). Still no mention of the cohabitee!

Those small advantages aside, it is the absence of any capital tax relief for transfers *inter se* which is the greatest disadvantage facing cohabitees. Elementary tax planning schemes are, as a result, fraught with difficulties. For income tax purposes, for instance, ensuring that a couple take full advantage of their individual allowances and lower and basic rate tax band will frequently involve an outright transfer of an income-producing asset. In the case of cohabitees, care must be taken to ensure that if that transfer is of a chargeable asset it falls within the transferor's annual CGT exemption whilst, for IHT purposes, if that transfer exceeds the £3,000 annual exemption it will constitute a potentially chargeable transfer. Will drafting for the cohabitor is likewise a problematic exercise: if everything is left to his cohabitee, the estate will be subject to a 40% tax levy once the £285,000 nil rate band has been exhausted. There is no exempt transfer to shelter behind in such cases: no simple channelling operation which can be performed to make any tax liability disappear as in the case of married couples.

A common trap which may arise is as follows. Assume that Terry and June cohabit in No 44 Railway Cuttings, a house which they own as joint tenants. Terry dies without having made a will (a negligent death) with the result that his free estate (ie his property other than his share of Railway Cuttings) passes to his parents. June is not entitled to any property on his intestacy although she could bring an action for reasonable financial provision under the Inheritance (Provision for Family and Dependants) Act 1975 provided she can show that she was financially dependent on Terry. In cases where both cohabitees have had full-time jobs this is unlikely to be the case. To return to the example, assume that the total value of Terry's estate exceeds the IHT nil rate threshold: say, for instance, that Terry's half share in the house is worth £180,000 and that his free estate is likewise worth £180,000. (It may in passing be noticed that in valuing Terry's half share in the house a discount on the basis of the joint occupation should be allowed. Such a discount is not, of course, available in the case of a half share owned by husband and wife because of the related property rules in IHTA 1984 s 161: see **Chapter 28**.) The IHT Bill (£30,000 assuming that Terry had an intact nil rate band) will result in an estate rate of 8.3% and June will be accountable for the £15,000 attributable to Terry's share in the house since the burden of IHT charged on joint property falls on that property. She has received nothing under Terry's intestacy and given that his parents may be unwilling to make any contribution towards the IHT charge on Railway Cuttings, the end result is that unless she can afford to raise a mortgage or alternatively to pay the tax in instalments (with interest) she will end up being forced to sell the house.

The recent Law Commission Consultation Paper (No 179, 2006) is specifically confined to the financial consequences of the termination of cohabiting relationships, whether by separation or by death, and does not amount to comprehensive review of all the law as it applies to cohabitees. Moreover, it explicitly excludes matters of taxation. Given this, and in light of the equal tax treatment of spouses and civil partners, it is likely that cohabitees may argue even more forcibly for their position to be reconsidered. That this argument will succeed is unlikely: for its part, the government has made it very clear that it will not entertain the idea of equating cohabitation of heterosexual couples with marriage. Moreover, a Special Commissioner has explained (in an *obiter dictum*: see *Holland v IRC* (2002)) that the treatment of cohabitees is not in breach of the European Convention on Human Rights and that it is permissible for Parliament to legislate for different tax provisions to apply to married persons, since this reflected the mutual rights and obligations brought about by marriage (see **[55.42]–[55.60]**).   **[51.131]**

# 52 Matrimonial breakdown

*Written and updated by Natalie Lee, Barrister, Senior Lecturer in Law, University of Southampton*

---

I     Income tax **[52.2]**
II    Capital gains tax **[52.21]**
III   Inheritance tax **[52.41]**
IV   The matrimonial home **[52.61]**

---

Matrimonial breakdown necessarily has financial and tax repercussions. The financial implications of divorce have been the recent subject of two high-profile decisions of the House of Lords. In *Miller v Miller* (2006), the question that needed to be determined was how capital assets should be divided following only a brief marriage. In contrast, the issue in *McFarlane v McFarlane* (2006) concerned the role of periodical payments in circumstances where, following a marriage lasting 16 years, the available capital, although substantial, was not sufficient to enable an immediate clean break, but the husband was a very high-earner and would continue to be so in the coming years. What is important to note is that, although matters of taxation may have led the parties to take certain decisions during the marriage (see particularly the High Court decision in *McFarlane v McFarlane* (2003), they are no longer an issue on matrimonial breakdown. Where once it used to be an occasion that afforded scope for tax planning, such opportunities have, in the main, been removed altogether since, from 5 April 2000, income tax relief on maintenance payments is no longer available at all unless one or both of the parties to the marriage was over the age of 65 on or before 5 April 2000. It should be noted that, since 5 December 2005, references to 'marriage' and associated terms include 'civil partnerships' and the term 'spouses' will include 'civil partners' (see **[51.130]**). Cohabitees, however, are treated as single people with a lack of legal remedies on separation (and on death as well). This position may well change following the publication of the Law Commission's Consultation Paper 179 (2006), which puts forward proposals that would enable eligible cohabiting couples who had provided the necessary contributions or sacrifices to the relationship to obtain financial relief.        **[52.1]**

## I   INCOME TAX

### 1   General principles

On the breakdown of a marriage the parties revert to single status. For income tax purposes marriage ends when the parties separate 'in such circumstances that the separation is likely to be permanent'. Because of independent taxation, both parties will, in any event, have been taxed separately whilst married, so that each will have been entitled to the personal allowance (£5,035 for 2006–07) and, prior to 6 April 2000, the couple would also have received the benefit of the relief in respect of the married couple's allowance. Where separation took place before 6 April 2000, relief in respect of the married couple's allowance continued to be given for the tax year of separation, but thereafter each party would normally have received merely the personal allowance. Where separation takes place after 5 April 2000, unless one of the spouses is aged 65 or more at that time, no such relief will be available since the married couple's allowance was withdrawn for 2000–01 and subsequent years of assessment. Where one or both of the separating spouses was born on or before 5 April 1935, relief in respect of the age-related married couple's allowance (see [51.24]) will continue to be given for the tax year of separation. Relief in respect of the additional personal allowance that was previously payable to the parent who had custody of any infant children was abolished for 2000–01 and subsequent years. From 6 April 2003, Child Tax Credit may be claimed in respect of children under the age of 16, or of young persons under the age of 19 who remain in full-time secondary education. The tax credit will be paid to the 'main carer' (see [51.29]).   [52.2]

## 2   The treatment of maintenance payments prior to 5 April 2000

Prior to 5 April 2000, relief for maintenance payments depended upon whether they were made under 'existing obligations' (which can loosely be defined as 'arrangements' entered into before 15 March 1988) or whether they were 'new' maintenance payments made on or after 15 March 1988.
   [52.3]

a)   *Existing obligations*

In the case of existing obligations, where the payment was made to a former spouse under a legal obligation, the sum paid was fully deductible by the payer in arriving at his income tax computation and was taxed as the income of the recipient under the former Schedule D Case III. Technically, the payment constituted a charge on the payer's income with basic rate income tax being collected at source under the provisions in TA 1988 s 348 (see **Chapter 14**). A similar result followed if a court order was obtained directing the payment to be made to any child of the marriage: the payment would then constitute a charge on the income of the payer, would be made net of basic rate income tax and the recipient child was then entitled to recover income tax deducted at source to the extent of any unused personal allowance. Details of the treatment of maintenance payments made under arrangements entered into before 15 March 1988 may be found in earlier editions of this book.   [52.4]

b)   *Maintenance payments made under arrangements set up on or after 15 March 1988*

In contrast to existing obligations, 'new' maintenance payments were made out of the taxed income of the payer, who received only limited compensation by means of a tax credit based upon a percentage of the married couple's allowance. Details of the treatment of maintenance payments made after 15 March 1988 (which will continue to apply to maintenance payments after 5 April 2000 where one or both of the parties to the marriage is aged 65 or over on or before 5 April 2000) are considered below (see [52.8]). [52.5]

## 3 The treatment of maintenance payments after 5 April 2000

a) *Where neither party to the marriage is aged 65 or over on or before 5 April 2000*

Tax relief for maintenance payments is withdrawn altogether from 5 April 2000 where neither party to the marriage was born on or before 5 April 1935. Where payments are being made under existing obligations (see [52.4]) recipients will no longer be taxable on the payments they receive.      [52.6]

b) *Where one or both of the parties to the marriage is aged 65 or over on 5 April 2000*

Tax relief for maintenance payments is retained where one or both of the parties to the marriage was born on or before 5 April 1935. All payments made on or after 6 April 2000 will be treated in the same way as 'new' maintenance arrangements (henceforth referred to as current maintenance payments and see [52.8], including payments made under 'existing obligations').      [52.7]

c) *Tax treatment of current maintenance payments (TA 1988 s 347B)*

Payments of 'new' maintenance, whether to spouses or children, differ substantially from payments under existing obligations with the following three results. *First*, the payer is not entitled to deduct the sum paid as a charge on his income and is therefore forced to make the payment out of taxed income. *Secondly*, the sum is paid over gross to the recipient: there is no question of deducting income tax at source. *Finally*, the sum is received free from income tax: ie it does not fall under ITTOIA 2005 s 683 (formerly Schedule D Case III) as an annual payment. The position is the same in respect of payments arising outside the UK (see ITTOIA 2005 s 730). Only limited compensation for the payer is offered, whereby the payer's tax liability on his total income is reduced by a percentage (10% for 2006–07) of a specified amount (£2,350) or, if lower, the actual amount of the maintenance paid. If the payer's income tax liability is insufficient to offset the whole of the reduction, relief is given by reducing the liability to nil; he cannot claim any repayment of tax. In determining what a payer's income tax liability is for this purpose, tax at the basic rate that the claimant is entitled to deduct or retain out of charges on income is excluded. Further, any income tax reduction to which he may be entitled by reason of the age-related married couple's allowance, or the widow's bereavement allowance (which has been abolished with respect to deaths on or after 6 April 2000) is ignored. It should be noted that this relief is only available in the case of payments to a former or separated spouse: it is not available in the case of maintenance payments made directly to children. Nor is it sufficient merely that such payments are made directly to the former or separated spouse; the court order or agreement under which such payments are made must specify that the payments are to be made to the other parent for the maintenance of the child and not to the child itself (*Billingham v John* (1998)). Remarriage by the former recipient spouse precludes the payer from obtaining relief, and it is immaterial that the second marriage may also have ended in divorce (*Norris v Edgson* (2000)). The payments must be made under a UK court order or agreement or under court orders of countries that are members of the EU or assessed by the Child Support Agency (see *Otter v Andrews* (1999): voluntary payments of mortgage interest were not qualifying maintenance payments).                                                    **[52.8]**

### EXAMPLE 52.1

Under a court order made on 1 July 1991 Eric, who celebrated his 65th birthday on 14 December 1999, is obliged to make annual payments of £3,500 to his former wife Erica. Eric's income for the year 2005–06 is £40,000.

|  |  | £ |
|---|---|---:|
| Income | | 40,000.00 |
| *Deduct:* personal allowance (age allowance restricted because of total income) | | 5,035.00 |
| | | £34,965.00 |
| Income tax liability: | £2,150 at 10% = £215.00 | |
| | £31,149 at 22% = £6,852.78 | |
| | £1,665 at 40% = £ 666.00 | 7,733.78 |
| *Deduct:* relief in respect of maintenance payment, subject to a maximum amount of £2,350 = £2,350 × 10% | | 235.00 |
| Net income tax liability | | £7,498.78 |

### EXAMPLE 52.2

Under a court order made in February 1988 Andrew, who celebrated his 65th birthday on 1 December 1999, is obliged to make payments of £10,000 to his former wife Sarah, who has no other income. .. Andrew's income for the year 2006–07 is £60,000. Andrew's tax treatment in respect of these payments in 2006–07 is as follows:

|  | £ |
|---|---:|
| Income | 60,000.00 |
| *Deduct:* personal allowance (age allowance restricted because of total income) | 5,035.00 |
| | £54,965.00 |

| Income tax liability: | £2,150 at 10% = £215.00 | |
|---|---|---|
| | £31,149 at 22% = £6,852.78 | |
| | £21,665 at 40% = £8,666.00 | 15,733.78 |
| *Deduct:* relief in respect of maintenance payments, subject to a maximum amount of £2,350 = £2,350 × 10% | | 23500 |
| Net income tax liability | | £15,498.78 |

(1)   In spite of the fact that the maintenance arrangements were made before 15 March 1988, Andrew cannot deduct any of the payments in computing his total income and therefore will have to meet the payments out of income that will have suffered tax at the higher rate of 40%.

(2)   The sum is not treated as Sarah's income.

(3)   Only limited relief is provided in that Andrew is entitled to a reduction in his income tax liability in respect of payments made to his former spouse.

## 4   Effect of withdrawal of relief for maintenance payments

The major changes that were made by FA 1988 in the treatment of maintenance payments had serious repercussions. Crucially, new maintenance payments were largely removed from the tax system. The result was that payments in favour of children no longer attracted tax relief, whilst payments to a former spouse only afforded the payer limited relief by way of a tax credit based upon a percentage of the then-existing married couple's allowance. Whilst poorer families remained largely unaffected by these important changes, couples in the middle-income bracket did suffer. The changes appear to have resulted in a reduction in the amounts paid under maintenance arrangements. For the wealthy, a switch to outright transfers of capital instead of income payments has been discernible. Accordingly, the withdrawal from 5 April 2000 of the very limited relief available to maintenance payments is unlikely to have any greater impact upon a system that had already undergone this radical change.                                  **[52.9]**

## 5   Pensions and divorce

Apart from the matrimonial home, the asset of greatest value to a married couple is the accumulated pension provision of the money earner. For the older divorcing couple, the financial arrangements made for their retirement will need adjusting since they will no longer be living in one household. How to treat pensions on divorce has, in the past, proved to be a major problem, stemming from the fact that, on divorce, the accrued pension rights of the parties are not usually equal: the spouse who has remained at home to care for the family is less likely to have built up pension entitlement than the working spouse.

This position has changed considerably in recent years due, in the main, to three factors: *first,* the high profile given to the problem by the case of *Brooks v Brooks* (1995) and the innovative way in which it was approached; *secondly,* the Pensions Act 1995 and the 'pension attachment' provisions and *thirdly,* the Welfare Reform and Pensions Act (WRPA) 1999 and 'pension sharing'.
                                  **[52.10]**

## a)   *Brooks v Brooks and the variation of settlements*

In *Brooks v Brooks*, the House of Lords held that a pension fund set up by the husband's company during the course of the marriage, and which specifically provided for a pension for his spouse, was a post-nuptial settlement which could be varied by the court in order to provide the wife with an immediate annuity and a pension on the termination of the marriage. In a previous case, *Griffiths v Dawson & Co* (1993), the court had held a solicitor, acting on behalf of a wife who was being divorced, negligent for failure to hold up the proceedings in order to investigate any possible rights she may have had in the pension fund linked to her husband's employment. (It is also arguable that a pension established prior to the marriage may be varied as an ante-nuptial settlement.) Provided both that the rules of the pension fund allow for the other spouse (frequently the wife) to claim such benefits and that the wife is of an age to take advantage of those benefits, and that third party rights are not prejudiced, these cases seem to provide an alternative means of providing income for a divorced spouse through contributions paid by the employed spouse which had not suffered tax. (It would seem that a variation of settlement order may be available in relation to any type of pension scheme apart from an unfunded statutory scheme. A retirement annuity contract or personal pension can only be varied insofar as the benefits will be approved by the Revenue.)

It should be noted that, with respect to petitions on or after 1 December 2000 (when the pension sharing provisions came into effect), this solution will no longer be available except as a consent incorporated in the preamble of the consent order by way of undertaking (WRPA 1999 Sch 3 para 3).

**[52.11]**

## b)   *Pensions Act 1995 and 'pension attachment'*

The courts now have a duty to consider the loss of pension rights in a divorce settlement (or on judicial separation) and can require the trustees of an occupational scheme to make a payment to the other party to the marriage when payment under the scheme becomes due to the party with the pension rights (see PA 1995 ss 166, 167 inserting into the Matrimonial Causes Act 1973 new ss 25B–25D). Periodical payments under a pension attachment order (formerly known as earmarking orders and renamed pension attachment orders by WRPA 1999) are regarded as deferred maintenance for income tax purposes. Such payments are therefore not taxable in the hands of the payee, but are regarded as the income of the scheme member.

**[52.12]**

## c)   *Welfare Reform and Pensions Act 1999 and pension sharing*

Pension sharing was introduced by WRPA 1999. The provisions are not retrospective, and only apply to petitions for divorce issued on or after 1 December 2000 (although, if the petition for divorce (say, by the husband) was issued prior to 1 December 2000, but no decree absolute had been granted by 1 December 2000, it is open to the wife to issue her own second petition for divorce).

Pension sharing enables the court to split a pension into any percentage at the time of divorce so that, for example, the wife may either become a member of the husband's scheme in her own right or, as an alternative, may take a transfer of an amount into her own pension scheme. It has been stated that provision for, say, a wife from a husband's pension did not introduce an 'entitlement-driven' system of pension-loss compensation (*T v T (Financial Relief: Pensions)* (1998); *Burrow v Burrow* (1999)); rather, their application should be based upon the needs of the claimant. However, in light of the decision in *White v White* (2001) and, more recently, *Miller v Miller* and *McFarlane v McFarlane* (2006), it is suggested that the court, in operating the principles of fairness, equality and non-discrimination, should consider not just the needs of the claimant, but also the requirement of compensation for any economic disadvantage generated by the relationship and the sharing of the fruits of the matrimonial partnership. In contrast to periodical payments under a pension attachment order, periodic pension payments under a pension sharing order are taxable at the payee's marginal rate of tax. It will therefore be appreciated that 'sharing' carries a considerable tax advantage, with each spouse having allowances/starting and lower rates of tax to set against the income resulting from the split.                    **[52.13]**

## 6  Life insurance policies and divorce

Where a court makes an order for ancillary relief under MCA 1973 which results in *either* a transfer of rights under a life insurance policy, capital redemption policy or a purchased life annuity from one spouse to the other *or* a formal ratification of an agreement reached by the divorcing parties that deals with the transfer of assets including a life insurance policy etc, the Revenue view is that the transfer of ownership of the policy is not for money or money's worth. As a consequence, no gain arises upon which income tax could be chargeable. This revised interpretation represents a change of view on the part of the Revenue (see *Tax Bulletin*, December 2003).        **[52.14]**

## 7  Tax credits

Where a joint claim for an award of tax credits is made either by a husband and wife or civil partners, or by a couple living together as husband and wife or as civil partners, the award will come to an end when the couple separates or when they cease to live together as husband or wife or as civil partners. There is a formal requirement to notify HMRC of such a change in circumstances if it occurs during the year for which an award has been made (Tax Credits Act 2002 s 6(3); The Tax Credit (Claims and Notification) Regulations 2002 (SI 2002/2014) reg 21 as amended). The penalty for not making the required notification is a fine not exceeding £300. Once the couple stop living together, a new claim must then be made, if appropriate, by each party, and any new award of the child tax credit and the childcare element of the working tax credit will only be made to the person who is the main carer of the child.                    **[52.15]–[52.20]**

## II  CAPITAL GAINS TAX

### 1  **The parameters of s 58**

Disposals between spouses are not subject to CGT and are treated as made for a consideration that will produce neither gain nor loss (see TCGA 1992 s 58 and **Chapter 19**). Once the spouses separate this provision ceases to apply and the ordinary rules of CGT operate (but note *Gubay v Kington* (1984)). Hence, a transfer of chargeable assets between spouses after their separation may be subject to CGT (see, for instance, *Aspden v Hildesley* (1982)). It is therefore crucial that the reorganisation of capital assets on the breakdown of a marriage should be arranged, so far as possible, to come within s 58. That section only applies in cases where the disposal is between spouses who 'in that year of assessment' were living together. Accordingly, if assets are not transferred in the year of separation, the no gain/no loss rule will be inapplicable. It also follows that, on a subsequent disposal of assets by the transferee spouse, taper relief will not operate with reference to the combined holding period of the spouses but, rather, to the holding period of the transferee spouse only. Although the exemption for inter-spouse transfers is lost in the tax year following separation, the couple remain connected persons until final divorce so that disposals between separation and divorce are deemed not to be bargains at arm's length, but are treated as for a consideration equal to the market value of the property (TCGA 1992 s 18). However, following the decision of *G v G* (2002), where there is a transfer of business assets pursuant to a court order, HMRC will now permit hold over relief (see **[24.21]**), thereby deferring any CGT liability to the recipient on a future disposal. This new policy will not apply to the transfer of business assets between spouses without recourse to the courts, unless the parties are able to demonstrate that there was a substantial gratuitous element in the transfer and that no consideration passed in the form of a surrender of rights. Since taper relief for business assets is available after a mere two years of ownership, resulting in an effective CGT rate of only 10%, this policy is of far less importance than it might otherwise have been.                    **[52.21]**

### 2  **The annual exemption**

For the year 2005–06 husband and wife are each entitled to their own annual CGT exemption (£8,800) and this entitlement will remain unaffected by separation.                                                                        **[52.22]**

### 3  **Orders for the payment of a lump sum under MCA 1973 s 31(7B)**

Under MCA 1973 s 31, the court has the power to vary, discharge or suspend an order for financial provision for a party to a marriage or former marriage. It may, for instance, under s 31(7A) discharge an order for periodical payments and then under s 31(7B) make a supplemental provision, for example for the payment of a lump sum. The Revenue accepts that in awarding the lump sum the court is exercising its discretion afresh and hence that sum is not derived from an asset (namely the now discharged right to periodical payments). Hence, TCGA 1992 s 22(1) (see **[19.112]**) does not apply and the lump sum is free of CGT (see *Tax Bulletin*, April 2001, p 840).

**[52.23]–[52.40]**

## III INHERITANCE TAX

For IHT purposes marriage continues until the final divorce so that transfers between spouses after separation and before divorce continue to be exempt. After final divorce, the general rules operate, unless the dispositions are exempt under IHTA 1984 s 11 (see **Chapter 31**). Maintenance payments fall within s 11 and are, therefore, exempt from IHT. However, s 11 is probably not wide enough to cover maintenance paid by way of a transfer of a capital sum or of a capital asset which may, therefore, be chargeable unless it does not reduce the transferor's estate (for example because it is in satisfaction of outstanding financial claims by the former spouse), or lacks gratuitous intent. In most cases the absence of gratuitous intent ensures no tax charge for transfers between former spouses that result from the breakdown of the marriage (see the statement of the Senior Registrar of the Family Division made with the agreement of the Revenue (1975) 119 SJ 396).

**[52.41]–[52.60]**

## IV THE MATRIMONIAL HOME

### 1 The difficulties

The matrimonial home will often be the only valuable asset owned by a couple so that its destination on divorce poses a number of tax problems. Before considering these, however, it is important to discover who owns the home. One spouse may be the sole owner at law but the other spouse may have acquired an equitable interest in the property either expressly (eg by agreement between the parties in writing) or under a resulting trust arising from that spouse's monetary contribution to the purchase of the property (see, for example, *Gissing v Gissing* (1971)), or under a constructive trust. A constructive trust may arise in one of two ways. *First*, there may be evidence of an express agreement or an express representation that the property is to be shared beneficially and that the other spouse has acted to his or her detriment in relying on that agreement or representation. *Alternatively* there may be evidence based on the conduct of the parties from which can be inferred a common intention to share the property beneficially, such conduct normally being a direct financial contribution by the spouse who is not the legal owner (*Lloyds Bank plc v Rosset* (1991)). If the house is to be sold on divorce, or its ownership transferred in whole or in part from one (former) spouse to the other, problems of income tax, CGT and (exceptionally) IHT may arise.

**[52.61]**

### 2 Income tax

Usually the property will be subject to a mortgage in favour of either a building society or a bank. Opportunities to maximise family resources on a marriage breakdown by the use of mortgage interest relief disappeared with the abolition of this relief in 2000–01. For an explanation of those opportunities, see earlier editions of this book.                                                **[52.62]**

## 3   CGT

Before separation any disposal of the matrimonial property will be exempt from CGT if it is the spouses' main residence. Once the parties separate, however, an absent spouse who has an interest in the property may incur a CGT liability on a disposal of it (for the availability of hold-over relief under TCGA 1992 s 165 (gifts of business assets) when the transfer is ordered by the court, see *Tax Bulletin*, August 2003 p 1051). Difficulties principally arise in two cases: assume in each case that the husband owns the house which he has left, and that the wife remains in occupation throughout.           **[52.63]**

*Case 1* The house is to be transferred to the wife. This disposal by the husband will not fall within the no gain/no loss rules of TCGA 1992 s 58 since the parties have been separated throughout the relevant tax year. Further, the husband has been absent from the house since the date of separation. So long as the disposal occurs within three years of that date, no charge will arise on any part of the gain (TCGA 1992 s 223(1)), but once that three-year period expires, the proportion of the total gain that is deemed to have accrued from the end of that period may be chargeable (the appropriate calculation is described at **[23.83]**). Any charge is, however, avoided if ESC D6 applies:

> 'Where a married couple separate or are divorced and one partner ceases to occupy the matrimonial home and subsequently as part of a financial settlement disposes of the home, or an interest in it, to the other partner, the home may be regarded for the purpose of sections [222 to 224 of TCGA 1992] as continuing to be a residence of the transferring partner from the date his or her occupation ceases until the date of transfer, provided that it has throughout this period been the other partner's only or main residence. Thus, where a husband leaves the matrimonial home while still owning it, the usual capital gains tax exemption or relief for a taxpayer's only or main residence would be given on the subsequent transfer to the wife, provided she has continued to live in the house and the husband has not elected that some other house should be treated for capital gains tax purposes as his main residence for this period.'

Provided that the wife has continuously occupied the house as her only or main residence and the husband has not elected for another house to be his main residence, the disposal of the house may, therefore, occur many years after the separation.                                                              **[52.64]**

*Case 2* The house is to be sold. If the sale occurs more than three years after the separation, ESC D6 (because the disposal is not to the wife) is not available, so that there will be a charge on a proportion of the total gain, subject to taper relief.                                                    **[52.65]**

## 4   IHT and stamp duty land tax

Transactions involving the matrimonial home will not usually involve IHT. Either the inter-spouse exemption still applies or, after divorce, there is no gratuitous intent (see **Chapter 28**). Moreover, provided that a transfer of assets on divorce to a former spouse is pursuant to a court order, transferors should escape any possible liability under the pre-owned asset regime (see **[29.141]**). The transfer of property between spouses and former spouses as a result of the breakdown of marriage are not subject to stamp duty land tax whether the transfer is made pursuant to a court order or by the agreement of the parties alone (see FA 2003 Sch 3 para 3). Furthermore, if the appropriate certificate is given there is no fixed duty and no adjudication requirement (SI 1987/516 as amended).                      **[52.66]**

## 5  The taxation consequences of typical court orders

In order to consider the taxation implications of four typical court orders dealing with the matrimonial home on divorce, assume throughout that the spouse who has left (H) owns the matrimonial home.                 **[52.67]**

### a)  *The order for outright transfer (the 'clean-break')*

H is ordered to transfer the entire ownership of the house to W (see *Hanlon v Hanlon* (1978)). H may also be ordered to make maintenance payments covering, *inter alia*, any mortgage payments to be made by W.         **[52.68]**

*Income tax* Relief is no longer obtainable on any mortgage interest payments that she makes.                                     **[52.69]**

*CGT* The disposal to W attracts no charge if it occurs within three years of separation; if it occurs later, there is no charge if ESC D6 applies.     **[52.70]**

*IHT* No charge arises as a transfer pursuant to a court order lacks gratuitous intent.                                          **[52.71]**

### b)  *H and W become joint owners of the house with sale postponed*

H is ordered to transfer an interest in the house to W. The couple will be tenants in common. W will be entitled to live in the house to the exclusion of H and the sale will be postponed until (for instance) the children reach 18 (see *Mesher v Mesher* (1980)).                           **[52.72]**

*Income tax* Although W has an interest in the house, there is no longer any entitlement to mortgage interest relief on the payments that she makes.
                                                          **[52.73]**

*CGT* When the half interest in the house is transferred to W the result is as in a) above. On the eventual sale of the house, a proportion of the gain on H's share will be chargeable (corresponding to his period of absence and subject to taper relief), unless it can be argued that the effect of the order is to create a settlement. Normally, jointly owned land is not settled (TCGA 1992 s 60; *Kidson v MacDonald* (1974) and **Chapter 25**). It may, however, be argued that because W has an exclusive right to occupy under the terms of the order the parties are not 'jointly absolutely entitled' since they do not have identical interests in the property. Accordingly, if the property is settled, no CGT will be charged upon its disposal, because it will have been occupied by W 'under the terms of the settlement' (see TCGA 1992 s 225). This is understood to be the current Revenue view.    **[52.74]**

*IHT* The property is not settled as there is no succession of interests (IHTA 1984 s 43). Hence if either party died their estate at death would include the half share of the house valued with a discount of (usually) 10–15%.    **[52.75]**

c)    *Settling the house*

W is given the right to live in the house for her life, or until remarriage, or until voluntary departure, whichever happens first. Thereafter, the house is to be sold and the proceeds divided equally between H and W (see *Martin v Martin* (1977)).    **[52.76]**

*Income tax* W is no longer able to claim tax relief on the mortgage payments.    **[52.77]**

*CGT* The creation of the settlement will not be chargeable (as in a) above) and on the termination of the life interest although a deemed disposal under TCGA 1992 s 71(1) will occur (see **[25.47]**), no charge to CGT will arise because of either the main residence exemption (TCGA 1992 s 225) or because of the death exemption (TCGA 1992, s 73).    **[52.78]**

*IHT* There will be no charge on the creation of the settlement (see **[52.71]**). W has an interest in possession and is, accordingly, deemed to own the house (IHTA 1984 s 50(5) and **[33.1]**). However, pursuant to the FA 2006, the property within the settlement will become relevant property and will be subject to the periodic charge (**[34.26]**) and, when W's interest comes to an end, the exit charge (**[34.23]**). If H is still alive, the other half share is excluded from charge under the reverter to settlor provisions (**[33.34]**). If H dies before W, his reversionary interest in the proceeds of sale is not excluded property, however, and is, therefore, chargeable (IHTA 1984 s 48(1); **[33.61]**) and a further charge will arise when the life interest ends in that half share on W's death since the reverter to settlor exemption does not apply.    **[52.79]**

d)    *Outright transfer subject to a charge over the property in favour of the transferor*

H transfers the house to W, but is granted a charge over the property either for a specific sum (as in *Hector v Hector* (1973)), or for a proportion of the sale proceeds (as in *Browne v Pritchard* (1975)). Sale and payment may be postponed until the children attain 18 or until W dies or wishes to leave the house.    **[52.80]**

*Income tax* Even if W makes the mortgage payments, she is no longer entitled to any relief.    **[52.81]**
*IHT* The property is not settled, but belongs to W—no charge.    **[52.82]**

*CGT* The transfer to W should not be chargeable on the principles in a) above. On the eventual sale, the position is not entirely clear. If H's charge is for a specific sum, this must be a debt due to H. Therefore, when the house is

finally sold and the debt repaid there will be no charge to CGT on the repayment (TCGA 1992 s 251; see **[22.42]**). If the charge is for a proportionate share of the proceeds of sale, however, H's right is not a debt, but a *chose in action*, ie the right to a future uncertain sum; see *Marren v Ingles* (1980) and **Chapter 19**. As a result, when the house is eventually sold and a sum of money paid to H, there will be a chargeable disposal of that *chose in action*.
**[52.83]**

e)  *Conclusions*

It must be stressed that taxation factors are not the most important considerations to be borne in mind when considering financial adjustments upon a matrimonial breakdown. The outright transfer may currently be the ideal for tax purposes, but it leaves the husband with no interest in the former matrimonial home and so deprives him of any capital appreciation. Further, the court has no power to adjust property orders once made, so they must be correct at the start. Finally, a transfer of the house or an interest therein is quite different from a declaration (normally under the Married Women's Property Act 1882) that a woman owns, and has always owned, a share in the asset. No transfer is involved in such cases and the taxation consequences of transfers discussed above are irrelevant.          **[52.84]**

# Section 10    Charities

**Chapters**

# 53 Tax treatment of charities

*Updated by Alison Paines and David Goepel, Withers LLP*

Charity law has been undergoing a fundamental reassessment in recent years. For centuries the law had been governed with reference to the Preamble to the Statute of Elizabeth of 1601, as interpreted by the dicta of Lord Macnaghten in *IRC v Pemsel* (1891). However, the first years of the twenty-first century have seen a major review, triggered by the NCVO Report of July 2001, and culminating in the publication of the draft Charities Bill in May 2004. The Bill was delayed by the 2005 General Election, but was reintroduced into the House of Commons in November 2005. As at July 2006, it had completed its Second Reading in the Commons and indications are that it may be enacted before the end of 2006. Although the changes proposed in the Bill do not specifically amend the taxation of charities, they will inevitably impact widely on the content of this chapter. Nevertheless, at the time of writing, charity law remains as described below, and is a complex area in relation to which the adviser will need to refer to the standard works on the subject, for example, Tudor, Picarda or *Tolley's Charities Manual.*

There have, however, been many changes to the tax treatment of charities in recent years, in particular in relation to the revision of Gift Aid in FA 2000 and the extension of income tax relief to gifts of quoted shares and land in FA 2001 and 2002. In addition, FA 2006 has introduced a number of further measures affecting the taxation of charities and their donors. [**53.1**]–[**53.20**]

## I   QUALIFYING CHARITIES

### 1   General

Tax reliefs are only available to bodies which are, in English law, charities. In general, the large majority of charities in England and Wales are now obliged to register with the Charity Commission, (and registration is widely seen as a 'badge' of charitable status). At present, however, charities which have failed to register may still have satisfied HMRC that they are established for charitable purposes only. There are also some charities which do not need to register with the Commission (Charities Act 1993 s 3(5)), and these include exempt charities under Charities Act 1993 Sch 2, any charity which is excepted by order or regulations and any charity which has neither any permanent endowment nor the use or occupation of any land and whose income does not amount to more than £1,000 a year. Clause 9 of the Charities Bill proposes to widen the class of charities which do not need to register with the Commission to include, for example, any charity whose gross income does not exceed £5,000 (subject to some exceptions). **[53.21]**

## 2   Definition of charity

The legal definition of charity in English law as it remains at present is complex, depending as it does on a voluminous body of case law.

The principal themes were drawn together by Lord Macnaghten (in *Income Tax Special Purposes Commissioners v Pemsel* (1891)), who classified charitable purposes under the following four headings, which form the generally-accepted legal definition as it stands in 2006:

i)   the relief of poverty
ii)  the advancement of education
iii) the advancement of religion
iv)  other purposes beneficial to the community.

In addition, there is a general requirement that charities must be for the benefit of the public at large, or a sufficient section of the public—the 'public benefit test'. Under the law as it stands, there is a (rebuttable) presumption that a charity promoting any of the first three heads will be for the public benefit, whereas charities seeking to qualify under the fourth head must actively show that they will benefit the public.

The fourth category is of course a very broad sweep-up head. For some, this simply causes confusion and undermines the purpose of a categorisation at all; for others it represents the beauty of a common law system, and allows flexibility for the definition to change with the times. It is certainly true that case law has allowed numerous additional purposes to qualify as charitable under the fourth head, for example, the relief of unemployment, the protection of the environment and the promotion of amateur sport, provided of course that they are deemed to satisfy the public benefit test mentioned above.

All of this is likely to be changed if the draft Charities Bill proceeds as planned. The Bill proposes a new definition of 'charitable purposes', comprising a two-stage test. First, to qualify as charitable, a purpose would have to come under one of the following 13 heads:

a)   the prevention or relief of poverty;
b)   the advancement of education;
c)   the advancement of religion;
d)   the advancement of health or the saving of lives;
e)   the advancement of citizenship or community development;
f)   the advancement of the arts, culture, heritage or science;
g)   the advancement of amateur sport;
h)   the advancement of human rights, conflict resolution or reconciliation or the promotion of religious or racial harmony or equality and diversity;

i) the advancement of environmental protection or improvement;
j) the relief of those in need, by reason of youth, age, ill-health, disability, financial hardship or other disadvantage;
k) the advancement of animal welfare;
l) the promotion of the efficiency of the armed forces of the Crown; and
m) a sweep-up category including:

    1    any purposes not within (a)–(l) but recognised as charitable purposes under existing charity law or by virtue of the Recreational Charities Act 1958 s 1;

    2    any purposes that may reasonably be regarded as analogous to any purposes within paragraphs (a)–(l) or (1) above; and

    3    any purposes that may reasonably be regarded as analogous to or within the spirit of, any purposes which have been recognised under charity law as falling within paragraph (2) above or this paragraph.

Secondly, all charities in the future would also need to satisfy the public benefit test on an equal basis, thereby effectively removing the presumption of public benefit which currently applies to some charities as mentioned above.

Many of the new 13 purposes are of course very similar to existing recognised purposes (and paragraphs (d) to (l) largely codify existing fourth head purposes, although there is likely to be some debate in future as to the scope of (e) and (h) for example). An important element is likely to be the 13th head, which retains a sweep-up provision, and which importantly will include any other existing recognised purposes and also purposes 'analogous to, or within the spirit of', any existing purpose, which should allow the Courts and the Charity Commission flexibility to continue to develop the law in future. **[53.22]**

## 3  Charitable work outside the UK and foreign charities

The charitable purposes do not have to be carried out exclusively in the UK: the Charity Commissioners accept charitable purposes abroad on the assumption that 'the relief of poverty and the advancement of education and religion are charitable in all parts of the world', and state that they 'test the public benefit issue in the same way for organisations intending to operate in whole or in part in other countries as we do for organisations operating in England and Wales'.

The Charity Commissioners are limited in their operations to England and Wales. In Scotland, a register of charities has in the past been maintained by HMRC, but the Charities and Trustee Investment (Scotland) Act 2005 has established an independent regulator, the Office of the Scottish Charity Regulator, whose responsibilities now include the maintenance of a register of Scottish charities. Further, the Commissioners' jurisdiction is restricted to charities which are defined in the Charities Act 1993 s 96(1) as 'any institution, corporate or not, which is established for charitable purposes and is subject to the control of the High Court in the exercise of the Court's jurisdiction with respect to charities'. Overseas charities will, in practice, only come within this definition if a majority of the trustees or the bulk of the funds are subject to the control of the High Court and therefore to supervision by the Attorney-General.

Despite 'charity' being defined in the TA 1988 as 'any body of persons established for charitable purposes only' the House of Lords decided in *Camille and Henry Dreyfus Foundation Inc v IRC* (1956) that these words had to be limited to a body of persons or trusts established for such purposes *in the UK*. In that case a foundation established in the State of New York and which carried on all its activities in the USA was not entitled to exemption (under the forerunner of s 505) for substantial royalties which it received from a company resident in the UK. The later case of *Gaudiya Mission v Brahmachary* (1997) confirmed that a corporate body whose objects were charitable under English law, but which was established and registered in India, was not subject to the jurisdiction of the High Court, and therefore not a 'charity' within the meaning of the 1993 Act. To ensure that this requirement is met a charitable trust should be subject to UK proper law and have a majority of UK resident trustees and a charitable company should be incorporated under the Companies Acts.    **[53.23]**

### 4  Non-charitable purpose trusts

English law has generally refused to accept that non-charitable purpose trusts are valid. Amongst the reasons given for this attitude are that, in a number of cases, the purposes have been so imprecisely drafted that it would be difficult to control the trustees in the exercise of their functions; in other cases the purposes would continue forever and therefore breach the perpetuity rule; whilst certain purposes have been stigmatised as useless or capricious (see, for instance, *McCaig v University of Glasgow* (1907) in which the court set aside a will trust that would have involved building statues of the deceased and other 'artistic towers' at prominent points on his estate).    **[53.24]**

### 5  The policy of conferring tax reliefs on all charities

There has been debate in the past as to whether all charities should automatically receive the uniform tax benefits available and there have been suggestions that only some charities should qualify, for example, those whose operation is for the public benefit to a sufficient degree (see Lord Cross of Chelsea in *Dingle v Turner* (1972)). As the Charities Bill proposes a uniform public benefit test for all charities, it is likely that this debate will be less important. Certainly there is no current legislative proposal to distinguish between charities in fiscal terms although community amateur sports clubs (which are not of themselves charitable) have a slightly different tax treatment from fully-qualifying charities—see **[53.100]**.    **[53.25]–[53.40]**

## II   TAX RELIEF ON CHARITABLE INCOME AND GAINS

### 1  Relief from direct taxes

TA 1988 s 505 and TCGA 1992 s 256 confer relief from income tax, CGT and corporation tax in respect of:

(1)   rent from land and property;
(2)   interest and dividends;
(3)   single gifts by companies and individuals (Gift Aid);
(4)   grants from other charities; and
(5)   chargeable gains.

In cases where tax has been deducted at source, the recipient charity is normally entitled to a refund by application to HMRC Charities division (the special position of charities which receive distributions (including dividends) from companies is discussed in **Chapter 42**). The relevant income must form part of the income of a charity or be applicable, and applied, for charitable purposes only (TA 1988 s 505 and see *IRC v The Helen Slater Charitable Trust Ltd* (1982)).

FA 2006 has made some changes to the mechanism for providing relief to charities (see **[53. 61]–[53.80]**) and added some further rules which deny relief to charities involved in 'transactions with substantial donors' – see **[53.44]–[53.60]** for more detail.                                                    **[53.41]**

## 2   Trading

Trading income is only exempt from tax in the following circumstances:
(1)   Where the trade carries out a primary purpose of the charity (eg an educational charity running a school).
(2)   Where the work is done mainly by beneficiaries of the charity (eg a charity set up to provide work for the disabled).
(3)   Where profits are from a fund-raising event, such as a ball or concert, which has exemption from VAT under VATA 1994 Sch 9 Group 12 (see **[53.127]**). The event must be organised primarily to raise money for the charity and the exemption only applies if not more than 15 events of the same type are held in the same location in a financial year. Events where weekly gross takings do not exceed £1,000 do not count towards the 15 events allowed for the purposes of this exemption. (See ESC C4.)
(4)   Where the total annual turnover of trades which are not otherwise exempt does not exceed £5,000 (or 25% of all the charity's incoming resources if greater—maximum £50,000). The exemption also applies if at the beginning of the period the charity had a reasonable expectation that the annual turnover would not be exceeded. (FA 2000 s 46).

Where charities carry out mixed trades (ie where some of the trade qualifies for relief and some does not), they previously had to rely on an HMRC concession to the effect that relief would be allowed pro rata, so that the non-qualifying element of the trade did not taint the qualifying element. FA 2006 s 56 (inserting a new s 505(1B) TA 1988 ) has regularised the position by ensuring that the practice is given a statutory footing, by treating the qualifying element as a separate trade from the non-qualifying element.

In those cases where the proposed trade does not satisfy the tests mentioned above, the device that has been commonly adopted by charities is to incorporate a company to carry out the work and for the profits thereby produced to be paid as Gift Aid payments to the charity. The result of so doing is that the taxable profits of the company are kept at zero and the sums received by the charity do not themselves attract tax. It is important that the right amount is paid by the company for if the Gift Aid payment turns out to be *less than* the profit, the company is left with a corporation tax liability: if *more than* the profit is paid, the excess has to be refunded by the charity (which also has to repay HMRC any excess tax refunded). To avoid this problem it is now provided that if a Gift Aid payment is made within nine months after the end of an accounting period and the paying company is wholly owned by a charity, the company can claim to treat the Gift Aid payment as made in that accounting period (TA 1988 s 339(7AA)–(7AC)). This means that a company, which is wholly owned by a charity, may calculate its profits for an accounting period and then make a Gift Aid payment to the charity within nine months of the end of the period, and thereby reduce its taxable profits to nil. An alternative method, for the profits to be paid to the charity by means of a dividend, is not recommended since not all the tax suffered by the company is recovered (see generally *Trading by Charities*, HMRC website).

The use of trading subsidiaries came under scrutiny in the recent case of *Noved Investment Co v HMRC* [2006] SSCD 120 (SpC 521). However, FA 2006 s 57 has clarified that the treatment mentioned above will continue to apply, and indeed has offered a concession, effectively extending the relief by allowing the Gift Aid mechanism described above to apply where a trading subsidiary company is jointly owned by a number of charities.

On the other hand, the abolition of the corporation tax nil rate band in FA 2006 will have a knock-on effect for charities and their trading subsidiary companies, which had previously been able to make use of this to build up working capital up to the nil rate band limit.                    **[53.42]**

### 3  Land transactions

It is worth noting that although charities are exempt from the usual charge to income tax on receipts representing rents and profits from land, they are not automatically exempt from the charge to income tax on gains of a capital nature realised from transactions in land which fall within TA 1988 s 776 (see **[13.101]–[13.113]**).                    **[53.43]**

### 4  Transactions with substantial donors

FA 2006 has introduced an entirely new set of rules under which charities can be denied tax relief on their income and gains. The rules operate to remove some of a charity's tax relief if the charity enters into certain transactions (listed below) with any of its 'substantial donors'.

The definition of a 'substantial donor' for these purposes is:
(1)   a person who has donated at least £25,000 to a charity in any period of 12 months; or
(2)   a person who has donated at least £100,000 to a charity over a period of six years

in which the relevant tax year falls in each case.

The new rules target certain transactions between a charity and any of its substantial donors and apply to transactions occurring on or after 22 March 2006 (irrespective of when the substantial donor has made his gift(s) to the charity). Where a transaction is caught under the rules, any payment by the charity to the substantial donor is deemed to be non-charitable expenditure by the charity. Similarly, if there is a difference between the actual price paid for the transaction and the market price and this favours the substantial donor, then this amount will also be treated as non-qualifying expenditure in the hands of the charity.

Under the new rules introduced in FA 2006, this means that tax relief is denied to the charity on a pound-for-pound basis with reference to the amount of the non-charitable expenditure incurred (see **[13.61]–[13.80]** below).

Transactions that will be caught under the new rules include the following:

(1)  the sale or letting of property by a charity to a substantial donor or vice-versa;
(2)  the provision of services by a charity to a substantial donor or vice-versa;
(3)  the exchange of property between a charity and a substantial donor;
(4)  the provision of financial assistance (including loans, guarantees or indemnities) by a charity to a substantial donor or vice-versa; and
(5)  investment by a charity in the business of a substantial donor, if the business is not listed on a recognised stock exchange.

There are some exemptions, the most important being that the new rules will generally not apply where a transaction is on arm's length terms and not part of tax avoidance arrangements (though where a donor is providing services, this must be in the course of a business being carried on by the donor).

Similarly, the rules will not apply to transactions between a charity and its wholly-owned trading subsidiary company.

If the exemptions are applied sensibly by HMRC and the Charity Commission, the new rules should not unduly restrict most donors from activities they would reasonably wish to undertake. Nevertheless, the rules do represent a surprising further encroachment on charity tax reliefs, focussing on the charity's own tax position rather than the traditional approach of restricting the application of Gift Aid or other tax reliefs where a donor benefits from his dealings with a charity (see **[53.84]**).          **[53.44]–[53.60]**


## III  EXPENDITURE BY A CHARITABLE BODY

To qualify for the tax benefits set out in this chapter, the charity must spend its money *only for charitable purposes*. Such expenditure will, of course, include the cost of its own charitable activities; buying assets to be used in activities; administrative and fund-raising costs; and the payment of money to bodies established to carry out the work of the charity. It is crucial to bear in mind, however, that spending money on non-charitable purposes, or investing or lending money in ways which are not for the benefit of the charitable objects, will not only result in a withdrawal of tax relief so far as both the charity and (in certain cases) its donors are concerned, but may also involve the appropriate trustees in committing a breach of trust.

It should be noted that a charity can also be treated as incurring non-charitable expenditure to the extent that it makes any investment which is not a qualifying investment (as defined in TA 1988, Sch 20, Part I), or makes a loan which is not a qualifying loan (as defined in TA 1988, Sch 20, Part II).

The precise mechanism for denying tax relief for non-charitable expenditure was altered by FA 2006 s 55, which has replaced the previous formula by making a direct link between non-charitable expenditure incurred by a charity and loss of tax relief, so that income and gains eligible for tax relief will be restricted by £1 for every £1 of non-charitable expenditure. The new provisions allow for excess non-charitable expenditure to be carried back to be set off against previous income and gains of the charity for up to the six previous tax years if necessary. In addition, until 2006, these rules did not apply to charities whose relevant income and gains were less than £10,000 per year. This limit has now been removed, bringing smaller charities directly within the ambit of the restrictions.The effect of incurring non-charitable expenditure was illustrated in *IRC v Educational Grants Association Ltd* (1967). In that case, the Educational Grants Association had been established for the advancement of education and had a close relationship with the Metal Box Company Ltd in that the bulk of its income came from a deed of covenant executed in its favour by that company. On a repayment claim for income tax deducted at source being made, it transpired that between 76% and 85% of the income of the charity was applied for the education of children of persons connected with the Metal Box Company Ltd. Accordingly the claim for repayment failed since the court was not convinced that the income of the charity was being applied for 'charitable purposes only'. In deciding that the organisation had expended money for non-charitable purposes, the judge accepted that this involved concluding that the managers had acted *ultra vires* in spending the Association's income: he therefore concluded: 'it is of course open to a comparable body to frame its objects so as to make clear that its income may be applied for private as well as public purposes, but in that case it may not obtain tax relief. It does not seem to me that such a body can have it both ways.'                          **[53.61]–[53.80]**

## IV   EFFECTIVE CHARITABLE GIVING

Tax relief for charitable giving was radically overhauled in FA 2000. Before that date:
(1)   Gift Aid was available for large one-off donations of £250 or more; and
(2)   deeds of covenant could be made which involved a legally enforceable obligation to make payments to a charity over a period which had to be capable of exceeding three years. There were no maximum or minimum limits.
As a measure of simplification the Gift Aid scheme was extended by FA 2000 and donations under deed of covenant brought within the scheme.
                                                                     **[53.81]**

## 1   Gift Aid (FA 1990 ss 25, 26 amended by FA 2000)

### a)   *Gift Aid after FA 2000*

The changes made by FA 2000 achieve a large measure of simplification as well as extending the scope of the relief. As from 6 April 2000 the £250 minimum payment has been abolished and *any* gift to charity is entitled to income tax relief provided:

(1)   it is a gift of money;

(2)   the donor makes a Gift Aid declaration;

(3)   any benefits to the donor are within the limits discussed at **[53.84]** below;

(4)   it is not associated with the purchase of property from the donor (so the donor cannot make a Gift Aid gift to a charity to enable the charity to purchase property from him); and

(5)   the donor is UK resident, or has sufficient income charged to UK tax.

If the gift qualifies for Gift Aid relief the donor is treated as having deducted income tax at the basic rate from his gift. Thus if he makes a gift of £78 to a charity he is treated as having made a gift of £100 from which tax of £22 has been deducted. The 22% tax deemed to have been deducted by the donor can be recovered by the charity from HMRC.

The donor's basic rate tax limit (ie his higher rate threshold) is increased by the gross amount of the gift. Thus if the donor makes a gift of £78 (gross value £100), the higher rate threshold will be increased from the usual figure (£33,300 in 2006–07) by £100 to £33,400. This means that if the donor is a higher rate taxpayer, he will pay income tax at 22% instead of 40% on taxable income between £33,300 and £33,400 (see diagram below). This will save him 18% of £100 (£18) on his tax bill. These provisions also apply to CGT. Thus if a taxpayer had £33,200 of income, and additional capital gains, £100 of the capital gains would be charged to CGT at 20% rather than 40%.

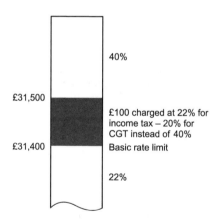

If the taxpayer pays less income tax and CGT than the amount recovered by the charity, he will be assessed for tax equal to the difference. Thus if the donor has given £78 to the charity (£100 gross), but has only paid £10 income tax and CGT, he will be required to refund to HMRC the difference between the £22 tax recovered by the charity and the £10 tax he has paid, ie a further £12 will be added to his tax bill.                **[53.82]**

b)   *Gift Aid declarations (see the standard form declaration below)*

The donor must make a written or electronic declaration (it can be made over the Internet). In addition, an oral declaration can be made (eg over the telephone).

*( 1)   Oral declarations*

New rules relating to oral Gift Aid declarations were introduced in November 2005 (by SI 2005/2790 amending the Donations to Charity (Appropriate Declarations) Regulations 2000 (SI 2000/2074)). Prior to these changes, where a donor made an oral Gift Aid declaration, the charity had to follow this up by sending the donor a written notification of his gift and a statement that the donor must pay income tax or CGT equal to the tax deducted from his donation. The new rules provide an alternative by allowing charities to receive oral Gift Aid declarations without sending a follow-up statement, thus substantially reducing spending on postage. However, in such cases, there remains an onerous duty on charities to maintain auditable records of declarations made and HMRC guidelines suggest that for oral declarations, the auditable record must be a recording of the donor making their declaration or of the donor responding to a pre-recorded declaration, which must be held by the charity for at least six years.

*( 2)   Written declarations*

Where a written declaration is used, other points to note include the following:
(1)   it must contain the donor's name and address;
(2)   it must contain the charity's name and a description of the donation to which it relates;
(3)   it must declare that the donation is to be treated as a Gift Aid donation and there must be a note explaining that the donor must pay income tax or CGT equal to the tax deducted from his donation;
(4)   there is no need for the donor's signature, national insurance number or tax reference. The declaration need not be dated unless the date is needed to identify the donations to which it applies. A single declaration may cover any number of donations already made or intended to be made in the future (hence it replaces the deed of covenant although, unlike a deed of covenant, the declaration is not legally binding).

| **Gift Aid declaration** |
|---|
| Name of Charity<br>............................................................................................ |
| Details of donor<br>Title ........ Forename(s) ................................ Surname<br>......................................<br><br>Ad-dress          ..............................................................................................<br><br>                  ..............................................................................................<br>                  .................................................. Post Code<br>                  ...................................... |

I want the charity to treat

    *the enclosed donation of £........................ as a Gift Aid donation

    *the donation(s) of £................... which I made on ............./ ............./ .............. as a Gift Aid donation(s)

    *all donations I make from the date of this declaration until I notify you otherwise as Gift Aid donations

    * all donations I have made for the six years prior to this year, (but no earlier than 6/4/2000) **and** all donations I make from the date of this declaration until I notify you otherwise, as Gift Aid donations.

You must pay an amount of Income Tax and/or Capital Gains Tax at least equal to the tax that the charity reclaims on your donations in the appropriate tax year (currently 28p for each £1 you give).

*delete as appropriate*

Signature ...................................................... Date ............./ ............./ ..............

Notes
(1)    You can cancel this declaration at any time by notifying the charity.
(2)    If in the future your circumstances change and you no longer pay tax on your income and capital gains equal to the tax that the charity reclaims, you can cancel your declaration.
(3)    If you pay tax at the higher rate you can claim further tax relief in your Self Assessment tax return.
(4)    If you are unsure whether your donations qualify for Gift Aid tax relief, ask the charity. Or, refer to help sheet IR65 on the HMRC website.
(5)    Please notify the charity if you change your name or address.   **[53.83]**

c)   *Receipt of benefits*

There are limits on benefits which a donor may receive in return for his donations. These rules have always applied to individual donors and to close companies, but FA 2006 has extended them to apply to all corporate donors (see **[53.86]**). The rules are surprisingly complicated. If the donation is to qualify for Gift Aid any benefits must satisfy both the 'relevant value' test and the 'aggregate value' test.

    The 'relevant value test' means that benefits to donors must not exceed the amounts below:

| | |
|---|---|
| Gifts up to £100 | 25% of gifts |
| Gifts of £100 to £1,000 | £25 |
| Gifts over £1,000 | 2.5% of gifts |

These limits are applied separately to each unconnected gift. Thus if the donor makes four unconnected gifts to a charity in a year, and only one gift exceeds the above limit, the remainder of the gifts can qualify for Gift Aid. However, connected gifts to the same charity in the same year must be considered together, and adjustments are made if the gifts are made for a period of less than a year. Thus if a £5 monthly subscription is paid to a charity for six months, this will be adjusted since it is only payable for half a year.

**EXAMPLE 53.1**

Subscription of £5 a month paid to charity under an open-ended standing order. This will be 'annualised' and treated as a gift of £60 (12/1 × £5). A one-off benefit up to £15 would be within the relevant value test.

Where the benefits are received for a period of less than 12 months, both the benefits and the gifts are adjusted.

**EXAMPLE 53.2**

Donor gives a gift of £240 to charity. He is given a six-month subscription to a computer magazine worth £15 (not just a magazine publicising the work of the charity which would not count as a benefit). The benefit is annualised £15 × 12/6 = £30. The gift is also annualised £240 × 12/6 = £480. The maximum benefit allowed is £25 so the relevant value test is not satisfied.

In addition to the relevant value test, the gifts must also satisfy the 'aggregate value' test. This means that if the aggregate value of benefits given by a charity to any one donor exceeds £250, gifts made from the time the £250 figure is reached will not qualify for Gift Aid.

It is worth noting that while the benefit rules apply to restrict the availability of Gift Aid, there could in some cases be a degree of overlap with the new rules relating to transactions with substantial donors (see **[53.44]–[53.60]**), in which case the charity could also lose tax relief on some of its income and gains.

The benefit rules may be avoided if a donor specifies that part of his payment to a charity is for benefits and part is a donation. This must be specified at or before the time the donation is made. It is too late to specify this after the gift. This can only be done where the item received by the donor has an easily ascertainable value and the excess paid by the donor has a clear donative purpose. The charity and the donors should keep evidence of how the payment was made. Alternatively, separate payments could be made.

The restrictions discussed above do not apply to the benefit of any right of admission to view property, the preservation of which is the sole or main purpose of the charity; or to observe wildlife, the conservation of which is its sole or main purpose, provided that the opportunity to make such gifts is available to members of the public (FA 1990 s 25(5E)). Thus if a member of a zoological society is given the right of free entry to the zoo, this does not count as a benefit.

However, in the 2005 Budget, the Government stated its intention to stop charities reclassifying admission fees as donations in order to benefit from Gift Aid, on the basis that this is outside the spirit and purpose of the Gift Aid rules, which were introduced with the intention of encouraging additional donations to charity. New provisions were enacted in F(No 2)A 2005 s 11 and have the effect that, from 6 April 2006, if a visitor makes a donation to a charity in order to view property falling within the exemption *instead* of paying the admission charge, Gift Aid will only apply in the following two alternative situations:

- where a right of admission given in return for the gift is valid for a period of at least one year at all times that the general public can gain admission; or
- if the right of admission is for less than one year, the gift must be at least 10% more than the amount that any member of the public would have to pay to gain the same right of admission.

However, the scope of the exemption has been broadened to apply to any charity which charges the public to view property *preserved, maintained, kept or created* by the charity in relation to its charitable work. 'Property' for these purposes includes plants, animals and works of art (but not performances).

Although the amendment has resulted in a reduction in the income of some charities, this has to some extent been offset by the benefits being extended to a broader range of charities.                    **[53.84]**

d)   *The 'Double-Dip' and St Dunstan's case*

It had been thought that Gift Aid could be employed to achieve a 'cake and eat it' result. For IHT purposes there are certain situations where 'reading back fictions' are available. For instance, a deed of variation falling within IHTA 1984 s 142 may be read back into the will of the testator (and therefore taxed as if that testator had made the relevant disposition of property) and, similarly, a precatory gift, falling within IHTA 1984 s 143, attracts IHT reading back. The fiction in both these cases holds good for IHT but not for income tax where the analysis remains that the original gift became the property of the named beneficiary who then in turn transferred that property to another person.

Assume, therefore, that Berta, who has just died, has left the residue of her estate (worth £300,000) to her daughter Janice. Janice now wishes to make a substantial donation to charitable causes. She enters into an instrument of variation whereby Berta's will is amended to provide for a gift of £50,000 to the charity (IHT free: if the tax has been paid a refund is in order) with the remaining £250,000 being paid to Janice. She may seek full income tax relief for the £50,000 under Gift Aid by combining Gift Aid with an instrument of variation. Unfortunately the Revenue successfully challenged the availability of Gift Aid relief on the basis that to qualify 'neither the donor or any person connected with him [must] receive a benefit in consequence of making [the gift]'. In an unsatisfactory judgment a Special Commissioner decided that the saving in IHT amounted to such a benefit thereby preventing relief (*St Dunstan's Educational Foundation v Major* (1997)).

However, it would seem that the variation of a non-residuary legacy would not give a benefit to the donor (since any tax saving would swell the residue), and would be eligible for Gift Aid provided that no one connected with the donor benefits from the IHT saving. In addition the provisions for 'Share Aid' (see **[53.98]**) and 'Land Aid' (**[53.99]**) have different benefit rules: in simple terms the amount on which relief is given is reduced by the value of any benefit received. Hence if 40% IHT relief is obtained which benefits the donor, 60% of the value of the gifted property is still capable of attracting Share Aid or Land Aid.                    **[53.85]**

*e)    Corporate Gift Aid*

From 1 April 2000, FA 2000 effected major simplification for corporate gifts similar to those already considered for individuals. The key provisions are:

(1)    companies no longer deduct income tax from their Gift Aid donations (including covenanted payments which now fall under the scheme);

(2)    companies no longer have to give the charity a Gift Aid declaration. The full sum is paid to the charity (which does not therefore reclaim tax from HMRC) and the company deducts the sum paid when calculating its profits for corporation tax;

(3)    as with individuals, payments under deed of covenant are within the Gift Aid scheme and the £250 limit was removed;

(4)    the requirement that the donation has to be made by a UK resident company was removed.

There are also restrictions on benefits received in respect of gifts made by a close company, which are similar to those applying to donations made by individuals (see [53.84]). FA 2006 s 58 has extended these restrictions to gifts made by any company, meaning that charities will in future have to take care that reciprocal sponsorship arrangements are carefully monitored to avoid falling foul of the new rules.

It is common for charities to engage in trading activities as a means of fundraising. However, income produced by such activities will normally attract income tax (see [53.42] for the exceptions). The problems arising are usually solved by carrying on the trade through a separate company which is wholly owned by the charity. Corporate profits may then be donated to the charity so that an exception from corporation tax is available. Such donations were commonly made by deed of covenant but from 1 April 2000 the Gift Aid scheme caters for such payments (see [53.42]).                              [53.86]

## 2    Deeds of covenant

Sums paid to charity under deed of covenant were tax effective (ie they reduced the income of the payer) provided that the covenant was capable of lasting for more than three years. This requirement could be satisfied if either a fixed period in excess of three years was chosen (hence the popularity of the four-year covenant) or, alternatively, if a period of uncertain duration was chosen which might exceed three years.

FA 2000 removed the separate tax relief for payments made under deed of covenant. Tax relief for such payments is now given under the Gift Aid scheme. As a transitional measure payments made under deeds in existence on 6 April 2000 will not require a Gift Aid declaration: the deed of covenant will in effect perform this function. To obtain tax relief for payments made under covenants executed after 5 April 2000, or to cover gifts larger than the amount covenanted, a Gift Aid declaration is required.            [53.87]

## 3    Payroll giving (TA 1988 s 202)

The so-called 'payroll deduction scheme' is discussed in **Chapter 8**. In broad terms, it involves employers who wish to set up a scheme for their employees entering into a contract with an agency approved by HMRC. Employees who wish to join the scheme authorise their employer to deduct the relevant amount from their pay before calculating PAYE tax due and to pay over the relevant amount to the agency. The function of the agency is to act as a clearing house, distributing the appropriate sums to the individual charities which have been nominated by the employees. The upper limit (£1,200 pa) was abolished as from 6 April 2000 and the Treasury paid a supplement of 10% on all donations via the payroll deduction scheme made between April 2000 and April 2004. **[53.88]**

## 4　Relief from capital taxes

### a)　*CGT*

TCGA 1992 s 257 provides that for CGT purposes gifts to charity are at no gain/no loss (compare the similar rule for inter-spouse gifts under TCGA 1992 s 58). In appropriate cases it may be better, however, to sell the asset (perhaps to realise a capital loss) and then gift the cash to charity taking advantage of the Gift Aid rules. HMRC accepts that the CGT exemption in TCGA 1992 s 256 applies to capital payments received from trusts which have stockpiled gains (on 'stockpiled gains' see further **[27.122]**). **[53.89]**

### b)　*IHT*

For IHT purposes, charitable gifts are exempt transfers of value under IHTA 1984 s 23. Relief under this section is given in the following terms:

> 'transfers of value are exempt to the extent that the values transferred by them are attributable to property which is given to charities.'

However, HMRC accepts that relief will be given in a case where the fall in value of the donor's estate exceeds the benefit received by the charity:

> 'Where the value transferred (i.e. the loss to transferor's estate as a result of the disposition) exceeds the value of the gift in the hands of a charity, etc, the Board take the view that the exemption extends to the whole value transferred.' (See SP E13.)

Three points may be made in connection with gifts to charity by will. **[53.90]**

### i)　*Gift to a foreign charity*

Assume that a will provides:

> 'I leave the residue of my estate to the X Foundation (a New York charity).'

No IHT relief is available: consider solving the problem by a deed of variation redirecting the gift to an English sub-charity. **[53.91]**

### ii)　*Drafting the will/making a lifetime gift*

Assume that the client wishes to make the following gift:

> 'I wish to give £50,000 to the University of Pennsylvania.'

Consider making the gift to a UK charity (eg the Charities Aid Foundation) whose objects allow it to carry on charitable activities abroad. It may, in due course, transfer the property to a foreign charity without loss of IHT relief (in the case of a gift by will beware IHTA 1984 s 143: 'precatory trusts').

**[53.92]**

### iii)   *Residuary gifts to charity and chargeable persons*

When the residue of an estate is to be split between one or more charities on the one hand and chargeable persons (eg relatives of the deceased) on the other, problems have arisen in calculating the IHT payable on the chargeable portion (this is often referred to as a '*Benham*' problem). This matter is considered in detail in **Chapter 30** and it is felt that *Re Ratcliffe* (1999) now affords general guidance which will apply in all save exceptional cases.

**[53.93]**

### 5   **Gifts in kind**

Businesses can obtain tax relief for the cost of gifts of trading stock and equipment which they sell or use in the course of their business (typical examples are computers, photocopiers, minibuses and furniture). The relief is, however, restricted as explained below.

**[53.94]**

### a)   *Equipment given to educational establishments*

TA 1988 s 84 provides relief for gifts of equipment by businesses to UK schools and other educational establishments. The relief applies to gifts by companies and unincorporated businesses of items of equipment either manufactured, sold or used in the course of their trade. It applies where such equipment is given to educational establishments, whether schools or higher educational institutions. The company or unincorporated business is allowed a deduction for the cost of acquiring or manufacturing the item of plant and machinery in calculating its taxable profits. This means that the business will be given full relief for the cost of the item and there will be no charge on the profit forgone by reason of the gift. Further, items of equipment used in the course of the donor's trade, and on which capital allowances have been given, are treated as having been disposed of at nil value, so that the balance of allowances due on the asset will be given to the business in the normal way. This relief brings the tax treatment of gifts of equipment to schools etc into line with the treatment of gifts of cash used by the recipient to purchase equipment.

**[53.95]**

### b)   *Trading stock and assets (TA 1988 s 83A)*

A person carrying on a trade, profession or vocation obtains tax relief on gifts to any charity of:
(1)   trading stock: the taxpayer is not required to account for any disposal value as a trading receipt (TA 1988 s 83A(3)(a));
(2)   used machinery and plant: again there is no obligation to account for any disposal value—in this case for capital allowance purposes (TA 1988 s 83A(3)(b)).

**[53.96]**

c)   *Other gifts of assets*

In its Consultation Document ('Review of Charity Taxation': March 1999) the government indicated that it wished to encourage gifts of assets to charity by businesses but did not favour giving individual donors income tax relief on the value of items so given. However relief for gifts of qualifying investments was introduced in FA 2000 and for gifts of land by FA 2002 (see **[53.98]** and **[53.99]** below).

Although the law in this area has not changed, HMRC have recently published practical guidance clarifying that Gift Aid can apply where a donor appoints a charity as his agent to sell an asset on his behalf and then voluntarily makes a gift of the sale proceeds to the charity. However, care will need to be taken to ensure that the gift is a voluntary gift of cash in order to qualify for Gift Aid, so that, for example, the donor must be given the chance to change his mind or donate only part of the proceeds once the sale has gone through. It would be preferable to have a written agreement between the charity and the donor in advance.                                             **[53.97]**

## 6   Gifts of qualifying investments—'Share Aid'

Qualifying investments comprise quoted stocks and shares on recognised stock exchanges (which include many exchanges around the world); units in an authorised unit trust; shares in an open-ended investment company and an interest in an offshore fund. The relief applies to gifts on or after 6 April 2000 in the case of individuals (see TA 1988 s 587B(2)(a)(i)) and on or after 1 April 2000 in the case of companies (TA 1988 s 587B(2)(a)(ii)). The donor obtains an income tax (or corporation tax) deduction for the full market value of the qualifying investment at the date of the gift (plus incidental costs of transfer). If the charity pays any money for the shares, or gives any other benefits, this is deducted from the tax relief.

The assets on which this relief is available benefit from an easily discoverable value, thereby minimising the costs of obtaining a valuation and reducing the possibilities of abuse.

In addition to this income tax relief, the usual CGT exemption (see **[53.89]**) also applies. This means that it can be very tax efficient to give shares to charity.

Amendments were incorporated in the FA 2004 to counter income tax avoidance by individuals using complex arrangements of offshore trusts and options to manipulate the value of gifts donated to charities, while potentially returning the whole value of the gift to the control of the donor. The changes prevent individuals from obtaining income tax relief in excess of the benefit received by a charity from the donation of shares or securities by providing that where a person places an obligation on the charity that results in the value of the gift in the hands of the charity being less than the gift in the hands of the donor, the income tax relief that can be claimed by the donor is restricted to the lower amount.                                     **[53.98]**

### EXAMPLE 53.3

Arthur purchased shares in A plc for £4,000. He sells them to a charity for £4,000 when they are worth £10,000. Arthur pays no CGT and can deduct £6,000 gift element from his income. If Arthur is a higher rate taxpayer who has used his CGT annual exemption this will save him £6,000 × 40% = £2,400 CGT *and* £6,000 × 40% = £2,400 income tax. It follows that it has only cost Arthur £1,200 (£6,000–£4,800) to give a £6,000 benefit to the charity.

## 7   Gifts of land—'Land Aid'

FA 2002 s 97 has extended tax relief to gifts of land similar to 'Share Aid' discussed in the previous section. It applies where a freehold or leasehold interest in the UK is given to charity on or after 6 April 2002 (on or after 1 April if the gift is by a company). Although the donor must usually dispose of the whole of his interest in the land, it is specifically provided that the grant of a lease for a term of years absolute in the whole or part of the land qualifies for the relief. Where land is owned jointly all owners must dispose of their interests if the gift is to qualify.

In order to claim the relief the donor must receive a certificate from the charity describing the interest in land, giving the date of the disposal and stating that the charity has acquired the interest. There are provisions for cancelling the tax relief if the donor becomes entitled to an interest in the land, or enjoys rights over it, before the 31 January which falls more than five years after the gift (in the case of a company before the sixth anniversary of the end of the accounting period in which the gift was made). Thus if an individual gives land to a charity on 1 June 2002, the tax relief will be cancelled if he enjoys any rights over the land before 31 January 2008. The cancellation provisions do not apply if the donor gives full consideration in money or money's worth for the interest or right he enjoys.          **[53.99]**

## 8   Community amateur sports clubs (FA 2002 Sch 18)

Amateur sports clubs, which are open to the whole community and which provide facilities for and promote participation in one or more eligible sports (for a list of eligible sports please visit www.hmrc.gov.uk/casc/casc_guidance.htm), may register with HMRC for the following corporation tax exemptions:
(1)   Exemption for trading income which does not exceed £30,000 a year.
(2)   Exemption for interest and Gift Aid payments.
(3)   Exemption for property income which does not exceed £20,000 a year.
(4)   Exemption for chargeable gains.
    Where the club incurs expenditure for non-qualifying purposes the amount of income or gains exempted is reduced. If a club ceases to be registered, or ceases to hold property for qualifying purposes, there is a deemed disposal and the capital gain may be chargeable to corporation tax.
    Gifts of money to the club qualify as Gift Aid donations, so the club will be able to reclaim basic rate tax on the gross amount of the gift, and the donors will be able to claim higher rate tax relief as if the sports club was a charity. However, membership fees do not count as gifts, so no tax relief is available to members or the club on membership fees. Gifts to sports clubs also qualify for exemption from inheritance tax. Gifts by a business of trading stock and used machinery and plant are given the same relief as applies to similar gifts to a charity (see **[53.96]** above).

As an alternative to registering with HMRC, an amateur sports club may register with the Charity Commission as a charity and qualify for all the usual charitable exemptions. The advancement of amateur sport has recently been recognised as a 'fourth head' charitable purpose by the Charity Commission, and was expressly included in the Charities Bill as one of the 13 charitable purposes proposed in the Bill. Registering as a charity may be more favourable to the club from a tax point of view as the payroll deduction scheme and 'Share Aid' and 'Land Aid' discussed above do not apply to sports clubs registered with HMRC. However, registration with the Charity Commission is still likely to be more onerous for the club with the need to submit to Charity Commission jurisdiction and to submit accounts and reports to them.

**[53.100]**

### 9  Gifts treated as made in previous tax year

Where a gift is made on or after 6 April 2003, the taxpayer may elect to treat the gift as made in the previous tax year for the purposes of claiming higher rate tax relief (FA 2002 s 98). The election can be made up to the date the taxpayer submits his income tax return for the previous year (but not after 31 January). The election will not affect claims made by the charity.

This provision means that a taxpayer can make a gift to charity before he submits his tax return and then get immediate higher rate tax relief against the income in the return. However, it may encourage delay in submitting tax returns as once the return is submitted it will not be possible to backdate gifts to the previous year.

**[53.101]**

### 10  Gifts of tax repayments to charity

Since 6 April 2004, taxpayers have been able to nominate a charity on their self-assessment tax returns to receive all or part of a tax repayment. The taxpayer will have to choose from a list of participating charities published by HMRC on its website. The list will be updated on a quarterly basis. A Gift Aid donation may be made anonymously or the taxpayer may agree to disclose his identity.

**[53.102]–[53.120]**

### V  VALUE ADDED TAX

Unlike other taxes, there are only a few special VAT exemptions which apply to charities and most of the VAT rules which apply to commercial organisations will continue to be relevant (see generally **Chapters 30–38**). Further useful guidance on this topic can be found in HMRC Notice 701/1 (May 2004).

**[53.121]**

### 1  Inputs—supplies made to the charity

Supplies made to the charity are usually taxable if they would be taxable when made to a non-charity. Taxable supplies are either charged to VAT at 17.5%, or some other rate including zero. Where the supply is zero-rated, the charity is not charged to VAT and the supplier is able to recover any VAT he has paid. Some supplies are exempt from VAT. This is less favourable as although the charity will not be charged VAT, the supplier will not be able to recover the VAT he has had to pay. It may thus result in a higher price paid by the charity.                                                                                    **[53.122]**

a)   *Zero-rated supplies to charities*

The following supplies are zero-rated if supplied to a charity (VATA 1994 Sch 8). In many cases the charity must make an eligibility declaration to the supplier that the goods are being purchased or imported by a charity (for examples of declarations see HMRC Notice 701/6 (Supplement) (April 1997)).

(1)   Advertising by charities whatever its purpose (VATA 1994 Sch 8 Group 15 Items 8–8C as substituted by SI 2000/805). Before 2000, zero-rating only applied if the advert was intended to raise money or publicise the charity's aims. The zero-rating extends to advertisement design and production services but excludes advertising where members of the public are 'selected' (ie by direct mailing, or telephone sales) website creation and design, and internal overheads related to advertising. By ESC the relief will also apply to goods used by charities for the purposes of collecting monetary donations, ie collection boxes, lapel badges, and pre-printed giving envelopes.

(2)   Equipment supplied to charities for producing talking newspapers and books for the blind, and radios and recorders supplied to charities for free loan to the blind (VATA 1994 Sch 8 Group 4).

(3)   The supply, repair and maintenance of lifeboats (VATA 1994 Sch 8 Group 8).

(4)   The donation of goods by a VAT registered person if made to a charity (or a company which has agreed in writing to pay all its profits to charity) for the purpose of sale, hire or export by the charity (or company) (VATA 1994 Sch 8 Group 15 item 2 as substituted by SI 2000/805).

(5)   The construction of a new building, or purchase of a freehold or lease exceeding 21 years of a new building if the building is used for relevant charitable purposes (ie for non-business purposes or as a village hall) (VATA 1994 Sch 8 Group 5). By ESC (and in some cases with HMRC's approval) minor non-qualifying use can be disregarded provided 90% of the building is used for charitable purposes.

(6)   Medical and scientific equipment and ambulances, if purchased with charitable or voluntary funds for donation to health authorities and charities providing rescue services or care for the sick and disabled (VATA 1994 Sch 8 Group 15 item 4).

(7)   Medicines given to a charity caring for patients or animals (VATA 1994 Sch 8 Group 15 item 9).

(8)   Goods and services designed for the disabled and certain building alterations for the disabled (eg bathroom adaptations) (see VATA 1994 Sch 8 Group 12 items 2, 10 and 11).                                                **[53.123]**

b)   *Supplies of fuel and power*

The supply of fuel and power for a qualifying use, such as in a residential care home or for use in charitable non-business activities, benefits from the 5% rather than standard rate. If the supply does not exceed the *de minimis* limits (eg 1,000 kilowatt hours of electricity or 2,300 litres of gas oil a month), it is automatically treated as being for a qualifying use. Where the use is part qualifying and part not, provided at least 60% is for qualifying use, VAT is also charged at 5% instead of at the standard rate. Where these limits are exceeded an apportionment must be made between business and non-business use, and an apportioned part is chargeable at 5%.                 **[53.124]**

**EXAMPLE 53.4**

A charity uses 50% of its building for non-business activities but 50% for business purposes. The supply of fuel exceeds the *de minimis* limits. One half of its supply of fuel would be charged at 5%, the remainder at the standard rate.

## 2   Outputs—supplies made by the charity

A charity, like anyone else, is generally liable to VAT on supplies made by it if the charity is a taxable person, and the supply is in the course of business and not exempt. A charity is a taxable person if its taxable supplies exceed the registration threshold (£61,000 a year from 1st April 2006). It must then register for VAT.                 **[53.125]**

a)   *Supplies must be in the course of business*

Some supplies by a charity are not in the course of business and are therefore outside the scope of VAT. Thus donations and grants freely given to the charity are not business receipts. By ESC, charges for advertisements in charity brochures are regarded as outside the scope of VAT provided at least 50% of the advertisements are private rather than trade. Further, welfare services supplied at least 15% below cost for the relief of distress, such as soup supplied to the poor, are regarded as non-business supplies. Voluntary services supplied free of charge, such as first aid, rescue at sea and rights of worship, are also regarded as outside the scope of VAT, even if a voluntary donation is received.

On the other hand, the receipt of subscriptions by a charity for which the charity provides goods or services is usually regarded as a supply in the course of business. This does not apply if the only benefits received are a right to vote at meetings and reports. Thus if a charity receives more than the registration threshold in the form of subscriptions and other taxable supplies, it will usually have to register for VAT and account for VAT on the subscriptions it receives.

The sale or letting of goods by a charity is in the course of business. However, the sale or hire by a charity of donated goods are zero-rated even where the sales are not to the general public as a whole but to specific categories of people (VATA 1994 Sch 8 Group 15 items 1 and 1A as substituted by SI 2000/805). However, sales of bought-in goods do not qualify for zero-rating and will be taxed at the standard rate of VAT (unless of course they are zero-rated by law such as children's clothes). Sales from a hospital trolley to patients in hospital are VAT exempt, but sales to members of the staff are standard-rated.

Where welfare services are supplied at a price which is more than 15% below cost (see above), the supply is in the course of business, but will be exempt if provided otherwise than for profit (VATA 1994 Sch 9 Group 7 item 9). Goods and services supplied incidental to the provision of spiritual welfare by a religious community are in the course of business, but are similarly exempt if supplied otherwise than for profit (VATA 1994 Sch 9 Group 7 item 10).

Examples of other supplies made by a charity in the course of business include admission fees, (generally standard rated), the hiring of charity buildings (usually exempt) and sponsorship payments for which the business receives advertisement or promotion (standard rated). Part of the initial payment made to a charity under an affinity credit card scheme (at least 20%) can be treated as standard rated and the remainder outside the scope of VAT.                                                                          **[53.126]**

b)    *Exemption for fund-raising events*

Fund-raising events organised for charitable purposes by a charity are, subject to certain conditions, exempt from VAT if the primary purpose is the raising of money and the events are promoted for that purpose. The exemption extends to events organised by a company which is wholly owned by the charity and has agreed in writing to transfer all its profits to the charity. The exemption does not apply if more than 15 events of the same kind are held by the charity in the same location in one financial year. Although events do not count towards this limit if gross takings from all similar events at the location do not exceed £1,000 a week, eg coffee mornings. However, if such coffee mornings are regular activities carried out more than once or twice a week they may not be 'events' and therefore may not qualify for exemption. Events where more than two nights' accommodation are provided are excluded, as are all events which are likely to distort competition with VAT registered traders (VATA 1994 Sch 9 Group 12 substituted by SI 2000/802).

Fund-raising events over the Internet qualify as exempt if the same conditions are met. For these purposes the whole of a charity's website is regarded as a single location.

If a fund-raising event does not qualify for exemption it is worth considering selling tickets for a lower price, and inviting voluntary donations. So long as the price of the tickets is not less than the usual price charged for a commercial event (in the case of events such as theatre performances), or is sufficient to cover the organiser's total costs (in the case of events such as dances) and, provided the position is reflected in the publicity material, VAT will not be charged on the voluntary donation.                                 **[53.127]**

### 3    Payment of VAT

Like any other business, a charity which makes taxable supplies pays VAT each quarter which is calculated by taking its output tax (the tax on its outputs, ie on supplies made *by* the charity) and deducting its input tax (the tax on its inputs, ie on supplies made *to* the charity). If its input tax exceeds its output tax it may claim a repayment of VAT. If the charity makes supplies which are exempt or outside the scope of VAT it can only deduct part of its input tax (see **Chapter 38**).

It may be possible for a small charity to join a flat rate scheme whereby VAT is calculated as a fixed percentage of its turnover (including VAT). The fixed percentage depends on the type of business activity, but has been specified as 5.5% for a membership organisation, or 10% for activities not specifically mentioned in the regulations (from 1 April 2004—SI 2004/767). Such a scheme may save a considerable amount of administrative work, but the VAT calculation is not so exact as under the normal scheme and could result in the charity paying more VAT. On the other hand, the VAT might work out to be less than under the usual scheme. This would need careful consideration by the charity. See HMRC Notice 733 (February 2004) and SI 2002/1142 (and amending SIs) for details of the flat rate scheme.

Subject to certain conditions, it may be possible for a charity and its trading subsidiaries to register as a VAT group (see HMRC Notice 700/2 (December 2004)). **[53.128]**

## VI  STAMP DUTY LAND TAX

Charities will be exempt from stamp duty land tax provided the conditions in FA 2003 Sch 8 para 1 are met. Firstly, the charity must intend to use the purchased land for qualifying charitable purposes (ie in furtherance of its charitable purposes or as an investment the profits of which are applied towards its charitable purposes). Secondly, the transaction must not have been entered into in order to avoid tax.

The first requirement creates some uncertainty. For example, while premises purchased for running as a care home or for the administration of the charity would clearly qualify as being used in furtherance of a charity's objects, what if a charity were to purchase a shop from which to sell goods, thereby using the premises in furtherance of the charity's business purposes (for example, where the charity is carrying on de minimis trade directly not using a trading company) rather than direct charitable purposes? Although it is currently understood that the Stamp Taxes Office will extend the exemption to property used for business or other activities the profits of which are applied for the charity's charitable purposes, there has been no formal clarification of this.

The exemption will be withdrawn if a 'disqualifying event' occurs within three years of the transaction (FA 2003 Sch 8 para 2). A disqualifying event would include the charity ceasing to be established for charitable purposes or the land ceasing to be used for a qualifying charitable purpose. **[53.129]**

# Section 11   European Law

**Chapters**

# 54   The impact of EC Law

*Written by Hartley Foster, Partner, DLA Piper Rudnick Gray Cary UK LLP*

## I   INTRODUCTION

The United Kingdom became a member of the European Economic Community (EEC) and a party to the treaties establishing the Community with effect from 1 January 1973. It took some time for the full legal effect of this (and the UK's implementing legislation) to become clear. However, it is now beyond doubt that the UK Parliament no longer has complete power to determine the laws in force in the UK. UK legislation, even if validly passed by Parliament, is now ineffective to the extent that it conflicts with EC law.

This has very wide-reaching implications for UK revenue law, just as it does for all other areas of UK law. Community law now increasingly acts as an important restraint on the UK's fiscal sovereignty. VAT (which is dealt with in **Chapter 37**) and customs duties (which are outside the scope of this work) are directly governed by detailed Community legislation passed under the provisions of the treaties. But even where there is no detailed legislation (such as in the case of direct tax), EC law has a very significant role to play. Although the European Court of Justice has reiterated consistently that direct taxation 'is a matter that falls within the competence of Member States' (see, for example, *Gschwind (1999)*) it has also made clear that Member States must exercise that competence 'in accordance with EC law'. The effect of this is that, where there is a conflict between EC law and domestic direct tax law, EC law will prevail and the relevant domestic rule will have no effect.

The rules of EC law that particularly affect the UK direct tax code are the 'fundamental freedoms' set out in Arts 25–31 and 39–60 of the EC Treaty itself. These rules require Member States to enable goods, services, persons and capital to move freely within the Community, in order to ensure the creation of an internal market. Ever since the treaties first came into force, the fundamental freedoms have been interpreted broadly, so as to strike down domestic legal rules incompatible with an internal market. In a succession of more recent cases, the freedoms have been applied specifically in the context of direct tax.

The chapter comprises 11 sections. After this introductory section, the next two sections comprise a brief overview of the EU institutions, and the sources of EC law respectively. The next six sections deal primarily with the impact of the EC case law on the UK direct tax code, considering both the tax cases and (to the extent necessary) the general law cases. Sections IX and X deal with two other areas of EC law: State aid and the tax directives; and the final section deals with a new structure that could lead, ultimately, to the introduction of a common set of rules for calculating EU-wide tax profits: the European Company or Societas Europea (SE).

Before proceeding, it is necessary to make one short explanatory point. The Treaty of Rome that established the EEC in 1957 was renamed the European Community Treaty by The Treaty on European Union signed at Maastricht on 7 February 1992 (the TEU). It is referred to as the 'EC Treaty' in this chapter. All references to Article numbers in the EC Treaty are to the post-Maastricht numbers.                                    **[54.1]**

## II    THE INSTITUTIONS OF THE EU

The main institutions of the EU that were set up by the EC Treaty to carry out the Community's tasks are:
  (i)   the Parliament;
  (ii)  the Council;
  (iii) the European Commission; and
  (iv)  the Court of Justice of the European Communities (known universally as the ECJ).

There are different powers ascribed to each of the institutions; and the way that they interact is designed to ensure that checks and balances prevent any one institution from becoming too powerful. The powers of the respective institutions have evolved over time and each revision of the treaties has seen an increase in the power of the Parliament in comparison to the other institutions.

A number of other institutions – such as the European Central Bank – have been established that have specific roles in the EU: these are outside the focus of this chapter.                                    **[54.2]**

### a)    *The European Parliament*

The European Parliament is directly elected, with the number of members of the Parliament per country being based on the population of each Member State. Currently, there are 732 MEPs, who represent 457 million citizens.

The European Parliament shares legislative power equally with the Council of the European Union. With regard to the adoption of new legislation, there is a distinction between the ordinary legislative procedure ('the co-decision procedure'), where the Parliament is on an equal footing with the Council, and the special legislative procedures that apply in specific cases where Parliament has only a consultative role ('the consultation procedure'). The co-decision procedure was introduced by The Treaty on European Union and extended by the Amsterdam Treaty (1999). Approximately two-thirds of European laws are adopted through the co-decision procedure. However, taxation matters are dealt with under the consultation procedure; here the European Parliament will give only an advisory opinion. **[54.3]**

b)  *The Council of the European Union*

The Council's task is to ensure that the objectives set out in the Treaty are attained. To that end, it shall 'ensure co-ordination of the general economic policies of the Member States; have power to take decisions ... and confer on the Commission, in the acts which the Council adopts, powers for the implementation of those rules which the Council lays down' (Art 202). The Council has the final power of decision in relation to most secondary legislation. However, in most cases, it may act only on the basis of a proposal from the Commission.

The Council consists of one representative from each Member State. The representative must be 'at ministerial level, authorised to commit the government of that Member State.' In the case of tax legislation, the Council of Ministers will comprise ministers from national governments with fiscal responsibility. This composition of the Council is known as 'ECOFIN'. The number of areas where qualified majority voting is used has been increased significantly. However, fiscal measures still require unanimous approval. **[54.4]**

c)  *European Commission*

The European Commission was created to represent the European interest that is common to all Member States. The Commission is responsible for implementing common policies (such as the common agricultural policy); and it administers the budget. Although the Commission has the right to take any step that it considers is appropriate in order to attain the objectives of the treaties, most proposals that it puts forward will be in response to a specific request for action from another institution, a Member State or from interested parties.

The Commission is the only body authorised to put forward proposals for legislation. The fundamental EC principles of subsidiarity and proportionality must be respected – the Commission should only propose legislation if it is more effective to do so on the EU level than at the domestic level and it should ensure that the legislation goes no further than is necessary to achieve the desired objectives. In preparing early drafts, it consults with national governments and civil servants, representatives of trade and professional bodies and other interested parties. When the text of a draft is settled, it will be formally adopted by the full Commission and will be published in all EU languages in the *Official Journal* ('OJ') as a formal proposal. At that stage, the Economic and Social Committee and the European Parliament will consider the proposal and, in doing so, will listen to the views of third parties. **[54.5]**

d)    *The European Court of Justice*

The jurisdiction of the European Court of Justice (ECJ) is defined in the EC treaties. It has jurisdiction on the following matters:
(1)    failure by a Member State to fulfil an obligation under the EC Treaty;
(2)    legality of acts of the Council and Commission;
(3)    failure to act by the Council or Commission; and
(4)    preliminary rulings.
    Under Art 234, the ECJ has jurisdiction to give preliminary rulings concerning:
(a)    the interpretation of the EC Treaty;
(b)    the validity and interpretation of acts of institutions of the Community; and
    (c)    the interpretation of the statutes of bodies established by an act of the Council.
    The ECJ comprises 15 judges and 8 Advocates-General. The Court may sit as a full court, in a Grand Chamber of 13 judges or in Chambers of three or five judges. It is rare for the ECJ to sit as a full court. It may do so where a case of exceptional importance is concerned; and there are particular cases prescribed by the Statute of the Court (such as proceedings to dismiss the European Ombudsman or a Member of the European Commission who has failed to fulfil his or her obligations) where it must. It sits in a Grand Chamber when a Member State or an institution which is a party to the proceedings so requests, and in particularly complex or important cases. The court makes a single decision. Decisions of the ECJ are always preceded by a detailed report ('opinion') from an Advocate-General ('A-G')) that also carries authoritative weight (but is not binding on the ECJ). When deciding a case, it is usual for the ECJ to follow the A-G's opinion. All cases before the ECJ are allocated a number, the last two digits of which refer to the year in which the action was started.
    In matters of EC law, all domestic courts and tribunals must refer points of dispute relating to EC law to the ECJ if they consider that a decision of the ECJ is necessary to enable them to give judgment. Decisions of the ECJ will bind domestic courts on the interpretation of EC law.
    The general rule is that, where a question concerning EC law arises before a national court or tribunal, the matter may be referred to the ECJ if a decision on the question is necessary to enable the national court to give judgment. However, under Art 234, the matter *must* be referred if there is no right of appeal from a decision of the court or tribunal. Thus, courts of last resort (typically the House of Lords in the UK) do not have a discretion as to whether to make a reference on an EC law issue which it is necessary to resolve before judgment can be given (although the court in question retains its discretion to decide whether a decision on a question of EC Law is necessary to enable it to give judgment (see *R v Henn and Darby* (Case 34/79) [1981] AC 850)). If the answer to the EC law point is 'acte clair' (in essence so obvious that there is no scope for any reasonable doubt), then there is no obligation to refer.
    The decision to make a reference is a matter for the national court, not for the parties to the case. Thus, if one of the parties disagrees with the decision, he or she must appeal under national law—there is no direct right of access

to the ECJ (see for example, *Marks and Spencer v Halsey*. The Special Commissioners declined to refer; that decision was appealed to the High Court, where Park J referred questions to the ECJ).

The ECJ's sole function under Art 234 is to decide what the EC law is. This has three important consequences. First, if a reference is made, the ECJ will not concern itself with the question of whether or not a reference was necessary; it will give a decision. Secondly, the ECJ will not interpret national law or apply its interpretation of EC law to the facts of the case. Thirdly, the ECJ will leave it to the national courts to implement its ruling (see eg *Naturally Yours Cosmetics Ltd v C & E Comrs* (1988), a case on the value of supplies to the company's agents at a discount where it was held that the discount was the value of the service provided by the agent; *Boots Co plc v C & E Comrs* (1990), a case on the effect of the customer obtaining a discount in the price by tendering a voucher, where it was held that the company had correctly accounted for VAT on the cash received only; and *Card Protection Plan v C & E Comrs* (2001), where the distinction between a single and a mixed supply was examined).  **[54.6]–[54.10]**

## III  SOURCES OF EC LAW

EC law comprises:
(1)  the various treaties;
(2)  regulations, directives and decisions made by EU institutions; and
(3)  decisions of the ECJ.

   EC law, in effect, imposes obligations on Member States to amend national law and, in certain instances, creates rights and obligations having direct effect in the legal systems of Member States without separate enactment by national legislatures. The following general conclusions can be drawn:
(1)  EC law affects both Member States and their nationals. Provisions having direct effect in Member States create rights and impose obligations on individuals, which may be enforced in national courts. Other provisions affect the relations of Member States, inter se, or impose obligations upon them to enact national legislation giving effect to common policies.
(2)  EC law has a uniform application in all Member States. The ECJ is the only body competent to give an authoritative ruling on the interpretation and application of the treaties. Member States cannot restrict the operation of EC law by failing to implement or repeal national legislation, or by passing legislation, which is inconsistent with it.
(3)  EC law takes precedence over national law. Inconsistent national legislation is overridden by EC law, and directly enforceable rights are to be given effect as part of national law whether or not national legislation has been implemented. However, a Member State cannot rely on such directly enforceable rights as against an individual national.  **[54.11]**

### a)  *The treaties*

The original Treaty of Rome that established the EEC in 1957 was primarily an economic treaty that was concerned with creating a single market in Europe. However, as well as traditional free-trading aims, it expressly included a number of purely social goals. The Single European Act ('SEA') (which entered into force on 1 July 1987) further extended the scope of Community competence. One of the key objectives of the SEA was to ensure that the EC's internal market would be completed by the end of 1992. It included a formal framework for co-operation by Member States which led ultimately to Maastricht. On 1 November 1993, the TEU, which had been signed at Maastricht on 7 February 1992, brought into being a new legal and political entity – the European Union.

The Treaty of Amsterdam ('TA') was signed in October 1997 and entered into force on 1 May 1999. Its aim was to change the composition and functioning of the institutions, which was considered politically necessary in order to enable enlargement of the EU, particularly with regard to applicants from central and eastern Europe. TA adopted the principle of 'closer co-operation', which provides that a limited number of Member States may establish rules that, in relation to a certain matter, apply only to themselves and not to any non-participating Member States, but nonetheless are within the institutional framework of the EU.

Articles 2 and 3 of the EC Treaty set out the main objectives of the Community and identify the means by which those objectives are to be met. They do not impose any particular legal obligations on Member States. They have interpretative value and may be used to clarify the parameters of the more specific treaty provisions that do impose legal obligations on Member States. The general aims of the EC Treaty (as variously amended) are set out in Art 2:

'The Community shall have as its task, by establishing a common market and an economic and monetary union and by implementing common policies or activities referred to in Articles 3 and 4, to promote throughout the Community a harmonious, balanced and sustainable development of economic activities, a high level of employment and of social protection, equality between men and women, sustainable and non-inflationary growth, a high degree of competitiveness and convergence of economic performance, a high level of protection and improvement of the quality of the environment, the raising of the standard of living and quality of life, and economic and social cohesion and solidarity among Member States.'

Article 3 provides:

'For the purposes set out in Article 2, the activities of the Community shall include, as provided in this Treaty and in accordance with the timetable set out therein:

(a)   the prohibition, as between Member States, of customs duties and quantitative restrictions on the import and export of goods, and of all other measures having equivalent effect;
(b)   a common commercial policy;
(c)   an internal market characterised by the abolition, as between Member States, of obstacles to the free movement of goods, persons, services and capital;
(d)   measures concerning the entry and movement of persons as provided for in Title IV;
(e)   a common policy in the sphere of agriculture and fisheries;
(f)   a common policy in the sphere of transport;
(g)   a system ensuring that competition in the internal market is not distorted;

(h)    the approximation of the laws of Member States to the extent required for the functioning of the common market;

(i)     the promotion of coordination between employment policies of the Member States with a view to enhancing their effectiveness by developing a coordinated strategy for employment;

(j)     a policy in the social sphere comprising a European Social Fund;

(k)    the strengthening of economic and social cohesion;

(l)     a policy in the sphere of the environment;

(m)   the strengthening of the competitiveness of Community industry;

(n)    the promotion of research and technological development;

(o)    encouragement for the establishment and development of trans-European networks;

(p)    a contribution to the attainment of a high level of health protection;

(q)    a contribution to education and training of quality and to the flowering of the cultures of the Member States;

(r)     a policy in the sphere of development cooperation;

(s)     the association of the overseas countries and territories in order to increase trade and promote jointly economic and social development;

(t)     a contribution to the strengthening of consumer protection;

(u)    measures in the spheres of energy, civil protection and tourism.'    **[54.12]**

b)   *Secondary legislation*

There are two forms of secondary legislation that may be adopted at Community level by the Council of Ministers or the Commission acting under a specific provision of the EC Treaty or by the Commission acting under powers delegated to it by the Council of Ministers:

(1)   *regulations:* this form of legislation has automatic effect in all Member States, without the need for any endorsement at national level. Regulations override inconsistent national legislation, whether adopted before or after the regulation; and

(2)   *directives:* these are addressed to Member States and are binding as to the result, but leave to the individual Member States responsibility for taking decisions about the manner and form of their implementation.

Directives specify the regime to apply and require Member States to adjust their national laws and administrative practices accordingly. A directive shall 'leave to the national authorities the choice of form and methods' as to the result to be achieved. Each directive specifies the period within which national laws must be amended. Legal action may be taken by the Commission against the Member State in question under Art 226 or by another Member State under Art 227 for failure to implement a Directive.

Article 226 provides that:

'If the Commission considers that a Member State has failed to fulfil an obligation under this Treaty, it shall deliver a reasoned opinion on the matter after giving the State concerned the opportunity to submit its observations.

If the State concerned does not comply with the opinion within the period laid down by the Commission, the latter may bring the matter before the Court of Justice.'

Article 227 further provides that:

'A Member State which considers that another Member State has failed to fulfil an obligation under this Treaty may bring the matter before the Court of Justice.

> Before a Member State brings an action against another Member State for an alleged infringement of an obligation it shall bring the matter before the Commission.
>
> The Commission shall deliver a reasoned opinion after each of the States concerned has been given the opportunity to submit its own case and its observations on the other party's case both orally and in writing.
>
> If the Commission has not delivered an opinion within three months of the date on which the matter was brought before it, the absence of such opinion shall not prevent the matter from being brought before the Court of Justice.'

A Member State which is found by the ECJ to be in breach of its obligations must, under Art 228 take measures to comply with the judgment. If a Member State does not comply with a judgment of the ECJ, the Commission may ask the ECJ to fine it for non-compliance. The first stage involves the Commission issuing a letter of formal notice. This is a request to the government of the member state to notify it of what measure has been taken to comply with the judgment of the ECJ. Failure to comply can result in daily penalties being imposed (up to 100,000 a day).

Directives have 'vertical' direct effect, ie they may be invoked by private individuals against Member States (and emanations of Member States, such as HMRC) where the Member State has failed properly to implement the provision within the period prescribed for that purpose. Directives cannot be invoked against private individuals (ie they do not have 'horizontal' direct effect).                                                                    **[54.13]–[54.20]**


## IV   UNDERLYING PRINCIPLES

### 1   The relevance of EC law to UK law

EC law matters in the UK for the simple reason that the UK Parliament has passed an Act requiring it to be taken into account. As a matter of UK law, international treaties do not give rise to enforceable rights as between the UK state and private individuals. Treaties (and other rules of international law) do not take effect in that way unless and until specifically incorporated into domestic law by a domestic statute. In other words, from a theoretical Public International Law perspective the UK has a 'dualist' system. Accordingly, in order to give legal effect in the UK to the treaties establishing the Community, Parliament passed legislation implementing them. The relevant statute is the European Communities Act 1972 (EC Act 1972).

The two key provisions of the EC Act 1972 are s 2(1) and (4). EC Act 1972 s 2(1) provides for all 'rights, powers, obligations and restrictions' under the relevant treaties to take effect as a matter of UK domestic law. EC Act 1972 s 2(4) provides that all UK legislation, whether passed before or after the introduction of EC Act 1972, shall have effect subject to s 2(1) and to the other provisions of s 2. Some (though not all) parts of EC law are expressed so as to give rise to enforceable rights (they are 'directly effective'). Therefore, EC Act 1972 s 2 has the effect of requiring that directly effective provisions of EC law have the force of law in the UK, and prevail over any inconsistent UK legislation.

Despite some initial doubts as to the acceptability of this interpretation under traditional constitutional law theory, the English Courts, from 1990 onwards, have adopted it. In *Factortame Ltd v Secretary of State for Transport* (1990) Lord Bridge said that EC Act 1972 s 2(4) has 'precisely the same effect as if a section were incorporated in [the relevant legislation] which in terms enacted that the provisions [set out there] were to be without prejudice to the directly enforceable Community rights of nationals of any Member State of the EEC'. A number of questions were referred to the ECJ and in a subsequent related case (*R v Secretary of State for Transport, ex p Factortame Ltd* (1991)) the House of Lords swept away any final constitutional doubts by saying that it was the implied intention of Parliament, by enacting EC Act 1972, to limit its sovereignty by accepting the supremacy of EC law. Since that time, there has been no doubt that unless and until the UK Parliament denounces the EC Treaty, the UK courts will accord supremacy to directly effective EC law by applying it directly in priority to inconsistent UK law.

**[54.21]**

## 2  The impact of EC law on UK law

The substantive provisions relating to the fundamental freedoms are discussed below. However, first, a few key underlying propositions stated by the ECJ are set out. It should be understood that this is nothing more than the briefest summary of the key rules with regard to the impact of EC law. For a fuller understanding, reference should be made to a specialist legal text.

(1)  In order for the aims of the EC to be achieved, it is necessary for there to be uniformity of application of EC law throughout the EC, and that requires EC law always to be supreme (see *Costa v ENEL* (1964) and *Internationale Handelsgesellschaft mbH* (1970)).

(2)  A domestic national court that is required to apply provisions of EC law is under a duty to give full effect to those provisions by refusing to apply any conflicting national legislation; the domestic court should not wait for such conflicting national legislation to be set aside by legislative or other means (*Simmenthal SpA* (1978)).

(3)  A finding that a national provision is inapplicable because of incompatibility with EC law does not mean that that domestic provision is *ultra vires* and thus is to be disregarded in its entirety. The ECJ has made it clear that national courts are to disapply national measures in order to safeguard enforceable Community law rights only to the extent that those measures are incompatible with Community law (See *IN CO GE '90 Srl* (1998) and *ICI v Colmer* (1996)). Otherwise, the offending national provisions remain in force.

(4)  The obligation to give full effect to EC law applies not only to national courts, but also to domestic administrative agencies such as, for example, HMRC (see *Gervais Larsy v INASTI* (2001)).  **[54.22]–[54.30]**

## V  THE FUNDAMENTAL FREEDOMS: INTRODUCTION

The four 'fundamental freedoms' (or, simply, 'freedoms') first appear in the EC Treaty Art 3. That Article provides that the broad aim of the EC Treaty is to ensure the creation of 'an internal market characterised by the abolition, as between Member States, of obstacles to the free movement of goods, persons, services and capital'. In other words, the freedoms are central to the treaty and its aims. Detailed rules for each of them are set out in Arts 28 to 60 EC, and they are each described more fully in paras **[54.42]–[54.50]** below. The freedoms primarily play an economic role, namely to assist in the abolition of barriers to the internal market. Although the four freedoms are addressed to Member States, the relevant Articles have been held by the ECJ to be directly effective. Accordingly, individuals and companies have the right to invoke any one or more of those freedoms to challenge the validity of domestic law provisions (including tax law) that represent an obstacle to their utilisation of such freedom(s).

However, in any such challenge, it is necessary to identify the particular freedom that it is asserted that a provision breaches. This is partly because the freedoms are somewhat different in scope. It is also because, as described below, there are certain grounds on which an obstacle to a freedom may be justified, so as to be protected from challenge, and those grounds are not identical for each of the four freedoms.

In certain circumstances, it is very clear which freedom is in play. The dividing line between, for example, 'goods' and 'persons' is very easy to identify. However, other boundaries, particularly the ones between 'goods' and 'capital' and between 'goods' and 'services' are less distinct. The ECJ cases suggest that in such cases there are no hard and fast rules: rather, it is a matter of degree. For example, the ECJ has held that, although collectors' coins are 'goods', legal tender in circulation falls within the provisions relating to 'capital' (*Bordessa* (1995)).

In other circumstances, although the freedoms are mutually exclusive in scope, it will be clear that a single domestic rule may represent an obstacle to two or more freedoms. In such circumstances, it is necessary to determine whether the rule should be tested against each of those freedoms, or only one of them. The position seems to be that any freedom that is only affected in an indirect or ancillary way is to be ignored in these circumstances (this, of course, has much in common with the test in the VAT case of *Card Protection Plan Ltd v C & E Comr* (1999) see **[30.72]**). This rule emerges from *C & E Comr v Schindler* (1994), a case where both 'goods' and 'services' were potentially relevant. In that case, the ECJ said that if goods are supplied in a form that is not an end in itself, but is ancillary to the supply of a service (such as advertising materials) then the activity should be treated as the movement of services, but not the movement of goods. A similar approach was recommended by A-G Tesauro in *Safir* (1998) in relation to the boundary between 'capital' and 'services'. He opined that, where possible, the domestic rule should be considered only in relation to the freedom that it restricts 'directly', and not as an obstacle to any other freedoms that it affects indirectly. Although the ECJ has not, to date, expressed a view on this part of his opinion, this passage was cited and relied upon by A-G Alber in *Baars* (2000) and by *A-G Geelhoed in Reisch* (2004).

The ECJ has not always been so punctilious, however. In *Svensson & Gustavvson* (1995), the ECJ held that certain aspects of Luxembourg law breached both the free movement of capital and services provisions, but it did so without providing an analysis of how each provision applied to the relevant law. That approach has, unsurprisingly, been criticised (particularly in the opinion of Advocate-General Tesauro in *Safir* (1998), noted above).

**[54.31]–[54.40]**

## VI THE FUNDAMENTAL FREEDOMS: SCOPE

As noted above, the EC Treaty provides four fundamental freedoms on which individuals and companies can rely, in accordance with the framework described above. However, although the framework is constant, each of those four freedoms applies in slightly different ways. This section addresses the specific circumstances in which specific tax rules have fallen (or will fall) within the scope of one of the freedoms, so as to be disapplied in order to give effect to the Member State's duties and the taxpayers' rights under that freedom.

It should be noted that at this stage that, in certain circumstances, rules that appear to fall within the scope of a fundamental freedom may nonetheless be considered to be justified, in which case they will not be disapplied (similarly, rules which are wholly non-discriminatory, both in theory and practice, will generally be permitted). Any justification will either be by reference to one of a list of overriding objectives set out in the Treaty itself, or by reference to one of a (separate, and open-ended) class of objectives which do not appear in the EC Treaty but which have been inferred by the ECJ. The justifications set out in the EC Treaty are dealt with in this section. The rather more important issues associated with the class of justifications clarified by the ECJ are discussed (together with the question of wholly non-discriminatory rules) in **Section IV** below. **[54.41]**

### 1 Free movement of goods (Arts 23–31)

As the EEC originated as a free trade area, the free movement of goods is often regarded by Community lawyers as the most important of the fundamental freedoms.

However, although many of the principles of the application of the fundamental freedoms were developed in the context of the free movement of goods, from a substantive point of view it is of little relevance to direct tax (being rather more concerned with indirect taxes such as customs and excise duties, which are beyond the scope of this work, and with VAT, which is discussed in the self-contained section in **Chapters 37–40**). Accordingly, specific instances of its application are not discussed here. **[54.42]**

### 2 Free movement of persons (Arts 39–48)

Uniquely amongst the four fundamental freedoms, free movement of persons comprises two quite distinct limbs: (i) the freedom of workers to travel to other Member States and to be able to accept employment there (Art 39); and (ii) the freedom of establishment for citizens of Member States (Art 43) and companies and firms incorporated in the EU or with their central administration here (a similar, but not identical, test to that set out in paras [**12.10**] and [**34.153**]): (the benefit of Art 43 is extended to such companies by Art 48).

Of the four freedoms, free movement of persons (particularly the 'establishment' arm) has had perhaps the most significant impact on direct tax. This is because most European tax systems were set up, prior to the advent of the EEC, in a way whose underlying philosophy is in direct conflict with the requirements of Art 43. In accordance with conventional international tax theory, the UK and most (if not all) of the Member States have proceeded on the basis that resident taxpayers are to be treated differently from non-resident taxpayers. They have also assumed that, from a 'parent company' perspective, branches and subsidiaries within the state can be treated differently from those that are abroad (and that branches owned locally can be treated differently from those parented in another jurisdiction). Finally, their laws tend to provide for cross-border transactions or activities to be taxed differently to purely domestic ones, principally to avoid the loss of tax to the particular state's fisc. However, the clear result of the obligation on Member States to ensure free movement of persons within the EC is that there are very serious restrictions on a state's ability to do any of these things. [**54.43**]

a)    *Free movement of workers: Art 39*

As noted above, this Article guarantees the freedom of workers to travel to other Member States and to be able to accept employment there. There is no definition of 'worker' in the Treaty; and the ECJ has interpreted the term in a wide sense. In *Levin* (1982), it said that if what is proposed involves: 'the pursuit of effective and genuine activities to the exclusion of activities on such a small scale as to be regarded as purely marginal and ancillary', then the person is a 'worker'; to define the term more restrictively would be contrary to the overarching principles of the treaty set out in Arts 2 and 3 EC.

The main set of issues that have arisen in this context relate to personal tax advantages, such as personal allowances (see [**4.101**]) that are expressed to be dependent upon residence. Broadly, subject to questions of discrimination and justification (see below), the ECJ has held that Member States are required to treat migrant workers as if they were residents. It should be noted that there is no corresponding right for companies to move their central management to another Member State under Art 39 (see *ex p Daily Mail and General Trust plc* (1999), though following *Centros* (1999) (see [**54.32**] below) and *de Lasteyrie* (2004), this may be protected by the right to freedom of establishment).

The leading case in relation to personal tax advantages for migrant workers is *Schumacker* (1995). Mr. Schumacker was a Belgian resident employed in Germany. Over 90% of his income was earned in Germany and he was exempted from Belgian tax on this foreign-source income. As there was no Belgian tax due in respect of which he could credit his Belgian personal allowances and deductions, he instead sought similar allowances from the German state. Under German law, he would only have been entitled to such allowances if he were a German resident. The ECJ agreed that he should be entitled to such allowances. Other cases are discussed below in relation to the question of discrimination.                          [**54.44**]

b)    *Freedom of establishment: Arts 43 and 48*

The right enshrined in Arts 43 and 48 is a right to establish a business in a Member State (whether by way of branch or subsidiary of an existing business, or otherwise) and to do so on terms that that business undertaking will not be discriminated against on the ground of the owner's nationality (or in the case of a company, its seat). Where the 'establisher' has only a part-interest in the establishment, this freedom will be engaged only if that interest allows him to participate in the management or control of entity or business and allows him to exercise definite influence (*Baars* (2000)). This is generally considered to be a non-numerical test, though the better view is that large minority holdings would qualify, provided that the 'establisher' does actually involve himself in the management or control of the establishment. This article has been considered to disapply domestic tax rules in each of the following situations.

1)    More stringent taxation on an individual resident abroad with a local business than a local resident:

*Wielockx (1995)*—a rule confining to residents the right to deduct payments to a pension scheme when computing business profits.

2)    More stringent taxation on a branch than a locally-incorporated subsidiary:

*Commission v France* (1986) (the 'avoir fiscal' case)—the inability of a French branch of a German company to claim a tax credit that would have been available to a French company in corresponding circumstances (this was, in fact, the first direct tax case to reach the ECJ);*Compagnie de Saint-Gobain* (1999)—the unavailability of treaty relief on dividend income received by a German branch of a French company, in circumstances that a German company would have been entitled to such relief; and
*Royal Bank of Scotland plc v Greek State* (1999)—the application of a flat rate of corporation tax to branches of overseas companies, when a lower rate was available in certain circumstances to Greek companies.

3)    More stringent taxation on a foreign-owned company than one that is domestically-owned:

*Metallgesellschaft/Hoechst* (2001)—the inability of the UK subsidiary of a non-resident company to make a group income election, which would have enabled it to pay a dividend to its parent companies without having to account for advance corporation tax (very broadly speaking, a collection mechanism for corporation tax triggered by the payment of a dividend); *and*
*Lankhorst-Hohorst* (2003)—the application of German thin capitalisation rules to a loan received by the German subsidiary of a Dutch parent company, which rules would not have applied had the loan been granted by a German-resident parent company.

4)    More stringent taxation on a person or entity with foreign establishments than one with local establishments:

*Imperial Chemicals Industries plc v Colmer* (1996)—the application of a UK rule that consortium relief for losses was conditional on the holding company being a company whose business consisted wholly or mainly of the holding of shares of companies that are its 90% subsidiaries and that in determining this only UK resident companies could be considered;

*Baars* (2000)—the denial of the Netherlands wealth tax exemption to holdings in foreign companies, when it applied to holdings in domestic companies;

*Bosal Holding BV (2001)*—the denial of relief for interest expenses in relation to monies borrowed to acquire shares in a non-Netherlands company;

*X&Y* (2002)—the denial of a CGT deferral on transfer of an asset to an associated but non-resident company, when that deferral would have been available on the transfer to an associated resident company; and

*de Baeck* (2004)—imposition of a CGT charge on transfer of an asset to an associated but non-resident company (this case is much the same as *X&Y* (2002) except that the domestic rule allowed for the transfer to be wholly tax-free).

5)    A tax charge applying directly on transfer of residence of the person or business abroad:

*De Lasteyrie (2003)*—a deemed disposal for French CGT purposes of assets when the individual moved his residence from France (although see *N v Inspecteur van de Belastingdienst Oost* (2006), where A-G Kokott opined that, although the exit charge regime in The Netherlands restricted the exercise of freedom of establishment, it could be justified as it pursued the legitimate objective of maintaining a proportional tax system based on the principles of territoriality and coherence).

It will be noted that Art 43 will disapply any establishment-related rule of more stringent taxation, whether that taxation applies to the establisher or the establishment itself. It will also be noted that in some of these cases, the right of establishment has disapplied not only rules which affect the establishment itself, but also rules which affect subsequent dealings between the establisher and the establishment (see, in particular, *X&Y* (2002) and *Lankhorst-Hohorst* (2003)). This is now a relatively uncontroversial proposition.                                                                                  **[54.45]**

*Derogations under Art 46*

Article 46 provides a list of exceptions to the free movement of workers and the freedom of establishment. They are of limited application in the context of direct tax: the right of persons to move freely does not override domestic rules providing for special treatment of foreign nationals based on public policy, public security or public health. Further, it is expected that these exceptions would be construed narrowly. Article 46 also exempts activities which are connected 'with the exercise of official authority'. This derogation has also been given a very narrow interpretation and a similar set of exceptions in relation to the free movement of goods has been narrowly construed, in particular to refuse protection to any rule which has even an economic objective, even if that is wholly ancillary: see *ex p Evans Medical Ltd* (1995).                                                                                  **[54.46]**

### 3  Freedom to provide services (Art 49)

Article 49 sets out the third freedom. It provides that nationals of Member States are guaranteed the right freely to provide services cross-border. As with freedom of establishment, the right is accorded to EC nationals and to companies that have either their registered office, central administration or place of business in a Member State. The freedom to provide services is a subsidiary freedom to the three other fundamental freedoms: the services in question are those 'normally provided for remuneration, insofar as they are not governed by the provisions relating to freedom of movement for goods, capital and persons' (Art 50(1)). Again, where domestic law provides that a cross-border provider of services is subject to more stringent taxation than a domestic provider, the relevant domestic rule will be disapplied.

It is frequently said that the right to provide services includes the right to receive services (see *Eurowings Luftverkehrs AG* (1999)). In that case, German companies leasing assets could claim a certain tax deduction only if they leased the assets from a domestic lessor. The ECJ held that this amounted to a restriction on the freedom to receive services from other Member States, and that the taxpayer should be entitled to such a deduction, even if it leased the assets from a foreign lessor. However, this is simply a manifestation of the fact that the more stringent tax treatment tends to apply in the hands of the recipient of the services rather than the provider. Therefore, in *Laboratoires Fournier* (2005) the limitation of an increased deduction for R&D expenditure to expenditure incurred in France was held to affect the right of non-French subcontractors to supply their services, even though the limitation applied to the tax position of the French company that had (or could have) sub-contracted the services in the first place. Further, this freedom can even affect an unfavourable tax treatment in the hands of a third party: in *Commission v Spain* (2004) the ECJ held that a rule which granted more favourable tax treatment to dealings in shares listed on the Spanish stock market restricted the right of other stock markets to provide their services to Spanish undertakings, thereby benefiting neither the stock market nor the undertaking, but an owner of shares in the undertaking.

As with free movement of persons and free movement of goods, the freedom to provide services is subject to derogation on the grounds of 'public policy, public security or public health' (under Art 56). Again, it is expected that these derogations would be construed narrowly, and (in particular) so as to exclude economic aims.                               **[54.47]**

### 4  Free movement of capital (Arts 56–60)

The final freedom is set out in Art 56. Article 56(1) provides that: 'within the framework of the provision set out in this Chapter, all restrictions on the movement of capital between Member States and between Member States and third countries shall be prohibited.' These current provisions have been in force only since 1 January 1994; before that date, the provisions on free movement of capital were much narrower in scope. The current provisions on movement of capital, like the provisions in respect of the free movement of goods, are expressed by reference to the object of protection, namely 'capital', rather than by reference to the rights of a given entity.

These provisions apply to all measures that impose a more stringent tax regime on or in respect of cross-border movements of capital. In *Lenz* (2004) and *Manninen* (2004), the ECJ held that a tax system that taxed dividends from local shares (Austrian and Finnish, respectively) more favourably than dividends from shares in non-resident companies was within Art 56, the cross-border capital movement being the original investment in the shares. In *Weidert & Paulus* (2004), a rule which allowed the acquisition costs of shares in domestic companies to be deducted from taxable income (but not the acquisition costs of shares in non-resident companies) also fell within Art 56 (it will be noted that this is a very similar case to *Bosal* (2001), but applying in circumstances where the level of investment was insufficient to create an establishment). As with freedom of establishment, Art 56 can disapply rules in either state: in *Fokus Bank* (2004), a case very similar to *Lenz* (2004) and *Manninen* (2004), the EFTA court found that the free movement of capital was impeded even though the tax regime in question applied in the state of the dividend payer, rather than in the shareholder's state.

Article 58(1)(b) provides for similar derogations to those in play for free movement of goods, services and persons. Again, it is to be expected that they will be construed narrowly.

However, although, so far, free movement of capital seems to apply in very much the same way as the other three freedoms, there are four significant points of difference.

First, Art 58(1) contains specific additional grounds on which measures that affect the free movement of capital can be justified. These must be considered in each case, not withstanding that the ECJ currently restricts their scope. Article 58(1)(a) allows Member States to apply tax provisions which restrict free movement of capital within the Community, in so far as they discriminate between 'tax-payers who are not in the same situation with regard to their place of residence or with regard to the place where their capital is invested'. However, although this ground appears to be quite wide-ranging in its scope, the Court has made clear that as Art 58(1)(a) is a derogation from a fundamental freedom, it is interpreted strictly (in an analogous way to Art 30). Thus, Art 58(1)(a) absolutely does not mean that any tax legislation that distinguishes between taxpayers by reference to the place where they invest their capital is automatically compatible with the Treaty. Further, by virtue of Art 58(3), in order to justify differential tax treatment under this provision, there must be an underlying difference that justifies the differing treatment. The decisions of the ECJ in *Manninen* (2004) and, particularly, *Weidert & Paulus* (2004) have put it almost beyond doubt that the effect of this is that Art 58(1)(a) adds nothing to the case law on justifications, discussed below. Article 58(1)(b) indicates that measures which affect the free movement of capital can be justified to the extent necessary 'to prevent infringements of national law and regulations, in particular in the field of taxation and the prudential supervision of financial institutions, or to lay down procedures for the declaration of capital movements for purposes of administrative or statistical information'. However, again, Art 58(3), applies and as appears from *Verkooijen* (2001), this restricts the impact of Art 58(1)(b) in much the same way as it restricts Art 58(1)(a).

Secondly, there is a further provision in Art 56(2), which is in identical terms to Art 56(1), but applies to 'payments', rather than 'movements of capital'. Although certain questions turn on the distinction between 'payment' and 'movement of capital', an analysis of that distinction is beyond the scope of this work. Further, there is much overlap between the two. In *NEC Semi-Conductors Ltd v IRC* (2003), Park J in the High Court held that that Art 57 (below) applies both to 'movements of capital' and 'payments', the Court of Appeal disagreed (2006); and it is likely that the question will be referred to the ECJ for resolution.

Thirdly, it is obvious that, in certain cases, there is a real overlap between free movement of capital and the other freedoms (particularly freedom of establishment) and it is now clear that Art 56 is to be treated as a subsidiary freedom, not to be considered where any impact on the free movement of capital arises indirectly from a limitation on another freedom (as in, for instance, *X&Y* (2002)). This seems to be a matter of administrative convenience only (and where, for example, both capital and establishment are engaged, it is necessary for the domestic rules to comply with both freedoms (as A-G Alber said in *Baars* (2000), relying on *Konle* (1999)). But as a practical matter, and as described above, where a domestic measure is a direct obstacle to another freedom, then free movement of capital will generally be left out of account, only to be invoked in respect of direct impediments to the actual transfer of funds (see A-G Alber in *Safir* (1998)). The priority as between capital and services (both of which consider themselves to be subsidiary freedoms) is not considered to be a significant issue in practice.

Finally, uniquely amongst the four freedoms, Art 56 applies even in respect of transactions with non-EU countries (as in *Ospelt* (2003)). The scope of this rule is currently somewhat uncertain, though for the reasons stated above, it should apply even in circumstances where the transaction is one to which (in a purely-EU context) the rules on freedom of establishment would be given effective priority. This was certainly the decision that the Amsterdam Tax Court of Appeal reached in a case in March 2005. The key substantive limitation is that found in Art 57(1), which permits the retention of any national or Community law measures that existed on 31 December 1993 that affect movements of capital to or from third countries 'involving direct investment (including investment in real estate), establishment, the provision of financial services or the admission of securities to capital markets'. In *Sanz de Lera* (1995) the ECJ held that this derogation is to be construed strictly: no new restrictions on the movement of capital to or from third countries can be created by Member States and the only permissible exceptions are in respect of the types of movements specified in the Article (although they also found that rules of equal application to EU and non-EU transactions will be protected by this standstill provision for non-EU transactions). There is no direct guidance on the existence or otherwise of any further limitations on the scope of Art 56 to affect the tax treatment of cross-border transactions with non-EU countries (A-G Kokott in *Manninen* (2004) went out of her way to express no view on this point), but a number of cases have been referred to the ECJ. In the meantime, it should be assumed that, subject to the effect of Art 57(1), the rules should apply in just the same way as for intra-Community transactions. **[54.48]–[54.50]**

## VII    THE FUNDAMENTAL FREEDOMS: BREACH AND JUSTIFICATION

### 1    Introduction

The previous section discussed the content of the fundamental freedoms, and specific carve-outs to them as set out in the EC treaties. Generally speaking, a domestic rule that affects the exercise of one of the freedoms and is not protected by a carve-out will be disapplied. However, as noted above, it is not necessarily the case that all such rules will be disapplied in this way. Certain rules will be permitted because they apply in a wholly non-discriminatory way. Even those that are not permitted for that reason may nonetheless be permitted on the basis that they are justified as a means of achieving one of the 'overriding objectives', which do not appear in the treaty, but which have been approved by the ECJ.    **[54.51]**

#### a)    *Barriers to market*

Measures which are wholly non-discriminatory and apply (in practice, as well as in theory) equally to cross-border taxpayers and transactions as they do to domestic ones will only be disapplied to the extent that they act as a genuine barrier preventing access to the market of one or more Member States. This was resolved first in the context of the free movement of goods where, after some equivocation, the ECJ held in *Keck and Mithouard* (1994) that non-discriminatory measures would be struck down only if they 'prevented' (or, according to Advocate-General Jacobs in *Leclerc-Siplec* (1995) 'substantially impeded') access to market. Similar questions subsequently arose in respect of the other fundamental freedoms; and in the 1990s the ECJ started gradually to apply this principle across the board. In the context of free movement of workers under Art 39, *Bosman* (1995) and *Graf* (2000) establish that non-discriminatory restrictions will be prohibited only if they have an effect akin to actual exclusion from a particular market. In the context of freedom to supply services, in *Alpine Investments* (1995) the ECJ referred only to provisions which 'directly affect' access to the market. In other words, these cases establish that a relatively severe test must be satisfied for such a restriction to be prohibited. Therefore, although the existence of corporation tax in the UK is a disincentive to doing business here, it is not (at least at 30%) a barrier to the UK market that the ECJ would disapply. Other than in exceptional circumstances, it is not considered likely that a tax rule would be disapplied under this heading.    **[54.52]**

#### b)    *Discrimination and restrictions*

However, the position is different for discriminatory rules (ie those which apply differently to domestic and cross-border situations). Rules that impose any sort of discriminatory disincentive (in the words of the ECJ an 'unjustified difference in treatment') will be disapplied even if their actual impact is slight. There is not even any need for evidence that, on the facts of the case, the rule in question actually affected the decision making process of the relevant persons. In *Gebhard* (1995) the ECJ said that the rule need only 'liable to hinder or make less attractive the exercise of the fundamental freedoms'. In *de Lasteyrie* (2004) the ECJ considered it to be uncontroversial that a rule would be disapplied even if it was of limited scope or minor importance (albeit, that in this case, the ECJ did say that, on the facts, there was a substantial effect). Indeed, even a difference in treatment that is purely procedural in nature can lead to the disapplication of a rule. In *Vestergaard* (2000) the ECJ held that a rule which introduced a rebuttable presumption that travel to conferences abroad was partly holiday (so that the reimbursement of expenses by the employer should be seen as a taxable benefit) fell foul of the provisions on free movement of services. In *de Lasteyrie* (2004) itself, the fact that the desired treatment was only available on the making of an application and the payment of a security deposit meant that the rule fell foul of EU law.

It was thought initially that only rules that discriminate directly on the grounds of nationality (or, in practice in every case other than *Gilly* (1998), residence) could be struck down if they did not act as a substantial barrier to market access. However, the case law of the ECJ now shows that there are also two other types of discriminatory disincentive to the exercise of the fundamental freedoms that may be prohibited: 'indirect discrimination' and (if different) 'restriction'. The distinction here is important for the following reason. If a measure is 'directly discriminatory', then it will be prohibited, unless it is permitted by one of the specific carve-outs provided in the EC Treaty, described above. However, if it is only 'indirectly discrimination' or a 'restriction', then it will be capable of being saved by a general justification, in the way and subject to the rules described in 3 below (including particularly the principle of proportionality, which is dealt with separately in 4 below). It is considered that it is now accepted that the case of *Royal Bank of Scotland* (1999), which indicated that only an express derogating provision could justify an indirectly discriminatory provision, is incorrect.        **[54.53]**

## 2   Discrimination and Restrictions

### a)   *Discrimination in general*

The first question to be answered, in determining whether a rule, which is not a substantial barrier to market but nonetheless acts as an obstacle to a fundamental freedom, will be disapplied, is whether the rule is discriminatory. In general terms, discrimination can arise in one of two ways. The first is where persons in a comparable situation are treated in a dissimilar way. The second is where two persons, not in a comparable position, are treated in a similar way. Discrimination in the context of direct tax is generally not within the 'traditional' framework of sex, nationality, colour or race: rather, it proceeds by reference to nationality, residence, or place of doing business.

The key issue here is to determine whether two people are in a comparable situation. However, this exercise is not always straightforward in an international tax context. This is very largely because many of the rules which fall within the scope of a fundamental freedom apply differently to residents and non-residents, because conventional international tax theory recognises that there is a distinction between residents and non-residents with regard to tax burden. A resident benefits from the public expenditure of his home State and enjoys the benefits of its laws for the protection of his person and his property. Thus, residents of a country are taxable in that state in respect of all income, no matter where it arises ('residence taxation'). If a person earns income in a country other than the country of his residence, then that country also is entitled to tax that person, because it provides the local infrastructure for him to earn that income, but only in respect of that locally-earned income ('source taxation'): see, for a general discussion *Whitney v IRC* (1926).

*Comparability and Territoriality.* The ECJ has recognised these principles and will, in certain cases, allow distinctions between resident and non-resident taxpayers to be made if this can be justified by objective differences between them. It invariably refers to this as the 'fiscal principle of territoriality'. The leading case here is *Futura* (1997). There, Luxembourg law dictated that for Luxembourg purposes a loss-making Belgian-resident company with a Luxembourg branch could carry forward only the Luxembourg element of its losses for set-off against Luxembourg profits. It also required the company to prepare Luxembourg-specific accounts to demonstrate those losses. The ECJ upheld the rule in question. As an entity that was objectively only properly taxable in Luxembourg according to its local income (A-G Maduro in *Marks and Spencer* (2004) considered that the objective standard was the consensus within the international tax community on the matters noted above), Futura was held to be in an objectively different position to a Luxembourg-resident company, and so Luxembourg was entitled to insist that only its Luxembourg losses be brought into account, even though those rules did not apply to Luxembourg residents.

However, there are three key limitations on this doctrine. First, it certainly does not permit Member States to apply different rules to cross-border transactions across the board, even if those transactions only apply differently to residents and non-residents. This point has been argued (and rejected) repeatedly, most recently in *Laboratoires Fournier* (2005). A-G Jacobs noted that it was an essential part of the rationale of *Futura* that non-resident companies were treated no less favourably than resident ones.

Secondly, it appears from the opinion of A-G Maduro in *Marks & Spencer* (2005), that this rule only applies to the state in whose favour the freedom has been exercised. That state is not obliged to give advantages to the person exercising their freedom that are not 'objectively justified'. However, the state from where the freedom was exercised has no choice—it is obliged in all circumstances to treat the person exercising the freedom as though he had undertaken a domestic transaction. Although this analysis is far from settled law, the only other authoritative statement (by A-G Kokott in *Manninen* (2004)) adopts a very similar approach.

Finally, this rule seems restricted to situations where the taxpayer is genuinely subject to taxation on only part of his income in the state in question. Therefore, in *Schumacker* (1995), the Court relied (in striking down the domestic rule denying personal allowances to migrant workers) on the proposition that, as he earned almost his entire income in Germany, Mr Schumacker was in a substantially comparable position to a German resident with regard to personal allowances and deductions. In the subsequent cases of *Gschwind* (1999), *Asscher* (2002) and *de Groot (2002), the* Court seemed to have moved to a more sensitive test, under which such a migrant worker will be in a comparable position to a local resident for these purposes only if by deriving the main part of his taxable income locally he was missing out on a corresponding benefit from his home State, but the Opinion of A-G Léger in *Ritter-Coulais* (2005) indicates that a person in substantially the same position as a resident should be entitled to the same benefits, regardless of whether that benefit would have been available at home. However, in *D v Inspecteur van be Belastingdienst* (2005), the ECJ held (contrary to the Opinion of its A-G), in the context of Art 56, that an individual, who had only 10% of his wealth in a State in which he was not resident, was not in a comparable situation to the residents of that State.

It should also be noted that A-G Maduro in *Marks & Spencer* (2005) treated the doctrine of territoriality as a potential justification, rather than as going to whether there had been a 'difference in treatment' in the first place. However, not only did the ECJ not adopt his reasoning in making its decision, the weight of authority (as well as principle) is against him on this: see in particular the Opinion of A-G Jacobs in *Laboratoires Fournier* (2004) and the judgment of the ECJ in *Manninen* (2004).

*Comparability by reference to other issues.* There are also indications in the case law of other circumstances in which taxpayers will or will not be treated as in comparable positions. This typically depends on the nature of a given enterprise (or facts applying to it: see *Schumacker* above) and the qualitative nature of the rules which apply to it in the particular context. Therefore, although (as noted above under freedom of establishment, see eg *'Avoir Fiscal'* (1986)) branches and subsidiaries are typically considered to be in comparable positions (and so to be treated the same), this is probably not the case when dealing with the ability of a given enterprise to use or surrender losses: the fact that a company with a branch in state X is taxable in that country on its local income, whereas a company incorporated there is taxable on its worldwide income, may well mean that the two are not in a comparable position for these purposes (see, for instance, the Opinion of A-G Maduro in *Marks and Spencer* (2005)). The relevant rules can be rules of local law (as in *Marks and Spencer* (2004)) or the law of another state: see the statements in *Manninen* (2004) that the comparability of a local and cross-border situation might depend on the effectiveness of the law of the other state to mitigate double taxation. However, differences in applicable tax rates will generally not lead to non-comparability (see A-G Tizzano in *Lenz* (2004)) because the taxpayers are in principle in the same situation: full taxpayers in their local Member State.                                                                                         **[54.54]**

b)   *Direct discrimination*

Article 12 of the EC Treaty provides a fundamental guarantee for EU nationals which prohibits direct discrimination on the grounds of nationality. It is now also clear that each of the fundamental freedoms also carries with it a specific right for discriminatory domestic rules not to be enforced in the area of that freedom. This prohibition on overt discrimination on grounds of nationality ('direct discrimination') is a cornerstone of the EU. In a tax context, direct discrimination occurs where the domestic tax provision expressly confers or denies a different tax treatment on the grounds of nationality (or, in practice, residence) in circumstances where there are no material differences for those purposes between a resident and a non-resident (as in *Schumacker* (1995)). Any such direct discrimination will be prohibited.

For completeness, it should be noted that there is some suggestion that a regime which discriminates between different cross-border situations, treating dealings with nationals of one state less well than dealings with those of another state, will also be prohibited, and the Revenue will be required to extend the more favourable treatment in both situations. This question (the so-called most-favoured nation (MFN) issue) was referred to the ECJ in *Hoechst/Metallgesellschaft* (2001), but not answered. In *D* (2005), although A-G Colomer said that the issue of discrimination here was not one of MFN, ie in the sense of between tax treaties, but was actually in the sense of residence, he lent some support to the MFN argument. However, the ECJ rejected the argument based on MFN. It held that it is inherent in a bilateral tax treaty that the reciprocal rights and obligations under the treaty apply only to persons resident in either of the two contracting Member States. Thus, a national of a Member State that is not party to the treaty is not in a comparable situation to a national of a contracting Member State.    **[54.55]**

c)    *Indirect discrimination*

It is now clear that a measure will be prohibited if, even though not expressly discriminatory by reference to nationality (or residence), it does have that effect in practice ('indirect discrimination'). An indirectly discriminatory provision is one that does not expressly include nationality (or residence) as a criterion for its application, but has the consequence that non-nationals (or residents) are treated less favourably than nationals.

The prospect of such measures being prohibited first arose in the context of the free movement of goods (under Art 28) in the seminal '*Cassis de Dijon*' case (*Rewe* (1979)). In this case, the ECJ had to consider a measure that was discriminatory on the grounds of nationality in practice only. German law specified a minimum alcohol content of 15–20% for certain spirits, including cassis. German cassis complied with this stipulation, but French cassis did not. The German rules were not directly discriminatory: they applied without distinction to domestic and imported goods. However, the result of the rules was effectively to ban French cassis from the German market. The issue was whether Germany could prevent the importation of goods lawfully marketed in France on the grounds that they did not comply with German product regulations. The ECJ concluded that the disparity between the French and German product regulations was, in principle, an obstacle to free movement of goods, within the scope of Art 28. Therefore, even though not directly discriminatory, it was capable of being disapplied.    **[54.56]**

d)    *Restrictions*

The 22nd edition of this work dealt at some length with the analysis of when a difference in treatment would be treated as discriminatory. Generally, the key issue there was identification of the relevant domestic comparator. However, it is now quite clear that the ECJ does not require the taxpayer to identify a comparator. A gradual shift since the opinion of A-G Jacobs in *Danner* (2001), means that the burden of proof of proving discrimination has effectively switched from the taxpayer to the Revenue. All that the taxpayer needs to do is establish a difference in treatment between a cross-border situation and a purely domestic situation. It then falls to the Revenue to seek to demonstrate that the difference is justified by some objective difference between the domestic and cross-border situation (see, most recently, *Laboratoires Fournier* (2005)) or, failing that, one of the true justifications dealt with in the next section. But, in any event, the ECJ no longer frames its judgments in terms of 'discrimination' but 'differences in treatment' or 'restrictions'.

It is understood that this approach grew up as a matter of administrative convenience, since it almost always transpired that there was no objective justification for the difference in treatment (and so discrimination was established). In this way, the ECJ could avoid the difficult questions of whether a measure is directly or indirectly discriminatory: it dealt with this question only when it absolutely has to (such as in *Haahr Petroleum Ltd* (1997)). However, the position here is now extremely clear. The taxpayer need only point to a difference in treatment. Unless the Member State can demonstrate that it involves no discrimination, or is justified, then the relevant rule will be disapplied. In fact, the Opinion of A-G Maduro in *Marks and Spencer* (2005) goes further, suggesting that, once a difference in treatment has been established based on the cross-border status of any situation, then that concludes irrevocably that a barrier to intra-community trade has been established. He treated the issue of fiscal territoriality as a justification rather than an element in constructing discrimination. While the decision of the ECJ in *Marks and Spencer* does not support the correctness of that analysis, discrimination is limited. In essence, once a difference in treatment is established, it will be disapplied unless the Member State can identify a 'justification'.                                                      **[54.57]**

## 3   The 'Rule of Reason' and Justifications

If it can be established that a restriction has arisen, the next question is whether it is capable of being justified. As noted above, the list of justifications is no longer confined to those set out in the EC Treaty. Over the past 20 years, a doctrine has emerged from the ECJ that, in some circumstances, such measures may be justified on general principles, rather than as a matter of a specific provision in the EC Treaty. This particularly has been by the adoption from US competition law (and application to the fundamental freedoms) of the concept of 'rule of reason': that certain measures, even though in principle prohibited, will be permitted if they are justified by pressing matters of public importance.

The application of the concept of the 'rule of reason' can be taken, for present purposes, to stem from the *Cassis de Dijon* case noted above. In this case, as outlined above, the indirectly discriminatory measures were found to breach Art 28, and not be protected by Art 30. However, the ECJ recognised that this could be harsh in its effects on member States. The ECJ held that certain measures, even if prohibited in principle, will, in appropriate circumstances, be upheld if 'recognised as being necessary in order to satisfy mandatory requirements relating in particular to the effectiveness of fiscal supervision, the protection of public health, the fairness of commercial transactions and the defence of the consumer'. In *Cassis de Dijon*, the ECJ made clear that the 'rule of reason' would not apply to directly discriminatory measures. This was later applied to services in *Säger* (1991). Then, in *Gebhard* (1995) (a case that involved the freedom of establishment) the ECJ indicated that a uniform approach should be followed in respect of all the freedoms. Since that case, it is clear that a measure will be treated as justified under the rule of reason only if:

(a)    it is applied in a non-discriminatory (ie, not directly discriminatory) manner;

(b)    it is justified by imperative reasons in the public interest;

(c)    it is suitable for securing the attainment of the objective pursued; and

(d)    it does not go beyond what is necessary to attain that objective (the so-called 'proportionality test'.

The first of these criteria was discussed in the last section. The second is discussed here. The third and fourth (suitability and proportionality) are discussed in the next section.

Outside the context of direct tax, the 'rule of reason' has been invoked to save measures from prohibition on a number of occasions. However, in the direct tax field, such an argument has only succeeded once (in the case of *Bachmann* (1992)), and it is not thought that that case would be decided the same way today. In particular, the following ideas have been rejected as not amounting to 'imperative reasons in the public interest': lack of reciprocity on the part of other Member States by not granting corresponding tax treatment to non-residents (*Eurowings (1999)* and *Commission v France* (1986)); economic aims such as the need to encourage investment in domestic companies (*Verkooijen* (2000) and, particularly, prevention of loss of tax revenue for that Member State (see *St Gobain* (1999) and, most recently, *Weidert & Paulus* (2004)). In the tax sphere, the only overriding require-ments in the public interest capable of justifying restrictions on the exercise of fundamental freedoms that the ECJ has recognised even as potentially applicable are: (1) fiscal cohesion; (2) prevention of tax avoidance; and (3) fiscal supervision. These are discussed in turn below.

It should be noted that the class of justifications is not closed. In *Labora-toires Fournier* (2005), both A-G Jacobs and the ECJ considered the prospect that the promotion of research and development might be an overriding requirement of general interest. However, no decision had to be taken on the facts of the case. In any event, A-G Jacobs noted that any such objective would have to be pursued on a Community-wide basis to be capable of justifying an obstacle to a fundamental freedom. It is likely that that analysis will apply also to any further justifications that may be mooted in the future.          **[54.58]**

a)    *Fiscal cohesion*

Fiscal cohesion is the only purpose for discriminatory tax measures that has been upheld as sufficient justification by the ECJ; and it has been upheld in only one instance—*Bachmann* (1992). Until 2005, it was thought widely that fiscal cohesion had had its day and that it would not be applied again. However, the principle seems to have been resurrected, at the A-G level at least. In *Manninen* and *Marks and Spencer* (2005) A-G Kokott and A-G Maduro respectively indicated that the doctrine has been construed too narrowly and may be due a revival.

*The facts of Bachmann:* Mr. Bachmann was a German national, resident and employed in Belgium. Prior to his move to Belgium, he had taken out sickness, invalidity and life insurance policies with German insurance com-panies. Belgian tax law provided, first, that the contributions paid on such policies were deductible only if they were paid 'within Belgium' (ie to a Belgian resident undertaking); and, secondly, that sums subsequently payable by insurance companies (whether resident in Belgium or abroad) under such policies were liable to tax in the hands of the recipients, unless there had been no deduction of contributions.

*The decision in Bachmann:* The ECJ ruled that such provisions amounted to indirect discrimination on the ground of nationality and so were capable of contravening the rules on the free movement of workers (Art 39) and freedom to provide services (Art 49). However, it also accepted the justification offered by Belgium, namely the need to maintain the coherence of its national tax system. In the Belgian system, there was a direct link between the deductibility of contributions and the taxation of benefits. The loss of revenue resulting from the deduction of insurance contributions was offset by the taxation of the sums payable by the insurers. Belgium could not tax the benefits paid to non-residents under policies with foreign insurers; and so if the Belgian system of tax allowed deductions for contributions in respect of such policies, then fiscal coherence would be disrupted.

*The subsequent retreat:* Since Bachmann, the fiscal coherence justification has been widely criticised and until very recently it has not been applied in any subsequent ECJ case. Broadly speaking, the ECJ has imposed two key restrictions on the principle. First, if there is a double taxation convention (see **[13.17]**) in force between the two relevant states, the defence of fiscal cohesion cannot be invoked, since the State is taken to have addressed any such concerns in that convention (see *Wielockx* (1995), where the failure in *Bachmann* to consider the relevance of double taxation conventions was criticised, and *Danner* (2001), where a case on almost identical facts to *Bachmann* was decided in favour of the taxpayer, at least in part on the grounds of the existence of a double taxation convention). Secondly, the requirement for a direct link (a 'symmetry') between the fiscal advantage and the corresponding fiscal disadvantage has been rigidly applied: in addition, the advantage and disadvantage must relate to the same tax and the same taxpayer (*Verkooijen* (2000) and *Lankhorst-Hohorst* (2003)). In both *Manninen* (2004) and *Weidert & Paulus* (2004) there was a strong indication that coherence must be judged on an EU-wide (or, possibly, even world-wide) basis; any argument that a disadvantage is linked to a corresponding advantage, but that corresponding advantage is simply that the Member State has relinquished taxing power in a related situation in favour of another member state, will be treated as an argument not as to fiscal cohesion, but as to reduction in tax revenue.

*The position at the start of 2005:* At the start of 2005 it was considered that the circumstances when the fiscal cohesion defence would be upheld by the ECJ were extremely limited. Indeed, in *Hoechst/Metallgesellschaft* (1991), A-G Fennelly described the case of *Bachmann* as 'unique'. The restrictive approach of the ECJ suggested that, even if circumstances arose where the defence may be applicable, the scope of the principle would be further circumscribed to preclude its application.

*A brief reprise.* In *Manninen* (2004) and, particularly, *Marks and Spencer* (2005) the respective Advocate-Generals indicated that the scope of fiscal cohesion may have been misunderstood. The opinion of A-G Kokott in *Manninen* (2004) attracted relatively little attention, but the view of A-G

Maduro in *Marks and Spencer* (2005) brought the issue right back to the fore. There is some indication that – as the English courts did with *Furniss v Dawson* (1984) – the ECJ had taken statements of how the doctrine might apply in specific cases, and erroneously elevated them to binding statements of general principle. Both A-Gs Maduro and Kokott said that, in their view, it would be necessary to relax the criteria which have been considered applicable to date (and, in particular, A-G Kokott thought that the 'same taxpayer' point was erroneous). On their analysis, provided the aim of the overall legislation is not one offensive to EU law (in *Marks and Spencer* (2005) ensuring fiscal neutrality of the effects of creating a group of companies, in *Manninen* (2004) avoiding double taxation) and provided that the rule which is subject to challenge is proportionate to deal with any additional difficulty in pursuing that aim which may arise because of the cross-border situation and appropriate for doing so, then, in the future, fiscal cohesion may apply to justify the difference in treatment. This approach was supported also by A-G Léger in *CLT-UFA* (2005). However, this expansion of the traditional analysis has not been accepted at the ECJ level: the ECJ in all three cases (*Manninen, Marks and Spencer* and *CLT-UFA*) (and (perversely) A-G Léger in *Ritter-Coulais* (2005)) adopted the traditional analysis and rejected the expansive new approach to the fiscal cohesion defence. As *Marks and Spencer* is an exceptional case in that, for the first time, the ECJ had to consider a case where, in reliance on Art 43, it may have been possible for a taxpayer to obtain a 'double benefit' (ie use of the losses against more than one set of profits) (and this fact decisively influenced the ECJ, and A-G Maduro in their analyses), it is considered that the circumstances when the fiscal cohesion defence will be upheld by the ECJ remain extremely limited.    **[54.59]**

### b)    *Fiscal supervision*

This possible justification was mentioned specifically in *Cassis de Dijon*. In the direct tax field, its role as a possible justification has been repeatedly confirmed (see, most recently, the opinion of A-G Jacobs in *Laboratoires Fournier* (2004)), but the leading case is still *Futura* (1997) in relation to direct taxes. The facts of this case are set out above. In *Laboratoires Fournier* the ECJ recognised that adequate fiscal supervision could be an imperative reason in the public interest to justify the requirement for Luxembourg accounts to be kept and Luxembourg losses to be computed on local principles, so justify the restriction of a fundamental freedom. However, the ECJ did not uphold the domestic rule on this ground. This was because the rule failed to meet one of the other *Gebhard* criteria: proportionality. The ECJ concluded that, in this case, the stringency and retro-active nature of the evidence requirements were not proportionate and, therefore, that the defence could not apply. Fiscal supervision has not succeeded as a justification in any other case (again, principally on the grounds of proportionality). In *de Lasteyrie* (2004) the ECJ said that the only substantive tax rules that may be justified are those that have the specific object of excluding any tax advantage from purely artificial schemes having the purpose of circumventing the law. Measures intended to allow the data underlying a return or claim to be ascertained clearly and precisely can also (*Laboratoires Fournier* (2005), confirming *Baxter* (1999), and see also A-G Kokott in *Manninen* (2004)) be justified under this ground. If the ECJ comes to consider a measure that is appropriately framed, so as to satisfy the requirements of appropriateness and proportionality, then it may well treat it as justified under this heading.

**[54.60]**

c)   *Prevention of tax avoidance*

This was first asserted as a defence in *Commission v France* (1986), where it was rejected by the ECJ without consideration. In later cases, the ECJ has recognised that the need to prevent tax avoidance could be a justification for restrictions. The first case in which the ECJ analysed the defence (and referred to the concept of a 'wholly artificial arrangement') was *Imperial Chemicals Industries plc v Colmer* Case C-264/96 [1998] STC 874. In that case, the ECJ said at para 26:

> 'As regards the justification based on the risk of tax avoidance, suffice it to note that the legislation at issue in the main proceedings does not have the specific purpose of preventing wholly artificial arrangements, set up to circumvent United Kingdom tax legislation, from attracting tax benefits, but applies generally to all situations in which the majority of a group's subsidiaries are established, for whatever reason, outside the United Kingdom. However, the establishment of a company outside the United Kingdom does not, of itself, necessarily entail tax avoidance, since that company will in any event be subject to the tax legislation of the state of establishment.'

The approach of the ECJ in *ICI* was that only legislation introduced for the specific purpose of precluding tax avoidance by preventing the setting up of wholly artificial arrangements that were designed to avoid domestic legislation for tax reasons could be justified by reference to the defence of 'prevention of tax avoidance'. Its existence as a valid defence has been confirmed most recently by the decision in *de Lasteyrie* (2004), citing *Hoechst/Metallgesellschaft* (2001), and *X&Y* (2000). In *de Lasteyrie*, the ECJ clarified that tax avoidance, for these purposes, means obtaining a tax advantage from a purely artificial scheme that has the purpose of circumventing the law. The ECJ said at para 50:

> 'As regards justification based on the aim of preventing tax avoidance, referred to by the national court in its question, it should be noted that Article 167a of the CGI is not specifically designed to exclude from a tax advantage purely artificial arrangements aimed at circumventing French tax law, but is aimed generally at any situation in which a taxpayer with substantial holdings in a company subject to corporation tax transfers his tax residence outside France for any reason whatever (see, to that effect, *ICI*, paragraph 26, and *X and Y*, paragraph 61).'

In *de Lasteyrie* the ECJ suggested very clearly that the principle can extend to tax evasion or fraud. The rule in question was found not to be justified on the basis of anti-avoidance, by virtue of failing the *Gebhard* (1995) appropriateness and proportionality tests.

The reasoning of the ECJ in cases such as *Eurowings* (1999) and *de Lasteyrie* suggests that, provided an item of profit remains capable of being taxed in one of the Member States, a rule which seeks to tax that profit in a given Member State will not be capable of justification on this ground. At this stage, the defence lapses into the illegitimate 'reduction of tax' argument.

In no case has the ECJ accepted it as an applicable defence. The basis of this jurisprudence is that the 'wholly artificial' doctrine is limited – that is, it is only where legislation has the specific purpose of ensuring that artificial arrangements aimed at circumventing the domestic law for a tax advantage that, potentially, that legislation may be capable of being defended; and then it must be analysed whether that legislation meets the *Gebhard test* of proportionality.

In *Cadbury Schweppes* (2006) (which concerned the UK's CFC regime), A-G Léger noted that the language used in the description of the anti-avoidance justification reproduced the wording of the abuse of rights doctrine. Whether the justification of anti-avoidance will be developed by the ECJ into a special ground that may justify a restriction, ie either a stand-alone doctrine of 'abuse' or a sub-set of the doctrine of 'abuse of rights', is currently an open question. The question that was referred to the ECJ in *Cadbury Schweppes* was whether the company,in establishing and capitalising companies in another Member State solely because of a more favourable tax regime available in that Member State,was exercising the fundamental freedoms, or whether it is an abuse of such freedoms. For that reason, this issue is analysed in the abuse of rights section below.                                                       **[54.61]**

d)   *Conclusion*

The list of possible justifications is certainly not closed. However, it is becoming increasingly clear, in practice, that, subject to the development of the anti-avoidance principle into a general abuse doctrine, any taxing rule that is, in principle, an impediment to the internal market, is likely to be struck down. In particular, the only justification for which the ECJ has shown any sustained sympathy is that described in the opinion of A-G Fennelly in *Hoechst/Metallgesellschaft* (2001), namely the prospect of tax evasion in both relevant countries ('it would seem that the true scope for fiscal cohesion as a justification for the differentiated treatment of non-residents would concern only situations in which there is a real and substantial risk that extending equal treatment in respect of a particular benefit would potentially facilitate tax evasion in both the host Member State and the Member State of residence of the claimant non-resident taxpayer'.). Little seems to turn on whether that is to be called fiscal cohesion, fiscal supervision, or restriction of tax avoidance. Indeed in *Marks and Spencer*, the ECJ considered the three justifications (preserving a balanced allocation of the power to impose taxes (tax sovereignty); guarding against the danger of double usage of losses ('double-dipping'); and guarding against the risk of tax avoidance through relieving losses in high-tax jurisdictions together.                       **[54.62]**

### 4   Justifications (2): Suitability and Proportionality

As noted above, even if a rule is justifiable in principle, it will nonetheless be struck down (as it was in *Futura Participations*) if it is not suitable for the objective that it seeks to meet, and is not proportionate to that objective: that is to say, if it goes beyond what is absolutely necessary in order to pursue the aim in question. As will be seen, the two criteria are somewhat similar in nature.                                                                         **[54.63]**

a) *Suitability*

This criterion has been considered particularly in the context of the prospective justification of 'tax avoidance'. The ECJ has repeatedly indicated that measures intended to prevent tax evasion will be considered disproportionate if they are not directly aimed at avoidance transactions (see *Futura Participations* (1997) and also *Lankhorst-Hohorst* (2003)). Therefore, in *de Lasteyrie* (2004), a purported anti-avoidance rule that sought to approximate tax avoidance intention by reference to the period for which certain assets were held was struck down. However, the criterion applies equally across all prospective justifications. **[54.64]**

b) *Proportionality*

Proportionality is a fundamental principle of EC law, developed as long ago as in *Internationale Handelsgesellschaft mbH* (above). No matter how important the end, if the means used to achieve it is not proportionate to that end, then the relevant measure will be prohibited. In determining this, the ECJ will consider whether the particular measure is necessary by analysing whether the end could have been achieved by other, less restrictive, measures (see A-G Tizzano in *Lenz* (2004)). Thus, for example, in the *Cassis de Dijon* case, the aims pursued by the German Government potentially could have been achieved merely by labelling the bottles with their alcohol content. As the regulations were not proportionate, they could not be justified.

In the direct tax context, in *Laboratoires Fournier* (2005) the ECJ held that a measure that imposed a blanket disallowance of foreign expenditure could not be justified on the grounds of fiscal supervision (the argument being that it was difficult for the local tax authority to prove to its satisfaction that foreign expenditure had been validly incurred). Similarly, both the A-G and the ECJ in *Lenz* (2004) suggest that withholding tax arrangements are unlikely to be considered proportionate. In *de Lasteyrie* (2004) the ECJ said that *Hoechst/Metallgesellschaft* (2001) is authority for the proposition that fiscal cohesion can never justify the collection of taxes in advance in respect of non-residents; and in the context of a defence which can only be invoked in the event of tax evasion or fraud, A-G Mischo said that it is disproportionate to have a presumption of tax evasion in a cross-border context, although the tax authorities should be free to seek to demonstrate it on a case-by-case basis.

Both the ECJ in *Laboratoires Fournier* (2005) and A-G Maduro in *Marks and Spencer* (2005) indicated that a measure that made the desired tax treatment conditional upon the provision of information might well be proportionate. This will, of course, mean that obtaining the desired tax treatment in a cross-border situation will involve some additional procedural steps, but it appears that that is acceptable, provided that the steps imposed are the minimum necessary in view of the difference in situation (see A-G Kokott in *Manninen* (2004), where she said there that the principal limitation was to ensure that those proof requirements did not prevent the cross-border taxpayer from having an 'effective' and 'equivalent' remedy (as required by *Cassis de Dijon* (1979) and *Grundig Italia* (2002)). There are practical difficulties here, associated with enforcing the collection of data or tax liabilities assessed on non-residents. However, the ECJ has not directly addressed the status of such difficulties. It should also be noted that, in relation to fiscal supervision, the ECJ has shown, on a number of occasions, such as *Schumacker* (1995) (and most recently in the Opinion of A-G Maduro (albeit not expressly in the judgment of the ECJ) in *Marks and Spencer* (2005)), a distinct lack of sympathy to arguments based on the difficulties involved in monitoring the tax affairs of non-residents. It has also drawn attention to the existence of possibilities for administrative co-operation between Member States offered by the Mutual Assistance Directive (77/799), and indicated that the prospect of taking advantage of that undermines any arguments that the Member States may have as to why provisions which impede the internal market should be upheld. Finally, it should be said that the concept of proportionality in EC law is similar to the concept in European human rights law, where the European Court of Human Rights (ECHR) has held that the interpretation of the Articles of the Convention must aim to strike a balance between: 'the demands of the general interests of the community, and the requirements of the protection of the individual's fundamental rights' (*Soering v UK* (1989)) (see **Chapter 52**). The balancing test essentially involves weighing up the impact of the restriction imposed, and evaluating whether this is justified by the importance of the end to be achieved. Central to this doctrine of proportionality is the idea that there must be a 'fair balance' between the societal interest and the individual's rights, which is analogous to the balancing in Community law between the matter of general interest and the fundamental freedom. Accordingly, it may be that, in the future, it will be possible to take guidance from the case law under European human rights law.                                                    **[54.65]–[54.70]**

## VIII   THE FUNDAMENTAL FREEDOMS: ABUSE OF RIGHT

### 1   Introduction

Given the extensive rights granted by EC law for individuals and companies to engage in cross-border activities without fear of disadvantageous tax treatment, it is clear that an opportunity exists for companies and individuals to rely on EC law as part of their tax planning. Profits are taxed in different ways in the different Member States, and it may well advantageous to arrange for particular profits to taxed in one state rather than another; an obvious, though very broad-brush, an example is the current low rates of corporation tax (10% and 12.5%) in the Republic of Ireland, which makes it clearly desirable to arrange for business profits to be taxed there rather than in (say) the UK. Further (as is clear from cases such as *Lankhorst-Hohorst* (2003), above), domestic anti-avoidance provisions designed to prevent this kind of behaviour may well themselves fall foul of EC law and so be ineffective.

However, in cases of abuse, there may well be a limitation on the rights granted by EC law under the doctrine of 'abuse of right'. Under this doctrine, in at least some circumstances, a taxpayer that purports to exercise his rights, but does so solely for tax avoidance reasons, will be unable to rely on those rights. Abuse of right is a well-developed concept in many European civil law systems that has come to be applied by the ECJ to rules of EC law. It is a protective doctrine that qualifies rights that are defined in broad terms. The basis of the doctrine is that rights granted by the law can be relied upon only to the extent that they are used for the purposes they were designed for (the classic formulation is by the French writer Plainiol in his *Traité e élémentaire de droit civil*, (Vol 2, p 871) 'la droit cesse là où l'abus commence': this is notoriously difficult to render adequately in English but 'the right ceases where abuse begins' is a reasonable approximation).

It seems that the application of the principle by the ECJ has been intended to ensure the operation of the single market. If transactions have no genuine economic purpose, and are carried out purely to obtain a beneficial treatment that should not be available in such circumstances, then they do not assist the operation of the single market, and so are not entitled to the protection of the rules regulating the market. Thus, the purpose of the doctrine is to prevent a distortion of competition. However, whether the doctrine is simply an aspect of a purposive interpretation of the fundamental freedoms (ie the fundamental freedoms apply only to the extent that they are exercised for a Community (ie a genuine economic) purpose) or exists as a stand-alone general principle of EC law, such as proportionality, remains an open question. **[54.71]**

## 2   The relevant case law

### a)   *The basic rule:* **Emsland-Stärke**

Probably the leading case on abuse of right in Community law is the customs duty case of *Emsland-Stärke GmbH* (2000). The taxpayer there exported goods from Germany to Switzerland and received export refunds from Germany (on the basis of EC Regulation 2730/79). Immediately after the goods had been released for home use in Switzerland, they were transported back into the EC where they entered free circulation after payment of import customs duties, which were about half of the amount of the export refunds paid by Germany. The ECJ held that the German tax authority was entitled to revoke its decision granting the export refund. It said that rights under EC law could not be relied upon where (1) although the conditions for the application of those rights had been met in form, they had not been met in substance, and (2) the taxpayer had an intention to obtain an advantage from the Community rules by creating artificially the conditions to formally come within the scope of a right. This formulation appears to have been restated by the ECJ in *Centros* (1999) in the following way: if a person is seeking to exercise an EC right 'unreasonably to derive, to the detriment of others, an improper advantage, manifestly contrary to the objective pursued by the legislator in conferring that particular right on the individual' then that person will be denied the benefit of the relevant EC law (see also *Holleran v Daniel Thwaites plc* (1989)). **[54.72]**

### b)   *Centros and its possible limitations*

The scope of the principle has not yet been substantially explored by the ECJ in the context of direct tax. The most directly relevant cases arise in the context of company law, where a person resident in Member State A has wished to avoid certain rules of local company law (such as minimum capital requirements (*Centros* (1999) or reporting requirements (*Inspire Art Ltd*

(2003)) and so has set up a company in Member State B with a view to conducting business in Member State A through that company. In both *Centros* (1999) and *Inspire Art* (2003), the ECJ held that efforts by Member State A to make such steps ineffective were contrary to Art 43, and so impermissible. In particular, the ECJ found that there had been no 'abuse of right' sufficient to prevent the Member State B company from relying on Art 43, even though the structure as a whole had no purpose other than circumvent the company law rules in question. However, the doctrine may not be quite as weak as would appear from this. In both cases, the ECJ relied on the fact that the rules of Member State A sought to inhibit the activities of the company incorporated in Member State B, and that the company itself genuinely wished to exercise its right of establishment for its own economic aims. Therefore, the conditions for the application of Art 43 had been met in both form and substance. Neither case addressed the legitimacy of a rule affecting the ability of the resident of Member State A to set up the shell company in Member State B in the first place. It is considered that a rule restricting that right could well apply, despite the impact of any fundamental freedom, to prevent abusive activities.

In *Marks and Spencer*, A-G Maduro hinted, at paragraph 67, that the use of the right of establishment can not be made: 'abusively to ... artificially exploit ... differences' between Member States' laws; and that 'free movers' should be prevented from being transformed, thanks to the freedoms conferred on them by the single market, into 'free riders'. However, he did not develop his analysis of how the abuse of rights doctrine could apply in that case.                                                                          **[54.73]**

c)    *The VAT experience*

In the UK, Customs & Excise has recently started to use the abuse of right principle as a means to challenge VAT avoidance arrangements. The underlying basis of Customs' approach to these cases is that VAT avoidance is not an economic activity under EC law. Thus, as VAT law is directed only to activities carried on with a business purpose, any 'abusive' steps are to be ignored. This approach was first raised in *BUPA Hospitals Ltd and Goldsborough Developments Ltd* (2002); and is analysed more fully in the later VAT Tribunal case of *Blackqueen Ltd* (2002). A number of questions on the point have been referred to the ECJ in various cases. However, the ECJ declined to deal with the point in *RAL (Channel Islands) Ltd* (2005), and the decisions of the ECJ in *Bond House Systems* (2005) and *Halifax/BUPA/University of Huddersfield* (2005) indicate that, although the *Emsland-Stärke (2000)* formulation remains good law, there are features of the VAT system (in particular that the taxpayer's 'right' arises under a provision of EC law (namely under the Sixth Directive)), which require the doctrine to be applied there rather differently than in the context of direct tax. In *Halifax*, the ECJ confirmed that the abuse of rights doctrine can apply to VAT. The ECJ held that it may apply if the transactions 'result in the accrual of a tax advantage the grant of which would be contrary to the purpose of [the legal provisions]' and it is apparent 'from a number of objective factors that the essential aim of the transactions concerned is to obtain a tax advantage.' However, the prohibition of abuse is not relevant 'where the economic activity carried out may have some explanation other than the mere attainment of tax advantages'. If abuse is present, then the transactions involved must be 'redefined so as to re-establish the situation that would have prevailed in the absence of the transactions constituting abusive practice'. That may give rise to practical difficulties. **[54.74]**

d) *Cadbury-Schweppes v IRC*

In the UK, three references to the ECJ have been made with regard to the impact of EC law on the controlled foreign companies rules: *Cadbury Schweppes plc v Commissioners of Inland Revenue* (Case C-196/04); *The CFC Group Litigation Order* (Case C-201/05); and *Vodafone 2 v HMRC* [2005] STC (SCD) 549. In each of the references, a question regarding abuse has been included.

The Opinion of A-G Léger in the first of these references (*Cadbury Schweppes*) was released on 2 May 2006. He answered the question whether the establishment by a parent company of a subsidiary in another Member State for the purpose of enjoying the more favourable tax regime of that other state constitutes, in itself, an abuse of freedom of establishment negatively. Such a decision could not, by itself, be an abuse of EC law. As the ECJ held in *Kamer van Koophandel en Fabrieken voor Amsterdam v Inspire Art Ltd* (Case C-167/01 [2003] ECR I-10155), the reason why a company chooses to incorporate in a Member State is irrelevant with regard to the application of the freedom of establishment. *A contrario*, in assessing whether there is abuse, the starting point is whether the objective pursued by the EC law provision relied upon is fulfilled. Establishment within the meaning of Art 43 involves the actual pursuit of an economic activity in the host state. Thus, if the subsidiary carries on a genuine economic activity, the purpose of Art 43 is met – it cannot be abusive. In terms of deciding whether there is 'genuine and actual pursuit of an activity' by the subsidiary in the Member State in which it was established, A-G Léger set out certain objective criteria that are to be applied on a case-by-case basis. These are:

- the degree of physical presence of the subsidiary in the foreign country;
- the genuine nature of the activity provided by the subsidiary; and
- the economic value of that activity with regard to the parent company/group. **[54.75]–[54.80]**

## IX   PROHIBITION OF STATE AID

There is one further provision of the EC Treaty that must be borne in mind in appropriate cases: Art 87, which deals with State aid. The State funding a particular undertaking, in principle, can give rise to a distortion of the free market and thus hinder its efficiency. However, it is recognised by the EU that the freedom for an individual Member State to aid particular sectors or undertakings must be maintained. State aid is an important economic and social tool that may be particularly necessary in areas of high employment or sectors that face localised economic difficulties, both in terms of economic growth and social cohesion. Moreover, it has been argued that even if certain State aid measures distort the competitive balance between Member States these measures may, nonetheless, be beneficial for the competitiveness of the EU as a whole in the global market-place. Thus, for example, the introduction of measures that aim to develop the economies of the States that acceded to the EU in May 2004 potentially may be sought to be justified on the ground that strengthening the economic development of these States will increase the economic power of the EU. The regulation of State aid is sensitive and the provisions in the EC Treaty aim to balance the competing interests of individual member States and the internal free market. This balancing act is achieved in two ways.

First, the granting of State aid that, 'distorts or threatens to distort competition by favouring certain undertakings or the production of certain goods', is broadly prohibited (under Art 87(1)), but this is subject to express and extensive derogations in Art 87(2) and (3), which allow aid that serves the purpose of protecting legitimate economic and social goals. Art 87(2) specifies the categories of aid that are compatible with the common market (such as, for example, 'aid having a social character, granted to individual consumers, provided that such aid is granted without discrimination related to the origin of the products concerned'); and Art 87(3) lists those aids that may be compatible (such as, for example, 'aid to facilitate the development of certain economic activities or of certain economic areas, where aid does not adversely affect trading conditions to an extent contrary to the common market').

The second limb of the balancing act is regulation of all State aid by the Commission. The Commission is required to keep 'under constant review all systems of aid'; and must 'be informed, in sufficient time to enable it to submit its comments, of any plans to grant or alter aid' (under Art 88(3)). Thus if a State wishes to introduce a tax measure that constitutes a State aid prohibited under Art 87, then it must notify the Commission prior to its implementation. Failure to notify the Commission timeously renders the aid illegal.

The term 'State aid' is not defined in the EC Treaty. The understanding of its scope, in practice, comes primarily from reports by the Commission and judgments of the ECJ. Each has construed it broadly. The Commission has indicated that four cumulative elements must be shown for a measure to constitute fiscal State aid: There must be: (1) favourable tax treatment (such as a reduction in the tax base); (2) granted by a Member State or through State resources (which includes the State foregoing revenue that it would otherwise have collected); (3) that actually or potentially affects trade between Member States; (4) by favouring certain undertakings or the production of certain goods.

For a measure to be classified as State aid, it must be specific in terms of its application. Any measure intended to exempt firms in a particular sector will be caught, no matter how broadly that identifiable sector is defined; whereas a mere propensity for a measure to favour one sector rather than another can not amount to selectivity. Thus, States remain free to take such measures as, for example, abolishing capital gains tax, even though the impact of this measure would be greater in certain sectors of the economy.

The boundary between a measure that is aimed at benefiting only certain sectors and a measure that may have that consequence is, however, often hard to discern. In order to determine whether a fiscal measure is specific, the common tax system must be determined. Then, it must be examined whether the measure is justified 'by the nature or general scheme' of the tax system, ie whether it 'derive[s] generally from the basic or guiding principles of the tax system in the Member State concerned. If this is not the case, then State Aid is involved.' (Commission Notice on State aid, OJ C384 10 December 1998, p 3). If the measure is a general one, but the State retains a discretionary power in respect of the administration of that rule, then that measure will be treated as if it is specific (*Ecotrade Srl v Altiformi e Ferriere di Servola SpA* (1998). For example, on 19 January 2005, the European Commission started an investigation into the UK's system of business rates that applies to the telecommunications industry. One of the bases of complaint was that there exist a number of different methods of valuation of hereditaments within the UK rating system and that there is discretion given to the Valuation Officer to choose the methodology to use.

Aid that falls within Art 87(1) is not limited to direct subsidies; it may be in 'any form whatsoever'. Thus any preferential tax treatment, consisting of a tax concession or a relief, gives rise to aid (*De Gezamenlijke Steenkolenmijnen in Limburg* (1961). Also, the imposition of a detriment in the form of a tax on one party can amount to aid elsewhere (this is often referred to as 'negative State aid'), if its imposition gives rise to a corresponding advantage to identifiable business competitors of those who have to bear the detriment (see *R (on the application of Professional Contractors Group Ltd) v IRC* (2002)). Thus, for example, a windfall tax on privatised industries could constitute State aid. Similarly, in *Weidert & Paulus* (2004), the ECJ noted that the Luxembourg provision giving beneficial tax treatment for investments in Luxembourg companies, which was unlawful for not being extended to non-resident companies, could alternatively have been prohibited as a state aid (subject to Commission approval under Art 88(3)).

The consequence of a measure being unlawful State aid is that the measure must be stopped. A business that has been the recipient of unlawful State Aid will be required to repay the aid even if this has consequence that the business must be wound up (*Commission v Belgium* (1986)). Therefore, in the *Weidert & Paulus* (2004) situation, State aid proceedings would have involved the aid being clawed back, instead of (in the case of proceedings for breach of a fundamental freedom) the benefit being extended to other taxpayers. The Commission publishes an annual survey of its proceedings relating to State aid in the *Official Journal* and publishes details in its annual report on competition policy. Due to this openness, a recipient of unlawful State aid will not, save in exceptional circumstances, be able to challenge repayment on the ground that it had a legitimate expectation that the aid had been granted in accordance with Art 88. **[54.81]–[54.90]**

## X DIRECTIVES

In addition to the impact of the fundamental freedoms and state aid, there is one other key article of the EC Treaty relevant to direct tax: Art 94. This allows for the adoption of harmonising measures in the field of direct tax. To date, there have been only three substantive direct tax directives adopted under Art 94. These are the Merger Directive (Directive 90/434/EEC) and the Parent-Subsidiary Directive (Directive 90/435/EEC), both of which were adopted on 23 July 1990, and the Interest and Royalties Directive (Directive 2003/49/EC) of 3 June 2003. There are also two directives that primarily concern the exchange of information between Member States: the Mutual Assistance Directive (Directive 77/799/EEC) and the Savings Directive (Directive 2003/48/EC).                                    **[54.91]**

## 1    The Merger Directive

The Merger Directive seeks to address the tax problems that can arise from the joining together of two (or more) companies from different Member States. Nearly every Member State's tax system contains rules that allow capital gains to be deferred on a takeover of or merger with another company. However, cross-border mergers would not benefit from this treatment. The aim of the Merger Directive is to ensure that there is no difference in tax treatment between domestic and cross-border mergers, as any difference could hinder the cross-border expansion of groups of companies. It provides for a common system for deferral of capital gains tax on four types of operation: (i) legal merger (where one company transfers all its assets and liabilities to another company, which company becomes legal successor to it, and then 'dissolves'); (ii) legal division (where one company transfers all its assets and liabilities to two or more companies, which companies become legal successors to it, and then dissolves); (iii) transfer of assets (a company transfers one or more branches to another company in return for shares in that company, but remains in existence); and (iv) exchange of shares (a company acquires a majority of shares in another company in return for its shares, but remains in existence).

The Directive contains a general anti-abuse provision, which provides that Member States may deny the beneficial capital gains treatment if one of the principal aims of the operation is tax avoidance. Such an aim may be presumed if the operation is 'not carried out for valid commercial reasons.' The scope of the anti-abuse clause was considered by the ECJ in *Leur-Bloem* (1997). The ECJ said that, although the domestic legislation may stipulate that if the operation is not carried out for valid commercial reasons, a presumption of tax avoidance arises, national authorities must still examine each particular transaction and can not simply apply predetermined general criteria. Thus, a general rule that automatically excluded certain categories of operations from the tax advantage is not allowed; it would not be proportionate. The ECJ also said that in order for an operation to be carried out for a valid commercial reason, it cannot be entered into only for the attainment of a purely fiscal advantage.

One particular area of difficulty in the United Kingdom is that UK company law does not allow for 'legal merger' or 'division' as those terms are defined in the Directive (as a matter of UK company law, a company that has transferred its assets and liabilities to another company still exists unless and until it is subsequently dissolved). Forming an SE may, however, assist. The Mergers Directive was recently amended by Directive 2005/19/EC so as: (i) to expand the list of companies to which the Mergers Directive applies to include SEs; and (ii) to introduce measures that deal with transfers of registered office by an SE where the assets remain connected with a permanent establishment in the relevant Member State. The provisions of Directive 2005/19/EC that apply to SEs are to have effect from 1 January 2006.                                    **[54.92]**

## 2 The Parent/Subsidiary Directive

If a subsidiary company remits its profits to its parent company in another Member State, then there are two potential tax charges that may arise. The first is a withholding tax on the payment of the dividends by the subsidiary; and the second is a tax on the parent company on the receipt of the dividends. The Parent-Subsidiary Directive seeks to abolish these potential hindrances to the free movement of capital and the freedom of establishment. The Directive applies to all the States that acceded to the EU in 2004, absent Estonia, which has been granted permission not to introduce the Directive until 31 December 2008.

The main features of the Directive are, first, that it, generally requires a full exemption from withholding tax on dividends paid by a subsidiary in one Member State to its parent company in another Member State; and secondly, it requires that Member States either should exempt parent companies from corporate tax on such dividends (exemption method), or give parent companies a credit against their tax liability for the corporate tax paid by the subsidiary (indirect credit method). The Directive applies to qualifying EU parent companies holding an interest of at least 10% in qualifying EU subsidiary companies.

The Directive is designed not to affect imputation systems that seek to prevent economic double taxation of the same profit (ie in the hands of the company that generated the profit and again in the hands of a parent company receiving a distribution representing that profit). Article 7(1) provides that the requirement for advance payment of corporation tax in a subsidiary's state of residence is not a withholding tax; and Art 7(2) provides that the Directive will not affect agreements among member states that are designed to mitigate economic double taxation of dividends (including the payment of tax credits to recipients of dividends). In *Océ van der Grinten NV* (2003) the ECJ held Art 7 is to be construed in a broad-brush way, so that provisions that form part of a body of rules protected by Art 7 will themselves be protected, even if, when considered alone, they would fall outside that protection.

As with the Merger Directive, the Parent Subsidiary Directive contains an anti-abuse provision. It is considered that this provision should be interpreted in accordance with the decision of the ECJ in *Leur-Bloem* (1997).

**[54.93]**

## 3 The Interest and Royalties Directive

The Interest and Royalty Directive requires exemption from withholding taxes on interest and royalty payments paid between certain related EU companies. It was adopted in June 2003 and Member States are required to apply it from 1 January 2004.

In the UK, FA 2004 ss 97–105 implements it with retrospective effect from 1 January 2004. These sections provide that certain interest or royalty payments are exempt from income tax exemption, provided that: (i) the person making the payment is either a UK company, or a UK permanent establishment of an EU-resident company; (ii) the beneficial owner of the income is either an EU company, or its permanent establishment (other than one in the UK or outside the EU); (iii) both companies are 25% associates (both companies are 25% associates if one directly holds at least 25% capital or voting rights in the other, or alternatively if a third company directly holds at least 25% capital or voting rights in each of them); (iv) and HMRC has issued an exemption notice.    **[54.94]**

### 4   The Mutual Assistance Directive

The Mutual Assistance Directive applies in relation to direct taxes, certain excise duties and insurance premium tax. It requires Member States to exchange information in order to enable each State to 'effect a correct assessment of taxes'. Information can and should be 'spontaneously' provided by a tax authority of one Member State to that of another Member State if the first Member State suspects a loss of tax in the other Member State. Similar restrictions as to whom the information can be passed apply under the Mutual Assistance Directive as apply under individual double taxation conventions (in particular that similarly strict standards of confidentiality will be observed by the tax authority in the other Member State).

FA 1990 s 125 extended the powers in TMA 1970 s 20 to allow for the issue of a s 20 notice to provide documents and information necessary to determine liability to tax on income or capital in another Member State.

**[54.95]**

### 5   The Savings Directive

The powers imposed by the Mutual Assistance Directive are to be enhanced by the new Savings Directive. It requires banks and other financial institutions to disclose details of the recipients of interest paid by such institutions in circumstances where the recipient of the interest is resident outside the Member State where the bank is situated.

The Directive allows for the levying of a withholding tax as an alternative to exchanges of information. However, this is only available to three Member States (Austria, Belgium and Luxembourg) who have 'opted out' of the disclosure requirements for a transitional period. Although these States are exempt from the requirement to disclose, they may still receive disclosures from other Member States or their dependencies during the opt-out period. The UK dependencies (in particular, the Channel Islands, and the Isle of Man) have all indicated that they also will opt for the withholding tax. However, they will, in addition, put in place a mechanism that allows for the exchange of information in respect of customers who have elected voluntarily for information about their accounts to be exchanged.

One of the main issues related to the Savings Directive has been the position of the so-called 'Third Countries', such as Switzerland, Andorra, Liechtenstein, Monaco and San Marino; Luxembourg and Austria, in particular, insisted that these non-Member States countries had to put into practice equivalent regulations at the same time as the EU countries. The ECOFIN Meeting approved the separate draft agreement negotiated with Switzerland, which included the extension of the benefits of the Parent/ Subsidiary and the Interest and Royalty Directives to Swiss persons. The EU has now reached agreements regarding all matters of relevance with Switzerland, Liechtenstein, Andorra, Monaco and San Marino. The agreement between the EU and Switzerland will serve as the basis for the agreements between the EU and Liechtenstein, Andorra, Monaco and San Marino. On 19 July 2004 the EU Council formally adopted the decision of the European Commission to delay implementation of the EU Savings Directive from 1 January 2005 until 1 July 2005.                                        **[54.96]**

## XI   EUROPEAN COMPANIES

On 8 October 2004, a new legal entity (which had a gestation period of over 30 years) was finally born: the SE. An SE is a European public limited company that is available in all Member States (and the EEA). The intention is that an SE will allow companies incorporated in different Member States to merge or form a holding company or joint subsidiary, whilst avoiding the legal and practical constraints that arise from the existence of numerous different legal systems. Use of an SE will allow companies operating in several Member States to operate with a unified management and reporting structure, and under one set of rules. Although an SE is not intended to be a tax saving vehicle (there are no specific tax rules provided in the SE regulation or directive), it is thus clear that it has, at least, the potential to assist with the Commission's proposal to work towards a common set of rules for calculating EU-wide tax profits. However, to date, the effect that SEs have had is limited. Most Member States had not introduced the necessary implementing measures by the due date and few non-EU countries (particularly the US) have indicated that a branch of an SE will have access to the benefits under double tax treaties.

F (No 2) A 2005 ss 51–65 introduce provisions relating to the SE. Broadly, these sections provide that if an SE is resident in the UK, then it will be subject to UK tax and they seek to ensure that an SE can be formed without giving rise to a significant tax cost. The intention is that a UK company's decision to merge with a company in another Member State to form an SE is not disadvantaged (or driven) by tax considerations. However, the provisions, unsurprisingly, do not address the underlying incompatibility of much of the UK tax system with EC law; and, to date, the SE is very far from providing a solution to this issue.                                        **[54.97]**

# 55   Human rights and taxation

*Written and updated by Natalie Lee, Barrister, Senior Lecturer in Law,
University of Southampton*

## I   INTRODUCTION

### 1   Background to the Human Rights Act 1998

The European Convention for the Protection of Human Rights and Fundamental Freedoms (the European Convention) is a treaty of the Council of
Europe. The Council, established at the end of the Second World War, was
established before the European Union and, although many nations are
members of both, the two bodies are quite separate. Over the years, the
European Convention has become one of the foremost agreements defining
standards of behaviour across Europe and indeed the acceptance of the
Convention by most European countries meant incorporation into their own
domestic law. Until the last few years, it was believed by the UK that the rights
and freedoms guaranteed by the Convention could be delivered under the
common law. That this is no longer sufficient has now been recognised both
by the increasing need of applicants to take their case to the European Court
of Human Rights (ECtHR) and by the passing of the Human Rights Act 1998.
The effect of this Act is to incorporate into UK law, from October 2000, a
major part of the European Convention. The aim is to guarantee a wide
range of rights and freedoms for everyone, whether individuals or corporate
entities, guaranteed in writing and enforceable in domestic courts.     [**55.1**]

### 2   The Human Rights Act 1998 and incorporation

It can be said that there has been incorporation of Convention rights by HRA
1998 only insofar as it is consistent with parliamentary sovereignty. Thus,
whereas the Constitution of the USA enables the US Supreme Court to strike
down Federal statutes that are inconsistent with human rights principles,

HRA 1998 does not give the courts a power to strike down primary legislation that is inconsistent with the Convention and Parliament may, if it chooses, maintain in force such legislation. Moreover, the Act can be repealed in the normal way.                                                                  **[55.2]**

### 3  Main principles of the Human Rights Act 1998

The Act operates on three main principles. *First*, courts and tribunals are required to construe both primary and secondary legislation in a way that is compatible with the Convention rights insofar as that is possible (s 3). This is in contrast to the pre-Act position when the domestic court was only obliged to construe *ambiguous* legislation in accordance with the Convention; now the possibility exists for a claimant to challenge *any* legislation on the basis that it is not compatible with Convention rights. This process was summarised by Lord Hoffmann in *R v IRC, ex p Wilkinson* (2005):

> 'The important change in the process of interpretation which was made by section 3 was to deem the Convention to form a significant part of the background against which all statutes, whether passed before or after the 1998 Act came into force, had to be interpreted. Just as the 'principle of legality' meant that statutes were construed against the background of human rights subsisting at common law ... so now, section 3 requires them to be construed against the background of Convention rights. There is a strong presumption, arising from the fundamental nature of Convention rights, that Parliament did not intend a statute to mean something which would be incompatible with those rights. This, of course, goes far beyond the old-fashioned notion of using background to 'resolve ambiguities' in a text which had notionally been read without raising one's eyes to look beyond it. The Convention, like the rest of the admissible background, forms part of the primary materials for the process of interpretation. But, with the addition of the Convention as background, the question is still one of *interpretation*, i.e. the ascertainment of what, taking into account the presumption created by section 3, Parliament would reasonably be understood to have meant by using the actual language of the statute.'

*Secondly*, the Act requires all public authorities to act in accordance with the Convention (s 6), and courts will be at liberty to strike down any exercise of power that infringes the Convention. This is subject to the doctrine of the 'margin of appreciation' which requires the court to consider not only whether the relevant authority acted 'reasonably, carefully and in good faith', but in addition whether the authority's action was 'proportionate to the aim pursued' and supported by 'relevant and sufficient' reasons, including 'an acceptable assessment of the relevant facts.' *Thirdly*, although no court is able to strike down or disregard primary legislation that conflicts with the Convention, the higher courts may make a 'declaration of incompatibility', which is a first step towards correcting the primary legislation (s 4, and see **[55.42]**).                                                                  **[55.3]**

### 4  The courts and human rights

It should be remembered that findings of the ECtHR have to be applied in about 40 states, all having very different cultures and politics. Accordingly, when dealing with human rights issues, domestic courts and tribunals will take into consideration the jurisprudence of the ECtHR, indeed they are obliged to do so by HRA 1998 s 2(1) but, like the ECtHR itself, they are not bound by any of its previous decisions. This was spelt out by Potter LJ in *Han (t/a Murdishaw Supper Bar) v C & E Comrs* (2001):

> 'Since s 2(1) of the HRA requires the court or tribunal to take into account the Strasbourg case law of the European Court of Human Rights (the Strasbourg Court) when determining a question which has arisen in connection with a Convention right, that case law provides the starting point for the domestic court or tribunal's deliberations and the court or tribunal has a duty to consider such case law for the purpose of making its adjudication. It is not bound to follow such case law (which itself has no doctrine of precedent) but, if study reveals some clear principle, test or autonomous meaning consistently applied by the Strasbourg Court and applicable to a Convention question arising before the English courts, then the court should not depart from it without strong reason.' **[55.4]**

## 5 Human rights and tax

How, then, have tax matters been affected by the HRA 1998? Given that EC law has applied in the UK for nearly three decades, but that it is only fairly recently that its implications for income tax and corporation tax have begun to be understood (see, for example, *ICI plc v Colmer* (2000)), it is difficult to make any accurate predictions. Commentators believe that it will have a substantial impact, particularly in relation to indirect taxation and, to a certain extent, that view has already been borne out (see *Han v C & E Comrs* (2001) (at **[55.82]**)). However, a recent judgment of the ECtHR shows a distinct lack of enthusiasm on the part of the majority sitting in the case for restricting state power in taxation matters (*Ferrazzini v Italy* (2001) (see **[55.83]**)), although that view is tempered by the fact that there was a strong and reasoned opinion by the dissenting judges. Accordingly, the precise circumstances in which Convention rights might be invoked in respect of fiscal matters remains a matter of speculation.

That cases will be brought is recognised by the fact that public funding (formerly legal aid) is now available for cases before the General and Special Commissioners of Income Tax where the proceedings concern penalties which the courts have declared to be criminal in the terms specified by the European Convention or where an applicant seeks to argue that issue, *and* it is in the interests of justice for an applicant to be legally represented. Funding is available for both legal advice prior to any hearing and for legal representation at the tribunal. This is subject to the applicant being financially eligible, with applicants on income support and income-based jobseekers allowance being automatically eligible. **[55.5]–[55.20]**

## II THE RIGHT TO PROPERTY: ART 1 OF PROTOCOL NO 1

### 1 Ambit of the provision

Article 1 of Protocol No 1 to the European Convention guarantees, in substance, the right to property and, in effect, comprises three elements. The first contains the general principle of peaceful enjoyment of property; the second deals with deprivation of property and subjects that to certain conditions; the third recognises that contracting states are entitled to control the use of property, expressly reserving the right of contracting states to pass laws that they deem necessary to secure the payment of taxes. This was explained by the ECtHR in *National and Provincial Building Society v UK* (1997) in the following terms:

> 'According to the Court's well established case law, an interference, including one resulting from a measure to secure the payment of taxes, must strike a fair balance between the demands of the general interest of the Community and the require-ments of the protection of the individual's fundamental rights. The concern to achieve this balance is reflected in the structure of Art 1 as a whole, including the second paragraph: there must therefore be a reasonable relationship of propor-tionality between the means employed and the aims pursued. Furthermore in determining whether this requirement has been met, it is recognised that a Contracting State, not least when framing and implementing policies in the area of taxation, enjoys a wide margin of appreciation and the Court will respect the Legislature's assessment in respect of such matters unless it is devoid of reasonable foundation.' (See also *Georgiou v UK* (2001) on the question of the wide margin of appreciation.)                                                                          **[55.21]**

## 2   IR35 and the Professional Contractors Group

Article 1 of Protocol No 1 was one of the arguments invoked in the high profile judicial review case brought against the Inland Revenue by *inter alia* the Professional Contractors Group in respect of the imposition of the notorious IR35 legislation relating to personal service companies (*R (on the application of Professional Contractors Group Ltd) v IRC* (2001)). The later appeal by the taxpayers did not concern the issue of human rights (see **[8.31]**)). Companies subject to the IR35 legislation are primarily one-man companies, which charge out the services of the owner, ('the service contractor'), to a client for fees paid by the client to the service company in circumstances where the service contractor would be an employee of the client if he had provided his services directly to it. Out of this remuneration, the service contractor is paid a small salary, from which income tax and employees' national insurance contributions (NICs) are deducted, and the service company pays employers' NICs. From the balance will be deducted allowable expenses, and a substantial dividend out of the profit may eventually be paid to the service contractor which will not attract NICs, and in respect of which income tax will only be payable as and when the dividend is declared. Any retained profit will be assessable to corporation tax, but (usually) at the special low rate applicable to small companies. The aim of IR35 is to treat the fees as income from employment with income tax and NICs being deduct-ible.

The claimants' case was that a right to enjoy the benefit of a shareholding in a service company is a right of property and, by virtue of the IR35 legislation, enjoyment of that right was interfered with contrary to Art 1 of Protocol No 1 for two reasons. *First*, the imposition of income tax and NICs on the notional remuneration together with the way in which expenses are treated, meant that the 'right' was rendered more expensive. *Secondly*, the uncertainty as to whether a particular service contractor would be classified as an employee if he had rendered his services directly to the client would result either in a loss of enjoyment of the shareholding or it put the very existence of service companies in jeopardy. In holding that the impact of IR35 was insufficient to amount to a breach of Art 1 of Protocol No 1, Burton J considered the Strasbourg jurisprudence in relation to the claimant's first argument, and said:

> 'A financial liability arising out of the raising of taxes or contributions may adversely affect the guarantee of ownership if it places an excessive burden on the person concerned or fundamentally interferes with his financial position. However, it is in the first place for the national authorities to decide what kind of taxes or contributions are to be collected. Furthermore the decisions in this area will commonly involve the appreciation of political, economic and social questions which the Convention leaves within the competence of the Contracting States. The power of appreciation of the Contracting States is therefore a wide one.'

Accordingly, he concluded that even if the full amount of a service company's earnings (without any allowance for expenses) in a given year were treated as the remuneration of the service contractor, this would not amount to a confiscation of property, nor to a fundamental interference with the claimants' financial position, and nor would it amount to an abuse of the UK's rights to levy taxes. As to the second argument in respect of uncertainty, Burton J was of the opinion that the effect of IR35 was to submit service contractors to the same common law test of employment with respect to each engagement to which they would have been subject but for the interposition of the service company. With that in mind, he concluded that it could not offend against the concept of certainty for the common law of employment to apply to a service contractor.　　　　　　　　　　　　　　　　　　**[55.22]**

## 3　Use of Art 1 of Protocol No 1

Article 1 of Protocol No 1 may also be invoked in the following cases:

(1)　*Recovery of overpaid tax* A taxpayer who has overpaid income or corporation tax by reason of an error or mistake in a return, has a statutory right to make a claim for repayment (TMA 1970 s 33). Relief is restricted by the fact that (a) HMRC is entitled to give only such relief as is 'reasonable and just'; (b) where a return is made in accordance with the 'prevailing practice' at the time, recovery is prevented; and (c) any claim is subject to time limits. The statutory right to the recovery of overpaid VAT is restricted if the claimant would thereby be unjustly enriched (VATA 1994 s 80). Each of the restrictions on recovery is capable of challenge under Art 1 of Protocol No 1. The claimant would have to show that the restrictions to reclaiming the overpaid tax (a possession of the taxpayer) could not be justified in the general interest and that they were disproportionate to the state's aim in providing for them.

(2)　*Seizure of property* Whilst the seizure of goods and documents would appear to infringe Art 1 of Protocol No 1, this may be justified depending upon the facts of each particular case. (Search and seizure may also infringe Art 8 (see **[55.61]**)). In deciding whether such provisions are necessary and proportionate, the claimant's case will largely depend upon whether the exercise of such powers is subject to effective judicial supervision and a right of appeal (see *AGOSI v United Kingdom* (1986), and also *Lindsay v C & E Comrs* (2002), and *R (on the application of Hoverspeed) v C & E Comrs* (2002), both cases concerning the seizure of vehicles following allegations of illegal importation of goods).

(3)    *Imposition of a one-off tax* It is possible that the levying of a tax such as the windfall tax on a particular taxpayer, or one type of taxpayer, may be in violation of Art 1 of Protocol No 1. To succeed, a claimant would have to show that the imposition of the tax interfered with that taxpayer's rights of ownership of its assets or its financial situation to such an extent that the tax could be considered disproportionate or an abuse of the state's right under Art 1 of Protocol No 1 to levy taxes (see *Wasa Liv Omsesidigt v Sweden* (1988) where the argument failed on the facts of the case). The imposition could also possibly be challenged under Arts 14 and 6(1) (see **[55.41]** and **[55.81]**).

(4)    *Imposition of retrospective legislation* In the area of taxation, retrospective legislation is used most often as an anti-avoidance measure by plugging a loophole. Such legislation does not automatically infringe the European Convention, but it is certainly capable of challenge under Art 1 of Protocol No 1 since it undermines the rule of law and legal certainty. It has been argued that the recent changes to the inheritance taxation of trusts and, in particular, interest in possession trusts (see **[33.1]**), could be the subject of a challenge on these grounds. The new provisions only bite on a death on or after 22 March 2006 and, generally, people can alter their wills to take account of the new legislation. To this extent, it must be doubtful whether such a challenge would be successful. However, for those estates where the testator actually died on 22 March 2006 or very soon thereafter, it may well be an important issue. Moreover, the uncertainty surrounding this particular legislation, affecting rather more people than the Revenue will admit, can only make a challenge more likely. A claimant would have to show that the legislation in question, whatever it might be, was not objectively justifiable and was disproportionate (for a discussion of this issue, see [2005] BTR 1).                                                  **[55.23]–[55.40]**

## III   ENJOYMENT OF CONVENTION RIGHTS WITHOUT DISCRIMINATION: ART 14

### 1   Article 14 is not a substantive provision

There is no general prohibition on discrimination in the European Convention. Article 14 requires that the enjoyment of the rights set out in the Convention are to be secured without discrimination. What this means is that in every case, Art 14 must be accompanied by a substantive provision. Although the application of Art 14 does not presuppose a breach of those substantive provisions, in order for it to be applied, the facts of the case must come within the ambit of one or more of them. It is likely that in the area of taxation, the substantive right that will most often be alleged to have been violated is Art 1 of Protocol No 1 (see, for example, *R (on the application of Wilkinson) v IRC* (2005) at [**55.42**]), although it should be noted that the connection between a substantive right and Art 14 may be somewhat tenuous!   [**55.41**]

## 2   Scope of Art 14

A challenge under Art 14 may be made in the following cases:

(1)   *Discrimination between similarly situated taxpayers* The imposition, for example, of a windfall tax on one, or only some, of a number of companies in the same sector may be challenged on the basis that it draws an arbitrary distinction between a similar group of taxpayers. The application for judicial review of a refusal by HMRC to make a widower's bereavement payment to an applicant was unsuccessful (see (3) below)). One of the applicant's claims was that it was irrational or an abuse of power to treat him differently from certain other taxpayers who, unlike him, had previously petitioned the court in Strasbourg and had come to a friendly settlement with HMRC. The House of Lords dismissed this claim on the basis that, having decided that there was no justification whatever for extending the widows' bereavement allowance to men, the applicant would not be entitled to damages in either a domestic court, or at Strasbourg; that HMRC did not take this point with the other taxpayers did not mean that they were not entitled to take the point against the applicant (*R IRC ex parte Wilkinson* (2005)). However, in *PM v UK* (2005) (see (2) below), the ECtHR was of the opinion that the Government had breached Convention rights by drawing a distinction between married and unmarried fathers for the purpose of qualifying maintenance payments.

(2)   *Discrimination on the grounds of marriage* UK legislation that provided for allowances discriminating between single and married people has been held not to be an infringement of the Convention on the grounds that it was within the discretion allowed to contracting states and that the distinction was objectively justifiable (*Lindsay v UK* (1986)). It was this case that the Government relied upon in response to the challenge in *PM v UK* (2005). Following the separation of an unmarried couple who had previously lived and had a daughter together, it was agreed under the terms of a deed of separation that the applicant, the father, would pay weekly maintenance for his daughter. He was granted tax relief for the maintenance payments made during the tax year in which they began, but it was later claimed by the UK Government that this was an error on the part of the Revenue. The applicant was refused relief for later years on the basis that he had never been married to his daughter's mother, and that, accordingly, his payments could not be qualifying maintenance payments within TA 1988, s 347(B) (the relief claimed by the applicant is no longer available unless one of the parties to the marriage or former marriage was aged 65 or over on the 5 April 2000; see [**52.6**]–[**52.12**]). Before the ECtHR, the applicant argued that there had been a violation of Art 14 in conjunction with Art1 of Protocol No 1 on the basis that he was being treated differently from a married (or previously married) father, and that there was no objective

or reasonable justification for the difference in treatment. Bearing in mind Governmental policy (manifested through the powers vested in the Child Support Agency) that parents, and fathers in particular, should be responsible for the maintenance of their children irrespective of their marital status, he was in an analogous position with a married father, since their legal obligations with respect to their children were identical. For its part, the Government submitted that, for the purpose of s 347B, paternity was not relevant in determining whether a payment was a qualifying maintenance payment; rather, it 'was the relationship of marriage that was at the core of the legislation', and that *Lindsay* precluded any argument denying the right of a government to distinguish between married and unmarried persons. The Government's alternative argument was that, in any event, there was an objective and reasonable justification for the difference in treatment, based on a policy of promoting the institution of marriage, even after the breakdown of the marriage. Holding that there had been a violation of Convention rights, the ECtHR was of the opinion that the applicant was not seeking to compare himself to a couple in a subsisting marriage, but to a married *father*; in terms of a child's welfare, a married and an unmarried father were in a relatively similar position. This case should, therefore, be more correctly placed in (1) above. The Court was of the further view that there was no justification for the difference in treatment. It said:

> 'Given that he has financial obligations towards his daughter, which he has duly fulfilled, the Court perceives no reason for treating him differently from a married father, now divorced and separated from the mother, as regards the tax deductibility of those payments. The purpose of the tax deductions was purportedly to render it easier for married fathers to support a new family; it is not readily apparent why unmarried fathers, who undertook similar new relationships, would not have similar financial commitments equally requiring relief.'

Generally, however, the ability to legislate on the basis of a distinction between married and unmarried persons remains within a government's competence. Whether the distinction will remain justifiable with the changing attitudes of society to marriage remains to be seen. It is interesting to note that the Working Tax Credit and Child Tax Credit draw no distinction between those who are married and those who are not. The issue has recently been tested in the context of Inheritance Tax that allows for an exemption for gifts between spouses. In *Holland v IRC* (2002), the Special Commissioners dismissed the appellant's argument that, although she and the deceased were not legally married, they had lived together as husband and wife for 31 years before his death and so she should be treated as his spouse for IHT purposes. The Revenue having accepted that marriage was a question of status within Art 14, and that the facts of the appeal fell within both Art 1 of the First Protocol and Art 8, the commissioners held (albeit *obiter*, the human rights issue having been determined on the basis that the Act had not come into force at the time of the death) that it was permissible for Parliament to legislate for different tax provisions to apply to married persons, since this reflected the fact that marriage is accompanied by mutual rights and obligations between the spouses relating to maintenance both during their lives and after their deaths. It was believed that further challenges might come from same-sex couples, traditionally treated in the same way as cohabitees for tax purposes and, additionally, ineligible as a couple to claim tax credits. The prospect of such challenges has now receded since, from 5 December 2005, same-sex couples who have registered their partnership under the Civil Partnership Act 2004 enjoy the same rights, and are subject to the same restrictions, as married couples under both tax and the tax credit legislation (see **[51.111]**). Given that heterosexual couples do not fall within the ambit of the Act, despite efforts on their behalf during the passage of the Civil Partnership Bill through Parliament, it is undoubtedly the case that this issue remains a live one, and that challenges may yet be brought before the higher courts.

(3)   *Discrimination on the grounds of gender* Such discrimination would appear to be hard to justify. A provision (now abolished) which allowed for a widow's bereavement allowance but not a widower's, has now been the subject of two challenges, one before the ECtHR and the other before the domestic courts. In the first case, in order to avoid a hearing before the court, the UK Government conceded the point and reached a settlement of the case. This involved paying out the same amount to the widower as would have been given to a widow (*Crossland v IRC* (1999)). However, in the wake of the Revenue's refusal to provide the same treatment for other widowers in the same position, an unsuccessful application to the High Court for judicial review of this refusal was made (*R (on the application of Wilkinson) v IRC* (2002)). Further appeals to the Court of Appeal (2003) and to the House of Lords (2005) were also unsuccessful. (It is interesting to note that, although each court reached the same ultimate conclusion, the reasoning and conclusions on particular claims differed.) In the higher courts, it was common ground that the offending provision was discriminatory, with no objective justification for the discrimination resulting from the widow's bereavement allowance, and thus incompatible with Art 14. *Prima facie*, the refusal of the allowance amounted to an unlawful act on the part of HMRC (HRA 1998 s 6(1)). The issues remaining to be decided were *first*, whether the Revenue had power to afford to the taxpayer an extra-statutory concession by way of income tax deduction equivalent to the allowance in question: if there was no such power, the Revenue could not have acted differently than it had done (HRA 1998 s 6(2)(a)), and this would provide an exclusion from s 6(1); *secondly*, if it did have such power, whether it was *obliged* to grant such a reduction to the taxpayer on the basis that the action was necessary to give effect to provisions which were not compatible with Convention rights (HRA 1998 s 6(2)(b)); and *thirdly*, whether the Revenue was obliged at common law, as a matter of fairness, to give the allowance to widowers in the light of the settlement of Mr Crossland's case before the ECtHR. In respect of the first issue, the House of Lords were in total agreement with the Court of Appeal which, having reviewed the authorities dealing with both the Revenue's powers to care for, manage and collect the

various taxes under TMA 1970 s 1, and their ability to make extra-statutory concessions, held that they were not authorised to grant the taxpayer an extra-statutory allowance in the form of a tax reduction.

Lord Hoffmann said:

'This discretion enables the commissioners to formulate policy in the interstices of the tax legislation, dealing pragmatically with minor or transitory anomalies, cases of hardship at the margins or cases in which a statutory rule is difficult to formulate or its enactment would take up a disproportionate amount of Parliamentary time. The commissioners publish extra-statutory concessions for the guidance of the public and Miss Rose drew attention to some which she said went beyond mere management of the efficient collection of the revenue. I express no view on whether she is right about this, but if she is, it means that the commissioners may have exceeded their powers under section 1 of TMA. It does not justify construing the power so widely as to enable the commissioners to concede, by extra-statutory concession, an allowance which Parliament could have granted but did not grant, and on grounds not of pragmatism in the collection of tax but of general equity between men and women.' (*R v IRC ex parte Wilkinson* (2005)).

Although the conclusion reached in respect of the first issue made argument in respect of the second untenable, the courthouse of Lords nevertheless dealt with it briefly, taking the view that, had the Revenue the power to grant an extra-statutory allowance to widowers to match the widow's bereavement allowance, they would not have been obliged to exercise that power in order to avoid a breach of Convention rights. Lord Hoffmann said:

'The reason why the commissioners are protected by section 6(2)(b) is not because they were "giving effect" to section 1 of TMA by insisting that it was a discretion and not a duty. They are protected because they were giving effect to section 262 by giving the allowance only to widows. If section 6(1) "does not apply" to what they did under section 262, there is no basis for saying that a failure to make an allowance to widowers was (as a matter of domestic law) in breach of Convention rights."

This was the decision reached in *R (on the application of Hooper & Ors) v Secretary of State for Work and Pensions* (2005) where, despite a statutory provision in respect of certain widows' benefits, there also existed a common law power that enabled the Secretary of State to make benefits payments to widowers). As far as the third issue was concerned, the House of Lords was unable to accept the taxpayer's argument that, in the light of the friendly settlement of *Crossland*, the HMRC's refusal to make a settlement in similar terms in the present case had caused the claimant to suffer a pecuniary loss that should be compensated by payment of damages. An award of damages is permissible under the HRA 1998, but only if it is necessary to afford the claimant 'just satisfaction'. Lord Hoffmann said that there was no justification what-ever for extending the widow's allowance to men. If Parliament had paid proper regard to Art 14, it would have abolished the allowance for widows. In that event, Mr Wilkinson would not have received an allowance and no damages were therefore necessary to put him in the position in which he would have been if there had been compliance with his Convention rights.

It is quite clear that, despite the elation from commentators following the decision of the ECtHR in *Willis v UK* (2002), in which the court held that the difference in treatment between men and women regarding entitlement to a Widow's Payment and a Widowed Mother's allowance (both social security payments) was not based on any objective and reasonable justification, and was, therefore, in violation of Art 14 of the Convention taken in conjunction with Art 1 of Protocol No 1, this case will have little bearing on the issue under discussion. Whilst it is necessary to take the decision into account, it carries little weight because it did not concern a tax allowance and, further, the UK did not deny its obligation to pay pecuniary compensation in that case, so that the principle of 'just satisfaction' was not in issue. A further provision (now amended, see **[7.104]**) allowing for an increased allowance to a *man* married to and living with a totally incapacitated wife with a dependent child but not to a woman was similarly challenged before European Commission of Human Rights (now abolished) (*MacGregor v UK* (1997)). The Commission found that the friendly settlement of the case had been secured on the basis of respect for human rights as defined in the Convention.

(4) *Discrimination between employees and self-employed persons* Different tax provisions apply to the employed (ITEPA 2003) and to the self-employed (ITTOIA 2005). One such provision permits employers to obtain a deduction for childcare expenses for employees as the provision of a benefit to its employees. Subject to certain conditions, an employee is not taxed on that benefit. In contrast, self-employed persons can make no such deduction in respect of expenses incurred in respect of childcare. The taxpayer, a self-employed person, argued in *Carney v Nathan* (2002) that the disallowance of such expenditure constituted discrimination within Art 14 in relation to Art 1 of the First Protocol. Her argument was dismissed by the Special Commissioner, whose brief view was that the taxpayer, as a self-employed person paying childcare expenses for herself, was not in a similar situation to an employer paying for the employee. Given that the rules allowing for deduction of expenditure are generally more generous to the self-employed than to the employed, this must be seen as a pragmatic decision.

(5) *Discrimination in the exercise of a discretion in relation to a published statement of practice or extra-statutory concession* Domestic law already provides for redress on the part of a taxpayer when the Revenue refuses either to apply a published practice to a particular taxpayer, or to abide by an undertaking given after full disclosure. In light of the comments in respect of extra-statutory concessions made by both the Court of Appeal and the House of Lords in the *Wilkinson* case, it is debatable whether Art 1 of the Protocol No 1 and Art 14 would provide an additional ground for redress. It is now highly unlikely that this would be the case where extra-statutory concessions are not published.

(6) *Discrimination as to prosecution* The Revenue's policy of selecting who to prosecute in cases of tax fraud has been held legitimate on the ground that the primary objective of the Board is to collect tax (*R v IRC, ex p Mead and Cook* (1992)). A taxpayer, aggrieved at being prosecuted when another guilty of a similar offence was not, may challenge the policy under Art 14. Presumably, however, the Revenue would seek to demonstrate that the policy was proportionate to the objective of collecting tax and that it was objectively justifiable.    **[55.42]–[55.60]**

## IV  RESPECT FOR PRIVACY: ART 8

Article 8 is concerned with issues of compliance. The primary protection in Art 8 is that everyone is entitled 'to respect for his private and family life, his home and his correspondence'. This does not provide a comprehensive privacy provision, and the right that is granted is subject to the limitations that any interference must be: (a) in accordance with the law; and (b) necessary in a democratic society in the interests of national security, public safety, the economic well-being of the country, the prevention of crime, the protection of health and morals and the protection of the rights and freedoms of others. In the context of taxation, a challenge to HMRC may be brought under Art 8 in respect of oppressive demands for information (*X v Belgium* (1982) and *Tamosius v UK* (2002)) and searches without warrant (*Funke v France* (1993)). In *X v Belgium*, whilst the European Commission of Human Rights held that the taxpayer had suffered an interference with his privacy in having to divulge all items of his expenditure and of his receipts, it had been in the interest of the economic well-being of the country, and thus outside Art 8. In contrast, in *Funke v France*, searches were made by customs officers at a time when no judicial sanctions were in place. The taxpayer agreed to give up certain documents, but subsequently retracted. As a consequence of the searches, fines were imposed upon the taxpayer. The ECtHR held that the searches were a direct interference of privacy and that, accordingly, this was an infringement of Art 8. In looking at whether the searches were necessary and proportionate, the court took into consideration the need for adequate judicial supervision in addition to the requirement in the Article itself. In the same context is the question of legal professional privilege, considered in *R (on the application of Morgan Grenfell & Co Ltd) v Special Commissioner of Income Tax* (2002), where the issue was whether the taxpayer was protected against a notice under TMA 1970 s 20(1)) requiring production of documents covered by legal professional privilege. (It should be noted that breach of a Convention right had not been pleaded—the issue centred on the specific words of s 20(1)). In holding that it was, the House of Lords, citing the ECtHR case of *Foxley v UK* (2000), confirmed that privilege is a fundamental human right which can be derogated from only in exceptional circumstances. Lord Hoffmann doubted that these exceptional circumstances would include the public interest in the collection of financial information by the Revenue and suggested that if new information-gathering legislation were to be passed, then any interference with privilege would have to be shown to have a legitimate aim necessary in a democratic society. (In fact, one of two new pieces of information-gathering legislation has already been the subject of a recent challenge. In *Bowman v Fels* (2005), the Court of

Appeal had to consider the effect of the PCA 2002 s 328. The purpose of the Act generally was to tackle major fraud and terrorism; but certain provisions (to be found in Part 7 of the Act) were thought to oblige solicitors, in effect, to abandon client confidentiality and report any suspected illegality to the National Criminal Intelligence Service (NCIS)). Lord Justice Brooke said that the Court of Appeal was of the firm opinion that Parliament never intended that a solicitor, in breach of his duty to the court and his client, should disclose to the NCIS suspicions aroused from studying documents released under compulsion by the other party. To hold otherwise, would be to act contrary to the driving principles behind EC law, ECtHR law and UK domestic law, which are seen to be virtually identical and encompass the notion that access to legal advice on a private and confidential basis is a fundamental principle that should not lightly be interfered with. In respect of the other piece of legislation (FA 2004 ss 306–319: see **[42.49]–[42.70]**, which requires the 'promoter' of certain tax avoidance schemes to notify HMRC of any proposal or arrangements falling within the disclosure rules set out in attendant regulations), solicitors have been advised by the Law Society that advice to clients on tax measures is protected by legal professional privilege and does not have to be revealed to HMRC). Such legitimate aim was tested in *Tamosius v UK* (2002), in which case the ECtHR rejected the complaint that the issue and execution of search warrants in connection with an IR investigation into an alleged tax fraud were in breach of Art 8, particularly in regard to documents covered by legal professional privilege. Whilst there was no dispute that the search constituted an interference with the applicant's rights under Art 8, because it had been carried out in accordance with the law and in pursuit of the prevention of crime and disorder, such interference was to be regarded as 'necessary in a democratic society' within the terms of Art 8(2). Scrutiny by the judge issuing the warrant, along with the prohibition on removing documents protected by legal professional privilege, provided sufficient safeguards against possible abuse.                                                    **[55.61]–[55.80]**

## V   THE RIGHT TO A FAIR HEARING: ART 6

One of the cornerstones of the Convention, Art 6(1) entitles everyone to a 'fair and public hearing within a reasonable time by an independent and impartial tribunal established by law' in the determination of their civil rights and obligations or in respect of criminal charges against them. In the context of taxation, several issues arise. These include:
(1)   the extent to which tax-related obligations are within Art 6(1), which requires either that a claimant is the subject of a criminal charge or that his 'civil rights and obligations' must have been affected;
(2)   the question of the burden of proof in respect of a criminal charge;
(3)   the problems concerning the privilege against self-incrimination; and
(4)   whether judicial review will be found to provide a fair enough hearing to satisfy the requirements of Art 6(1).                                    **[55.81]**

## 1   Tax-related obligations and Art 6(1)

### a)   *What amounts to a criminal charge?*

The importance of establishing that a charge is a criminal one lies in the fact that the more generous protections given in Art 6 to criminal proceeding will apply (see **[55.84]**). Whilst it is clear that, for example, a charge under FA 2000 s 144 (evading income tax) is a criminal charge, certain other provisions imposing penalties leave room for doubt. A spate of recent decisions has been concerned with the question of whether certain tax, and ostensibly civil, penalties give rise to criminal charges within the meaning of Art 6(1). That such a penalty could be criminal in nature was confirmed by the ECtHR in *Georgiou v UK* (2001), and was applied in the High Court by Jacob J in *King v Walden* (2001), who held that the system for imposing penalties for fraudulent or negligent delivery of incorrect tax returns was criminal for the purposes of Art 6(1) because the system was punitive. In *Han v C & E Comrs* (2001), the Court of Appeal had to decide whether or not civil penalties imposed against Han and others for alleged dishonest evasion of tax provided for in the VATA 1994 s 60 (see **[38.61]**) gave rise to criminal charges. In upholding the decision of the Chairman of the VAT and Duties Tribunal that the penalties were 'criminal charges' for the purposes of Art 6 by a majority of two to one, the Court of Appeal's starting point was to consider the Strasbourg case law on the issue. According to the Strasbourg jurisprudence, the concept of criminal charge within the meaning of Art 6 is an autonomous one and, effectively, three criteria are applied to determine whether a criminal charge has been imposed (see *Engel v The Netherlands* (1976); *AP, MP and TP v Switzerland* (1998)). These are (a) the classification of the proceedings in domestic law; (b) the nature of the offence; and (c) the nature and degree of severity of the penalty that the person concerned risked incurring. In applying these criteria, Potter LJ noted that:

> '... the Strasbourg Court does not in practice treat these three requirements as analytically distinct or as a three stage test, but as factors together to be weighed in seeking to decide whether, taken cumulatively, the relevant measure should be treated as criminal. When coming to such decision ... factors (b) and (c) carry substantially greater weight than factor (a).'

This means that the categorisation of the charge in domestic law is not decisive of the nature of the charge and provides only a starting point for the classification. Rather, Art 6 impels the court to look behind the appearances and examine the realities of the procedure in question. This is done by considering the second and third criteria in the cumulative rather than in the alternative. Applying the three criteria to the facts before them, the Court of Appeal was of the opinion that:

(1)   the national classification of the penalties as 'civil' was merely a starting point and, moreover, that classification (which came about through the implementation of the proposals contained in the *Report of the Committee on Enforcement of Powers of Revenue Departments*, 'the Keith Report' (1983)), did not represent a decision on the part of the legislature to de-criminalise dishonest evasion of VAT;

(2)   the relevant provisions applied in principle to all citizens as taxpayers and not merely to a restricted group, and sought to deter and punish rather than compensate Customs and Excise; and

(3)   it was sufficient that the penalty was substantial and its purpose was punitive and deterrent, and there was no requirement that it should involve imprisonment.

Accordingly, looking at the substance rather than merely the form of the penalty, it was evident that it amounted to a criminal charge to which Art 6 applied. This approach has recently been followed in *Sharkey v R & C Commrs* (2006), in which case a fixed penalty of £50 for the non-production of documents was held not to amount to a criminal charge. Although there was an element of punishment in the penalty, the High Court said that its primary function was to secure documents for the Revenue. Moreover, it was held that the possibility of further daily penalties in the future for a continued failure to produce the documents in question could not affect the classification of the fixed penalty. For its part, the ECtHR has also taken the view that 20% or 40% civil penalties were criminal for the purposes of Art 6, irrespective of the fact that no criminal intent had to be established before the penalties could be imposed (*Vastberga Taxi Association & Vulic v Sweden* (2002), and *Janosevic v Sweden* (2002). It is interesting to note that in both of these cases, the ECtHR took the view that the three criteria should be viewed as alternatives and not cumulative unless, after an analysis of each, it was impossible to reach a conclusion as to the existence of a criminal charge). A number of cases involving dishonesty penalties had been stood over pending the Court of Appeal decision in the case of *Han* and, in one such case, *Ali & Begum v C & E Comrs* (2002), the VAT Tribunal decided that serious misdeclaration penalties, default surcharges and late registration penalties were *not* criminal for the purposes of Art 6. Seemingly at odds with the decisions of the ECtHR, it may be instructive that the penalties imposed were 15%, lower than those in the two Swedish cases (see also *Bankcroft v Cruchfield* (2002) [**55.83**], where the surcharge of 5% of unpaid tax under TMA 1970, s 59C was too small to be considered a criminal penalty). The question that has to be asked is how are any future cases concerning penalties for misdeclaration, default surcharge, belated VAT registration, demand for security and refusal to restore seized excise, together with those involving direct tax civil penalties, likely to be decided? Prior to the amalgamation of the Revenue with Customs and Excise, as far as Customs and Excise were concerned, there was little change to existing procedures, with a mere amendment to their existing explanation to a taxpayer involved in 'civil' investigations to take account of human rights. In contrast, the Inland Revenue seemed more aware of the possible impact of the HRA 1998, and issued guidance to their staff so as to avoid the possibility of infringing the taxpayer's right of non-incrimination and right to silence although, in doing so, they did not concede that their civil penalties were criminal in nature but said that 'it is not clear' (*Guidance to Inland Revenue Staff on Human Rights and Penalties*, Inland Revenue, 11 September 2002, see [**55.85**]). This guidance has since been incorporated into individual manuals (see, eg., IHTM 36401, dealing with human rights and penalties in connection with inheritance tax, and EM 1360, dealing with the obligations of employers).                    [**55.82**]

b)   *Civil rights and obligations*

As far as 'civil' rights are concerned, Strasbourg jurisprudence indicates that a taxpayer's obligations are outside the scope of Art 6(1) because they are 'public in nature'. It would appear that public law rights and obligations are not civil rights and obligations, whereas private law rights and obligations are. Thus, the obligations to make social security payments and to pay taxes are 'public' obligations since they derive from the citizen's 'normal civic duties in a democratic society' (see *Schouten and Meldrum v Netherlands* (1994)). Accordingly, in cases where the issue is one of assessment to tax, there would appear to be no guarantee of a fair hearing under Art 6(1). In *Ferrazzini v Italy* (2001), the view of the majority of the ECtHR (sitting as the Grand Chamber of 17 judges, giving an indication of the importance of the issue) was that:

> 'tax matters still form part of the hard core of public-authority prerogatives, with the public nature of the relationship between the taxpayer and the tax authority remaining predominant'.

Nonetheless, there was a strong dissenting opinion from six members of the Grand Chamber, and an indication that this might not always be the view of the court. The view was put that:

> 'as long as a dividing line between "civil" and "non-civil" rights and obligations is maintained in respect of proceedings between individuals and governments, it is important to ensure that the relevant criteria for determining what is "civil" are applied in a logical and reasonable manner—and that may make it necessary from time to time to adjust the case law in order to make it consistent in the light of recent developments.'

This decision was recently affirmed by the ECtHR in *Vastberga Taxi Association Vulic v Sweden* (2002), and *Janosevic v Sweden* (2002), and was followed in *Bankcroft v Crutchfield* (2002), in which case the Special Commissioner held that an appeal against a surcharge under TMA 1970, s 59C did not relate to civil rights, and in *Taylor v IRC* (2003), where the same Special Commissioner dismissed a claim by a personal representative that an appeal against a notice of determination to inheritance tax was not within a reasonable time of the death of the testator. Where the issue goes beyond that of liability to tax and quantum of tax assessed, Art 6 may be invoked where a taxpayer is given no right of appeal against a particular decision, or the right of appeal is so restricted that it is impossible to exercise, or where a taxpayer is subject to an unacceptably onerous burden of proof (see *Hodgson v C E Comrs* (1997)).

**[55.83]**

## 2   **Rights guaranteed by Art 6: the burden of proof**

The importance of the question at issue in cases such as *Han* lies in the protection afforded to taxpayers by the various minimum rights provided for by Art 6(2) and (3). That everyone charged with a criminal offence shall be presumed innocent until proved guilty is confirmed by Art 6(2). Article 6(3) guarantees certain minimum rights to everyone charged with a criminal offence. These ensure that defendants are able to defend themselves either personally or with legal assistance, that there is adequate time to prepare a defence, the right to secure the attendance of witnesses, and that they understand the charges brought against them and have the assistance of an interpreter if necessary. This last 'right' is particularly pertinent where penalties have been raised against non-English or inadequate English speakers, as in *Han* itself. Of great importance in this context is the question of the burden of proof. It might be assumed that where it has been concluded that a penalty amounts to a criminal charge, the Revenue would have to prove its case beyond all reasonable doubt, rather than on the balance of probabilities. That this is not the case was spelt out by Mance LJ in *Han*:

> 'The classification of a case as criminal for the purpose of Art 6(3) of the Convention on Human Rights … is a classification for the purposes of the Convention only. It entitles the defendant to the safeguards provided expressly or by implication by that Article. It does not make the case criminal for all domestic purposes. In particular, it does not, necessarily, engage protections such as those provided by the Police and Criminal Evidence Act 1984.'

However, in *Ajay Chandubhai Kumar Patel v C & E Comrs* (2001) (17248), the VAT tribunal, citing the House of Lords decision in *Khawaja v Secretary of State for Home Department* (1984), considered that:

> 'The standard is the civil standard of the balance of probabilities; however, under Art 6(2) the appellant is innocent until proved guilty. In any event, clear evidence is needed for a finding of dishonesty; the more serious the allegation, the more cogent the evidence must be.'  **[55.84]**

## 3   The privilege against self-incrimination and the right to silence

Issues concerning a breach of Art 6 may arise where the Revenue obtains information from the taxpayer either under threat of penalty for non-compliance, or where the *Hansard* procedure has been adopted, and that information is subsequently used in criminal proceedings against the taxpayer. (The *Hansard* procedure is adopted by the Revenue in cases of tax fraud, and permits the Board to accept a money settlement in lieu of instituting criminal proceedings in respect of the alleged fraud. Prior to the recent changes made to the procedure (see below) no undertaking was given that such a settlement would be accepted, even if the taxpayer had made a full confession, and the Revenue's decision to exercise its discretion in favour of the taxpayer would have been influenced by the amount of co-operation given by him.) In these circumstances, the taxpayer may well argue that his right to a fair trial has been breached because, by providing sensitive information under threat of a penalty, he has been forced to incriminate himself. This issue was considered by the House of Lords, albeit *obiter*, in *R v Allen* (2001). In that case the taxpayer, who was being investigated for tax fraud, had failed to comply with a notice (under TMA 1970 s 20(1)) requiring him to furnish the Revenue with certain information. The *Hansard* procedure having been adopted, the taxpayer answered the Revenue's questions and furnished it with, albeit false, information. He was subsequently charged with the criminal offence of cheating the public revenue and, in the House of Lords, he argued that the demands made upon him both by s 20(1) and the *Hansard* procedure had caused the information to be given involuntarily, and was a breach of his right not to incriminate himself, thus violating his right to a fair trial under Art 6 of the Convention. In fact, the trial and conviction took place before the relevant sections of the HRA 1998 had come into force on 2 October 2000. The House of Lords held that, despite the fact that the appeal was being heard after that date, the Act did not operate retrospectively to make unsafe by reason of a breach of Art 6 a conviction which was safe under English law at the time the conviction took place. Despite this, Lord Hutton gave his opinion on the issue, and he distinguished *Allen* from *Saunders v United Kingdom* (1996), a case not concerning taxation, in which the ECtHR stated that the right to silence and the right not to incriminate oneself are 'generally recognised international standards which lie at the heart of a notion of a fair procedure under Art 6'. In Lord Hutton's opinion, just as the state would be perfectly at liberty to prosecute a taxpayer for cheating the Revenue by furnishing a standard tax return containing false information:

> '... viewed against the background that the state, for the purpose of collecting tax, is entitled to require a citizen to inform it of his income and to enforce penalties for failure to do so, the s 20(1) notice requiring information cannot constitute a violation of the right against self-incrimination'.

Moreover, to the extent that there was an inducement to provide information contained in the *Hansard* procedure, it was to give true and accurate information to the Revenue. In *Allen*, the defendant failed to respond to the inducement and gave false information. Accordingly, his argument that he was induced to provide certain information in the hope of non-institution of criminal proceedings held out by the Revenue, and that its provision was therefore involuntary and in breach of Art 6(1), was invalid. However, Lord Hutton did conclude that:

> 'If, in response to the *Hansard* Statement, the appellant had given true and accurate information which disclosed that he had earlier cheated the Revenue and had then been prosecuted for that earlier dishonesty, he would have had a strong argument that the criminal proceedings were unfair and an even stronger argument that the Crown should not rely on evidence of his admission ...'

In the light of Lord Hutton's concluding words, changes have now been made to the *Hansard* procedure (see *Tax Bulletin No 62*). As a consequence, a taxpayer making a full confession under this procedure is now assured that HMRC will not pursue a criminal prosecution; the discretion previously enjoyed by the Revenue as to the course of action it would take following such a confession has effectively been removed. However, in addition to giving both a full and complete confession, the taxpayer must also offer full co-operation during the investigation, including the giving of full facilities for investigation into his affairs and for examination of such books, papers, documents or information as the Board may consider necessary. Without such co-operation, the taxpayer remains at risk of prosecution. Just as the changes to the *Hansard* procedure were a direct result of the HRA, so also is the fact that taxpayers suspected of fraud must now be interviewed under caution. The Revenue had always maintained that the *Hansard* interview was part of the civil process designed to gather in money, and was not a criminal investigation. However, in *R v Gill and Gill* (2003), taxpayers charged with cheating the Revenue challenged the use made of answers given by them during the *Hansard* opening interview. The Court of Appeal held that tax fraud involves the commission of a criminal offence or offences, with the result that the investigation of tax fraud must involve the investigation of a criminal offence. Accordingly, in contrast to the views of Potter and Mance LLJ in *Han*, the provisions of the Police and Criminal Evidence Act 1984 should be applied to the *Hansard* interview. Despite this, the court held further that, on the facts of the case, the admission of the evidence provided during the *Hansard* investigation would not have had such an adverse effect on the fairness of the proceedings that ht e court ought not to have admitted it. Although it was thus possible that the Revenue could have continued as normal using the new *Hansard* procedure introduced as a result of *R v Allen* with the hope of surviving any subsequent challenge on the lines of *R v Gill and Gill*, they have now started to interview under caution and to tape interviews.

In addition to the changes made to the *Hansard* procedure, the Revenue, whilst not conceding that their penalties are criminal in nature, have also issued guidance to their staff so as to avoid the possibility of infringing the taxpayer's right of non-incrimination (and also the right to silence). Revenue staff must make the taxpayer fully aware of (i) the need to provide information; (ii) the penalties that may attach if this is not done; (iii) the formal powers that can be used to obtain the necessary information should the taxpayer be unwilling to answer questions directed to him; (iv) the fact that the extent to which the taxpayer has freely and fully offered information may be taken into account in calculating the penalty; and (v) the fact that, in the event that the Revenue are unable to agree with the taxpayer, information or documents provided during the enquiry may be used in any appeal proceedings. **[55.85]**

## 4 Judicial review and Art 6(1)

The issue of whether judicial review will be found to provide a fair enough hearing to satisfy the requirements of Art 6(1) is fundamental. Tribunals, such as the Special Commissioners and the VAT and Duties Tribunals, face a further, and overriding, difficulty. Even in cases where the taxpayer is given no rights of appeal, unless the tribunal is able to construe the domestic legislation in such a way so as to comply with Art 6(1), it will be powerless under the HRA 1998. Whilst the Act enables a 'court' to make a declaration that domestic legislation is incompatible with the European Convention (which, ultimately, paves the way for remedial action), a tribunal is not a 'court' for these purposes. Tribunals may, however, resort to EC law to ensure enforceability of the right to a fair hearing. **[55.86]–[55.100]**

## VI HUMAN RIGHTS AND EC LAW

If the area of law in question is governed by EC law, all the principles of the European Convention, which underpin EC law, will apply in any event and every court and tribunal has power to take the provisions of the European

Convention into account. This principle has been restated in *Marks & Spencer v C E Comrs* (2002) (although, on the facts of the case, it was unnecessary to consider the arguments based on this principle). Provided that it applies, EC law is not subject to the limitations imposed by the HRA 1998 on tribunals (see **[55.86]**). This means that arguments about incompatibility of domestic law with the European Convention can be made before the Special Commissioners and the VAT and Duties Tribunals (see also *Ali v Begum* (2002) where the VAT Tribunal recognised that there might be circumstances where the Community protection of human rights confers greater procedural protection than Art 6 of the Convention). **[55.101]**

# Index

[*all references are to paragraph number*]